SECOND

The Making of the West

PEOPLES AND CULTURES

SECOND EDITION

The Making of the West

PEOPLES AND CULTURES

Volume I: To 1740

Lynn Hunt
University of California,
Los Angeles

Thomas R. Martin
College of the Holy Cross

Barbara H. Rosenwein
Loyola University Chicago

R. Po-chia Hsia
Pennsylvania State University

Bonnie G. Smith
Rutgers University

BEDFORD/ST. MARTIN'S
Boston ◆ New York

FOR BEDFORD/ST. MARTIN'S

Executive Editor for History: Mary Dougherty
Director of Development for History: Jane Knetzger
Developmental Editor: Sara Wise
Senior Production Editor: Anne Noonan
Senior Production Supervisor: Dennis Conroy
Senior Marketing Manager: Jenna Bookin Barry
Editorial Assistant: Rachel L. Safer
Production Assistant: Kristen Merrill
Copyeditor: Janet Renard
Text Design: Wanda Kossak
Page Layout: DeNee Reiton Skipper
Photo Researchers: Elsa Peterson and Judy Brody
Cover Design: Billy Boardman
Cartography: Mapping Specialists Limited
Composition: TechBooks
Printing and Binding: R.R. Donnelley & Sons Company

President: Joan E. Feinberg
Editorial Director: Denise B. Wydra
Director of Marketing: Karen Melton Soeltz
Director of Editing, Design, and Production: Marcia Cohen
Managing Editor: Elizabeth M. Schaaf

Library of Congress Control Number: 2004102164

For information, write: Bedford/St. Martin's, 75 Arlington Street, Boston, MA 02116
(617-399-4000)

ISBN: 0-312-40959-1 (hardcover edition)   EAN: 978-0-312-40959-3
ISBN: 0-312-41740-3 (paperback Vol. I)   EAN: 978-0-312-41740-6
ISBN: 0-312-41761-6 (paperback Vol. II)   EAN: 978-0-312-41761-1
ISBN: 0-312-41767-5 (paperback Vol. A)   EAN: 978-0-312-41767-3
ISBN: 0-312-41768-3 (paperback Vol. B)   EAN: 978-0-312-41768-0
ISBN: 0-312-41769-1 (paperback Vol. C)   EAN: 978-0-312-41769-7

Cover Art: Illumination by the Master of the Cité des Dames (fl. c. 1400–15) from *Le Chevalier Errant* (Ms. FR. 12559) by Thomas de Saluces (1240–1296). Courtesy of Bibliothéque nationale de France.

Preface

THE IDEA OF "THE WEST" is now urgently under discussion. The end of the cold war after 1989 presented new challenges for historical interpretation, but these had hardly been digested when the shock of September 11, 2001, reverberated throughout the world. These momentous events present extraordinary challenges for authors of Western civilization textbooks. We welcome the challenges, for they have deepened our commitment to our project's basic goal and approach. From the very beginning, we have insisted on an expanded vision of the West that includes the United States, fully incorporates eastern Europe, and emphasizes Europe's relationship with the rest of the world, whether through trade, colonization, migration, cultural exchange, or religious and ethnic conflict.

Every generation of students needs new textbooks that synthesize recent findings. Textbooks conceived during the era of the cold war are, of course, oriented toward explaining the clash between a West unquestionably identified as western Europe and the United States and its eastern-bloc opponents, eastern Europe and the Soviet Union. Since much of eastern Europe has now joined the European Union, the notion of Europe—and the West—has to change. Conflict now takes place on a global stage, and globalization of the economy and culture has become a subject of passionate debate. Nowhere is that debate more crucial than over relations between the West and Islam precipitated by the September 11, 2001, attacks by Islamic radicals. How to respond to such global threats sharply divides the West. The United States and Great Britain's decision to invade Iraq despite strong opposition from allies in western Europe tests long-standing alliances and suggests significant international realignments. New histories must reflect these dramatic changes, and we feel confident that ours meets the challenge. In every chapter, we develop these new perspectives and show how they offer a more coherent and convincing view of the important issues in the making of the West.

Central Themes and Approach

Our title, *The Making of the West: Peoples and Cultures*, makes two enduring points about our themes and approach: (1) that the history of the West is the story of a process that is still ongoing, not a finished result with only one fixed meaning; and (2) that "the West" includes many different peoples and cultures, that is, that there is no one Western people or culture that has existed from the beginning until now. To understand the historical development of the West and its position in the world today, it is essential to place the West's emergence in a larger, global context that reveals the cross-cultural interactions fundamental to the shaping of the Western identity. Our task as authors, moreover, is to integrate the best of social and cultural history with the enduring developments of political, military, and diplomatic history, offering a clear, compelling narrative that sets all the key events and stages of the West's evolution in a broad, meaningful context.

We know from our own teaching that introductory students need a solid chronological framework, one with enough familiar benchmarks to make the material readily assimilable, but also one with enough flexibility to incorporate the new varieties of historical research. That is one reason why we present our account in a straightforward, chronological manner. Each chapter treats all the main events, people, and themes of a period in which the West significantly changed; thus students are not required to learn about political events in one chapter, then backtrack to concurrent social and cultural developments in the next. The chronological organization also accords with our belief that it is important, above all else, for students to see the interconnections among varieties of historical experience—between politics and cultures, between public events and private experiences, between wars and diplomacy and everyday life. Our chronological synthesis allows students to appreciate these relationships while it, we hope, captures the spirit of each age and sparks students' historical imaginations. For teachers, our chronological approach ensures a balanced account, allows the flexibility to stress themes of one's own choosing, and perhaps best of all, provides a text that reveals history not as a settled matter but as a process that is constantly alive, subject to pressures, and able to surprise us. In writing *The Making of the West: Peoples and Cultures*, it has been our aim to communicate the vitality and excitement as well as the fundamental importance of history. If we have succeeded in conveying some of the vibrancy of the past and the thrill of historical investigation, we will be encouraged to start rethinking and revising—as historians always must—once again.

Pedagogy and Features

More and more is required of students these days, and not just in Western civilization courses. We know from our own teaching that students need all the help they can get in assimilating information, acquiring skills, learning about historical debate, and sampling the newest approaches to historical thinking. With these goals in mind, we retained the class-tested learning and teaching aids that contributed to the first edition, but we have also added more such features.

Each chapter begins with a ***vivid anecdote*** that draws readers into the atmosphere and issues of the period and raises the chapter's main themes, supplemented by a full-page illustration that echoes the anecdote and similarly reveals the temper of the times. We have added ***new chapter outlines*** and ***timelines*** to introduce students to each chapter. As they read, students now encounter ***review questions*** strategically placed at the end of each major section to check their comprehension of main ideas, plus bolded ***key terms*** in the text with corresponding ***glossary*** definitions at the end of the book and a running ***pronunciation guide***. Each chapter closes with a strong ***chapter conclusion*** that reviews main topics and ties together the chapter's thematic strands. An all-new ***chapter review*** section provides a clear study plan with a table of important events, list of key terms, review questions, and "Making Connections" questions, which encourage students to analyze chapter material or make comparisons within or beyond the chapter.

But like a clear narrative synthesis, strong pedagogical support is not enough on its own to encourage active learning. To reflect the richness of the themes in the text and to enliven the past with many more original sources, in the second edition we have added ***sixty new single-source documents*** (two per chapter). Nothing can give a more direct experience of the past than original voices, and we have each endeavored, sometimes through our own retranslation, to let those voices speak, whether it is Seneca describing everyday life in the Roman Empire, Frederick Barbarossa replying to the Romans when they offer him the emperor's crown, or an ordinary person's account of one of Stalin's pogroms. At the same time, we have retained our unique, proven features that extend the narrative by revealing the process of interpretation, providing a solid introduction to the principles of historical argument, and capturing the excitement of historical investigation:

- ***Contrasting Views*** provide three or four often conflicting eyewitness accounts of a central event, person, or development, such as Martin Luther, the English Civil War, and late-nineteenth-century migration.
- ***New Sources, New Perspectives*** show students how historians continue to develop

new kinds of evidence about the past, from tree rings to Holocaust museums.

- *Terms of History* explain the meanings of some of the most important and contested terms in the history of the West and show how those meanings have developed—and changed—over time. For example, the discussion of *progress* shows how the term took root in the eighteenth century and has been contested in the twentieth.
- *Did You Know?* is a short, illustrated feature that emphasizes the interactions between the West and the broader world, offering unexpected and sometimes startling examples of cultural interchange, from the invention of "smoking" (derived from the New World) to the creation of polo (adapted from South Asia).
- *Taking Measure* highlights a chart, table, graph, or map of historical statistics that illuminates an important political, social, or cultural development.

The map program of the first edition was widely praised as the most comprehensive in any survey text. In each chapter we offer a set of three types of maps, each with a distinct role in conveying information to students. Four to five *full-size maps* show major developments, two to four *"spot" maps*—small maps that emphasize a detailed area from the discussion—aid students' understanding of specific but crucial issues, and *"Mapping the West"* summary maps at the end of each chapter provide a snapshot of the West at the close of a transformative period and help students visualize the West's changing contours over time. For this edition, we have carefully considered each map, improved the colors for better contrast, and clarified and updated borders and labels where needed.

It has been our intention to integrate art as fully as possible into the narrative and to show its value for teaching and learning. *Over 400 illustrations*, carefully chosen to reflect this edition's broad topical coverage and geographic inclusion, reinforce the text and show the varieties of visual sources from which historians build their narratives and interpretations. All artifacts, illustrations, paintings, and photographs are contemporaneous with the chapter; there are no anachronistic illustrations—no fifteenth-century peasants

tilling fields in a chapter on the tenth century! We know that today's students are very attuned to visual sources of information, yet they do not always receive systematic instruction in how to "read" or think critically about such visual sources. Our substantive captions for the maps and art help them learn how to make the most of these informative materials, and now in the second edition, we have frequently included specific questions or suggestions for comparisons that might be developed. Specially designed visual exercises in the *Online Study Guide* supplement this approach in an especially thought-provoking fashion. A new page design for the second edition supports our goal of intertwining the art and the narrative and lends more interest and dynamism to the page.

Textual Changes

A textbook, unlike most scholarly books, offers historians the rare chance to revise the original work, to keep it fresh, and to make it better. It has been a privilege to bring our own scholarship and teaching to bear on this rewriting. In this second edition, we have kept our emphasis on a strong central story line that incorporates the best of new research, but we have worked to make the narrative even more focused and accessible by reviewing every line of text and recrafting the headings to provide better signposts for readers.

Our book now begins with a new prologue that examines the lives of early human beings in the Paleolithic and Neolithic eras. Here we discuss the archeological evidence that points to the technology, trade, religious practices, and social traditions of people who left no written history. The prologue is designed for maximum flexibility. It contains full chapter pedagogy to support instructors who choose to assign this period. Alternatively, it can be used as introductory or extra reading for those instructors who begin their courses with Mesopotamia.

To illustrate our conception of the history of the West as an ongoing process, the first chapter opens with a new section on the origins and contested meaning of *Western civilization.* In this conversation, we emphasize our theme of cultural borrowing between the peoples of Europe and their neighbors that has characterized Western civilization from the beginning. We continue to incorporate the experiences of borderland regions and the importance of global interactions into the historical narrative and in many of our new art selections.

Of course, the recent past is the most pressing arena in which to examine the West as an evolving construct. The impact of recent events is reflected most dramatically in the last two chapters, which have been completely rewritten and now divide at 1989, the year that marks the beginning of a new era after the cold war.

Throughout each chapter, we've added new material and drawn on new scholarship on topics such as the demise of the Akkadian Empire and the succeeding Ur III dynasty (Chapter 1); Zoroastrianism and the influence of Persian religion on later faiths (Chapter 2); criticisms of radical democracy (Chapter 3); diversity among the non-Roman peoples who flooded into the Roman Empire (Chapter 7); the origins of Islam (Chapter 8); Byzantine court culture and the *dynatoi* (Chapter 9); the prominence of the flagellant movement (Chapter 13); Spanish exploration of the Pacific Coast of North America (Chapter 16); the promotion of women's emigration to the new colonies (Chapter 17); sugar grinding in the colonies (Chapter 18); the role of peasants in the French Revolution (Chapter 20); nineteenth-century French efforts to transform Saigon (Chapter 23); Japan's imperialist activity in the 1920s (Chapter 26); discontent in the colonies during the depression (Chapter 27); postwar recovery in Scandinavia and the contributions of immigrants to postwar European economies (Chapter 28); the rise in the study of social sciences (Chapter 29); and the impact of global outsourcing (Chapter 30).

Supplements

As with the first edition, a well-integrated ancillary program supports *The Making of the West: Peoples and Cultures.* Each print and electronic resource has been carefully revised to provide a host of practical teaching and learning aids.

For Students

***Sources of* The Making of the West, Second Edition**—Volumes I (to 1740) and II (since 1500)—by Katharine J. Lualdi, University of Southern Maine. For each chapter in *The Making of the West*, this companion sourcebook features four or five important political, social, and cultural documents that reinforce or extend discussions in the textbook, encouraging students to make connections between narrative history and primary sources. Short chapter summaries and document headnotes contextualize the wide array of sources and perspectives represented, while discussion and comparative questions guide students' reading and promote historical thinking skills. The second edition provides instructors with even more flexibility, as the nearly one-third new selections feature visual sources for the first time. This edition also features more attention to geographic areas beyond Europe and includes an improved balance between traditional documents and selections that provide a fresh perspective.

***Study Guide to Accompany* The Making of the West, Second Edition**—Volumes I (to 1740) and II (since 1500)—by Victoria Thompson, Arizona State University, and Eric Johnson, University of California, Los Angeles. For each chapter in the textbook, the *Study Guide* offers overview questions; a chapter summary; an expanded timeline with questions; a glossary of key terms with a related exercise; multiple-choice and short-answer questions; plus map, illustration, and source exercises that help students synthesize information and practice analytical skills. Answers for all exercises are provided.

***Online Study Guide* at bedfordstmartins.com/hunt** The popular *Online Study Guide* for *The Making of the West* is a free and uniquely personalized learning tool to help students master themes and information in the textbook and improve their historical skills. Instructors can monitor student progress through the online *Quiz Gradebook* or receive e-mail updates.

The Bedford Series in History and Culture—Advisory Editors Natalie Zemon Davis, Princeton University; Ernest R. May, Harvard University; David W. Blight, Yale University; and Lynn Hunt, University of California, Los Angeles. European titles in this highly praised series combine first-rate scholarship, historical narrative, and important primary documents for undergraduate courses. Each book is brief, inexpensive, and focused on a specific topic or period. Packaged discounts are available. European titles include *Spartacus and the Slave Wars, Utopia, Candide, The French Revolution and Human Rights, The Enlightenment,* and *The Communist Manifesto.*

DocLinks at bedfordstmartins.com/ doclinks This Web site provides over 400 annotated Web links with single-click access to primary documents online, including speeches, legislation, treaties, social commentary, essays, travelers' accounts, personal narratives and testimony, newspaper articles, visual artifacts, songs, and poems. Searchable by topic, date, or specific chapter of *The Making of the West.*

HistoryLinks at bedfordstmartins.com/ historylinks HistoryLinks directs instructors and students to over 500 carefully selected and annotated history-related Web sites, including those containing image galleries, maps, and audio and video clips for supplementing lectures or making assignments. Searchable by date, subject, medium, keyword, or specific chapter in *The Making of the West.*

A Student's Online Guide to History Reference Sources at bedfordstmartins .com/benjamin This collection of links provides access to history-related electronic reference sources such as databases, indexes, and journals, plus contact information for state, provincial, local, and professional history organizations. Based on the appendix to Jules Benjamin's *A Student's Guide to History,* Ninth Edition.

For Instructors

Instructor's Resource Manual to Accompany **The Making of the West, Second Edition**—Volumes I (to 1740) and II (since 1500)—by Dakota Hamilton, Humboldt State University. This helpful manual offers both first-time and experienced teachers a wealth of tools for structuring and customizing Western civilization history courses of different sizes. For each chapter in the textbook, the *Instructor's Resource Manual* includes an outline of chapter themes; a chapter summary; lecture and discussion topics; film and literature suggestions; writing and class-presentation assignments; research topic suggestions; and in-class exercises for working with maps, illustrations, and sources.

Transparencies A set of over 200 full-color acetate transparencies for *The Making of the West* includes all full-sized maps and many images from the text.

Computerized Test Bank—by Joseph Coohill, Pennsylvania State University at New Kensington, and Frances Mitilineos, Loyola University Chicago; available on CD-ROM. This fully updated test bank offers over 80 exercises per chapter, including multiple-choice, identification, timelines, map labeling and analysis, source analysis, and full-length essay questions. Instructors can customize quizzes, edit both questions and answers, as well as export them to a variety of formats, including WebCT and Blackboard. The disc includes answer keys and essay outlines.

Instructor's Resource CD-ROM This disc provides instructors with ready-made and easily customized PowerPoint multimedia presentations built around chapter outlines, maps, figures, and selected images from the textbook. The disc also contains images in JPEG format, an electronic version of the *Instructor's Resource Manual,* outline maps in PDF format for quizzing or handouts, and quick-start guides to the *Online Study Guide.*

Book Companion Site at bedfordstmartins .com/hunt The companion Web site for

The Making of the West gathers all the electronic resources for the text, including the *Online Study Guide* and related *Quiz Gradebook*, at a single Web address. It provides convenient links to such helpful lecture and research materials as PowerPoint chapter outlines from the textbook, DocLinks, HistoryLinks, and Map Central.

Map Central at bedfordstmartins.com/mapcentral   Map Central is a searchable database of more than 750 maps from Bedford/St. Martin's history texts for classroom presentations and more than 50 basic political and physical outline maps for quizzes or handouts.

***Using the Bedford Series in History and Culture with* The Making of the West, Second Edition**   This short guide gives practical suggestions for using the volumes in The Bedford Series in History and Culture in conjunction with *The Making of the West.* This reference supplies connections between the text and the supplements and ideas for starting discussions focused on a single primary-source volume. Available in print as well as online at bedfordstmartins.com/usingseries.

Blackboard and WebCT content is available for *The Making of the West.*

Videos and Multimedia   A wide assortment of videos and multimedia CD-ROMs on various topics in European history is available to qualified adopters.

Acknowledgments

In the vital process of revision, the authors have benefited from repeated critical readings by many talented scholars and teachers. Our sincere thanks go to the following instructors, whose comments often challenged us to rethink or justify our interpretations and who always provided a check on accuracy down to the smallest detail.

Stephen J. Andrews, *Albuquerque Technical Vocational Institute*

Laetitia Argenteri, *San Diego Mesa College*

Sharon Arnoult, *Midwestern State University*

Wayne C. Bartee, *Southwest Missouri State University*

S. Jonathan Bass, *Samford University*

Joel D. Benson, *Northwest Missouri State University*

Marjorie Berman, *Red Rocks Community College*

Lyn A. Blanchfield, *Le Moyne College*

Stephen Blumm, *Montgomery County Community College*

Ronald G. Brown, *College of Southern Maryland*

J. Laurel Carrington, *St. Olaf College*

Joseph Coohill, *Pennsylvania State University, New Kensington*

Cassandra B. Cookson, *Brazosport College*

Paul Cullity, *Keene State College*

Marianne Eve Fisher, *South Dakota State University*

Malia Formes, *Western Kentucky University*

James Genova, *Indiana State University*

Karen Graubert, *Cornell University*

William G. Gray, *Texas Tech University*

Ginger Guardiola, *Colorado State University*

David Halahmy, *Cypress College*

Paul Halsall, *University of North Florida*

Dakota Hamilton, *Humboldt State University*

Carmen Harris, *University of South Carolina, Spartanburg*

L. Edward Hicks, *Faulkner University*

Christine Holden, *University of Southern Maine*

David Hood, *California State University, Long Beach*

Chris Howell, *Red Rocks Community College*

David Hudson, *California State University, Fresno*

Paul J. Hughes, *Sussex County Community College*

Marsh W. Jones, *Parkland College*

Erin Jordan, *University of Northern Colorado*

Gerald Kadish, *State University of New York, Binghamton*

Ruth Mazo Karras, *University of Minnesota*

Frances A. Kelleher, *Grand Valley State University*

Jason Knirck, *Humboldt State University*

Anne Kelly Knowles, *Middlebury College*
John Krapp, *Hofstra University*
David Kutcha, *University of New England*
Ann Kuzdale, *Chicago State University*
Michelle Laughran, *Saint Joseph's College of Maine*
Alison Williams Lewin, *St. Joseph's University*
Janice Liedl, *Laurentian University*
Paul Douglas Lockhart, *Wright State University*
David W. Madsen, *Seattle University*
Steven G. Marks, *Clemson University*
Andrew McMichael, *Western Kentucky University*
Gary M. Miller, *Southern Oregon University*
Eva Mo, *Modesto Junior College*
David B. Mock, *Tallahassee Community College*
Scott Morschauser, *Rowan University*
Johanna Moyer, *State University of New York, Oswego*
Peter Parides, *New York City College of Technology*
Paulette L. Pepin, *University of New Haven*
Norman Raiford, *Greenville Technical College*
Salvador Rivera, *State University of New York, Cobleskill*
Kenneth W. Rock, *Colorado State University*
Anna Marie Roos, *University of Minnesota, Duluth*
Patricia C. Ross, *Columbus State Community College*
Jon Rudd, *Prince George's Community College*
Brian Rutishauser, *Fresno City College*
Daniella Sarnoff, *Xavier University*
Lynn Schibeci, *University of New Mexico*
Kim Schutte, *Missouri Western State College*
David Shafer, *California State University, Long Beach*
Jessica A. Sheetz-Nguyen, *Oklahoma City Community College*
William A. Sherrard, *Creighton University*
Charlie R. Steen, *University of New Mexico*
Nicholas Steneck, *Ohio State University*
Robert E. Stiefel, *University of New Hampshire*

Ann Sullivan, *Tompkins Cortland Community College*
Paul Teverow, *Missouri Southern State College*
Michael E. Thede, *Florida Gulf Coast University*
Frances Titchener, *Utah State University*
Tracey Trenam, *Aims Community College*
David G. Troyansky, *Texas Tech University*
Timothy Vogt, *University of San Francisco*
James J. Ward, *Cedar Crest College*
Theodore Weeks, *Southern Illinois University*
Michael Weiss, *Linn-Benton Community College*
Stephen J. White Sr., *College of Charleston*
Anne Will, *Skagit Valley College*
Andrea Winkler, *Whitman College*
Robinson Yost, *Kirkwood Community College*

Each of us has also benefited from the close readings and valuable criticisms of our coauthors, though we all assume responsibility for our own chapters. Thomas Martin has written Chapters 1–7; Barbara Rosenwein, Chapters 8–12; Ronnie Hsia, Chapters 13–15; Lynn Hunt, Chapters 16–22; and Bonnie Smith, Chapters 23–30.

Many colleagues, friends, and family members have helped us develop this work as well. They know how grateful we are. We also wish to acknowledge and thank the publishing team at Bedford/St. Martin's who did so much to bring this revised edition to completion: Joan Feinberg, Denise Wydra, Elizabeth Welch, Mary Dougherty, Jane Knetzger, Sara Wise, Anne Noonan, Kristen Merrill, Jenna Bookin Barry, Rachel Safer, Bryce Sady, Jan Fitter, Dale Anderson, Gretchen Boger, Elsa Peterson, and Judy Brody.

Our students' questions and concerns have shaped much of this work, and we welcome all our readers' suggestions, queries, and criticisms. Please contact us at our respective institutions or via history@bedfordstmartins.com.

L.H. T.R.M. B.H.R. R.P.H. B.G.S.

Brief Contents

Contents

The Transformation of the Roman Empire, 284–c. 600 C.E.   243

The Heirs of the Roman Empire, 600–750   283

Unity and Diversity in Three Societies, 750–1050 *319*

The Medieval Search for Order and Harmony, 1215–1320   435

The Crisis of Late Medieval Society, 1320–1430   467

A Century of Crisis, 1560–1648   *581*

State Building and the Search for Order, 1648–1690   *621*

The Atlantic System and Its Consequences, 1690–1740   665

Maps and Figures

Maps

Figures

Special Features

Individual Documents

Contrasting Views

To the Student

This guide to your textbook introduces the unique features that will help you understand the fascinating story of Western civilization.

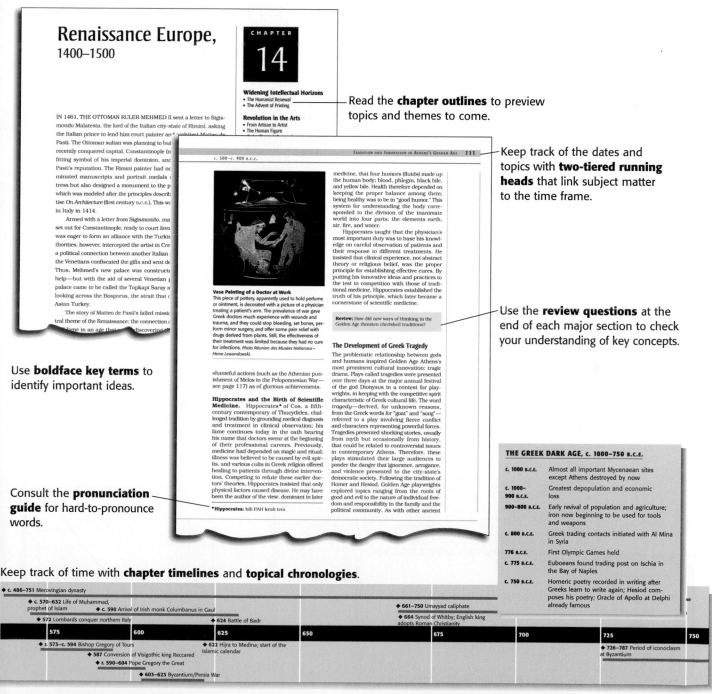

Read the **chapter outlines** to preview topics and themes to come.

Keep track of the dates and topics with **two-tiered running heads** that link subject matter to the time frame.

Use the **review questions** at the end of each major section to check your understanding of key concepts.

Use **boldface key terms** to identify important ideas.

Consult the **pronunciation guide** for hard-to-pronounce words.

Keep track of time with **chapter timelines** and **topical chronologies**.

Special features show you how historians think and work.

The document program reveals the range of sources that historians use to learn about the past and to draw conclusions.

Numerous **individual documents** offer direct experiences of the past including personal letters, poems, songs, political statements, and speeches.

Contrasting Views provide three or four often-conflicting eyewitness accounts of a central event, person, or development.

New Sources, New Perspectives show how new evidence leads historians to fresh insights—and sometimes new interpretations.

A Merchant's Advice to His Sons

Giovanni Rucellai, one of the most successful merchants of fifteenth-century Florence, kept an extensive diary that reveals life among the city's urban elite. In this selection, Rucellai warns his sons against pursuing political power for self-serving reasons. Rucellai's comments on political of- in order to convert the treasure of the state into your own, for such an action is not good and I shall not approve it. He who aspires to a political position with this goal in mind has always been destroyed by the state itself regardless of the power of ingenuity which he might command. Everyone who ...

CONTRASTING VIEWS

Christians in the Empire: Conspirators or Faithful Subjects?

Ancient Romans worried that new religions might disrupt the long-standing "peace with the gods" that guaranteed their national safety and prosperity. Groups whose religious creed seemed likely to offend the traditional deities could therefore be accused of treason, but Christians insisted that they were loyal subjects who prayed for the safety of the em... Looking up to heaven, the Christians—with hands outspread, because innocent, with head bare because we do not blush, yes! and without a prompter because we pray from the heart—are ever praying for all the emperors. We pray for a fortunate life for them, a secure rule, a safe house, brave armies, a faithful senate, a virtuous people ...

faced a
policy th
to those
(Docume

**1. TERT
HIS FELL

NEW SOURCES, NEW PERSPECTIVES

The Cairo Geniza

What do historians know about the daily life of ordinary people in the Middle Ages? Generally speaking, very little. We have writings from the intellectual elite and administrative documents from monasteries, churches, and courts. But these rarely mention ordinary folk, and if they do, it is always from the standpoint of those who are not ordinary themselves. Glimpsing the concerns, occupations, and family relations of medieval people as they went about their daily lives is very difficult—except at old Cairo (now called Fustat), in Egypt.

Cairo is exceptional because of a cache of un-

Many of these documents were purchased by American and English collectors and ended up in libraries in New York, Philadelphia, and Cambridge, England, where they remain. As is often the case in historical research, the questions that scholars ask are just as important as the sources themselves. At first, historians did not ask what the documents could tell them about everyday life. They wanted to know how to transcribe and read them; they wanted to study the evolution of their writing style (a dicipline called paleography). They also needed to organize the material. Dispersed among various libraries, the documents were a

Other engaging features investigate historical terms, evidence of cultural exchange, and qualitative data.

Terms of History identify a term central to history writing yet hotly debated.

Did You Know? features offer unexpected examples of cultural interchange between the West and the wider world.

Taking Measure data reveal how individual facts add up to broad trends and introduce important quantitative analysis skills.

TERMS OF HISTORY

Progress

Believing as they did in the possibilities of improvement, many Enlightenment writers preached a new doctrine about the meaning of human history. They challenged the traditional Christian belief that the original sin of Adam and Eve condemned human beings to un- you was a bottomless pit." In the movement toward postmodernism, which began in the 1970s, critics argued that we should no longer be satisfied with the modern; the modern brought us calamity and disaster, not reason and freedom. They wanted to go beyond the modern, hence The most influential Frenchman Michel 970s and 1980s that

DID YOU KNOW?

Tobacco and the Invention of "Smoking"

In the early seventeenth century, a "new astonishing fashion," wrote a German ambassador, came to the Dutch Republic from the New World. The term *smoking* gradually evolved in the seventeenth century out of "a fog-drinking bout," "drinking smoke," or "drinking tobacco." One Jesuit preacher called it "dry drunkenness." The analogy to inebriation is not entirely far-fetched, for nicotine (named after the French ambassador to Portugal panded their exports of tobacco sixfold between 1663 and 1699. Until 1700, Amsterdam dominated the curing process; half the tobacco factories in Amsterdam were owned by Jewish merchants of Spanish or Portuguese descent.

Smoking spread geographically from western to eastern Europe, socially from the upper classes downward, and from men to women. At first the Spanish preferred cigars, the British pipes, and

TAKING MEASURE

Read the **art and map captions** to help you analyze images and place events.

The Exotic as Consumer Item
This painting by the Venetian artist Rosalba Carriera (1675–1757) is titled *Africa*. The young black girl wearing a turban represents the African continent. Carriera was known for her use of pastels. In 1720, she journeyed to Paris where she became an associate of Antoine Watteau and helped inaugurate the rococo style in painting. Why did the artist choose to paint an African girl for this picture? **For more help analyzing this image,** see the visual activity for this chapter in the Online Study Guide at **bedfordstmartins.com/hunt.** *Staatliche Kunstsammlungen Dresden, Gemaldegalerie Alte Meister.*

Web references direct you to visual activities at the Online Study Guide.

MAP 17.2 State Building in Central and Eastern Europe, 1648–1699
The Austrian Habsburgs had long contested the Ottoman Turks for dominance of eastern Europe, and by 1699 they had pushed the Turks out of Hungary. In central Europe, the Austrian Habsburgs confronted the growing power of Brandenburg-Prussia, which had emerged from relative obscurity after the Thirty Years' War to begin an aggressive program of expanding its military and its territorial base. As emperor of the Holy Roman Empire, the Austrian Habsburg ruler governed a huge expanse of territory, but the emperor's control was in fact only partial because of guarantees of local autonomy.

Full-size maps show major historical developments and carry informative captions.

Mapping the West summary maps provide a snapshot of the West at the close of each chapter.

"Spot" maps offer geographic details right where you need them.

officers, in fact the dukes of Benevento and Spoleto ruled on their own behalf. Although many Lombards were Catholics, others, including important kings and dukes, were Arian. The "official" religion of **Lombard Italy** varied with the ruler in power. Rather than signal a major political event, the conversion of the Lombards to Catholic Christianity occurred gradually, ending only around the mid-seventh century. Partly as a result of this slow development, the Lombard kings, unlike the Visigoths, Franks, or even the

Lombard Italy, Early Eighth Century

MAPPING THE WEST Europe and Byzantium, C. 1215
The major transformation in the map of the West between 1150 and 1215 was the conquest of Constantinople and the setting up of European rule there until 1261. The Byzantine Empire was now a mere shell. A new state, Epirus, emerged in the power vacuum to dominate Thrace. Bulgaria once again gained its independence. If Venice had hoped to control the Adriatic by conquering Constantinople, it must have been disappointed, for Hungary became its rival over the ports of the Dalmatian coast.

Organize your study plans with review sections at the end of each chapter.

Chapter conclusions tie together the chapter's thematic strands, review main topics, and point you onward.

Annotated lists of suggested references provide print and web resources for papers, research projects, or further study.

39 CHAPTER 1 • FOUNDATIONS OF WESTERN CIVILIZATION
c. 4000–c. 1000 B.C.E.

UNITY AND DIVERSITY IN EARLY SOCIETIES 39
c. 4000–c. 1000 B.C.E.

forced them to wander abroad in search of new places to settle. Like people from the earliest times, these devastated ancestors of Western civilization had to move to build a better life.

Review: How did war determine the fates of the early civilizations of Crete, Anatolia, and Greece?

Conclusion

Western civilization emerged in Mesopotamia and Egypt; these cultures in turn influenced the later civilization of Greece. Cities first arose in Mesopotamia by around 3000 B.C.E. Hierarchy characterized society to some degree from the very beginning, but it grew more pronounced once civilization emerged.

Trade and war were constants, both aiming in different ways at profit and glory. Indirectly, they often generated energetic cultural interaction by putting civilizations into close contact to learn from one another. Technological innovation was also a prominent characteristic of this long period. The invention of metallurgy, monumental architecture, mathematics, and alphabetic writing greatly affected the future. Religion was at the center of people's lives, with the gods seen as demanding just and righteous conduct from everyone. The emergence of monotheism set the stage for the leading faiths of later Western history.

have seemed destined for irreversible economic and social decline, even oblivion. Chapter 2 shows how wrong this prediction would have been. After a dark period of economic and population decline called the Dark Age, Greeks invented a new form of social and political organization and breathed renewed life into their culture, inspired by their neighbors in the Near East and Egypt.

Suggested References

Mesopotamia, Home of the First Civilization, c. 4000–c. 1000 B.C.E.

Archaeological exploration in Mesopotamia (present-day Iraq) has been almost completely halted for more than a decade. Scholars have therefore been limited to studying already excavated material and texts. Modern translations have made Mesopotamian myths more accessible to today's readers.

Alcock, Susan, et al., eds. *Empires.* 2001.
Ancient Near East: http://www.etana.org/abzu.
Aruz, Joan, ed. *Art of the First Cities: The Third Millennium B.C. from the Mediterranean to the Indus.* 2003.
Bertman, Stephen. *Handbook to Life in Ancient Mesopotamia.* 2003.
Bienkowski, Piotr, and Alan Millard, eds. *Dictionary of the Ancient Near East.* 2000.
Bottéro, Jean. *Everyday Life in Mesopotamia.* Trans. Antonia Nevill. 2001.
Collins, Billie Jean. *A History of the Animal World in the Ancient Near East.* 2002.
...ord, Harriet. *Sumer and the Sumerians.* ...1.
...y, Stephanie, trans. *Myths from Mesopotamia: Creation, The Flood, Gilgamesh, and ...ers.* 1991.
...ews, Roger. *Archaeology of Mesopotamia: ...ories and Approaches.* 2003.
...ardson, M. E. J. *Hammurabi's Laws: Text, ...nslation and Glossary.* 2000.
...ng, William H., Jr. *Ancient Near Eastern ...tory and Culture.* 2003.
...rian literature. http://www-etcsl.orient ...ac.uk.
...ry sources.

CHAPTER REVIEW

Important Events lists help you review key happenings at a glance.

IMPORTANT EVENTS

c. 500–323 B.C.E.	Classical Age of Greek History
499–479 B.C.E.	Wars between Persia and Greece
490 B.C.E.	Battle of Marathon
480–479 B.C.E.	Xerxes' invasion of Greece
480 B.C.E.	Battle of Salamis
479 B.C.E.	Battles of Plataea and Mycale
461 B.C.E.	Ephialtes reforms the Athenian court system
Early 450s B.C.E.	Pericles introduces pay for office holders in Athenian democracy
454 B.C.E.	Catastrophic defeat of Athenian fleet by Persians in Egypt kills tens of thousands of oarsmen
451 B.C.E.	Pericles sponsors law to restrict Athenian citizenship to children whose parents are both citizens
c. 450 B.C.E.	Protagoras and other Sophists begin to move to Athens to teach
446–445 B.C.E. (winter)	Peace treaty between Athens and Sparta; intended to last thirty years
431 B.C.E.	Euripides presents the tragedy *Medea*
431–404 B.C.E.	Peloponnesian War
420s B.C.E.	Herodotus finishes *Histories*, the first great Greek work of history writing
415–413 B.C.E.	Enormous Athenian military expedition against Sicily
411 B.C.E.	Aristophanes presents the comedy *Lysistrata*
404–403 B.C.E.	Rule of the Thirty Tyrants at Athens
403 B.C.E.	Restoration of democracy

Key terms highlight important concepts with page references that point to the text discussion. Each term is defined in the **glossary** at the end of the book.

KEY TERMS

agora (93)
Delian League (88)
frieze (95)
hetaira (99)
hubris (114)
metic (97)
mystery cult (97)
ostracism (91)
radical democracy (90)
Socratic method (109)
Sophists (106)
subjectivism (106)
symposium (plural "symposia") (99)
trireme (89)

Review Questions offer section-by-section comprehension prompts.

REVIEW QUESTIONS

1. What differences in Greek and Persian political and military organization determined the course of the Persian Wars?
2. What factors prompted political change in fifth-century B.C.E. Athens?
3. How did new ways of thinking in the Golden Age threaten cherished traditions?
4. How did unexpected events contribute to the outcome of the Peloponnesian War?

MAKING CONNECTIONS

1. What were the most significant differences between Greece in the Archaic Age and in the Golden Age?
2. What did Greeks of the Golden Age believe it was worth spending public funds to pay for and why?

FOR FURTHER EXPLORATION

To assess your mastery of the material in this chapter, see the Online Study Guide at bedfordstmartins.com/hunt.

To read additional primary-source material from this period, see Chapter 3 in *Sources of The Making of the West,* Second Edition.

Making Connections analytical questions help you link ideas within or across chapters.

For Further Exploration points you to free online activities that help you master the chapter material and to additional chapter-related primary sources.

See the preface for a full list of student resources, including the Online Study Guide, that accompany *The Making of the West: Peoples and Cultures,* Second Edition.

How to Read Primary Sources

In each chapter of this textbook you will find many primary sources to broaden your understanding of the development of the West. Primary sources refer to firsthand, contemporary accounts or direct evidence about a particular topic. For example, speeches, letters, diaries, song lyrics, and newspaper articles are all primary sources that historians use to construct accounts of the past. Nonwritten materials such as maps, paintings, artifacts, and even architecture and music can also be primary sources. Both types of historical documents in this textbook—written and visual—provide a glimpse into the lives of the men and women who influenced or were influenced by the course of Western history.

    To guide your interpretation of any source, you should begin by asking several basic questions, listed below, as starting points for observing, analyzing, and interpreting the past. Your answers should prompt further questions of your own.

1. **Who is the author?** Who wrote or created the material? What was his or her authority? (Personal? institutional?) Did the author have specialized knowledge or experience? If you are reading a written document, how would you describe the author's tone of voice? (Formal, personal, angry?)

2. **Who is the audience?** Who were the intended readers, listeners, or viewers? How does the intended audience affect the ways that the author presents ideas?

3. **What are the main ideas?** What are the main points that the author is trying to convey? Can you detect any underlying assumptions of values or attitudes? How does the form or medium affect the meaning of this document?

4. **In what context was the document created?** From when and where does the document originate? What was the interval between the initial problem or event and this document, which responded to it? Through what form or medium was the document communicated? (For example, a newspaper, a government record, an illustration.) What contemporary events or conditions might have affected the creation of the document?

5. **What's missing?** What's missing or cannot be learned from this source, and what might this omission reveal? Are there other sources that might fill in the gaps?

Now consider these questions as you read the following document, "Columbus Describes His First Voyage, 1493." Compare your answers to the sample observations provided.

Columbus Describes His First Voyage, 1493

In this famous letter to Raphael Sanchez, treasurer to his patrons, Ferdinand and Isabella, Columbus recounts his initial journey to the Bahamas, Cuba, and Hispaniola (today Haiti and the Dominican Republic), and tells of his achievements. This passage reflects the first contact between Native Americans and Europeans; already the themes of trade, subjugation, gold, and conversion all emerge in Columbus's own words.

Indians would give whatever the seller required; …Thus they bartered, like idiots, cotton and gold for fragments of bows, glasses, bottles, and jars; which I forbad as being unjust, and myself gave them many beautiful and acceptable articles which I had brought with me, taking nothing from them in return; I did this in order that I might the more easily conciliate them, that they might be led to become Christians, and be inclined to entertain a regard for the King and Queen, our Princes and all Spaniards, and that I might induce them to take an interest in seeking out, and collecting, and delivering to us such things as they possessed in abundance, but which we greatly needed. They practise no kind of idolatry, but have a firm belief that all strength and power, and indeed all good things, are in heaven, and that I had descended from thence with these ships and sailors, and under this impression was I received after they had thrown aside their fears. Nor are they slow or stupid, but of very clear understanding; and those men who have crossed to the neighbouring islands give an admirable description of everything they observed; but they never saw any people clothed, nor any ships like ours. On my arrival at that sea, I had taken some Indians by force from the first island that I came to, in order that they might learn our language, and communicate to us what they know respecting the country; which plan succeeded excellently, and was a great advantage to us, for in a short time, either by gestures and signs, or by words, we were enabled to understand each other. These men are still travelling with me, and although they have been with us now a long time, they continue to entertain the idea that I have descended from heaven.

Source: Christopher Columbus, *Four Voyages to the New World*. Translated by R. H. Major (New York: Corinth Books, 1961), 8–9.

1. **Who is the author?** The title and headnote that precede each document contain information about the authorship and date of its creation. In this case, the Italian explorer Christopher Columbus is the author. His letter describes events in which he was both an eyewitness and a participant.

2. **Who is the audience?** Columbus sent the letter to Raphael Sanchez, treasurer to Ferdinand and Isabella—someone who Columbus knew would be keenly interested in the fate of his patrons' investment. Because the letter was also a public document written to a crown official, Columbus would have expected a wider audience beyond Sanchez. How might his letter have differed had it been written to a friend?

3. **What are the main ideas?** In this segment, Columbus describes his encounter with the native people. He speaks of his desire to establish good relations by treating them fairly, and he offers his impressions of their intelligence and naiveté—characteristics he implies will prove useful to Europeans. He also expresses an interest in converting them to Christianity and making them loyal subjects of the crown.

4. **In what context was the document was created?** Columbus wrote the letter in 1493, within six months of his first voyage. He would have been eager to announce the success of his endeavor.

5. **What's missing?** Columbus's letter provides just one view of the encounter. We do not have a corresponding account from the Native Americans' perspective nor from anyone else travelling with Columbus. With no corroboration evidence, how reliable is this description?

Note: You can use these same questions to analyze visual images. Start by determining who created the image—whether it's a painting, photograph, sculpture, map, or artifact—and when it was made. Then consider the audience for whom the artist might have intended the work and how viewers might have reacted. Consult the text for information about the time period, and look for visual cues such as color, artistic style, and use of space to determine the central idea of the work. As you read, consult the captions in this book to help you evaluate the images and to ask more questions of your own.

Authors' Note

The B.C.E./C.E. Dating System

"When were you born?" "What year is it?" We customarily answer questions like these with a number, such as "1987" or "2004." Our replies are usually automatic, taking for granted the numerous assumptions Westerners make about how dates indicate chronology. But to what do numbers such as 1987 and 2004 actually refer? In this book the numbers used to specify dates follow a recent revision of the system most common in the Western secular world. This system reckons the dates of solar years by counting backward and forward from the traditional date of the birth of Jesus Christ, over two thousand years ago.

Using this method, numbers followed by the abbreviation B.C.E., standing for "before the common era" (or, as some would say, "before the Christian era"), indicate the number of years counting backward from the assumed date of the birth of Jesus Christ. B.C.E. therefore indicates the same chronology marked by the traditional abbreviation B.C. ("before Christ"). The larger the number following B.C.E. (or B.C.), the earlier in history is the year to which it refers. The date 431 B.C.E., for example, refers to a year 431 years before the birth of Jesus and therefore comes earlier in time than the dates 430 B.C.E., 429 B.C.E., and so on. The same calculation applies to numbering other time intervals calculated on the decimal system: those of ten years (a decade), of one hundred years (a century), and of one thousand years (a millennium). For example, the decade of the 440s B.C.E. (449 B.C.E. to 440 B.C.E.) is earlier than the decade of the 430s B.C.E. (439 B.C.E. to 430 B.C.E.). "Fifth century B.C.E." refers to the fifth period of 100 years reckoning backward from the birth of Jesus and covers the years 500 B.C.E. to 401 B.C.E. It is earlier in history than the fourth century B.C.E. (400 B.C.E. to 301 B.C.E.), which followed the fifth century B.C.E. Because this system has no year "zero," the first century B.C.E. covers the years 100 B.C.E. to 1 B.C.E. Dating millennia works similarly: the second millennium B.C.E. refers to the years 2000 B.C.E. to 1001 B.C.E., the third millennium to the years 3000 B.C.E. to 2001 B.C.E., and so on.

To indicate years counted forward from the traditional date of Jesus' birth, numbers are followed by the abbreviation C.E., standing for "of the common era" (or "of the Christian era"). C.E. therefore indicates the same chronology marked by the traditional abbreviation A.D., which stands for the Latin phrase *anno Domini* ("in the year of the Lord"). A.D. properly comes before the date being marked. The date A.D. 1492, for example, translates as "in the year of the Lord 1492," meaning 1492 years after the birth of Jesus. Under the B.C.E./C.E. system, this date would be written as 1492 C.E. For dating centuries, the term "first century C.E." refers to the period from 1 C.E. to 100 C.E. (which is the same period as A.D. 1 to A.D. 100). For dates C.E., the smaller the number, the earlier the date in history. The fourth century C.E. (301 C.E. to 400 C.E.) comes before the fifth century C.E. (401 C.E. to 500 C.E.). The year 312 C.E. is a date in the early fourth century C.E., while 395 C.E. is a date late in the same century. When numbers are given without either B.C.E. or C.E., they are presumed to be dates C.E. For example, the term *eighteenth century* with no abbreviation accompanying it refers to the years 1701 C.E. to 1800 C.E.

No standard system of numbering years, such as B.C.E./C.E., existed in antiquity. Different people in different places identified years with varying names and numbers. Consequently, it was difficult to match up the years in any particular local system with those in a different system. Each city of ancient Greece, for example, had its own method for keeping track of the years. The ancient Greek historian Thucydides, therefore, faced a problem in presenting a chronology for the famous Peloponnesian War between Athens and Sparta, which began (by our reckoning) in 431 B.C.E. To try to explain to as many of his readers as possible the date the war had begun, he described its first year by three different local systems: "the year when Chrysis was in the forty-eighth year of her priesthood at Argos, and Aenesias was overseer at Sparta, and Pythodorus was magistrate at Athens."

A Catholic monk named Dionysius, who lived in Rome in the sixth century C.E., invented the system of reckoning dates forward from the birth of Jesus. Calling himself *Exiguus* (Latin for "the little" or "the small") as a mark of humility, he placed Jesus' birth 754 years after the foundation of ancient Rome. Others then and now believe his date for Jesus' birth was in fact several years too late. Many scholars today calculate that Jesus was born in what would be 4 B.C.E. according to Dionysius's system, although a date a year or so earlier also seems possible.

Counting backward from the supposed date of Jesus' birth to indicate dates earlier than that event represented a natural complement to reckoning forward for dates after it. The English historian and theologian Bede in the early eighth century was the first to use both forward and backward reckoning from the birth of Jesus in a historical work, and this system gradually gained wider acceptance because it provided a basis for standardizing the many local calendars used in the Western Christian world. Nevertheless, B.C. and A.D. were not used regularly until the end of the eighteenth century. B.C.E. and C.E. became common in the late twentieth century.

The system of numbering years from the birth of Jesus is far from the only one in use today. The Jewish calendar of years, for example, counts forward from the date given to the creation of the world, which would be calculated as 3761 B.C.E. under the B.C.E./C.E. system. Under this system, years are designated A.M., an abbreviation of the Latin *anno mundi*, "in the year of the world." The Islamic calendar counts forward from the date of the prophet Muhammad's flight from Mecca, called the *Hijra*, in what is the year 622 C.E. The abbreviation A.H. (standing for the Latin phrase *anno Hegirae*, "in the year of the Hijra") indicates dates calculated by this system. Anthropology commonly reckons distant dates as "before the present" (abbreviated B.P.).

History is often defined as the study of change over time; hence the importance of dates for the historian. But just as historians argue over which dates are most significant, they disagree over which dating system to follow. Their debate reveals perhaps the most enduring fact about history—its vitality.

Elevation

Feet	Meters
Over 13,120	Over 4,001
6,561–13,120	2,001–4,000
1,641–6,560	501–2,000
661–1640	201–500
0–660	0–200
Below sea level	Below sea level

⊛ National capital

● Major city

0   150   300 miles
0   150   300 kilometers

ATLANTIC OCEAN

North Sea

Baltic Sea

NORWAY
Bergen
Oslo
SWEDEN
Stockholm
Göteborg

SCOTLAND
Glasgow
Edinburgh

NORTHERN IRELAND
Belfast

IRELAND
Dublin
Cork

UNITED KINGDOM
Liverpool
Birmingham
WALES
ENGLAND
Thames R.
London

Aarhus
DENMARK
Copenhagen

Gdańsk

NETHERLANDS
Amsterdam
Rotterdam
Antwerp
Brussels
BELGIUM

Elbe R.
Berlin
POLAND

GERMANY
Frankfurt
Rhine R.
Oder R.

English Channel

Paris
Seine R.
Luxembourg
LUXEMBOURG

Prague
CZECH REP.
Brno

Loire R.

FRANCE

LIECHTENSTEIN
Munich
Vienna
Bratislava
Danube R.
Zürich
Vaduz
Bern
Innsbruck
AUSTRIA
SWITZERLAND
Graz
Budapest

Bay of Biscay

Lyon

Milan
Rhône R.
Po R.
SLOVENIA
Ljubljana
Zagreb
CROATIA

Oporto
PORTUGAL
Ebro R.
PYRENEES
ANDORRA
Andorra la Vella
Marseille
MONACO

San Marino
SAN MARINO
APENNINES
Adriatic Sea
Split
BOSNIA AND HERZEGOVINA
Sarajevo

Lisbon
SPAIN
Madrid
Barcelona

Corsica
Sardinia
Tyrrhenian Sea
Rome
ITALY
Naples

Seville

BALEARIC IS.

Gibraltar (Br.)

Algiers

Palermo
Sicily

Ionian Sea

Rabat

Tunis

Valletta
MALTA

MOROCCO

TUNISIA

Tripoli

ALGERIA

LIBYA

N
W   E
S

80 N

Greenland
(Den.)

ICELAND

Alaska

60 N

CANADA

UNITED
KINGDOM

IRELAND

FRANCE

SPAIN

40 N

UNITED STATES

PORTUGAL

Azores
(Port.)

ATLANTIC
OCEAN

MOROCCO

Canary Is.
(Sp.)

Western Sahara
(Mor.)

BAHAMAS

DOMINICAN
REPUBLIC

HAITI

Puerto Rico (U.S.)

MEXICO

MAURITANIA

20 N

Hawaii

CUBA

JAMAICA

BELIZE

CAPE
VERDE

ST. KITTS AND NEVIS

ANTIGUA AND BARBUDA

Guadeloupe (Fr.)

DOMINICA

SENEGAL

MALI

GUATEMALA

HONDURAS

Martinique (Fr.)

ST. VINCENT AND THE GRENADINES

GAMBIA

EL SALVADOR

NICARAGUA

ST. LUCIA

BARBADOS

GUINEA-BISSAU

GRENADA

GUINEA

COSTA RICA

TRINIDAD AND TOBAGO

SIERRA LEONE

PACIFIC OCEAN

PANAMA

VENEZUELA

GUYANA

SURINAME

LIBERIA

CÔTE D'IVOIRE

COLOMBIA

French Guiana (Fr.)

BURKINA FASO

0

Equator

GHANA

Galápagos Is.
(Ec.)

ECUADOR

BRAZIL

SAMOA

PERU

TONGA

20 S

BOLIVIA

Easter I.
(Chile)

PARAGUAY

CHILE

ATLANTIC
OCEAN

URUGUAY

0   1,500   3,000 miles

0   1,500   3,000 kilometers

ARGENTINA

40 S

Falkland Is.
(U.K.)

60 S

80 S

160 W   140 W   120 W   100 W   80 W   60 W   40 W   20 W

ARCTIC OCEAN

NORWAY
SWEDEN
FINLAND
DEN.
NETH.
BEL.
LUX.
GERMANY
POLAND
CZ. REP.
ESTONIA
LATVIA
LITHUANIA
BELARUS
UKRAINE
MOLDOVA
AUS.
SLK.
SLN.
HUNG.
SWITZ.
CR.
ITALY
S.M.
ROMANIA
B.H.
MAC.
BULGARIA
ALB.
GREECE
TUNISIA
MALTA
CYPRUS
ISRAEL
LEBANON
SYRIA
JORDAN
GEORGIA
ARMENIA
AZERBAIJAN
TURKEY
IRAQ
IRAN
KUWAIT
BAHRAIN
SAUDI ARABIA
QATAR
UNITED ARAB
EMIRATES
OMAN

RUSSIAN FEDERATION

KAZAKHSTAN

UZBEKISTAN
KYRGYZSTAN
TURKMENISTAN
TAJIKISTAN
AFGHANISTAN
PAKISTAN

MONGOLIA

N. KOREA
S. KOREA
JAPAN

CHINA

TAIWAN

PACIFIC OCEAN

ERIA
LIBYA
EGYPT

NIGER
CHAD
SUDAN
ERITREA
DJIBOUTI
YEMEN

NEPAL
BHUTAN
BANGLADESH
INDIA
MYANMAR
(BURMA)
THAILAND
LAOS
VIETNAM
CAMBODIA

PHILIPPINES

Mariana Is.
(U.S.)

Guam
(U.S.)

MARSHALL
IS.

NIGERIA
BENIN
TOGO
CENTRAL
AFRICAN REP.
ETHIOPIA
SOMALIA

CAMEROON
EQ.
GUINEA
GABON
SÃO TOMÉ
& PRÍNCIPE
CONGO
DEM. REP. OF
THE CONGO
RWANDA
BURUNDI
UGANDA
KENYA
TANZANIA

MALDIVES

SRI
LANKA

BRUNEI

MALAYSIA

SINGAPORE

PALAU

FEDERATED STATES
OF MICRONESIA

NAURU

KIRIBATI

TUVALU

COMOROS
SEYCHELLES

INDIAN OCEAN

INDONESIA

PAPUA
NEW
GUINEA

EAST
TIMOR

SOLOMON
IS.

ANGOLA
ZAMBIA
MALAWI
ZIMBABWE
MADAGASCAR

NAMIBIA
BOTSWANA

MAURITIUS

VANUATU

FIJI

New Caledonia
(Fr.)

SOUTH
AFRICA
MOZAMBIQUE
SWAZILAND
LESOTHO

AUSTRALIA

NEW
ZEALAND

Tasmania
(Aust.)

N
W   E
S

Abbreviations	
ALB.	ALBANIA
AUS.	AUSTRIA
BEL.	BELGIUM
B.H.	BOSNIA AND HERZEGOVINA
CR.	CROATIA
CZ. REP.	CZECH REPUBLIC
DEN.	DENMARK
HUNG.	HUNGARY
LUX.	LUXEMBOURG
MAC.	MACEDONIA
NETH.	NETHERLANDS
S.M.	SERBIA AND MONTENEGRO
SLK.	SLOVAKIA
SLN.	SLOVENIA
SWITZ.	SWITZERLAND

ANTARCTICA

20 E   40 E   60 E   80 E   100 E   120 E   140 E   160 E

About the Authors

LYNN HUNT, Eugen Weber Professor of Modern European History at the University of California, Los Angeles, received her B.A. from Carleton College and her M.A. and Ph.D. from Stanford University. She is the author of *Revolution and Urban Politics in Provincial France* (1978); *Politics, Culture, and Class in the French Revolution* (1984); and *The Family Romance of the French Revolution* (1992). She is also the coauthor of *Telling the Truth about History* (1994); coauthor of *Liberty, Equality, Fraternity: Exploring the French Revolution* (2001, with CD-ROM); editor of *The New Cultural History* (1989); editor and translator of *The French Revolution and Human Rights* (1996); and coeditor of *Histories: French Constructions of the Past* (1995), *Beyond the Cultural Turn* (1999), and *Human Rights and Revolutions* (2000). She has been awarded fellowships by the Guggenheim Foundation and the National Endowment for the Humanities and is a fellow of the American Academy of Arts and Sciences. She served as president of the American Historical Association in 2002.

THOMAS R. MARTIN, Jeremiah O'Connor Professor in Classics at the College of the Holy Cross, earned his B.A. at Princeton University and his M.A. and Ph.D. at Harvard University. He is the author of *Sovereignty and Coinage in Classical Greece* (1985) and *Ancient Greece* (1996, 2000) and one of the originators of *Perseus 1.0: Interactive Sources and Studies on Ancient Greece* (1992, 1996, and www.perseus.tufts.edu), which, among other awards, was named the EDUCOM Best Software in Social Sciences (History) in 1992. He also wrote the lead article on ancient Greece for the revised edition of the *Encarta* electronic encyclopedia. He serves on the editorial board of STOA (www.stoa.org) and as codirector of its DEMOS project (online resources on ancient Athenian democracy). A recipient of fellowships from the National Endowment for the Humanities and the American Council of Learned Societies, he is currently conducting research on the comparative historiography of ancient Greece and ancient China.

BARBARA H. ROSENWEIN, professor of history at Loyola University Chicago, earned her B.A., M.A., and Ph.D. at the University of Chicago. She is the author of *Rhinoceros Bound: Cluny in the Tenth Century* (1982); *To Be the Neighbor of Saint Peter: The Social Meaning of Cluny's Property, 909–1049* (1989); *Negotiating Space: Power, Restraint, and Privileges of Immunity in Early Medieval Europe* (1999); and *A Short History of the Middle Ages* (2001). She is the editor of *Anger's Past: The Social Uses of an Emotion in the Middle Ages* (1998) and coeditor of *Debating the Middle Ages: Issues and Readings* (1998) and *Monks and Nuns,*

Saints and Outcasts: Religion in Medieval Society (2000). A recipient of Guggenheim and National Endowment for the Humanities fellowships, she is currently working on a history of emotions in the early Middle Ages.

R. PO-CHIA HSIA, Edwin Erle Sparks Professor of History at Pennsylvania State University, received his B.A. from Swarthmore College and his M.A. and Ph.D. from Yale University. He is the author of *Society and Religion in Münster, 1535–1618* (1984); *The Myth of Ritual Murder: Jews and Magic in Reformation Germany* (1988); *Social Discipline in the Reformation: Central Europe 1550–1750* (1989); *Trent 1475: Stories of a Ritual Murder Trial* (1992); and *The World of the Catholic Renewal* (1997). He has edited *The German People and the Reformation* (1998); *In and Out of the Ghetto: Jewish-Gentile Relations in Late Medieval and Early Modern Germany* (1995); *Calvinism and Religious Toleration in the Dutch Golden Age* (2002); and *A Companion to the Reformation World* (Blackwell Companion Series, 2004). An academician at the Academia Sinica, Taiwan, he has also been awarded fellowships by the Woodrow Wilson International Society of Scholars, the National Endowment for the Humanities, the Guggenheim Foundation, the Davis Center of Princeton University, the Mellon Foundation, the American Council of Learned Societies, and the American Academy in Berlin. Currently he is working on the cultural contacts between Europe and Asia between the sixteenth and eighteenth centuries.

BONNIE G. SMITH, Board of Governors Professor of History at Rutgers University, earned her B.A. at Smith College and her Ph.D. at the University of Rochester. She is the author of *Ladies of the Leisure Class* (1981); *Confessions of a Concierge: Madame Lucie's History of Twentieth-Century France* (1985); *Changing Lives: Women in European History Since 1700* (1989); *The Gender of History: Men, Women, and Historical Practice* (1998); and *Imperialism* (2000). She is also the coauthor and translator of *What Is Property?* (1994); editor of *Global Feminisms since 1945* (2000); and coeditor of *Objects of Modernity: Selected Writings of Lucy Maynard Salmon, Gendering Disability* (2004) and the forthcoming *Oxford Encyclopedia of Women in World History*. She has received fellowships from the Guggenheim Foundation, the National Endowment for the Humanities, the National Humanities Center, the Davis Center of Princeton University, and the American Council of Learned Societies. Currently she is studying the globalization of European culture since the seventeenth century.

SECOND EDITION

The Making of the West

PEOPLES AND CULTURES

Prologue:
Before Civilization,
to c. 4000 B.C.E.

IN 1997, A TEAM OF ARCHAEOLOGISTS IN ETHIOPIA spied pieces of fossilized bone embedded in hard sand. They scraped away the dirt to reveal the fragments, which fit together to form an adult skull, missing its lower jaw. Deep cut marks scarred the surface of the skull. The archaeologists soon found pieces of other skulls, including a much smaller one. Radioisotope analysis of the bones produced a startling analysis: dated to about 160,000 years ago, they were the oldest remains ever found of the species **Homo sapiens** ("wise human being")—people whose brains and appearances were similar (though not identical) to ours today. Before this, no one had ever discovered fossils near as old as these that could be securely identified as *Homo sapiens*. The discovery excited scientists because it seemed to confirm what previously had been only a theory: that *Homo sapiens* first appeared in Africa around 160,000 to 200,000 years ago and spread from there all over the world.

New discoveries keep making new history, which means that answers to important questions, such as those concerning human origins, can change. Also, past discoveries can be reinterpreted through new research, which means that historians regularly open new debates over the meaning of what has already been found. As part of doing history, therefore, experts argue and often disagree over the significance of evidence. Some scientists, for example, contest the "out of Africa" theory of human origins, arguing for a multiregional model according to which human beings arose in different parts of the world. They hope that future discoveries of fossilized human bones in widely different places will prove them correct. Research concerning the periods, locations, and ways in which human beings came into existence and populated the world thus fuels one of the hottest topics in contemporary archaeology and anthropology.

**The Paleolithic Age,
c. 200,000–c. 10,000 B.C.E.**
- The Life of Hunter-Gatherers
- Trade, Technology, Religion, and Hierarchy

**The Neolithic Age,
c. 10,000–c. 4000 B.C.E.**
- The Neolithic Revolution
- Neolithic Origins of Modern Life
- Daily Life in the Neolithic Village of Çatalhöyük
- Social Change in the Neolithic Age

Stone Age Handaxe
Archaeologists found this stone cutting tool, called a handaxe, at the site in Ethiopia where they also discovered the bones of the oldest known ancestors of the species Homo sapiens—people closely resembling modern human beings. These early people probably used a hammer made from bone or wood to chip off flakes from the stone to create knifelike edges for cutting. This sharp tool would have been especially useful for butchering animals, such as the hippopotamuses that these hunter-gatherers killed for meat. Shown here at its full size (seven and a half inches top to bottom), the tool would have fit into the palm; perhaps users wrapped it in a piece of hide to protect their hands from cuts. *Paleoanthropology Laboratory, National Museum of Ethiopia, Addis Ababa. Photo © 2001 David L. Brill/Atlanta.*

A crucial point on which researchers agree is that the deepest roots of human history tunnel far into the past. The scientific dating of fossilized bones supports genetic studies on human mitochondrial DNA to suggest that human beings developed slowly over millions of years before the emergence of *Homo sapiens*. Researchers disagree on precisely how long it took for the descendents of *Homo sapiens* to become the most recent type of human being—people exactly like us. They call this modern type *Homo sapiens sapiens* ("wise, wise human being"). Originating in sub-Saharan Africa more than fifty thousand years ago, bands of these modern-type human beings had moved out of Africa by some forty-five thousand years ago to settle across the Near East,[1] Europe, and Asia, becoming the ancestors of everyone alive today.

---

[1]The term *Near East*, like *Middle East*, has undergone several changes in meaning over time. Both terms reflect the geographical point of view of Europeans. Today, the term *Middle East*, more commonly employed in politics and journalism than in history, usually refers to the area encompassing the Arabic-speaking countries of the eastern Mediterranean region, Israel, Iran, Turkey, Cyprus, and much of North Africa. Ancient historians, by contrast, generally use the term *ancient Near East* to designate Anatolia (often called Asia Minor, today occupied by the Asian portion of Turkey), Cyprus, the lands around the eastern end of the Mediterranean, the Arabian peninsula, Mesopotamia (the lands north of the Persian Gulf, today Iraq and Iran), and Egypt. In this book we will observe the common usage of the term *Near East* to mean the lands of southwestern Asia and Egypt.

❖ The Paleolithic Age, c. 200,000–c. 10,000 B.C.E.

Archaeology is our only source of information about the extended period of human history before 10,000 B.C.E.; there are no documents to inform us about the lives of early human beings because people did not invent writing until about 4000–3000 B.C.E. For this reason, historians sometimes label the time before the invention of writing as "prehistory," because "history" traditionally implies having written sources about the past. It is also possible to label this period "precivilization" because these early people did not live in cities, the main characteristic that historians use to distinguish the word *civilization*. (The first cities emerged about the same time as writing, as we will see in Chapter 1.) Both *prehistory* and *precivilization* are contested terms because they can be taken to mean that people without writing or cities were "primitive," when in fact they developed complex ways of life.

The period in which these early peoples lived is called the Stone Age because they made their most durable tools from stone. The Stone Age saw the most significant change in all of ancient human history: people learned how to produce their own food by farming instead of only hunting for it in the wild. This discovery changed almost everything about how people have lived since. To mark this momentous turning point, archaeologists divide the Stone Age into two periods, one before people farmed for a living—the **Paleolithic** ("Old Stone") period and one after, the **Neolithic** ("New Stone") period.

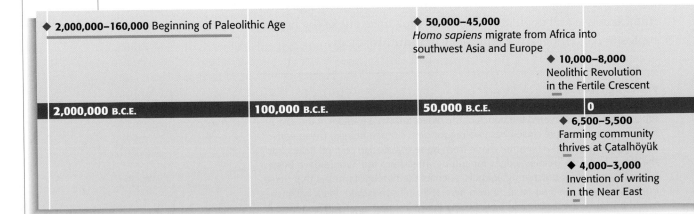

◆ 2,000,000–160,000 Beginning of Paleolithic Age

◆ 50,000–45,000
Homo sapiens migrate from Africa into southwest Asia and Europe

◆ 10,000–8,000
Neolithic Revolution in the Fertile Crescent

| 2,000,000 B.C.E. | 100,000 B.C.E. | 50,000 B.C.E. | 0 |

◆ 6,500–5,500
Farming community thrives at Çatalhöyük

◆ 4,000–3,000
Invention of writing in the Near East

The Life of Hunter-Gatherers

Paleolithic peoples lived a radically different life from the settled existence most of us now take for granted: they roamed all their lives, never settling permanently in one place, always moving around because they had to hunt and gather their food in the wild. Although they knew a great deal about how to survive in the natural environment, they had not yet learned to produce their own food by growing crops and raising animals. Instead, they hunted wild game for meat, fished in lakes and rivers, collected shellfish along the shore, and gathered wild grains, fruits, and nuts. Historians refer to human beings who obtained their food in these ways as **hunter-gatherers**.

Archaeology reveals that the movement of the later *Homo sapiens sapiens* out of Africa around 50,000–45,000 B.C.E. was a crucial period in human history because it coincided with what some scientists call an explosion of inventiveness. People began devising new forms of tools, weapons, and jewelry and more elaborate burial customs. Climate change probably impelled people to leave Africa. Long periods without rain would have driven game animals into southwest Asia and then Europe to find water, and at least some of the mobile human populations who hunted them in African lands would have followed this moving food into new continents. There is no evidence explaining why some hunter-gatherers left Africa in the Paleolithic period while others stayed behind.

When *Homo sapiens sapiens* first appeared in Europe and Asia, they encountered earlier types of human beings that had migrated out of Africa long before, such as the heavy-browed, squat-bodied Neanderthal type (named after the Neander Valley in Germany, where their fossil remains were first found; their body type is often used to represent "cave men" in popular art). Eventually *Homo sapiens sapiens* completely replaced all earlier types of people around the globe, traversing then-existent land bridges to reach the Americas and Australia.

Archaeological exploration of early humans' campsites tells us about their lives on the move. In addition, anthropologists speculate about the lives of ancient hunter-gatherers on the basis of comparative study of the scattered groups of people who lived on as hunter-gatherers into modern times, such as the !Kung♦ San of Africa's Kalahari Desert in southern Africa, the Aborigines in Australia, and the Coahuiltecans♦ in the American Southwest. These two categories of evidence suggest that Paleolithic hunter-gatherers banded together in groups numbering around twenty or thirty people to hunt and forage for food that they shared with each other. Their average life expectancy was about twenty-five to thirty years. Since they had not learned to domesticate animals or to make wheels for carts, they walked everywhere. Because women of childbearing age had to carry and nurse their babies, they would have found it difficult to roam far from camp. They and the smaller children therefore gathered edible plants, fruits, and nuts close to camp and caught small animals such as frogs and rabbits. The plant food that they gathered provided the majority of the group's diet. Men did most of the hunting of large animals, which frequently took them a great distance away from camp to kill prey at close range with rocks and spears; butchered hippopotamus bones found near the skulls in Ethiopia show that early humans hunted these large and dangerous animals. Women probably participated in some hunts, especially when the group used large nets to ensnare game.

Although early people tended to divide their main labor—finding food—by gender, they recognized that both women and men did essential work in feeding their band. In fact, hunter-gatherers probably lived originally in societies that we would characterize as egalitarian, meaning that all adults enjoyed a general equality in making decisions for the group. Nevertheless, differences in social status probably existed. Older people of both genders gained prestige because of their wisdom, gained from long experience of life in an era when most people died of illness or accidents before they were thirty years old. Women past childbearing age earned respect by helping out wherever needed around camp, while strong and clever men may have also enjoyed higher status from their prominent role in hunting dangerous game.

♦**!Kung:** (clicking sound) kung
♦**Coahuiltecans:** koh uh WEEL tehk uhns

Paleolithic hunter-gatherers did not roam randomly in their search for food. Each group tended to stay within its own territory. If they behaved anything like the hunter-gatherers of modern times, they ranged over an area that averaged roughly sixty miles across in any one direction. Their constant walking, bending, and lifting kept them in robust condition, but they counted on their knowledge as well as their strength. Most important, they planned ahead for cooperative hunts at favorite spots, such as river crossings or lakes with shallow banks, where experience taught they were likely to find herds of large game animals fording the stream and drinking water.

They also used their knowledge to establish makeshift camps year after year in the locations that experience showed to be particularly good spots for gathering wild plants to eat. They took shelter from the weather in caves or rough dwellings made from branches and animal skins. On occasion, they built more elaborate shelters, such as the dome-like hut found in Ukraine that was constructed from the bones of mammoths. Nevertheless, their temporary dwellings could never become permanent homes; they had to roam to survive.

Trade, Technology, Religion, and Hierarchy

Over time, Paleolithic people developed skill at shaping tools such as hammers and blades from stone, wood, and bone. When they encountered other bands, they could exchange these worked goods or valued natural objects such as flint or seashells. The objects exchanged in this way could travel great distances from their point of origin: for example, ocean shells worn as jewelry made their way inland through repeated swaps from one group to another. This process of exchange, for which there is archaeological evidence from the late Paleolithic period, foreshadowed the development of long-distance trade that would forge connections among distant parts of the world in later times.

Technological innovation helped Paleolithic people increase their chances for survival. Learning how to chip sharp edges and points in stone created better cutting tools and weapons for hunting, digging out roots, and making clothes from animal skins. The discovery of how to kindle fire proved invaluable, especially because Paleolithic people had to endure the cold of extended ice ages, when the northern European glaciers moved much farther south than usual. The coldest part of the most recent Ice Age started about twenty thousand years ago and created a harsh climate in much of Europe for nearly ten thousand years. Their control of fire also helped hunter-gatherers to flourish by making it possible for them to cook. Cooking was a crucial innovation because it turned indigestible wild plants, such as grains, into edible and nutritious food.

Archaeological discoveries hint that Paleolithic hunter-gatherers had religious beliefs that began very long ago. Researchers interpret the missing jaws and the marks on the skulls found in Ethiopia and elsewhere as evidence that these early people cut away the flesh from dead persons' heads as part of a careful burial ritual (and not for cannibalism, as some have said). Even the small Ethiopian skull, that of a child six or seven years old, received this treatment. Another indication of belief is the care with which later Paleolithic bands buried their dead, decorating the corpses with red paint, flowers, and seashells. This elaborate procedure points to a concern with the mystery of death and perhaps some notions about an afterlife.

Important evidence for early religious beliefs also comes from the discovery of striking female figurines in excavations of late Paleolithic sites all over Europe. These statuettes of women with extra-large breasts,

A Paleolithic Shelter

This is a reconstruction of a hut that Paleolithic people built around fifteen thousand years ago from the bones of giant mammoths in what is now Ukraine. Animal hides would have been used to cover the poles. It was structure, like a tent on big enough for a small group to huddle inside to survive cold weather. *Novosti* (London).

abdomens, buttocks, and thighs were called Venus figurines by modern archaeologists after the Roman goddess of sexual love (see the Venus of Willendorf, shown here). These sculptures' exaggerated features suggest that the people who made them had a special set of beliefs and rituals about fertility and birth. Comparative evidence from early Japan suggests that women played a role in these religious activities.

The colorful late Paleolithic cave paintings found in Spain and France hint at hunter-gatherers' religious ideas and display their artistic ability. Using strong, dark lines and earthy colors, Paleolithic artists painted on the walls of caves that were set aside as special places, not used as day-to-day shelters. The paintings, which depict primarily large animals, suggest that these powerful beasts and the dangerous hunts for them played a significant role in the life and religion of Paleolithic hunter-gatherers. Still, there remains a great deal we cannot yet understand about their beliefs, such as the meaning of the dots, rectangles, and hands that they often drew beside their paintings of animals.

Burials reveal more than religious beliefs: they show that by late Paleolithic times hunter-gatherers recognized differences in status and marked them with physical objects.

Prehistoric Venus Figurine
This limestone statuette, eleven centimeters high, was found at Willendorf in Austria. Carved in the later Paleolithic period and originally colored red, it probably was meant to have symbolic power expressing the importance of women's fertility. The striking depiction of the woman's breasts and pubic area have led scholars to call such statuettes Venus figurines after the Roman goddess of love and sex; archaeologists have uncovered many of them all across Europe. Since no contemporary texts exist to explain the significance of the figurine's hairstyle, obesity, and pronounced sexual characteristics, we can only speculate about the complex meanings that prehistoric peoples extracted from it. How would you explain the figurine's appearance? *SuperStock.*

People who were buried with weapons, tools, animal figurines, ivory beads, and bracelets must have had special social standing for their band to bury these valuable items along with the body. These object-rich burials suggest that some late Paleolithic groups organized themselves into **hierarchies**,

Bison Painting in the Cave at Lascaux
Stone Age people painted these bison on the rock walls of a large cave at Lascaux in central France about 15,000 B.C.E., to judge from radiocarbon dating of charcoal found on the floor. Using black, red, yellow, and white pigments, the artists made the deep cave into an art gallery by filling it with pictures of large animals such as these European buffaloes, horses, deer, bears, and wooly rhinoceroses. Some scholars have suggested that the scenes were meant to symbolize the importance of hunting to the people who painted them, but this guess seems wrong because the bones from butchered animals found in the cave are 90 percent reindeer, while no reindeer pictures exist in the cave. **For more help analyzing this image,** see the visual activity for this chapter in the Online Study Guide at **bedfordstmartins.com/hunt**. *Bridgeman Art Library.*

social systems that ranked certain people as more important and more dominant than others. This is the earliest evidence for social differentiation, the marking of certain people as wealthier, more respected, or more powerful than others in their group.

Despite their varied knowledge and technological skill, prehistoric hunter-gatherers lived precarious lives that were dominated by the relentless search for something to eat. Survival was a risky business at best. The only groups to survive were those that learned to cooperate effectively in securing food and shelter, to profit from technological innovations like the use of fire and toolmaking, and to teach their children the knowledge, beliefs, and social traditions that had helped make their society viable.

> **Review:** How would you describe the daily activities of Paleolithic hunter-gatherers, male and female?

❖ The Neolithic Age, c. 10,000–c. 4000 B.C.E.

Daily life as we know it depends on agriculture and the domestication of animals, developments that began about 10,000–8000 B.C.E. This era is considered the beginning of the Neolithic period. These radical innovations in the way humans acquired their food caused such fundamental changes in the ways they lived that together they are called the **Neolithic Revolution**.

The Neolithic Revolution

How early peoples learned to sow and harvest crops and to raise animals for food remains mysterious in many ways. Recent archaeological research, however, indicates that it took thousands of years for people to invent farming. The process began in the part of southwestern Asia we call the Fertile Crescent because, unlike most regions of the earth, its hillier regions happened to have the right combination of soil, water, temperature, and wild mammals for the invention of agriculture and the domestication of animals. The Fertile

Crescent stretches in an arc, or crescent, along the foothills and lowlands that run northward from modern Israel across Syria and then turn in a southeasterly direction down to the plain of the lower stretches of the Tigris and Euphrates rivers in what is now southern Iraq (Map 1 opposite).

Climate change in the Fertile Crescent probably put in motion the long process of trial and error through which people learned to farm. About ten to twelve thousand years ago, the long-term weather pattern in this region became milder and rainier than it had been during the Ice Age that had just ended. This change promoted the growth of luxuriant fields of wild grains. The hunter-gatherer populations living in the Fertile Crescent began to gather more and more of their food from these now easily available and increasingly abundant stands of wild cereal grains. This regular supply of food in turn promoted fertility, which led to a growth in population, a process that might have already begun as a result of the new milder climate. The more children that were born, the greater the corresponding need to exploit the food supply efficiently. Over centuries of repeated trial and error, people learned to plant part of the seeds from one crop of grain to produce another crop. Since Neolithic women did most of the foraging for plant food, they had the greatest knowledge of plant life and therefore probably played the major role in the invention of agriculture and the tools needed to turn grains into food, such as grinding stones for making flour. For a long time thereafter, women and children did most of the agricultural labor, while men continued to hunt.

During this early part of the Neolithic period, people also learned to breed and herd animals that they could eat, a development that helped replace the meat formerly supplied by the hunting of large mammals, many of which had been hunted to extinction. Fortunately for the people in the Fertile Crescent, their region was home to large mammals whose temperaments made domestication possible. Unlike African animals such as the zebra or the hippopotamus, the wild sheep, goats, and cattle of the Fertile Crescent could, over the span of generations, be turned into animals accustomed to live closely and interdependently with human beings. The sheep was the

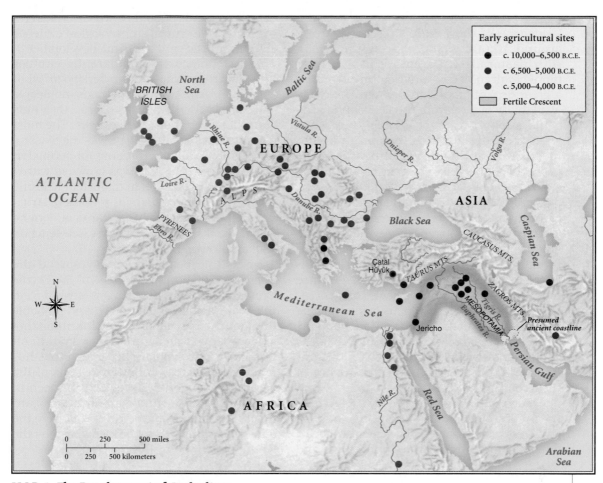

MAP 1 The Development of Agriculture

From around 10,000 to 8000 B.C.E., people first learned to plant seeds to grow nourishing plants in the foothills of the semicircle of mountains that curved up and around from the eastern end of the Mediterranean down to Mesopotamia, where reliable rainfall and moderate temperatures prevailed. The invention of irrigation later allowed them to grow lush crops in the hot plains below, providing resources that eventually spurred the emergence of the first large cities by about 4000 B.C.E.

first animal to be domesticated as a source of meat, beginning about 8500 B.C.E. (The dog had been domesticated much earlier but was not usually eaten.) By about 7000 B.C.E., domesticated animals had become common throughout the Near East. In this early period of domestication, some people continued to move around to find grazing land for their animals, living as what are called pastoralists. They also cultivated small temporary plots from time to time when they found a suitable area. Other people, relying more and more on growing crops for their livelihood, kept small herds close to their settlements. Men, women,

and children alike could therefore tend the animals. These earliest domesticated herds seem to have been used only as a source of meat, not for products such as milk or wool.

Neolithic Origins of Modern Life

The Neolithic Revolution, in which people came to support themselves as farmers instead of hunter-gatherers, laid the foundation of our modern way of life. First, to be able to raise crops on a permanent basis, people had to cease roaming and settle in one place with adequate land and water. Farming communities thus sprang up across the landscape of the Fertile Crescent starting around 10,000 B.C.E., sharing the region with pastoralists. Parents began to have more children because agriculture required a great deal of labor and because the ready availability of food from the fields and herds could support a larger population. At the same time, living in close quarters with domesticated animals, who might well be penned right next to or even inside the house, exposed people in these settlements to new epidemic diseases transmitted from animals to humans. Hunter-gatherers had largely escaped this danger because they had no groups of animals around them every day, although they could sometimes become infected by eating diseased wild animals. Since many viruses that afflict people today originate in domesticated animals before moving into the human population—as happens when humans today contract flu from flocks of chickens—we are still living with this unintended and unfortunate consequence of the Neolithic Revolution.

Much larger and more densely packed than the fleeting settlements of Paleolithic hunter-gatherers, early farming villages featured permanent houses built from mud bricks and containers made of pottery (whose broken remains provide crucial archaeological evidence for chronology and cultural development). The first homes were apparently circular huts, like those known from Jericho (in what is today Israel). Around two thousand people had settled in Jericho by 8000 B.C.E., their huts sprawling over about twelve acres. The most striking feature of the village was the massive fortification wall surrounding its perimeter. Ten feet thick, the wall was crowned with a stone tower ten meters in diameter enclosing an internal flight of stairs; this massive structure implies that the inhabitants of Jericho feared attacks by their neighbors (see Jericho's wall and tower, below).

Neolithic people gradually spread the knowledge of agriculture beyond the Fertile Crescent. Farmers migrating westward from the Near East looking for more land probably brought the new technology of farming into areas where it was not previously known. Although recent scholarship argues that human beings in several other regions of the world independently developed the techniques of agriculture and domestication of animals, migrants from the Near East were the ones who spread this knowledge across the length of Europe by 4000 B.C.E.

Tower in the Stone Wall of Neolithic Jericho

The circular mass in the center of this photograph is the base of a tower in the stone wall that the people of Jericho (today in Israel) built to protect their community around 8000–7000 B.C.E. This is one of the earliest such structures ever discovered: most of the people in this era still lived in unwalled collections of mud huts, but the inhabitants of Jericho had reached a more complex level of social organization that allowed them to collaborate on major building projects. The agricultural fields that lay outside the walls supplied the overwhelming majority of Jericho's economy, while the defensive wall provided security for the residents' homes and storehouses and thus protected their improving standard of living. *Photo: Zev Radovan.*

The remarkable new technologies underlying the changes of the Neolithic Revolution emerged as innovative human responses to the link between environmental change and population growth (See "New Sources, New Perspectives," page P-12). Furthermore, the Neolithic Revolution reveals the importance of **demography**—the study of the size, growth, density, distribution, and vital statistics of the human population—in understanding historical change.

Daily Life in the Neolithic Village of Çatalhöyük

The most intriguing evidence yet discovered for the vast changes in human life that took place during the Neolithic period comes from an archaeological site northwest of the Fertile Crescent, in the region later called Anatolia by the Greeks and Asia Minor by the Romans (now Turkey). There, on an upland plain near a river, a large mound rises from the surrounding open countryside. Known to us only by its modern Turkish name, Çatalhöyük◆ (meaning "Fork Mound"), this site was home to a population whose settled agricultural lifestyle illustrates Neolithic daily life. By 6500 B.C.E., the farmers of Çatalhöyük had erected a settlement of mud-brick houses nestled chock-a-block with one another. They constructed their dwellings in the rectangular shape that we retain in our domestic architecture to this day, with one striking difference: they had no doors in their outer walls. Instead, they entered their homes by climbing down a ladder through a hole in the flat roof. Since this hole also served as a vent for smoke from the family fire, getting into a house at Çatalhöyük could be a grimy business. But the absence of exterior doors also meant that the walls of the community's outermost houses served as a fortification wall for the community.

◆**Çatalhöyük:** chah TAHL hoo YOOK

Wall Painting of a Neolithic Hunter at Çatalhöyük
This running hunter armed with a bow and wearing a flaring leopard-skin loincloth appears in a wall painting from the Neolithic settlement at Çatalhöyük in central Anatolia, which flourished from around 6500 to 5500 B.C.E. The people of Çatalhöyük depicted such hunters chasing wild bulls, an animal that evidently had special significance for the villagers; bull horns and skulls decorated the walls of rooms at Çatalhöyük that archaeologists suggest are shrines. Why do you think people whose living depended mainly, though not exclusively, on agriculture instead of hunting and gathering would devote such attention in their art and perhaps their religion to hunting a powerful wild animal? *Photo: James Mellaart.*

The people of Çatalhöyük knew how to feed themselves by producing their own food instead of having to forage for it. In the fields stretching out below the mound, the villagers planted and harvested wheat, barley, and vegetables such as field peas, and they diverted water from the nearby river to increase their harvests. Beyond their cultivated fields they pastured the domesticated cattle that provided their main supply of meat and, by this time, hides and milk. They continued to hunt, too, as we can tell from the paintings of hunting scenes they drew on the walls of some of their buildings, reminiscent of the cave paintings of much earlier times. Unlike hunter-gatherers, however, these villagers no longer had to depend on the hit-or-miss luck of the hunt or risk being killed by wild animals to acquire meat and leather. At its height, the village's population reached perhaps six thousand people.

The diversity of occupations practiced at Çatalhöyük marked another significant change

NEW SOURCES, NEW PERSPECTIVES

Daily Bread, Damaged Bones, and Cracked Teeth

The invention of agriculture radically changed human life in many ways. Above all, Neolithic agricultural technology helped people to produce a more predictable and abundant supply of food, which in turn allowed the population to expand. Since not everybody had to be a farmer for there to be enough food to support the community, some people could become specialists in crafts and trades. Eventually, this revolution in the way humans fed themselves promoted the development of cities.

This change came at a price. Recent scientific research in biological anthropology and osteological archaeology (the study of ancient bones and teeth) has uncovered dramatic evidence of the physical stress endured by some of the individuals who first made agriculture the basis of daily subsistence. Excavators at Tell Abu Hureyra in Syria have found bones and teeth from people living around 6000 B.C.E. that offer startling indications of the pain that the new technology could cause. Their big toes especially show proof of extreme and prolonged dorsiflexion—bending the front of the foot up toward the shin. Dorsiflexion made the ends of the toe bones become flatter and broader than normal through the constant pressure of being bent in the same position for long periods of time.

What activity could the people have been pursuing so doggedly that it deformed their bones? The only posture that creates such severe bending of the foot is kneeling for extended periods. Osteologists confirmed that kneeling was common in this population by finding several cases of arthritic changes in knee joints and lower spines in skeletons at the site.

But why were the people kneeling for so long? Other bone evidence offered the first clue to solving this mystery. The skeletons showed strongly developed attachment points for the deltoid muscle on the humerus (the bone in the upper arm) and prominent growth in the lower arm bones. These characteristics mean that the people had especially strong deltoids for pushing their shoulders back and forth and powerful biceps for rotating their forearms. Whatever they were doing made them use their shoulders and arms vigorously.

Bones from Tell Abu Hureyra, Syria
These big toes from a middle-aged man reveal severe arthritic changes to the joint. Osteologists interpret this damage as evidence of extreme and prolonged dorsiflexion, or bending, of the foot. *The Natural History Museum, London.*

from the past and hinted at the economic complexity of later societies. Since the community could produce enough food to support itself without everyone having to work in the fields or herd cattle, some people could take the time to develop crafts as full-time occupations. Just as others in the community produced food for them, craft specialists produced goods for those who produced the food. Craft specialists continued to fashion tools,

The skeletons' teeth provided the next clue. Everyone except the very youngest individuals had deeply worn and often fractured teeth. This damage indicated that they regularly chewed food full of rock dust, which probably resulted from grain being ground in rock bowls.

The final clue came from art. Later paintings and sculptures from the region show people, usually women, kneeling down to grind grain into flour by pushing and rotating a stone roller back and forth on heavy grinding stones tilted away from them. This posture is exactly what would cause deformation of the big toes and arthritis in the knees and lower back. People grinding grain this way would have to push off hard from their toes with every stroke down the stone, as well as vigorously use the muscles of their shoulders and forearms to apply pressure to the roller. In ad-

dition, the flour would pick up tiny particles from the wearing down of the stones used to grind it; bread made from it would have a sandy consistency hard on teeth. That Neolithic people worked so constantly and so hard at processing the grain they grew, no matter the toll on their bones and their teeth, shows how vital this supply of food had become to them.

At this Syrian site, everyone's bones—men's, women's, and even children's—show the same signs of the kneeling and grinding activity. Evidently the production of flour for bread was so crucial that no gender division of this labor was possible or desirable, as it seems to have become in later times. Regardless of who performed it, this new technology that provided the stuff of life for the community took its toll in individual pain and hardship.

Sculpture from Giza, Egypt
In this statuette, a woman grinds grain into flour. The sculptor shows her rubbing her severely flexed left foot with the toes of her right foot, probably trying to ease the throbbing resulting from hours of kneeling. *The Oriental Institute, University of Chicago.*

QUESTIONS TO CONSIDER

1. Does the introduction of new technology to increase productivity and better human life usually involve new pains and stresses as well?

2. How do you decide what price—financial, physical, emotional—is worth paying for new technology? Who will make those decisions?

FURTHER READING

Hillman, G. "Traditional Husbandry and Processing of Archaic Cereals in Recent Times: The Operations, Products, and Equipment Which Might Feature in Sumerian Texts." *Bulletin on Sumerian Agriculture* 1 (1984): 114–52.

Molleson, Theya. "Seed Preparation in the Mesolithic: The Osteological Evidence." *Antiquity* 63 (1989): 358.

Moore, A. M. T. "The Excavation of Tell Abu Hureyra in Syria: A Preliminary Report." *Proceedings of the Prehistoric Society* 41 (1975): 50–71.

containers, and ornaments in the traditional way—from wood, bone, hide, and stone—but they now also worked with the material of the future: metal. So far, archaeologists are certain only that metalworkers at Çatalhöyük

knew how to fashion lead into pendants and to hammer naturally occurring lumps of copper into beads and tubes for jewelry. Since traces of slag have been found on the site, however, the workers may also have begun to develop the technique of smelting metal from ore. This tricky process—the basis of true metallurgy and the foundation of much modern technology—required temperatures of seven hundred degrees centigrade, and it took centuries for metalworkers to perfect. Other workers at Çatalhöyük specialized in weaving textiles, and the scraps of cloth discovered there are the oldest examples of this craft ever found. Like other early technological innovations, metallurgy and the production of cloth apparently also developed independently in other places.

In addition to craft specialization, trade also figured prominently in the economy of this early farming community. Trade allowed the people of Çatalhöyük to acquire goods from far away, such as shells from the Mediterranean Sea to wear as ornaments and a special flint from far to the east to shape into ceremonial daggers. The villagers acquired these prized materials by offering obsidian in exchange, a local volcanic glass whose glossy luster and capacity to hold a sharp edge made it valuable. The trading contacts the Neolithic villagers made with other settlements increased the level of economic interconnection among far-flung communities that had begun in the Paleolithic period.

The nearby volcano that provided obsidian for the villagers to trade proved in the end to be as dangerous as it had been profitable. Çatalhöyük never recovered from a volcanic eruption that overwhelmed it about a thousand years after its foundation. A remarkable wall painting suggests that the people of Çatalhöyük regarded the volcano as an angry god whom they needed to propitiate, and shrines uncovered by archaeologists show how much their religious beliefs meant to the villagers. They outfitted these special rooms with representations of bulls' heads and female breasts, perhaps as symbols of male and female elements in their religion. Like the hunter-gatherers before them, they sculpted figurines depicting amply endowed women, who perhaps represented goddesses of birth. This evidence for their fascination with the secret of life and fertility, so essential to maintain their population, finds its mirror image in the evidence for their deep interest in the mystery of death: skulls displayed in the shrines and wall paintings of vultures devouring headless corpses.

We cannot tell whether the village had priests or priestesses with special authority for religious matters, just as we cannot tell what sort of political organization the villagers had for making decisions. We can feel confident, however, that the people of Çatalhöyük had a social and political hierarchy. The need to plan and regulate irrigation, trade, and the exchange of food and goods between farmers and crafts producers created a need for leaders with more authority than was required to maintain peace and order in hunter-gatherer bands. Furthermore, households that were successful in farming, herding, crafts production, and trade generated surpluses in wealth that distinguished them from others whose efforts proved less fortunate. In short, the villagers did not live in an undifferentiated, egalitarian, or leaderless society.

Social Change in the Neolithic Age

The equality between men and women that existed in hunter-gatherer society had also disappeared by the late Neolithic period. The reasons for this shift remain uncertain, but they perhaps involved gradual changes in agriculture and herding over many centuries. Plows pulled by animals began to be used after about 4000 B.C.E. to cultivate land that was more difficult to sow than the areas cultivated in the earliest period of agriculture. Men apparently operated this new technology of plowing, probably because it required more physical strength than digging with sticks and hoes. They also predominated in the tending of the larger herds that had become more common in settled communities; people were now keeping cattle as sources of milk and raising sheep for wool. The herding of a community's large groups of animals tended to take place at a distance from the home settlement because the animals continually needed new grazing land. As with hunting in hunter-gatherer populations, men, free from having to nurse children, took on this task that required ranging a long way from home.

Women, on the other hand, probably became more tied to the central settlement because they had to bear and raise more children to support agriculture as it became more intensive and therefore required more and more labor than had foraging for food or the earliest forms of farming. The responsibility for new labor-intensive tasks related to processing the secondary products of larger herds also fell to women. For example, they now turned milk into cheese and yogurt and made cloth by spinning and weaving wool. The predominance of men in agriculture in the late Neolithic period combined with women's lessened mobility and decreased time away from housebound tasks apparently led to women's loss of equality with men. The changes in people's lives that occurred during the Neolithic Revolution prepared the way for the first civilizations.

All these transformations of human life eventually combined to create cities and **political states**, people living in a definite territory and organized under a system of government with powerful leaders, officials, and judges. These marks of civilization first appeared in the Near East, but they subsequently emerged at various other distant places around the world, including India, China, and the Americas—whether through independent development or some process of mutual influence we cannot yet say. Either way, the innovations in human life created by the Neolithic Revolution spurred the development of civilization as we know it today.

Review: In what major ways did the Neolithic Revolution change people's lives?

Conclusion

Permanent homes, relatively reliable food supplies from agriculture and animal husbandry, specialized occupations, and hierarchical societies in which men have held the most power have characterized Western history from the Neolithic period forward. For this reason, the broad outlines of the life of Neolithic villagers might seem unremarkable to us today. But the Neolithic way of life in built environments surrounded by cultivated fields and herds would have seemed astounding, we can guess, to Paleolithic hunter-gatherers, such as the roaming African hippopotamus hunters who now rank as the earliest known *Homo sapiens*. The Neolithic Revolution was the most pivotal change in the early history of human beings; it literally overturned the ways in which people related to and affected the natural environment and the ways in which they related to and affected one another. Now that farmers and herders could produce a surplus of food to support other people, specialists in art, architecture, crafts, religion, and politics could multiply as never before. Hand in hand with these developments came an increasing social differentiation and a new division of labor by gender that saw men begin to take over agriculture and women to take up new tasks at home. These developments reflected the apportionment of power in the society.

Suggested References

Çatal Höyük archaeological site: `http://catal.arch.cam.ac.uk/index.html`.

Clark, J. Desmond, et al. "Stratigraphic, Chronological and Behavioural Contexts of Pleistocene *Homo Sapiens* from Middle Awash, Ethiopia," *Nature* 423 (June 12, 2003): 747–52.

Diamond, Jared. *Guns, Germs, and Steel: The Fates of Human Societies.* 1999.

Fagan, Brian M. *People of the Earth: An Introduction to World Prehistory.* 10th ed. 2000.

Klein, Richard G. *The Dawn of Human Culture.* 2002.

Lewis-Williams, David. *The Mind in the Cave: Consciousness and the Origins of Art.* 2002.

Rudgley, Richard. *The Lost Civilizations of the Stone Age.* 1999.

Wenke, Robert J. *Patterns in Prehistory: Humankind's First Three Million Years.* 4th ed. 1999.

White, Tim D., et al. "Pleistocene *Homo Sapiens* from Middle Awash, Ethiopia," *Nature* 423 (June 12, 2003): 742–47.

CHAPTER REVIEW

IMPORTANT EVENTS

c. 200,000–160,000 B.C.E.	Beginning of the Paleolithic ("Old Stone") Age
c. 50,000–45,000 B.C.E.	*Homo sapiens* migrate from Africa into southwest Asia and Europe
c. 10,000–8000 B.C.E.	The Neolithic ("New Stone") Revolution in the Fertile Crescent
c. 8000 B.C.E.	Walled settlement at Jericho (in modern Israel)
c. 6500–5500 B.C.E.	Farming community thrives at Çatal-höyük (in modern Turkey)
c. 4000–3000 B.C.E.	Invention of writing in the Near East

KEY TERMS

demography (P–11)

hierarchies (P–7)

Homo sapiens (P–3)

hunter-gatherers (P–5)

Neolithic (P–4)

Neolithic Revolution (P–8)

Paleolithic (P–4)

political states (P–15)

REVIEW QUESTIONS

1. How would you describe the daily activities of Paleolithic hunter-gatherers, male and female?

2. In what major ways did the Neolithic Revolution change people's lives?

MAKING CONNECTIONS

1. Explain whether you think human life was more stressful in the Paleolithic period or the Neolithic period.

2. What do you think were the most important differences and similarities between Stone Age life and modern life? Why?

FOR FURTHER EXPLORATION

To assess your mastery of the material in this prologue, see the Online Study Guide at **bedfordstmartins.com/hunt**.

Foundations of Western Civilization, c. 4000–c. 1000 B.C.E.

ANCIENT EGYPTIANS BELIEVED that the gods judged them after death, to decide their fate in the afterlife, and that the stakes were high. In *Instructions for Merikare*, for example, written sometime around 2100–2000 B.C.E., Merikare's father, the king, warns his son to rule with justice because even a king would face a day of judgment when divine inquisitors would determine whether his choices had been good or evil: "Make secure your place in the cemetery by being upright, by doing justice, upon which people's hearts rely.... When a man is left over after mourning, his deeds are piled up next to him as treasure." Being judged pure of heart led to an eternal reward; if the dead king reached the judges "without doing evil," he would be transformed so that he would "abide [in the afterlife] like a god, roaming [free] like the lords of time."

Being judged impure, however, meant disaster for all eternity. The illustrated manual containing instructions for mummies on how to travel safely in the underworld, commonly called the *Book of the Dead*, explained that on the day of judgment the jackal-headed god Anubis would weigh the dead person's heart in a scale against the goddess Maat◆ and her feather of Truth, with the ibis-headed god Thoth carefully writing down the result (see the illustration at left). Pictures in the *Book of the Dead* also show the "Swallower of the"

◆**Maat:** MAH aht

Weighing of the Heart on Judgment Day
This painting on papyrus (paper made from a river reed) from about 1275 B.C.E. illustrates a main concern of ancient Egyptian religious belief: the day of judgment when the gods decided a person's fate after death. Here, a man named Any is having his heart (in the left balance) weighed against the feather of Truth of the goddess Maat. The feather stands for "What Is Right." The jackal-headed god Anubis works the scales, while the bird-headed god Thoth records the result. The standing male figure on the left symbolizes Any's destiny, and the seated figures above are the jury of gods. The painting formed part of Any's copy of the *Book of the Dead*, a collection of instructions and magic spells to help the dead person in the afterlife, on the assumption that the verdict would be positive and bestow a blessed eternal life. *British Museum, London, UK/Bridgeman Art Library.*

Damned"—a hybrid monster featuring a crocodile's head, a lion's body, and a hippopotamus's hind end—who crouched behind Thoth ready to devour the heart of anyone who failed the test of purity. These stories, like the many others with a similar message preserved in Egyptian mythology, taught that living a just life was the highest human goal because it was the key to a blessed existence after death.

The Egyptians' neighbors in the ancient Western world—the Mesopotamians, those inhabiting the eastern Mediterranean coast (called the Levant,[1] today Syria, Lebanon, Palestine, and Israel), the Cretans, and the Greeks—did not all share this optimism about the chances for a delightful afterlife. Some, like the Greeks, believed that most people could expect only a gloomy, shadow-like existence following their deaths. All these peoples, however, agreed that justice was the ideal by which they should organize their societies and guide their personal lives. At the same time, they disagreed over whether the gods paid close attention to how human beings treated one another.

These are the peoples whose beliefs, customs, and accomplishments historians call the foundations of Western civilization. It is essential to acknowledge from the start that these early peoples living around the Mediterranean Sea and in the Near East had diverse ideas on issues as fundamental as the

---

[1] The term *Levant*, French for "rising (sun)"—that is, the East—reflects the European perspective on the region's location. It is the term commonly used in professional writing to refer to these lands.

nature of justice. This sort of cultural diversity has always characterized what historians call Western civilization. It is also true that trade and travel kept these peoples in frequent contact with other populations elsewhere on the globe, exchanging goods, technologies, and ideas. This tendency toward interconnectivity raises the question of what historians mean by the concept *Western civilization*, a term that is sometimes taken to imply separateness or even isolation from the rest of the world.

❖ The Controversial Concept of Western Civilization

Technically, a study of the history of Western civilization focuses on the peoples living on and near the continent of Europe from ancient to modern times, beginning with the history of Sumer in Mesopotamia and of Egypt in Africa. In practice, the historical idea of Western civilization mixes together three ambiguous topics: the contested historical concept of civilization, the geographic notion of the West, and—most controversial of all—the value of Western culture (that is, the West's particular ways of life and ideas).

Debating the Meaning of Western Civilization

Historians traditionally define the term **civilization** as a way of life that includes political states based on cities with dense populations, large buildings constructed for communal activities, diverse economies,

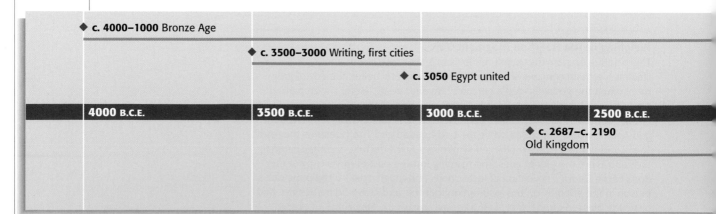

a sense of local identity, and some knowledge of writing. The implications of this definition are controversial (see "Terms of History," page 6). Although we often use *civilization* and related terms such as *civilized behavior* as if everyone agreed that civilization was not a problematic idea, some social critics of modern life ask whether civilization in fact represents a better and more just way of life than does human history "before civilization." They argue that people were healthier, more equal in power, and more peaceful before civilization. Such comparisons are hard to evaluate meaningfully because there is so little evidence about life before civilization (see the Prologue, pages P-3–P-16). If there were indeed fewer conflicts then, it might be simply because so many fewer people existed and they were spread so much farther apart.

The geographic notion of the West comes to us from the Greeks. Building on ideas they probably derived from their Near Eastern neighbors, they gave us the term *Europe* to indicate the West (where the sun sets) as distinct from the East (where the sun rises). The Greeks, like modern historians, were not sure exactly where to draw the boundaries of the West because the geographical content of the term was, and is, too open-ended to allow precise definition. The boundaries shift depending on what era is being described, and the *West* in *Western civilization* sometimes refers to peoples and places beyond Europe and sometimes not. For example, the region that is today Turkey was certainly part of Western civilization at the time of the Roman empire; yet in the opening years of the

twenty-first century, Europeans and Turks alike are debating what changes in Turkish life and politics it would take—and what the financial and cultural costs would be—for Turkey to be judged Western enough to join the European Union.

The idea that one culture might be superior in value to another is the most contested issue surrounding the concept of Western (or indeed any) civilization. This idea is old. The Greeks inherited from their neighbors in the Near East the idea that regional differences meant that one people's way of life was better than another's. Merikare's father, for instance, sternly warned him to beware of the "miserable Asiatic [Near Easterner], wretched because of where he's from, a place with no water, no wood.... He doesn't live in one place, hunger propels his legs.... He doesn't announce the day of battle, like a thief darting around a crowd."

Modern commentators continue to argue over the relative merits of different cultures as part of the murky debate over the meaning of *Western* (or, for that matter, *Eastern*) *civilization*. One thing, however, is clear about the story of Western civilization: cultural borrowing between the peoples of Europe and their neighbors near and far has characterized Western civilization from the beginning, whether that borrowing involved ideas, technologies, or goods. In fact, the story of Western civilization concerns cultural and political interaction both among the West's diverse peoples and between them and the peoples of the rest of the globe. Therefore, we should not understand the word *Western* to mean "fenced off in the West from the rest of the world."

◆ **c. 2350** First empire in Akkadia   ◆ **c. 1600** Canaanites invent the alphabet

◆ **c. 2300–2200** Enheduanna's poetry   ◆ **c. 1400** Mycenaeans take Crete

◆ **c. 2200** Minoan palaces   ◆ **c. 1569–1081** New Kingdom

◆ **c. 1900** Hebrews enter Canaan   ◆ **c. 1190** Pharaoh Ramesses III defeats the invading Sea Peoples

2000 B.C.E.   **1500 B.C.E.**   **1000 B.C.E.**   **500 B.C.E.**

◆ **2112–2004** Ur III dynasty   ◆ **c. 1700–1500** Hebrews enter Egypt

◆ **c. 2061–1665** Middle Kingdom   ◆ **c. 1274** Battle of Kadesh

◆ **c. 1792–1750** Hammurabi's code   ◆ **c. 1250** Hebrew exodus

◆ **c. 1750** Hittite kingdom   ◆ **c. 1200–1000** Period of calamities

TERMS OF HISTORY

Civilization

Our term *civilization* comes from the Latin word *civilis*. For ancient Romans, civilis meant "suitable for a private citizen" and "behaving like an ordinary, unpretentious person." To be "un-civilis" was to behave in a showy and arrogant way that suggested you thought yourself superior to others.

Ironically, then, the modern term *civilization* expresses the judgment that becoming civilized meant achieving a superior way of life. Consider, for example, these definitions from a widely used reference work, *The Random House Webster's College Dictionary.*[1]

civilization: 1. an advanced state of human society, in which a high level of culture, science, and government has been reached. 2. those people or

[1] *The Random House Webster's College Dictionary*, 2nd ed. (New York, 1997), 240.

nations that have reached such a state. 3. any type of culture, society, etc. of a specific place, time, or group: *Greek civilization.* 4. the act or process of civilizing or being civilized. 5. cultural and intellectual refinement. 6. cities or populated areas in general, as opposed to unpopulated or wilderness areas. 7. modern comforts and conveniences, as made possible by science and technology.

civilize: to bring out of a savage, uneducated, or rude state; make civil; enlighten; refine: *Rome civilized the barbarians.*

civilized: 1. having an advanced or humane culture, society, etc. 2. polite, well-bred; refined.

The common thread among these definitions is the idea that *civilization* implies an "advanced" or "refined" way of life compared to a "savage" or "rude" way. Ancient peoples often drew this sort of comparison between themselves and others whom

Locating Western Civilization's Foundations

If we accept the traditional definition of *civilization*, Western civilization's deepest foundations lie in two places: (1) Mesopotamia (the region pierced by the Euphrates◆ and Tigris◆ Rivers in modern Iraq), where the people of Sumer had developed an urban society by c. 3000 B.C.E., and (2) Egypt, in northeastern Africa, whose civilization emerged beginning around 3050 B.C.E., when a strong ruler unified the country along the Nile River under a central authority. The Sumerians, who built the world's first cities, believed that divinely imposed justice required humans to serve the gods by building them temples, worshiping them, and

◆**Euphrates:** yu FRAY teez
◆**Tigris:** TY gruhs

bringing them gifts, even though the deities seemed unpredictable and arbitrary. The Egyptians employed their extraordinary architectural skills and their country's natural wealth in agriculture and minerals to build magnificent temples and pyramids that expressed their religious devotion to the gods whom they believed lovingly provided them with life's delights. Their concept of justice revolved around the complicated significance of Maat.

The story of Western civilization next spreads beyond Mesopotamia and Egypt. By around 2000–1900 B.C.E., civilizations had also appeared in Anatolia◆ (today Turkey), the Levant, the island of Crete in the eastern Mediterranean Sea, and Greece. All these peoples learned from the older civilizations of Mesopotamia and Egypt, and they all shared

◆**Anatolia:** a nuh TOH lee uh

they saw as crude; the urban dwellers of the Near East, Greece, and Rome, for example, applied this judgment to those who did not build cities. Much later, this notion of superiority became especially prominent in European thought after voyagers to the New World and colonial settlers reported on what they saw as the savage or barbarous life of the peoples they called Indians. Because Europeans of the times saw Indian life as lacking discipline, government, and, above all, Christianity, it seemed to them to be primitive and raw and therefore an inversion of their idea of civilized life.

Thus, the term *civilization* entered the English language in a "sense opposed to *barbarity*," as James Boswell in 1772 advised Samuel Johnson to define it in the latter's famous and influential *Dictionary of the English Language*. It became common to compare "the lower races of man" with "civilized peoples."[2] The word's built-in sense of comparative superiority became so accepted that it could even be used to express this notion in nonhuman contexts, such as in the following startling comparison: "some communities of ants are more advanced in civilization than others."[3]

Historians in recent times have been reluctant to confront explicitly the difficult issues that the term raises. For example, they shy away from the troubling question of how, or indeed whether, to evaluate the relative merits of one civilization versus another. Tellingly, there is no mention of the topic in the standard guide to scholarly work issued by the major professional organization for historians.[4]

Ultimately, the failure to consider what the term should mean can lead to its being used without much definitional content at all, as in the Random House dictionary's third definition under *civilization*. Does the term have any deep meaning if it can be used to mean "any type of culture, society, etc. of a specific place, time, or group"? This empty definition reveals that studying civilization still presents daunting challenges to students of history today. It should be their task to make *civilization* a term with intellectual content and a reality with meaning for improving human life, as those who first used the word thought that it was.

---

[2] Sir John Lubbock, *The Origin of Civilisation and The Primitive Condition of Man. Mental and Social Condition of Savages*, 5th ed. (New York, 1889), 1–2.

[3] Sir John Lubbock, *On the Origin and Metamorphoses of Insects*, 2nd ed. (London, 1874), 13.

[4] *The American Historical Association's Guide to Historical Literature*, 3rd ed. (New York, 1995).

the sense that nothing in life was more important than religion. Comparably complex societies also emerged in India, China, and the Americas in different eras starting around 2500 B.C.E.; however, these societies pursued independent paths of development before coming in contact with people from Europe and the Mediterranean in much later times.

Early civilizations developed and changed both intentionally and unintentionally. The invention of increasingly sophisticated metallurgical technology, for example, led to the creation of ever better tools and weapons, but it also turned out to be one factor promoting differences in social status; that is, people constructed status for themselves in part by acquiring metal objects. In every known civilization people insisted on establishing hierarchies, or status differences, among themselves. Some contemporary scientists claim that this development was inevitable because human beings are by nature "status-protecting organisms." In any case, early civilizations evolved to a large extent through cultural interaction provoked by international trade and war. Contact with unfamiliar ways and technologies spurred people to learn from one another and to adapt for themselves the traditions, beliefs, and inventions of others.

Understanding the history of Western civilization therefore requires us to trace the mingling and conflicts of diverse peoples and regions. We will begin with the early civilizations of Mesopotamia, Egypt, the Levant, Crete, and Greece. We will be reminded of the potential fragility of what we traditionally call civilization when we see that a mysterious era of widespread violence lasting from about 1200 to 1000 B.C.E. nearly put an early end to civilization in the West.

❖ Mesopotamia, Home of the First Civilization, c. 4000–c. 1000 B.C.E.

The Neolithic Revolution (see the Prologue, pages P-3–P-16) opened the way to civilization, as historians define it, by creating the first permanent settlements that, over millennia, grew into cities and by providing enough surplus agricultural resources to allow many people to work full-time at crafts, not just farming. Metal became an ever more important component of wealth and power from around 4000 to 1000 B.C.E. Historians label this period the Bronze Age because bronze, an alloy of copper and tin, was the most important metal for weapons and tools. The ownership of objects produced by the new technology of metallurgy increased the division in society between men and women and rich and poor. Long-distance commerce developed to satisfy people's desire for goods and materials not available in their homelands, while rulers created systems of law to convince their subjects that their power had divine backing and to show the gods that they were promoting justice in their increasingly complex societies.

Early farming villages gradually grew larger until, by around 3000 B.C.E., the people of Sumer, the name for southern Mesopotamia, built settlements big enough to be called the first cities. Each of these large urban communities controlled its surrounding territory and remained politically independent. The cities' residents grew bounteous crops by irrigating marginal land, built great temples to honor their gods, lived in a hierarchical society with slaves at the bottom and kings at the top, and invented writing to keep track of economic transactions and record their stories and beliefs. The rulers of these cities constantly battled one another for glory, territory, trade, and, especially, access to metal ores.

Cities and Society, c. 4000–c. 2350 B.C.E.

The first cities and thus the first civilization emerged in Sumer because its inhabitants figured out how to raise crops on the fertile but dry land between and around the Tigris and Euphrates Rivers (Map 1.1). Agriculture had begun in the well-watered hills of the Fertile Crescent, but these slopes offered too little habitable land to support the growth of cities. The plains along the rivers were huge, but they presented serious challenges to farmers: little rain fell, temperatures soared to 120 degrees Fahrenheit, and devastating floods occurred unpredictably. First Sume-

The "Standard of Ur" of Sumer
This wooden box, about twenty inches long and eight inches high, was found in a large grave in the Royal Cemetery at Ur dating to about 2600–2400 B.C.E. Its pictures, inlaid in white shell, red limestone, and blue lapis lazuli on all sides of the box, have made this mysterious object famous because they provide some of our earliest visual evidence for Sumerian life. This side shows animals being led to a banquet scene, where a musician playing a lyre entertains men in their characteristic woolen fleeces or fringed skirts. The large figure at the left is probably the king, here celebrating his role as the gods' representative to his subjects. The other side shows a Sumerian army. **For more help analyzing this image**, see the visual activity for this chapter in the Online Study Guide at **bedfordstmartins.com/hunt**.
British Museum.

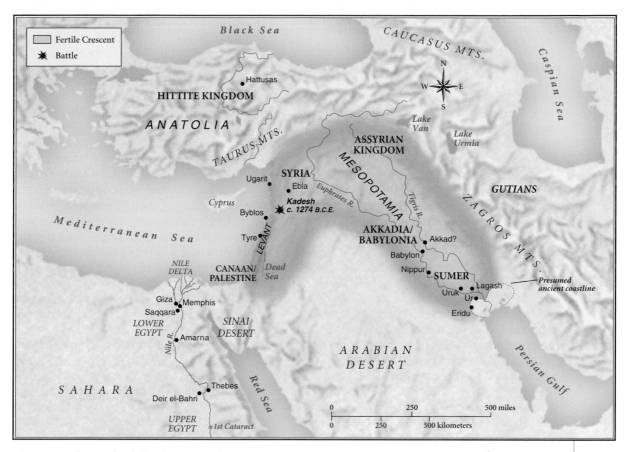

MAP 1.1 The Ancient Near East, c. 4000–3000 B.C.E.
The diverse region we call the ancient Near East encompassed many different landscapes, climates, peoples, and languages. Kings ruled its independent city-states, the centers of the world's first civilizations, beginning around 4000–3000 B.C.E. Trade by land and sea for natural resources, especially metals, and wars of conquest kept the peoples of the region in constant contact and conflict with one another.

rians and then other Mesopotamians turned this marginal environment into lush farmland by using the Tigris and Euphrates to irrigate the plains. Intricate canal systems that required constant maintenance turned the desert green and helped limit flooding. The surpluses of food produced by Mesopotamian farmers allowed the population to swell, the number of crafts producers to increase rapidly, and cities to emerge. The necessity of organizing labor to maintain the canals promoted the growth of monarchy to exercise centralized authority in Mesopotamian cities. Each city controlled agricultural land outside its fortification walls and built large temples inside them. Historians call this arrangement—an urban center

exercising political and economic control over the countryside around it—a **city-state**.

The Cities of Sumer. The origins of the Sumerians are obscure; unlike many other Mesopotamian peoples, they spoke a language whose background remains unknown, except that it was not one of the Semitic languages (which include Akkadian, Hebrew, and Arabic). By around 3000 B.C.E. the Sumerians lived in twelve independent city-states—including Uruk, Eridu,◆ and Ur—which remained fiercely separate communities warring over land and natural resources. By around 2500 B.C.E., each of the Sumerian

---

◆ **Eridu:** EHR ih doo

cities had expanded to twenty thousand residents or more.

Travelers from one city-state to another would first come to the irrigated green fields on the outskirts of the city, then the villages housing agricultural workers, and finally the city's fortress walls and the high buildings looming behind. Outside the gates, travelers would find a bustling center of trade, either a harbor on the river or a marketplace on the overland routes leading to the city. Once they were inside the walls, their eyes would be drawn to the royal family's palace and, above all, to the immense temples. To be close to the gods, Sumerians built great **ziggurats**◆ (see The Ziggurat of Ur in Sumer below), temple towers with a stair-step design, which soared up to ten stories high and dominated the urban skyline.

City dwellers lived in mud-brick houses constructed around an open court. Most houses had only one or two rooms, but the wealthy constructed two-story dwellings that had a dozen or more rooms. Rich and poor alike suffered the ill effects of a domestic water supply often contaminated by sewage because no system of waste disposal existed. Pigs and dogs scavenged in the streets and areas where garbage was unceremoniously dumped.

Agriculture and trade made Sumerians prosperous. They constantly bartered grain, vegetable oil, woolens, and leather with one another and with foreign regions, from which

they acquired natural resources not found in Sumer, such as metals, timber, and precious stones. Sumerian traders traveled as far east as India, sailing for weeks to reach that distant land, where the Indus civilization's large cities emerged about five hundred years after Sumer's. Technological innovation strengthened the early Mesopotamian economy, especially beginning around 3000 B.C.E., when Sumerians invented the wheel in a form sturdy enough to be used on carts for transport.

Religious officials predominated in the early Sumerian economy because they controlled large farms and gangs of laborers, whose work for the gods supported the ziggurats and their related activities. Priests and priestesses supervised considerable property and economic activity. By around 2600 B.C.E., however, the kings had leveraged their war leadership to achieve dominance over the economy; some private households also amassed significant wealth by working large fields.

Kings in Sumer.   Kings and their royal families topped the Sumerian social hierarchy. A king formed a council of older men as his advisers and acknowledged the gods as his ruler and the guarantors of his power. This claim to divinely justified power gave priests and priestesses political influence. Patriarchy—domination by men in political, social, and economic life—was already the rule in these first cities. Although a Sumerian queen was respected because she was the

---

◆**ziggurats:** ZIH guh rats

The Ziggurat of Ur in Sumer

King Ur-Nammu and his son Shulgi built this massive temple as an architectural marvel for their city of Ur (in what is today southern Iraq) in the early twenty-first century B.C.E. Its three massive terraces, one above another and connected by stairways, were constructed with a mud-brick core covered by a skin of baked brick, glued together with tar. Compare the angular outline of its structure with that of the minaret of the Great Mosque at Samarra. The ziggurat's walls were more than seven feet thick to sustain its enormous weight. Its original height is uncertain, but the first terrace alone soared some forty-five feet above the ground. The enormous bulk of the Great Pyramid in Egypt, however, dwarfed it (see page 22). *Hirmer Fotoarchiv.*

wife of the king and the mother of the royal children, the king held the supreme power. Still, women had more legal rights under Sumerian law than they would in later Mesopotamian societies; only Egypt would give women a greater legal standing than Sumer.

The king's supreme responsibility was to ensure justice, which meant pleasing the gods, developing law, keeping order among the people, and defending his city-state from attacks by rival rulers eager to seize its riches and irrigated land. In return, the king extracted surpluses from the working population as taxes to support his family, court, palace, army, and officials. If the surpluses came in regularly, the king mostly left the people alone to live their daily lives.

As befitted his status atop the hierarchy, a Sumerian king and his family lived in an elaborate palace that rivaled the scale of the great temples. The palace served as the city-state's administrative center and the storehouse for the ruler's enormous wealth. Members of the royal family dedicated a significant portion of the community's economic surplus to displaying their superior status. Archaeological excavation of the immense royal cemetery in Ur, for example, has revealed the dazzling extent of the rulers' riches—spectacular possessions crafted in gold, silver, and precious stones. These graves also yielded grislier evidence of the exalted status of the king and queen: the bodies of the servants sacrificed to serve their royal masters after death. The spectacle of wealth and power that characterized Sumerian kingship reveals how great the gap was between the upper and lower ranks of Sumerian society.

Slaves in Sumer. Sumerian society confined slaves to its lowest level. No single description of slavery covers all its diverse forms or its social and legal consequences. Both the gods (through their temple officials) and private individuals could own slaves. People lost their freedom by being captured in war, by being born to slaves, by voluntarily selling themselves or their children to escape starvation, or by being sold by their creditors to satisfy debts. Foreigners enslaved as captives in war or by raiding parties were considered inferior to citizens who fell into slavery to pay off debts. Children whose parents dedicated them as servants to the gods, although counted as slaves, could rise to prominent positions in the temple administrations.

In general, slaves existed in a state of near-total dependency on other people. Legally, they were excluded from normal social relations, usually worked without compensation, and lacked almost all rights. Although slaves sometimes formed relationships with free persons and frequently married each other and had families, their masters could sell their family members at will. Their masters could buy, sell, beat, or even kill them because slaves counted as property, not humans. Sumerians, like later Mesopotamians, apparently accepted slavery as a fact of nature, and there is no evidence of any sentiment for abolishing it.

Slaves worked in domestic service, craft production, and farming, but historians dispute their economic significance compared with that of free workers. Most state labor seems to have been performed by free persons who paid their taxes through labor rather than with money (which consisted of measured amounts of food or precious metal; coins were not invented until around 700 B.C.E. in Anatolia). Under certain conditions slaves could gain their freedom: masters' wills could liberate them, or they could purchase their freedom from the earnings they could sometimes accumulate.

The Invention of Writing. Beginning around 3500 B.C.E. the Sumerians invented writing to do accounting because their economic transactions had increased in complexity as their populations swelled. Before writing, people drew small pictures on clay tablets to represent objects. At first, these pictographs symbolized concrete objects only, such as a cow. Over several centuries of development, nonpictorial symbols and marks were added to the pictographs to stand for the sounds of spoken language. The final version of Sumerian writing was not an alphabet, in which a symbol represents the sound of a single letter, but a mixed system of phonetic symbols and pictographs that represented the sounds of entire syllables or entire words.

c. 3100 B.C.E.	c. 3000 B.C.E.	c. 2500 B.C.E.	c. 2100 B.C.E.	c. 700 B.C.E. (Neo-Assyrian)	Sumerian reading + meaning
					SAG Head
					NINDA bread
					GU₇ eat
					AB₂ cow
					APIN plough
					SUHUR carp

FIGURE 1.1 Cuneiform Writing
The earliest known form of writing developed in different locations in Mesopotamia in the 3000s B.C.E. when people began linking meaning and sound to signs such as these. The scribes who mastered the system used sticks or reeds to press dense rows of small wedge-shaped marks into damp clay tablets or chisels to engrave them on stone. Cuneiform was used for at least fifteen Near Eastern languages and continued to be written for three thousand years. Written about 1900 B.C.E., this cuneiform text records a merchant's complaint that a shipment of copper contained less metal than he had expected. His letter, impressed on a clay tablet several inches long, was enclosed in an outer clay shell, which was then marked with the sender's private seal. This envelope (photo above) protected the inner text from tampering or breakage. *British Museum.*

Archaeologists call the Sumerians' fully developed script **cuneiform**♦ (from *cuneus*, Latin for "wedge") because they used wedge-shaped marks impressed into clay tablets to record spoken language (Figure 1.1). Other Mesopotamian peoples subsequently adopted cuneiform to write their own languages. For a long time, only a few professionally trained men and women, known as scribes, mastered the new technology of writing. Schools sprang up to teach aspiring scribes, who could then find jobs as accountants. Kings, priests, and wealthy landowners employed scribes to keep records that let them control their workers carefully by keeping precise track of who had paid their taxes, who still owed, and how much.

Writing soon proved useful for purposes other than accounting. The scribal schools extended their curriculum to cover nature lore, mathematics, and foreign languages. Writing also created a new way to hand down stories and beliefs previously preserved only in memory and speech. This written literature provided a powerful new tool for passing on a culture's traditions to later generations. Enheduanna,♦ an Akkadian woman of the twenty-third century B.C.E., composed the world's oldest written poetry whose author is known. She was a priestess, prophetess, and princess, the daughter of King Sargon♦ of the city of Akkad.♦ Her poetry, written in Sumerian, praised the awesome power of the life-giving goddess of love, Inanna: "the great gods scattered from you like fluttering bats, unable to face your intimidating gaze... knowing and wise queen of all the lands, who makes all creatures and people multiply." Later princesses, who wrote love songs, lullabies, dirges, and prayers, continued the Mesopotamian tradition of royal women as authors and composers.

Mesopotamian Mythology and Religion.
Writing was a crucial technology for passing down Mesopotamian myths about the gods and their actions toward human beings. Mesopotamian religion was a form of **polytheism** (the worship of multiple gods). Various gods were thought to have power in different areas affecting human existence, such as war,

---

♦**cuneiform:** kyoo NEE uh fawrm

♦**Enheduanna:** en hed oo AH na
♦**Sargon:** SAHR gahn
♦**Akkad:** AH kahd

fertility, and the weather. The more critical a divinity's sphere of influence over people's well-being, the more important the god. Each city-state honored a particular major deity as its special protector.

Realizing that human beings could not control nature, Mesopotamians viewed the gods as absolute masters to whom they owed total devotion. They believed that their deities looked like human beings and had human emotions, especially anger and an arbitrary will. Myths emphasized the gods' awesome but unpredictable power and the limits of human control over what the gods might do to them. If human beings offended them, Mesopotamian divinities such as Enlil, god of the sky, and Ishtar (also called Inanna♦), goddess of love and war, would punish worshipers by causing disasters, like floods and famine.

The *Epic of Gilgamesh*, a long poem usually read today as a combination of its many versions, relates the adventures of the hero Gilgamesh, who sought to cheat death and achieve immortality. As king of the city of Uruk,♦ he forced the city's young men to construct a temple and fortification wall and all the young women to sleep with him. When the distressed inhabitants implored Anu, lord of the gods, to grant them a rival to Gilgamesh, Anu called on Aruru, the mother of the gods, to create a man of nature, Enkidu,♦ "hairy all over... dressed as cattle are." A week of sex with a prostitute tamed this brute, preparing him for civilization: "Enkidu was weaker; he ran slower than before. But he had gained judgment, was wiser." After wrestling to a draw, Enkidu and Gilgamesh became friends and set out to conquer Humbaba (or Huwawa), the ugly, giant monster of the Pine Forest. Gilgamesh later insulted the goddess Ishtar, however, who sent the Bull of Heaven to challenge him and Enkidu. The two comrades prevailed, but when Enkidu made matters worse by hurling the dead bull's haunch at Ishtar, the gods condemned him to death. In despair over human failure and frailty, Gilgamesh tried to find the secret of immortality, only to have his quest foiled by a thieving snake. He subsequently realized that

immortality for human beings comes only from the fame generated by their achievements, above all building a great city such as Uruk, which encompassed "three square miles and its open ground." Only memory and gods live forever, he found.

A late version of the *Epic of Gilgamesh* includes a description of a huge flood that covered the earth, recalling the devastating inundations that often struck Mesopotamia. When the gods sent the flood, they warned one man, Utnapishtim, of the impending disaster, telling him to build a boat. He loaded his vessel with his relatives, artisans, possessions, domesticated and wild animals, and "everything there was." After a week of torrential rains, he and his passengers disembarked to repopulate and rebuild the earth. This story foreshadows the biblical account of the flood and the story of Noah's ark. The themes of Mesopotamian mythology, which lived on in poetry and song, also powerfully influenced the mythology of distant peoples, most notably the Greeks.

Since religion meant so much to Mesopotamians, the priest or priestess of a city's chief deity enjoyed extremely high status. The most important duty of Mesopotamian priests was to discover the will of the gods by divination. To perform this function, they studied natural signs by tracking the patterns of the stars, interpreting dreams, and cutting open animals to examine their organs for deformities signaling trouble ahead. These inspections helped the people decide when and how to please their fickle gods, whether by placing wondrous gifts in their sanctuaries or by celebrating festivals in their honor. During the New Year holiday, for example, the reenactment of the mythical marriage of the goddess Inanna and the god Dumuzi was believed to ensure successful reproduction by the city's residents, animals, and plants for the coming year.

Metals, the Akkadian Empire, and the Ur III Dynasty, c. 2350–c. 2000 B.C.E.

The drive to acquire metals from distant sources was one important factor impelling the kings of the Akkadians,♦ a Mesopotamian

---

♦**Inanna:** in AH na
♦**Uruk:** OO ruk
♦**Enkidu:** EHN kee doo

♦**Akkadians:** uh KAY dee uhns

people from the city-state of Akkad, to create the world's first **empire**, a political unit in which one or more formerly independent territories or peoples are ruled by a single sovereign power. Pursuing wealth and glory, the aggressive Akkadian monarchs led their armies on brutal campaigns to subdue their neighbors.

Wealth of course meant more than just metal—agricultural production was perhaps the greatest source of riches—but the history of early metallurgy presents a clear example of a recurrent theme in history since the Neolithic Revolution: technological change impacting social norms. Akkadian kings and the social elite prized the new luxury goods and the improved tools for agriculture, construction, and, above all, war that the Bronze Age smiths devised. These craftsmen invented ways to smelt ore and to make metal alloys at high temperatures. Pure copper, which had been available for some time, easily lost its shape and edge; bronze, by contrast, a copper-tin alloy hard enough to hold a razor edge, enabled smiths to produce durable and deadly swords, daggers, and spearheads. Soon every warrior wanted bronze weaponry as his standard equipment.

Rich men soon began to display their wealth and status by commissioning metalworkers to decorate their swords and daggers with lavish and expensive engravings and inlays, as on costly guns today. Metal weapons also underscored the differences between men and women in society, because they signified the masculine roles of hunter and warrior that had emerged long before in the division of labor among hunter-gatherers. The development of metallurgy had other social consequences as well. People now expected to acquire wealth not just in foodstuffs, animals, or land but also in metals. Their desire to accumulate wealth and to possess status symbols stimulated demand for metals and for the skilled workers who could create lavishly adorned weapons for

The Akkadian Empire, c. 2350–2200 B.C.E.

men and exquisitely crafted jewelry made from exotic materials for both women and men. Growing numbers of crafts workers swelled the size of Bronze Age cities.

Mesopotamian monarchs who craved a reliable supply of metals to support their quest for status, glory, and power spawned the development of empires. If a king lacked deposits of ore in his territory, he could acquire it in either of two ways: trade or conquest. Ambition induced rulers to seize rather than to trade, and they started wars to capture territory where ore mines could be found. The first empire began around 2350 B.C.E., when Sargon, king of Akkad, launched invasions far to the north and south of his homeland in mid-Mesopotamia. His violent campaigns overcame Sumer and the regions all the way westward to the Mediterranean Sea. Since Akkadians expressed their ideas about their own history in poetry and believed that the gods determined their fate, it was fitting that a poet of around 2000 B.C.E. credited Sargon's success to the favor of the god Enlil: "to Sargon the king of Akkad, from below to above, Enlil had given him lordship and kingship."

Sargon's energetic grandson Naram-Sin continued the family tradition of conquering distant places. By around 2250 B.C.E., he had severely damaged Ebla, a large city whose site has only recently been discovered in modern Syria, more than five hundred miles from Naram-Sin's home base in Mesopotamia. Archaeologists have unearthed many cuneiform tablets at Ebla, some of them in more than one language. These discoveries suggest that Ebla thrived as an early center for learning as well as a trading station.

The process of building an empire by force had the unintended consequence of spreading Mesopotamian literature and art throughout the Near East. The Akkadians, like many other peoples of the Near East, spoke a Semitic language unrelated to Sumerian, but in conquering Sumer they took over most of the characteristics of that region's religion, literature, and culture. The other peoples whom the Akkadians overran were then exposed to Sumerian beliefs and traditions, which they in turn adapted to suit their own purposes. In this way, war promoted cultural interaction between peoples, although that was not the goal of the Akkadian empire builders.

The Akkadian empire failed to last. The traditional explanation for its fall has been that the Gutians,♦ a neighboring hill people, overthrew the Akkadian dynasty around 2200 B.C.E. by swooping down from, in the words of a poet, "their land that rejects outside control, with the intelligence of human beings but with the form and stumbling words of a dog." Research has revealed, however, that civil war is a more likely explanation for the Akkadian empire's demise. A newly resurgent Sumerian dynasty, called Ur III (2112–2004 B.C.E.), then seized power in Sumer and presided over a flourishing of Sumerian literature as "high culture." The Ur III rulers created a centralized economy, published the earliest preserved law code, and justified their rule by proclaiming the king to have a divine nature. The best-preserved ziggurat was built in their era. Royal hymns, a new literary form, glorified the king; one example reads: "Your commands, like the word of a god, cannot be reversed; your words, like rain pouring down from heaven, are without number."

Neither the Ur III kings' control of the economy nor their new royal ideology could protect them from monarchy's fatal weakness—its tendency to inspire powerful and ambitious internal rivals to conspire to overthrow the ruling dynasty and take power themselves. When civil war weakened the regime, Amorite marauders from nearby took advantage to conduct damaging raids. The Ur III dynasty collapsed after only a century of rule.

Assyrian and Babylonian Achievements, c. 2000–c. 1000 B.C.E.

New kingdoms developed in Assyria and Babylonia in the second millennium B.C.E. to fill the power vacuum that the ruin of the Akkadian empire and the Sumerian Ur III dynasty created. Assyrian innovations in commerce and Babylonian achievements in law have had lasting fame in Western civilization. These accomplishments are especially remarkable because they occurred while

♦**Gutians:** GOOT ee uhns

Mesopotamian city-states were experiencing prolonged troubles caused by agricultural pollution. Intensive irrigation had helped create populous cities and centralized government, but over time this technology had the unintended consequence of increasing the salt level of the soil so much that crop yields declined. By around 2000 B.C.E. the resulting economic stress had undermined the political stability in Mesopotamia; the trouble persisted for centuries.

The Assyrians and Long-Distance Capitalism. The Assyrians inhabited northern Mesopotamia, just east of Anatolia. They took advantage of their geography to build an independent kingdom whose prosperity depended on long-distance trade conducted by private entrepreneurs. The city-states of Anatolia supplied Mesopotamian states with wood, copper, silver, and gold. By acting as intermediaries in this trade between Anatolia and Mesopotamia, the Assyrians became

The Kingdom of Assyria, c. 1900 B.C.E.

the leading merchants of the Near East. They produced woolen textiles to export to Anatolia in exchange for its raw materials, which they in turn sold to the rest of Mesopotamia.

Centralized state monopolies had previously dominated the economies of Mesopotamian city-states. Instead of relying on a free market in the domestic economy, the king's officials managed international trade and redistributed goods according to their notions of who needed what. This **redistributive economy** never disappeared in Mesopotamia, but by 1900 B.C.E. the Assyrian kings were allowing individuals to transact large commercial deals on their own initiative. Private Assyrian investors provided funds to traders to purchase an export cargo of cloth. The traders then formed donkey caravans to travel the hundreds of rocky and dangerous miles to Anatolia, where, if they survived the journey, they could make huge profits to be split with their investors. Royal regulators settled complaints of trader fraud and losses in transit. This trade was not the first time in history that private entrepreneurs conducted business in a way that we might label early capitalism—maximizing profits as a reward for the risk of business—but it provides the best-known example from this period.

Hammurabi of Babylon and Written Law. The expansion of private commerce and property ownership in Mesopotamia created a pressing need to guarantee fairness and reliability in contracts and other business agreements. The king had the sacred duty to make divine justice known to his subjects by rendering judgments in all sorts of cases, from commercial disputes to crime. Once written down, the record of the king's decisions amounted to what historians today call a law code, even though the Mesopotamians did not use that term. King Hammurabi♦ (r. c. 1792–c. 1750 b.c.e.) of Babylon, a great city on the Euphrates River in what is today Iraq, built an empire rivaling that of Sargon. The fifth king of the Babylonian Amorite dynasty, he instituted the most famous law code of the era by building on earlier Mesopotamian legal traditions, such as those of the Akkadian monarchs and the Ur III dynasty. Hammurabi's code stands as a prime example of the sophistication that Mesopotamian legal traditions achieved (see "Hammurabi's Laws for Physicians," page 17).

In his code Hammurabi proclaimed that his goals as ruler were to support "the principles of truth and equity" and to protect the less powerful members of society from exploitation. The code legally divided society into three categories: free persons, commoners, and slaves. We do not know what made the first two categories different, but they reflect a social hierarchy in which some people were assigned a higher value than others. An attacker who caused a pregnant woman of the free class to miscarry, for example, paid twice the fine levied for the same offense against a commoner. In the case of physical injury between social equals, the code specified "an eye for an eye" (an expression still used today). But a member of the free class who killed a commoner was not executed, only fined.

♦**Hammurabi:** ha muh RAH bee

Most of the laws concerned the king's interests as a property owner who leased many tracts of land to tenants in return for rent or services. The laws imposed severe penalties for offenses against property, including mutilation or a gruesome death for crimes as varied as theft, wrongful sales, and careless construction. Women had only limited legal rights in this patriarchal society, but they could make business contracts and appear in court. A wife could divorce her husband for cruelty; a husband could divorce his wife for any reason. The inequality of the divorce laws was tempered in practice, however, because a woman could recover the property she had brought to her marriage, a considerable disincentive for a man to end his union.

Hammurabi's laws publicized a royal ideal of justice guaranteed by a righteous king; they did not necessarily reflect everyday reality. Indeed, Babylonian documents show that legal penalties were often less severe than the code specified. The people themselves assembled in courts to determine most cases by their own judgments. Why, then, did Hammurabi have his laws written down? He announces his reasons at the beginning and end of his code: to show Shamash, the Babylonian sun god and god of justice, that he had fulfilled the social responsibility imposed on him as a divinely installed monarch—to ensure justice and the moral and material welfare of his people: "So that the powerful may not oppress the powerless, to provide justice for the orphan and the widow ... let the victim of injustice see the law which applies to him, let his heart be put at ease." The king's moral responsibility for his society's welfare corresponded to the strictly hierarchical and religious vision of society accepted by all Mesopotamian peoples.

City Life and Learning. The situations covered by Hammurabi's laws illuminate many aspects of the lives of city dwellers in Mesopotamia's Bronze Age kingdoms. For example, crimes of burglary and assault apparently plagued urban residents. The bride's father and the groom arranged a marriage, sealing the agreement with a legal contract. The detailed laws on surgery make clear that doctors practiced in the cities.

Hammurabi's Laws for Physicians

In Hammurabi's collection of 282 laws, the following statutes set the fees for successful operations and the punishment for physicians' errors. The prescription of mutilation of a surgeon as the punishment for mutilation of a patient from the highest social class (law number 218) squares with the legal principle of equivalent punishment ("an eye for an eye") that pervades Hammurabi's collection.

215. If a physician performed a major operation on a freeman with a bronze scalpel and has saved the freeman's life, or he opened up the eye-socket of a freeman with a bronze scalpel and has saved the freeman's eye, he shall receive ten shekels[1] of silver.

216. If it was a commoner, he shall receive five shekels of silver.

217. If it was a freeman's slave, the owner of the slave shall give two shekels of silver to the physician.

218. If a physician performed a major operation on a freeman with a bronze scalpel and has caused the freeman's death, or he opened up the eye-socket of a freeman and has destroyed the freeman's eye, they shall cut off his hand.

219. If a physician performed a major operation on a commoner's slave with a bronze scalpel and has caused his death, he shall make good slave for slave.

220. If he opened up [the slave's] eye-socket with a bronze scalpel and has destroyed his eye, he shall pay half his value in silver.

[1] A shekel is a measurement of weight (about 3/10 oz.), not a coin. A hired laborer earned about a shekel per week. The average price of a slave was about twenty shekels.

Source: Adapted from James B. Pritchard, *Ancient Near Eastern Texts Relating to the Old Testament*, 3rd ed. with supplement (Princeton, NJ: Princeton University Press, 1969), 175.

Because people believed that angry gods or evil spirits caused serious diseases, Mesopotamian medicine included magic as well as treatment with potions and diet. A doctor might prescribe an incantation as part of his therapy. Magicians or exorcists offered medical treatment that depended primarily on spells and on interpreting signs, such as the patient's dreams or hallucinations.

Archaeological evidence supplements the information on urban life found in Hammurabi's code. City dwellers evidently enjoyed alcoholic drinks in a friendly setting because cities had many taverns and wine shops, often run by women proprietors. Contaminated drinking water caused many illnesses because sewage disposal was rudimentary. Relief from the odors and crowding of the streets could be found in the city's open spaces. The oldest known map in the world, an inscribed clay tablet showing the outlines of the Babylonian city of Nippur about 1500 B.C.E., indicates a substantial area set aside as a city park.

Creating maps required sophisticated techniques of measurement and knowledge of spatial relationships. Mesopotamian achievements in mathematics and astronomy had a profound effect that endures to this day. Mathematicians used algebra to solve complex problems, and they could derive the roots of numbers. They invented place-value notation, which makes a numeral's position in a number indicate ones, tens, hundreds, and so on. We have also inherited from Mesopotamia the system of reckoning based on sixty, still used in the division of hours and minutes and degrees of a circle. Mesopotamian expertise in recording the paths of the stars and planets probably arose from the desire to make predictions about the future, in accordance with the astrological belief that the movement of celestial bodies directly affects human life. Astrology never lost its popularity in Mesopotamia, and the charts and tables compiled by Mesopotamian stargazers laid the foundation for later advances in astronomical knowledge.

> **Review:** How did life change for people in Mesopotamia when they began to live in cities?

❖ The Egyptians, Canaanites, and Hebrews, c. 3050–c. 1000 B.C.E.

Africa was home to the second great civilization to shape the West—that of the Egyptians. Egypt was located close enough to Mesopotamia to learn from its peoples but geographically protected enough to develop its own distinct culture. Egyptians created a wealthy, profoundly religious, and strongly traditional civilization ruled by kings. Unlike Mesopotamia, Egypt became a united state whose prosperity and stability depended on the king's success in maintaining strong central authority. The Egyptians' deep concern for the immortality of their souls and the afterlife motivated the construction of some of the most imposing tombs in history, the pyramids, while their architecture and art inspired later Mediterranean peoples, especially the Greeks.

The early civilizations of the Levant never rivaled Egypt's splendor, but they transmitted lasting legacies to Western civilization, especially the Canaanites' alphabet and the monotheism of the Hebrews (or Israelites). The Hebrews' religion, known as Judaism, took a long time to develop and reflected influences from their polytheistic neighbors in Canaan (ancient Palestine), but it initiated the most important religious movements in Western history.

From Egyptian Unification to the Old Kingdom, c. 3050–c. 2190 B.C.E.

Geography treated the Egyptians kindly: the Nile River irrigated their farms, the deserts beyond their rich fields yielded metal ores and protected them from invasion, their Mediterranean ports supported seaborne commerce, and their southern neighbors in Africa offered trade and cultural interaction. The first large-scale Egyptian state began to emerge about 3050 B.C.E., when King Narmer (also called Menes)[2] united the previously separate territories of Upper (southern) Egypt and Lower (northern) Egypt. (*Upper* and *Lower* derive from the direction of the Nile River, which begins south of Egypt and flows northward to the Mediterranean.) The Egyptian ruler therefore referred to himself as "King of the Two Lands." By around 2687 B.C.E., the monarchs had forged a strong, centralized state, called the Old Kingdom by historians, which lasted until around 2190 B.C.E. (Map 1.2). The Old Kingdom's rulers established Egypt as an international power and a cultural beacon for the ancient world.

Narmer's unification created a state from a territory resembling a long green ribbon, zigzagging seven hundred miles southward from the Mediterranean Sea along the Nile. Lush agricultural fields extending several miles away from the river's banks formed this fertile strip. Under normal weather conditions, the Nile created Egypt's fertility by overflowing its channel for at least several weeks each year, when melting snow from the mountains of central Africa swelled its volume of water. This annual flood enriched the soil with nutrients from the river's silt and prevented the accumulation of harmful deposits of mineral salts. Unlike the random and catastrophic floods of the Mesopotamian

---

[2]Representing ancient Egyptian names and dates presents serious problems. Since the Egyptians did not include vowel sounds in their writing, we are not sure how to spell their names. The spelling of names here is taken from *The Oxford Encyclopedia of Ancient Egypt*, edited by Donald B. Redford (2001), with alternate names given in cases where they might be more familiar. Dates are approximate and controversial; the scattered evidence for Egyptian chronology embroils scholars in "a world of uncertainty and acrimonious debate" (Redford, *The Oxford Encyclopedia*, vol. 1, p. xi; for an explanation of the problems, see the article on "Chronology and Periodization," vol. 1, pp. 264–68). The dates appearing in this book are compiled with as much consistency as possible from articles in *The Oxford Encyclopedia* and in the "Egyptian King List" given at the back of each of its volumes.

rivers, the flooding of the Nile was predictable and beneficial. Trouble came only if dry weather in the mountains kept the flood from occurring and therefore reduced the year's crops to dust.

Deserts east and west of the river protected Egypt from attack by land, except through the Nile's delta at its mouth and its valley on the southern frontier with Nubia. The surpluses that a multitude of hardworking farmers produced in the lush Nile valley made Egypt prosperous. Date palms, vegetables, grass for pasturing animals, and grain grew in abundance. From their ample supplies of grain the Egyptians made bread and beer, a staple beverage.

Egypt comprised a diversity of people, whose skin color ranged from light to very dark. A significant proportion of Egyptians would be regarded as black by modern American racial classification, a distinction ancient people did not observe. The heated modern controversy over whether Egyptians were people of color is therefore anachronistic; if asked, ancient Egyptians would presumably have answered that they identified themselves by geography, language, religion, and traditions. Like many ancient groups, the Egyptians called themselves simply "The People." Later peoples, especially the Greeks, admired Egyptian civilization for its great antiquity and piety. There is merit to the modern accusation that some nineteenth-century historians minimized the Egyptian contribution to Western civilization, but it is important to remember that ancient peoples did not.

Early Egyptians learned from both the Mesopotamians and their southern African neighbors the Nubians.♦ Egyptians may have originally learned the technology of writing from the Sumerians, but they developed their own scripts rather than using cuneiform. To write formal and official texts they used an ornate pictographic script known as **hieroglyphs**♦ (Figure 1.2, page 20). They also developed other scripts for everyday purposes.

Some historians believe that Nubian society deeply influenced early Egypt. At places

---

♦**Nubians:** NOO bee uhns
♦**hieroglyph:** HY ruh glihf

MAP 1.2 Ancient Egypt
Arid deserts closely embraced the Nile River, which provided Egyptians with water to irrigate their fields and a highway for traveling north to the Mediterranean Sea and south to Nubia. The only easy land route into and out of Egypt lay through the northern Sinai peninsula into the coastal area of the eastern Mediterranean; Egyptian kings therefore always fought to control this region to secure the safety of their land.

such as Afyeh, near the Nile's First Cataract, a Nubian social elite lived in dwellings much grander than the small huts housing most of the population. Egyptians interacted with Nubians while trading for raw materials such as gold, ivory, and animal skins, and some scholars argue that a hierarchical political and social organization in Nubia influenced the development of Egypt's politically centralized Old Kingdom. Eventually, however, Egypt's power overshadowed that of its southern neighbor.

Hieroglyph	Meaning	Sound value
	vulture	glottal stop
	flowering reed	consonantal I
	forearm and hand	ayin
	quail chick	W
	foot	B
	stool	P
	horned viper	F
	owl	M
	water	N
	mouth	R
	reed shelter	H
	twisted flax	slightly guttural
	placenta (?)	H as in "loch"
	animal's belly	slightly softer than h
	door bolt	S
	folded cloth	S
	pool	SH
	hill	Q
	basket with handle	K
	jar stand	G
	loaf	T

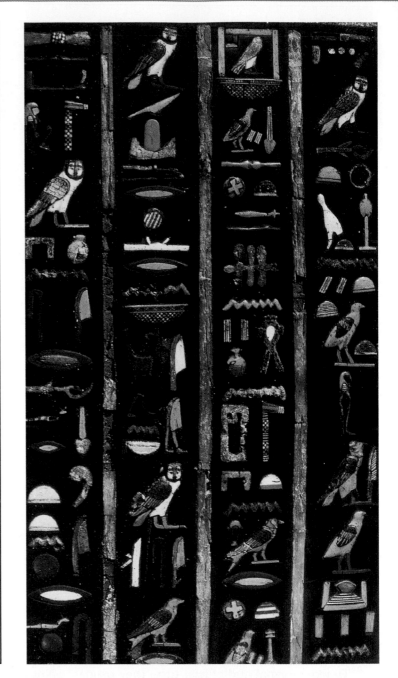

FIGURE 1.2 Egyptian Hieroglyphs

Ancient Egyptians used pictures such as these to develop their own system of writing about 3000 B.C.E. Egyptian hieroglyphs employ around seven hundred pictures in three categories: ideograms (signs indicating things or ideas), phonograms (signs indicating sounds), and determinatives (signs clarifying the meaning of the other signs). Because Egyptians employed this formal script mainly for religious inscriptions on buildings and sacred objects, Greeks referred to it as *ta hieroglyphica* ("the sacred carved letters"), from which comes the modern word *hieroglyphic,* used for this system of writing. Eventually, Egyptians also developed the handwritten cursive script called demotic (Greek for "of the people"), a much simpler and quicker form of writing. The hieroglyphic writing system continued until about 400 C.E., when it was replaced by the Coptic alphabet. The Egyptian language continued to be widely spoken until Arabic displaced it in medieval times. (It is preserved today in the liturgy of the Coptic Church.) Compare hieroglyphic writing with cuneiform (see page 12). *Victor Boswell, Jr. © National Geographic Society Image Collection. Giraudon/Art Resource, NY.*

Religion and the Old Kingdom's Central Authority.

The waxing and waning of strong central authority determined the course of Egyptian political history. When the kings were strong, as during the Old Kingdom, the country was stable and rich, with flourishing international trade, especially along the eastern Mediterranean coast. However, political instability resulted when the governors of different regions refused to support the king.

The king's power and success depended on his properly fulfilling his religious obligations. Like the Mesopotamians, Egyptians both royal and ordinary centered their lives on religion. They worshiped a great variety of gods, who were often shown in paintings and sculpture as creatures with both human and animal features, such as the head of a jackal or a bird atop a human body. This style of depicting deities did not mean that people worshiped animals but rather that they believed the gods each had a particular animal through which they revealed themselves to mortals. A picture or a statue of a divinity included the animal so that the depiction would have meaning to the human observer. Egyptian religion told complicated stories about the daily lives of the gods to explain their powers and their significance for human beings. At the most basic level, deities were associated with powerful natural objects, emotions, qualities, and technologies—examples are Re, the sun god; Isis, the goddess of love and fertility; and Thoth, the god of wisdom and the inventor of writing.

Egyptians regarded their king as a divinity in human form, identified with the hawk-headed god Horus.♦ In the Egyptian view, the king's rule was divine because it represented on earth the supernatural, eternal force that created harmony and stability in human life. The goddess **Maat** (literally, "What Is Right"), who stood for cosmic order, embodied this force; for Egyptians, order brought justice. As a divine being, the king had the heavy responsibility of ruling according to Maat's principles, which meant promoting law and keeping the forces of nature in balance for the benefit of his people.

This included regulating his daily activities very strictly: he had to have a specific time to take a bath, go for a walk, or make love to his wife. Most crucially, he had to ensure fertility and prosperity. These depended on a proper flooding of the Nile, which he guaranteed by performing his duties justly and in accordance with traditional order. A failure to make the flood happen could gravely weaken the king's authority.

Pyramids and the Afterlife.

Successful Old Kingdom rulers used expensive building programs to demonstrate their piety and exhibit their status atop the social hierarchy. Unlike their Mesopotamian counterparts ruling independent states in a divided land, Egyptian kings built only a few large cities in their united country. The first capital of the united country, Memphis (south of modern Cairo), grew into a metropolis packed with mammoth structures. In the desert outside Memphis, the Old Kingdom rulers erected the most stunning manifestations of their status and their religion—their huge tombs.

These tombs—the pyramids (see The Pyramids at Giza)—formed the centerpieces of elaborate groups of buildings for royal funerals and religious ceremonies. Although the pyramids were not the first monuments in the world built from enormous worked stones (that honor goes to temples on the Mediterranean island of Malta), they rank as the grandest. Old Kingdom rulers spent vast resources on these huge complexes to proclaim their divine status and protect their mummified bodies for existence in the afterlife. Imhotep, chief architect of King Djoser (r. 2687–2668 B.C.E.), became famous for overseeing the construction of the first large stone pyramid, the Step Pyramid at Saqqara.♦ King Khufu♦ (r. 2609–2584 B.C.E.; also known as Cheops♦) commissioned the hugest of them all—the Great Pyramid at Giza. At about 480 feet high, it stands taller than a forty-story skyscraper. Covering more than thirteen acres and 760 feet long on each side, it required more than two million

♦**Horus:** HAWR uhs

♦**Saqqara:** suh KAHR uh
♦**Khufu:** KOO foo
♦**Cheops:** CHEE ahps

blocks of limestone, some of which weighed fifteen tons apiece. Its fine exterior blocks were quarried along the Nile and then floated to the site on barges. Free workers (not slaves) dragged them up ramps into position using rollers and sleds.

The kings' lavish preparations for death reflect the strong Egyptian belief in an afterlife. More than any other ancient people, the Egyptians devoted material resources to preparing for eternity. A hieroglyphic text addressed to the god Atum◆ expresses the hope that the ruler will have a secure afterlife: "O Atum, put your arms around King Neferkare Pepy II [r. c. 2300–2206 B.C.E.], around this construction work, around this pyramid. . . . May you guard lest anything happen to him evilly throughout the course of eternity." The royal family equipped their tombs with elaborate delights for their existence in the world of the dead. Gilded furniture, sparkling jewelry, exquisite objects of all kinds—the dead kings had all this and more placed beside their coffins, in which rested

---

◆**Atum:** AH tuhm

their mummies. Archaeologists have even uncovered two full-sized cedar ships buried next to the Great Pyramid, meant to carry King Khufu on his journey into eternity.

Hierarchy and Order in Egyptian Society. Old Kingdom rulers organized Egyptian society into a tightly structured hierarchy to preserve their authority and therefore support what they regarded as the proper order. The king and queen, whose roles included producing children to continue the ruling dynasty, topped the social order. Brothers and sisters in the royal family could marry each other, perhaps because such matches were believed necessary to preserve the purity of the royal line or to imitate the marriages of the gods. The priests, royal administrators, provincial governors, and commanders of the army came next in the hierarchy, but they ranked far below the king and queen. The common people, who mostly worked in agriculture, constituted the massive base of this figurative pyramid of free people in Egypt. Although not slaves, workers had heavy obligations to the state. For example, in a system

The Pyramids at Giza in Egypt
The kings of the Egyptian Old Kingdom constructed massive stone pyramids for their tombs, the centerpieces of large complexes of temples and courtyards stretching down to the banks of the Nile or along a canal leading to the river. The inner burial chambers lay at the end of long, narrow tunnels snaking through the pyramids' interiors. The biggest pyramid shown here is the so-called Great Pyramid of King Khufu (aka Cheops), erected at Giza (in the desert outside what is today Cairo) in the twenty-sixthcentury B.C.E. and soaring almost 480 feet high, several times taller than the famous Parthenon temple in fifth-century B.C.E. Athens (see page 93). © *John Lawrence/Super Stock.*

called corvée labor, the kings could and did command commoners to work on the pyramids during slack times for agriculture. The state fed, housed, and clothed them while they performed this seasonal work, but their labor was a way of paying taxes. Rates of taxation reached 20 percent on the produce of free farmers. Slaves captured in foreign wars served the royal family and the priests in the Old Kingdom, but privately owned slaves working in free persons' homes or on their farms did not become prevalent until after the Old Kingdom.

Women generally enjoyed the same legal rights as free men in ancient Egypt. They could own land and slaves, inherit property, pursue lawsuits, transact business, and initiate divorces. Old Kingdom portrait statues show the equal status of wife and husband: each figure is the same size and sits on the same kind of chair. Men dominated public life, while women devoted themselves mainly to private life, managing their households and property. When their husbands went to war or were killed in battle, however, women often took on men's work. Some women could therefore serve as priestesses, farm managers, or healers.

The formalism of Egypt's art illustrates how much the civilization valued order and predictability. Almost all Egyptian sculpture and painting comes from tombs or temples, testimony to its people's consuming interest in maintaining proper relations with the gods. Old Kingdom artists excelled in stonework, from carved ornamental jars to massive portrait statues of the kings. These statues represent the subject either standing stiffly with the left leg advanced or sitting on a chair or throne, stable and poised. The concern for decorum also appears in the Old Kingdom literature the Egyptians called instructions, known today as **wisdom literature**. These texts conveyed instructions for appropriate behavior for high officials. In the *Instruction of Ptahhotep,*♦ for example, the royal minister Ptahhotep instructs his son, who will succeed him in office, not to be arrogant or overconfident just because he is well educated and to seek advice from ignorant people as well as the wise.

♦**Ptahhotep:** tah HOH tehp

The Middle and New Kingdoms in Egypt, c. 2061–c. 1081 B.C.E.

The Old Kingdom's ordered stability began to disintegrate in the late third millennium B.C.E. The causes remain mysterious. One suggestion is that climate changes caused the annual Nile flood to shrink and the ensuing agricultural failure discredited the regime— it had betrayed Maat. Economic hard times probably fueled rivalry for royal rule between ambitious families, and civil war between a northern and a southern dynasty then ripped apart the Kingdom of the Two Lands. This destruction of the Old Kingdom's unity allowed regional governors to increase their power. Some governors, who had supported the kings while times were good, seized independence for their regions. It was the troubles of this period that made Merikare's father's advice so pressing: famine and civil unrest during the so-called First Intermediate Period (c. 2190–c. 2061 B.C.E.) thwarted all attempts to reestablish political unity.

The Middle Kingdom. The monarchs of what historians label the Middle Kingdom (c. 2061–c. 1665 B.C.E.) gradually restored the strong central authority their Old Kingdom predecessors had lost. They pushed the boundaries of Egypt farther south, while to the north they expanded diplomatic and trade contacts in Canaan and Syria and with the island of Crete.

Middle Kingdom literature reveals that the reclaimed national unity contributed to a deeply felt pride in the homeland. The Egyptian narrator of the famous tale *The Story of Sinuhe*, for example, reports that he lived luxuriously during a forced stay in Syria but still longed to return: "Whichever deity you are who ordered my exile, have mercy and bring me home! Please allow me to see the land where my heart dwells! Nothing is more important than that my body be buried in the country where I was born!" For this lost soul, love for Egypt outranks even personal riches.

From the Hyksos Invasion to the New Kingdom. The Middle Kingdom lost its unity during the Second Intermediate Period (c. 1664– c. 1570 B.C.E.), when the kings proved too weak to repel foreign invaders who violently disrupted the Egyptians' ordered world. A Semitic people from the eastern Mediterranean coast expanded into Lower Egypt around 1664 B.C.E. The Egyptians called these foreigners Hyksos♦ (literally, "rulers of the foreign countries"). Recent archaeological discoveries have emphasized the role of Hyksos settlers in transplanting elements of foreign culture to Egypt: their capital, Avaris, boasted wall paintings done in the Minoan style current on the island of Crete. Some historians think the Hyksos also introduced such innovations as bronze-making technology, horses and war chariots, more powerful bows, new musical instruments, humpbacked cattle, and olive trees; they certainly promoted frequent contact with other Near Eastern states. As with the empire of the Akkadians, violent invasion indirectly promoted cultural interchange.

Eventually, the leaders of Thebes in southern Egypt reunited the kingdom by overcoming the Hyksos in a long struggle; their dynasties are called the New Kingdom (c. 1569–c. 1081 B.C.E.). The kings of this period, known as *pharaohs* (meaning "the great house" and referring to the royal palace and estate) rebuilt central authority by restricting the power of regional governors and promoted a renewed sense of national identity. To prevent invasions, the pharaohs created a standing army and a military elite to lead it. Recognizing from the Hyksos invasion that knowledge of the rest of the world was necessary for safety, they engaged in regular diplomacy with neighboring monarchs to increase their cosmopolitan contacts. In fact, the pharaohs regularly exchanged letters on matters of state with their "brother kings," as they called them, in Mesopotamia, Anatolia, and the eastern Mediterrranean region.

Warrior Pharaohs. The New Kingdom pharaohs sent their reorganized military into foreign wars to promote Egypt's interests. They earned the epithet *warrior pharaohs* by waging many campaigns abroad and modifying their royal religious stature by presenting themselves as the incarnations of warrior gods. They invaded Nubia and the Sudan to the south to win access to gold and

other precious materials, and they fought in the lands of the Levant to control the land route to Egypt.

Massive riches supported the power of the warrior pharaohs. Egyptian traders exchanged local fine goods, such as ivory, for foreign luxury goods, such as wine and olive oil transported in painted pottery from Greece. Egyptian royalty displayed its wealth most conspicuously in the enormous sums spent to build stone temples. Queen Hatshepsut♦ (opposite) (r. 1502–1482 B.C.E.), for example, built her massive mortuary temple at Deir el Bahri near Thebes, including a temple dedicated to the god Amun (or Amen), to buttress her claim to divine birth and the right to rule. After her husband (who was also her half brother) died, Hatshepsut proclaimed herself "female king" as co-ruler with her young stepson. In this way, she shrewdly sidestepped Egyptian political ideology, which made no provision for a queen to reign in her own right. She therefore often had herself represented in official art as a man, sporting a king's beard and male clothing.

Religious Tradition and Upheaval. The many gods of Egyptian polytheism oversaw all aspects of life and death, with particular emphasis on the afterlife. Glorious temples honored the traditional gods, and their cults (that is, worship traditions and rituals) enriched the religious life of the entire population. The principal festivals of the gods, for example, involved lavish public celebrations. A calendar based on the moon governed the dates of religious ceremonies. (The Egyptians also developed a calendar for administrative and fiscal purposes that had 365 days, divided into 12 months of 30 days each, with the extra 5 days added before the start of the next year. Our modern calendar derives from it.)

The early New Kingdom pharaohs from Thebes promoted their state god Amun-Re♦ until he overshadowed the other gods. This Theban cult incorporated and subordinated the other gods without denying either their existence or the continued importance of their priests. The pharaoh Akhenaten♦

♦**Hyksos:** HIHK sahs

♦**Hatshepsut:** hat SHEHP soot
♦**Amun-Re:** AH muhn RAH
♦**Akhenaten:** AH kehn AH tehn

(r. 1372–1355 B.C.E.) went a step further, however; because he believed so fervently that traditional belief was misguided, he forcibly reformed official religion by making Aten, who represented the shining disk of the sun, the only true god. Some scholars identify Akhenaten's religion as the first **monotheism** (belief in only one god, as in Judaism, Christianity, and Islam). Akhenaten made the king and the queen the only people with direct access to the cult of Aten, using his new religion as a tool to reassert power over the nobles. Ordinary people had no part in the cult.

To showcase the royal family and the concentration of power that he sought, Akhenaten built a new capital for his god at Tell el-Amarna (see Map 1.2). He tried to force his revised religion on the priests of the old cults, but they resisted stubbornly. Historians have blamed Akhenaten's religious zeal for leading him to neglect the practical affairs of ruling the kingdom, weakening its defense, but recent research on international correspondence found at Tell el-Amarna has shown that the pharaoh used diplomacy to try to pit foreign enemies against each other to prevent them from becoming strong enough to threaten Egypt. His policy failed, however, when the Hittites defeated the Mitanni, Egypt's allies in eastern Syria. His religious reform also died with him. During the reign of Akhenaten's successor, Tutankhamun♦ (r. 1355–1346 B.C.E.)—famous today through the discovery in 1922 of his rich, unlooted tomb—the cult of Amun-Re reclaimed its leading role. The crisis created by Akhenaten's attempted reform emphasizes the overwhelming importance of religious conservatism in Egyptian life and the control of religion by the ruling power.

Life and Belief in the New Kingdom. Despite the period's many upheavals, the rhythm of ordinary Egyptians' daily lives still revolved around their labor and the annual flood of the Nile. During the months when the river stayed between its banks, they worked their fields, rising early in the morning to avoid the searing heat. Their obligation to labor on royal building projects came due when the flooding halted agricultural work

♦**Tutankhamun:** too tang KAH muhn

Queen Hatshepsut of Egypt as Pharaoh
This famous New Kingdom monarch of the fifteenth century B.C.E. had to adopt the male trappings of Egyptian kingship to claim legitimacy because her land's tradition had no place for women as sole rulers. Here she is depicted wearing the distinctive garb of a pharaoh. She had this statue placed in a temple she built outside Thebes in Upper Egypt. *Metropolitan Museum of Art, Rogers Fund and contribution from Edward Harkness, 1929.*

Declaring Innocence on Judgment Day in Ancient Egypt

The Egyptian collection of spells known today as the Book of the Dead *instructed the dead person how to make a declaration of innocence to the gods and demons judging the person's fate on the day of judgment. The declaration listed evils that the person denied having committed; presumably the divine judges could tell whether the deceased was speaking truthfully. This selection of denials, each directed to a specific deity, reveals what Egyptians regarded as just and proper behavior.*

Wide-of-Stride who comes from On: I have not done evil.

Flame-grasper who comes from Kheraha: I have not robbed.

Long-nosed who comes from Khmun: I have not coveted.

Shadow-eater who comes from the cave: I have not stolen.

Savage-faced who comes from Rostau: I have not killed people.

Lion-Twins who come from heaven: I have not trimmed the measure.

Flint-eyed who comes from Kehm: I have not cheated.

Fiery-one who comes backward: I have not stolen a god's property.

Bone-smasher who comes from Hnes: I have not told lies.

Flame-thrower who comes from Memphis: I have not seized food.

Cave-dweller who comes from the west: I have not sulked.

White-toothed who comes from Lakeland: I have not trespassed.

Blood-eater who comes from slaughterplace: I have not slain sacred cattle.

Entrail-eater who comes from the tribunal: I have not extorted.

Lord of Maat who comes from Maaty: I have not extorted.

Wanderer who comes from Bubastis: I have not spied.

Pale-one who comes from On: I have not prattled.

Villain who comes from Anjdty: I have contended only for my goods.

Fiend who comes from slaughterhouse: I have not committed adultery.

Examiner who comes from Min's temple: I have not defiled myself.

Chief of the nobles who comes from Imu: I have not caused fear.

Wrecker who comes from Huy: I have not trespassed.

Disturber who comes from the sanctuary: I have not been violent.

Child who comes from the nome of On: I have not been deaf to Maat.

Foreteller who comes from Wensi: I have not quarreled.

Bastet who comes from the shrine: I have not winked.

Backward-face who comes from the pit: I have not copulated with a boy.

Flame-footed who comes from the dusk: I have not been false.

Dark-one who comes from darkness: I have not reviled.

[More denials follow.]

Source: Translation from Miriam Lichtheim, *Ancient Egyptian Literature* (Berkeley: University of California Press, 1978), Vol. 2, 126–27.

and freed them to move to workers' quarters erected next to the building sites. Although slaves became more common as household workers in the New Kingdom, free workers, performing labor instead of paying taxes in money, did most of the work on this period's mammoth royal construction projects. Written texts reveal that workers lightened their burden by singing songs and telling adventure stories. They labored extensively: the majority of temples remaining in Egypt today come from the New Kingdom. The architecture of these rectangular stone buildings studded with soaring, sculpted columns anticipated the style of the later temples of Greece.

Ordinary people remained devoted to deities outside the royal cults, especially to gods they hoped would protect them in their daily lives. They venerated Bes, for instance, a dwarf with the features of a lion, as a protector of the household. They carved his image on amulets, beds, headrests, and the handles of mirrors. People also spent lots of time and effort preparing for the next life. Those who could afford it arranged to have their tombs outfitted with all the goods needed for the journey to their new existence. Most important, they had their corpses mummified so that they could have a body in the afterlife. Making a mummy required removing the brain and internal organs, drying the body with mineral salts to the consistency of old leather, and wrapping it in linen soaked with unguents. Every mummy had to travel to the afterlife with a copy of the *Book of the Dead*, whose collection of magical instructions warded off dangers and coached the dead person through his or her trial before the gods. Particularly powerful spells would be labeled "truly excellent, proved a million times." The text enumerated a long list of sins that the dead person had to be able to deny, including "I have not committed crimes against people; I have not mistreated cattle; I have not robbed the poor; I have not caused pain; I have not caused tears" (see "Declaring Innocence on Judgment Day in Ancient Egypt," page 26).

Magic, both written and oral, played a large role in the lives of Egyptians. They sought spells and charms from professional magicians to ward off demons, smooth the rocky course of love, exact revenge on enemies, and find relief from disease and injury. Egyptian doctors knew many medicinal herbs (knowledge that was passed on to later civilizations), and they could perform demanding surgeries, including opening the skull. Still, no doctor could cure severe infections; as in the past, sick people continued to rely on the help of supernatural forces through prayers and spells.

Canaanite Innovation and Hebrew Origins, c. 3000–c. 1000 B.C.E.

The peoples living along the coast of the eastern Mediterranean Sea played a large role in the history of Western civilization because their location put them at a crossroads of cultural interaction, which energized their inventiveness. In particular, the Canaanites' innovation in writing technology and the Hebrews' innovation in religion made them enduringly influential, even though they never rivaled the political and military power of their neighbors in Anatolia, Mesopotamia, and Egypt.

Canaanites, Commerce, and the Alphabet. The Canaanites originally dominated the lands of the Levant. By around 3000 B.C.E., they had built an urban civilization. Their independent city-states, especially the bustling ports of Ugarit, Byblos,◆ and Tyre, grew rich from maritime commerce in the second millennium B.C.E. by trading metals and exporting timber from the Lebanese foothills; they expanded their populations by absorbing merchants from many lands. Some scholars believe that the political structure of the Canaanite communities provided an antecedent for the later city-states of Greece.

The interaction of traders and travelers from many different cultures encouraged innovation in the recording of business transactions. This lively, multilingual environment produced an overwhelmingly important innovation in writing technology about 1600 B.C.E.: the alphabet. In this new system of writing, a simplified picture—a letter—stood for only one sound in the language, a dramatic change from complicated cuneiform and hieroglyphic scripts. The alphabet developed in the Canaanite cities later became the basis for the Greek and Roman alphabets and, hence, of modern Western alphabets.

The Ancient Levant

◆**Byblos:** BIH bluhs

Pottery Stand with Sculpted Musicians from the Levant
This sculpted stand from about 1000 B.C.E., a little over a foot high, has five musicians playing different wind and perhaps small stringed instruments, leaning out from "windows" in the pedestal. The traces of incised and painted decoration preserved on this stand reflect a mixture of Canaanite and Mycenaean artistic styles, the result of the kind of cultural interchange that took place along the eastern Mediterranean coast, the crossroads of the ancient Near East. Since music played an important role in religion and court ceremonies, this piece may have belonged to a temple or a palace. *Israel Museum, Jerusalem. Artifact Collection of the Israel Antiquities Authority.*

The Canaanite alphabet therefore ranks as one of the most important legacies contributing to the foundation of Western civilization.

The Hebrews and the Bible.   The enduring legacy of the Hebrews to Western civilization comes from the significance of the book that became their sacred scripture, the Hebrew Bible (known to Christians as the Old Testament). This book deeply affected the formation of not only Judaism but also Christianity and, later, Islam. Unfortunately, no source provides definitive information on the historical background of the Hebrews or their religion. The Bible tells stories to explain God's moral plan for the universe, not to give a full account of Hebrew origins, and archaeology has not yielded a clear picture.

The Bible's account of Hebrew origins reports that the patriarch Abraham and his followers left the Mesopotamian city of Ur to migrate to Canaan, at the southeast corner of the Mediterranean Sea. Because other Semitic peoples, such as the Amorites, are known to have moved throughout the Fertile Crescent in the early second millennium, the story of Abraham's journey perhaps reflects this era; if so, it would be dated around 1900 B.C.E. Once in Canaan, the Hebrews continued their traditional existence as semi-nomads, tending flocks of animals on the region's scanty grasslands and living in temporary tent settlements. They occasionally planted barley or wheat for a season or two and then moved on to new pastures. Traditionally believed to have been divided into twelve tribes, they never settled down or formed a political state in this period. Organized political and military power in the region remained in the hands of the Canaanites.

Abraham's son Isaac moved his pastoral people to various locations to try to avoid disputes with local Canaanites over grazing rights. Isaac's son Jacob, the story continues, moved to Egypt late in life when his son Joseph brought Jacob and other relatives there to escape famine in Canaan. Joseph had previously used his intelligence and charisma to rise to an important position in the Egyptian administration. The biblical story of the movement of a band of Hebrews to Egypt represents a crucial event in their early history, possibly reflecting a time when drought forced some Hebrews to migrate gradually from southwest Asia into the Nile delta of Egypt. They probably drifted in gradually during the seventeenth or sixteenth century B.C.E. as part of the movement of peoples into Egypt under the Hyksos. By the thirteenth century B.C.E., the pharaohs had conscripted the Hebrew men into slave-labor gangs for farming and for construction work on large building projects.

According to the book of Exodus, the Hebrew deity, Yahweh,♦ instructed Moses to lead the Hebrews out of bondage in Egypt against the will of the king, perhaps Ramesses♦ II, around the mid-thirteenth century B.C.E. Yahweh sent ten plagues to compel the pharaoh to free the Hebrews, but the king still tried to recapture them during their flight. Yahweh therefore miraculously parted the Red Sea to allow them to escape eastward; the water swirled back together as the pharaoh's army tried to follow, drowning the Egyptians.

♦**Yahweh:** YAH way
♦**Ramesses:** RAM seez

Covenant and Hebrew Law. The biblical narrative then relates the crucial event in the history of the Hebrews: the formalizing of a covenant between them and their deity, who revealed himself to Moses on Mount Sinai in the desert northeast of Egypt. The covenant consisted of an agreement between the Hebrews and Yahweh that, in return for their promise to worship him exclusively as their only God and to live by his laws, God would make them his chosen people and lead them into a promised land of safety and prosperity. This binding agreement demanded human obedience to divine law and promised punishment for unrighteousness. God described himself to Moses as "compassionate and gracious, patient, ever constant and true...forgiving wickedness, rebellion, and sin, and not sweeping the guilty clean away; but one who punishes sons and grandsons to the third and fourth generation for their fathers' iniquity" (Exodus 34:6–7).

The Hebrew Bible set forth the religious and moral code the Hebrews had to follow. The Pentateuch◆ (the first five books of the Hebrew Bible) recorded numerous laws for righteous living. Most famous are the Ten Commandments, which required Hebrews to worship Yahweh, honor their parents, observe the seventh day of the week (the Sabbath) as a day free of work, and abstain from murder, adultery, theft, lying, and covetousness. Many Pentateuchal laws shared the traditional form and content of earlier Mesopotamian laws, such as those of Hammurabi: if someone did a certain thing to another person, then a specified punishment was imposed on the perpetrator. For example, both Hammurabi's and Hebrew law covered the case of an ox that had gored a person; the owner was penalized only if he had been warned about his beast's tendency to gore and had done nothing to restrain it. Also like Hammurabi's laws, Hebrew law expressed an interest in the welfare of the poor as well as the rich. In addition, it secured protection for the lower classes and people without power, such as strangers, widows, and orphans.

Hebrew law and thus Hebrew justice differed significantly from Mesopotamian precedent, however, in applying the same rules and punishments to everyone, without regard to a person's social ranking. Hebrew law also eliminated vicarious punishment—a Mesopotamian tradition ordering, for example, that a rapist's wife be raped or that the son of a builder be killed if his father's negligent work caused the death of someone else's son. Hebrew women and children had certain legal protections, although their rights were less extensive than men's. For example, wives had less freedom to divorce their husbands than husbands had to divorce their wives, much as in the laws of Hammurabi. Crimes against property did not carry the death penalty, as they frequently did in other Near Eastern societies. Hebrew laws also protected slaves against flagrant mistreatment by their masters. Slaves who lost an eye or even a tooth from a beating were to be freed. Like free people, slaves enjoyed the right to rest on the Sabbath, the holy day of the seven-day Hebrew week.

Hebrew Monotheism. The Hebrews' innovation in developing a monotheistic religion makes them a principal building block in the foundations of Western civilization. Because the earliest parts of the Hebrew Bible were probably composed about 950 B.C.E., more than three hundred years after the exodus from Egypt, their account of the Hebrew covenant and laws deals with a distant, undocumented time. Many uncertainties persist in our understanding of the process by which the Hebrews acquired their distinctive religion and way of life, but it seems clear that both took much longer to evolve than the biblical account describes. Like their neighbors in Canaan, the early Hebrews worshiped a variety of gods, including spirits believed to reside in natural objects such as trees and stones. Yahweh may have originally been the deity of the tribe of Midian, to which Moses's father-in-law belonged. The form of the covenant with Yahweh conformed to the ancient Near Eastern tradition of treaties between a superior and subordinates, but its content differed from that of other ancient Near Eastern religions because it made Yahweh the exclusive deity of his people. In the time of Moses, Yahweh religion was not yet the pure monotheism it would later

---

◆**Pentateuch:** PEN tah took

become because it did not deny the existence of other gods. Because in the ensuing centuries some Hebrews worshiped other gods as well, such as Baal of Canaan, it seems that the covenant with Yahweh and fully formed Hebrew monotheism did not emerge until well after 1000 B.C.E.

The Hebrews who fled from Egypt with Moses made their way back to Canaan, but they were still exposed to attacks by the Egyptian army. The first documentation of their return to Canaan comes from an inscribed monument erected by the pharaoh Merneptah in the late thirteenth century B.C.E. to commemorate his victory in a military expedition there. The Hebrew tribes joined their relatives who had remained in Canaan and somehow carved out separate territories for themselves there. The twelve tribes remained politically distinct under the direction of separate leaders, called judges, until the eleventh century, when their first monarchy emerged. Their monotheism gradually developed over the succeeding centuries.

Review: How did religion guide the lives of people in the early civilizations of Egypt and the Levant?

❖ The Hittites, Minoans, and Mycenaeans, c. 2200–c. 1000 B.C.E.

The first civilizations in the central Mediterranean region emerged in Anatolia, dominated by the warlike Hittite kingdom (see Map 1.1); on the large island of Crete, home to the famously artistic Minoan civilization; and on the Greek mainland, where Mycenaean civilization grew rich from raiding and trade (Map 1.3).

These peoples enjoyed advanced technologies, elaborate architecture, striking art, a marked taste for luxury, and extensive trade contacts with Egypt and the Near East. They also inhabited a dangerous world in which regional disruptions from around 1200 to 1000 B.C.E. ultimately overwhelmed their prosperous cultures. Nevertheless, their accomplishments paved the way for the later civilization of Greece, which would dramatically influence the course of Western history.

The earliest central Mediterranean civilizations arose on islands located on antiq-

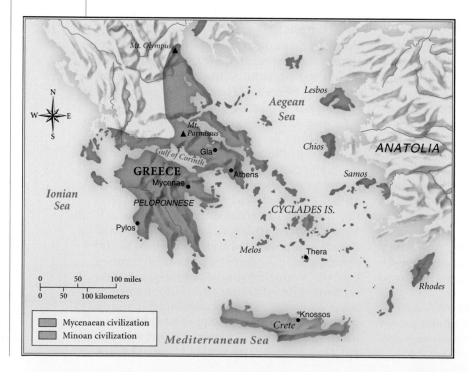

MAP 1.3 Greece and the Aegean Sea, c. 1500 B.C.E.
A closely packed jumble of mountains, islands, and seas defined the geography of Greece. The distances between settlements were mostly short, but rough terrain and seasonally stormy sailing made travel a chore. The distance from the mainland to the largest island in this region, Crete, where Minoan civilization arose, was sufficiently long to keep Cretans isolated from the turmoil of most of later Greek history.

Hittite Royal Couple Worshiping the Weather God
This relief sculpture from Alaca Höyük in north central Anatolia shows a Hittite king and queen worshiping the weather god, as he was called, who is represented here by his sacred animal, the bull, standing on an altar. In Hittite mythology, the weather god was thought to ride over the mountains in a chariot pulled by bulls. He was a divine hero who overcame evil by slaying a great dragon. At first the monster defeated him, but the goddess Inaras tricked the dragon into getting drunk so that the weather god could kill him. What characteristics of bulls and dragons made them relevant for expressing religious ideas?
Hirmer Fotoarchiv.

uity's interstate highway, the sea. People, trade goods, and ideas from other places could reach islands easily. As early as 6000 B.C.E., people from Anatolia began migrating westward and southward to inhabit islands in the Mediterranean Sea. By around 2200 B.C.E., the rich civilization of the Minoans had emerged on the island of Crete. The Anatolian peoples who stayed on the mainland also developed civilizations, of which the most aggressive and ambitious was the kingdom of the Hittites, who came into conflict with New Kingdom Egypt.

The Hittite Kingdom, c. 1750–c. 1200 B.C.E.

By around 1750 B.C.E. the Hittites had made themselves the most powerful people of central Anatolia. They had migrated from the Caucasus area, between the Black and Caspian Seas, and overcome indigenous peoples to set up their kingdom. It flourished because they inhabited a fertile upland plateau in the peninsula's center, excelled in war and diplomacy, and controlled trade in their region and southward. The Hittites' military campaigns knifing into the Levant threatened Egypt's possessions in Syria.

Since the Hittites spoke an Indo-European language, they belonged to the linguistic family that eventually populated most of Europe. The original Indo-European speakers, who were pastoralists and raiders, had migrated as separate groups into Anatolia and Europe, including Greece, from somewhere in western Asia. Recent archaeological discoveries there of graves of women buried with weapons suggest that women in these groups originally occupied positions of leadership in war and peace alongside men; the prominence of Hittite queens in documents, royal letters, and foreign treaties perhaps sprang from that tradition.

As in other early civilizations, rule in the Hittite kingdom depended on religion. Hittite religion combined worship of the gods of Indo-European religion with worship of deities inherited from the original Anatolian population. The king served as high priest of the storm god, and Hittite belief therefore demanded that he maintain a strict purity in his life as a demonstration of his justice and guardianship of social order. His drinking water, for example, always had to be strained. So strong was this insistence on purity that the king's water carrier was executed if so much as one hair was found in the water. Like Egyptian kings, Hittite rulers felt responsible for maintaining the gods' goodwill toward their subjects. King Mursili♦ II (r. 1321–1295 B.C.E.), for example, issued a set of prayers begging the gods to end a plague: "What is this, o gods, that you have done? Our land is dying. . . . We have lost our wits, and we can do nothing right. O gods, whatever sin you behold, either let a prophet come forth to identify it . . . or let us see it in a dream!"

The kings conducted many religious ceremonies in their capital, Hattusas, which grew into one of the most impressive cities of its era. Ringed by massive defensive walls and towers of stone, it centered on huge palaces aligned along straight, gravel-paved streets. Sculptures of animals, warriors, and, especially, the royal rulers decorated public spaces. The Hittite kings maintained their rule by forging personal alliances—cemented by marriages and oaths of loyalty—with the noble families of the kingdom.

These rulers aggressively employed their troops to expand their power. In the periods during which ties between the kings and the nobles remained strong and the kingdom therefore preserved its unity, they launched extremely ambitious military campaigns. In 1595 B.C.E., for example, the royal army raided as far as Babylon, destroying that kingdom. Scholars no longer accept the once popular idea that the Hittites owed their success in war to a special knowledge of making weapons from iron, although their craftsmen did smelt iron, from which they made ceremonial implements. (Weapons made from iron did not become common in the Mediterranean world until well after 1200 B.C.E.—at the end of the Hittite kingdom.) Their army excelled in the use of chariots, and perhaps this skill gave them an edge.

The economic strength of the Hittite kingdom flowed from control over long-distance trade routes for essential raw materials, especially metals. The Hittites worked mightily to dominate the lucrative trade moving between the coast and inland northern Syria. The Egyptian New Kingdom pharaohs fiercely resisted Hittite expansion and power in this region. The Anatolian kingdom proved too strong, however, and in the bloody battle of Kadesh,♦ around 1274 B.C.E., the Hittites checked the Egyptians in Syria, leading to a stalemate. Fear of Assyria eventually led the Hittite king Hattusili♦ III to negotiate with his Egyptian rival Ramesses II, and the two war-weary kingdoms became allies sixteen years after the battle of Kadesh by agreeing to a treaty that is a landmark in the history of international diplomacy. Remarkably, both Egyptian and Hittite copies of the treaty survive. In it, the two monarchs pledged to be "at peace and brothers forever." The alliance lasted, and thirteen years later the Hittite king gave his daughter to his Egyptian "brother" as his wife.

Minoan Crete, c. 2200–c. 1400 B.C.E.

Study of early Greek civilization traditionally begins with the people today known as Minoans, who inhabited the island of Crete by the late third millennium. The word *Minoan* was applied after a famous archaeologist, Arthur Evans (1851–1941), searched the island for traces of King Minos, renowned in Greek myth as a fierce ruler who built the first great navy. Scholars today are not sure whether to count the Minoans as Greek ancestors because they are uncertain whether the Minoan language, whose decipherment remains controversial, was related to Greek.

Cretans wrote in a script today called Linear A. Recent research suggests that, despite the long-held assumption to the contrary, Minoan may have been a member of the Indo-European family of languages, the ancestor of many languages, including Greek, Latin, and, much later, English. If this idea is confirmed by future research, then Minoan history will confidently rank as the earliest Greek history. Unfortunately, no Minoan literature survives, nor do any documents revealing Cretan ideas about the nature of justice.

Crete's large, fertile plains, adequate rainfall, and sheltered ports for fishing and

---

♦**Mursili:** mur SIHL ih

♦**Kadesh:** KAH dehsh
♦**Hattusili:** hat uh SIHL ih

Wall Painting from Akroteri on Thera

Minoan artists painted with vivid colors on plaster to enliven the walls of buildings. They depicted a wide variety of subjects, from lively animals and flowering plants to young boxers and women of the court in splendid dress. Unfortunately, time and earthquakes have severely damaged most Minoan wall paintings, and the versions we see today are largely reconstructions painted around surviving fragments of the originals. The fragmentary paintings from Akroteri on the island of Thera, south of Crete, were preserved by deep layers of ash spewed out by a massive volcanic eruption. *Julia M. Fair.*

seaborne trade offered a fine home for settlers. By around 2200 B.C.E., the Minoans had exploited these natural resources to create what scholars call a **palace society**, in recognition of its sprawling, many-chambered buildings that apparently housed both the rulers and their political, economic, and religious administration. The Cretan rulers combined the functions of chief and priest, dominating both politics and religion but without the unchallenged power of kings. The palaces seem to have been largely independent, with no one imposing unity on the island. Minoan rulers, their families, and their servants lived in the palaces. The general population clustered around the palaces in houses adjacent to one another; some of these settlements reached the size of cities, with thousands of inhabitants. Knossos♦ is the most famous such palace complex, which Evans thought had been Minos's headquar-

ters. Other, smaller settlements dotted outlying areas of the island.

The emergence in Minoan farming of what is called **Mediterranean polyculture**—the cultivation of olives, grapes, and grains in a single, interrelated agricultural system—profoundly affected Minoan society. The idea was to make the best use of a farmer's labor by growing crops together that required intense work at different seasons. This system, which still dominates Mediterranean agriculture, had two major consequences. First, the combination of crops provided a very healthy diet (the "Mediterranean diet," as it is called in today's medical community), which in turn stimulated population growth. Second, agriculture became both more diversified and more specialized, increasing production of the valuable products olive oil and wine.

The production of agricultural surpluses on Minoan Crete led to growth in specialized crafts, just as it had in Mesopotamia and

♦**Knossos:** NAH suhs

Egypt. Because old methods were inadequate for storing and transporting surplus food, Cretan artisans began to invent and manufacture huge storage jars (the size of a modern refrigerator) that could accommodate these products, in the process creating another specialized industry. Crafts workers, producing their sophisticated wares using time-consuming techniques, no longer had time to grow their own food or make the goods, such as clothes and lamps, they needed for everyday life. Instead, they had to exchange the products they made for food and other goods. In this way, Cretan society experienced increasing economic interdependence.

The vast storage areas in Cretan palaces suggest that Minoan rulers, like some Mesopotamian kings before them, controlled this interdependence through a redistributive economic system. The Knossos palace, for example, held hundreds of gigantic jars capable of storing 240,000 gallons of olive oil and wine. Bowls, cups, and dippers crammed storerooms nearby. Palace officials would have decided how much each farmer or crafts producer had to contribute to the palace storehouse and how much of those contributions would then be redistributed to each person in the community for basic subsistence or as an extra reward. In this way, people gave the products of their labor to the local authority, which redistributed them as it saw fit. There would have been almost no free markets.

The Minoan economy apparently worked peacefully until at least 1400 B.C.E. Although contemporary settlements elsewhere around the Aegean Sea and in Anatolia had elaborate defensive walls, Crete had none. The palaces, towns, and even isolated country houses apparently saw no need to fortify themselves. The remains of the newer palaces—such as the one at Knossos, with its hundreds of rooms in five stories, indoor plumbing, and colorful scenes painted on the walls—have led some historians to the controversial conclusion that Minoans spurned war. Others object to the romanticizing of Minoans as peaceful because they dominated neighboring Aegean islands. Recent discoveries of tombs have revealed weapons caches, and a find of bones cut by knives has raised the possibility of human sacrifice. The promi-

nence of women in palace frescoes and the numerous figurines of buxom goddesses found on Cretan sites have also prompted speculation that Minoan society was female-dominated, but no texts have come to light to verify this. Minoan art certainly depicts women prominently and nobly, but the same is true of contemporary civilizations that men controlled. More archaeological research is needed to resolve the controversies about the nature of Minoan civilization.

Mycenaean Greece, c. 1800–c. 1000 B.C.E.

The Greeks were Indo-European speakers whose ancestors had moved into the region by 8000 B.C.E.; the first mainland civilization definitely identified as Greek because of its language arose about the same time as the Hittite kingdom, in the early second millennium B.C.E. These early Greeks are called Mycenaeans, a name derived from the hilltop site of Mycenae,◆ famous for its rich graves, multiroomed palace, and massive fortification walls. Located in the Peloponnese◆ (the large peninsula forming southern Greece; see Map 1.3), Mycenae dominated its local area, but neither it nor any other settlement ever ruled all of Bronze Age Greece. Instead, the independent communities of what we call Mycenaean civilization vied with one another in a fierce competition for natural resources and territory.

Since the hilly terrain of Greece had little fertile land but many useful ports, settlements tended to spring up near the coast. Greeks from the earliest times depended on the sea: for food, for trade with one another and foreign lands, and for naval raids on rich targets. Palace records inscribed on clay tablets reveal that the Mycenaeans had a redistributive economy. Scribes wrote on the tablets to make detailed lists of goods received and goods paid out, tirelessly recording stored material, livestock, land holdings, and personnel. They recorded everything from chariots to perfumes, even broken equipment taken out of service. The records of goods distributed from the storerooms

---

◆**Mycenae:** my SEE nee
◆**Peloponnese:** PEH luh puh nee

covered ritual offerings to the gods, rations to personnel, and raw materials for crafts production, such as metal issued to bronze smiths. As on Minoan Crete, however, no written documents have survived to tell us about Mycenaean literature or ideas of justice.

The first excavator of Mycenae, a nineteenth-century German millionaire named Heinrich Schliemann, made the site famous by discovering treasure-filled graves there. The burial objects revealed a warrior culture organized in independent settlements and ruled by aggressive kings. Constructed as stone-lined shafts, the graves contained entombed dead, who had taken hordes of valuables with them: golden jewelry, including heavy necklaces festooned with pendants, gold and silver vessels, bronze weapons decorated with scenes of wild animals inlaid in precious metals, and delicately painted pottery.

In his excitement at finding treasure, Schliemann proudly informed the international press that he had found the grave of Agamemnon, the legendary king who commanded the Greek army against Troy, a city in northwestern Anatolia, in the Trojan War. Homer, Greece's first and most famous poet, immortalized this war in his epic poem *The Iliad*. Archaeologists now know the shaft graves date to around 1700–1600 B.C.E., long before the Trojan War could have taken place. Schliemann, who paid for his own excavation at Troy to prove to skeptics that the city had really existed, infuriated scholars with his self-promotion. But his passion to confirm that Greek myth preserved a kernel of historical truth spurred him on to the work at Mycenae, which provided the most spectacular evidence for mainland Greece's earliest civilization.

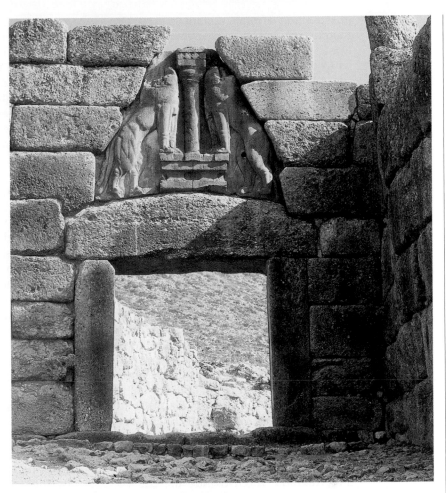

The Lion Gate to the Citadel at Mycenae
The hilltop fortress and palace at Mycenae was the capital of Bronze Age Greece's most famous kingdom. Above its main gate stood a sculpture of lions flanking a column, a design imitating the royal art of the Near East that shows that the Mycenaean kings admired the power and traditions of that region. What do you think the column between the lions signifies? In the circle of graves beyond the gate, Heinrich Schliemann found a treasure that he thought had belonged to King Agamemnon, the leader of the Greeks in the Trojan War. *Dimitrios Harissiades/© Photographic Archive, Benaki Museum Athens.*

Mycenaean Interaction with Minoan Crete. Mycenaean rulers enriched themselves by dominating local farmers, conducting raids near and far, and participating in seaborne trade. Underwater archaeology has disclosed that international commerce in this period promoted vigorous cultural interaction. Divers have discovered, for example, that a late-fourteenth-century B.C.E. shipwreck off Uluburun♦ in Turkey carried such a mixed cargo and varied personal

♦**Uluburun:** ou lou boor UHN

possessions—from Canaan, Cyprus, Greece, Egypt, Babylon, and elsewhere in the Near East—that attaching a single nationality to this tramp freighter makes no sense.

A special kind of burial chambers, called *tholos* tombs—spectacular underground domed chambers built in beehive shapes with closely fitted stones—shows that some Mycenaeans had become very rich by about 1500 B.C.E. The architectural details of the tholos tombs and the style of the burial goods placed in them testify to the far-flung raiding and trading that Mycenaean rulers conducted throughout the eastern Mediterranean. Above all, however, they show a close connection with the civilization of Minoan Crete because they display many motifs clearly inspired by Cretan designs.

Yet the Mycenaean and Minoan civilizations remained distinctly different in important ways. The Mycenaeans spoke Greek and made burnt offerings to the gods; the Minoans did neither. The Minoans scattered sanctuaries across the landscape in caves, on mountaintops, and in country villas; the mainlanders did none of this. When the Mycenaeans started building palaces in the fourteenth century B.C.E., unlike the Minoans they designed them around *megarons*—rooms with prominent ceremonial hearths and thrones for the rulers. Some Mycenaean palaces had more than one megaron, which could soar two stories high with columns to support a roof above the second-floor balconies.

This evidence demonstrates that the Mycenaeans were originally a separate people from the Minoans. A startling find of documents in the palace at Knossos shows, however, that Mycenaeans eventually achieved dominance over Crete, possibly in a war over commerce in the Mediterranean. The documents were tablets written in a script called **Linear B**, which was a pictographic script based on Minoan Linear A. A brilliant twentieth-century architect named Michael Ventris proved that Linear B was used to write not Minoan, but a different language: Greek. Because the Linear B tablets date from before the final destruction of Knossos in about 1370 B.C.E., they indicate that the palace administration had been keeping its records in a foreign language for some time

and, therefore, that Mycenaeans were controlling Crete well before the end of Minoan civilization.

In the end, then, the Mycenaeans conquered the Minoan culture whose art they had so highly admired, and by the middle of the fourteenth century B.C.E., they had displaced the Cretans as the Aegean region's preeminent civilization. The Greeks later recalled this reversal of power in the myth about Theseus♦ and the Minotaur:♦ The Cretan king Minos had forced Athenian youths, sent to him as a form of tribute, into his labyrinth, where the half-man, half-bull Minotaur devoured them. Theseus of Athens, however, slew the beast in its lair and backtracked to freedom through the labyrinth's dark corridors, guided by the thread that the king's daughter Ariadne, who had fallen in love with the dashing hero, had told him to leave to mark his way in the maze.

War in Mycenaean Society. By the time Mycenaeans took over Crete, war at home and abroad was the principal concern of well-off Mycenaean men, a tradition that they passed on to later Greek civilization. Contents of Bronze Age tombs in Greece reveal that no wealthy man went to his grave without his war equipment. The expense of these grave goods shows that armor and weapons were so central to a Mycenaean male's identity that he could not do without them, even in death. Warriors rode into battle in expensive hardware—lightweight, two-wheeled chariots pulled by horses. These revolutionary vehicles, perhaps introduced by Indo-Europeans migrating from Central Asia, first appeared in various Mediterranean and Near Eastern societies not long after 2000 B.C.E.; the first picture of such a chariot in the Aegean region occurs on a Mycenaean grave marker from about 1500 B.C.E. Wealthy people evidently desired this new form of transportation not only for war but also as proof of their social status.

The Mycenaeans seem to have spent more on war than on religion. In any case, they did not construct any giant religious buildings like Mesopotamia's ziggurats or

♦**Theseus:** THEE see uhs
♦**Minotaur:** MIH nuh tawr

Egypt's pyramids. Their most important deities were male gods concerned with war. The names of gods found in the Linear B tablets reveal that Mycenaeans passed down many divinities to the Greeks of later times.

The Period of Calamities, c. 1200–c. 1000 B.C.E.

A state of political equilibrium, in which kings corresponded with one another and traders traveled all over the area, characterized the Mediterranean and Near Eastern world around 1300 B.C.E. Within a century, however, calamity had struck not only small, loosely organized groups such as the Hebrews but also almost every major political state in the region, including Egypt, some kingdoms of Mesopotamia, and the Hittite and Mycenaean kingdoms. Explaining all the catastrophes that occurred around 1200–1000 B.C.E. remains one of the most fascinating puzzles in ancient Western history.

The best clue to what happened comes from Egyptian and Hittite records. They document many foreign invasions in this period, especially from the sea. According to an inscription, the pharaoh Ramesses III around 1190 B.C.E. defeated a fearsome coalition of seaborne invaders from the north, who had fought their way to the edge of Egypt. These **Sea Peoples**, as historians call them, comprised many different groups. Some had been mercenary soldiers in the armies of rulers whom they deserted; some were raiders by profession. Many may have been Greeks. The famous story of the Trojan War probably recalls this period of calamities because it portrays a seaborne Greek army attacking Troy and the surrounding region in Anatolia.

Apparently no single, unified group of Sea Peoples launched a tidal wave of violence. Rather, many different bands devastated the region. A chain reaction of attacks and flights in a recurring and expanding cycle put even more bands on the move. The turmoil reached far inland. The Kassite kingdom in Babylonia collapsed, and the Assyrians were confined to their homeland. Invasions by the Semitic peoples known as Aramaeans and Chaldeans devastated western Asia and Syria.

The reasons for these widespread calamities remain mysterious, but their dire consequences for the eastern Mediterranean region are clear. The once mighty Hittite kingdom fell about 1200 B.C.E., when raiders cut off its trade routes for raw materials. Invaders razed its capital city, Hattusas, which never revived. Egypt's New Kingdom repelled the Sea Peoples with a tremendous military effort, but these raiders reduced the Egyptian long-distance trade network to a shambles. Power struggles between the pharaohs and the priests only made the situation worse. By the end of the New Kingdom, around 1081 B.C.E., Egypt had shrunk to its original territorial core along the Nile's banks. The calamities ruined Egypt's credit. For example, when the eleventh-century B.C.E. Theban temple official Wenamun traveled to Byblos in Phoenicia to buy cedar for a ceremonial boat, the city's ruler demanded cash in advance. Although the Egyptian monarchy struggled on, ongoing power struggles between pharaohs and priests, made worse by frequent attacks from abroad, prevented the reestablishment of centralized authority. No Egyptian dynasty ever again became an aggressive international power.

The calamities of this time also afflicted the copper-rich island of Cyprus in the eastern Mediterranean and the flourishing cities of the eastern Mediterranean coast. Raiders from the north, called Philistines, settled in Canaan and attacked the Canaanites and the Hebrews repeatedly in the eleventh century B.C.E. The Hebrew tribes appointed rulers called judges in an attempt to unify their loose confederation during this period of near anarchy. One of these judges, Deborah, led an Israelite coalition force to victory over a Canaanite army, but the Hebrews remained weak militarily.

In Greece, the troubles were homegrown. The Mycenaeans reached the zenith of their power around 1400–1250 B.C.E. The enormous domed tomb at Mycenae, called the Treasury of Atreus, testifies to the riches of this period. The tomb's elaborately decorated facade and soaring roof reveal the self-confidence of the Mycenaean warrior princes. The last phase of the extensive palace at Pylos♦ on

♦**Pylos:** PY lahs

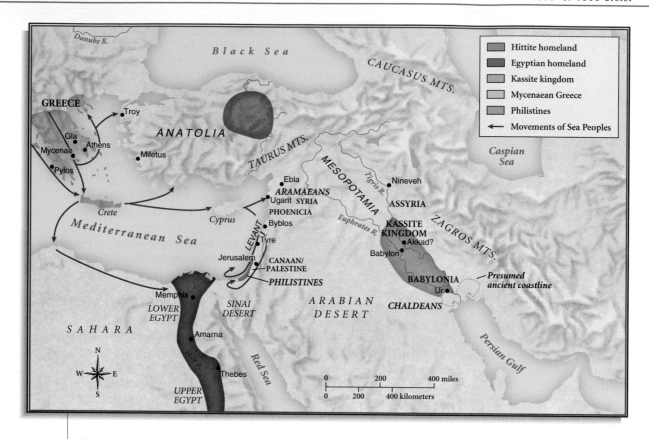

MAPPING THE WEST The Period of Calamities, c. 1200–1000 B.C.E.
Bands of wandering warriors and raiders set the eastern Mediterranean aflame at the end of the Bronze Age. This violence displaced many people and ended the power of the kingdoms of the Egyptians, the Hittites, and the Mycenaeans. Even some of the Near Eastern states well inland from the eastern Mediterranean coast felt the effects of this period of unrest, whose causes remain mysterious.

the west coast of the Peloponnese also dates from this time. It boasted glorious wall paintings, storerooms bursting with food, and a royal bathroom with a built-in tub and intricate plumbing. But these prosperous Mycenaeans did not escape the widespread calamities that began around 1200 B.C.E. Linear B tablets record the disposition of troops to the coast to guard the palace at Pylos at this time. The palace inhabitants of eastern Greece now constructed such massive defensive walls that the later Greeks thought giants had built them. These fortifications would have protected coastal palaces against seafaring attackers, who could have been either outsiders or Greeks. The wall around the inland palace at Gla in central Greece, however, which foreign raiders could not easily reach, confirms that, above all,

the Mycenaeans had to defend themselves against other Mycenaeans.

In Greece itself, then, the Sea Peoples apparently did relatively little damage. Rather, internal turmoil and major earthquakes destroyed Mycenaean civilization. Archaeology offers no evidence for the ancient tradition that Dorian Greeks invading from the north caused the destruction. Near-constant civil war by jealous local rulers overburdened the elaborate administrative balancing act necessary for the palaces' redistributive economies and hindered recovery from earthquake damage. The violence killed many Mycenaeans and put many others on the road to starvation through the disappearance of the palace-based redistributive economy. The calamity uprooted many of the remaining Greeks from their homes and forced them to wander abroad in search of new places to settle. Like people from the earliest times, these devastated ancestors of Western civilization had to move to build a better life.

> **Review:** How did war determine the fates of the early civilizations of Crete, Anatolia, and Greece?

Conclusion

Western civilization emerged in Mesopotamia and Egypt; these cultures in turn influenced the later civilization of Greece. Cities first arose in Mesopotamia by around 3000 B.C.E. Hierarchy characterized society to some degree from the very beginning, but it grew more pronounced once civilization emerged.

Trade and war were constants, both aiming in different ways at profit and glory. Indirectly, they often generated energetic cultural interaction by putting civilizations into close contact to learn from one another. Technological innovation was also a prominent characteristic of this long period. The invention of metallurgy, monumental architecture, mathematics, and alphabetic writing greatly affected the future. Religion was at the center of people's lives, with the gods seen as demanding just and righteous conduct from everyone. The emergence of monotheism set the stage for the leading faiths of later Western history.

The Mediterranean Sea was a two-edged sword for the early civilizations that grew up around and near it: as a highway for transporting goods and ideas, it was a boon; as an artery for conveying attackers, it was a bane. Ironically, the raids of the Sea Peoples that smashed the prosperity of the eastern Mediterranean region around 1200–1000 B.C.E. also set in motion the forces that led to the next step in our story, the resurgence of Greece. Strife among Mycenaean rulers turned the regional unrest of those centuries into a local catastrophe; fighting each other for dominance, they so weakened their monarchies that they could not recover after natural disasters. To an outside observer, Greek society by around 1000 B.C.E. might have seemed destined for irreversible economic and social decline, even oblivion. Chapter 2 shows how wrong this prediction would have been. After a dark period of economic and population decline called the Dark Age, Greeks invented a new form of social and political organization and breathed renewed life into their culture, inspired by their neighbors in the Near East and Egypt.

Suggested References

Mesopotamia, Home of the First Civilization, c. 4000–c. 1000 B.C.E.

Archaeological exploration in Mesopotamia (present-day Iraq) has been almost completely halted for more than a decade. Scholars have therefore been limited to studying already excavated material and texts. Modern translations have made Mesopotamian myths more accessible to today's readers.

Alcock, Susan, et al., eds. *Empires.* 2001.

Ancient Near East: http://www.etana.org/abzu.

Aruz, Joan, ed. *Art of the First Cities: The Third Millennium B.C. from the Mediterranean to the Indus.* 2003.

Bertman, Stephen. *Handbook to Life in Ancient Mesopotamia.* 2003.

Bienkowski, Piotr, and Alan Millard, eds. *Dictionary of the Ancient Near East.* 2000.

Bottéro, Jean. *Everyday Life in Mesopotamia.* Trans. Antonia Nevill. 2001.

Collins, Billie Jean. *A History of the Animal World in the Ancient Near East.* 2002.

Crawford, Harriet. *Sumer and the Sumerians.* 1991.

*Dalley, Stephanie, trans. *Myths from Mesopotamia: Creation, The Flood, Gilgamesh, and Others.* 1991.

Matthews, Roger. *Archaeology of Mesopotamia: Theories and Approaches.* 2003.

*Richardson, M. E. J. *Hammurabi's Laws: Text, Translation and Glossary.* 2000.

Stiebing, William H., Jr. *Ancient Near Eastern History and Culture.* 2003.

Sumerian literature. http://www-etcsl.orient .ox.ac.uk.

*Primary sources.

The Egyptians, Canaanites, and Hebrews, c. 3050–c. 1000 B.C.E.

Research and writing on ancient Egypt continue at a furious pace, while scholars studying the eastern Mediterranean region increasingly emphasize the interaction of its various cultures in trade and in war.

Assmann, Jan. *The Search for God in Ancient Egypt*. Trans. David Lorton. 2001.

Baines, John. *Religion and Society in Ancient Egypt*. 2003.

Dever, William. *Who Were the Early Israelites and Where Did They Come From?* 2003.

Hawass, Zahi. *Silent Images: Women in Pharaonic Egypt*. 2000.

Healy, John F. *The Early Alphabet*. 1990.

*Lichtheim, Miriam. *Ancient Egyptian Literature*. 3 vols. 1973.

Meskell, Lynn. *Private Life in New Kingdom Egypt*. 2002.

Morkot, Robert G. *The Black Pharaohs: Egypt's Nubian Rulers*. 2000.

Partridge, Robert B. *Fighting Pharaohs: Weapons and Warfare in Ancient Egypt*. 2002.

Redford, Donald B., ed. *The Oxford Encyclopedia of Ancient Egypt*. 2000.

*Simpson, William Kelly, ed. *The Literature of Ancient Egypt. An Anthology of Stories, Instructions, and Poetry*. 3rd ed. 2003.

Thebes in ancient Egypt: **http://www.thebanmappingproject.com**.

Tubb, Jonathan N. *Canaanites*. 1998.

Tyldesley, Joyce. *Hatshepsut: The Female Pharaoh*. 1996.

Virtual Museum of Nautical Archaeology (including the Uluburun shipwreck): **http://ina.tamu.edu/vm.htm**.

The Hittites, Minoans, and Mycenaeans, c. 2200–c. 1000 B.C.E.

Archaeology provides the securest evidence for the emergence of Greek and Anatolian civilizations. It has not yet, however, revealed what initiated the period of calamities around 1200–1000 B.C.E.

Bryce, Trevor. *Life and Society in the Hittite World*. 2002.

Crete and the Aegean Islands: **http://harpy.uccs.edu/greek/crete.html**.

Dickinson, Oliver. *The Aegean Bronze Age*. 1994.

Drews, Robert. *The End of the Bronze Age: Changes in Warfare and the Catastrophe ca. 1200 B.C.* 1993.

Farnoux, Alexandre. *Knossos: Searching for the Legendary Palace of King Minos*. Trans. David J. Baker. 1996.

Minoan civilization: **http://www.culture.gr/2/21/211/21123m/e211wm01.html**.

Mycenaean civilization: **http://harpy.uccs.edu/greek/mycenae.html**.

Sanders, N. K. *The Sea Peoples: Warriors of the Ancient Mediterranean, 1250–1150 B.C.* Rev. ed. 1985.

*Singer, Itamar. *Hittite Prayers: Writings from the Ancient World*. 2002.

CHAPTER REVIEW

IMPORTANT EVENTS

c. 4000–1000 B.C.E.	Bronze Age in southwestern Asia, Egypt, and Europe
c. 3500–3000 B.C.E.	Mesopotamians invent writing and establish first cities
c. 3050 B.C.E.	Narmer (Menes) unites Upper and Lower Egypt into one kingdom
c. 2687–c. 2190 B.C.E.	Old Kingdom in Egypt
c. 2350 B.C.E.	Sargon establishes the world's first empire in Akkadia
c. 2300–2200 B.C.E.	Enheduanna, princess of Akkad, composes poetry
c. 2200 B.C.E.	Minoans build their first palaces on Crete
2112–2004 B.C.E.	Ur III dynasty rules in Sumer
c. 2061–1665 B.C.E.	Middle Kingdom in Egypt
c. 1900 B.C.E.	Hebrews migrate from Ur in Mesopotamia to Canaan
c. 1792–1750 B.C.E.	Hammurabi rules the kingdom of Babylon and issues his law code
c. 1750 B.C.E.	Hittites establish their kingdom in Anatolia
c. 1700–1500 B.C.E.	Hebrews migrate from Canaan into Egypt
c. 1569–c. 1081 B.C.E.	New Kingdom in Egypt
c. 1600 B.C.E.	Canaanites invent the alphabet
c. 1400 B.C.E.	The Mycenaeans build their first palaces in Greece and take over Minoan Crete
c. 1274 B.C.E.	The Hittites war with Pharaoh Ramesses II at Kadesh in Syria
c. 1250 B.C.E.	Hebrews leave Egypt on their Exodus back to Canaan
c. 1200–1000 B.C.E.	Period of Calamities ends many kingdoms
c. 1190 B.C.E.	Pharaoh Ramesses III defeats an invasion of Egypt by Sea Peoples

KEY TERMS

city-state (9)

civilization (4)

cuneiform (12)

empire (14)

hieroglyphs (19)

Linear B (36)

Maat (21)

Mediterranean polyculture (33)

monotheism (25)

palace society (33)

polytheism (12)

redistributive economy (15)

Sea Peoples (37)

wisdom literature (23)

ziggurat (10)

REVIEW QUESTIONS

1. How did life change for people in Mesopotamia when they began to live in cities?
2. How did religion guide the lives of people in the early civilizations of Egypt and the Levant?
3. How did war determine the fates of the early civilizations of Crete, Anatolia, and Greece?

MAKING CONNECTIONS

1. Compare and contrast the environmental factors affecting the emergence of the world's first civilizations in Mesopotamia and Egypt.
2. What were the similarities and the differences in the notion of justice in the earliest civilizations?

FOR FURTHER EXPLORATION

To assess your mastery of the material in this chapter, see the Online Study Guide at **bedfordstmartins.com/hunt**.

To read additional primary-source material from this period, see Chapter 1 in *Sources of The Making of the West*, Second Edition.

New Paths for Western Civilization, c. 1000–500 B.C.E.

HOMER, THE MOST FAMOUS GREEK POET, told violent stories from the period of calamities (c. 1200–c. 1000 B.C.E) in his epic poem *The Iliad*, composed in the eighth century B.C.E. His bloody tale of the Trojan War was rich with legends born from mingled Greek and Near Eastern traditions, such as the story of the Greek hero Bellerophon.✦ Driven from his home by a false charge of sexual assault, Bellerophon had to serve as "enforcer" for a king in Lycia (a region south of Troy), combating the king's most dangerous enemies. He had to fight—and kill— fierce tribesmen, Amazons, and even the king's own warriors, but his most famous contest pitted him against a monster. As Homer tells it, Bellerophon was ordered "to defeat the Chimera,✦ an inhuman freak created by the gods, horrible with its lion's head, goat's body, and dragon's tail, breathing fire all the time." Bellerophon triumphed by swooping down on the beast in an aerial attack, riding on the winged horse Pegasus. So amazing were Bellerophon's heroics that the king gave him his daughter in marriage and half his kingdom.

Both the multiform Chimera in Homer and the horse-headed, hawk-bodied, lion-footed beast painted on the vase from Corinth shown in the chapter opening illustration were creatures from Near Eastern myth taken over by Greeks. They provide evidence for the intercultural contact that characterized the far-flung world of ancient Western civilization. People were eager to trade and to discover new technology in other places. Inevitably, contact exposed people

---

✦**Bellerophon:** buh LEHR uh fahn
✦**Chimera:** ky MIHR uh

From Dark Age to Empire in the Near East, c. 1000–500 B.C.E.

- The New Empire of Assyria, c. 900–612 B.C.E.
- The Neo-Babylonian Empire, c. 605–562 B.C.E.
- The Persian Empire, c. 557–500 B.C.E.
- The Consolidation of Hebrew Monotheism, c. 1000–539 B.C.E.

Remaking Greek Civilization, c. 1000–750 B.C.E.

- The Greek Dark Age, c. 1000–750 B.C.E.
- The Values of the Olympic Games
- Homer, Hesiod, and Divine Justice in Greek Myth

The Creation of the Greek Polis, c. 750–500 B.C.E.

- The Physical Environment of the Greek City-State
- Trade and "Colonization," c. 750–580 B.C.E.
- Citizenship and Freedom in the Greek City-State

New Directions for the Polis, c. 750–500 B.C.E.

- Oligarchy in Sparta, c. 700–500 B.C.E.
- Tyranny in Corinth, c. 657–585 B.C.E.
- Democracy in Athens, c. 632–500 B.C.E.
- New Ways of Thought and Expression, c. 630–500 B.C.E.

Black-Figure Vase from Corinth

This vase was made in Corinth about 600 B.C.E. and then shipped to the island of Rhodes, where it was found. The drawing is in the so-called black-figure style, in which artists carved details into the dark-baked clay. In the late sixth century B.C.E., this style gave way to red-figure, in which artists painted details in black on a reddish background instead of engraving them; the result was finer detail (compare this vase painting with that on page 55). The animals and mythical creatures on this vase follow Near Eastern models, which inspired Archaic Age Greek artists to put people and animals into their designs again after their absence during the Dark Age. Why do you think the artist depicted the animal at the lower right with two bodies but only one head? *British Museum.*

not only to others' products but also to their ideas. New paths for civilization emerged as people traded, traveled, innovated, and adapted for their own purposes things that they had learned or acquired from foreigners.

Even the turmoil and economic distress that ended the Bronze Age around 1000 B.C.E. did not suppress people's craving for trade and cross-cultural interaction. This drive only increased as conditions slowly improved in the following centuries. The Near East recovered more quickly than Greece, retaining monarchy as its traditional form of social and political organization. Following the model of the earlier Assyrian and Babylonian empires, Near Eastern kings in this period extracted surpluses from subject populations to support their palaces and their armies. They also continually sought new conquests to win glory, exploit the labor of conquered peoples, seize raw materials, and conduct long-distance trade.

In Greece, by contrast, politics and society in the period after 1000 B.C.E. emerged in radically different forms. The wars and subsequent economic collapse of 1200–1000 B.C.E. had destroyed the political and social organization of Minoan and Mycenaean Greece. Powerful rulers controlling the population no longer existed. During Greece's slow recovery from poverty and depopulation from about 1000 to 750 B.C.E., its Dark Age, Greeks maintained trade and cross-cultural contact with the older civilizations of the Near East. Their mythology, as in Homer, and their art, as on the Corinthian vase, reveal that they imported ideas as well as goods during this difficult era.

By the eighth century B.C.E., Greeks had begun to create the polis as a new form of political and social organization in the city-state. It was novel because it made citizenship the basis for society and politics, with legal—but not political—rights for women and with slavery for some. With the exception of occasional tyrannies, Greek city-states depended on the agreement among male citizens to share power in governing and in contributing surpluses to the state for common purposes. The extent of the power sharing varied, with small groups of upper-class men dominating in some places. In other places, however, the polis shared power among all free men, even the poor, creating the world's first democracy (literally, " rule by the people"). The invention of the democratic polis stands as a landmark in the history of Western civilization.

One experience that Greeks and Near Eastern peoples shared during this period of recovery was frequent warfare. In Greece, the gradual process of creating independent city-states created violent clashes over the mainland's limited supply of fertile land, while in the Near East the desire for empire and the control of trade made war as common as sunshine in that arid region. With the clash of arms constantly ringing in their ears, thinkers in the Near East and Greece developed new patterns in religion and philosophy that make up the foremost legacies of this period to later Western civilization: the Persians' Zoroastrian beliefs about life as a struggle between good and evil, the monotheism of the Hebrews, and the Greeks' development of philosophic rationalism to compete with mythological explanations of nature.

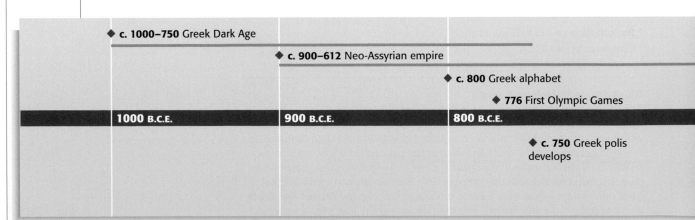

◆ **c. 1000–750** Greek Dark Age

◆ **c. 900–612** Neo-Assyrian empire

◆ **c. 800** Greek alphabet

◆ **776** First Olympic Games

| **1000 B.C.E.** | **900 B.C.E.** | **800 B.C.E.** |

◆ **c. 750** Greek polis develops

❖ From Dark Age to Empire in the Near East, c. 1000–500 B.C.E.

The widespread violence in 1200–1000 B.C.E. had weakened or obliterated many communities and populations in the eastern Mediterranean. We know little about the period of recovery that followed because few sources exist to supplement archaeological evidence. Both because economic conditions were so gloomy for so many people and because our view of what happened is so obscured, historians refer to the era in which conditions were hardest for a particular region as its **Dark Age**. Recent archaeological excavation suggests that the Dark Age in the Near East lasted less than a century, a much shorter period than Greece experienced.

By 900 B.C.E., a powerful and centralized Assyrian kingdom had once again emerged in Mesopotamia. From this base, the Assyrians ruthlessly carved out a new empire even larger than before. The riches and power of this Neo-Assyrian empire inspired first the Babylonians and then the Persians to build their own empires when Assyrian power collapsed. The traditional strife for empire remained constant in the Near East. The relatively powerless Hebrews, however, established a new path for civilization during this period by changing their religion. They developed monotheism and produced the Hebrew Bible, known to Christians as the Old Testament.

The New Empire of Assyria, c. 900–612 B.C.E.

When the Hittite kingdom fell around 1000 B.C.E., the Neo-Assyrian empire gained power by seizing supplies of metal and controlling trade routes in the eastern Mediterranean (Map 2.1). By 900 B.C.E., its armies were

MAP 2.1 Expansion of the Neo-Assyrian Empire, c. 900–650 B.C.E.
Like their Akkadian, Assyrian, and Babylonian predecessors, the Neo-Assyrian kings dominated a vast region of the Near East to secure a supply of metals, access to trade routes on land and sea, and imperial glory. In so doing, they built the largest empire the world had yet seen. Also like their predecessors, they treated disobedient subjects harshly and intolerantly to try to prevent their diverse territories from rebelling.

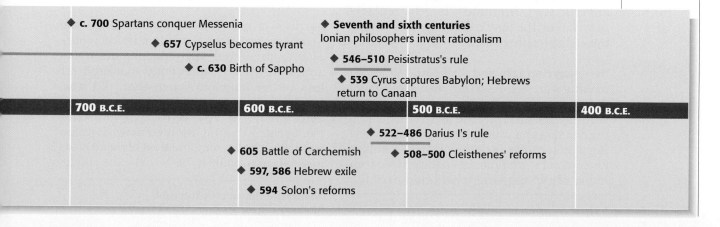

◆ **c. 700** Spartans conquer Messenia

◆ **657** Cypselus becomes tyrant

◆ **c. 630** Birth of Sappho

◆ **Seventh and sixth centuries**
Ionian philosophers invent rationalism

◆ **546–510** Peisistratus's rule

◆ **539** Cyrus captures Babylon; Hebrews return to Canaan

| **700 B.C.E.** | **600 B.C.E.** | **500 B.C.E.** | **400 B.C.E.** |

◆ **522–486** Darius I's rule

◆ **605** Battle of Carchemish

◆ **508–500** Cleisthenes' reforms

◆ **597, 586** Hebrew exile

◆ **594** Solon's reforms

striking westward against the Aramaean states in Syria until they punched through to the coast. In the eighth century B.C.E., the Neo-Assyrian kings extended their control into southern Mesopotamia by conquering Babylon, and they added Egypt to their empire in the seventh century. The weakness that had plagued Egypt since the New Kingdom's collapse in 1081 B.C.E. made this conquest possible.

Neo-Assyrian Militarism and Imperial Brutality. A warrior culture pervaded Neo-Assyrian society. Forsaking tradition, the Neo-Assyrians made foot soldiers their main strike force in place of cavalry. Trained infantrymen excelled in using military technology such as siege towers and battering rams, while swift chariots carried archers. Campaigns against foreign lands brought in revenues supplementing the domestic economy, which centered on agriculture, animal husbandry, and long-distance trade. Neo-Assyrian kings treated conquered peoples brutally, torturing and executing captives to keep order by instilling fear. Conquered peoples left in their homelands had to pay annual tribute to support the Assyrians' prosperity; these tributes included raw materials and luxury goods such as incense, wine, dyed linens, glasswork, and ivory. Worse was the fate of the large number of defeated people whom the kings routinely deported to Assyria for work on huge building projects—temples and palaces—in main cities. One unexpected consequence of this harsh policy was that the kings undermined their native language: so many Aramaeans, for example, were deported from Canaan to Assyria that Aramaic◆ largely replaced Assyrian as the land's everyday language by the eighth century B.C.E.

Neo-Assyrian Life and Religion. When not making war, Neo-Assyrian men spent much time hunting wild animals; the more dangerous the quarry, the better. The king hunted lions as proof of his vigor and power. Royal lion hunts provided a favorite subject for sculptors, who mastered the artistic technique of carving long relief sculptures that

◆**Aramaic:** ar uh MAY ihk

Neo-Assyrian Guardian Creature
This human-headed bull and lion creature (called a lamassu) stood guard over a gate at the palace of the Neo-Assyrian King Ashurnasirpal (r. 883–859 B.C.E.) in his capital city Kalhu (today Nimrud). Carved from alabaster, the guardian stood ten feet tall, with a cap to signify its divine power. The sculptor gave it five legs so it would look natural when viewed either from the side or the front. Ashurnasirpal reported in an inscription that he hosted 69,574 people at a party celebrating his new capital: "I feasted, wined, bathed, and honored them for ten days before sending them home in peace and joy." *Gift of John D. Rockefeller Jr., 1932 (32.143.1-.2). Photograph (c) 1981 The Metropolitan Museum of Art.*

narrated a connected story. Although the Neo-Assyrian imperial administration meticulously preserved many documents in its archives, literacy apparently mattered far less to the kingdom's men than did war, hunting, and practical technology. King Sennacherib◆ (r. 704–681 B.C.E.), for example, boasted that he invented new irrigation equipment and a novel method of metal casting. Ashurbanipal◆ (r. 680–626 B.C.E.) is the

◆**Sennacherib:** suh NA kuh ruhb
◆**Ashurbanipal:** ah shur BAH nuh pahl

only Assyrian ruler to proclaim his scholarly accomplishments: "I have read complicated texts, whose versions in Sumerian are obscure and in Akkadian hard to understand. I do research on the cuneiform texts on stone from before the Flood." Women of the social elite probably had a chance to become literate, but they were excluded from the male dominions of hunting and war.

Public religion, which included deities adopted from Babylonian religion, reflected the prominence of war in Assyrian culture: even the cult of Ishtar (the Babylonian name for Inanna), the goddess of love and fertility, glorified warfare. The Neo-Assyrians' passion for monumental architecture led them to build huge temples for the gods. The temples' staffs of priests and slaves grew so numerous that the revenues from temple lands could no longer support them, so the kings had to supply extra funds from the spoils of conquest.

The Neo-Assyrian kings' harshness made even their own people, especially the social elite, dislike their rule. Rebellions were common throughout the history of the kingdom; a seventh-century B.C.E. revolt fatally weakened it. The Medes,♦ an Iranian people, and the Chaldeans,♦ a Semitic people who had driven the Assyrians from Babylonia, combined forces to invade the tottering kingdom. When they destroyed its capital at Nineveh in 612 B.C.E., they forever blotted out the Neo-Assyrian kings' dreams of empire.

The Neo-Babylonian Empire, c. 605–562 B.C.E.

Since the Chaldeans had captained the allies who overthrew the Neo-Assyrian empire, they seized the lion's share of territory. Sprung from seminomadic herders along the Persian Gulf, they established the Neo-Babylonian empire, the most powerful in Babylonian history. King Nebuchadnezzar♦ II (r. 605–562 B.C.E.) made the Neo-Babylonians the Near East's leading power by driving the Egyptian army from Syria at the battle of Carchemish in 605 B.C.E.

♦**Medes:** meeds
♦**Chaldeans:** kal DEE uhns
♦**Nebuchadnezzar:** neh byuh kuhd NEH zur

Nebuchadnezzar spent lavishly to turn Babylon into an architectural showplace, rebuilding the great temple of its chief god, Marduk, creating the famous Hanging Gardens—so named because lush plants drooped over its terraced sides—and constructing an elaborate city gate dedicated to the goddess Ishtar. Blue-glazed bricks and lions molded in yellow, red, and white decorated the gate's walls, which soared thirty-six feet high.

The Chaldeans adopted traditional Babylonian culture and preserved much Mesopotamian literature, such as the *Epic of Gilgamesh*. They also created many new works of prose and poetry, which the educated minority would often read aloud publicly for the enjoyment of the illiterate. Particularly popular were fables, proverbs, essays, and prophecies teaching morality and proper behavior. This so-called wisdom literature, a Near Eastern tradition going back at least to the Egyptian Old Kingdom, would greatly influence the later religious writings of the Hebrews.

The Chaldeans also passed on their knowledge to others outside their region. Their advances in astronomy became so influential that the Greeks used the word *Chaldean* to mean "astronomer." As in the past, the Chaldeans' primary motivation for observing the stars was the belief that the gods communicated their will to humans through natural phenomena, such as celestial movements and eclipses, abnormal births, the way smoke curled upward from a fire, and the trails of ants. The interpretation of these phenomena as messages from the gods exemplified the mixture of science and religion characteristic of ancient Near Eastern thought and proved influential on the Greeks.

The Persian Empire, c. 557–500 B.C.E.

Cyrus (r. c. 557–530 B.C.E.) founded the Near East's next great kingdom in Persia (today Iran) through his skills as a general and a diplomat who respected others' religious beliefs. He continued the region's tradition of kings warring to gain territorial empires when he conquered Babylon in 539 B.C.E.; a rebellion there had weakened the Chaldean dynasty when King Nabonidus (r. c. 555–539 B.C.E.) provoked a revolt among the priests of Marduk by promoting the cult of Sin, the moon god of the Mesopotamian city of Harran. Cyrus capitalized on this religious strife by presenting himself as the restorer of traditional Babylonian religion, thereby winning local support. An ancient inscription has him proclaim: "Marduk, the great lord, caused Babylon's generous residents to adore me."

His successors expanded Persian rule on the same principles of military strength and cultural tolerance. At its greatest extent, the empire extended from Anatolia (today Turkey), the eastern Mediterranean coast, and Egypt on the west to Pakistan on the east (Map 2.2). The kings' faith that they had a divine right to rule everyone in the world could provoke great conflicts, above all the war between Persians and Greeks that would break out around 500 B.C.E.

Persian Royal Magnificence and Decentralized Rule. The Persian monarchy's revenues produced wealth beyond imagination, and everything about the king emphasized his grandeur. His purple robes outshone everyone else's; only he could step on the red carpets spread for him to walk on; his servants held their hands before their mouths in his presence so that he would not have to breathe the same air as they; he appeared larger than any other person in the sculpture adorning his immense palace at Persepolis. To display his concern for his loyal subjects, as well as the gargantuan scale of his resources, the king provided meals for fifteen thousand nobles, courtiers, and followers every day—although he himself ate hidden from his guests' view. Those who committed serious offenses against his laws or his dignity the king punished brutally, mutilating their bodies and executing their families. Contemporary Greeks, in awe of the Persian

The Great King of Persia
Like their Assyrian predecessors, the Persian kings decorated their palaces with large relief sculptures emphasizing royal dignity and success. This one from Persepolis shows officials and petitioners giving the king proper respect when entering his presence. To symbolize their elevated status, the king and his son, who stands behind the throne, are depicted as larger than everyone else. Do you think the way the sculptors portrayed the figures from the side is more or less artistic than the way the Egyptian painters did it in the picture of the day of judgment on page 2? Why?
For more help analyzing this image, see the visual activity for this chapter in the Online Study Guide at **bedfordstmartins.com/hunt**. *Courtesy of the Oriental Institute of the University of Chicago.*

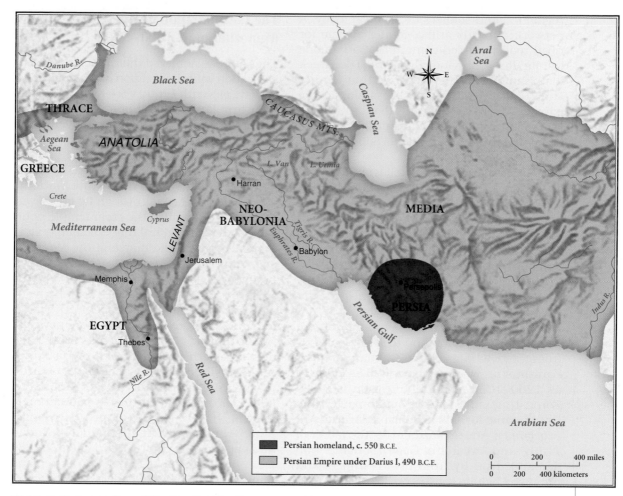

MAP 2.2 Expansion of the Persian Empire, c. 550–490 B.C.E.
Cyrus (r. c. 557–530 B.C.E.) initiated the Persian empire, which his successors expanded to be even larger than the Neo-Assyrian empire that it replaced. The Persian kings pressed hard outward from their inland center to gain coastal possessions for access to seaborne trade and naval bases. By the later years of Darius's reign (r. 522–486 B.C.E.), the Persian empire had expanded eastward as far as the western edge of India, while to the west it reached Thrace, the eastern edge of Europe. Unlike their imperial predecessors, the Persian kings won their subjects' loyalty with tolerance and religious freedom, although they treated rebels very harshly.

monarch's power and his lavish lifestyle, called him the Great King.

So long as his subjects—numbering in the millions and of many different ethnicities—remained peaceful, the king left them alone to live and worship as they pleased. The empire's smoothly functioning administrative structure sprang from Assyrian precedents: **satraps**◆ (regional governors) ruled enormous territories with little interference from

the kings. In this decentralized system, the governors' duties included keeping order, enrolling troops when needed, and sending revenues to the royal treasury.

Darius I (r. 522–486 B.C.E.) vastly extended Cyrus's conquests by pushing Persian power eastward to the Indus valley and westward to Thrace. Organizing this vast territory into provinces, he assigned each region taxes payable in the medium best suited to its local economy—precious metals, grain, horses, slaves. He also required each

◆**satraps:** SAY trap

region to send soldiers to the royal army. A network of roads and a courier system for royal mail provided communication among the far-flung provincial centers. The Greek historian Herodotus◆ reported that neither snow, rain, heat, nor darkness slowed the couriers from completing their routes as swiftly as possible, a feat transformed centuries later into the U.S. Postal Service motto.

Zoroastrian Religion.   Ruling as absolute autocrats, the Persian kings believed themselves superior to everyone. They claimed not to be gods but rather to be the agents of Ahura Mazda◆ (literally, "Wise Lord"), the supreme god of Persia. As Darius said in his autobiography, carved into a mountainside in three languages, "Ahura Mazda gave me kingship. . . . By the will of Ahura Mazda the provinces respected my laws."

Persian religion made Ahura Mazda the center of its devotion and took its doctrines from the teachings of the legendary prophet Zarathustra, who may have lived as long ago as 1200–1000 B.C.E. (The religion is called Zoroastrianism◆ today from Zoroaster, the Greek name for this holy man.) Zarathustra proclaimed Ahura Mazda to be "the father of Truth" and "creator of Good Thought," who demanded purity from his worshipers and promised help to those who lived with truthfulness and justice. The most important doctrine of Zoroastrianism was its monotheism, which explained the origin of evil through **moral dualism**: perceiving the world as the arena of an ongoing battle between the opposing divine forces of good and evil. Ahura Mazda as the embodiment of good and light constantly struggled against the evil darkness represented by the Satan-like figure Ahriman. Human beings had to choose between the way of the truth and the way of the lie, between purity and impurity. Only those judged righteous after death made it across "the bridge of separation" to heaven and avoided falling from its narrow span into hell. The Persian religious emphasis on ethical behavior had a lasting influence on others, especially the Hebrews.

◆**Herodotus:** heh RAH duh tuhs
◆**Ahura Mazda:** ah hur uh MAZ duh
◆**Zoroastrianism:** zor oh AHS tree uhn iz uhm

The Consolidation of Hebrew Monotheism, c. 1000–539 B.C.E.

The Hebrews achieved their first national organization with the creation of a monarchy in the late eleventh century B.C.E. Saul became their first king by fighting to limit Philistine power in Palestine (the southern Levant), and his successors David (r. 1010–970 B.C.E.) and Solomon (r. c. 961–922 B.C.E.) brought the nation to the height of its prosperity. The kingdom's wealth, based on international commerce conducted through its cities, was displayed above all in the great temple richly decorated with gold leaf that Solomon built in Jerusalem to be the house of the Hebrews' god, Yahweh. This temple was the Hebrews' premier religious monument.

After Solomon's death, the monarchy split into two kingdoms: Israel in the north and Judah in the south. The more powerful Mesopotamians later subjugated these kingdoms. Tiglath-pileser III of Assyria forced much of Palestine to become a tribute-paying, subject territory, destroying Israel in 722 B.C.E. and deporting its population to Assyria. In 597 B.C.E., the neo-Babylonian king Nebuchadnezzar II conquered Judah and captured its capital, Jerusalem. In 586 B.C.E. he destroyed its temple to Yahweh and banished the Hebrew leaders and much of the population to Babylon. The Hebrews always remembered the sorrow of this exile.

When the Persian king Cyrus overthrew the Babylonians in 539 B.C.E., he permitted the Hebrews to return to their part of Canaan, which was called Yehud from the name of the southern Hebrew kingdom Judah. From this geographical term came the word *Jew*, a designation for the Hebrews after their Babylonian exile. Cyrus allowed them to rebuild their main temple in Jerusalem and to practice their religion. After returning from exile, the Jews were forever a people subject to the political domination of various Near Eastern powers, save for a period of independence during the second and first centuries B.C.E.

Jewish prophets, both men and women, preached that their defeats were divine punishment for neglecting the Sinai covenant and mistreating their poor. Some prophets also predicted the coming end of the present world following a great crisis, a judgment by Yahweh, and salvation leading to a new and better world. This **apocalypticism** ("uncovering" of the future), reminiscent of Babylonian prophetic wisdom literature, would greatly influence Christianity later. Yahweh would save the Hebrew nation, the prophets thundered, only if Jews strictly observed divine law.

Jewish leaders therefore developed complex religious laws to maintain ritual and ethical purity in all aspects of life. Marrying non-Jews was forbidden, as was working on the Sabbath (the week's holy day). Fathers had legal power over the household, subject to intervention by the male elders of the community; women gained honor as mothers. Only men could initiate divorce proceedings. Ethics applied not only to obvious crimes but also to financial dealings; cheating in business transactions was condemned. Jews had to pay taxes and offerings to support and honor the sanctuary of Yahweh, and to forgive debts every seventh year.

The Jews' hardships had taught them that their religious traditions and laws gave them the strength to survive even when separated from their homeland. Gradually, they came to believe that Yahweh was the only god and that to abide by divine will they had to behave ethically toward everyone, rich and poor alike. They thus created the first complete monotheism, with laws based on ethics. Jews retained their identity by following this religion, regardless of their personal fate or their geographical location. A remarkable outcome of these religious developments was that Jews who did not return to their homeland, instead choosing to remain in Babylon or Persia or Egypt, could maintain their Jewish identity while living among foreigners. In this way, the **Diaspora** ("dispersion of population") came to characterize the history of the Jewish people.

Hebrew monotheism made the preservation and understanding of a sacred text, the Bible, the center of religious life. The chief priests compiled an authoritative scripture by forming the **Torah** (also referred to as the Pentateuch, or first five books of the Hebrew Bible), to which were eventually added the books of the prophets, such as Isaiah, and other writings, including Psalms

Goddess Figurines from Judah
Many small statues of this type, called Astarte figurines after a popular Canaanite goddess, have been found in private houses in Judah dating from about 800 to 600 B.C.E. Hebrews evidently kept them as magical tokens to promote fertility and prosperity. The prophets fiercely condemned the worship of such figures as part of the development of Hebrew monotheism and the abandoning of polytheism. Compare the shape of these figurines to the body shape of the Venus figurine on page P-5. What do you think these shapes represented? © *Israel Museum, Jerusalem. Artifact Collection of the Israel Antiquities Authority.*

and wisdom literature. Making scripture the focus of religion proved the most crucial development for the history not only of Judaism but also of Christianity and Islam, because these later religions made their own sacred texts, the Christian Bible and the Qur'an, respectively, the centers of their belief and practice.

Although the ancient Hebrews never formed a militarily powerful nation, their religious ideas created a new path for Western civilization. Through the continuing vitality of Judaism and its impact on the doctrines of Christianity and Islam, the early Jews passed on ideas—the belief in monotheism and the notion of a covenant bestowing a divinely ordained destiny on a people if they obey divine will—whose effects have endured to this day. These religious concepts constitute one of the most significant legacies to Western civilization from the Near East in the period 1000–500 B.C.E.

Review: In what ways did religion affect the history of the Near East from c. 1000 B.C.E. to c. 500 B.C.E.?

❖ Remaking Greek Civilization, 1000–750 B.C.E.

The period of calamities of 1200–1000 B.C.E. cost the Greeks the distinguishing marks of civilization: they no longer had unified states, large settlements, or writing. These losses underlay their Dark Age (c. 1000–750 B.C.E.), during which they had to remake their civilization by emerging from poverty and depopulation. Trade, cultural interaction, and technological innovation led to recovery: contact with the Near East promoted intellectual, artistic, and economic revival, while the introduction of metallurgy for making iron made farming more efficient. As conditions improved, a social elite distinguished by wealth and the competitive pur-

suit of individual excellence proclaimed in Homeric poetry replaced the lost hierarchy of Mycenaean times. In the eighth century B.C.E., the creation of the Olympic Games and the emphasis on justice in the poetry of Hesiod◆ promoted the communal values that fueled the remaking of Greek civilization following the Dark Age.

The Greek Dark Age, c. 1000–750 B.C.E.

The fall of Mycenaean civilization in the period of calamities brought to Greece the depressed economic conditions that so many people in other regions experienced during the worst years of their Dark Ages. One of the most startling indications of the severity of life in the Dark Age in Greece is that Greeks apparently lost their knowledge of writing when Mycenaean civilization fell. The Linear B script they had used to write Greek was difficult to master and probably known only by a few scribes, who used writing exclusively to track the flow of goods in and out of the palaces. When the Mycenaean states collapsed, the Greeks no longer needed scribes or writing. Oral transmission kept Greek cultural traditions alive.

Archaeology reveals that the Greeks, although spread across roughly the same geographical area as in Mycenaean times, cultivated much less land and had many fewer settlements in the early Dark Age (Map 2.3). No longer did powerful rulers ensconced in stone fortresses control redistributive economies providing a stable standard of living for their subjects. The number of ships carrying Greek adventurers, raiders, and traders dwindled. Developed political states ceased to exist, and the people eked out their existence as herders, shepherds, and subsistence farmers bunched in tiny settlements—as few as twenty people in many cases. The decimated population produced less food than before, causing its numbers to drop further. These two processes reinforced each other in a vicious circle, multiplying the negative effects of both.

The Greek agricultural economy remained complex despite the withering away

MAP 2.3 Dark Age Greece
Recent archaeological research indicates that Greece was not as impoverished or as depopulated after the fall of the Mycenaean kingdoms as once assumed. The many small ports along Greece's jagged coastline and the short distances between its islands allowed seafaring trade and communication to continue. By island hopping, boats could make it safely across the Aegean Sea and beyond, keeping the routes open to the Near East. Still, during the Dark Age, Greeks lived in significantly fewer and smaller population centers than in the Bronze Age. It took centuries for the region as a whole to revive.

◆**Hesiod:** HEE see uhd

of many traditional forms of agriculture. Since more Greeks than ever before made their living by herding animals, people became more mobile: they needed to move their herds to new pastures once the animals had overgrazed their current location. Lucky herders might find a new spot where they could grow a crop of grain if they stayed long enough. In this transient lifestyle, people built only simple huts and kept few possessions. Unlike their Bronze Age forebears, Greeks in the Dark Age had no monumental architecture, and they even lost an old tradition in their everyday art: they stopped painting people and animals in their principal art form, ceramics.

Trade, Innovation, and Recovery in Greece. The Greeks kept trading with the civilizations of the eastern Mediterranean even during the Dark Age. From this contact, the Greeks learned to write again about 800 B.C.E. They learned the alphabet from the Phoenicians,♦ seafaring traders from Canaan (whose name may have derived from the Greek term for the valuable purple dye they extracted from shellfish). Greeks changed and added letters to achieve independent representation of vowel sounds so that they could express their language and record their literature, beginning with Homer's and Hesiod's poetry in the eighth century B.C.E. Near Eastern art inspired Greeks to resume depicting animals and people in their paintings (as on the Corinthian vase on page 42). Seaborne commerce encouraged elite Greeks to produce surpluses to trade for luxuries such as gold jewelry and gems from Egypt and Syria.

Most important, trade brought the new technology of iron metallurgy. The violence of the period of calamities had interrupted the traditional trading routes for tin, imported from eastern sources by Assyrian middlemen. Without tin, metalsmiths could not forge bronze weapons and tools. To make up for this loss, metal workers in the eastern Mediterranean devised technology to smelt iron ore. Greeks then learned this skill through their eastern trade contacts and mined their own ore, which was common in

THE GREEK DARK AGE, c. 1000–750 B.C.E.

c. 1000 B.C.E.	Almost all important Mycenaean sites except Athens destroyed by now
c. 1000– 900 B.C.E.	Greatest depopulation and economic loss
900–800 B.C.E.	Early revival of population and agriculture; iron now beginning to be used for tools and weapons
c. 800 B.C.E.	Greek trading contacts initiated with Al Mina in Syria
776 B.C.E.	First Olympic Games held
c. 775 B.C.E.	Euboeans found trading post on Ischia in the Bay of Naples
c. 750 B.C.E.	Homeric poetry recorded in writing after Greeks learn to write again; Hesiod composes his poetry; Oracle of Apollo at Delphi already famous

Greece. Iron eventually replaced bronze in many uses, above all for agricultural tools, swords, and spear points. Bronze was still used for shields and armor, however, because it was easier to shape into thinner, curved pieces.

Eventually, the iron tools' lower cost meant that more people could afford them; and because iron is harder than bronze, implements now kept their sharp edges longer. Better and more plentiful farming implements of iron eventually helped increase food production, which supported a larger population. In this way, imported technology improved the people's chances for survival and thus helped Greece recover from the Dark Age's depopulation.

The Greek Social Elite and the Homeric Ideal. With no Mycenaean rulers to dominate, leadership was competitive in Dark Age Greece. Individuals who proved themselves excellent in action, words, charisma, and religious knowledge became the social elite. Excellence—**aretê♦** in Greek—was a competitive value: a family's high social status stemmed from its members' outdoing others. Men displayed aretê through prowess

♦**Phoenicians :** fih NEE shuhns

♦**aretê:** ah ruh TAY

A Rich Woman's Model Granary from the Dark Age

This clay model of storage containers for grain was found in a woman's tomb in Athens from about 850 B.C.E. It apparently symbolizes the surpluses that the woman and her family were able to accumulate and indicates that she was wealthy by the standards of her time. We can therefore deduce that economic conditions had begun to improve for at least some Athenians already at this point in the Dark Age. The geometric designs painted on the pottery are characteristic of Greek art in this period, when human and animal figures were left out. By the Archaic Age, this had changed under Near Eastern influence. Contrast the lively animals painted some two hundred years later on the Corinthian vase illustrated at the opening of this chapter (page 42). *American School of Classical Studies at Athens: Agora Excavation.*

in war and persuasiveness in speech; the highest aretê for women was savvy management of a bustling household of children, slaves, and the family's storerooms. Members of the elite also accumulated wealth by controlling agricultural land, which people of lower status worked for them as tenants or slaves.

Homer's poems, which became Greece's most famous literature, reflect the elite's ideals. The Greeks believed that Homer was a blind poet from the region called Ionia (today Turkey's western coast), who composed the epics *The Iliad* and *The Odyssey*. Most modern scholars believe that Homer was the last in a long line of poets who, influenced by Near Eastern mythology, had been singing these stories for centuries, orally transmitting cultural values from one generation to the next. *The Iliad* tells the story of the Greek

army in the Trojan War. Camped before the walls of Troy for ten years, the heroes of the army compete for glory and riches by raiding the countryside, dueling Troy's best fighters, and quarreling with one another over status and booty. The greatest Greek hero is Achilles, who proves his surpassing excellence by choosing to die young in battle rather than accept the gods' offer to return home safely but without glory. *The Odyssey* recounts the hero Odysseus's ten-year adventure finding his way home after the fall of Troy and the struggle of his wife, Penelope, to protect their household from the schemes and threats of their family's rivals for status and wealth. Penelope proves her aretê by outwitting envious neighbors to preserve her family's prosperity for her husband's return.

Homer reveals that the white-hot emotions inflamed by an individual quest for excellence could provoke a disturbing level of inhumanity. As he prepares to duel Hector, the prince of Troy, Achilles brutally rejects the Trojan's proposal that the winner return the loser's corpse to his family and friends: "Do wolves and lambs agree to cooperate? No, they hate each other to the roots of their being." The victor, Achilles, mutilates Hector's body. When Hecuba,♦ the queen of Troy, sees this outrage, she bitterly shouts, "I wish I could sink my teeth into his liver in his guts to eat it raw." The endings of Homer's poems suggest that the gods could help people achieve reconciliation after violent conflict, but the depth of human suffering makes it clear that excellence comes at a high price.

As in Homer, the real world of the Greek Dark Age had a small but wealthy social elite. At Lefkandi on the island of Euboea, for example, archaeologists have discovered the tenth-century B.C.E. grave of a couple who took such enormous riches with them to the next world that the woman's body was dripping with gold ornaments. About 900 B.C.E., a man at Athens had many weapons of iron buried with him. Fifty years later, an Athenian woman had her grave filled with jewelry from the Near East and a model of the storehouse for all her grain. These people had done well in the competition for status and wealth; most people of the time were, by

♦**Hecuba:** HEH kyuh buh

Athletic Competition
Greek vase painters loved to depict male athletes in action or training, perhaps in part because they were customers who would buy pottery with such scenes. As in this scene of an Athenian foot race from around 530 B.C.E., the athletes were usually shown nude, which is how they competed, revealing their superb physical condition and strong musculature. Being in excellent shape was a man's ideal for several reasons: it was regarded as beautiful, it enabled him to strive for individual glory in athletic competitions, and it allowed him to fulfill his community responsibility by fighting as a well-conditioned soldier in the city-state's citizen militia. Why do you think the figure at the far left does not have a full beard? (See the caption on page 76 for a hint.)
The Metropolitan Museum of Art, Rogers Fund, 1914.

comparison, paupers. They had to scratch out a living as best they could, while only dreaming of the heroic deeds and rich goods they heard about in Homer's poems.

The Values of the Olympic Games

Greece's recovery was assured by the eighth century B.C.E. The most vivid evidence is the founding of the Olympic Games, traditionally dated to 776 B.C.E. This international religious festival showcased the competitive value of aretê, as the fifth-century B.C.E. poet Pindar made clear in praising a family of victors: "Hiding the nature you are born with is impossible. The seasons rich in their flowers have many times bestowed on you, sons of Aletes, the brightness that victory brings, when you achieved the heights of excellence in the sacred games."

Every four years, the games took place in a huge sanctuary dedicated to Zeus, the king of the gods, at Olympia in the northwest Peloponnese. Athletes from elite families vied in sports imitating the aretê needed for war: running, wrestling, jumping, and throwing. Horse and chariot racing were added to the program later, but the main event remained a two-hundred-yard sprint, the *stadion*.♦ Athletes competed as individuals, not on national teams as in the modern Olympic Games. Winners received only a garland made from wild olive leaves to symbolize the prestige of victory.

Crowds of men flocked to the games; women were barred on pain of death. Women had their own separate Olympic festival on a different date in honor of Hera, queen of the

---

♦ *stadion:* STAHD ee ahn

gods, in which only unmarried women could compete. Eventually, full-time athletes dominated the Olympics, earning their living from appearance fees and prizes at games held throughout the Greek world. The most famous winner was Milo,♦ from Croton♦ in Italy. Six-time Olympic wrestling champion, he stunned audiences with demonstrations of strength such as holding his breath until his veins expanded to snap a cord tied around his head.

Although the Olympics existed to glorify individual excellence, their organization reveals an important trend under way in Greek society: the games were open to any socially elite Greek male good enough to compete and to any male spectator who could journey there. These rules represented beginning steps toward a concept of collective Greek identity. Remarkably for a land so often torn by war, once every four years an international truce of several weeks was declared so that competitors and fans from all Greek communities could travel to and from Olympia in security. By the mid-eighth century B.C.E., the Olympic Games channeled the competition for excellence—an individual, not a communal, value—into a new context of social cooperation and communal interest, essential preconditions for the creation of Greece's new political form, the city-state.

Homer, Hesiod, and Divine Justice in Greek Myth

Greeks' belief in divine justice inspired them to develop the communal and cooperative values that remade their civilization. This idea came not from scripture—Greeks had none—but from poetry telling myths about the gods and goddesses and their relationships to humans.

Homer's poems reveal that the gods had a plan for human existence; Zeus's will, for example, motivated the Trojan War's tragic events. Homer did not reveal, however, whether the divine plan was just. Bellerophon, the wronged hero whose brave efforts won him a princess bride and a kingdom, ended up losing everything. He became, in Homer's

words, "hated by the gods and wandering the land alone, eating his heart out, a refugee fleeing from the haunts of men." The story gives no explanation for this tragedy and no reason to believe that justice underlay the divine plan (see "Homer's Vision of Justice in the Polis," on the opposite page).

Hesiod's poetry, by contrast, reveals how religious myths about justice contributed to the feeling of community that motivated the creation of Greece's emerging new social and political structure. Hesiod told vivid stories originating in Near Eastern creation myths. They show that existence, even for deities, entailed struggle, sorrow, and violence. The stories also reveal, however, that the divine order of the universe included a concern for justice that persisted in Hesiod's own time.

Hesiod's epic poem *Theogony*♦ (Genealogy of the Gods) recounted the birth of the race of gods from primeval Chaos ("void" or "vacuum") and Earth, the mother of Sky (Uranus) and numerous other offspring. Hesiod explained that when Sky began to imprison his siblings, Earth persuaded her fiercest son, Kronos, to overthrow him violently because "Sky first contrived to do shameful things." When Kronos later began to swallow his own children to avoid sharing power with them, his wife, Rhea (who was also his sister), had their son Zeus forcefully depose his father in retribution.

In his poem on conditions in his own world, *Works and Days*, Hesiod identified Zeus as the source of justice in human affairs and justice as a divine quality punishing evildoers: "For Zeus ordained that fishes and wild beasts and birds should eat each other, for they have no justice; but to human beings he has given justice, which is far the best." Men from the social elite dominated the distribution of justice in Hesiod's day. They controlled their family members and household servants. Hesiod insisted that a leader should demonstrate excellence by employing persuasion instead of force: "When his people in their assembly get on the wrong track, he gently sets matters right, persuading them with soft words."

Hesiod complained that many elite leaders in his time fell short of this ideal, creating

♦**Milo:** MY loh
♦**Croton:** KROH tahn

♦*Theogony:* thee AH guh nee

Homer's Vision of Justice in the Polis

Homer's epics mainly tell tales of individual excellence from the heroic past of the Trojan War era, but he also hints at the development of communal values in the polis, which Greeks were creating at about the same time that he composed his works, around 750 B.C.E. We see this in one of the most striking passages in his Iliad, *which describes the pictures of a polis at war and a polis at peace that Hephaestus, the technology god, sculpted on a new shield for Achilles. Homer portrays the figures in the scenes as moving and talking, as if in a magical filmstrip. The picture of the polis at peace concerns finding a just resolution to a man's death. Homer doesn't tell us whether the death was accidental or criminal, or where the gold came from that would be the victorious arbitrator's reward for the best judgment, the one that would restore harmony to the community through justice.*

In the [polis at peace], weddings and celebrations were in full swing. Blazing torches lit the way for youthful brides being brought out from their homes and through the polis center. People sang the wedding song in loud, clear voices. The young men twirled in a lively dance to the music of flutes and lyres. The women lingered smilingly on their doorsteps, taking it all in with deep pleasure. Their husbands had gone off as a group to the polis's gathering place (agora), where a dispute was being conducted between two men over another's death and the payment of compensation. One of the two was proclaiming for all to hear that he would pay full compensation, while the other insisted that he would not accept any of it; both of them were declaring that arbitrators should settle the case. Each man had numerous supporters there yelling for him to prevail, and the heralds were trying hard to keep the crowd from rioting. The elders [i.e., the arbitrators] sat in a circle on sacred stone seats. The clear-voiced heralds handed them scepters, which each stepped forward with when it was his turn to say what he thought was a just resolution. A heap of gold lay in front of them as a reward for whichever elder pronounced the best decision.

Source: Homer, *Iliad* Book 18, lines 490–508. Translation by Thomas R. Martin.

---

strife between themselves and the peasants— free proprietors of small farms owning a slave or two, oxen to work their fields, and a limited amount of goods acquired by trading the surplus of their crops. Hesiod warned that justice's divine origin should deter "bribe-devouring chiefs," who use "crooked judgements" to settle disputes among their followers and neighbors. The feeling of outrage that commoners felt at not receiving equal treatment served as a stimulus for the gradual movement toward a new form of social and political organization in Greece.

Review: What factors proved most important in the Greek recovery from the economic troubles of the Dark Age?

❖ The Creation of the Greek Polis, c. 750–500 B.C.E.

The Greek Dark Age gave way to what historians call the Archaic Age (c. 750–500 B.C.E.). This new era saw the creation of the **polis**, the Greek city-state, an independent community of citizens inhabiting a city and the countryside around it. The polis differed from earlier, monarchical city-states because it was a community of citizens, not subjects, who usually governed themselves under various different political systems. Greece's geography, dominated by mountains and islands, promoted the creation of hundreds of separate, independent city-states in its heartland in

DID YOU KNOW?

The First Money with Pictures

Minotaur, Crete
(American Numismatic Society)

Satyr Carrying off Nymph, Thasos
(American Numismatic Society)

When someone today asks "Do you have any money on you?" he or she is referring to currency: coins and bills with pictures and words identifying their source and value. As familiar as this form of money now seems, people got along without it for thousands of years before the first currency, coins minted about 650–600 B.C.E. at the intersection of Near Eastern and Greek culture in Anatolia. Before that, Near Eastern civilization used money in many other forms, from measured amounts of grain to small, unmarked pieces or rings of weighed metal.

Coinage soon became the principal form of money in ancient Greece, but it did not replace the noncoinage money of the Near East while that region's traditional kingdoms remained strong. The reason for earlier use in Greece lay in the contrasting political structures of the two regions and their traditions in regulating exchanges. Images and letters on coins indicated, among other things, the states that minted them. That informa-

The Goddess Athena, Athens
(American Numismatic Society)

tion told people where they could be certain the money would be honored. Greeks needed this guarantee because they lacked a central political authority like Near Eastern monarchy, which could enforce the integrity of unmarked precious metal traditionally used for payments. Greeks lived under a more freewheeling system of exchange and took up the use of coinage to provide more secure transactions.

The identity of the minting state was not the only information provided on Greek coins. They displayed a dizzying diversity of images, from gods and goddesses, to monsters such as the half-man, half-bull Minotaur, to scenes of satyrs ravishing nymphs. Realizing that coinage had enormous potential to promote both prosperity and crime, the Greeks punished counterfeiting with death and locked away false coins in temples so that the gods could keep them forever out of human society.

and around the Aegean Sea. From these original locations, Greeks dispersed widely around the Mediterranean to settle hundreds more trading communities that often grew into new city-states. Individuals' entrepreneurial drive for profit from trade, especially in raw materials, and free farmland probably started this process of founding new settlements.

Greeks drew on their ideas of divine justice to make citizenship the defining char-

acteristics of their city-states, which distinguished theirs from the Mesopotamian city-states, whose inhabitants were the king's subjects. Surprisingly for the ancient world, poor citizens in Greek city-states enjoyed a rough legal and political equality with the rich. Not so surprisingly, women failed to attain equality with men, and slaves remained completely excluded from the benefits of the city-state's new emphasis on communal interests. Nevertheless, this new direction for politics and society failed to eliminate tension between the interests of the elite and those of ordinary people.

The Physical Environment of the Greek City-State

The ancient Greeks never constituted a nation in the modern political sense because their many city-states lacked a unifying organization. Greeks identified with one another culturally, however, because they spoke the same language and worshiped the same deities. (See "Did You Know?" opposite.) Their homeland lay in and around the Aegean Sea, a section of the Mediterranean between modern Greece and Turkey dotted with large and small islands (Map 2.4).

The mountainous geography of Greece tended to isolate its communities and contributed to the city-states' feisty separateness. A single island could be home to multiple city-states; Lesbos, for example, had five. Because few city-states had enough farmland to support a large population, settlements numbering only several hundred to several thousand were the rule even after the rise in the population at the end of the Dark Age.

Only the sea offered practical long-distance travel in Greece. Greek rivers were little more than creeks, while land transport was slow and expensive because rudimentary dirt paths and dry riverbeds provided the only roads. The most plentiful resource was timber from the mountains for building houses and ships. Deposits of metal ore were scattered throughout Greek territory, as were clays suitable for pottery and sculpture. Various quarries of fine stone such as marble provided material for special buildings and works of art. The uneven distribution of these resources meant that some areas were considerably wealthier than others.

MAP 2.4 Archaic Greece, c. 750–500 B.C.E.
The Greek heartland lay in and around the Aegean Sea, in what is today the nation of Greece and the western edge of the nation of Turkey (ancient Anatolia). The "mainland," where Athens, Corinth, and Sparta are located, is the southernmost tip of the mountainous Balkan peninsula. The many islands of the Aegean area were home mainly to small city-states, with the exception of the large islands just off the western Anatolian coast, which were home to populous ones.

None of the mountains wrinkling the Greek landscape rose higher than ten thousand feet, but their steep slopes restricted agriculture. Only 20 to 30 percent of the total land area could be farmed. The scarcity of level terrain in most areas ruled out large-scale herds of cattle and horses; pigs, sheep, and goats were the common livestock. The domestic chicken had been introduced from the Near East by the seventh century B.C.E. The Mediterranean climate (intermittent heavy rain during a few months and hot, dry summers) limited a farmer's options, as did the fragility of the environment: grazing livestock, for example, could be so hard on plant life that winter downpours would wash away the limited topsoil. Because the amount of annual precipitation varied greatly, farming was a precarious business of boom and bust. Farmers grew more barley, the cereal staple of the Greek diet, than wheat, which people preferred but which was more expensive to cultivate. Wine grapes and olives were the other most important crops.

Trade and "Colonization," c. 750–580 B.C.E.

The polis emerged when Greeks were once again in frequent contact with Egypt and the Near East. Greeks in this period gained many opportunities for cross-cultural contact as the desire for trade and land roused them to move around the Mediterranean. Greece's jagged coastline made sea travel practical: almost every community lay within forty miles of the Mediterranean Sea. But sailing meant dangers from pirates and, especially, storms; in

fact, prevailing winds and fierce gales almost ruled out sea travel during winter. Sailors tried to hug the coast, hopping from island to island and putting in to shore at night, but sometimes the drive for profit made long, non-stop voyages necessary over the open waters. As Hesiod commented, merchants needing to make a living took to the sea "because an income means life to poor mortals, but it is a terrible fate to die among the waves."

The desire for metals and other scarce resources drove traders far from home in this era, as it had for centuries. The *Odyssey* describes the basic strategy of this commodity trading, when the goddess Athena appears disguised as a metal trader: "I am here…with my ship and crew on our way across the wine-dark sea to foreign lands in search of copper; I am carrying iron now." By

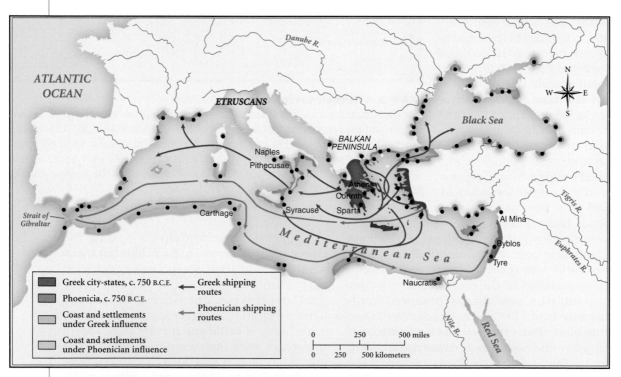

MAP 2.5 Phoenician and Greek Expansion, c. 750–500 B.C.E.
The Phoenicians, setting out from their homeland on the Mediterranean's eastern edge, were early explorers and settlers of the western Mediterranean; by 800 B.C.E. they had already founded the city of Carthage, which would become the main commercial power in the region. During the Archaic Age, groups of adventurous Greeks followed the Phoenicians' lead and settled all around the Mediterranean, hoping to improve their economic prospects by trade and farming. Sometimes they moved into previously established Phoenician settlements; sometimes they founded their own. Eventually, some Greek city-states in the heartland established formal ties with new settlements or sent out their own expeditions to try to establish "colonies" (new independent city-states that were supposed to remain loyal to their mother city).

800 B.C.E., the Mediterranean swarmed with entrepreneurs of many nationalities. The Phoenicians established footholds as far west as Spain's Atlantic coast to gain access to inland mines there. Their North African settlement at Carthage (modern Tunis) would become one of the Mediterranean's most powerful cities in later times, dominating commerce west of Italy.

Greeks energetically joined this wave-tossed contest for profit as the scale of trade soared near the end of the Dark Age: archaeologists have found only two tenth-century B.C.E. Greek pots that were carried abroad, while eighth-century pottery has turned up at more than eighty foreign sites. By 750 B.C.E. (or earlier—the evidence is hard to date), Greeks had begun to settle far from their homeland, sometimes living in others' settlements, such as those of the Phoenicians in the western Mediterranean, and sometimes establishing trading posts of their own, as at Pithecusae in the Bay of Naples. Everywhere they traded energetically with the local populations, such as the Etruscans in central Italy, who imported large amounts of Greek goods, as the vases found in their tombs reveal. Greeks staying abroad for the long term would also cultivate vacant land, gradually building permanent communities. A shortage of arable territory in Greece drove some poor citizens abroad to find farmland of their own. Because apparently only males left home on trading and land-hunting expeditions, they had to find wives in the areas where they settled, either through peaceful negotiation or by kidnapping.

By about 580 B.C.E., Greeks had settled in practically every available location in Spain, present-day southern France, southern Italy and Sicily, North Africa, and the Black Sea coast (Map. 2.5). The settlements in southern Italy and Sicily, such as Naples and Syracuse, eventually became so large and powerful that this region was called Magna Graecia (literally, "Great Greece"), and its communities became rivals of Carthage for commercial dominance in the western Mediterranean.

Fewer Greeks settled in the eastern Mediterranean, perhaps because the monarchies there restricted foreign immigration. Still, a trading station had sprung up at Al Mina in Syria by 800 B.C.E., while King

Archaic Age Sculpture of a Dead Athenian Warrior
This Athenian marble statue dating from about 530–520 B.C.E. shows the stiff posture and smiling expression that Archaic Age Greek sculptors used for "heroic nudes" depicting dead young men. These kouros ("young male") statues had a striding stance recalling the style of Egyptian art and were painted in bright colors; this one retains traces of red paint. A base probably belonging to this six-foot four-inch tall statue bore an inscription addressed to people passing by: "Stand and mourn at this monument of Croesus, now dead; raging Ares [the Greek war god] destroyed him as he battled in the front ranks." *The Art Archive/National Archeological Museum Athens/Dagli Orti.*

Psammetichus I of Egypt (r. 664–610 B.C.E.) permitted a similar foundation at Naucratis. These close contacts with eastern Mediterranean civilizations paid cultural as well as economic dividends. In addition to inspiring Greeks to reintroduce figures into their painting, Near Eastern art gave them models for statues: they began sculpting images that stood

Cyrene Records Its Foundation as a Greek Colony

The Greeks living in Cyrene in North Africa (in modern Libya) set up this inscription recording the foundation of their polis by colonists dispatched about 630 B.C.E. from Thera (a polis on an island north of Crete). The text we have, which is damaged and therefore uncertain in places (marked by brackets), comes from the fourth century B.C.E., but it was based on earlier documents. Cyrene was one of the few colonies originally established by a polis instead of entrepreneurs.

The Oath of the Colonists

The assembly of Thera decided:

Since the god Apollo of Delphi spontaneously instructed Battus and the Therans to settle Cyrene, the Therans decided to send Battus to North Africa as leader and king and for the Therans to sail as his companions. They are to sail on equal and fair terms according to their households and one adult son [from each household] is to be selected, and grown young men [are to be selected], and of the other Therans only those who are free can sail. And if the colonists establish a colony, a man from the households who subsequently sails to North Africa shall share in citizenship and public office and shall be given a portion from land that has no owner. But if they do not establish a colony and the Therans are unable to provide aid, but the colonists suffer hardship for five years, they are allowed to leave the land without fear and return to Thera and their property and to be citizens. If any man is not willing to sail when the polis sends him, he will be subject to the death penalty and his property shall be confiscated. Any man who harbors or hides such a man, whether a father his son, or a brother his brother, will be subject to the same penalty as the man who is not willing to sail. Those who stayed at home and those who sailed to found the colony swore oaths on these terms, and they invoked curses against those who break the oaths and fail to keep them, whether they were those who settled in North Africa or those who remained at home.

Source: R. Meiggs and D. Lewis, eds., *A Selection of Greek Historical Inscriptions to the End of the Fifth Century B.C.* (1969), no. 5. Translation by Thomas R. Martin.

stiffly and stared straight ahead, imitating Egyptian statuary. When the improving economy of the later Archaic Age allowed Greeks again to afford monumental architecture in stone, their rectangular temples on platforms with columns reflected Egyptian architectural designs.

Historians have traditionally called the settlement process of this era Greek colonization, but recent research questions this term's accuracy because the word *colonization* implies the process by which modern European governments officially installed colonies abroad. The evidence for these Greek settlements suggests rather that private entrepreneurship initiated most of them; official state involvement was minimal, at least in the beginning. Most commonly, a Greek city-state in the homeland would establish ties with a settlement originally set up by its citizens privately and then claim it as its colony only after the community had grown into an economic success. Few instances are clearly recorded in which a Greek mother city officially sent out a group to establish a formally organized colony abroad.

Citizenship and Freedom in the Greek City-State

The creation of the polis filled the political vacuum left by Mycenaean civilization's fall. The Greek city-state was unique because it was based on the concept of citizenship for all its free inhabitants. Moreover, except in tyrannies, at least some degree of shared governance was common; this power sharing reached its purest form in democratic Greek city-states. Some historians argue that knowledge of the older cities of the island of Cyprus and of Phoenicia influenced the Greeks in creating their new political systems; since monarchs dominating subjects ruled those eastern states, however, this theory cannot explain the origin of citizenship in all Greek city-states and the sharing of power in many, especially democracies. The most famous ancient analyst of Greek politics and society, the philosopher Aristotle (384–322 B.C.E.), insisted that the forces of nature had created the city-state: "Humans are beings who by nature live in a city-state." Anyone who existed outside such a community, Aristotle remarked, must be either a simple fool or superhuman.

Religion in the Greek City-State.   Greek city-states were officially religious communities: as well as worshiping many deities, each city-state honored a particular god or goddess, such as Athena at Athens, as its special protector. Different communities could choose the same deity: Sparta, Athens's chief rival in later times, also chose Athena as its defender. Greeks envisioned the twelve most important gods banqueting atop Mount Olympus, the highest peak in mainland Greece. Zeus headed this pantheon; the others were Hera, his wife; Aphrodite,♦ goddess of love; Apollo, sun god; Ares, war god; Artemis, moon goddess; Athena, goddess of wisdom and war; Demeter, earth goddess; Dionysus, god of pleasure, wine, and disorder; Hephaestus, fire god; Hermes, messenger god; and Poseidon, sea god. Like Homer's proud warriors, the Olympian gods resented any slights to their honor. "I am well aware that the gods are competitively envious and disruptive towards humans," remarked the sixth-century Athenian statesman Solon. The Greeks believed that their gods occasionally experienced temporary pain or sadness in their dealings with one another but were immune to permanent suffering because they were immortal.

Greek religion's core belief was that humans, both as individuals and as communities, must honor the gods to thank them for bless-

ings received and to receive more blessings in return. Furthermore, the Greeks believed that the gods sent both good and bad into the world. The relationship between gods and humans generated sorrow as well as joy, punishment in the here and now, and an uncertain hope for favored treatment in this life and in the underworld after death. Greeks did not expect to reach paradise at some future time when evil forces would finally be vanquished forever.

The idea of reciprocity between gods and humans underlay the Greek understanding of the nature of the gods. Deities did not love humans. Rather, they supported people who paid them honor and did not offend them. Gods offended by humans could punish them by sending calamities such as famine, earthquake, epidemic disease, or defeat in war.

City-states honored gods by sacrificing animals such as cattle, sheep, goats, and pigs, decorating their sanctuaries with works of art, and celebrating festivals with songs, dances, prayers, and processions. A seventh-century B.C.E. bronze statuette, which a man named

A Greek Woman at an Altar
This red-figure vase painting (contrast the black-figure vase on page 55) from the center of a large drinking cup shows a woman in rich clothing pouring a libation to the gods onto a flaming altar. In her other arm, she carries a religious object that we cannot securely identify. This scene illustrates the most important and frequent role of women in Greek public life: participating in religious ceremonies, both at home and in community festivals. Greek women (and men) commonly wore sandals; why do you think they are usually depicted without shoes in vase paintings? *The Toledo Museum of Art, Toledo, Ohio; Purchased with funds from the Libbey Endowment, Gift of Edward Drummond Libbey.*

♦**Aphrodite:** a fruh DY tee

Mantiklos◆ gave to a sanctuary of Apollo to honor the god, makes clear why individuals gave such gifts. On its legs Mantiklos inscribed his understanding of the transaction: "Mantiklos gave this from his share to the Far Darter of the Silver Bow [Apollo]; now you, Apollo, do something for me in return."

People's greatest religious difficulty lay in anticipating what might offend a deity. Mythology hinted at the gods' expectations of proper human behavior. For example, the Greeks told stories of the gods demanding hospitality for strangers, proper burial for family members, and punishment for human arrogance and murderous violence. Oracles, dreams, divination, and the prophecies of seers were all regarded as clues to what humans might have done to anger the gods. Offenses could be acts such as performing a sacrifice improperly, violating the sanctity of a temple area, or breaking an oath or sworn agreement. People believed that the deities were attentive to some wrong doings, such as violating oaths, but generally uninterested in common crimes, which humans had to police themselves. Homicide was such a serious offense, however, that the gods were thought to punish it by casting a miasma (ritual contamination) on the murderer and on all those around him or her. Unless the members of the affected group purified themselves by punishing the murderer, they could all expect to suffer divine punishment, such as bad harvests or disease.

The community and individuals alike paid homage and respect to the deities through cults, the prescribed sets of publicly funded religious activities for each deity overseen by priests and priestesses. To carry out their duties, people prayed, sang hymns of praise, offered sacrifices, and presented gifts at the deity's sanctuary. In these holy places a person could honor and thank the deities for blessings and beg them for relief when misfortune struck the community or the petitioner. Individuals could also offer sacrifices at home with the household gathered around; sometimes the family's slaves were allowed to participate.

Priests and priestesses chosen from the citizen body conducted the sacrifices of public

cults; they did not use their positions to influence political or social matters. Their special knowledge consisted in knowing how to perform traditional religious rites. They were not guardians of correct religious thinking because Greek polytheism had no scripture or uniform set of beliefs and practices. It required its adherents only to support the community's local rituals and to avoid religious pollution.

Citizenship for Rich and Poor. Greeks devised the concept of citizenship to organize their city-states; it meant free people agreeing to form a political community that was supposed to be a partnership of privileges and duties in common affairs under the rule of law. Citizenship was a distinctive political concept because, even in Greek city-states organized as tyrannies or oligarchies, it bestowed a basic level of political and legal equality. Most important, it carried the expectation (although not always the fulfillment) of equal treatment under the law for male citizens regardless of their social status or wealth. Women had the protection of the law, but they were barred from participation in politics on the grounds that female judgment was inferior to male. Regulations governing sexual behavior and control of property were stricter for women than for men.

The most dramatic version of political equality was having all free, adult male citizens in an oligarchic or democratic Greek city-state share in governance by attending and voting in a political assembly, where the laws and policies of the community were ratified. The degree of power sharing was closer to equality in some places than in others. In city-states where the social elite had a stranglehold on politics, small groups or even a single family could dominate the process of legislating. Other city-states introduced the revolutionary innovation of direct democracy, which gave all free men the right to propose laws and policies in the assembly and to serve on juries. Even in democratic city-states, however, citizens did not enjoy perfect political equality. The right to hold office, for example, could be restricted to citizens possessing a certain amount of property. Equality prevailed most strongly in the justice system,

---

◆**Mantiklos:** MAN tee klahs

in which all male citizens were treated the same, regardless of wealth or status.

Because monarchy and legal inequality had characterized the history of the ancient Near East and Greece in earlier times, it is remarkable that a notion of equality became a principle for the reorganization of Greek society and politics in the Archaic Age. The polis—with its emphasis on equal protection of the laws for rich and poor alike—remained the preeminent form of political and social organization in Greece until the beginning of Roman control six centuries later.

The Greek city-states' free poor enjoyed the privileges and duties of citizenship alongside the rich throughout this long period. How the poor gained that status remains an important mystery. The greatest population increase in the late Dark Age and the Archaic Age came in the ranks of the poorer section of the population. These families raised more children to help farm more land, which had been vacant after the depopulation brought on by the worst of the Dark Age. (See "Taking Measure," below.) There was no precedent for extending the principle of even

TAKING MEASURE

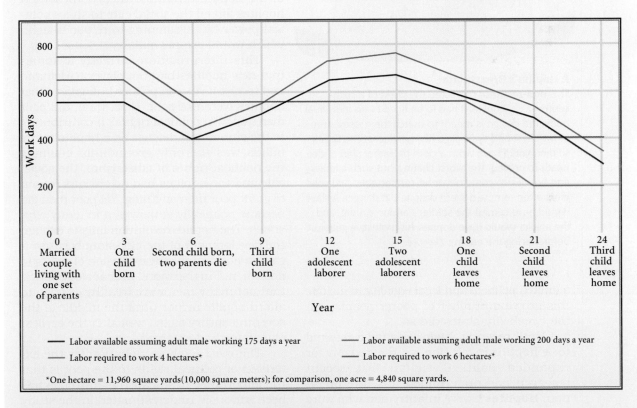

Labor available assuming adult male working 175 days a year
Labor required to work 4 hectares*
Labor available assuming adult male working 200 days a year
Labor required to work 6 hectares*

*One hectare = 11,960 square yards (10,000 square meters); for comparison, one acre = 4,840 square yards.

Greek Family Size and Agricultural Labor in the Archaic Age

Modern demographers have calculated the changing relationship in the Archaic Age between a farm family's productive capacity to work the land and the number of people in the family over time. The graph shows how valuable healthy teenage children were to the family's well-being. When the family had two adolescent laborers available, it could farm over 50 percent more land, increasing its productivity significantly and thus making life more prosperous. *Adapted from Thomas W. Gallant,* Risk and Survival in Ancient Greece: Reconstructing the Rural Domestic Economy *(1991), Fig. 4.10. Reprinted with the permission of Stanford University Press.*

A Hoplite's Breastplate
This bronze armor protected the chest of a sixth-century B.C.E. hoplite. It had to be fitted to his individual body; the design is meant to match the musculature of his chest and symbolize his manliness. The Greek soldier would have worn a cloth or leather shirt underneath to prevent the worst chafing, but such a heavy and hot device could never be comfortable, and soldiers often removed them despite the danger. A slave would have carried the soldier's armor for him, and the soldier would have donned his protective gear just before facing the enemy. *Ekdotike.*

a limited political and legal equality to include this growing number of poorer people, but the Greek city-states did so.

Until recently, historians have referred to a hoplite revolution as the reason for expanded political rights, but recent research has undermined this interpretation. **Hoplites**◆ were infantrymen who wore metal body armor; they constituted the main strike force of the militia that defended each city-state; there were no permanent Greek armies at this period. Hoplites marched into combat arrayed in a rectangular formation called a phalanx. Staying in line and working as part of the group were the secrets to suc-

◆**hoplites:** HAHP lyts

cessful phalanx tactics. In the words of the seventh-century B.C.E. poet Archilochus, a good hoplite was "a short man firmly placed upon his legs, with a courageous heart, not to be uprooted from the spot where he plants his feet." Greeks had fought in phalanxes for a long time, but until the eighth century B.C.E. only the elite could afford hoplite equipment. In the eighth century B.C.E., however, a growing number of men had become prosperous enough to buy metal weapons, especially because the use of iron had made them more readily available. Presumably these new hoplites, because they bought their own equipment and trained hard to learn phalanx tactics to defend their community, felt they should also enjoy political rights. According to the hoplite revolution theory, these new hoplites forced the social elite to share political power by threatening to refuse to fight, which would cripple military defense.

This interpretation correctly assumes that new hoplites had the power to demand and receive a voice in politics but ignores that hoplites were not poor. How, then, did poor men, too, win political rights? If contributing to the city-state's defense as a hoplite in the militia was the only grounds for claiming the political rights of citizenship, the social elite and the hoplites had no obvious reason to grant poor men anything. Yet poor men did become politically empowered in many city-states. The hoplite revolution fails to explain the development of the city-state because it cannot account for the extension of rights to poor men. Furthermore, archaeology shows that not many men were wealthy enough to afford hoplite armor until the middle of the seventh century B.C.E., well after the earliest city-states had emerged.

The most likely explanation for the extension of political rights to the poor is that the importance of so-called light troops has been seriously underestimated in the study of Greek warfare and that poor men earned respect by fighting to defend the community, just as hoplites did. The poor fought as lightly armed skirmishers, able to disrupt an enemy's heavy infantry by slinging barrages of rocks or shooting arrows. It is also possible that tyrants—sole rulers who seized power for their families unconstitutionally in some city-states (see discussion on page

72)—boosted the status of poor men. Tyrants may have granted greater political rights to poor or disfranchised men as a means of marshaling popular support.

In any case, the wealthier elements in society did not extend rights of citizenship to the poor out of any romanticized vision of poverty as spiritually noble. As one contemporary put it, "Money is the man; no poor man ever counts as good or honorable." Tension between haves and have-nots never disappeared in the city-state. Nevertheless, in whatever way the poor became citizens who possessed a rough equality of political and legal rights with the rich, this unprecedented decision constituted Greek society's most daring innovation in the Archaic Age.

The Expansion of Greek Slavery. Even as the idea of a free citizenry took root, the practice of slavery also grew in Greece. Many slaves were war captives; pirates or raiders seized others in the rough regions to the north and east of Greek territory. The fierce bands in these areas also captured and sold one another to slave dealers. Rich families prized Greek-speaking and educated slaves because they could use them to tutor their children, since no schools existed in this period.

City-states as well as individuals owned slaves. Public slaves enjoyed limited independence, living on their own and performing specialized tasks. In Athens, for example, special slaves were trained to detect counterfeit coinage. Temple slaves "belonged" to the deity of the sanctuary, for whom they worked as servants.

Slaves made up about one-third of the total population in some city-states by the fifth century B.C.E. They became cheap enough that even middle-class people could afford one or two. Still, small landowners and their families continued to do much work themselves, sometimes hiring free laborers. Not even wealthy Greek landowners acquired large numbers of agricultural slaves because maintaining gangs of hundreds of enslaved workers year-round would have been uneconomical. Most crops required short periods of intense labor punctuated by long stretches of inactivity, and owners did not want to feed slaves who had no work.

Slaves did all kinds of jobs. Household slaves, often women, had the safest lives: they cleaned, cooked, fetched water from public fountains, helped the wife with the weaving, watched the children, accompanied the husband as he did the marketing, and performed other domestic chores. Neither they nor their male counterparts could refuse if their masters demanded sexual favors. Owners often labored alongside their slaves in small manufacturing businesses and on farms, although rich landowners might appoint a slave supervisor to oversee work in the fields. Slaves toiling in the narrow, landslide-prone tunnels of Greece's silver and gold mines had the worst lot: many died doing this dangerous, dark, back-breaking work.

Since slaves existed as property, not people, owners could legally beat or even kill them. But hurting or executing slaves was probably limited because it made no economic sense—the master would be crippling or destroying his own property. Under the best conditions, household workers with humane masters lived lives free of violent punishment; they might even be allowed to join their owners' families on excursions and attend religious rituals. However, without the right to a family of their own, without property, and without legal or political rights, slaves remained alienated from regular society. In the words of an ancient commentator, slaves lived lives of "work, punishment, and food." Sometimes owners liberated their slaves, and some promised freedom at a future date to encourage their slaves to work hard. Those slaves who gained their freedom did not become citizens in Greek city-states but instead mixed into the population of *metics*—noncitizens officially allowed to live in the community. Freed slaves were still expected to help out their former masters when called on.

Greek slaves rarely revolted on a large scale, except in Sparta, because they were usually of too many different origins and nationalities and too scattered to organize. No Greek called for the abolition of slavery. The expansion of slavery in the Archaic Age reduced more and more unfree persons to a state of absolute dependence; as Aristotle later put it, slaves were "living tools."

Greek Women's Lives. Women counted as citizens legally, socially, and religiously, although only men had the right to participate in city-state politics and to vote. Women's citizenship gave them an important source of security and status because it guaranteed access to the justice system and a respected role in official religious activity. Citizen women had legal protection against being kidnapped for sale into slavery, and they had recourse to the courts in disputes over property, although they usually had to have a man speak for them. Before her marriage, a woman's father served as her legal guardian; after marriage, her husband assumed the same role. The traditional paternalism of Greek society, with men acting as "fathers" to regulate the lives of women and safeguard their interests as defined by men demanded that all women have male guardians to protect them physically and legally.

The emergence of widespread slavery in the city-state made households bigger and added new responsibilities for women. While their husbands farmed, participated in politics, and met with their male friends, well-off wives managed the household: raising the children, supervising the preservation and preparation of food, keeping the family's financial accounts, weaving fabric for clothing, directing the work of the slaves, and tending them when they were ill. Poor women worked outside the home, hoeing and reaping in the fields and selling produce and small goods such as ribbons and trinkets in the market that occupied the center of every settlement. Women's labor ensured the family's economic self-sufficiency and allowed the male citizens the time to participate in public life.

Women's religious functions gave them freedom of movement and prestige. Women left the home to attend funerals, state festivals, and public rituals. They had access, for example, to the initiation rights of the popular cult of Demeter at Eleusis, near Athens. Women had control over cults reserved exclusively for them and also performed important duties in other official cults; in fifth-century B.C.E. Athens, for example, women officiated as priestesses for more than forty different deities, with benefits including salaries paid by the state.

Marriage. Marriages were arranged, and everyone was expected to marry. A woman's guardian—her father or, if he was dead, her uncle or her brother—would often engage her to another man's son while she was still a child, perhaps as young as five. The engagement was an important public event conducted in the presence of witnesses. The guardian on this occasion repeated the phrase that expressed the primary aim of the marriage: "I give you this woman for the plowing [procreation] of legitimate children." The wedding itself took place when the girl was in her early teens and the groom ten to fifteen years older. Hesiod advised a man to marry a virgin in the fifth year after her first menstruation, when he himself was "not much younger than thirty and not much older." A legal wedding consisted of the bride moving to her husband's dwelling; the procession to his house served as the ceremony. The woman brought to the marriage a dowry of property (perhaps land yielding an income, if she was wealthy) and personal possessions that formed part of the new household's assets and could be inherited by her children. Her husband was legally obliged to preserve the dowry and to return it in case of a divorce. A husband could expel his wife from his home; a wife could legally leave her husband to return to the guardianship of her male relatives, but her husband could force her to stay.

Except in certain cases in Sparta, monogamy was the rule in ancient Greece, as was a nuclear family (husband, wife, and children living together without other relatives in the same house). Citizen men, married or not, were free to have sexual relations with slaves, foreign concubines, female prostitutes, or willing pre-adult citizen males. Citizen women, single or married, had no such freedom. Sex between a wife and anyone other than her husband carried harsh penalties for both parties, except in Sparta.

Greek citizen men placed Greek citizen women under their guardianship both to regulate marriage and procreation and to maintain family property. According to Greek mythology, women were a necessary evil: men needed them to have a family but could expect troubles as the price. Zeus supposedly created the first woman, Pandora, as a pun-

A Bride's Preparation

This special piece of pottery was an epinetron, designed to fit over a woman's thigh to protect it while she sat down to spin wool. As a woman's tool, it appropriately carried a picture from a woman's life: a bride being helped to prepare for her wedding by her family, friends, and servants. The inscriptions indicate that this fifth-century B.C.E. epinetron shows the mythological bride Alcestis, famous for sacrificing herself to save her husband and then being rescued from Death by the hero Heracles. *Deutsches Archaologisches Institut-Athen. DAI Neg No. INM5126. Photo: E.M. C2aKo.*

ishment for men in his vendetta against Prometheus for giving fire to humans. Like the biblical Eve giving Adam forbidden fruit from the Tree of Knowledge, Pandora loosed "evils and diseases" into the previously trouble-free world when curiosity overcame her. To see what was in a container that had come as a gift from the gods, Pandora lifted its lid and accidentally freed the evils that had been penned inside. When she finally slammed the lid back down, only hope still remained in the container. The poet Hesiod described women as "big trouble" but thought any man who refused to marry to escape the "troublesome deeds of women" would come to "destructive old age" alone, with no heirs. In other words, a man needed a wife so that he could sire children who would later care for him and preserve his property after his death. This paternalistic attitude allowed men to control human reproduction and consequently the distribution of property.

Review: What degrees of freedom existed for the different categories of people in the Greek city-state?

❖ New Directions for the Polis, c. 750–500 B.C.E.

Greek city-states developed three forms of society and government: oligarchy, tyranny, and democracy. Sparta, for example, provided Greece's most famous example of an oligarchy, in which a small number of men dominated policymaking in an assembly of male citizens. For a time Corinth had the best-known tyranny, in which one man seized control of the city-state, ruling it for the advantage of his family and loyal supporters, while acknowledging the citizenship of all. And Athens developed Greece's best-known democracy by allowing all male citizens to participate in governing. Although assemblies of men had influenced some ancient Near Eastern kings, Greek democracies gave their male citizens an amount of equality and political power never before seen in world history.

The Archaic Age polis is justly famous because it became the incubator for democratic politics; it also provided the environment in which Greeks created new ways of thought. In this period they formulated innovative ways of understanding the physical world, their relations to it, and their relationships with one another.

Oligarchy in Sparta, c. 700–500 B.C.E.

Military readiness overrode all other concerns in Sparta. This city-state developed the mightiest infantry force in Greece during the Archaic Age. Its citizens were renowned for their militaristic self-discipline. Sparta's urban center nestled in an easily defended valley on the Peloponnese peninsula twenty-five miles from the Mediterranean coast. This separation from the sea kept the Spartans from becoming adept sailors; their strength lay on land.

The Spartan version of oligarchy included three components of rule. First came the two hereditary, prestigious military leaders called kings, who served as the state's religious heads and the generals of its army. Despite their title, they were not monarchs but only part of the ruling oligarchy. The other two parts were a council of twenty-eight men over sixty years old (the elders) and five annually elected magistrates called *ephors* (overseers).

In principle, legislation had to be approved by an assembly of all Sparta's free adult males, who were called the Alike to stress their common traditions. The assembly had only limited power to amend the proposals put before it, however, and the council would withdraw a proposal when the assembly's reaction proved negative. "If the people speak crookedly," according to Spartan tradition, "the elders and the leaders of the people shall be withdrawers." The council would then resubmit the proposal after marshaling support for its passage.

Spartan society demanded strict compliance with all laws. When the ephors took office, for example, they issued an official proclamation to Sparta's males: "Shave your

Sparta and Corinth, c. 750–500 B.C.E.

mustache and obey the laws." The laws' importance was emphasized by the official story that the god Apollo had given them to Sparta. Unlike other Greeks, the Spartans never wrote down their laws. Instead, they preserved their system with a unique, highly structured way of life. All Spartan citizens were expected to put service to their city-state before personal concerns because their state's survival was continually threatened by its own economic foundation: the great mass of Greek slaves, called Helots,◆ who did almost all the work for citizens.

The Helots. Helots were captives from neighboring parts of Greece that the Spartans conquered. Most Helots came from Messenia to the west, which Sparta conquered by around 700 B.C.E. Sparta's Helot population outnumbered its free citizens. Helots lived bitter lives, as reflected in the Messenian legend of Aristodemus.◆ During the Spartan invasion of his homeland, Aristodemus sacrificed his beloved daughter to the gods of the underworld in an attempt to enlist their aid against the invaders and prevent the Messenians from being enslaved. When Messenia fell to Sparta, he killed himself on his daughter's grave. Deprived of their freedom and their city-states, Helots craved the chance to revolt against their Spartan overlords.

Helots were not owned by individual Spartans but rather belonged to the whole community, which alone could free them. Helots had a semblance of family life because they were expected to produce children to maintain their population, and they could own some personal possessions and practice their religion. They labored as farmers and household slaves so that Spartan citizens would not have to do such nonmilitary work. Spartan men in fact wore their hair very long to show they were warriors rather than laborers, for whom long hair was inconvenient.

Helots lived under the constant threat of officially sanctioned violence. Every year the ephors formally declared war between Sparta and the Helots, allowing any Spartan to kill a Helot without legal penalty or fear of offending the gods by unsanctioned murder. By

◆**Helots:** HEH luhts
◆**Aristodemus:** ar i sto DEE muhs

beating the Helots frequently, forcing them to get drunk in public as an object lesson to young Spartans, and humiliating them by making them wear dog-skin caps, the Spartans consistently emphasized the slaves' "otherness." In this way Spartans created a moral barrier to justify their harsh abuse of fellow Greeks. Contrasting the freedom of Spartan citizens from ordinary work with the lot of the Helots, the later Athenian Critias observed, "Sparta is the home of the freest of the Greeks, and of the most enslaved."

Spartan Communal Life. Because Helots worked the fields, male citizens could devote their whole lives to full-time preparation for war, training to protect their state from hostile neighbors and its own slaves. Boys lived at home only until their seventh year, when they were sent to live in communal barracks with other males until they were thirty. They spent most of their time exercising, hunting, practicing with weapons, and being acculturated to Spartan values by listening to tales of bravery and heroism at common meals, where adult males ate most of the time instead of at home. Discipline was strict, and the boys were purposely underfed so that they would learn stealth by stealing food. If they were caught, punishment and disgrace followed immediately. One famous Spartan tale shows how seriously boys were supposed to fear such failure: having successfully stolen a fox, which he was hiding under his clothing, a Spartan youth died because he let the panicked animal rip out his insides rather than be detected in the theft. Spartan males who could not survive the tough conditions of their childhood training fell into social disgrace and were denied Alike status.

Spending so much time in shared quarters schooled Sparta's young men in their society's values. This communal existence took the place of a Spartan boy's family and school when he was growing up and remained his main social environment even after he reached adulthood. There he learned to call all older men Father to emphasize

that his primary loyalty was to the group instead of his biological family. The environment trained him for the one honorable occupation for Spartan men: obedient soldier. The seventh-century B.C.E. poet Tyrtaeus expressed the Spartan male ideal: "Know that it is good for the city-state and the whole people when a man takes his place in the front row of warriors and stands his ground without flinching."

An adolescent boy's life often involved what in today's terminology would be called

Hunt Painting in a Spartan Cup
This black-figure drinking cup with a picture of a hunt on its interior was made in Sparta about 560 B.C.E. Hunting large, dangerous wild game was an important way for Spartan men to show their courage and acquire meat for their communal meals. The painter has chosen a "porthole" style, as if we were looking through a circular window at the scene beyond. The alignment of the figures' legs, torsos, and heads reflect the influence of Egyptian art on the Greeks. The fish below the ground line may indicate a seashore, or they may just be a way for the painter to fill open space decoratively, a technique characteristic of Greek art in this period. By the classical period, Spartans had largely stopped creating art, reflecting the strongly military focus of their society. *Photo Reunion Des Musées Nationaux—H. Lewandowski.*

a homosexual relationship, although the ancient concepts of heterosexuality and homosexuality did not match modern notions. An older male would choose a teenager as a special favorite, in many cases engaging him in sexual relations. Their bond of affection was meant to make each ready to die for this other man at whose side he would march into battle. The sexual customs of numerous city-states included this form of homosexuality, but some forbade it. Evidently, this sort of physical relationship was controversial; the Athenian author Xenophon (c. 430–355 B.C.E.) in fact wrote a work on the Spartan way of life denying that sex with boys existed there because he thought it demeaning to the Spartans' reputation for virtue. However, the evidence shows this homosexuality did exist (the first modern histories of Greece suppressed discussion of this relationship because their writers saw it as a form of child abuse).

In such relationships the elder partner (the "lover") was supposed to help educate the young man (the "beloved") in politics and community values and not just exploit him for physical pleasure. The relationship would not be lasting or exclusive: beloveds would grow up to get married, as their lovers were, and would eventually become the older member of a new pair. Homoerotic sex was considered disgraceful between adult males, as it was for women of all ages (at least according to men).

Spartan women were known throughout the Greek world for their personal freedom. Since their husbands were so rarely at home, women directed the households, which included servants, daughters, and sons until they left for their communal training. Consequently, Spartan women exercised more power in the household than did women elsewhere in Greece. They could own property, including land. Wives were expected to use their freedom from farm labor provided by the Helot system to keep themselves physically fit so that they could bear healthy children to keep up the population. They were also expected to drum Spartan values into their children. One mother became legendary for handing her son his shield on the eve of battle and admonishing him, "Come back with it or on it."

Demography determined Sparta's long-term fate. Its population was never large; adult males—who made up the army—numbered between eight and ten thousand in the Archaic period. Over time, the problem of producing enough children to keep the Spartan army from shrinking became desperate, probably because losses in war far outnumbered births. Men became legally required to marry, with bachelors punished by fines and public ridicule. If everyone agreed, a woman could legitimately have children by a man other than her husband. The seventh century B.C.E. poet Alcman expressed the male ideal for Spartan women in a song he wrote about the leader of a women's chorus: "She stands out as if, among a herd of cows, someone placed a firmly built horse with ringing hooves, a prize winner from winged dreams."

Because the Spartans' survival depended on the exploitation of enslaved Greeks, they believed changes in their way of life must be avoided because any change might make them vulnerable to internal revolts. Some Greeks criticized the Spartan way of life as repressive and monotonous, but everyone admired the Spartans' respect for their laws.

Tyranny in Corinth, c. 657–585 B.C.E.

In some city-states, competition between members of the social elite for political leadership became so bitter that a single family would suppress all its rivals and establish itself in rule for a time. The family's leader thus became a tyrant, a dictator backed by his relatives and other supporters who gained political dominance by force. Tyrants usually rallied support by promising privileges to poor citizens in city-states where they lacked full citizenship or felt disfranchised in political life. Successful tyrants kept their elite rivals at bay by cultivating the goodwill of the masses with economic policies favoring their interests, such as public employment schemes. Since few tyrants successfully passed their popularity on to their heirs, their tyrannies tended to be short-lived.

Tyrants usually preserved their city-states' existing laws and political institutions. If a city-state had an assembly, for example, the tyrant would allow it to continue to meet, expecting it to follow his direction. Although today the English word *tyrant* indicates a brutal or unwanted leader, tyrants in Archaic Greece did not always fit that description. Ordinary Greeks evaluated tyrants according to their behavior, opposing the ruthless and violent ones but welcoming the fair and helpful ones.

The most famous early tyranny arose at Corinth in 657 B.C.E., when the family of Cypselus◆ rebelled against the city's harshly oligarchic leadership. This takeover attracted wide attention in the Greek world because Corinth was such an important city-state. Its location on the isthmus controlling land access to the Peloponnese and a huge amount of seaborne trade made it the most prosperous city-state of the Archaic Age (see Map 2.4). Cypselus gained support for his political coup by rallying popular support. "He became one of the most admired of Corinth's citizens because he was courageous, prudent, and helpful to the people, unlike the oligarchs in power, who were insolent and violent," according to a later historian. He later ruthlessly suppressed rivals, but his popularity remained so great that he could govern without a bodyguard to protect him.

Cypselus's son Periander◆ succeeded him at his death in 625 B.C.E. Like his father, Periander aggressively continued Corinth's economic expansion by founding colonies to increase trade. He also pursued commercial contacts with Egypt. Unlike his father, however, Periander lost popular support by ruling harshly. He held on to power until his death in 585 B.C.E., but the hostility he had provoked soon led to the overthrow of his heir,

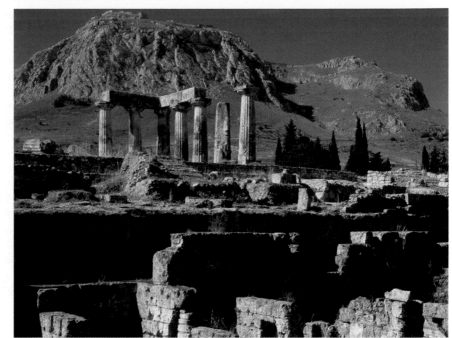

The Archaic Temple of Apollo at Corinth
This temple was built in the sixth century B.C.E. near the base of Corinth's acropolis, the massive rock formation soaring in the background. One of the earliest stone temples from Greece, it was constructed in Doric style, with its fluted columns resting directly on the foundation and topped by flattened disks. Earthquakes over the centuries have toppled most of the temple's columns and all its walls. (The walls in the foreground are from later buildings.) *The Art Archive/Dagli Orti.*

Psammetichus. The social elite installed a government based on a board of magistrates and a council to forestall further tyrants.

Democracy in Athens, c. 632–500 B.C.E.

Only democracy, which Greeks invented, instituted genuine political power sharing in the polis. Athens, located at the southeastern corner of central Greece, became the most famous of the democratic city-states because its government gave political rights to the greatest number of people, financed magnificent temples and public buildings, and became militarily strong enough to force numerous other city-states to follow Athenian leadership. Athenian democracy did not reach its full development until the mid-fifth century B.C.E., but its first steps in the Archaic Age were remarkable because they allowed all male citizens to participate meaningfully in making

◆**Cypselus:** KIHP suh luhs
◆**Periander:** pehr ee AN dur

laws and administering justice. Democracy has remained so important in Western civilization that understanding why and how Athenian democracy worked remains a vital historical quest.

Athens's early development of a populous middle class was a crucial factor in opening this new path for Western civilization. The Athenian population apparently expanded at a phenomenal rate when economic conditions improved rapidly from about 800 to 700 B.C.E. The ready availability of good farmland in Athenian territory and opportunities for seaborne trade along the long coastline allowed many families to achieve modest prosperity. These hardworking entrepreneurs evidently felt that their self-won economic success entitled them to a say in government. The cohesiveness forged by the Athenian masses was evident as early as 632 B.C.E., when the people rallied "from the fields in a body," according to Herodotus, to foil the attempt by an elite Athenian named Cylon to install a tyranny.

Athens and Central Greece, c. 750–500 B.C.E.

By the seventh century B.C.E., all freeborn adult male citizens of Athens had the right to vote on public matters in the assembly. They also elected magistrates called archons, who headed the government and the judicial system by rendering verdicts in disputes and criminal accusations. Members of the elite dominated these offices at the time because they carried no pay, meaning poor men could not afford to serve.

An extended economic crisis beginning in the late seventh century B.C.E. almost suffocated Athens's infant democracy. The first attempt to solve the problem was the emergency appointment around 621 B.C.E. of a man named Draco (literally, "the Serpent") to revise the laws. Like the Mesopotamian kings before them, Athens's leaders believed that reforming and clarifying the laws would bring social harmony through justice. Unfortunately, Draco's changes proved too harsh to work because they made death the penalty

for even minor crimes; later Greeks said he had written his laws in blood, not ink. By 600 B.C.E., the situation had become critical, with poorer farmers forced to borrow constantly from richer neighbors and deeply mortgage their land. Finally, the crisis became so bad that impoverished citizens were sold into slavery to pay off debts. Civil war seemed next.

Solon's Democratic Reforms.   Desperate, the Athenians appointed another emergency official in 594 B.C.E., a war hero named Solon. To head off violence, Solon gave both rich and poor something of what they wanted, a compromise called the "shaking off of obligations" that canceled private debts, which helped the poor but displeased the rich; Solon's decision not to redistribute land had the opposite effect. He also banned selling citizens into slavery to settle debts and liberated citizens who had become slaves in this way. His elimination of debt slavery was a significant recognition of what today would be called citizen rights, and Solon celebrated his success in poetry: "To Athens, their home established by the gods, I brought back many who had been sold into slavery, some justly, some not."

Solon balanced political power between rich and poor by reforming Athens's traditional ranking of citizens into four groups. Most important, he made the top-ranking division depend solely on wealth, not birth. This change eliminated formal aristocracy at Athens. The groupings did not affect a man's treatment at law, only his eligibility for government office. The higher a man's ranking, the higher the post to which he could be elected; men at the poorest level, called laborers, were not eligible for any office. Solon did, however, confirm the laborers' right to participate in the legislative assembly. His revised classification scheme was another step toward democracy because it allowed for upward social mobility: if a man increased his wealth, he could move up the scale of eligibility for office.

To make the assembly more efficient, Solon created a council of four hundred men to prepare the assembly's agenda. He prevented the social elite from capturing too many places by having council members chosen annually by lottery. Over time, the council became the institution that kept Athenian direct democracy functioning efficiently; it organized the assembly's deliberations while preserving its freedom of action.

Even more than his changes to the government, Solon's two changes in the judicial system promoted democratic principles of equality. First, he mandated that any male citizen could bring charges on behalf of any crime victim. Second, he gave people the right to appeal a magistrate's judgment to the assembly. With these two measures, Solon empowered ordinary citizens in the administration of justice. Characteristically, he balanced these democratic reforms by granting broader powers to the "Council which meets on the Hill of the god of war Ares," a judicial body we call the Areopagus♦ Council. This select body, limited to ex-archons, wielded great power because its members judged the most important cases concerning public justice—accusations against archons themselves.

Solon's reforms broke the traditional pattern of government limited to the elite; they extended power broadly through the citizen body and created a system of law applying more equally than before to all the community's free men. An anecdote reported by the later biographer Plutarch offers a glimpse of how remarkable Solon's innovations seemed at the time: when a visiting foreign king, Anacharsis from Scythia,♦ discovered what Solon was doing, he burst into laughter, scoffing at Athenian democracy. Observing the procedure in the Athenian assembly, the king expressed his amazement that elite politicians could only recommend policy in their speeches, while the male citizens as a whole voted on what to do. "I find it astonishing," he remarked, "that here wise men speak on public affairs, while fools decide them." The king then added, "Do you actually believe your fellow citizens' injustice and greed can be kept in check this way? Written laws are more like spiders' webs than anything else: they tie up the weak and the small fry who get stuck in them, but the rich and the powerful tear them to shreds." Solon replied that communal values assure

the rule of law: "People abide by their agreements when neither side has anything to gain by breaking them. I am writing laws for the Athenians in such a way that they will clearly see it is to everyone's advantage to obey the laws rather than to break them."

Some elite Athenians vehemently disagreed with Solon because they wanted oligarchy. Their jealousy of one another kept them from uniting, and the unrest they caused opened the door to tyranny at Athens. Peisistratus,♦ helped by his upper-class friends and the poor whose interests he championed, made himself tyrant in 546 B.C.E. Like the Corinthian tyrants, he promoted the economic, cultural, and architectural development of Athens and curried the masses' favor. He helped poorer men, for example, by hiring them to build roads, a huge temple to Zeus, and fountains to increase the supply of drinking water. He boosted Athens's economy and its image by minting new coins stamped with Athena's owl and organizing a great annual festival honoring the god Dionysus that attracted people from near and far to see its musical and dramatic performances.

Peisistratus's family could not maintain public goodwill after his death. When Hippias, his eldest son, ruled harshly, a rival family, the Alcmaeonids,♦ denounced him as unjust toward the people. They convinced the Spartans, the self-proclaimed champions of Greek freedom, to "liberate" Athens from tyranny by expelling Hippias and his family in 510 B.C.E.

Cleisthenes, "Father of Athenian Democracy." Expelling the tyrants opened the way to the most important step in developing Athenian democracy, the reforms of Cleisthenes.♦ Himself a member of the social elite, in 508 B.C.E. he promised greater democracy to the masses to win political support for his election to office. Ordinary people favored his plan so strongly that they spontaneously rallied to repel a Spartan army that Cleisthenes' bitterest rival had convinced Sparta's leaders to send to block the reforms.

♦**Areopagus:** a ree AH puh guhs
♦**Scythia:** SIH thee uh

♦**Peisistratus:** pie SIS truh tuhs
♦**Alcmaeonids:** alk MEE uhn ihds
♦**Cleisthenes:** KLYS thuh neez

Vase Painting of a Music Lesson
This sixth-century B.C.E. red-figure vase shows a young man (seated on the left, without a beard) holding a lyre and watching an older, bearded man play the same instrument, while an adolescent boy and an older man listen. They all wear wreaths to show they are in a festive mood. The youth is evidently a pupil learning to play. Instruction in performing music and singing lyric poetry was considered an essential part of an upper-class Greek male's education. The teacher's lyre has a sounding board made from a turtle shell, as was customary for this instrument. *Staatliche Antikensammlungen und Glyphothek.*

By about 500 B.C.E. Cleisthenes had ensured direct participation in government by as many adult male citizens as possible. First he assembled constituent units for the city-state's new political organization by grouping country villages and urban neighborhoods into units called demes♦ ("peoples"). The demes chose council members annually by lottery in proportion to the size of their populations. To allow for greater participation, Solon's Council of Four Hundred was expanded to five hundred members. Finally, Cleisthenes required candidates for public office to be spread widely throughout the demes.

Cleisthenes helped his reforms succeed by basing them in preexisting social conditions favorable to democracy. Using demes, most of which were country villages, suggests that democratic notions stemmed from traditions of village life. There, each man was entitled to his say in running local affairs and had to persuade, not force, others to

agree. Cleisthenes' reforms caused Athenians to remember him as the father of their democracy, but it took another fifty years of political struggle before Athenian democracy reached its full development.

New Ways of Thought and Expression, c. 630–500 B.C.E.

The idea that persuasion, rather than force or status, should drive political decisions in democracy matched the spirit of intellectual change rippling through Greece in the late Archaic Age. In city-states all over the Greek world, new ways of thought inspired artists, poets, and philosophers. The Greeks' ongoing contacts with the Near East supplied traditions to learn from and, in some cases, to alter dramatically.

Archaic Age Art and Literature. Early in the Archaic period Greek artists took inspiration from the Near East. By the sixth century B.C.E., they had introduced innovations of their own. In ceramics, painters experimented with different clays and colors to depict vivid scenes from mythology and daily life. They became expert at rendering fully three-dimensional figures in an increasingly realistic style. Sculptors gave their statues balanced poses and calm, smiling faces.

Greek poets built on the Near Eastern tradition of poetry expressing personal emotions by creating a new form, called **lyric poetry**. This poetry sprang from popular song and was always performed to the accompaniment of the lyre (a kind of harp that gives its name to the poetry). Greek lyric poems were short, rhythmic, and diverse in subject. Lyric poets wrote songs both for choruses and for individual performers. Choral poems honored deities on public occasions, celebrated famous events in a city-state's history, praised victors in athletic contests, and enlivened weddings.

Solo lyric poems generated controversy because they valued individual expression and opinion over conventional views. Solon wrote poems justifying his reforms. Other poets criticized traditional values, such as strength in war. Sappho,♦ a lyric poet from

♦**demes:** deems

♦**Sappho:** SA foh

Lesbos born about 630 B.C.E. and famous for her poems on love, wrote, "Some would say the most beautiful thing on our dark earth is an army of cavalry, others of infantry, others of ships, but I say it's whatever a person loves." In this poem Sappho was expressing her longing for a woman she loved, who was now far away. Archilochus of Paros,♦ who probably lived in the early seventh century B.C.E., became famous for poems mocking militarism, lamenting friends lost at sea, and regretting love affairs gone wrong. He became infamous for his lines about throwing away his shield in battle so that he could run away to save his life: "Oh, the hell with it; I can get another one just as good." When he taunted a family in verse after the father had ended Archilochus's affair with one of his daughters, the power of his ridicule reportedly caused the father and his two daughters to commit suicide.

Greek Philosophy and Science.   The discipline of philosophy (literally, "love of wisdom") began in the seventh and sixth centuries B.C.E. when Greek thinkers whom we call pre-Socratic ("before Socrates") philosophers created prose writing to express their innovative ideas. These thinkers developed radically new explanations of the human world and its relation to the gods. Most pre-Socratic philosophers lived in Ionia, on Anatolia's western coast. This location gave them contact with Near Eastern knowledge in astronomy, mathematics, and myth. Because there were no formal schools in the Archaic Age, philosophers communicated their ideas by teaching privately and giving public lectures. Some also composed poetry to explain their theories. People who studied with these philosophers or heard their presentations helped spread the new ideas.

Working from Babylonian discoveries about the regular movements of the stars and planets, Ionian philosophers such as Thales♦ (c. 625–545 B.C.E.) and Anaximander♦ (c. 610–540 B.C.E.), both of Miletus, reached the revolutionary conclusion that unchang-

ing laws of nature governed the universe rather than gods' whims. Pythagoras,♦ who emigrated from the island of Samos to the Greek city-state Croton in southern Italy about 530 B.C.E., taught that numerical relationships explained the world and initiated the Greek study of mathematics and the numerical aspects of musical harmony.

Ionian philosophers insisted that natural phenomena were neither random nor arbitrary. They applied the word *cosmos*—meaning "an orderly arrangement that is beautiful"—to the universe. The cosmos encompassed not only the motions of heavenly bodies but also the weather, the growth of plants and animals, and human health. Because the universe was ordered, it was knowable; because it was knowable, thought and research could explain it. Philosophers therefore looked for the first or universal cause of all things, a problem that scientists still pursue. These first philosophers firmly believed

Ionia and the Aegean, c. 750–500 B.C.E.

they needed to give reasons for their conclusions and to persuade others by arguments based on evidence; that is, they believed in logic. This new way of thought, called **rationalism**, became the foundation for the study of science and philosophy. This rule-based view of the causes of events and physical phenomena contrasted sharply with the traditional mythological view. Naturally, many people had difficulty accepting such a startling change in their understanding of the world, and the older tradition explaining events as the work of deities lived on alongside the new approach. Magic remained an important preoccupation in the lives of most people.

The first Greek philosophers deeply influenced later times by separating scientific thinking from myth and religion. Their idea that people must give reasons to justify their beliefs, rather than just make assertions that others must believe without evidence, was their

---

♦**Archilochus of Paros:** ahr KIHL uh kuhs (of) PAR ahs
♦**Thales:** THAY leez
♦**Anaximander:** an nak suh MAN dur

♦**Pythagoras:** pie THAG uhr ahs

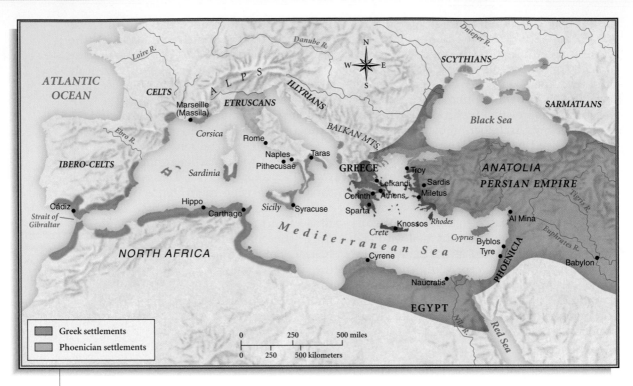

MAPPING THE WEST Mediterranean Civilizations, c. 500 B.C.E.
At the end of the sixth century B.C.E., the Persian empire was far and away the most powerful civilization touching the Mediterranean. Its riches and its unity gave it resources that no
Phoenician or Greek city could match. The Phoenicians dominated economically in the western Mediterranean, while the Greek city-states in Sicily and southern Italy rivaled the power of
those in the heartland. In Italy, the Etruscans were the most powerful civilization; the Romans
were still a small community struggling to replace monarchy with a republic.

most important achievement. This insistence
on rationality, coupled with the belief that the
world could be understood as something other
than the plaything of divine caprice, gave
people hope that they could improve their
lives through their own efforts. As Xenophanes
of Colophon♦ (c. 580–480 B.C.E.) concluded,
"The gods have not revealed all things from
the beginning to mortals, but, by seeking, human beings find out, in time, what is better."
This saying expressed the value Archaic Age
philosophers gave to intellectual freedom,
corresponding to the value that citizens gave
to political freedom in the city-state.

> **Review:** What were the main differences between
> the various forms of government in the Greek
> city-states?

♦**Xenophanes of Colophon:** zih NAH fuh neez (of)
KAH luh fuhn

Conclusion

Over different spans of time and with different results, both the Near East and Greece
recovered from their Dark Ages, which the
calamities of the period 1200–1000 B.C.E.
had caused. After its Dark Age the Near East
quickly revived its traditional pattern of social
and political organization: empire with a strong
central authority. The Neo-Assyrians, the Neo-
Babylonians, and the Persians succeeded
one another as imperial powers. The moral
dualism of Persian religion, Zoroastrianism,
influenced later religions. The Jews developed
their monotheism based on scripture.

Greece's recovery from its Dark Age produced the polis, a city-state based on citizenship as a new form of political and social
organization. The rapidly growing population of the Archaic Age developed the sense
of communal interests, personal freedom,

and divine justice that underlay the city-state. Greek city-states were ruled by tyranny, oligarchy, and—for the first time in history—democracy. Athens developed the most thoroughgoing democracy, but it took more than a century to do so.

Just as revolutionary as the invention of democracy were the new ways of thought that Greek philosophers developed. Arguing that laws of nature controlled the universe and that humans could discover these laws through reason and research, they established rationalism as the conceptual basis for science and philosophy.

The political and intellectual innovations of the Greek Archaic Age, which so profoundly affected later Western civilization, were almost lost to history. The grave threat to the Greek world and its new values came from Persia's awesome empire by about 500 B.C.E.

Suggested References

From Dark Age to Empire in the Near East, c. 1000–500 B.C.E.

Recent surveys of ancient Near Eastern history take an integrative approach to the subject, treating its various empires comparatively. The significance of Persian religion for later faiths has also been an active field of study.

Briant, Pierre. *From Cyrus to Alexander: A History of the Persian Empire.* 2002.

Brown, John Pairman. *Ancient Israel and Ancient Greece: Religion, Politics, and Culture.* 2003.

Brosius, Maria. *Women in Ancient Persia, 559–331 B.C.* 1996.

Cohn, Norman. *Cosmos, Chaos, and the World to Come: The Ancient Roots of Apocalyptic Faith.* 1993.

Kugel, James. *The God of Old: Inside the Lost World of the Bible.* 2003.

*Lieber, David L., ed. *Etz Hayim: Torah and Commentary.* 2001.

*Malandra, William W. *An Introduction to Ancient Iranian Religion: Readings from the Avesta and the Achaemenid Inscriptions.* 1983.

Nigosian, S. A. *The Zoroastrian Faith: Tradition and Modern Research.* 1993.

Persepolis and Ancient Iran: http://www.oi.uchicago.edu/OI/MUS/PA/IRAN/PAAI/PAAI_Persepolis.html.

Silberman, Neil, and Israel Finkelstein. *The Bible Unearthed: Archaeology's New Vision of Ancient Israel and the Origin of Its Sacred Texts.* 2002.

Snell, Daniel C. *Life in the Ancient Near East, 3100–332 B.C.E.* 1997.

Stiebing, William H., Jr. *Ancient Near Eastern History and Culture.* 2003.

Remaking Greek Civilization, c. 1000–750 B.C.E.

Scholarship on the Dark Age, such as by Sarah Morris, emphasizes that it was not as dark as sometimes asserted in the past because Greece was never completely cut off from contact with the Near East. Scholars agree that the Archaic Age was a period of tremendous activity and change, but they dispute the trustworthiness of the (later) ancient sources that inform us about it. The date of the first Olympic Games, for example, is much debated (see the article by Hugh Lee in the collection edited by Rashcke).

Hanson, Victor Davis. *The Other Greeks: The Family Farm and the Agrarian Roots of Western Civilization.* 1995.

*Hesiod. *Theogony; Works and Days.* Trans. M. L. West. 1999.

Kriwaczek, Paul. *In Search of Zarathustra: The First Prophet and the Ideas That Changed the World.* 2003.

Miller, Stephen G. *Ancient Greek Athletics.* 2004.

Morris, Sarah P. *Daidalos and the Origins of Greek Art.* 1992.

Olympia: http://harpy.uccs.edu/greek/olympia.html.

Osborne, Robin. *Greece in the Making, 1200–479 B.C.* 1996.

Raschke, Wendy J., ed. *The Archaeology of the Olympics: The Olympics and Other Festivals in Antiquity.* 1988.

Snodgrass, Anthony. *The Greek Dark Age.* 1971.

Social justice in Homer's *Odyssey:* http://www.fas.harvard.edu/%7Echs/HCJ/index.html.

The Creation of the Greek Polis, c. 750–500 B.C.E.

The Greek city-state did not spring up in a cultural vacuum, but the scarcity of sources for this period makes it difficult to evaluate the

*Primary source.

importance of various influences on it. Recent research persuasively argues for a greater role for individual entrepreneurs in what is usually regarded as state-initiated colonization (see the article by Robin Osborne in the collection edited by Fisher and van Wees).

Burkert, Walter. *The Orientalizing Revolution: The Near Eastern Influence on Greek Culture in the Early Archaic Age.* Trans. Margaret E. Pinder and Walter Burkert. 1992.

Fisher, Nick, and Hans van Wees, eds. *Archaic Greece: New Approaches and Evidence.* 1998.

Garlan, Yvon. *Slavery in Ancient Greece.* Rev. ed. Trans. Janet Lloyd. 1988.

Garland, Robert. *Religion and the Greeks.* 1994.

Starr, Chester. *Individual and Community: The Rise of the Polis, 800–500 B.C.* 1986.

Wees, Hans van, ed. *War and Violence in Ancient Greece.* 2000.

New Directions for the Polis, c. 750–500 B.C.E.

Contemporary scholarship stresses the diversity of city-state governance and customs, but, as always in ancient history, the scarcity of hard evidence hinders our gaining a clear picture.

Anhalt, Emily Katz. *Solon the Singer: Politics and Poetics.* 1993.

Archaic Greek sculpture: **http://harpy.uccs.edu/greek/archaicsculpt.html**.

*Barnes, Jonathan. *Early Greek Philosophy.* 1987.

*Campbell, David A. *Greek Lyric.* Five volumes. 1982–1993.

Cartledge, Paul. *Spartan Reflections.* 2001.

Emlyn-Jones, C. J. *The Ionians and Hellenism: A Study of the Cultural Achievements of Early Greek Inhabitants of Asia Minor.* 1980.

Gottlieb, Anthony. *The Dream of Reason: A History of Philosophy from the Greeks to the Renaissance.* 2000.

Halperin, David M. *One Hundred Years of Homosexuality and Other Essays on Greek Love.* 1990.

Hurwitt, Jeffrey M. *The Art and Culture of Early Greece, 1100–480 B.C.* 1985.

Kennell, Nigel M. *The Gymnasium of Virtue: Education and Culture in Ancient Sparta.* 1995.

McGlew, James F. *Tyranny and Political Culture in Ancient Greece.* 1993.

*Robinson, Eric W. *Ancient Greek Democracy: Readings and Sources.* 2003.

CHAPTER REVIEW

IMPORTANT EVENTS

c. 1000–750 B.C.E.	Greece experiences its Dark Age
c. 900 B.C.E.	Neo-Assyrian empire emerges
c. 800 B.C.E.	Greeks learn to write with an alphabet
776 B.C.E.	Olympic Games founded in Greece
c. 750 B.C.E.	Greeks begin to create the polis
c. 700 B.C.E.	Spartans conquer Messenia and enslave its inhabitants
700–500 B.C.E.	Ionian philosophers invent rationalism
657 B.C.E.	Cypselus becomes tyrant in Corinth
c. 630 B.C.E.	The lyric poet Sappho is born
612 B.C.E.	Medes and Chaldean destroy Neo-Assyrian empire
605 B.C.E.	Neo-Babylonian King Nebuchadnezzar II defeats the Egyptians at the battle of Carchemish in Syria
597 and 586 B.C.E.	Nebuchadnezzar II deports Hebrews to exile in Babylon
594 B.C.E.	Solon's reforms promote early democracy in Athens
546–510 B.C.E.	Peisistratus's family rules Athens as tyrants
539 B.C.E.	Persian King Cyrus captures Babylon and permits the Hebrews to return to Canaan
522–486 B.C.E.	Rule of Persian king Darius I
508–500 B.C.E.	Cleisthenes' reforms secure democracy at Athens

KEY TERMS

apocalypticism (51)
aretê (53)
Dark Age (45)
Diaspora (51)
hoplite (66)
lyric poetry (76)
moral dualism (50)
polis (57)
rationalism (77)
satrap (49)
Torah (51)

REVIEW QUESTIONS

1. In what ways did religion affect the history of the Near East from c. 1000 B.C.E. to c. 500 B.C.E.?
2. What factors proved most important in the Greek recovery from the economic troubles of the Dark Age?
3. What degrees of freedom existed for the different categories of people in the Greek city-state?
4. What were the main differences between the various forms of government in the Greek city-states?

MAKING CONNECTIONS

1. What made the Greek city-state a new form of political and social organization?
2. How were the ideas of the Ionian philosophers different from mythic traditions?

FOR FURTHER EXPLORATION

To assess your mastery of the material in this chapter, see the Online Study Guide at **bedfordstmartins.com/hunt**.

To read additional primary-source material from this period, see Chapter 2 in *Sources of The Making of the West*, Second Edition.

The Greek Golden Age, c. 500–c. 400 B.C.E.

A DIPLOMATIC FIASCO FUELED THE GREATEST FOREIGN DANGER ever to threaten Greece. In 507 B.C.E. Athens feared an attack from Sparta, its more powerful rival. The Athenian assembly therefore sent ambassadors to the Persian king, Darius I (r. 522–486 B.C.E.), to plead for a defensive alliance. The Athenian diplomats wrangled an audience with the king's governor in Ionia (the western coast of modern Turkey), who controlled the Greeks living in that region. After the Athenians made their plea to the governor, his first words were, "But who in the world are these people and where do they live that they want an alliance with the Persians?" The mutual misunderstandings that ensued from this confused meeting helped start a prolonged conflict between mainland Greece and Persia in the early fifth century B.C.E.

This incident reveals external and internal reasons why war dominated Greece's history throughout that century, first with Greeks fighting Persians and then with Greeks fighting Greeks. The Persian king was eager to subject more Greek city-states (those in Ionia had been his subjects for forty years) because their trade and growing wealth made them desirable prizes and because the Persians' traditions encouraged their kings to expand their empire. Unity seemed the Greeks' best defense to protect their states' treasured political independence, but the mainland city-states so deeply distrusted each other that they had never yet been able to come together to combat

---

Greek against Persian in Hand-to-Hand Combat (detail)
This red-figure painting appears on the interior of the shallow kind of cup that Greeks used to drink wine. Painted about 480 B.C.E. (during the Persian Wars), it shows a Greek armored infantryman (hoplite) about to kill a Persian warrior at the ultimate moment in battle—hand-to-hand combat with swords. The Greek has lost his principal weapon, a spear, and the Persian can no longer shoot his, the bow and arrow. The Greek artist has composed the scene to express multiple messages: the realistic rendering of the Persian's colorful outfit with sleeves and pants stresses the "otherness" of the enemy in Greek eyes; representing the fighters without shoes is an artistic convention to make the scene more heroic; and their serene expressions at a moment of extreme stress dignify the horror of killing in war. Greek warriors often had heroic symbols painted on their shields, such as the winged horse Pegasus, an allusion to the brave exploits of Bellerophon.
© The Trustees of the National Museums of Scotland.

the Persians, not even to try to liberate the Greek city-states in Ionia from Persian control. Athens and Sparta suspected each other so badly, the incident shows, the Athenians appealed to foreigners for help against Greeks.

Conflicting interests and mutual misunderstandings between Persia and Greece ignited a great conflict at the start of the fifth century B.C.E.: the so-called Persian Wars, in which Persia invaded Greece. The Persian invasions threatened the independence of the Greek mainland and Aegean islands. So dire was the threat that thirty-one Greek states (out of hundreds) temporarily formed an alliance to defeat the Persians; in victory, however, they lost their unity and fell to fighting one another. In the midst of this nearly constant warfare spanning the century, Greeks (especially in Athens) created what later ages judged to be their most famous innovations in architecture, art, and theater. These cultural achievements have led historians to call this period from around 500 to around 400 B.C.E. a Golden Age. This Golden Age is the first part of the period called the Classical Age of Greece, which lasted from around 500 B.C.E. to the death of Alexander the Great in 323 B.C.E.

Athens provides almost all of the surviving evidence for the Golden Age because most of the cultural achievements took place there and because the surviving literary and archaeological sources preserve few details about this period in other important city-states, such as Corinth and Syracuse. Many famous plays, histories, inscriptions, buildings, and sculptures survive from fifth-century

B.C.E. Athens. For these reasons, studying the Greek Golden Age primarily means studying the Athenian Golden Age.

The confidence derived from repelling the Persian invasions encouraged Greeks in the Golden Age to make innovations in education and philosophy that were hotly controversial at the time but that have had a lasting influence on Western civilization. These new ways of thought angered many people because the changes seemed to attack ancient traditions, especially religion; they feared the gods would punish them for abandoning ancestral ways.

Political change also characterized the Athenian Golden Age. First, Athenian citizens made their city-state government more democratic than ever. Second, Athens also grew internationally powerful by using its navy to establish rule over other Greeks in a system dubbed "empire" by modern scholars. This naval power also promoted seaborne trade, and revenues from rule and trade brought enormous prosperity. This newfound wealth supported cultural and political innovation because Athens's citizens voted to use the funds to finance new public buildings, art, and theater festivals, and to pay for poorer men to serve as officials and jurors in an expanded democratic government.

The Golden Age ended when Sparta defeated Athens in the Peloponnesian War (431–404 B.C.E.) and the Athenians then fought a brief but bloody civil war (404–403 B.C.E.). The fifth century B.C.E., so famous for its cultural innovation, therefore both began and ended with fierce wars, with Greeks standing together in the first one and tearing

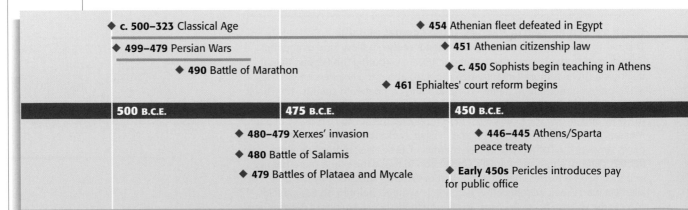

◆ **c. 500–323** Classical Age

◆ **499–479** Persian Wars

◆ **490** Battle of Marathon

◆ **454** Athenian fleet defeated in Egypt

◆ **451** Athenian citizenship law

◆ **c. 450** Sophists begin teaching in Athens

◆ **461** Ephialtes' court reform begins

| **500 B.C.E.** | **475 B.C.E.** | **450 B.C.E.** |

◆ **480–479** Xerxes' invasion

◆ **480** Battle of Salamis

◆ **479** Battles of Plataea and Mycale

◆ **446–445** Athens/Sparta peace treaty

◆ **Early 450s** Pericles introduces pay for public office

each other apart in the concluding one. The victory of the Persian Wars spurred the growth of Athens's naval power and seaborne trade; the added income from military victories and international commerce financed political and cultural development; losing the Peloponnesian War bankrupted and divided Athens, turning its Golden Age to lead.

❖ Wars between Persia and Greece, 499–479 B.C.E.

The Persian Wars had their roots in Athens's request for help from Persia in 507 B.C.E. The Athenian ambassadors agreed to the standard Persian requirement for an alliance: presenting tokens of earth and water to acknowledge submission to the Persian king. The Athenian assembly erupted in outrage at this capitulation but failed to inform King Darius that it rejected his terms; he therefore continued to believe that Athens remained loyal to him. This misunderstanding planted the seed for two Persian invasions of Greece. Since the Persian Empire far outstripped the Greek city-states in soldiers and money, the conflict pitted the equivalent of a huge bear against a pack of undersized dogs.

From the Ionian Revolt to the Battle of Marathon, 499–490 B.C.E.

When the Ionian Revolt led to the Persian Wars, the lesser conflict sparked a greater one—a common occurrence in the history of war. In 499 B.C.E., the Greek city-states in Ionia revolted against their Persian-installed tyrants, who were ruling harshly and unjustly, and the king's demand that the Ionians send still more soldiers for his army. The Spartans refused to help the Ionian rebels, but the Athenians sent troops because they regarded the Ionians as close kin. A Persian counterattack sent the Athenians fleeing home and crushed the revolt by 494 B.C.E. (Map 3.1, page 86). King Darius erupted in anger when he learned that the Athenians had attacked in Ionia; after all, he thought they were faithful allies. So bitter was this perceived betrayal that, according to the historian Herodotus, Darius ordered a slave to repeat three times at every meal, "Lord, remember the Athenians."

In 490 B.C.E., Darius ordered his fleet to punish Athens with an invasion to install a puppet tyrant. The king expected Athens to surrender without a fight. The Athenians refused to back down, however, confronting the invaders near the village of Marathon. The Athenian soldiers were stunned at the sight of the Persians' foreign appearance—they wore colorful pants instead of the short tunics and bare legs that Greeks regarded as proper dress—but their commanders innovated tactically by spurring the hoplites (armored infantry) to charge the enemy at a dead run instead of their usual slow advance. This new tactic minimized the time the Athenians could be hit by the numerically superior Persian archers. The Greeks clanked across the Marathon plain in their metal armor (seventy pounds each) under a hail of arrows. In the hand-to-hand combat, the

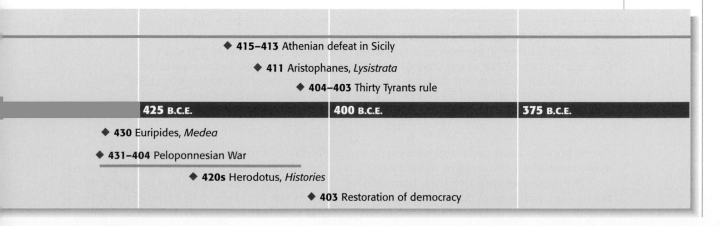

◆ **415–413** Athenian defeat in Sicily

◆ **411** Aristophanes, *Lysistrata*

◆ **404–403** Thirty Tyrants rule

| **425 B.C.E.** | **400 B.C.E.** | **375 B.C.E.** |

◆ **430** Euripides, *Medea*

◆ **431–404** Peloponnesian War

◆ **420s** Herodotus, *Histories*

◆ **403** Restoration of democracy

MAP 3.1 The Persian Wars, 499–479 B.C.E.
Following the example of the founder of the Persian kingdom, Cyrus the Great (d. 530 B.C.E.),
Cambyses (r. 530–522 B.C.E.) and Darius (r. 522–486 B.C.E.) energetically worked to expand their
empire eastward and westward. Darius invaded Thrace more than fifteen years before the conflict
against the Greeks that we call the Persian Wars. The Persians' unexpected defeat in Greece put
an end to their attempt to extend their power into Europe.

Greek hoplites used their heavier weapons to
overwhelm the Persian light infantry.

The Athenian infantry then hurried the
twenty-six miles from Marathon to Athens
to guard the city against the Persian navy.

(Today's marathon races commemorate the
legend of a runner speeding ahead to announce the victory, and then dropping dead.)
When the Persians sailed home, the Athenians rejoiced in disbelief; thereafter, a family's

greatest honor was to count a "Marathon fighter" among its ancestors.

Their unexpected success at Marathon evidently strengthened the Athenians' sense of community. When a fabulously rich strike was made in Athens's publicly owned silver mines in 483 B.C.E., a far-sighted leader named Themistocles♦ convinced the assembly to spend the money on doubling the size of the navy to defend against possible foreign attack instead of distributing the money to the citizens to spend on themselves.

The Persian Invasion of 480–479 B.C.E.

Themistocles' foresight proved valuable when Darius's son Xerxes♦ I (r. 486–465 B.C.E.) assembled an immense force to invade Greece in 480 B.C.E. to avenge his father's defeat and add the mainland city-states to the many lands paying him tribute. So huge was Xerxes' army, the Greeks claimed, that it required seven days and seven nights to cross the Hellespont, the strip of sea between Anatolia and Greece. Xerxes thought the Greek city-states would immediately surrender; some did, but thirty-one made a decision new in Greek history: to unite as allies to defend their city-states' political freedom.

Their coalition became known as the Hellenic League, but it hardly represented the entire Greek world. The allies desperately wanted the major Greek city-states in Italy and Sicily to join the league because these western states were rich naval powers, but they refused. Syracuse, for example, the most powerful Greek state at the time, controlled a regional empire built on agriculture in Sicily's plains and seaborne commerce through its harbors astride the Mediterranean's western trading routes. Gelon, who ruled Syracuse as a tyrant, rejected the league's appeal for help because he was fighting his own foreign war against Carthage, a Phoenician city in North Africa, over control of the trade routes.

The Hellenic League chose Sparta as its leader because Spartans had the best

♦**Themistocles:** thuh MIHS tuh kleez
♦**Xerxes:** ZURK seez

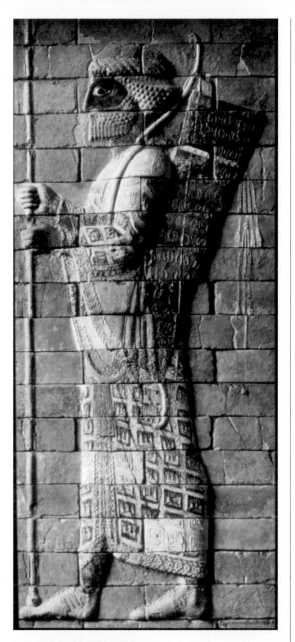

A Persian Royal Guard
This six-foot-high panel of polychrome glazed brick formed part of the decoration of a courtyard in the palace at Susa built by the Persian king Darius I (r. 522–486 B.C.E.). Susa was the most important administrative center of the Persian Empire, and the king and his court spent part of each year there. The warrior shown here perhaps represents one of the royal guards known as "immortals." An inscription reports that the craftsmen who made these colorful panels came from Babylon, where there was a long tradition of this sort of architectural decoration. *The Granger Collection, NY.*

reputation for military valor. The Spartans demonstrated their mettle in 480 B.C.E. when three hundred of their infantry blocked Xerxes' army for several days at the narrow pass called Thermopylae♦ ("Gate of Hot Springs") in central Greece. When told the Persian archers were so numerous that their arrows darkened the sun, one Spartan reportedly remarked, "That's good news; we'll get to fight in the shade." They did—to the death. Their tomb's memorial proclaimed, "Go tell the Spartans that we lie buried here obedient to their orders."

When the Persians marched south, the Athenians, knowing they could not defend the city, evacuated its residents to the Peloponnese rather than surrender; the Persians then burned Athens. In the summer of 480 B.C.E. Themistocles tricked the Persian king into sending his navy into battle against the coalition Greek fleet in the channel between the island of Salamis and the west coast of Athens. The narrowness of the channel prevented the Persians from deploying all their warships at the same time; the heavier Greek warships prevailed by ramming the flimsier Persian craft in the tight space. The following summer (479 B.C.E.), the Spartans as the Hellenic League commanders led the Greek infantry to dual victories over the Persian land forces at Plataea♦ on the mainland and, now on the offensive against the enemy, at Mycale in Anatolia. Superior generalship brought these successes.

The Greeks won their battles against the Persians because their generals, especially Themistocles, had better strategic foresight, their soldiers had stronger body armor, their warships were more effective in close combat, and their tactics minimized the Persian advantage in numbers of troops and ships. Above all, the Greeks won the war because enough of them took the innovative step of uniting in a coalition to fight together for their independence. Because the Greek forces included not only the social elites but also thousands of poorer men who rowed the warships, the victory against the Persians showed that rich and poor Greeks alike trea-

sured the ideal of political freedom for their city-states that had earlier emerged in the Archaic Age.

Review: What differences in Greek and Persian political and military organization determined the course of the Persian Wars?

❖ Athenian Confidence in the Golden Age, 478–431 B.C.E.

The struggle against the Persians was one of the rare occasions when at least some city-states cooperated. Victory fractured this alliance, however, because the allies resented the harshness of Spartan command and the Athenians had gained the confidence to replace the Spartans as leaders. From this change arose the so-called Athenian Empire; no longer were Athenians satisfied to be followers of Sparta. Now they dreamed of a much grander role for themselves. The growth of Athenian power over other Greeks inspired yet more confidence, which created a broader democracy willing to spend vast amounts on pay for officials and jurors, public buildings, art, and festivals.

The Establishment of Athenian Empire

After the Persian Wars, Sparta and Athens built up competing alliances to strengthen their own positions. Sparta led strong infantry forces from the Peloponnese region, and its ally Corinth had a sizable navy. Called the Peloponnesian League, the Spartan alliance had an assembly to decide policy, but Sparta dominated it.

Athens, led by the aristocrat Aristides (c. 525–465 B.C.E.), allied with city-states in northern Greece, on the islands of the Aegean Sea, and along the Ionian coast—the places most in need of protection from Persian retaliation. This alliance was built on naval power and today is called the **Delian League**

♦**Thermopylae:** thur MAH puh lee
♦**Plataea:** plah TEE uh

because its treasury was originally located on the Aegean island of Delos.

Athens controlled the Delian League through its allies' willingness to cede the leadership and the financing arrangements for the league's fleet. Each ally paid dues (called tribute) according to its size. Larger city-states paid by sending **triremes**◆ (warships propelled by 170 rowers on three levels and equipped with a ram) complete with trained crews and their pay; smaller states could share the cost of one ship—or contribute cash instead.

Over time, more and more Delian League members voluntarily paid cash because it was easier. Athens then used their tribute to construct triremes and pay men to row them; oarsmen who brought a slave to row alongside them earned double pay. Drawn primarily from the poorest citizens, rowers gained both income and political influence in Athenian democracy because the navy became the city-state's main force. These benefits made poor citizens eager to expand Athenian international power.

The increase in Athenian naval power thus promoted the development of a wider democracy at home, but it undermined the democracy of Athens's international alliance. Since most Delian League allies had not kept up their own navies, the Athenian assembly could use the league fleet to compel disobedient allies to pay tribute. As the Athenian historian Thucydides◆ commented, rebellious allies "lost their independence, and the Athenians became no longer as popular as they used to be." Athens's heavy-handed dominance of the Delian League, backed up

The Delian and Peloponnesian Leagues

◆**triremes:** TRY reems
◆**Thucydides:** thoo SIH duh deez

FIGURE 3.1 Triremes, the Foremost Classical Greek Warships

Innovations in military technology and training fueled a naval arms race in the fifth century B.C.E. when Greek shipbuilders devised larger and faster ramming ships powered by 170 rowers seated in three rows, one above each other. (See the illustration of the rowers, from behind, at the top of this page.) Called triremes, these ships' radical new design with triple banks of oars, as shown in the drawing, made them expensive to build and required extensive crew training. Only wealthy and populous city-states such as Athens could afford to build and man large fleets of triremes. No ancient trireme survives to show exactly how such a warship was built, but this relief sculpture found on the Athenian acropolis and dating from about 400 B.C.E. gives a glimpse of what a trireme looked like from the side when being rowed into battle. (Sails were only used to power the ship when not in combat.) *The Art Archive/ Acropolis Museum Athens/Dagli Orti.*

by the threat of force, has led modern historians to label it the Athenian empire.

Unpopularity among most allies was the price Athens paid for making itself the major naval power in the eastern Mediterranean: by about 460 b.c.e. the Delian League's fleet had expelled remaining Persian garrisons from northern Greece and driven the enemy fleet from the Aegean Sea. This sweep eliminated the Persian threat for the next fifty years and proved the Athenian leadership's effectiveness.

Military success made Athens prosperous by bringing in spoils and tribute, making seaborne trade safe, and benefiting rich and poor alike—the poor men who rowed the Delian League's navy earned good pay, while elite commanders enhanced their chances for election to high office by spending their spoils on public festivals and buildings. The assembly debated how to employ Athens's international power in treating the league allies, but the majority consistently rejected complaints on the grounds that the league was fulfilling its original duty by protecting everyone from Persian attack.

Radical Democracy and Pericles' Leadership, 461–431 b.c.e.

As the Delian League grew, the Athenian fleet's oarsmen realized that they provided the cornerstone for Athens's new power and prosperity. By the late 460s b.c.e. they decided that the time had come to increase their political power by making the court system of Athens just as democratic as the process of passing laws in the assembly, in which all free adult male citizens could already participate. They wanted laws and political institutions that would make Cleisthenes' promise of *isonomia* (equal treatment under the law) a reality for everyone so that they would no longer be liable to unfair verdicts at the hands of the elite in criminal cases and civil suits. Members of the elite stepped up to lead this push for judicial reform, hoping to win popular support for election to high office by speaking out for the interests of the masses. A member of one of Athens's most distinguished families, Pericles (c. 495–429 b.c.e.), became Golden Age Athens's dominant politician by spearheading reforms to democratize its judicial system and provide pay for many public offices.

Creating Radical Democracy. The changes to Athenian democracy in the 460s and 450s b.c.e. have led historians to label the system *radical* (literally, "from the roots") because it gave direct political power and participation in the court system to the mass of adult male citizens. Athens's **radical democracy** balanced two competing principles: participation by as many ordinary male citizens as possible in direct, not representative, democracy and selective leadership by elite citizens. To achieve the first, Athenian voters established (1) random selection by lottery for most public offices, term limits, shared power, and pay for most officials and members of the Council of Five Hundred (which prepared the assembly's agenda and supervised public matters); (2) open investigation and punishment of corruption; (3) equal protection under the law for citizens regardless of wealth; and (4) pay and random selection for jurors. To achieve the second principle, radical democracy selected its higher-level officials by election, not lottery. The top officials (the board of ten generals, who oversaw military and financial affairs) ran for election every year, could be reelected an unlimited number of times, and received no pay so that they would not seek election just for financial rewards. A successful general could stay in office indefinitely; Pericles, for example, won reelection fifteen years in a row in one stretch of his political career.

The changes in the judicial system did the most to create radical democracy. Previously, magistrates and ex-magistrates, who were members of the elite, had decided most legal cases. As with Cleisthenes, reform took place when an elite man proposed it to support ordinary men's political rights and simultaneously win their votes against his rivals: in 461 b.c.e. Ephialtes♦ won popular support by getting the assembly to establish a new court system. To make it more democratic and prevent bribery, jurors were selected by lottery from male citizens over thirty years old. They received a daily stipend to serve on juries numbering from several hundred to several thousand members. No judges or lawyers existed, and jurors voted by secret ballot after hearing speeches from the

♦**Ephialtes:** ehf ee AL teez

persons involved. As in the assembly, a majority vote decided matters; no appeals of verdicts were allowed.

Ostracism and Majority Rule. Athenian radical democracy included notions of privacy and legal protection for individuals, but majority rule could override them on matters of public policy. A striking example was **ostracism** (from *ostrakon*, a piece of broken pottery used as a ballot). Once a year, all male citizens could cast a ballot on which they scratched the name of one man they thought should be exiled for ten years. If at least six thousand ballots were cast, the man whose name appeared on the greatest number was expelled from Athens. He suffered no other penalty; his family and property remained undisturbed.

Usually a man was ostracized because he had become so popular that a majority feared he would overthrow the democracy to rule as a tyrant. There was no guarantee of voters' motives, however, as a story about Aristides illustrates. He was nicknamed "the Just" because he had proved himself so fair-minded in setting the original level of dues for Delian League members. On the day of an ostracism, an illiterate citizen handed him a pottery fragment and asked him to scratch a name on it:

> "Certainly," said Aristides. "Which name shall I write?"
>
> "Aristides," replied the man.
>
> "All right," said Aristides as he inscribed his own name, "but why do you want to ostracize Aristides? What has he done to you?"
>
> "Oh, nothing. I don't even know him," sputtered the man. "I just can't stand hearing everybody refer to him as 'the Just.'"

True or not, this tale demonstrates that most Athenians believed the right way to protect democracy was to trust a majority vote regardless of its possible injustice to a particular individual.

Not all citizens approved of radical democracy, however. Some socially elite citizens expressed bitter criticism of what they saw as its disregard for social merit in giving political power to the poor. One anonymous author, for example, blasted democracy because its equality promoted the interests of what he saw

Potsherd Ballots for Ostracism
These two shards (ostraka) were broken from the same pot (as the breakage line shows) to be inscribed for use as ballots in an ostracism at Athens in the Classical Age. They come from unpainted—and therefore cheaper—pieces of pottery than those such as the cup shown on page 82. The lower fragment carries the name of Themistocles, the controversial Athenian leader who engineered the Greek fleet's successful stand against the Persian navy off the island of Salamis in 480 B.C.E.; the upper one bears the name of the Delian League's most famous general against the Persians, Cimon. Political strife led to Themistocles' ostracism sometime in the late 470s B.C.E. and Cimon's in 461 B.C.E. Therefore, if these two ballots were intended for the same ostracism, it must have been that of Themistocles or an earlier one when he was still in Athens. *Deutsches Archäologisches Institut—Athens.*

as the "wicked" (i.e., the poor) over the interests of "useful" citizens (i.e., the rich):

> The Athenian political system allows the wicked people to do better than the useful people.... Throughout the whole world the best part of the citizenry is opposed to democracy. For the best people have the least lack of self-discipline and injustice, while they give the greatest care to what is useful. The masses, by contrast, display the greatest lack of learning, lack of order, and wickedness because their poverty inclines them to disgraceful behavior, and some of them are uneducated and ignorant from their lack of money.

Opponents of democracy never disappeared; in fact, they became particularly vocal when Athens's democracy suffered periods of crisis, as at certain points in the great war with Sparta that was to erupt at the end of the Golden Age. As the Athenian writer quoted above implied, they insisted that oligarchy—the rule of the few—was morally superior to radical democracy because, as the writer quoted above implied, the poor lacked the education and moral values needed for leadership and would use their majority rule to strip the rich of their wealth by passing laws to make them pay for expensive public programs.

Pericles' Leadership. Pericles became the most influential leader of his era by using his political vision and spellbinding skills in public speaking to convince the assembly to pass reforms strengthening the equality that poor citizens prized. He began his career by supporting Ephialtes's reform of the court system. Then, in the early 450s B.C.E., he boosted mass participation in democracy by introducing pay for service in the public offices filled by lottery. This reform used public funds to pay men for serving in numerous government posts, the Council of Five Hundred, and on juries. Previously, because these offices had been unpaid, only wealthy men could afford to fill them. Now, poor citizens could serve. In 415 B.C.E. Pericles shattered tradition by sponsoring a law to restrict citizenship to those whose mother and father were both Athenian by birth. Previously, wealthy men had often married foreign women from elite families. This change both increased the status of Athenian women, rich or poor, as potential mothers of citizens and limited the number of people eligible for citizenship's legal and financial benefits. In a complementary measure to enforce exclusiveness, officials reviewed everyone's citizenship and, some sources report, struck thousands from the rolls.

Pericles also promoted aggressive naval campaigns (and thus provided poor Athenians an income as rowers) when war with Sparta broke out in the 450s over Athenian actions against Peloponnesian League states. He also supported sending the fleet against Persian garrisons in Cyprus, Egypt, and the eastern Mediterranean to expand the Delian League's power and win war spoils. Enthusiasm for his plans reached such a fever pitch that the assembly authorized up to three major expeditions at the same time. This exuberant militarism slowed in the late 450s B.C.E. only after a horrendous defeat at the hands of Persian forces in Egypt in 454 B.C.E. killed tens of thousands of oarsmen; the Athenians had sent a large naval force to aid an Egyptian rebellion against Persian rule, hoping to weaken Persian power in the eastern Mediterranean. In the winter of 446–445 B.C.E., Pericles engineered a peace treaty with Sparta with the goal of stabilizing the balance of power in Greece for thirty years and thus preserving Athenian control of the Delian League.

> **Review:** What factors prompted political change in fifth-century B.C.E. Athens?

The Urban Landscape

Golden Age Athens prospered from Delian League dues, war plunder, and taxes on booming international seaborne trade. Its Piraeus harbor promoted cross-Mediterranean commerce, its navy made its empire's numerous ports safe for merchants and travelers from far-flung locations, and its courts resolved legal disputes. Its artisans produced goods traded far and wide; the Etruscans in central Italy, for example, imported countless painted vases for wine drinking at Greek-style dinner parties. The economic activity and international traffic of the mid-fifth century B.C.E. boosted Athens to its greatest prosperity ever.

Athenians spent their new riches not just on broadening participation in democratic government but also on their city's public buildings, art, and festivals. In private life, rich urban dwellers splurged on luxury goods influenced by Persian designs, but most houses retained their traditional modest size and plainness. Farmhouses could cluster in villages or stand isolated, while homes and apartments in the city wedged tightly against one another along narrow, winding streets. Recent archaeological study of the city of Olynthus in northeastern Greece shows that urban single-family homes were built on varying patterns, but one favorite plan grouped bedrooms, storerooms, and dining rooms around open-air courtyards. Poor city residents rented small apartments. Wall paintings or decorative artworks were rare, furnishings sparse. Toilets consisted of pots and a pit outside the front door; the city paid collectors to dump the dung outside its fortification walls.

Generals who wanted to display their excellence (*aretê*) and also win the people's favor spent their war spoils on running tracks, shade trees, and public buildings. A popular building project was a stoa, a narrow structure open along one side that offered shelter from the weather. The super-rich commander Cimon, for example, paid for the Painted Stoa to be built on the edge of Athens's **agora,**♦ the central market square. There, crowds of shoppers could admire the stoa's bright paintings depicting his family's military exploits, especially his father's leadership in the battle of Marathon. This sort of contribution was voluntary, but the laws required wealthy citizens to pay for festivals and equipping warships. This financial obligation on the rich was essential because Athens, like most Greek city-states, had no regular property or income taxes.

♦**agora:** a guh RAH

The Parthenon.   On Athens's acropolis (the rocky hill at the city's center, Map 3.2, page 94), Pericles had the two most famous buildings of Golden Age Athens erected during the 440s and 430s B.C.E.: a mammoth gateway and an enormous marble temple of Athena called the Parthenon. Comparing a day's wage then and now, we can estimate that these buildings together cost more than the equivalent of a billion dollars, a phenomenal sum for a Greek city-state; Pericles' political rivals slammed him for spending too much public money on the project and diverting Delian League funds to domestic uses.

The Parthenon (literally, "the virgin goddess's house") has become the foremost symbol

The Acropolis of Athens

Most Greek city-states, including Athens, sprang up around a prominent rocky hill, called an acropolis ("height of the city"; compare the picture of Corinth on page 73). The summit of the acropolis usually housed sanctuaries for the city's protective deities and could serve as a fortress of last resort for the population during an enemy attack. Athens's acropolis boasted several elaborately decorated marble temples honoring the goddess Athena; the largest one was the Parthenon, seen here from its west (back) side. Recent research suggest that the ruins of a temple burned by the Persians when they captured Athens in 480 B.C.E. remained in place right next to the Parthenon; the Athenians did not clear away its charred remains to remind themselves of the sacrifices they had made in defending their freedom. (The walls in the lower foreground are from a theater built in Roman times.) © AKG-Images, London.

MAP 3.2 Fifth-Century B.C.E. Athens

The urban center of Athens, with the agora and acropolis at its heart, measured about one square mile, surrounded by a stone wall with a circuit of some four miles. Gates guarded by towers and various smaller entries allowed traffic in and out of the city; much of the Athenian population lived in the many villages (demes) of the surrounding countryside. Most of the city's water supply came from wells and springs inside the walls, but, unusually for a Greek city, Athens also had water piped in from outside. Most streets were narrow (no more than fifteen or twenty feet wide) and winding, with houses crowding in on both sides.

of Athens's Golden Age. As the city's patron deity, Athena already had another sanctuary on the acropolis honoring her as protector of the citizens' prosperity, as well as the ruins of her temple burned by the Persians in 480 B.C.E., left standing as a memorial. The Parthenon honored her as the divine champion of Athenian military power and proclaimed that she had an immanent presence in the city. Inside the temple soared a gold-and-ivory statue nearly forty feet high depicting the goddess in armor, holding in her outstretched hand a six-foot statue of Nike, the goddess of victory.

Like all Greek temples, the Parthenon was meant as a house for its divinity, not as a gathering place for worshipers. Its design followed standard temple architecture: a rectangular box on a raised platform studded with columns, a plan the Greeks probably derived from the stone temples of Egypt. The Parthenon's soaring columns fenced in a porch surrounding the interior chamber on all sides. They were carved in

FIGURE 3.2 Styles of Greek Capitals

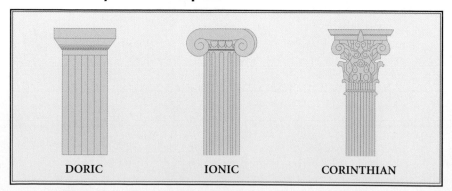

DORIC   IONIC   CORINTHIAN

The Greeks decorated the capitals, or tops, of columns in these three styles to fit the different architectural "canons" (their word for precise mathematical systems of proportions) that they devised for designing buildings. These styles were much imitated in later times, as on many U.S. state capitols and the U.S. Supreme Court Building in Washington, D.C.

Scene from the Parthenon Frieze
The Parthenon, the Athenian temple honoring Athena as a warrior goddess and patron of the Delian League, dominated the summit of the city's acropolis. A frieze (band of sculpture in relief), of which this is a small section, ran around the top of the temple's outside wall. Here, the deities observe the citizens participating in the Pan-Athenaic festival's procession to the Parthenon; Athenian confidence in divine goodwill explains why the frieze shows ordinary people in close association with the gods. The original blazed with bright colors and details fashioned from metal. The elaborate folds of the figures' garments display the rich style characteristic of clothed figures in Classical Age sculpture. How would you explain the differences between the poses of this relief's figures and those on the Persian relief on page 87? *British Museum.*

the simple style called Doric, in contrast to the more elaborate Ionic and Corinthian styles often imitated in columns on modern buildings (Figure 3.2).

The Parthenon's massive size and innovative style proclaimed Golden Age Athens's self-confidence. Constructed from twenty thousand tons of Attic marble, the temple stretched some 230 feet in length and 100 feet wide, with eight columns across the ends instead of the six normally found in Doric style and seventeen instead of thirteen along the sides. The temple's sophisticated architecture demonstrated the Athenian ambition to use human skill to improve nature: because perfectly rectilinear architecture appears curved to the human eye, subtle curves and inclines were built into the Parthenon to produce an illusion of completely straight lines and emphasize its massiveness.

The Parthenon's many sculptures communicated confident messages: the gods en-

sure triumph over the forces of chaos, and Athenians enjoy the gods' goodwill more than any other city-state's citizens. The sculptures in each pediment (a triangular space atop the columns at either end of the temple) portrayed Athena as the city-state's benefactor. The metopes (panels sculpted in relief above the outer columns around all four sides) portrayed victories over hostile centaurs and other enemies of civilization. Most strikingly of all, a **frieze**✦ (a continuous band of figures carved in relief) ran around the top of the walls inside the porch and was painted in bright colors (which have since faded) to make it more visible. The Parthenon's frieze was special because usually only Ionic-style buildings had one. The frieze portrayed Athenian men, women, and children in a parade in the presence of the gods, depicting the procession in motion like the pictures in a graphic novel or cartoon today.

✦**frieze:** freez

The Parthenon frieze made a striking statement about how Athenians perceived their relationship to the gods—no other Greeks had ever adorned a temple with representations of themselves. Its sculpture staked a claim of unique intimacy between the city-state and the gods, reflecting the Athenians' confidence after helping turn back the Persians, achieving leadership of a powerful naval alliance, and amassing great wealth. Their success, the Athenians believed, proved that the gods were on their side, and their fabulous buildings signaled their gratitude.

Sculpture's New Message.   Like the unique Parthenon frieze, the innovations that Golden Age artists made in representing the human body in freestanding sculpture shattered tradition. Archaic Age (c. 750–500 B.C.E.) statues stood stiffly balanced, staring straight ahead in imitation of Egyptian sculpture's unchanging style. Striding forward on their left legs, arms held rigidly at their sides, they projected an image of stability; not even a hard shove seemed likely to budge them. By the time of the Persian Wars, however, Greek sculptors had begun to put statues into motion in new poses. This style of movement in stone expressed an energetic balancing of competing forces, echoing a theme evident in radical democracy's principles.

Sculptors also began carving anatomically realistic but perfect-looking bodies, suggesting that humans could be confident in their potential for beauty and perfection. Female statues, for example, now displayed the shape of the curves underneath their clothing, while male ones showed bodybuilders' muscles. The faces showed a self-confident reserve rather than the smiles of archaic statues.

As with the Parthenon's relief sculptures, Golden Age freestanding statues were erected to be seen by the public, whether they were paid for with private or government funds. Privately commissioned statues of gods were placed in sanctuaries as symbols of devotion. Wealthy families commissioned statues of their deceased members, especially if they had died young in war, to be placed above their graves as memorials of their virtue.

❖ Tradition and Innovation in Athens's Golden Age

Golden Age Athens's prosperity and international contacts created unprecedented innovations in architecture, art, drama, and intellectual life, but central aspects of its social and religious customs remained traditional, as such customs did throughout Greece. This contrast between cultural change and social continuity generated tension between the desire to innovate and the pressure to preserve traditional ways, especially with regard to religion and the conduct of women. In keeping with tradition, Athenians, along with other Greeks, continued to expect women to limit their role in public life to participating in religious ceremonies but to make an essential contribution to private life by managing their households and, if they were poor, by working to help support their families. The startling new ideas on religion of competitive philosophers and teachers called Sophists and the Athenian philosopher Socrates' views on personal morality and responsibility created the greatest tension because many people feared that these new ways of thought would anger the gods. The most famous response to the clash between innovation and tradition was the development of publicly funded drama festivals, whose tragic and comic plays examined problems in city-state life, especially the social and personal hardships caused by war.

Religious Tradition in a Period of Change

Greeks maintained religious tradition publicly by participating in the city-state's sacrifices and festivals and privately by seeking a personal relationship with the gods in the rituals of hero cults and mystery cults. Each cult—the set of prayers and other forms of worship connected with a particular divinity—had its own rituals, including sacrifices ranging from the slaughter of large animals to bloodless offering of fruits, vegetables, and small cakes. The speechwriter Lysias (c. 445–380 B.C.E.), a Syracusan residing in Athens, explained the reason for publicly funded sacrifices:

Our ancestors handed down to us the most powerful and prosperous community in Greece by performing the prescribed sacrifices. It is therefore proper for us to offer the same sacrifices as they, if only for the sake of the success which has resulted from those rites.

The public sacrifice of a large animal provided an occasion for the community to reaffirm its ties to the divine world and for the worshipers to benefit by feasting on the roasted meat of the sacrificed beast. For poor people, the free food provided at religious festivals might be the only taste of meat they ever got.

Golden Age Athens used its riches to pay for more festivals than any other city-state; nearly half the days of the year included one. The biggest festivals featured parades as well as contests with valuable prizes in music, dancing, poetry, and athletics. Laborers' contracts specified how many days off they received to attend such ceremonies. Some festivals were for women only, such as the three-day festival for married women in honor of Demeter,♦ goddess of agriculture and fertility.

Privately, people took a keen interest in actions meant to improve their own personal relations with the divine. Families marked significant moments such as birth, marriage, and death with prayers, rituals, and sacrifices. They honored their ancestors with offerings made at their tombs, consulted seers about the meanings of dreams and omens, and paid magicians for spells to improve their love lives or curses to harm their enemies. Particularly important were hero cults and mystery cults. Hero cults included rituals performed at the tomb of an extraordinarily famous man or woman. Heroes' remains were thought to retain special power to reveal the future by inspiring oracles, healing sickness, and providing protection in battle. The strongman Herakles (or Hercules, as the Romans spelled his name) had cults all over the Greek world because his superhuman reputation gave him international appeal. **Mystery cults** involved a set of prayers, hymns, ritual purification, sacrifices, and other forms of worship undertaken to gain divine protection. Each cult was connected with a particular divinity and cen-

tered on initiation into secret knowledge about the divine and human worlds.

The Athenian mystery cult of Demeter and her daughter Kore♦ (also called Persephone) attracted worshipers from all parts of the world because it offered hope for protection on earth and in the afterlife. The cult's central rite was the Mysteries: a series of initiation ceremonies into secret knowledge. So important were these Mysteries that the Greek states observed an international truce—as with the Olympic Games—to allow travel even from distant corners of the world to attend them. The Mysteries were open to any free, Greek-speaking individuals— women and men, adults and children—if they were free of ritual contamination (for example, if they had not been convicted of murder, committed sacrilege, or had recent contact with a corpse or blood from a birth). Some slaves who worked in the sanctuary were also eligible. The main stage of initiation took almost two weeks, culminating in the revelation of Demeter's central secret after a day of fasting. So seriously did Greeks take the initiation that no one ever revealed the secret during the cult's thousand-year history. Indirect reports reveal that it promised initiates a better life on earth (for example, with protection from ghosts or shipwreck) as well as a better fate after death. In the words of the poem *The Hymn to Demeter*, "Richly blessed is the mortal who has seen these rites; but whoever is not an initiate and has no share in them, that one never has an equal portion after death, down in the gloomy darkness."

Mystery cults reveal that ancient Greeks thought their gods required action from their worshipers to receive blessings. Preserving religious tradition mattered deeply to most people because they saw it as a safeguard against the precariousness of life.

Women, Slaves, and Metics in Traditional Society

Women, slaves, and **metics** (foreigners granted permanent residence permits in return for obligations to pay taxes and do military service) together made up the majority

♦**Demeter:** dih MEE tur

♦**Kore:** KOH ray

of Athens's population, but they lacked political rights. Women who were citizens enjoyed legal privileges and social status denied slaves and foreigners, and they earned respect through their roles in the family and in religion. Upper-class women managed their households, visited female friends, and participated in religious cults at home and in public. Poor women worked as small-scale merchants, crafts producers, and agricultural laborers. Slaves' and metics' work also contributed much to Athens's prosperity, but they always remained outsiders in the city-state.

Property, Inheritance, and Marriage.
Bearing children in marriage earned women status because it was literally the source of family—the heart of Greek society. To defend this fundamental social institution, men were expected to respect and support their wives. Childbirth was dangerous under the medical conditions of the time. In *Medea*, a play of 431 B.C.E. by Euripides, the heroine shouts in anger at her husband, who has selfishly betrayed her: "People say that we women lead a safe life at home, while men have to go to war. What fools they are! I would much rather fight in battle three times than give birth to a child even once."

Athenian wives were expected to be partners with their husbands in owning and managing the household's property to help the family thrive. (See "Contrasting Views," page 100.) Rich women acquired property, including land—the most valued possession in Greek society because it could be farmed or rented out for income—through inheritance and dowry (the family property a daughter received at marriage). The husband was legally required to preserve the dowry and use it to support his wife and their children. A man often had to put up valuable land of his own as collateral to guarantee the safety of his wife's dowry.

Like fathers, mothers were expected to hand down property to their children to keep it in the family line. This expectation shows up most clearly in Athenian law about heiresses (daughters whose fathers died without any sons, which happened in about one in every five families): the heiress's father's closest male relative—her official guardian

after her father's death—was required to marry her. The goal was to produce a son to inherit the father's property himself. This rule applied regardless of whether the heiress was already married (unless she had sons) or whether the male relative already had a wife; the heiress and the male relative were both supposed to divorce their present spouses and marry each other. In real life, however, people often used legal technicalities to get around this requirement so that they could remain with their loves.

Requiring property to be passed down in this way met two traditional goals of male-dominated Greek society: continuing the father's blood line and preventing property from piling up in the hands of unmarried women (and therefore out of the control of men). At Sparta, the renowned scholar Aristotle (384–322 B.C.E.) reported, the inheritance laws were different (and in his opinion deficient); he claimed that women came to own 40 percent of Spartan territory.

Women's Daily Lives. Tradition restricted women's freedom of movement in public; men claimed this restriction protected women by limiting opportunities for seducers and rapists. Men wanted to ensure that their children were truly theirs, that family property went only to genuine heirs, and that the city had only legitimate citizens. Well-off women in the city were expected to avoid contact with men outside their family and to spend most of their time at home or with women friends in their houses. Recent research has exploded the idea that Greek homes had a set "women's quarter" to which women were confined; rather, women were granted privacy in certain rooms. If the house included an interior courtyard, women could walk there in the open air and talk with other members of the household, male and female. In the safety of her home a well-to-do woman would spin wool for clothing, converse with visiting friends, direct her children, supervise the slaves, and present her opinions on various matters, including politics, to the men of the house as they came and went. Poor women had little time for such activities because they—like their husbands, sons, and brothers—had to leave their homes, usually crowded rental apartments, to set up small stalls to sell bread, vegetables, simple clothing, or trinkets they had made.

An elite woman careful of her reputation left home only for appropriate reasons, such as religious festivals, funerals, childbirths at the houses of relatives and friends, and trips to workshops to buy shoes or other domestic articles. Often her husband escorted her, but sometimes she took only a slave, setting her own itinerary.

Women who bore legitimate children merited increased respect and freedom, as an Athenian man explained in his speech (written by Lysias) defending himself for having killed his wife's adulterer:

> After my marriage, I initially refrained from bothering my wife very much, but neither did I allow her too much independence. I kept an eye on her....But after she had a baby, I started to trust her more and put her in charge of all my things, believing we now had the closest of relationships.

Bearing male children brought special honor to a woman because sons meant security. They could appear in court to support their parents in lawsuits and protect them in the streets of Athens, which for most of its history had no regular police force. By law, sons were required to support elderly par-

ents. So intense was the pressure to produce sons that stories circulated of women who smuggled in male babies born to slaves and passed them off as their own. Substitution was possible, if unlikely, because husbands customarily stayed away at childbirth.

Most upper-class women probably viewed their limited contact with men outside the household as a badge of superior social status. For example, a pale complexion, from staying inside so much, was much admired as a sign of an enviable life of leisure and wealth. Unaware of the health risk, many women used powdered white lead as makeup to give themselves a fashionable pallor.

Extraordinary Women. A few women in Athens escaped traditional restrictions by working as what Greeks called a **hetaira**♦ (literally, "companion"). Companions, usually foreigners, were physically attractive, witty in speech, and skilled in music and poetry. Men hired them to entertain at *symposia* (drinking parties to which wives were not invited) with their playful conversation. Their much-admired skill at clever taunts and verbal snubs allowed companions a freedom of speech denied to "proper" women; they

---

♦**hetaira:** heh TYE rah

Vase Painting of a Woman Buying Shoes

Greek vases were frequently decorated with scenes from daily life instead of mythological stories. Here, a woman is being fitted for a pair of custom-made shoes by a craftsman and his apprentice. Her husband has accompanied her, as was often the case for shopping; and, to judge from his gesture, he is participating in the discussion of the purchase. This vase was painted in so-called black-figure technique, in which the figures are dark and have their details incised on a background of red clay. Over time, this technique was replaced by the red-figure style, as seen in the vase on page 111. **For more help analyzing this image**, see the visual activity for this chapter in the Online Study Guide at **bedfordstmartins.com/hunt**. *Museum of Fine Arts, Boston. Henry Lillie Pierce Fund. Photograph © 2004 Museum of Fine Arts, Boston (01. 80 35).*

CONTRASTING VIEWS

The Nature of Women and Marriage

Greeks believed that women had different natures from men and that both genders were capable of excellence, but in their own ways (Documents 1 and 2). Marriage was supposed to bring these natures together in a partnership of complementary strengths and obligations to each other (Document 3). Marriage contracts (Document 4), similar to modern prenuptial agreements, became common to define the partnership's terms.

1. THE POLITICAL LEADER PERICLES ADDRESSING THE ATHENIANS AT THE FUNERAL OF SOLDIERS KILLED IN THE FIRST YEAR OF THE PELOPONNESIAN WAR (WINTER OF 431–430 B.C.E.)

According to Thucydides, the famously stern Pericles concluded his Funeral Oration, a solemn public occasion commemorating the valor and virtues expected of citizens, with these terse remarks to the women in the audience. His comments reveal two ancient Greek assumptions: that women had a different nature from men and that women best served social harmony by not becoming subjects of gossip. He kept these comments to a bare minimum in his long speech.

If it is also appropriate now for me to say something about what constitutes excellence for women, I will signal all my thinking with this short piece of advice to those of you present who are now widows of the war dead: your reputation will be great if you don't fall short of your innate nature and men talk about you the least whether in praise of your excellence or blaming your faults.

Source: Thucydides, *History of the Peloponnesian War*, Book 2.45. Translation by Thomas R. Martin.

2. MELANIPPE, THE HEROINE OF *MELANIPPE THE CAPTIVE*, A LATE-FIFTH-CENTURY B.C.E. TRAGEDY BY EURIPIDES, EXPLAINING WHY MEN'S CRITICISM OF WOMEN IS BASELESS

The Athenian playwright Euripides often portrayed female characters as denouncing men for misunderstanding and criticizing women. In mythology, Melanippe is a mother who overcomes hardship and treachery to save her family and fight for justice. Preserved only on damaged papyrus scraps, Melanippe's speech unfortunately breaks off before finishing.

Men's blame and criticism of women are empty, like the twanging sound a bow string makes without an arrow. Women are superior to men, and I'll demonstrate it. They make contracts with no need of witnesses [to swear they are honest]. They manage their households and keep safe the valuable possessions, shipped from abroad, that they have inside their homes; without a woman, no household is elegant or happy. And then in the matter of people's relationship with the gods—this I judge to be most important of all—there we have the greatest role. For women prophesy the will of Apollo in his oracles, and at the hallowed oracle of Dodona by the sacred oak tree a woman reveals the will of Zeus to all Greeks who seek it. And then there are the sacred rites of initiation performed for the Fates and the Goddesses Without Names: these can't be done with holiness by men, but women make them flourish in every way. In this way women's role in religion is right and proper.

Therefore, should anyone put down women? Won't those men stop their empty fault-finding, the ones who strongly believe that all women should be blamed if a single one is found to be bad? I will make a distinction with the following argument: nothing is worse than a bad woman, but nothing is more surpassingly superior than a worthy one.

Source: Euripides, *Melanippe the Captive*, fragment 660 Mette. Translation by Thomas R. Martin.

3. THE PHILOSOPHER SOCRATES DISCUSSING GENDER ROLES IN MARRIAGE WITH A NEW HUSBAND TOWARD THE END OF THE FIFTH CENTURY B.C.E.

Socrates, who was dedicated to discovering the nature of human virtue, often discussed family life because it revealed the qualities of women as well as men. When his upper-class friend Ischomachus♦ married a young wife, as was common, the philosopher quizzed him about their marriage; the new husband, according to Xenophon, explained that it was a partnership based on the complementary natures of male and female.

ISCHOMACHUS: I said to her:...I for my sake and your parents for your sake [arranged our marriage] by considering who would be the best partner for forming a household and having children. I chose you, and your parents chose me as the best they could find. If god should give us children, we will then plan how to raise them in the best possible way. For our partnership provides us this good: the best mutual support and the best maintenance in our old age. We have this sharing now in our household, because I've contributed all that I own to the common resources of the household, and so have you. We're not going to count up who brought more property, because the one who turns out to be the better partner in a marriage has made the greater contribution.

ISCHOMACHUS'S WIFE (no name is given): But how will I be able to partner you? What ability do I have? Everything rests on you. My mother told me my job was to behave with thoughtful moderation.

ISCHOMACHUS: Well, my father told me the same thing. Thoughtful moderation for a man as for a woman means behaving in such a way that their possessions will be in the best possible condition and will increase as much as possible by good and just means....So, you must do what the gods made you naturally capable of and what our law requires....With great forethought the gods have yoked together male and female so that they can form the most beneficial partnership. This yoking together keeps living creatures from disappearing by producing children, and it provides offspring to look after parents in their old age, at least for people. [He then explains that human survival requires outdoor work—to raise crops and livestock—and indoor work—to preserve food, raise infants, and manufacture clothing.]...And since the work both outside and inside required effort and care, god, it seems to me, from the start fashioned women's nature for indoor work and men's for outdoor. Therefore he made men's bodies and spirits more able to endure cold and heat and travel and marches, giving them the outside jobs, while assigning indoor tasks to women, it seems, because their bodies are less hardy....

But since both men and women have to manage things, [god] gave them equal shares in memory and attentiveness; you can't tell which gender has more of these qualities. And god gave both an equal ability to practice self-control, with the power to benefit the most from this quality going to whoever is better at it—whether man or woman. Precisely because they have different natures, they have greater need of each other and their yoking together is the most beneficial, with the one being capable where the other one is lacking. And as god has made them partners for their children, the law makes them partners for the household.

Source: Xenophon, *Oeconomicus* 7.10–30. Translation by Thomas R. Martin.

♦**Ischomachus:** iss KAH muh kuhs

(Continued)

(Continued)

4. A GREEK MARRIAGE CONTRACT FROM ELEPHANTINE IN EGYPT STATING THE LEGAL OBLIGATIONS OF HUSBAND AND WIFE (311–310 B.C.E.)

Greeks living abroad customarily drew up written contracts to define the duties of each partner in a marriage because they wanted their traditional expectations to remain legally binding regardless of the local laws. The earliest surviving such contract comes from the site of a Greek military garrison far up the Nile.

Marriage contract of Heraclides and Demetria.

Heraclides [of Temnos] takes as his lawful wife Demetria of Cos from her father Leptines of Cos and her mother Philotis. He is a free person; she is a free person. She brings a dowry of clothing and jewelry worth 1,000 drachmas. Heraclides must provide Demetria with everything appropriate for a freeborn wife. We will live together in whatever location Leptines and Heraclides together decide is best.

If Demetria is apprehended doing anything bad that shames her husband, she will forfeit all her dowry; Heraclides will have to prove any allegations against her in the presence of three men, whom they both must approve. It will be illegal for Heraclides to bring home another wife to Demetria's harm or to father children by another woman or to do anything bad to Demetria for any reason. If he is apprehended doing any of these things and Demetria proves it in the presence of three men whom they both approve, Heraclides must return her dowry in full and pay her 1,000 drachmas additional. Demetria and those who help her in getting this payment will have legal standing to act against Heraclides and all his property on land and sea....Each shall have the right to keep a personal copy of this contract. [A list of witnesses follows.]

Source: *Elephantine Papyri*, ed. O. Rubensohn (Berlin, 1907), no. 1. Translation by Thomas R. Martin.

QUESTIONS TO CONSIDER
1. What evidence and arguments for differing natures for men and women do these documents offer?
2. Do you think Athenian women would have found these arguments convincing? Why or why not?

---

nevertheless lacked the social respectability and status that wives and mothers possessed.

Sometimes companions also sold sex for a high price, and they got to control their own sexuality by choosing their clients. Athenian men (but not women) could buy sex as they pleased without legal hindrance. "Certainly you don't think men father children out of sexual desire?" wrote the upper-class author Xenophon.♦ "The streets and the brothels are swarming with ways to take care of that." Men (but, again, not women) could also have sex freely with female or male slaves, who could not refuse their masters.

Less successful companions lived precarious lives of exploitation and even violence at the hands of their male customers, but the most skilled of them attracted admirers from the highest levels of society and earned enough to live in luxury on their own. The most famous companion in Athens was Aspasia from Miletus, who became Pericles's lover and bore him a son. She dazzled men with her brilliant talk and wide knowledge; Pericles fell so deeply in love with her that he wanted to make her an "honest woman" by marrying her, despite his own law of 451 B.C.E. restricting citizenship, which meant their children could not be citizens without a special law passed by the assembly.

Great riches could also free women from tradition, allowing them to speak to men openly and bluntly. The most outspoken Athenian woman of wealth was Elpinike, Cimon's sister. When controversy erupted over a speech by Pericles supporting Athens's attack on a rebellious Delian League ally, she publicly rebuked him by sarcastically remarking in front of a band of women who were praising him, "This really is wonderful, Pericles.... You have caused the loss of

♦**Xenophon:** ZEH nuh fuhn

many good citizens, not in battle against Phoenicians or Persians...but in suppressing an allied city of fellow Greeks."

Other sources, especially comic drama and fourth-century B.C.E. oratory, imply that not-so-rich women, too, had strong opinions about politics and foreign policy. They customarily expressed their views to their husbands and male relatives at home in private.

Slaves and Metics. Traditional social and legal restrictions in Golden Age Athens made outsiders of slaves and metics, despite all the work they did in and for the city-state. Individuals and the city-state alike owned slaves, who could be purchased from traders or bred in the household. Unwanted newborns abandoned by their parents (the practice called infant exposure) were often picked up by others and raised as slaves. Athens's commercial growth in this period increased the demand for slaves, who in Pericles' time made up around 100,000 of the city-state's total of perhaps 250,000 inhabitants (an estimate compiled from ancient reports of the army's numbers and probable household sizes). Slaves worked in homes, on farms,

and in crafts shops; rowed alongside their owners in the navy; and, if they were really unlucky, toiled in Athens's dangerous silver mines. Unlike those at Sparta, Athens's slaves almost never rebelled, probably because they originated from too many different places to be able to unite. Many mining slaves did run away to the Spartan base established in Athenian territory during the Peloponnesian War; the Spartans resold them.

Golden Age Athens's wealth and cultural vitality attracted many metics, who flocked to the city from all around the Mediterranean, hoping to make money as importers, crafts producers, entertainers, and laborers. By the start of the Peloponnesian War in 431 B.C.E., metics constituted perhaps 50,000 to 75,000 of the approximately 150,000 free men, women, and children in the city-state. Metics paid for the privilege of living and working in Athens through a special foreigners' tax and military service. Athenians valued metics' contributions to the city's prosperity, but their insistence on exclusive citizenship meant they were unwilling to share its legal and financial benefits with immigrants.

Vase Painting of a Symposium
Upper-class Greek men often spent their evenings at symposia, drinking parties that always included much conversation and usually featured music and entertainers; wives were not included. The discussions could range widely, from literature to politics to philosophy. The man on the right is about to fling the dregs of his wine, playing a messy game called *kottabos*. The nudity of the female musician indicates she is a hired prostitute. *Reproduction by permission of the Syndics of the Fitzwilliam Museum, Cambridge. Master and Fellows of Corpus Christi College, Cambridge, The Parker Library.*

The Masculine Ideal
This sculpture of a male warrior/athlete was cast in bronze in the fifth century B.C.E.; bronze was preferred over marble for top-rank statues, but not many have survived because they were usually melted down in much later times to reuse their metal (e.g., to make guns). The relaxed pose displays the asymmetry—the head looking to one side, the arms in different positions, the torso tilted—that made Greek statues from the Classical Age appear less stiff than Archaic Age ones or their Egyptian predecessors (compare the illustration on pages 25 and 61). The body displays the ideal build that Greek men worked to achieve through daily workouts. For male statues, nudity indicated a heroic ideal. What do you think a female statue indicated depending on whether it was clothed (as on page 95) or nude (as on page 151)? *Erich Lessing/Art Resource, NY.*

Intellectual Innovation

New ways of thinking challenged accepted ideas about how people should live, creating social tension in the Golden Age. Innovative concepts in education, philosophy, historical writing, and medicine thrilled some fifth-century Greeks, but they deeply upset others, who feared that these startling changes from the old ways would undermine the traditions that held society together, especially religion, thereby provoking punishment from the angry gods. These controversial innovations had major consequences for Western civilization.

Education and philosophy provided the hottest battles between tradition and innovation. Earlier, education had stressed the preservation of old ways; parents controlled what children learned at home and from hired tutors (there were no public schools). Controversy erupted when Sophists appeared in the mid-fifth century B.C.E. and offered, for pay, classes to teenaged and young-adult males that taught nontraditional philosophic and religious doctrines and novel techniques for public speaking. Some philosophers' ideas about the nature of the cosmos challenged traditional religious views. The philosopher Socrates expounded ethical views on personal morality and responsibility and thus provoked an equally fierce controversy even though he did not work as a Sophist. In historical writing and medicine, innovators created models of interpretation and scientific method that also stimulated argument over how to understand human experience and the body.

Disagreement over whether these changes in intellectual life were dangerous for Athenian society contributed to the political tension that had arisen at Athens by the 430s B.C.E. concerning Athens's harsh treatment of its own allies and its economic sanctions against those allied with Sparta. This interaction occurred because the political, intellectual, and religious dimensions of life in ancient Athens were closely intertwined. Athenians would make connections between philosophic ideas about the nature of justice and decisions concerning what the city-state should do in domestic and foreign policy, while also being concerned about the attitude

Athenian Regulations for a Rebellious Ally

The city-state of Chalcis on the island of Euboea rebelled from the Athenian-dominated Delian League in 446 B.C.E. After defeating the rebels, the Athenians forced the Chalcidians to swear compliance with new regulations, which were inscribed on stone in both cities. The text reveals that the terms were not the same for the two sides.

The Athenian Council and the jurors shall swear an oath in this form: "I will not expel Chalcidians from Chalcis nor will I reduce the city to ruins nor deprive any individual of his citizen rights nor punish him with exile nor imprison him nor kill him nor take property from anyone who has not had a trial without approval from the People [i.e., the assembly] of the Athenians, nor will I have a vote taken against the community or any single individual without their being called to trial, and when an embassy arrives, I will introduce them to the Council and People within ten days when I am in charge of the procedure, so far as I am able. These things I will guarantee the Chalcidians if they obey the People of the Athenians."

The Chalcidians shall swear an oath in this form: "I will not rebel from the People of the Athenians either by cunning or by any way at all either by word or by deed, and I will not obey anyone who rebels, and if anyone does rebel, I will denounce him to the Athenians, and I will pay the tribute to the Athenians which I persuade the Athenians [to levy on me], and as an ally I will be the best and most just that I am able, and I will give support to and defend the People of the Athenians, if anyone wrongs the People of the Athenians, and I will obey the People of the Athenians."

Source: *Inscriptiones Graecae*, 3rd ed. (1981), no. 40. Translation by Thomas R. Martin.

of the gods toward the community. (See "Athenian Regulations for a Rebellious Ally," above.)

Education. The only formal education available came from private teachers, to whom well-to-do families sent their sons to learn to read, write, play a musical instrument or sing, and practice athletic skills suitable for war. Physical training was considered a vital part of men's education because it both made their bodies beautiful and prepared them for service in the militia (to which they could be summoned from age eighteen to sixty). Therefore, men exercised nude every day in public open-air facilities paid for by wealthy families. Men frequently discussed politics and exchanged news at these gymnasia.♦ The daughters of wealthy families usually received instruction at home from educated slaves, who were expensive because they were rare. The young girls learned reading, writing, and arithmetic so that they would be ready to help their future husbands by managing the household.

Poor girls and boys received no formal education; they learned a trade and perhaps a little reading, writing, and calculating by assisting their parents in their daily work or by serving as apprentices to skilled crafts workers. Scholars disagree about how many people could read well, but most likely they were a minority. Weak reading skills were less of a problem then than they are today because Greeks could always find someone to read aloud any written text; in fact, oral communication was at the center of Greek life, whether in speeches about politics or in songs, plays, and stories from literature and history.

Traditionally, young men from prosperous families learned how to participate in Athenian democracy by observing their fathers, uncles, and other older men as they

♦**gymnasia:** jihm NAY zee uh

debated in the Council of Five Hundred and the assembly, served in public office, and spoke in court. Often an older man would choose an adolescent boy as his special favorite to educate. The teenager would learn about public life by spending time with the older man. During the day the boy would listen to his mentor talking politics in the agora, help him perform his duties in public office, and work out with him in a gymnasium. They would spend their evenings at a symposium, whose agenda could range from serious political and philosophical discussion to riotous partying.

This older mentor–younger favorite relationship could lead to sexual relations between the youth and the older male, who would usually be married. Sex between mentors and favorites was considered acceptable in elite circles in many city-states, including Athens and Thebes; other places banned this behavior because they believed, as the Athenian author Xenophon suggests, that it sprang from a man's shameful inability to control his lustful desires. Sex between free adult men outside this sort of relationship was evidently regarded as disgraceful throughout the Greek world (too little evidence survives to reveal general Greek attitudes toward sex between women). These complicated attitudes about male homoerotic relations reflected the complexity of Greek ideas of masculinity—about what made a man a man and what unmade him. In any case, a mentor was expected never to exploit his younger companion just for pleasure, nor to neglect his political education.

Sophists and Philosophers as a Threat to Tradition.   By the time of radical democracy in Athens, young men eager to develop the essential political skill of public speaking could pay a new kind of teacher to train them. **Sophists**, or "men of wisdom," sparked controversy because they strongly challenged traditional beliefs by teaching new skills of persuasion in speaking and new ways of thinking about philosophy and religion. The term sophist later acquired a negative connotation (preserved in the English word sophistry) because the Sophists were so clever in debate that they could make deceptive arguments using complex reasoning.

Starting about 450 B.C.E. Athens's booming economy and lively intellectual activity attracted Sophists from around the Greek world. They were individual entrepreneurs vying with one another to attract pupils who could pay the hefty prices they charged for their innovative courses. As in every part of Greek intellectual life, the competition for prominence was intense. Sophists competed by offering specialized training in rhetoric—the skill of speaking persuasively. Every ambitious young man craved rhetorical training because it promised power in Athens's assembly, council, and courts. The Sophists alarmed many tradition-minded Athenians, who feared their teachings would undermine established social and political traditions. Speakers trained by silver-tongued Sophists, they believed, might be able to mislead the assembly by persuading it to take bad decisions promoting their private interests.

Young men were not the only Athenians frequenting the Sophists; prominent leaders, Pericles among them, joined the Sophists for discussions of their new philosophical ideas. The most notorious sophist was Protagoras, a contemporary of Pericles from Abdera, in northern Greece. Protagoras moved to Athens around 450 B.C.E., when he was around forty, and spent most of his career there. His views on the nature of truth and morality outraged many Athenians: he denied that there could be an absolute standard of truth, asserting that every issue had two irreconcilable sides. For example, if one person feeling a breeze thinks it warm whereas another person thinks it cool, neither judgment can be absolutely correct because the wind simply is warm to one and cool to the other. Protagoras summed up this **subjectivism**—the belief that there is no absolute reality behind and independent of appearances—in the much-quoted opening of his work *Truth*: "The human being is the measure of all things, of the things that are that they are, and of the things that are not that they are not." The term *human being* (*anthropos* in Greek, hence our word *anthropology*) in this passage refers to the individual, male or female, whom Protagoras makes the sole judge of his or her own impressions.

The subjectivism of Protagoras and other Sophists contained two main ideas: (1) human

Sophists Arguing Both Sides of a Case

The Sophist Protagoras taught his students to argue both sides of any case, but he insisted he did not teach this skill for immoral purposes. Some teachers following in his footsteps were less ethical. This excerpt comes from an anonymous handbook of the late fifth century B.C.E. entitled Double Arguments, *which provided examples of how Sophists could make arguments in the fashion of Protagoras.*

Greek philosophers put forward double arguments concerning the good and the bad. Some say that the good is one thing and the bad another, but others say that they are the same, and that a thing might be good for some persons but bad for others, or at one time good and at another time bad for the same person. I myself agree with those who hold the latter opinion, which I shall examine using as an example human life and its concern for food, drink, and sexual pleasures: these things are bad for a man if he is sick but good if he is healthy and needs them. And, further, overindulgence in these things is bad for the one who overindulges but good for those who make a profit by selling these things. And again, sickness is bad for the sick but good for the doctors. And death is bad for those who die but good for the undertakers and makers of grave monuments.... Shipwrecks are bad for the ship owners but good for the ship builders. When tools are blunted and worn away it is bad for others but good for the blacksmith. And if a pot gets smashed, this is bad for everyone else but good for the potter. When shoes wear out and fall apart it is bad for others but good for the shoemaker.... In the *stadium* race for runners, victory is good for the winner but bad for the losers.

Source: *Dissoi Logoi* 1.1–6. Translation adapted from Rosamund Kent Sprague, ed., *The Older Sophists* (Columbia: University of South Carolina Press, 1972), 279–80.

institutions and values are only matters of convention, custom, or law (*nomos*) and not creations of nature (*physis*), and (2) since truth is subjective, speakers should be able to argue either side of a question with equal persuasiveness. The first view implied that traditional human institutions were arbitrary and transient rather than natural and permanent, whereas the second made questions of right and wrong seem irrelevant. (See "Sophists Arguing Both Sides of a Case," above.)

The Sophists' critics therefore charged them with teaching moral relativism and threatening the shared public values of the democratic city-state. Aristophanes,◆ author of comic plays, satirized Sophists for harming Athens by instructing students in persuasive techniques "to make the weaker argument the stronger." Protagoras, for one, energetically responded that his doctrines were not hostile to democracy, arguing that every person had a natural capability for excellence and that human society depended on the rule of law based on a sense of justice. Members of a community, he explained, must be persuaded to obey the laws, not because they were based on absolute truth, which did not exist, but because it was advantageous for everyone to be law-abiding. A thief, for example, who might claim that stealing was a part of nature, would have to be persuaded that a man-made law forbidding theft was to his advantage because it protected his own property and the community in which he, like all humans, had to live in order to survive.

Even more disturbing than the Sophists' ideas about truth were their ideas about religion. Protagoras angered people with his agnosticism (the belief that supernatural phenomena are unknowable): "Whether the gods exist I cannot discover, nor what their

◆**Aristophanes:** a ruh STAH fuh neez

form is like, for there are many impediments to knowledge, [such as] the obscurity of the subject and the brevity of human life." This statement implies that conventional religion had no meaning; people therefore worried that Protagoras's words might provoke divine anger against the community that gave him a home.

The fifth-century B.C.E. philosophers Anaxagoras♦ of Clazomenae♦ and Leucippus♦ of Miletus, though not working as Sophists, also propounded unsettling new theories about the nature of the cosmos that offended believers in traditional religion. Anaxagoras, for example, argued that the sun was nothing more than a lump of flaming rock, not a god. Leucippus, whose doctrines were made famous by his pupil Democritus of Abdera, invented an atomic theory of matter to explain how change was constant in the universe. Everything, he argued, consisted of tiny, invisible particles in eternal motion. Their random collisions caused them to combine and recombine in an infinite variety of forms, with no divine purpose guiding their collisions and combinations. This physical explanation of change, like Anaxagoras's analysis of the nature of the sun, seemed to invalidate traditional religion, which explained events as governed by the gods' will.

The Sophists' techniques of persuasion and ways of thought enabled a man to advance his political opinions forcefully and defend himself staunchly in court. But because only wealthy men could afford their classes, the Sophists threatened Athenian democracy's egalitarian principles by giving yet another advantage to the rich in the assembly's debates or speeches in court. In addition, moral relativism and the physical explanation of the universe struck many Athenians as dangerous: they feared that such teachings, by offending the gods, would destroy the divine goodwill they believed Athens enjoyed. These ideas so infuriated some Athenians that in the 430s B.C.E., Plutarch reports, they sponsored a law allowing citizens to bring charges of impiety against "those who fail to respect divine

things or teach theories about the cosmos." The philosopher Anaxagoras was brought to trial under this procedure and apparently convicted; his close friend Pericles arranged a comfortable exile for him in another city-state.

Socrates on Ethics. Socrates♦ (469–399 B.C.E.), the most famous philosopher of the Golden Age, became well known in his home state of Athens during this troubled time of the 430s, when people were anxious not just about the Sophists but also about the growing threat of war with Sparta. Socrates devoted his life to questioning people about their beliefs, but he insisted he was not a Sophist because he offered no courses and took no pay. Above all, he fought against the view that justice should be equated with power over others. By insisting that true justice was better than injustice under any and all circumstances, he gave a new direction to Greek philosophy: an emphasis on ethics (the study of ideal human values and moral duties). Although other thinkers before him (especially poets and authors of plays) had dealt with similar issues, Socrates was the first philosopher to make ethics his central concern.

Socrates lived an eccentric life that attracted constant attention. Sporting a stomach, in his words, "a bit too big to be convenient," he wore the same cheap cloak summer and winter and scorned shoes no matter how cold the weather. His physical stamina—including both his tirelessness as a soldier in Athens's infantry and his ability to outdrink anyone at a symposium—was legendary. Unlike the high-priced Sophists, he lived in poverty and disdained material possessions, somehow managing to support a wife and several children; he probably inherited some money and accepted gifts from wealthy admirers.

Socrates spent his time in conversations all over Athens: participating in a symposium, strolling in the agora, or watching young men exercise in a gymnasium. In this behavior he resembled his fellow Athenians, who placed great value on the importance and pleasure of speaking with one another at length. He wrote nothing; our knowledge

♦**Anaxagoras:** a nak SA guh ruhs
♦**Clazomenae:** kluhd ZAH muh nee
♦**Leucippus:** loo KIP us

♦**Socrates:** SAH kruh teez

of his ideas comes from others' writings, especially those of his famous follower Plato (c. 428–348 B.C.E.). Plato portrays Socrates as a relentless questioner of his fellow citizens, foreign friends, and leading Sophists. Socrates' questions had the goal of making his conversational partners examine the basic assumptions of their way of life. Giving few answers, Socrates never directly instructed anyone; instead, he led them to draw conclusions in response to his probing questions and refutations of their cherished assumptions. Today this procedure is called the **Socratic method**.

Socrates often upset and even outraged people because his method made them feel ignorant and baffled. Socrates' questions forced them to admit that they did not in fact know what they had assumed they knew very well. Even more painful to them was Socrates' fiercely argued view that the way they lived their lives—pursuing success in politics or business or art—was merely an excuse for avoiding the hard work of understanding and developing genuine virtue. Socrates insisted that he was ignorant of the best definition of virtue but that his wisdom consisted of knowing that he did not know. He vowed he was trying to improve, not undermine, people's ethical beliefs, even though, as a friend put it, a conversation with Socrates made a man feel numb—just as if a jellyfish had stung him.

Socrates especially wanted to use reasoning to discover universal, objective standards that justified individual ethics. He attacked the Sophists for their relativistic claim that conventional standards of right and wrong were merely "the fetters that bind nature." This view, he protested, equated human happiness with power and "getting more."

Socrates passionately believed that the only way to achieve true happiness was to behave justly in accordance with a universal, transcendent standard of just behavior. Essentially, he argued that just behavior, or virtue, was identical to knowledge and that true knowledge of justice would inevitably lead people to choose good over evil. They would therefore have truly happy lives, regardless of how rich or poor they were. Since Socrates believed that ethical knowledge was all a person needed for the good life, he

Statuette of the Philosopher Socrates
The controversial Socrates, the most famous philosopher of Athens in the fifth century B.C.E., joked that he had a homely face and a bulging stomach. This small statue is an artist's impression of what Socrates looked like; we cannot be sure of the truth. Socrates was renowned for his irony, and he may have purposely exaggerated his physical unattractiveness to show his disdain for ordinary standards of beauty and his own emphasis on the quality of one's soul as the true measure of one's worth. Compare his body to that of the athletes shown in the vase painting on page 55 or of the statue of the warrior/athlete on page 104. *British Museum.*

argued that no one knowingly behaved unjustly and that behaving justly was always in the individual's interest. It was simply ignorant to believe that the best life was the life of unlimited power to pursue whatever one desired. The most desirable human life was concerned with virtue and guided by reason, not by dreams of personal gain.

Socrates' ideas proved as disturbing as the Sophists' very different doctrines because they rejected the Athenians' usual, traditional way of life. His ridicule of commonly accepted ideas about the importance of wealth and public success infuriated many people. Unhappiest of all were the fathers whose sons, after listening to Socrates' questions reduce someone to utter bewilderment, came home to try the same technique on their parents by arguing that the accomplishments their family held dear were old-fashioned and worthless. Men who experienced this reversal of the traditional educational hierarchy— the father was supposed to educate the son— felt that Socrates was undermining the stability of society by making young men question Athenian traditions. Socrates evidently did not teach women, but Plato portrays him as ready to learn from exceptional women, such as Pericles' hyperintelligent companion Aspasia.

The worry that Socrates' ideas presented a danger to conventional society inspired Aristophanes to write his comedy *The Clouds* (423 B.C.E.). This play portrays Socrates as a cynical Sophist who, for a fee, offers instruction in the Protagorean technique of making the weaker argument the stronger. When the curriculum of Socrates' school ("The Thinkery") transforms a youth into a public speaker who argues that a son has the right to beat his parents, his father burns the place down. None of these plot details seems to have been real; what was genuine was the fear that Socrates' radical views on individual morality endangered the city-state's traditional practices. This anxiety only grew worse as the Peloponnesian War dragged on with ever more casualties and many citizens began to feel that their best hope for victory lay in strengthening tradition, not weakening it.

Historical Writing. Just as the Sophists and Socrates antagonized many people with their new ideas, the inventors of historical writing drew attention because they took a critical attitude in their descriptions of the past. Herodotus of Halicarnassus♦ (c. 485–425 B.C.E.) and Thucydides of Athens (c. 455–399 B.C.E.) became Greece's most

famous historians and established Western civilization's tradition of history writing. The fifth-century B.C.E.'s unprecedented events— a coalition Greek victory over the world's greatest power and then the longest war ever between Greeks—apparently inspired them to create history as a subject based on strenuous research. They explained that they wrote histories because they wanted people to remember the past and to understand why wars had taken place. In the 420s B.C.E., Herodotus finished a long, groundbreaking work called *Histories* (meaning "inquiries" in Greek) to explain the Persian Wars as a clash between the cultures of the East and West; by Roman times he had been dubbed the "Father of History." A typically competitive Greek intellectual, Herodotus made the justifiable claim that he surpassed all previous recording of the past by taking an in-depth and investigative approach to evidence, being interested in the culture of non-Greeks as well as Greeks, and expressing explicit and implicit judgments about people's actions. Because Herodotus recognized the necessity (and the delight) of studying other cultures for doing his historical research, he pushed his inquiries deep into the past, looking for long-standing cultural differences that helped explain the Persian-Greek conflict. Unlike poets and playwrights, he did not make the gods the driving force in history, instead putting the focus on human psychology and interaction.

Thucydides redirected historical inquiry— and overtly competed with Herodotus—by writing contemporary history and inventing the kind of analysis of power that today informs political science. His *History of the Peloponnesian War*, published after the end of the war, made power politics, not divine intervention, history's primary force. Deeply affected by the war's brutality, he used his experiences as a politician and failed military commander (he was exiled for losing a key outpost) to make his narrative vivid and frank in describing human moral failings. His insistence that historians should spare no effort in seeking out the most reliable sources and evaluating their testimony with objectivity set a high standard for later writers. Like Herodotus, he challenged tradition by revealing that Greek history was just as full of

♦**Halicarnassus:** ha luh kahr NA suhs

Vase Painting of a Doctor at Work
This piece of pottery, apparently used to hold perfume or ointment, is decorated with a picture of a physician treating a patient's arm. The prevalence of war gave Greek doctors much experience with wounds and trauma, and they could stop bleeding, set bones, perform minor surgery, and offer some pain relief with drugs derived from plants. Still, the effectiveness of their treatment was limited because they had no cure for infections. *Photo Réunion des Musées Nationaux— Herve Lewandowski.*

shameful actions (such as the Athenian punishment of Melos in the Peloponnesian War— see page 117) as of glorious achievements.

Hippocrates and the Birth of Scientific Medicine. Hippocrates♦ of Cos, a fifth-century contemporary of Thucydides, challenged tradition by grounding medical diagnosis and treatment in clinical observation; his fame continues today in the oath bearing his name that doctors swear at the beginning of their professional careers. Previously, medicine had depended on magic and ritual; illness was believed to be caused by evil spirits, and various cults in Greek religion offered healing to patients through divine intervention. Competing to refute these earlier doctors' theories, Hippocrates insisted that only physical factors caused disease. He may have been the author of the view, dominant in later

♦**Hippocrates:** hih PAH kruh teez

medicine, that four humors (fluids) made up the human body: blood, phlegm, black bile, and yellow bile. Health therefore depended on keeping the proper balance among them; being healthy was to be in "good humor." This system for understanding the body corresponded to the division of the inanimate world into four parts: the elements earth, air, fire, and water.

Hippocrates taught that the physician's most important duty was to base his knowledge on careful observation of patients and their response to different treatments. He insisted that clinical experience, not abstract theory or religious belief, was the proper principle for establishing effective cures. By putting his innovative ideas and practices to the test in competition with those of traditional medicine, Hippocrates established the truth of his principle, which later became a cornerstone of scientific medicine.

Review: How did new ways of thinking in the Golden Age threaten cherished traditions?

The Development of Greek Tragedy

The problematic relationship between gods and humans inspired Golden Age Athens's most prominent cultural innovation: tragic drama. Plays called tragedies were presented over three days at the major annual festival of the god Dionysus in a contest for playwrights, in keeping with the competitive spirit characteristic of Greek cultural life. The word *tragedy*—derived, for unknown reasons, from the Greek words for "goat" and "song"— referred to a play involving fierce conflict and characters representing powerful forces. Tragedies presented shocking stories, usually from myth but occasionally from history, that could be related to controversial issues in contemporary Athens. Therefore, these plays stimulated their large audiences to ponder the danger that ignorance, arrogance, and violence presented to the city-state's democratic society. Following the tradition of Homer and Hesiod, Golden Age playwrights explored topics ranging from the roots of good and evil to the nature of individual freedom and responsibility in the family and the political community. As with other ancient

Theater of Dionysus at Athens
Tragedies, satyr plays, and comedies were produced at Athens during the daytime in this outdoor theater honoring the god Dionysus. The seating and stone stage building foundations that are visible today come from later eras; the seating, the stage, and the scenery were temporary, wooden installations during the Classical Age. The theater seated about fourteen thousand or more people, and subsidies kept ticket prices reasonable. Since Athens's drama festivals featured multiple plays each day, spectators spent long hours in the theater to see them all. *John Elk III/Bruce Coleman, Inc., New York.*

texts, most tragedies have not survived: only thirty-three still exist from the hundreds that were produced at Athens.

The competition took place every year, with a magistrate choosing three authors from a pool of applicants. Each of these finalists presented four plays during the festival: three tragedies in a row (a trilogy), followed by a semicomic play featuring satyrs (mythical half-man, half-animal beings) to end the day on a lighter note. Tragedies were written in verses of solemn language; they were often based on stories about the violent possibilities when gods and humans interacted. The plots often ended with a resolution to the trouble—but only after prolonged suffering.

Athenian tragedies in performance bore little resemblance to modern plays. They took place during the daytime in an outdoor theater sacred to Dionysus, built into the southern slope of Athens's acropolis. This theater held about fourteen thousand spectators overlooking an open, circular area in front of a slightly raised stage. A tragedy had eighteen cast members, all of whom were men: three actors to play the speaking roles (both male and female characters) and fifteen chorus members. Although the chorus leader sometimes engaged in dialogue with the actors, the chorus primarily performed songs and dances in the circular area in front of the stage, called the orchestra.

A successful tragedy offered a vivid spectacle. The chorus wore elaborate costumes and performed intricate dance routines. The actors, who wore masks, used broad gestures and booming voices to reach the upper tier of seats. A powerful voice was crucial to a tragic actor because words represented the heart of the plays, in which dialogue and long speeches predominated over physical action. Special effects were part of the spectacle. For example, a crane allowed actors playing the roles of gods to fly suddenly onto the stage. The actors playing lead roles, called the protagonists (literally, "first competitors"), competed against one another for the designation of best actor. So important was a first-rate protagonist to a play's success that actors were assigned by lottery to the competing playwrights to give all three an equal chance to have a winning cast. Great protagonists became enormously popular, although they were not usually members of the social elite.

Playwrights were from the elite because only men of some wealth could afford the amount of time and learning this work demanded: as author, director, producer, musical composer, choreographer, and sometimes even actor. As citizens, playwrights also fulfilled the normal military and political obligations of Athenian men. The best-known Athenian tragedians—Aeschylus◆ (525–456 B.C.E.), Sophocles◆ (c. 496–406 B.C.E.), and Euripides (c. 485–406 B.C.E.)—all served in the army, and Sophocles was elected to Athens's highest public office. Authors of plays competed from a love of honor, not money: the prizes, determined by a board of judges, awarded high prestige but little cash. The competition was regarded as so important that any judge who took a bribe to award a prize was put to death.

Athenian tragedy was a public art form subsidized by tax revenues and mandatory contributions by the rich. Tragedy's plots explored the difficulties of telling right from wrong when humans came into conflict with one another in the city-state and the gods became involved. Even though most tragedies were based on stories that referred to a legendary time before city-states existed, such as the period of the Trojan War, the moral issues the plays illuminated always pertained to the society and obligations of citizens in a city-state. To take only a few examples: Aeschylus in his trilogy *Oresteia*◆ (458 B.C.E.) uses the story of how the gods stopped the

murderous violence in the family of Orestes, son of Agamemnon, the Greek leader against Troy, to explain the divine origins of democratic Athens's court system. The plays suggest that human beings learn only by suffering but that the gods provide justice in the long run. Sophocles' *Antigone* (441 B.C.E.) presents the story of the cursed family of Oedipus of Thebes as a drama of harsh conflict between a courageous woman, Antigone, and the city-state's stern male leader, her uncle Creon. After her brother dies in a failed rebellion, Antigone insists on her family's

Theaters of Classical Greece

moral obligation to bury its dead in obedience to divine command, while Creon takes harsh action to preserve order and protect community values by prohibiting the burial of his nephew the traitor. In a horrifying story of raging anger and suicide that features one of the most famous heroines of Western literature, Sophocles exposes the right and wrong on each side of the conflict. His play offers no easy resolution of the competing interests of divinely sanctioned moral tradition and the state's political rules. Euripides' *Medea* (431 B.C.E.) reveals that the stability and prosperity of the city-state depend on men treating their wives and families with honor and trust: when Medea's husband, Jason, betrays her to marry a younger woman in a deal to gain political leadership, she takes revenge on him by using her magical powers to destroy the new bride and, in utter desperation, murders her own children to express her hatred of Jason.

Ancient sources tell us that the audiences reacted strongly to the messages of the tragedies presented in the drama competition of the Dionysian festival. For one thing, they could see that the central characters of the plays were figures who fell into disaster even though they held positions of power and prestige. The characters' reversals of fortune came about not because they were absolute villains but because, as humans, they were susceptible to a lethal mixture of error, ignorance,

---

◆**Aeschylus:** EHS kuh luhs
◆**Sophocles:** SAH fuh kleez
◆**Oresteia:** awr ehs TYE uh

and **hubris**✦ (violent arrogance). The Athenian Empire was at its height when audiences at Athens attended the tragedies of these three great playwrights. Thoughtful spectators could reflect on the possibility that Athens's current power and prestige, managed as they were by humans, might fall prey to the same kind of mistakes and conflicts that brought down the heroes and heroines of tragedy. Thus, tragedies not only entertained through their spectacle but also educated through their stories and words. In particular, they reminded male citizens, who governed the city-state in its assembly, council, and courts, that success created complex moral problems that self-righteous arrogance never solved.

The Development of Greek Comedy

Golden Age Athens developed comedy as its second distinctive form of public theater. Like tragedies, comedies were written in verse, performed in a competition in the city's large outdoor theater during festivals honoring the god Dionysus, and subsidized with public funds and contributions from the rich. Unlike tragedies, comedies made direct comments about public policy and criticized current politicians and intellectuals. They did this with plots and casts presenting outrageous fantasies of contemporary life. For example, comic choruses, which had twenty-four dancing singers, could be colorfully dressed as talking birds or dancing clouds, or an actor could fly up on a giant dung beetle to visit the gods.

Comic playwrights competed for the honor of winning the award for the festival's best comedy by creating beautiful poetry, raising laughs with constant jokes and puns, and skewering pretentious citizens and political leaders. Much of the humor concerned sex and bodily functions, delivered in a stream of imaginative profanity. Well-known men of the day were targets for insults as

✦**hubris:** HYOO brihs

Statuettes of Comic Actors Although these little statues portray comic actors dressed in the kinds of masks and costumes that came into vogue later than the style of comedy that Aristophanes and his contemporaries wrote in the fifth century B.C.E. (for which no such pieces exist), they give a vivid sense of the exaggerated buffoonery that characterized the acting in Greek comedy. In Aristophanes' day, the grotesque unreality of comic costumes would have been even more striking because the male actors wore large leather phalluses (penises) attached below their waists that could be props for all sorts of ribald jokes. The use of masks in certain kinds of theater performances continued into Roman times. *Staatliche Museen zu Berlin-Bildarchiv Preussischer Kulturbesitz/Art Resource, NY.*

cowards or effeminate weaklings. Women characters portrayed as figures of fun and ridicule seem to have been fictional, to protect the dignity of actual female citizens.

Athenian comedies often made fun of political leaders. As the leading politician of radical democracy, Pericles came in for fierce criticism in comedy. Comic playwrights mocked his policies, his love life, even the shape of his skull ("Old Turnip Head" was a favorite insult). So fiercely did Aristophanes (c. 455–385 B.C.E.), Athens's most famous comic playwright, ridicule Cleon, the city's most prominent leader early in the Peloponnesian War, in his comedy *Babylonians* in 426 B.C.E. that Cleon sued him. A citizen jury upheld free speech by returning the verdict in Aristophanes' favor. The author responded by pitilessly parodying Cleon as a scheming foreign slave in *The Knights* of 424 B.C.E., calling him a "mud-churning fraud who threw the whole city into chaos."

Several of Aristophanes's comedies have powerful women as their main characters, who compel the men of Athens to change their policy to preserve family life and the city-state. These plays even criticize the assembly's policy during wartime. Most famous is *Lysistrata* (411 B.C.E.), named after the female lead character of the play. In this fantasy, the women of Athens and Sparta unite to force their husbands to end the Peloponnesian War. To make the men agree to a peace treaty, they first seize the acropolis, where Athens's financial reserves are kept, to prevent the men from squandering them further on the war. They then use sarcasm and pitchers of cold water to beat back an attack on their position by the old men who have remained in Athens while the younger men are out on campaign. Although the women eagerly look forward to sex with their husbands, they steel themselves to refuse to sleep with those who were returning from battle. The effects of their strike on the men, portrayed in a series of sexually explicit comic episodes, finally compel the warriors to make peace.

Lysistrata presents women acting bravely and aggressively against men who seem bent on destroying their traditional family life—they are staying away from home for long stretches while on military campaign and are ruining the city-state by prolonging a pointless war. Lysistrata insists that women have the intelligence and judgment to make political decisions: "I am a woman, and, yes, I have brains. And I'm not badly off for judgment. Nor has my education been bad, coming as it has from my listening often to the conversations of my father and the elders among the men." Her old-fashioned training and good sense allow her to see what needs to be done to protect the community. Like the heroines of tragedy, Lysistrata is a conservative, even a reactionary; she wants to put things back the way they were before the war ruined family life. To do that, however, she has to act like an impatient revolutionary. That irony sums up the challenge that fifth-century Athens faced in trying to resolve the tension between the dynamic innovation of its Golden Age and the importance of tradition in Greek life.

The remarkable freedom of speech of Athenian comedy allowed frank, even brutal, commentary on current issues and person-alities. It cannot be an accident that this energetic, critical drama emerged in Athens at the same time as radical democracy, in the mid-fifth century B.C.E. The feeling that all citizens should have a stake in determining their government's policies evidently fueled a passion for using biting humor to keep the community's leaders from becoming arrogant and aloof.

❖ The End of the Golden Age, 431–403 B.C.E.

A war between Athens and Sparta that lasted a generation (431–404 B.C.E.) ended the Golden Age; it is called the Peloponnesian War today because it pitted Sparta's Peloponnese-based alliance against Athens and its allies. The war started, according to Thucydides, because the growth of Athenian power alarmed the Spartans, who feared that their interests and allies would fall to the Athenians' restless drive. Pericles, the most powerful politician in Athens at the time, persuaded its assembly to take a hard line when the Spartans demanded that Athens ease restrictions on city-states allied with Sparta. Corinth and Megara, crucial Spartan allies, complained bitterly to Sparta about Athens; finally, Corinth told Sparta to attack Athens, or else Corinth and its navy would change sides to the Athenian alliance. Sparta's leaders therefore gave Athens an ultimatum—stop mistreating our allies—that Pericles convinced the Athenian assembly to reject on the grounds that Sparta had refused to settle the dispute through the third-party arbitration process called for by the 446–445 B.C.E. treaty. Pericles's critics claimed he was insisting on war against Sparta to revive his fading popularity; his supporters replied that he was defending Athenian honor and protecting foreign trade, a linchpin of the economy. By 431 B.C.E. these disputes had shattered the thirty-year peace between Athens and Sparta that Pericles had made in 446–445 B.C.E.

The Peloponnesian War, 431–404 B.C.E.

Lasting longer than any previous war in Greek history, the Peloponnesian War (Map 3.3) took place above all because Spartan

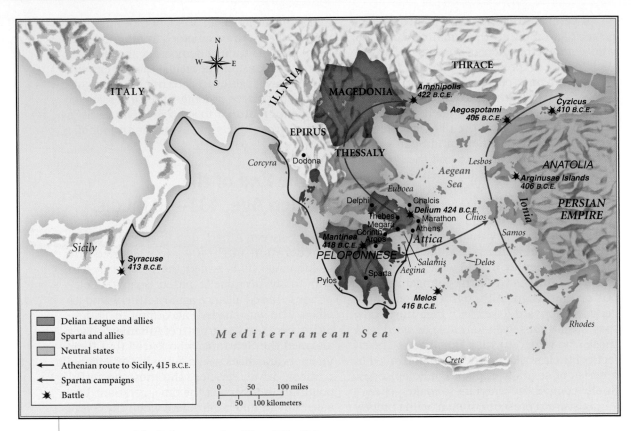

MAP 3.3 The Peloponnesian War, 431–404 B.C.E.
For the first ten years, the Peloponnesian War's battles took place largely in mainland Greece. Sparta, whose armies usually avoided distant campaigns, shocked Athens when its general Brasidas led successful attacks against Athenian forces in northeast Greece. Athens stunned the entire Greek world in the war's next phase by launching a huge naval expedition against Spartan allies in far-off Sicily. The last ten years of the war saw the action move to the east, on and along the western coast of Anatolia and its islands, on the boundary of the Persian Empire, which helped the Spartans build a navy there to defeat the famous Athenian fleet.

leaders believed they had to fight now to keep the Athenians from using their superior long-distance offensive weaponry—the Delian League's naval forces—to destroy Sparta's control of the Peloponnesian League. (See "Taking Measure," opposite.) The war opened with a Spartan first strike, but it dragged on so long because the Athenian assembly failed to negotiate and maintain peace with Sparta when it had the chance and because the Spartans were willing to deal with Persia to gain money to build a fleet to win the war.

Dramatic evidence for how angry the feelings were that fueled the war comes from Thucydides's version of Pericles's stern

oration to the Athenian assembly about not yielding to Spartan pressure:

If we do go to war, harbor no thought that you went to war over a trivial affair. For you this trifling matter is the assurance and the proof of your determination. If you yield to their demands, they will immediately confront you with some larger demand, since they will think that you only gave way on the first point out of fear. But if you stand firm, you will show them that they have to deal with you as equals. . . . When our equals, without agreeing to arbitration of the matter under dispute, make claims on us as neighbors and state those claims as commands, it would be no better than slavery to give in to them, no matter how large or how small the claim may be.

When Sparta began hostilities by invading Athenian territory, Pericles advised a two-pronged strategy to win what he saw would be a long war: (1) use the navy to raid the lands of Sparta and its allies, and (2) avoid large infantry battles with the superior land forces of the Spartans, even when the enemy hoplites plundered the Athenian countryside outside the city. The citizens could retreat to safety behind Athens's impregnable fortification walls, massive barriers of stone that encircled the city and the harbor, with the Long Walls protecting the land corridor between the urban center and the port. He insisted that Athenians should sacrifice their country property, which was vast and valuable, to save their population. In the end, he predicted, the superior resources of Athens would enable it to win a war of attrition, especially because without a base in Athenian territory the Spartans could not support long invasions.

Backed by Pericles' unyielding leadership, this strategy might have made Athens the winner in the long run, but chance intervened to deprive Athens of his guidance: an epidemic disease that struck Athens in 430 B.C.E. killed Pericles the next year. This plague ravaged Athens's population for four years, killing thousands as it spread like wildfire among the people packed in behind the walls to avoid Spartan attacks. Despite their losses and the fears of many that the gods had sent the epidemic to punish them, the Athenians fought on; over time, however, they abandoned the disciplined strategy that Pericles' prudent plan had required. The generals elected after his death pursued a much more aggressive strategy, but they failed to protect Athens's possessions in northern Greece, crippling the supply of timber and precious metals from this crucial region.

The most innovative and confident new general, Alcibiades,♦ persuaded the assembly to reject a peace that had been made in 421 B.C.E. and to attack Spartan allies in 418 B.C.E. In 416–415 B.C.E. the Athenians and their allies overpowered the tiny and strategically meaningless Aegean island of Melos because it refused to abandon its allegiance to Sparta. Thucydides dramatically represents Athe-

nian messengers telling the Melians they had to be conquered to show that Athens permitted no defiance to its dominance. Following their victory the Athenians executed the Melian men, sold the women and children into slavery, and colonized the island.

TAKING MEASURE

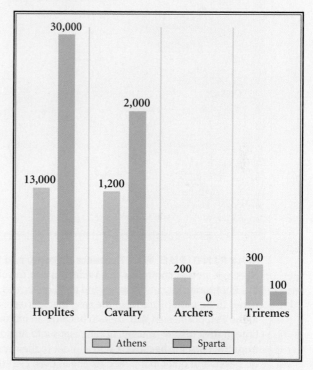

Military Forces of Athens and Sparta at the Beginning of the Peloponnesian War (431 B.C.E.) These figures give estimates of the relative strengths of the military forces of the Athenian side and the Spartan side when the Peloponnesian War broke out in 431 B.C.E. The numbers come from ancient historical sources, above all the Athenian general and historian Thucydides, who fought in the war. The bar graphs starkly reveal the different characteristics of the competing forces: Athens relied on its navy of triremes and its archers (the fifth-century equivalent of artillery and snipers), while Sparta was preeminent in the forces needed for pitched land battles, hoplites (heavily armed infantry) and cavalry (shock troops used to disrupt opposing phalanxes). These differences dictated the differing strategies and tactics of the two sides, Athens trying guerrilla-fashion by launching surprise raids from the sea and Sparta trying to force decisive confrontations on the battlefield. *From Pamela Bradley,* Ancient Greece: Using Evidence *(Melbourne: Edward Arnold, 1990), 229.*

♦**Alcibiades:** al suh BY uh deez

MAPPING THE WEST Greece, Europe, and the Mediterranean, c. 400 B.C.E.
No single power controlled the Mediterranean region at the end of the fifth century B.C.E. In the west, the Phoenician city of Carthage and the Greek cities of Sicily and southern Italy were rivals for the riches to be won by trade. In the east, the Spartans, emboldened by their recent victory over Athens in the Peloponnesian War, tried to become an international power outside the mainland for the first time in their history by sending campaigns into Anatolia. This aggressive action aroused stiff opposition from the Persians because it was a threat to their westernmost imperial provinces. There was to be no peace and quiet in the Mediterranean even after the twenty-seven years of the Peloponnesian War.

The turning point in the war came soon thereafter when in 415 B.C.E. Alcibiades persuaded the Athenian assembly to launch the greatest and most expensive campaign in Greek history. The expedition of 415 B.C.E. was directed against Sparta's allies in Sicily, far to the west; Alcibiades had dazzled his fellow citizens with the dream of conquering that rich island and especially its greatest city, Syracuse. Alcibiades' political rivals had him deposed from his command, however, and lesser generals blundered into catastrophic defeat in Sicily in 413 B.C.E. (see Map 3.3). The victorious Syracusans destroyed the allied invasion fleet and packed the survivors like human sardines into quarries under the blazing sun, with no toilets and only half a pint of drinking water and a handful of grain a day.

On the advice of Alcibiades, who had deserted to their side in anger at having lost his command, the Spartans seized a permanent base of operations in the Athenian countryside for year-round raids, now that Athens was too weak to drive them out. Athenian agriculture was then devastated by constant Spartan attacks, and twenty thousand slave workers crippled production in Athens's silver mines by deserting to the enemy. The democratic assembly became so upset over these losses that in 411 B.C.E. it voted itself out of existence in favor of an emergency government run by the wealthier citizens. When an oligarchic group illegally took charge, however, the citizens restored the traditional radical democracy and kept fighting. The end came when Persia gave the Spartans money to build a navy; the Persian king thought it was in his interest to see Athens defeated. Aggressive Spartan action at sea forced Athens to surrender in 404 B.C.E. After twenty-seven years of near-continuous war, the Athenians were at their enemy's mercy.

> **Review:** How did unexpected events contribute to the outcome of the Peloponnesian War?

Athens Humbled: Tyranny and Civil War, 404–403 B.C.E.

Following Athens's surrender, the Spartans installed a regime of antidemocratic Athenians who were willing to collaborate with the victors; they were members of the social elite, and some had been well-known pupils of Sophists. They became known as the Thirty Tyrants. Brutally suppressing democratic opposition, these oligarchs embarked on an eight-month period of terror and plundering in 404–403 B.C.E. The speechwriter Lysias, for example, reported that Spartan henchmen seized his brother for execution as a way of stealing the family's valuables, even ripping the gold earrings from the ears of his brother's wife. Outraged at the violence and greed of the Thirty Tyrants, citizens who wanted to restore democracy banded together outside the city to fight to regain control of Athens. Fortunately for them, the Spartans were paralyzed by a feud between their two most important leaders and did not send help to their Athenian collaborators. The democratic rebels defeated the forces of the Thirty Tyrants in a series of bloody street battles in Athens.

Democracy was therefore restored, but the city-state seethed with anger and unrest in the aftermath of the defeat by Sparta and the horrors the Thirty Tyrants perpetrated on their fellow citizens. To settle the internal strife that threatened to tear Athens apart, the newly restored democratic assembly voted the first known amnesty in Western history, a truce agreement forbidding any official charges or recriminations stemming from the crimes of 404–403 B.C.E. Agreeing not to pursue grievances in court was the price of peace. As would soon become clear, however, some Athenians harbored grudges that no amnesty could dispel. In addition, Athens's financial and military strength had been shattered. The end of the Golden Age left Athenians worriedly wondering how to remake their lives and restore the luster that their city-state's innovative accomplishments had produced.

Conclusion

When some Greek city-states temporarily united to resist the Persian Empire at the beginning of the fifth century B.C.E., they surprised themselves in the Persian Wars by defeating the invasion that had threatened their political independence. When the Persians retreated, so, too, did Greek unity. Athens's part in the victory made it a rival of Sparta for international power; the Athenian Golden Age that followed the war was based on empire and trade, and the city's riches funded the widening of democracy and cultural accomplishments that have remained influential ever since.

As the money poured in, the city-state built glorious temples, instituted pay for service in many government offices to strengthen democracy, and assembled the Mediterranean's most powerful navy. The poor men who rowed the ships demanded greater democracy; such demands led to legal reforms that guaranteed fair treatment for all. Pericles became the most famous politician of the Golden Age by leading the drive for radical democracy.

Religious practice and women's lives reflected the strong effect of tradition on everyday life, but intellectual life saw dramatic innovation that created tension in the society. Art and architecture broke out of old forms, promoting an impression of balanced motion rather than stability. Tragedy and comedy developed at Athens as public art forms commenting on contemporary social and political issues. The Sophists' relativistic views disturbed tradition-minded people, as did Socrates' definition of virtue, emphasizing his questioning of ordinary people's love of wealth and success.

Wars framed the Golden Age. The Persian Wars sent the Athenians soaring to imperial power and prosperity, but their high-handed treatment of allies and enemies combined with Spartan fears about Athenian power to bring on the disastrous Peloponnesian War.

Its nearly three decades of battle brought the stars of the Greek Golden Age crashing to earth: by 400 B.C.E. the Athenians found themselves in the same situation as in 500 B.C.E., fearful of Spartan power and worried whether the world's first democracy could survive. As it turned out, the next great threat to Greek stability and independence would once again come from a neighboring monarchy, this time not from Persia to the east but from Macedonia to the north.

Suggested References

Wars between Persia and Greece, 499–479 B.C.E.

Like many groups in history, the ancient Greeks defined their own identity by contrasting themselves with others, especially non-Greek-speaking peoples ("barbarians"). The Persian Wars strengthened their sense of difference from other peoples ruled by kings.

Georges, Pericles. *Barbarian Asia and the Greek Experience: From the Archaic Period to the Age of Xenophon.* 1994.

Hall, Jonathan M. *Ethnic Identity in Greek Antiquity.* 1997.

Hanson, Victor Davis. *The Wars of the Ancient Greeks.* 1999.

*Herodotus. *The Histories.* Translated Aubrey de Sélincourt. Revised by John Marincola. New edition, 1996.

Persian art: http://www.oi.uchicago.edu/OI/MUS/GALLERY/PERSIAN/New_Persian_Gallery.html.

Wees, Hans van, ed. *War and Violence in Ancient Greece.* 2000.

Athenian Confidence in the Golden Age, 478–431 B.C.E.

Athenian government remains significant for modern scholars in debates over direct versus representative democracy and the nature of citizenship. Online resources are also now available and important for studying the full context of Golden Age Athenian history.

Athenian democracy: http://www.stoa.org/projects/demos/home.

Camp, John M. *The Archaeology of Athens.* 2001.

*Primary source.

Cohen, Edward E. *The Athenian Nation.* 2000.

Ober, Josiah, and Charles W. Hedrick, eds. *Demokratia: A Conversation on Democracies, Ancient and Modern.* 1996.

Parthenon: http://www.perseus.tufts.edu/cgi-bin/vor?x=16&y=13&lookup=parthenon.

Tradition and Innovation in Athens's Golden Age

Lively debates continue about how to measure and evaluate the difference between ancient Greek and modern Western customs. Davidson, for example, has rebutted the recent idea that Greeks considered sex a game of aggressive domination.

Blundell, Sue. *Women in Ancient Greece.* 1995.

Brunschwig, Jacques and Geoffrey E. R. Lloyd, eds. *Greek Thought: A Guide to Classical Knowledge.* 2000.

Davidson, James. *Courtesans and Fishcakes: The Consuming Passions of Classical Athens.* 1998.

Fisher, N. R. E. *Slavery in Classical Greece.* 1995.

Greek gods: http://www.getty.edu/art/collections/subjects/s23-1.html.

Parker, Robert. *Athenian Religion: A History.* 1996.

Patterson, Cynthia B. *The Family in Greek History.* 1998.

Plutarch on Sparta. Trans. Richard J. A. Talbert. 1988.

The End of the Golden Age, 431–403 B.C.E.

Controversy still exists over whether to explain the Athenian defeat in the Peloponnesian War as caused by political disunity and failure of leadership at Athens, or by Persia's financial support of Sparta; Strassler's edition of Thucydides is the best resource for assessing the evidence of the most important ancient source.

Kagan, Donald. *The Peloponnesian War.* 2003.

Lazenby, J. F. *The Spartan Army.* 1985.

Munn, Mark. *The School of History. Athens in the Age of Socrates.* 2000.

The Peloponnesian War and Athenian Life: http://www.perseus.tufts.edu/cgi-bin/ptext?doc=Perseus%3Atext%3A1999.04.0009%3Ahead%3D%23212.

*Strassler, Robert B., ed. *The Landmark Thucydides: A Comprehensive Guide to the Peloponnesian War.* 1996.

*Pseudo-Xenophon, *Constitution of the Athenians.* Trans. G. W. Bowersock, in *Xenophon VII. Scripta Minora.* 1971.

CHAPTER REVIEW

IMPORTANT EVENTS

c. 500–323 B.C.E.	Classical Age of Greek History
499–479 B.C.E.	Wars between Persia and Greece
490 B.C.E.	Battle of Marathon
480–479 B.C.E.	Xerxes' invasion of Greece
480 B.C.E.	Battle of Salamis
479 B.C.E.	Battles of Plataea and Mycale
461 B.C.E.	Ephialtes reforms the Athenian court system
Early 450s B.C.E.	Pericles introduces pay for office holders in Athenian democracy
454 B.C.E.	Catastrophic defeat of Athenian fleet by Persians in Egypt kills tens of thousands of oarsmen
451 B.C.E.	Pericles sponsors law to restrict Athenian citizenship to children whose parents are both citizens
c. 450 B.C.E.	Protagoras and other Sophists begin to move to Athens to teach
446–445 B.C.E. (winter)	Peace treaty between Athens and Sparta; intended to last thirty years
431 B.C.E.	Euripides presents the tragedy *Medea*
431–404 B.C.E.	Peloponnesian War
420s B.C.E.	Herodotus finishes *Histories*, the first great Greek work of history writing
415–413 B.C.E.	Enormous Athenian military expedition against Sicily
411 B.C.E.	Aristophanes presents the comedy *Lysistrata*
404–403 B.C.E.	Rule of the Thirty Tyrants at Athens
403 B.C.E.	Restoration of democracy

KEY TERMS

agora (93)

Delian League (88)

frieze (95)

hetaira (99)

hubris (114)

metic (97)

mystery cult (97)

ostracism (91)

radical democracy (90)

Socratic method (109)

Sophists (106)

subjectivism (106)

symposium (plural "symposia") (99)

trireme (89)

REVIEW QUESTIONS

1. What differences in Greek and Persian political and military organization determined the course of the Persian Wars?

2. What factors prompted political change in fifth-century B.C.E. Athens?

3. How did new ways of thinking in the Golden Age threaten cherished traditions?

4. How did unexpected events contribute to the outcome of the Peloponnesian War?

MAKING CONNECTIONS

1. What were the most significant differences between Greece in the Archaic Age and in the Golden Age?

2. What did Greeks of the Golden Age believe it was worth spending public funds to pay for and why?

FOR FURTHER EXPLORATION

To assess your mastery of the material in this chapter, see the Online Study Guide at **bedfordstmartins.com/hunt**.

To read additional primary-source material from this period, see Chapter 3 in *Sources of The Making of the West*, Second Edition.

From the Classical to the Hellenistic World,
c. 400–30 B.C.E.

ABOUT 255 B.C.E., AN EGYPTIAN CAMEL TRADER far from home paid a scribe to write his Greek employer, Zeno, back in Egypt, to protest how Zeno's assistant, Krotos, was cheating him:

> You know that when you left me in Syria with Krotos I followed all your instructions concerning the camels and behaved blamelessly towards you. But Krotos has ignored your orders to pay me my salary; I've received nothing despite asking him for my money over and over. He just tells me to go away. I waited a long time for you to come, but when I no longer had life's necessities and couldn't get help anywhere, I had to run away . . . to keep from starving to death. . . . I am desperate summer and winter. . . . They have treated me like dirt because I am not a Greek. I therefore beg you, please, command them to pay me so that I won't go hungry just because I don't know how to speak Greek.

The trader's name and ethnic identity have been lost, but his desperate plea shows that his not being Greek hurt him. His plight—needing help from a foreigner holding power in his homeland—reflects the challenges that characterized the eastern Mediterranean world in the Hellenistic period (323–30 B.C.E.). The movement of Greeks into the Near East and their interaction with local peoples changed both the Greek and the Near Eastern worlds. War fueled this population shift. First, following the Peloponnesian War (431–404 B.C.E.), thousands

---

The Rosetta Stone
The writing on this black stone found near Rosetta in the Nile River delta allowed nineteenth-century European scholars to unlock the lost secrets of hieroglyphics; knowledge of how to read the ancient Egyptian script writing had been lost in antiquity. The three bands of text repeat the same message (praise for King Ptolemy V decreed by priests in 196 B.C.E.) in three different scripts: at the top, hieroglyphs (Egypt's oldest writing system, from around 3100 or 3000 B.C.E.), then demotic (a cursive form of Egyptian invented around 600 B.C.E.), and finally a translation into Greek. Scholars deciphered the hieroglyphs by comparing them to the Greek version, which they knew how to read. They started with royal names, which, they already guessed, were surrounded by an oval (cartouche) in hieroglyphic writing. Most Egyptians, like the badly treated camel trader stuck in Syria, could not read Greek, and most Greeks living in Egypt under the rule of the Ptolemaic kings could not read Egyptian, so bilingual texts such as the Rosetta Stone were necessary to reach the widest audience in Hellenistic Egypt. *Art Resource, NY.*

of Greeks became mercenary soldiers serving Near Eastern rulers. Later in the fourth century B.C.E., the number of Greeks living in the Near East exploded when Alexander the Great (356–323 B.C.E.) conquered the Persian Empire and planted colonies of Greeks.

Alexander's successors revived monarchy in the Greek world by carving out territories to rule. The wealth of these new kingdoms made them the dominant political powers of a new era: the Hellenistic Age. **Hellenistic**, meaning "Greek-like," suggests the blending of Greek and Near Eastern cultures that occurred in the eastern Mediterranean in this period. The dominance of the new Hellenistic kingdoms demoted Greece's city-states to second-rate status in international politics; the city-states retained local rule but lost their independence in foreign policy, which the Hellenistic kings now controlled. They imported Greeks to fill royal offices, man their armies, and run businesses. This demographic change created tension with the kings' non-Greek subjects, such as the forlorn camel trader. Immigrant Greeks, such as Zeno in Egypt, formed a social and political elite that lorded it over the kingdoms' local populations. Egyptians, Syrians, or Mesopotamians who wanted to rise in society had to win the support of these Greeks and learn their language. Otherwise, they were likely to find themselves as powerless as the hungry camel merchant.

Over time, the Near East's local cultures interacted with the Greek overlords' culture to spawn a multicultural synthesis. Locals married Greeks, shared their religious traditions with the newcomers, taught them their agricultural and scientific knowledge, and learned Greek to win administrative jobs. Although Hellenistic royal society always remained hierarchical, with Greeks at the top, and never eliminated tension between rulers and ruled, it did promote innovations in art, science, philosophy, and religion by combining Near Eastern and Greek traditions. The Hellenistic kingdoms fell in the second and first centuries B.C.E. when the Romans overthrew them one by one.

The Hellenistic period's cultural interaction provided its greatest legacy to later times. Its mixing of peoples and ideas influenced Roman civilization and therefore later Western civilization. Artistic, scientific, philosophical, and religious innovations persisted even after the glory of Greece's Golden Age had faded, especially since Hellenistic religion provided the background for Christianity.

❖ Classical Greece's Decline, c. 400–350 B.C.E.

The Peloponnesian War (431–404 B.C.E.) destroyed Greece's Golden Age. The defeated Athenians regained a tolerable standard of living in the early fourth century B.C.E., but many remained bitter toward fellow citizens, whom they blamed for the Thirty Tyrants' murderous rule in 404–403 B.C.E. This tension culminated in the execution of Socrates, whose death spurred Plato and Aristotle to develop Greece's most famous philosophies about right and wrong and how human beings should live.

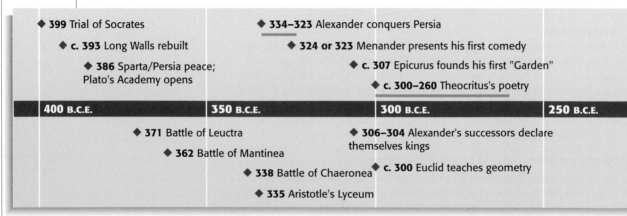

◆ **399** Trial of Socrates

◆ **c. 393** Long Walls rebuilt

◆ **386** Sparta/Persia peace; Plato's Academy opens

◆ **334–323** Alexander conquers Persia

◆ **324 or 323** Menander presents his first comedy

◆ **c. 307** Epicurus founds his first "Garden"

◆ **c. 300–260** Theocritus's poetry

| **400 B.C.E.** | **350 B.C.E.** | **300 B.C.E.** | **250 B.C.E.** |

◆ **371** Battle of Leuctra

◆ **362** Battle of Mantinea

◆ **338** Battle of Chaeronea

◆ **335** Aristotle's Lyceum

◆ **306–304** Alexander's successors declare themselves kings

◆ **c. 300** Euclid teaches geometry

The Spartans tried to turn their Peloponnesian War victory into international power. Their collaboration with the Persian Empire, along with their aggressive policy toward other Greek states, stirred up violent resistance from Thebes and Athens. By the 350s B.C.E., this bloody squabbling had so weakened the Greek city-states that they failed to counter the expansion of the Macedonian kingdom (Alexander the Great's homeland). This decline in power precipitated the fall of Classical Greece.

Restoring Daily Life in Postwar Athens

Spartan invaders during the Peloponnesian War had ruined the lives and farms of many Athenians who lived in the countryside. The devastation of the economy and overcrowding in wartime Athens produced friction between rural refugees and city dwellers. Middle-class women whose husbands and brothers had died during the conflict saw their lives change against their will. Traditionally they had woven cloth for their families and supervised the household slaves, but the men had earned the family's income by farming or working at a trade. Now, with no man to provide for them and their children, many war widows had to work outside the home. The only possibilities open to them were low-paying jobs such as wet nursing, weaving, or laboring in Athens's vineyards.

Resourceful Athenians found ways to profit from women's skills. The family of Socrates' friend Aristarchus,♦ for example, became

♦**Aristarchus:** ar uh STAHR kuhs

Vase Painting of Women Fetching Water
This vase painting depicts a scene from everyday life in a Greek city: women filling water jugs from the gushing spouts of a public fountain to take back to their homes. Both freeborn and slave women fetched water for their households' drinking, cooking, washing, and cleaning needs, as almost no Greek homes had running water. Prosperous cities built attractive fountain houses such as this one, which dispensed fresh water from springs or piped it in through small aqueducts. (compare the large Roman aqueduct on page 181). Women often gathered at fountains for conversation with people from outside their household. The women in this scene wear the long robes and hair coverings characteristic of the time. *Museum of Fine Arts, Boston. William Francis Warden Fund. Photograph © 2004 Museum of Fine Arts, Boston (61.195).*

poverty-stricken when several widowed sisters, nieces, and female cousins moved in. Aristarchus complained to Socrates that he had too little income to support his new family of fourteen plus their slaves. Socrates replied that the women knew how to make men's and women's cloaks, shirts, capes,

◆ **c. 195** Laodice funds dowries

◆ **167** Maccabee revolt

◆ **30**
Death of
Cleopatra

| 200 B.C.E. | 150 B.C.E. | 100 B.C.E. | 50 B.C.E. |

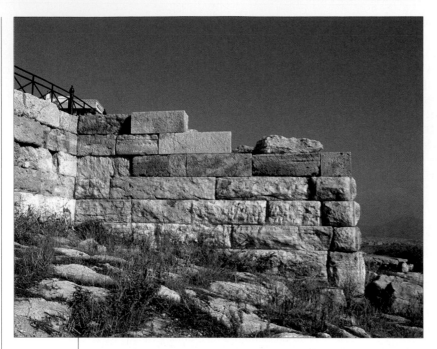

The Long Walls of Athens

In the fifth century B.C.E., at the height of its naval power, Athens had made itself impregnable to attack by extending its fortification walls in a corridor called the Long Walls that stretched from the ring around the city center to the harbor of Piraeus several miles to the west. This section, which stood near the water where the walls protected the port entrance, shows the close-fitting blocks forming the exterior of the walls. The victorious Spartans forced the Athenians to demolish the Long Walls after the Peloponnesian War ended in 404 B.C.E. When the Athenians regained their freedom in the following year, they set out to repair the walls. When they finished in 393 B.C.E., their city had regained its ability to defend itself against invasion, and the Athenians soon embarked on rebuilding their naval empire. *Craig and Marie Mauzy, mauzy@otenet.gr.*

and smocks, "the work considered the best and most fitting for women." He suggested they begin to sell the clothes outside the home. This plan succeeded financially, but the women complained that Aristarchus was the household's only member who ate without working. Socrates advised his friend to reply that the women should think of him as sheep did a guard dog— he earned his share of the food by keeping the wolves away.

Athens's postwar economy recovered strength because private business owners and households engaged in trade and produced manufactured goods in their homes and small shops, such as metal foundries and pottery workshops. Greek businesses, usually run by families, never grew large; the largest known was a shield-making company employing 120 slaves. The return of prosperity, coupled with the greater flexibility in work roles for men and women that the war had produced, led to some change in occupations formerly defined by gender. For example, men began working alongside women in cloth production in this period, when the first commercial weaving shops outside the home sprang up. Later in the fourth century B.C.E., some women made careers in the arts, especially painting and music, which men had traditionally dominated.

The rebuilding by 393 B.C.E. of Athens's Long Walls, which connected the city to the port and had been destroyed at war's end, boosted the economy. These fortifications protected the ships importing grain to feed the population and made conducting business safe for international traders. A brisk commerce therefore resumed in grain, wine, pottery, and some silver from Athens's mines. The refortified harbor also allowed Athens to begin to rebuild its navy, which increased employment opportunities for poor men.

Daily life remained tough for working people even in an improving economy. Most workers earned only enough to feed and clothe their families. They usually ate two meals a day, a light one at midmorning and a heavier evening meal. Bread baked from barley provided their main food; only rich people could afford wheat bread. A family bought bread from small bakery stands, often run by women, or made it at home, with the

Athens's Long Walls as Rebuilt after the Peloponnesian War

wife directing the slaves in grinding the grain, shaping the dough, and baking it in a pottery oven heated by charcoal. People topped their bread with greens, beans, onions, garlic, olives, fruit, and cheese. Most people had meat only after animal sacrifices paid for by the state; the few households wealthy enough to afford meat at home boiled or grilled it over a fire. Everyone of all ages drank wine, diluted with water, with every meal. Women and slaves fetched drinking water in jugs from public fountains.

The Execution of Socrates, 399 B.C.E.

Even though most Athenians' daily lives returned to old patterns after the war, people remembered the horror of the reign of the Thirty Tyrants. Their bitter feelings created tensions that economic improvement did not relieve. The Athenian philosopher Socrates became the most famous victim of this bitterness. Since an amnesty prohibited prosecutions for crimes committed under the Thirty Tyrants, angry citizens had to find other charges against those they hated. Several prominent democratic Athenians felt this way about Socrates: they blamed him because his follower Critias had been one of the Thirty's most violent members.

Socrates's opponents charged him with impiety, a crime under Athenian law. His accusers said Socrates's philosophy angered the gods and therefore threatened divine punishment for the city. They argued their case in 399 B.C.E. before a jury of 501 male citizens, who had been chosen by lottery from that year's pool of eligible men. Their case presented religious and moral arguments: Socrates, they claimed, rejected the city-state's gods, introduced new divinities, and lured young men away from Athenian moral traditions. When Socrates spoke in his own defense, he refused to beg for sympathy, as was usual; instead, he repeated his dedication to goading his fellow citizens into examining their moral preconceptions. He vowed to remain their stinging gadfly no matter what.

When the jurors narrowly voted to convict, standard Athenian legal procedure required them to decide between alternative penalties proposed by the prosecutors and

the defendant. The prosecutors proposed death. Everyone expected Socrates to offer exile as an alternative and the jury to accept it. The philosopher, however, said that he deserved a reward rather than a punishment, until his friends made him propose a fine as his penalty. The jury chose death. Socrates accepted his sentence calmly because, as he put it, "no evil can befall a good man either in life or in death." He was executed with a poisonous drink concocted from powdered hemlock. Executing Socrates did not resolve Athens's postwar tension. Ancient sources report that many Athenians soon came to regret his punishment as a tragic mistake and a severe blow to their reputation.

The Philosophy of Plato and Aristotle

Socrates' death made his most famous follower, Plato (c. 429–348 B.C.E.), hate democracy. From a well-to-do family, Plato started out trying to right what he saw as democracy's wrongs by promoting the rule of philosopher-tyrants as the best form of government. He served as political adviser to Dionysius, ruler of Syracuse in Sicily, but when he failed to turn him into an ideal ruler, Plato gave up hope that everyday politics could stop violence and greed. Instead, he devoted himself to talking and writing about philosophy as the guide to life and established a philosophical school, the Academy, in Athens around 386 B.C.E. It was not a school in the modern sense but rather an informal association of people who studied philosophy, mathematics, and theoretical astronomy under the leader's guidance. The Academy attracted intellectuals to Athens for the next nine hundred years, and Plato's ideas about the nature of reality, ethics, and politics have remained central to philosophy and political science to this day.

Plato's legacy also includes inspiring his most famous pupil, Aristotle (384–322 B.C.E.). The son of a wealthy doctor in northern Greece, Aristotle came to study in Plato's Academy at the age of seventeen. From 342 to 335 B.C.E. he earned a living by tutoring the young Alexander the Great in Macedonia. Returning to Athens, Aristotle founded his

Mosaic Depicting Plato's Academy

This Roman-era mosaic depicts philosophers—identified by their beards—at Plato's school (called the Academy after the name of a local mythological hero) in Athens holding discussions among themselves. The Academy, founded about 386 B.C.E., became one of Greece's most famous and long-lasting institutions, attracting scholars and students for more than nine hundred years until it closed under the Byzantine emperor Justinian in 529 C.E. The columns and the tree in the mosaic express the harmonious blend of the natural and built environment of the Academy, which was meant to promote productive and pleasant discussions. What message do the philosophers' bare chests convey? Compare the style of dress of the Spartan men on a hunt on page 71 and the Athenian men at a music lesson on page 76. *Erich Lessing/Art Resource, NY.*

own school, the Lyceum,✦ and taught his own life-guiding philosophy, based on logic, scientific knowledge, and practical experience. His vast writings made him one of the world's most influential thinkers.

Plato's Ethical Thought. Plato's intellectual interests covered astronomy, mathematics, political philosophy, ethics, and **metaphysics** (ideas about the ultimate nature of reality beyond the reach of the human senses). His innovative views on the nature of

reality underlay his ethics. He presented his ideas in dialogues, which usually featured Socrates conversing with a variety of people. Plato wrote to provoke readers into thoughtful reflection, not to prescribe a set of beliefs; nowhere did he offer a single set of doctrines. Nevertheless, he always maintained one essential idea based on his view of reality: ultimate moral qualities are universal, unchanging, and absolute, not relative.

Plato's dialogues teach that ethical qualities such as justice, goodness, beauty, or equality exist on their own outside our world and are not defined by our experience of them in our daily lives. Any earthly examples of them can always display the opposite quality. For example, returning what you have borrowed might seem like justice. But what if you borrow a friend's weapon and then discover your friend wants the weapon back to commit murder? Returning the borrowed item would then support injustice. For Plato, every virtue and every quality is relative in the context of the world that we humans experience with our senses.

Plato used the term *Forms* (or *Ideas*) to describe the abstract and ultimate realities of ethical qualities. Goodness, Justice, Beauty, Equality and exist as Forms. Forms are invisible, invariable, and eternal entities located in a higher realm beyond the daily world. According to Plato, the Forms are the only genuine reality; the qualities and other things that we perceive with our senses on earth are only dim and imperfect copies of these metaphysical realities. Our experiences, he said, are like us watching shadows of ultimate realities cast on the wall of a cave. The difficult notion of Forms, which made metaphysics an important issue for philosophers, exemplifies the complexity of Plato's philosophy.

Plato's ideas about the soul also had a profound influence on later thought. He believed that humans possess immortal souls distinct from their bodies; this idea established the concept of **dualism**, a separation between spiritual and physical being. Plato furthermore explained that the human soul possesses preexisting knowledge put there by a deity. Plato called this god the Demiurge✦ (literally, "craftsman") because the deity uses

✦**Lyceum:** lye SEE uhm

✦**Demiurge:** DEH mee urj

the Forms as his guide in crafting living beings out of raw matter. The world has order because a knowing, rational god created it. Furthermore, living beings have goals, such as animals adapting to their environments to survive. The Demiurge wanted to reproduce the Forms' perfect order in the material world, but the world turned out imperfect because matter is imperfect.

Plato believed our life's goal is to seek perfect order and purity in our own souls by using rational thought to control our irrational and therefore harmful desires. The desire to drink excessive alcohol, for example, is irrational and harmful because the one who binges fails to consider the hangover that follows. People who yield to irrational desires fail to consider the future of their body and soul. Finally, our present, impure existence is only a temporary stage in our cosmic existence because while the body does not last, the soul is immortal.

Plato's *Republic*.   Plato presented his most famous ideas on politics in his dialogue *The Republic*. This work, whose Greek title actually means "System of Government," primarily concerns the nature of justice and the reasons people should be just instead of unjust. For Plato, democracy cannot create justice because people on their own cannot rise above narrow self-interest to knowledge of any universal truth. Justice can come only under the rule of an enlightened oligarchy or monarchy. Therefore, a just society requires a strict hierarchy.

Plato's *Republic* envisions an ideal society stratified into three classes of people distinguished by their ability to grasp the truth of Forms. The highest class constitutes the rulers, or "guardians," who must be educated in mathematics, astronomy, and metaphysics. Next come the "auxiliaries," who defend the community. "Producers" make up the bottom class; they grow food and make objects for the whole population. Each class contributes to society by fulfilling its proper function in the hierarchy.

Women as well as men can be guardians because they possess the same virtues and abilities as men, except for a disparity in physical strength between the average woman and the average man. To minimize

distraction, guardians are to have neither private property nor nuclear families. Male and female guardians are to live in houses shared in common, to eat in the same mess halls, and to exercise in the same gymnasiums. They are to have sexual relations with various partners so that the best women can mate with the best men to produce the best children. The children are to be raised together in a common environment by special caretakers. The guardians who achieve the highest level of knowledge in Plato's ideal society qualify to rule as philosopher-kings.

Plato did not think that human beings could actually create this ideal society, but he did believe that imagining it was an important way to help people learn to live justly. That is, he passionately believed that philosophy mattered to human life.

Aristotle, Scientist and Philosopher.
Aristotle's reputation rests on his scientific investigation of the natural world and development of rigorous systems of logical argument. He regarded science and philosophy not as abstract subjects isolated from the concerns of ordinary existence but as the disciplined search for knowledge in every aspect of life. That search brought the good life and genuine happiness. Like Plato, Aristotle criticized democracy because it allowed uneducated instead of "better" people to control politics. He nevertheless chose Athens as the site of his school,

Aristotle's Lyceum, established 335 B.C.E.

the Lyceum (founded 335 B.C.E.), because the city's cosmopolitan atmosphere attracted the wealthy young men he needed as pupils. Later called the Peripatetic School after the covered walkway (*peripatos*) where his students conversed as they strolled, Aristotle's school became world famous. He lectured with dazzling intelligence on biology, medicine, anatomy, psychology, meteorology, physics, chemistry, mathematics, music, metaphysics, rhetoric, literary criticism, political science, and ethics. He also invented a system of logic for precise argumentation. By creating ways to identify valid arguments, Aristotle established grounds for distinguishing a logically sound case from a merely persuasive one.

Aristotle required explanations to be based on common sense rather than metaphysics. He denied the validity of Plato's theory of Forms because, he said, the separate existence Plato postulated for Forms was not subject to demonstrable logic or proof. Furthermore, Aristotle believed that the best way to understand anything was to observe it in its natural setting. He coupled detailed investigation with perceptive reasoning in biology, botany, and zoology. He was the first investigator to try to collect and classify all the available information on the animal species, recording facts and advancing knowledge about more than five hundred different kinds of animals, including insects. His recognition that whales and dolphins are mammals, for example, was overlooked by later writers on animals and not rediscovered for another two thousand years.

Some of Aristotle's views justified inequalities characteristic of his time. He regarded slavery as natural, arguing that some people were slaves by nature because their souls lacked the rational part that should rule in a human. He also concluded, on the basis of faulty biological observations, that nature made women inferior to men. He wrongly believed, for example, that in procreation the male's semen actively gave the fetus its design, whereas the female passively provided its matter. He justified his assertion that females were less courageous than males by mistaken evidence about animals, such as the report that a male squid would stay by as if to help when its mate was speared but that a female squid would swim away when the male was impaled. Erroneous biological information led Aristotle to evaluate females as incomplete males, a conclusion with disastrous results for later thought. At the same time, he believed that human communities could be successful and happy only if women and men both contributed. (See "Aristotle on the Nature of the Greek Polis," opposite.)

In ethics, Aristotle emphasized the need to develop practical habits of just behavior. People should achieve self-control by training their minds to win out over instincts and passions, as Plato believed. Self-control did not mean denying human desires and appetites; rather, it meant finding the **mean**, or balance, between suppressing and heedlessly indulging physical yearnings. Aristotle claimed that the mind should rule in finding this balance because the intellect is the finest human quality and the mind is the true self—indeed, the godlike part of a person.

Aristotle helped the study of ethics by insisting that standards of right and wrong have merit only if they are grounded in character and aligned with the good in human nature; they cannot work if they consist of lists of abstract reasons for behaving in one way rather than another. That is, an ethical system must be relevant to the actual moral situations people experience. In his ethical thought, as in all his scholarship, Aristotle distinguished himself by insisting that the life of the mind and experience of the real world are inseparable in defining a worthwhile existence for human beings.

> **Review:** What were the major differences between Plato's philosophical ideas and Aristotle's?

Greek Political Disunity

During the same period in which Plato taught and Aristotle began his studies—the fifty years following the Peloponnesian War—the rival city-states of Sparta, Thebes,♦ and Athens each in turn fought to dominate Greece. None succeeded. Their wars sapped their strength, leaving Greek independence susceptible to external threat.

The Spartans provoked fatal disunity by trying to conquer other city-states. Their general Lysander pursued an aggressive policy in Anatolia and northern Greece in the 390s B.C.E., and other Spartan commanders meddled in Sicily. Thebes, Athens, Corinth, and Argos then formed an anti-Spartan coalition. The Spartans checkmated the alliance by coming to terms with the Persian king. In a blatant renunciation of their traditional claim to defend Greek freedom, the Spartans

---

♦**Thebes:** theebs

Aristotle on the Nature of the Greek Polis

Aristotle's famous book Politics *probably represents his lecture notes on the origins of political states and his analysis of the different ways to organize them. In this excerpt, Aristotle argues that the origin of the polis, the most common Greek political state after the Dark Age, is found in nature. This approach reveals Aristotle's method of examining things by starting with their most fundamental characteristics.*

Since we see that every city-state [polis] is a type of partnership and that every partnership is established for the sake of some good, for everything that everyone does is motivated by what seems to them to be a good, it is clear that, with all partnerships aiming at some good, the most authoritative partnership, which includes all other partnerships, does this the most of all and aims at the most authoritative of all goods. This one is what is called the polis, that is, the political partnership....

If one looks at things as they grow from the beginning, one will make the best observations, on this topic and all others. Necessity first brings together those who cannot exist without each other, that is, on the one hand, the female and the male for the purpose of reproduction, and this not a matter of choice, but just as with the other animals and with plants, it is a matter of nature to desire to leave behind another of the same kind; on the other hand, [necessity brings together] the ruler and the one who is naturally ruled for the sake of security, for the one who is able to foresee things with his mind is by nature a ruler and by nature a master, while the one who is able to do things with his body is the one who is ruled and is by nature a slave. For this reason the same thing benefits master and slave. Nature distinguishes between the female and the slave,...but among the barbarians the female and the slave have the same status. The reason is that they do not have rule by nature, but there exists a partnership of them as female slave and male slave. For this

reason the poets say, "It is fitting for Greeks to rule barbarians,"[1] on the grounds that being a barbarian and being a slave are by nature the same.

From these two partnerships comes first the household, and Hesiod spoke correctly, saying, "First of all, [get yourself] a house and a wife and an ox for plowing,"[2] because the ox is a household slave for a poor man. Therefore, the partnership that is established first by nature for everyday purposes is the household....

The partnership that first arises from multiple households for the sake of more than everyday needs is the village. The village especially seems by nature to be a colony from the household....

The final partnership of multiple villages is the city-state, which possesses the limit of self-sufficiency, so to speak. It comes into being for the sake of living, but it exists for the sake of living well. Every city-state therefore exists by nature, if it is true that the first partnerships do. For the city-state is the goal or end of the others, and nature is a goal or end, because, that which each thing is when its growth is at an end, is what we say is the nature of each thing, whether a human being, or a horse, or a household. And that for which something exists is its best goal or end. Self-sufficiency is a goal or an end and is best. From these things it is clear that the city-state belongs to the things existing by nature, and that humans are beings who by nature live in a city-state, and that the one who has no city-state by nature and not by chance is either a simple fool or superhuman....So, indeed, the city-state is by nature prior to the household and to each of us.

---

[1] A quotation from Euripides, *Iphigenia at Aulis*, line 1400.
[2] A quotation from *Works and Days*, line 405.

Source: Aristotle, *Politics*, Book 1.1–2, 1252a1–1253a19. Translation by Thomas R. Martin.

acknowledged the Persian ruler's right to control the Greek city-states of Anatolia—in return for permission to pursue their own interests in Greece without Persian interference. This agreement of 386 B.C.E., called the King's Peace, effectively sold out the Greeks of Anatolia, returning them to their dependent status of a century earlier in the days before the Greek victory in the Persian Wars.

The Athenians rebuilt their military strength to combat Sparta. The reconstructed Long Walls restored Athens's invulnerability to invasion, and a new kind of light infantry—the *peltast*, armed with a small leather shield, javelins, and sword—fighting alongside hoplites gave Athenian ground forces more tactical mobility and flexibility. Most important, the navy regained its offensive strength, and by 377 B.C.E. Athens had again become the leader of a naval alliance of Greek city-states. This time the league members insisted that their rights be specified in writing to prevent a recurrence of high-handed Athenian behavior.

The Thebans, fighting hard to block Spartan power, became Greece's main power in the 370s B.C.E. through brilliant generalship. They dashed Sparta's dreams by crushing its invasion force at Leuctra◆ in Boeotia◆ in 371 B.C.E. and then attacking the Spartan homeland in the Peloponnese. They destroyed Spartan power forever by freeing many Helots. This Theban success so frightened the Athenians, whose city was only forty miles from Thebes, that they made a temporary alliance with their hated enemies the Spartans. Their combined armies confronted the Thebans in the Peloponnese in 362 B.C.E., in the battle of Mantinea.◆ Thebes won the battle but lost the war when its best general was killed and no capable replacement could be found.

The battle of Mantinea left the Greek city-states in impotent disunity. The contemporary historian Xenophon succinctly summed up the situation after 362 B.C.E.: "Everyone had supposed that this battle's winners would become Greece's rulers and its losers their subjects; but there was only

more confusion and disturbance in Greece after Mantinea than before." This judgment was confirmed when the Athenian naval alliance fell apart in a war between Athens and its allies over the close ties some allies were developing with Persia and Macedonia.

By the mid 350s B.C.E., then, no Greek city-state had the power to rule anything except its own territory. This state of mutual weakness crippled foreign policy, which depended on military power. The Greek city-states' struggle for supremacy over one another, begun long before in the Peloponnesian War, had thus finally petered out in a stalemate of exhaustion. By failing to cooperate, the Greeks opened the way for the rise of a new power—the kingdom of Macedonia—that ended their independence.

❖ The Rise of Macedonia, 359–323 B.C.E.

The kingdom of Macedonia, located north of the Greek heartland, made itself an international superpower by taking advantage of the Greek city-states' constant wars. That this formerly minor kingdom seized the leadership of Greece and conquered the Persian Empire counts as one of the greatest surprises in ancient military and political history. Two aggressive and charismatic Macedonian kings produced this transformation: Philip II (r. 359–336 B.C.E.) and his son Alexander the Great (r. 336–323 B.C.E.). Their conquests ended the Greek Classical Age and began the Hellenistic Age's cultural changes.

The Roots of Macedonian Power

The Macedonians' power sprang from the characteristics of their monarchy and their people's ethnic pride. Macedonian kings did not rule in isolation—they had to listen to their people, who had freedom of speech to tell their monarchs what needed improvement. The king could govern only by winning the nobles' support because they ranked as the king's social equals and controlled large bands of followers. Macedonian men spent their time training for war, hunting, and drinking heavily. The king had to excel in

---

◆**Leuctra:** LOOK truh
◆**Boeotia:** bee OH shah
◆**Mantinea:** man tih NEE uh

these activities to show that he was capable of leading the state. Queens and royal mothers received respect because they came from powerful families in the nobility or the ruling houses of lands bordering Macedonia. In the king's absence these royal women could wield power at court.

Macedonians thought of themselves as Greek by blood and took great pride in their identity. They spoke their own language, related to Greek but not comprehensible to Greeks, and Macedonian nobles routinely learned to speak Greek. Nevertheless, Macedonians looked down on Greeks as too soft to survive life in their northern land. The Greeks reciprocated this scorn. The famed Athenian orator Demosthenes♦ (384–322 B.C.E.) lambasted Philip II as "not only not a Greek nor related to the Greeks, but not even a barbarian from a land worth mentioning; no, he's a pestilence from Macedonia, a region where you can't even buy a slave worth his salt." These mutually hostile attitudes made cooperation between Macedonians and Greeks difficult.

The Rule of Philip II, 359–336 B.C.E.

King Philip II forged Macedonia into an international power against heavy odds. Before his reign, frequent strife between royals and nobles had pre-

♦**Demosthenes:** dih MAHS thuh neez

vented the kingdom from reaching its military potential. Indeed, kings so feared their own countrymen that they stationed bodyguards outside the royal bedroom. Princes married earlier than did ordinary men, soon after the age of twenty, because the instability of the kingship demanded male heirs as soon as possible.

A military disaster in 359 B.C.E. had brought Philip to the throne at a desperate moment. The Illyrians, hostile neighbors to the north, had slaughtered the previous king and four thousand troops. Philip immediately persuaded the nobles to recognize him as king in place of his infant nephew. He then restored the army's confidence by teaching the hoplites an unstoppable new tactic with their thrusting spears, which reached sixteen feet long and took two hands to wield: arranging them in the traditional phalanx formation, he created deep blocks of soldiers whose front

Gilded Wine Bowl

This large metal bowl was discovered at Derveni in Macedonia. Its artistic style dates it to the 330s B.C.E. Wealthy Macedonian men attending Greek-style drinking parties (symposia) used these expensive vessels to dilute wine with water so that they could imbibe greater quantities. The excited states of the two figures—a satyr and a female worshiper of Dionysus, the god of wine and pleasure (page 63)—expressed the ecstatic joy the partygoers wanted to achieve. Since erect penises are depicted frequently in Greek and Macedonian art connected with Dionysus, probably to represent hopes for fertility and sexual enjoyment, pictures of them evidently were not regarded as obscene. *Thessalonike, Archaeological Museum, © Archaeological Receipts Fund.*

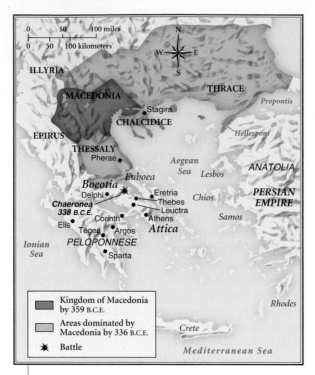

MAP 4.1 Expansion of Macedonia under Philip II, 359–336 B.C.E.
Geographic and cultural factors drove Macedonian expansion southward: mountainous terrain and war-like people blocked the way northward, while the Macedonian royal house saw itself as ethnically Greek and therefore rightfully linked to Greece to the south. King Philip II made himself the leader of Greece by convincing the Thessalians to follow his leadership in the 340s B.C.E. and then by defeating a Greek coalition led by Athens at the battle of Chaeronea in 338 B.C.E. Sparta, far from Macedonia in the southern Peloponnese, kept out of the fray; its dwindling population had made it too weak to matter.

lines bristled with outstretched spears like a lethal porcupine. Then he trained them to move around in battle in different directions without losing their formation. By moving as a unit, a mobile phalanx armed with such long spears could shove opposing forces aside. Deploying cavalry as a strike force to soften up the enemy while also protecting the infantry's flanks, Philip used his reorganized army to rout the Illyrians in the field, while at home he eliminated his local rivals for the kingship.

Philip promptly embarked on a whirl-wind of diplomacy, bribery, and military ac-

tion to force the Greek city-states to follow his lead in foreign policy. A Greek contemporary, the historian Theopompus of Chios,◆ labeled Philip "insatiable and extravagant; he did everything in a hurry…he never spared the time to reckon up his income and expenditure." By the late 340s B.C.E., Philip had cajoled or coerced most of northern Greece to fall into line behind him. Seeking glory for Greece and fearing the instability his reinvigorated army would create in his kingdom if the soldiers had nothing to do, he set his sights on leading a united Macedonian and Greek army to conquer the Persian Empire.

Philip turned to Greek history to justify attacking Persia: revenge for the Persian invasion in the Persian Wars 150 years earlier. Some Greeks remained unconvinced. At Athens, Demosthenes used stirring rhetoric to criticize Greeks for not resisting Philip. They stood by, he thundered, "as if Philip were a hailstorm, praying that he would not come their way, but not trying to do anything to head him off." Moved by his words, Athens and Thebes rallied a coalition of southern Greek city-states to combat Philip, but in 338 B.C.E. the Macedonian king and his Greek allies trounced the coalition's forces at the battle of Chaeronea◆ in Boeotia (Map 4.1). The defeated city-states retained their internal freedom, but Philip compelled them to join the alliance under his undisputed leadership. The battle of Chaeronea was a decisive turning point in Greek history: never again would the city-states of Greece be independent actors in international politics. City-states remained Greece's central social and economic units, but they were always looking over their shoulders, worrying about the powerful kings who wanted to control them.

The Rule of Alexander the Great, 336–323 B.C.E.

Philip's son Alexander III stepped onto center stage in 336 B.C.E. when a Macedonian assassinated Philip. Rumors swirled that Alexander's mother, Olympias, had instigated the murder to procure the throne for her son.

◆**Theopompus of Chios:** thee oh PAHM puhs (of) KY ahs

◆**Chaeronea:** kehr uh NEE uh

Mosaic of Alexander the Great at the Battle of Issus
This large mosaic, which served as a floor in an upscale Roman house, was a copy of a famous
painting of the battle of Issus of 333 B.C.E. It shows Alexander the Great on his warhorse Bucephalus
confronting the Persian king Darius in his chariot. Darius reaches out in compassion for the warriors
who are selflessly throwing themselves in the way to protect him. The original artist was an extremely
skilled painter, as revealed by the dramatic foreshortening of the horse right in front of Darius and by
the startling effect of the face of the dying warrior reflected in the polished shield just to the right of
the horse. Do you think the painting expresses more about Alexander or about Darius? *Erich Lessing/
Art Resource, NY.*

The twenty-year-old Alexander murdered his
rivals, forcing the nobles to recognize him as
king. Next, he subdued Macedonia's enemies
to the west and north with several lightning-
fast strikes. Finally, Alexander compelled
the southern Greeks, who had defected from
the alliance at the news of Philip's death, to
rejoin. To demonstrate the price of disloyalty,
in 335 B.C.E. Alexander destroyed Thebes for
having rebelled.

Conquering the Persian Empire. In 334
B.C.E. Alexander launched the most astonishing military campaign in ancient history by
leading a Macedonian and Greek army
against the Persian king Darius III to fulfill
Philip's dream of avenging Greece. Alexander's feat in conquering all the lands from
Turkey to Egypt to Uzbekistan while still in

his twenties earned him the title "the Great"
in later ages. In his own time his greatness
flowed from his motivating his men to follow
him into hostile, unknown regions and deploying cavalry charges to disrupt the enemy's
infantry.

Alexander inspired his troops by reckless
disregard for his own safety in battle. He often led the charge against the enemy's front
line, riding his warhorse Bucephalus◆ (literally, "Oxhead"). Everyone saw him speeding
ahead wearing his plumed helmet, vividly
colored cloak, and armor polished to reflect
the sun. He was so intent on conquering
distant lands that he rejected advice to delay
his departure from Macedonia until he had
married and fathered an heir. He further

◆**Bucephalus:** byoo SEHF uh luhs

alarmed his principal adviser by giving away virtually all his land and property to strengthen the army, thereby creating new landowners who would furnish troops. "What," the adviser asked, "do you have left for yourself?" "My hopes," Alexander replied. Alexander's hopes centered on making himself a warrior as splendid as the incomparable Achilles of Homer's *Iliad*; he always kept a copy of the *Iliad* under his pillow—along with a dagger.

Alexander displayed his heroic ambitions as his army advanced relentlessly through Persian territory. In Anatolia, he visited Gordion, where an oracle had promised the lordship of Asia to whoever could untie a massive knot of rope tying the yoke of an ancient chariot. The young king, so the story goes, cut the Gordian knot with his sword. When Alexander later captured King Darius's wives and daughters, he treated the women with respect. His honorable behavior toward the Persian royal women enhanced his reputation among the Persians.

Alexander complemented his personal qualities with an engineer's eye for better military technology. When Tyre, a heavily fortified city on an island off the eastern Mediterranean, refused to surrender to him in 332 B.C.E., he built a massive stone pier out into the sea as a platform for artillery towers, armored battering rams, and catapults flinging boulders to breach Tyre's walls. The successful use of this siege technology against Tyre showed that walls alone could no longer protect city-states. The knowledge that a technologically equipped army could break through their defenses made enemies much readier to negotiate a deal.

After Alexander conquered Egypt and the Persian heartland, he revealed his strategy for ruling this vast empire: establishing cities of Greeks and Macedonians in conquered territory while keeping an area's traditional administrative system. In Egypt, he established his first new city, naming it Alexandria after himself. In Persia, he proclaimed himself the king of Asia and left the existing governing units intact, retaining various Persian administrators. For the Persian Empire's local populations, therefore, the Macedonian Alexander's becoming the Per-

sian king changed their lives not a bit. They continued to send the same taxes to a remote master, whom they rarely if ever saw.

Marching to India and Back. So fierce was Alexander's heroic love of conquest and adventure that he led his army past the Persian heartland farther east into territory hardly known to the Greeks (Map 4.2). He apparently aimed to outdo the heroes of legend by marching to the end of the world. Paring his army to reduce the need for supplies, he led it northeast into the trackless steppes of Bactria and Sogdiana (modern Afghanistan and Uzbekistan). On the Jaxartes◆ River (Syr Darya), he founded a city called Alexandria the Furthest to show that he had penetrated deeper into this region than even Cyrus, the founder of the Persian Empire. When it proved impossible to subdue the highly mobile locals, however, Alexander settled for an alliance sealed by his marriage to the Bactrian princess Roxane.

Alexander then headed east into India. Seventy days of marching through monsoon rains extinguished his soldiers' fire for conquest. In the spring of 326 B.C.E., they mutinied on the banks of the Hyphasis◆ River in western India and forced Alexander to turn back. The return journey through southeastern Iran's scorching deserts cost many casualties from hunger and thirst; the survivors finally reached safety back in the Persian heartland in 324 B.C.E. Alexander immediately began planning an invasion of the Arabian peninsula and, after that, of all North Africa west of Egypt.

Alexander ruled more harshly after his return and began treating the Greeks as subjects instead of allies. Despite his earlier promise to respect the city-states' internal freedom, he ordered them to restore citizenship to the many exiles created by war, whose status as wandering, stateless persons was causing unrest. Even more striking was Alexander's announcement that he wished to receive the honors due a god. Initially dumbfounded by this request, most Greek city-states soon complied by sending honorary religious delegations to him. The Spartan

◆**Jaxartes:** jak SAHR teez
◆**Hyphasis:** Hy FAH sihs

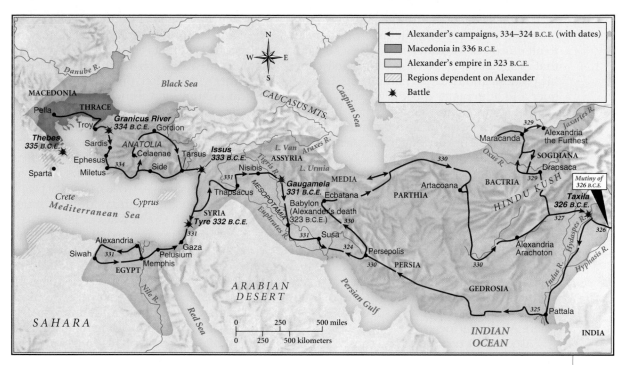

MAP 4.2 Conquests of Alexander the Great, 336–323 B.C.E.
The scale of Alexander's military campaigns in Asia made him a legend; from the time he led his army out of Macedonia and Greece in 334 B.C.E. until his death in Babylon in 323 B.C.E., he was continually on the move. His careful intelligence gathering combined with his charismatic and fearless generalship generated an unbroken string of victories, while his skillful choice of regional administrators, founding of garrison cities, and preservation of local governing structures kept his conquests stable after he moved on.

Damis pithily expressed the only prudent position on Alexander's deification: "If Alexander wishes to be a god, then we'll agree that he be called a god."

Personal rather than political motives best explain Alexander's announcement. He had come to believe he was actually the son of Zeus; after all, Greek mythology reported that Zeus had mated with many human females who produced children. Most of Zeus's legendary offspring were mortal, but Alexander's superhuman conquests proved that he had surpassed them. Since Alexander's accomplishments demonstrated that he had achieved godlike power, he therefore must be a god himself. Alexander's divinity was, in ancient terms, a natural consequence of his power.

Alexander's premature death from a fever and heavy drinking on June 10, 323 B.C.E., aborted his plan to conquer Arabia and North Africa. His death followed months of depression provoked by the death of his best friend, Hephaistion.♦ Close since their boyhood, Alexander and Hephaistion were probably lovers. Like Pericles, Alexander had made no plans about what should happen if he died unexpectedly. Roxane gave birth to their first child a few months after Alexander's death. The story goes that, when at Alexander's deathbed his commanders asked him to whom he bequeathed his kingdom, he replied, "To the most powerful."

Alexander's Impact. Modern scholars disagree on almost everything about Alexander, from whether his claim to divinity was meant to justify his increasingly authoritarian attitude toward the Greek city-states, to what his expedition was meant to achieve. They also offer different assessments of his character, ranging from bloodthirsty monster obsessed

---

♦**Hephaistion:** hih FEHST ee uhn

with endless conquest to romantic visionary intent on creating a multiethnic world open to all cultures. The ancient sources suggest that Alexander had interlinked goals reflecting his restless and ruthless nature: both to conquer and administer the known world and to explore and colonize new territory beyond.

The ancient world agreed that Alexander was a marvel. The Athenian orator Aeschines♦ (c. 397–322 B.C.E.) expressed the bewildered reaction many people had to the events of Alexander's lifetime: "What strange and unexpected event has not occurred in our time? The life we have lived is no ordinary human one, but we were born to be an object of wonder to posterity." Alexander's fame only increased after his death. Stories of fabulous exploits attributed to him became popular folktales throughout the ancient world, even in distant regions, such as southern Africa, where Alexander never set foot.

Alexander's conquests had consequences in many areas. His explorations benefited scientific fields from geography to botany because he took along knowledgeable writers to collect and catalog new knowledge. He had vast quantities of scientific observations dispatched to his old tutor Aristotle. Alexander's new cities promoted trade in valuable goods, such as spices, exported to the Mediterranean region and also brought Greece and the Near East into closer cultural contact than ever before. It was this contact that represented his career's most enduring impact.

> **Review:** How did innovation and tradition combine to sustain Macedonia's power during the reigns of Philip II and Alexander the Great?

❖ The Hellenistic Kingdoms, 323–30 B.C.E.

Nineteenth-century scholars coined the adjective *Hellenistic* (see page 124) to designate the period from Alexander's death in 323 B.C.E. to the death of Cleopatra VII, the last Macedonian queen of Egypt, in 30 B.C.E. The word conveys the idea that a mixed form of social and cultural life combining Greek and indigenous traditions emerged in the eastern Mediterranean region in the aftermath of Alexander's expedition, producing innovative political, cultural, and economic developments. War stirred up this cultural mixing, and tension persisted between conquerors and subjects. The process promoted regional diversity: Greek ideas and practices had their greatest impact on the urban populations of Egypt and southwestern Asia, while the many people who farmed in the countryside had much less contact with Greek ways of life.

New kingdoms formed the Hellenistic period's dominant political structures. They reintroduced monarchy into Greek culture, kings having been rare in Greece since the fall of Mycenaean civilization nearly a thousand years earlier. Commanders from Alexander's army created the kingdoms after his death by seizing portions of his empire and proclaiming themselves kings in these new states. This process of state formation took more than twenty years of war. The would-be kings had to transform their families into dynasties and accumulate enough power to compel the Greek city-states to conduct their foreign policies in accordance with the kings' wishes.

Creating Successor Kings

Alexander left his succession as an open question at his death. As noted earlier, his only legitimate son, Alexander IV, was born a few months later. Alexander's mother, Olympias, tried for several years to establish her grandson as the Macedonian king under her protection, but her plan failed because Alexander's former army commanders wanted to rule instead. In 316 B.C.E., they executed Olympias for rebellion and in about 311 B.C.E. they murdered the boy and his mother, Roxane; having eradicated the royal family, they divided Alexander's conquests among themselves. Antigonus (c. 382–301 B.C.E.) took over Anatolia, the Near East, Macedonia, and Greece; Seleucus♦ (c. 358–281 B.C.E.) seized Babylonia and the East as far as India;

♦**Aeschines:** EHS kuh neez

♦**Seleucus:** sel OU kuhs

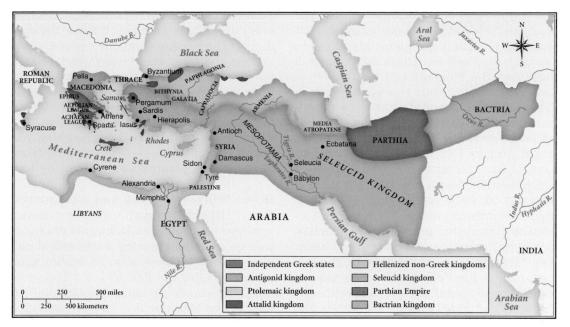

MAP 4.3 Hellenistic Kingdoms, c. 240 B.C.E.
Although the traditional Greek city-states retained their formal independence in the Hellenistic period, monarchy became the dominant political system in the areas of Alexander's former conquests. By about eighty years after his death in 323 B.C.E., the most striking changes to the three major kingdoms originally established by his successors were that the Seleucids had given up their easternmost territories and the kingdom of Pergamum had carved out an independent local reign in western Anatolia.

and Ptolemy◆ (c. 367–282 B.C.E.) grabbed Egypt. Because these men controlled the largest parts of Alexander's conquests, they were referred to as the **successor kings**.

These new rulers—the Hellenistic kings—had to create their own form of kingship because they did not inherit their positions legitimately: they were self-proclaimed monarchs with neither a blood relationship to Alexander's royal line nor any inherited claim to a particular territory. For this reason historians often characterize their type of rule as "personal monarchy." They transformed themselves and their sons into kings by relying on military might, prestige, and ambition.

In the beginning, the new kings' biggest enemies were one another. They fought constantly in the decades after Alexander's death, trying to annex more territory to their individual kingdoms. By the middle of the third century B.C.E., the three Hellenistic kingdoms reached a balance of power that precluded their further expansion (Map 4.3). The Antigonids had been reduced to a kingdom in Macedonia, but they also controlled mainland Greece, whose city-states had to follow royal foreign policy, though they retained their internal freedom. The Seleucids ruled in Syria and Mesopotamia, but they had been forced to cede their easternmost territory early on to the Indian king Chandragupta (r. 323–299 B.C.E.), founder of the Mauryan dynasty. They also lost most of Persia to the Parthians, a northern Iranian people. The Ptolemies ruled the rich land of Egypt.

These territorial arrangements were never completely stable because Hellenistic monarchs never stopped competing. Conflicts frequently arose over contested border areas. The Ptolemies and the Seleucids, for example, repeatedly fought to control the eastern Mediterranean coast, just as the Egyptians

◆**Ptolemy:** TAH luh mee

and Hittites had done centuries earlier. The struggles between the major kingdoms left openings for smaller, regional kingdoms to establish themselves. The most famous of these was the kingdom of the Attalids◆ in western Anatolia, with the wealthy city of Pergamum as its capital. In Bactria in Central Asia, the Greeks—originally colonists settled by Alexander—broke off from the Seleucid kingdom in the mid-third century B.C.E. to found their own regional kingdom, which flourished for a time from the trade in luxury goods between India and China and the Mediterranean world.

The Hellenistic kings adopted different strategies to meet the goal shared by all new political regimes: establishing a tradition of legitimacy to justify their rule. They needed legitimacy to found a royal line with any chance of enduring beyond their deaths. The kings tried to incorporate local traditions into their rule to help build legitimacy. The Seleucids combined Macedonian with Near Eastern royal customs, while the Ptolemies mixed Macedonian with Egyptian. All the kingdoms buttressed their legitimacy from the female as well as the male side. Hellenistic queens therefore enjoyed a high social status as the representatives of distinguished families and as the mothers of a line of royal descendants. In the end, of course, the rulers' positions ultimately rested on their personal ability and their power. A letter from the city of Ilion (on the site of ancient Troy) summed up the situation by praising the Seleucid king Antiochus◆ I (c. 324–261 B.C.E.): "His rule depends above all on his own excellence [aretê], and on the goodwill of his friends, and on his forces."

The Structure of Hellenistic Kingdoms

The Hellenistic kingdoms imposed foreign rule by kings and queens of Macedonian descent on indigenous populations. Royal power was the ultimate source of control over the kingdoms' subjects, in keeping with the Near Eastern monarchical tradition that Hellenistic kings adopted. This tradition persisted above all in defining justice.

◆**Attalids:** AT uhl ihds
◆**Antiochus:** an TY uh kuhs

Seleucus claimed the right to judge as a universal truth of monarchy: "It is not the customs of the Persians and other people that I impose upon you, but the law which is common to everyone, that what is decreed by the king is always just." Hellenistic kings of course had to do more to survive than simply assert a right to rule. The survival of their dynasties depended on their ability to foster strong armies, effective administrations, and cooperative urban elites.

Royal Military Forces and Administration. Hellenistic royal armies and navies provided security against internal unrest as well as external enemies. Professional soldiers manned these forces. To develop their military might, the Seleucid and Ptolemaic kings vigorously promoted immigration by Greeks and Macedonians, who received land grants in return for military service. When this source of manpower gave out, the kings had to employ more local men as troops. Military competition put tremendous financial pressure on the kings not only to pay growing numbers of mercenaries but also to purchase expensive new military technology. To compete effectively, a Hellenistic king had to provide giant artillery, such as catapults capable of flinging a 170-pound projectile up to two hundred yards. His navy cost a fortune because warships were now huge, requiring several hundreds of men as crews. War elephants, which became popular after Alexander's encounters with them in India, were also extremely costly to maintain.

Hellenistic kings had to create large administrations to collect the revenues they needed. Initially, they recruited mostly Greek and Macedonian immigrants to fill high-level administrative posts. Following Alexander the Great's example, however, the Seleucids and the Ptolemies also employed non-Greeks in the middle and lower levels of their administrations, where it was necessary for officials to be able to deal with the subject populations and speak their languages. Local men who wanted a government job bettered their chances if they learned to read and write Greek in addition to their native language. This bilingualism qualified them to fill positions communicating the orders of the highest-ranking officials, all Greeks and

Macedonians, to the indigenous farmers, builders, and crafts producers. Even if non-Greeks had successful government careers, however, they were rarely admitted to the highest ranks of royal society because Greeks and Macedonians saw themselves as too superior to mix with locals. Greeks and non-Greeks therefore tended to live in separate communities. (See "Ethnic Tension in Ptolemaic Egypt," below.)

In many ways the goals and structures of Hellenistic royal administrations recalled those of the earlier Assyrian, Babylonian, and Persian empires. Administrators' principal responsibilities were to maintain order and to direct the kingdoms' tax systems. Officials kept order by mediating disputes whenever possible, but they could call on soldiers to serve as police if necessary. The complex Ptolemaic administration used methods of central planning and control inherited from earlier Egyptian history. Its officials continued to administer royal monopolies, such as that on vegetable oil, to maximize the king's revenue. They also decided how much land farmers could sow in oil-bearing plants, supervised production and distribution of the oil, and set prices for every stage of the oil business. The king, through his officials, also often entered into partnerships with private investors to produce more revenue.

Cities and Urban Elites. Cities were the Hellenistic kingdoms' economic and social hubs. Many Greeks and Macedonians lived in new cities founded by Alexander and the Hellenistic kings in Egypt and the Near East, and they also immigrated to existing cities there. Hellenistic kings promoted this urban immigration to build a supportive constituency. They adorned their new cities with the traditional features of classical Greek city-states, such as gymnasia and theaters.

Ethnic Tension in Ptolemaic Egypt

This papyrus document from 221 B.C.E. records the complaint of Tetosiris, an Egyptian woman, about intimidation of witnesses in a legal dispute. Her report illustrates the tension between Egyptians and Greeks in the Ptolemaic kingdom. The regional administrator, a Greek named Diophanes, would have handled her case, as was customary. Damage to the papyrus, which was reused as mummy wrapping, has obliterated his response.

Greetings to King Ptolemy from Tetosiris. I have a lawsuit pending ... against [the Greek]* Apollodorus over a house. ... Needing witnesses for the trial, I obtained from the clerk of the court a letter instructing the town police chief, Herakleodorus, to take sworn depositions from the witnesses I would bring to him. Apollodorus, bringing a gang [?] with him, burst in and terrorized all my witnesses, saying he would beat them and me within an inch of our lives and drive us out of the village. He even abused [a Greek], a landholder who was going to testify for me, and he said he would beat him up too. Therefore, he did not testify for me. As the others who were going to testify for me are Egyptians, they were intimidated and ran away and did not testify. I therefore ask and beg you, O king, not to allow justice to be delayed in this way ... but to instruct Diophanes, the regional administrator, to write to Herakleodorus to send to Diophanes those who, as I will inform him, built this house—laborers, carpenters, masons [?]—so that he may take their sworn depositions. ... When that has been done I, O king, fleeing for refuge with you, the common benefactor of all, will experience your benevolence. Farewell.

*Brackets indicate damaged spots in the text.

Source: Translation adapted from Naphtali Lewis, *Greeks in Ptolemaic Egypt* (Oxford: Clarendon Press, 1986), 60–61.

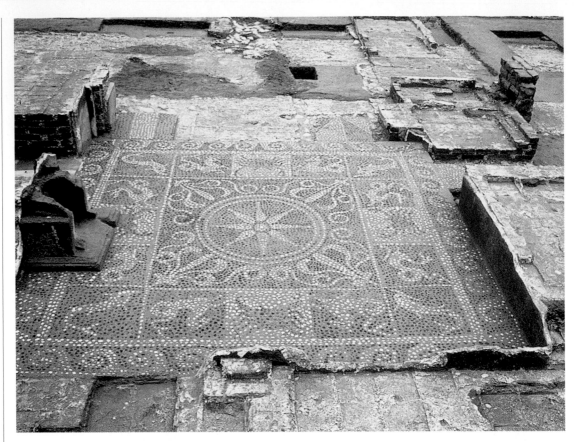

Mosaic Floor from Ai Khanoum◆
Archaeologists discovered this mosaic floor at the site of a city founded by Greeks and Macedonians in Afghanistan about 300 B.C.E.; since the city's original name is lost, it is referred to by its modern one, Ai Khanoum. Decorating floors with designs constructed from pebbles or colored pieces of stone was a favorite technique for giving visual interest to a room, while also providing a very durable surface. Like the other cities that Alexander the Great and the successor kings founded in the Near East and Asia, this one functioned as a defense point and an administrative center. To make their immigrant population feel more at home, its architects designed its buildings to replicate the Greek way of life. *Paul Bernard/Hellenisme et Civilizations Orientales.*

The price of these amenities was dependence on the king. Although Hellenistic cities often retained the polis's political institutions, such as councils and assemblies for citizen men, the requirement that they follow royal policy limited their freedom; they certainly made no independent decisions on international affairs. In addition, the cities also often taxed their citizens to send money demanded by the king.

Monarchy's reemergence in the Greek world therefore severely circumscribed the self-sufficiency and independence of the tradi-

tional city-states. At the same time, monarchy created a new relationship between rulers and the social elites, because the crucial element in the Hellenistic kingdom's political and social structure was the system of mutual rewards by which the kings and their leading urban subjects became partners in government and public finance. Wealthy people in the cities had the crucial responsibility of collecting taxes from the surrounding countryside as well as from their city and sending the money on to the royal treasury; the royal military and the administration were too small to perform these duties themselves. The kings therefore treated the cities con-

◆**Ai Khanoum:** aye kah NOOM

siderately because they needed the goodwill of the wealthiest and most influential city dwellers—the Greek and Macedonian urban elites—to ensure a steady flow of tax revenues. The kings honored and flattered the members of the cities' social elites to secure their help. When writing to a city's council, the king would express himself in the form of a polite request, but the recipients knew he expected his wishes to be fulfilled as commands.

This system continued the Greek tradition of requiring the wealthy elite to contribute to the common good, through the social interaction of the kings and the urban upper classes. Cooperative cities received gifts from the king to pay for expensive public works like theaters and temples or for reconstruction after natural disasters such as earthquakes. Wealthy men and women in the urban elites in turn helped keep the general population peaceful by subsidizing teachers and doctors, building public works, and providing donations and loans that secured a reliable supply of grain to feed the city's residents.

This organizational system also required the kings to establish relationships with well-to-do non-Greeks living in the old cities of Anatolia and the Near East, such as Sardis, Tyre, and Babylon. The kings had to develop cordial relations with the leading citizens of such indigenous cities because they could not keep their vast kingdoms peaceful and profitable without the help of local elites. In addition, non-Greeks and non-Macedonians from eastern regions began moving westward to the new Hellenistic Greek cities in increasing numbers. Jews in particular moved from their ancestral homeland to Anatolia, Greece, and Egypt. The Jewish community eventually became an influential minority in Egyptian Alexandria, the most important Hellenistic city. In Egypt the king also had to negotiate with the priests who controlled the temples of the traditional Egyptian gods because the temples owned large tracts of rich land worked by tenant farmers.

The Layers of Hellenistic Society

Hellenistic monarchy reinforced social hierarchy. The royal family and the king's friends topped the ranks. The Greek and Macedonian elites of the major cities ranked next.

Just under them came indigenous urban elites, leaders of large minority urban populations, and local lords in rural regions. Merchants, artisans, and laborers made up the free population's bottom layer. Slaves remained where they had always been, without social status at all.

The kingdoms' growth increased the demand for slave labor throughout the eastern Mediterranean; the centrally located island of Delos established a market where up to ten thousand slaves a day were bought and sold. The fortunate ones were purchased as servants for the royal court and lived physically comfortable lives, so long as they pleased their owners; the luckless ones toiled, and often died, in the mines. Enslaved children could be taken far from home to work: for example, a sales contract from 259 B.C.E. shows that Zeno, to whom the camel trader wrote, bought a girl about seven years old named Sphragis ("Gemstone") to make her labor in an Egyptian textile factory. Originally from Sidon in the Levant, she had previously worked as the slave of a Greek mercenary soldier employed by a Jewish cavalry commander in the Transjordan region.

The Poor. Most people continued to live where the majority always had—in country villages. Poor people performed almost all the labor required to support the Hellenistic kingdoms' economies. Agriculture remained the economic base, and working conditions for farmers and laborers changed little over time. Many worked on the royal family's huge agricultural estates, but free peasants still worked their own small plots in addition to laboring for wealthy landowners. Rural people rose with the sun and began working before the heat became unbearable, raising the same kinds of crops and animals as their ancestors had with the same simple hand tools. Perhaps as many as 80 percent of all adult men and women, free as well as slave, had to work the land to produce enough food to sustain the population. In the cities, poor women and men could work as small merchants, peddlers, and artisans, producing and selling goods such as tools, pottery, clothing, and furniture. Men could sign on as deckhands on the merchant ships that sailed the Mediterranean Sea and Indian Ocean.

Poverty often meant hunger, even in fertile lands such as Egypt. Papyrus documents reveal that villagers at Kerkeosiris in the late second century B.C.E. had enough food for about 2,200 calories each per day in grain, supplemented by some lentils, onions, and other vegetables. They thus risked starvation: physically active adults require about 2,500 to 3,600 or more calories depending on size, gender, and the intensity of their activity. By comparison, slaves in the American South in 1860 received an average of 4,185 calories daily on a diet of mostly corn and pork (showing they could be worked harder than Hellenistic laborers); the general U.S. population in 1879 consumed about 3,741 calories per day (showing they were much richer than Hellenistic villagers).

A large portion of the rural population in the Seleucid and Ptolemaic kingdoms existed in a state of dependency between free and slave. The peoples, as they were called, were compulsory tenants who farmed the estates belonging to the king. Although they could not be sold like slaves, they were not allowed to move away or abandon their tenancies. They owed a certain quota of produce per area of land to the king, similar to rent to a landlord. The rent was so heavy that these tenant farmers had little chance to escape poverty.

Women's Lives. Hellenistic women's social and political status depended on their rank in the kingdom's hierarchy. Hellenistic queens, like their Macedonian predecessors, commanded enormous riches and honors. They usually exercised power only to the extent that they could influence their husbands' decisions, but they ruled on their own when no male heir existed. Because the Ptolemaic royal family observed the Egyptian royal tradition of brother-sister marriage, daughters as well as sons could rule. For example,

Emotion in Hellenistic Sculpture
Hellenistic sculptors introduced a new style into Greek art by depicting people not at the height of their glory or beauty but in realistic emotional terms. This statue of an elderly woman, for example, shows her with pain etched on her face, her clothing disheveled, and her body stooped from age and the burden of carrying her load of chickens and vegetables in a basket. The statue probably is intended to portray a poor woman desperately trying to survive by hawking food in the street. The artist apparently wanted to show the stress and strain caused by poverty. This new sort of art strove to produce an emotional response in its viewers. The statue's date is uncertain; this version may be a later copy of a Hellenistic original. *Rogers Fund, 1909 (09.39). Photograph © 1997 The Metropolitan Museum of Art.*

Arsinoe◆ II (c. 316–270 B.C.E.), the daughter of Ptolemy I, first married the Macedonian successor king Lysimachus, who gave her four towns as her personal domain. After Lysimachus's death she married her brother Ptolemy II of Egypt and exerted at least as much influence on policy as he did. The virtues publicly praised in a queen reflected traditional Greek values for women. When the city of Hierapolis◆ around 165 B.C.E. passed a decree honoring Queen Apollonis of Pergamum, it praised her piety toward the gods, reverence toward her parents, distinguished conduct toward her husband, and harmonious relations with her "beautiful children born in wedlock."

Some queens paid special attention to the condition of women. About 195 B.C.E., for example, the Seleucid queen Laodice◆ gave a ten-year endowment to the city of Iasus in

◆**Arsinoe:** ahr SIHN oh ee
◆**Hierapolis:** hy uh RA puh luhs
◆**Laodice:** lay AHD uh see

southwestern Anatolia to provide dowries for needy girls. That Laodice funded dowries shows that she recognized the importance to women of controlling property, the surest guarantee of respect in their households.

Most women still remained under the control of men. "Who can judge better than a father what is to his daughter's interest?" remained the dominant creed of fathers with daughters; once a woman married, the words *husband* and *wife's* replaced *father* and *daughter's* in the creed. Most of the time, elite women continued to be separated from men outside of their families, while poor women still worked in public. Greeks continued to abandon infants they could not or would not raise—girls more often than boys—but other populations, such as the Egyptians and the Jews, did not practice abandonment, or exposure, as it is often called. Exposure differed from infanticide because the parents expected someone else to find the child and rear it, albeit usually as a slave. The third-century B.C.E. comic poet Posidippos overstated the case by saying, "A son, one always raises even if one is poor; a daughter, one exposes, even if one is rich." Daughters of wealthy parents were not usually abandoned, but it has been estimated that up to 10 percent of other infant girls were.

In some ways, however, women achieved greater control over their lives in the Hellenistic period than in earlier periods. The rare woman of exceptional wealth could enter public life by making donations or loans to her city and in return be rewarded with an official post in her community's government. In Egypt, women acquired greater say in married life because the customary marriage contracts (see page 102) gradually evolved from an agreement between the bride's parents and the groom to one in which the bride made her own arrangements with the groom.

The Wealthy.   Rich people showed increasing concern for the welfare of the less fortunate during the Hellenistic period. They were following the lead of the royal families, who emphasized philanthropy to build a reputation for generosity that would buttress their legitimacy. On the island of Samos, wealthy citizens funded a foundation to distribute free grain to all the citizens to

Egyptian-Style Statue of Queen Arsinoe II

Arsinoe II (c. 316–270 B.C.E.), daughter of Alexander's general Ptolemy, was one of the most remarkable women of the Hellenistic period. After surviving twenty-five years of political turmoil, dynastic intrigue, and family murders, she married her brother Ptolemy II to unify the monarchy. Hailed as Philadelphoi ("Brother-Loving"), the couple set a precedent for brother-sister marriages in the Macedonian dynasty, the Ptolemies, that ruled Egypt until the death of Cleopatra VII in 30 B.C.E. Arsinoe was the first Ptolemaic ruler whose image was placed in Egyptian temples as a "temple-sharing goddess." This eight-foot-tall, red granite statue portrays her in the traditional sculptural style of the pharaohs. Compare the statue of the Egyptian queen Hatshepsut on page 25. Why would a Hellenistic queen wish to be depicted in traditional Egyptian royal dress? *Vatican Museums.*

eliminate food shortages. Wealthy citizens also funded state-sponsored schools for children in various Hellenistic cities. In some places, girls as well as boys could attend school. Many cities also began sponsoring doctors to improve medical care: patients still had to pay, but at least they could count on finding a doctor.

The donors funding these services were repaid by the respect and honor they earned from their fellow citizens. Philanthropy even touched international relations. When an earthquake devastated Rhodes, many cities joined kings and queens in sending donations to help the Rhodians recover. In return, Rhodes's citizens showered honors on their benefactors by appointing them to prestigious municipal offices and erecting inscriptions expressing the city's gratitude. In this system, the masses' welfare depended more and more on the voluntary generosity of the rich; without democracy, the poor had no political power to demand support.

The End of the Hellenistic Kingdoms

All the Hellenistic kingdoms eventually fell to the Romans. The trouble began when Philip V (238–179 B.C.E.), descendant of Antigonus and king of Macedonia, made a treaty in 215 B.C.E. to aid Hannibal of Carthage in a war against Rome (the Second Punic War). After the Romans won in 201 B.C.E., they sent an army to punish Philip. Rome repeatedly intervened in the squabbles of the Greek city-states to try to maintain peace on its eastern frontier, causing wars that established Roman dominance over Macedonia and Greece by the middle of the second century B.C.E. The city-state of Rhodes and the Attalid kings in Pergamum then convinced the Romans that preserving Rome's safety required Roman intervention farther east in the Mediterranean, to counterbalance Seleucid and Ptolemaic power.

The Seleucid kingdom finally fell to the Romans in 64 B.C.E. The Ptolemaic kingdom in Egypt survived a bit longer. By the 50s B.C.E., its royal family had split into warring factions; the resulting disunity and weakness forced the rivals for the throne to seek Roman support. The end came when the famous queen Cleopatra, a descendant of Ptolemy and the last Macedonian to rule Egypt, chose the losing side in the civil war between Mark Antony and the future emperor Augustus in the late first century B.C.E. An invading Roman army ended her reign and the long succession of Ptolemaic rulers in 30 B.C.E. Rome thus became the heir to all the Hellenistic kingdoms (see Map 4.3).

> **Review:** What were the biggest challenges facing the Hellenistic kings?

❖ Hellenistic Culture, 323–30 B.C.E.

Hellenistic culture reflected three principal characteristics: the overwhelming impact of royal wealth, increased emphasis on private life and emotion, and the increased interaction of diverse peoples. The fabulously rich kings drove developments in literature, art, science, and philosophy by deciding which scholars and artists to put on the royal payroll. Their obligation to the kings meant that authors and artists did not have freedom to criticize public policy; they therefore concentrated on everyday life and individual emotion.

Cultural interaction between Greek and Near Eastern traditions occurred most prominently in language and religion. These developments deeply influenced the Romans as they took over the Hellenistic world; the Roman poet Horace (65–8 B.C.E.) described the effect of Hellenistic culture on his own by saying that "captive Greece captured its fierce victor."

The Arts under Royal Patronage

Hellenistic kings became the patrons of scholarship and the arts on a vast scale, competing with one another to lure the best scholars and artists to their capitals with lavish salaries. They spent money supporting intellectual activity because they wanted to boost their reputations by having these famous people produce books, poems, sculptures, and other prestigious creations at their courts.

The Ptolemies assembled the Hellenistic world's most intellectually distinguished court by turning Alexandria into the Mediterranean's leading arts and sciences center. There the kings established the world's first scholarly research institute and a massive library to support its work. The librarians were instructed to collect all the books (that is, manuscripts) in the world. The library grew to hold half a million scrolls, an enormous number for the time. Linked to it was the building in which scholars hired to do research dined together and produced encyclopedias of knowledge such as *The Wonders of the World* and *On the Rivers of Europe* by Callimachus,♦ a learned prose writer as well as a poet. We still use the name of the research institute's building, the Museum (meaning "place of the Muses," the Greek goddesses of learning and the arts), to designate institutions preserving knowledge. The Alexandrian scholars produced prodigiously. Their champion was Didymus♦

♦**Callimachus:** kuh LIH muh kuhs
♦**Didymus:** DIH duh muhs

(c. 80–10 B.C.E.), nicknamed "Brass Guts" for writing nearly four thousand books. Sadly, not a single one has survived.

Literature at Court. The writers and artists whom Hellenistic kings paid necessarily had to please their patrons with their works. The poet Theocritus (c. 300–260 B.C.E.) spelled out the deal underlying royal patronage in a poem expressly praising his patron, King Ptolemy II: "The spokesmen of the Muses [that is, poets] celebrate Ptolemy in return for his benefactions." Poets such as Theocritus succeeded by avoiding overtly political subjects and stressing the division in society between the intellectual elite—to which the kings belonged—and the uneducated masses. They filled their new poetry with erudite references to make it difficult to understand and therefore exclusive. Only people with a deep literary education could appreciate the mythological allusions that studded these authors' elaborate poems.

Theocritus was the first Greek poet to express the divide between town and countryside, a poetic stance corresponding to a growing Hellenistic reality. His *Idylls* emphasized the discontinuity between urban life and the country bumpkins' bucolic existence, reflecting the Ptolemaic social division between the food consumers in the town and the food producers in the countryside. Theocritus presented a city dweller's idealized dream that country life was peaceful and stress-free, a fiction that deeply influenced later literature.

No Hellenistic women poets seem to have enjoyed royal patronage, but they practiced their art nevertheless. They excelled in writing **epigrams**, a style of short poem originally used for funeral epitaphs. Elegantly worded poems by women from diverse regions of the Hellenistic world—Anyte of Tegea♦ in the Peloponnese, Nossis of Locri♦ in southern Italy, Moero of Byzantium♦—still survive. They often wrote about women, from courtesans to respectable matrons, and their personal feelings. Love was their favorite subject.

Nossis's poem on the power of Eros, for example, proclaimed, "Nothing is sweeter than Eros. All other delights are second to it—from my mouth I spit out even honey. And this Nossis says: whoever Aphrodite has not kissed knows not what sort of flowers are her roses." No other Hellenistic literature better conveys the depth of human emotion than the epigrams of women poets.

The Hellenistic theater, too, largely shifted its focus to stories about individual emotion; no longer did dramatists openly criticize political leaders, as they had in the Classical period. Comic dramatists now presented plays with timeless plots concerning the trials and tribulations of fictional lovers. These comedies of manners, as they are called, proved enormously popular because, like modern situation comedies, they offered a humorous view of situations from daily life. Recent papyrus finds have allowed us to recover comedies of Menander (c. 342–289 B.C.E.), the most famous Hellenistic playwright, and to appreciate his skill in depicting human personality. He presented his first comedy at Athens in 324 or 323 B.C.E. (See "New Sources, New Perspectives," page 148.) Hellenistic tragedy could take a multicultural approach: Ezechiel, a Jew living in Alexandria, wrote *Exodus*, a tragedy in Greek about Moses leading the Hebrews out of captivity in Egypt.

Emotion in Sculpture and Painting. Like their literary contemporaries, Hellenistic sculptors and painters featured personal feelings prominently in their works. Classical artists had consistently imbued their subjects' faces with an idealized serenity. Hellenistic sculptures, usually surviving only in later copies, depicted individual emotions. In portrait sculpture, Lysippus's famous bust of Alexander the Great captured the young commander's passionate dreaminess. A sculpture from Pergamum (page 150) by an unknown artist commemorated the third-century B.C.E. Attalid victory over the plundering Gauls (one of the Celtic peoples from what is now France) by showing a defeated Celtic warrior stabbing himself after having killed his wife to prevent her enslavement by the victors. A large-scale painting of Alexander battling with the Persian king Darius (see

---

♦**Anyte of Tegea:** ahn EE tay (of) TEH jee uh
♦**Nossis of Locri:** NAH sis (of) LOH kry
♦**Moero of Byzantium:** MAH ee ro (of) buh ZAN tee uhm

NEW SOURCES, NEW PERSPECTIVES

Papyrus Discoveries and Menander's Comedies

Fourth-century B.C.E. Greek playwrights invented the kind of comedy that is today's most popular entertainment—the sitcom. In the Peloponnesian War's aftermath, they wrote comic plays that concentrated on the conflicts between human personality types as their characters suffered through everyday trials and tribulations. The rocky course of love and marriage drove most plots. Forsaking the bawdy political satire of earlier Greek comedy, comedians now created stereotypical characters such as addled lovers, cantankerous fathers, rascally servants, and boastful soldiers. Confusions of identity leading to hilarious misunderstandings were a frequent plot device, while jokes about marriage were another staple. The following is a typical exchange:

> FIRST MAN: "He's married, you know."
> SECOND MAN: "What's that you say? Actually married? How can that be? I just left him alive and walking around!"

The comedies' titles hinted at their tone: *The Country Boob, Pot-Belly, The Stolen Girl, The Bad-Tempered Man.*

By the end of the fourth century, these comedies had become wildly popular. Greek comic plays about daily life and social mix-ups inspired many imitations, especially Roman comedies, which eventually inspired William Shakespeare (1564–1616) in England and Molière (1622–1673) in France; their comedies, in turn, led to today's sitcoms.

The most famous author of this kind of comedy was Menander (343–291 B.C.E.) of Athens. Ancient critics ranked him as "second only to Homer" for his poetry's quality, and they praised his plots as "a mirror of life." Despite antiquity's unanimous "two thumbs up," none of Menander's comedies survived into modern times. Works of Greek and Roman literature had to be copied over and over by hand for centuries if they were to survive, until finally the invention of the printing press in the fifteenth century made mass production of books possible. For unknown reasons, people at some point stopped recopying comedies, including Menander's. Thus, although we knew Menander

Pompeian Wall Painting Depicting Menander
Four centuries after Menander's death, a wealthy Roman commissioned this painting of the playwright for a wall in his house at Pompeii, near Naples. Evidently the owner meant to proclaim his love for Greek drama because the room's other walls—now very damaged—were probably decorated with images of the tragedian Euripides and possibly the Muses of Tragedy and Comedy. This figure was identified by faded lettering on the scroll: "Menander: he was the first to write New Comedy." The ivy wreath on his head symbolizes the poet's victory in the contests of comedies presented at the festivals of the god Dionysus, the patron of drama. *Scala/Art Resource, NY.*

had been a star, we could not read the plays that made him so famous—until quite recently.

The situation changed dramatically when scholars in the late eighteenth century C.E. began finding ancient paper—papyrus—buried in Egypt's dry sands. In antiquity, Egyptians processed the reeds of the papyrus plant to make a thick, brownish paper for writing down everything from literature to letters to tax receipts. When papyrus texts were damaged or no longer needed, they were thrown out with the garbage or used to wrap mummies to help preserve the dried-out corpses for the afterlife. The super-arid climate of the Egyptian desert kept this waste paper from rotting away. The French emperor Napoleon's occupation of Egypt in 1798–1801 inspired a European mania for collecting papyrus. By excavating ancient Egyptian trash dumps and unwrapping mummies, scholars have discovered thousands and thousands of texts of all kinds. Papyrus experts estimate that the original production of papyrus texts was so enormous that it was more than 150,000 times greater than what has survived.

Incredibly, these discoveries have returned Menander to us from more than two thousand years ago: over the last several decades, painstaking study of often severely damaged papyrus sheets has uncovered texts of his comedies. When the so-called Bodmer Papyrus proved to contain a nearly complete copy of *The Bad-Tempered Man*, we could once again enjoy a Menander comedy for the first time since antiquity. Further detective work has yielded more, and today we can also read most of *The Girl from Samos* and parts of other plays. In this way, Menander's memorable and influential characters, stories, and jokes have been restored from the dead.

Rediscovering ancient comedy (or any other kind of writing) on papyrus is challenging. The handwriting is often crabbed and difficult to decipher, there are no gaps between words, punctuation is minimal at best, changes in speakers are indicated just by colons or dashes rather than by names, and there are no stage directions. The papyrus can be burned or torn into pieces or chewed by mice and insects. One part of a play can turn up in the wrapping of one mummy and another part in a different one. Incompletely preserved scenes and lines can be hard to understand.

The hard work required to make sense of papyrus texts pays off wonderfully, however, with

Books on Papyrus
Menander's works were written on sheets of papyrus like these that were glued together to make scrolls, the form of books used until the later Roman period. Holes and tears caused by age and use can destroy letters and words, making reconstruction of the original text a difficult task. The writing can also be hard to decipher; compared to most papyrus books from antiquity, this example is well preserved and has a very clear script. (Its words and drawings come from the works of the fourth-century B.C.E. astronomer and mathematician Eudoxus of Cnidos.) *Réunion des Musées Nationaux/ Art Resource, NY/Photo: Herve Lewandowski.*

discoveries like those that recovered Menander's comedies. In this case, the collaboration of archaeologists, historians, and literary scholars has brought back to life the distant beginnings of what remains our most enduring and crowd-pleasing form of comedy.

QUESTIONS TO CONSIDER
1. What makes situation comedy so appealing?
2. Why would Greeks living in the fourth century B.C.E. prefer situation comedy to political satire or darker forms of humor?

FURTHER READING
Roger Bagnall, *Reading Papyri, Writing Ancient History.* 1995.
Menander: Plays and Fragments. Translated with an introduction by Norma Miller. 1987.
Richard Parkinson and Stephen Quirke, *Papyrus.* 1995.

page 135) portrayed Alexander's intense concentration and Darius's horrified expression. The artist, who was probably either Philoxenus of Eretria◆ or a Greek woman from Egypt named Helena (one of the first female painters known), used foreshortening (sizing objects according to the rules of perspective to look real) and strong contrasts between shadows and highlights to accentuate the picture's emotional impact.

Hellenistic sculptors and painters created their works mainly on commission from royalty and from the urban elites who wanted to show they had artistic taste like their social superiors in the royal family. The increasing diversity of subjects that emerged in Hellenistic art presumably represented a trend approved by kings, queens, and the elites. Sculpture best reveals this new preference for depiction of humans in a wide variety of poses, mostly from private life (in

◆**Philoxenus of Eretria:** fih LAHK suh nuhs (of) eh RET tree uh

Dying Celts

Hellenistic artists excelled in portraying deeply emotional scenes, such as this murder-suicide of a Celtic warrior who is in the act of slaying himself after killing his wife, to prevent their capture by the enemy after defeat in battle. Celtic women followed their men to the battlefield and willingly exposed themselves to the same dangers. The original of this composition was in bronze, forming part of a large sculptural group that Attalus I, king of Pergamum from 241 to 197 B.C.E., set up on his acropolis to commemorate his defeat around 230 B.C.E. of the Celts, called Galatians, who had moved into Anatolia in the 270s B.C.E. to conduct raids throughout the area. It is striking that Attalus celebrated his victory by erecting a monument portraying the defeated enemy as brave and noble. **For more help analyzing this image**, see the visual activity for this chapter in the Online Study Guide at **bedfordstmartins.com/hunt**.
Erich Lessing/Art Resource, NY.

contrast with classical art). Hellenistic sculptors portrayed subjects never before shown: sympathetic enemies (such as the dying Celts), drunkards, battered athletes, wrinkled old people. The female nude became a particular favorite. A statue of Aphrodite by Praxiteles,◆ which portrayed the goddess completely nude for the first time, became renowned as a religious object and tourist attraction in the city of Cnidos,◆ which had commissioned it. The king of Bithynia◆ offered to pay off the citizens' entire public debt if he could have the work of art. They refused.

Philosophy for a New Age

New philosophies arose in the Hellenistic period, all asking the same question: What is the best way to live? They recommended different paths to the same answer: individuals must attain personal tranquility to achieve freedom from the turbulence of outside forces, especially chance. It is easy to see why these philosophies had appeal: outside forces—the Hellenistic kings—had robbed Greek city-states of freedom in foreign policy, and their citizens' fates ultimately rested in the hands of distant, often capricious monarchs. More than ever before, human life and opportunities for free choice seemed out of individuals' control. It therefore made sense, at least for those wealthy enough to spend time philosophizing, to look for personal, private solutions to the unsettling new conditions of Hellenistic life.

Hellenistic philosophers concentrated on **materialism**, the doctrine that only things made of matter truly exist. Materialism denied Plato's metaphysical concept of the soul and indeed of all nonmaterial

◆**Praxiteles:** prak SIH tuh leez
◆**Cnidos:** kuh NY duhs
◆**Bithynia:** buh THIH nee uh

phenomena, following up Aristotle's doctrine that only things identified through logic or observation exist. Hellenistic philosophy was divided into three related areas: (1) logic, the process for discovering truth; (2) physics, the fundamental truth about the nature of existence; and (3) ethics, how humans should achieve happiness and well-being as a consequence of logic and physics. The era's philosophical thought greatly influenced Roman thinkers and thus the many important Western philosophers who later read their works.

Epicureanism. One of the two most significant new Hellenistic philosophies was **Epicureanism**. It took its name from its founder, Epicurus (341–271 B.C.E.), who about 307 B.C.E. settled his followers in Athens in a house amid a verdant garden (hence "the Garden" as the name of his school). Epicurus broke with tradition by admitting women and slaves to study philosophy in his group. His lover, the courtesan Leontion, became famous for her treatise criticizing the ideas of Theophrastus◆ (c. 370–285 B.C.E.), Aristotle's most famous pupil.

Epicurus's key idea was that people should be free of worry about death. Because all matter consists of tiny, invisible, and irreducible pieces called atoms (Greek for "indivisible things") in random movement, death is nothing more than the painless separating of the body's atoms. Moreover, all human knowledge must be empirical, that is, derived from experience and perception. Phenomena that most people perceive as the work of the gods, such as thunder, do not result from divine intervention in the world. The gods live far away in perfect tranquillity, ignoring human affairs. People therefore have nothing to fear from the gods, in life or in death.

◆**Theophrastus:** thee uh FRAS tuhs

Epicurus believed people should pursue pleasure, but he had a particular definition of true pleasure: it meant an "absence of disturbance." That is, we should live free from the daily turbulence, passions, and desires of ordinary existence. A sober life spent with friends and separated from the cares of the common world provided Epicurean "pleasure." Epicureanism therefore represented a serious challenge to Greek citizenship's traditional ideal of men actively participating in politics and women in public religious cults.

Stoicism. The other important new Hellenistic philosophy, **Stoicism**, recommended a less isolationist life. Its name derives from the Painted Stoa in Athens, where Stoic philosophers discussed their doctrines. Zeno (c. 333–262 B.C.E.) from Citium, on Cyprus, founded Stoicism, but Chrysippus◆ (c. 280–206 B.C.E.) from Cilicia, in Anatolia, made it a comprehensive guide to life. Stoics believed that fate controls

◆**Chrysippus:** kry SIHP uhs

Praxiteles's Statue of Aphrodite
The Athenian sculptor Praxiteles, whose career spanned approximately 375–330 B.C.E., became internationally renowned for his marble statues. He excelled at making stone resemble the softness of flesh and producing perfect surface finishes, which he employed the painter Nicias to enliven with color. His masterpiece was the Aphrodite made for the city-state of Cnidos in southwestern Anatolia; the original is lost, but many Hellenistic-era copies of the type illustrated here were made. The statue was displayed in a colonnaded, circular shrine set in a garden. It was the first time that the goddess of love had been portrayed completely nude, and gossips spread the rumor that Praxiteles had used his lover Phryne as his model for the world-famous statue. Given that there was a long tradition of nude male statues, why do you think it took until the Hellenistic period for Greek sculptors to portray female statues in the nude? *Nimatallah/Art Resource, NY.*

Gemstone Showing Diogenes in His Jar
This engraved gem from the Roman period shows the famous philosopher Diogenes (c. 412–c. 324 B.C.E.) living in a large storage jar and having a discussion with a man who holds a scroll. Diogenes was born at Sinope on the Black Sea but was exiled in a dispute over monetary fraud; he spent most of his life at Athens and Corinth, becoming famous as the founder of Cynic ("doglike") philosophy. He espoused an ascetic life of poverty ruled by nature, not law or tradition. In his defiance of social convention he was said to live like a dog, hence the name given to his philosophical views and the dog usually shown beside him in art, as in this engraving. What kind of person do you think would have wanted this gemstone as a piece of jewelry?
Thorvaldsen Museum, Copenhagen.

people's lives but that individuals should still make the pursuit of virtue their goal. Stoic virtue meant putting oneself in harmony with the divine, rational force of universal Nature by cultivating good sense, justice, courage, and temperance. These doctrines applied to women as well as men. In fact, some Stoics advocated equal citizenship for women and abolition of the conventions of marriage and families as the Greeks knew them. Zeno even proposed unisex clothing as a way to obliterate unnecessary distinctions between women and men.

The Stoic belief in fate created the question of whether humans truly have free will. Relying on subtle reasoning, Stoic philosophers concluded that purposeful human actions do have significance even if fate rules. Nature, itself good, does not prevent vice from occurring, because virtue would otherwise have no meaning. What matters in life is the striving for good, not the result. A person should therefore take action against evil by, for example, participating in politics. To be a Stoic also meant to shun desire and anger while enduring pain and sorrow calmly, an attitude that yields the modern meaning of the word *stoic*. Through endurance and self-control, adherents of Stoic philosophy at-

tained tranquillity. They did not fear death because they believed that people live the same life over and over again. This repetition occurred because the world is periodically destroyed by fire and then re-formed.

Competing Philosophies. Other Hellenistic philosophies competed with Epicureanism and Stoicism for people's minds and hearts. Some of these philosophies built on the work of earlier giants such as Plato and Pythagoras. Others struck out in idiosyncratic directions. Skeptics, for example, aimed at the same state of personal calm as did Epicureans, but from a completely different premise. Following the doctrines of Pyrrho (c. 360–270 B.C.E.) from Elis, in the Peloponnese, Skeptics believed that secure knowledge about anything was impossible because the human senses yield contradictory information about the world. All we can do, they insisted, is depend on appearances while suspending judgment about their reality. Pyrrho's thought had been influenced by the Indian ascetic wise men (the magi) he met while on Alexander the Great's expedition.

The philosophers called Cynics ostentatiously rejected every convention of ordinary life, especially wealth and material comfort.

They believed that humans should aim for complete self-sufficiency. Whatever was natural was good and could be done without shame before anyone; therefore, even public defecation and fornication were acceptable. Women and men alike were free to follow their sexual inclinations. Above all, Cynics disdained life's comforts. The most famous early Cynic, Diogenes (d. 323 B.C.E.) from Sinope, on the Black Sea, wore borrowed clothing and slept in a storage jar. Almost as notorious was Hipparchia,♦ a Cynic of the late fourth century B.C.E. She once bested an obnoxious philosophical opponent named Theodorus the Atheist with the following remarks: "That which would not be considered wrong if done by Theodorus would also not be considered wrong if done by Hipparchia. Now if Theodorus strikes himself, he does no wrong. Therefore, if Hipparchia strikes Theodorus, she does no wrong." The name *Cynic*, which meant "like a dog," reflected the common evaluation of this ascetic and unconventional way of life.

In the Hellenistic period, Greek philosophy reached a wider audience than ever before. Although the working poor had neither the leisure nor the resources to attend philosophers' lectures, the well-off members of society studied philosophy in growing numbers. Theophrastus lectured to crowds of two thousand in Athens. Most philosophy students continued to be men, but women could now join some groups. Kings competed to attract famous philosophers to their courts, and Greek settlers took their interest in philosophy with them to even the most remote Hellenistic cities. Archaeologists excavating a city located thousands of miles from Greece on the Oxus River in Afghanistan uncovered a Greek philosophical text as well as inscriptions of moral advice imputed to Apollo's oracle at Delphi.

Scientific Innovation

Scientific investigation was separated from philosophy in the Hellenistic period. Science so benefited from its widening divorce from philosophy that historians have called this era ancient science's golden age. Various factors

contributed to a flourishing of scientific innovation: Alexander's expedition had encouraged curiosity and increased knowledge about the world's extent and diversity, royal patronage supported scientists financially, and the concentration of scientists in Alexandria promoted a fertile exchange of ideas.

Advances in Geometry and Mathematics. The greatest advances in scientific knowledge came in geometry and mathematics. Euclid, who taught at Alexandria around 300 B.C.E., made revolutionary discoveries in analyzing two- and three-dimensional space. The utility of Euclidean geometry still endures. Archimedes of Syracuse (287–212 B.C.E.) was a mathematical genius who calculated the approximate value of pi and devised a way to manipulate very large numbers. He also invented hydrostatics (the science of the equilibrium of fluid systems) and mechanical devices such as a screw for lifting water to a higher elevation. Archimedes's shout of delight when he solved a problem while soaking in his bathtub has been immortalized in the modern expression "Eureka!" (*heurêka* in Greek), meaning "I have found it!"

Advances in Hellenistic mathematics energized other fields that required complex computation. Aristarchus of Samos early in the third century B.C.E. became the first to

Bronze Astronomical Calculator

These fragments of a Hellenistic bronze astronomical calculator were discovered underwater in an ancient shipwreck off Anticythera, below the Peloponnese in southern Greece. The device was being transported to Italy in the early first century B.C.E. as part of a shipment of metalwork and other valuable objects. The product of sophisticated applied engineering and astronomical knowledge, it used a complex set of intermeshed gears, turned by hand, to control rotating dials that indicated the position of celestial phenomena. *National Archaeological Museum, Athens. Archaeological Receipts Fund.*

♦**Hipparchia:** hip ARK ee uh

propose the correct model of the solar system: the earth revolves around the sun, which is far larger and more distant than it appears. Later astronomers rejected Aristarchus's heliocentric model in favor of the traditional geocentric one (with the earth at the center) because calculations based on the orbit he calculated for the earth failed to correspond to the observed positions of celestial objects. Aristarchus had assumed a circular orbit instead of an elliptical one, an assumption not corrected until much later. Eratosthenes of Cyrene (c. 275–194 B.C.E.) pioneered mathematical geography. He calculated the circumference of the earth with astonishing accuracy by simultaneously measuring the length of the shadows of widely separated but identically tall structures. Together, these researchers gave Western scientific thought an important start toward its fundamental procedure of reconciling theory with observed data through measurement and experimentation.

Scientific Discoveries. Hellenistic science flourished despite the enormous difficulties imposed by technical limitations. Rigorous scientific experimentation was not possible because no technology existed for the precise measurement of very short intervals of time. Measuring tiny quantities of matter was also next to impossible. The science of the age was as quantitative as it could be given these limitations. Ctesibius♦ of Alexandria (b. c. 310 B.C.E.), a contemporary of Aristarchus, invented pneumatics by creating machines operated by air pressure. He also built a working water pump, an organ powered by water, and the first accurate water clock. A later Alexandrian, Hero, continued the Hellenistic tradition of mechanical ingenuity by building a rotating sphere powered by steam. As in most of Hellenistic science, these inventions did not lead to viable applications in daily life. The scientists and their royal patrons were more interested in new theoretical discoveries than in practical results, and the metallurgical technology to produce the pipes, fittings, and screws needed to build powerful machines did not yet exist.

Hellenistic science did produce noteworthy new military technology. The kings hired engineers to design powerful catapults and wheeled siege towers many stories high; these weapons could batter down the defenses of walled cities. The most famous large-scale application of technology for nonmilitary purposes was the construction of the Pharos, a lighthouse three hundred feet tall, for the harbor at Alexandria. Using polished metal mirrors to reflect the light from a large bonfire, the Pharos shone many miles out over the sea. Awestruck sailors called it one of the wonders of the world.

The Origins of Anatomy. Medicine also benefited from the Hellenistic quest for new knowledge. Increased contact between Greeks and people of the Near East made Mesopotamian and Egyptian medical knowledge better known in the West and promoted research on human health and illness. Around 325 B.C.E., Praxagoras♦ of Cos discovered the value of measuring the pulse in diagnosing illness. A bit later, Herophilus of Chalcedon♦ (b. c. 300 B.C.E.), working in Alexandria, became the first Western scientist to study anatomy by dissecting human cadavers and, it was rumored, condemned criminals while they were still alive; he had access to these subjects because the king authorized his research. Some of the anatomical terms Herophilus invented are still used. Other Hellenistic advances in anatomy included the discovery of the nerves and nervous system.

Like scientists of the time, Hellenistic medical researchers were limited by the lack of technology to detect and measure phenomena not visible to the naked eye. Unable to see what really occurred under the skin in living patients, doctors thought that many illnesses in women were caused by displacements of the womb, which they wrongly believed could move around in the body. These mistaken ideas could not be corrected because the technology to evaluate them was absent.

♦**Ctesibius:** teh SIHB ee uhs

♦**Praxagoras:** prak SAG uh ruhs
♦**Herophilus of Chalcedon:** huh RAHF uh luhs (of) KAL suh dahn

Cultural and Religious Transformations

Wealthy non-Greeks increasingly adopted Greek habits as they adapted to the Hellenistic world's social hierarchy. Diotimus of Sidon, for example, took a Greek name and pursued the premier Greek sport, chariot racing. He traveled to Nemea in the Peloponnese to enter his chariot in the race at the prestigious festival of Zeus. He announced his victory in an inscription written in Greek, which had become the Hellenistic world's common language for international commerce and cultural exchange. The explosion in the use of the Greek language in the form called **Koine**◆ (literally, "shared" or "common") reflected the emergence of an international culture based on Greek models; this was the reason that the Egyptian camel trader stranded in Syria had to communicate in Greek with a high-level official in Egypt. The most striking evidence of this cultural development comes from Afghanistan. There, King Ashoka (r. c. 268–232 B.C.E.), who ruled most of the Indian subcontinent, used Greek as one of the languages in his public inscriptions. These texts announced his plan to teach his subjects Buddhist traditions of self-control, such as abstinence from eating meat. Local languages did not disappear in the Hellenistic kingdoms, however. In one region of Anatolia, for example, people spoke twenty-two different languages. This sort of diversity remained the norm in the world that the Hellenistic kings ruled.

Changes in Greek and Egyptian Religion. The diversity of religious practice matched the variety in so many other areas of Hellenistic life. The traditional cults of Greek religion remained popular, but new cults, above all those that deified ruling kings, reflected changing political and social conditions. Preexisting cults that previously had only local significance, such as that of the Greek healing deity Asclepius◆ or the mystery cult of the Egyptian goddess Isis, gained adherents all over the Hellenistic world. In many cases, Greek cults and local cults from the eastern Mediterranean influenced each other. Their beliefs meshed well because these cults shared many assumptions about how to remedy the troubles of human life. In other instances, local cults and Greek cults existed side by side and even overlapped. The inhabitants of villages in the Fayum◆ district of Egypt, for example, continued worshiping their traditional crocodile god and mummifying their dead according to the old ways but also paid homage to Greek deities. Since they were polytheists (believers in multiple gods), people could worship in both old and new cults.

New cults incorporated a prominent theme of Hellenistic thought: concern for the relationship between the individual and what seemed the controlling, arbitrary power of the divinities such as Tychê (literally "Chance"). The chaotic course of Greek history after the Peloponnesian War made human existence appear more unpredictable than ever. Since advances in astronomy revealed the mathematical precision of the celestial sphere of the universe, religion now had to address the seeming disconnection between that heavenly uniformity and the shapeless chaos of life on earth. One increasingly popular approach to bridging that gap was to rely on astrology for advice deduced from the movement of the stars and planets, thought of as divinities. Another very common choice was to worship Tychê as a god in the hope of securing good luck in life.

The most revolutionary approach in seeking protection from the capricious tricks of chance or luck was to pray for salvation from deified kings, who enjoyed divine status in what are now called **ruler cults**. Various populations established these cults in recognition of great benefactions. The Athenians, for example, deified the Macedonian Antigonus and his son Demetrius as savior gods in 307 B.C.E., when they liberated the city and bestowed magnificent gifts on it. Like most ruler cults, this one expressed both spontaneous gratitude and a desire to flatter the rulers in the hope of obtaining

◆**Koine:** koy NAY
◆**Asclepius:** as KLEE pee uhs

◆**Fayum:** fa yoom

additional favors. Many cities in the Ptolemaic and Seleucid kingdoms instituted ruler cults for their kings and queens. An inscription put up by Egyptian priests in 238 B.C.E. concretely described the qualities appropriate for a divine king and queen:

> King Ptolemy III and Queen Berenice, his sister and wife, the Benefactor Gods, . . . have provided good government . . . and [after a drought] sacrificed a large amount of their revenues for the salvation of the population, and by importing grain . . . they saved the inhabitants of Egypt.

As these words make clear, the Hellenistic monarchs' tremendous power and wealth gave them the status of gods to the ordinary people who depended on their generosity and protection. The idea that a human being could be a god, present on earth to be a savior who delivered people from evils, was now firmly established and would prove influential later in Roman imperial religion and Christianity.

Healing divinities offered another form of protection to anxious individuals. Scientific Greek medicine had rejected the notion of supernatural causes and cures for disease ever since Hippocrates had established his medical school on the Aegean island of Cos in the late fifth century B.C.E. Nevertheless, the cult of the god Asclepius, who offered cures for illness and injury at his many shrines, grew popular during the Hellenistic period. Suppliants seeking Asclepius's help would sleep in special dormitories at his shrines to await dreams in which he prescribed healing treatments. These prescriptions emphasized diet and exercise, but numerous inscriptions commissioned by grateful patients also testified to miraculous cures and surgery performed while the sufferer slept. The following example is typical:

> Ambrosia of Athens was blind in one eye. . . . She . . . ridiculed some of the cures [described in inscriptions in the sanctuary] as being incredible and impossible. . . . But when she went to sleep, she saw a vision; she thought the god was standing next to her. . . . He split open the diseased eye and poured in a medicine. When day came she left cured.

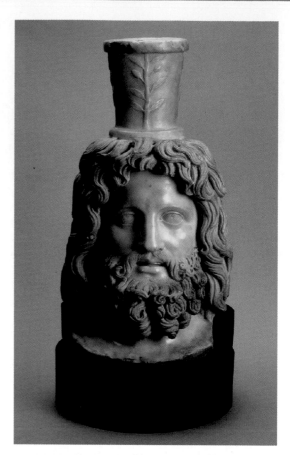

Bust of the Greco-Egyptian God Sarapis
This marble head was found in a Roman-era temple in England, demonstrating the enduring and widespread appeal of this Egyptian deity. Originally a conjunction of Osiris, the consort of Isis, and the sacred Apis bull, Sarapis was adopted in the early Hellenistic period by the Ptolemaic royal family as its patron god guaranteeing their rule. Eventually, the cult of Sarapis was spread around the Hellenistic world by groups of devotees who met for worship and feasting. They identified him as a transcendent god combining the powers of Zeus with those of other divinities and looked to him for miracles. He was commonly portrayed with a food container or measure on his head, as here, to signify his concern for human prosperity in this world and in the afterlife. *Museum of London Photographic Library.*

People's faith in divine healing gave them hope that they could overcome the constant danger of illness, which seemed to strike at random.

Mystery cults proffered secret knowledge as a key to worldly and physical salvation.

MAPPING THE WEST Roman Takeover of the Hellenistic World, to 30 B.C.E.
By the death of Cleopatra VII, the last Ptolemaic monarch of Egypt, in 30 B.C.E., the Roman
republic had conquered or absorbed the Hellenistic kingdoms of the eastern Mediterranean.
Compare the political divisions on this map with those on the map at the end of Chapter 3
to see the differences from the Classical Age. Competition for the tremendous wealth that this
expansion captured helped fuel bitter and divisive feuds between Rome's most ambitious
generals and political leaders. This territory became the eastern half of the Roman Empire,
with only minor changes in extent over time.

The cults of the Greek god Dionysus and, in particular, the Egyptian goddess Isis attracted many followers in this period. Isis was beloved because her powers protected her worshipers in all aspects of their lives. King Ptolemy I boosted her popularity by establishing a headquarters for her cult in Alexandria. He also refashioned the Egyptian deity Osiris in a Greek mold as the new god Sarapis, whose job was to serve as Isis's consort. Sarapis reportedly performed miracles of rescue from shipwreck and illness. The cult of Isis, who became the most popular female divinity in the Mediterranean, involved extensive ceremonies, rituals and festivals incorporating features of Egyptian religion mixed with Greek elements. Disciples of Isis apparently hoped to achieve personal purification as well as the aid of the goddess in overcoming the demonic influence of Tychê on human life. That an Egyptian deity like Isis could achieve enormous popularity among Greeks (and Romans in later times) alongside the traditional gods of Greek religion is the best evidence of the cultural cross-fertilization of the Hellenistic world.

Hellenistic Judaism. Cultural interaction between Greeks and Jews produced important changes in Judaism during the Hellenistic period. King Ptolemy II made the Hebrew Bible accessible to a wide audience by having his Alexandrian scholars produce a Greek translation—the Septuagint—in the early third century B.C.E. Many Jews, especially those in the large Jewish communities that had grown up in Hellenistic cities outside their homeland, began to speak Greek and adopt Greek culture. These Hellenized Jews did, however, retain traditional Judaism's rituals and rules, and they did not worship Greek gods. In other words, they did not simply become Greek but instead mixed Jewish and Greek customs.

Internal dissension among Jews erupted in second-century B.C.E. Palestine over how much Greek tradition was acceptable for traditional Jews. The Seleucid king Antiochus IV (r. 175–163 B.C.E.) intervened in the conflict to support an extreme Hellenizing faction of Jerusalem Jews, who had taken over the high priesthood that ruled the Jewish community with royal approval. In 167 B.C.E., Antiochus converted the great Jewish temple in Jerusalem into a Greek temple and outlawed the practice of Jewish religious rites, such as observing the Sabbath and circumcision. This provoked a revolt led by Judah the Maccabee, which won Jewish independence from Seleucid control after twenty-five years of war. The most famous episode in this revolt was the retaking of the Jerusalem temple and its rededication to the worship of the Jewish god, Yahweh, commemorated by the Hanukkah holiday. That Greek culture attracted some Jews in the first place provides a striking example of the transformations that affected many—though far from all—people of the Hellenistic world. By the time of the Roman Empire, one of those transformations would be Christianity, whose theology had roots in the cultural interaction of Hellenistic Jews and Greeks and their ideas on apocalypticism and divine human beings.

Review: How did the political changes of the Hellenistic period affect art and science?

Conclusion

The Peloponnesian War's violence and the decades of war that followed in the early fourth century B.C.E. led ordinary people as well as philosophers like Plato and Aristotle to question the basis of morality. The disunity of Greek international politics allowed Macedonia's aggressive leaders Philip II (r. 359–336 B.C.E.) and Alexander the Great (r. 336–323 B.C.E.) to make themselves the masters of the squabbling city-states. Inspired by Greek heroic ideals, Alexander the Great conquered the Persian Empire and set in motion the Hellenistic period's momentous political, social, and cultural changes.

When Alexander's generals transformed themselves into Hellenistic kings, they not only made use of the conquered lands' existing administrative structures but also added an administrative layer staffed by Greeks and Macedonians. Local elites as well as Greeks and Macedonians cooperated with the Hellenistic monarchs in governing and financing their society, which was divided along hierarchical ethnic lines. To enhance their own magnificence, the kings and queens of the Hellenistic world supported writers, artists, scholars, philosophers, and scientists, thereby energizing Hellenistic intellectual life. The traditional city-states continued to exist in Hellenistic Greece, but their freedom extended only to local governance; the Hellenistic kings determined international affairs.

Cultural diversity in the Hellenistic world encompassed much that was new, because interaction between different peoples became more common than ever before. Artists and writers expressed emotion in their works in novel ways, philosophers discussed ways to achieve true happiness, and scientists explored the mysteries of nature and the human body more deeply than ever before. Political and cultural change increased people's uncertainty and therefore their anxiety about the role of chance in life. In response, people looked for new religious experiences to satisfy their yearning for protection from perils. In the midst of so much novelty, however, the ancient world's fundamental elements remained unchanged—the labor, the poverty, and the necessarily limited horizons of the mass of ordinary people working in its fields, vineyards, and pastures.

What changed most of all was the Romans' culture once they took over the Hellenistic kingdoms' territory and came into close contact with their diverse peoples' traditions. Rome's rise to power took centuries, however, because Rome originated as a tiny, insignificant place that no one except Romans ever expected to amount to anything on the world stage.

Suggested References

Classical Greece's Decline, c. 400–350 B.C.E.

The works of Plato and Aristotle, unlike those of many ancient authors, have survived in quantity so that we can study their thought in detail. Xenophon's *Hellenica* and *Anabasis* offer action-packed accounts of the wars of the early fourth century B.C.E.

*Aristotle. *Complete Works.* Ed. Jonathan Barnes. 1985.

Barnes, Jonathan. *Aristotle.* 1982.

Garnsey, Peter. *Ideas of Slavery from Aristotle to Augustine.* 1996.

Greek archaeology: http://archnet.uconn.edu/regions/europe.php3.

*Plato. *The Collected Dialogues* (including *Apology, Crito,* and *Republic*). Eds. Edith Hamilton and Huntington Cairns. 1963.

Strauss, Barry S. *Athens after the Peloponnesian War: Class, Faction, and Policy, 403–386 B.C.* 1986.

Tritle, Lawrence A., ed. *The Greek World in the Fourth Century: From the Fall of the Athenian Empire to the Successors of Alexander.* 1997.

*Xenophon. *A History of My Times (Hellenica).* Trans. Rex Warner. 1979.

———.*The Persian Expedition (Anabasis).* Trans. Rex Warner. 1972.

The Rise of Macedonia, 359–323 B.C.E.

Modern scholars energetically debate Alexander's character; Bosworth, for example, brands him a natural-born killer, while O'Brien sees him as overcome by alcoholism.

*Primary source.

*Arrian. *The Campaigns of Alexander (Anabasis).* Trans. Aubrey de Sélincourt. 1971.

Borza, Eugene N. *In the Shadow of Olympus: The Emergence of Macedon.* 1990.

Bosworth, A. B. *Alexander and the East: The Tragedy of Triumph.* 1996.

———. *Conquest and Empire: The Reign of Alexander the Great.* 1988.

Carney, Elizabeth Donnelly. *Women and Monarchy in Macedonia.* 2000.

Macedonian royal tombs at Vergina: http://alexander.macedonia.culture.gr/2/21/211/21117a/e211qa07.html.

O'Brien, John Maxwell. *Alexander the Great, the Invisible Enemy: A Biography.* 1992.

*Plutarch. *The Age of Alexander.* Trans. Ian Scott-Kilvert. 1973.

Stoneman, Richard. *Alexander the Great.* 1997.

The Hellenistic Kingdoms, 323–30 B.C.E.

Recent research stresses the innovative responses of the successor kings to the challenges of ruling multicultural empires. Underwater archaeology has begun to reveal ancient Alexandria in Egypt, whose harbor district has sunk below the level of today's Mediterranean Sea.

*Austin, M. M. *The Hellenistic World from Alexander to the Roman Conquest: A Selection of Ancient Sources in Translation.* 1981.

*Burstein, Stanley M. *The Hellenistic Age from the Battle of Ipsos to the Death of Kleopatra VII.* 1985.

Ellis, Walter M. *Ptolemy of Egypt.* 1994.

Empereur, Jean-Yves. *Alexandria: Jewel of Egypt.* 2002.

Lewis, Naphtali. *Greeks in Ptolemaic Egypt.* 1986.

Ptolemaic Egypt: http://www.houseofptolemy.org.

Sherwin-White, Susan, and Amélie Kuhrt. *From Samarkhand to Sardis: A New Approach to the Seleucid Empire.* 1993.

Shipley, Graham. *The Greek World After Alexander 323–30 B.C.* 2000.

Hellenistic Culture, 323–30 B.C.E.

Old scholarship viewed Hellenistic culture as "impure" and less valuable than Classical Age culture because it mixed traditions. Scholars today identify the imaginative ways in which Hellenistic thinkers and artists combined the old and the new, the familiar and the foreign. Studying Hellenistic philosophers for the intrinsic interest of their ideas has become an important activity in the history of philosophy and ethics.

Ancient Alexandria in Egypt: **http://ce.eng .usf.edu/pharos/alexandria**.

*Bartlett, John R. *Jews in the Hellenistic World: Josephus, Aristeas, The Sibylline Oracles, Eupolemus.* 1985.

Chamoux, François. *Hellenistic Civilization.* Trans. Michel Roussel. 2003.

Inwood, Brad, ed. *The Cambridge Companion to the Stoics.* 2003.

Long, A. A. *Hellenistic Philosophy: Stoics, Epicureans, Sceptics.* 2nd ed. 1986.

*Menander. *The Plays and Fragments.* Trans. Maurice Balme. 2002.

Mikalson, Jon D. *Religion in Hellenistic Athens.* 1998.

Pollitt, J. J. *Art in the Hellenistic Age.* 1986.

Pomeroy, Sarah B. *Women in Hellenistic Egypt: From Alexander to Cleopatra.* Rev. ed. 1990.

Schäfer, Peter. *Judeophobia: Attitudes toward the Jews in the Ancient World.* 1997.

Sharples, R. W. *Stoics, Epicureans, and Sceptics: An Introduction to Hellenistic Philosophy.* 1996.

Snyder, Jane M. *The Woman and the Lyre: Women Writers in Classical Greece and Rome.* 1989.

Walker, Susan, and Peter Higgs, eds. *Cleopatra of Egypt: From History to Myth.* 2001.

CHAPTER REVIEW

IMPORTANT EVENTS

399 B.C.E.	Trial and execution of Socrates at Athens
c. 393 B.C.E.	Athens's Long Walls rebuilt
386 B.C.E.	Sparta makes a peace with Persia ceding control over the Anatolian Greek city-states; Plato founds the Academy in Athens
371 B.C.E.	Thebes defeats Sparta at the battle of Leuctra in Boeotia
362 B.C.E.	Power vacuum in Greece after the battle of Mantinea in the Peloponnese
338 B.C.E.	Philip II defeats a Greek alliance at the battle of Chaeronea to become the leading power in Greece
335 B.C.E.	Aristotle founds the Lyceum in Athens
334–323 B.C.E.	Alexander the Great leads an army of Greeks and Macedonians in a conquest of the Persian Empire
324 or 323 B.C.E.	The dramatist Menander presents his first comedy at Athens
c. 307 B.C.E.	Epicurus founds his philosophical group "the Garden" in Athens
306–304 B.C.E.	The successors of Alexander declare themselves to be kings
c. 300–260 B.C.E.	Theocritus writes poetry at the Ptolemaic court
c. 300 B.C.E.	Euclid teaches geometry at Alexandria in Egypt
c. 195 B.C.E.	Seleucid queen Laodice endows dowries for girls in Iasus
167 B.C.E.	Maccabee revolt after Antiochus IV converts the Jewish temple in Jerusalem to a Greek sanctuary
30 B.C.E.	Death of Cleopatra VII, queen of Egypt, and takeover of the Ptolemaic empire by Rome

KEY TERMS

dualism (128)

Epicureanism (151)

epigrams (147)

Hellenistic (124)

Koine (155)

materialism (150)

mean (130)

metaphysics (128)

ruler cults (155)

Stoicism (151)

successor kings (139)

REVIEW QUESTIONS

1. What were the major differences between Plato's philosophical ideas and Aristotle's?
2. How did innovation and tradition combine to sustain Macedonia's power during the reigns of Philip II and Alexander the Great?
3. What were the biggest challenges facing the Hellenistic kings?
4. How did the political changes of the Hellenistic period affect art and science?

MAKING CONNECTIONS

1. For people of all social classes, how did life in the Hellenistic kingdoms compare to that in the Greek city-state of the Classical Age?
2. What are the advantages and disadvantages of governmental support of the arts and sciences? Compare such support in the Hellenistic kingdoms to that in the United States today (e.g., through the National Endowment for the Humanities, National Endowment for the Arts, and the National Science Foundation).

FOR FURTHER EXPLORATION

To assess your mastery of the material in this chapter, see the Online Study Guide at **bedfordstmartins.com/hunt**.

To read additional primary-source material from this period, see Chapter 4 in *Sources of The Making of the West*, Second Edition.

The Rise of Rome,
c. 753–44 B.C.E.

THE ROMANS TREASURED LEGENDS describing their state's transformation from a tiny village to a world power. They especially loved stories about their legendary first king, Romulus, famous as a hot-tempered and shrewd leader. According to the legend later called the "Rape of the Sabine◆ Women," Romulus's Rome needed more women to bear children to increase its population and build a strong army. The king therefore begged Rome's neighbors for permission for Romans to marry their women. Everyone turned him down, scorning Rome's poverty and weakness. Enraged, Romulus hatched a plan to use force where diplomacy had failed. Inviting the neighboring Sabines to a religious festival, he had his men kidnap the unmarried women. The Roman kidnappers promptly married the Sabine women, promising to cherish them as beloved wives and new citizens. When the Sabine men attacked Rome to rescue their kin, the women rushed into the midst of the bloody battle, begging their brothers, fathers, and new husbands either to stop slaughtering one another or to kill them to end the war. The men immediately made peace and agreed to merge their populations under Roman rule.

This legend emphasizes that Rome, unlike the city-states of Greece, expanded by absorbing outsiders into its citizen body, sometimes violently, sometimes peacefully. Rome's growth became the ancient world's most dramatic expansion of population and territory, as a people originally housed in a few huts gradually created a state that swallowed up most of Europe, North Africa, Egypt, and the eastern Mediterranean lands. The social, cultural, political, legal, and economic traditions that Roman society and government developed

---

◆**Sabine:** SAY byn

Roman Social and Religious Traditions
- Roman Moral Values
- The Patron-Client System
- The Roman Family
- Education for Public Life
- Public and Private Religion

From Monarchy to Republic, c. 753–287 B.C.E.
- Roman Society During the Monarchy, c. 753–509 B.C.E.
- The Early Roman Republic, 509–287 B.C.E.

Roman Imperialism and Its Consequences, Fifth to First Centuries B.C.E.
- Expansion in Italy, c. 500–c. 220 B.C.E.
- Wars with Carthage and in the East, 264–121 B.C.E.
- Hellenism in Roman Literature and Art, Third to First Centuries B.C.E.
- Stresses on Republican Society, Third and Second Centuries B.C.E.

Upheaval in the Late Republic, c. 133–44 B.C.E.
- The Gracchi and Factional Politics, 133–121 B.C.E.
- Gaius Marius and the Origin of Client Armies, 107–100 B.C.E.
- Sulla and Civil War, 91–78 B.C.E.
- The Republic's Downfall, 83–44 B.C.E.

The Wolf Suckling Romulus and Remus
This silver coin, dating from 269–268 B.C.E., belongs to the earliest issues of Roman coinage. A head of the Greek hero Hercules is on the other (front) side, while this side, the reverse, depicts the myth that a she-wolf suckled the twin brothers Romulus and Remus, the offspring of the war god Mars and the future founders of Rome. Romans treasured this story because it implied that Mars loved their city so dearly that he dispatched a wild animal to nurture its founders after a cruel tyrant had forced their mother to abandon the infants. The myth also taught Romans that their state had been born in violence: Romulus killed Remus in an argument over who would lead their new settlement. The word below the picture means "of the Romans."

in ruling this vast area created closer inter-connections between its diverse peoples than ever before or since. Unlike the Greeks and Macedonians, the Romans maintained the unity of their state for centuries. Its political longevity meant that Rome deeply affected the course of later Western civilization.

Roman culture sprang from the traditions of ancient Italy's many peoples, but Greek literature, art, and philosophy influenced Rome's culture most of all. Some historians charge that Romans mindlessly took over the older civilization's traditions and changed them only in superficial ways, such as giving Latin names to Greek gods. It is more accurate, however, to think of the cross-cultural contact that so deeply influenced Rome as a kind of competition in innovation between equals rather than as imagining Greek culture to have been "superior" and improving "inferior" Roman culture. Like other ancient peoples, Romans often copied their neighbors, but they adapted whatever they learned to their own purposes and determined their own cultural identity.

The kidnapping legend belongs to Rome's earliest history, when kings ruled (c. 753–509 B.C.E.). Rome's most important history comes afterward, divided into two major periods of about five hundred years each—the republic and the empire. These terms refer only to the system of government in place at the time: under the republic (founded 509 B.C.E.), an oligarchy of the social elite governed; under the empire, monarchs once again ruled. Rome's greatest expansion came during the republic. The confidence that fueled this tremendous

growth stemmed from Romans' belief in a divine destiny: the gods willed that the Romans should rule the world by military might and law and improve it through social and moral values. Their unshakable faith that heaven backed them is illustrated by the legend of the Sabine women, in which the earliest Romans used a religious festival as a ruse to commit kidnapping. Their firm belief that values should drive politics showed in their determination to persuade the Sabine women that loyalty and love would wipe out the crime that had forcibly turned them from captives into wives and Romans.

In addition to a determination to establish families, Roman values under the republic emphasized selfless service to the community, individual honor and public status, the importance of the law, and shared decision making. Unfortunately, these values conflicted with one another in the long run. During most of the republic, the conflicts never became fierce enough to threaten Rome's stability. By the first century B.C.E., however, power-hungry leaders such as Sulla and Julius Caesar had plunged Rome into civil war and destroyed the republic by putting their personal ambition before the good of the state.

❖ Roman Social and Religious Traditions

Roman social and religious traditions shaped the history of the Roman republic. Its citizens believed that eternal moral values connected them to one another and required them

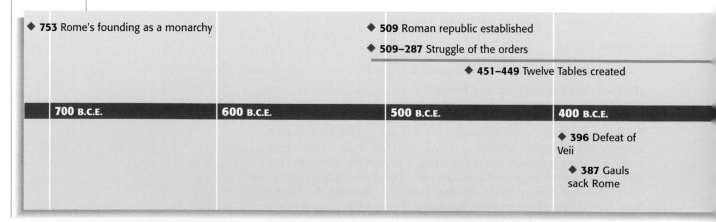

◆ **753** Rome's founding as a monarchy

◆ **509** Roman republic established

◆ **509–287** Struggle of the orders

◆ **451–449** Twelve Tables created

700 B.C.E.	600 B.C.E.	500 B.C.E.	400 B.C.E.

◆ **396** Defeat of Veii

◆ **387** Gauls sack Rome

to honor the gods in return for divine support. Hierarchy affected every aspect of their lives: people in all social levels were obligated to patrons or clients; in families, fathers dominated; in religion, the gods' superiority demanded that people pray to them to protect the state and their families.

Roman Moral Values

Roman values involved complex ideas and often overlapped. Most important, they determined relationships with other people and with the gods. Romans guided their lives by the **mos maiorum** (literally, "the way of the elders"), or values handed down from their ancestors. The Romans treasured the antiquity of these values because, for them, *old* equaled "tested by time" whereas *new* implied "dangerous." Roman morality emphasized virtue, faithfulness, and respect; moral conduct earned public respect.

Virtus (literally, "virtue") was a primarily masculine quality comprising courage, strength, and loyalty. It also included wisdom and moral purity, qualities that members of the social elite were expected to display in their public and private lives. In this broader sense, virtus applied to women as well as men. In the second century B.C.E., the Roman poet Lucilius defined it in this way:

> Virtue is to know the human relevance of each thing,
> To know what is humanly right and useful and honorable,
> And what things are good and what are bad, useless, shameful, and dishonorable. . . .
> Virtue is to pay what in reality is owed to honorable status

> To be an enemy and a foe to bad people and bad values
> But a defender of good people and good values. . . .
> And, in addition, virtue is putting the country's interests first,
> Then our parents', with our own interests third and last.

Faithfulness (*fides*, from which our word *fidelity* derives) meant keeping one's obligations no matter the cost, whether the obligation was formal or informal. To fail to meet an obligation was to offend the community and the gods. Faithful women remained virgins before marriage and monogamous afterward. Men demonstrated faithfulness by never breaking their word, paying their debts, and treating everyone with justice—which did not mean treating everyone the same, but rather treating each person appropriately according to whether he or she was an equal, a superior, or an inferior.

Religious activity was a crucial part of faithfulness. Showing devotion to the gods and to one's family was its supreme form. Women and men alike respected the superior authority of the gods and of the elders and ancestors of their families. Performing religious rituals properly and regularly was crucial: Romans believed that they had to worship the gods faithfully and respectfully to maintain the divine favor that protected their community.

Roman values demanded that each person maintain self-control and limit displays of emotion. So strict was this value that not even wives and husbands could kiss in public without seeming emotionally out of control.

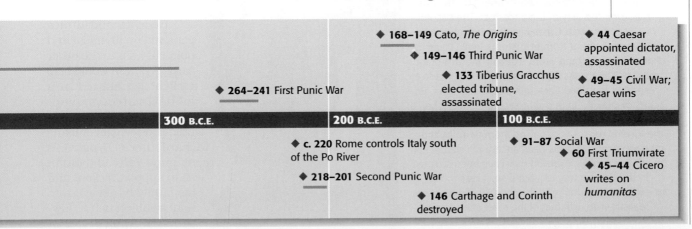

- ♦ **168–149** Cato, *The Origins*
- ♦ **149–146** Third Punic War
- ♦ **133** Tiberius Gracchus elected tribune, assassinated
- ♦ **44** Caesar appointed dictator, assassinated
- ♦ **49–45** Civil War; Caesar wins
- ♦ **264–241** First Punic War

| **300 B.C.E.** | **200 B.C.E.** | **100 B.C.E.** |

- ♦ **c. 220** Rome controls Italy south of the Po River
- ♦ **218–201** Second Punic War
- ♦ **146** Carthage and Corinth destroyed
- ♦ **91–87** Social War
- ♦ **60** First Triumvirate
- ♦ **45–44** Cicero writes on *humanitas*

It also meant that a person should never give up no matter how hard the situation. Persevering and doing one's duty were thus basic Roman values.

The reward for living these values was respect from other people. Women earned respect by bearing legitimate children and educating them morally; their reward was a good reputation among their families and friends. Respected men relied on their reputations to help them win election to government posts. A man of the highest reputation commanded so much respect that others would obey him regardless of whether he held an office with formal power over them. A man with this much prestige was said to enjoy "authority."

The concept of authority based on respect reflected the Roman belief that some people were inherently superior to others; that is, they believed that society should be hierarchical. They therefore divided people up according to status, determined both by the history of their family and their wealth. Romans believed that aristocrats, or people born into the best families, automatically deserved high respect. In compensation, however, aristocrats were supposed to live strictly by the highest values and serve the community.

A Patrician Holding Death Masks of His Ancestors

This marble statue shows an elderly patrician man holding two death masks of his ancestors. It illustrates the Romans' commitment to the *mos maiorum*, the way of the ancestors. The second-century B.C.E. Greek historian Polybius, who learned about Roman customs while living in Rome for seventeen years, explains the use of the masks: "The masks are portraits, carefully made to resemble the dead person in shape and form. Romans display them at public sacrifices, and when a prominent family member dies, they carry them in the funeral procession, having them worn by those who most resemble the dead ancestor in stature and build." This particular version may have been sculpted in the first century C.E., but if so, it was a copy of an earlier statue dating to the republic. Compare its realistic style with that of the relief of an ex-slave family on page 167. *Scala/Art Resource, NY.*

In Roman legends about the early days, a person could be poor and still remain a proud aristocrat. Over time, however, money became overwhelmingly important to the Roman elite, for spending on showy luxuries, large-scale entertaining, and lavish gifts to the community. In this way, wealth became necessary to maintain high social status. By the later centuries of the Roman republic, ambitious men often trampled on other values to acquire riches and the status they now conveyed.

The Patron-Client System

The **patron-client system** provided the legal and moral basis for the status differences so key to Roman society. It was an interlocking network of personal relationships that obligated people to one another. A patron was a man of superior status who could provide benefits, as they were called, to lower-status people who paid him special attention. These were his clients, who in return owed him duties. In this hierarchical system, a patron was often himself the client of a more distinguished man. The Romans called the patron-client relationship a friendship; a patron would greet a social inferior as "my friend," not as "my client." A client, however, would honor his superior by addressing him as "my patron."

Benefits and duties centered on financial and political help to the other party. A patron would help a client get started in a political career by supporting his candidacy and would provide gifts or loans in hard times. A patron's most important obligation was to support a client and his family if they got into legal trouble, such as lawsuits involving property.

Sculpted Tomb of a Family of Ex-Slaves
The inscription on this tomb monument, which may date to the first century B.C.E., reveals that the husband and wife depicted on it started life as slaves but gained their freedom and thus became Roman citizens. Their son, shown in the background holding a pet pigeon, was a free person. One of the remarkable features of Roman civilization, and a source of its demographic strength, was the wholesale incorporation of ex-slaves into the citizen body. This family had done well enough financially to afford a sculpted tomb, and the tablets the man is holding and the carefully groomed hairstyle of the woman are meant to show that their family was literate and stylish. Compare the man's realistically lined face with the woman's softer, more idealized one. *German Archeological Institute/ Madeline Grimoldi.*

Clients had to aid their patrons' campaigns for public office by swinging votes their way. They also had to lend money when patrons serving as officials incurred large expenses to provide public works and fund their daughters' lavish dowries. Furthermore, a patron expected his clients to gather at his house early in the morning to accompany him to the forum, the city's public center, because it was a mark of great status to have numerous clients thronging around him. A Roman leader needed a large, fine house to hold this throng and to entertain his social equals; a crowded house signified social success.

Patrons' and clients' mutual obligations were supposed to endure over generations. Ex-slaves, who automatically became the clients for life of the masters who freed them, often passed this relationship on to their children. Romans with contacts abroad could acquire clients among foreigners; particularly distinguished Romans sometimes had entire foreign communities obligated to them. With its emphasis on duty and permanence, the patron-client system enshrined the Roman view that social stability and well-being were achieved by faithfully maintaining the established ties.

The Roman Family

The family was Roman society's bedrock because it taught values and determined the ownership of property. Men and women shared the duty of teaching their children values, though by law the father possessed the ***patria potestas♦*** (literally, "father's power") over his children, no matter how old, and his slaves. This power made him the sole owner of all his dependents' property. As long as he was alive, no son or daughter could officially own anything, accumulate money, or possess any independent legal standing. Unofficially, however, adult children did acquire personal property and money, and favored slaves could build up savings. Fathers also held legal power of life and death over these members of their households, but they rarely exercised this power on anyone except newborns. Abandoning unwanted babies (a practice called exposure)—so that they would die, be adopted, or be raised by strangers as slaves—was accepted to control the size of families and dispose of physically imperfect infants. Baby girls probably suffered this fate more often

---

♦***patria potestas:*** PAH tree uh poh TEHS tahs

than boys because a family enhanced its power by investing its resources in its sons.

Since their values had a strong communal aspect, Romans regularly conferred with others to seek consensus on important family issues. Each Roman man had a council, a circle of friends and relatives whom he consulted before making significant decisions. A man contemplating the drastic decision to execute an adult member of his household, for example, would not have made the decision on his own. A father's council would certainly have advised him to think again if he proposed killing his adult son, except for an extremely compelling reason. In a rare instance of the violent exercise of a father's power, one outraged Roman had his son put to death in 63 b.c.e. because the youth had committed treason by joining a conspiracy to overthrow the government.

The patria potestas did not allow a husband to control his wife because "free" marriages—in which the wife formally remained under her father's power as long as the father lived—eventually became the most common. But in the ancient world, few fathers lived long enough to oversee the lives of their married daughters or sons; four out of five parents died before their children reached thirty. A woman without a living father was relatively independent. Legally she needed a male guardian to conduct her business, but guardianship was largely an empty formality by the first century b.c.e. Upper-class women could even on occasion demonstrate to express their opinions. In 195 b.c.e., for example, a group of women blocked Rome's streets for days, until the men rescinded a wartime law meant to reduce tensions between rich and poor by limiting the amount of gold jewelry and fine clothing women could wear and where they could ride in carriages. A later legal expert commented on women's freedom of action: "The common belief, that because of their instability of judgment women are often deceived and that it is only fair to have them controlled by the authority of guardians, seems more false than true. For women of full age manage their affairs themselves."

A Roman woman had to grow up fast to assume her duties as teacher of values to her children and manager of her household's resources. Tullia (c. 79–45 b.c.e.), daughter of the renowned politician and orator Marcus Tullius Cicero♦ (106–43 b.c.e.), was engaged at twelve, married at sixteen, and widowed by twenty-two. Like every other married woman of wealth in Rome, she oversaw the household slaves, monitored the nurturing of the young children by wet nurses, kept account books to track the property she personally owned, and accompanied her husband to dinner parties—something a Greek wife never did.

A mother's responsibility for shaping her children's values constituted the foundation of female virtue in Roman eyes. Women like Cornelia, a famous aristocrat of the second century b.c.e., won enormous respect for their accomplishments in raising outstanding citizens. When her distinguished husband died, Cornelia refused an offer of marriage from the Ptolemaic king of Egypt so that she could continue to oversee the family estate and educate her surviving daughter and two sons. (Her other nine children had died.) The boys, Tiberius♦ and Gaius Sempronius Gracchus,♦ grew up to be among the most influential and controversial political leaders in the late republic. The number of children she bore exemplified the fertility and stamina required of a Roman wife to ensure the survival of her husband's family line. Cornelia also became renowned for entertaining important people and for her stylish letters, which were still being read by the educated public a century later.

Roman women had no official political role, but wealthy women like Cornelia could wield indirect political influence by expressing their opinions privately to their husbands, male children, and other relatives. Marcus Porcius Cato♦ (234–149 b.c.e.), a famous politician and author, described the behind-the-scenes reality of women's influence: "All mankind rule their wives, we [Roman men] rule all mankind, and our wives rule us."

Women helped themselves and their families by accumulating property through in-

---

♦**Cicero** SIH suh roh
♦**Tiberius:** ty BEER ee uhs
♦**Gaius Sempronius Gracchus:** GAY uhs sehm PROH nee uhs GRAK uhs
♦**Porcius Cato:** PAWR key uhs KAY toh

Sculpture of a Woman Running a Store
This relief sculpture portrays a woman selling food from behind the counter of a small shop while customers make purchases or converse with each other. Since Roman women could own property, it is possible that the woman is the store owner. The man immediately to the left, behind the counter, could be her husband or a servant. The market areas in Roman towns were packed with small, family-run stores like this that sold everything imaginable, much like malls of today. Poor people did not own stores; they hawked cheap goods in the street. *Art Resource, NY.*

heritance and entrepreneurship; recent archaeological discoveries reveal that by the end of the republic some women owned large businesses. Most poor women, like poor men, had to toil for a living; often they held small-scale sales jobs, hawking vegetables, amulets, or ribbons from a stand (see illustration on this page). Women and men together performed the predominant form of Roman manufacturing: production in the home. The men worked the raw materials, cutting, fitting, and polishing wood, leather, and metal, while the women sold the finished goods. The poorest women often could earn money through prostitution, which was legal but considered disgraceful. Because both women and men could control property, prenuptial agreements determining the property rights of husband and wife were common. Divorce was legally simple, with fathers usually keeping the children.

Education for Public Life

Roman education aimed to make men and women exponents of traditional values and, for different purposes, effective speakers. As in Greece, most children received their education in the family; only the rich could afford to pay teachers. Wealthy parents bought literate slaves to educate their children; by the late republic, they often chose Greek slaves so that their children could learn to speak Greek and read that culture's literary classics, which most Romans regarded as the world's best. Wealthy parents might also send their children, from about seven years old, to classes offered by independent schoolmasters in their lodgings. Lessons usually consisted of rote memorization, and teachers frequently used corporal punishment to keep pupils attentive. In upper-class families, both daughters and sons learned to read. The girls were also taught literature and perhaps some music; they especially learned how to make educated conversation at dinner parties. The principal aim of women's education was to prepare them to instill traditional social and moral values in their children.

Sons received physical training and learned to fight with weapons—courage being a fundamental value—but the principal aim of a boy's education was to learn rhetoric—the skill of persuasive public speaking. Rhetorical training dominated an upper-class Roman boy's curriculum because it was crucial to a successful public career. A boy would hear rhetoric in action by accompanying his male relatives to public meetings, assemblies, and court sessions. By listening to the speeches, he would learn to imitate winning techniques. Cicero, Rome's most famous orator, agreed that young men must learn to "excel in public speaking. It is the tool for controlling men at Rome, winning them over to your side, and keeping them from harming you. You fully realize your own power when you are a man who can cause your rivals the greatest fears of meeting you in a trial." Wealthy parents paid advanced teachers to instruct their sons in the knowledge an effective speaker required, the same sort of education that the Sophists had offered in Greece. Roman rhetoric owed much to Greek techniques, and many Roman orators studied with Greek teachers. This was only one of the crucial ways in which Greek culture influenced Rome.

Public and Private Religion

Romans also followed Greek models in religion, worshiping many divinities identified with those of Greece. Romans viewed their chief deity, Jupiter, who corresponded to the Greek god Zeus, as a powerful, stern father. Juno (Greek Hera), queen of the gods, and Minerva (Greek Athena), goddess of wisdom, joined Jupiter to form the state religion's central triad. These three deities shared Rome's most revered temple on the Capitoline, the city's acropolis.

Guarding Rome's physical safety and prosperity was the gods' major function. Above all, they were supposed to help Rome defeat enemies in war, but divine support for agriculture was also indispensable. Many official prayers requested the gods' aid in ensuring good crops, warding off disease, and promoting healthy reproduction for animals and people. In times of crisis, Romans even sought foreign gods to protect them, such as when the government imported the cult of the healing god Asclepius from Greece in 293 B.C.E., hoping he would save Rome from a plague. Similarly, the Senate in 204 B.C.E. voted to bring to Rome the pointed

black stone representing Cybele♦ ("the Great Mother"), whose chief sanctuary was in Phrygia♦ in Asia Minor (the Roman term for Anatolia). Her cult was believed to promote fertility.

The republic supported many other cults with special guardian features. The shrine of Vesta (Greek Hestia), the goddess of the hearth and therefore a protector of the family, housed Rome's official eternal flame, which guaranteed the state's permanent existence. The Vestal Virgins, six unmarried women sworn to chastity at ages six to ten for terms of thirty years, tended Vesta's shrine. Their chastity symbolized protection of the Roman family structure and thus the preservation of the republic itself. As members of Rome's only female priesthood, the Vestal Virgins earned high status and freedom from their fathers' control by performing their most important duty: keeping the flame from going out. As the Greek historian Dionysius of Halicarnassus♦ reported in the first century B.C.E., "The Romans dread the extinction of the fire above all misfortunes, looking upon it as an omen which portends the destruction of the city." On the rare occasions when the flame went out, the Romans assumed that one of the Vestal Virgins had broken her vow of chastity and buried her alive as the penalty.

Religion occupied a prominent place in Roman family life. Each household maintained a sacred space for small shrines housing statuettes of its Penates♦ (spirits of the household stores) and Lares♦ (spirits of the ancestors), who were believed to keep the family well and its moral traditions alive (see Household Shrine from Pompeii). Upper-class families kept death masks of distinguished ancestors hanging in the main room and wore them at funerals to commemorate the family's heritage and the current generation's responsibility to live up to the ancestors' values. This strong sense of family

♦**Cybele:** SIH buh lee
♦**Phrygia:** FRIH jee uh
♦**Dionysius of Halicarnassus:** dy uh NIH see uhs of ha luh kahr NA suhs
♦**Penates:** peh NAY teez
♦**Lares:** LAHR eez

tradition and instruction from parents (especially mothers) underlay Roman morality. The shame of losing public esteem, not the fear of divine punishment, was the strongest deterrent to immoral behavior.

Because Romans believed that divine spirits participated in crucial events such as birth, marriage, and death, they performed many rituals seeking protection from dangers. Rituals also accompanied everyday activities, such as breast-feeding babies or fertilizing crops. Many public religious gatherings promoted the community's health and stability. For example, during the February 15 Lupercalia festival (whose name recalled the wolf, *luper* in Latin, who legend said had reared Romulus and his twin, Remus), naked young men streaked around the Palatine hill, lashing any woman they met with strips of goatskin. Women who had not yet borne children would run out to be struck, believing this would help them to become fertile. The December 17 Saturnalia festival, honoring the Italian deity of liberation, Saturnus, temporarily inverted the social order to release tensions caused by the inequalities between masters and slaves. As the playwright and scholar Accius♦ (c. 170–80 b.c.e.) described the occasion, "People joyfully hold feasts all through the country and the towns, each owner acting as a waiter to his slaves." This social inversion reinforced the slaves' ties to their owners by symbolizing a benefit from the latter, which the former had to repay with faithful service.

Like the Greek gods, Rome's deities had few direct connections with human morality because Roman tradition did not regard the gods as the originators of society's moral code. Cicero's description of Jupiter's official titles explained public religion's closer ties to national security and prosperity than to individual morality: "We call Jupiter the Best (*Optimus*) and Greatest (*Maximus*) not because he makes us just or sober or wise but, rather, healthy, unharmed, rich, and prosperous." In keeping with this belief, Roman officials preceded important actions with the ritual called taking the auspices—seeking Jupiter's approval for their plans by observing natural signs such as the direction of the

♦**Accius:** AK key uhs

Household Shrine from Pompeii
This colorfully painted shrine stood inside the entrance to a house at Pompeii known as the House of the Vettii, from the name of its owners. Successful businessmen, the Vettii spared no expense in decorating their home: with 188 frescoes (paintings done by applying pigments to damp plaster) adorning its walls, the interior blazed in a riot of color. This type of shrine, found in every Roman house, is called a *lararium* after the *lares* (deities protecting the household), who are shown here flanking a central figure. He portrays the spirit (*genius*) of the father of the family. What do you think it signifies that the lares seem to be dancing? The snake below, which is about to drink from a bowl probably holding milk set out for it, also symbolizes a protective force, the good daimon. The whole scene sums up the role Romans expected their gods to play: staving off harm and bad luck. *Scala/Art Resource, NY.*

flights of birds, their eating habits, or the appearance of thunder and lightning. Action proceeded only if the signs were favorable.

Romans linked values and religion by regarding central values as divine forces. *Pietas* (literally, "piety") for example, which meant devotion and duty to family, friends, the state, and the gods, had a temple at Rome. It housed a statue personifying pietas as a female divinity in human form. This personification of abstract moral qualities provided a focus for cult rituals. The religious aura attached to the cults of moral qualities emphasized that they were ideals to which every Roman should aspire.

The duty of Roman religious officials, or priests, was to ensure the gods' goodwill toward the state; this the Romans called *pax deorum* (literally, "peace of or with the gods"). Men from the top of the social hierarchy served as priests by conducting frequent sacrifices, festivals, and other rituals conforming strictly to ancestral tradition. These priests were not professionals devoting their lives solely to religious activity; rather, they were citizens performing public service in keeping with Roman values. The most important official, the *pontifex maximus*◆ (literally, "highest priest"), served as the head of state religion and the ultimate authority on religious matters affecting government. The political powers of this priesthood motivated Rome's most prominent men to seek it.

Disrespect for religious tradition brought punishment. Naval commanders, for example, took the auspices by feeding sacred chickens on their ships: if the birds ate energetically before a battle, Jupiter favored the Romans and an attack could begin. In 249 B.C.E., the commander Publius Claudius Pulcher◆ grew frustrated when his chickens, probably seasick, refused to eat. Determined to attack, he finally hurled the birds overboard in a rage, sputtering, "Well then, let them drink!" When he promptly suffered a huge defeat, he was fined very heavily.

> **Review:** What was the most important common theme in Roman traditional values?

❖ From Monarchy to Republic, c. 753–287 B.C.E.

Rome's communal values provided the unity and stability necessary for its astounding growth from a tiny settlement into the Mediterranean's greatest power. This growth took place over centuries, as the Romans developed the republic's government and expanded their territory and population. Politically, Rome in the eighth through the sixth century B.C.E. adopted the ancient world's most common kind of political system: rule by kings. Disturbed by the later kings' violence, members of the social elite overthrew the monarchy to create a new political system—the republic—which lasted from the fifth through the first century B.C.E. The republic (from the Latin **res publica**, "the people's matter" or "the public business") distributed power more widely by electing officials in open meetings of male citizens. Rome gained land and population by winning aggressive wars and by absorbing other peoples. Its economic and cultural growth depended on contact with many other peoples around the Mediterranean.

Roman Society During the Monarchy, c. 753–509 B.C.E.

Legend taught that Rome's original government had seven kings, ruling in succession from 753 (the most commonly given date for the city's founding) to 509 B.C.E. The kings created Rome's most famous and enduring government body: the Senate, a group of distinguished men chosen as the king's personal council. The Senate helped the king rule in accordance with the Roman principle that important decisions should be thoroughly discussed with one's wisest friends. It played the same role—advising government leaders—for a thousand years, as Rome changed from a monarchy to a republic and back to a monarchy (the empire).

The kings laid the foundation for Rome's expansion by fighting enemies and taking in outsiders whom they conquered, as reflected in the story of Romulus's absorbing the Sabine women and their relatives into the Roman state. This inclusionary policy of making others into citizens, which contrasted sharply with the exclusionary laws of the contemporary Greek city-states, promoted ethnic diversity in early Rome and proved crucial for Rome's tremendous growth in power. Another important part of Roman policy—also different from Greek practice—was to grant citizenship to freed slaves. These freedmen and freedwomen, as they were called, still owed special obligations to their former owners, and they could not hold elective office or serve in the army. In all other

---

◆*pontifex maximus:* PAHN tih fehks MAK sih muhs
◆**Publius Claudius Pulcher:** PUHB lee uhs KLAW dee uhs PUHL kur

ways, however, ex-slaves enjoyed full civil rights, such as legal marriage. Their children possessed citizenship without any limitations. By the late republic, many Roman citizens were descendants of freed slaves.

Expansion and Cross-Cultural Contact.
Over the 250 years of the monarchy, Rome's inclusionary policy produced tremendous expansion. By around 550 b.c.e., the Romans controlled three hundred square miles of the area around Rome, called Latium;♦ the tiny original settlement had grown to between thirty and forty thousand people. This growth under the kings foreshadowed Rome's future as a powerful imperialist state.

Rome's geography and contact with other cultures, especially Greek, helped propel its expansion and rise to power. Rome lay at the natural center of both Italy and the Mediterranean world. The historian Livy♦ (59 b.c.e.–17 c.e.), who became famous for depicting Rome's early history as heroic, summed up the city's geographical advantages: "With reason did gods and men choose this site: all its advantages make it of all places in the world the best for a city destined to grow great." These advantages were fertile farmland, control of a river crossing on the major north–south route along the peninsula, and a nearby harbor on the Mediterranean Sea. Most important, Rome was ideally situated for contact with the outside world: the peninsula it was on stuck so far out into the Mediterranean that east–west traffic naturally encountered it (Map 5.1). The Romans' geographic term for the peninsula, Italia, came from an indigenous word meaning "calf land" and originally designated only the southern portion. Gradually Italia, or Italy, came to mean the entire peninsula south of the Alps.

The early Romans' contact with their diverse neighbors profoundly influenced their cultural development. Their closest neighbors, the people of Latium, were poor villagers like the Romans and spoke the same Indo-European language, an early form of Latin. To the south, however, lived Greeks, and contact with them had the greatest effect

MAP 5.1 Ancient Italy, c. 500 b.c.e.
When the Romans ousted the monarchy to found a republic in 509 b.c.e., they inhabited a relatively small territory in central Italy between the western coast and the mountain range that bisects the peninsula from north to south. Many different peoples lived in Italy at this time, with the most prosperous occupying fertile agricultural land and sheltered harbors on the peninsula's west side. The early republic's most urbanized neighbors were the Etruscans to the north and the Greeks in the city-states to the south, including on the island of Sicily. Immediately adjacent to Rome were the people of Latium, called Latins.

on Roman cultural development. Greeks had established colonies on the Campanian♦ plain as early as the 700s b.c.e. These settlements, such as Naples, grew prosperous and populous thanks to their location in a fertile area and their participation in international trade. Greek culture reached its most famous

♦**Latium:** LAY shee uhm
♦**Livy:** LIH vee

♦**Campanian:** kam PAY ny uhn

Banquet Scene Painted in an Etruscan Tomb
Painted about 480–470 B.C.E., this brightly colored fresco decorated a wall in an Etruscan tomb (known today as the Tomb of the Leopards, from the animals painted just above this scene) at Tarquinia. Wealthy Etruscans filled their tombs with pictures such as these, which, some scholars suggest, simultaneously represented the funeral feasts held to celebrate the life of the dead person and also the social pleasures experienced in this life and expected in the next. Here the banqueters recline on their elbows in Greek style, one of the many ways in which Etruscans were influenced by Hellenic culture. The Greeks themselves had probably adopted their dining customs from Near Eastern precedents. Why do you think the mens' robes are more colorful than those worn by the men in the mosaic depicting Plato's Academy on page 128? *Scala/Art Resource, NY.*

flowering in the fifth century B.C.E., at the time when the Roman republic was just taking shape after the end of the monarchy and centuries before Rome had its own literature, theater, or monumental architecture. Romans developed a love-hate relationship with Greece, admiring its literature and art but despising its lack of military unity. They adopted many elements from Greek culture—from ethical values to deities for their national cults, from the model for their poetry and prose to architectural design and style.

The Etruscans.   Cross-cultural influence also flowed to Rome from the Etruscans,◆ a people just to the north. Etruscan culture itself remains poorly known because the language has not yet been fully deciphered. The Etruscans became a prosperous people living in independent towns nestled on central Italian hilltops. Magnificently colored wall paint-

ings, which survive in some of their tombs, portray funeral banquets and games testifying to the splendor of their society (see the illustration on this page). While producing their own fine artwork, jewelry, and sculpture, the Etruscans nevertheless had a passion for importing luxurious objects from Greece and other Mediterranean lands. Most of the intact Greek vases known today, for example, were found in Etruscan tombs.

The Etruscans' international trade encouraged cultural interaction: gold tablets inscribed in Etruscan and Phoenician and discovered in 1964 at the port of Pyrgi◆ (thirty miles northwest of Rome) reveal that in about 500 B.C.E. the Etruscans dedicated a temple to the Phoenician goddess Astarte, whom they had learned about from trade with Carthage. That rich city, founded in western North Africa (modern Tunisia) by Phoenicians about 800 B.C.E., dominated seaborne commerce in the western Mediterranean.

◆**Etruscans:** ih TRUHS kuhns

◆**Pyrgi:** PEER ghee

The relationship between Etruscan and Roman culture remains a controversial topic. Until recently, scholars thought that the Etruscans had a huge influence on early Rome, assuming that the Etruscans conquered Rome and dominated it politically in the sixth century b.c.e. They also thought that the Etruscans were more culturally refined than the early Romans, mainly because archaeologists found so much Greek art at Etruscan sites. In short, they believed the Etruscans completely reshaped Roman culture during a period of supposed domination. New scholarship, however, stresses the Romans' independence in developing their own cultural traditions: they borrowed from the Etruscans, as from the Greeks, whatever appealed to them and revised these borrowings to fit their own circumstances.

Scholars agree that the Romans adopted ceremonial features of Etruscan culture, such as magistrates' elaborate garments, musical instruments, and procedures for religious rituals. The Romans also learned from the Etruscans to divine the will of the gods by looking for clues in the shapes of the vital organs of slaughtered animals. And they may have gotten their tradition of wives joining husbands at dinner parties from the Etruscans.

Other features of Roman culture formerly seen as deriving from Etruscan influence were probably part of the ancient Mediterranean's shared cultural environment. Rome's first political system, monarchy, was widespread in that world. The organization of the Roman army, a citizen militia of heavily armed infantry troops (hoplites) fighting in formation, reflected not just Etruscan precedent but that of many other peoples in the region. The alphabet, which the Romans certainly first learned from the Etruscans and used to write their own language, was actually Greek; the Greeks had gotten it through their contact with the earlier alphabets of eastern Mediterranean peoples. Trade with other areas of the Mediterranean and civil engineering leading to urbanization are other features of Etruscan life that Romans are said to have assimilated, but it is too simplistic to assume that cultural developments of this breadth resulted from one superior culture instructing another, less developed one. Rather, at this time in Mediterranean history, similar cultural developments were under way in many places. The Romans, like so many others, found their own way in navigating through this common cultural sea.

The Early Roman Republic, 509–287 b.c.e.

The Roman social elite's hatred of monarchy motivated the creation of the republic as a new political system. Aristocrats believed that a sole ruler and his family would inevitably become tyrannical and misuse their rule. This belief was enshrined in the most famous legend about the birth of the republic, Livy's story of the rape of Lucretia. Like most of Livy's stories about Roman history, it stressed moral virtue's role in the republic's founding. (See "Livy on Liberty in the Founding of the Roman Republic," page 176.) The end of the monarchy came when King Tarquin♦ the Proud's swaggering son raped Lucretia, a chaste wife in the social elite, to flaunt his superior power. Despite pleas from her husband and father not to blame herself, Lucretia committed suicide after denouncing her attacker and calling Roman women to remain faithful.

Declaring themselves Rome's liberators from tyranny, her relatives and their friends, led by Lucius Junius Brutus,♦ drove out Tarquin in 509 b.c.e. to end royal abuse of power. They then created the republic to ensure the sharing of power. Thereafter, the Romans prided themselves on having created a freer political system than that of many of their neighbors. The legend of the warrior Horatius at the bridge, for example, advertised the republic's dedication to national freedom. As Livy told the story, Horatius singlehandedly blocked the Etruscan army's access to Rome over a bridge crossing the Tiber♦ River when they tried to reimpose a king on the city (Map 5.2). While hacking at his opponents, Horatius berated them as slaves who had lost their freedom because they

---

♦**King Tarquin:** [King] TAHR kwihn
♦**Lucius Junius Brutus:** LOO shuhs JOO nyuhs BROOT uhs
♦**Tiber:** TY bur

Livy on Liberty in the Founding of the Roman Republic

The Roman historian Livy, writing in the late first century B.C.E. at the time of Augustus (the first Roman emperor), describes the foundation of the Roman republic in 509 B.C.E. as successful because it did not occur before Rome's early kings had prepared the masses for liberty. Livy dates the first Roman king to 753 B.C.E., which implies that this preparation to live in liberty took two hundred years or more.

From this point I will be writing the history of the Roman people as a liberated people—their deeds in peace and war, their officials elected annually, and their rule of laws with greater power than human beings possessed. The excess pride of Rome's last king [Tarquin the Proud] made their liberty all the more full of joy. The earlier kings had ruled in such a way that they are deservedly counted certainly as founders of parts of the city, which they built as new residences for the population which they added. There is no doubt that the same Brutus who deserves so much glory for having driven out King Tarquin the Proud would have done the worst thing for the Roman people if he had torn away rule from one of the earlier kings through a desire for premature liberty. What would have happened, if that mass of shepherds and immigrants, all renegades from their own peoples and having gained liberty, or at least impunity, under the protection of an inviolable sanctuary, had been released from their fear of royal rule and began to be stirred up by stormy tribunes and instigate political fights with the senators in a city not their own, before their obligations to wives and children and love of the soil itself—which comes about only over a long time—had united their hearts? Their community, not yet grown to adulthood, would have been broken apart by disagreements, the very community that the peaceful moderation of the early kings' rule had fostered and nurtured to the point that with its mature strength it could bear the good fruit of liberty.

Moreover, one may count the origin of liberty as created more by fixing the consuls' term of office at a single year rather than by any lessening of royal authority. The first consuls possessed all the rights and all the insignia [of the kings]. . . . Brutus [one of the first consuls] guarded liberty just as fiercely as he had won it. First of all, while the people were eager for their new liberty, he impelled them to swear an oath that they would never allow anyone to rule Rome as a king, so that later they could not be won over by the pleas or gifts of a [would-be] king. Next, to make the Senate stronger from the number of its members—Tarquin had shrunk it by murdering "Fathers" [senators under the kings]—he filled out its ranks to three hundred by appointing leading men from the equestrian class. It is said that from that time on there was the tradition of convoking the Senate by summoning the "Fathers" and the "Enrolled," the latter being those senators who had been appointed. This proved marvelously positive for the concord of the citizen community and for linking the hearts of the masses to the "Fathers."

Source: Livy, *From the Foundation of the City*, Book 2.1. Translation by Thomas R. Martin.

were ruled by haughty kings. This legend made clear that the compelling reason to found the republic was to prevent monarchy's abuses.

The Struggle of the Orders. The Romans struggled for nearly 250 years to shape a stable government for the republic after its foundation in 509 B.C.E. Roman social hierarchy split the population into two **orders**—the patricians◆ (a small group of the most aristocratic families) and the plebeians◆ (the rest of the citizens). Bitter turmoil over political and legal power pitted the orders against one another in the republic's early centuries; historians call this turmoil the

◆**patricians:** puh TRIH shuhns
◆**plebeians:** plih BEE uhns

struggle of the orders. Finally, in 287 B.C.E., the plebeians forced the patricians to grant them the right to make laws in their own assembly.

Social and economic disputes fueled the struggle. Patricians constituted a tiny percentage of the population—numbering only about 130 families in all—but their inherited status entitled them to control essential religious activities. Soon after the republic's founding they used their religious importance to monopolize political office. In this early period, many patricians were much wealthier than most citizens. Some plebeians, however, were also rich, and they resented the patricians' dominance. They especially hated the patricians' ban on intermarriage with plebeians because it seemed a humiliating assertion of superiority. Patricians enflamed tensions by wearing special red shoes to set themselves apart; later they changed to black shoes adorned with a small metal crescent.

The struggle began when rich plebeians clamored for the right to marry patricians as social equals, while poor plebeians demanded an equitable distribution of farmland and relief from crushing debts. To pressure the patricians, the plebeians periodically left the city for a temporary settlement and then refused military service. This tactic of secession worked because Rome's army depended on plebeian manpower; the patricians were too few to defend Rome by themselves. The patricians therefore agreed to written laws guaranteeing greater equality and social mobility. The earliest Roman law code, the **Twelve Tables** (so named from the bronze tablets on which the laws were engraved for all to see), was enacted between 451 and 449 B.C.E. in response to a secession brought on by a patrician's violence against a plebeian woman. The Tables encapsulated early Rome's prevailing legal customs in simply worded provisions such as "If plaintiff calls defendant to court, he shall go," or "If a wind causes a neighbor's tree to be bent and lean over your farm, action may be taken to have that tree removed." These laws prevented the patrician public officials who judged most legal cases from, as Livy puts it, "arbitrarily giving the force of law to their own preferences." The laws contained in the Twelve Tables became so important a symbol of the commitment to justice for all citizens that

MAP 5.2 The City of Rome during the Republic
Roman tradition said that King Servius Tullius built Rome's first defensive wall in the sixth century B.C.E., but archaeology shows that the first wall completely encircling the city's center and seven hills on the east bank of the Tiber River belongs to the fourth century B.C.E. and covered a circuit of about seven miles. By the second century B.C.E. the wall had been extended to soar fifty-two feet high and had been fitted with catapults to protect the large gates. Like the open agora surrounded by buildings at the heart of a Greek city, the forum remained Rome's political and social heart.

children were required to memorize them. The Roman belief in clear, fair laws as the best protection against social unrest helped keep the republic united until Tiberius and Gaius Gracchus provoked murderous turmoil in the late second century B.C.E.

The Consuls, the Ladder of Offices, and the Senate. Elected officials ran Roman republican government. All posts operated as panels, numbering from two to more than a dozen members, in accordance with the Roman value that rule should be shared. The highest officials were called consuls; two were elected each year. Their most important duty was commanding the army. Winning a consulship not only was the highest political honor a Roman man could achieve but also bestowed high status on his descendants forever.

To gain the consulship, a man traditionally had to win elections all the way up a **ladder of offices**. First, however, came ten years of military service from about age twenty to thirty. The ladder's first step was getting elected quaestor,♦ a financial administrator. Continuing to climb the ladder, an ambitious man would gain election as one of Rome's aediles,♦ who supervised the city's streets, sewers, aqueducts, temples, and markets. Few men reached the next level, the office of praetor.♦ The board of praetors performed judicial and military duties. The most successful praetors competed for the consulship. Ex-consuls competed to become one of the censors, elected every five years to conduct censuses of the citizen body and to select new senators so that the Senate membership stayed at about three hundred men. To be eligible for selection to the Senate, a man had to have won election as a quaestor.

The patricians tried to monopolize the highest offices, but the plebeians resisted fiercely. After violent struggle from about 500 to 450 B.C.E., the plebeians forced the patricians to create a special panel of ten annually elected plebeian officials, called tribunes, whose only responsibility was to stop actions that would harm plebeians and their property. The tribunate did not count as a regular ladder office, and tribunes derived their power from the plebeians' sworn oath to protect them against all attacks. This inviolability, called *sacrosanctity*,♦ gave tribunes veto (a Latin word meaning "forbid") power to block officials' actions, prevent laws from being passed, suspend elections, and—most controversially—contradict the Senate's advice. The tribunes' extraordinary power to veto government action often made them the catalysts for bitter political disputes. By 367 B.C.E., the plebeians had smashed their way into the competition for high public office

by forcing passage of a law requiring that at least one consul every year be a plebeian.

Roman values were supposed to motivate men to compete for high public office to win respect and glory, not money. Only well-off men could run for election because officials earned no salaries. In fact, they were expected to spend their own money lavishly to win popular support by paying for expensive public shows featuring gladiators (trained fighters) and wild beasts, such as lions imported from Africa. Financing such exhibitions could put a candidate deeply in debt. Once elected, a magistrate had to spend his money to subsidize public works, such as roads, aqueducts, and temples.

Early republican officials' only rewards were the esteem they won by service to the res publica. As the Romans gradually conquered more and more overseas territory, however, their desire for money to finance electoral campaigns overcame their emphasis on faithfulness and honesty. By the second century B.C.E., military officers enriched themselves not only legally by seizing booty from foreign enemies but also illegally by extorting bribes as administrators of newly conquered territories. Over time, acquiring money became more important than winning respect by upright public service.

The Senate under the republic retained the role it had enjoyed under the monarchy: shaping government policy by giving advice to its highest officials. Strictly speaking, the Senate did not make law. The senators' high social standing gave their opinions the moral force of law, however. If a consul rejected or ignored the Senate's advice, a political crisis ensued. The Senate thus guided the republic in every area: decisions on war, domestic and foreign policy, state finance, official religion, and all types of legislation. In keeping with the Roman tradition that status should be visible, the senators wore special black high-top shoes and robes embroidered with a broad purple stripe.

The Assemblies.   Male citizens meeting in a complicated system of differing assemblies officially determined legislation, government policy, election outcomes, and judgment in certain trials. Assemblies met outdoors and were only for voting, not discussion; a public gathering with speeches by leading men

---

♦**quaestor:** KWEH stur
♦**aediles:** EE dials
♦**praetor:** PREE tur
♦**sacrosanctity:** sa kroh SANK tuh tee

about the issues preceded every assembly. Everyone, including women and noncitizens, could listen to these speeches. The crowd expressed its agreement or disagreement with the speeches by applauding or hissing. Speakers therefore heard public opinion while forming the proposals that they put before the assemblies, which gave a small measure of democracy to the republic's oligarchic government. This was the extent of what some historians call the republic's mixed constitution. A significant restriction on democracy in the assemblies, however, was that voting took place by group, not individuals. Each assembly was divided into different groups, whose size was determined by status and wealth; a small group had the same vote as a large group.

The struggle of the orders led to a complex organization of the assemblies. Legend dated the earliest major one, the Centuriate Assembly, to the sixth century B.C.E., under the reign of Servius Tullius, Rome's fifth king. Its division into voting groups matched the army's organization and stuck the huge group of people too poor to afford military weapons, the **proletarians**,♦ into one group exercising only 1 vote out of the total of 193 votes. The groups of patricians and richer citizens therefore dominated this assembly. Conducting the elections for consuls and praetors became its main function.

To counterbalance the Centuriate Assembly, the plebeians in the fifth century B.C.E. created the Plebeian Assembly, which excluded patricians, divided plebeians into thirty-five groups according to where they lived, and elected tribunes. As plebeians gradually prevailed in the struggle of the orders, their assembly became more important; in 287 B.C.E., its resolutions, called *plebiscites*, became legally binding on all Romans. Soon after the Plebeian Assembly emerged, the Tribal Assembly was created to mix patricians with plebeians in voting groups according to where they lived. This assembly, in which plebeians greatly outnumbered patricians, eventually became the republic's most important institution for making policy, passing laws, and, until separate courts were created, conducting judicial trials.

♦**proletarians:** proh luh TEHR ee uhns

The Judicial System. The republic's judicial system developed slowly and with overlapping institutions. The praetors originally decided many legal cases, after listening to advice from their personal council; especially serious trials could be transferred to the assemblies. A separate jury system arose only in the second century B.C.E., and senators repeatedly clashed with other upper-class Romans over whether these juries should be manned only by Senate members.

As in Greece, Rome had no state-sponsored prosecutors or defenders. Accusers and accused had to speak for themselves in court or have friends speak for them. People of lower social status suffered a distinct disadvantage if they lacked a distinguished patron to plead their case. Priests dominated in legal knowledge procedures until the third century B.C.E. At that time, senators with legal expertise began to play a central role. Called jurists (from the Latin *juris*, "of the law"), they operated as private citizens, not as officials, in offering legal advice. Jurists' importance in the republican judicial system reflected the Roman tradition of consulting one's council in making decisions. Romans had a simple criminal law, but they formulated sophisticated civil law to regulate disputes over property and personal interests. Developed over centuries and gradually incorporating laws from other peoples, Roman civil law became the basis for many Western legal codes still in use today.

The republic's jumbled network of political and judicial institutions evolved in response to conflicts over power. Many different political bodies enacted laws, and legal cases could be decided in various ways. Rome had no highest judicial authority, such as the U.S. Supreme Court, to settle disputes about conflicting laws or controversial cases. The republic's stability therefore depended on a reverence for the mos maiorum. This tradition ensured that the most socially prominent and richest Romans dominated government and society—because they defined the way of the elders.

Review: Disputes over what issues fueled the struggle of the orders?

❖ Roman Imperialism and Its Consequences, Fifth to First Centuries B.C.E.

Expansion through war made conquest and military service central to Romans' lives. During the fifth, fourth, and third centuries B.C.E., the Romans fought war after war in Italy until they became the most powerful state on the peninsula. In the third and second centuries B.C.E., they also warred far from home in all directions, above all against Carthage to the south. Their success in these campaigns made Rome the premier power in the Mediterranean by the first century B.C.E.

Fear and the desire for wealth propelled Roman imperialism under the republic. The senators' worries about national security made them recommend preemptive attacks against foreign peoples they thought might attack Rome, while everyone longed to capture riches through conquest. Poorer soldiers hoped to pull their families out of poverty; the elite, who commanded the armies, expected to promote their chances for office by acquiring glory and greater wealth.

Nearly constant warfare in Italy and abroad transformed Roman life. Culturally, the contact with others that conquest brought stimulated the first Roman history and poetry; astonishingly, Rome had no literature until around 240 B.C.E. War's harsh reality also deeply influenced Roman art, especially portraiture. On the social side, endless military service away from home created stresses on small farmers and undermined the stability of Roman society; so, too, did the importation of huge numbers of war captives to work as slaves on rich people's estates. Rome's great victories in the third and second centuries B.C.E. thus turned out to be a two-edged sword: they brought expansion and wealth, but their unexpected social and political consequences disrupted traditional values and the community's stability.

Expansion in Italy, c. 500–c. 220 B.C.E.

The Romans believed they were successful militarily because they respected the gods' will. Cicero claimed, "We have overcome all the nations of the world, because we have realized that the world is directed and governed by the gods." Believing that the gods supported defensive wars as just, the Romans always insisted they fought only in self-defense, even when they attacked first.

After defeating their Latin neighbors in the 490s B.C.E., the Romans spent the next hundred years warring with the Etruscan town of Veii,◆ a few miles north of the Tiber River. Their 396 B.C.E. victory doubled Roman territory. By the fourth century B.C.E., the Roman infantry legion of five thousand men had surpassed the Greek and Macedonian phalanx as an effective fighting force. A devastating sack of Rome in 387 B.C.E. by marauding Gauls (Celts) from beyond the Alps proved only a temporary military setback, though it made Romans forever fearful of foreign invasion. By around 220 B.C.E., Rome controlled all of Italy south of the Po River.

The Romans combined brutality with diplomacy to control conquered people and territory. Sometimes they enslaved the defeated or forced them to surrender large parcels of land. Other times they struck generous peace terms with former enemies. Some defeated Italians immediately became Roman citizens, others gained limited citizenship without the right to vote, and still other communities received treaties of alliance. No conquered Italian peoples had to pay taxes to Rome. All, however, had to render military aid in future wars, for which they received a share of the booty, chiefly slaves and land, from victorious campaigns against a new crop of enemies. In this way, the Romans co-opted their former opponents by making them partners in the spoils of conquest, an arrangement that in turn enhanced Rome's wealth and authority.

Rome and Central Italy, Fifth Century B.C.E.

◆**Veii:** VAY

Aqueduct at Nîmes♦ in France

Like the Greeks, the Romans met the challenge of supplying drinkable water to towns by constructing aqueducts; they excelled at building complex delivery systems of tunnels, channels, bridges, and fountains to transport it from far away. Compare the Greek city fountain shown in the vase painting on page 125. One of the best-preserved sections of a major aqueduct is the so-called Pont-du-Gard near Nîmes♦ (ancient Nemausus) in France, erected in the late first century B.C.E. to serve the flourishing town there. Built of stones fitted together without clamps or mortar, the span soars 160 feet high and 875 feet long, carrying water along its topmost level from thirty-five miles away in a channel constructed to fall only one foot in height for every three thousand feet in length so that the flow would remain steady but gentle. What sort of social and political organization would be necessary to construct such a system? **For more help analyzing this image**, see the visual activity for this chapter in the Online Study Guide at **bedfordstmartins.com/hunt**. *Hubertus Kanus/Photo Researchers, Inc.*

To buttress homeland security, the Romans planted colonies of citizens and constructed roads up and down the peninsula to allow troops to march faster. By connecting Italy's diverse peoples, these roads hastened the creation of a more unified culture dominated by Rome. Latin became the common language, although local tongues lived on, especially Greek in the south. The wealth captured in the first two centuries of expansion attracted hordes of people to the capital because it financed new aqueducts to provide fresh, running water—a treasure in the ancient world—and a massive building program that employed the poor. By 300 B.C.E., about 150,000 people lived within Rome's walls. Outside the city, around 750,000 free Roman citizens inhabited various parts of Italy on land taken from local peoples. Much conquered territory was declared public land, open to any Roman for grazing cattle.

Rich patricians and plebeians cooperated to exploit the expanding Roman territories; the old distinction between the orders had become largely a technicality. This merged elite derived its wealth mainly from agricultural land and plunder acquired during military service. Since Rome levied no regular income or inheritance taxes, families could pass down this wealth from generation to generation. Those who at some point had

Roman Roads, c. 110 B.C.E.

♦**Nîmes:** neem

a consul in the family enjoyed the highest status. They called themselves the nobles to set themselves apart from the rest of the elite.

Wars with Carthage and in the East, 264–121 B.C.E.

Since most of Rome's leaders, remembering the Gauls' attack, feared foreign invasions and also saw imperialism as the route to riches, it is hardly surprising that the republic fought its three most famous wars against the wealthy city of Carthage in North Africa. Governed, like Rome, as a republic, by the third century B.C.E. Carthage controlled an empire encompassing the northwest African coast, part of Libya, Sardinia, Corsica, Malta, and the southern portion of Spain. Geography decreed that an expansionist Rome would sooner or later infringe on Carthage's interests, which depended on the sea. The Carthaginians♦ possessed a large fleet but had to hire mercenaries to field a strong infantry. To Romans, Carthage seemed both a dangerous rival and a fine prize because it had grown so prosperous from agriculture and international trade. Roman hostility was also fueled by horror at the Carthaginian tradition of incinerating infants in the belief it would placate their gods in times of trouble.

First Wars Abroad.   A coincidence finally ignited conflict with Carthage, drawing Roman troops outside Italy for the first time; the three wars that ensued are called the Punic Wars, from the Roman term for Phoenicians, *Punici*. The First Punic War (264–241 B.C.E.) exploded when a desperate band of mercenaries in Messana at Sicily's northeastern tip appealed both to Rome and Carthage to aid them against their enemies. Both states sent troops. The Carthaginians wanted to protect their revenue from Sicilian trade; the Romans wanted to keep Carthaginian troops from moving close to their territory and to acquire war spoils. The Roman and Carthaginian forces clashed, starting a war that lasted a generation. Its bloody battles revealed why the Romans won wars: the Italian population provided deep manpower re-

serves, and the Roman government was prepared to sacrifice as many troops, spend as much money, and fight as long as it took to prevail. Previously unskilled at naval warfare, the Romans expended vast sums to build warships to combat Carthage's experienced navy; they lost more than five hundred ships and 250,000 men while learning how to win at sea. (See "Taking Measure," opposite.)

The Romans' victory in the First Punic War made them masters of Sicily, where they set up their first province (a foreign territory ruled and taxed by Roman officials). This innovation proved so profitable that they soon seized the islands of Sardinia and Corsica from the Carthaginians to create another province. These first successful foreign conquests whetted their appetite for more (Map 5.3). Fearing a renewal of Carthage's power, they cemented alliances with local peoples in Spain, where the Carthaginians were expanding from their southern trading posts.

A Roman ultimatum forbidding further expansion convinced the Carthaginians that another war was inevitable, so they decided to strike back. In the Second Punic War (218–201 B.C.E.), the daring Carthaginian general Hannibal (247–182 B.C.E.) astonished the Romans by marching troops and war elephants from Carthaginian territory in Spain over the snowy Alps into Italy. Slaughtering more than thirty thousand at Cannae in 216 B.C.E. in the bloodiest Roman loss ever, Hannibal tried to convince Rome's Italian allies to desert. But disastrously for him, most Italians remained loyal to Rome. His alliance in 215 B.C.E. with King Philip V of Macedonia (238–179 B.C.E.) forced the Romans to fight on a second front in Greece, but they refused to crack despite Hannibal's ravaging Italy from 218 to 203 B.C.E. The Romans finally won by turning the tables: invading the Carthaginians' homeland, the Roman general Scipio crushed them at the battle of Zama♦ in 202 B.C.E. and was dubbed "Africanus" to commemorate the victory. The Senate imposed a punishing settlement on the enemy in 201 B.C.E., forcing Carthage to scuttle its navy, pay huge war indemnities scheduled to last fifty years, and hand over its lucrative

♦**Carthaginians:** kahr thuh JIH nyuhns

♦**Zama:** ZAH muh

TAKING MEASURE

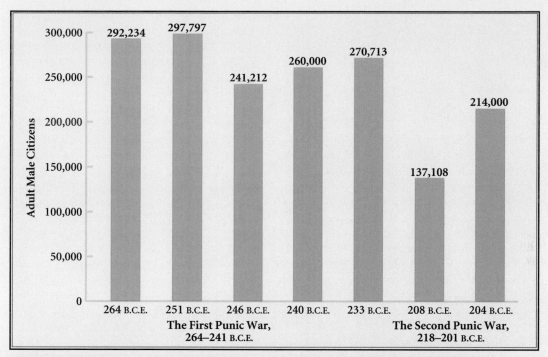

Census Records of Adult Male Roman Citizens during the First and Second Punic Wars
Livy (59 B.C.E.–17 C.E.) and Jerome (c. 347–420 C.E.) provide these numbers from Rome's censuses, which counted only adult male citizens (the men eligible for Rome's regular army), conducted during and between the first two wars against Carthage. The drop in the total for 246 B.C.E., compared with the total for 264 B.C.E., reflects losses in the First Punic War. The low total for 208 B.C.E. reflects both losses in battle and defections of citizenship-holding communities such as Capua in 216 B.C.E. Since the census did not include the Italian allies fighting on Rome's side, the census numbers understate the wars' total casualties; scholars estimate that they took the lives of nearly a third of Italy's adult male population, which would have meant perhaps a quarter of a million soldiers killed. *Tenney Frank,* An Economic Survey of Ancient Rome, *Vol. I (New York: Farrar, Straus, and Giroux, 1959), 56.*

holdings in Spain, which Rome made into provinces prosperous from their mines.

Dominance in the Mediterranean. The Third Punic War (149–146 B.C.E.) began when the Carthaginians, who had revived financially, retaliated against the aggression of their neighbor, the Numidian king Masinissa, who was a Roman ally. After winning the war, the Romans heeded the crusty senator Cato's repeated opinion, "Carthage must be destroyed!" They razed the city and converted its territory into a province. This dis-

aster did not obliterate Punic culture, however, and under the Roman empire this part of North Africa flourished economically and intellectually, displaying a synthesis of Roman and Punic traditions.

The Punic War victories extended Roman power beyond Spain and North Africa to Macedonia, Greece, and western Asia Minor. King Philip's alliance with Hannibal had brought Roman troops east of Italy for the first time. After thrashing Philip for revenge and to prevent any threat of his invading Italy, the Roman commander Flamininus

MAP 5.3   Roman Expansion, c. 500–44 B.C.E.
During the first two centuries of its existence, the Roman republic used war and diplomacy
to extend its power north and south in the Italian peninsula. In the third and second centuries B.C.E., conflict with Carthage in the south and west and the Hellenistic kingdoms in
the east extended Roman power far outside Italy and led to the creation of provinces from
Spain to Greece. The first century B.C.E. saw the conquest of Syria by Pompey and of Gaul
by Julius Caesar (d. 44 B.C.E.).

proclaimed the "freedom of the Greeks" in
196 B.C.E. to show respect for Greece's glorious
past. The Greek cities and federal leagues understood the proclamation to mean that they
could behave as they liked. They misunder-
stood. The Romans expected them to behave
as clients and follow their new patrons' advice, while the Greeks thought, as "friends" of
Rome, that they were truly free. Trouble developed because the two sides failed to realize
that common and familiar words like *freedom*
and *friendship* could carry very different implications in different societies.

The Romans repeatedly intervened to
make the kingdom of Macedonia and the

Greeks observe their obligations as clients;
faced with continuing resistance, the Senate
in 146 B.C.E. ordered Corinth destroyed for
asserting its independence and converted
Macedonia and Greece into a province. In
133 B.C.E., the Attalid king Attalus III of Pergamum increased Roman power with a stu-
pendous gift: he left his Asia Minor kingdom
to Rome in his will. In 121 B.C.E., the Romans
made the lower part of Gaul across the Alps
(modern France) into a province. By the late
first century B.C.E., then, Rome governed
and profited from two-thirds of the Mediterranean region; only the easternmost Mediterranean lay outside its control (see Map 5.3).

Hellenism in Roman Literature and Art, Third to First Centuries B.C.E.

Roman imperialism generated extensive cross-cultural contact with Greece. Although Romans looked down on Greeks for their military impotence, they felt awe before Hellenic literature and art. Roman authors and artists looked to Greek models. Tellingly, about 200 B.C.E. the first Roman historian, Fabius Pictor, used Greek to write his narrative of Rome's foundation and the wars with Carthage. The earliest Latin poetry was a translation of Homer's *Odyssey* by a Greek ex-slave, Livius Andronicus, composed sometime after the First Punic War.

Greek Influences on Roman Literature. Roman literature gained vitality by combining the foreign and the familiar. Many famous early Latin authors were not native Romans. The poet Naevius (d. 201 B.C.E.) came from Campania in southern Italy; the poet Ennius (d. 169 B.C.E.) from even farther south, in Calabria; the comic playwright Plautus♦ (d. 184 B.C.E.) from north of Rome, in Umbria; his fellow comedy writer Terence♦ (c. 190–159 B.C.E.) from North Africa. They all found inspiration in Greek literature. Roman comedies, for example, took their plots and stock characters from Hellenistic Greek comedy, which made jokes about family life and stereotyped personalities, such as the braggart warrior and the obsessed lover. (See Actors in a Comedy on this page.)

Not all Romans applauded Greek influence. Cato, although he studied Greek himself, thundered against the influence the "effete" Greeks had on the "sturdy" Romans. He established Latin prose by publishing a history of Rome, *The Origins* (written between 168 and 149 B.C.E.), and instructions on running a large farm, *On Agriculture* (published about 160 B.C.E.). He glumly predicted that if the Romans ever adopted Greek values, they would lose their power. In truth, despite its debt to Greek literature, early Latin literature reflected traditional Roman values. Ennius, for example, was inspired by Greek epic poetry to compose his path-

♦**Plautus:** PLAW tuhs
♦**Terence:** TEHR unts

Actors in a Comedy
This relief sculpture dating to the first century C.E. shows actors portraying characters in one of the various kinds of comedy popular during the Roman republic. In this variety, which derived from Greek New Comedy of the Hellenistic period, the actors wore exaggerated masks designating stock personality types and strove for broad, slapstick comedy. The plots ranged from burlesques of famous mythological stories to stereotypes of common family problems. Here, on the right, an irresponsible son returns home drunk after a night of binge drinking, supported by his slave and preceded by a hired female musician. On the left, his enraged father is being restrained by a friend from beating the prodigal son with his cane. *Scala/Art Resource, NY.*

breaking Latin epic *Annals*, a poetic version of Roman history. Its contents, however, praised ancestral Roman traditions, as a famous line demonstrates: "On the ways and the men of old rests the Roman commonwealth."

Later Roman writers took inspiration from Greek literature in both content and style. The poet Lucretius (c. 94–55 B.C.E.) wrote a long poem, *On the Nature of Things*, to argue that people should not fear death, a terror that only inflamed "the running sores of life." His ideas reflected Greek philosophy's "atomic theory," which said that matter was composed of tiny, invisible particles. Dying, the poem taught, simply meant the dissolution of the union of atoms, which had come together temporarily to make up a person's body. There could be no eternal punishment or pain after death, indeed no existence at all, because a person's soul, itself made up of atoms, perished along with the body.

COMPARISON OF ANCIENT GREEK AND ROMAN DEVELOPMENTS, C. 750 B.C.E. – 146 B.C.E.

	GREECE	ROME
c. 750 B.C.E.	Polis begins to develop	
c. 750-700 B.C.E.	First Greek poetry (Homer and Hesiod)	
753 B.C.E.		Traditional date for the founding of Rome
509 B.C.E.		Overthrow of monarchy and establishment of the republic
508-c. 500 B.C.E.	Cleisthenes's reforms to strengthen Athenian democracy	
c. 500-c. 450 B.C.E.		Struggle to establish office of tribune to protect the people
461 B.C.E.	Ephialtes's reforms to democratize Athens's courts	
451-449 B.C.E.		Rome's first law code established (Twelve Tables)
420s B.C.E.	The first Greek history (Herodotus)	
c. 200 B.C.E.		First Roman history in Greek (Fabius Pictor)
c. 240-c. 210 B.C.E.		First poetry in Latin (Livius Andronicus's translation of Homer's Odyssey)
168-149 B.C.E.		First Roman history in Latin (Cato)
146 B.C.E.	Greece forced to become a Roman province	

Hellenistic Greek authors inspired Catullus♦ (c. 84–54 B.C.E.) to write witty poems that savaged prominent politicians for their sexual behavior and lamented his own disastrous love life. His most famous series of love poems detailed his passion for a married woman named Lesbia, whom he begged to think only of immediate pleasures:

♦**Catullus:** kuh TUH luhs

Let us live, my Lesbia, and love;
the gossip of stern old men is not worth a cent.
Suns can set and rise again;
we, when once our brief light has set,
must sleep one never-ending night.
Give me a thousand kisses, then a hundred,
then a thousand more.

The great orator Cicero wrote speeches, letters, and treatises on political science, philosophy, ethics, and theology building on Greek philosophy. He adapted Hellenic ideas to Roman life and infused his writings with an appreciation of each human personality's uniqueness. His doctrine of **humanitas** (literally, "humanness, the quality of humanity") combined various strands of Greek philosophy, especially Stoicism, to express an ideal for human life based on generous and honest treatment of others and a commitment to morality based on natural law (the inherent rights of all people, independent of the differing laws and customs of different societies). The spirit of humanitas that he passed on to later ages was one of the ancient world's most attractive ideals.

Realistic Portraiture. Greece also influenced Rome's art and architecture, from the style of sculpture and painting to the design of public buildings. Romans adapted Greek models to their own purposes, as portrait sculpture reveals. Hellenistic sculptors had pioneered a realistic style showing the ravages of age and infirmity on the human body. They portrayed only stereotypes, however, such as the "old man" or the "drunken woman," not specific people. Individual portrait sculpture presented actual individuals in the best possible light, much like a retouched photograph today.

Roman artists in the later republic applied Greek realism to male portraiture, as contemporary Etruscan sculptors also did. They sculpted men without hiding their unflattering features: long noses, receding chins, deep wrinkles, bald heads, careworn looks. Portraits of women, by contrast, were more idealized, probably representing the traditional vision of the bliss of family life (see the image of the sculpted family tomb on page 167). Portraits of children were uncommon during the republic, perhaps because offspring were not seen as contributing to public life until they were grown. Because the men depicted in the portraits (or their families) paid for the busts, they must have wanted their faces sculpted realistically—showing the toll of age and effort—to emphasize how hard they had worked to serve the res publica.

Stresses on Republican Society, Third and Second Centuries B.C.E.

The republic faced grave social and economic difficulties when the successful wars of the third and second centuries B.C.E. produced disastrous side effects on small farmers. The long deployments abroad disrupted Rome's agricultural system, the economy's foundation. Before this time, Roman warfare had followed a pattern of short campaigns timed not to interfere with the fluctuating labor needs of farming. Now, however, a farmer absent on protracted military service had two unhappy choices: rely on a hired hand or slave to manage his crops and animals, or have his wife work in the fields in addition to her usual domestic tasks.

The story of the consul Regulus,♦ who led a Roman army to victory in Africa in 256 B.C.E., revealed the severe problems a man's prolonged absence could cause. When the man who managed Regulus's 4⅓-acre farm died while the consul was away fighting Carthage, a hired hand stole all the farm's tools and livestock. Regulus implored the Senate to send a general to replace him so that he could return home to save his wife and children from starving. The senators sent help to preserve Regulus's family and property because they wanted to keep him in the field, but ordinary soldiers' families could expect no such rescue. The republic's unceasing wars caused many of them to face disaster.

The Poor.   These troubles hit poor farmers particularly hard. When their families fell into debt, they were forced to sell their only source of income—their farmland. Not all regions of Italy suffered as severely as others, and some impoverished farmers managed to stay in the countryside by working as day laborers for others. Many ruined families, however, migrated to Rome, where the men looked for work as menial laborers and the

women did piecework making cloth—or became prostitutes.

This influx of desperate people swelled the poverty-level population at Rome, and the landless poor became an explosive element in Roman politics. They backed any politician who promised to address their need for food, and the government had to feed them to avert riots. Like Athens in the fifth century B.C.E., Rome by the late second century B.C.E. needed to import grain to feed its swollen urban population. The poor's demand for low-priced (and eventually free) food distributed at state expense became one of the most contentious issues in late republican politics.

The Rich.   Rome's elite reaped rich political and material rewards from imperialism. The increased need for commanders to lead military campaigns abroad created opportunities for successful generals to enrich themselves and their families. By using their gains to finance public works and services, the elite enhanced their reputations by benefiting the general population. Building new temples, for example, was thought to increase everyone's security because the Romans believed it pleased their gods to have many shrines. In 146 B.C.E., the victorious general Caecilius Metellus paid for Rome's first marble temple, finally bringing this Greek style to the capital city.

The economic distress plaguing farmers in Italy suited rich landowners because they could buy bankrupt small farms to create large estates. They further increased their holdings by illegally occupying public land carved out of the territory seized from defeated enemies. The rich worked their huge farms, called **latifundia**,♦ with slaves as well as free laborers. They had a ready supply of slaves in the huge number of captives taken in the same wars that displaced Italy's small farmers; as it turned out, the victories won by free but poor Roman soldiers created a slave workforce with which the poor could not compete. The growing size of the slave crews working on latifundia was a mixed blessing for their wealthy owners because the presence of so many slave workers in one place led to periodic revolts that required military intervention.

♦**Regulus:** REH gyuh luhs

♦**latifundia:** la tuh FUHN dee uh

Mosaic of the Riches of the Sea
Created in Pompeii about 100 B.C.E., this colorful mosaic was typical of the kind of exuberant decoration that Romans liked in their houses. It depicts the wide range of seafood popular at banquets in seaside towns like Pompeii. The details of the creatures shown, from fish to cephalopods to a spiny lobster, are accurate enough for scientists to identify their species. Super-wealthy Romans spent huge sums to build artificial salt-water ponds to raise favorite varieties of fish and eels to impress their guests at dinner parties. *Alinari/Art Resource, NY.*

Manius Curius◆ (d. 270 B.C.E.) became legendary for his life's simplicity: despite glorious military victories, he boiled turnips for his meals in a humble hut. Now, in the second century B.C.E., the elite acquired showy luxuries, such as large country villas for entertaining friends and clients. Money had become more valuable to them than the ancestral values of the res publica.

> **Review:** What were the unintended consequences of Rome's victories over foreign peoples?

❖ Upheaval in the Late Republic, c. 133–44 B.C.E.

In the late republic some ambitious members of the Roman elite set the republic on the road to war with itself by placing their own interests ahead of traditional communal values. When Tiberius and Gaius Gracchus used their powers as tribunes to agitate for reforms to help small farmers, the backbone of the army, the brothers' opponents in the Senate resorted to murder to curb them. When a would-be member of the elite, Gaius Marius,◆ opened military service to the poor to boost his personal status, his creation of "client armies" undermined faithfulness to the general good of the community. When the people's unwillingness to share citizenship with Italian allies sparked a war in Roman territory and then the clashing ambitions of the "great men" Sulla, Pompey, and Julius Caesar burst into civil war, the republic fractured, never to recover.

The Gracchi and Factional Politics, 133–121 B.C.E.

The upper-class brothers Tiberius and Gaius Sempronius Gracchus based their political careers on pushing the rich to make concessions to strengthen the state. They came from the acme of Roman society: their grandfather was the Scipio who had defeated Hannibal, and their mother was the Cornelia whom

The elite profited from Rome's expansion because they filled the governing offices in the new provinces and could get much richer than they already were if they ruled corruptly. Since provincial officials ruled by martial law, no one in the provinces could curb a greedy governor's appetite for graft, extortion, and plunder. Some governors ruled honestly, but others used their unsupervised power to squeeze all they could from the provincials. Often such offenders faced no punishment because their colleagues in the Senate excused one another's crimes.

The new opportunities for rich living strained the traditional values of moderation and frugality. Previously, a man like

◆**Manius Curius:** MAH nee uhs KOOR ee uhs
◆**Gaius Marius:** GAY uhs MAR ee uhs

the Ptolemaic king of Egypt had courted after their father died. Their policies supporting the poor angered many of their fellow elite. Tiberius, the older of the Gracchi (the plural of Gracchus), eloquently dramatized the tragic circumstances that motivated them politically, according to the biographer Plutarch (c. 50–120 C.E.):

> The wild beasts that roam over Italy have their dens. . . . But the men who fight and die for Italy enjoy nothing but the air and light; without house or home they wander about with their wives and children. . . . They fight and die to protect the wealth and luxury of others; they are styled masters of the world, and have not a clod of earth they call their own.

When Tiberius won election as a tribune in 133 B.C.E., his opponents blocked his attempts at reform. He therefore took the radical step of disregarding the Senate's advice by having the plebeian assembly pass reform laws to redistribute public land to landless Romans. He further broke with tradition by circumventing the senators to finance his agrarian reform: before they could decide whether to accept the king of Pergamum's bequest of his kingdom, Tiberius had the people pass a law to use the gift to equip new farms on the redistributed land.

Tiberius then announced he would run for reelection as tribune for the following year, violating the traditional prohibition against consecutive terms. His senatorial opponents boiled over: Tiberius's cousin Scipio Nasica, an ex-consul, led a band of senators and their clients in a sudden attack on him, shouting, "Save the republic." Pulling up their togas over their left arms so they would not trip in a fight, these illustrious Romans clubbed the tribune to death, along with many of his followers. Their assault made murder a political tactic.

Gaius, whom the people elected tribune for 123 B.C.E. and, contrary to tradition, again for the next year, followed his brother's lead by pushing measures that outraged the reactionary members of the elite: more agrarian reform, subsidized prices for grain, public works projects throughout Italy to provide employment for the poor, and colonies abroad with farms for the landless. His most revolutionary measures proposed Roman citizenship for

many Italians and new courts to try senators accused of corruption as provincial governors. The new juries would be manned not by senators but by **equites**♦ (literally, "equestrians" or "knights"). These were landowners who, in the earliest republic, had been what the word suggests—men rich enough to provide horses for cavalry service—but were now wealthy businessmen, whose careers in commerce instead of government set them at odds with senators. Because they did not serve in the Senate, the equites could convict criminal senators free of peer pressure. Gaius's proposal marked the equites' emergence as a political force in Roman politics, to the senators' dismay.

When in 121 B.C.E. the senators blocked Gaius's plans, he assembled an armed group to threaten them. They responded by telling the consuls "to take all measures necessary to defend the republic," meaning the use of force. To escape arrest and certain execution, Gaius had one of his slaves cut his throat; the senators then killed hundreds of his supporters and their servants.

The violence provoked by the Gracchi introduced factions (strongly aggressive interest groups) into Roman politics. From that point on, members of the elite identified themselves either as supporters of the people, the **populares** faction, or supporters of "the best," the **optimates** faction. Some chose a faction from genuine allegiance to its policies; others based their choice on political expediency, supporting whichever side better promoted their own political advancement. The elite's splintering into bitterly hostile factions remained a source of violent conflict until the end of the republic.

Gaius Marius and the Origin of Client Armies, 107–100 B.C.E.

The republic needed imaginative commanders to combat slave revolts and foreign invasions in the late second and early first centuries B.C.E. A new kind of leader arose to meet this need: the upper-class man without a consul among his ancestors, who relied on sheer ability to force his way to fame, fortune, and—his ultimate goal—the consulship. Called new men, these leaders challenged the nobles' political dominance.

♦**equites:** EHK wih tehs

Polybius on Roman Military Discipline in the Republic

In Histories, *Polybius, a Greek military officer of the second century* B.C.E. *who spent years on campaign with Roman armies, describes the ideal centurion— an experienced soldier appointed to discipline the troops—and the importance of harsh punishments and the fear of disgrace for maintaining discipline.*

The Romans want centurions not so much to be bold and eager to take risks but rather to be capable of leadership and steady and solid in character. Nor do they want them to initiate attacks and precipitate battle. They want men who will hold their position and stay in place even when they are losing the battle and will die to hold their ground. . . . Soldiers [convicted of neglecting sentry duty] who manage to live [after being beaten or stoned as punishment] don't thereby secure their safety. How could they? For they are not permitted to return to their homeland, and none of their relatives would dare to accept such a man into their households. For this reason men who have once fallen into this misfortune are completely ruined. . . . Even when clearly at risk of being wiped out by enormously superior enemy forces, troops in tactical reserve units are not willing to desert their places in the battle line, for fear of the punishment that would be inflicted by their own side. Some men who have lost a shield or sword or another part of their arms in battle heedlessly throw themselves against the enemy, hoping either to recover what they lost, or to escape the inevitable disgrace and the insults of their relatives by suffering [injury or death].

Source: Polybius, *Histories*, Book 6.24, 37. Translation by Thomas R. Martin.

Gaius Marius (c. 157–86 B.C.E.) set the pattern for this new kind of leader. He came from the equites class in Arpinum in central Italy. Ordinarily, a man of Marius's status had no chance to crack the ranks of Rome's ruling oligarchy of noble families. Fortunately for Marius, however, Rome at the end of the second century B.C.E. had a pressing need for men who could lead an army to victory. Capitalizing on his military record as a junior officer and on popular dissatisfaction with the nobles' war leadership, Marius won election as one of the consuls for 107 B.C.E. In Roman terms this election made him a new man— that is, the first man in his family's history to become consul. Marius's continuing success as a commander in great crises, first in North Africa and next against German tribes who attacked southern France and then Italy, led the people to elect him consul six times, an unprecedented honor.

Marius's victories led the Senate to vote him a triumph, Rome's ultimate military honor. On the day of his triumph, the successful general rode in a chariot through the streets of Rome. His face was painted red for reasons Romans could no longer remember. Huge crowds cheered him, while his army pricked him with off-color jokes, to ward off the evil eye at this moment of supreme glory. For a similar reason, a slave rode with him to keep whispering in his ear, "Look behind you, and remember that you are a mortal." For a former small-town member of the equites class like Marius to be granted a triumph was a supreme social coup.

Despite his triumph, the optimates faction never accepted Marius because they viewed him as an upstart and a threat to their preeminence. His support came from the common people, whom he had won over with his reform of entrance requirements for the army. Previously, only men with property could enroll as soldiers. Marius opened the ranks even to proletarians, men who owned little or nothing. For them, serving in the army under a successful general meant an opportunity to better their lot by acquiring booty and a grant of land to retire on. (See "Polybius on Roman Military Discipline in the Republic," above.)

Marius's reform changed Roman history by creating armies more loyal to their commander than to the republic. Proletarian troops felt immense goodwill toward a commander who led them to victory and then divided the spoils with them generously. The crowds of poor Roman soldiers thus began to behave like an army of clients following their commander as patron. In keeping with the patron-client system, they supported his personal ambitions. Marius was the first to promote his own career in this way. He lost his political importance after 100 B.C.E. when he was no longer consul and foolishly tried to win favor with the optimates. When commanders after Marius used client armies to advance their political careers more ruthlessly than he had, they accelerated the republic's disintegration.

Sulla and Civil War, 91–78 B.C.E.

An unscrupulous noble named Lucius Cornelius Sulla♦ (c. 138–78 B.C.E.) took advantage of uprisings in Italy and Asia Minor in the early first century B.C.E. to use his client army to seize Rome's highest offices and compel the Senate to support his policies. (See Bust of the General Lucius Cornelius Sulla.) His career revealed the dirty secret of politics in the late republic: traditional values no longer restrained commanders who prized their own advancement and the enrichment of their troops above peace and the good of the community.

The Social War. The uprisings in Italy occurred because Rome's Italian allies mostly lacked Roman citizenship and therefore had no vote in decisions concerning their own interests. They became increasingly unhappy as wealth from conquests piled up in the late republic; their upper

♦**Lucius Cornelius Sulla:** LOO shuhs kawr NEEL eeuhs SULL uh

classes wanted a greater share of the luxurious prosperity that war had brought the citizen elite. Romans rejected the allies' demand for citizenship, from fear that sharing that status would lessen their economic and political power.

The Italians' discontent finally erupted in 91–87 B.C.E. in the Social War (so named because the Latin word for "ally" is *socius*). Forming a confederacy to fight Rome, the allies demonstrated their commitment by the number of their casualties—300,000 dead. Although Rome's army eventually prevailed, the rebels won the political war: the Romans granted citizenship and the vote to all freeborn peoples in Italy south of the Po River. The Social War's bloodshed therefore reestablished Rome's tradition of strengthening the state by granting citizenship to outsiders. The war's other significant outcome was that Sulla's successful generalship against the allies won him election as consul for 88 B.C.E.

Plunder Abroad and Violence at Home. Sulla gained supreme power by taking advantage of events in Asia Minor in 88 B.C.E., when Mithradates♦ VI (120–63 B.C.E.), king of Pontus on the Black Sea's southern coast, instigated a murderous rebellion against Roman control. The peoples of Asia Minor hated Rome's rapacious tax collectors, who tried to make provincials pay much more than was required. After denouncing the Romans as "the common enemies of all mankind,"

♦**Mithradates:** mihth ruh DAY teez

Bust of the General Lucius Cornelius Sulla
Sulla (c. 138–78 B.C.E.) was the Roman commander who lit the match to the dynamite that was the political situation in the late republic. When he marched on Rome in 88 B.C.E., employing violence against his own countrymen to make the Senate give him the command in Asia Minor, he smashed beyond repair the Roman tradition that leading citizens should put the interests of the commonwealth ahead of their private goals. This bust, now in the Venice Archaeological Museum, is usually identified as Sulla—its harsh gaze at least corresponds to what the ancient sources report of his personality.
Scala/Art Resource, NY.

Mithradates persuaded the locals to kill all the Italians there—tens of thousands of them—in a single day.

As retaliation for this treachery, the Senate advised a military expedition; victory would mean unimaginable booty because Asia Minor held many wealthy cities. Born to a patrician family that had lost much of its status and all of its money, Sulla craved the command against Mithradates. When the Senate gave it to him, his jealous rival Marius, now an old man, immediately connived to have it transferred to himself by plebiscite. Outraged, Sulla marched his client army against Rome itself. All his officers except one deserted him in horror at this unthinkable outrage, but his common soldiers followed him to a man. Neither they nor their commander shrank from starting a civil war. After capturing Rome, Sulla killed or exiled his opponents and let his men rampage through the city. He then led them off to fight Mithradates, ignoring a summons to stand trial and sacking Athens on the way to Asia Minor.

Sulla's ruthless violence only bred more. In Sulla's absence, Marius embarked on his own reign of terror in Rome to try to regain his former preeminence. In 83 B.C.E., Sulla returned after defeating Mithradates, having allowed his soldiers to strip Asia Minor bare. Civil war recommenced for two years until Sulla crushed his Roman enemies and their Italian allies. The climactic battle of the war took place in late 82 B.C.E. before the gates of Rome. An Italian general whipped his troops into a frenzy against Sulla's army by shouting, "The last day is at hand for the Romans! These wolves that have made such ravages upon our liberty will never vanish until we have cut down the forest that harbors them."

This passionate cry for freedom failed to carry the day. Sulla won and proceeded to exterminate everyone who had opposed him. To speed the process, he devised a horrific procedure called **proscription**—posting a list of those supposedly guilty of treasonable crimes

The Kingdom of Mithradates VI, c. 88 B.C.E.

so that anyone could hunt them down and execute them. (See "Contrasting Views," page 194.) Because proscribed men's property was confiscated, the victors fraudulently added to the list anyone's name whose wealth they coveted. The terrorized Senate appointed Sulla dictator—an emergency office supposed to be held only temporarily—without any limitation of term. He used the office to reorganize the government in the interest of the optimates—his social class—by making senators the only ones allowed to judge cases against their colleagues and forbidding tribunes to sponsor legislation or hold any other office after their term.

The Effects of Sulla's Career.   Convinced by a prophecy that he would die soon, Sulla surprised everyone by retiring to private life in 79 B.C.E. and indeed dying in 78 B.C.E. His murderous career had uncovered the strengths and weaknesses of the republic's values. First, success in war had long ago changed its meaning from defense of the community to acquiring profits for common soldiers and commanders alike. Second, the patron-client system and its promise of material rewards led poor soldiers to feel stronger ties of obligation to their generals than to the republic.

Finally, the traditional desire to achieve status worked both for and against political stability. When that value motivated men to seek office to promote the community's welfare—the traditional ideal of a public career—it exerted a powerful force for social unity and prosperity. But pushed to its extreme, as in the case of Sulla, the drive for prestige and wealth could overshadow all considerations of public service. Sulla in 88 B.C.E. could not bear to lose the personal glory that a victory over Mithradates would bring, preferring to initiate a civil war rather than to see his status diminished.

The republic was doomed once its leaders and its followers forsook the mos maiorum, which had emphasized respect for the peace, prosperity, and traditions of the republic above personal gain. Sulla's career reveals that the republic's traditional values were not enough by themselves to restrain violently ambitious leaders who lusted after a dictator's power.

The Republic's Downfall, 83–44 B.C.E.

Powerful generals after Sulla took him as their model: while professing allegiance to the state, they ruthlessly pursued their own advancement. Their reasoning—that a Roman noble could never have too much glory or too much wealth—was a corruption of the republic's ancient values. Two Roman nobles' competition for power and money flared into a brutal civil war that ruined the republic and opened the way for the return of monarchy after an absence of nearly five hundred years. Those nobles were Pompey and Caesar.

Pompey's Irregular Career. The career of Gnaeus Pompey♦ (106–48 B.C.E.) reveals how the traditional restraints on an individual's power ceased operating in the first century B.C.E. At twenty-three years old, Pompey gathered a private army from his father's clients to win victories for Sulla in the civil war in 83 B.C.E. So frightening was Pompey's power that Sulla could not refuse his astonishing demand for a triumph. Awarding the supreme honor to such a young man, who had held not a single public office, shattered the republic's ancient traditions. But as Pompey told Sulla, "People worship the rising, not the setting, sun."

In 71 B.C.E. Pompey won the final victories over a massive slave rebellion led by a fugitive gladiator named Spartacus, stealing the glory from the real victor, Marcus Licinius Crassus♦ (c. 115–53 B.C.E.). (For two years, Spartacus had terrorized southern Italy and defeated consuls with his army of 100,000 escaped slaves.) Pompey demanded and won election to the consulship in 70 B.C.E., years before he had reached the legal age of forty-two or even won any other office. Three years later, he received a command with unlimited powers to exterminate the pirates then infesting the Mediterranean, a task he accomplished in a matter of months. This success made him wildly popular with the urban poor, who depended on a steady flow of imported grain; with the wealthy commercial and shipping interests, which depended on safe sea lanes; and with coastal

♦**Gnaeus Pompey:** GNEE uhs PAHM pee
♦**Licinius Crassus:** lih SIHN ee uhs   KRAS uhs

communities that had suffered from the pirates' raids. In 66 B.C.E., he defeated Mithradates, who was still stirring up trouble in Asia Minor. By annexing Syria as a province in 64 B.C.E., Pompey ended the Seleucid kingdom and extended Rome's power to the Mediterranean's eastern coast. In 63 B.C.E., Pompey captured the Jewish capital, Jerusalem. Jews had lived in Rome since the second century B.C.E., but most Romans knew little about Judaism; Pompey inspected the Jerusalem temple to satisfy his curiosity and confiscate its treasures.

Pompey's victories were so spectacular that people compared him to Alexander the Great and nicknamed him Magnus ("the Great"). He boasted that he had increased Rome's provincial revenues by 70 percent and distributed spoils equal to twelve and a half years' pay to each of his soldiers. His actions show the degree to which Roman foreign policy had become the personal business of "great men." On his eastern campaigns he ignored the tradition of commanders consulting the Senate about conquering and administering foreign territories, behaving like an independent king rather than a Roman official. He summed up his attitude when replying to some foreigners who criticized his actions as unjust: "Stop quoting the laws to us," he told them. "We carry swords."

Pompey's enemies at Rome sought popular support by proclaiming their concern for the common people's plight. By the 60s B.C.E., Rome's urban population had soared to more than half a million. Hundreds of thousands of the poor lived crowded together in slum apartment buildings and lived off subsidized food distributions. Jobs were scarce. Danger haunted the streets because the city had no police force. Even property owners were in trouble: Sulla's confiscations had caused land values to plummet and produced a credit crunch by flooding the real estate market with properties for sale. Overextended investors were trying to borrow their way back to liquidity, with no success.

The First Triumvirate. Pompey's return to Rome in 62 B.C.E. lit the fuse to this political time bomb. The Senate, eager to curb his independence, blocked Pompey's eastern arrangements and his reward of land to his

The Proscription Edict of 43 B.C.E.

Lucius Cornelius Sulla (c. 138–78 B.C.E.) initiated the brutal punishment known as proscription (from the Latin for "publishing a notice"). To take revenge on his enemies and raise money after capturing Rome in 82 B.C.E., he posted lists of Romans who were declared outlaws and whose property could therefore be confiscated. Those named in these notices could be killed by anyone with impunity; rewards were offered for their deaths, and their descendants were barred from public office. Sulla's associates added the names of innocent people to settle grudges or seize valuable properties. The victors in the civil wars of the later first century B.C.E. continued this practice (Document 1), making it difficult to achieve a secure peace because proscription caused such bitterness among its victims' families (Documents 2 and 3).

1. THE WINNERS IN THE CIVIL WAR JUSTIFY THEIR PROSCRIPTION EDICT OF 43 B.C.E.

Following the assassination of Julius Caesar in 44 B.C.E., Octavian (the future Augustus), Mark Antony, and Lepidus formed a triumvirate (coalition of three men) to rule Rome; their most infamous action was a proscription. Here, the second-century C.E. historian Appian reports the triumvirate's public justification for proscribing fellow citizens.

The proscription edict was in the following words: "Marcus Lepidus, Marcus Antonius, and Octavius Caesar [Octavian], chosen by the people to set in order and regulate the Republic, declare as follows:

"Had not perfidious traitors begged for mercy and when they had obtained it become the enemies of their benefactors and conspired against them, neither would Julius Caesar have been slain by those whom he saved by his clemency after capturing them in war, whom he admitted to his friendship, and upon whom he heaped offices, honors, and gifts, nor should we have been compelled to use this widespread severity against those who have in-

sulted us and declared us public enemies. Now, seeing that the malice of those who have conspired against us and by whose hands Julius Caesar perished cannot be mollified by kindness, we prefer to anticipate our enemies rather than suffer at their hands. Let no one who sees what both Caesar and we ourselves have suffered consider our action unjust, cruel, or immoderate. . . .

"Some of them we have punished already; and by the aid of divine providence you shall presently see the rest punished. . . . One task still remains, and that is to march against Caesar's assassins beyond the sea. On the eve of undertaking this foreign war for you, we do not consider it safe, either for you or for us, to leave other enemies behind to take advantage of our absence and watch for opportunities during the war; nor again do we think that in such great urgency we should delay on their account, but that we ought rather to sweep them out of our pathway once and for all, seeing that they began the war against us when they voted us and the armies under us public enemies.

"What vast numbers of citizens have they, on their part, doomed to destruction with us, disregarding the vengeance of the gods and the reprobation of mankind! We shall not deal harshly with any multitude of men, nor shall we count as enemies all who have opposed or plotted against us, or those distinguished for their riches merely, their abundance or their high position, or as many as another man [i.e., Sulla] slew who held the supreme power before us when he too was regulating the commonwealth in civil convulsions, and whom you named the Fortunate on account of his success; and yet necessarily three persons will have more enemies than one. We shall take vengeance only on the worst and most guilty. This we shall do for your interest no less than for our own, for while we keep up our conflicts you will all be involved necessarily in great dangers, and it is necessary for us also to do something to quiet the army, which has been insulted, irritated, and decreed a public enemy by our common foes.

Although we might arrest on the spot whomsoever we had determined on, we prefer to proscribe rather than seize them unaware—and this too on your account, so that it may not be in the power of enraged soldiers to exceed their orders against persons not responsible, but that they may be restricted to a certain number designated by name and spare the others according to order.

"So be it then! Let no one harbor anyone of those whose names are appended to this edict, or conceal them, or send them away anywhere, or be corrupted by their money. Whoever shall be detected in saving, aiding, or conniving with them we will put on the list of the proscribed without allowing any excuse or pardon. Let those who kill the proscribed bring us their heads and receive the following rewards: to a free man 25,000 Attic drachmas per head, to a slave his freedom and 10,000 Attic drachmas and his master's right of citizenship. Informers shall receive the same rewards. In order that they may remain unknown the names of those who receive the rewards shall not be inscribed in our records."

Source: Appian, *Civil Wars*, Book 4.2.8–11, Loeb Classical Library (Cambridge: Harvard University Press, 1913).

2. THE FUTURE AUGUSTUS BETRAYS CICERO

The most famous victim of the proscription of 43 B.C.E. was the orator and politician Cicero, who had helped Octavian (the future Augustus) to power. Cicero had desperately underestimated Octavian's determination and ruthlessness when he planned to use the young man to promote the Senate's interest against Antony and then discard him. When Antony and Octavian unexpectedly united in the triumvirate, Cicero lost his gamble, with fatal consequences, as the Greek biographer Plutarch relates in this work from about 100 C.E.

Here, indeed, more than at any other time, Cicero was led on and cheated, an old man by a young man. He assisted Caesar [i.e., Octavian, Julius Caesar's adopted son] in his canvass and induced the Senate to favour him. For this he was blamed by his friends at a time, and shortly afterwards he perceived that he had ruined himself and betrayed the liberty of the people. For after the young man had waxed strong and obtained the consulship, he dropped Cicero, and after making friends with Antony and Lepidus and uniting his forces with theirs, he divided the sovereignty with them, like any other piece of property. And a list was made out by them of men who must be put to death, more than two hundred in number. The proscription of Cicero, however, caused most strife in their debates, Antony consenting to no terms unless Cicero should be the first man to be put to death, Lepidus siding with Antony, and Caesar holding out against them both. They held secret meetings by themselves near the city of Bononia for three days, coming together in a place at some distance from the camps and surrounded by a river. It is said that for the first two days Caesar kept up his struggle to save Cicero, but yielded on the third and gave him up. The terms of their mutual concessions were as follows. Caesar was to abandon Cicero, Lepidus his brother Paulus, and Antony Lucius Caesar, who was his uncle on the mother's side. So far did anger and fury lead them to renounce their human sentiments, or rather, they showed that no wild beast is more savage than man when his passion is supplemented by power.

Source: Plutarch, *Life of Cicero*, 46, Loeb Classical Library (Cambridge: Harvard University Press, 1919).

3. A GRIEVING HUSBAND DESCRIBES HIS DEAD WIFE'S VALOR

This eulogy emotionally describes the loss a husband felt at the death of his wife, who had saved his life during the proscription, first by helping him escape and then by confronting Lepidus when he tried to void her husband's pardon. Their story shows the victim's side of this notorious episode.

Rare indeed are marriages of such long duration, which are ended by death, not divorce. We had the good fortune to spend forty-one years together with no unhappiness. I wish that our long marriage had come finally to an end by *my* death,

(*Continued*)

(Continued)

since it would have been more just for me, who was older, to yield to fate.

Why should I mention your personal virtues—your modesty, obedience, affability, and good nature, your tireless attention to wool-working, your performance of religious duties without superstitious fear, your artless elegance and simplicity of dress? Why speak about your affection toward your relatives, your sense of duty toward your family (for you cared for my mother as well as you cared for your parents)? Why recall the countless other virtues which you have in common with all Roman matrons worthy of that name? The virtues I claim for you are your own special virtues; few people have possessed similar ones or been known to possess them. The history of the human race tells us how rare they are. . . .

When my political enemies were hunting me down, you aided my escape by selling your jewelry; you gave me all the gold and pearls which you were wearing and added a small income from household funds. We deceived the guards of my enemies, and you made my time in hiding an "enriching" experience. . . .

Why should I now disclose memories locked deep in my heart, memories of secret and concealed plans? Yes, memories—how I was warned by swift messages to avoid present and imminent dangers and was therefore saved by your quick thinking; how you did not permit me to be swept away by my foolhardy boldness; how, by calm consideration, you arranged a safe place of refuge for me and enlisted as allies in your plans to save me your sister and her husband, Gaius Cluvius, even though the plans were dangerous to all of you. If I tried to touch on all your actions on my behalf, I could go on forever. For us let it suffice to say that you hid me safely.

Yet the most bitter experience of my life came later. . . . I was granted a pardon by Augustus, but his colleague Lepidus opposed the pardon. When you threw yourself on the ground at his feet, not only did he not raise you up, but in fact he grabbed you and dragged you along as if you were a slave. You were covered with bruises, but with unflinching determination you reminded him of Augustus Caesar's edict of pardon. . . . Although you suffered insults and cruel injuries, you revealed them publicly in order to expose him as the author of my calamities. . . .

When the world was finally at peace again and order had been restored in the government, we enjoyed quiet and happy days.

Source: H. Dessau, ed., *Inscriptiones Latinae Selectae*, No. 8393 (Berlin, 1892–1916). Translation Jo-Ann Shelton, *As The Romans Did* (1988).

QUESTIONS TO CONSIDER
1. Can violence be justified if it is meant to bring peace?
2. What controls are possible to prevent the victors in war from abusing their defeated enemies?

army veterans. Pompey therefore negotiated with his fiercest political rivals, Crassus and Julius Caesar (100–44 B.C.E.). In 60 B.C.E., these three formed an unofficial arrangement called the **First Triumvirate** (*triumvirate* means "group of three"). Pompey then forced through laws confirming his eastern arrangements and land for his veterans, thus affirming his status as a great patron. Caesar got the consulship for 59 B.C.E. and a special command in Gaul,◆ where he could seize booty to build his own client army, and Crassus received financial breaks for the Roman tax collectors in Asia Minor, who supported him politically and financially.

This informal coalition of former political enemies revealed how weak the republic's values had become. In the triumvirate, private relationships replaced communal values as the glue of republican politics. To cement their political bond, Caesar married his daughter, Julia, to Pompey in 59 B.C.E., even though she had been engaged to another man. Pompey soothed Julia's jilted fiancé by having him marry his own daughter, who had been engaged to yet somebody else. Through these marital machinations, the two powerful antagonists now had a common

◆**Gaul:** gawl

interest: the fate of Julia, Caesar's only daughter and Pompey's new wife. (He had earlier divorced his second wife after Caesar allegedly seduced her.) Pompey and Julia apparently fell deeply in love in their arranged marriage. As long as Julia lived, Pompey's affection for her kept him from breaking with her father.

Caesar's Civil War. During the 50s B.C.E. Caesar won his soldiers' loyalty with year after year of victories and plunder in central and northern Gaul, which he added to the Roman provinces, and where he awed his troops with his daring by crossing the channel to campaign in Britain. His political enemies at Rome dreaded him even more as his military successes mounted, and the bond linking him to Pompey shattered in 54 B.C.E. when Julia died in childbirth. The two leaders' rivalry then exploded into violence: gangs of their supporters roamed the streets of Rome searching for opponents to beat up or murder. Street fighting reached such a pitch in 53 B.C.E. that it was impossible to hold elections; no consuls could be chosen until the year was half over. The triumvirate completely dissolved that same year when Crassus died in battle at Carrhae♦ in northern Mesopotamia fighting the Parthians, an Iranian people who ruled a vast territory stretching from the Euphrates to the Indus River. A year later, Caesar's enemies convinced the Senate to make Pompey consul by himself, a political trick that violated the republican tradition against sole rule.

The crisis exploded into civil war when the Senate ordered Caesar to surrender his command and thus open himself to prosecution by his enemies. Like Sulla, Caesar led his army against Rome. As he crossed the Rubicon River, the official northern boundary of Italy, in early 49 B.C.E., he uttered the famous words signaling that he had made an irrevocable choice: "The die is cast." His troops followed him without hesitation, and the people in the countryside cheered him on. He had many backers in Rome, too: the

Coin Portrait of Julius Caesar

Julius Caesar (100–44 B.C.E.) was the first living Roman to have his portrait depicted on a coin, defying the tradition of showing only dead persons (the same rule applies to United States currency). After he won the civil war in 45 B.C.E. Caesar broke that tradition, as he did many others, to show that he was Rome's supreme leader. Here he wears the laurel wreath of a conquering general (a *triumphator*). The portrait conforms to late republican style, in which the subject is shown realistically. Caesar's wrinkled neck and careworn expression emphasize the suffering he had endured— and imposed on others—to reach the pinnacle of success. *Bibliothèque Nationale, Paris.*

masses counting on his legendary generosity for handouts and impoverished members of the elite hoping to recoup their fortunes through proscriptions of the rich.

The support for Caesar induced Pompey and most senators to flee to Greece to prepare for war. Caesar entered Rome peacefully, soon departed to defeat the army his enemies had raised in Spain, and then sailed to Greece in 48 B.C.E. There he nearly lost the war when his supplies ran out, but his soldiers stuck with him even when they were reduced to eating bread made from roots. When Pompey saw what Caesar's men were willing to subsist on, he lamented, "I am fighting wild beasts." Caesar's nail-hard troops defeated the army of Pompey and the Senate at the battle of Pharsalus in central Greece in 48 B.C.E. Pompey fled to Egypt, where the ministers of the boy-king Ptolemy♦ XIII (63–47 B.C.E.) treacherously murdered him.

Caesar next invaded Egypt, winning a difficult campaign that ended when the young pharaoh drowned in the Nile and Caesar restored Cleopatra VII (69–30 B.C.E.) to the throne of Egypt. As ruthless as she was intelligent, Cleopatra charmed Caesar into sharing her bed and supporting her rule. Their love affair shocked the general's friends and enemies alike: they thought Rome should seize power from foreigners, not yield it to them.

Caesar's Dictatorship and Murder. By 45 B.C.E., Caesar had defeated the final holdouts in the civil war. He now had to decide how

♦**Carrhae:** KAR eye

♦**Ptolemy:** TAH luh mee

Ides of March Coin
Celebrating Caesar's Murder

Roman coins were the most widely distributed form of art and communication in the Roman world. Usually the messages they carried expressed the mint officials' pride in their own ancestry, but during the crisis of the late republic, they became topical and contemporary. Caesar's assassins, led by Marcus Junius Brutus (85–42 B.C.E.), issued this coin celebrating the murder and their claim to be liberators. The daggers refer to their method, while the conical cap stands for liberation—it was the kind of headgear worn by slaves who had won their freedom. The inscription gives the date of the assassination, the Ides of March (March 15), according to the Roman calendar. What political message was intended by puting picture of murder weapons on coins? *British Museum.*

to rule a shattered republic. He apparently believed that only a sole ruler could end the chaotic violence of factional politics, but the republic's oldest tradition prohibited monarchy. The second-century B.C.E. senator Cato, notorious for his advice about destroying Carthage, had best expressed the Roman elite's view: "A king," he quipped, "is an animal that feeds on human flesh."

Caesar decided to rule as a king without the title. First, he made himself dictator in 48 B.C.E., using the traditional Roman title for a temporary emergency ruler. In 44 B.C.E., he said he would continue as dictator without a term limit. "I am not a king," he insisted. The distinction, however, was meaningless. As dictator, he controlled the government. Elections for offices continued, for example, but Caesar manipulated the results by recommending candidates to the assemblies, which his supporters dominated.

Caesar's policies as dictator were wide-ranging: a moderate cancellation of debts; a cap on the number of people eligible for subsidized grain; a large program of public works, including public libraries; colonies for his veterans in Italy and abroad; rebuilding Corinth and Carthage as commercial centers; and citizenship for more non-Romans, such as the Cisalpine Gauls (those on the Italian side of the Alps). He also admitted non-Italians to the Senate when he expanded its membership from six hundred (the number after Sulla) to nine hundred.

Unlike Sulla, Caesar did not proscribe his enemies. Instead, he exercised clemency; its beneficiaries were obligated to be his grateful clients. His not taking revenge earned him unprecedented honors, such as a special golden seat in the Senate house and the renaming of the seventh month of the year after him (our July). He also regularized the Roman calendar by having each year include 365 days, a calculation based on an ancient Egyptian calendar that roughly forms the basis for our modern one.

Caesar's dictatorship suited the people but outraged the optimates faction. They resented being dominated by one of their own, a "traitor" who had deserted to the people's faction. A conspiracy arose among a band of senators, led by Caesar's former close friend Marcus Junius Brutus and inspired by the memory of Brutus's ancestor Lucius Junius Brutus, who headed the overthrow of Rome's first monarchy five hundred years before. The conspirators cut Caesar to pieces with daggers in a shower of blood in the Senate house on March 15 (the Ides of March in the Roman calendar), 44 B.C.E. When his friend Brutus stabbed him, Caesar gasped his last words—in Greek: "You, too, child?" He collapsed dead at the foot of a statue of Pompey.

The "liberators," as they styled themselves, had no new plans for governing Rome. They apparently believed that the traditional republic would revive automatically after Caesar's murder; in their profound naïveté, they ignored the grisly political violence of the previous forty years and the deadly imbalance reigning in Roman values, with ambitious individuals valuing their private interests over the community's. The liberators were stunned when the people rioted at Caesar's funeral to vent their anger against the upper class that had robbed them of their generous patron. Instead of then forming a united front, the elite resumed their vendettas with one another to secure personal political power. By 44 B.C.E., the republic had suffered damage beyond repair.

Review: Who were the most important leaders in the republic's downfall and what were their policies?

MAPPING THE WEST **The Roman World at the End of the Republic, c. 44 B.C.E.**
Upon Julius Caesar's assassination in 44 B.C.E., the territory that Rome would control during the coming centuries of the empire was almost complete. Caesar's young relative Octavian (the future Augustus) would conquer and add Egypt in 30 B.C.E. Geography and distance were the primary factors inhibiting further expansion, which Romans never stopped thinking of as desirable, even when practical difficulties rendered it purely theoretical. The deserts of Africa and the Near East worked against expansion southward or eastward against the often formidable powers located beyond, while trackless forests and fierce resistance from local inhabitants made expansion into central Europe and the British Isles impossible to maintain.

Conclusion

The most remarkable features of the Roman republic's history were its phenomenal expansion and its violent disintegration. Rome expanded because it incorporated outsiders, its small farmers produced agricultural surpluses to support a growing population and army, and its leaders respected its values stressing the common good. The Romans' willingness to endure great loss of life and property—the proof of their faithfulness—made their army unstoppable in prolonged conflicts: Rome might lose battles, but never wars. Because wars of conquest brought profits to leaders and the common people alike, peace seemed a wasted opportunity.

But the republic's victories against Carthage and in Macedonia and Greece had unexpected consequences. Long military service ruined many farming families. Flocking to Rome to live on subsidized food, they became an unstable political force. Members of the upper class escalated their competition with each other for the increased career opportunities presented by constant war. These rivalries became unmanageable when successful generals began acting as patrons to client armies of poor troops. In this dog-eat-dog atmosphere, violence and murder became the preferred means for settling political disputes. Communal values were drowned in the blood of civil war. No reasonable Roman could have been optimistic about the chances for an enduring peace following Caesar's assassination in 44 B.C.E.; that Caesar's adopted son Octavian—a teen-aged student at the time of the murder—would eventually forge peace by devising a new political system as Augustus would have seemed an impossible dream.

Suggested References

Roman Social and Religious Traditions

Recent scholarship on Roman culture emphasizes how Roman values were grounded in religious belief. In addition, study of legends about Rome's foundation shows how Romans in the late republic relied on those stories to define their national identity.

Ancient Rome: http://www.vroma.org.

Beard, Mary, et al. *Religions of Rome.* 2 vols. 1998.

Bradley, Keith. *Slavery and Society at Rome.* 1994.

*Cicero, *On Duties.* Eds. M. T. Griffin and E. M. Atkins. 1991.

Gardner, Jane. *Women in Roman Law and Society.* 1986.

Pallottino, Massimo. *A History of Earliest Italy.* Trans. M. Ryle and K. Soper. 1991.

Rawson, Beryl, ed. *The Family in Ancient Rome: New Perspectives.* 1986.

Wiseman, T. P. *Remus: A Roman Myth.* 1995.

From Monarchy to Republic, c. 753–287 B.C.E.

Instead of seeing early Rome as shaped largely by Etruscan influence, contemporary scholarship stresses the Romans' own efforts at shaping their state and culture. Recent interpretation of the struggle of the orders has concentrated on the effects of the overlapping interests of patricians and plebeians.

Cornell, T. J. *The Beginnings of Rome: Italy and Rome from the Bronze Age to the Punic Wars (c. 1000–264 B.C.).* 1995.

Ladder of offices: http://www.vroma.org/~bmcmanus/romangvt.html.

*Livy, *From the Founding of the City*, Books 1–5. From *The Early History of Rome.* Trans. Aubrey de Sélincourt. 2002.

MacNamara, Ellen. *The Etruscans.* 1991.

Miles, Gary B. *Livy: Reconstructing Early Rome.* 1992.

Stewart, Roberta. *Public Office in Early Rome: Ritual Procedure and Political Practice.* 1998.

*Primary source.

Roman Imperialism and Its Consequences, Fifth to First Centuries B.C.E.

Roman imperialism remains a major emphasis in scholarship. Works on Roman warfare now offer a vivid sense of what life on the ground was like during Rome's wars of expansion.

Conte, Gian Biagio. *Latin Literature: A History.* Trans. Joseph B. Solodow; rev. Don Fowler and Glenn W. Most. 1994.

Daly, Gregory. *Cannae. The Experience of Battle in the Second Punic War.* 2002.

Etruscan art and objects: http://mv.vatican.va/3_EN/pages/MGE/MGE_Main.html.

Harris, William V. *War and Imperialism in Republican Rome, 327–70 B.C.* 1985.

Lancel, Serge. *Carthage: A History.* Trans. Antonia Nevill. 1995.

*Livy, *From the Founding of the City*, Books 6–10, 21–45. From *Rome and Italy.* Trans. Betty Radice. 1986.

Toynbee, J. M. C. *Roman Historical Portraits.* 1978.

Upheaval in the Late Republic, c. 133–44 B.C.E.

For the late republic, Cicero's many letters and speeches and Caesar's memoirs supplement the ancient narrative accounts (which date to the later period of empire). Arguments about the failure of the republic now tend to reject the traditional view that destructive rivalries were based more on family and group loyalties than on political issues.

Beard, Mary, and Michael Crawford. *Rome in the Late Republic.* 1985.

*Caesar, *The Gallic War.* Trans. Carolyn Hammond. 1998.

*Caesar, *The Civil War.* Trans. John Carter. 1997.

*Catullus, *The Poems.* Trans. Guy Lee. 1998.

*Cicero, *Philippic Orations.* From *Philippics.* Trans. Walter C. Ker. 1969.

Gruen, Erich. *The Last Generation of the Roman Republic.* 1995.

Jiménez, Ramon L. *Caesar Against Rome: The Great Roman Civil War.* 2000.

Julius Caesar: http://www.vroma.org/bmmanus/caesar.html.

Keaveney, Arthur. *Sulla: The Last Republican.* 1982.

Shaw, Brent D. *Spartacus and the Slave Wars: A Brief History with Documents.* 2001.

Southern, Pat. *Cleopatra.* 1999.

Stockton, David. *The Gracchi.* 1979.

CHAPTER REVIEW

IMPORTANT EVENTS

753 b.c.e.	Traditional date of Rome's founding as a monarchy
509 b.c.e.	Roman republic established
509–287 b.c.e.	Struggle of the orders
451–449 b.c.e.	Creation of the Twelve Tables, Rome's first written law code
396 b.c.e.	Defeat of the Etruscan city of Veii; first great expansion of Roman territory
387 b.c.e.	Gauls sack Rome
264–241 b.c.e.	First Punic War between Rome and Carthage
c. 220 b.c.e.	Rome controls Italy south of the Po River
218–201 b.c.e.	Second Punic War between Rome and Carthage
168–149 b.c.e.	Cato writes *The Origins*, the first history of Rome in Latin
149–146 b.c.e.	Third Punic War between Rome and Carthage
146 b.c.e.	Carthage and Corinth destroyed
133 b.c.e.	Tiberius Gracchus elected tribune; assassinated in same year
91–87 b.c.e.	Social War between Rome and its Italian allies
60 b.c.e.	First Triumvirate of Caesar, Pompey, and Crassus
49–45 b.c.e.	Civil war, with Caesar the victor
45–44 b.c.e.	Cicero writes his philosophical works on *humanitas*
44 b.c.e.	Caesar appointed dictator for life; assassinated in same year

KEY TERMS

equities (189)
First Triumvirate (196)
humanitas (186)
ladder of offices (178)
latifundia (187)
mos maiorum (165)
optimates (189)
orders (176)
patria potestas (167)
patron-client system (166)
plebiscites (179)
populares (189)
proletarians (179)
proscription (192)
res publica (172)
Twelve Tables (177)

REVIEW QUESTIONS

1. What was the most important common theme in Roman traditional values?
2. Disputes over what issues fueled the struggle of the orders?
3. What were the unintended consequences of Rome's victories over foreign peoples?
4. Who were the most important leaders in the republic's downfall and what were their policies?

MAKING CONNECTIONS

1. How do the political and social values of the Roman republic compare to those of the Classical Greek city-state?
2. What were the positive and the negative consequences of war for the Roman republic?

FOR FURTHER EXPLORATION

To assess your mastery of the material in this chapter, see the Online Study Guide at bedfordstmartins.com/hunt.

To read additional primary-source material from this period, see Chapter 5 in *Sources of The Making of the West*, Second Edition.

The Roman Empire, c. 44 B.C.E.—284 C.E.

IN 203 C.E., VIBIA PERPETUA,◆ wealthy and twenty-two years old, nursed her infant in a Carthage jail while awaiting execution; she had received the death sentence for refusing to sacrifice to the gods for the Roman emperors' health and safety. One morning the jailer dragged her off to the city's main square, where a crowd had gathered. Perpetua described in a journal what happened when the local governor tried to persuade her to save her life:

> My father came carrying my son, crying "Perform the sacrifice; take pity on your baby!" Then the governor said, "Think of your old father; show pity for your little child! Offer the sacrifice for the imperial family's welfare." "I refuse," I answered. "Are you a Christian?" asked the governor. "Yes." When my father would not stop trying to change my mind, the governor ordered him flung to the earth and whipped with a rod. I felt sorry for my father; it seemed they were beating me. I pitied his pathetic old age.

The brutality of Perpetua's punishment failed to break her: gored by a wild cow and stabbed by a gladiator, she died professing her faith.

Perpetua went to her death as a martyr because she believed that her faith in Christ required her not only to disregard the traditional Roman value of faithfulness to her family obligations but even to refuse the state's demand for a demonstration of loyalty to the "way of the elders" in public religion. Her decision to put her personal religious commitment ahead of her civic duty was a different version of the republic's commanders' fighting civil wars because they valued their individual success above service to the common good.

◆**Vibia Perpetua:** VIB ee uh   per PET you ah

Executing a Criminal in the Amphitheater
This mosaic shows a condemned man being mauled by a leopard in the arena of an amphitheater. Romans believed that especially despicable criminals deserved disgraceful deaths before crowds of spectators. "Being condemned to the beasts," as the execution was called, was the most spectacularly gruesome of punishments. Martyrs charged with treason, such as Perpetua, were often executed in this way. Here the prisoner is tied to a stake on a small chariot so the handlers can propel him into the face of the leopard to provoke an angry leap; wild animals did not always attack without such provocation. This scene formed part of a larger mosaic showing gladiators and other performers in a huge show held in the arena. Dated to about 200 C.E., the mosaic covered a villa floor near the coast of North Africa in what is today Libya; it therefore belonged to the same time and general region of the Roman empire as did Perpetua. The villa's owner perhaps ordered these subjects for the mosaic to commemorate his sponsorship of the expensive public spectacle that included this grisly execution. *Roger Wood / Corbis.*

In the aftermath of Julius Caesar's assassination in 44 B.C.E., Augustus (63 B.C.E.–14 C.E.) eventually restored peace by developing a special kind of monarchy to reorient Romans' communal loyalty toward the ruling family. Ever after, however, Rome's rulers feared disloyalty above all because it threatened to reignite the fires of civil war that had consumed the republic. The refusal of Christians such as Perpetua to perform traditional sacrifice was considered treason—the ultimate disloyalty—because Romans believed the gods would punish the entire community for harboring such impious people.

The Roman Empire, the usual modern name applied to the period from Augustus onward, opened with a bloodbath: seventeen years of civil war followed Caesar's funeral. Finally, in 27 B.C.E., Augustus created his disguised monarchy—the ***principate***—to end the violence. He ingeniously masked his creation as a restoration of the republic. He retained the republic's institutions for sharing power—the Senate, the consuls, the courts—while in truth making himself sole ruler. He enshrouded his monarchy in deft language: instead of calling himself *rex* ("king"), he used *princeps*◆ ("first man"), a traditional honorary title designating the leading senator. Princeps became the office that today we call emperor (from the Latin *imperator*, "commander"). Each new princeps was supposed to be designated only with the Senate's approval, but in practice each ruler chose his own successor. Augustus's arrangement thus made Rome into a monarchy—without the name.

This transformed political system brought stability for two hundred years, except for a few brief interludes of fighting between generals competing to become princeps. Worn out by war with each other, Romans welcomed this period of peace, which historians call the **Pax Romana** ("Roman peace"). In the early third century C.E., however, violent rivalries over rule reignited prolonged civil war that generated political and economic crisis. By the 280s C.E., Roman government desperately needed again to transform its political institutions to keep from disintegrating. The most pressing question remained how to retain the traditional values of citizen loyalty and public service by the wealthy. Coming to power in 284, C.E. the emperor Diocletian◆ began that transformation.

❖ Creating the Pax Romana

Inventing tradition takes time. Augustus founded his new political system gradually; as the biographer Suetonius◆ (c. 70–130) expressed it, Augustus "made haste slowly." He succeeded because he won the struggle for power, reinvented government, and built loyalty by communicating an image of himself as a dedicated leader. His professed respect for tradition and his reign's length decisively established monarchy as Rome's

◆***princeps:*** PRIHN kehps

◆**Diocletian:** dy uh KLEE shuhn
◆**Suetonius:** swee TOH nee uhs

◆ **30** Octavian conquers Egypt

◆ **27** Augustus inaugurates principate

◆ **c. 46** Paul begins seeking converts to Christianity

◆ **64** Rome burns; Nero blames Christians

◆ **69** Civil war during Year of the Four Emperors

50 B.C.E.	0	50 C.E.	100 C.E.

◆ **c. 30** Jesus crucified

◆ **70** Titus destroys Jewish temple

◆ **c. 70–90** New Testament Gospels

◆ **80s** Domitian's campaigns against invaders

future political system and saved the state from anarchy. Succeeding where Caesar had failed, he did it by making the new look old.

From Republic to Principate, 44–27 B.C.E.

The gruesome infighting among those who hoped to fill the political vacuum created by Caesar's assassination in 44 B.C.E. transformed the republic into the principate. The main competitors for power were Caesar's close friend Mark Antony and Caesar's eighteen-year-old grandnephew and adopted son, Octavian (the future Augustus). Octavian won the support of Caesar's soldiers by promising them rewards from their murdered general's wealth, which he had inherited. Marching these troops to Rome, the teenager demanded that the Senate make him consul in 43 B.C.E. As with Pompey previously, fearful senators granted Octavian's demand, disregarding the rule that a man had to climb the ladder of offices before becoming consul. Once again, force trumped tradition.

Octavian, Antony, and a general named Lepidus joined forces to eliminate Caesar's assassins, their supporters, and anyone else they deemed dangerous. In late 43 B.C.E., the trio formed the so-called Second Triumvirate and forced the Senate to recognize them as an official panel for reconstituting the state. They then ruthlessly proscribed their enemies and confiscated their property. (See "Contrasting Views," page 194 in Chapter 5.)

Octavian and Antony, too ambitious to cooperate for long, forced Lepidus into retirement and began fighting each other. Antony based his forces in the eastern Mediterranean, allying with the Ptolemaic queen Cleopatra VII (69–30 B.C.E.), who had earlier allied with Caesar. Dazzled by her wit and intelligence, Antony, who was already married to Octavian's sister, fell deeply in love with Cleopatra. Octavian then rallied support by claiming that Antony planned to make this foreign woman their ruler. He made the residents of Italy and the western provinces his clients by having them swear a personal oath of allegiance to him. His victory in the naval battle of Actium in northwest Greece in 31 B.C.E. won the war. Cleopatra and Antony fled to Egypt, where they both committed suicide in 30 B.C.E. The general first stabbed himself, bleeding to death in his lover's embrace. The queen then ended her life by allowing a poisonous serpent, a symbol of Egyptian royal authority, to bite her. Octavian's capture of Egypt made him Rome's richest citizen and its unrivaled leader.

Augustus's Restoration, 27 B.C.E.–14 C.E.

Following up his victory by distributing land to army veterans and creating colonies in the provinces, Octavian formally announced in 27 B.C.E. that he had restored the republic. The Senate and the Roman people, he proclaimed, should decide how to preserve it. There followed a turning point in Roman history: recognizing that Octavian possessed overwhelming

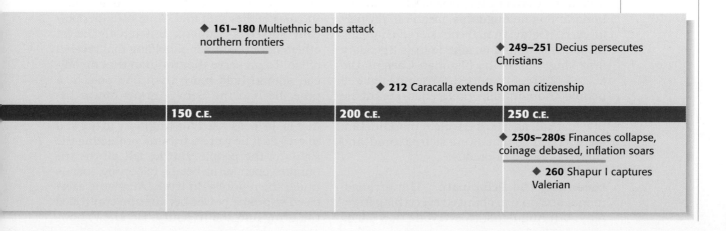

◆ **161–180** Multiethnic bands attack northern frontiers

◆ **249–251** Decius persecutes Christians

◆ **212** Caracalla extends Roman citizenship

150 C.E.	200 C.E.	250 C.E.

◆ **250s–280s** Finances collapse, coinage debased, inflation soars

◆ **260** Shapur I captures Valerian

Priests on the Altar of Augustan Peace
Augustus dedicated the Altar of Augustan Peace in northwest Rome on his wife's birthday in 9 B.C.E.
The altar resided inside a four-walled enclosure, open to the sky, about thirty-four feet long, thirty-eight feet wide, and twenty-three feet high. Relief sculptures covered the marble walls. This section shows a religious procession, headed by the imperial family (out of the picture to the left) and completed by a representation of Rome's senators. The figures wearing leather caps with spikes are priests called *flamines*, whose special headgear was part of the complex ritual of their positions. The hooded man at the right, veiled for performing sacrifice, is probably Marcus Agrippa, Augustus's greatest general. Mythological figures were also sculpted on the walls, expressing the same message as the Prima Porta statue (page 217): Augustus, with his divine family origins, was the patron who brought peace and prosperity to Rome while respecting its republican traditions. The altar can be seen today in its original form because it was reconstructed by Benito Mussolini, Fascist dictator of Italy from 1926 to 1943, who wanted to appropriate Augustan glory for his regime. *Scala/Art Resource, NY.*

power, the senators implored him to safeguard the restored republic, granted him special civil and military powers, and bestowed on him the honorary name **Augustus**, meaning "divinely favored." Octavian had considered changing his name to Romulus, after Rome's legendary first king, but as the historian Cassius Dio (c. 164–230 C.E.) reported, "When he realized people thought this preference meant he longed to be their king, he accepted the other title instead, as if he were more than human; for everything that is most treasured and sacred is called *augustus.*"

Inventing the Principate.   The arrangements of 27 B.C.E. changed everything in reality, but Augustus, as everyone now called

him, kept up the appearance of republican government. Consuls were elected every year, the Senate tendered its advice, and the assemblies still met. Augustus periodically served as consul, but mostly he let others have the honor of holding that revered office. To preserve the tradition that no official should hold more than one post at a time, he had the Senate grant him a tribune's powers without holding the office; that is, he possessed the authority to act and to veto as if he were a tribune protecting the rights of the people, but he left all the tribunates open for plebeians to occupy, just as under the republic. In truth, Augustus exercised supreme power because he controlled the army and the treasury. He knew, however, that symbols affect people's perception of reality, so he dressed and acted modestly, like a regular republican citizen, not a haughty monarch. Livia, his wife, played a prominent role under his regime as his very visible partner in upholding old-fashioned values.

Augustus's choice of princeps as his only official title was a brilliant symbolic move. In the republic, the princeps had guided Rome only by the respect and **auctoritas**♦ ("moral authority") he merited; he had no more *potestas*♦ ("formal power") than any other leader. By appropriating this title, Augustus claimed to carry on this valued tradition. He invented the principate to disguise a monarchy as a corrected and improved republic, headed by an emperor cloaked as a princeps ruling only by auctoritas. In reality, he revised the underlying power structure: no one previously could have exercised the powers of both consul and tribune simultaneously while also controlling the state's money and troops.

Augustus made the military the foundation of his moral authority by turning the republic's citizen militia into a full-time professional force. He established regular lengths of service for soldiers and a substantial retirement benefit, changes that made the princeps the soldiers' patron and solidified their loyalty to him. To pay the added costs, Augustus imposed Rome's first inheritance tax on citizens, angering the rich. His other major military innovation was to station troops in Rome for the first time ever. These soldiers—the **praetorian**♦ **guard**—would later play a crucial role in imperial politics by sometimes determining who the princeps should be. Augustus meant them to prevent rebellion in the capital by serving as a visible reminder that the princeps's superiority was grounded in the threat of force.

♦ *auctoritas:* auk TORE ih tahs
♦ *potestas:* poh TEHS tahs
♦ *praetorian:* pree TAWR ee uhn

Temple of Mars Ultor   Colonnades (porches) lined with columns   Statues of Roman heroes

Unroofed area

FIGURE 6.1 Cutaway Reconstruction of the Forum of Augustus
Augustus built this large forum (120 x 90 yards) to commemorate his victory over the assassins of his adoptive father, Julius Caesar. Dedicated in 2 B.C.E., its centerpiece was a marble temple dedicated to the god Mars Ultor ("The Avenger"). Inside the temple he placed statues of Mars, Venus (the divine ancestor of Julius Caesar), and Julius Caesar (as a god), as well as Caesar's sword and works of art. The two apses flanking the temple featured statues of Aeneas and Romulus, Rome's founders. The porches stretching along the open courtyard housed other statues of Roman heroes. The ceremony marking teenaged boys' passage into adult status took place here, where they were surrounded by images of the valorous and glorious men whom they were expected to emulate. The high stone wall behind the temple was a barrier protecting it from fire, which was a constant threat in the crowded and poor neighborhood that lay just on the other side.

Communicating the Emperor's Image. In keeping with his policy of always complementing displays of force with displays of symbols, Augustus constantly communicated his image as patron and public benefactor (see "Augustus, *Res Gestae*," page 208). He used media as small as coins and as large as buildings. The only mass-produced medium for official messages, Roman coins functioned like modern political advertising. They proclaimed slogans such as "Father of His Country" to remind Romans of the princeps's moral authority or "Roads have been built" to emphasize his generosity in paying for highway construction.

Augustus also erected public buildings in Rome paid for by his personal fortune. The huge Forum of Augustus he dedicated in

Augustus, *Res Gestae* (My Accomplishments)

Augustus, the first Roman emperor, had stone inscriptions with an autobiographical report of his accomplishments displayed around the empire. These excerpts reveal his justifications for his rule. Many of the sections not included here list his numerous and expensive contributions to public works.

1. At the age of nineteen, on my own initiative and at my own expense, I raised an army, which I used to liberate the republic, which had been oppressed by the tyranny of a faction. For this reason the Senate passed honorary votes for me and made me a member [in 43 B.C.E.], at same time granting me the rank of a consul in its voting, and it gave me the power of military command [*imperium*]. It ordered me as propraetor to see to it, along with the consuls, that no harm came to the state. Moreover, in the same year, when both consuls had died in the war, the people elected me consul and a triumvir with the duty of establishing the republic. . . .

3. I waged many wars, civil and foreign, throughout the whole world by land and by sea, and as victor I spared all citizens who asked for pardons. Foreign peoples who could safely be pardoned I preferred to spare rather than destroy. Approximately 500,000 Roman citizens swore military oaths to me. A little more than 300,000 of these, when their terms of service were ended, I settled in colonies or sent back to their own municipalities; I allotted lands or granted money to all of them as rewards for military service. . . .

4. . . . At the time I wrote this, I had been consul thirteen times, and I was in the thirty-seventh year of my tribunician power [14 C.E.].

5. I refused to accept the dictatorship offered to me [in 22 B.C.E.] by the people and by the senate, both in my absence and my presence. During a severe scarcity of grain I accepted the supervision of the grain supply, which I so administered that within a few days I freed the whole people from imminent panic and danger by my expenditures and effort. The consulship, too, which was offered to me at that time as an annual office for life, I refused to accept.

2 B.C.E. best illustrates his skill at sending messages with bricks and stone. This public gathering space centered on a temple to Mars, the Roman god of war. Two-story colonnades extended from the temple like wings, sheltering statues of famous Roman heroes to serve as inspirations to future leaders. Augustus's forum provided space for religious rituals and the ceremonies marking the passage into adulthood of upper-class boys, but it also stressed the themes he wanted to communicate to justify his rule: peace restored through victory, the foundation of a new age, devotion to the gods who protected Rome, respect for tradition, and his unselfishness in spending money for public purposes.

Augustus's Motives. Augustus never revealed his motives for establishing the principate. Was he a cynical despot suppressing the republic's freedoms? Or did he have to impose a veiled monarchy to stabilize a society crippled by anarchy? Or did his motives lie somewhere in between? Most likely he was a revolutionary bound by tradition. His problem was the one always facing a Roman leader—how to balance society's need for peace, its traditional commitment to its citizens' freedom of action, and his own ambitions. Augustus's solution was to employ traditional values in making changes, as with his inspired reinvention of the meaning of the word "princeps." Above all, he transferred the traditional paternalism of social relations—the patron-client system—to politics by making the princeps everyone's most important patron with the moral authority to guide their lives. This process culminated in 2 B.C.E. when the Senate joined the Roman people in formally proclaiming him "Father of His Country."

6. [In 19, 18, and 11 B.C.E.], although the Roman senate and people in unison agreed that I should be elected sole guardian of the laws and morals with supreme power, I refused to accept any office offered to me that was contrary to our ancestors' traditions [*mos maiorum*]. The measures that the senate desired me to take at that time I carried out under the tribunician power. While holding this power I five times voluntarily requested and was given a colleague by the senate.

7. . . . I have been ranking senator [*princeps senatus*] for forty years, up to the day on which I wrote this document. [There follows a list of priesthoods he held, including that of "the greatest priest," *pontifex maximus.*]

8. . . . By new legislation that I sponsored I restored many precedents from our ancestors that were becoming dead letters in our generation, and I myself handed down precedents in many spheres for posterity to imitate. . . .

34. In my sixth and seventh consulships [28 and 27 B.C.E.], after I had put an end to the civil wars, having gained possession of everything through the consent of everyone, I transferred the state from my own power [*potestas*] to the control of the Roman Senate and the people.

As reward for this meritorious service, I received the title of Augustus by vote of the senate, and the doorposts of my house were publicly decked with laurels, the civic crown was affixed over my doorway, and a golden shield was set up in the Julian senate house, which, as the inscription on this shield testifies, the Roman senate and people gave me in recognition of my valor, clemency, justice, and devotion. After that time I excelled all in authority [*auctoritas*], but I possessed no more power [*potestas*] than the others who were my colleagues in each magistracy.

35. When I held my thirteenth consulship [2 B.C.E.], the senate, the equestrian order, and the entire Roman people gave me the title of "father of the country" [*pater patriae*] and voted that this title should be inscribed in the vestibule of my house, in the Julian senate house, and in the Augustan Forum on the pedestal of the chariot which was set up in my honor by vote of the senate. At the time I wrote this document I was in my seventy-sixth year.

Source: Herbert W. Benario, ed. *Caesaris Augusti Res Gestae et Fragmenta*, 2nd ed. (1990). Translation by Thomas R. Martin.

Suetonius quotes Augustus as responding, "Fathers of the Senate, I have at last achieved my highest ambition. What more can I request from the immortal gods than that they will let me keep your approval until I die?" The title emphasized that the principate gave Romans a sole ruler who governed them like a father: stern but caring, expecting obedience and loyalty from his children, and obligated to nurture them in return. The goal of such an arrangement was a combination of stability and order, not political freedom.

Augustus ruled as emperor (to use the modern equivalent of the word "princeps") until his death at age seventy-five in 14 C.E. The length of his reign—forty-one years—solidified his transformation of Roman government. As the Roman historian Tacitus♦

♦**Tacitus:** TA suh tuhs

(c. 56–120) remarked, by the time Augustus died, "almost no one was still alive who had seen the republic." Through his longevity, command over the army, rapport with the capital's urban masses, and manipulation of the republic's political symbols and vocabulary to mask his power, Augustus restored stability to society and transformed republican Rome into imperial Rome.

Augustan Rome

A crucial factor in Augustus's success was his attention to citizens' everyday lives. The worst problems were in Rome, a metropolis teeming with a population approaching a million people, many of whom had no job and too little to eat. Archaeological and literary sources reveal a composite picture of life in Augustan Rome. Although some of the sources

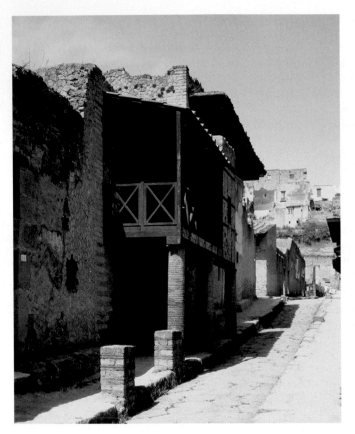

Downtown Street in Herculaneum
Like Pompeii, the prosperous town of Herculaneum on the shore of the Bay of Naples was frozen in time by the massive eruption of the neighboring volcano, Mount Vesuvius, in 79 C.E. A flood of mud from the eruption buried the town and preserved its buildings until they were excavated beginning in the eighteenth century. Typical of a Roman town, it had straight roads paved with large, flat stones and flanked by sidewalks. Balconies jutted from the upper stories of houses, offering residents a shady viewing point for the lively traffic in the urban streets. Instead of having yards in front or back, houses often enclosed a garden courtyard open to the sky. Why do you think urban homes had this arrangement?
Scala/Art Resource, NY.

refer to times after Augustus and to cities other than Rome, they nevertheless help us understand this period, as economic and social conditions were essentially the same in Roman cities throughout the empire's early centuries.

Augustan Rome's population was vast for the ancient world. No European city would have this many people again until London in the 1700s. The streets were packed: "One man jabs me with his elbow, another whacks me with a pole; my legs are smeared with mud, and big feet step on me from all sides" was how the poet Juvenal♦ described walking in Rome in the early second century. To ease congestion in the narrow streets, the city banned carts and wagons in the daytime. This regulation made nights noisy with the creaking of axles and the shouting of drivers caught in traffic jams.

The Precariousness of City Life. Most urban residents lived in small apartments in multistoried buildings called *insulae*♦ ("islands," so named because in early times each building had an open strip around it). Outnumbering private houses by more than twenty to one, the apartment buildings' first floors housed shops, bars, and simple restaurants. Graffiti of all kinds—political endorsements, the posting of rewards, personal insults, and advertising—decorated the exterior walls. The higher the floor, the cheaper the rent. Well-off tenants occupied the lower stories, while the poorest people lived in single rooms rented by the day on the top floors. Aqueducts delivered a plentiful supply of fresh water to public fountains, but apartment dwellers had to lug jugs up the stairs. The wealthy few had piped-in water at ground level. Most tenants lacked bathrooms and had to use the public latrines or pots for toilets at home. Some buildings had cesspits, but most people had to carry buckets of excrement down to the streets to be emptied by sewage collectors. Lazy tenants flung these containers' foul-smelling contents out the window. Sanitation was an enormous problem because the city generated about sixty tons of human waste every day.

To keep clean, residents used public baths. Because admission fees were low, almost everyone could afford to go to the baths daily. Baths existed all over the city; like modern health clubs, they served as centers for exercising and socializing as well as washing (see "The Scene at a Roman Bath," page 211). Bath patrons progressed through a series of increasingly warm, humid areas until they reached a sauna-like room. Bathers swam naked in their choice of hot or

♦**Juvenal:** JOO vuh nuhl
♦*insulae:* IHN suh lie

The Scene at a Roman Bath

The Roman philosopher Seneca (4 B.C.E.–65 C.E.) wrote to a friend describing the commotion that he had to endure to keep up his studies while living in a rented apartment over a public bath. He offers a lively picture of the range of people using and working in and around the baths, which existed in every sizable community in the Roman Empire.

I am staying in an apartment directly above a public bath house. Imagine all the kinds of voices that I hear, enough to make me hate having ears! When the really strong guys are working out with heavy lead weights, when they are working hard or at least pretending to work hard, I hear their grunts; and whenever they exhale the breath they've been holding in, I hear them hissing and panting harshly. When I happen to notice some sluggish type getting a cheap rubdown, I hear the slap of the hand pounding his shoulders, changing its sound according to whether it's a blow with an open or a closed fist. If a serious ball-player comes along and starts keeping score out loud, then I'm done for. Add to this the bruiser who likes to pick fights, the pickpocket who's been caught, and the man who loves to hear the sound of his own voice in the bath. And there are those people who jump into the swimming pool with a tremendous splash and lots of noise. Besides all the ones who have awful voices, imagine the "armpit hair plucker-outer" with his high, shrill voice—so he'll be noticed—always chattering and never shutting up, except when he is plucking armpits and making his customer yell instead of yelling himself. And there are also all the different cries from the sausage seller, and the fellow hawking pastries, and all the food vendors screaming out what they have to sell, all of them with their own special tones.

Source: Seneca, *Moral Epistles*, 56.1–2. Translation by Thomas R. Martin.

---

cold pools. Women had full access to the public baths, but men and women bathed apart, either in separate rooms or at different times of the day. Since bathing was thought to be particularly valuable for sick people, communal baths contributed to the spread of communicable diseases.

Augustus did all he could to improve public health. By 33 B.C.E., his general Agrippa♦ had vastly improved the city's main sewer, but its contents still emptied untreated into the Tiber River in the city's midst. The technology for sanitary disposal of waste simply did not exist. People regularly left human and animal corpses in the streets, to be gnawed by vultures and dogs. The poor were not the only people affected by such conditions: a stray mutt once brought a human hand to the table where Vespasian,♦ who would be emperor from 69 to 79, was eating lunch. Flies buzzing everywhere and a lack of mechanical refrigeration contributed to frequent gastrointestinal ailments: the most popular jewelry of the time was supposed to ward off stomach trouble. Although the wealthy could not eliminate such discomforts, they made their lives more pleasant with luxuries such as snow rushed from the mountains to ice their drinks and slaves to clean their airy houses, which were built around courtyards and gardens.

City residents faced unpredictable hazards beyond infectious disease. Apartment dwellers often hurled broken pots and household debris out their windows, where it rained down like missiles on unwary pedestrians. "If you are walking to a dinner party in Rome," Juvenal warned, "you would be foolish not to make out your will first. For every open window is a source of potential disaster." The insulae could be dangerous to their inhabitants as well as to passersby because they were in constant danger of collapsing.

♦**Agrippa:** uh GRIH puh
♦**Vespasian:** veh SPAY zhee uhn

Roman engineers, despite their expertise in using concrete, brick, and stone as building materials, lacked the technology to calculate precisely how much stress their constructions could stand. Crooked builders cut costs by cheating on structural materials. Augustus tried to improve the situation by imposing a height limit of seventy feet on new apartment buildings. Fire presented the greater risk to city dwellers; one of Augustus's most important achievements was providing Rome with the first public fire department in Western history. He also established the first permanent police force, despite his reported fondness for stopping to watch the frequent brawls in Rome's crowded streets.

As Rome's patron, Augustus also worked to ensure an adequate food supply for the urban poor. He freely spent his personal fortune to pay for imported grain. Distributing subsidized or free grain to the capital's poor had long been a tradition, but the extent of his dole broke all precedents: 250,000 recipients. When we include the recipients' families, this statistic suggests that more than 700,000 people depended on the government for their dietary staple. Poor Romans cooked this grain into a watery porridge, which they washed down with cheap wine. If they were lucky, they might have some beans, leeks, or cheese on the side. The rich, as we learn from an ancient cookbook, ate more delectable dishes, such as spiced roast pork or crayfish, often flavored with sweet-and-sour sauce concocted from honey and vinegar.

More and more wealthy Romans spent money on luxuries and political careers instead of raising families. Fearing that a scarcity of children would destroy the elite on which Rome relied for public service, Augustus granted special legal privileges to the parents of three or more children. To strengthen marriages, he made adultery a criminal offense and supported this reform so strongly that he exiled his own daughter—his only child—and a granddaughter after sex scandals. His legislation had little effect, however, and the prestigious old families dwindled over the coming centuries. Recent research suggests that up to three-quarters of senatorial families either lost their official

status by spending all their money or died out every generation by failing to have children. Equestrians and provincials who won imperial favor took their places in the social hierarchy and the Senate.

Roman Slavery. Unlike other ancient states, Rome gave citizenship to freed slaves. All slaves could hope to acquire the rights of a free citizen, and their descendants, if they became wealthy, could become members of the social elite. This policy gave slaves reason to persevere and cooperate with their masters. It also meant that most Romans had slave ancestors.

The harshness of slaves' lives varied widely. Slaves in agriculture and manufacturing lived a grueling existence. Most such workers were men, although women might assist the foremen who managed gangs of rural laborers. The second-century novelist Apuleius◆ penned this grim description of slaves in a flour mill: "Through the holes in their ragged clothes you could see all over their bodies the scars from whippings. Some wore only loincloths. Letters had been branded on their foreheads and irons manacled their ankles." Worse than the mills were the mines, where the foremen constantly whipped the miners to keep them working in such a dangerous environment.

Household slaves lived better. Most Romans owned slaves as home servants; modestly well-off families had one or two, while rich houses and, above all, the imperial palace had hordes. Domestic slaves were often women, working as nurses, maids, kitchen helpers, and clothes makers. Some male slaves ran businesses for their masters, and they were often allowed to keep part of the profits as an incentive; they saved to purchase their freedom someday. Women had less opportunity to earn money, though masters sometimes granted tips for sexual favors. Many female prostitutes were slaves working for a master. Slaves with savings would sometimes buy other slaves, especially to have a mate. They could then live as a shadow family, barred from legal marriage because they and their children remained their master's property. Fortunate slaves

◆**Apuleius:** ahp you LAY uhs

could buy themselves from their masters or be freed in their masters' wills. Some tomb inscriptions record a master's affection for a slave, but even household slaves endured inhumane treatment if their masters were cruel. Slaves had no legal recourse, and if they attacked their owners, the punishment was death.

Violence in Public Entertainment. Potential violence defined slaves' lives; actual violence defined much Roman public entertainment. The emperors regularly provided spectacles featuring "hunters" killing fierce beasts, wild African animals of all kinds mangling condemned criminals, mock naval battles in flooded arenas, blood-drenched gladiatorial combats, and wreck-filled chariot races. Spectators packed arenas for these shows, seated according to their social rank and gender following an Augustan law; the emperor and senators sat close to the action, while women and the poor were relegated to the upper tiers. Roman spectacles had a political context, demonstrating that the ruler was generous in providing expensive entertainment, powerful enough to command life-and-death exhibitions, and dedicated to preserving the social hierarchy.

War captives, criminals, slaves, and free volunteers fought as gladiators; most were men, though women sometimes competed. Daughters trained by their gladiator fathers had first competed during the republic, and women continued to compete occasionally until the emperor Septimius Severus◆ (r. 193–211) banned their appearance. Gladiatorial shows had originated as part of extravagant funerals, but Augustus made them popular entertainment for tens of thousands of spectators. Gladiators were often wounded but rarely fought to the death, unless they were captives or criminals; professional fighters could have extended careers.

◆**Severus:** suh VEHR uhs

To make the fights more unpredictable, pairs of gladiators often competed with different weapons. One favorite bout pitted a lightly armored "net man," who used a net and a trident, against a more heavily armored "fish man," so named from the design of his helmet crest. Betting was popular, the crowds rowdy. As the Christian theologian Tertullian◆ (c. 160–240) complained: "Look at the mob coming to the show—already they're out of their minds! Aggressive, heedless, already in an uproar about their bets! They all share the same suspense, the same madness, the same voice."

Gladiatorial champions won riches and celebrity but not social respectability. Early in the first century C.E., the senators became alarmed when some members of the upper class became gladiators—they regarded this choice as a disgrace to the class. They therefore banned the elite and all free-born women under twenty from appearing in gladiatorial shows.

Public festivals featuring gladiatorial shows, chariot races, and theater productions became a way for ordinary citizens to express their wishes to the emperors, who were expected to attend. Poorer Romans

◆**Tertullian:** tur TUHL yuhn

Gladiators Sculpted on a Tomb

This relief sculpture, which adorned a tomb near Rome dating to about 30–10 B.C.E., shows gladiators competing in games held to honor the person buried there. Gladiatorial combats originated as part of funeral ceremonies because they portrayed with dramatic energy the violent and inevitable struggle to avoid death. Hiring gladiators was very expensive, and only the very wealthy could afford to have them perform at their funerals or in spectacles meant to win the people's favor. These gladiators represent a traditional form of fighting called *provocator* ("challenger"). A challenger, who only fought gladiators of the same type, used a short sword (*gladius*), curved shield, greaves, a metal belt cinching up a loincloth, a forearm guard, a partial chest protector, and a plumed helmet. These men's muscular bodies show the great strength required to be a successful fighter.

© *Alinari/Art Resource, NY.*

Literacy and Social Status

This twenty-six-inch-high wall painting of a woman and her husband was found in an alcove off the central room of a comfortable house in Pompeii, the town in southern Italy buried by a volcanic explosion in 79 C.E. The couple may have owned the bakery that adjoined the house. Both are depicted with items meant to indicate that they were literate and therefore deserving of social status. She holds the notepad of the time, a hinged wooden tablet filled with wax for writing on with the stylus (thin stick) that she touches to her lips; he holds a scroll, the standard form for books in the early Roman Empire. Her hairstyle was one popular in the mid-first century C.E., which hints that this picture was painted not many years before Mount Vesuvius erupted and covered Pompeii in twelve feet of ash. *Erich Lessing/Art Resource, NY.*

rioted at festivals to protest shortfalls in the free grain supply. In this way, public entertainment served as two-way communication between ruler and ruled.

Arts and Letters Fit for an Emperor

Elite culture changed in the Augustan age to serve the same goal as public entertainment: legitimizing and strengthening the transformed political system. Oratory—the highest

attainment of Roman arts and letters—lost its bite for this reason. Under the republic, the ability to make stirring speeches criticizing political opponents had been such a powerful weapon that it could catapult a "new man" like Cicero to a leadership role. Under the principate, the emperor's supremacy ruled out freewheeling political debate. Now ambitious men required rhetorical skills primarily to praise the emperor on the numerous public occasions that promoted his image as a competent and compassionate ruler. Political criticism was out.

Imperial Education. Education in oratory remained a privilege of the wealthy. Rome had no free public schools, so the poor received no formal education. Most people had time only for learning practical skills. A character in *Satyricon*,♦ a satirical literary work of the first century by Petronius,♦ expresses this utilitarian attitude: "I didn't study geometry and literary criticism and worthless junk like that. I just learned how to read the letters on signs and how to work out percentages, and I learned weights, measures, and the values of the different kinds of coins."

Servants looked after rich boys and girls, who attended private elementary schools from age seven to eleven to learn reading, writing, and basic arithmetic. Teachers used rote methods in the classroom, inflicting physical punishment for mistakes. Some children went on to the next three years of school, in which they studied literature, history, and grammar. Only a few boys then proceeded to the study of rhetoric.

Advanced studies concerned literature, history, ethical philosophy, law, and dialectic (reasoned argument). Mathematics and science were rarely studied as separate subjects, but engineers and architects became proficient at calculation despite the difficulty of using Roman numerals for complex math. Rich men and women employed slaves to read aloud to them. Books were continuous scrolls made from papyrus or animal skin. A reader had to unroll the scroll with one hand while rolling it up with the other.

♦**Satyricon:** sa TIHR ih kahn
♦**Petronius:** puh TROH nee uhs

Ideals in Literature and Sculpture. So much literature blossomed during Augustus's era that modern critics call it the Golden Age of Latin literature. The emperor, who himself composed verse and prose, supported the arts by serving as patron for writers and artists. His favorites were Horace (65–8 B.C.E.) and Virgil (70–19 B.C.E.). Horace entranced audiences with the rhythms and irony of his short poems on public and private subjects. His poem celebrating Augustus's victory at Actium became famous for its opening line: "Now we have to drink [a toast]!"

Virgil became the most famous Roman poet for his epic poem *The Aeneid,*◆ which both praised and criticized the emperor—very gently. He composed so painstakingly that he spent a decade writing it, and the poem remained unfinished at his death. He wanted it burned, but Augustus preserved it. Inspired by Homer's poetry, *The Aeneid* told the legend of the Trojan Aeneas, the legendary founder of the Roman people. Virgil tempered his praise for Rome with a profound recognition of the price in freedom to be paid for peace. *The Aeneid* therefore revealed the complex mix of gain and loss created by Augustus's transformation of Roman politics. Above all, it expressed a moral code for all Romans: no matter how tempting the emotional pull of revenge and pride, be merciful to the conquered but lay low the haughty.

Authors with a more independent streak had to be careful. The historian Livy (54 B.C.E.–17 C.E.) composed an enormous history of Rome in which he refused to hide Augustus's ruthlessness in the civil war after Caesar's murder. The emperor chided but did not punish Livy because the history did proclaim that success and stability depended on traditional values of loyalty and self-sacrifice. The poet Ovid◆ (43 B.C.E.–17 C.E.) fared worse.

◆*Aeneid:* ih NEE ihd
◆*Ovid:* AH vihd

An irreverent wit, in *Art of Love* and *Love Affairs* he implicitly mocked the emperor's moral legislation with tongue-in-cheek tips for conducting love affairs and picking up other men's wives at festivals. His book *Metamorphoses* undermined the idea of hierarchy as natural by telling bizarre stories of supernatural shape-changes, with people becoming animals and confusion between the human and the divine. In 8 B.C.E., after Ovid became embroiled in a scandal involving Augustus's daughter, the emperor exiled the poet to a bleak town on the Black Sea.

Public sculpture also reflected the emperor's influence. When Augustus was growing up, portraits were starkly realistic. The sculpture that Augustus commissioned displayed a more idealized style, reminiscent of classical Greek models. In renowned works such as the Prima Porta ("First Gate") statue

Marble Statue of Augustus from Prima Porta
At six feet eight inches high, this imposing sculpture of Rome's first emperor stood a foot taller than its subject. Found at his wife Livia's country villa at Prima Porta ("First Gate") just outside the capital, the marble statue was probably a copy of a bronze original sculpted about 20 B.C.E., when Augustus was in his early forties. The sculptor has depicted him as a younger man, using the idealizing techniques of classical Greek art. Compare his smooth face to Sulla's realistic wrinkles in the bust on page 191. The sculpture is crowded with symbols communicating the image Augustus wished to present: the bare feet hint he is a near-divine hero, the Cupid refers to the Julian family's descent from the goddess Venus, and the design on the breastplate shows a Parthian surrendering to a Roman soldier under the gaze of personified cosmic forces admiring the peace Augustus's regime has created. **For more help analyzing this image,** see the visual activity for this chapter in the Online Study Guide at **bedfordstmartins.com/hunt**. *Scala/Art Resource, NY.*

of him or the sculpted frieze on his Altar of Peace (finished in 9 B.C.E.), Augustus had himself portrayed as serene and dignified, not careworn and sick, as he often was. As with his monumental architecture, Augustus used sculpture to project a calm and competent image of himself as the "restorer of the world" and founder of a new age for Rome.

> **Review:** What were Augustus's most important actions in bringing peace to Rome and transforming its political system?

❖ Maintaining the Pax Romana

A serious problem confronted Augustus's restored republic: how to avoid a violent struggle for power when the emperor died, given that officially no successor could inherit power, only be awarded it by the Senate. Augustus's solution was to train an heir to take over as princeps after his death, with the Senate giving its blessing and awarding the same powers it had conferred on Augustus. This strategy kept rule in his family, called the Julio-Claudians,♦ until the death in 68 C.E. of Augustus's last descendent, the infamous Nero. It established the tradition that family dynasties ruled imperial Rome.

Under the Augustan system, the emperor's main goals were preventing unrest, building loyalty, and financing the administration while governing a vast territory of diverse provinces. Augustus set the pattern for effective imperial rule: taking special care of the army, communicating the emperor's image as a just and generous ruler, and promoting Roman law and culture as universal standards while allowing as much local freedom as possible. The citizens, in return for their loyalty, expected the emperors to be generous patrons—but, for better or worse, the difficulties of long-range communication imposed practical limits on imperial intervention in the lives of the residents of the provinces.

♦**Julio-Claudians:** JOOL yoh KLAW dee uhns

Making Monarchy Permanent, 14–180 c.e.

To avoid civil war, Augustus wanted to make his disguised monarchy Rome's permanent government, but his fiction that the republic continued meant that he needed the Senate's cooperation to give legitimacy to his successor. Already in the 20s B.C.E. he started looking for a relative to designate as the next princeps (he had no son), but one after another they died before he did. Finally, in 4 C.E., he adopted a relative who would survive him, Livia's son (by a previous marriage), Tiberius (42 B.C.E.–37 C.E.). Since Tiberius had a distinguished record as a general, the army supported Augustus's choice. The senators prudently recognized Tiberius as princeps when Augustus died in 14 C.E. The Julio-Claudian dynasty had begun.

The First Dynasty: The Julio-Claudians, 14–68. The stern and irascible Tiberius (r. 14–37) held power for twenty-three years because he had the most important qualification for succeeding as emperor: the army's respect. He built the praetorian guard a fortified camp in Rome so that its soldiers could better protect the emperor, which had the unintended consequence of guaranteeing them a de facto role in determining all future successions—no new emperor could succeed without their support.

Tiberius's long reign provided the stable transition period that the principate needed, establishing the compromise on power between the elite and the emperor on which imperial stability depended. On the one hand, the traditional offices of consul, senator, and so forth continued, with elite Romans filling them and basking in their prestige; on the other hand, the emperors decided who filled the offices and controlled law and government policy. In this way, everyone saved face by pretending that republican government's remaining traces still mattered.

Tiberius paid a bitter price for becoming emperor. To strengthen their family tie, Augustus forced Tiberius to divorce his beloved wife Vipsania to marry Augustus's daughter, Julia—and the marriage proved disastrously unhappy. Tiberius's reign revealed the problems that an unhappy emperor could create. When his personal torments led him to spend his reign's last decade in seclusion far from Rome, his neglect of routine governing permitted abuses by subordinates in Rome and kept him from grooming a decent successor.

Tiberius designated Gaius (r. 37–41), better known as Caligula,♦ to be the next emperor because Gaius was Augustus's great-grandson and Tiberius's fawning supporter, not because he exhibited the qualities a ruler needed or had any training for rule. Still, the third Julio-Claudian emperor might have been successful because he knew about soldiering: Caligula means "baby boots," the nickname the soldiers gave him as a child because he wore little leather shoes like theirs when he was growing up in the military garrisons his father commanded. Unfortunately, Gaius had feeble virtues but enormous appetites. Ruling with cruelty and violence, he bankrupted the treasury to humor his whims. Suetonius labeled him a monster for his murders and sexual crimes. He outraged social tradition by fighting in mock gladiatorial combats and appearing in public in women's clothing or costumes imitating gods. Two praetorian commanders murdered him in 41 to avenge personal insults.

The senators debated the idea of truly restoring the republic by refusing to choose a new emperor. They capitulated, however, when Claudius (r. 41–54), Augustus's grand-nephew and Caligula's uncle, bribed the praetorian guard to back him. Claudius's succession made it clear that the soldiers would insist on there always being an emperor so that they would have a patron to pay them. It also revealed that senatorial yearnings for the republic's return would never be fulfilled.

Claudius opened the way for provincial elites to expand their participation in governing by enrolling men from Transalpine Gaul, a province outside Italy, in the Senate. In return for keeping their regions peaceful and paying taxes, they would receive offices at Rome and imperial patronage. Claudius also transformed imperial bureaucracy by employing freed slaves as powerful administrators; since they owed their great advancement to the emperor, they could be expected to be loyal.

Absolute power's temptations corrupted Claudius's teen-aged successor, Nero (r. 54–68). Emperor at sixteen, he loved music and acting, not governing. The lavish spectacles he sponsored and the cash he distributed kept him popular with Rome's poor. A giant fire in 64 (the incident that led to the legend that Nero fiddled while Rome burned), however, aroused suspicions that he ordered the conflagration to clear the way for a new palace. Nero scandalized the senatorial class by appearing onstage to sing to captive audiences, and he emptied the treasury by spending outrageous sums on a sumptuous palace (his Golden House) and a trip to perform in Greece. To raise money he faked treason charges against senators and equites to seize their property. When rebellious commanders in the provinces toppled his regime, Nero had a servant help him cut his own throat as he dug his grave, wailing, "I'm dying reduced to a laborer's status!"

The Flavian Dynasty and the Imperial Cult, 69–96. Nero's fall sparked a year of civil war in which four generals vied for power (69, the Year of the Four Emperors). Vespasian (r. 69–79) won. His victory proved that the monarchy would continue because the ruling class and the army demanded it. To give his new dynasty—the Flavian,♦ from his family name—legitimacy, Vespasian had the Senate recognize him as ruler. Second, he encouraged the spread of the imperial cult (worship of the emperor as a living god and sacrifices for his household's welfare) in the provinces outside Italy, where most of the empire's population resided.

Vespasian built on local traditions to promote the imperial cult. In the eastern Mediterranean, the Hellenistic kingdoms had established the precedent of subjects worshiping their ruler; inhabitants of Roman provinces there had treated the emperor as a living god since Augustus's era. The imperial cult communicated the same image of the emperor to the provinces as the city's architecture and sculpture did in the capital: he was larger than life, deserved loyal respect,

♦**Caligula:** kuh LIH gyuh luh

♦**Flavian:** FLAY vee uhn

and provided benefactions. Because emperor worship was already well established in Greece and the ancient Near East, Vespasian promoted it in Spain, southern France, and North Africa. Traditional Romans scorned the imperial cult as a provincial aberration, and Vespasian evidently did not believe in his own divinity, to judge from the witty remark Suetonius reports he muttered as he lay dying in 79: "Oh me! I think I'm becoming a god." He allowed emperor worship in the provinces, however, because it was traditional there.

Following their father's lead, Titus (r. 79–81) and Domitian◆ (r. 81–96) conducted hardheaded fiscal policy, professional administration, and high-profile military campaigns. Titus, for example, suppressed a Jewish revolt in Judaea by capturing Jerusalem in 70. He sent relief to Pompeii and Herculaneum when in 79 Mount Vesuvius's massive volcanic eruption buried these towns. He also provided a state-of-the-art site for public entertainment by finishing Rome's **Colosseum**, outfitting the giant amphitheater with awnings to shade the crowd. The Colosseum was deliberately constructed on the site of the former fishpond in Nero's Golden House to demonstrate the new dynasty's public-spiritedness. Domitian balanced the budget and campaigned against Germanic tribes threatening the frontier regions along the Rhine and Danube Rivers.

In the end, Domitian failed because he alienated the Senate. His arrogance made the senators hate him; once he sent them a letter announcing, "Our lord god, myself, orders you to do this." Embittered by a general's rebellion in Germany, he executed numerous upper-class citizens as conspirators. Fearful that they, too, would become victims, his wife and members of his court murdered him in 96.

The Five "Good Emperors," 96–180. As Domitian's fate showed, the principate had not solved monarchy's inevitable weakness: rivalry for rule that could explode into murderous conspiracy. The danger of civil war persisted, whether generated by ambitious generals or the emperor's heirs. No one could predict whether a good ruler or bad would emerge from the struggle over succession. As Tacitus acidly commented, emperors were like the weather: "We just have to wait for bad ones to pass and hope for good ones to appear." Fortunately for Rome, fair weather dawned with the next five emperors—Nerva◆ (r. 96–98), Trajan◆ (r. 98–117), Hadrian◆ (r. 117–138), Antoninus Pius◆ (r. 138–161), and Marcus Aurelius◆ (r. 161–180). Following the influential eighteenth-century historian Edward Gibbon, historians dub these five emperors' period of rule the empire's Golden Age because it was marked by peaceful transfers of power for nearly a century. The period was, however, full of war and strife, as Roman history always was: Trajan fought fierce campaigns to expand Roman power northward across the Danube River into Dacia (today Romania) and eastward into Mesopotamia (Map 6.1); Hadrian earned the Senate's hatred by executing several senators as alleged conspirators and punished a Jewish revolt by turning Jerusalem into a military colony; and Marcus Aurelius spent miserable years on campaign protecting the Danube region from outside attacks.

Still, the five "good emperors" did preside over a political and economic Golden Age. They succeeded one another without murder or conspiracy—the first four, having no surviving sons, used adoption to find the best possible successor. Enough money came in through taxes to pay their expenses, and the army remained obedient. Their reigns marked Rome's longest stretch without a civil war since the second century B.C.E.

Life in the Golden Age, 96–180 C.E.

Peace and prosperity in Rome's Golden Age depended on defense by a loyal military, public-spiritedness by provincial elites in local administration and tax collection, common laws enforced throughout diverse territories, and a healthy population reproducing itself. The empire's size and the relatively

◆**Domitian:** duh MIH shuhn

◆**Nerva:** NUR vuh
◆**Trajan:** TRAY juhn
◆**Hadrian:** HAY dree uhn
◆**Antoninus Pius:** an tuh NY nuhs PY uhs
◆**Aurelius:** aw REEL i uhs

MAP 6.1 The Expansion of the Roman Empire, 30 B.C.E.–117 C.E.
When Octavian (the future Augustus) captured Egypt in 30 B.C.E. after the suicides of Mark Antony and Cleopatra, he greatly boosted Rome's economic strength. The land of the Nile yielded prodigious amounts of grain and gold, and Roman power now effectively encircled the Mediterranean Sea (indigenous kings ruled Mauretania with Roman approval until about 44 C.E. in the reign of Claudius). When the emperor Trajan took over the southern part of Mesopotamia in 114–117 C.E., imperial conquest reached its height; Rome's control had never extended so far east. Egypt remained part of the empire until the Arab conquest in 642 C.E., but Mesopotamia was immediately abandoned by Hadrian, Trajan's successor, probably because it seemed too distant to defend.

small numbers of soldiers and imperial officials in the provinces meant that emperors had only limited control over these factors.

Imperial Military Aims and the Army. In theory, Rome's military goal remained infinite expansion, because conquest brought glory. Virgil expressed this notion in *The Aeneid* by portraying Jupiter, the king of the gods, as promising Rome "imperial rule without limit."

In reality, the emperors were content to have other kingdoms and peoples recognize their authority and not disturb the frontier regions; imperial territory never expanded permanently much beyond what Augustus had controlled.

Most provinces were peaceful and had no need for garrisons, so soldiers were a rare sight in many places. Even Gaul, which had originally resisted imperial control with a suicidal frenzy, was, according to a contemporary witness, "kept in order by 1,200 troops—hardly more soldiers than it has towns." Most legions (a unit of five thousand troops) were stationed on the northern and eastern frontiers, facing hostile neighbors. The Pax Romana guaranteed by the army allowed commerce to operate smoothly in imperial territory, and the Golden Age's prosperity promoted long-distance trade for luxury goods, such as spices and silk, that came from as far away as India and China.

The army reflected the population's diversity because it included many auxiliary units of noncitizens from the provinces. Serving under Roman officers, they could pick up some Latin and Roman customs, and they contributed to improving life in the provinces by helping construct public works. Upon discharge, they received Roman citizenship. In this way the army served as an instrument for spreading a common way of life.

Financing Government and Defense. Paying for imperial government became an insoluble problem. The problem's deepest root was that the army was no longer making conquests to fund the treasury. In the past, foreign wars had brought in huge amounts of capital through booty and prisoners of war sold into slavery. Conquered territory also provided additional tax revenues. Now, there were no new sources of income, but the emperors' standing army had to be paid regularly to maintain discipline. To fulfill their obligations as the army's patrons, emperors at their accession and other special occasions supplemented soldiers' regular pay with substantial bonuses. These rewards made a soldier's career desirable.

A tax on agricultural land in the provinces (Italy was exempt) now provided the principal source of revenue for imperial government and defense. The administration required relatively little money because it was small compared with the size of the territory being governed: no more than several hundred top officials governed a population of about fifty million. Most locally collected taxes stayed in the provinces for expenditures there. Senatorial and equestrian governors with small staffs ran the provinces, which eventually numbered about forty. In Rome,

the emperor employed a substantial palace staff, while equestrian officials called prefects managed the city itself.

The decentralized tax system required public service by the provincial elites; the central and local governments' financial well-being absolutely depended on it. As **decurions♦** (municipal senate members, later called *curiales*), the local officials were required to collect taxes and personally guarantee that their town's public expenditures were covered. If there was a shortfall in tax collection or local finances, these wealthy men had to make up the difference from their own pockets. Wise emperors kept taxes moderate. As Tiberius put it when refusing a request for tax increases from provincial governors, "I want you to shear my sheep, not skin them alive."

The financial liability could make civic office expensive, but the positions' prestige made the elite willing to take the risk. Some received priesthoods in the imperial cult as a reward, an honor open to both men and women. All expected their service to help them secure imperial disaster aid for their area after an earthquake or a flood.

The system worked because it observed tradition: the local social elites were their communities' patrons and the emperor's clients. As long as there were enough rich, public-spirited provincials participating in the system, the principate functioned by fostering the republican ideal of communal values.

The Impact of Roman Culture on the Provinces. The principate changed the Mediterranean world profoundly but unevenly. The provinces contained a wide diversity of peoples speaking different languages, observing different customs, dressing in different styles, and worshiping different divinities (Map 6.2). In the remote countryside, Roman conquest had only a modest effect on local customs. Where new cities sprang up around Roman forts or from settlements of army veterans, Roman influence prevailed. Roman culture had the greatest effect on western Europe, permanently rooting Latin (and the languages that would emerge from it) and Roman law and customs there. Modern cities

♦**decurions:** dih KYUR ee uhns

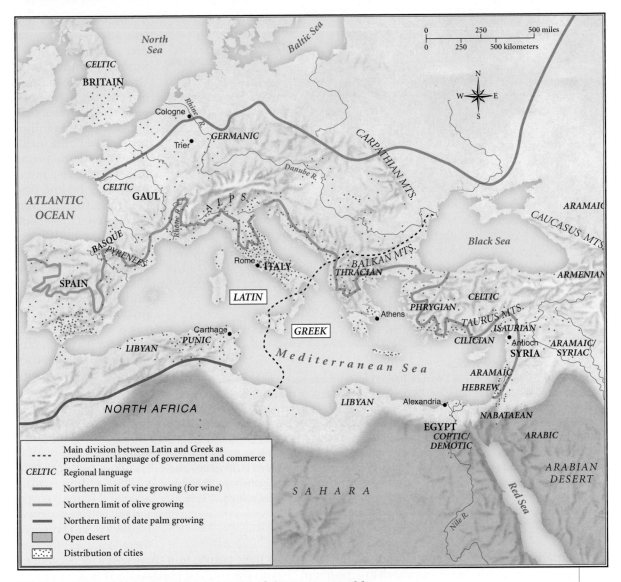

MAP 6.2 Natural Features and Languages of the Roman World

The environment of the Roman world included a large variety of topography, climate, and languages. The inhabitants of the Roman world, estimated to have numbered as many as 50 million, spoke dozens of different tongues, many of which survived well into the late empire. The two predominant languages were Latin in the western part of the empire and Greek in the eastern. Latin remained the language of law even in the eastern empire. Vineyards and olive groves were important agricultural resources because wine was regarded as an essential beverage, and olive oil was the principal source of fat for most people, as well as being used to make soap, perfume, and other products for daily life. Dates were a popular sweet in the Roman world, which had no sugar.

such as Trier♦ and Cologne♦ in Germany started as Roman towns. Over time, social and cultural distinctions lessened between the provinces and Italy. Eventually, emperors came from the provinces; Trajan, from Spain, was the first.

Romanization, as historians call the spread of Roman rule and culture in the provinces, raised the standard of living for

♦**Trier:** trihr
♦**Cologne:** kuh LOHN

Roman Architecture in North Africa

The Roman town of Thysdrus (today El Djem in Tunisia) built this massive amphitheater for public entertainment in the early third century C.E. Its design imitated that of the larger Colosseum in Rome and made it the seventh biggest such building in the empire. Its arched walls soared more than a hundred feet high; its storerooms under the arena floor had three elevators to lift wild animals to the surface; and its seats accommodated nearly 32,000 spectators. Since this seating capacity was several thousand more than the total population of the town, it is apparent that the citizens of Thysdrus planned to attract outside visitors to their spectacular sports facility; they also built a track for chariot racing and a smaller amphitheater for more intimate gatherings. Their big spending for public spectacle put them in the mainstream of Roman imperial culture. © *Erich Lessing/Art Resource.*

many by providing roads and bridges, increasing trade, and establishing peaceful conditions for agriculture. The army's need for supplies meant business for farmers and merchants. The prosperity that provincials enjoyed under Roman rule made Romanization easier for them to take. In addition, Romanization was not a one-way street culturally. In western regions as diverse as Gaul, Britain, and North Africa, interaction between the local people and Romans produced new, mixed cultural traditions, especially in religion and art. Therefore, the process led to a gradual merging of Roman and local culture, not the unilateral imposition of the conquerors' way of life. (See the image, Roman Architecture in North Africa, above.)

Romanization had less effect on the eastern provinces, which largely retained their Greek and Near Eastern character. In much of this region, daily life continued to follow traditional Greek models. When Romans had taken over these areas in the second and first centuries B.C.E., they encountered urban cultures that had flourished for thousands of years. Huge Hellenistic cities such as Alexandria in Egypt and Antioch♦ in Syria rivaled Rome in size and splendor. In fact, compared with Rome, they boasted more individual houses for the well-to-do, fewer blocks of high-rise tenements, and equally magnificent temples.

The eastern provincial elites readily accepted Roman governance. Hellenistic royal traditions had prepared them to see the emperor as their patron and themselves as his clients, with the mutual obligations this ancient system required. Their willing cooperation in the task of governing the provinces was crucial for imperial stability and prosperity.

New Trends in Literature. The continuing vitality of Greek language and culture contributed to a flourishing of Roman literature. New trends, often harking back to classical literature, blossomed. Authors of the second century C.E. such as Chariton and Achilles Tatius wrote romantic adventure novels in Greek. Lucian (c. 117–180) composed satirical dialogues fiercely mocking both stuffy people and superstitious reli-

♦**Antioch:** AN tee ahk

giosity. As part of his enormous and varied literary output, the essayist and philosopher Plutarch (c. 50–120) wrote *Parallel Lives*, biographies of matching Greek and Roman men. His keen moral sense and lively taste for anecdotes made him favorite reading for centuries; William Shakespeare (1564–1616) based several plays on Plutarch's work.

Latin literature thrived as well; in fact, scholars rank the late first and early-to-mid-second centuries C.E. as Rome's Silver Age, second only to the Augustan Golden Age. Its most famous authors wrote with acid wit, verve, and imagination. Tacitus (c. 56–120) composed his *Annals* as a biting narrative about the Julio-Claudians, laying bare Augustus's ruthlessness and his successors' crimes. The satiric poet Juvenal (c. 65–130) skewered pretentious Romans and grasping provincials while bemoaning the indignities of living broke in the capital. Apuleius (c. 125–170) scandalized readers with his *Golden Ass*, a lusty novel about a man turned into a donkey who then regains his body and his soul by the kindness of the Egyptian goddess Isis.

Law and Order through Equity.   Unlike Augustus, second-century emperors never worried that scandalous literature posed a threat to the social order. They did, however, share his belief that law was crucial. Indeed, Romans prided themselves on their ability to order their society through law. As Virgil said, their mission was "to establish law and order within a framework of peace." Roman law influenced most systems of law in modern Europe. One distinctive characteristic was the recognition of the principle of equity, which meant accomplishing what was "good and fair" even if the letter of the law had to be ignored. This principle led legal thinkers to insist, for example, that people's intent in a contract outweighed the agreement's words, and that accusers should prove the accused guilty because it was often impossible for defendants to prove they had not committed the crime. The emperor Trajan ruled that no one should be convicted on the grounds of suspicion alone because it was better for a guilty person to go unpunished than for an innocent person to be condemned. (See "Contrasting Views," page 230.)

The Roman notion of hierarchy required formal distinctions among society's orders. The elites still constituted a tiny portion of the population. Only about one in every fifty thousand had enough money to qualify for the senatorial order, the highest-ranking class, while about one in a thousand belonged to the equestrian order, the second-ranking class. Different purple stripes on clothing identified these orders. The third-highest order consisted of decurions, the local officials in provincial towns.

Those outside the social elite faced greater disadvantages than snobbery. The republican distinction between "better people" and "humbler people" hardened under the principate, and by the third century C.E. it became a standard in Roman law. The legal class of "better people" included senators, equites, decurions, and retired army veterans. Everybody else—except slaves, who counted as property, not people—made up the vastly larger group of "humbler people." The latter faced their gravest disadvantage in court: the law imposed harsher penalties on them than on "better people" for the same crime. "Humbler people" convicted of capital crimes were regularly executed by being crucified or torn apart by wild animals before a crowd of spectators. "Better people" rarely suffered the death penalty; if they did, they received a quicker and more dignified execution by the sword. "Humbler people" could also be tortured in criminal investigations, even if they were citizens. Romans regarded these differences as fair on the grounds that an elite person's higher status required of him or her a higher level of responsibility for the common good. As one provincial governor expressed it, "Nothing is less equitable than mere equality itself."

Reproduction and Marriage.   Nothing, not even law, mattered more to the stability and prosperity of the empire than steady population levels. Concern about reproduction therefore permeated Roman society. The upper-class government official Pliny,♦ for example, sent the following report to the grandfather of his third wife, Calpurnia: "You will be very sad to learn that your granddaughter has suffered

♦**Pliny:** PLIH nee

Midwife's Sign
Childbirth was dangerous for women because of the danger of bleeding to death from an internal hemorrhage. This terra-cotta sign from Ostia, the ancient port city of Rome, probably hung outside a midwife's room to announce her expertise in aiding women in giving birth. It shows a pregnant woman clutching the sides of her chair, with an assistant supporting her from behind and the midwife crouched in front to help deliver the baby. Why do you think the woman is seated for delivery instead of lying down? Such signs were especially effective for people who were illiterate; a person did not have to read to understand the services that the specialist inside could provide. *Scala/ Art Resource, NY.*

a miscarriage. She is a young girl and did not realize she was pregnant. As a result she was more active than she should have been and paid a high price."

Ancient medicine could do little to promote healthy childbirth and reduce infant mortality. Complications in childbirth could easily lead to the mother's death because doctors could not stop internal bleeding or cure infections. They possessed sturdy instruments for surgery and physical examinations, but they were badly mistaken about the process of reproduction. Gynecologists such as Soranus, who practiced in early second century Rome, erroneously recommended the days just after menstruation as the best time to become pregnant, when the woman's body was "not congested." As in Hellenistic medicine, treatments were mainly limited to potions, poultices, and bleeding; Soranus recommended treating exceptionally painful menstruation by drawing blood "from the bend of the arm." Many doctors were freedmen from Greece and other provinces, usually with only informal training. People considered their occupation of low status, unless they served the upper class.

As in earlier times, girls often wed in their early teens or even younger and thus had as many years as possible to bear children. Wealthier women hired wet nurses to breast-feed their babies for them. Because so many babies died young, families had to produce numerous offspring to keep from disappearing. The tombstone of Veturia,♦ a soldier's wife married at eleven, tells a typical story: "Here I lie, having lived for twenty-seven years. I was married to the same man for sixteen years and bore six children, five of whom died before I did." The propertied classes usually arranged marriages between spouses who hardly knew each other, although husband and wife could grow to love each other in a partnership devoted to family.

Marriage's emphasis on childbearing brought many health hazards to women, but to remain single and childless represented social failure for Romans. When Romans wanted to control family size, they practiced contraception by obstructing the female organs or by administering drugs to the female partner. They also exposed infant girls more frequently than boys because sons were considered more valuable than daughters as future supporters and protectors of their families.

The emperors did their best to support reproduction. They aided needy children to encourage larger families. Following the emperors' lead, wealthy people often adopted

---

♦**Veturia:** veh TOUR ee ah

children in their communities. One North African man supported three hundred boys and three hundred girls each year until they grew up. The differing value afforded male and female children was also evident in these humanitarian programs: boys often received more aid than girls.

Review: What distinguished the rule of "bad" and "good" emperors?

❖ The Emergence of Christianity

Christianity began as a Jewish splinter group in Judaea, where, as elsewhere under Roman rule, Jews were allowed to practice their ancestral religion. The new faith was slow to attract believers; three centuries after the death of Jesus, Christians were still a small minority. Moreover, they faced constant suspicion and hostility; virtually every New Testament book decries the resistance the emerging faith encountered. It grew, if only gradually, because it had an appeal based on Jesus' charismatic career, its message of salvation, its early believers' sense of mission, and the strong bonds of community it inspired. Ultimately, Christianity's emergence proved the most significant development in Roman history.

Jesus of Nazareth and the Spread of His Teachings

The new religion sprang from the life and teachings of Jesus (c. 4 B.C.E.–30 C.E.), but its background lay in ancient Jewish history. Harsh Roman rule in Judaea had made the Jews restless and the provincial authorities anxious about rebellion. Jesus' career therefore developed in an unsettled environment. His execution reflected Roman readiness to eliminate perceived threats to peace and social order. In the two decades after his crucifixion, his devoted followers, particularly Paul of Tarsus, spread his teachings beyond Palestine's Jewish community into an unwelcoming wider world.

Jewish Apocalypticism and Christianity. Christianity offered an answer to a difficult question about divine justice prompted by the Jews' long history of oppression under the kingdoms of the ancient and Hellenistic Near East: how could a just God allow the wicked to prosper and the righteous to suffer? Nearly two hundred years before Jesus's birth, persecution by the Seleucid king Antiochus IV (r. 175–164 B.C.E.) had provoked the Jews into a bloody revolt; this protracted struggle gave birth to apocalypticism (see page 51, Chapter 2). According to this religious idea, evil powers, divine and human, controlled the world. The regime of these powers would end, however, when God revealed his plan to conquer the forces of evil by sending a **Christ** (Greek for "anointed one"; in Hebrew *Mashiach*, or in English *Messiah*). A final judgment would soon follow, punishing the wicked and rewarding the righteous for eternity. Apocalypticism especially influenced the Jews living in Judaea under Roman rule. It later inspired Christians and Muslims.

Apocalyptic doctrines had special appeal around the time of Jesus' birth because most Judaean Jews detested the Romans and disagreed among themselves about what form Judaism should take in such troubled times. Some favored accommodation with their overlords, while others preached rejection of the non-Jewish world and its spiritual corruption. Their local ruler, installed by the Romans, was Herod the Great (r. 37–4 B.C.E.). His flamboyant taste for a Greek style of life, flouting Jewish law, made him unpopular with many locals, despite his magnificent rebuilding of the holiest Jewish shrine, the great temple in Jerusalem. When a decade of unrest followed Herod's death, Augustus responded to local petitions for help by installing provincial government to deal with squabbling dynasts and competing religious factions. Judaea had thus turned into a powder keg by Jesus' lifetime.

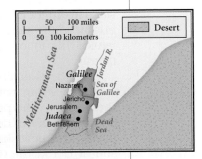

Palestine in the Time of Jesus, 30 C.E.

Catacomb Painting of Christ as the Good Shepherd

Catacombs (underground tombs), cut into soft rock outside various cities of the Roman Empire, served as vast underground burial chambers for Jews and Christians. Rome alone had 340 miles of catacombs. Painted in the third century C.E. on the wall of a Christian catacomb just outside Rome, this fresco depicts Jesus as the Good Shepherd (John 10:10–11). In addition to the tired or injured sheep, Jesus carries a pot of milk and perhaps honey, which new Christians received after their baptism as a symbol of their entry into the Promised Land of the Hebrew Bible. Such catacomb paintings were the earliest Christian art. By the fifth century C.E., the emperors' adoption of the new religion meant that Christians no longer had to make their tombs inconspicuous, and catacombs became sites of pilgrimage instead of burial. *Scala/Art Resource, NY.*

The Life of Jesus. Jesus began his career as a teacher and healer in his native Galilee, the northern region of Palestine, during the reign of Tiberius. The books that would later become the New Testament Gospels, composed between about 70 and 90 C.E., offer the earliest accounts of his life. Jesus wrote nothing down, and others' accounts of his words and deeds are varied and controversial. He taught not through direct instruction but by telling stories and parables that challenged his followers to reflect on what he meant.

All the Gospels say that Jesus' public ministry began with his baptism by John the Baptist, who preached a message of repentance before the approaching final judgment. The Jewish ruler Herod Antipas, a son of Herod the Great whom the Romans supported, executed John because he feared that John's apocalyptic preaching might instigate riots. After John's death, Jesus continued his mission by traveling around Judaea's countryside proclaiming the imminence of God's kingdom and the need to prepare spiritually for its coming. While many saw Jesus as the Messiah, his complex apoc-alypticism did not preach immediate revolt against the Romans. Instead, he taught that God's true kingdom was to be sought not on earth but in heaven. He stressed that this kingdom was open to believers regardless of their social status or apparent sinfulness. His emphasis on God's love for humanity and people's overriding responsibility to love one another reflected Jewish religious teachings, as in the interpretation of the Scriptures by the first-century rabbinic teacher Hillel.

Jesus realized that he had to reach the urban crowds to make an impact. Therefore, he took his message to the Jewish population of Jerusalem, the region's main city. His miraculous healings and exorcisms combined with his powerful preaching created a sensation. His popularity attracted the attention of the Jewish authorities, who assumed that he aspired to replace them. Fearing Jesus might ignite a Jewish revolt, the Roman governor Pontius Pilate (r. 26–36) ordered his crucifixion, the usual punishment for sedition, in Jerusalem in 30.

The Mission of Paul of Tarsus. Jesus' influence endured after his execution. His followers reported that they had seen him in person after his death, proclaiming that God had miraculously raised him from the dead. They convinced a few other Jews that he was the promised savior who would soon return to judge the world and usher in God's kingdom. At this point, his closest disciples, the twelve Apostles (Greek for "messengers"), still considered themselves faithful Jews and continued to follow the commandments of Jewish law.

A radical change took place with the conversion of Paul of Tarsus (c. 10–65), a pious Jew of the Diaspora and a Roman citizen who had been violently opposed to those who accepted Jesus as the Messiah. A spiritual vision on the road to Damascus in Syria, which Paul interpreted as a divine revelation, inspired him to become a follower of Jesus as the Messiah or Christ—a Christian, as members of the movement came to be known. Paul taught that accepting Jesus as divine and his crucifixion as the ultimate sacrifice for the sins of humanity was the only way of becoming righteous in the eyes of God. In this way alone could one expect to attain salvation in the world to come.

Seeking converts outside Judaea, beginning in about 46, Paul traveled to preach to the Jews of the Diaspora and Gentiles (non-Jews) who had adopted some Jewish practices in Syria, Asia Minor, and Greece. Although he stressed the necessity of ethical behavior along traditional Jewish lines, especially the rejection of sexual immorality and polytheism, Paul also taught that converts need not keep all the provisions of Jewish law. To make conversion easier, he did not require the males who entered the movement to undergo the Jewish initiation rite of circumcision. This tenet and his teachings that his congregations did not have to observe Jewish dietary restrictions or festivals led to tensions with Jewish authorities in Jerusalem as well as with the followers of Jesus living there, who still believed that Christians had to follow Jewish law. Roman authorities soon arrested Paul as a criminal troublemaker; he was executed in about 65.

Paul's mission was only one part of the turmoil afflicting the Jewish community in this period; hatred of Roman rule finally provoked the Jews in Palestine to revolt in 66. After crushing the rebels in 70, Titus as the victorious general destroyed the Jerusalem temple and sold most of the city's population into slavery. In the aftermath of this catastrophe, Christianity became separate from Judaism, giving birth to a separate religion now that the Jewish community had lost its religious center.

Paul's importance in early Christianity shows in the number of letters—thirteen—attributed to him among the twenty-seven Christian writings that were put together as the New Testament by around 200. Followers of Jesus regarded the New Testament as having equal authority with the Jewish Bible, which they then called the Old Testament. Since teachers like Paul preached mainly in the cities to reach large crowds, congregations of Christians sprang up in urban areas. Women could sometimes be leaders in the movement, but not without arousing controversy; some Christians believed that men should teach and women only listen. Still, early Christianity was diverse enough that the first head of a congregation named in the New Testament was a woman.

Growth of a New Religion

Christianity had to overcome serious hurdles to develop as a new religion. Imperial officials, suspecting Christians such as Vibia Perpetua of being politically subversive, prosecuted them for treason for refusing to perform traditional sacrifices. Christian leaders had to build an organization from scratch to administer their growing congregations. Finally, Christians had to settle the dispute over a leadership role for women.

The Rise of Persecution and Martyrdom. The emperors found Christians baffling and irritating. Unlike Jews, Christians espoused a novel faith rather than their ancestors' traditional religion; Roman law therefore granted them no special treatment. Most Romans felt hostile toward Christians because they feared that tolerating them would offend the gods of traditional Roman religion. Christians' denial of the old gods and the imperial cult seemed sure to provoke divine retribution. Christians furthermore aroused contempt because they proclaimed as divine king a man the imperial government had crucified as a criminal. Their secret rituals led to accusations of cannibalism and sexual promiscuity because they symbolically ate the body and drank the blood of Jesus during communal dinners, called Love Feasts, which men and women attended together. In short, Christians seemed a threat to peace with the gods.

Not surprisingly, then, Romans were quick to blame Christians for disasters. Following Rome's great fire in 64, Nero punished Christians as arsonists. As Tacitus reports,

Nero had them "covered with the skins of wild animals and mauled to death by dogs, or fastened to crosses and set on fire to provide light at night." The unusual cruelty of their punishment earned Christians sympathy from Rome's population.

Persecutions like Nero's were infrequent and ad hoc. No law forbade Christianity, but officials could punish Christians, just like other citizens, to maintain public order. Pliny's actions as a provincial governor in Asia Minor illustrated the predicament for both sides. (See "Contrasting Views," page 230.) In about 112, he asked some people accused of practicing this new religion if they were indeed Christians and urged those who confessed to reconsider. He freed those who denied Christianity, as well as those who stated they no longer believed, so long as they sacrificed to the gods, vowed allegiance to the imperial cult, and cursed Christ. He executed those who persisted in their faith. Advocates of Christianity such as Tertullian and Justin (c. 100–165) argued that Romans had nothing to fear from their faith. Far from spreading immorality and subversion, these writers insisted, Christianity taught an elevated moral code and respect for authority. It was not a foreign superstition but the true philosophy, combining the best features of Judaism and Greek thought.

Persecution did not stop Christianity. Christians like Perpetua regarded public trials and executions as an opportunity to become a **martyr** (Greek for "witness"), someone who dies for his or her religious beliefs. Martyrs' firm conviction that their deaths would lead directly to heavenly bliss allowed them to face excruciating tortures with courage; some even courted martyrdom. Tertullian proclaimed that "martyrs' blood is the seed of the Church." Ignatius (c. 35–107), bishop of Antioch, begged Rome's congregation, which was becoming the most prominent Christian group, not to ask the emperor to show him mercy after his arrest: "Let me be food for the wild animals [in the arena] through whom I can reach God," he pleaded. "I am God's wheat, to be ground up by the teeth of beasts so that I may be found pure bread of Christ." Most Christians tried their best to avoid becoming martyrs by keeping a low profile, but stories recounting the martyrs' courage inspired the faithful to endure hostility from non-Christians and helped shape the new religion's identity as a creed that gave its believers the spiritual power to overcome great suffering.

Bishops and Christian Hierarchy. First-century Christians expected Jesus to return to pass judgment on the world during their lifetimes. When he did not, they began transforming their religion from an apocalyptic Jewish sect expecting the immediate end of the world into one that could survive over the long term. They struggled to achieve unity in their beliefs and to create a hierarchical organization to impose order on the congregations.

Early Christians fiercely disagreed about what they should believe, how they should live, and who had the authority to decide these questions. Some insisted Christians should withdraw from the everyday world to escape its evil, abandoning their families and shunning sex and reproduction. Others believed they could live by Christ's teachings while retaining their jobs and ordinary lives. Many Christians questioned whether they could serve as soldiers without betraying their religious beliefs because the army participated in the imperial cult. This dilemma raised the further issue of whether Christians could remain loyal subjects of the emperor. Disagreement over these doctrinal questions raged in the many congregations that arose in the early empire around the Mediterranean, from Gaul to Africa to the Near East (Map 6.3).

The emergence of bishops with authority to define Christian doctrine became the most important institutional development in Christianity's early centuries. Bishops received their positions based on the principle later called **apostolic✦ succession**, which states that Jesus' Apostles appointed the first bishops as their successors, granting these new officials the authority Jesus had originally given to the Apostles. Those designated by the Apostles in turn appointed their own successors, and so on. Bishops had the authority to ordain priests with the holy power to administer the sacraments, above all baptism and communion, which believers regarded as

---

✦**apostolic:** a puh STAH lihk

c. 44 B.C.E.–284 C.E.

MAP 6.3 Christian Populations in the Late Third Century C.E.
Christians were still a distinct minority in the Roman world three hundred years after Jesus' crucifixion. Certain areas of the empire, however, especially Asia Minor (western Turkey), where Paul had preached, had a concentration of Christians. Most Christians lived in cities and towns, where the missionaries had gone to spread their message to crowds of curious listeners. *Paganus*, a Latin word for "country person" or "rural villager," was appropriated to mean a believer in traditional polytheistic cults—hence the term *pagan* often found in modern works on this period. Paganism lived on in rural areas for centuries.

necessary for achieving eternal life. Bishops also controlled their congregations' memberships and finances; the money financing the early church flowed from members' gifts.

The bishops worked to stifle the disagreements splintering the new religion. They claimed the authority to define what was true doctrine (**orthodoxy**) and what was not (heresy). The meetings of the bishops of different cities constituted the church's organization in this period. Today it is common to refer to this loose organization as the early Catholic (Greek for "universal") church. Since the bishops themselves often disagreed about doctrine, church unity remained a goal, not a reality.

Women in the Church. Early Christians argued about the role women should play in the church. In the first congregations, women held some leadership positions. When bishops were established atop the hierarchy, however, women were relegated to inferior positions. This demotion reflected the view that in Christianity women should be subordinate to men, just as in Roman imperial society in general.

Some congregations took a long time to accept the bishops' view, however, and women

still commanded positions of authority in some groups in the second and third centuries. Declaring themselves believers in the predictions of the imminent end of the world made by a mysterious preacher named Montanus,♦ the late-second-century prophetesses Prisca♦ and Maximilla,♦ for example, claimed the authority to prophesy and baptize. They spread the apocalyptic message that the heavenly Jerusalem would soon descend in Asia Minor.

After leadership posts were closed to women, many chose a life of celibacy to demonstrate their devotion to Christ. Their commitment to chastity gave these women the power to control their own bodies by removing their sexuality from men's command. Other Christians regarded women achieving this special closeness to God as holy and socially superior. By rejecting the traditional roles of wife and mother in favor of spiritual excellence, celibate Christian women achieved independence and authority denied them in the outside world.

♦**Montanus:** mahn TAN uhs
♦**Prisca:** PRIHS kah
♦**Maximilla:** max ih MILL ah

CONTRASTING VIEWS

Christians in the Empire: Conspirators or Faithful Subjects?

Ancient Romans worried that new religions might disrupt the long-standing "peace with the gods" that guaranteed their national safety and prosperity. Groups whose religious creed seemed likely to offend the traditional deities could therefore be accused of treason, but Christians insisted that they were loyal subjects who prayed for the safety of the emperors (Document 1). The early emperors faced a daunting challenge in trying to forge a policy that was fair both to Christian subjects and to those citizens who feared and detested them (Document 2).

1. TERTULLIAN'S DEFENSE OF HIS FELLOW CHRISTIANS, c. 197 C.E.

An eloquent theologian from North Africa, Tertullian insisted that Christians did indeed support the empire. Even though they refused to pray to the emperor, they prayed for him and thus for the community's health and safety, he explained.

So that is why Christians are public enemies—because they will not give the emperors vain, false, and rash honors; because, being men of a true religion, they celebrate the emperors' festivals more in heart than in frolic. . . .

On the contrary, the name faction may properly be given to those who join to hate the good and honest, who shout for the blood of the innocent, who use as a pretext to defend their hatred the absurdity that they take the Christians to be the cause of every disaster to the state, of every misfortune of the people. If the Tiber reaches the walls, if the Nile does not rise to water the fields, if the sky does not move [i.e., if there is no rain] or the earth does, if there is famine, if there is plague, the cry at once arises: "The Christians to the lions!"

For we invoke the eternal God, the true God, the living God for the safety of the emperors. . . .

Looking up to heaven, the Christians—with hands outspread, because innocent, with head bare because we do not blush, yes! and without a prompter because we pray from the heart—are ever praying for all the emperors. We pray for a fortunate life for them, a secure rule, a safe house, brave armies, a faithful senate, a virtuous people, a peaceful world. . . .

Should not our sect [i.e., Christianity] have been classed among the legal associations, when it commits no such actions as are commonly feared from unlawful associations? For unless I am mistaken, the reason for prohibiting associations clearly lay in forethought for public order—to save the state from being torn into factions, a thing very likely to disturb election assemblies, public gatherings, local senates, meetings, even the public games, with the clashing and rivalry of partisans. . . . We, however, whom all the passion for glory and rank leave cold, have no need to combine; nothing is more foreign to us than the state. One state we recognize for all—the universe.

Source: Tertullian, *Apology*, 10.1, 23.2–3, 35.1, 40.1–2. Translation by T. R. Glover, 1931.

2. PLINY ON EARLY IMPERIAL POLICY TOWARD CHRISTIANS, c. 112 C.E.

As governor of the province of Bithynia, Pliny had to decide the fate of Christians accused of crimes by their neighbors. Knowing of no precedent to guide him, he tried to be fair and wrote to the emperor Trajan to ask if he had acted correctly. The emperor's reply set out what passed for official policy concerning Christians in the early empire.

[Pliny to the emperor Trajan]

It is my practice, my lord, to refer to you all matters concerning which I am in doubt. For who can better give guidance to my hesitation or inform my ignorance? I have never participated in trials of Christians. I therefore do not know what offenses it is the practice to punish or investigate, and to what extent. . . .

In the case of those who were denounced to me as Christians, I have observed the following procedure: I interrogated these as to whether they were Christians; those who confessed I interrogated a second and a third time, threatening them with punishment; those who persisted I ordered executed. For I had no doubt that, whatever the nature of their creed, stubbornness and inflexible obstinacy surely deserve to be punished. There were others possessed of the same folly; but because they were Roman citizens, I signed an order for them to be transferred to Rome.

Soon accusations spread, as usually happens, because of the proceedings going on, and several incidents occurred. An anonymous document was published containing the names of many persons. Those who denied that they were or had been Christians, when they invoked the gods in words dictated by me, offered prayer with incense and wine to your image, which I had ordered to be brought for this purpose together with statues of the gods, and moreover cursed Christ—none of which those who are really Christians, it is said, can be forced to do—these I thought should be discharged. Others named by the informer declared that they were Christians, but then denied it, asserting that they had been but had ceased to be, some three years before, others many years, some as much as twenty-five years. They all worshiped your image and the statues of the gods, and cursed Christ.

They asserted, however, that the sum and substance of their fault or error had been that they were accustomed to meet on a fixed day before dawn and sing responsively a hymn to Christ as to a god, and to bind themselves by oath, not to some crime, but not to commit fraud, theft, or adultery, not to falsify their trust, nor to refuse to return a trust when called upon to do so. When this was over, it was their custom to depart and to assemble again to partake of food—but ordinary and innocent food. Even this, they affirmed, they had ceased to do after my edict by which, in accordance with your instructions, I had forbidden political associations. Accordingly, I judged it all the more necessary to find out what the truth was by torturing two female slaves who were called attendants. But I discovered nothing else but depraved, excessive superstition.

I therefore postponed the investigation and hastened to consult you. For the matter seemed to me to warrant consulting you, especially because of the number involved. For the contagion of this superstition has spread not only to the cities but also to the villages and farms. But it seems possible to check and cure it. It is certainly quite clear that the temples, which had been almost deserted, have begun to be frequented, that the established religious rites, long neglected, are being resumed, and that from everywhere sacrificial animals are coming, for which until now very few purchasers could be found. Hence it is easy to imagine what a multitude of people can be reformed if an opportunity for repentance is afforded.

[The emperor Trajan to Pliny]

You observed proper procedure, my dear Pliny, in sifting the cases of those who had been denounced to you as Christians. For it is not possible to lay down any general rule to serve as a kind of fixed standard. They are not to be sought out; if they are denounced and proved guilty, they are to be punished, with this reservation, that whoever denies that he is a Christian and really proves it—that is, by worshiping our gods—even though he was under suspicion in the past, shall obtain pardon through repentance. But anonymously posted accusations ought to have no place in any prosecution. For this is both a dangerous kind of precedent and out of keeping with [the spirit of] our age.

Source: Pliny, *Letters*, Book 10, nos. 96 and 97. Translation by Betty Radice, 1969.

QUESTIONS TO CONSIDER

1. Do you think that Pliny's procedure in dealing with the accused Christians respected the Roman legal principle of equity? Explain.
2. How should a society treat a minority of its members whose presence severely disturbs the majority?

Competing Beliefs

Even three or four centuries after Jesus' death, the overwhelming majority of the population still practiced polytheism. The clusters of beliefs that centered on deities worshiped in varying ways in different places never became a unified religion, as the modern term *paganism* (from *paganus*, Latin for country person) might suggest. The principate's success and prosperity gave traditional believers confidence that the old gods protected them and that the imperial cult added to their safety. Even those who preferred religious philosophy, such as Stoicism's idea of divine providence, nevertheless respected the old-style cults because they embodied Roman tradition. By the third century, spiritually inclined people had competing beliefs from which to choose. These beliefs appealed to people because they offered hope that they could change their lives for the better and, in some cults, look forward to an afterlife.

Polytheistic, or pagan, religion had as its goal gaining the favor of all the divinities who could affect human life. Its deities ranged from the state cults' major gods, such as Jupiter and Minerva, to spirits thought to inhabit groves and springs. Famous international cults such as the Mysteries of Demeter and Persephone at Eleusis outside Athens remained popular; the emperor Hadrian was initiated at Eleusis in 125.

Isis and Mithras. The cults of Isis and Mithras demonstrate how polytheistic rituals provided believers with a religious experience that aroused strong personal emotions and demanded a moral way of life. The Hellenized Egyptian goddess Isis had already attracted Romans by the time of Augustus, who tried to suppress her cult because it was Cleopatra's religion. But the stature of Isis as a kind, compassionate goddess who cared for her followers made her cult too popular to crush: the Egyptians said it was her tears for famished humans that caused the Nile to flood every year and bring them good harvests. Her image was that of a loving mother, and in art she was often depicted nursing her son. Her cult's central doctrine concerned the death and resurrection of her husband, Osiris; Isis promised her believers a similar life after death.

Isis required her followers to behave righteously. Many inscriptions expressed her high moral standards by listing her own civilizing accomplishments: "I broke down the rule of tyrants; I put an end to murders; I caused what is right to be mightier than gold and silver." The hero of Apuleius's novel *The Golden Ass*, whom Isis rescues from torturous enchantment, shouts out his intense joy after being spiritually reborn by the goddess: "O holy and eternal guardian of the human race, who always cherishes mortals and blesses them, you care for the troubles of miserable humans with a sweet mother's love. Neither day nor night, nor any moment of time, ever passes by without your blessings." Other cults also required worshipers to lead upright lives. Numerous inscriptions from remote villages in Asia Minor, for example, record people's confessions to sins such as sexual transgressions for which their local god had imposed severe penance.

Archaeology reveals that the cult of Mithras had many shrines under the empire, but no detailed texts survive explaining its rituals and symbols. Roman-era worshipers claimed the ancient Persian sage Zarathustra had founded the cult for, as they called him, the "unconquerable god Mithras." Modern scholars have found no evidence of an ancient Persian cult, however, and the archaeological evidence comes mostly from western Roman territory. Mithras's legend said that he killed a bull in a cave, apparently as a sacrifice for the benefit of his worshipers. As pictures show (see Mithras Slaying the Bull), this was not an ordinary sacrifice because the animal did not die without struggling. Initiates in Mithras's cult proceeded through rankings named, from bottom to top, Raven, Male Bride, Soldier, Lion, Persian, Sun-runner, and Father. The sources reveal little about what these grades meant, except that astrology may have been involved and that Father was a title of great honor. The poor state of the evidence prevents us from understanding clearly what Mithras's followers believed, except that they looked to what they thought was ancient Persian tradition as a guide to religious truth.

Mithras Slaying the Bull
Hundreds of shrines to the mysterious god Mithras have been found in the Roman Empire. Scholars strenuously debate the symbolic meaning of the bull slaying so prominent in art connected to Mithras's cult, as in this wall painting of about 200 C.E. from the shrine at Marino, south of Rome. Here, a snake and a dog lick the sacrificial animal's blood, while a scorpion pinches its testicles as it dies in agony. The ancient sources do not clarify the scene's meaning. What do you think could be the explanation for this type of sacrifice?
Scala/Art Resource, NY.

Philosophy as Guide. Many upper-class Romans guided their lives by a philosophy centered on religion. The most popular philosophy was Stoicism, which stressed self-discipline and duty (see Chapters 4 and 5). Philosophic individuals put together their own set of beliefs, such as those expressed by the emperor Marcus Aurelius in his memoirs, entitled *To Myself* (today known as *Meditations*).

Christian and polytheistic intellectuals meanwhile energetically debated Christianity's relationship to traditional Greek philosophy. The theologian Origen♦ (c. 185–255), for example, argued that Christianity was superior to Hellenic philosophical doctrines as a guide to correct living. At about the same time, however, philosophic belief achieved its most religiously influential formulation in the works of Plotinus (c. 205–270). Plotinus's spiritual philosophy, called **Neoplatonism** because it developed new doctrines based on Plato's philosophy, influenced many educated Christians as well as polytheists. Its religious doctrines focused on a human longing to return to the universal Good from which human existence derives. By turning away from the life of the body through the intellectual pursuit of philosophy, individual souls could ascend to the level of the universal soul; they would then become the whole of the universe. This mystical union

♦**Origen:** AWR uh juhn

War Scenes on Trajan's Column
Much of our knowledge of Roman military equipment, such as the intricate construction of chain-mail armor, comes from close study of Trajan's Column in Rome. The sculpted band depicting Trajan's Dacian wars that spiraled up his column (detail shown here) contained some 2,500 figures. The scenes were about three feet high at the bottom but grew to four feet at the top to accommodate the distance and angle of vision for spectators. The spiral's beginning shows the landscape of Dacia, with the following narrative scenes blending into one another without formal frames to separate them. They show the emperor leading his troops and making sacrifices to the gods, while his soldiers appear preparing to march, crossing the Danube, building sturdy camps, being stormed in their encampments by bands of Dacians, and fighting fierce hand-to-hand battles. *Scala/Art Resource, NY.*

with what the Christians called God could be achieved only through strenuous self-discipline in personal morality as well as intellectual life. Neoplatonism's stress on spiritual purity gave it a powerful appeal to Christian intellectuals. Like the cult of Isis or Stoicism, Neoplatonism provided guidance, comfort, and hope through good times and bad.

> **Review:** What beliefs and actions made Christians suspicious in the opinion of Roman officials?

❖ The Third-Century Crisis

Life turned grim for many people in the middle of the third century. Several factors combined to provoke a crisis. Invasions on the northern and eastern frontiers had forced the emperors to expand the army for defense, but no new revenues came in to meet the additional costs. The emperors' desperate schemes to raise money to pay and equip the troops damaged the economy and infuriated the population. The ensuing social unrest encouraged unscrupulous generals to imitate the behavior that had destroyed the republic: commanding client armies to seize power. The worst trouble came when civil war once again afflicted Rome. Earthquakes and scattered epidemics added to people's misery. By the end of the third century, this combination of troubles had shredded the Pax Romana.

Defending the Frontiers

Emperors since Domitian in the first century had combated invaders. The most aggressive attackers were the multiethnic bands that crossed the Danube and Rhine Rivers to raid Roman territory. Constant fighting against the Roman army helped these poorly organized northerners develop effective military discipline, and they mounted especially dangerous invasions during the reign of Marcus Aurelius (161–180). A major threat also appeared at the eastern edge of the empire, when a new dynasty, the Sassanids,❖ defeated the Parthian Empire and reenergized the ancient Persian kingdom. By 227, Persia's military resurgence compelled the emperors to concentrate forces in the rich eastern provinces,

---

❖**Sassanids:** suh SAH nuhd

at the expense of the defense of the northern frontiers.

Recognizing the northern warriors' bravery, the emperors had begun hiring them as auxiliary soldiers for the Roman army in the late first century and settling them on the frontiers as buffers against other invaders. By around 200, the army had expanded to enroll perhaps as many as 450,000 legionary and auxiliary troops (the size of the navy remains unknown). Training constantly, soldiers had to be fit enough to carry forty-pound packs up to twenty miles in five hours, swimming rivers en route. Since Hadrian's reign in the early second century, the emperors had built many stone camps for permanent garrisons, but on the march an army constructed a fortified camp every night; soldiers transported all the makings of a wooden-walled city everywhere they went. As one ancient commentator noted, "Infantrymen were little different from loaded pack mules." At one temporary fort in a frontier area, archaeologists found a supply of a million iron nails—ten tons' worth. The same encampment required seventeen miles of timber for its barracks' walls. To outfit a single legion with tents required fifty-four thousand calves' hides.

The increased demand for pay and supplies strained imperial finances because successful conquests had dwindled over time. The army had become a source of negative instead of positive cash flow to the treasury, and the economy had not expanded to make up the difference. To make matters worse, inflation had driven up prices. A principal cause of inflation may have been, ironically, the principate's long period of peace that promoted increased demand for the Roman economy's relatively static production of goods and services.

In desperation, some emperors responded to inflated prices by debasing imperial coinage in a vain attempt to cut government costs. **Debasement of coinage** meant putting less silver in each coin without changing its face value; the emperors hoped this move would create more cash from the same amount of precious metal. (See "Taking Measure," opposite.) But merchants simply raised prices to make up for the debased coinage's reduced value; this in turn pro-

duced more inflation. By 200, this furious spiral of swiftly rising prices had spun into a financial tornado. Still, the soldiers demanded that their patrons, the emperors, pay them well. This pressure drove imperial finances into catastrophic collapse by the 250s.

TAKING MEASURE

The Value of Roman Imperial Coinage, 27 B.C.E.–300 C.E.
Ancient silver coinage derived its value from its metallic content; the less silver in a coin, the less the coin was worth. When they faced rising government and military expenses but had flat or falling revenues, emperors resorted to debasing the coinage by reducing the amount of silver and increasing the amount of other, cheaper metals in each coin. These pie charts reveal that there was a relatively gradual devaluation of the coinage until the third century, when military expenses apparently skyrocketed. By 300 C.E., only a trace amount of silver was left in coins. Debasement fueled inflation because merchants and producers had to raise their prices for goods and services when they were being paid with currency that was increasingly less valuable.
Adapted from Kevin Greene, *The Archeology of the Roman Empire* (London: B. T. Batsford, Ltd., 1986), 60. Reprinted with permission of Salamander Books Limited.

The Severan Emperors and Catastrophe

The Severan emperors—Septimius Severus (r. 193–211) and his sons, Caracalla♦ and Geta—put Rome's economic catastrophe in motion: the father drained the treasury to satisfy the army, while his sons' murderous rivalry and reckless spending destroyed the government's stability. A soldier's soldier who came from the large North African city of Lepcis Magna in what is today Libya, Severus became emperor in 193 when his predecessor proved hopelessly incompetent and set off a government crisis and civil war. To remedy the situation by restoring imperial prestige and acquiring money through foreign conquest, Severus vigorously pursued successful campaigns beyond the frontiers of the provinces in Mesopotamia and northern Britain.

Since inflation had reduced their wages to almost nothing after deductions for the costs of supplies and clothing, soldiers expected the emperors, as their patrons, to provide gifts of extra money. Severus spent large sums on gifts and tried to improve soldiers' conditions permanently by raising their pay by a third. The army's expanded size made this raise more expensive than the treasury could handle and further fueled inflation. His policy's dire financial consequences concerned Severus not at all. His deathbed advice to his sons in 211 was to "stay on good terms with each other, be generous to the soldiers, and pay no attention to anyone else."

Caracalla's Failure. Sadly for the principate, Severus's sons followed his advice only on the last two points. Caracalla (r. 211–217) seized power for himself by murdering his brother Geta. Caracalla's violent and profligate reign ended the Roman Golden Age of peace and prosperity. He increased the soldiers' pay by another 40 to 50 percent and spent gigantic sums on building projects, including the largest public baths Rome had ever seen, covering blocks and blocks of the city to display his munificence and win popular acclaim. His extravagant spending put

♦**Caracalla:** ka ruh KA luh

unbearable pressure on the local provincial officials responsible for collecting taxes and on the citizens, whom the officials in turn squeezed for ever larger payments.

In 212, Caracalla took his most famous step to try to fix the budget crisis: he granted Roman citizenship to almost every man and woman in imperial territory except slaves. Since only citizens paid inheritance taxes and fees for freeing slaves, an increase in citizens meant an increase in revenues, most of which was earmarked for the army. But too much was never enough for Caracalla, who contemporaries whispered was insane. He wrecked the imperial budget. Once when his mother upbraided him for his excesses he replied, as he drew his sword, "Never mind, we won't run out of money as long as I have this."

The Threat of Fragmentation. Financial troubles produced political instability. After the praetorian guard commander Macrinus murdered Caracalla in 217 to make himself emperor, Caracalla's female relatives convinced the army to overthrow Macrinus and make a young relative emperor. The restored dynasty soon ended with the assassination of the last Severan emperor in 235. This opened a half-century of civil war that, compounded by natural disasters, broke the principate's back. For fifty years, a parade of emperors and pretenders fought to rule; more than two dozen men, often several at a time, held or claimed power during that violent period. Their only qualification was their ability to command a frontier army and to reward the troops for loyalty to their general instead of to the state.

Territory of Zenobia, Queen of Palmyra, 269–272 C.E.

The mid-third century civil war exacted a tremendous toll on the population and the economy; violence and hyperinflation made life miserable in many regions. Agriculture withered as farmers found it impossible to keep up normal production in wartime, when battling armies damaged their crops searching for food. City council members faced constantly escalating demands for tax revenues from the swiftly changing emperors; the constant financial pressure destroyed their will to serve their communities.

Foreign enemies to the north and east took advantage of the Roman civil wars to attack. Roman fortunes hit bottom when Shapur I, king of the Sassanid Empire of Persia, invaded the province of Syria and captured the emperor Valerian (r. 253–260). Imperial territory was in constant danger of fragmenting by the later third century. Zenobia,◆ the warrior queen of Palmyra◆ in Syria, for example, seized Egypt and Asia Minor; the tough and experienced emperor Aurelian (r. 270–275) recovered these provinces only with great difficulty. He also had to encircle Rome with a massive wall to ward off surprise attacks from northern raiders, who were smashing their way into Italy from the north.

Historians dispute how severely these troubles were worsened by natural disasters, but devastating earthquakes and virulent epidemics did strike some of the provinces around the middle of the century. The population probably declined significantly as food supplies became less dependable, civil war killed soldiers and civilians alike, and infection flared over large regions. The loss of population meant fewer soldiers for the army, whose strength as a defense and police force had been gutted by political and financial chaos. This weakness made frontier areas more vulnerable to raids and allowed roving bands of robbers to range unchecked inside the borders.

Persecution.   Polytheists explained the horrible times of the third century in the traditional way: the state gods were angry about something. But what? The obvious answer was the presence of Christians, who denied the existence of the Roman gods and refused to participate in their worship. The emperor Decius◆ (r. 249–251) therefore launched a

systematic persecution to eliminate this contaminated group and restore the goodwill of the gods. He proclaimed himself Restorer of the Cults while declaring, "I would rather see a rival to my throne than another bishop of Rome." He ordered all the empire's inhabitants to prove their loyalty to the state's well-being by sacrificing to its gods. Christians who refused were killed.

This persecution did not stop the civil war, economic failure, and natural disasters that threatened Rome's empire. By the 280s, the principate was near to fragmenting. Remarkably, it was to be dragged back to unity in the same way it had begun: a dynamic leader would create a new form of authoritarian leadership to replace the failed old system. That leader was the emperor Diocletian (r. 284–305).

> **Review:** What disasters provoked the crisis in Roman government and society in the third century C.E.?

Conclusion

Augustus created the principate by installing a cloaked monarchy while insisting that he was restoring the republic to its traditional values. He succeeded because he ensured the army's loyalty and exploited the traditional patron-client system. The principate made the emperor the army's and the people's patron. Most provincials, especially in the eastern Mediterranean, found this arrangement acceptable because it replicated the familiar relationship between ruler and ruled inherited from the Hellenistic kingdoms.

So long as sufficient funds allowed the emperors to keep their millions of clients satisfied, stability prevailed. They spent money to provide food to the poor, build baths and arenas for public entertainment, and pay their troops. The emperors of the first and second centuries expanded the military to protect their distant territories stretching from Britain to North Africa to Syria. By the second century, peace and prosperity had created an imperial Golden Age. Long-term fiscal difficulties set in, however, because the

---

◆**Zenobia:** zuh NOH bee uh
◆**Palmyra:** pal MY ruh
◆**Decius:** DEE shuhs

MAPPING THE WEST The Roman Empire in Crisis, c. 284 C.E.
By the 280s C.E., fifty years of civil war had torn the principate apart. Imperial territory retained the outlines inherited from the time of Augustus (compare Map 6.1 on page 219), except for the loss of Dacia to the Goths during Aurelian's reign (270–275 C.E.). Attacks from the north and east had repeatedly penetrated the frontiers, however. What do you think would have been the greatest challenges in ruling such a vast empire in an age without swift communications or fast travel?

army, now concentrating on defense, no longer brought money into the treasury through conquest. Severe inflation made the situation desperate. Since the wealthy elites could no longer meet the demand for increased taxes without draining their fortunes, they lost their public-spiritedness and avoided their communal responsibilities. Loyalty to the state became too expensive.

The emergence of Christians added to the uncertainty because Roman officials doubted their dedication to the state. Their new religion evolved from Jewish apocalypticism to an increasingly hierarchical organization. Its believers disputed with each other and with the authorities; martyrs such as Vibia Perpetua impressed and worried the government with the depth of their convictions. Citizens placing loyalty to a divinity ahead of loyalty to the state was a new and inexplicable phenomenon for Roman officialdom.

When financial ruin, civil war, and natural disasters combined to weaken the imperial system in the mid-third century, the emperors lacked the money and the popular support to end the crisis. Not even persecutions of Christians could convince the gods to restore Rome's good fortunes. The empire instead had to be transformed politically and religiously. Against all expectations, that process began with Diocletian in 284.

Suggested References

Creating the Pax Romana

Whether scholars label Augustus tyrant or reformer, they agree that he was a brilliant visionary. Recent research on the ways Augustus and his successors communicated the meaning of empire to the public stresses the role of grandiose and often violent spectacles.

Barrett, Anthony A. *Livia: First Lady of Imperial Rome.* 2002.

Conlin, Diane Atnally. *The Artists of the Ara Pacis: The Process of Hellenization in Roman Relief Sculpture.* 1997.

Futrell, Alison. *Blood in the Arena: The Spectacle of Roman Power.* 1997.

Galinsky, Karl. *Augustan Culture.* 1996.

Horace's poetry and country house: http://www.humnet.ucla.edu/horaces-villa.

Potter, D. S., and D. J. Mattingly, eds. *Life, Death, and Entertainment in the Roman Empire.* 1999.

Roman emperors: http://www.roman-emperors.org.

Roman technology: http://www.unc.edu/courses/rometech/public/frames/art_set.html.

Southern, Pat. *Augustus.* 1998.

*Suetonius, *The Twelve Caesars.* Trans. Robert Graves. 1979.

*Virgil, *Aeneid.* Trans. Robert Fitzgerald. 1985.

Maintaining the Pax Romana

Research shows that the Pax Romana was made possible both by the devotion to duty of em-

*Primary source.

perors such as Marcus Aurelius and by the general prosperity that emerged during the absence of war in imperial territory.

*Apuleius, *The Golden Ass.* Trans. P. G. Walsh. 1995.

Ball, Warwick. *Rome in the East: The Transformation of an Empire.* 2001.

Champlin, Edward. *Nero.* 2003.

Garnsey, Peter, and Richard Saller. *The Roman Empire: Economy, Society, and Culture.* 1987.

Mattern, Susan. *Rome and the Enemy: Imperial Strategy in the Principate.* 1999.

*Marcus Aurelius, *Meditations.* Trans. A. L. Farguharson. 1998.

Roman towns, monuments, and historical texts: http://www.ukans.edu/history/index/europe/ancient_rome/E/Roman/home.html.

Treggiari, Susan. *Roman Marriage: Iusti Coniuges from the Time of Cicero to the Time of Ulpian.* 1991.

Wiedemann, Thomas. *The Julio-Claudian Emperors, A.D. 14–70.* 1989.

The Emergence of Christianity

Scholarly debate concerning early Christianity remains energetic. The sources' meanings are hotly contested because both the ancient authors and their modern interpreters usually have particular points of view.

Brown, Peter. *The Rise of Western Christendom: A.D. 200–1000.* 2nd ed. 2003.

Crossan, John Dominic, and Jonathan L. Reed. *Excavating Jesus: Beneath the Stones, Behind the Texts.* 2001.

Early Christianity: http://www.wabashcenter.wabash.edu/internet/early.htm.

*Ehrman, Bart D. *The New Testament and Other Early Christian Writings: A Reader.* 1998.

Kraemer, Ross Shephard. *Her Share of the Blessings: Women's Religion among Pagans, Jews, and Christians in the Greco-Roman World.* 1992.

Nickelsburg, George W. E. *Ancient Judaism and Christian Origins. Diversity, Continuity, and Transformation.* 2003.

Schürer, Emil. *The History of the Jewish People in the Age of Jesus Christ (175 B.C.–A.D. 135).* Rev. ed. 4 vols. 1973–1987.

Stambaugh, John E., and David L. Balch. *The New Testament in Its Social Environment.* 1986.

Torjesen, Karen Jo. *When Women Were Priests: Women's Leadership in the Early Church and the Scandal of Their Subordination in the Rise of Christianity.* 1993.

Turcan, Robert. *The Cults of the Roman Empire.* Trans. Antonia Nevill. 1996.

The Third-Century Crisis

The fundamental problem in the third century remained the same: the Roman monarchy's propensity to generate civil war and the inevitably disastrous effects on the economy. Hence, scholarly study of the crisis emphasizes military and political history.

Campbell, Brian. *Warfare and Society in Imperial Rome, 31 b.c.–a.d. 284.* 2002.

Decius, the persecutor of Christians: **http://www.roman-emperors.org/decius.htm**.

*Dodgeon, Michael H., and Samuel N. C. Lieu. *The Roman Eastern Frontier and the Persian Wars a.d. 226–363: A Documentary History.* 1994.

Elton, Hugh. *Frontiers of the Roman Empire.* 1996.

Grant, Michael. *The Collapse and Recovery of the Roman Empire.* 1999.

*Herodian, *The History (180 to 238 c.e.).* Trans. C. R. Whittaker, 1969.

Southern, Pat. *The Roman Empire from Severus to Constantine.* 2001.

CHAPTER REVIEW

IMPORTANT EVENTS

30 B.C.E.	Octavian (the future Augustus) conquers Ptolemaic Egypt
27 B.C.E.	Augustus inaugurates the principate
c. 30 C.E.	Jesus of Nazareth crucified in Jerusalem
c. 46 C.E.	Paul begins travels seeking converts to Christianity
64 C.E.	Much of Rome burns in mammoth fire; Nero blames Christians
69 C.E.	Civil war during the Year of the Four Emperors
70 C.E.	Titus captures Jerusalem and destroys the Jewish temple
c. 70–90 C.E.	New Testament Gospels are written
80s C.E.	Domitian leads campaigns against multiethnic invaders on northern frontiers
161–180 C.E.	Multiethnic bands attack the northern frontiers
212 C.E.	Caracalla extends Roman citizenship to almost all free inhabitants of the provinces
249–251 C.E.	Decius persecutes Christians
250s–280s C.E.	Imperial finances collapse from civil war, debased coinage, and massive inflation
260 C.E.	The Persian king Shapur I captures Emperor Valerian in battle in Syria

KEY TERMS

apostolic succession (228)

auctoritas (207)

Augustus (206)

Christ (226)

Colosseum (218)

debasement of coinage (235)

decurions (220)

martyr (228)

Neoplatonism (233)

orthodoxy (229)

Pax Romana (204)

praetorian guard (207)

principate (204)

Romanization (221)

REVIEW QUESTIONS

1. What were Augustus's most important actions in bringing peace to Rome and transforming its political system?
2. What distinguished the rule of "bad" and "good" emperors?
3. What beliefs and actions made Christians suspicious in the opinion of Roman officials?
4. What disasters provoked the crisis in Roman government and society in the third century C.E.?

MAKING CONNECTIONS

1. What were the similarities and differences between the crisis in the first century B.C.E. that undermined the republic and the crisis in the third century C.E. that undermined the principate?
2. If you had been a first-century Roman emperor under the principate, what would you have done about the Christians and why? What if you had been a third-century emperor?

FOR FURTHER EXPLORATION

To assess your mastery of the material in this chapter, see the Online Study Guide at **bedfordstmartins.com/hunt**.

To read additional primary-source material from this period, see Chapter 6 in *Sources of The Making of the West*, Second Edition.

The Transformation of the Roman Empire, 284–c. 600 C.E.

A THIRD-CENTURY Egyptian woman named Isis sent a letter to her mother that archaeologists discovered while exploring a village near the Nile River. The letter, written in Greek on papyrus, hints at the anxiety that people in the Roman Empire felt during the turmoil of that century.

> Every day I pray to the lord Sarapis and his fellow gods to watch over you. I want you to know that I have arrived in Alexandria safely after four days. I send affectionate greetings to my sister and the children and Elouath and his wife and Dioscorous and her husband and children and Tamalis and her husband and son and Heron and Ammonarion and…Sanpat and her children. And if Aion wants to be in the army, let him come—everybody is in the army!

This letter raises tantalizing questions about Isis's life, such as her relationship with the people she mentions, who have a mixture of Greek and Semitic names. It also poses many other unanswered questions. Did Isis know how to write or, as was common, had she hired a scribe? Why did she go to Alexandria? Why did Aion♦ want to become a soldier? Why was "everybody" in the army?

The answers lie in the third-century crisis that nearly destroyed the empire. Perhaps economic troubles forced Isis to leave her home to look for work in the largest city in her area. Perhaps Aion wanted to join the army to better his prospects; the emperors, like

---

♦**Aion:** AYE uhn

Emperor Honorius as Christian Victor
Both leaves of this ivory diptych ("folding tablet") made in 406 C.E. depict Honorius, emperor of the western Roman empire, as a military victor attributing his success to Christ. Petronius Probus presented this gift to the emperor to signify his gratitude for being awarded the consulship, the empire's highest honor. On the left, Honorius holds a standard (a sign on a post) that says, "You will always conquer, in the name of Christ," and a statuette of Victory astride the globe offers him a victor's wreath. On the right, he holds a shield and a scepter. His clothing and armor identify him as a military leader; the inscription above his head and the diadem of pearls on it proclaim him "Our Master, Always Augustus," while the circle (nimbus) around his head testifies to his holiness. As this carving shows, Honorius, like other emperors, believed that he had divine backing for his army. In his case, it was not enough: the Goths sacked Rome only four years later.
Cathedral Treasury. Aosta, Italy. © Alinari/Art Resource, NY.

Honorius◆ (r. 395–423) shown in the chapter-opening illustration in his military garb, were always looking for more soldiers. No wonder, then, that it seemed everybody was in the army: the political turmoil during the third century had erupted into fifty years of civil war.

By 284 C.E., decades of bloodshed, with Roman armies fighting Roman armies over who should be emperor, had presented the imperial government with a desperate challenge: how to resume its fundamental role of guaranteeing peace, order, and prosperity. In that year, the empire was saved from falling apart when Diocletian became emperor (r. 284–305) and proved to be a leader tough enough to impose peace and flexible enough to reorganize the administration through subdivision of power.

Regaining social stability was difficult because religious tensions were growing between Christians and followers of traditional polytheistic cults like the letter writer Isis, whose faith was visible in her namesake, an Egyptian goddess. Diocletian, a follower of traditional Roman religion, blamed the Christians for angering the gods and thus bringing on the third-century crisis; he and his partners in rule therefore embarked on the worst persecutions of Christians yet. Diocletian's successor Constantine (r. 306–337) unexpectedly ended this brutality by converting to Christianity and supporting it with imperial funds and a

◆**Honorius:** ah NOHR ee uhs

Miniature Portrait of Emperor Constantine
This eight-inch-high bust of Constantine is carved from chalcedony, a crystalline mineral prized for its milky translucence. The first Christian emperor is depicted as gazing upward, to link himself to his hero and model Alexander the Great, who had ordered his portrait done in this posture. Constantine also appears without a beard, a style made popular by Alexander and imitated by Augustus and Trajan, successful emperors with whom Constantine also wished to be associated. The cross at the top center of Constantine's breastplate makes the statuette one of the relatively few pieces of fourth-century Roman art to display overtly Christian symbols. The position of this sign of the emperor's religious choice recalls the design on Augustus's breastplate depicted on page 215; like the founder of the principate, Constantine communicated his image through art. *Bibliothèque Nationale.*

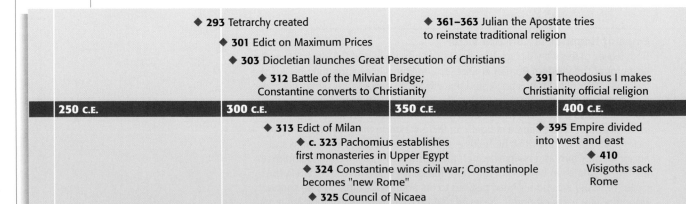

◆ **293** Tetrarchy created

◆ **301** Edict on Maximum Prices

◆ **303** Diocletian launches Great Persecution of Christians

◆ **361–363** Julian the Apostate tries to reinstate traditional religion

◆ **312** Battle of the Milvian Bridge; Constantine converts to Christianity

◆ **391** Theodosius I makes Christianity official religion

| 250 C.E. | 300 C.E. | 350 C.E. | 400 C.E. |

◆ **313** Edict of Milan

◆ **c. 323** Pachomius establishes first monasteries in Upper Egypt

◆ **324** Constantine wins civil war; Constantinople becomes "new Rome"

◆ **325** Council of Nicaea

◆ **395** Empire divided into west and east

◆ **410** Visigoths sack Rome

policy of religious toleration. Even with official support, however, it took nearly a hundred years more for the new faith to become the state religion. The social and cultural transformations produced by the Christianization of the Roman Empire settled in even more slowly because many traditional Romans clung to their ancestral beliefs; even visibly Christian emperors such as Honorius had to employ non-Christians if they wanted to get the best possible administrators and generals.

The political rescue of the empire engineered by Diocletian only postponed the splintering of imperial territory: at the end of the fourth century, Honorius's father split the empire into two geographic divisions, with Honorius ruling the west and his brother Arcadius the east. The co-emperors were supposed to cooperate, but in the long run this system of divided rule could not cope with the different pressures that affected the two regions. In the western empire, a variety of non-Roman peoples from eastern Europe (sometimes referred to as barbarians) moved in, radically transforming the region's society, culture, and politics by displacing Roman provincial government with their own new kingdoms. There the newcomers lived side by side with Romans, the different groups keeping some traditional customs intact but merging other parts of their cultures. The growing strength of these new non-Roman regimes in western Europe and the consequent decentralization of authority there during the fifth century transformed the region in ways that foreshadowed its later political states. In the east, the Roman provinces remained economically vibrant and politically united, becoming (in modern terminology) the Byzantine Empire in the sixth century. Despite financial pressures and the gradual loss of territory, this continuation of the Roman imperial structure endured until Turkish invaders conquered it in 1453. In this way, the empire lived on in the eastern Mediterranean for a thousand years beyond its transformation in the west.

❖ Reorganizing the Empire, 284–395

Diocletian and Constantine pulled Roman government out of the third-century crisis by making the emperors' authority more blatant than ever before, reorganizing the empire's defense, restricting workers' freedom, and changing the tax system to try to raise the money to pay for all this. The two emperors also believed that they had to win back divine favor to make their people safe. This traditional duty, however, was now complicated by the thorny issue of a growing Christian church and the worry about the gods' goodwill that it provoked among followers of Rome's ancient religion.

Diocletian and Constantine believed that the best solution for the empire's problems was to strengthen their authority. Since for Romans strength had to be seen to be effective, they transformed their appearance as rulers to make their power seem awesome beyond compare, hoping that this display of supremacy would help keep the empire united.

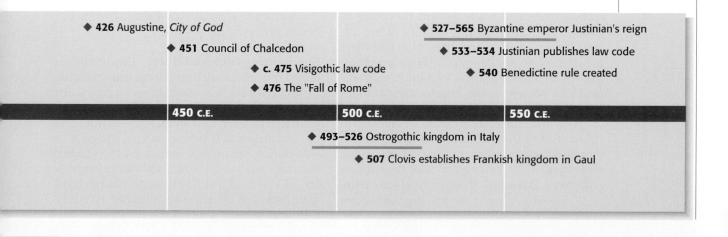

◆ **426** Augustine, *City of God*

◆ **451** Council of Chalcedon

◆ **c. 475** Visigothic law code

◆ **476** The "Fall of Rome"

◆ **527–565** Byzantine emperor Justinian's reign

◆ **533–534** Justinian publishes law code

◆ **540** Benedictine rule created

450 C.E.   **500 C.E.**   **550 C.E.**

◆ **493–526** Ostrogothic kingdom in Italy

◆ **507** Clovis establishes Frankish kingdom in Gaul

In the long run, however, their desire to preserve the empire on the scale created by Augustus proved to be an empty longing.

From Reform to Fragmentation

No one could have predicted Diocletian's success: he began life as an uneducated peasant in Dalmatia✦ in the Balkans, far from the center of power in Rome. In the third-century crisis, however, military talent counted for more than connections. Diocletian's talent for leadership, courage, and intelligence propelled him through the ranks until the army made him emperor in 284. He slammed the gate on half a century of anarchy by imposing the most autocratic system of rule in Roman history.

Inventing the Dominate. The foremost symbol of Diocletian's new system was the title that he took after becoming emperor: *dominus*, meaning "lord" or "master"—what slaves called their owners. This title replaced the one that Augustus had chosen from the traditions of the republic, *princeps* ("first man"). Historians therefore refer to Roman rule from Diocletian onward as the **dominate** because of its rulers' blatant claim of supreme power. Like the emperors before them, the emperors of the dominate continued to refer to their government as "the Roman republic," but they ruled as "lords and masters." This new system eliminated any sharing of authority with the Senate. Senators, consuls, and other vestiges of republican government continued to exist, but only as posts of honor; these officials had the responsibility to pay for public services, especially games and festivals, but no power to govern. Recalling the monarchies of the ancient Near East, the emperors of the dominate recognized no social equals. Their administrators were increasingly chosen from lower ranks of society according to their competence and their loyalty to the emperor.

The grandiose style of the dominate recalled that of the autocratic King of Persia a thousand years earlier rather than that of the emperors of the principate. The dominate's emperors flaunted their majesty by sur-

rounding themselves with courtiers and ceremony, presiding from a raised platform, and sparkling in jeweled crowns, robes, and shoes (see Honorius's garb in the illustration on page 242). Constantine initiated the tradition of the emperor's wearing a diadem, a purple headband blazing with gems, a visible boast of supremacy shunned by earlier emperors. To show the difference between the emperor and ordinary people, a series of veils separated the palace's waiting rooms from the interior room where the emperor listened to people's pleas for help or justice. Officials marked their rank in the fiercely hierarchical administration by wearing special shoes and belts and claiming grandiose titles such as "most perfect."

The dominate's emperors also aggressively asserted their supreme power through law and punishments. Their word alone made law; indeed, they came to be above the law because they were not bound even by the decisions of their predecessors. To promote order, they maintained harsh punishments from the past and raised others to brutal levels. Violent criminals were executed in traditional fashion: tied in a leather sack with poisonous snakes and drowned in a river. New punishments included Constantine's order that the "greedy hands" of officials who took bribes "shall be cut off by the sword." The guardians of a young girl who allowed a lover to seduce her were executed by having molten lead poured into their mouths. Penalties grew ever harsher for the majority of the population, who were legally designated as "humbler people," meaning they could be punished more severely than the "better people" for comparable offenses. In this way, the dominate strengthened the divisions between ordinary people and the rich.

Subdividing Imperial Rule. Diocletian realized that he needed to reform imperial rule to prevent civil war and defend against invaders from the north and the east. The principle underlying his reforms—subdivide the government's power to strengthen it—was daring because it increased the chance of more civil war between ambitious leaders. By 293 he had put the first part of his plan into practice by carving imperial territory into four loosely defined administrative dis-

---

✦**Dalmatia:** dal MAY shuh

MAP 7.1   Diocletian's Reorganization of 293
Anxious to avoid further civil war, Emperor Diocletian reorganized imperial territory for tighter control by placing the empire under the rule of the tetrarchy's four partners, each the head of a large district. He subdivided the preexisting provinces into smaller units and grouped them into twelve dioceses, each overseen by a regional administrator. The four districts as shown here reflect the arrangement mentioned by the imperial official Sextus Aurelius Victor in his book *On the Caesars*, a biographically oriented history of the empire inspired by Suetonius's biographies from the early second century, which Victor published around 360.

tricts, two in the west and two in the east. He appointed three "partners" to join him in this new subdivision of power, called a **tetrarchy** ("rule by four"). Each ruler controlled one of the four districts. Diocletian served as supreme ruler and was supposed to receive the loyalty of the others. This system was Diocletian's attempt to keep imperial government from being isolated at a distance from the empire's elongated frontiers.

Diocletian also subdivided the territory of the provinces themselves, thereby doubling their number to almost a hundred. He then grouped these smaller administrative units

into twelve regions (dioceses) under separate governors, who reported to the four emperors' first assistants, the praetorian prefects (Map 7.1). Finally, he tried to prevent provincial administrators from rebelling by beginning to subdivide their civil and military authority, granting them control only of legal and financial affairs while entrusting defense to separate commanders, a process that Constantine completed.

Although Diocletian's successors dropped the tetrarchy, his principle of subdivision endured in Roman imperial rule. It also ended Rome's thousand years as the capital city. Diocletian—who lived in Nicomedia,◆ in Asia Minor—did not even visit Rome until 303, nearly twenty years after becoming emperor. He chose his four new capitals for their utility as military command posts close to the frontiers: Milan in northern Italy, Sirmium◆ near the Danube River border, Trier near the Rhine River border, and Nicomedia. Italy became just another section of the empire, on an equal footing with the other provinces and subject to the same taxation system, except for the district of Rome itself—the last vestige of the city's traditional primacy.

Creating Eastern and Western Empires.

Diocletian's reforms failed to prevent civil war. After he abdicated in 305 for mysterious reasons, rivals for power fought off and on until 324, when Constantine finally defeated all contenders outside his own family. At the end of his reign in 337, Constantine designated his three sons as joint heirs, admonishing them to continue the new imperial system of co-emperorship. Plunging into war with one another, they failed to govern together as bloodily as had the sons of Septimius Severus a century earlier.

The Sections of the Empire, c. 395

When their gory rivalry ruined any chance of genuinely shared rule, geography led the opposing forces to take up positions roughly splitting the empire on a north–south line along the Balkan peninsula. This territorial division became official in 395, when Theodosius◆ I (r. 379–395) died, leaving his son Arcadius◆ as emperor in the eastern half and his son Honorius in the western. East and West were intended to cooperate, but the permanent division launched the empire's halves on different courses that would endure.

◆**Nicomedia:** nih kuh MEE dee uh

◆**Sirmium:** SEAR mee uhm

◆**Theodosius:** thee uh DOH shee uhs

◆**Arcadius:** ahr KAY dee uhs

Each half had its own capital city. Constantinople ("Constantine's City"), located at the mouth of the Black Sea, was the eastern capital. Formerly the ancient city of Byzantium (today Istanbul, Turkey), it had received its new name in 324 when Constantine renamed it after himself, boasting that it was a "new Rome." He had made it his capital because of its military and commercial possibilities: it lay on an easily fortified peninsula astride principal routes for trade and troop movements. To recall the glory of Rome and thus claim for himself the political legitimacy of the old capital, Constantine had beautified his refounded city with a forum, an imperial palace, a hippodrome for chariot races, and monumental statues of the traditional gods. Constantinople grew to be the greatest city in the empire, eventually giving its former name to what we call the Byzantine Empire.

Geography determined the site of the western capital as well. Honorius wanted his palace in a city that was easier to defend than Rome. In 404, he chose Ravenna,◆ a port on Italy's northeastern coast that housed a main naval base and was an important commercial center. Great marshes and walls protected it from attack by land, while access to the sea kept it from being starved out in a siege. The emperors enhanced Ravenna with churches covered in multicolored mosaics, but it never rivaled Constantinople in size or splendor.

The High Cost of Rescuing the Empire

Diocletian's rescue of the empire carried high costs, especially for a large army. Diocletian therefore imposed price controls and a new taxation system, hoping to control inflation and generate higher tax revenues.

Price Controls and Tax Increases. The third-century civil wars had created hyperinflation that Diocletian struggled to control. As inflated costs caused people to hoard whatever they could buy, prices were constantly driven higher. "Hurry and spend all my money you have; buy me any kinds of goods at whatever prices they are available," wrote one official to his servant, trying to salvage something of the value of his savings by converting his money into things.

◆**Ravenna:** rah VEN nah

In 301, the inflationary distress was so acute that Diocletian took the radical step of imposing a harsh system of wage and price controls in the worst-hit areas (see "Diocletian's Edict Controlling Prices and Wages" on page 250). His Edict on Maximum Prices, which blamed high prices on profiteers' "unlimited and frenzied avarice," forbade hoarding and set ceilings on what could legally be charged or paid for about one thousand goods and services. His edict soon became ineffective because merchants refused to cooperate and government officials were unable to enforce it, despite the threat of death or exile as the penalty for violations.

The civil wars that followed Diocletian's reign stoked the government's insatiable appetite for revenue. Taxes rose mostly to support the army, which required enormous amounts of grain, meat, salt, wine, vegetable oil, horses, camels, and mules. The major sources of payments were a tax on land, assessed according to its productivity, and a head tax on individuals. To supplement taxes paid in coin, the emperors began collecting some revenue in goods and services.

The empire was too large to enforce the tax system consistently. In some areas, both men and women from the age of about twelve to sixty-five paid the full tax, but in others women paid only one-half the tax assessment or none at all. Workers in cities probably owed taxes only on their property, perhaps to encourage crafts production. They periodically paid "in kind," that is, by laboring without pay on public works projects such as cleaning municipal drains or repairing buildings. Owners of urban businesses, from shopkeepers to prostitutes, still paid taxes in money, while members of the senatorial class were exempt from ordinary taxes but had to pay special levies.

Social Consequences. The new tax system depended on agricultural production remaining stable and the government keeping track of the people liable for the head tax (see "Taking Measure," below). Diocletian therefore

TAKING MEASURE

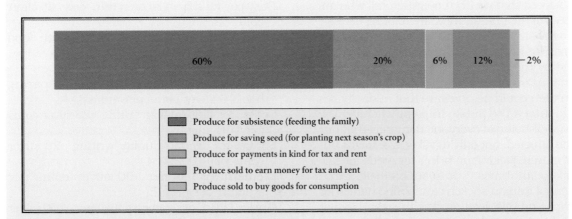

60%   20%   6%   12%   — 2%

  Produce for subsistence (feeding the family)
  Produce for saving seed (for planting next season's crop)
  Produce for payments in kind for tax and rent
  Produce sold to earn money for tax and rent
  Produce sold to buy goods for consumption

Peasants' Use of Farm Produce in the Roman Empire
This graph offers a hypothetical model of how peasants during the Roman Empire may have used what they produced as farmers and herders to maintain their families, pay rent and taxes, and buy things they did not produce themselves. The amounts are speculative because reliable and comprehensive statistics of this kind do not exist for the ancient world. Individual families would have had widely varying experiences, and this estimate applies only to the population of peasant producers as a whole. Still, it is very likely that most families did have to use most of their production just to maintain a subsistence level—a description of poverty by modern standards. *Adapted from Keith Hopkins, Conquerors and Slaves: Sociological Studies in Roman History (New York: Cambridge University Press, 1978), 17. Reprinted with permission of Cambridge University Press.*

Diocletian's Edict Controlling Prices and Wages

To try to stop rampant inflation caused by soaring government expenditures, Diocletian and his co-emperors in 301 C.E. issued an edict setting maximum prices and wages for the first time in Roman history. Their orders proved impossible to enforce across the vast empire. The bombastic language was typical of imperial bureaucracy under the dominate.

Recalling the wars that we have successfully waged, it is to the fortune of our republic, next to the immortal gods, that we owe the peaceful state of our world, located in the lap of the deepest tranquility, and the benefits of peace, which we worked for with great effort. Our honorable public and Rome's respectability and majesty long for this fortune to be faithfully established and suitably adorned. Therefore, we, who with the kind support of the gods in the past overcame the blazing raids of the barbarian peoples by slaughtering those nations, must fortify the tranquility that we established for eternity with the necessary defenses of justice. . . .

It is agreed that we [the co-emperors], who are the parents of the human race, are to bring decisive justice to the situation, so that, what humanity has long hoped for but not been able to provide will be conferred by the solutions of our foresight for the common improvement of everyone. . . .

Who then could be unaware that audacity lies in wait to attack the public interest wherever the common well-being of everyone demands that our armies be directed, not only in villages or towns but on every march, jacking up prices for goods for sale not four or eight times, but to such a height that the system of human speech cannot find names for this pricing and this deed. And so the result is that the sale of a single item deprives the soldier of his bonus and his pay, and that all the taxes paid by the entire world to support the armies fall victim to this detestable profit seeking. . . .

It is our decision that, if anyone makes an effort through daring to go against this edict, he shall be subject to capital punishment. . . .

Listed below are the prices for the sale of individual items; no one may exceed them.

[These examples are selections from the edict's long list of maximum allowed prices and wages. A sextarius was about half a liter; the Roman pound was about three-quarters of a U.S. pound. The silver coin was the denarius. A soldier at this date earned 1,800 silver coins per year.]

Prices for food

Sextarius of first-quality old wine   24 silver coins
Sextarius of country wine   8 silver coins
Sextarius of beer from Gaul   4 silver coins
Sextarius of beer from Egypt   2 silver coins
Pound of pork   12 silver coins
Pound of goat or sheep   8 silver coins
Fattened pheasant   250 silver coins
Pair of chickens   60 silver coins
Pound of second-quality fish   16 silver coins

Wages for workers

Daily pay for a farm laborer, with food   25 silver coins
Daily pay for a finish carpenter, with food   50 silver coins
Baker, with food   50 silver coins
Mule doctor, for trimming and preparing hoofs 6 silver coins per animal
Scribe, for first-quality writing   25 silver coins per 100 lines
Scribe, for second-quality writing   20 silver coins per 100 lines
Elementary teacher   50 silver coins per student per month
Greek, Latin, or geometry teacher   200 silver coins per student per month
Public speaking teacher   250 silver coins per student per month
Legal expert or speaker in court   1,000 silver coins per case

Source: *Diocletiani edictum de pretiis rerum venalium* (http://www.fh-augsburg.de/~harsch/dio_ep_i.html). Translation by Thomas R. Martin.

restricted the movement of tenant farmers, called *coloni*,♦ whose work provided the empire's economic base. Coloni had traditionally been free to move to another farm to work for a new landlord as long as their debts were paid. Now, male tenant farmers, as well as their wives in areas where women were assessed for taxes, were increasingly tied to a particular plot. Their children were also bound to the family plot, making farming a hereditary occupation.

The government also regulated other occupations deemed essential. Bakers, for example, could not leave their jobs, and anyone who acquired a baker's property had to assume that occupation. The bakers were needed to produce free bread for Rome's many poor, a tradition begun under the republic to prevent food riots. From Constantine's reign on, the military was another hereditary lifetime career: the sons of military veterans had to serve in the army.

The emperors decreed equally oppressive regulations for the propertied class in the cities and towns, the **curials**.♦ In this period, almost all men in the curial class were obliged to serve as unsalaried city council members, who had to spend their own funds to support the community. Their financial responsibilities ranged from maintaining the water supply to feeding troops, but their most expensive duty was paying for shortfalls in tax collection. The emperors' demands for more and more revenue now made this a crushing blow, compounding the damage that the third-century crisis had inflicted on local elites.

For centuries, the empire's welfare had depended on a steady supply of property owners filling crucial local posts in return for honor and the emperor's favor. Now this tradition broke down as wealthier people avoided public service to escape financial ruin. So distorted had the situation become that service on a municipal council could be imposed as punishment for a crime. Eventually, to prevent curials from escaping their obligations, imperial policy forbade them to move away from the town where they had been born; they even had to ask for official permission to travel. These laws made members of the elite feverish to win exemptions from public service by petitioning the emperor, bribing imperial officials, or taking up an occupation that freed them from curial obligations (the military, imperial administration, or church governance). The most desperate simply fled, abandoning home and property to avoid fulfilling their traditional duties.

The restrictions on freedom caused by the viselike pressure for higher taxes thus eroded the communal values that had motivated wealthy Romans for so long. The squeeze to increase revenues also produced social discontent among poorer citizens: when the tax rate on land eventually reached one-third of its gross yield, this burden impoverished the rural population. Conditions became so bad in fifth-century Spain that the peasants there rebelled against imperial control. Financial troubles, especially severe in the west, kept the empire from ever regaining the prosperity of its Golden Age and contributed to increasing friction between government and citizens.

The Emperors and Official Religion

Since traditional Romans sought religious explanations for disasters, Diocletian concluded that the gods' anger had caused the empire's third-century crisis. To restore divine goodwill, he called on citizens to follow the ancient gods who had guided Rome to power and virtue in the past: "Through the providence of the immortal gods, eminent, wise, and upright men have in their wisdom established good and true principles. It is wrong to oppose these principles or to abandon the ancient religion for some new one." Christianity was the novel faith he meant.

From Persecution to Conversion.   To eliminate what he saw as a threat to national security, Diocletian in 303 launched the so-called **Great Persecution** to suppress Christians. He expelled them from official posts, seized their property, tore down churches, and executed anyone who refused to participate in official religious rituals. His three partners in the tetrarchy applied the policy unevenly. In the western empire, violence against Christians stopped after about

♦**coloni:** kuh LOH ny
♦**curials:** KYUR ee uhls

The Edict of Milan on Religious Liberty

In 313 C.E., Constantine, a recent Christian convert, and his fellow emperor Licinius, a follower of traditional Roman religion, met at Milan to discuss official policy on religion. They agreed to abolish restrictions on Christianity and proclaim religious liberty. The Edict of Milan represents the message later sent to governors in the eastern provinces. The long sentences (which are shortened here) and convoluted expression reflect the official imperial style.

When I, Constantine Augustus, and I, Licinius Augustus, had a successful meeting at Milan and discussed everything pertaining to the public benefit and security, among other things that we regarded as going to be of use to many people, we believed that first place should go to those matters having to do with reverence for divinity, so that we might give the Christians and everyone the free power of worshiping in the religion that they wish. In this way, whatever divinity exists in the heavenly seat may be appeased and be kind to us and to all those who are established under our power. And thus, believing that we should initiate this policy on a wholesome and most upright basis, we thought that to no one whatsoever should the opportunity be denied, whether he dedicates his mind to the worship of the Christians or to that religion, which he felt best suited him. Our purpose is so that the highest divinity, whose religion we follow with free minds, may provide his customary favor and kindness in all things. Wherefore it has pleased us for your Devotedness [the provincial governor] to know that all the restrictions on the Christian name set forth in letters given to your office previously are completely removed and that whatever seemed utterly sinister and foreign to our clemency should be repealed, and that now any person of those also wishing to observe the religion of the Christians may strive to do so freely and plainly without any worry or interference. We believed that these things should be made completely clear to your Solicitude so that you would know that we have given a free and absolute permission to these Christians to practice their religion. When you see that we have granted this to them, your Devotedness will know that we have likewise conceded an open and free power to others to practice their religion for the sake of the tranquility of our age, so that each person may have free permission to worship in the manner he has chosen. We did this so that we shall not seem to have detracted from any observance or religion.

[The emperors next order people who bought or received Christians' property confiscated in the Great Persecution to return it at no cost and then to apply to an imperial representative for reimbursement through the emperors' "clemency."]

On all these matters you will be obligated to provide your most effectual aid to the body of Christians mentioned above, so that our orders may be carried out more quickly, whereby public tranquility may be served also by our clemency. In this way it will happen, as was explained above, that divine favor toward us, which we have experienced in so many things, will endure for all time to give prosperity to our successes in company with the public happiness. Moreover, so that the content of this ordinance and of our kindness may come to everyone's attention, it should be put up everywhere above an announcement of your own and brought to the knowledge of everyone, so that this ordinance of our kindness shall not be concealed.

Source: Lactantius, *On the Deaths of the Persecutors* 48, and Eusebius, *Ecclesiastical History* 10.5.2–14. Translation by Thomas R. Martin.

a year; in the east, it continued for a decade. So gruesome were the public executions of Christian martyrs that they aroused the sympathy of some polytheists. The persecution, like the Edict on Maximum Prices, failed: it undermined social stability without destroying Christianity.

Constantine changed the world's religious history forever by converting to the new faith. He chose Christianity for the same reason that Diocletian had persecuted it: to win divine protection for himself and the empire. During the civil war that he fought after Diocletian's abdication, Constantine experienced a dream vision promising him the support of the Christian God. His biographer, Eusebius◆ (c. 260–340), later reported that Constantine had also seen a vision of Jesus' cross in the sky surrounded by the words "In this sign you shall be the victor" (the slogan Honorius displays on the plaque he holds on page 242). When Constantine won a great victory in the civil war at the battle of the Milvian Bridge in Rome in 312, he attributed his success to the Christian God's miraculous power and goodwill. He therefore declared himself a Christian emperor.

Edict of Milan of 313.   Following his conversion to the new faith, Constantine neither outlawed polytheism nor made Christianity the official religion. Instead, he compelled all the rivals for power in the empire to allow religious toleration. A clear statement of this unprecedented policy survives in the **Edict of Milan** of 313 (see "The Edict of Milan on Religious Liberty" on page 252). It proclaimed free choice of religion for everyone and referred to the empire's protection by "the highest divinity"—an imprecise term meant to satisfy both polytheists and Christians.

Constantine tried to avoid angering traditional believers because they still greatly outnumbered Christians, but he also promoted his newly chosen religion. These conflicting goals called for a careful balancing act that continued the principle of subdividing power to achieve stability. In this case, he subdivided official support and respect for religion. For example, he returned all prop-

erty confiscated from Christians during the Great Persecution, but he had the treasury compensate those who had bought it. When in 321 he made the Lord's Day a holy occasion each week on which no official business or manufacturing work could be performed, he called it Sunday to blend Christian and traditional notions in honoring two divinities, God and the sun. When he adorned his new capital, Constantinople, he stationed many statues of traditional gods around the city. Most conspicuously, he respected tradition by continuing to hold the office of *pontifex maximus* ("chief priest"), which emperors had filled ever since Augustus.

Review: What changes did Diocletian and his successors make in their reorganization of the empire and why?

❖ Christianizing the Empire, 312–c. 540

Constantine's conversion in 312 set the empire on the path to Christianization. The process was gradual: not until the end of the fourth century was Christianity proclaimed the official religion, and even thereafter many people worshiped the traditional gods in private. Eventually, however, Christianity became the religion of the overwhelming majority by solidifying its hierarchical organization, attracting converts among women as well as men of all classes, assuring believers of personal salvation, nourishing a strong sense of community, and offering the social advantages and security of belonging to the emperors' religion. The transformation from polytheist empire into Christian state was the most influential legacy of Greco-Roman antiquity.

Changing Religious Beliefs

The empire's Christianization provoked passionate responses because ordinary people cared fervently about religion. Polytheists and Christians shared some similar beliefs. Both assigned a potent role to spirits and demons as ever-present influences on life.

◆**Eusebius:** yoo SEE bee uhs

Relief Sculpture of Saturn from North Africa

This sculpted and inscribed pillar depicts the solar divinity known to Romans as Saturn and to Carthaginians as Ba'al Hammon, from the cult of the Phoenician founders of Carthage. This syncretism (identifying deities as the same even though they carried different names in different places) was typical of ancient polytheism and allowed Roman and non-Roman cults to merge. The inscription dates the pillar to 323, a decade after Constantine's conversion to Christianity; such objects testifying to the prevalence of polytheistic cults remained common until the end of the fourth century, when the Christian emperors succeeded in suppressing most public manifestations of traditional religion. What in this sculpture indicates that it depicts a god? *Copyright Martha Cooper/ Peter Arnold, Inc.*

For some, it seemed safest to ignore neither faith. For example, a silver spoon used in the worship of the polytheist forest spirit Faunus has been found engraved with a fish, the common symbol whose Greek spelling (*ichthys*) was taken as an acronym for the Greek words "Jesus Christ the Son of God, the Savior."

The Persistence of Polytheism. The differences between polytheists' and Christians' beliefs far outweighed their similarities. People debated passionately whether there was one God or many and what kind of interest the divinity (or divinities) took in the world of humans. Polytheists still participated in frequent festivals and sacrifices to many different gods. Why, they asked, did these joyous occasions not satisfy everyone's yearnings for contact with divinity?

Equally incomprehensible to them was belief in a savior who had not only failed to overthrow Roman rule but had even been ex-

ecuted as a common criminal. The traditional gods, by contrast, had bestowed a world empire on their worshipers. Moreover, polytheists pointed out, cults such as that of the goddess Isis, after whom the worried letter writer had been named, and philosophies such as Stoicism insisted that only the pure of heart and mind could be admitted to their fellowship. Christians, by contrast, embraced sinners. Why, wondered perplexed polytheists, would anyone want to associate with them? In short, as the Greek philosopher Porphyry◆ (c. 234–305) argued, Christians had no right to claim they possessed the sole version of religious truth, for no one had ever discovered a doctrine that provided "the sole path to the liberation of the soul."

The slow pace of religious change revealed how strong polytheism remained in this period, especially at the highest social levels. In fact, the emperor known as Julian the Apostate (r. 361–363) rebelled against his family's Christianity—the word **apostate** means "renegade from the faith"—and tried to impose his philosophical brand of polytheism as the official religion. He believed in a supreme deity derived from Greek philosophy: "This divine and completely beautiful universe, from heaven's highest arch to earth's lowest limit, is tied together by the continuous providence of god, has existed ungenerated eternally, and is imperishable forever." Julian's restoration of traditional religion ended with his death during an attack on Persia.

Making Christianity Official. The Christian emperors after Julian tried to end polytheism by gradually removing its official privileges, dropping the title *pontifex maximus*, and ceasing government-funded

◆**Porphyry:** PAWR fuh ree

sacrifices. Symmachus♦ (c. 340–402), a polytheist senator who held the prestigious post of prefect ("mayor") of Rome, objected to this suppression of religious diversity. Speaking eloquently in a last public protest against the new religious order, he echoed Porphyry: "We all have our own way of life and our own way of worship.... So vast a mystery cannot be approached by only one path."

Christianity decisively replaced traditional polytheism as the state religion in 391 when Theodosius I successfully enforced a ban on polytheist sacrifices, even if private individuals paid for the animals, and announced that all polytheist temples had to close. Some ancient shrines, such as the Parthenon in Athens, remained open for a long time; temples were gradually converted to churches during the fifth and sixth centuries. Non-Christian schools were not forced to close—the Academy, founded by Plato in Athens in the early fourth century B.C.E., endured for 140 years after Theodosius's reign—but Christians received advantages in official careers.

Jews posed a special problem for the Christian emperors. They seemed entitled to special treatment because Jesus had been a Jew and because previous emperors had allowed Jews to practice their religion, but the Christian emperors loaded them with legal restrictions. Imperial decrees banned Jews from holding government posts but still required them to assume the financial burdens of curials without the status. By the late sixth century, the law barred Jews from marrying Christians, making wills, receiving inheritances, or testifying in court.

These restrictions began the long process that made Jews into second-class citizens in later European history, but they did not disable Judaism. Magnificent synagogues continued to exist in Palestine, where some Jews still lived, though most had been dispersed throughout the cities of the empire and the lands to the east. Jewish scholarship flourished in this period, culminating in the fifth century C.E. texts known as the Palestinian and the Babylonian Talmuds (collections of learned opinions on Jewish law) and the scriptural commentaries of the Midrash (explanation of the meaning of the Hebrew Bible), compiled from around 200 to 800. These works of religious scholarship laid the foundation for later Jewish life and practice.

Christianity's Growing Appeal.   Christianity's official status attracted new believers, especially in the military. Now soldiers could convert and still serve in the army; previously, Christians had sometimes created

Christ as Sun God
This heavily damaged mosaic comes from a burial chamber in Rome that is now in the Vatican under the basilica of St. Peter built by Constantine. It perhaps dates to the mid-third century. Christ appears in a guise traditional for polytheistic representations of the Sun god, especially the Greek Apollo: riding in a chariot pulled by horses with rays of light shining forth around his head. This symbolism—God is light—had a long history reaching back to ancient Egypt; Christian artists used it to portray Jesus because he had said "I am the light of the world" (John 8:12). Here the mosaic artist has carefully arranged the sunbeams to suggest the shape of the Christian cross. The cloak flaring from Christ's shoulder suggests the spread of his motion across the heavens. **For more help analyzing this image**, see the visual activity for this chapter in the Online Study Guide at **bedfordstmartins.com/hunt**. *Scala/Art Resource, NY.*

♦**Symmachus:** SIH muh kuhs

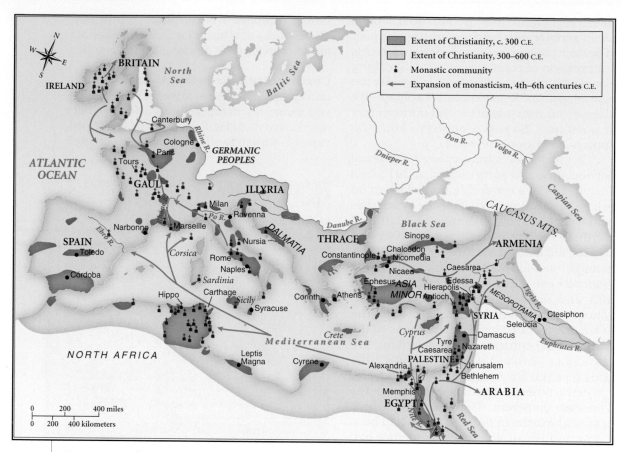

MAP 7.2   The Spread of Christianity, 300–600

Christians were distinctly a minority in the Roman Empire in 300, although congregations existed in many cities and towns, especially in the eastern provinces. The emperor Constantine's conversion to Christianity in the early fourth century gave a boost to the new religion; it gained further strength during that century as the Christian emperors supported it financially and eliminated subsidies for the polytheist cults that had previously made up the religion of the state. By 600, the preaching of the church's missionaries and the money of the emperors had spread Christianity from end to end of the empire's huge expanse of territory. From Henry Chadwick and G. R. Evans, *Atlas of the Christian Church* (Oxford: Andromeda Oxford Ltd., 1987), 28. Reproduced by permission of Andromeda Oxford Limited.

disciplinary problems by renouncing their military oath. As one senior infantryman had said at his court-martial in 298 for refusing to continue his duties, "A Christian serving the Lord Christ should not serve the affairs of this world." Once the emperors had become Christians, however, soldiers saw military duty as serving Christ's regime.

Christianity's religious and social values provided its main appeal. It offered believers a strong sense of community in this world as well as the promise of salvation in the next. Wherever they traveled, they could find a warm welcome in the local congregation

(Map 7.2). The faith also won adherents by promoting the tradition of charitable works characteristic of Judaism and some polytheist cults, which emphasized caring for the poor, widows, and orphans. By the mid-third century, for example, Rome's congregation was supporting fifteen hundred widows and poor people. The Christian practices of fellowship and philanthropy contributed to the faith's growth because it supported poor believers.

Women were deeply involved in the new faith. Augustine (354–430), bishop of Hippo in North Africa and perhaps the most influential theologian in Western history, eloquently recognized women's contribution to the strengthening of Christianity in a letter he wrote to the unbaptized husband of a baptized woman: "O you men, who fear all the burdens imposed by baptism! Your women easily best you. Chaste and devoted to the faith, it is their presence in large numbers that causes the church to grow." Women could win renown by giving their property to their congregation or by renouncing marriage to dedicate themselves to Christ. Consecrated virgins and widows who chose not to remarry thus joined large donors as especially respected women. These women's choices challenged the traditional social order, in which women were supposed to devote themselves to raising families. Even these sanctified women, however, were excluded from leadership positions as the church's organization evolved into a hierarchy more and more resembling the male-dominated world of imperial rule.

Solidifying Hierarchy. The Christianization of the Roman Empire depended on creating hierarchical leadership based on the authority of male bishops, who replaced early Christianity's relatively loose, communal form in which women could also lead. Bishops selected priests to conduct the church's sacraments, such as baptism and communion, the rituals that guaranteed eternal life. They also oversaw their congregations' memberships and finances. Over time, the bishops replaced the curials as the emperors' partners in local rule, in return earning the right to control the distribution of imperial subsidies to the people. Regional councils of bishops appointed new bishops and addressed doctrinal disputes. The bishops in the largest cities became the most powerful leaders in the church. The main bishop of Carthage, for example, oversaw at least one hundred local bishops in the surrounding area. The bishop of Rome eventually emerged as the church's supreme leader in the western empire, reserving for himself a title previously applied to many bishops: pope (from *pappas*, Greek for "father"), the designation still used for the head of the Roman Catholic church. Church leaders in the eastern empire never agreed that the bishop of Rome headed the Christian world.

The bishops of Rome justified their leadership over other bishops by citing the New Testament, where Jesus tells his apostle Peter: "You are Peter, and upon this rock I will build my church....I will entrust to you the keys of the kingdom of heaven. Whatever you bind on earth shall be bound in heaven. Whatever you loose on earth shall be loosed in heaven" (Matt. 16:18–19). Because Peter's name in Greek means "rock" and because Peter was believed to have been the first bishop of Rome, later bishops in Rome claimed that this passage recognized their direct succession from Peter and thus their supremacy in the church.

Establishing Christian Orthodoxy

Jesus himself left no written teachings, and the earliest Christians frequently argued over what their savior had meant them to believe. The church's expanding hierarchy pushed hard for uniformity in belief and worship to ensure its members' spiritual purity and to maintain its authority over them. Bishops as well as rank-and-file believers often disagreed about theology, however, and Christians never achieved uniformity in their doctrines.

Disputes centered on what constituted orthodoxy as opposed to heresy. (See Chapter 6, page 229.) After Christianity became official, the emperor was ultimately responsible for enforcing orthodox creed (a summary of beliefs) and could use force to compel agreement when disputes led to violence.

Arguing about God: Arianism. Subtle theological questions about the nature of the Christian Trinity—Father, Son, and Holy Spirit—seen by the orthodox as a unified, co-eternal, and identical divinity, caused the deepest divisions. The doctrine called **Arianism** generated fierce controversy for centuries. Named after its founder, Arius♦ (c. 260–336) a priest from Alexandria, it maintained that Jesus as God's son had not existed eternally; rather, God the Father "begot" (created) his son from nothing and bestowed on him his special status. Thus, Jesus was not co-eternal with God and not

♦**Arius:** AR ee uhs

identical in nature with his father. This view implied that the Trinity was divisible and that Christianity's monotheism was not absolute. Arianism found widespread support, perhaps because it eliminated the difficulty of understanding how a son could be as old as his father and because its subordination of son to father corresponded to the norms of family life. Arius used popular songs to make his views known, and people everywhere became engrossed in the controversy. "When you ask for your change from a shopkeeper," one observer remarked in describing Constantinople, "he harangues you about the Begotten and the Unbegotten. If you inquire how much bread costs, the reply is that 'the Father is superior and the Son inferior.'"

Many Christians became so incensed over this apparent demotion of Jesus that Constantine had to intervene to try to restore ecclesiastical peace and lead the bishops in determining religious truth. In 325, he convened 220 bishops at the Council of Nicaea◆ to settle the dispute over Arianism. The majority of bishops voted to come down hard on the heresy: they banished Arius to Illyria, a rough Balkan region, and declared that the Father and the Son were indeed "of one substance" and co-eternal. So difficult were the issues, however, that Constantine later changed his mind twice, first recalling Arius from exile and then reproaching him again not long after. The doctrine lived on: Constantine's third son, Constantius II (r. 337–361), favored Arianism, and his missionaries converted many of the non-Roman peoples who later poured into the empire.

Original Areas of Christian Splinter Groups

Monophysitism, Nestorianism, and Donatism.

Numerous other disputes about the nature of Christ roiled believers. The orthodox position held that Jesus' divine and human natures commingled within his per-

◆**Nicaea:** ny SEE uh

son but remained distinct. Monophysites◆ (a Greek term for "single-nature believers") argued that the divine took precedence over the human and that Jesus had essentially only a single nature. They split from the orthodox hierarchy in the sixth century to found independent churches in Egypt (the Coptic church), Ethiopia, Syria, and Armenia.

Nestorius, who became bishop of Constantinople in 428, disagreed with the orthodox version of how Jesus' human and divine natures were related to his birth, insisting that Mary gave birth to the human that became the temple for the indwelling divine. Nestorianism◆ enraged orthodox Christians by rejecting the designation *theotokos*◆ (Greek for "bearer of God") for Mary. The bishops of Alexandria and Rome had Nestorius deposed and his doctrines officially rejected at councils held in 430 and 431; they condemned his writings in 435. Refusing to accept these decisions, Nestorian bishops in the eastern empire formed a separate church centered in Persia, where for centuries Nestorian Christians flourished under the tolerance of non-Christian rulers. They later became important agents of cultural diffusion by establishing communities that still endure in Arabia, India, and China.

Donatism◆ best illustrates the level of ferocity that Christian disputes could generate. The conflict began in North Africa over whether to readmit to their old congregations those Christians who had cooperated with imperial authorities during the Great Persecution. The Donatists (followers of the North African priest Donatus) insisted that the church should not be polluted with such "traitors." So bitter was the clash that it even sundered Christian families. One son threatened his mother, "I will join Donatus's followers, and I will drink your blood."

With emotions at a fever pitch, the church promoted orthodoxy as religious truth. The Council of Chalcedon◆ (a suburb of Constantinople) in 451 was the most important attempt to forge agreement on or-

◆**Monophysites:** muh NAH fuh sytes
◆**Nestorianism:** neh STAWR ee uh nih zuhm
◆ *theotokos:* thee uh TOH kuhs
◆**Donatism:** DOH nuh tih zuhm
◆**Chalcedon:** KAL suh dahn

Mosaic of a Family from Edessa

This mosaic, found in a cave tomb, depicts an upper-class family of Edessa in the late Roman Empire. Their names are given in Syriac, the dialect of Aramaic spoken in their region, and their colorful clothing reflects local Iranian traditions. What indications does the mosaic give of the family's wealth and status? Edessa was the capital of the small kingdom of Osrhoëne,◆ between the Taurus Mountains and the Syrian desert. Rome annexed the kingdom in 216, and it became famous in Christian history because its king Agbar (r. 179–216) was remembered as the first monarch to convert to Christianity, well before Constantine. By the early fourth century, the story had emerged that after his death Jesus had sent one of his disciples to Edessa; the disciple painted a picture of Jesus that served as a talisman to protect the city from its enemies. The Byzantine emperors proclaimed themselves the heirs of King Agbar and the city's grant of divine protection.

Photo courtesy of Thames & Hudson Ltd., London, from Vanished Civilizations.

thodoxy. Its conclusions form the basis of what most Christians in the West still accept as doctrine. At the time, however, it failed to create unanimity, especially in the eastern empire, where Monophysites flourished.

Augustine on Order. The ideas of Augustine (354–430), bishop of Hippo in North Africa, became the foundation of Christian orthodoxy in the western empire. By around 500, Augustine and other influential theologians such as Ambrose (c. 339–397) and Jerome (c. 345–420) earned the informal title "church fathers" because their views were cited as authoritative in disputes over orthodoxy. Augustine became the most famous of this group of patristic (from the Greek for "father," *pater*) authors, and for the next thousand years his works would be the most influential texts in western Christianity, save for the Bible. He wrote so prolifically in Latin about religion and philosophy that a later scholar was moved to declare: "The man lies who says he has read all your works."

Augustine deeply affected later thinkers with his views on authority in human life, expressed in his book *City of God*, a "large and

arduous work," as he called it, published in 426 after thirteen years of writing. Its arguments refuted those who expected that Christianity guaranteed Christians safety and success on earth. In particular, Augustine argued that the sack of Rome by invading marauders in 410 was not divine retribution for the official abandonment of the traditional gods. At the same time, the book redefined the ideal state as a society of Christians. Not even Plato's doctrines teaching that people must subordinate their feelings to their reason offered a true path to purification, Augustine asserted, because the basic problem for humans was not between emotion and reasoning but between desire for earthly pleasures and spiritual purity. Emotion, especially love, was natural and desirable, but only when directed toward God. Humans were misguided to look for value in life on earth. Only life in God's eternal city had meaning.

Nevertheless, Augustine wrote, law and government were required on earth because humans are imperfect by nature. God's original creation was full of goodness, but humans lost their initial perfection by inheriting a permanently flawed nature after Adam and Eve disobeyed God. The doctrine of original sin—a subject of theological debate since at

◆**Osrhoëne:** os row EE neh

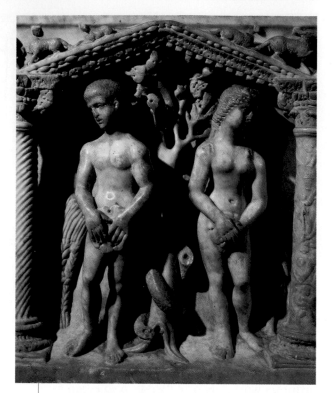

Adam and Eve on the Sarcophagus of Junius Bassus
This scene of the biblical first man and woman in the Garden of Eden is one image on the most spectacular surviving Christian sarcophagus. Dated by an inscription to 359, it holds the remains of Junius Bassus, the son of a consul and himself prefect of Rome. Carved from marble in a classical style, the scenes are all taken from the Bible and center on the story of Christ. The exclusion of scenes from polytheistic mythology, which had been standard on Christian sarcophaguses, illustrates Christians' growing confidence in their religious traditions. What explains the position of Adam's and Eve's hands? (Consider the section on Augustine and sexual desire beginning on this page.) *Erich Lessing/Art Resource, NY.*

least the second century—meant that people suffered from a hereditary moral disease that turned the human will into a disruptive force. This corruption necessitated governments that could suppress evil. The state therefore had a duty to compel people to remain united to the church, by force if necessary.

For Augustine, the purpose of secular authority was to maintain a social order based on a moral order. Order was so essential, Augustine argued, that it justified what he admitted was the unjust institu-

tion of slavery. While detesting slavery, he believed it was a lesser evil than the social disorder that he thought its abolition would create. To help maintain order, Christians had a duty to obey the emperor and participate in political life. Soldiers, too, had to follow their orders.

To make the *City of God* persuasive, Augustine argued that history has a divine purpose, even if people could not see it. All that Christians could know with certainty was that history progressed toward an ultimate goal, but only God could know the meaning of each day's events:

> To be truthful, I myself fail to understand why God created mice and frogs, flies and worms. Nevertheless, I recognize that each of these creatures is beautiful in its own way. For when I contemplate the body and limbs of any living creature, where do I not find proportion, number, and order exhibiting the unity of concord? Where one discovers proportion, number, and order, one should look for the craftsman.

The repeated *I* in this example indicates the intense personal engagement Augustine brought to matters of faith and doctrine. Many other Christians shared this intensity, a trait that energized their disagreements over orthodoxy and heresy.

Augustine and Sexual Desire.   Next to the nature of Christ, the question of how to understand and regulate sexual desire presented Christians with the thorniest problem in the search for religious truth. Augustine became the most influential source of the idea that sex enmeshed human beings in evil and that they should therefore strive for **asceticism**✦ (the practice of self-denial, from the Greek *askesis*, meaning "training"). Augustine knew from personal experience how difficult it was to accept this doctrine. In fact, he revealed in his autobiographical work *Confessions*, written about 397, that he felt a deep conflict between his sexual desire and his religious philosophy. Only after a long period of reflection and doubt, he explained, did he find the inner strength to pledge his future chastity as part of his conversion to Christianity.

✦**asceticism:** uh SEH tuh sih zuhm

He advocated sexual abstinence as the highest course for Christians because he believed that Adam and Eve's disobedience had forever ruined the perfect harmony God created between the human will and human passions. According to Augustine, God punished his disobedient children by making sexual desire a disruptive force that human will would always struggle to control. He reaffirmed the value of marriage in God's plan, but he insisted that sexual intercourse even between loving spouses carried the melancholy reminder of humanity's fall from grace. A married couple should "descend with a certain sadness" to the task of procreation, the only acceptable reason for sex; sexual pleasure could never be a human good.

This doctrine ennobled virginity and sexual renunciation as the highest virtues; in the words of the ascetic biblical scholar Jerome, they counted as "daily martyrdom." By the end of the fourth century, the importance of virginity to Christians as an ascetic virtue had grown so great that congregations began to call for virgin priests and bishops.

The Beginning of Christian Monasticism

Christian asceticism reached its peak with the development of monasticism. Monks (from the Greek *monos*, for "single, solitary") were men and women who withdrew from everyday society to live a life of extreme self-denial imitating Jesus' suffering, while praying for divine mercy on the world. The first monks lived alone, but soon communities of monks formed for mutual support in the pursuit of holiness.

The Appeal of Monasticism. Polytheists and Jews also had strong ascetic traditions, but Christian monasticism was distinctive for the huge numbers of people drawn to it and the high status that they earned in the Christian population. Monks' renown came from their total disregard for ordinary pleasures and comforts. They left their families and congregations, renounced sex, worshiped almost constantly, wore rough clothes, and ate only enough to survive. To achieve inner peace detached from daily concerns, monks fought a constant spiritual battle against fantasies of earthly delights—plentiful, tasty food and the joys of sex.

The earliest monks emerged in Egypt in the second half of the third century. Antony (c. 251–356), the son of a well-to-do family, was among the first to renounce regular existence. When he was eighteen he abruptly abandoned all his property after hearing a sermon stressing Jesus's command to a rich young man to sell his possessions and give the proceeds to the poor (Matt. 19:21). In about 285, Antony placed his sister in a home for unmarried women and fled alone into the desert for the rest of his life to worship God through extreme self-denial.

Antony achieved fame for his ascetic life, illustrating a principal appeal of monasticism: the chance to achieve excellence and recognition, a traditional ideal in the ancient Western world. This opportunity seemed especially valuable after the end of the Great Persecution. Becoming a monk—a living martyrdom—served as the substitute for dying a martyr's death and emulated the sacrifice of Christ. Individual, or eremitic,♦ monks (hence the word *hermit*) went to great lengths to secure fame for their dedication. In Syria, for example, "holy women" and "holy men" attracted great attention with feats of pious endurance; Symeon the Stylite (390–459), for one, lived atop a tall pillar (*stylos* in Greek) for thirty years, preaching to the people gathered at the foot of his perch. Egyptian Christians came to believe that their monks' supreme piety made them living heroes who ensured the annual flooding of the Nile, an event once associated with the pharaohs' religious power.

The influence of ascetics with reputations for exceptional holiness continued after their deaths. Their relics—body parts or clothing—became treasured sources of protection and healing. Projecting the enduring power of saints (people venerated after their deaths for their holiness), relics gave believers faith in divine favor. Christian reverence for relics continued a very long tradition: the fifth-century B.C.E. Athenians, for example, believed good fortune would follow from the recovery of bones identified as the remains of Theseus, their legendary founder.

♦**eremitic:** ehr uh MIH tihk

The Rise of Monastic Communities. In about 323, an Egyptian Christian named Pachomius♦ organized the first monastic community, establishing the tradition of single-sex settlements of male or female monks helping one another along the harsh path to holiness. This communal monasticism, called coenobitic (meaning "life in common"), dominated Christian asceticism ever after. Communities of men and women were often built close together to share labor, with women making clothing, for example, while men farmed.

All monastic groups imposed military-style discipline, but they differed in their degree of internal austerity and contact with the outside world (see Monastery of St. Catherine at Mount Sinai). Some strove for complete self-sufficiency to avoid transactions with outsiders. The most isolationist groups lived in the eastern empire, but the followers of Martin of Tours (c. 316–397), an ex-soldier famed for his pious deeds, founded communities in the west as austere as any. Basil of Caesarea♦ in Asia Minor (c. 330–379) started a competing tradition of monasteries in service to society. Basil (later dubbed "the Great") required monks to perform charitable deeds, especially ministering to the sick, a development that led to the foundation of the first hospitals, attached to monasteries.

A milder code of monastic conduct became the standard in the west, greatly influencing Catholic worship. It is called the Benedictine rule after its creator, Benedict of Nursia in central Italy (c. 480–553). Benedict created his code in about 540 to prescribe his monastery's daily routine of prayer, scriptural readings, and manual labor. The rule divided the day into seven parts, each with a compulsory service of prayers and lessons, called the office. Unlike the harsh regulations of other monastic communities, Benedict's code did not isolate the monks from the outside world or deprive them of sleep, adequate food, or warm clothing. Although it gave the abbot (the head monk) full authority, it instructed him to listen to what every member of the community had to say before deciding important matters. He was not allowed to beat disobedient monks, as sometimes happened under other systems. Communities of women, such as those founded by Basil's sister Macrina and Benedict's sister Scholastica, generally followed the rules of the male monasteries, with an emphasis on the decorum thought necessary for women.

The thousands upon thousands of Christians who joined monasteries from the fourth century onward abandoned the outside world for social as well as theological reasons. The glory of monastic piety held special appeal for women and the rich. Jerome wrote, "[As monks] we evaluate people's virtue not by their gender but by their character, and deem those to be worthy of the greatest glory who have renounced both status and riches." Some monks had not chosen their life; they had been given as babies to monasteries by parents who could not raise them or were fulfilling pious vows, a practice called oblation. Jerome once gave this advice to a mother who decided to send her young daughter to a monastery:

> Let her be brought up in a monastery, let her live among virgins, let her learn to avoid swearing, let her regard lying as an offense against God, let her be ignorant of the world, let her live the angelic life, while in the flesh let her be without the flesh, and let her suppose that all human beings are like herself.

When the girl reached adulthood as a virgin, he added, she should avoid the baths so she would not be seen naked or give her body pleasure by dipping in the warm pools. Jerome enunciated traditional values favoring males when he promised that God would reward the mother with the birth of sons in compensation for the dedication of her daughter.

Since monasteries were self-governing, they could find themselves in conflict with the church hierarchy. Bishops resented members of their congregations who withdrew into monasteries, especially because they then gave money and property to their new community instead of to their local churches. Moreover, monks represented a threat to bishops' authority because holy men and women earned their special status not by having it bestowed from the church hierarchy but through their own actions; strengthening

♦**Pachomius:** puh KOH mee uhs
♦**Basil of Caesarea:** BAAH zuhl (of) seh zuh REE uh

the bishops' right to discipline monks who resisted their authority was one of the goals of the Council of Chalcedon. At bottom, however, bishops and monks did share a spiritual goal—salvation and service to God. While polytheists had enjoyed immediate access to their gods, who were thought to visit the earth constantly, Christians worshiped a transcendent God removed from this world. Monks bridged the chasm between the human and the divine by interceding with God to ask mercy for the faithful.

> **Review:** What were the major spiritual disputes among early Christians and why were they so fierce?

❖ Non-Roman Kingdoms in the West, c. 370–550s

The residents of the western empire had special reason to pray for God's help because their territory came under great pressure from the often violent incursion of non-Roman peoples that took place in the fourth and fifth centuries. Migrations and invasions of peoples from east of the Rhine River and north of the Danube River transformed politics, society, and economy in the western half of the Roman world. The multiethnic groups that forced their way into the empire from the northeast had two strong motivations to move westward: to flee attacks by the Huns, nomads from central Asia, and to

Monastery of St. Catherine at Mount Sinai

The Byzantine emperor Justinian (r. 527–565) built a wall to enclose the buildings of this monastery in the desert at the foot of Mount Sinai (on the peninsula between Egypt and Arabia). Justinian supported the monastery to promote orthodoxy in a region dominated by Monophysite Christians. The monastery gained its name in the ninth century when the story was circulated that angels had recently brought the body of Catherine of Alexandria there. Catherine was said to have been martyred in the fourth century for refusing to marry the emperor because, in her words, she was the bride of Christ, though no contemporary sources record her story.
Erich Lessing/ Art Resource, NY.

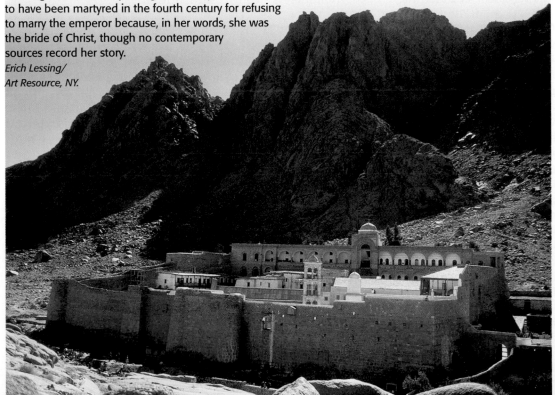

enjoy Roman prosperity. By the 370s this human tide had swollen to a flood, provoking violence and a loss of order in the western empire. Over the coming decades, the immigrants embarked on a remarkable transition, transforming themselves from loosely organized, multiethnic tribes into kingdoms with newly defined identities. By the 470s, one of their commanders ruled Italy—the political change that has been said to mark the so-called fall of the Roman Empire. In fact, the interactions of these non-Roman peoples with the empire's residents in western Europe and North Africa are better understood as causing a political, social, and cultural transformation that made them the heirs of the western Roman Empire and led to the formation of medieval Europe.

Non-Roman Migrations

The non-Roman peoples who flooded into the empire had diverse origins; scholars in the past referred to them generically as Germanic peoples, but this label misrepresents the variety of languages and customs among these multiethnic groups. Romans lumped them all together as barbarians, a term that some historians now use but whose negative implications impede fair-minded analysis. What we should remember is that they were a diverse population with no strongly established sense of ethnic identity; many of them had had previous contact with Romans through trade or employment as mercenary fighters. Fourth-century emperors at first encouraged the movement of non-Romans into imperial territory, recruiting the men to serve in the Roman army, as earlier emperors had done. By late in the century, these warriors' families had followed them into the empire. Hordes of men, women, and children crossed the Roman border as refugees. They came with no political or military unity and no clear plan. Loosely organized into tribes that often warred with one another, they shared only their terror of the Huns and their custom of conducting raids for a living.

The western government was fatally weakened by its inability to prevent the newcomers from crossing the border or to control them once they arrived. Persistent economic weakness rooted in the third-century crisis underlay this failure. Tenant farmers and landlords fleeing crushing taxes had left as much as 20 percent of arable territory unfarmed in the most seriously affected areas. The loss of revenue made the government unable to afford enough soldiers to control the situation. Over time the immigrating non-Roman peoples compelled Roman government to cede them territory in the empire. Remarkably, they then began to develop separate ethnic identities and formed new societies for themselves and the Romans living under their control.

Immigrant Traditions. The newcomers had to develop more tightly structured societies to govern the lands that the weak western government grudgingly granted them under threat of violence. The traditions they brought with them from their eastern homelands had ill prepared them for ruling others. There they had lived in small settlements whose economies depended on farming, herding, and ironworking; they had no experience with running kingdoms built on strong central authority.

Their original societies were chiefdoms, whose members could only be persuaded, not ordered, to follow the chief. The chiefs maintained their status by giving gifts to their followers and leading raids to capture cattle and slaves. They led clans—groups of households organized on kinship lines, following maternal as well as paternal descent. The members of a clan were supposed to keep peace among themselves, and violence against a fellow clan member was the worst possible offense. Clans in turn grouped themselves into tribes, very loose and fluctuating multiethnic coalitions that anyone could join. Tribes differentiated themselves by their clothing, hairstyles, jewelry, weapons, religious cults, and oral stories.

Family life was patriarchal: men headed households and held authority over women, children, and slaves. Warfare preoccupied men, as their ritual sacrifices of weapons preserved in northern European bogs have shown. Women were valued for their ability to bear children, and rich men could have more than one wife and perhaps concubines as well. A division of labor made women responsible for agriculture, pottery making, and the production of textiles, while men worked iron and herded cattle. Women enjoyed certain rights of inheritance and could control property, and married women received a dowry of one-third of their husband's property.

Assemblies of free male warriors provided the only traditional form of decision making among the tribes. Their leaders' authority was restricted mostly to religious and military matters. Tribes could be very unstable and prone to internal conflict—clans frequently feuded, with bloody consequences. Tribal law tried to determine what forms of violence were and were not acceptable in seeking revenge, but laws were oral, not written, and thus open to wide dispute.

Migrants Fleeing the Huns. The migrations avalanched when the Huns invaded eastern Europe in the fourth century. Distantly related to the Hiung-nu,♦ a central Asian people who had earlier attacked China and Persia, the Huns arrived on the Russian steppes shortly before 370 as the vanguard of Turkish-speaking nomads. Huns excelled as raiders, launching cavalry attacks far and wide. Their warriors' appearance terrified their victims, who reported skulls elongated from having been bound between boards in infancy, faces grooved with decorative scars, and arms fearsome with elaborate tattoos. Their prowess as horsemen made them legendary; they could shoot their powerful bows while riding full tilt and stay mounted for days, sleeping atop their horses and carrying snacks of raw meat between their thighs and the animal's back.

The Huns moved westward toward the Hungarian plain north of the Danube late in the fourth century, terrifying the peoples there and launching raids southward into the Balkans. The emperors in Constantinople began paying the Huns to spare their territory, so the most ambitious Hunnic leader, Attila (r. c. 440–453), pushed his domain westward toward the Alps. In 451, he led his forces as far west as central France, and in 452 into northern Italy. At Attila's death in 454, the Huns lost their fragile cohesiveness

and faded from history. By this time, however, the terror that they had inspired in the peoples living in eastern Europe had provoked the migrations that eventually transformed the western empire.

Visigoths: The First New Society. The first non-Roman group that coalesced to create a new society after entering imperial territory came to be called the Visigoths. Shredded by constant Hunnic raids, in 376 they obtained permission from the eastern emperor Valens♦ (r. 364–378) to move into the Balkans, so long as their warriors agreed to fight in the Roman army against the Huns (Map 7.3). Their history illustrates the pattern of the migrations: desperate people in barely organized groups seeking asylum from Roman government in return for service, being mistreated, and rebelling to form their own, new kingdom.

When greedy Roman officers charged with helping them instead extorted bribes, the refugees starved; the officials forced them to sell some of their own people into slavery to buy dogs to eat. The desperate band fought back. In 378, they defeated and killed Valens in the battle of Adrianople♦ in Thrace.♦ Theodosius I, Valens's successor, then had to agree to give them large annual payments, let them settle permanently inside the borders in a kingdom under their own laws, and designate them as federates (allies) helping protect the empire.

Realizing they could not afford to keep this agreement, the eastern emperors soon forced the newcomers to the west by cutting off the payments and threatening full-scale war unless the refugees left. The angry group moved violently into the western empire; neither they nor the western empire would ever be the same. In 410, they stunned the world by sacking Rome itself. For the first time since the Gauls eight hundred years before, a foreign force occupied the ancient capital. They terrorized the population: when their commander Alaric♦ demanded all the citizens' goods, the Romans asked, "What will be left to us?" "Your lives," he replied.

♦**Valens:** VAL ehnz
♦**Adrianople:** ay dree uh NOH puhl
♦**Thrace:** thrays
♦**Alaric:** A luh rihk

♦**Hiung-nu:** hee UNG new

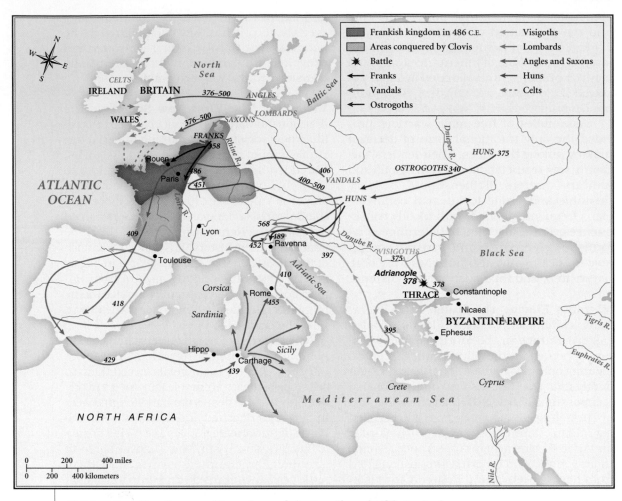

MAP 7.3   Migrations and Invasions of the Fourth and Fifth Centuries
The movements of non-Roman peoples into imperial territory transformed the Roman Empire. This phenomenon had begun as early as the reign of Domitian (r. 81-96), but in the fourth century it became a pressing problem for the emperors when the Huns' attacks pushed various multiethnic bands from their homelands in eastern Europe into the empire's northern provinces. Print maps can offer only a schematic representation of dynamic processes such as these migrations and invasions, but this map does convey a sense of the variety of peoples involved, the wide extent of imperial territory that they affected, and the concentration of their effects in the western section of the empire.

Too weak to fend off the invaders, the western emperor Honorius in 418 reluctantly agreed to settle the newcomers in southwestern Gaul (present-day France), where they completed their unprecedented transition from tribe to kingdom, organizing a political state and establishing their ethnic identity as Visigoths. In this process of creation they followed the only model available: Roman tradition. For one thing, they estab-lished mutually beneficial relations with local Roman elites, who used time-tested ways of flattering their new superiors to gain advantages. Sidonius Apollinaris, for example, a well-connected noble from Lyon♦ (c. 430–479), once purposely lost a backgammon game to the Visigothic king as a way of winning a favor.

♦**Lyon:** ly OHN

How the new non-Roman kingdoms raised revenues has become a much-debated question. Did the newcomers become landed proprietors by forcing Roman landowners to redistribute a portion of their lands, slaves, and movable property to them? Or did Romans directly pay the expenses of the kingdom's soldiers, who lived mostly in urban garrisons? Whatever the new arrangements were, the Visigoths found them profitable enough to expand into Spain within a century of establishing themselves in southwestern Gaul.

The Vandals and the Spiral of Violence. The western government's concessions to the Visigoths emboldened other groups to seize territory and create new kingdoms and identities. The violence spiraled to new levels in 406 when the Vandals, fleeing the Huns, crossed the Rhine into Roman territory. This huge group cut a swath through Gaul all the way to the Spanish coast. (The modern word *vandal*, meaning "destroyer of property," perpetuates their reputation for warlike ruthlessness.)

In 429, eighty thousand Vandals ferried to North Africa, where they soon broke their agreement to become federates and captured the region. They crippled the western empire by seizing North Africa's tax payments of grain and vegetable oil and disrupting the importation of food to Rome, and they frightened the eastern empire with their strong navy. In 455, they set the western government tottering by plundering Rome. The Vandals caused tremendous hardship for local Africans by confiscating property rather than (like the Visigoths) allowing owners to make regular payments to "ransom" their land.

The Anglo-Saxons at the Empire's Western Edge. Small non-Roman groups took advantage of the disruption caused by bigger bands to break off distant pieces of the weakened western empire. The most significant group for later history was the Anglo-Saxons. Composed of Angles from what is now Denmark and Saxons from northwestern Germany, this mixed group invaded Britain in the 440s after the Roman army had been recalled from the province to defend Italy against the Visigoths. They established their kingdoms by wresting territory away from the indigenous Celtic peoples and the remaining Roman inhabitants. Gradually, their culture replaced the local traditions of the island's eastern regions; the Celts there lost most of their language, and Christianity gave way to Anglo-Saxon beliefs, surviving only in Wales and Ireland.

The Fall of Rome and the Ostrogoths. Yet another non-Roman group, the Ostrogoths,♦ carved out a kingdom in Italy in the fifth century. By the time the Ostrogothic king Theodoric came to power (r. 493–526), there had not been a western Roman emperor for nearly twenty years, and there never would be again—the change that has traditionally, but simplistically, been called the fall of the Roman Empire. (See "New Sources, New Perspectives," page 268.) The story's details reveal the complexity of the political transformation of the western empire under the new kingdoms. The weakness of the western emperors' army had obliged them to hire foreign officers to lead the defense of Italy. By the middle of the fifth century, one non-Roman general after another decided who would serve as puppet emperor under his control. The employees were running the company.

The last such unfortunate puppet was only a child; his father, a former aide to Attila, tried to establish a royal house by proclaiming his young son as western emperor in 475. He gave the boy ruler the name Romulus Augustulus ("Romulus the Little Augustus") to match his tender age and recall both Rome's founder and its first emperor. In 476, following a dispute over pay, the emperor's non-Roman soldiers murdered his father and deposed him; pitied as an innocent child, Little Augustus was given safe refuge and a generous pension. The rebels' leader, Odoacer,♦ did not appoint another emperor, a move traditionally labeled the "fall of Rome." Instead, he had the Roman Senate petition Zeno, the eastern emperor, to recognize his leadership in return for his acknowledging Zeno as sole emperor over west and east. Odoacer thereafter oversaw Italy nominally as the eastern emperor's viceroy, but in fact he ruled as he liked.

♦**Ostrogoths:** AHS truh gahths
♦**Odoacer:** oh doh AH ker

Looking for the Decline and Fall of the Roman Empire

In 1776, the Englishman Edward Gibbon (1737–1794) became a celebrity by publishing the first installment of his best-selling, multi-volume work *The Decline and Fall of the Roman Empire*. The reading public loved his writing for its stinging style, though some people found Gibbon himself irritating for his flashy vanity and conceit.

Ironically, historians have found his title irritating for its enduring renown: the phrase grew so famous that, if there is anything commonly "known" about the Roman Empire, it is that it declined and fell. The trouble is that this idea is woefully misleading. Gibbon himself lived to regret his choice of a title because his work continued telling the empire's story far beyond 476 C.E., the year when a non-Roman general took over the western empire. His final volume (published in 1788) reached 1453, when the Turks toppled the Byzantine Empire by taking Constantinople.

Various sources of new information and analysis have revealed the inadequacies of the idea that the Roman Empire fell once and for all in 476. This is not to say that no disasters occurred in the fourth and fifth centuries: clearly some condi-tions of life—economic security and prosperity, opportunities for leisure and entertainment, and even nutrition—got worse for many people as non-Roman peoples entered the western empire and the center of power shifted to its eastern half. So, too, the Byzantine emperors regarded the political division of the old empire as a problem they wanted to remedy by conquering the new non-Roman kingdoms to reunite west and east. Still, these changes are far from the full story. To tell that entire story today, it is more accurate to describe the empire's fate as a complex transformation rather than as a simple decline and fall.

Art and archaeology have provided some of the most intriguing sources for this perspective, either looking at long-known objects in new ways or discovering new objects. Past scholars, for example, considered Gothic art inferior because, unlike classical art, its designs did not emphasize the human figure or symmetry. Instead, it focused on animal motifs and abstract patterns. This tendency did not mean that it could not communicate as powerfully as classical art; it just meant that observers had to be able to un-

In 488, Zeno plotted to rid himself of an ambitious non-Roman general then resident in Constantinople—Theodoric—by sending him to fight Odoacer, whom the emperor had found too independent. Successful in eliminating Odoacer by 493, Theodoric went on to establish his own Ostrogothic kingdom to rule Italy from the traditional capital at Ravenna.

Theodoric and his Ostrogothic nobles wanted to enjoy the luxurious life of the empire's elite, not destroy it, and to preserve the empire's prestige and status. They therefore left the Senate and consulships intact. An Arian Christian, Theodoric followed Constantine's example by announcing a policy of religious toleration: "No one can be forced to believe against his will." Like the other non-Romans, the Ostrogoths appropriated Roman traditions that supported the stability of their own rule. For these reasons, scholars consider it more accurate to speak of the western empire's "transformation" than of its "fall."

The Enduring Kingdom of the Franks. The Franks were the people who transformed Roman Gaul into Francia (from which the name France comes). Roman emperors had allowed some of the Franks to settle in a rough northern border region (now in the Netherlands) in the early fourth century; by the late fifth century they were a major pres-

Eagle Fibulae (Brooches) from Gothic Spain
Walters Art Gallery, Baltimore.

this style had not served to identify separate groups; now it said, "I am a Visigothic woman."

Above all, Gothic art expressed the transformation of the empire. A clear example comes in the spectacular eagle pins that elite Goths favored. Dazzlingly fashioned in gold and semiprecious stones, these small works of art took their inspiration from the traditions of the Huns and the Romans, both of whom highlighted the eagle as a symbol of power. Goths had never previously used eagles this way, but now they adapted the traditions of others to express their own transformation into powerful members of imperial politics and society. From their perspective, the empire's fate was hardly a decline and fall.

QUESTIONS TO CONSIDER

1. How do historical and aesthetic appreciations of art differ? What are the advantages of each approach?
2. How do people determine whether art is "superior" or "inferior"? Are such judgments important to make?

FURTHER READING

Greene, K. "Gothic Material Culture." In Ian Hodder, ed. *Archaeology as Long-Term History.* 1987. 117–42.
Heather, Peter. *The Goths.* 1996. Chapter 10.
Hoxie, Albert. "Mutations in Art." In Lynn White Jr., ed. *The Transformation of the Roman World: Gibbon's Problem after Two Centuries.* 1966. 266–90.

derstand the art's conventions and goals. Recent archaeological research has shown that Goths used everyday art objects to convey crucial meanings—in particular, assertions of the growing sense of ethnic identity that emerged during their migrations into the Roman Empire. When in the fifth century C.E. Visigoths took up permanent residence in Spain, the women expressed their identity by emphasizing an old custom from their traditional Danube region: wearing two artfully crafted brooches to fasten their clothes at the shoulders instead of just one. Previously,

ence in Gaul. Their king Clovis (r. 485–511) in 507 overthrew the Visigothic king in southern Gaul with support from the eastern Roman emperor. When the emperor named him an honorary consul, Clovis celebrated this ancient honor by having himself crowned with a diadem in the style of the emperors since Constantine. He carved out western Europe's largest new kingdom in what is today mostly France, overshadowing the neighboring and rival kingdoms of the Burgundians and Alemanni in eastern Gaul. Probably persuaded by his wife Clotilda, a Christian, to believe that God had helped him defeat the Alemanni, Clovis proclaimed himself an orthodox Christian and renounced Arianism,

which he had reportedly embraced previously. To build stability, he carefully fostered good relations with the bishops as the regime's intermediaries with the population.

Clovis's dynasty, called Merovingian♦ after the legendary Frankish ancestor Merovech, endured for another two hundred years, foreshadowing the kingdom that would emerge much later as the forerunner of modern France. The Merovingians survived so long because, better than any other kingdom, they created a workable symbiosis between their own traditions of military valor and Roman social and legal traditions, and because

♦**Merovingian:** mehr uh VIHN jee uhn

their location in far western Europe kept them out of the reach of the destructive invasions sent against Italy by the eastern emperor Justinian in the sixth century to reunite the Roman world.

Mixing Traditions

Western Europe's political transformation—the gradual replacement of imperial government by the new kingdoms—set in motion a social and cultural transformation (Map 7.4). The newcomers and their Roman subjects created novel ways of life by combining old traditions, as the Visigoth king Athaulf (r. 410–415) explained after marrying a Roman noblewoman:

> At the start I wanted to erase the Romans' name and turn their land into a Gothic empire, doing myself what Augustus had done. But I have learned that the Goths' freewheeling wildness will never accept the rule of law, and that state with no law is no state. Thus, I have more wisely chosen another path to glory: reviving the Roman name with Gothic vigor. I pray that future generations will remember me as the founder of a Roman restoration.

This process of social and cultural transformation promoted stability by producing new law codes but undermined long-term security by weakening the economic situation.

Visigothic and Frankish Law.   Roman law was the most influential precedent for the new kings in their efforts to construct stable states. Their original tribal societies never had written laws, but their new states required legal codes to create a sense of justice and keep order. The Visigothic kings were the first to issue a written law code. Published in Latin in about 475, it made fines and compensation the primary method for resolving disputes. Clovis also emphasized written law for the Merovingian kingdom. His code, also published in Latin between about 507 and 511, promoted social order through clear penalties for specific crimes. In particular, he formalized a system of fines intended to defuse feuds and vendettas between individuals and clans. The most prominent component of this system was **wergild**, the payment a murderer had to make as compensation for his crime. Most of the money was paid to the victim's kin, but the king received about one-third of the fine.

Since laws enshrine social values, the differing amounts of wergild in Clovis's code offer a glimpse of the relative values of different categories of people in his kingdom. Murdering a woman of childbearing age, a boy under twelve, or a man in the king's retinue incurred a massive fine of six hundred gold coins, enough to buy six hundred cattle. A woman past child-

Upper-Class Country Life
This fourth-century mosaic, fourteen by eighteen feet, covered a floor in a country villa at Carthage in North Africa. Like a set of cartoon strips, it portrays the life of an elite couple on their estate at different seasons of the year. Their home, resplendent with towers and a second-story colonnade, stands as a fortified retreat at the center. Above, the lady of the house sits in parklike surroundings while her servants and tenants tend to animals; winter activities are at the left, summer at the right. In the middle, hunters pursue game. Below left, the lady appears in springtime; below right, her husband in autumn. The servant to his left hands him a roll addressed "to the master Julius," revealing his name. Rural estates such as these provided prosperity and idyllic security for their owners in the western empire. They also made tempting targets for the Vandals during their invasion of North Africa; with the weakening of the provincial government in this period, these estates had to provide their own defense against raiders. *Le Musée du Bardo, Tunis.*

MAP 7.4 Peoples and Kingdoms of the Roman World, c. 526

The provinces of the Roman empire had always been home to a population diverse in language and ethnicity. By the early sixth century, the territory of the western empire had become a welter of diverse political units as well. Italy and most of the former western provinces were ruled by kingdoms organized by different non-Roman peoples, who had moved into former imperial territory over several centuries. The eastern empire, which we call the Byzantine Empire, remained under the political control of the emperor in Constantinople (formerly Byzantium until refounded by Constantine in 330).

bearing age (specified as sixty years), a young girl, or a freeborn man was valued at two hundred. Ordinary slaves rated thirty-five.

A Transformed Economic Landscape.
The migrations that transformed the west harmed its already weakened economy. The Vandals' violent sweep severely damaged many towns in Gaul, hastening the decline of urban communities that had been growing for some time. In the countryside, now outside the control of any central government, wealthy Romans built sprawling villas on extensive estates, staffed by tenants bound to the land like slaves. These establishments strove to operate as self-sufficient units by producing all they needed, defending themselves against raids, and keeping their distance from any authorities. Craving isolation, the owners shunned municipal offices and tax collection, the public services that had supplied the lifeblood of Roman administration. The vestiges of provincial government disappeared, and the new kingdoms never matured sufficiently to replace their services fully.

The situation only grew grimmer as the effects of these changes multiplied one another. The infrastructure of trade—roads and bridges—fell into disrepair with no public-spirited elite to maintain them. Nobles holed up on their estates could take care of themselves and their fortress-like households because they could be astonishingly rich. The very wealthiest boasted an annual income rivaling that of entire provinces in the old western empire.

In some cases, these fortunate few helped transmit Roman learning to later ages. Cassiodorus (c. 490–585), for one, founded a monastery on his ancestral estate in Italy in the 550s after a career in imperial administration. He gave the monks the task of copying manuscripts to keep their contents from disappearing as old ones disintegrated. His own book *Institutions* encapsulated the respect for tradition that kept classical traditions alive: listing the books a person of superior education should read, it included ancient secular texts as well as Scripture and Christian literature. The most strenuous effort to perpetuate the Roman past, however, came in the eastern empire.

> **Review:** What transformations took place in the society of the non-Romans who came into the Roman Empire from around 370 to the 550s?

❖ Byzantine Empire in the East, c. 500–565

The eastern empire avoided the massive transformations that reshaped western Europe. The east's trade and agriculture kept it from poverty, while its emperors employed force, diplomacy, and bribery to prevent invasions from the north and defeat attacks by the Sassanid kingdom in Persia, which was still making periodic attacks against the eastern empire. By about 500, the eastern empire had achieved such riches and ambition that historians have given it a new name, the **Byzantine empire**. Its emperors would rule in Constantinople until 1453, when a Turkish army finally captured the capital.

These rulers confidently saw themselves as perpetuating the Roman Empire and guarding its culture against barbarism; they regarded themselves as protectors of Constantine's "new Rome." The most famous early Byzantine emperor, Justinian (r. 527–565), took this mission so seriously that he waged war for decades against the non-Roman kingdoms in the west, aiming to reunite the empire and return it to its original scale as created by Augustus. Like Diocletian,

Justinian enlarged the authority of imperial rule and tried to purify religion to provide what he saw as the strong leadership and divine favor necessary in unsettled times. He and his successors in the Byzantine empire also contributed to later history by preserving much of classical literature.

Byzantine Society

The sixth-century Byzantine empire enjoyed a vitality that had vanished in the west. Its elite spent freely on silk, precious stones, and prized spices such as pepper imported from China and India. Markets in its large cities teemed with merchants from far and wide. Its churches' soaring domes testified to its confidence in God as its divine protector.

In keeping with Roman tradition, the Byzantine emperors sponsored religious festivals and entertainments on a massive scale to rally public support. Rich and poor alike crowded city squares, theaters, and hippodromes on these lively occasions. Chariot racing aroused the hottest passions. Constantinople's residents divided themselves into competitive factions called Blues and Greens after the racing colors of their favorite charioteers. These high-energy fans mixed religious competition with their sports rivalry: orthodox Christians joined the Blues, while Monophysites were Greens. They brawled with one another over theology as well as race results.

Preserving "Romanness." The Byzantine emperors ardently strove to maintain Roman tradition and identity, believing that "Romanness" was an important defense against what had happened to the western empire. They hired many foreign mercenaries, but they also tried to keep their subjects from adopting foreign ways. Styles of dress figured prominently in this struggle. Eastern emperors ordered Constantinople's residents not to wear barbarian-style clothing (especially heavy boots and clothing made from animal furs) instead of traditional Roman garb (sandals or light shoes and robes).

The quest for cultural unity was hopeless because Byzantine society was thoroughly multilingual and multiethnic. Byzantines regarded themselves as the heirs of ancient

Roman culture: they pointedly referred to themselves as Romans. At the same time, they spoke Greek as their native language and used Latin only for government and military communication. Many people retained their traditional languages, such as Phrygian and Cappadocian in western Asia Minor, Armenian farther east, and Syriac♦ and other Aramaic dialects along the eastern Mediterranean coast. The streets of Constantinople reportedly rang with seventy-two languages.

Romanness definitely included Christianity, but the Byzantines' theological diversity rivaled their ethnic complexity. Bitter controversies over doctrine divided eastern Christians; neither the emperors nor the bishops succeeded in imposing orthodoxy. Emperors used violence against heretics when persuasion failed. They had to resort to extreme measures, they believed, to save lost souls and preserve the empire's religious purity and divine goodwill. The persecution of Christian subjects by Christian emperors illustrates the disturbing consequences that the quest for a unitary identity required.

Women in Society and at Court. Most women in Byzantine society lived according to ancient Mediterranean tradition: they concentrated on the support of their households and minimized contact with men outside that circle. Law barred them from fulfilling many public functions, such as witnessing wills. Subject to the authority of their fathers and husbands, women veiled their heads (though not their faces) to show modesty. Since Christian theologians exceeded Roman tradition in restricting sexuality and reproduction, divorce became more difficult and remarriage was discouraged even for widows. Stiffer legal penalties for sexual offenses also were imposed. Female prostitution remained legal and common, but emperors raised the penalties for those who forced women under their control (children or slaves) into prostitution.

Women in the imperial family could achieve prominence unattainable for their workaday contemporaries. Theodora (d. 548), wife of the emperor Justinian, dramatically exhibited the influence women could achieve

in Byzantine monarchy. Uninhibited by her humble origins (she was the daughter of a bear trainer and had been an actress with a scandalous reputation), she came to rival anyone in influence and wealth (see the mosaic of Theodora on page 274). She had a hand in every aspect of Justinian's rule, advising him on personnel for his administration, pushing for her religious views in disputes over Christian doctrine, and rallying his courage at times of crisis. John Lydus, a contemporary government official and high-ranking administrator, judged her "superior in intelligence to any man."

Social Class and Government Services. Byzantine government aggravated social divisions because it provided services according to people's wealth. Officials demanded fees for countless activities, from commercial permits to legal grievances. Nothing got done without payment. People with money and status found this process easy: they relied on their social connections to get a hearing from the right official and on their wealth to pay bribes to move matters along quickly. Whether seeking preferential treatment or just spurring administrators to do what they were supposed to do, the rich could make the system work. The poor, by contrast, could not afford the hefty amounts that government officials extorted.

This fee-based system saved the emperors money to spend on other goals; they could pay their civil servants paltry salaries because the public paid them fees. John Lydus, for example, reported that he earned thirty times his annual salary in payments from petitioners during his first year in office. To keep the system from destroying itself through limitless extortion, the emperors published an official list of the maximum bribes that their employees could exact.

The Reign of Justinian, 527–565

Justinian, the most famous early Byzantine emperor, spent his regime's money trying to reverse the subdivision of the empire. Born in a small Balkan town, he rose rapidly in imperial service until 527, when he succeeded his uncle as emperor (see the mosaic of Justinian on page 275). During his reign he launched enormous military expeditions to

♦**Syriac:** SIHR ee ak

Theodora and Her Court in Ravenna
This resplendent mosaic shows the empress Theodora (c. 500–548) and members of her court presenting a gift to the church at San Vitale in Ravenna. It faced the matching scene of her husband Justinian and his attendants. Theodora wears the jewels, pearls, and rich robes characteristic of Byzantine monarchs. (Compare the style of the clothes in these two mosaics to those shown in the sculptural scene from Augustus's time on page 206. What were the different styles of dress meant to convey about the leaders in each period?) Theodora extends in her hands a gem-encrusted wine cup as her present; her gesture imitates the gift-giving of the Magi to the baby Jesus, the scene illustrated on the hem of her garment. The circle around her head, called a nimbus (Latin for "cloud"), indicates special holiness.
Scala/Art Resource, NY.

try to reunite the Roman Empire. His desire to perpetuate imperial glory also led him to embellish Constantinople with magnificent and costly architecture. The first intellectual on the throne since Julian in the 360s, Justinian was motivated by his deep interest in the law and theology to impose reforms with the same aims as all his predecessors: to preserve social order based on hierarchy and maintain divine goodwill. Unfortunately, the financial strains of his campaigns and programs instead led to social unrest.

Financial Distress and Social Unrest.
Justinian faced bitter resistance to his plans and their enormous cost. So unpopular were his taxes that they provoked a major riot in 532. Known as the Nika♦ Riot, it arose when the Blue and Green factions gathering to watch chariot races unexpectedly united against the emperor, shouting "Nika! Nika!" ("Win! Win!") as their battle cry. After nine days of violence that left much of Constantinople in ashes, Justinian was ready to abandon his throne and flee in panic. But Theodora sternly rebuked him: "Once born, no one can escape dying, but for one who has held im-

perial power it would be unbearable to be a fugitive. May I never take off my imperial robes of purple, nor live to see the day when those who meet me will not greet me as their ruler." Her husband then sent in troops, who quelled the disturbance by slaughtering thirty thousand rioters trapped in the racetrack.

Justinian's most ambitious goal was to restore the empire to a unified territory, religion, and culture. Invading the former western provinces, his brilliant generals Belisarius♦ and Narses♦ defeated the Vandals and Ostrogoths after campaigns that in some cases took decades to complete. With enormous effort and expense, imperial armies reoccupied Italy, the Dalmatian coast, Sicily, Sardinia, Corsica, part of southern Spain, and western North Africa by 562. These successes indeed restored the old empire's geography temporarily: Justinian's territory stretched from the Atlantic to the western edge of Mesopotamia.

These military triumphs came at a tragic cost: they destroyed the west's infrastructure and the east's finances. Italy endured the most physical damage; the war there against

♦**Nika:** NEE kah

♦**Belisarius:** beh luh SAWR ee uhs
♦**Narses:** NAHR seez

Justinian and His Court in Ravenna
This mosaic scene dominated by the Byzantine emperor Justinian (r. 527–565) stands across the chancel from Theodora's mosaic in San Vitale's church in Ravenna. The emperor is shown presenting a gift to the church. Justinian and Theodora finished building the church, which the Ostrogothic king Theodoric had started, to commemorate their successful campaign to restore Italy to the Roman Empire and reassert control of the western capital, Ravenna. The inclusion of the portrait of Maximianus, bishop of Ravenna, standing on Justinian's left and identified by name, stresses the theme of cooperation between bishops and emperors in ruling the world. What do you think the inclusion of the soldiers at the left is meant to indicate? *Scala/Art Resource, NY.*

the Goths spread death and destruction on a massive scale. The east suffered because Justinian squeezed even more taxes out of his already overburdened population to finance the western wars and bribe the Persian kingdom not to attack while his home defenses were depleted. The tax burden crippled the economy, leading to constant banditry in the countryside. Crowds poured into the capital from rural areas, seeking relief from poverty and robbers.

Natural disaster compounded Justinian's troubles. In the 540s, a horrific epidemic killed a third of his empire's inhabitants; a quarter of a million succumbed in Constantinople alone, half the capital's population. This was only the first of many pandemics that erased millions of people in the eastern empire over the next two centuries. Serious earthquakes, always a danger in this region, increased the death toll. The loss of so many people created a shortage of army recruits, requiring the hire of expensive mercenaries, and left countless farms vacant, reducing tax revenues.

Strengthening Monarchy.   The threats to his regime made Justinian crave stability, which he sought by strengthening his authority in two ways: emphasizing his close-

ness to God and increasing the autocratic power of his rule. These traits became characteristic of Byzantine emperors. His artists brilliantly recast the symbols of his rule in a Christian context. A gleaming mosaic in his church at San Vitale♦ in Ravenna, for example, displayed a dramatic vision of the emperor's role: Justinian standing at the center of the cosmos shoulder to shoulder with both Christ and the ancient Hebrew patriarch Abraham. Moreover, Justinian proclaimed the emperor the "living law," recalling the Hellenistic royal doctrine that the ruler's decisions defined law.

His building program in Constantinople communicated his overpowering supremacy and religiosity. Most spectacular of all was his reconstruction of Constantine's Hagia Sophia♦ (Church of the Holy Wisdom). Creating a new design for churches, his architects erected a huge building on a square plan capped by a dome 107 feet across and soaring 160 feet above the floor. Its interior walls glowed like the sun from the light reflecting off their four acres of gold mosaics. Imported marble of every color added to the sparkling

---

♦**San Vitale:** sahn vee TAHL eh
♦**Hagia Sophia:** HAH gee uh so FEE uh

effect. When he first entered his masterpiece, dedicated in 538, Justinian exclaimed, "Solomon, I have outdone you," claiming to have bested the glorious temple that the ancient king built for the Hebrews.

His more autocratic monarchy reduced the autonomy of the empire's cities. Their councils ceased to govern; imperial officials took over instead. Provincial elites still had to ensure full payment of their area's taxes, but they lost the compensating reward of deciding local matters. Now the imperial government determined all aspects of decision making and social status. Men of property from the provinces who aspired to power and prestige knew they could satisfy their ambitions only by joining the imperial administration in the capital.

Constantinople during the Rule of Justinian

Law and Religion.   To solidify his authority, Justinian codified the laws of the empire to bring uniformity to the confusing mass of decisions that earlier emperors had announced. The final version of his *Codex* appeared in 534. A team of scholars also condensed millions of words of regulations to produce the *Digest* in 533, intended to expedite legal cases and provide a syllabus for law schools. This collection, like the *Codex* written in Latin and therefore readable in the western empire, influenced legal scholars for centuries. Justinian's legal experts also compiled a textbook for students, the *Institutes*, which appeared in 533 and remained on law school reading lists until modern times.

To fulfill the emperor's sacred duty to secure the welfare of his people, Justinian acted to enforce their religious purity. Like the polytheist and Christian emperors before him, he believed his world could not flourish if its divine protector became angered by the presence of religious offenders. As emperor, Justinian decided who the offenders were. Zealously enforcing laws against polytheists, he compelled them to be baptized or forfeit their lands and official positions. He also relentlessly purged heretical Christians who re-

jected his version of orthodoxy. In pursuit of sexual purity, his laws made male homosexual relations illegal for the first time in Roman history. Homosexual marriage, apparently not uncommon earlier, had been officially prohibited in 342, but civil sanctions had never before been imposed on men engaging in homosexual activity. All the previous emperors, for example, had simply taxed male prostitutes. The legal status of homosexual activity between women is less clear; it probably counted as adultery when married women were involved and thus constituted criminal behavior.

A brilliant theologian in his own right, Justinian labored mightily to reconcile orthodox and Monophysite Christians by having the creed of the Council of Chalcedon revised. But the church leaders in Rome and Constantinople had become too bitterly divided and too jealous of the others' prominence to agree on a unified church; the eastern and western churches were by now firmly launched on the diverging courses that would result in formal schism five hundred years later. Justinian's own ecumenical council in Constantinople ended in disaster in 553 when he jailed Rome's defiant Pope Vigilius while also managing to alienate Monophysite bishops. Probably no one could have done better, but his efforts to compel religious unity only drove Christians further apart and undermined his vision of a restored Roman world.

Preserving Classical Literature

Christianization of the empire put the survival of classical literature—plays, histories, poems, speeches, and novels alike—at risk because these works were polytheist and therefore potentially subversive of Christian belief. The real danger to the classical tradition, however, stemmed not so much from active censorship as simple neglect. As Christians became authors, which they did in great numbers, their works displaced the ancient texts of Greece and Rome as the most important literature of the age. Fortunately for later times, however, the Byzantine Empire played a crucial role in preserving the brilliant intellectual legacy of the past.

Classical texts survived because Christian education and literature depended on non-Christian models, Latin and Greek. In the eastern empire, the region's original Greek culture remained the dominant influence, but Latin literature continued to be read because the administration was bilingual, with official documents and laws published in Rome's ancient tongue along with Greek translations. Latin scholarship in the east received a boost when Justinian's Italian wars impelled Latin-speaking scholars to flee for safety to Constantinople. Their labors in the capital helped to conserve many works that might otherwise have disappeared in the violence in the western empire. Byzantine scholars preserved classical literature because they regarded it as a crucial part of a high-level education, an attitude reflecting their deep regard for elite tradition. Much of the classical literature available today survived because it served as schoolwork for Byzantine Christians. At least a rudimentary knowledge of some pre-Christian classics was required for a good career in government service, the goal of every ambitious student. In the words of an imperial decree from 360, "No person shall obtain a post of the first rank unless it shall be shown that he excels in long practice of liberal studies, and that he is so polished in literary matters that words flow from his pen faultlessly."

Another factor promoting the preservation of classical literature was that the principles of classical rhetoric provided the guidelines for the most effective presentation of Christian theology. When Ambrose, bishop of Milan from 374 to 397, composed the first systematic description of Christian ethics for young priests, he consciously imitated the great classical orator Cicero. Theologians refuted heretical Christian doctrines by employing the dialogue form pioneered by Plato, and polytheist traditions of laudatory biography inspired the hugely popular genre on saints' lives. Similarly, Christian artists incorporated polytheist traditions in communicating their beliefs and emotions in paintings, mosaics, and carved reliefs. A favorite artistic motif of Christ with a sunburst surrounding his head, for example, took its inspiration from polytheist depiction of the radiant Sun as a god.

The proliferation of Christian literature generated a technological innovation used

The Soaring Architecture of Hagia Sophia
Golden mosaics originally reflected a dazzling light from the interior of Hagia Sophia ("Holy Wisdom"), the enormous church that the Byzantine emperor Justinian built in the 530s C.E. near his palace in Constantinople. A central dome, 184 feet high and supported by four arches resting on massive piers, capped the church's vast interior; the ring of windows at the base of the dome is just visible at the top of the picture. Hagia Sophia became a mosque after the Turks captured the city in 1453; the large medallions contain religious quotations in Arabic. Now a museum, Hagia Sophia continues to host people offering prayers. © *Adam Woolfitt/Corbis.*

also to preserve classical literature. Polytheist scribes had written books on sheets of thin animal skin or paper made from papyrus. They then glued the sheets together and attached rods at both ends to form a scroll. Readers faced a cumbersome task in unrolling scrolls to read. For ease of use, Christians produced their literature in the form of the codex—a book with bound pages that was less susceptible to damage from rolling and unrolling and contained text more efficiently than scrolls. Eventually the codex became the standard form of book production in the Byzantine world.

Despite the continuing importance of classical Greek and Latin literature in Byzantine education and rhetoric, its survival remained precarious in a war-torn world dominated by Christians. Knowledge of Greek in the turbulent west faded so drastically that by the sixth century almost no one there could read the original versions of Homer's *Iliad* and *Odyssey*, the traditional foundations

MAPPING THE WEST **The Byzantine Empire and Western Europe, c. 600**
The Byzantine emperor Justinian employed brilliant generals and expended huge sums of money
to reconquer Italy, North Africa, and part of Spain to reunite the western and eastern halves of
the former Roman Empire. His wars to regain Italy and North Africa eliminated the Ostrogothic
and Vandal kingdoms, respectively, but at a huge cost in effort, time—the war in Italy took twenty
years—and expense. The resources of the eastern empire were so depleted that his successors
could not maintain the reunification. By the early seventh century, the Visigoths had taken back
all of Spain. Africa, despite serious revolts by indigenous Berber tribes, remained under imperial
control until the Arab conquest of the seventh century, but within five years of Justinian's death
the Lombards had set up a new kingdom controlling a large section of Italy. Never again would
anyone attempt to reestablish a universal Roman empire.

of a classical literary education. Latin fared
better, and scholars such as Augustine and
Jerome knew Rome's ancient literature extremely well. But they also saw its classics as
potentially too seductive for a pious Christian
because the pleasure that came from reading
them could be a distraction from the worship
of God. Jerome in fact once had a night-
mare of being condemned on Judgment Day
for having been a Ciceronian instead of a
Christian.

The closing around 530 of the Academy
founded in Athens by Plato more than nine

hundred years earlier vividly demonstrated
the dangers for classical learning lurking in
the Byzantine world. This most famous of
classical schools finally went out of business when many of its scholars emigrated to
Persia to escape harsher restrictions on polytheists and its revenues dwindled because
the Athenian elite, its traditional supporters, were increasingly Christianized. The
Neoplatonist school at Alexandria, by contrast, continued; its leader John Philoponus◆

◆**Philoponus:** fy luh POH nuhs

(his name means "loves to work," c. 490–570) was a Christian. In addition to Christian theology, Philoponus wrote commentaries on the works of Aristotle published from 517 to around 530; some of his ideas anticipated those of Galileo a thousand years later. With his work, he achieved the kind of synthesis of old and new that was one of the fruitful possibilities in the ferment of the late Roman world—he was a Christian subject of the Byzantine Empire in sixth-century Egypt, heading a school founded long before by polytheists, studying the works of an ancient Greek philosopher as the inspiration for his forward-looking scholarship. The strong possibility that present generations could learn from the past would continue as Western civilization once again remade itself in medieval times.

Review: What role did the emperor Justinian see himself playing in Roman history?

Conclusion

The third-century civil wars brought the Roman Empire to a turning point. Military activity was so prominent that, as Isis wrote to her mother, it seemed as if everybody was in the army. Diocletian's creation of the dominate and reorganization of government delayed the empire's fragmentation, but his principle of subdivision opened the way to its separation in 395 into western and eastern halves. From this time on, Roman history increasingly divided into two regional streams, even though emperors as late as Justinian in the sixth century retained the dream of reuniting the empire and restoring it to the glory of its Golden Age.

Multiple disasters interacted to destroy the unity of the Roman world, beginning with the catastrophic losses of property and people during the third-century crisis, which hit the west harder than the east. In the late fourth century migrations of non-Roman peoples fleeing the Huns brought pressures on the central government. When the Roman authorities bungled the task of integrating the immigrant tribes into Roman society, the newcomers created kingdoms that eventually replaced imperial government in the west. This change transformed not only the west's politics, society, and economy but also the tribes themselves, as they developed a sense of ethnic identity while organizing themselves into kingdoms inside Roman territory. The economic deterioration accompanying these transformations drove a stake into the heart of the elite public-spiritedness that had been one of the foundations of imperial stability, as wealthy nobles retreated to self-sufficient country estates and shunned municipal office.

The eastern empire fared better economically and parried the worst violence of the migrations. As the Byzantine state, it self-consciously continued the empire both politically and culturally by working to preserve "Romanness." The financial drain of pursuing the goal of unity through war against the new kingdoms increased social discontent by driving tax rates to punitive levels, while the concentration of power in the capital weakened the local communities that had made the empire robust.

This period of increasing political and social division saw the official religious unification of the empire under the banner of Christianity. Constantine's conversion in 312 marked an epochal turning point in Western history. Christianization of the Roman world occurred gradually, and Christians disagreed among themselves, even to the point of violence, over fundamental doctrines of faith. The church developed a hierarchy to combat disunity, but believers proved remarkably recalcitrant in the face of authority. Many of them abandoned everyday society to live as monks attempting to come closer to God personally and praying daily for mercy for the world. Monastic life redefined the meaning of holiness by creating communities of God's heroes who withdrew from this world to devote their service to glorifying the next. In the end, then, the imperial vision of unity faded before the divisive forces of religious strife combined with the powerful dynamics of political and social transformation. Nevertheless, the memory of Roman power and culture remained potent and present, providing an influential inheritance to the peoples and states that would become Rome's heirs.

Suggested References

Reorganizing the Empire, 284–395

Scholars continue to debate the religious motives of Diocletian and Constantine. Understanding them is challenging because their religious sensibilities, markedly different from those of most modern believers, so deeply influenced their political actions.

Bowersock, G. W., Peter Brown, and Oleg Grabar, eds. *Late Antiquity: A Guide to the Postclassical World.* 1999.

Elsner, Jaś. *Imperial Rome and Christian Triumph: The Art of the Roman Empire* A.D. *100–450.* 1998.

*Grubbs, Judith Evans. *Women and Law in the Roman Empire: A Sourcebook on Marriage, Divorce, and Widowhood.* 2002.

Southern, Pat, and Karen R. Dixon. *The Late Roman Army.* 1996.

Christianizing the Empire, 312–c. 540

Recent research has deepened our appreciation of the emotional depths that the Christianization of the empire stirred for both polytheists and Christians. People's ideas about themselves changed as their ideas about divinity changed.

Brown, Peter. *Augustine of Hippo: A Biography.* Rev. ed. 2000.

Caner, Daniel. *Wandering, Begging Monks: Spiritual Authority and the Promotion of Monasticism in Late Antiquity.* 2002.

Curran, John. *Pagan City and Christian Capital: Rome in the Fourth Century.* 2000.

Drake, H. A. *Constantine and the Bishops: The Politics of Intolerance.* 2000.

*Early Christian literature: http://www.ocf.org/OrthodoxPage/reading/St.Pachomius/Welcome.html.

Glancy, Jennifer A. *Slavery in Early Christianity.* 2002.

*Lee, A. D. *Pagans and Christians in Late Antiquity: A Sourcebook.* 2000.

*Maas, Michael. *Readings in Late Antiquity, A Sourcebook.* 2000.

MacMullen, Ramsay. *Christianity and Paganism in the Fourth to Eighth Centuries.* 1997.

Trombley, Frank R. *Hellenic Religion and Christianization c. 370–529.* Vol. 2. 2001.

*Primary source.

Non-Roman Kingdoms in the West, c. 370–550s

Debate still thrives over how to categorize the social and cultural transformation of the Roman world in the fourth and fifth centuries and the ethnogenesis (development of a separate ethnic identity) of the non-Roman peoples who created new kingdoms inside the empire's borders.

Burns, Thomas. *Rome and the Barbarians.* 2003.

Carr, Karen Eva. *Vandals to Visigoths: Rural Settlement Patterns in Early Medieval Spain.* 2002.

*Drew, Katherine Fischer. *The Laws of the Salian Franks.* 1991.

Effros, Bonnie. *Merovingian Mortuary Archaeology and the Making of the Middle Ages.* 2003.

Geary, Patrick J. *The Myth of Nations: The Medieval Origins of Europe.* 2001.

Goffart, Walter. *Barbarians and Romans,* A.D. *418–584.* 1987.

Heather, Peter. *The Goths and Romans.* 1996.

Lançon, Bertrand. *Rome in Late Antiquity: Everyday Life and Urban Change,* A.D. *312–609.* Trans. Antonia Nevill. 2001.

MacGeorge, Penny. *Late Roman Warlords.* 2002.

*Mathisen, Ralph W. *People, Personal Expression, and Social Relations in Late Antiquity.* 2 vols. 2002.

Byzantine Empire in the East, c. 500–565

Scholars today recognize the Byzantine Empire as the continuation of the eastern Roman Empire, emphasizing the challenge posed to its rulers in trying to maintain order and prosperity for their distinctly multicultural and multilingual population.

Byzantine civilization: http://www.fordham.edu/halsall/byzantium.

Cavallo, Guglielmo, ed. *The Byzantines.* 1997.

*Geanakoplos, Deno J. *Byzantium: Church, Society, and Civilization Seen Through Contemporary Eyes.* 1986.

Haldon, John. *The Byzantine Wars.* 2001.

Kalavrezou, Ioli. *Byzantine Women and Their World.* 2003.

Mango, Cyril, ed. *The Oxford History of Byzantium.* 2002.

Moorhead, John. *The Roman Empire Divided, 400–700.* 2001.

Women in Byzantine history, bibliography: http://www.wooster.edu/Art/wb.html.

CHAPTER REVIEW

IMPORTANT EVENTS

293	Diocletian creates the tetrarchy
301	Diocletian issues the Edict on Maximum Prices
303	Diocletian launches Great Persecution of Christians
312	Constantine wins the battle of the Milvian Bridge and converts to Christianity
313	Constantine and Licinius proclaim religious toleration in the Edict of Milan
c. 323	Pachomius in Upper Egypt establishes the first monasteries for men and women
324	Constantine wins the civil war and refounds Byzantium as Constantinople, the "new Rome"
325	Council of Nicaea
361–363	Julian the Apostate tries to reinstate traditional religion as official state religion
391	Theodosius I makes Christianity the official state religion
395	Theodosius I divides the empire into western and eastern halves
410	Visigoths sack Rome
426	Augustine publishes *City of God*
451	Council of Chalcedon
c. 475	Visigothic law code published
476	The "Fall of Rome" (German commander Odoacer deposes the final western emperor, the boy Romulus Augustulus)
493–526	Ostrogothic kingdom in Italy
507	Clovis establishes Frankish kingdom in Gaul
527–565	Reign of Byzantine emperor Justinian
533–534	Justinian publishes law code and handbooks
c. 540	Benedict devises his rule for monasteries

KEY TERMS

apostate (254)

Arianism (257)

asceticism (260)

Byzantine empire (272)

coloni (251)

curials (251)

dominate (246)

Edict of Milan (253)

Great Persecution (251)

tetrarchy (247)

wergild (270)

REVIEW QUESTIONS

1. What changes did Diocletian and his successors make in their reorganization of the empire and why?
2. What were the major spiritual disputes among early Christians and why were they so fierce?
3. What transformations took place in the society of the non-Romans who came into the Roman Empire from around 370 to the 550s?
4. What role did the emperor Justinian see himself playing in Roman history?

MAKING CONNECTIONS

1. What were the main similarities and differences between the political reality and the political appearance of the principate and the dominate?
2. What were the main similarities and differences between traditional Roman religion and Christianity as official state religion?

FOR FURTHER EXPLORATION

To assess your mastery of the material in this chapter, see the Online Study Guide at **bedfordstmartins.com/hunt**.

To read additional primary-source material from this period, see Chapter 7 in *Sources of The Making of the West*, Second Edition.

The Heirs of the Roman Empire, 600–750

ACCORDING TO A WRITER who was not very sympathetic to the Byzantines, one night Emperor Heraclius♦ (r. 610–641) had a dream: "Verily [he was told] there shall come against thee a circumcised nation, and they shall vanquish thee and take possession of the land." Heraclius thought the vision foretold an uprising of the Jews, and he ordered mass baptisms in all his provinces. "But," continued the story,

> *after a few days there appeared a man of the Arabs, from the southern districts, that is to say, from Mecca or its neighborhood, whose name was Muhammad; and he brought back the worshipers of idols to the knowledge of the One God.... And he took possession of Damascus and Syria, and crossed the Jordan and dammed it up. And the Lord abandoned the army of the Romans before him.*

This tale, however fanciful, recalls the most astonishing development of the seventh century: the Arabs conquered much of the Roman Empire and became one of its heirs. The western and eastern parts of the empire, both diminished, were now joined by yet a third power—Arab and Muslim. The resulting triad has endured in various guises to the present day: the western third of the old Roman Empire became western Europe; the eastern third, occupying what is now Turkey, Greece, and some of the Balkans, became part of eastern Europe and helped to create Russia; and North Africa, together with the ancient Near East (now called the Middle East), remains the Arab world.

As diverse as these cultures are today, they share many of the same roots. All were heirs of Hellenistic and Roman traditions. All adhered to monotheism. The western and eastern halves of the empire had Christianity in common, although they differed at times

---

♦**Heraclius:** hehr uh KLY uhs

Mosque at Damascus
Islam conquered the Byzantines, then Islam was "conquered" in turn by Byzantine culture. For the grand mosque at Damascus, his capital city, the Umayyad caliph al-Walid employed mosaicists trained in the Byzantine style. They depicted classical motifs—buildings, animals, vegetation—but scrupulously avoided depicting human beings, in this way conforming to one strand of Islamic thought that argued against figural representations. *(Detail) Jean-Louis Nou.*

in interpreting it. The Arab world's religion, Islam, accepted the same one God that Christians did but considered Jesus one of God's prophets rather than his son.

The history of the seventh and eighth centuries is a story of adaptation and transformation. Historians consider the changes important enough to signal the end of one era—antiquity—and the beginning of another—the Middle Ages. (See "Terms of History," page 286.) During this period, all three heirs of the Roman Empire combined elements of their heritage with new values, interests, and conditions. The divergences among them resulted from disparities in geographical and climatic conditions, material and human resources, skills, and local traditions. But these differences should not obscure the fact that the Byzantine, Muslim, and western European worlds were sibling cultures.

❖ Byzantium: A Christian Empire under Siege

Emperor Justinian (r. 527–565) had tried to re-create the old Roman Empire. On the surface he succeeded. His empire once again included Italy, North Africa, and the Balkans. Vestiges of old Roman society persisted: an educated elite maintained its prestige, town governments continued to function, and old myths and legends were retold in poetry and depicted on silver plates and chests. By 600, however, the Byzantine Empire began to undergo a transformation as striking as the one that had earlier remade the western half. Almost constant war beginning in the last third of the sixth century shrank Byzantium's territory drastically. Cultural and political change came as well. Cities decayed, and the countryside became the focus of governmental and military administration. In the wake of these shifts, the old elite largely disappeared and classical learning gave way to new forms of education, mainly religious in content. The traditional styles of urban life, dependent on public gathering places and community spirit, faded away.

Wars on the Frontiers, c. 570–750

From about 570 to 750, the Byzantine Empire waged war against invaders. One key challenge came from an old enemy, Persia. Another involved many new groups—Lombards, Slavs, Avars,❖ Bulgars, and Muslims. In the wake of these onslaughts, Byzantium was transformed.

Invasions from Persia. The **Sassanid**❖ **Empire** of Persia was the superpower on the Byzantine doorstep. Since the third century, the Sassanid kings and Roman emperors had fought sporadically but never with decisive effect on either side. But in the middle of the sixth century, the Sassanids chose to concentrate their activities on their western half, Mesopotamia (today Iraq), nearer the Byzantine border (Map 8.1). They began to collect land taxes from the prosperous farmers of the

❖**Avars:** AY vahrz
❖**Sassanid:** suh SAH nihd

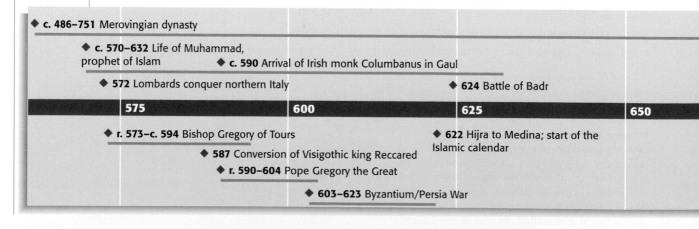

❖ **c. 486–751** Merovingian dynasty

❖ **c. 570–632** Life of Muhammad, prophet of Islam

❖ **c. 590** Arrival of Irish monk Columbanus in Gaul

❖ **572** Lombards conquer northern Italy

❖ **624** Battle of Badr

| 575 | 600 | 625 | 650 |

❖ **r. 573–c. 594** Bishop Gregory of Tours

❖ **622** Hijra to Medina; start of the Islamic calendar

❖ **587** Conversion of Visigothic king Reccared

❖ **r. 590–604** Pope Gregory the Great

❖ **603–623** Byzantium/Persia War

MAP 8.1 Byzantine and Sassanid Empires, c. 600
Justinian hoped to re-create the old Roman Empire, but just a century after his death Italy was largely conquered by the Lombards. Meanwhile, the Byzantine Empire had to contend with the Sassanid Empire to its east. In 600, these two major powers faced each other uneasily. Three years later, the Sassanid king attacked Byzantine territory. The resulting wars, which lasted until 627, exhausted both empires and left them open to invasion by the Arabs.

region, assuring their government of a steady, predictable income and turning Persia into a center of trade. Reforming the army, which previously had depended on nobles who could supply their own arms, the Sassanid kings began to pay and arm new warriors, drawn from the lower nobility.

The Sassanid rulers constructed their capital city at Ctesiphon◆ on the model of the great Byzantine city of Antioch (in fact, they gave it the title "Better-than-Antioch"). There they set up a bureaucracy of scribes tied to

◆**Ctesiphon:** TEH suh fahn

◆ **661–750** Umayyad caliphate

◆ **664** Synod of Whitby; English king adopts Roman Christianity

| **675** | **700** | **725** | **750** |

◆ **726–787** Period of iconoclasm at Byzantium

TERMS OF HISTORY

Medieval

How did the word *medieval* come into being, and why is it a derogatory term today? No one who lived in the Middle Ages thought of herself as "medieval." No one thought he lived in the "Middle Ages." The whole idea of the Middle Ages began in the sixteenth century. At that time, writers decided that their own age, known as the Renaissance (French for "rebirth"), and the ancient Greek and Roman civilizations were much alike. They dubbed the thousand-year period nearly in between—from about 600 to about 1400—with a Latin term: the *medium aevum,* or the "middle age." It was not a flattering term. Renaissance writers considered the middle age a single unfortunate, barbaric, and ignorant period.

Only with the Romantic movement of the nineteenth century and the advent of history as an academic discipline did writers begin to divide that middle age into several ages. Often, they divided it into three periods: early (c. 600–1100), high (c. 1100–1300), and late (c. 1300–1400). This categorization revealed a bias: the "high Middle Ages" was clearly considered more important—higher—than what came before or after. In the view of nineteenth-century historians, the high Middle Ages was important for two reasons. First, it saw the beginnings of modern institutions such as the common law, universities, and centralized states. Second, it fostered the development of typically medieval yet highly regarded institutions such as the Crusades, Gothic cathedrals, and scholasticism.

The period before the high Middle Ages was sometimes called the Dark Ages, a term that immediately brings to mind doom and gloom. The period after the high Middle Ages was more problematic for historians because the fourteenth century was not just the end of the Middle Ages but also the period in which the Renaissance began. Historians tended (and still tend) to ignore this fact. Instead, they fix on certain events, developments, and ideas within the period. If these seem modern and new—such as the rise of humanism and the development of diplomacy—historians call them part of the Renaissance. But if they seem retrograde or old—such as the ecstasies of mystics or knightly warfare—historians tend to call them late medieval.

One of the most remarkable recent developments in historians' view of the Middle Ages concerns the early Middle Ages. Since cultures in the period from about 400 to about 1100, with few exceptions, lacked centralized governments, organized institutions of higher learning, and well-developed legal systems, historians of the old school found little to praise in that time. However, in the 1960s some historians came to see the early Middle Ages differently. Rather than applaud the high Middle Ages for its bureaucratic states and its laws, they relished the variety of peoples, the informal methods of government, and the community involvement evident in the society of the early Middle Ages.

Today, newspaper reporters and others still sometimes use *medieval* as a pejorative term, for example, by calling a primitive prison system medieval. Little do they know that using the term in this way is as out-of-date as it was in the sixteenth century.

FURTHER READING

Freedman, Paul, and Gabrielle Spiegel. "Medievalisms Old and New: The Rediscovery of Alterity in North American Medieval Studies." *American Historical Review* 103 (1998): 677–704.

Little, Lester K., and Barbara H. Rosenwein. *Debating the Middle Ages: Issues and Readings.* 1998.

them by job and loyalty. They cultivated other writers and writings as well and thus opened their court to Byzantine and other Western influences and teachings. This openness accorded with their policy of maintaining good relations with the native population in Mesopotamia, many of whom were Nestorian Christians (see page 297), even though the Sassanid kings themselves still adhered to Zoroastrianism (see page 297).

These kings promoted an exalted view of themselves. They took the title "King of Kings" and gave the men at their court titles such as "priest of priests" and "scribe of scribes." (See A Sassanid King.) Royal glory was accompanied by military and imperial dreams. The Sassanid king Chosroes◆ II (r. 591–628) wanted to re-create the Persian empire of Xerxes and Darius, which had extended down through Syria all the way to Egypt. He began by invading the Byzantine Empire in 603, taking Damascus, Jerusalem, and even Egypt by 619. But the Byzantine emperor Heraclius reorganized his army and inspired his troops to avenge the sack of Jerusalem; by 627, the Byzantines had regained all their lost territory. The chief outcome of these fruitless confrontations was exhaustion on both sides.

Attack on All Fronts. Because Byzantium was preoccupied by war with the Sassanids, it was ill equipped to deal with other groups pushing into parts of the empire at about the same time (see Map 8.1). The Lombards, a Germanic people, arrived in northern Italy in 568 and by 572 were masters of the Po valley and some inland regions in Italy's south, leaving the Byzantines only Bari, Calabria, and Sicily as well as Rome and a narrow swath of land through the middle called the Exarchate◆ of Ravenna.

The Byzantine army could not contend any more successfully with the Slavs and other peoples just beyond the Danube River.

◆**Chosroes:** KAHZ ruh eez
◆**Exarchate:** EHKS ar kate

A Sassanid King
His head topped by a mighty horned headdress, this representation of a Sassanid ruler evokes the full majesty of a king of kings. A glance at "The Great King of Persia" on page 48 shows that traditional Persian sculpture was not, as here, in the round. The influence of Greek and Roman classical styles is evident in this sixth- or seventh-century bronze figure, despite the enmity between Sassanid Persia and Byzantium (heir of Greece and Rome) at the time. *Louvre/Agence Photographique de la réunion des musées nationaux.*

The Slavs conducted lightning raids on the Balkan countryside (part of Byzantium at the time); and, joined by the Avars, nomadic pastoralists and warriors, they attacked Byzantine cities as well. Meanwhile the Bulgars entered what is now Bulgaria in the 670s, defeating the Byzantine army and in 681 forcing the emperor to recognize their new state.

At the same time as the Byzantine Empire was being attacked on all fronts, its power was being whittled away by more peaceful means. For example, as Slavs and Avars, who were not subject to Byzantine rulers, settled in the Balkans, they often intermingled with the indigenous population, absorbing local agricultural techniques and burial practices while imposing their language and establishing religious cults.

Consequences of Constant Warfare. Byzantium's loss of control over the Balkans through both peaceful and military means meant the shrinking of its empire. More important over the long term was that the Balkans could no longer serve, as they had previously, as a major conduit between Byzantium and Europe. The loss of the Balkans exacerbated the increasing separation of the eastern and western parts of the former Roman Empire. The political division between the Greek-speaking and Latin-speaking halves had already begun in the fourth century. The events of the seventh century, however, made the split both physical and cultural. Avar and Slavic control of the Balkans effectively cut off trade and travel between Constantinople and the cities of the Dalmatian coast, while the Bulgar state threw a political barrier across the Danube. Perhaps as a result of this physical separation, Byzantine historians ceased to be interested in Europe, and Byzantine scholars no longer bothered to learn Latin. The two halves of the former Roman Empire, once united, communicated very little in the seventh century.

The principal outcome of Byzantium's wars with the Sassanid Empire was the sap-

ping of both Persian and Byzantine military strength. Exhausted, these empires were now vulnerable to attack by the Arabs, whose military prowess would create a new empire and spread a new religion, Islam. In the hundred years between 630 and 730, the Arabs succeeded in conquering much of the Byzantine Empire, at times attacking the very walls of Constantinople itself. No wonder the patriarch of Jerusalem saw in the Arab onslaught the impending end of the world: "Behold," he said, "the Abomination of Desolation, spoken of by the Prophet Daniel, that standeth in the Holy Place."

TAKING MEASURE

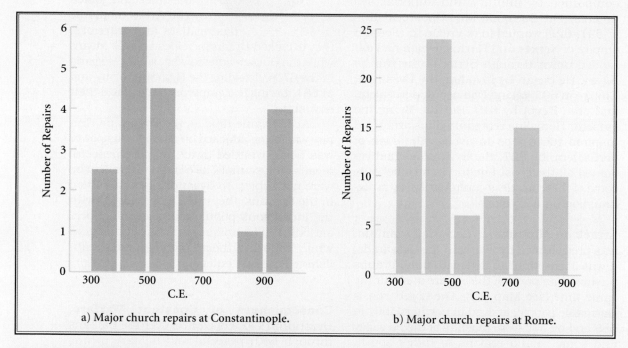

a) Major church repairs at Constantinople.

b) Major church repairs at Rome.

Church Repair, 600–900
The impoverishment of the period 600–750 is clear from graph (a), which shows a major slump in church repair at Constantinople during the period. If there had been any money to spend on building repairs, it would undoubtedly have gone to the churches first. By contrast, graph (b) shows that Rome was not so hard hit as Constantinople, even though it was part of the Byzantine Empire. There was, to be sure, a dramatic reduction in the number of church repairs in the period 500–600. But from 700 to 800, there was a clear, if small, increase. Taken together, the two graphs help show the toll taken by the invasions and financial hardships of the period 600–750. *Data adapted from Klavs Randsborg, "The Migration Period: Model History and Treasure,"* The Sixth Century: Production, Distribution and Demand, *eds. Richard Hodges and William Bowden (Leiden: Brill, 1998).*

From an Urban to a Rural Way of Life

As their borders shrank, Byzantines had to contend with new rulers and learn to accommodate to them. When Byzantine subjects in Syria and Egypt found themselves under Arab rule, they adapted to the new conditions, paying a special tax to their conquerors and practicing their Christian and Jewish religions in peace. In the countryside they were permitted to keep and farm their lands, and their cities remained centers of government, scholarship, and business.

Ironically, the most radical transformations for seventh- and eighth-century Byzantines occurred not in the territories lost but in the shrunken empire itself. Under the ceaseless barrage of invaders, many towns, formerly bustling nodes of trade and centers of the imperial bureaucratic network, vanished or became unrecognizable in their changed way of life. The public activity of large, open marketplaces, theaters, and town squares largely ended. City baths, once places where people gossiped, made deals, and talked politics and philosophy, disappeared in most Byzantine towns—with the significant exception of Constantinople. Warfare reduced some cities to rubble, and the limited resources available for rebuilding went to construct thick city walls and solid churches instead of marketplaces and baths. Traders and craftspeople moved to overcrowded streets that looked much like the open-air bazaars of the modern Middle East. People under siege sought protection at home or in a church rather than in community pastimes. One example is the Byzantine city of Ephesus,♦ where the citizens who built the new walls in the seventh century enclosed not the old public edifices but rather their homes and churches (Map 8.2). Despite the new emphasis on church buildings, many cities were too impoverished even to repair their churches. (See Taking Measure on page 288)

The pressures of war against the Arabs brought a change in Byzantine society parallel to that in the western half of the empire a few centuries before. Above all the class of town councilors (the *curiales*), the elite that

♦**Ephesus:** EH fuh suhs

MAP 8.2 Diagram of the City of Ephesus
The center of classical Ephesus had been the agora and the embolos (a wide street paved with marble and rimmed by shops and monuments). After the seventh century, the city was partially destroyed, its population declined, and the rebuilt city—without agora or embolos—was located to the north and protected by walls.

for centuries had mediated between the emperor and the people, disappeared. But an upper class nevertheless remained: as in western Europe, bishops and their clergy continued to form a rich and powerful upper stratum even within declining cities.

Despite the general urban decay, the capital of Constantinople and a few other urban centers retained some of their old vitality. The manufacture and trade of fine silk textiles continued. Even though Byzantium's economic life became increasingly rural and barter-based in the seventh and eighth centuries, the skills, knowledge, and institutions of urban workers remained. The full use of these resources, however, had to await the end of centuries of debilitating wars.

As urban life declined, agriculture, always the basis of the Byzantine economy, became the center of its social life as well. But unlike in Europe, where an extremely rich and powerful elite dominated the agricultural economy, the Byzantine Empire of the seventh century was principally a realm of free and semi-free peasant farmers, who grew food, herded cattle, and tended vineyards on small plots of land. In the shadow of decaying urban centers, the social world of the farmer was narrow. Two or three neighbors were enough to ratify a land transfer. Farmers interacted mostly with members of their families or with monks at local monasteries. On the other hand, when they came into contact with the state—to pay taxes, for example—they missed the protective buffer once provided by the curial class. Rural farmers now felt directly the impact of the emperor or his representatives.

The emphasis on local, domestic life was encouraged by emperors for both financial and religious reasons. Imperial legislation gave the nuclear family new institutional importance, narrowing the grounds for divorce and setting new punishments for marital infidelity. Husbands and wives who committed adultery were whipped and fined, and their noses were slit. Abortion was prohibited, and new protections were set in place against incest. Mothers were given equal power with fathers over their offspring and, if widowed, became the legal guardians of their minor children and controlled the household property.

New Military and Cultural Forms

The transformations of the countryside went hand in hand with military, political, and cultural changes. On the military front, the Byzantine navy found a potent weapon in "Greek fire," a combustible oil that floated on water and burst into flames upon hitting its target. Determined to win wars on land as well, the imperial government exercised greater autocratic control, hastening the decline of the curial class, wresting power from other elite families, and encouraging the formation of a middle class of farmer-soldiers.

David and Goliath
This large silver plate, nearly twenty inches in diameter, was made at Cyprus, a part of the Byzantine empire, in the first third of the seventh century. It formed part of a series of nine such plates, all showing scenes from the life of the biblical hero David. Here, in the center panel, armed only with his slingshot, David fights the champion of the Philistines, Goliath. In the bottom third, he cuts off Goliath's head. As the author of the Psalms, a king of Israel, and a victor in the battle against the Philistines, David was a particularly important figure for people whose education was largely religious.
Photograph © 2000 The Metropolitan Museum of Art.

In the seventh century an emperor, possibly Heraclius, divided the empire into military districts called *themes* and put all civil as well as military matters in each district into the hands of one general, a *strategos* (plural, *strategoi*). Landless men were lured to join the army with the promise of land and low taxes; they fought side by side with local farmers, who provided their own weapons and horses. The new organization effectively countered frontier attacks.

The new emphasis on the rural world affected Byzantine education and culture. Whereas the old curial elite had cultivated the study of the pagan classics, sending their children (above all, their sons) to schools or tutors to learn to read the works of Greek poets and philosophers, eighth-century parents showed far more interest in giving their children, both sons and daughters, a religious education. Even with the decay of urban centers, cities and villages often retained an elementary school. There teachers used the Book of Psalms (the Psalter) as their primer. Throughout the seventh and eighth centuries, secular, classical learning remained decidedly out of favor, whereas dogmatic writings, biographies of saints, and devotional works took center stage.

Religion, Politics, and Iconoclasm

The importance placed on religious learning and piety complemented both the autocratic imperial ideal and the powers of the bishops in the seventh century. Since the spiritual and secular realms were understood to be inseparable, the bishops wielded political power in their cities, while Byzantine emperors ruled as both religious and political figures. In theory, imperial and church power were separate but interdependent. In fact, the emperor exercised considerable power over the church; he influenced the appointment of the chief religious official, the patriarch of Constantinople; he called church councils to determine dogma; and he regularly used bishops as local governors. Beginning with Heraclius, the emperors considered it one of their duties to baptize Jews forcibly, persecuting those who would not convert. In the view of the imperial court, this was part of the ruler's role in upholding orthodoxy.

Powerful Bishops and Monks. Bishops functioned as state administrators in their cities. They acted as judges and tax collectors. They distributed food in times of famine or siege, provisioned troops, and set up military fortifications. As part of their charitable work, they cared for the sick and the needy. Byzantine bishops were part of a three-tier system: they were appointed by metropolitans, bishops who headed an entire province; and the metropolitans, in turn, were appointed by the patriarchs, bishops with authority over whole regions.

Theoretically, monasteries were under the limited control of the local bishop, but in fact they were enormously powerful institutions that often defied the authority of bishops and even emperors. Because monks commanded immense prestige as the holiest of God's faithful, they could influence the many issues of church doctrine that racked the Byzantine church.

Conflict over Icons. The most important issue of the Byzantine church in this period revolved around icons. Icons are images of holy people—Christ, his mother (Mary), and the saints (see the image, Icon of Virgin and Child, on this page). To Byzantine Christians,

Icon of Virgin and Child

Surrounded by two angels in the back and two soldier-saints at either side, the Virgin Mary and the Christ Child are depicted with still, otherworldly dignity. Working with hot pigmented beeswax, the sixth-century artist gave the angels transparent halos to emphasize their spiritual natures, while depicting the saints as earthly men, with hair and beards, and feet planted firmly on the ground. Icons such as this were used in private worship as well as in the religious life of Byzantine monasteries.

icons were far more than mere representations. They were believed to possess holy power that directly affected people's daily lives as well as their chances for salvation.

Many seventh-century Byzantines made icons the focus of their religious devotion. To them, the images were like the incarnation of Christ: they turned spirit into material substance. Thus, an icon manifested in physical form the holy person it depicted. Some

Byzantines actually worshiped icons; others, particularly monks, considered icons a necessary part of Christian piety. As the monk St. John of Damascus put it in a vigorous defense of holy images, "I do not worship matter, I worship the God of matter, who became matter for my sake, and deigned to inhabit matter, who worked out my salvation through matter."

Other Byzantines abhorred icons. Most numerous of these were the soldiers on the frontiers. Shocked by Arab triumphs, they found the cause of their misfortunes in the biblical injunction against graven images. When they compared their defeats to Muslim successes, they could not help but notice that Islam prohibited all representations of the divine. To these soldiers and others who shared their view, icons revived pagan idolatry and desecrated Christian divinity. As iconoclastic (anti-icon or, literally, icon-breaking) feeling grew, some churchmen became outspoken in their opposition to icons.

Byzantine emperors shared these religious objections, and they also had important political reasons for opposing icons. In fact, the issue of icons became a test of their authority. Icons diffused loyalties, setting up intermediaries between worshipers and God that undermined the emperor's exclusive place in the divine and temporal order. In addition, the emphasis on icons in monastic communities made the monks potential threats to imperial power; the emperors hoped to use this issue to break the power of the monasteries. Above all, though, the emperors opposed icons because the army did, and they wanted to support their troops.

After Emperor Leo III the Isaurian (r. 717–741) had defeated the Arabs besieging Constantinople at the beginning of his reign, he turned his attention to consolidating his political position. Officers of the imperial court tore down the great golden icon of Christ at the gateway of the palace and replaced it with a cross, while a crowd of women protested by going on a furious rampage in support of icons. But Leo would not budge. In 726 he ordered all icons destroyed, a ban that remained in effect, despite much opposition, until 787. This is known as the period of **iconoclasm** in Byzantine history. A modified ban would be revived in 815 and last until 843.

Iconoclasm had an enormous impact on daily life. At home, where people had their own portable icons, it forced changes in private worship: the devout had to destroy their icons or worship them in secret. The ban on icons meant ferocious attacks on the monasteries: splendid collections of holy images were destroyed; vast properties were confiscated; and monks, who were staunch defenders of icons, were ordered to marry and give up their vocation. In this way iconoclasm destroyed communities that might otherwise have served as centers of resistance to imperial power. Reorganized and reoriented, the Byzantine rulers were able to maintain themselves against the onslaught of the Arabs, who attacked under the banner of Islam.

> **Review:** What stresses did the Byzantine Empire endure in the seventh and eighth centuries, and how was iconoclasm a response to those stresses?

❖ Islam: A New Religion and a New Empire

In the sixth century, Arabia, today Saudi Arabia, witnessed the rise of Islam, a religion that called on all to submit to the will of one God. Islam, which means "submission to God," emerged under Muhammad (c. 570–632), a merchant-turned-holy-man from the city of Mecca. While the great majority of people living in Arabia were polytheists, Muhammad recognized one God, the same one worshiped by the Jews and the Christians. He saw himself as God's last prophet—and thus he is called the Prophet—the person to receive and in turn repeat God's final words to humans. Invited by the disunited and pagan people of the city of Medina to come and act as a mediator for them, Muhammad exercised the powers of both a religious and a secular leader. This dual role became the model for his successors, known as caliphs.◆ Through a combination of persuasion and force, Muhammad and his co-

---

◆**caliph:** KAY luhf

religionists, the Muslims, converted most of the Arabian peninsula. By the time Muhammad died in 632, conquest and conversion had begun to move northward, into Byzantine and Persian territories. In the next generation, the Arabs conquered most of Persia and all of Egypt and were on their way across North Africa to Spain. Yet within the territories they conquered, daily life went on much as before.

The Desert and the Cities

Before the seventh century, the great deserts of the Arabian peninsula were sparsely populated by Bedouins.◆ These were nomads who lived in tribes—loose confederations of clans, or kin groups—herding flocks for meat and milk and trading (or raiding) for grain, dates, and slaves. Poor tribes herded sheep, whereas richer ones kept camels—extremely hardy animals, splendid beasts of burden, and good producers of milk and meat. (*Arab* was the name camel nomads called themselves.)

Tribal makeup shifted as kin groups joined or left. Though continually changing, these associations nevertheless saw outsiders as rivals, and tribes constantly fought with one another. Yet this very rivalry was itself an outgrowth of shared values. Bedouin men prized "manliness," which meant far more than sexual prowess. They strove to be brave in battle and feared being shamed. Manliness also entailed an obligation to be generous, to give away the booty that was the goal of intertribal warfare. Women were often part of this booty, for Bedouins practiced polygyny (having more than one wife at the same time). Bedouin wars rarely involved much bloodshed; their main purpose was to capture people and take belongings.

Tribal, nomadic existence produced its own culture, including an Arabic poetry of striking delicacy, precision, and beauty. In the absence of written language, the Bedouins used oral poetry and storytelling to transmit their traditions, simultaneously entertaining, reaffirming values, and teaching new generations.

Dotting the Bedouins' desert world were cities that arose around oases—fertile, green areas. Here more settled forms of life and trade took place. Mecca, near the Red Sea, was one such commercial center. Meccan caravans crisscrossed the peninsula, selling slaves and spices. More important, Mecca played an important religious role because it contained a shrine, the Ka'ba. Long before Muhammad was born, the Ka'ba, a great rock surrounded by the images of 360 gods, served as a sacred place within which war and violence were prohibited. The tribe that dominated Mecca, the Quraysh,◆ controlled access to the shrine and was able to tax the pilgrims who flocked there as well as sell them food and drink. In turn, plunder was transformed into trade as the visitors bartered with one another on the sacred grounds, assured of their security.

The Prophet Muhammad and the Faith of Islam

Mecca, the birthplace of Muhammad, was a center with two important traditions—one religious, the other commercial. Muhammad's early years were inauspicious: orphaned at the age of six, he spent two years with his grandfather and then came under the care of his uncle, a leader of the Quraysh tribe. Eventually, Muhammad became a trader. At the age of twenty-five, he married Khadija, a rich widow who had once employed him. They had at least four daughters and lived (to all appearances) happily and comfortably. Yet Muhammad sometimes left home and spent some time on the nearby Mount Hira, devoting himself to prayer and contemplation.

In about 610, on one of these retreats, Muhammad heard a voice and had a vision that summoned him to worship Allah, the God of the Jews and Christians. (*Allah* means "the God" in Arabic.) He accepted the call as coming from God. Over the next years he received messages that he understood to be divine revelation. Later, when they had been written down and arranged—a process that was completed in the seventh century, but after Muhammad's death—these messages

◆**Bedouins:** BEHD oo ihns

◆**Quraysh:** kur RAYSH

Qur'an

More than a holy book, the Qur'an represents for Muslims the very words of God that were dictated to Muhammad by the angel Gabriel. Generally the Qur'an was written on pages wider than long, perhaps to differentiate it from other books. This example dates from the seventh or eighth century. It is written in Kufic script, a formal and majestic form of Arabic that was used for the Qur'an until the eleventh century. The round floral decoration on the right-hand page marks a new section of the text. *Property of the Ambrosian Library. All rights reserved.*

became the Qur'an,◆ the holy book of Islam. (See pages of a Qur'an above.) *Qur'an* means "recitation"; each of its chapters, or *suras,* is understood to be God's revelation as told to Muhammad by the archangel Gabriel, then recited in turn by Muhammad to others. It begins with the Fatihah, frequently also said as an independent prayer, and continues with suras of gradually decreasing length, which cover the gamut of human experience and the life to come (see "The Fatihah of the Qur'an," page 295). For Muslims (literally, "those who submit to Islam") the Qur'an contains the foundations of history, prophecy, and the legal and moral code by which men and women should live: "Do not set up another god with God.... Do not worship anyone but Him, and be good to your parents.... Give to your relatives what is their due, and to those who are needy, and the wayfarers."

The Qur'an emphasizes the nuclear family—a man, his wife (or wives), and children—as the basic unit of Muslim society. Islam cuts its adherents adrift from the protection and particularism of the tribe but gives them in return an identity as part of the **ummah**, the community of believers, who share both a belief in one God and a set of religious practices. Islam stresses individual belief in God and adherence to the Qur'an. Thus, Muslims have no priests, no mass, and no intermediaries between the divine and the individual. However, Islam does rec-

ognize authorities whose interpretations of the Qur'an and related texts are considered decisive. The Ka'ba, with its many gods, had gathered together tribes from the surrounding vicinity. Muhammad, with his one God, forged an even more universal religion.

Growth of Islam, c. 610–632

First to convert to Muhammad's faith was his wife, Khadija; then a few friends and members of his immediate family joined him; and, as Muhammad preached the new faith, eventually some others became adherents. Soon, however, the new faith polarized Meccan society. Muhammad's insistence that the cults of all other gods be abandoned in favor of one brought him into conflict with leading clan members of the Quraysh tribe, whose control over the Ka'ba, a polytheistic shrine, had given them prestige and wealth. Lacking political means to expel him, they insulted Muhammad and harassed his adherents.

Hijra: Journey to Medina. Disillusioned with Mecca and angry with his own tribe, Muhammad tried to find a place and a population receptive to his message. Most important, he expected support from Jews, whose monotheism, in Muhammad's view, prepared them for his own faith. When a few of Muhammad's converts from Medina promised to protect him if he would join them there, he eagerly accepted the invitation, in part because Medina had a significant Jewish popu-

◆**Qur'an:** Kur AN/Koo RAHN

lation. In 622, Muhammad made the **Hijra,**◆ or emigration, to Medina, an oasis about two hundred miles north of Mecca. This journey proved a crucial event for the fledgling movement. At Medina, Muhammad found followers ready to listen to his religious message and to regard him as the leader of their community. They expected him to act as a neutral and impartial judge in their interclan disputes. Muhammad's political position in the community set the pattern by which Islamic society would be governed afterward; rather than adding a church to political and cultural life, Muslims made their political and religious institutions inseparable. After Muhammad's death, the year of the Hijra was named the first year of the Islamic calendar; it marked the beginning of the new Islamic era.[1]

Although successful at Medina, the Muslims felt threatened by the Quraysh at Mecca, who actively opposed the public practice of Islam. For this reason Muhammad led raids against them. At the battle of Badr◆ in 624, aided by their position near an oasis, Muhammad and his followers killed forty-nine of the Meccan enemy, took numerous prisoners, and confiscated rich booty. At the battle of Badr, Bedouin plundering was grafted onto the Muslim duty of jihad (literally, "striving").[2]

The battle of Badr was a great triumph for Muhammad, who was now able to consolidate his position at Medina, gaining new adherents and silencing all doubters, including the Jews. Muhammad had first seen the Jews of Medina as allies, but they had not converted to Islam as he had expected. Suspecting them of supporting his enemies, Muhammad expelled two Jewish tribes from Medina and killed the male members of another. Although Muslims had originally prayed in the direction of Jerusalem, the center of Jewish worship, Muhammad now had them turn in the direction of Mecca.

---

[1]Thus, 1 A.H. (1 *anno Hegirae*) on the Muslim calendar is equivalent to 622 C.E.

[2]*Jihad* means "striving" and is used in particular in the context of striving against unbelievers. In that sense, it is often translated as "holy war." But it can also mean striving against one's worst impulses.

◆**Hijra:** HID jruh
◆**Badr:** BAHD ihr

The Fatihah of the Qur'an

The Fatihah (or Prologue) is the prayer that begins the Qur'an. It emphasizes God's oneness and the believer's recourse to God alone, without intermediaries of any sort. The "path that is straight" is the path of right worship.

The Fatihah
In the name of Allah, most benevolent, ever-merciful
All praise be to Allah
Lord of all the worlds,
2. Most beneficent, ever-merciful,
3. King of the Day of Judgement.
4. You alone we worship, and to You alone turn for help.
5. Guide us (O Lord) to the path that is straight,
6. The path of those You have blessed,
7. Not of those who have earned Your anger, nor those who have gone astray.

Source: *Al-Qur'an: A Contemporary Translation*, trans. Ahmed Ali (Princeton: Princeton University Press, 1993), 11.

Defining the Faith. As Muhammad broke with the Jews, he instituted new practices to define Islam as a unique religion. Among these were the *zakat*, a tax on possessions to be used for alms; the fast of Ramadan, which took place during the ninth month of the Islamic year, the month in which the battle of Badr had been fought; the *hajj*, the pilgrimage to Mecca during the last month of the year, which each Muslim was to make once in his lifetime; and the *salat*, formal worship at least three times a day (later increased to five), which could include the *shahadah*, or profession of faith—"There is no divinity but God, and Muhammad is the messenger of God." Detailed regulations for these practices, sometimes called the five pillars of Islam, were worked out in the eighth and early ninth centuries.

Meanwhile, Muhammad sent troops to subdue Arabs north and south. In 630, he entered Mecca with ten thousand men and took over the city, assuring the Quraysh of leniency and offering alliances with its leaders. By this time the prestige of Islam was enough to convince clans elsewhere to convert. Through a combination of force, conversion, and negotiation, Muhammad was able to unite many, though by no means all, Arabic-speaking tribes under his leadership by the time of his death two years later.

In so doing, Muhammad brought about important social transformations. The ummah included not only men but also women; as a result, women's status was enhanced. Islam prohibited all infanticide, a practice that had long been used largely against female infants; and at first, Muslim women joined men during the prayer periods that punctuated the day. Men were allowed to have up to four wives at one time, but they were obliged to treat them equally; their wives received dowries and had certain inheritance rights. But beginning in the eighth century, women began to pray apart from the men. Like Judaism and Christianity, Islam retained the practices of a patriarchal society in which women's participation in community life was circumscribed.

Even though Islamic society was a new sort of community, in many ways it did function as a tribe, or rather a "supertribe," obligated to fight common enemies, share plunder, and resolve peacefully any internal disputes. Muslims participated in group rituals, such as the salat and public recitation. The Qur'an was soon publicly sung by professional reciters, much as the old tribal poetry had been. Most significant for the eventual spread of Islam, Muslim men continued to be warriors. They took up where Meccan traders had been forced to leave off; along the routes once taken by caravans to Syria, their armies reaped

MAP 8.3 Expansion of Islam to 750
In little more than a century, Islamic armies conquered a vast region that included numerous different people, cultures, climates, and living conditions. Yet under the Umayyads, these disparate territories were administered by one ruler from the capital city at Damascus. The uniting force was the religion of Islam, which gathered all believers into one community, the *ummah*.

profits at the point of a sword. But this differed from intertribal fighting; it was the jihad of people who were carrying out the injunction of God against unbelievers. "Strive, O Prophet," says the Qur'an, "against the unbelievers and the hypocrites, and deal with them firmly. Their final abode is Hell: And what a wretched destination!"

The Caliphs, Muhammad's Successors, 632–750

In founding a new political community in Arabia, Muhammad reorganized traditional Arab society as he cut across clan allegiances and welcomed converts from every tribe. He forged the Muslims into a formidable military force, and his successors, the caliphs, moved into the Byzantine and Persian worlds, taking them by storm.

War and Conquest. To the west, the Muslims easily took Byzantine territory in Syria and moved into Egypt in the 640s (Map 8.3). To the east, they invaded the Sassanid Empire, defeating the Persians at the very gates of their capital, Ctesiphon, in 637. The whole of Persia was in Muslim hands by 651. During the last half of the seventh century and the beginning of the eighth, Islamic warriors extended their sway to Spain (in the west) and to India (in the east).

How were such conquests possible, especially in so short a time? First, the Islamic forces came up against weakened empires. The Byzantine and Sassanid states were exhausted from fighting each other. The cities of the Middle East that had been taken by the Persians and retaken by the Byzantines were depopulated, their few survivors burdened with heavy taxes. Second, the Muslims were welcomed into both Byzantine and Sassanid territories by discontented groups. Many Monophysite Christians (see p. 276) in Syria and Egypt had suffered persecution under the Byzantines and were glad to have new, Islamic overlords. In Persia, Jews, Monophysites, and Nestorian Christians were at best irrelevant to the Zoroastrian King of Kings and his regime. These were the external reasons for Islamic success. There were also internal reasons. Arabs had long been used to intertribal warfare; now they were

Arab Coin
The Arabs learned coinage and minting from those whom they conquered—the Persians and the Byzantines. Although one branch of Islam barred depicting the human form, others were less condemning. Thus, the Umayyads saw nothing wrong with imitating traditional numismatic models. The ruler depicted on this silver coin wears a headdress that echoes the one worn by the Sassanid ruler depicted on page 287. The word for this type of coin, *dirham,* is Greek, from *drachma.* The Umayyad fiscal system, which retained the old Roman land tax, was administered by Syrians, who had often served Byzantine rulers in the same capacity. *The British Museum.*

united as a supertribe. The tribes of the cities had been the first to convert to Islam; they then brought the Bedouins into the fold, consolidating all of Arabia under one Islamic state. Under the banner of jihad, these united tribes exercised their skills as warriors not against one another but rather against unbelievers. Fully armed, on horseback, employing camels as convoys, they conquered with amazing ease. Then, making their victories permanent, they built garrison cities from which soldiers requisitioned taxes and goods. Sometimes whole Arab tribes, including women and children, were imported to settle conquered territory, as happened in parts of Syria. In other regions, such as Egypt, a small Muslim settlement at Fustat sufficed to gather the spoils of conquest.

The Politics of Succession. Struck down by an illness in the midst of preparations for an invasion of Syria, Muhammad died quietly at Medina in 632. His death marked a crisis in the government of the new Islamic state and was the origin of tension between Shi'ite and Sunni Muslims that continues today. The choice of caliphs to follow Muhammad was difficult. They came not from the traditional tribal elite but rather from a new inner circle of men who had participated in the

Hijra and remained close to Muhammad. The first two caliphs ruled without serious opposition, but the third caliph, Uthman (r. 644–656), a member of the Umayyad✦ family and son-in-law (by marriage to two daughters) of Muhammad, aroused discontent among other clan members of the inner circle and soldiers unhappy with his distribution of high offices and revenues. Accusing Uthman of favoritism, they supported his rival, Ali, a member of the Hashim clan (to which Muhammad had belonged) and the husband of Muhammad's only surviving child, Fatimah. After a group of discontented soldiers murdered Uthman, civil war broke out between the Umayyads and Ali's faction. It ended when Ali was killed by one of his own erstwhile supporters, and the caliphate remained in Umayyad hands from 661 to 750.

Nevertheless, the *Shi'at Ali*, the faction of Ali, did not fade away. Ali's memory lived on among groups of Muslims (the Shi'ites) who saw in him a symbol of justice and righteousness. For them, Ali's death was the martyrdom of the only true successor to Muhammad. They remained faithful to his dynasty, shunning the mainstream caliphs of the other Muslims (Sunni Muslims, as they were later called, from *Sunna*, the practices of Muhammad). The Shi'ites awaited the arrival of the true leader—the imam—who in their view could come only from the house of Ali.

Under the **Umayyad caliphate**, which lasted from 661 to 750, the Muslim world became a state with its capital at Damascus, the historic capital of Syria—and today's as well. Borrowing from the institutions well known to the civilizations they had just conquered, the Muslims issued coins and hired former Byzantine and Persian officials. They made Arabic a tool of centralization, imposing it as the language of government on regions not previously united linguistically. For Byzantium, this period was one of unparalleled military crisis, the prelude to iconoclasm. For the Islamic world, now a multiethnic society of Muslim Arabs, Syrians, Egyptians, Iraqis, and other peoples, it was a period of settlement, new urbanism, and literary and artistic flowering.

✦**Umayyad:** oo MAH yuhd

Peace and Prosperity in Islamic Lands

Ironically, the Islamic warriors brought peace. While the conquerors stayed within their fortified cities or built magnificent hunting lodges in the deserts of Syria, the conquered went back to work, to study, to play, and—in the case of Christians and Jews, who were considered protected subjects—to worship as they pleased in return for the payment of a special tax. At Damascus, local artists and craftspeople worked on the lavish decorations for a mosque in a neoclassical style at the very moment Muslim armies were storming the walls of Constantinople. Leaving the Byzantine institutions in place, the Muslim conquerors allowed Christians and Jews to retain their posts and even protected dissidents.

During the seventh and eighth centuries, Muslim scholars wrote down the hitherto largely oral Arabic literature. They determined the definitive form for the Qur'an and compiled pious narratives about Muhammad (hadith literature). Scribes composed these works in exquisite handwriting; Arab calligraphy became an art form. A literate class, composed mainly of the old Persian and Syrian elite now converted to Islam, created new forms of prose writing in Arabic—official documents as well as essays on topics ranging from hunting to ruling. Umayyad poetry explored new worlds of thought and feeling. Patronized by the caliphs, who found in written poetry an important source of propaganda and a buttress for their power, the poets also reached a wider audience that delighted in their clever use of words, their satire, and their invocations of courage, piety, and sometimes erotic love:

> I spent the night as her bed-companion, each enamored of the other,
>
> And I made her laugh and cry, and stripped her of her clothes.
>
> I played with her and she vanquished me; I made her happy and I angered her.
>
> That was a night we spent, in my sleep, playing and joyful,
>
> But the caller to prayer woke me up.

Such poetry scandalized conservative Muslims, brought up on the ascetic tenets of the Qur'an. But this love poetry was a product of the new urban civilization of the Umayyad period, during which wealth, cultural mix, and the confidence born of conquest inspired diverse and experimental literary forms. By the close of the Umayyad period in 750, Islamic civilization was multiethnic, urban, and sophisticated, a true heir of Roman and Persian traditions.

> **Review:** How and why did the Muslims conquer so many lands in the very short period 632–750?

❖ Western Europe: A Medley of Kingdoms

With the demise of Roman imperial government in the western half of the empire, the region was divided into a number of kingdoms: various monarchs ruled in Spain, Italy, England, and Gaul. The primary foundations of power and stability in all of these kingdoms were kinship networks, church patronage, royal courts, and wealth derived from land and plunder. In contrast to Byzantium, where an emperor still ruled as the successor to Augustus and Constantine, drawing upon an unbroken chain of Roman legal and administrative traditions, political power in western Europe was more diffuse. There were kings, to be sure; but in some places churchmen and rich magnates were even more powerful than royalty. Power lodged too (as people believed) in the tombs and relics of saints, who represented and wielded the divine forces of God. Although the patterns of daily life and the procedures of government in western Europe remained recognizably Roman, they were also in the process of change,

borrowing from and adapting to local traditions and to the very powerful role of the Christian religion in every aspect of society.

Frankish Kingdoms with Roman Roots

The most important kingdoms in post-Roman Europe were Frankish. During the sixth century, the Franks had established themselves as dominant in Gaul, and by the seventh century the limits of their kingdoms roughly approximated the eastern borders of present-day France, Belgium, the Netherlands, and Luxembourg (Map 8.4). Moreover, the Frankish kings, known as the Merovingians♦ (the

♦**Merovingians:** Mehr oh VIN jians

MAP 8.4 The Merovingian Kingdoms in the Seventh Century
By the seventh century, there were three powerful Merovingian kingdoms: Neustria, Austrasia, and Burgundy. The important cities of Aquitaine were assigned to one of these major kingdoms, while Aquitaine as a whole was assigned to a duke or other governor. Kings did not establish capital cities; they did not even stay in one place. Rather, they continually traveled throughout their kingdoms, making their power felt in person.

TABLE 8.1   The Three Monotheistic Religions, c. 750*

RELIGION	FOUNDER/ PROPHET	CHIEF RELIGIOUS HEAD(S)	PLACE OF WORSHIP	IMPORTANT ELEMENTS OF WORSHIP	KEY RELIGIOUS TEXTS	MATERIAL AIDS TO WORSHIP
CHRISTIANITY Roman Catholic	Jesus	Bishops, increasingly pope at Rome	Church	Mass, prayer, fasting	Bible, especially the Psalms	Relics
Byzantine	Jesus	Patriarch of Constantinople	Church	Mass, prayer, fasting	Bible, especially the Psalms	Icons
JUDAISM	Abraham	Rabbis	Synagogue	Prayer, fasting	Hebrew Scriptures and rabbinic legal literature (Talmud)	Torah (first five books of the Bible)
ISLAM	Muhammad	Caliphs or, increasingly, religious scholars	Mosque	Prayer, fasting	Qur'an and commentaries on it	Qur'an

*None of these religions fixed remained in the form they had in 750. See Chapter 15, in particular, for changes in Christianity.

name of the dynasty derived from Merovech, a reputed ancestor), had subjugated many of the peoples beyond the Rhine, foreshadowing the contours of the western half of modern Germany. These northern and eastern regions were little Romanized, but the inhabitants of the rest of the Frankish kingdoms lived with the vestiges of Rome at their door.

Roman Ruins.   Travelers making a trip to Paris in the seventh century, perhaps on a pilgrimage to the tomb of St. Denis, would probably have relied on river travel, even though some Roman roads were still in fair repair. (They would have preferred water routes because land travel was very slow and because even large groups of travelers on the roads were vulnerable to attacks by robbers.) Like the roads, other structures in the landscape would have seemed familiarly Roman. Coming up the Rhône River from the south, voyagers would have passed Roman amphitheaters and farmlands neatly and squarely laid out by Roman land surveyors. The great stone palaces of villas would still

have dotted the countryside. (See Amphitheater at Arles, page 301.)

What would have been missing, to observant travelers, were thriving cities. Hulks of cities remained, of course, and they served as the centers of church administration; but gradually during the late Roman period, many urban centers had lost their commercial and cultural vitality. Depopulated, many survived as mere skeletons. Moreover, if the travelers had approached Paris from the northeast, they would have passed through dense, nearly untouched forests and land more often used as pasture for animals than for cereal cultivation. These areas were not much influenced by Romans; they represented far more the farming and village settlement patterns of the Franks. Yet even on the northern and eastern fringes of the Merovingian kingdoms, some structures of the Roman Empire remained. Fortresses were still standing at Trier (near Bonn, Germany, today), and great stone villas, such as the one excavated by archaeologists near Douai (today in France, near the Belgian border), loomed over the more humble wooden dwellings of the countryside.

The Social Scale. In the south, gangs of slaves still might occasionally be found cultivating the extensive lands of wealthy estate owners, as they had done since the days of the late Roman Republic. Scattered here and there, independent peasants worked their own small plots as they had for centuries. But for the most part, seventh-century travelers would have found semifree peasant families settled on small holdings, their manses—including a house, a garden, and cultivable land—for which they paid dues and owed labor services to a landowner. Some of these peasants were descendants of the *coloni* (tenant farmers) of the late Roman Empire; others were the sons and daughters of slaves, now provided with a small plot of land; and a few were people of free Frankish origin who for various reasons had come down in the world. At the lower end of the social scale, the status of Franks and Romans had become identical.

Amphitheater at Arles
In what is today southern France, the ruins of an amphitheater built by the Romans still dwarfs the surrounding buildings of the modern city of Arles. This huge stadium must have been even more striking in the seventh century, when the city was impoverished and depopulated. Plague, war, and the dislocation of Roman trade networks meant that most people abandoned the cities to live on the land. Only the bishop and his clergy— and those who could make a living servicing them—remained in the cities. *Jean Dieuzaide.*

Romans (or, more precisely, Gallo-Romans) and Franks had also merged at the upper end of the social scale. Although people south of the Loire River continued to be called Romans and people to the north Franks, their cultures were strikingly similar: they shared language, settlement patterns, and religious sensibilities. (See "New Sources, New Perspectives," page 302.) There were many dialects in the Frankish kingdoms in the seventh century, but most were derived from Latin, though no longer the Latin of Cicero. "Though my speech is rude," Gregory, bishop of Tours♦ (r. 573–c. 594), wrote at the end of the sixth century,

I have been unable to be silent as to the struggles between the wicked and the upright; and I have been especially encouraged because, to my surprise, it has often been said by men of our day, that few understand the learned words of the rhetorician but many the rude language of the common people.

Thus Gregory began his *Histories*, a valuable source for the Merovingian period (c. 486–751). He was trying to evoke the sympathies of his readers, a traditional Roman rhetorical device; but he also expected that his "rude" Latin—the plain Latin of everyday speech— would be understood and welcomed by the general public.

Whereas the Gallo-Roman aristocrat of the fourth and fifth centuries had lived in

♦**Tours:** TOO ur

NEW SOURCES, NEW PERSPECTIVES

Anthropology, Archaeology, and Changing Notions of Ethnicity

At the end of the nineteenth century, scholars argued that ethnicity was the same as race and that both were biological. They measured skeletal features and argued that different human groups—blacks, whites, Jews, and Slavs, for example—were biologically distinct and that some were better than others according to "scientific" criteria. This same view was shared by historians, who spoke of the various groups who entered the Roman Empire—Franks, Visigoths, Saxons, Lombards—as if these people were biologically different from Romans and from one another. They thought, for example, that there was a real biological group called the Lombards that had migrated into the Roman Empire and set up the "Lombard kingdom" in Italy by conquering another real biological group called the Romans.

Some anthropologists challenged this view. In the early 1900s, for example, the anthropologist Franz Boas showed that American Indians were not biologically different from any other human group; their "ethnicity" was cultural. Boas meant that the characteristics that made Indians "Indian" were not physical but rather a combination of practices, beliefs, language, dress, and sense of identity. Soon archaeologists came to realize that no physical difference distinguished a Frankish skeleton from a Lombard or a Roman or a Slav. It was only the artifacts associated with skeletons in grave excavations—jewelry, weapons—that revealed to what ethnicity a person belonged.

If ethnicity were biological, it would be fixed. No one could be a Lombard except if he or she had been born into the group. But since ethnicity is

isolated villas with his *familia*—his wife, children, slaves, and servants—aristocrats of the seventh century lived in more populous settlements: in small villages surrounded by the huts of peasants, shepherds, and artisans. The early medieval village, constructed mostly out of wood or baked clay, was generally built near a waterway or forest or around a church for protection. Intensely local in interests and outlook, the people in the Frankish kingdoms of the seventh and eighth centuries clustered in small groups next to protectors, whether rich men or saints.

The Living and the Dead. Tours—the place where Gregory was bishop—exemplified this new-style settlement. Once a Roman city, Tours's main focus was now outside the city walls, where a church had been built. The population of the surrounding countryside was pulled to this church as if to a magnet, for it housed the remains of the most important and venerated person in the locale: St. Martin. This saint, a fourth-century soldier-turned-monk, was long dead, but his relics—his bones, teeth, hair, and clothes—could be found at Tours, where he had served as bishop. There, in the succeeding centuries, he remained a supernatural force: a protector, healer, and avenger through whom God manifested divine power. In Gregory's view, for example, Martin's relics (or rather God *through* Martin's relics) had prevented armies from plundering local peasants. Martin was not the only human thought to have great supernatural power; all of God's saints were miracle workers.

cultural, "outsiders" can join, while "insiders" can be shed. Historians—especially those associated with the University of Vienna—have shown in detail how this was the case with the peoples that the Romans called barbarians. Walter Pohl, for example, has demonstrated how ethnic groups like the Lombards and Franks were made up of men and women from all sorts of backgrounds. Their sense of being Lombard or Frankish was a product of common myths that they accepted about themselves. The Lombards, for example, thought that their name came from a trick played by their women, who tied their long hair around their chins, humoring the war god Woden into calling them "Longbeards" and giving their men victory in battle. The Avars, for their part, were held together by their loyalty to their leader, the *khagan*. Avars who broke away from the khagan's political dominance were no longer considered part of the group. (They were considered Bulgarians instead.) In contrast, the less centrally organized Slavs recognized all sorts of people living in their territory as Slavs; their ethnicity was based on language and other cultural traditions, which could be learned even by newcomers.

Seeing ethnicity as cultural allows us to understand the origins of European states not as the result of the conquest of one well-defined group by another but rather as a historical process. France, Germany, and England were not created by fixed entities known for all time as, respectively, the Franks, the Germans, and the Angles. Rather, they were created and shaped by the will and imagination of men and women who intermingled, interacted, and adapted to one another over time.

QUESTIONS TO CONSIDER

1. The society of the United States has been called a melting pot. In what ways might the same be said about European societies?
2. How do common myths nourish contemporary notions of ethnicity?

FURTHER READING

Geary, Patrick J. *The Myth of Nations: The Medieval Origins of Europe.* 2002.

Pohl, Walter, with Helmut Reimitz. *Strategies of Distinction: The Construction of Ethnic Communities, 300–800.* 1998.

Wolfram, Herwig. "The Shaping of the Early Medieval Kingdom." *Viator* 1 (1970): 1–20.

Whereas in the classical world the dead had been banished from the presence of the living, in the medieval world the holy dead held the place of highest esteem. The church had no formal procedures for proclaiming saints in the early Middle Ages, but holiness was "recognized" by influential local people and the local bishop. When, for example, miracles were observed at the site of a tomb in Dijon, the common people went there regularly to ask for help. But the nearby bishop was convinced that St. Benignus inhabited the tomb only after the martyr himself came to visit the bishop in a vision. At St. Illidius's tomb in Clermont, it was reported that "the blind are given light, demons are chased away, the deaf receive hearing, and the lame the use of their limbs." Even a few women were so esteemed: "[Our Savior] gave us as models [of sanctity] not only men, who fight [against sinfulness] as they should, but also women, who exert themselves in the struggle with success," wrote Gregory as a preface to his story of the nun Monegund, who lived with a few other ascetic women and whose miracles included curing tumors and prompting paralyzed limbs to work again. No one at Tours doubted that Martin had been a saint, and to tap into the power of his relics the local bishop

Tours, c. 600

Nancy Gauthier and Henri Galinié, eds., Grégoire de Tours et l'espace gaulois (Tours: Actes du congrés internationale, 1997), 70.

built a church in the cemetery directly over his tomb. For a man like Gregory of Tours and his flock, the church building was above all a home for the relics of the saints.

Economic Activity in a Peasant Society

As a bishop, Gregory was aware of some of the sophisticated forms of economic activity in early medieval Europe, such as long-distance trade. Yet most people lived on the very edge of survival. Studies of Alpine peat bogs show that from the fifth to the mid-eighth century glaciers advanced and the mean temperature in Europe dropped. This climatic change spelled shortages in crops. Chronicles, histories, and biographies of saints also describe crop shortages, famines, and diseases as a normal part of life. For the year 591 alone, Gregory reported that

> *a terrible epidemic killed off the people in Tours and in Nantes.... In the town of Limoges a number of people were consumed by fire from heaven for having profaned the Lord's day by transacting business.... There was a terrible drought which destroyed all the green pasture. As a result there were great losses of flocks and herds.*

Early Medieval Accounting
In the seventh century, peasants in western Europe were lucky to produce more grain than they sowed. To make sure that it got its share of this meager production, at least one enterprising landlord, the monastery of St.-Martin at Tours, kept a kind of ledger. This extremely unusual parchment sheet, dating from the second half of the seventh century, lists the amount of grain and wood owed to St.-Martin by its tenants. *Bibliothèque Nationale, Paris.*

Subsistence and Gift Economies. An underlying reason for the calamities of the Merovingian period was the weakness of the agricultural economy. Even the meager population of the Merovingian world was too large for its productive capacities. The dry, light soil of the Mediterranean region was easy to till, and wooden implements were no liability. But the northern soils of most of the Merovingian world were heavy, wet, and difficult to turn and aerate. Technological limitations meant a limited food supply, and agricultural work was not equitably or efficiently allocated and managed. A leisure class of landowning warriors and churchmen lived off the work of peasant men, who tilled the fields, and peasant women, who wove cloth, gardened, brewed, and baked.

Occasionally surpluses developed, either from peaceful agriculture or plunder in warfare, and these were traded, although not in an impersonal, commercial manner. Most economic transactions of the seventh and eighth centuries were part of a gift economy, a system of give and take: booty was taken, tribute demanded, harvests hoarded, and coins minted, all to be redistributed to friends, followers, and dependents. Kings and other rich and powerful men and women amassed gold, silver, ornaments, and jewelry in their treasuries and grain in their storehouses to mark their power, add to their prestige, and demonstrate their generosity. Those benefiting from the largesse of the rich included religious people and institutions: monks, nuns, and bishops, monasteries and churches. We still have a partial gift economy today. At holidays, for example, goods change hands for social purposes: to consecrate a holy event, to express love and friendship, to show off wealth and status. In the Merovingian world, the gift economy was the dynamic behind most of the moments when goods and money changed hands.

Trade and Traders. Some economic activity in this period was purely commercial and impersonal, especially long-distance trade, for which Europe supplied slaves and raw materials such as furs and honey, and in return received luxuries and manufactured goods such as silks and papyrus. Trading voyages, diplomatic ventures, and pilgrimages were the ways in which the Byzantine, Islamic, and western European descendants of the Roman Empire kept in tenuous contact with one another. Seventh- and eighth-century sources speak of Byzantines, Syrians, and Jews as the chief intermediaries of any long-distance trade that existed. Many of these intermediaries lived in the still-thriving port cities of the Mediterranean. Gregory of Tours associated Jews with commerce, complaining that they sold things "at a higher price than they were worth."

Contrary to Gregory's view, however, Jews were not involved only, or even primarily, in trade. Rather, they were almost entirely integrated into every aspect of secular life in many regions of Europe. They used Hebrew in worship, but otherwise they spoke the same languages as Christians and used Latin in their legal documents. Their children were often given the same names as Christians (and, in turn, Christians often took Old Testament biblical names); they dressed as everyone else dressed; and they engaged in the same occupations. Many Jews planted and tended vineyards, in part because of the importance of wine in synagogue services and in part because the surplus could easily be sold. Some Jews were rich landowners, with slaves and dependent peasants working for them; others were independent peasants of modest means. Whereas some Jews lived in towns with a small Jewish quarter where their homes and synagogues were located, most Jews, like their Christian neighbors, lived on the land. Only much later, in the eleventh century, would the status of Jews change, setting them markedly apart from Christians.

Nor were women as noticeably set apart from men in the Merovingian period as they had been in Roman times. As in the Islamic world, western women received dowries and could inherit property. In some parts of western Europe, they could be entrepreneurs as well; documents reveal at least one enterprising peasant woman who sold wine at Tours to earn additional money.

The Powerful in Merovingian Society

Monarchs and aristocrats were the powerful people of Merovingian society. Merovingian aristocrats—who included monks and bishops

as well as laypeople—did not form a separate legal group but held power through hereditary wealth, status, and political influence.

The Aristocrats. Many aristocrats were extremely wealthy. The will drawn up by one aristocrat, Bertram of Le Mans, shows that he had estates—some from his family, others obtained by royal largesse—scattered over much of Gaul. They were tilled by tenants and slaves.

Along with administering their estates, lay male aristocrats of the period spent their time honing their proficiency as warriors. To be a great warrior in Merovingian society, just as in the otherwise very different world of the Bedouin, meant more than just fighting: it meant perfecting the virtues necessary for leading armed men. Aristocrats affirmed their skills and comradeship in the hunt, they proved their worth in the regular taking of booty, and they rewarded their followers afterward at generous banquets. At these feasts, following the dictates of the gift economy, the lords combined fellowship with the redistribution of wealth as they gave abundantly to their dependents.

Merovingian aristocrats also valued bedtime. The bed—and the production of children—was the focus of their marriage. Because of its importance to the survival of aristocratic families and to the transmission of their property and power, marriage was an expensive institution. There was more than one form: in the most formal, the man gave a generous dowry of clothes, livestock, and land to his bride, while after the marriage was consummated, he gave her a "morning gift" of furniture. Very wealthy men also might support one or more concubines, who enjoyed a less formal type of marriage, receiving a morning gift but no dowry. In this period, churchmen had many ideas about the value of marriages, but in practice they had little to do with the matter. Marriage was a family decision and a family matter; no one was married in a church.

Some sixth-century aristocrats still patterned their lives on those of the Romans, teaching their children classical Latin poetry and writing to one another in phrases borrowed from Virgil. But already in the seventh century their spoken language had become

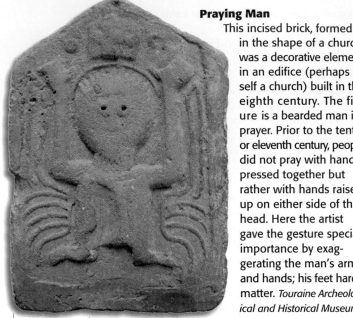

Praying Man

This incised brick, formed in the shape of a church, was a decorative element in an edifice (perhaps itself a church) built in the eighth century. The figure is a bearded man in prayer. Prior to the tenth or eleventh century, people did not pray with hands pressed together but rather with hands raised up on either side of the head. Here the artist gave the gesture special importance by exaggerating the man's arms and hands; his feet hardly matter. *Touraine Archeological and Historical Museum, Hotel Gouin, Tours, France.*

very different from literary Latin. Some still learned Latin, but they cultivated it mainly to read the Psalms. A religious culture emphasizing Christian piety over the classics was developing in Europe at the same time as in Byzantium.

This new religious sensibility was given powerful impetus by the arrival (c. 590) on the continent of the Irish monk St. Columbanus (d. 615). The Merovingian aristocracy was much taken by Columbanus's brand of monasticism, which stressed exile, devotion, and discipline. The monasteries St. Columbanus established in both Gaul and Italy attracted local recruits from the aristocracy, some of them grown men and women. Others were young children, given to the monastery by their parents. This practice, called oblation, was not only accepted but also often considered essential for the spiritual well-being of both the children and their families. Irish monasticism introduced aristocrats on the continent to a deepened religious devotion. Those aristocrats who did not join or patronize a monastery still often read (or listened to others read) books about penitence, and they chanted the Psalms.

Bishops were generally aristocrats—Bertram of Le Mans, the man of many estates, was one. They ranked among the most pow-

erful men in Merovingian society. Gregory of Tours, for example, considered himself the protector of "his citizens" at Tours. When representatives of the king came to collect taxes, Gregory stopped them in their tracks, warning them that St. Martin would punish anyone who tried to tax his people. "That very day," Gregory reported, "the man who had produced the tax rolls caught a fever and died."

Like other aristocrats, many bishops were married, even though church councils demanded celibacy. As the overseers of priests, however, bishops were expected to be moral supervisors and refrain from sexual relations with their wives. Since bishops were ordinarily appointed late in life, long after they had raised a family, this restriction did not threaten the ideal of a procreative marriage.

Women of Power. Noble parents determined whom their daughters were to marry, for such unions bound together whole extended families rather than simply husbands and wives. As was true for brides of the lower classes, aristocratic wives received a dowry (usually land) over which they had some control; if they were widowed without children, they were allowed to sell, give away, exchange, or rent out their dowry estates as they wished. Moreover, men could give their women kinfolk property outright in written testaments. Fathers so often wanted to share their property with their daughters that an enterprising author created a formula for scribes to follow when drawing up wills in such cases. It began:

> *For a long time an ungodly custom has been observed among us that forbids sisters to share with their brothers the paternal land. I reject this impious law: I make you, my beloved daughter, an equal and legitimate heir in all my patrimony [inheritance].*

Because of such bequests, dowries, and other gifts, many aristocratic women were very rich. Childless widows frequently gave generous gifts to the church from their vast possessions. But a woman need not have been a widow to control enormous wealth. In 632, for example, the nun Burgundofara, who had never married, drew up a will giving her monastery the land, slaves, vineyards, pastures, and forests she had received from her two brothers and her father. In the same will, she gave other property near Paris to her brothers and sister.

Though legally under the authority of her husband, a Merovingian woman often found ways to take control of her life. Tetradia, wife of Count Eulalius, left her husband, taking all his gold and silver, because, as Gregory of Tours tells us,

> he was in the habit of sleeping with the women-servants in his household. As a result he neglected his wife....As a result of his excesses, he ran into serious debt, and to meet this he stole his wife's jewelery and money.

In a court of law, Tetradia was sentenced to repay Eulalius four times the amount she had taken from him, but she was allowed to keep and live on her own property. Other women were able to exercise behind-the-scenes control through their sons. Artemia, for example, used the prophecy that her son Nicetius would become a bishop to prevent her husband from taking the bishopric himself. Although the prophecy eventually came to pass, Nicetius remained at home with his mother well into his thirties, working alongside the servants and teaching the younger children of the household to read the Psalms.

Some women exercised direct power. Rich widows with fortunes to bestow wielded enormous influence. Some Merovingian women were abbesses, rulers in their own right over female monasteries and sometimes over "double monasteries," with separate facilities for men and women. Monasteries under the control of abbesses could be very substantial centers of population: the convent at Laon, for example, had three hundred nuns in the seventh century. Because women lived in populous convents or were monopolized by rich men able to support several wives or mistresses at one time, unattached aristocratic women were scarce in society and therefore valuable.

The Power of Kings. Atop the aristocracy were the Merovingian kings, rulers of the Frankish kingdoms. The **Merovingian dynasty** (c. 486–751) owed its longevity to good political sense: it had allied itself with local lay aristocrats and ecclesiastical authorities. The kings relied on these men to bolster their power derived from other sources: their lead-

Relic of Queen Balthild
A slave purchased in England by a Frankish mayor of the palace, Balthild soon caught the eye of the Frankish king himself, who made her his queen. This seventh-century Cinderella story did not end with the marriage: when her husband died, Balthild played an important role as regent, acting as the ruler on behalf of her young son. Later she retired to a monastery, where she was revered as a saint. This shirt is one of her relics. Tradition has it that Balthild distributed her jewels to the poor and contented herself by wearing their images in embroidery. *Musée de Chelles/photographers: E. Mittard and N. Georgieff.*

ership in war and access to the lion's share of plunder; and their takeover of the taxation system, public lands, and legal framework of Roman administration. The kings' courts functioned as schools for the sons of the aristocracy, tightening the bonds between royal and aristocratic families and loyalties. And when kings sent officials—counts and dukes—to rule in their name in various regions of their kingdoms, these regional governors worked with and married into the aristocratic families who had long controlled local affairs.

Both kings and aristocrats had good reason to want a powerful royal authority. The king acted as arbitrator and intermediary for the competing interests of the aristocrats while taking advantage of local opportunities to appoint favorites and garner prestige by giving out land and privileges to supporters and religious institutions. Gregory of Tours's history of the sixth century is filled with stories of bitter battles between Merovingian kings, as royal brothers fought continuously over territories, wives, and revenues. Yet what seemed to the bishop like royal weakness and violent chaos was in fact one way the kings focused local aristocratic enmities, preventing them from spinning out of royal control. By the beginning of the seventh century, three relatively stable Frankish kingdoms had emerged: Austrasia◆ to the northeast; Neustria to the west, with its capital city at Paris; and Burgundy, incorporating the southeast (see Map 8.4). These divisions were so useful to local aristocrats and the Merovingian dynasty alike that even when royal power was united in the hands of one king, Clothar II (r. 613–623), he made his son the independent king of Austrasia.

The very power of the kings in the seventh century, however, gave greater might to their chief court official, the mayor of the palace. In the following century, allied with the Austrasian aristocracy, one mayoral family would displace the Merovingian dynasty and establish a new royal line, the Carolingians.

Christianity and Classical Culture in the British Isles

The Merovingian kingdoms exemplify some of the ways in which Roman and non-Roman traditions combined. The British Isles show others. Ireland had never been part of the

◆**Austrasia:** aw STRAY zhuh

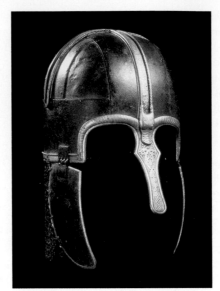

York Helmet
This fine helmet, once belonging to a very wealthy warrior living near York, England, in the second half of the eighth century, was intended for both display and real battle. The helmet, made of iron, and the back flap, made of flexible chain mail, gave excellent protection against sword blades. The cheek pieces were probably originally pulled close to the warrior's face by a leather tie. The nose piece, decorated with interlaced animals, protected his nose. Over the top, two bands of copper meet at the middle. They were inscribed "In the name of our Lord Jesus, the Holy Spirit, God, and with all, we pray. Amen. Oshere. Christ." *York Castle Museum/City of York Museum Services.*

Roman Empire, but it was early converted to Christianity, as were Roman Britain and parts of Scotland. Invasions by various Celtic and Germanic groups—particularly the Anglo-Saxons, who gave their name to England, "the land of the Angles"—redrew the religious boundaries. Ireland, largely free of invaders, remained Christian; Scotland, also relatively untouched by invaders, was slowly evangelized by the Irish from the west and the British from the south; England, which emerged from the invasions as a mosaic of about a dozen kingdoms ruled by separate Anglo-Saxon kings, became largely pagan.

Two Competing Forms of Christianity in Anglo-Saxon England. Christianity was introduced to **Anglo-Saxon England** from two directions. In the north of England, Irish monks brought their own brand of Christianity. Converted in the fifth century by St. Patrick and other missionaries, the Irish had rapidly evolved a church organization that corresponded to its rural clan organization. Abbots and abbesses, generally from powerful dynasties, headed monastic *familiae*, communities composed of blood relatives, servants, slaves, and of course monks or nuns. Bishops were often under the authority of abbots, since the monasteries rather than cities were the centers of population settlement in Ireland. The Irish missionaries to England were monks, and they set up monasteries on the model of those at home.

In the south of England, Christianity came via missionaries sent by Gregory the Great (r. 590–604) in 597. The missionaries, under the leadership of Augustine (not the same Augustine as the bishop of Hippo), intended to convert the king and people of Kent, the southernmost kingdom, and then work their way northward. But Augustine and his party brought with them Roman practices at odds with those of Irish Christianity, stressing ties to the pope and the organization of the church under bishops rather than abbots. Using the Roman model, they divided England into territorial units called dioceses headed by an archbishop and bishops. Augustine, for example, became archbishop of Canterbury. As he was a monk, he set up a monastery right next to his cathedral, and it became a peculiar characteristic of the English church to have a community of monks attached to the bishop's church. Later a second archbishopric was added at York.

A major bone of contention between the Roman and Irish churches involved the calculation of the date of Easter. The Roman church insisted that Easter fall on the first Sunday following the first full moon after the spring equinox. The Irish had a different method of determining when Easter should fall, and therefore they celebrated Easter on a different day. Because everyone agreed that believers could not be saved unless they observed Christ's resurrection properly and on the right date, the conflict was bitter. It was resolved by Oswy, king of Northumbria, who organized a meeting of churchmen, the Synod of Whitby in 664. Convinced by the synod that Rome spoke with the voice of St. Peter, who was said in the New Testament to hold the keys of the kingdom of heaven, Oswy chose the Roman date. His decision paved the way for the triumph of the Roman brand of Christianity in England.

Literary Culture. St. Peter was not the only reason for favoring Rome. To many English churchmen, Rome had great prestige because it was a treasure trove of knowledge, piety, and holy objects. Benedict Biscop♦ (c. 630–690), the founder of two important English monasteries, made many arduous trips to Rome, bringing back relics, liturgical vestments, and even a cantor to teach his monks the proper melodies in a time before written musical notation. Above all, he went to Rome to get books. At his monasteries in the north of England, he built up a grand library. In Anglo-Saxon England, as in Scotland and Ireland, all of which lacked a strong classical tradition from Roman times, a book was considered a precious object, to be decorated as finely as a garnet-studded brooch.

The British Isles

The Anglo-Saxons and Irish Celts had a thriving oral culture but extremely limited uses for writing. Books became valuable only when these societies converted to Christianity. Just as Islamic reliance on the Qur'an made possible a literary culture under the Umayyads, so Christian dependence on the Bible, liturgy, and the writings of the church fathers helped make England and Ireland centers of literature and learning in the seventh and eighth centuries. Archbishop Theodore (r. 669–690), who had studied at Athens and was one of the most learned men of his day, founded a school at Canterbury where students studied Latin and even some Greek manuscripts to comment on biblical texts. Men like Benedict Biscop soon sponsored other centers of learning, using the texts from the classical past. Although women did not establish famous schools, many abbesses ruled over monasteries that stressed Christian learning. Here as elsewhere, Latin writings, even pagan texts, were studied diligently, in part because Latin was

♦**Biscop:** BIS cup

Lindisfarne Gospels
The lavishly illuminated manuscript known as the Lindisfarne Gospels, of which this is one page, was probably produced in the first third of the eighth century. For the monks at Lindisfarne and elsewhere in the British Isles, books were precious objects, to be decorated much like pieces of jewelry. To introduce each of the four Gospels, the artist—who was also the scribe—produced three elaborate pages: the first was a "portrait" of the evangelist, the second a decorative "carpet" page, and the third the beginning of the text. The page depicted here is the beginning of the Gospel according to St. Matthew, which begins with the words "Liber generationis." Note how elaborately the first letter, L, is treated and how the decoration gradually recedes, so that the last line, while still very embellished, is quite plain in comparison with the others. In this way the very layout of the book led the reader slowly and reverently into the text of the Gospels itself. *British Library.*

so foreign a language that mastering it required systematic and formal study. One of Benedict Biscop's pupils was Bede♦ (673–735), an Anglo-Saxon monk and a historian of extraordinary breadth. Bede in turn taught a new generation of monks who became advisers to eighth-century rulers.

The vigorous pagan Anglo-Saxon oral tradition was only partially suppressed; much of it was adapted to Christian culture. Bede encouraged and supported the use of Anglo-Saxon, urging Christian priests, for example, to use it when they instructed their flocks. In contrast to other European regions, where the vernacular was rarely written, Anglo-Saxon came to be a written language used in every aspect of English life, from government to entertainment.

♦**Bede:** beed

After the Synod of Whitby, the English church was tied by doctrine, friendship, and conviction to the church of Rome. An influential Anglo-Saxon monk and bishop, Wynfrith, even changed his name to the Latin Boniface to symbolize his loyalty to the Roman church. Preaching on the continent, Boniface (680–754) worked to set up churches in Germany and Gaul that, like those in England, looked to Rome for leadership and guidance. His zeal would give the papacy new importance in Europe.

Unity in Spain, Division in Italy

In contrast to the British Isles, southern Gaul, Spain, and Italy had long been part of the Roman Empire and preserved many of its traditions. Nevertheless, as they were settled and fought over by new peoples, their histories came to diverge dramatically. When the Merovingian king Clovis defeated the Visigoths in 507, their vast kingdom, which had sprawled across southern Gaul into Spain, was dismembered. By midcentury, the Franks came into possession of most of the Visigothic kingdom in southern Gaul.

In Spain the Visigothic king Leovigild (r. 569–586) established territorial control by military might. But no ruler could hope to maintain his position in **Visigothic Spain** without the support of the Hispano-Roman population, which included both the great landowners and leading bishops; and their backing was unattainable while the Visigoths remained Arian (see page 257). Leovigild's son Reccared (r. 586–601) took the necessary step in 587, converting to Catholic Christianity. Two years later, at the Third Council of Toledo, most of the Arian bishops followed their king by announcing their conversion to Catholicism.

Thereafter the bishops and kings of Spain cooperated to a degree unprecedented in other regions. While the king gave the churchmen free rein to set up their own hierarchy (with the bishop of Toledo at the top) and to meet regularly at synods to regulate and reform the church, the bishops in turn supported their Visigothic king, who ruled as a minister of the Christian people. Rebellion against him was tantamount to rebellion against Christ. The Spanish bishops reinforced this idea by anointing the king, daubing him with holy oil in a ritual that paralleled the ordination of priests and demonstrated divine favor. Toledo, the city where the highest bishop presided, was also where the kings were "made" through anointment. While the bishops in this way made the king's cause their own, their lay counterparts, the great landowners, helped supply the king with troops, allowing him to maintain internal order and repel his external enemies.

Ironically, it was precisely the centralization and unification of the Visigothic kingdom that proved its undoing. When the Arabs arrived in 711, they needed only to kill the king, defeat his army, and capture Toledo to deal the kingdom a crushing blow.

By contrast, in Italy the Lombard king constantly faced a hostile papacy in the center of the peninsula and virtually independent dukes in the south. Theoretically royal officers, in fact the dukes of Benevento and Spoleto ruled on their own behalf. Although many Lombards were Catholics, others, including important kings and dukes, were Arian. The "official" religion of **Lombard Italy** varied with the ruler in power. Rather than signal a major political event, the conversion of the Lombards to Catholic Christianity occurred gradually, ending only around the mid-seventh century. Partly as a result of this slow development, the Lombard kings, unlike the Visigoths, Franks, or even the Anglo-Saxons, never enlisted the wholehearted support of any particular group of churchmen.

Lacking strong and united ecclesiastical favor, Lombard royal power still had buttresses. Chief among these were the traditions of leadership associated with the royal dynasty, the kings' military ability and their control over large estates in northern Italy, and the Roman institutions that survived in Italy. Although the Italian peninsula had been devastated by the wars between the Ostrogoths and the Byzantine Empire, the Lombard kings took advantage of the still-urban organization of Italian society and economy, assigning dukes to city bases and setting up a royal capital at Pavia. Recalling emperors like Constantine and Justinian, the kings built churches, monasteries, and other places of worship in the royal capital, maintained the walls, issued laws, and minted coins. Revenues from tolls, sales taxes, port duties, and court fines filled their coffers, although their inability to revive the Roman land tax was a major weakness. The greatest challenge for the Lombard kings came not from their own institutions but from sharing the peninsula with Rome. As soon as the kings began to make serious headway into southern Italy against the duchies of Spoleto and Benevento, the pope began to fear for his own position and called on the Franks for help.

Lombard Italy, Early Eighth Century

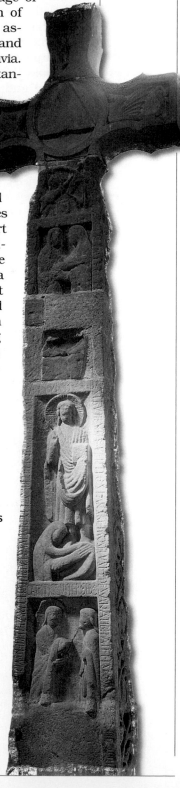

Ruthwell Cross
Originally not a cross at all (the top was added later), the Ruthwell Cross is one of a number of monumental carved stone pillars constructed in the north of England in the eighth century. Nothing quite like it exists on the Continent. Containing a fascinating mixture of Latin and runic inscriptions, vine scrolls, and biblical scenes, the Ruthwell Cross includes the text of the poem "Dream of the Holy Rood," which purports to be the "dream" of the wood on which Christ was crucified. What purposes might have been served by monuments such as this? *Edwin Smith/RIBA Library Photographs Collection, London.*

Political Tensions and Reorganization at Rome

By 600, the pope's position was ambiguous: he was both a ruler and a subordinate. On the one hand, believing he was the successor of St. Peter and head of the church, he wielded real secular power. Pope Gregory the Great in many ways laid the foundations for the papacy's spiritual and temporal ascendancy. (See A Portrait of Pope Gregory the Great, page 313.) During his tenure, the pope became the greatest landowner in Italy; he organized the defenses of Rome and paid for its army; he heard court cases, made treaties, and provided welfare services. The missionary expedition he sent to England was only a small part of his involvement in the rest of Europe. For example, Gregory maintained close ties with the church-men in Spain who were working to convert the Visigoths from Arianism to Catholicism. A prolific author of spiritual works and biblical commentaries, Gregory digested and simplified the ideas of church fathers like St. Augustine of Hippo, making them accessible to a wider audience. His practical handbook for the clergy, *Pastoral Rule*, was matched by practical reforms within the church: he tried to impose in Italy regular elections of bishops and to enforce clerical celibacy.

Yet the pope was not independent. He was only one of many bishops in the Roman Empire, which was now ruled from Constantinople, and he was therefore subordinate to the emperor and Byzantium. For a long time the emperor's views on dogma, discipline, and church administration prevailed at Rome. This authority began to unravel in the seventh

Mosaic at Santo Stefano Rotondo

The church of Santo Stefano, built by Pope Simplicius (r. 468–483), was round, like a classical temple. It made up part of the papal Lateran palace complex, in the southeastern zone of Rome. Later popes continued to beautify and adorn Santo Stefano, drawing on the artistic styles of their own time. Pope Theodore (r. 642–649) moved the relics of two Roman martyrs, Primus and Felician, from a small church outside of Rome to Santo Stefano. To celebrate the event, he commissioned the mosaic shown here, in which the figures of Primus and Felician flank a giant cross. The heavy outlines and gold surroundings echo mosaics done at Byzantium around the same time, attesting to political, cultural, and theological links between Rome and Constantinople. **For more help analyzing this image**, see the visual activity for this chapter in the Online Study Guide at **bedfordstmartins.com/hunt**. *Madeline Grimoldi.*

A Portrait of Pope Gregory the Great by Bishop Gregory of Tours

At the end of the sixth century, the pope at Rome had no jurisdiction over bishops outside of Italy, though Gregory's mission to England meant that his handpicked man would become archbishop there. Elsewhere the pope had no power to appoint or depose bishops; Gregory of Tours himself was named bishop by a Merovingian king and queen. Nevertheless, the bishop of Tours was well aware—and a great admirer—of the pope at Rome. This passage from his Histories *begins with a description of an attack of plague at Rome in 590 that resulted in the death of Pope Pelagius and many others.*

The people then unanimously chose as Pope the deacon Gregory,[1] for the Church could not be left without a leader. He was descended from one of the leading senatorial families. From his youth upwards had been devoted to God's service. He founded six monasteries in Sicily from his own re-

sources, and he established a seventh inside the walls of the city of Rome. He endowed them with sufficient land to provide the monks with their daily sustenance; then he sold the rest of his possessions, including all his household goods, and he gave the proceeds to the poor. He who until then had been in the habit of processing through the city in silken robes sewn with glittering gems [when he was Prefect of the City] now served at the Lord's altar in a fustian gown. He was appointed as seventh among the deacons who served the Pope. His abstinence in taking food, his vigils and his prayers, the severity of his fasting, were such that his weakened stomach could scarce support his frame. He was so skilled in grammar, dialectic and rhetoric that he was held second to none in the entire city. He wanted very much to avoid the highest honor, lest as a result of his being elected the worldly pomp which he had renounced should invade once more his public life.

[1]The pope was served by seven deacons, one for each of the seven districts into which Rome was divided for church administration. Gregory, so soon to become Pope Gregory the Great, was the least of these.

Source: Excerpt from Gregory of Tours, *The History of the Franks,* trans. Lewis Thorpe (London: Penguin Books, 1974), 543–44. Some footnotes have been omitted, and the spellings have been Americanized.

century. In 691, Emperor Justinian II convened a council that determined 102 rules for the church, and he sent them to Rome for papal endorsement. Most of the rules were unobjectionable, but Pope Sergius I (r. 687 or 689–701) was unwilling to agree to the whole because it permitted priestly marriages (which the Roman church did not want to allow) and prohibited fasting on Saturdays in Lent (which the Roman church required). Outraged by Sergius's refusal, Justinian tried to arrest the pope, but Italian armies (theoretically under the emperor) came to the pontiff's aid, while Justinian's arresting officer cowered under the pope's bed. The incident reveals that some local forces were already willing to rally to the side of the pope against the emperor. By now Constantinople's influence and

authority over Rome was tenuous at best. Sheer distance, as well as diminishing imperial power in Italy, meant that the popes were in effect the leaders of the parts of Italy not controlled by the Lombards.

The gap between Byzantium and the papacy widened in the early eighth century as Emperor Leo III tried to increase the taxes on papal property to pay for his all-consuming war against the Arab invaders. The pope responded by leading a general tax revolt. Meanwhile, Leo's fierce policy of iconoclasm collided with the pope's tolerance of images. In Italy, as in other European regions, Christian piety focused not so much on icons as on relics. Nevertheless, the papacy was not willing to allow sacred images and icons to be destroyed. The pope argued that holy images

MAPPING THE WEST Europe and the Mediterranean, c. 750
The major political fact of the period 600–750 was the emergence of Islam and the creation of an Islamic state that reached from Spain to the Indus River. The Byzantine Empire, once a great power, was dwarfed—and half swallowed up—by its Islamic neighbor. To the west were fledgling barbarian kingdoms, mere trifles on the world stage. The next centuries, however, would prove their resourcefulness and durability.

could and should be venerated—but not worshiped. His support of images reflected popular opinion as well. A later commentator wrote that iconoclasm so infuriated the inhabitants of Ravenna and Venice that "if the pope had not prohibited the people, they would have attempted to set up a [different] emperor over themselves."

These difficulties with the emperor were matched by increasing friction between the pope and the Lombards. The Lombard kings had gradually managed to bring under their control the duchies of Spoleto and Benevento as well as part of the Exarchate of Ravenna. By the mid-eighth century, the popes feared that Rome would fall to the Lombards,

and Pope Zachary (r. 741–752) looked northward for friends. He created an ally by sanctioning the deposition of the last Merovingian king and his replacement by the first Carolingian king, Pippin III (r. 751–768). In 753, a subsequent pope, Stephen II (r. 752–757), called on Pippin to march to Italy with an army to fight the Lombards. Thus, events at Rome had a major impact on the history not only of Italy but of the Frankish kingdom as well.

Review: What were the roles, projects, and powers of the pope in early medieval Europe? On balance, how important was the papacy?

Conclusion

The three heirs of the Roman Empire—Byzantines, Muslims, and western Europeans—built on three distinct legacies. Byzantium directly inherited the central political institutions of Rome: its people called themselves Romans; its emperor was the Roman emperor; and its capital, Constantinople, was the new Rome. Sixth-century Byzantium also inherited the cities, laws, and religion—Christianity—of Rome. The changes of the seventh and eighth centuries—contraction of territory, urban decline, disappearance of the old elite, a ban on icons—whittled away at this Roman character. By 750, Byzantium was less Roman than it was a new, resilient political and cultural entity, a Christian polity on the borders of the new Muslim empire.

Muslims were the newcomers to the Roman world, but Islam was influenced by both Jewish and Christian monotheism, each with roots in Roman culture. Under the guidance of Muhammad (the Prophet), Islam became both a coherent theology and a tightly structured way of life. Once the Muslim Arabs embarked on military conquests, they too became heirs of Rome, preserving its cities, hiring its civil servants, and adopting its artistic styles. Drawing on Roman and Persian traditions, the Muslims created a powerful Islamic state, with a capital city in Syria, regional urban centers elsewhere, and a culture that generally tolerated a wide variety of economic, religious, and social institutions so long as the conquered paid taxes to their Muslim overlords.

Western Europe also inherited Roman institutions and transformed them with great diversity. Frankish Gaul built on Roman traditions that had long been transformed by provincial and Germanic custom. In England, however, once the far-flung northern outpost of the Roman Empire, the Roman legacy had to be reimported in the seventh century. In Spain, the Visigothic kings allied themselves with a Hispano-Roman elite that maintained elements of the organization and vigorous intellectual traditions of the late empire. In Italy and at Rome itself, the traditions of the classical past remained living parts of the fabric of life. The roads remained, the cities of Italy survived (although depopulated), and both the popes and the Lombard kings ruled in the traditions of Roman government.

All three heirs to Rome suffered the ravages of war. In all three societies, the social hierarchy became simpler, with the loss of "middle" groups like the *curiales* at Byzantium and the near-suppression of tribal affiliations among Muslims. As each of the three heirs shaped Roman institutions to its own uses and advantages, each also strove to create a religious polity. In Byzantium, the emperor was a religious force, presiding over the destruction of images. In the Islamic world, the caliph was the successor to Muhammad, a religious and political leader. In western Europe the kings allied with churchmen in order to rule. Despite their many differences, all these leaders had a common understanding of their place in a divine scheme: they were God's agents on earth, ruling over God's people.

Suggested References

Byzantium: A Christian Empire under Siege

While some scholars (Ousterhout and Brubaker, Weitzmann) concentrate on religion, culture, and the role of icons, others (Treadgold, Whittow) tend to stress politics and war.

*The Byzantine Studies Page: http://www.bway.net/~halsall/ byzantium.html.

*Geanakoplos, Deno John, ed. and trans. *Byzantium: Church, Society, and Civilization Seen through Contemporary Eyes*. 1986.

Haldon, J. F. *Byzantium in the Seventh Century: The Transformation of a Culture*. 1990.

Norwich, John Julius. *Byzantium: The Early Centuries*. 1989.

Ousterhout, Robert, and Leslie Brubaker. *The Sacred Image East and West*. 1995.

Treadgold, Warren. *A History of the Byzantine State and Society*. 1997.

Weitzmann, Kurt. *The Icon: Holy Images, Sixth to Fourteenth Century*. 1978.

Whittow, Mark. *The Making of Byzantium, 600–1025*. 1996.

*Primary sources.

Islam: A New Religion and a New Empire

The classic (and as yet unsurpassed) discussion is in Hodgson. Crone's book is considered highly controversial. Berkey's book is balanced and up-to-date.

Ahmed, Leila. *Women and Gender in Islam: Historical Roots of a Modern Debate.* 1992.

Berkey, Jonathan P. *The Formation of Islam: Religion and Society in the Near East, 600–1800.* 2003.

Crone, Patricia. *Meccan Trade and the Rise of Islam.* 1987.

Donner, Fred McGraw. *The Early Islamic Conquests.* 1981.

Hodgson, Marshall G. S. *The Venture of Islam: Conscience and History in a World Civilization.* Vol. 1, *The Classical Age of Islam.* 1974.

*Islamic Sourcebook: http://www.fordham.edu/halsall/islam/islamsbook.html.

Kennedy, Hugh. *The Prophet and the Age of the Caliphates: The Islamic Near East from the Sixth to the Eleventh Century.* 1986.

*Lewis, Bernard, ed. and trans. *Islam: From the Prophet Muhammad to the Capture of Constantinople.* 2 vols. 1987.

Waddy, Charis. *Women in Muslim History.* 1980.

Western Europe: A Medley of Kingdoms

Geary and Wood provide complementary guides to the Merovingian world. Recent keen historical interest in the role of the cults of the saints in early medieval society is reflected in Van Dam. While interest in Anglo-Saxon England has not diminished, other parts of the British Isles are receiving new attention, as Smyth demonstrates.

*Bede. *A History of the English Church and People.* Trans. Leo Sherley-Price. 1991.

Collins, Roger. *Early Medieval Spain: Unity in Diversity, 400–1000.* 1983.

*Fouracre, Paul, and Richard A. Gerberding. *Late Merovingian France: History and Hagiography, 640–720.* 1996.

Geary, Patrick. *Before France and Germany: The Creation and Transformation of the Merovingian World.* 1988.

*Gregory of Tours. *The History of the Franks.* Trans. Lewis Thorpe. 1976.

*Gregory of Tours: http://www.unipissing.ca/department/history/4505/show.htm.

Heinzelmann, Martin, *Gregory of Tours: History and Society in the Sixth Century.* 2001.

Smyth, A. P. *Warlords and Holy Men: Scotland, AD 80–1000.* 1984.

Van Dam, Raymond. *Saints and Their Miracles in Late Antique Gaul.* 1993.

Wood, Ian. *The Merovingian Kingdoms, 450–751.* 1994.

Wickham, Chris. *Early Medieval Italy: Central Power and Local Society 400–1000.* 1981.

CHAPTER REVIEW

IMPORTANT EVENTS

c. 486–751	Merovingian dynasty
c. 570–632	Life of Muhammad, prophet of Islam
572	Lombards conquer northern Italy
r. 573–c. 594	Bishop Gregory of Tours
587	Conversion of Visigothic king Reccared
c. 590	Arrival of Irish monk Columbanus in Gaul
r. 590–604	Papacy of Pope Gregory the Great
603–623	War between Byzantium and Persia
622	Hijra to Medina; the beginning date of the Islamic calendar
624	Muhammad and Meccans fight Battle of Badr
661–750	Umayyad caliphate
664	Synod of Whitby; English king opts for Roman form of Christianity
726–787	Period of iconoclasm at Byzantium

KEY TERMS

Anglo-Saxon England (308)

Hijra (294)

iconoclasm (291)

Lombard Italy (311)

Merovingian dynasty (307)

Sassanid Empire (284)

Umayyad caliphate (298)

ummah (294)

Visigothic Spain (310)

REVIEW QUESTIONS

1. What stresses did the Byzantine Empire endure in the seventh and eighth centuries, and how was iconoclasm a response to those stresses?

2. How and why did the Muslims conquer so many lands in the very short period 632–750?

3. What were the roles, projects, and powers of the pope in early medieval Europe? On balance, how important was the papacy?

MAKING CONNECTIONS

1. What were the similarities and what were the differences between the three heirs of the Roman Empire?

2. Which of the heirs seemed most poised for success (economic, political, cultural) around the year 750, and why?

FOR FURTHER EXPLORATION

To assess your mastery of the material in this chapter, see the Online Study Guide at **bedfordstmartins.com/hunt**.

To read additional primary-source material from this period, see Chapter 8 in *Sources of The Making of the West*, Second Edition, Volume I.

Unity and Diversity in Three Societies, 750–1050

IN 841, A FIFTEEN-YEAR-OLD BOY NAMED WILLIAM went to serve at the court of the king of the Franks, Charles the Bald. William's father was Bernard, an extremely powerful noble. His mother was Dhuoda,◆ a well-educated, pious, and able woman; she administered the family's estates in the south of France while her husband occupied himself in court politics and royal administration. In 841, however, politics had become a dangerous business. King Charles, named after his grandfather Charlemagne,◆ was fighting with his brothers over his portion of the Carolingian Empire, and Bernard (who had been a supporter of Charles's father, Louis the Pious) held a precarious position at the young king's court. In fact, William was sent to Charles's court as a kind of hostage, to ensure Bernard's loyalty. Anxious about her son, Dhuoda wanted to educate and counsel him, so she wrote a handbook of advice for William, outlining what he ought to believe about God; about politics and society; about obligations to his family; and, above all, about his duties to his father, which she emphasized even over loyalty to the king:

> In the human understanding of things, royal and imperial appearance and power seem preeminent in the world, and the custom of men is to account those men's actions and their names ahead of all others....But despite all this...I caution you to render first to him whose son you are special, faithful, steadfast loyalty as long as you shall live....So I urge you again, most beloved son William, that first of all you love God....Then love, fear, and cherish your father.

William heeded his mother's words, with tragic results: when Bernard ran afoul of Charles and was executed, William died in a failed attempt to avenge his father.

Dhuoda's handbook reveals the volatile political atmosphere of the mid-ninth century, and her advice to her son points to one of its

---

◆**Dhuoda:** doo OH duh
◆**Charlemagne:** SHAHR luh mayn

Carolingian Mother
This depiction of a nursing mother is a detail from a full-page illustration of the biblical story of the Creation and Fall in a Carolingian Bible manuscript made in the ninth century. The mother is Eve, cast out of the Garden of Eden and suckling her first born, Cain. Christian mothers had an important model in Mary, the mother of Jesus, and Eve's dignified placement within a bower of garlands may reflect this association. *By permission of the British Library.*

causes: a crisis of loyalty. Loyalty to emperors, caliphs, and kings—all of whom were symbols of unity cutting across regional and family ties—competed with allegiances to local authorities; and those, in turn, vied with family loyalties. The period 600–750 had seen the startling rise of Islam, the whittling away of Byzantium, and the beginnings of stable political and economic development in an impoverished Europe. The period 750–1050 would see all three societies contend with internal issues of diversity even as they became increasingly conscious of their unity and uniqueness. At the beginning of this period, rulers built up and dominated strong, united political communities. By the end, these realms had fragmented into smaller, more local units. While men and women continued to feel some loyalty toward faraway kings, caliphs, or emperors, their most powerful allegiances often focused on authorities closer to home.

At Byzantium, the military triumphs of the emperors brought them enormous prestige. A renaissance (that is, an important revival) of culture and art took place at Constantinople. Yet at the same time new elites began to dominate the Byzantine countryside. In the Islamic world, a dynastic revolution in 750 ousted the Umayyads from the caliphate and replaced them with a new family, the Abbasids. The new caliphs moved their capital east, away from Damascus, and they adopted some of the trappings of the Sassanid King of Kings. Yet their power too began to ebb as regional Islamic rulers came to the fore. In western Europe, Charlemagne—a Frankish king from a new dynasty, the Carolingians—forged a huge empire. Yet this newly unified kingdom was

fragile, disintegrating within a generation of Charlemagne's death. In western Europe, even more than in the Byzantine and Islamic worlds, power fell into the hands of local leaders.

All along the borders of these realms, new political entities began to develop, conditioned by the religion and culture of their more dominant neighbors. Russia grew up in the shadow of Byzantium, as did Bulgaria and Serbia. Western Europe was more crucial in the development of central Europe. By the year 1050, the contours of what were to become modern Europe and the Middle East were dimly visible.

❖ Byzantium: Renewed Strength and Influence

In the hundred years between 750 and 850, Byzantium staved off Muslim attacks in Asia Minor and began to rebuild. After 850, it went on the attack. Military victories brought new wealth and power to the imperial court, and the emperors supported a vast program of literary and artistic revival—the Macedonian renaissance—at Constantinople. But while the emperor dominated at the capital, a new landowning elite began to control the countryside. On its northern front, Byzantium helped create new Slavic realms.

Imperial Power

While the *themes,* with their territorial military organization, took care of attacks on Byzantine territory, new mobile armies made up of the best troops—*tagmata* (singular, *tagma*)—

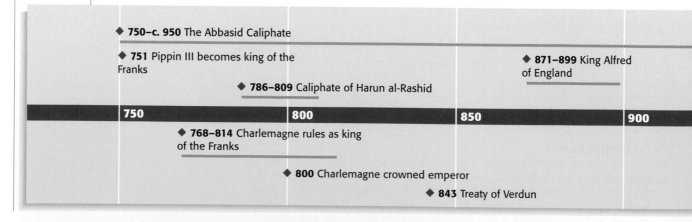

♦ **750–c. 950** The Abbasid Caliphate

♦ **751** Pippin III becomes king of the Franks

♦ **786–809** Caliphate of Harun al-Rashid

♦ **871–899** King Alfred of England

| 750 | 800 | 850 | 900 |

♦ **768–814** Charlemagne rules as king of the Franks

♦ **800** Charlemagne crowned emperor

♦ **843** Treaty of Verdun

moved aggressively outward, beginning around 850. By 1025, the empire had expanded to the Danube in the north and the Euphrates in the south (Map 9.1). The Byzantines had not controlled so much territory since their wars with the Sassanids four hundred years earlier.

Victories such as these gave new prestige and wealth to the army and to the imperial court. The emperors drew revenues from vast and growing imperial estates. They could tax and demand services from the general population at will—requiring citizens to build bridges and roads, to offer lodging to the emperor and his attendants, and to pay taxes in cash. Supported by their wealth, the emperors created a lavish court culture, surrounding themselves with servants, slaves, family members, and civil servants. Eunuchs, castrated men who could not pose a threat to the imperial line, were entrusted with some of the highest posts in government. From this powerful position, the emperors negotiated with other rulers, exchanging ambassadors and receiving and entertaining diplomats with elaborate ceremonies. One such diplomat, Liutprand, bishop of the northern Italian city of Cremona, reported on his audience with Emperor Constantine VII Porphyrogenitos♦ (r. 913–959) as follows:

Leaning upon the shoulders of two eunuchs I was brought into the emperor's presence. At my approach [mechanical] lions began to roar and birds to cry out, each according to its kind. . . . After I had three times [bowed] to the emperor with my face upon the ground, I lifted my head, and behold! the man whom just before I had

seen sitting on a moderately elevated seat had now changed his [clothing] and was sitting on the level of the ceiling. How it was done I could not imagine, unless perhaps he was lifted up by some such sort of device as we use for raising the timbers of a wine press.

Although Liutprand mocked this elaborate court ceremonial, it had a real function: to express the serious, sacred, concentrated power of imperial majesty.

The emperor's wealth relied on the prosperity of an agricultural economy organized for trade. State regulation and entrepreneurial enterprise were delicately balanced in Byzantine commerce. Although the emperor controlled craft and commercial guilds to ensure imperial revenues and a stable supply of valuable and useful commodities, entrepreneurs organized most of the markets held throughout the empire. Foreign merchants traded within the empire, either at Constantinople (where they were lodged at state expense) or in border cities. Because this international trade intertwined with foreign policy, the Byzantine government considered trade a political as well as an economic matter. Emperors issued privileges to certain "nations" (as, for example, the Venetians, Russians, and Jews were called), regulating the fees they were obliged to pay and the services they had to render. At the end of the tenth century, for example, the Venetians bargained to reduce their customs dues per ship from thirty *solidi*♦ (coins) to two; in return they promised to transport Byzantine soldiers to Italy whenever the emperor wished.

♦**Porphyrogenitos:** pohr fuh roh JEHN uht uhs

♦*solidi:* SAH luh dy

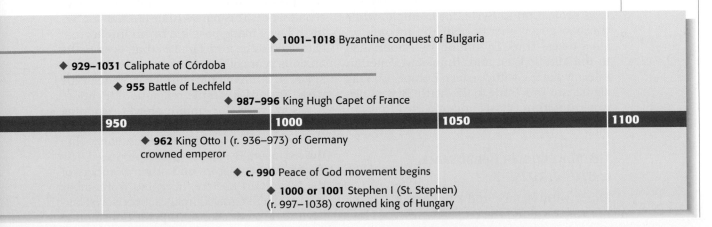

♦ **1001–1018** Byzantine conquest of Bulgaria

♦ **929–1031** Caliphate of Córdoba

♦ **955** Battle of Lechfeld

♦ **987–996** King Hugh Capet of France

950 | **1000** | **1050** | **1100**

♦ **962** King Otto I (r. 936–973) of Germany crowned emperor

♦ **c. 990** Peace of God movement begins

♦ **1000 or 1001** Stephen I (St. Stephen) (r. 997–1038) crowned king of Hungary

MAP 9.1 The Expansion of Byzantium, 860–1025
In 860, the Byzantine Empire was only a fraction of its former size. To the west, it had lost most of Italy, to the east, it held only part of Asia Minor. On its northern flank, the Bulgarians had set up an independent state. By 1025, however, it had ballooned, its western half embracing the whole Balkans, its eastern arm extending around the Black Sea, and its southern fringe reaching nearly to Tripoli. The year 1025 marked the Byzantine Empire's greatest size after the rise of Islam.

At the same time, the emperors negotiated privileges for their own traders in foreign lands. Byzantine merchants were guaranteed protection in Syria, for example, while the two governments split the income on sales taxes. Thus, Byzantine trade flourished in the Middle East and, thanks to Venetian intermediaries, with western Europe. Equally significant was trade to the north. Byzantines wore furs from Russia and imported Russian slaves, wax, and honey.

The Macedonian Renaissance, c. 870–c. 1025

Flush with victory and thinking of Byzantium's past glory, the emperors revived clas-sical intellectual pursuits. Basil I (r. 867–886) from Macedonia founded the imperial dynasty that presided over the so-called Macedonian renaissance. This renaissance (French for "re-birth") was made possible by an intellectual elite, who came from families that, even in the anxious years of the eighth century, had persisted in studying the classics in spite of the trend toward a simple religious education.

Now, with the empire slowly regaining its military eminence and with icons permanently restored in 843, this scholarly elite thrived again. Byzantine artists produced new works, and emperors and other members of the new court society, liberated from sober taboos against graven images, sponsored lavish artistic productions. Emperor Constantine

Porphyrogenitos (see the image on this page), wrote books of geography and history and financed the work of other scholars and artists. He even supervised the details of his craftspeople's products, insisting on exacting standards: "Who could enumerate how many artisans the Porphyrogenitos corrected? He

The Macedonian Renaissance

This manuscript illumination, made at Constantinople in the mid-ninth century, combines Christian and classical elements in a harmonious composition. David, author of the Psalms, sits in the center. Like the classical Orpheus, he plays music that attracts and tames the beasts. In the right-hand corner a figure labeled "Bethlehem" is modeled on a lounging river or mountain god. Compare this image of David with the one on the Cyprus plate on page 290. *Cliché Bibliotheque Nationale de France, Paris.*

The Crowning of Constantine Porphyrogenitos

The figures of this ivory relief were carved at Constantinople in the mid-tenth century. The artist wanted to emphasize hierarchy and symbolism, not nature. Christ is shown crowning Emperor Constantine Porphyrogenitos (r. 913–959). What message do you suppose the artist wanted to telegraph by making Christ higher than the emperor and by having the emperor slightly incline his head and upper torso to receive the crown? **For more help analyzing this image**, see the visual activity for this chapter in the Online Study Guide at **bedfordstmartins.com/hunt**. *Hirmer Fotoarchiv, München.*

corrected the stonemasons, the carpenters, the goldsmiths, the silversmiths, and the blacksmiths," wrote a historian supported by the same emperor's patronage.

The emperors were not alone. Other members of the imperial court also sponsored writers, philosophers, and historians. Scholars wrote summaries of classical literature, encyclopedias of ancient knowledge, and commentaries on classical authors. Some copied manuscripts of religious and theological commentaries, such as homilies, liturgical texts, Bibles, and Psalters. The merging of classical and Christian traditions is clearest in manuscript illuminations (painted illustrations or embellishments in hand-copied manuscripts). Both at Byzantium and in the West, artists chose their subjects by considering the texts they were to illustrate and the ways in which previous artists had handled particular themes. They drew on traditional models to make their subjects identifiable. Like modern illustrators of Santa Claus who rely on a tradition dictating a plump man with a bushy white beard—Santa's "iconography"—medieval artists depended on particular visual cues to alert viewers to the identity of their subjects. For example, to illustrate King David, the supposed poet of the Psalms, an artist illuminating a Psalter turned to a model of Orpheus, the enchanting musician of ancient Greek mythology.

The Dynatoi:
A New Landowning Elite

At Constantinople the emperor reigned supreme. But outside the capital, especially in the border regions of Anatolia, where army leaders of the tagmata became famous as military heroes, extremely powerful military families established themselves and began to compete with imperial power. The **dynatoi,**♦ as this new hereditary elite was called, got rich on booty and new lands taken in the aggressive wars of the tenth century. They took over or bought up whole villages, turning the peasants' labor to their benefit. For the most part they exercised their power locally, but they also sometimes occupied the imperial throne.

The Phocas♦ family is a good example of the strengths as well as the weaknesses of the dynatoi. Probably originally from Armenia, they possessed military skills and exhibited loyalty to the emperor that together brought them high positions in both the army and at court in the last decades of the ninth century. But in the tenth century, with new successes in the east, the Phocas family gained independent power. In fact, after some particularly brilliant wars, Nicephorus♦ Phocas was declared emperor by his armies and ruled at Constantinople from 963 to 969. But opposing factions of the dynatoi brought him down. The mainstay of Phocas family power, as of that of all the dynatoi, was outside the capital, on the family's great estates.

With the development of the dynatoi, the social hierarchy of Byzantium began to resemble that of western Europe, where land owned by aristocrats was farmed by a subject peasantry whose tax and service obligations bound them to the fields they cultivated.

♦**dynatoi:** DY nuh toy
♦**Phocas:** FOH kuhs
♦**Nicephorus:** ny SEH fuh ruhs

In Byzantium's Shadow:
Bulgaria, Serbia, Russia

The shape of what was to become modern eastern Europe was created during the period 850–950. By 800, Slavic settlements dotted the area from the Danube River down to Greece and from the Black Sea to Croatia. The ruler of the Bulgarians, called a *khagan,*♦ presided over the largest realm, northwest of Constantinople. Under Khagan Krum♦ (r. c. 803–814) and his son, Bulgarian rule stretched west all the way to the Tisza♦ River in modern Hungary. At about the same time as Krum's triumphant expansion, however, the Byzantine Empire began its own campaigns to conquer, convert, and control these Slavic regions.

Bulgaria and Serbia. The Byzantine offensive to the north and west began under Emperor Nicephorus I (r. 802–811), who waged war against the Slavs of Greece in the Peloponnesus, set up a new Christian diocese there, organized it as a new military theme, and forcibly resettled Christians in the area to counteract Slavic paganism. The Byzantines followed this pattern of conquest as they pushed northward. By 900, Byzantium ruled all of Greece.

The Balkans, c. 850–950

Still under Nicephorus, the Byzantines launched a massive attack against the Bulgarians, took the chief city of Pliska,♦ plundered it, burned it to the ground, and then marched against Krum's encampment in the Balkan mountains. Krum, however, took advantage of his position, attacked the imperial troops, killed Nicephorus, and brought home the em-

---

♦**Khagan:** KAG an
♦**Khagan Krum:** KAG an kruhm
♦**Tisza:** TIH saw
♦**Pliska:** PLEE skah

peror's skull in triumph. Cleaned out and lined with silver, the skull served as the victorious Krum's drinking goblet. In 816, the two sides agreed to a peace that lasted for thirty years. But hostility remained, and the intermittent skirmishes between the Bulgarians and Byzantines gave way to longer wars throughout the tenth century. The Byzantines advanced in a slow, methodical conquest (1001–1018) led by Emperor Basil II (r. 976–1025). Aptly called the Bulgar-Slayer, Basil subjected the entire region to Byzantine control and forced its ruler to accept the Byzantine form of Christianity. Similarly, the Serbs, encouraged by Byzantium to oppose the Bulgarians, began to form the political community that would become Serbia, in the shadow of Byzantine interest and religion.

Religion played an important role in the Byzantine offensive. In 863, two brothers, Cyril◆ and Methodius,◆ were sent as Christian missionaries from the Byzantines to the Slavs. Well educated in both classical and religious texts, they spoke one Slavic dialect fluently and devised an alphabet for Slavic (until then an oral language) based on Greek forms. It was the ancestor of the modern Cyrillic◆ alphabet used in Bulgaria, Serbia, and Russia today.

Kievan Russia. Russia in the ninth and tenth centuries lay outside the sphere of direct Byzantine rule, but like Serbia and Bulgaria it came under increasingly strong Byzantine cultural and religious influence. In the ninth century the Vikings—Scandinavian adventurers who ranged over vast stretches of ninth-century Europe seeking trade, booty, and land—had penetrated Russia from the north and imposed their rule over the Slavs inhabiting the broad river valleys. Like the Bulgars in Bulgaria, the Scandinavian Vikings gradually blended into the larger Slavic population. At the end of the ninth century, one Dnieper◆ valley chief, Oleg, established control over most of the tribes in southwestern Russia and forced peoples far-

◆**Cyril:** SIH ruhl
◆**Methodius:** meh THOH dee uhs
◆**Cyrillic:** suh RIH lihk
◆**Dnieper:** NEE pur

ther away to pay tribute money. The tribal association he created formed the nucleus of Kievan Russia, named for Kiev, the city that had become the commercial center of the region and today is the capital of Ukraine.

Kievan Russia and Byzantium began their relationship with war, developed it through trade agreements, and finally sustained it by religion. Around 905, Oleg launched a military expedition to Constantinople, forcing the Byzantines to pay him a large fee and open their doors to Russian traders in exchange for peace. At the time, only a few Christians lived in Russia, along with Jews and probably some Muslims. The Russians' conversion to Christianity was spearheaded by a Russian ruler later in the century. Vladimir (r. c. 980–1015), the grand prince of Kiev and all Russia, and the Byzantine emperor Basil II agreed that Vladimir should adopt the Byzantine form of Christianity. Vladimir took a variant of the name Basil in honor of the emperor and married the emperor's sister Anna; then he reportedly had all the people of his realm baptized in the Dnieper River.

Vladimir's conversion represented a wider pattern. Along with the Christianization of Slavic realms such as Old Moravia, Serbia, and Bulgaria under the Byzantine church, the rulers and peoples of Poland, Hungary, Denmark, and Norway were converted under the auspices of the Roman church. Russia's conversion to Christianity was especially significant, because Russia was geographically as close to the Islamic world as to the Christian and could conceivably have become an Islamic land. By converting to Byzantine Christianity, Russians made themselves heir to Byzantium and its church, customs, art, and political ideology. Adopting Christianity linked Russia to the Christian world, but choosing the Byzantine (Greek) form of Christianity, rather than the Roman Catholic, served later on to isolate Russia from western Europe, as in the course of the centuries the Greek and Roman churches became estranged.

Russian rulers at times sought to cement relations with central and western Europe, which were tied to Catholic Rome. Prince Iaroslav the Wise (r. 1019–1054) forged such links through his own marriage and those of his sons and daughters to rulers and princely families in France, Hungary, and Scandinavia. Iaroslav encouraged intellectual and artistic developments that would connect Russian culture to the classical past. At his own church of St. Sophia, at Kiev, which copied the one at Constantinople, Iaroslav created a major library.

When Iaroslav died, his kingdom was divided among his sons. Civil wars broke out between the brothers and eventually between cousins, shredding what unity Russia had known. Massive invasions by outsiders, particularly from the east, further weakened Kievan rulers, who were eventually displaced by princes from northern Russia. At the crossroads of East and West, Russia could meet and absorb a great variety of traditions; but its situation also opened it to unremitting military pressures.

Review: What were the effects of expansion on the power of the Byzantine emperor?

❖ The Islamic World: From Unity to Fragmentation

A new dynasty of caliphs—the Abbasids—first brought unity and then, in their decline, fragmentation to the Islamic world. Caliphs continued to rule in name only as regional rulers took over the real business of government in Islamic lands. Local traditions based on religious and political differences played an increasingly important role in people's lives. Yet, even in the eleventh century, the Islamic world had a clear sense of its own unity, which came from language, commercial life, and vigorous intellectual debate across regional boundaries.

The Abbasid Caliphate, 750–c. 950

In 750, a civil war ousted the Umayyads and raised the **Abbasids**◆ to the caliphate. The Abbasids found support in an uneasy coalition of Shi'ites (the faction of Islam loyal to

Ali's memory) and non-Arabs who had been excluded from Umayyad government and now demanded a place in political life. The new regime signaled a revolution. The center of Islamic rule shifted from Damascus, with its roots in the Roman tradition, to Baghdad, a new capital city, built by the Abbasids right next to Ctesiphon, which had been the Sassanid capital. Here the Abbasid caliphs imitated the Persian King of Kings (whose image they knew from sculptures such as the one on page 287) and adopted the court ceremony of the Sassanids. Their administration grew more and more centralized: the caliph's staff grew, and he controlled the appointment of regional governors.

The Abbasid caliph Harun al-Rashid◆ (r. 786–809) presided over a flourishing empire from Baghdad. His contemporary Frankish ruler, Charlemagne, was very impressed with the elephant Harun sent him as a gift, along with monkeys, spices, and medicines. But these items were mainstays of everyday commerce in Harun's Iraq. For example, a mid-ninth-century list of imports inventoried "tigers, panthers, elephants, panther skins, rubies, white sandal, ebony, and coconuts" from India, as well as "silk, chinaware, paper, ink, peacocks, racing horses, saddles, felts [and] cinnamon" from China.

The Abbasid dynasty began to decline after Harun's death. Obliged to support a huge army and increasingly complex civil service, the Abbasids found their tax base inadequate. They needed to collect revenues from their provinces, such as Syria and Egypt, but the governors of those regions often refused to send the revenues. After Harun's caliphate, ex-soldiers seeking better salaries recognized different caliphs and fought for power in savage civil wars. The caliphs tried to bypass the regular army, made up largely of free Muslim foot soldiers, by turning to slaves, bought and armed to serve as mounted cavalry. This tactic failed, however, and in the tenth century the caliphs became figureheads only. Religious leadership was now in the hands of religious scholars. Political leadership fell into the hands of independent rulers, who established themselves in the various Islamic regions. To sup-

◆**Abbasids:** A buh suhds

◆**Harun al-Rashid:** huh ROON ahl ruh SHEED

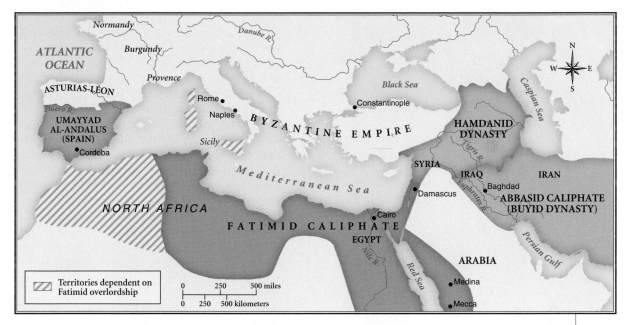

MAP 9.2 Islamic States, c. 1000
A glance back at Map 8.3 on page 296 will quickly demonstrate the fragmentation of the once united Islamic caliphate. In 750, one caliph ruled territory stretching from Spain to India. In 1000, there was more than one caliphate as well as several other ruling dynasties. The most important were the Fatimids, who began as organizers of a movement to overthrow the Abbasids. By 1000, they had conquered Egypt and claimed hegemony over all of North Africa.

port themselves militarily, many of these new rulers came to depend on independent military commanders who led armies of Mamluks♦—Turkish slaves or freedmen trained as professional mounted soldiers. Mamluks were well paid to maintain their mounts and arms, and many gained renown and high positions at the courts of regional rulers.

Thus, in the Islamic world, as in the Byzantine, a new military elite arose. But the Muslim and Byzantine elites differed in key ways. Whereas the Byzantine dynatoi were rooted in specific regions—tied to their estates and extended families—the Mamluks were highly mobile. They were not supported by land but rather were paid from taxes collected by local rulers. Organized into tightly knit companies bound together by devotion to a particular general and by a strong camaraderie, they easily changed employers, moving from ruler to ruler for pay.

Regional Diversity

A faraway caliph could not command sufficient allegiance from local leaders once he demanded more in taxes than he gave back in favors. The forces of fragmentation were strong in the Islamic world: it was, after all, based on the conquest of many diverse regions, each with its own deeply rooted traditions and culture. The Islamic religion, with its Sunni/Shi'ite split, also became a source of polarization. Western Europeans knew almost nothing about Muslims, calling all of them Saracens♦ (from the Latin for "Arabs") without distinction. But, in fact, Muslims were of different ethnicities, practiced different customs, and identified with different regions. With the fragmentation of political and religious unity, each of the tenth- and early-eleventh-century Islamic states built on local traditions under local rulers (Map 9.2).

♦**Mamluks:** MAM looks

♦**Saracens:** SAIR uh suhns

**Dome of the Mihrab of
the Great Mosque at Córdoba**
The mihrab is the prayer niche of the mosque, located so that the worshiper facing it is thereby facing Mecca. For the one at Córdoba, built between 961 and 976 by the Andalusian caliph al-Hakam, Byzantine mosaicists were imported to produce a decoration that would recall the mosaics of the Great Mosque at Damascus (see page 282). Why would this caliph, a Umayyad, be particularly interested in reminding Andalusians of the Damascus mosque? *Institut Amatller d'Art Hispanic, Barcelona.*

The Fatimid Dynasty. In the tenth century, one group of Shi'ites, calling themselves the Fatimids♦ (after Fatimah, Muhammad's only surviving child and wife of Ali), began a successful political movement. Allying with the Berbers in North Africa, the Fatimids established themselves in 909 as rulers in the region now called Tunisia. The Fatimid Ubayd Allah♦ claimed to be not only the true imam,♦ descendant of Ali, but also the *mahdi*,♦ the "divinely guided" messiah, come to bring justice on earth. In 969, the Fatimids declared

themselves rulers of Egypt. Their dynasty lasted for about two hundred years. Fatimid leaders also controlled North Africa, Arabia, and even Syria for a time.

The Spanish Emirate. Whereas the Shi'ites dominated Egypt, Sunni Muslims ruled al-Andalus,♦ the Islamic central and southern heart of Spain. Unlike the other independent Islamic states, which were forged during the ninth and tenth centuries, the Spanish emirate of Córdoba♦ (so called because its ruler took the secular title *emir*,♦ "commander," and fixed his capital at Córdoba) was created near the start of the Abbasid caliphate, in 756. During the Abbasid revolution, Abd al-Rahman—a member of the Umayyad family—fled to Morocco, gathered an army, invaded Spain, and was declared emir after only one battle. He and his successors ruled a broad range of peoples, including many Jews and Christians. After the initial Islamic conquest of Spain, the Christians adopted so much of the new language and so many of the customs that they were called Mozarabs,♦ that is, "like Arabs." The Arabs allowed them freedom of worship and let them live according to their own laws. Some Mozarabs were content with their status, others converted to Islam, and still others intermarried—most commonly, Christian women married Muslim men and raised their children as Muslims, since the religion of the father determined that of the children.

Abd al-Rahman♦ III (r. 912–961) was powerful enough to take the title of caliph; the caliphate of Córdoba that he created lasted from 929 to 1031. Under Abd al-Rahman's rule members of all religious groups in al-Andalus were given absolute freedom of worship and equal opportunity to rise in the civil service. The caliph also initiated important diplomatic contracts with Byzantine and European rulers, ignoring the weak and tiny Christian kingdoms squeezed into northern Spain. His successor, al-Hakam, built a splendid mihrab at Córdoba (see Dome of the

♦**Fatimids:** FAT ih mihds
♦**Ubayd Allah:** ub EYED a LAH
♦**imam:** ih MAHM
♦ *mahdi:* MAH dee

♦**al-Andalus:** al AND uh loos
♦**Córdoba:** KAWR duh buh
♦ *emir:* ih MIHR
♦**Mozarabs:** moh ZAR ruhbs
♦**Abd al-Rahman:** uhb dur rahk MAHN

Mihrab at Córdoba, page 328). Yet under later caliphs, al-Andalus, too, experienced the same political fragmentation that was occurring everywhere else. The caliphate of Córdoba broke up in 1031, and rulers of small, independent regions, called *taifas,*◆ took power.

Unity of Commerce and Language

Although the regions of the Islamic world were diverse culturally and politically, they maintained a measure of unity through trade networks and language. Their principal bond was Arabic, the language of the Qur'an. At once poetic and sacred, Arabic was also the language of commerce and government from Baghdad to Córdoba. Moreover, despite political differences, borders were open: an artisan could move from Córdoba to Cairo; a landowner in Morocco might very well own property in al-Andalus; a young man from North Africa would think nothing of going to Baghdad to find a wife; a young girl purchased as a slave in Mecca might become part of a prince's household in Baghdad. With few barriers to commerce (though every city and town had its own customs dues), traders regularly dealt in various, often exotic, goods.

Although the primary reason for these open borders was Islam itself, the openness extended to non-Muslims as well. We happen to know a good deal about the Tustari◆ brothers, Jewish merchants from southern Iran. The Tustaris' commercial activities were typical in the Arabic-speaking world. By 1026, they had established a flourishing business in Egypt. They did not have "branch offices," but informal contacts allowed them many of the same advantages and much flexibility: friends and family in Iran shipped the brothers fine textiles to sell in Egypt, and the Tustaris exported Egyptian fabrics to sell in Iran. Dealing in fabrics could yield fabulous wealth, for cloth was essential not only for clothing but also for home decoration: textiles covered walls; curtains separated rooms. The Tustari brothers held the highest rank in Jewish society and had contacts with Muslim rulers. The son of one of the brothers con-verted to Islam and became **vizier** (chief minister) to the Fatimids in Egypt. But the sophisticated Islamic society of the tenth and eleventh centuries supported networks even more vast than those represented by the Tustari family. Muslim merchants brought tin from England; salt and gold from Timbuktu in west-central Africa; amber, gold, and copper from Russia; and slaves from every region.

The Islamic Renaissance, c. 790–c. 1050

The dissolution of the caliphate into separate political entities multiplied the centers of learning and intellectual productivity. Unlike the Macedonian renaissance, which was concentrated in Constantinople, a renaissance of Islam occurred throughout the Islamic world. It was particularly dazzling in capital cities such as Córdoba, where tenth-century rulers presided over a brilliant court culture, patronizing scholars, poets, and artists. The library at Córdoba contained the largest collection of books in Europe at that time.

Elsewhere, already in the eighth century, the Abbasid caliphs endowed research libraries and set up centers for translation where scholars culled the writings of the ancients, including the classics of Persia, India, and Greece. Many scholars read, translated, and commented on the works of ancient philosophers. Others worked on astronomy (see Andromeda C, page 330), and still others wrote on mathematical matters. Al-Khwarizmi's◆ book on equations, written around 825, became so well known in the West that the word *al-jabr* in the title of his book became the English word *algebra.* Muhammad ibn Musa◆ (d. 850) used numerals such as 1, 2, and 3, which had been created in India, in his treatise on arithmetical calculations. Inventing the crucial placeholder zero, Musa was for the first time able to manipulate very large numbers (something impossible with Roman numerals). When these numerals were introduced into western Europe in the twelfth century, they were known as Arabic, as they are still called today.

◆*taifas:* TY fuhs
◆**Tustari:** tus TAR ee

◆**Al-Khwarizmi:** al KWAHR ihz mee
◆**Muhammad ibn Musa:** moh HAM uhd

Andromeda C. (11ᵗʰ century)
The study of sciences such as medicine, physics, and astronomy flourished in the tenth and eleventh centuries in the cosmopolitan Islamic world. This whimsical depiction of Andromeda C, a constellation in the Northern Hemisphere, illustrates the *Book of Images of the Fixed Stars,* an astronomical treatise written around 965 by al-Sufi at the request of his "pupil," the ruler of Iran. Since the Muslim calendar was lunar and the times of Muslim prayer were calculated by the movement of the sun, astronomy was important for religious as well as secular purposes. Al-Sufi drew from classical treatises, particularly the *Almagest* by Ptolemy. This copy of his book, probably made by his son in 1009, also draws on classical models for the illustrations; but instead of Greek clothing, Andromeda wears the pantaloons and skirt of an Islamic dancer. *Reference (shelfmark) MS Marsh 144. Bodleian Library. University of Oxford.*

The newly independent Islamic rulers supported science as well as mathematics. Ibn Sina◆ (980–1037), known in Christian Europe as Avicenna,◆ wrote books on logic,

the natural sciences, and physics. His *Canon of Medicine* systematized earlier treatises and reconciled them with his own experience as a physician. Active in the centers of power, he served as vizier to various rulers. In his autobiography he spoke with pleasure and pride about his intellectual development:

> One day I asked permission [of the ruler] to go into [his doctors'] library, look at their books, and read the medical ones. He gave me permission, and I went into a palace of many rooms, each with trunks full of books, back-to-back. In one room there were books on Arabic and poetry, in another books on jurisprudence, and similarly in each room books on a single subject. . . . When I reached the age of eighteen, I had completed the study of all these sciences.

Long before there were universities in Europe, there were important institutions of higher learning in the Islamic world. Rich Muslims, often members of the ruling elite, demonstrated their piety and charity by establishing schools for professors and students. Each school, or **madrasa,**◆ was located within or attached to a mosque. Professors held classes throughout the day on the interpretation of the Qur'an and other literary or legal texts. Students, all male, attended the classes that suited their achievement level and interest. Most students paid a fee for learning, but there were also scholarship students. One tenth-century vizier was so solicitous of the welfare of all scholars that each day he set out iced refreshments, candles, and paper for them in his own kitchen.

The use of paper, made from flax and hemp or rags and vegetable fiber, points to a major difference among the Islamic, Byzantine, and (as we shall see) Carolingian renaissances. Byzantine scholars worked to enhance the prestige of the ruling classes. Their work, written on expensive parchment (made from animal skins), kept manuscripts out of the hands of all but the very rich. This was true of scholarship in Europe as well. By contrast, Islamic scholars had goals that cut

---

◆**Ibn Sina:** ihb uhn SEE nah
◆**Avicenna:** a vuh SEH nuh

◆**madrasa:** muh DRA suh

across all social classes: to be physicians to the rich, teachers to the young, and contributors to passionate religious debates. Their writings, on paper (less expensive than parchment), were widely available.

> **Review:** What forces led to the fragmentation of the Islamic world in the tenth and eleventh centuries?

❖ The Creation and Division of a New European Empire

Just as in the Byzantine and Islamic worlds, so too in Europe the period 750–1050 saw first the formation of a strong empire, ruled by one man, and then its fragmentation as local rulers took power into their own hands. A new dynasty, the Carolingians, came to rule in the Frankish kingdom at almost the very moment (c. 750) that the Abbasids gained the caliphate. Charlemagne, the most powerful Carolingian monarch, conquered new territory, took the title of emperor, and presided over a revival of Christian classical culture known as the Carolingian renaissance. He ruled at the local level through counts and other military men. Nevertheless, the unity of this empire—based largely on conquest, a measure of prosperity, and personal allegiance to Charlemagne—was shaky. Its weaknesses were exacerbated by attacks from invaders—Vikings, Muslims, and Magyars. Charlemagne's successors divided his empire among themselves and saw it divided further as local leaders took defense—and rule—into their own hands.

The Rise of the Carolingians

The Carolingians were among many aristocratic families on the rise during the Merovingian period, but they gained exceptional power by monopolizing the position of "palace mayor" under the Merovingian kings. Charles Martel, mayor 714–741, gave the name

Carolingian (from *Carolus*, the Latin for "Charles") to the dynasty. Renowned for defeating an invading army of Muslims from al-Andalus between Poitiers◆ and Tours in 732, he also contended vigorously against other aristocrats who were carving out independent lordships for themselves. Charles and his family turned aristocratic factions against one another, rewarded supporters, crushed enemies, and dominated whole regions by supporting monasteries that served as focal points for both religious piety and land donations.

The Carolingians also allied themselves with the Roman papacy and its adherents. They supported Anglo-Saxon missionaries like Boniface,◆ who went to areas on the fringes of the Carolingian realm as the pope's ambassador. Reforming the Christianity that these regions had adopted, Boniface set up a hierarchical church organization and founded monasteries dedicated to the Benedictine rule. His newly appointed bishops were loyal to Rome and the Carolingians. Pippin III (d. 768), Charles Martel's son, turned to the pope even more directly. When he deposed the Merovingian king in 751, taking over the kingship himself, Pippin petitioned Pope Zachary to legitimize the act. The pope agreed. The Carolingians readily returned the favor a few years later when the pope asked for their help in defense against hostile Lombards. That papal request signaled a major shift. Before 754, the papacy had been part of the Byzantine Empire; after that, it turned to Europe for protection. Pippin launched a successful campaign against the Lombard king that ended in 756 with the so-called Donation of Pippin, a peace accord between the Lombards and the pope. The treaty gave back to the pope cities that had been ruled by the Lombard king. The new arrangement recognized what the papacy had long ago created: a territorial "republic of St. Peter" ruled by the pope, not by the Byzantine emperor. Henceforth, the fate of Italy would be tied largely to the policies of the pope and the Frankish kings to the north, not to the emperors of the East.

◆**Poitiers:** pwah tee AY
◆**Boniface:** BAH nuh fuhs

The Carolingian partnership with the Roman church gave the dynasty a Christian aura, expressed in symbolic form by anointment. Bishops rubbed holy oil on the foreheads and shoulders of Carolingian kings during the coronation ceremony, imitating the Old Testament kings who had been anointed by God.

Charlemagne and His Kingdom, 768–814

The most famous Carolingian king was Charles (r. 768–814), called the Great (*le Magne* in Old French) by his contemporaries. Epic poems portrayed Charlemagne as a just, brave, wise, and warlike king. In a biography written by Einhard,♦ his friend and younger contemporary, and patterned closely on Suetonius's♦ *Lives of the Caesars*, Charlemagne appeared as the very model of a Roman emperor. Some scholars at his court described him as another David, the anointed Old Testament king. Modern historians are less dazzled than his contemporaries were, noting that Charlemagne was complex, contradictory, and sometimes brutal. He loved listening to St. Augustine's *City of God* as it was read aloud, and he supported major scholarly enterprises; yet he never learned to write. He was devout, building a beautiful chapel at his major residence at Aachen♦ (see Charlemagne's Throne on this page), yet he flouted the advice of churchmen when they told him to convert pagans rather than force baptism on them. He admired the pope, yet he was furious when a pope placed the imperial crown on his head. He waged many successful wars, yet he thereby destroyed the buffer states surrounding the Frankish kingdoms, unleashing a new round of invasions even before his death.

Behind these contradictions, however, lay a unifying vision. Charlemagne dreamed of an empire that would unite the martial and learned traditions of the Roman and Germanic worlds with the legacy of Christianity. This vision lay at the core of his

---

♦**Einhard:** EYN hard
♦**Suetonius:** swee TOH nee uhs
♦**Aachen:** AH kuhn

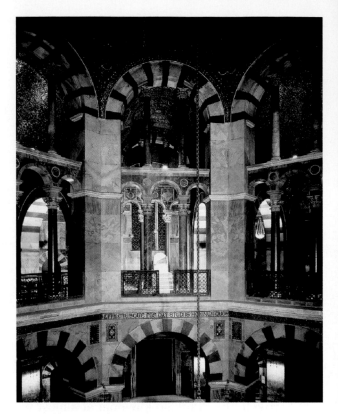

Charlemagne's Throne
Charlemagne was the first Frankish king to build a permanent capital city. The decision to do so was made in 789, and the king chose Aachen because of its natural warm springs. There he built a palace complex that included a grand living area for the king and his retinue and a church, still standing today, modeled on the Byzantine church of San Vitale in Ravenna. In the balcony above the altar of the church, Charlemagne placed his throne. Consider that Charlemagne had conquered northern Italy in 774. What aspirations might Charlemagne have been expressing by imitating a northern Italian Byzantine church? What idea of himself was he conveying by placing his own throne above the main altar? *Ann Munchow/Das Domkapital, Aachen.*

political activity, his building programs, and his active support of scholarship and education.

Territorial Expansion.   Charlemagne spent the early years of his reign conquering lands in all directions and subjugating the conquered peoples (Map 9.3). He invaded Italy, seizing the crown of the Lombard kings and annexing northern Italy in 774. He then moved northward and began a long and dif-

MAP 9.3 Expansion of the Carolingian Empire under Charlemagne
The conquests of Charlemagne temporarily united almost all of western Europe under one ruler. Although this great empire broke apart (see the inset showing the divisions of the Treaty of Verdun), the legacy of that unity remained, even serving as one of the inspirations behind today's European Union.

ficult war against the Saxons, concluded only after more than thirty years of fighting, during which he forcibly annexed Saxon territory and converted the Saxon people to Christianity through mass baptisms at the point of the sword. To the southeast, Charlemagne waged a campaign against the Avars. Einhard exulted, "All the money and treasure that had been amassed over many years was seized, and no war in which the Franks have ever engaged within the memory of man brought them such riches and such booty." To the southwest, Charlemagne led an ex-

pedition to al-Andalus. Although suffering a notable but local defeat at Roncesvalles♦ in 778 (immortalized later in the medieval epic *The Song of Roland*), he did set up a march, or military buffer region, between al-Andalus and his own realm.

By the 790s, Charlemagne's kingdom stretched eastward to the Saale♦ River (today in eastern Germany), southeast to what is today Austria, and south to Spain and Italy.

♦**Roncesvalles:** rawn tsuhs VA Luh
♦**Saale:** ZAH luh

Such power in the West was unheard of since the time of the Roman Empire. Charlemagne began to follow the old Roman model: he sponsored building programs to symbolize his authority, standardized weights and measures, and acted as a patron of intellectual and artistic efforts. He built a capital city at Aachen, complete with a church patterned on one built by Justinian at Ravenna.

To discourage corruption, Charlemagne appointed special officials, called *missi dominici*◆ (meaning "those sent out by the lord king"), to oversee his regional governors—the counts—on the king's behalf. The missi—lay aristocrats or bishops— traveled in pairs to make a circuit of regions of the kingdom. As one of Charlemagne's capitularies (summaries of royal decisions) put it, the missi "are to make diligent inquiry wherever people claim that someone has done them an injustice, so that the missi fully carry out the law and do justice for everyone everywhere, whether in the holy churches of God or among the poor, orphans, or widows."

Imperial Coronation. While Charlemagne was busy imitating Roman emperors through his conquests, his building programs, his legislation, and his efforts at church reform, the papacy was beginning to claim imperial power for itself. At some point, perhaps in the mid-750s, members of the papal chancery (writing office) created a document called the Donation of Constantine, which declared the pope the recipient of the fourth-century emperor Constantine's crown, cloak, and military rank along with "all provinces, palaces, and districts of the city of Rome and Italy and of the regions of the West." (The document was much later proved a forgery.) The tension between the imperial claims of the Carolingians and those of the pope was heightened by the existence of an emperor at Constantinople who also had rights in the West.

Pope Hadrian◆ I (r. 772–795) maintained a balance among these three powers. But Hadrian's successor, Leo III (r. 795–816), tipped the balance. In 799, accused of adultery and perjury by a faction of the Roman aristocracy, Leo narrowly escaped being

blinded and having his tongue cut out. He fled northward to seek Charlemagne's protection. Charlemagne had him escorted back to Rome under royal protection and arrived there himself to an imperial welcome orchestrated by Leo. On Christmas Day, 800, Leo put an imperial crown on Charlemagne's head and the clergy and nobles who were present acclaimed the king Augustus, the title of the first Roman emperor. The pope hoped in this way to exalt the king of the Franks, to downgrade the Byzantine ruler, and to enjoy the role of "emperor maker" himself.

About twenty years later, when Einhard wrote about this coronation, he said that the imperial title at first displeased Charlemagne "so much that he stated that, if he had known in advance of the pope's plan, he would not have entered the church that day." In fact, Charlemagne did not use any title but king for more than a year afterward. But it is unlikely that he was completely surprised by the imperial title; his advisers certainly had been thinking about it for him. He might have hesitated to adopt the title because he feared the reaction of the Byzantines, as Einhard went on to suggest, or he might have objected to the papal role in his crowning rather than to the crown itself. When Charlemagne finally did call himself emperor, after establishing a peace with the Byzantines, he used a long and revealing title: "Charles, the most serene Augustus, crowned by God, great and peaceful Emperor who governs the Roman Empire and who is, by the mercy of God, king of the Franks and the Lombards." According to this title, Charlemagne was not the Roman emperor crowned by the pope but rather God's emperor, who governed the Roman Empire along with his many other duties.

The Carolingian Renaissance, c. 790–c. 900

Charlemagne inaugurated—and his successors continued to support—a revival of learning designed to enhance the glory of the kings, educate their officials, reform the liturgy, and purify the faith. Like the renaissances of the Byzantine and Islamic worlds, the Carolingian renaissance resuscitated the learning of the past. Scholars studied Roman im-

---

◆*missi dominici:* MEE si dom IN i kee
◆**Hadrian:** HAY dree uhn

perial writers such as Suetonius and Virgil, read and commented on the works of the church fathers, and worked to establish complete and accurate texts of everything they read and prized.

The English scholar Alcuin♦ (c. 732–804), a member of the circle of scholars whom Charlemagne recruited to form a center of study, brought with him the traditions of Anglo-Saxon scholarship that had been developed by men such as Benedict Biscop and Bede. Invited to Aachen, Alcuin became Charlemagne's chief adviser, writing letters on the king's behalf, counseling him on royal policy, and tutoring the king's household, including the women and girls. He also prepared an improved edition of the Vulgate,♦ the Latin Bible read in all church services by the clergy.

The Carolingian renaissance depended on an elite staff of scholars such as Alcuin, yet its educational program had broader appeal. In one of his capitularies, Charlemagne ordered that the cathedrals and monasteries of his kingdom teach reading and writing to all who were able to learn. Some churchmen expressed the hope that schools for children (perhaps they were thinking of girls as well as boys) would be established even in small villages and hamlets. Although this dream was never realized, it shows that, at just about the same time as the Islamic world was organizing its madrasas, the Carolingians were thinking about the importance of religious education for more than a small elite.

Art, like scholarship, served Carolingian political and religious goals. Carolingian artists turned to models from Byzantium (perhaps some refugees from Byzantine iconoclasm joined them) and Italy to illustrate gospels, psalters, scientific treatises, and literary manuscripts.

The Carolingian program was ambitious and lasting, even after the Carolingian dynasty had faded to a memory. The work of locating, understanding, and transmitting models of the past continued in a number of monastic schools. In the materials they studied, the questions they asked, and the answers they suggested, the Carolingians offered a mode of inquiry fruitful for subse-

St. Matthew
The Carolingian renaissance produced art of extraordinary originality. Although the artist of this picture was inspired by classical models, his frenetic, emotional lines and uncanny colors are something new. This illustration, a depiction of St. Matthew writing (with an ink horn in his left hand and a quill in his right hand), precedes the text of St. Matthew's Gospel in a book of Gospels made around 820. Compare it to the Psalter illumination from Constantinople on page 323. What does this comparison tell you about the similarities and differences between the Macedonian and Carolingian renaissances?
La Médiathèque, Ville d'Epernay.

quent generations. In the twelfth century, scholars would build on the foundations laid by the Carolingian renaissance. The very print of this textbook depends on one achievement of the period: modern letter fonts are based on the clear and beautiful letter forms, called Caroline miniscule,♦

♦**Alcuin:** AL kwuhn
♦**Vulgate:** VUHL gayt

♦**Caroline miniscule:** KAR uh lyn MIHN his kyool

invented in the ninth century to standardize manuscript handwriting—and make it more readable—across the whole empire.

Charlemagne's Successors, 814–911

Charlemagne's son Louis the Pious (r. 814–840) took his role as leader of the Christian empire even more seriously than his father did. He brought the monastic reformer Benedict of Aniane◆ to court and issued a capitulary in 817 imposing a uniform way of life, based on the Benedictine rule, on all the monasteries of the empire. Although some monasteries opposed this legislation, and in the years to come the king was unable to impose his will directly, this moment marked the effective adoption of the Benedictine rule as the monastic standard in Europe.

In a new development of the coronation ritual, Louis's first wife, Ermengard◆, was crowned empress by the pope in 816. In 817, their firstborn son, Lothar, was given the title emperor and made co-ruler with Louis. Their other sons, Pippin and Louis (later called Louis the German), were made sub-kings under imperial rule. Louis the Pious hoped in this way to ensure the unity of the empire while satisfying the claims of all his sons. Should any son die, only his firstborn could succeed him, a measure intended to prevent further splintering. But Louis's hopes were thwarted by events. Ermengard died, and Louis married Judith, the daughter of one of the most powerful families in the kingdom. In 823, she and Louis had a son, Charles (later known as Charles the Bald, to whose court Dhuoda's son William was sent). The sons of Ermengard, bitter over the birth of another royal heir, rebelled against their father and fought one another for more than a decade. Finally, after Louis's death in 840, the Treaty of Verdun◆ (843) divided the empire among the three remaining brothers (Pippin had died in 838) in an arrangement that would roughly define the future political contours of western Europe (see Map 9.3). The western third, bequeathed to Charles the Bald (r. 843–877), would eventually be-

come France; the eastern third, handed to Louis the German (r. 843–876), would become Germany. The "Middle Kingdom," which was given to Lothar (r. 840–855) along with the imperial title, had a different fate: parts of it were absorbed by France and Germany, and the rest eventually formed what were to become the modern states of the Netherlands, Belgium, Luxembourg, Switzerland, and Italy.

By 843, the European-wide empire of Charlemagne had dissolved. Forged by conquest, it had been supported by a small group of privileged aristocrats with lands and offices stretching across the whole of it. Their loyalty—based on shared values, real friendship, expectations of gain, and sometimes formal ties of vassalage◆ and fealty◆ (see page 342)—was crucial to the success of the Carolingians. The empire had also been supported by an ideal, shared by educated laymen and churchmen alike, of conquest and Christian belief working together to bring good order to the earthly state. But powerful forces operated against the Carolingian Empire. Once the empire's borders were fixed and conquests ceased, the aristocrats could not hope for new lands and offices. They put down roots in particular regions and began to gather their own followings. Powerful local traditions such as different languages also undermined imperial unity. Finally, as Dhuoda revealed, some people disagreed with the imperial ideal. Asking her son to put his father before the emperor, she demonstrated her belief in the primacy of the family and the personal ties that bound it together. Her ideal represented a new sensibility that saw real value in the breaking apart of Charlemagne's empire into smaller, more intimate local units. (See "Dhuoda's Handbook for Her Son on page 337")

Land and Power

The Carolingian economy, based on trade and agriculture, contributed to both the rise and the dissolution of the Carolingian Empire. At the onset, the empire's wealth came from land and plunder. After the booty from war

---

◆**Aniane:** ahn YAHN
◆**Ermengard:** EHR mehn gahrd
◆**Verdun:** vur DUHN

◆**vassalage:** VA suh lihj
◆**fealty:** FEE uhl tee

Dhuoda's Handbook for Her Son

Dhuoda's handbook, written in the mid-ninth century, is a rare example of writing by a woman from this period. Yet the excellent education that her handbook reveals cannot have been hers alone; it is likely that most of the female members of the aristocracy in the Carolingian period knew how to read and write. In the following passage she shows her concern for her son's moral character and religious faith.

It is I, Dhuoda, who give you direction, my son William. I wish that, as you grow patiently in worthy virtues among those who fight alongside you, you may always be "slow to speak, and slow to anger" [James 1:19]. If you grow angry, do so without sin. May it never happen that our merciful God grows angry in turn with you or—and may this also never befall—that you stray in your anger from the true path.

Therefore I direct you that, with gentleness, justice, and holiness, you perform your worldly service to him who, admonishing his faithful ones to shine with patience, says, "In your patience you shall possess your souls" [Luke 21:19]. If you are patient, and if you restrain your thoughts and your tongue, you will be blessed. . . .

If you encounter a poor man, offer him as much help as you can, not only in words but also in deeds. I direct you likewise to offer generous hospitality to pilgrims, widows and orphans, children and indigents and to be quick to lift your hand to help those who you see are in need. As Scripture says, "we are sojourners," immigrants and "strangers, as were all our fathers" [1 Par 29:5] who passed upon the earth. . . .

We know that poverty and want are found not only among the least of men but also frequently, for many reasons, among the great. So it is that a rich man too may be in need. Why? Because his soul is wretchedly needy. And then there is the poor man who gathers riches with great ease. Or the rich man who envies the poor man, or the poor man who wishes to become rich, just as an unlettered man wishing to become learned may desire this completely but never accomplish it.

Source: Dhuoda, Handbook for William: A Carolingian Woman's Counsel for Her Son, trans. Carol Neel (Washington, DC: Catholic University of America Press, 1991), 54–55.

ceased to pour in, the Carolingians still had access to money and goods. To the north, in Viking trading stations such as Haithabu◆ (today Hedeby, in northern Germany), archaeologists have found Carolingian glass and pots alongside Islamic coins and cloth, which tells us that the Carolingian economy intermingled with that of the Abbasid caliphate. Silver from the Islamic world probably came north up the Volga River through Russia to the Baltic Sea. There the coins were melted down, the silver traded to the Carolingians in return for wine, jugs, glasses, and other manufactured goods. The Carolingians turned the silver into coins of their own, to be used throughout the empire for small-scale local trade. The weakening of the Abbasid caliphate in the mid-ninth century, however, disrupted this far-flung trade network and contributed to the weakening of the Carolingians at about the same time.

Land provided the most important source of Carolingian wealth and power. Like the landholders of the late Roman Empire and the Merovingian period, Carolingian aristocrats held many estates, scattered throughout the Frankish empire. But in the Carolingian period these estates were reorganized and their productivity carefully calculated. Modern historians often call these estates **manors**.

Typical was the manor called Villeneuve◆ St.-Georges, which belonged to the monastery

◆**Haithabu:** HATH uh boo

◆**Villeneuve:** veel NUHV

of St.-Germain-des-Prés♦ (today in Paris) in the ninth century. Villeneuve consisted of arable fields, vineyards, meadows where animals could roam, and woodland, all scattered about the countryside rather than connected in a compact unit. The land was not tilled by slave gangs, as had been the custom on great estates of the Roman Empire, but by peasant families, each one settled on its own manse, which consisted of a house, a garden, and small pieces of the arable land. The families farmed the land that belonged to them and also worked the demesne,♦ the very large manse of the lord (in this case the abbey of St.-Germain).

These peasant farms, cultivated by households, marked a major social and economic development. Slaves had not been allowed to live in family units. By contrast, the peasants on Villeneuve and on other Carolingian estates could not be separated involuntarily from their families or displaced from their manses. In this sense, the peasant household of the Carolingian period was the precursor of the modern nuclear family.

Peasants at Villeneuve practiced the most progressive sort of plowing, known as the three-field system, in which they farmed two-thirds of the arable land at one time. They planted one-third with winter wheat and one-third with summer crops and left one-third fallow, to restore its fertility. The crops sown and the fallow field then rotated so that land use was repeated only every three years. This method of organizing the land produced larger yields (because two-thirds of the land was cultivated each year) than the still prevalent two-field system, in which only half of the arable land was cultivated one year, the other half the next.

All the peasants at Villeneuve were dependents of the monastery and owed dues and services to St.-Germain. Their obligations varied enormously. One family, for example, owed four silver coins, wine, wood, three hens, and fifteen eggs every year, and the men had to plow the fields of the demesne land. Another family owed the intensive labor of working the vineyards. One woman was required to weave cloth and feed the chickens.

Peasant women spent much time at the lord's house in the *gynaeceum*♦—the women's workshop, where they made and dyed cloth and sewed garments—or in the kitchens, as cooks. Peasant men spent most of their time in the fields.

Estates organized on the model of Villeneuve were profitable. Like other lords, the Carolingians benefited from their extensive estates. Nevertheless, farming was still too primitive to return great surpluses, and as the lands belonging to the king were divided up in the wake of the partitioning of the empire and new invasions, Carolingian dependence on manors scattered throughout their kingdom proved to be a source of weakness.

Vikings, Muslims, and Magyars Invade, c. 790–955

Carolingian kings and counts confronted new groups—Vikings, Muslims, and Magyars—along their borders (Map 9.4). As royal sons fought one another and as counts and other powerful men sought to carve out their own principalities, some allied with the newcomers, helping to integrate them swiftly into European politics.

Vikings. About the same time as they made their forays into Russia, the Vikings moved westward as well. The Franks called them Northmen; the English called them Danes. They were, in fact, much less united than their victims thought. When they began their voyages at the end of the eighth century, they did so in independent bands. Merchants and pirates at the same time, Vikings followed a chief, seeking profit, prestige, and land. Many traveled as families: husbands, wives, children, and slaves.

The Vikings perfected the art of navigation. In their longships they crossed the Atlantic, settling Iceland and Greenland and (about 1000 C.E.) landing on the coast of North America. Other Viking bands navigated the rivers of Europe. The Vikings were pagans, and to them monasteries and churches—with their reliquaries, chalices, and crosses—were simply storehouses of booty.

♦**St.-Germain-des-Prés:** san jair MAN duh PRAY
♦**demesne:** dih MAYN

♦*gynaeceum:* gy nuh SEE uhm

MAP 9.4 Muslim, Viking, and Magyar Invasions of the Ninth and Tenth Centuries
Bristling with multicolored arrows, this map suggests that western Europe was continually and thoroughly pillaged by outside invaders for almost two centuries. That impression is only partially true; it must be offset by several factors. First, not all the invaders came at once. The Viking raids were nearly over when the Magyar attacks began. Second, the invaders were not entirely unwelcome. The Magyars were for a time enlisted as mercenaries by the king of Italy, and some Muslims were allied to local lords in Provence. Third, the invasions, though widespread, were local in effect. Note, for example, that the Viking raids were largely limited to rivers or coastal areas.

TAKING MEASURE

Viking Coin Hoards, c. 865–895

We know from chronicles and other written sources that the Vikings invaded and settled in parts of the British Isles. But where, exactly? And how many people were involved? Counting buried coins from the period can help answer these questions. Before safe-deposit boxes and banks, people buried their money in times of trouble. From Viking coin hoards in the British Isles archaeologists can see that the area called Danelaw was fairly thickly populated by Vikings, with a scattering in other regions as well. The Viking impact was not so much political—no Viking chief took it over—as demographic. After 900, England, in particular, was as much Scandinavian as it was Anglo-Saxon. The lack of Viking coin hoards in Ireland suggests that the Scandinavians did not settle there permanently. *From David Hill*, An Atlas of Anglo-Saxon England (Toronto, 1981).

Parts of the British Isles were especially hard hit. (See "Taking Measure," on this page.) In England, for example, the Vikings raided regularly in the 830s and 840s; by midcentury, they were spending winters there. The Vikings did not just destroy. In 876, they settled in the northeast of England, plowing the land and preparing to live on it. The region where they settled and imposed their own laws was later called the *Danelaw.*♦ (See the spot map England in the Age of King Alfred, on page 350.)

In Wessex, the southernmost kingdom of England, King Alfred the Great (r. 871–899) bought time and peace by paying tribute and giving hostages. Such tribute, later called *Danegeld,*♦ was collected as a tax that eventually became the basis of a relatively lucrative taxation system in England. Then in 878, Alfred led an army that, as his biographer put it, "gained the victory through God's will. He destroyed the Vikings with great slaughter and pursued those who fled . . . hacking them down." Thereafter the pressures of invasion eased as Alfred reorganized his army, set up strongholds, and deployed new warships.

On the continent, too, the invaders set up trading emporia and settled where originally they had raided. Beginning about 850, their attacks became well-organized expeditions for regional control. At the end of the ninth century, one contingent settled in the region of France that soon took the name Normandy, the land of the Northmen. The new inhabitants converted to Christianity during the tenth century. Rollo, the Viking leader in Normandy, accepted Christianity in 911; at the same time, Normandy was formally ceded to him by the Frankish king Charles the Simple.

Normandy was not the only new Christian polity created in the north during the tenth and eleventh centuries. Scandinavia itself was transformed with the creation of the powerful kingdom of Denmark. There had been kings in Scandinavia before the tenth century, but they had been weak, their power challenged by nearby chieftains. The Vikings had been led by these chieftains,

---

♦*Danelaw*: DAYN law
♦*Danegeld*: DAYN gehld

each competing for booty to win prestige, land, and power back home. During the course of their raids, they and their followers came into contact with new cultures and learned from them. Meanwhile the Carolingians and the English supported missionaries in Scandinavia. By the middle of the tenth century, the Danish kings and their people had become Christian. And, following the model of the Christian kings to their south, they built up an effective monarchy, with a royal mint and local agents who depended on them. By about 1000, the Danes had extended their control to parts of Sweden, Norway, and even England under King Cnut◆ (r. 1017–1035).

Muslims. The dynasty that preceded the Fatimids in Egypt developed a navy that, in the course of the ninth and tenth centuries, gradually conquered Sicily, which had formerly been under Byzantine rule. By the middle of the tenth century, independent Islamic princes ruled all of Sicily. Around the same time, other raiders from North Africa set up bases on other Mediterranean islands, while pirates from al-Andalus built a stronghold in Provence (in southern France). Liutprand◆ of Cremona was outraged:

> [Muslim pirates from al-Andalus], disembarking under cover of night, entered the manor house unobserved and murdered—O grievous tale!— the Christian inhabitants. They then took the place as their own…[fortified it and] started stealthy raids on all the neighboring country…. Meanwhile the people of Provence close by, swayed by envy and mutual jealousy, began to cut one another's throats, plunder each other's substance, and do every sort of conceivable mischief…. [Furthermore, they called upon the Muslims] and in company with them proceeded to crush their neighbors.

In this way the Muslims, although outsiders, were drawn into local Provençal disputes.

Magyars. The Magyars,◆ a nomadic people and latecomers to Europe, arrived around 899 into the Danube basin. Until then the region

◆**Cnut:** kuh NOOT
◆**Liutprand:** LEE ut
◆**Magyars:** MAH jahrs

had been predominantly Slavic, but the Magyars came from the East and spoke a language unrelated to any other in Europe (except Finnish). Their entry drove a wedge between the Slavs near the Frankish kingdom and those bordering on Byzantium; the Bulgarians, Serbs, and Russians were driven into the Byzantine orbit, while the Slavs nearer the Frankish kingdom came under the influence of Germany.

From their bases in present-day Hungary, the Magyars raided far to the west, attacking Germany, Italy, and even southern Gaul frequently between 899 and 955. Then one marauding party of Magyars was met at the Lech River by the German king Otto I (r. 936–973), whose army defeated them in the battle of Lechfeld◆ in 955. Otto's victory, his subsequent military reorganization of his eastern frontiers, and the cessation of Magyar raids around this time made Otto a great hero to his contemporaries. However, histo-

◆**Lechfeld:** LEHK fehlt

Viking Picture Stone

Picture stones, some very elaborate, others with simple incisions, were made on the island of Gotland, today part of Sweden, from the fifth to the twelfth century. This one, dating from the eighth or ninth century, has four interrelated scenes. At the bottom is a battle between people defending a farm (note the cattle tied to the walls of the enclosure) and archers outside. Above is another enclosure with a woman at its wall. She is either Gudrun mourning her brother Gunnar, who was thrown into a snake pit, or Sigyn, the faithful wife of the god Loke, catching in a bowl the venom that a snake pours down on her chained husband. Next comes a ship, a typical motif on picture stones; it is the ship of death that takes heroes to heaven. At the very top is heaven, or Valhalla, itself, where the heroes hunt and feast for all eternity.
Photo: Raymond Hejdstrom.

rians today think the containment of the Magyars had more to do with their internal transformation from nomads to farmers than with their military defeat.

The Viking, Muslim, and Magyar invasions were the final onslaught western Europe experienced from outsiders. In some ways they were a continuation of the invasions that had rocked the Roman Empire in the fourth and fifth centuries. Loosely organized in warbands, the new groups entered western Europe looking for wealth but stayed on to become absorbed in the region's post-invasion society.

Review: What were the strengths and weaknesses of Carolingian institutions of government, warfare, and defense?

❖ After the Carolingians: The Emergence of Local Rule

The Carolingian Empire was too diverse to cohere. Although Latin was the language of official documents and most literary and ecclesiastical text, few people spoke it; instead they used a wide variety of different languages and dialects. The king demanded loyalty from everyone, but most people knew only his representative, the local count. The king's power ultimately depended on the count's allegiance, but as the empire ceased to expand and was instead attacked by outsiders, the counts and other powerful men stopped looking to the king for new lands and offices and began to develop and exploit what they already had. They became powerful lords, commanding allegiance from vassals, building castles, setting up markets, collecting revenues, keeping the peace, and seeing themselves as independent regional rulers. They dominated the local peasantry. In this way, a new warrior class of lords and vassals came to dominate post-Carolingian society.

Yet it would be wrong to imagine that all of Europe came under the control of rural leaders. In northern and central Italy, where cities had never lost their importance, urban elites ruled over the surrounding countryside. Everywhere kings retained a certain amount of power; indeed, in some places, such as

Germany and England, they were extremely effective. Central European monarchies formed under the influence of Germany.[1]

Public Power and Private Relationships

The key way in which both kings and less powerful men commanded others was to ensure personal loyalty. In the ninth century, the Carolingian kings had their *fideles*,♦ their "faithful men." Among these were the counts. In addition to a share in the revenues of their administrative district, the county, the counts received benefices, later also called fiefs,♦ temporary grants of land given in return for service. These short-term arrangements often became permanent, however, once a count's son inherited the job and the fiefs of his father. By the end of the ninth century, fiefs were often properties that could be passed on to heirs.

Lords and Vassals.   In the wake of the invasions, more and more warriors were drawn into similar networks of dependency, but not with the king: they became the faithful men—the vassals—of local lords. From the Latin word for fief comes the word *feudal*, and some historians use the term **feudalism** to describe the social and economic system created by the relationship among vassals, lords, and fiefs. (See "Terms of History," page 343.)

It was frequently said by medieval people that their society consisted of three groups: those who prayed, those who fought, and those who worked. All of these people were involved in a hierarchy of dependency and linked by personal bonds, but the upper classes—the prayers (monks) and the fighters (the knights)—were free. Their brand of dependency was prestigious, whether they were vassals, lords, or both. In fact, a typical warrior was lord of several vassals even while serving as the vassal of another lord. Monas-

[1] Terms such as *Germany*, *France*, and *Italy* are used here for the sake of convenience. They refer to regions, not the nation-states that would eventually become associated with those names.

♦ *fideles*: fee DAY lays
♦ **fiefs:** feefs

TERMS OF HISTORY

Feudalism

Feudalism is a modern word, like *capitalism* and *communism*. No one in the Middle Ages used it, or any of its related terms, such as *feudal system* or *feudal society*. Many historians today think that it is a misleading word and should be discarded. The term poses two serious problems. First, historians have used it to mean different things. Second, it implies that one way of life dominated the Middle Ages, when in fact there were numerous varieties of social, political, and economic arrangements.

Consider the many different meanings that *feudalism* has had. Historians influenced by Karl Marx's powerful communist theory used (and still use) *feudalism* to refer to an economic system in which nobles dominated subservient peasant cultivators. When they speak of feudalism, they are speaking of manors, lords, and serfs. Other historians, however, call that system *manorialism*. They reserve the term *feudalism* for a system consisting of vassals (who never did agricultural labor but only military service), lords, and fiefs. For example, in an influential book written in the mid-1940s, *Feudalism*, F. L. Ganshof considered the tenth to the thirteenth centuries to be the "classical age of feudalism" because during this period lords regularly granted fiefs to their vassals, who fought on their lord's behalf in return.

But, writing around the same time, Marc Bloch included in his definition of *feudalism* every aspect of the political and social life of the Middle Ages, including peasants, fiefs, knights, vassals, and the fragmentation of royal authority yet the survival of the state, which "was to acquire renewed strength" in the course of the feudal period. Some historians, reacting to this broad definition, have tried to narrow it by considering *feudalism* to be a political term that refers to the decline of the state and the dispersal of political power. Others, while also trying to narrow the definition, use *feudalism* to mean a system by which kings controlled their men. These definitions are opposites.

Whatever the definition, they all stress certain institutions that some recent historians argue were very peripheral to medieval life. The fief, for example, a word whose Latin form (*feodum*) gave rise to the word *feudalism*, was by no means important everywhere. And even where it was important, it did not necessarily have anything to do with lords, vassals, or military obligations. "Nobles and free men," writes the historian Susan Reynolds, "did not generally owe military service before the twelfth century because of the grant of anything like fiefs to them or their ancestors. . . . They owed whatever service they owed, not because they were vassals of a lord, but because they were subjects of a ruler." For Reynolds, feudalism is a myth.

Mythical or not, all these views, even that of Reynolds, have one thing in common: a stress on vertical hierarchies, such as lords over peasants or kings over their subjects. Some recent historians, however, point out that not all of medieval society was hierarchical. Horizontal relations—such as those that created peasant communities, urban corporations, and the comradeship of knightly troops—were equally, if not more, important.

For all of these reasons, many historians have stopped using the word *feudalism*, preferring to stress the variety of medieval social and political arrangements. How many times have you encountered the term in this history book?

FURTHER READING

Bloch, Marc. *Feudal Society*. 2 vols. Trans. L. A. Manyon, 1961.

Ganshof, F. L. *Feudalism*. Trans. Philip Grierson, 1961.

Reynolds, Susan. *Fiefs and Vassals: The Medieval Evidence Reinterpreted*. 1994.

Two Cities Besieged

In about 900, the monks of the monastery of St. Gall produced a Psalter with numerous illuminations. The illustration for Psalm 59, which tells of King David's victories, used four pages. This page was the fourth. On the top level, David's army besieges a fortified city from two directions. On the right are foot soldiers, one of whom holds a burning torch to set the city afire; on the left are horsemen—led by their standard-bearer—with lances and bows and arrows. Note their chain-mail coats and their horses' stirrups. Within the city, four soldiers protect themselves with shields, but another has fallen and hangs upside down from the city wall. The dead and wounded on the ground are bleeding. Four other men seem to be cowering behind the city. In the bottom register, a different city burns fiercely (note the towers on fire). This city lacks defenders; the people within it are unarmed. Although this illumination purports to show David's victories, in fact it nicely represents the equipment and strategies of ninth-century warfare. *Stiftsbibliothek St. Gallen, Switzerland.*

teries normally had vassals to fight for them, and their abbots in turn were often vassals of a king or other powerful lord (see Two Cities Beseiged, on this page).

Vassalage grew up as an alternative to public power and at the same time as a way to strengthen what little public power there was. Given the impoverished economic conditions of western Europe, its primitive methods of communication, and its lack of unifying traditions, kings came to rely on vassals personally loyal to them to muster troops, collect taxes, and administer justice. When in the ninth century the Frankish empire broke up politically and power fell into the hands of local lords, those lords, too, needed "faithful men" to protect them and carry out their orders. And vassals needed lords. At the low end of the social scale, poor vassals looked to their lords to feed, clothe, house, and arm them. They hoped that they would be rewarded for their service with a fief of their own, with which they could support themselves and a family. At the upper end of the social scale, vassals looked to lords to give them still more land. (For more on the mutual obligations of lords and vassals, see Fulbert of Chartres (c. 960–1028), "Letter to William of Aquitaine," page 345).

A few women were vassals, and some were lords (or, rather, ladies, the female counterpart); and many upper-class laywomen participated in the society of fighters and prayers as wives and mothers of vassals and lords. Other aristocratic women entered convents and became members of the social group that prayed. Through its abbess or a man standing in for her, convents often had vassals as well.

Becoming the vassal of a lord often involved both ritual gestures and verbal promises. In a ceremony witnessed by others, the vassal-to-be knelt and, placing his hands between the hands of his lord, said, "I promise to be your man." This act, known as homage,◆ was followed by the promise of fealty—fidelity, trust, and service—which the vassal swore with his hand on relics or a Bible. Then the vassal and the lord kissed. In an age when many people could not read, a public ceremony such as this represented a

---

◆**homage:** AH mihj

visual and verbal contract. Vassalage bound the lord and vassal to one another with reciprocal obligations, usually military. Knights, as the premier fighters of the day, were the most desirable vassals.

Lords and Peasants. At the bottom of the social scale were those who worked—the peasants. In the Carolingian period, many peasants were free; they did not live on a manor or, if they did, they owed very little to its lord. But as power fell into the hands of local rulers, fewer and fewer peasants remained free. Rather, they were made dependent on lords, not as vassals but as **serfs**. A serf's dependency was separate from and completely unlike that of a vassal. Serfdom was not voluntary but rather inherited. No serf did homage or fealty to his lord; no serf kissed his lord as an equal. And the serf's work as a laborer was not prestigious. Peasants constituted the majority of the population, but unlike knights, who were celebrated in song, they were barely noticed by the upper classes—except as a source of revenue.

New methods of cultivation and a burgeoning population helped transform the

Fulbert of Chartres, "Letter to William of Aquitaine" (1020)

Duke William of Aquitaine, a very powerful lord in France, often found himself in conflict with his vassals. To clarify his and their obligations, he asked Fulbert, bishop of Chartres, to advise him on the matter. Fulbert's letter, reproduced in full here, shows that many of the obligations were, like the Ten Commandments, negative ones.

Fulbert, bishop, to the glorious duke of the Aquitainians William

Invited to write something concerning the form of fealty, I have briefly noted for you the following things from the authority of books. He who swears fealty to his lord must always remember these six things: harmless, safe, honorable, useful, easy, possible. Harmless, that is, he must not harm his lord in his body. Safe, he must not harm him in his secrets or in the fortifications by which he is able to be safe. Honorable, so that he must not harm him in his justice or in other affairs which are seen to pertain to his honor. Useful, that he might not be harmful to him in his possessions. Easy or possible, so that he not make difficult any good which his lord could easily do nor make anything impossible

that is difficult. It is just that the vassal avoid these evils, but he does not merit his holding [fief] for so doing, for it is not enough that he abstain from evil unless he does what is good.

Therefore it remains that he should give his lord counsel and aid in these same six above mentioned things if he wishes to be seen worthy of his benefice [fief] and to be safe in the fealty he has sworn. The lord should act toward his vassal reciprocally in all these things. If he does not do so, he deserves to be considered of bad faith, just as the vassal, if he were caught in collusion or in doing or in consenting to them, would be perfidious or perjured.

I would have written to you at greater length if I had not been occupied with many other things, both the restoration of our city and of our church which have recently been totally consumed by a horrendous fire. Although for a time we could not be turned away from this loss, through the hope in the consolation of God and of you we once more breathe.

Source: From Patrick J. Geary, *Readings in Medieval History,* 2nd ed. (Peterborough, Ontario: Broadview Press, 1998), 366.

Hard Work in January

During the cold month of January, peasants had to put on their warm clothes, harness their oxen to the plow, and turn over the heavy soil to loosen and aerate it for planting. This illustration of January's peasant labor comes from a calendar—a text useful to clergy because it listed the saints' feasts for each day of each month. In this case the artist was an Anglo-Saxon working in the second quarter of the eleventh century. Normally, medieval artists followed painted models rather than nature; nevertheless, this miniature probably represents contemporary reality fairly well. One peasant guides the heavy plow as it makes a deep furrow, another drives the animals, and a third drops the seeds. Farmwork was cooperative, and peasant solidarity was an important aspect of village life. *British Library.*

rural landscape and make it more productive. With a growing number of men and women to work the land, the lower classes now had more mouths to feed and faced the hardship of food shortage. Landlords began reorganizing their estates to run more efficiently. In the tenth century, the three-field system became more prevalent; heavy plows which could turn the heavy northern soils came into wider use; and horses (more effective than oxen) were harnessed to pull the plows. (See the image, Hard Work in January, on this page.) The result was surplus food and a better standard of living for nearly everyone.

In search of greater profits, some lords lightened the dues and services of peasants temporarily to allow them to open up new lands by draining marshes and cutting down forests. Some landlords converted dues and labor services into money payments, a boon for both lords and peasants. Lords now had

money to spend on what they wanted rather than hens and eggs they might not need or want. Peasants benefited because their dues were fixed despite inflation. Thus, as the prices of their hens and eggs went up, they could sell them, reaping a profit in spite of the payments they owed their lords.

By the tenth century, many peasants lived in populous rural settlements, true villages. In the midst of a sea of arable land, meadow, wood, and wasteland, these villages developed a sense of community. Boundaries—sometimes real fortifications, sometimes simple markers—told nonresidents to keep out and to find shelter in huts located outside the village limits.

The church often formed the focal point of local activity. There people met, received the sacraments, drew up contracts, and buried their parents and children. Religious feasts and festivals joined the rituals of farming to mark the seasons. The church dominated the village in another way: men and women owed it a tax called a **tithe**◆ (equivalent to one-tenth of their crops or income, paid in money or in kind), which was first instituted on a regular basis by the Carolingians.

Village peasants developed a sense of common purpose based on their practical interdependence, as they shared oxen or horses for the teams that pulled the plow or turned to village craftsmen to fix their wheels or shoe their horses. A sense of solidarity sometimes encouraged people to band together to ask for privileges as a group. Near Verona, in northern Italy, for example, twenty-five men living around the castle of Nogara joined together in 920 to ask their lord, the abbot of Nonantola, to allow them to lease plots of land, houses, and pasturage there in return for a small yearly rent and the promise to defend the castle. The abbot granted their request.

Village solidarity could be compromised, however, by conflicting loyalties and obligations. A peasant in one village might very well have one piece of land connected with a certain manor and another bit of arable field on a different estate; and he or she might owe several lords different kinds of dues. Even peasants of one village working for one lord might owe him varied services and taxes.

Layers of obligations were even more striking across the regions of Europe than in particular villages. The principal distinction was between free peasants, such as small landowners in Saxony and other parts of Germany, and unfree peasants, who were especially common in France and England. In Italy, peasants ranged from small independent landowners to leaseholders (like the tenants at Nogara); most were both, owning a parcel in one place and leasing another nearby.

As the power of kings weakened, this system of peasant obligations became part of a larger system of local rule. When landlords consolidated their power over their manors, they collected not only dues and services but also fees for the use of their flour mills, bake houses, and breweries. Some built castles, fortified strongholds, and imposed the even wider powers of the **ban**: the rights to collect taxes, hear court cases, levy fines, and muster men for defense.

In France, for example, as the king's power waned, political control fell into the hands of counts and other princes. By 1000, castles had become the key to their power. In the south of France, power was so fragmented that each man who controlled a castle—a **castellan**◆—was a virtual ruler, although often with a very limited reach. In northwestern France, territorial princes, basing their rule on the control of *many* castles, dominated much broader regions. For example, Fulk Nera,◆ count of Anjou (987–1040), built more than thirteen castles and captured others from rival counts. By the end of his life, he controlled a region extending from Blois◆ to Nantes◆ along the Loire◆ valley.

Castellans extended their authority by subjecting everyone near their castle to their ban. Peasants, whether or not they worked on his estates, had to pay the castellan a variety of dues for his "protection" and judicial rights over them. Castellans also established links with the better-off landholders in the region, tempting or coercing them to become vassals. Lay castellans often supported local monasteries and controlled the appointment of local priests. But churchmen themselves sometimes held the position of territorial lord, as did, for example, the archbishop of Milan in the eleventh century.

The development of virtually independent local political units, dominated by a castle and controlled by a military elite, marks an important turning point in western Europe. Although this development did not occur everywhere simultaneously (and in some places it hardly occurred at all), the social, political, and cultural life of Europe was now dominated by landowners who saw themselves as military men and regional leaders.

◆**tithe:** tyth

◆**castellan:** KAS tuh luhn
◆**Fulk Nera:** FULK nehr rah
◆**Blois:** blwah
◆**Nantes:** naHnt
◆**Loire:** luh WAHR

Warriors and Warfare

Not all warriors were alike. At the top of the elite were the kings, counts, and dukes. Below them, but on the rise, were the castellans; and still further down the social scale were ordinary knights. Yet all shared in a common lifestyle.

Knights and their lords fought on horseback. High astride his steed, wearing a shirt of chain mail and a helmet of flat metal plates riveted together, the knight marked a military revolution. The war season started in May, when the grasses were high enough for horses to forage. Horseshoes allowed armies to move faster than ever before and to negotiate rough terrain previously unsuitable for battle. Stirrups, probably invented by Asiatic nomadic tribes, allowed the mounted warrior to hold his seat. This made it possible for knights to thrust at their enemy with heavy lances. The light javelin of ancient Roman warfare was abandoned.

Lords and their vassals often lived together. In the lord's great hall they ate, listened to entertainment, and bedded down for the night. They went out hunting together, competed with one another in military games, and went off to the battlefield as a group as well. Of course there were powerful vassals—counts, for example—who lived on their own fiefs. They hardly ever saw their lord (probably the king), except when doing homage and fealty—once in their lifetime—or serving him in battles, for perhaps forty days a year (as was the custom in eleventh-century France). But they themselves were lords of knightly vassals who were not married and who lived and ate and hunted with them.

No matter how old they might be, unmarried knights who lived with their lords were called youths by their contemporaries. Such perpetual bachelors were something new, the result of a profound transformation in the organization of families and inheritance. Before about 1000, noble families had recognized all their children as heirs and had divided their estates accordingly. In the mid-ninth century, Count Everard◆ and his wife, for example, willed their large estates,

scattered from Belgium to Italy, to their four sons and three daughters (although they gave the boys far more than the girls, and the oldest boy far more than the others).

By 1000, however, adapting to diminished opportunities for land and office, and wary of fragmenting the estates they had, French nobles changed both their conception of their family and the way property passed to the next generation. Recognizing the overriding claims of one son, often the eldest, they handed down their entire inheritance to him. (When the heir is indeed the eldest son, this system of inheritance is called **primogeniture.◆**) The heir, in turn, traced his lineage only through the male line, backward through his father and forward through his own eldest son. Such patrilineal◆ families left many younger sons without an inheritance and therefore without the prospect of marrying and founding a family; instead, the younger sons lived at the courts of the great as youths, or they joined the church as clerics or monks. The development of territorial rule and patrilineal families went hand in hand, as fathers passed down to one son undiminished not only manors but also titles, castles, and the authority of the ban.

Patrilineal inheritance tended to bypass daughters and so worked against aristocratic women, who lost the power that came with inherited wealth. In families without sons, however, widows and daughters did inherit property. And wives often acted as lords of estates when their husbands were at war. Moreover, all aristocratic women played an important role in this warrior society, whether in the monastery (where they prayed for the souls of their families) or through their marriages (where they produced children and helped forge alliances between their own natal families and the families of their husbands).

Efforts to Contain Violence

Warfare benefited territorial rulers in the short term, but in the long run their revenues suffered as armies plundered the countryside and sacked walled cities. Bishops, who were themselves from the class of lords and war-

◆**Everard:** EHV rahrd

◆**primogeniture:** Pry moh JEH nih chur
◆**patrilineal:** pa truh LIH nee uhl

riors, worried about the dangers to church property. Peasants cried out against wars that destroyed their crops or forced them to join regional infantries. Monks and religious thinkers were appalled at violence that was not in the service of an anointed king. By the end of the tenth century, all classes clamored for peace.

Sentiment against local violence was united in a movement called the **Peace of God**, which began in the south of France around 990 and by 1050 had spread over a wide region. Meetings of bishops, counts, and lords and often crowds of lower-class men and women set forth the provisions of this peace: "No man in the counties or bishoprics shall seize a horse, colt, ox, cow, ass, or the burdens which it carries. . . . No one shall seize a peasant, man or woman," ran the decree of one early council. Anyone who violated this peace was to be excommunicated: cut off from the community of the faithful, denied the services of the church and the hope of salvation.

The peace proclaimed at local councils like this limited some violence but did not address the problem of conflict between armed men. A second set of agreements, the Truce of God, soon supplemented the Peace of God. The truce prohibited fighting between warriors at certain times: on Sunday because it was the Lord's day, on Saturday because it was a reminder of Holy Saturday, on Friday because it symbolized Good Friday, and on Thursday because it stood for Holy Thursday. Enforcement of the truce fell to the local knights and nobles, who swore over saints' relics to uphold it and to fight anyone who broke it.

The Peace of God and Truce of God were only two of the mechanisms that attempted to contain or defuse violent confrontations in the tenth and eleventh centuries. At times, lords and their vassals mediated wars and feuds in assemblies called *placita*.♦ In other instances, monks or laymen tried to find solutions to disputes that would leave the honor of both parties intact. Rather than establishing guilt or innocence, winners or losers, these methods of adjudication often resulted in compromises on both sides.

♦*placita:* PLAH kiht uh

Political Communities in Italy, England, and France

The political systems that emerged in the wake of the breakup of the Carolingian empire were as varied as the regions of Europe. In northern and central Italy, cities were the centers of power, still reflecting, if feebly, the political organization of ancient Rome. In England, strong kings came to the fore. In France, as we have seen, great lords dominated the countryside; there the king was relatively weak.

Urban Power in Northern and Central Italy. Unlike their counterparts in France, where great landlords built their castles in the countryside, Italian elites tended to construct their family seats within the walls of cities such as Milan and Lucca. Also built within the city walls were churches, as many as fifty or sixty, the proud work of rich laymen and laywomen or of bishops. From their perch within the cities, the great landholders, both lay and religious, dominated the countryside.

Italian cities also functioned as important marketplaces. Peasants sold their surplus goods there, artisans and merchants lived within the walls, and foreign traders offered their wares. These members of the lower classes were supported by the noble rich, who depended, here even more than elsewhere, on cash to satisfy their desires. In the course of the ninth and tenth centuries, both servile and free tenants became renters who paid in currency.

The social and political life in Italy was conducive to a familial organization somewhat different from the patrilineal families of France. To stave off the partitioning of their properties among heirs, families organized themselves by formal contract into *consorteria*,♦ in which all male members shared the profits of the family's inheritance and all women were excluded. The consorterial family became a kind of blood-related corporation, a social unit on which early Italian businesses and banks would later be modeled.

♦*consorteria:* cohn sawr TEHR ee uh

Alfred and His Sucessors: Kings of All the English. Whereas much of Italy was urban, most of England was rural. In the face of the Viking invasions in England, King Alfred the Great of Wessex (r. 871–899) developed new mechanisms of royal government, instituting reforms that his successors continued. He fortified settlements throughout Wessex and divided the army into two parts, one with the duty of defending these fortifications (or burhs◆), the other operating as a mobile unit. Alfred also started a navy. These military innovations cost money, and the assessments fell on peasants' holdings.

Alfred sought to strengthen his kingdom's religious integrity as well as its regional fortifications. In the ninth century, people interpreted invasions as God's punishment for sin, the real culprit. Hence Alfred began a program of religious reform by bringing scholars

to his court to write and to educate others. Above all, Alfred wanted to translate key religious works from Latin into Anglo-Saxon (or Old English). He was determined to "turn into the language that we can all understand certain books which are the most necessary for all men to know." Alfred and scholars under his guidance translated works by church fathers such as Gregory the Great and St. Augustine. Even the Psalms, until now sung only in Hebrew, Greek, and Latin, were rendered into Anglo-Saxon. In most of ninth- and tenth-century Europe, Latin remained the language of scholarship, government, and writing, separate from the language people spoke. In England, however, the vernacular—the common spoken language— was also a literary language. With Alfred's work giving it greater legitimacy, Anglo-Saxon came to be used alongside Latin for both literature and royal administration.

England in the Age of King Alfred, 871–899

◆**burhs:** Burhs

Alfred's reforms strengthened not only defense, education, and religion but also royal power. He consolidated his control over Wessex and fought the Danish kings, who by the mid-870s had taken Northumbria, northeastern Mercia, and East Anglia. Eventually, as he successfully fought the Danes who were pushing south and westward, he was recognized as king of all the English not under Danish rule. He issued a law code, the first by an English king since 695. Unlike earlier codes, drawn up for each separate kingdom of England, Alfred drew his laws from and for all of the English kingdoms. In this way Alfred became the first king of all the English.

Alfred's successors rolled back the Danish rule in England. "Then the Norsemen departed in their nailed ships, bloodstained survivors of spears," wrote one poet about a battle the Vikings lost in 937. But many Vikings remained. Converted to Christianity, their great men joined Anglo-Saxons in attending the English king at court. As peace returned, new administrative subdivisions were established throughout England: shires and hundreds, districts for judicial and taxation purposes. The powerful men of the kingdom swore fealty to the king, promising to be enemies of his enemies, friends of his friends. England was united and organized to support a strong ruler.

Alfred's grandson Edgar (r. 957–975) commanded all the possibilities early medieval kingship offered. He was the sworn lord of all the great men of the kingdom. He controlled appointments to the English church and sponsored monastic reform. In 973, following the continental fashion, he was anointed king. The fortifications of the kingdom were in his hands, as was the army, and he took responsibility for keeping the peace by proclaiming certain crimes—arson and theft—to be under his special jurisdiction and mobilizing the machinery of the shire and hundred to find and punish thieves.

Despite its apparent centralization, England was not a unified state in the modern sense, and the king's control was often tenuous. Many royal officials were great landowners who (as on the continent) worked for the king because it was in their best interest. When it was not, they allied with different claimants to the throne. This political fragility may have helped the Danish king Cnut (or Canute) to conquer England. King there from 1017 to 1035, Cnut reinforced the already strong connections between England and Scandinavia while keeping intact much of the administrative, ecclesiastical, and military apparatus already established in England by the Anglo-Saxons. By Cnut's time, Scandinavian traditions had largely merged with those of the rest of Europe and the Vikings were no longer an alien culture.

Capetian Kings of Franks: Weak but Prestigious. French kings had a harder time than the English coping with the invasions because their realm was much larger. They had no chance to build up their defenses slowly from one powerful base. During most of the tenth century, Carolingian kings alternated on the throne with kings from a family that would later be called the Capetian.♦ As the Carolingian dynasty waned, the most powerful men of the kingdom — dukes, counts, and important bishops—came together to elect Hugh Capet (r. 987–996), a lord of considerable prestige yet relatively little power. His choice marked the end of Carolingian rule and the beginning of the new Capetian dynasty that would hand down the royal title from father to son until the fourteenth century.

The Kingdom of the Franks under Hugh Capet, 987–996

In the eleventh century, the reach of the Capetian kings was limited by territorial lordships in the vicinity. The king's scattered but substantial estates lay in the north of France, in the region around Paris—the Île-de-France (literally, "island of France"). His castles and his vassals were there. Independent castellans, however, controlled areas nearby. In the sense that he was a neighbor of castellans and not much more powerful militarily than they, the king of the Franks— who would only later take the territorial title of king of France—was just another local leader. Yet the Capetian kings had considerable prestige. They were anointed with holy oil, and they represented the idea of unity inherited from Charlemagne. Most of the counts, at least in the north of France, became their vassals. They did not promise to obey the king, but they did vow not to try to kill or depose him.

Emperors and Kings in Central and Eastern Europe

In contrast with the development of territorial lordships in France, Germany's fragmentation hardly began before it was reversed. The Ottonian♦ kings of Germany consolidated their rule there; took the title emperor; and then, hand in hand with the papacy, fostered the emergence of new Christian monarchies. Aligned with the Roman church, these new kingdoms were the ancestors of today's Czech and Slovak Republics, Poland, and Hungary.

Ottonian Power in Germany. Five duchies♦ (regions dominated by dukes) emerged in Germany in the late Carolingian period, each much larger than the counties and castellanies of France. With the death in 911 of the last Carolingian king in Germany, Louis the Child, the dukes elected one of themselves as king. Then, as the Magyar invasions increased, the dukes gave the royal title to the duke of Saxony, Henry I (r. 919–936), who proceeded to set up fortifications and reorganize his army, crowning his efforts with a major defeat of a Magyar army in 933.

Otto I, the son of Henry I, was an even greater military hero. In 951, he marched into Italy and took the Lombard crown. His defeat of the Magyar forces in 955 at Lechfeld gave him prestige and helped solidify his dynasty. Against the Slavs, with whom the Germans shared a border, Otto set up marches from

---

♦**Capetian:** kuh PAY shuhn

♦**Ottonian:** ah TOH neean
♦**duchies:** DUH cheez

which he could make expeditions and stave off counterattacks. After the pope crowned him emperor in 962, Otto claimed the Middle Kingdom carved out by the Treaty of Verdun and cast himself as the agent of Roman imperial renewal.

Otto's victories brought tribute and plunder, ensuring him a following but also raising the German nobles' expectations for enrichment. He and his successors, Otto II (r. 973–983), Otto III (r. 983–1002)—for which reason the dynasty is called the Ottonian♦— and Henry II (r. 1002–1024), were not always able or willing to provide the gifts and inheritances their family members and followers expected. To maintain centralized rule, for example, the Ottonians did not divide their kingdom among their sons: like castellans in France, they created a patrilineal pattern of inheritance. But the consequence was that younger sons and other potential heirs felt cheated, and disgruntled royal kin led revolt after revolt against the Ottonian kings. The rebels found followers among the aristocracy, where the trend toward the patrilineal family prompted similar feuds and thwarted expectations.

Relations between the Ottonians and the German clergy were more harmonious. With a ribbon of new bishoprics along his eastern border, Otto I appointed bishops, gave them extensive lands, and subjected the local peasantry to their overlordship. Like Charlemagne, Otto believed that the well-being of the church in his kingdom depended on him. The Ottonians placed the churches and many monasteries of Germany under their control. They gave bishops the powers of the ban, allowing them to collect revenues and call men to arms. Answering to the king and furnishing him with troops, the bishops became royal officials, while also carrying out their pastoral and religious duties. German

kings claimed the right to select bishops, even the pope at Rome, and to "invest" them by participating in the ceremony that installed them in office. The higher clergy joined royal court society. Most came to the court to be schooled; in turn, they taught the kings, princes, and noblewomen there.

Like all the strong rulers of the day, whether in Europe or the Byzantine and Islamic worlds, the Ottonians presided over a renaissance of learning. For example, the tutor of Otto III was Gerbert, the best-educated man of his time. Placed on the papal throne as Sylvester II (r. 999–1003), Gerbert knew how to use the abacus and to calculate with Arabic numerals. He spent "large sums of money to pay copyists and to acquire copies of authors," as he put it. He studied the Latin classics as models of rhetoric and argument, and he reveled in logic and debate. Not only did churchmen and kings support Ottonian scholarship, but to an unprecedented extent noblewomen in Germany also acquired an education and participated in the intellectual revival. Aristocratic women spent much of their wealth on learning. Living at home with their kinfolk and servants or in convents that provided them with comfortable private apartments, noblewomen wrote books and occasionally even Roman-style plays. They also supported other artists and scholars.

Despite their military and political strength, the kings of Germany faced resistance from dukes and other powerful princes, who hoped to become regional rulers themselves. The Salians,♦ the dynasty that succeeded the Ottonians, tried to balance the power among the German dukes but could not meld them into a corps of vassals the way the Capetian kings tamed their counts. In Germany vassalage was considered beneath the dignity of free men. Instead of relying on vassals, the Salian kings and their bishops used ministerials, men who were legally serfs, to collect taxes, administer justice, and fight on horseback. Ministerials retained their servile status even though they often rose to wealth and high position. Under the Salian kings, ministerials became the mainstay of the royal army and administration.

The Ottonian Empire, 936–1002

The extent of the Empire under Otto I

The extent of the Empire under Otto III

Marcher regions

Dependent on Ottonians

★ Battle

Saxony

GERMANY

POLAND

BOHEMIA

Danube R.

FRANCE

KINGDOM OF BURGUNDY

★ Lechfeld 955

HUNGARY

CROATIA

ITALY

Rome

0   250   500 miles

0   250   500 kilometers

♦**Salians:** SAY leeans

Otto III Receiving Gifts
This triumphal image is in a book of Gospels made for Otto III. The crowned women on the left are personifications of the four parts of Otto's empire: Sclavinia (the Slavic lands), Germania (Germany), Gallia (Gaul), and Roma (Rome). Each offers a gift in tribute and homage to the emperor, who sits on a throne holding the symbols of his power (orb and scepter) and flanked by representatives of the church (on his right) and of the army (on his left). Why do you suppose that the artist separated the image of the emperor from that of the women? What does the body language of the women indicate about the relations Otto wanted to portray between himself and the parts of his empire? Can you relate this manuscript, which was made in 997–1000, to Otto's conquest over the Slavs in 997? *Pro Biblioteca Academiae Scientiarum, Hungaricae.*

Supported by their prestige, their churchmen, and their ministerials, the German kings expanded their influence eastward, into the region from the Elbe River to Russia. Otto I was so serious about expansion that he created an extraordinary "elastic" archbishopric: it had no eastern boundary, so it could increase as far as future conquests and conversions to Christianity would allow.

The Emergence of Catholic Bohemia, Poland, Hungary, and Croatia. Hand in hand with the popes, German kings insisted on the creation of new, Catholic polities along their eastern frontier. The Czechs, who lived in the region of Bohemia, converted under the rule of Václav♦ (r. 920–929), who thereby gained recognition in Germany as the duke of Bohemia. He and his successors did not become kings, remaining politically within the German sphere. Václav's murder by his younger brother made him a martyr and the patron saint of Bohemia, a symbol around which later movements for independence rallied.

The Poles gained a greater measure of independence than the Czechs. In 966, Mieszko♦ I (r. 963–992), the leader of the Slavic tribe known as the Polanians, accepted baptism to forestall the attack that the

♦**Václav:** VAHT slahv
♦**Mieszko:** MYEHSH kaw

MAPPING THE WEST Europe and the Mediterranean, c. 1050
The clear borders and bright colors of the "states" on this map distort an essential truth: none of them had centralized governments that controlled whole territories, as in modern states. Instead, there were numerous regional rulers within each, and there were numerous overlapping claims of jurisdiction. The next centuries would show both the weaknesses and surprising strengths of this fragmentation.

Germans were already mounting against pagan Slavic peoples along the Baltic coast and east of the Elbe River. Busily engaged in bringing the other Slavic tribes of Poland under his control, he adroitly shifted his alliances with various German princes to suit his needs. In 991, Mieszko placed his realm under the protection of the pope, establishing a tradition of Polish loyalty to the Roman church. Mieszko's son Boleslaw◆ the Brave (r. 992–1025) greatly extended Poland's boundaries, at one time or another holding sway from the Bohemian border to Kiev. In 1000, he gained a royal crown with papal blessing.

◆**Boleslaw:** baw LEH slahf

Hungary's case is similar to that of Poland. The Magyars settled in the region known today as Hungary. They became landowners, using the native Slavs to till the soil and imposing their language. At the end of the tenth century, the Magyar ruler Stephen I (r. 997–1038) accepted Roman Christianity. In return, German knights and monks helped him consolidate his power and convert his people. According to legend, the crown placed on Stephen's head when he was crowned king (in late 1000 or early 1001) was sent to him by the pope. To this day, the crown of St. Stephen (Stephen was canonized in 1083) remains the most hallowed symbol of Hungarian nationhood.

Symbols of rulership such as crowns, consecrated by Christian priests and accorded a prestige almost akin to saints' relics, were among the most vital sources of royal power in central Europe. The economic basis for the power of central European rulers gradually shifted from slave raids to agriculture. This change encouraged a proliferation of regional centers of power that challenged monarchical rule. From the eleventh century onward, all the medieval Slavic realms faced the constant problem of internal division.

Review: How and why did the different states of central and eastern Europe—Russia, Hungary, Serbia, Croatia, and so on—emerge?

Conclusion

In 800, the three heirs of the Roman Empire all appeared to be organized like their parent: centralized, monarchical, imperial. Byzantine emperors writing their learned books, Abbasid caliphs holding court in their new resplendent palace at Baghdad, and Carolingian emperors issuing their directives for reform to the *missi dominici* all mimicked the Roman emperors. Yet they confronted tensions and regional pressures that tended to decentralize political power. Byzantium felt this fragmentation least, yet even there the emergence of a new elite, the *dynatoi*, led to the emperor's loss of control over the countryside. In the Islamic world, economic crisis, religious tension, and the ambitions of powerful local rulers

decisively weakened the caliphate and opened the way to separate successor states. In Europe, powerful independent landowners strove with greater or lesser success (depending on the region) to establish themselves as effective rulers. By 1050, the states that would become those of modern Europe began to form.

In western Europe, local conditions determined political and economic organizations. Between 900 and 1000, for example, French society was transformed by the development of territorial lordships, patrilineal families, and ties of vassalage. These factors figured less prominently in Germany, where a central monarchy remained, buttressed by churchmen, ministerials, and conquests to the east.

After 1050, however, the German king would lose his supreme position as a storm of church reform whirled around him. The economy changed, becoming more commercial and urban, and new learning, new monarchies, and new forms of religious expression came to the fore.

Suggested References

Byzantium: Renewed Strength and Influence

Recent studies of Byzantium stress the revival in the arts and literature, but Whittow is excellent on political, social, and religious issues. Almost nothing was available in English on eastern Europe and Russia until the 1980s.

*Byzantine art: http://gallery.sjsu.edu/artH/ byzantine/mainpage.html.

Fine, Jon V. A., Jr. *The Early Medieval Balkans: A Critical Survey from the Sixth to the Late Twelfth Century.* 1983.

Franklin, Simon, and Jonathan Shepard. *The Emergence of Rus, 750–1200.* 1996.

Garland, Lynda. *Byzantine Empresses: Women and Power in Byzantium, AD 527–1204.* 1999.

Maguire, Henry, ed. *Byzantine Court Culture from 829 to 1204.* 1997.

*Psellus, Michael. *Fourteen Byzantine Rulers: The Chronographia.* Trans. E. R. A. Sewter. 1966.

Whittow, Mark. *The Making of Byzantium, 600–1025.* 1996.

*Primary sources.

The Islamic World: From Unity to Fragmentation

The traditional approach to the Islamic world is political (Kennedy). Glick is unusual in taking a comparative approach. The newest issue for scholars is the role of women in medieval Islamic society (Spellberg).

Berkey, Jonathan P. *The Formation of Islam: Religion and Society in the Near East, 600–1800.* 2003.

Glick, Thomas. *Islamic and Christian Spain in the Early Middle Ages: Comparative Perspectives on Social and Cultural Formation.* 1979.

Kennedy, Hugh. *The Prophet and the Age of the Caliphates: The Islamic Near East from the Sixth to the Eleventh Century.* 1986.

Makdisi, George. *The Rise of Colleges.* 1981.

Spellberg, Denise. *Politics, Gender, and the Islamic Past.* 1994.

The Creation and Division of a New European Empire

Huge chunks of the primary sources for the Carolingian world are now available in English translation, thanks in large part to the work of Dutton. Hodges and Whitehouse provide the perspective of archaeologists. The Carolingian renaissance is increasingly recognized as a long-term development rather than simply the achievement of Charlemagne.

*Carolingian studies: **http://www.fordham.edu/ halsall/sbooklh.html**.

*Dutton, Paul Edward. *Carolingian Civilization: A Reader.* 1993.

*———. *Charlemagne's Courtier: The Complete Einhard.* 1998.

*Einhard and Notker the Stammerer. *Two Lives of Charlemagne.* Trans. Lewis Thorpe. 1969.

Hodges, Richard, and David Whitehouse. *Mohammed, Charlemagne, and the Origins of Europe.* 1983.

McKitterick, Rosamond. *Carolingian Culture: Emulation and Innovation.* 1994.

Nelson, Janet. *Charles the Bald.* 1987.

Riche, Pierre. *Daily Life in the World of Charlemagne.* Trans. J. A. McNamara. 1978.

After the Carolingians : The Emergence of Local Rule

Historians used to lament the passing of the Carolingian Empire. More recently, however, they have come to appreciate the strengths and adaptive strategies of the post-Carolingian world. Duby speaks of the agricultural "takeoff" of the period, whereas Head and Landes explore new institutions of peace.

Duby, Georges. *The Early Growth of the European Economy: Warriors and Peasants from the Seventh to the Twelfth Century.* Trans. H. B. Clark. 1974.

Engel, Pál. *The Realm of St. Stephen: A History of Medieval Hungary, 895–1526.* Trans. Tamás Pálosfalvi. 2001.

Frantzen, Allen. *King Alfred.* 1986.

Head, Thomas, and Richard Landes, eds. *The Peace of God: Social Violence and Religious Response in France around the Year 1000.* 1992.

Jones, Gwyn. *A History of the Vikings.* Rev. ed. 1984.

*Medieval and Renaissance manuscripts: **http:// www.columbia.edu/cu/libraries/indiv/rare/ images**.

Reuter, Timothy. *Germany in the Early Middle Ages, c. 800–1056.* 1991.

Sweeney, Del, ed. *Agriculture in the Middle Ages: Technology, Practice, and Representation.* 1995.

*Whitelock, Dorothy, ed. *English Historical Documents*, Vol. 1. 2nd ed. 1979.

Wilson, David. *The Vikings and Their Origins: Scandinavia in the First Millennium.* 1970.

CHAPTER REVIEW

IMPORTANT EVENTS

750–c. 950	The Abbasid Caliphate
751	Pippin III becomes king of the Franks, establishing Carolingians on the throne
768–814	Charlemagne rules as king of the Franks
786–809	Caliphate of Harun al-Rashid
800	Charlemagne crowned emperor at Rome
843	Treaty of Verdun
871–899	King Alfred of England
929–1031	Caliphate of Córdoba
955	Battle of Lechfeld
962	King Otto I (r. 936–973) of Germany crowned emperor
987–996	Reign of King Hugh Capet of France
c. 990	Peace of God movement begins
1000 or 1001	Stephen I (St. Stephen) (r. 997–1038) crowned king of Hungary
1001–1018	Byzantine conquest of Bulgaria

KEY TERMS

Abbasids (326)

ban (347)

castellan (347)

dynatoi (324)

feudalism (343)

madrasa (330)

manor (337)

Peace of God (349)

primogeniture (348)

serfs (345)

tithe (347)

vassalage (344)

REVIEW QUESTIONS

1. What were the effects of expansion on the power of the Byzantine emperor?
2. What forces led to the fragmentation of the Islamic world in the tenth and eleventh centuries?
3. What were the strengths and weaknesses of Carolingian institutions of government, warfare, and defense?
4. How and why did the different states of central and eastern Europe—Russia, Hungary, Serbia, Croatia, and so on—emerge?

MAKING CONNECTIONS

1. How were the Byzantine, Islamic, and European economies similar? How did they differ? How did these economies interact?
2. How were the powers and ambitions of castellans similar to, and how were they different from, those of the dynatoi of Byzantium and of Muslim provincial rulers?
3. Compare the effects of the barbarian invasions into the Roman Empire with the effects of the Viking, Muslim, and Magyar invasions into Carolingian Europe.

FOR FURTHER EXPLORATION

To assess your mastery of the material in this chapter, see the Online Study Guide at **bedfordstmartins.com/hunt**.

To read additional primary-source material from this period, see Chapter 9 in *Sources of The Making of the West*, Second Edition, Volume I.

Renewal and Reform, 1050–1150

BRUNO OF COLOGNE WAS HEADED for a successful career in the church. An esteemed teacher at the prominent French cathedral school of Reims, he was a likely choice for promotion to bishop or even archbishop. But around 1084, he abandoned it all. He was disgusted with the new archbishop of Reims,◆ Manasses, who had purchased his office and was so uninterested in religious matters that he once reportedly said, "The archbishopric of Reims would be a good thing, if one did not have to sing Mass for it." Bruno quit his post at the school and left the city. But he did not do what ethical and morally outraged men of the time were expected to do—join a monastery. Rejecting both the worldly goals of secular clerics like Manasses and the communal goals of Benedictine monks, Bruno set up a hermitage—an isolated retreat—at Chartreuse,◆ high in the Alps. The hermits who gathered there lived in seclusion and poverty. One of Bruno's contemporaries marveled: "They do not take gold, silver, or ornaments for their church from anyone." This unworldliness was matched, however, with keen interest in learning: for all its poverty, Chartreuse had a rich library.

Thus began La Chartreuse, the chief house of the Carthusians, a monastic order still in existence. The Carthusian monks lived as hermits, eschewed material wealth, and emphasized learning. In some ways their style of life was a reaction against the monumental changes rumbling through their age: their solitude ran counter to the burgeoning cities, and their austerity contrasted sharply with the opulence and power of princely courts. Their reverence for the written word, however, reflected the growing interest in scholarship and learning.

The most salient feature of the period 1050–1150 was increasing wealth. Cities, trade, and agricultural production swelled. The resulting worldliness met with a wide variety of responses. Some

---

◆**Reims:** RANS
◆**Chartreuse:** shahr TROOZ

La Chartreuse
The impulse behind the foundation of La Chartreuse was withdrawal from the world. Yet the world came to the Carthusians' high perch. One of the abbots of Cluny made it his custom to visit every year. He said that the new monks reminded him of the desert hermits. He did not mean that the Alps looked like Egypt but rather that the monks, living in separate cells, practiced the heroically ascetic life of the first monks. *Photo © Gary Kleinschmidt.*

people, like Bruno, fled the world; others tried to reform it; and still others embraced, enjoyed, or tried to understand it.

Within one century, the development of a profit-based economy transformed western European communities. Many villages and fortifications became cities where traders, merchants, and artisans conducted business. Although most people still lived in less-populated, rural areas, their lives were touched in many ways by the new cash economy. Economic concerns drove changes within the church, where a movement for reform gathered steam. Money helped redefine the role of the clergy and, elaborating new political ideas, popes, kings, and princes came to exercise new forms of power.

At the same time, city dwellers began to demand their own governments. Monks and clerics reformulated the nature of their communities and, like Bruno of Cologne, sought intense spiritual lives. All of these developments inspired (and in turn were inspired by) new ideas, forms of scholarship, and methods of inquiry. The rapid pace of religious, political, and economic change was matched by new developments in thought, learning, and artistic expression.

❖ The Commercial Revolution

As the population of Europe continued to expand in the eleventh century, cities, long-distance trade networks, local markets, and new business arrangements meshed to create a profit-based economy. With improve-

ments in agriculture and more land in cultivation, the great estates of the eleventh century produced surpluses that helped feed—and therefore make possible—a new urban population.

Commerce was not new to the history of western Europe, but the **commercial revolution** of the Middle Ages spawned the institutions that would be the direct ancestors of modern businesses: corporations, banks, accounting systems, and, above all, urban centers that thrived on economic vitality. Whereas ancient cities had primarily religious, social, and political functions, medieval cities were centers of production and economic activity. Wealth meant power: it allowed city dwellers to become self-governing.

Cities, Towns, and Fairs

The new commercial centers—cities and towns—developed around castles and monasteries and within the walls of ancient Roman towns. Great lords in the countryside—and this included monasteries—were eager to take advantage of the profits that their estates generated. In the late tenth century, they had reorganized their lands for greater productivity, encouraged their peasants to cultivate new land, and converted services and dues to money payments. Now with ready cash, they not only fostered the development of sporadic markets where they could sell their surpluses and buy luxury goods but even encouraged traders and craftspeople to settle down near them. The lords gained at each step: their purchases brought them an enhanced lifestyle and greater prestige, while

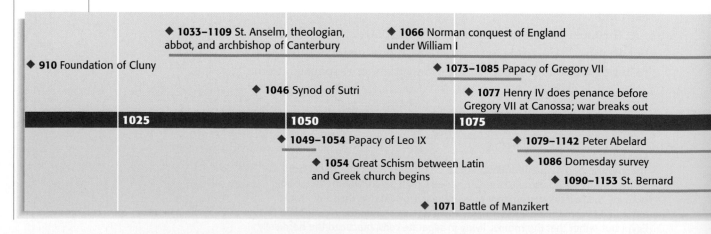

◆ **1033–1109** St. Anselm, theologian, abbot, and archbishop of Canterbury

◆ **1066** Norman conquest of England under William I

◆ **910** Foundation of Cluny

◆ **1073–1085** Papacy of Gregory VII

◆ **1046** Synod of Sutri

◆ **1077** Henry IV does penance before Gregory VII at Canossa; war breaks out

1025   **1050**   **1075**

◆ **1049–1054** Papacy of Leo IX

◆ **1079–1142** Peter Abelard

◆ **1054** Great Schism between Latin and Greek church begins

◆ **1086** Domesday survey

◆ **1090–1153** St. Bernard

◆ **1071** Battle of Manzikert

Medieval Besalú

The bridge leading to Besalú, a town in Catalonia (Spain), was constructed, like the town's walls and many of its other buildings, during the eleventh and twelfth centuries. The high fortified entrance was added in the fourteenth century. Already in the ninth century Besalú was the center of a county, and in the eleventh century it briefly became the seat of a bishopric. At the same time it was home to a thriving Jewish population, whose mikvah, or ritual bath house, still stands today. *AKG Images/Scheutze/Rodemann.*

they charged merchants tolls and sales taxes, in this way profiting even more from trade.

Traders. At Bruges◆ (today in Belgium), the local lord's castle became the magnet around which a city formed. As a medieval chronicler observed:

◆**Bruges:** broozh

To satisfy the needs of the people in the castle at Bruges, first merchants with luxury articles began to surge around the gate; then the wine-sellers came; finally the innkeepers arrived to feed and lodge the people who had business with the prince. . . . So many houses were built that soon a great city was created.

Other commercial centers clustered around monasteries and churches. Still other markets

◆ **1095** Council of Clermont; Pope Urban II calls the First Crusade

◆ **1122** Concordat of Worms

◆ **c. 1140** Gratian, *Decretum*

◆ **1108–1137** Reign of Louis VI

◆ **1151** Hildegard of Bingen, *Scivias*

◆ **1097** Establishment of commune at Milan

1100   **1125**   **1150**

◆ **1109** Establishment of the Crusader States

◆ **1096–1099** First Crusade

◆ **1147–1149** Second Crusade

◆ **1098** Foundation of Cîteaux

MAP 10.1   Medieval Trade Routes in the Eleventh and Twelfth Centuries
In the medieval world, bulk goods from the north (furs, fish, and wood) were traded for luxury goods from the south (ivory and spices, including medicines, perfumes, and dyes). Already regions were beginning to specialize. England, for example, supplied raw wool, but Flanders (Ypres, Ghent) specialized in turning that wool into cloth and shipping it farther south, to the fairs of Champagne (whose capital was Troyes) or Germany. Italian cities channeled goods from the Muslim and Byzantine worlds northward and exported European goods southward and eastward.

formed just outside the walls of older cities; these gradually merged into new and enlarged urban communities as town walls were built around them to protect their inhabitants. Sometimes informal country markets might eventually be housed in permanent structures. Along the Rhine and in other river valleys, cities sprang up to service the merchants who traversed the route between Italy and the north.

Many such long-distance traders were Jews and Italians. They supplied the fine wines, spices, and fabrics beloved by lords and ladies, their families, and their vassals. Jews had often been involved at least part-time in long-distance trade as vintners; and as lords reorganized the countryside, driving out Jewish landowners, most Jews were forced to turn to commerce full-time. Italians took up long-distance trade because of their proximity to Byzantine and Islamic ports; their opportunities for plunder and trade on the high seas; and their never entirely extinguished urban traditions (Map 10.1).

Many other traders were local, like one Benedictine monk who supervised a manor twenty miles to the south of his monastery in France and sold its surplus horses and grain at a local market. At Reims, the city Bruno left, the middle of a forum dating back to the Roman Empire became a new commercial center. As early as 1067, the king of France was writing about the many fairs in his realm—great markets held at regular intervals that attracted large crowds. Around the marketplace at Reims grew a network of streets whose names (many of which still exist) revealed their essentially commercial functions: Street of the Butchers, Street of the Wool Market, Street of the Wheat Market. The shoemaker's sign on this page originally hung in a street full of other shoe stores.

The Building Boom. The look and feel of such developing cities varied enormously, but nearly all included a marketplace, a castle, and several churches. Most had to adapt to increasingly crowded conditions. Archaeologists have discovered that at the end of the eleventh century in Winchester, England, city plots were still large enough to accommodate houses parallel to the street; but the swelling population soon necessitated destroying these houses and building instead long, narrow, hall-like tenement houses, constructed at right angles to the thoroughfare. These were built on a frame made from strips of wood filled with wattle and daub—twigs woven together and covered with clay. If they were like the stone houses built in the late twelfth century (a period about which we know a good deal), they had two stories: a shop or warehouse on the lower floor and living quarters above. Behind this main building was the kitchen and perhaps also enclosures for livestock, as archaeologists have found at Southampton, England. Even city dwellers clung to rural pursuits, living largely off the food they raised themselves.

The construction of houses and markets was part of a building boom that began in the tenth century and continued at an accelerated pace through the thirteenth. Specialized buildings for trade and city government were put up—charitable houses for the sick and indigent, community houses, and warehouses. In addition, medieval cities surrounded them-

Shoemaker
By the twelfth century, a fortified village (a burg) had developed around the monastery of Cluny to cater to the monks' material needs. This carving of a shoemaker at his bench, which was displayed above his shop at Cluny, is an example of the sorts of signs that merchants used to advertise their services. *Musée d'Art et d' Archéologie (Musée Ochier), Cluny, France.*

selves with walls. By 1100, Speyer (today in Germany) had three: the first had been put up around its cathedral, the second went just beyond the parish church of St. Moritz, and the last was built still farther out to protect the marketplace. Within the walls lay a network of streets—often narrow, dirty, dark, and winding—made of packed clay or gravel. New bridges were built to span the rivers. Before the eleventh century, Europeans had depended on boats and waterways for bulky long-distance transport; now carts could haul items overland because new roads through the countryside linked the urban markets.

Although commercial centers developed throughout western Europe, they grew fastest and became most dense in regions along key waterways: the Mediterranean coasts of Italy, France, and Spain; northern Italy along the Po River; the river system of the Rhône-Saône-Meuse;♦ the Rhineland; the English Channel; the shores of the Baltic Sea. During the eleventh century these waterways became part of a single interdependent economy.

♦**Rhône-Saône-Meuse:** rohn / sohn / meyz

Business Arrangements

The development of commercial centers reflected changing attitudes toward money. The new mode of commerce transformed the social relations involved in economic transactions. In the gift economy, exchanges of coins, gold, and silver were components of ongoing relationships. In the new market economy, which thrived on the profit motive, arrangements were less personal. They often relied on written contracts and calculations of the profitability of a particular business venture.

Partnerships, Contracts, and the Rise of Industry. In the course of the eleventh and twelfth centuries, people created new kinds of business arrangements through partnerships, contracts, and large-scale productive enterprises. Although they took many forms, all new business agreements had the common purpose of bringing people together to pool their resources and finance larger initiatives. Short-lived partnerships were set up for the term of one sea voyage; longer-term partnerships were created for land trade. In northern and central Italy, for example, these long-term ventures took the form of a *compagnia,*◆ formed by extended families. Everyone who contributed to the compagnia bore joint and unlimited liability for all losses and debts. This provision enhanced family solidarity, because each member was responsible for the debts of all the others, but it also risked bankrupting everyone in the family.

The commercial revolution also fostered the development of contracts for sales, exchanges, and loans. Loans were the most problematic. In the Middle Ages, as now, interest payments were the chief inducement for an investor to supply money. To circumvent the church's ban on usury (profiting from loans), interest was often disguised as a "penalty for late payment" under the rules of a contract. The new willingness to finance business enterprises with loans signaled a changed attitude toward credit: risk was acceptable if it brought profit.

Contracts and partnerships made large-scale productive enterprises possible. In fact,

◆*compagnia:* kahm puh NEE yuh

light industry began in the eleventh century. One of the earliest products to benefit from new industrial technologies was cloth. Water mills powered machines such as flails to clean and thicken cloth and presses to extract oil from fibers. Machines were also used to exploit raw materials more efficiently: new deep-mining technology provided Europeans with hitherto untapped sources of metals. At the same time, forging techniques improved, and iron was for the first time regularly used for agricultural tools and plows. This, in turn, made for better farming, which in turn fed the commercial revolution. Metals were also used for weapons and armor or fashioned into ornaments or coins.

Self-Government for the Towns

Both to themselves and to outsiders, townspeople seemed different. Tradespeople, artisans, ship captains, innkeepers, and money changers did not fit into the old categories of medieval types—those who pray, those who fight, and those who labor. Just knowing they were different gave townspeople a sense of solidarity with one another. But practical reasons also contributed to their feeling of common purpose: they lived in close quarters, and they shared a mutual interest in reliable coinage, laws to facilitate commerce, freedom from servile dues and services, and independence to buy and sell as the market dictated. Already in the early twelfth century, the king of England granted to the citizens of Newcastle-upon-Tyne the privilege that any unfree peasant who lived there unclaimed by his lord for a year and a day would thereafter be a free person. To townspeople, freedom meant having their own officials and law courts. They petitioned the political powers that ruled them—bishops, kings, counts, castellans—for the right to govern themselves. Often they had to fight for this freedom and, if successful, paid a hefty sum for the privilege. Town institutions of self-government were called **communes**; they were sworn associations of citizens who formed a legal corporate body.

Communes were especially common in northern and central Italy, France, and Flanders. Italian cities were centers of regional political power even before the commercial revolution. Castellans constructed their fortifications and bishops ruled the countryside from such cities. The commercial revolution swelled the Italian cities with tradespeople, whose interest in self-government was often fueled by religious as well as economic concerns. At Milan in the second half of the eleventh century, popular discontent with the archbishop, who effectively ruled the city, led to numerous armed clashes. In 1097, the Milanese succeeded in transferring political power from the archbishop and his clergy to a government of leading men of the city, who called themselves consuls. The title recalled the government of the ancient Roman republic, affirming the consuls' status as representatives of the people. Like the archbishop's power before, the consuls' rule extended beyond the town walls, into the *contado,*♦ the outlying countryside.

Outside Italy, movements for city independence took place within the framework of larger kingdoms or principalities. Such movements were sometimes violent, as at Milan, but at other times they were peaceful. For example, William Clito, who claimed the county of Flanders (today in Belgium), willingly granted the citizens of St. Omer the rights they asked for in 1127 in return for their support of his claims: he recognized them as legally free, gave them the right to mint coins, allowed them their own laws and courts, and lifted certain tolls and taxes. Whether violently or peacefully, the men and women of many towns and cities gained a measure of self-rule.

Review: What new professions and institutions arose as a result of the commercial revolution?

❖ Church Reform and Its Aftermath

The commercial revolution affected the church no less than it affected other institutions of the time. Bishops ruled over many cities. Kings appointed many bishops. Local lords installed priests in their parish churches. Churchmen gave gifts and money to these

secular powers for their offices. The impulse to free the church from "the world"—from rulers, wealth, sex, and power—was as old as the origins of monasticism; but, beginning in the tenth century and increasing to fever pitch in the eleventh, reformers demanded that the church as a whole remodel itself and become free of secular entanglements.

This freedom was from the start as much a matter of power as of religion. Most people had long believed that their ruler—whether king, duke, count, or castellan—reigned by the grace of God and had the right to control the churches in his territory. But by the second half of the eleventh century, more and more people saw a great deal wrong with secular power over the church. They looked to the papacy to lead the movement of church reform. The matter came to a head under Pope Gregory VII, whose clash with Emperor Henry IV ushered in a major civil war in Germany and a great upheaval in the distribution of power across western Europe. By the early 1100s, a reformed church—with the pope at its head—had become an institution, penetrating into areas of life never before touched by churchmen. Church reform began as a way to free the church from the world, but in the end the church was equally involved in the new world it had helped to create.

Beginnings of Reform

The project of freeing the church from the world began in the tenth century with no particular plan and only a vague idea of what it might mean. Some early steps were taken by local reformers—both clerical and lay—to make the clergy celibate and independent of laymen. But the policy of the reformers did not take final shape until it was taken up by the papacy and turned into a recipe for reorganizing the church under papal leadership. The movement to "liberate the church" in fact began in unlikely circles: with the very rulers who were controlling churches and monasteries, appointing churchmen, and using bishops as their administrators.

Cluniac Reform. The Benedictine monastery of Cluny may serve to represent the early phases of the reform. Cluny was founded in

♦*contado:* cahn TA doh

910 by the duke and duchess of Aquitaine, who endowed it with property but then gave it and its worldly possessions to Saints Peter and Paul. In this way they put control of the monastery into the hands of the two most powerful heavenly saints. They designated the pope, as the successor of St. Peter, to be the monastery's worldly protector if anyone should bother or threaten it. The whole notion of "freedom" at this point was very vague. But Cluny's prestige was great because of its status as St. Peter's property and the elaborate round of prayers that the monks carried out there with scrupulous devotion. The Cluniac monks fulfilled the role of "those who pray" in a way that dazzled their contemporaries. Through their prayers they seemed to guarantee the salvation of all Christians. Rulers, bishops, rich landowners, and even serfs (if they could) gave Cluny donations of land, joining their contributions to the land of St. Peter. Powerful men and women called on the Cluniac monks to reform other monasteries along the Cluniac model.

The abbots of Cluny came to see themselves as reformers of the world as well. They believed in clerical celibacy, arguing against the prevailing norm in which parish priests and even bishops were married. They also thought that the laity could be reformed, become more virtuous, and cease its oppression of the poor. In the eleventh century, the Cluniacs began to link their program of internal monastic and external worldly reform to the papacy. When their lands were encroached on by bishops and laypeople, they appealed to the popes to help them. At the same time the papacy itself was becoming interested in reform.

Church Reform in the Empire. Around the time the Cluniacs were joining their fate to that of the popes, a small group of clerics and monks in the empire began calling for systematic reform within the church. They buttressed their arguments with new interpretations of canon law—the laws decreed over the centuries at church councils and by bishops and popes. They concentrated on two breaches of those laws: clerical marriage and **simony**◆ (buying church offices).

Most of the men who promoted these ideas lived in the most commercialized regions of the empire—Italy and the regions along the northern half of the Rhine River. Their familiarity with the impersonal practices of a profit economy led them to interpret as crass purchases the gifts that churchmen were used to giving in return for their offices.

Emperor Henry III (r. 1039–1056) supported the reformers. Taking seriously his position as the anointed of God, Henry felt responsible for the well-being of the church in his empire. He denounced simony and personally refused to accept money or gifts when he appointed bishops to their posts. When in 1046 three men, each representing a different faction of the Roman aristocracy, claimed to be pope, Henry, as ruler of Rome, traveled to Italy to settle the matter. The Synod of Sutri (1046), over which he presided, deposed all three popes and elected another. In 1049, Henry appointed Leo IX (r. 1049–1054), a bishop from the Rhineland, to the papacy. But this appointment did not work out as Henry had expected, for Leo set out to reform the church under his own, not the emperor's, control.

Leo IX and the Expansion of Papal Power. During Leo's tenure, the pope's role expanded. (For one artist's image of Leo, see the picture on the next page.) He traveled to France and Germany, holding councils to condemn bishops guilty of simony. He sponsored the creation of a canon law textbook—the *Collection in 74 Titles*—which emphasized the pope's power. To the papal court Leo brought the most zealous reformers of his day: Humbert of Silva Candida, Peter Damian, and Hildebrand (later Gregory VII).

At first, Leo's claims to new power over the church hierarchy were complacently ignored by clergy and secular rulers alike. The Council of Reims, which Leo called in 1049, for example, was attended by only a few bishops and boycotted by the king of France. Nevertheless, the pope made it into a forum for exercising his authority. Placing the relics of St. Remegius◆ (the patron saint of Reims) on the altar of the church, he demanded that the attending bishops and ab-

---

◆**simony:** SY muh nee

◆**Remegius:** reh MEE gee uhs

Leo IX

This eleventh-century manuscript shows not so much a portrait of Leo IX as an idealized image of his power and position. What does the halo signify? Why do you suppose he stands at least three heads taller than the other figure in the picture, Warinus, the abbot of St. Arnulf of Metz? What is Leo doing with his right hand? With his left hand he holds a little church (symbol of a real one) that is being presented to him by Warinus. Compare these figures to those of emperor and Christ on page 323. What did the artist intend to convey about the relationship of this church to papal power? *Burgerbibliothek Bern cod. 292f.#72r.*

bots say whether or not they had purchased their offices. A few confessed they had, some did not respond, and others gave excuses. New and extraordinary was the fact that all present felt accountable to the pope and accepted his verdicts.

In his last year as pope, Leo sent Humbert of Silva Candida to Constantinople on a diplomatic mission to argue against the patriarch of Constantinople on behalf of the new, lofty claims of the pope. Furious at the contemptuous way he was treated by the patriarch, Humbert excommunicated him. In retaliation the patriarch excommunicated Humbert and his party, threatening them with eternal damnation. Clashes between the two churches had occurred before and had been patched up, but this one, called the **Great Schism** (1054), proved insurmountable.[1] Thereafter, the Roman Catholic and the Greek Orthodox churches were largely separate.

The popes who followed Leo continued his program to expand papal power. When military adventurers from Normandy began carving out states for themselves in southern Italy, the popes in nearby Rome felt threatened. After waging unsuccessful war against the interlopers, the papacy made the best of a bad situation by granting the Normans Sicily and parts of southern Italy as a fief, turning its former enemies into vassals.

As leader of the Christian people, the papacy also participated in wars in Spain, where it supported Christians against the dominant Muslims. The political fragmentation of al-Andalus into small and weak *taifas* (see page 329) made it fair game to the Christians to the north. Slowly the idea of the *reconquista*,♦ the Christian reconquest of Spain, took shape, fed by religious fervor as well as greed for land and power.

The Gregorian Reform and the Investiture Conflict, 1073–1122

The papal reform movement is above all associated with Pope Gregory VII (r. 1073–1085) and is therefore often called the **Gregorian reform**. He began as a lowly Roman cleric, named Hildebrand, with the job of administering the papal estates and rose slowly in the hierarchy. A passionate advocate of papal primacy (the theory that the pope was the head of the church), Gregory was not afraid to clash head-on with Emperor Henry IV (r. 1056–1106) over leadership of the church. In his view—and it was astonishing at the time, given

---

[1]Despite occasional thaws and liftings of the sentences, the mutual excommunications of pope and patriarch largely remained in effect until 1965, when Pope Paul VI and the Greek Orthodox patriarch, Anthanagoras I, publicly deplored them.

♦*reconquista:* ray con KEE stuh

the religious and spiritual roles associated with rulers—the emperor was just a layman who had no right to meddle in church affairs.

Gregory was and remains an extraordinarily controversial figure. He certainly thought that as pope he was acting as the vicar, or representative, of St. Peter on earth. Describing himself, he declared, "I have labored with all my power that Holy Church, the bride of God, our Lady Mother, might come again to her own splendor and might remain free, pure, and Catholic." He thought the reforms he advocated and the upheavals he precipitated were necessary to free the church from the Satanic rulers of the world. But his great nemesis, Henry IV, had a very different view of Gregory. He considered him an ambitious and evil man who "seduced the world far and wide and stained the Church with the blood of her sons." Not surprisingly, modern historians are only a bit less divided in their assessment of Gregory. Few deny his sincerity and deep religious devotion, but many speak of his pride, ambition, and single-mindedness. He was not an easy man.

Henry IV was less complex. He was brought up in the traditions of his father, Henry III, a pious church reformer who considered it part of his duty to appoint bishops and even popes to ensure the well-being of both church and state. The emperor believed that he and his bishops—who were, at the same time, his most valuable supporters and administrators—were the rightful leaders of the church. He had no intention of allowing the pope to become head of the church.

The Investiture Conflict.[2]

The great confrontation between Gregory and Henry that

The World of the Investiture Conflict, c. 1070–1122

---

[2]This movement is also called the Investiture Controversy, Investiture Contest, or Investiture Struggle. The epithets all refer to the same thing: the disagreement between popes and emperors regarding the right to invest churchmen in particular and power over the church hierarchy in general.

historians call the **Investiture Conflict** began over the appointment of the archbishop of Milan. Gregory disputed Henry's right to "invest" churchmen. In the investiture ritual, the emperor or his representative symbolically gave the church and the land that went with it to the priest or bishop or archbishop chosen for the job. When, in 1075, Henry insisted on investing a new archbishop of Milan, the emperor and the pope began hurling denunciations at each other. The next year Henry called a council of German bishops who demanded that Gregory, that "false monk," resign. In reply, Gregory called a synod that both excommunicated and suspended Henry from office:

I deprive King Henry, son of the emperor Henry, who has rebelled against [God's] Church with unheard-of audacity, of the government over the whole kingdom of Germany and Italy, and I release all Christian men from the allegiance which they have sworn or may swear to him, and I forbid anyone to serve him as king.

It was this part of the decree that made it politically explosive, because it authorized anyone in Henry's kingdom to rebel against him. Henry's enemies, mostly German princes (as German aristocrats were called), now threatened to elect another king. They were motivated partly by religious sentiments, as many had established links with the papacy through their support of reformed monasteries, and partly by political opportunism, as they had chafed under the strong German king, who had tried to keep their power in check. Some bishops joined forces with Gregory's supporters, however. This was a great blow to royal power because Henry desperately needed the troops supplied by his churchmen.

Attacked from all sides, Henry traveled to intercept Gregory, who was journeying northward to visit the rebellious princes. In early 1077, king and pope met at Canossa, high in central Italy's snowy Apennine◆ Mountains. Gregory was inside a fortress there; Henry stood outside as a penitent, begging forgiveness. Henry's move was astute, for no priest could refuse absolution to a penitent; Gregory had to lift the excommunication and receive Henry back into the church. But Gregory

---

◆**Apennine:** A puh nyn

Matilda of Tuscany
Matilda, countess of Tuscany and key supporter of Pope Gregory VII, here sits on a throne. She is the dominant figure in this picture, which was made around 1115 to illustrate a book about her life. To her right is Hugh, the abbot of Cluny. Beneath them both, in a gesture of supplication, is Emperor Henry IV, who asks them to intervene with the pope on his behalf.
© *Biblioteca Apostalica Vaticana (Vatican).*

now had the advantage of enjoying the king's humiliation before the majesty of the pope.

Although Henry was technically back in the church's fold, nothing of substance had been resolved, and civil war began. The princes elected an antiking (a king chosen illegally), and Henry and his supporters elected an antipope. From 1077 until 1122, papal and imperial armies and supporters waged intermittent war in both Germany and Italy.

Outcome of the Investiture Conflict. The Investiture Conflict was finally resolved long after Henry IV and Gregory VII had died. The Concordat of Worms♦ of 1122 ended the fighting with a compromise that relied on a conceptual distinction between two parts of investiture—the spiritual (in which a man re-

♦**Worms:** vuhrms

ceived the symbols of his clerical office) and the secular (in which he received the symbols of the material goods that would allow him to function). Under the terms of the concordat, the ring and staff, the symbols of church office, were to be given by a churchman in the first part of the ceremony. In the second part, the emperor or his representative would touch the bishop with a scepter, a symbolic gesture that stood for the land and other possessions that went with church office. Elections of bishops in Germany would take place "in the presence" of the emperor—that is, under his influence. In Italy, the pope would have a comparable role.

Superficially, nothing much had changed; secular rulers would continue to have a part in choosing and investing churchmen. In fact, however, few people would now claim that a king could act as head of the church. Just as the new investiture ceremony broke the ritual into spiritual and secular parts, so too it implied a new notion of kingship that separated it from priesthood. The Investiture Conflict did not produce the modern distinction between church and state—that would develop very slowly—but it set the wheels in motion.

The most important changes brought about by the Investiture Conflict, however, were on the ground: the political landscape in both Italy and Germany was irrevocably transformed. In Germany, the princes consolidated their lands and their positions at the expense of royal power. In Italy, the emperor lost power to the cities. The northern and central Italian communes were formed in the crucible of the war between the pope and the emperor. In fierce communal struggles, city factions, often created by local grievances but claiming to fight on behalf of the papal or the imperial cause, created their own governing bodies. In the course of the twelfth century, these Italian cities became accustomed to self-government.

The Sweep of Reform

Church reform involved much more than the clash of popes, emperors, and their supporters. It penetrated into the daily lives of ordinary Christians, inspired new forms of legal scholarship, and changed the way the church operated.

A Byzantine View of Papal Primacy

A continual source of friction between the Roman and Greek churches was the question of papal primacy (the pope's place at the head of the church). Even after the Great Schism of 1054, the two sides continued to argue over the matter. In 1136 a debate at Constantinople pitted a German bishop, Anselm of Havelburg—who argued that the pope had jurisdiction over the Greek church—against Nicetas, the Greek bishop of Nicomedia. In the following passage, Nicetas presents a moderate view.

I neither deny nor do I reject the Primacy of the Roman Church whose dignity you have extolled. As a matter of fact, we read in our ancient histories that there were three patriarchal sees closely linked in brotherhood, Rome, Alexandria, and Antioch, among which Rome, the highest see in the empire, received the primacy. . . .

But the Bishop of Rome himself ought not to be called the Prince of the Priesthood, nor the Supreme Priest nor anything of that kind, but only the Bishop of the first see. Thus it was that Boniface III [607], who was Roman by nationality, and the son of John, the Bishop of Rome, obtained from the Emperor Phocas confirmation of the fact that the apostolic see of Blessed Peter was the head of all the other Churches, since at that time, the Church of Constantinople was saying that it was the first see because of the transfer of the Empire. . . .

But the Roman Church to which we do not deny the Primacy among her sisters, and whom we recognize as holding the highest place in any general council, the first place of honor, that Church has separated herself from the rest by her pretensions. She has appropriated to herself the monarchy which is not contained in her office and which has divided the bishops and the churches of the East and the West since the partition of the Empire. When, as a result of these circumstances, she gathers a council of the Western bishops without making us (in the East) a part of it, it is fitting that her bishops should accept its decrees and observe them with the veneration that is due to them . . . but although we are not in disagreement with the Roman Church in the matter of the Catholic faith, how can we be expected to accept these decisions which were taken without our advice and of which we know nothing, since we were not at that same time gathered in council? If the Roman Pontiff, seated upon his sublime throne of glory, wishes to fulminate against us and to launch his orders from the height of his sublime dignity, if he wishes to sit in judgment on our Churches with a total disregard of our advice and solely according to his own will, as he seems to wish, what brotherhood and what fatherhood can we see in such a course of action? Who could ever accept such a situation? In such circumstances we could not be called nor would we really be any longer sons of the Church but truly its slaves.

Source: Deno John Geanakoplos, *Byzantium: Church, Society, and Civilization Seen through Contemporary Eyes* (Chicago: University of Chicago Press, 1984), 214–15, quoting in turn from F. Dvornik, *Byzantium and the Roman Primacy*, trans. Edwin A. Quain, S.J. (New York: Fordham University Press, 1966/1979), 145–46. Footnote omitted.

New Emphasis on the Sacraments. According to the Catholic church, the sacraments were the regular means by which God's heavenly grace infused mundane existence. But this did not mean that Christians were clear about how many sacraments there were, how they worked, or even what their significance was. Eleventh-century church reformers began the process—which would continue into the thirteenth century—of emphasizing the importance of the sacraments and the special nature of the priest, whose chief role was to administer them.

In the sacrament of marriage, for example, the effective involvement of the church in the wedding of husband and wife came only after the Gregorian reform. Before the twelfth century, priests had little to do with weddings, which were family affairs. After the twelfth century, however, priests were expected to consecrate the marriage. When the knight Arnulf of Ardres got married in 1194, for example, priests blessed and sprinkled him and his wife with holy water as the couple lay in their nuptial bed. Churchmen also began to assume jurisdiction over marital disputes, not simply in cases involving royalty (as they had always done) but also in those involving lesser aristocrats. The clergy's prohibition of marriage partners as distant as seventh cousins (marriage between such cousins was considered incest) had the potential to control dynastic alliances. Because many noble families kept their inheritance intact through a single male heir, the heirs' marriages took on great significance.

At the same time, churchmen began to stress the sanctity of marriage. Hugh of St. Victor, a twelfth-century scholar, dwelled on the sacramental meaning of marriage:

> Can you find anything else in marriage except conjugal society which makes it sacred and by which you can assert that it is holy? . . . Each shall be to the other as a same self in all sincere love, all careful solicitude, every kindness of affection, in constant compassion, unflagging consolation, and faithful devotedness.

Hugh saw marriage as a matter of Christian love.

The reformers also proclaimed the special importance of the sacrament of the Mass, holy communion through the body and blood of Christ. Gregory VII called the Mass "the greatest thing in the Christian religion." No layman, regardless of how powerful, and no woman of any class or status at all could perform anything equal to it, for the Mass was the key to salvation.

Clerical Celibacy. The new emphasis on the sacraments, which were now more thoroughly and carefully defined, along with the desire to set priests clearly apart from the laity, led to vigorous enforcement of an old element of church discipline: the celibacy of priests. The demand for a celibate clergy had far-reaching significance for the history of the church. It distanced western clerics even further from their eastern Orthodox counterparts (who did not practice celibacy), ex-

acerbating the Great Schism of 1054. It also broke with traditional local practices, as clerical marriage was customary in some places. Gregorian reformers exhorted every cleric in higher orders, from the humble parish priest to the exalted bishop, to refrain from marriage or to abandon his wife. Naturally many churchmen resisted. The historian Orderic Vitalis♦ (1075–c. 1142) reported that one zealous archbishop in Normandy

> fulfilled his duties as metropolitan with courage and thoroughness, continually striving to separate immoral priests from their mistresses [and wives]: on one occasion when he forbade them to keep concubines he was stoned out of the synod.

Undaunted, the reformers persisted, and in 1123 the pope proclaimed all clerical marriages invalid. With its new power, the papacy was largely able to enforce the rule.

The "Papal Monarchy." Part of the new powers of the papacy rested on its consolidation and imposition of canon law. These laws had begun simply as rules determined at church councils. Later they were supplemented with papal declarations. Several attempts to gather together and organize these laws had been made before the eleventh century. But the proliferation of rules during that century, along with the desire of Gregory's followers to clarify church law as they saw it, made a systematic collection of rules even more necessary. This was achieved around 1140 by a landmark synthesis, the *Decretum,*♦ written by a teacher of canon law named Gratian. Collecting nearly two thousand passages from the decrees of popes and councils as well as the writings of the church fathers, Gratian intended to demonstrate their essential agreement. In fact, the book's original title was *Harmony of Discordant Canons.* If he found any "discord" in his sources, Gratian usually imposed the harmony himself by arguing that the passages dealt with different situations. A bit later another legal scholar revised and expanded the *Decretum,* adding ancient Roman law to the mix.

♦**Orderic Vitalis:** awr duh REEK vy TAY luhs
♦***Decretum:*** duh KREET uhm

Already while Gratian was writing, the papal curia, or government, centered in Rome, resembled a court of law with its own collection agency. The papacy had developed a bureaucracy to hear cases and rule on petitions, such as disputed elections of bishops. Churchmen not involved in litigation went to Rome for other sorts of benefits: to petition for privileges for their monasteries or to be consecrated by the pope. All these services were also expensive, requiring lawyers, judges, hearing officers, notaries, and collectors. The lands owned by the papacy were not sufficient to support the growing cost of its administrative apparatus, and the petitioners and litigants themselves had to pay, a practice they resented. A satire written about 1100, in the style of the Gospels, made bitter fun of papal greed:

> There came to the court a certain wealthy clerk, fat and thick, and gross. . . . He first gave to the dispenser, second to the treasurer, third to the cardinals. But they thought among themselves that they should receive more. The Lord Pope, hearing that his cardinals had received many gifts, was sick, nigh unto death. But the rich man sent to him a couch of gold and silver and immediately he was made whole. Then the Lord Pope called his cardinals and ministers to him and said to them: "Brethren, look, lest anyone deceive you with vain words. For I have given you an example: as I have grasped, so you grasp also."

The pope, with his law courts, bureaucracy, and financial apparatus, had become a monarch.

Early Crusades and Crusader States

Asserting itself as head of the Christian church and leader of its reform, the papacy sometimes supported and proclaimed holy wars to advance the cause of Christianity. The most important of these were the crusades. Combinations of war and pilgrimage—the popular practice of making a pious voyage to a sacred shrine to petition for help or cure—the early crusades sent armed European Christians into battle against Muslims in the Holy Land, the place where Christ had lived and died. The crusaders established several tiny states along the coast of the eastern

Mediterranean Sea, holding on to them precariously until 1291.

Although the crusades ultimately "failed" in the sense that the crusaders did not succeed in permanently retaining the Holy Land for Christendom, they were a pivotal episode in Western civilization. They marked the first stage of European overseas expansion, which would later become imperialism.

Calling the First Crusade. The First Crusade began with the entry of the Seljuk♦ Turks into Asia Minor (Map 10.2). In the 900s, the Muslim world had splintered into numerous small states; by the 1050s, the fierce, nomadic Sunni Muslim **Seljuk Turks** had captured Baghdad, subjugated the caliphate, and begun to threaten Byzantium. The difficulties the Byzantine emperor Romanus IV had in pulling together an army to attack the Turks in 1071 reveal how weak his position had become. Unable to muster Byzantine troops—which were either busy defending their own districts or led by *dynatoi* (see page 324) wary of sending support to the emperor—Romanus had to rely on a mercenary army made up of Normans, Franks, Slavs, and even Turks. This motley force met the Seljuks at Manzikert♦ in what is today eastern Turkey. The battle was a disaster for Romanus: the Seljuks, under Sultan Alp Arslan,♦ routed his army and captured him. The battle at Manzikert (1071) marked the end of Byzantine domination in the region.

The Turks, gradually settling in Asia Minor, extended their control across the empire and beyond, all the way to Jerusalem, which had been under Muslim control since the seventh century. In 1095, the Byzantine emperor Alexius Comnenus (Alexius I) appealed for help to Pope Urban II, hoping to get new mercenary troops for a fresh offensive.

Urban II chose to interpret the request in his own way. At the Council of Clermont (in France) in 1095, after finishing the usual business of proclaiming the Truce of God (prohibition of fighting on various days of the week for various reasons) and condemn-

---

♦**Seljuk:** SEL jook
♦**Manzikert:** MAN zuh kurt
♦**Alp Arslan:** ahlp ahr SLAHN

MAP 10.2   The First Crusade, 1096–1098
The First Crusade was a major military undertaking that required organization, movement over both land and sea, and enormous resources. Four main groups were responsible for the conquest of Jerusalem. One began at Cologne, in northern Germany; a second group started out from Blois, in France; the third originated just to the west of Provence; and the fourth launched ships from Brindisi, at the heel of Italy. All joined up at Constantinople, where their leaders negotiated with Alexius for help and supplies in return for a pledge of vassalage to the emperor.

ing simony among the clergy, Urban moved outside the church and addressed an already excited throng:

> Oh, race of Franks, race from across the mountains, race beloved and chosen by God. . . . Let hatred depart from among you, let your quarrels end, let wars cease, and let all dissensions and controversies slumber. Enter upon the road to the Holy Sepulcher; wrest that land from the wicked race, and subject it to yourselves.

The crowd reportedly responded with one voice: "God wills it." Historians remain divided over Urban's motives for his massive call to arms. Certainly he hoped to win Christian control of the Holy Land. He was also anxious to fulfill the goals of the Truce of God

by turning the entire "race of Franks" into a peace militia dedicated to holy purposes, an army of God. Just as the Truce of God mobilized whole communities to fight against anyone who broke the truce, so the First Crusade mobilized armed groups sworn to free the Holy Land of its enemies. Finally, Urban's call placed the papacy in a new position of leadership, one that complemented in a military arena the position the popes had gained in the church hierarchy.

Heeding the Call.   Both men and women, rich and poor, young and old heeded Urban's call to go on the First Crusade (1096–1099). They abandoned their homes and braved the rough journey to the Holy Land to fight for

CONTRASTING VIEWS

The First Crusade

When Urban II preached the First Crusade at Clermont in 1095, he unleashed a movement that was seen and interpreted in many different ways. Document 1 is an early and almost official account begun around 1100 by Fulcher of Chartres, who considered the crusade a wonderful historical movement and participated in it himself. Jews in the Rhineland who experienced the virulent attacks of some of the crusading forces had a very different view (Document 2). Document 3 presents an Arab view of the crusaders' capture of Jerusalem.

1. THE CHRONICLE OF FULCHER OF CHARTRES (EARLY TWELFTH CENTURY)

Fulcher of Chartres, a chaplain for one of the crusade leaders, wrote his account of the First Crusade for posterity. His chronicle is ordinarily very accurate, and he is careful to note the different experiences of different participants. It is all the more significant, therefore, that he expresses the public view of the First Crusade by making liberal use of biblical quotations and imagery to describe the event. He saw it as the fulfillment of God's plan for humanity.

In March of the year 1096 from the Lord's Incarnation, after Pope Urban had held the Council, which has been described, at Auvergne in November, some people, earlier prepared than others, hastened to begin the holy journey. Others followed in April or May, June or July, and also in August, September, or October, whenever the opportunity of securing expenses presented itself.

In that year, with God disposing, peace and a vast abundance of grain and wine overflowed through all the regions of the earth, so that they who chose to follow Him with their crosses according to His commands did not fail on the way for lack of bread. [Fulcher then names the "leaders of the pilgrims."] . . .

So, with such a great band proceeding from western parts, gradually from day to day on the way there grew armies of innumerable people coming together from everywhere. Thus a countless multitude speaking many languages and coming from many regions was to be seen. However, all were not assembled into one army until we arrived at the city of Nicaea.

What more shall I tell? The islands of the seas and all the kingdoms of the earth were so agitated that one believed that the prophecy of David was fulfilled, who said in his Psalm: "All nations whom Thou hast made shall come and worship before Thee O Lord" [Ps. 86:9]; and what those going all the way there later said with good reason: "We shall worship in the place where His feet have stood" [Ps. 132:7]. We have read much about this in the Prophets which it is tedious to repeat.

Source: Edward Peters, ed., *The First Crusade: The Chronicle of Fulcher of Chartres and Other Source Materials* (Philadelphia: University of Pennsylvania Press, 1971), 35–37.

2. THE JEWISH EXPERIENCE AS TOLD BY SOLOMON BAR SIMSON (MID-TWELFTH CENTURY)

Around 1140, Solomon Bar Simson, a Jew from Mainz, published a chronicle of the First Crusade. This excerpt shows that the Jewish community interpreted the coming of the crusaders as a punishment from God; hence their prayers and fasting and their conviction that those killed by the crusaders were martyrs for God.

At this time arrogant people, a people of strange speech, a nation bitter and impetuous, Frenchmen and Germans, set out for the Holy City, which had been desecrated by barbaric nations, there to seek their house of idolatry and banish the Ishmaelites [Muslims] and other denizens of the land and conquer the land for themselves. . . . Now it came to pass that as they passed through the towns where Jews dwelled, they said to one another: "Look now, we are going a long way to seek out the profane shrine and to avenge ourselves on the Ishmaelites, when here, in our very midst, are the Jews—they whose forefathers murdered and crucified [Christ] for no reason. Let us first avenge ourselves on them and exterminate them from among the nations so that the name of Israel will no longer be remembered, or let them adopt our faith and acknowledge the offspring of promiscuity."

When the Jewish communities became aware of their intentions, they resorted to the custom of our ancestors, repentance, prayer, and charity. The hands of the Holy Nation turned faint at this time, their hearts melted, and their strength flagged. They hid in their innermost rooms to escape the swirling sword. They subjected themselves to great endurance, abstaining from food and drink for three consecutive days and nights, and then fasting many days from sunrise to sunset, until their skin was shriveled and dry as wood upon their bones. And they cried out loudly and bitterly to God. . . .

On the eighth day of Iyar, on the Sabbath, the foe attacked the community of Speyer and murdered eleven holy souls who sanctified their Creator on the holy Sabbath and refused to defile themselves by adopting the faith of their foe. There was a distinguished, pious woman there who slaughtered herself in sanctification of God's name. She was the first among all the communities of those who were slaughtered. The remainder were saved by the local bishop without defilement [baptism], as described above.

On the twenty-third day of Iyar they attacked the community of Worms. The community was then divided into two groups; some remained in their homes and others fled to the local bishop seeking refuge. Those who remained in their homes were set upon by the steppe-wolves who pillaged men, women, and infants, children and old people. They pulled down the stairways and destroyed the houses, looting and plundering; and they took the Torah Scroll, trampled it in the mud, and tore and burned it.

Source: Patrick J. Geary, ed., *Readings in Medieval History* (Peterborough, Ontario, Canada: Broadview Press, 1989), 433–34.

3. THE SEIZURE OF JERUSALEM AS TOLD BY IBN AL-ATHIR (EARLY THIRTEENTH CENTURY)

Ibn Al-Athir (1160–1233) was an Arab historian who drew on earlier accounts for this recounting of the crusaders' conquest of Jerusalem. He stresses the greed and impiety of the crusaders, who pillaged Muslim holy places, and their pitiless slaughter.

After their vain attempt to take Acre by siege, the Franks moved on to Jerusalem and besieged it for more than six weeks. They built two towers, one of which, near Sion, the Muslims burnt down, killing everyone inside it. It had scarcely ceased to burn before a messenger arrived to ask for help and to bring the news that the other side of the city had fallen. In fact Jerusalem was taken from the north on the morning of Friday 22 sha'ban 492 [July 15, 1099]. The population was put to the sword by the Franks who pillaged the area for a week. A band of Muslims barricaded themselves into the Oratory of David and fought on for several days. They were granted their lives in return for surrendering.

The Franks honored their word, and the group left by night for Ascalon. In the Masjid al-Aqsa [a mosque] the Franks slaughtered more than 70,000 people, among them a large number of Imams and Muslim scholars, devout and ascetic men who had left their homelands to live lives of pious seclusion in the Holy Place. The Franks stripped the Dome of the Rock [a place holy to the Muslims, upon which was built the mosque that the Crusaders plundered] of more than forty silver candelabra, each of them weighing 3,600 drams, and a great silver lamp weighing forty-four Syrian pounds, as well as a hundred and fifty smaller silver candelabra and more than twenty gold ones, and a great deal more booty. Refugees from Syria reached Baghdad in ramadan [the month of fasting].

Source: Patrick J. Geary, ed., *Readings in Medieval History* (Peterborough, Ontario, Canada: Broadview Press, 1989), 443.

QUESTIONS TO CONSIDER
1. What commonalities, if any, do you detect between the religious ideas of the crusaders and those whom they attacked?
2. What were the similarities and what were the differences in the experiences of the Jews in Rhineland cities and the Arabs in Jerusalem.
3. What were the motives of the crusaders?

A Crusader and His Wife
How do we know that the man on the left is a crusader? On his shirt is a cross, the sign worn by all men going on the crusades. In his right hand is a pilgrim's staff, a useful reminder that the crusades were sometimes considered less a matter of war than of penance and piety. What does the crusader's wife's embrace imply about marital love in the twelfth century? *Musée Lorrain, Nancy/photo: P. Mignot.*

their God. They also went—especially younger sons of aristocrats, who could not expect an inheritance because of primogeniture—because they wanted land. Some knights took the cross because they were obligated to follow their lord. Others hoped for plunder. Although women were discouraged from going on the crusades (one, who begged permission from her bishop, was persuaded to stay home and spend her wealth on charity instead), some crusaders were accompanied by their wives. (See the image, A Crusader and His Wife, at left.) Other women went as servants; a few may have been fighters. Children and old men and women, not able to fight, made the cords for siege engines—giant machines used to hurl stones at enemy fortifications. As more crusades were undertaken during the twelfth century, the transport and supply of these armies became a lucrative business for the commercial classes of maritime Italian cities such as Venice, which was strategically located on the route eastward.

The armies of the First Crusade were organized not as one military force but rather as separate militias, each commanded by a different individual. Fulcher of Chartres♦ (c. 1059–c.1127), an eyewitness, reported: "There grew armies of innumerable people coming together from everywhere. Thus a countless multitude speaking many languages and coming from many regions was to be seen." Fulcher was speaking of the armies led by nobles and authorized by the pope.

Attacking the Jews. One band, not authorized by the pope, consisted of commoners. This People's (or Peasants') Crusade, which started out before the others under the leadership of an eloquent but militarily unprepared French preacher, Peter the Hermit, took a route through the Rhineland in Germany before going on to Asia Minor, where most of its participants were slaughtered.

The Rhineland route was no mistake. Peter went there because he meant to attack the Jews. By this time, most Jews—forced off the land by castellans and other landlords—lived in cities, many in the flourishing commercial region of the Rhineland. Under Henry IV,

♦**Chartres:** shahrt

the Jews in the empire gained a place within the political system by receiving protection from the local bishop (an imperial appointee) in return for paying a tax. Within these cities the Jews lived in their own neighborhoods, where their tightly knit communities focused around the synagogue, which was a school and community center as well as a place of worship. Nevertheless, Jews also participated in the life of the larger Christian community. Archbishop Anno of Cologne, for example, dealt with Jewish moneylenders, and other Jews in Cologne were allowed to trade their wares at the fairs there.

It was against such Jewish communities that Peter's group, joined by local nobles and militias, vented its fury. As one commentator put it, the crusaders considered it ridiculous to attack Muslims when other infidels lived in their own backyards: "That's doing our work backward." The Rhineland Jews faced either forced conversion or death. Some of their persecutors relented when the Jews paid them money; others, however, attacked. Jews sometimes found refuge with bishops or in the houses of Christian friends, but in many cities — Metz,✦ Speyer,✦ Worms, Mainz,✦ and Cologne✦ — they were massacred.

Reorganizing the Holy Land. The main objective of the First Crusade — to wrest the Holy Land from the Muslims and subject it to Christian rule — was accomplished largely because of Muslim disunity. After nearly a year of ineffectual attacks, the crusaders took Antioch on June 28, 1098, killing every Turk in the city; on July 15, 1099, they seized Jerusalem. By 1109 they had carved out several tiny states in the Holy Land.

Because the crusader states were created by conquest, they were treated as lordships. The rulers granted fiefs to their own vassals, and some of these men in turn gave portions of their holdings as fiefs to some of their own vassals. Many other vassals simply lived in the households of their lords. Since most Europeans went home after the First Crusade, the rulers who remained learned to coexist with the indigenous population, which included Muslims, Jews, and Greek Orthodox Christians. They encouraged a lively trade at their ports, to which came merchants from Italy, Byzantium, and Islamic cities (see "Genoese Traders in Palestine," page 378).

Jewish Communities Attacked during the First Crusade

Adapted from Angus Mackay with David Ditchburn, eds., Atlas of Medieval Europe (New York: Routledge, 1997).

✦**Metz:** mets
✦**Speyer:** SHPY ur
✦**Mainz:** mynts
✦**Cologne:** kuh LOHN

Jewish Cemetery at Worms
There was a large Jewish community at Worms in the eleventh century, and Emperor Henry IV granted the Jews there the right to travel and trade within the empire. He also exempted them from various tolls and taxes. Lured by the size and wealth of its Jewish population, one crusading contingent massacred about eight hundred Jews at Worms in 1096. The slaughtered men, women, and children were no doubt buried in this cemetery, which dates to the completion of the synagogue in 1034. It contains about two thousand gravestones; the oldest one extant was put up in 1076. *Erich Lessing/Art Resource, NY.*

The main concern of these rulers, however, was military. They set up castles and recruited knights from Europe. So organized for war was this society that it produced a new and militant kind of monasticism: the Knights Templar. Like Bruno's Carthusians, the Templars vowed themselves to poverty and chastity. But rather than withdraw to a hermitage on a mountaintop, the Templars, whose name came from their living quarters in

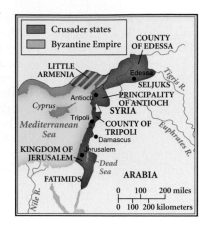

The Crusader States in 1109

the area of the former Jewish Temple at Jerusalem, devoted themselves to warfare. Their first mission—to protect the pilgrimage routes from Palestine to Jerusalem—soon diversified. They manned the town garrisons of the crusader states, and they transported money from Europe to the Holy Land. In this way, the Templars became enormously wealthy, with branch "banks" in major cities across Europe.

Genoese Traders in Palestine

The First Crusade yielded rich booty for the crusading armies and navies. In the entry for 1101 in the Annals of Genoa, *written by a chronicler named Caffaro, the Genoese, who sent a navy on the expedition, are shown fighting at Caesarea. Some of the officers and sailors later returned, turning their plunder into capital for trade or investment in land.*

The Genoese, wearing the cross on their right shoulders, climbed a palm tree leaning against the wall of the city and, calling Christ to their aid, at once crossed swords with the Saracens [the term that Europeans used for Muslims]. The Saracens, however, dropped their swords and other weapons on the spot and began to flee to their mosque. But before the Saracens could reach the mosque, the Genoese struck dead all men fighting on the walls, in the city [streets], and at every corner. And all the Christian [inhabitants of the city] in company with the patriarch [Daiberto, archbishop of Pisa] rushed without delay to the mosque. And a thousand wealthy merchants, who had gone up into the tower of the mosque, began to cry out to the patriarch: "Sir, sir, give us a safe conduct so that we shall not die, because

we hold to the rule of Christ, your God, and we shall give you everything we have." And the patriarch asked permission from the Genoese to grant the safe conduct. The Genoese then granted this permission to the patriarch. And immediately after the permission was granted [the Genoese] went through the city, seizing men and women and much money, and they took possession of everything that was inside. . . .

Later the Genoese with their galleys and the entire expeditionary force went to the beach of San Parlerio near Solino [probably al-Suwaydiyya, harbor of the ancient city of Antioch] and encamped there. First, they set aside from the money [pooled together] in the encampment one tenth and one fifth [which was due] to the [owners of the] galleys. But all the remaining money they divided among the eight thousand men. And they gave 48 solidi Poitevin and 2 pounds of pepper to each as his share.

Source: Robert S. Lopez and Irving W. Raymond, *Medieval Trade in the Mediterranean World: Illustrative Documents Translated with Introductions and Notes* (New York: W. W. Norton, n.d.), 88–89. Footnotes have been incorporated into the text itself in brackets.

Krak-des-Chevaliers
This imposing castle was built in 1142 on the site of a Muslim fortification in Syria by the Hospi-tallers, a religious military order much like the Knights Templar. A large community of perhaps fifty monk-knights and their hired mercenaries lived there. To the northeast (in back of the com-plex seen here) was a fortified village that in part served the needs of the castle. Peasants raised grain, which was ground by a windmill on one wall of the castle. For water, there were reservoirs to catch the rain, wells, and an aqueduct (on the right). Twelve toilets connected to a common drain. The monks worshiped in a chapel within the inner walls. The outer walls, built of masonry, completely enclosed the inner buildings, making Krak one of the most important places for refuge and defense in the crusader states. *Maynard Williams/NGS Image Collection.*

The Disastrous Second Crusade. The pres-ence of the Knights Templar did not prevent a new Seljuk chieftain, Zengi, from taking one of the crusader states, Edessa, in 1144. The slow but steady shrinking of the crusader states began. The Second Crusade (1147–1149) came to a disastrous end. After only four days of besieging the walls of Damascus, the crusaders, whose leaders could not keep the peace among themselves, gave up and went home. Thereafter, despite numerous new crusades—fully eight major crusades were fought between the first in 1096 and the last at the end of the thirteenth century—most Europeans were simply not willing to commit the vast resources and personnel that would have been necessary to main-tain the crusader states. They fell to the Muslims permanently in 1291.

Review: What were the causes and conse-quences of the Gregorian Reform?

❖ The Revival of Monarchies

Even as the papacy was exercising its new authority, kings and other rulers were en-hancing and consolidating their own power. They created new ideologies and dusted off old theories to justify their hegemony, they hired officials to work for them, and they found vassals and churchmen to support them. Money gave them greater effective-ness, and the new commercial economy sup-plied them with increased revenues.

Reconstructing the Empire at Byzantium

In 1081, ten years after the disastrous battle at Manzikert, the energetic dynatoi Alexius Comnenus seized the Byzantine throne. It is no wonder that an artist of his times hopefully pictured him receiving Christ's blessing, for Alexius faced considerable unrest in Constantinople, whose populace suffered from a combination of high taxes and rising living costs. In addition, his empire was under attack on every side—from Normans in southern Italy, Seljuk Turks in Asia Minor, and new groups in the Balkans. But Alexius I (r. 1081–1118) managed to turn actual and potential enemies against one another, staving off immediate defeat.

Alexius Comnenus Stands before Christ
In this twelfth-century manuscript illumination, the Byzantine emperor Alexius is shown in the presence of Christ. Note that both are almost exactly the same height, and the halos around their heads are the same size. What do you suppose is the significance of Christ sitting on a throne while the emperor is standing? Compare this image of the emperor with that on page 323. What statement is the twelfth-century artist making about the relationship between Christ and Alexius? *Biblioteca Apostolica Vaticana.*

When Alexius asked Pope Urban II to supply him with some European troops to fight his enemies, he was shocked and disappointed to learn that crusaders rather than mercenaries were on the way. His daughter, Anna Comnena (1083–c. 1148), who wrote an account of the crusades from the Byzantine perspective in a book about her father, the *Alexiad*, considered the crusaders barbarians:

> The Latin race [the Europeans] at all times is unusually greedy for wealth, but when it plans to invade a country, neither reason nor force can restrain it. They set out helter-skelter, regardless of their individual companies. Near the Drakon [River] they fell into the Turkish [ambush] and were miserably slaughtered. . . . Some men of the same race as [those] slaughtered barbarians later . . . used the bones of the dead as pebbles to fill up the cracks [of a wall].

To wage all the wars he had to fight, Alexius relied on mercenaries and allied dynatoi, who were armed and mounted like European knights and accompanied by their own troops. In return for their services he gave these nobles lifetime possession of large imperial estates and their dependent peasants. Meanwhile, Alexius satisfied the urban elite by granting them new offices. He normally got on well with the patriarch and Byzantine clergy, for emperor and church depended on each other to suppress heresy and foster orthodoxy. The emperors of the Comnenian dynasty (1081–1185) thus gained a measure of increased power, but at the price of important concessions to the nobility.

In the eleventh and early twelfth centuries, Constantinople remained a rich, sophisticated, and highly cultured city. Sculptors and other artists strove to depict ideals of human beauty and elegance. Churches built during the period were decorated with elaborate depictions of the cosmos. Significant innovations occurred in the realm of Byzantine scholarship and literature. The neo-Platonic tradition of late antiquity had always influenced Byzantine religious and philosophical thought, but now scholars renewed their interest in the wellsprings of classical Greek philosophy, particularly Plato and Aristotle. The rediscovery of ancient culture inspired Byzantine writers to reintroduce old forms into the grammar, vocabulary, and rhetorical style of Greek literature. Anna Comnena wrote her *Alexiad* in this newly learned Greek and prided herself on "having read thoroughly the treatises of Aristotle and the dialogues of Plato." The revival of ancient Greek writings, especially Plato's, in eleventh- and twelfth-century Byzantium had profound consequences for both eastern and western European civilization in centuries to come, as their ideas slowly penetrated European culture.

England under Norman Rule

In the twelfth century the kings of England were the most powerful monarchs of Europe because they ruled their whole kingdom by right of conquest. When the Anglo-Saxon king Edward the Confessor (r. 1042–1066) died childless in 1066, three main contenders desired the English throne: Harold, earl of Wessex, an Englishman close to the king but not of royal blood; Harald Hardrada,♦ the king of Norway, who had unsuccessfully attempted to conquer the Danes and now turned hopefully to England; and William, duke of Normandy, who claimed that Edward had promised him the throne fifteen years earlier. On his deathbed, Edward had named Earl Harold to succeed him, and the witan, a royal advisory committee that had the right to choose the king, had confirmed the nomination.

The Norman Invasion, 1066. When he learned that Harold had been anointed and crowned, William (1027–1087) prepared for battle. Appealing to the pope, he received the banner of St. Peter, and with this symbol of God's approval William launched the invasion of England, filling his ships with warriors recruited from many parts of France. About a week before William's invasion force landed, Harold defeated Harald Hardrada at Stamford Bridge, near York, in the north of England. When he heard of William's arrival, Harold turned his forces south, marching them 250 miles and picking up new soldiers along the way to meet the Normans.

♦**Hardrada:** HAWR raw duh

The two armies clashed at Hastings on October 14, 1066, in one of history's rare decisive battles. Both armies had about seven or eight thousand men, Harold's in defensive position on a slope, William's attacking from below. All the men were crammed into a very small space as they began the fight. Most of Harold's men were on foot, armed with battle-axes and stones tied to sticks, which could be thrown with great force. William's army consisted of perhaps three thousand mounted knights, a thousand archers, and the rest infantry. At first William's knights broke rank, frightened by the deadly battle-axes thrown by the English; but then some of the English also broke rank as they pursued the knights. William removed his helmet so his men would know him, rallying them to surround and cut down the English who had broken away. Similar skirmishes lasted the entire afternoon, and gradually Harold's troops were worn down, particularly by William's archers, whose arrows flew a hundred yards, much farther than an Englishman could throw his battle-ax. (Some of the archers are depicted on the lower margin of the Bayeux "Tapestry" on the following page.) By dusk, King Harold was dead and his army utterly defeated. No other army gathered to oppose the successful claimant.

Norman Conquest of England, 1066

Some people in England gladly supported William, considering his victory a verdict from God and hoping to gain a place in the new order themselves. But William—known to posterity as William the Conqueror—wanted to replace, not assimilate, the Anglo-Saxons. In the course of William's reign, families from the continent almost totally supplanted the English aristocracy. And although the English peasantry remained—now with new lords—they were severely shaken. A twelfth-century historian claimed to record William's deathbed confession:

Bayeux "Tapestry" (detail)
This famous "tapestry" is misnamed; it is really an embroidery, 231 feet long and 20 inches wide, that was made to tell the story of the Norman conquest of England from William's point of view. In this detail, the Norman archers are lined up along the lower margin, in a band below the armies. In the central band, the English warriors are on foot (the one at the farthest right holds a long battle-ax), while the Norman knights are on horseback. Who seems to be winning? Compare the armor and fighting gear shown here with that shown on page 344. **For more help analyzing this image**, see the visual activity for this chapter in the Online Study Guide at **bedfordstmartins .com/hunt**. *Tapisserie de Bayeux. By special permission of the City of Bayeux, France.*

> *I have persecuted [England's] native inhabitants beyond all reason. Whether gentle or simple, I have cruelly oppressed them; many I unjustly disinherited; innumerable multitudes, especially in the county of York, perished through me by famine or the sword.*

Modern historians estimate that one out of five people in England died as a result of the Norman conquest and its immediate aftermath.

Institutions of Norman Kingship. Although the Normans destroyed a generation of English men and women, they preserved and extended many Anglo-Saxon institutions. For example, the new kings used writs—terse written instructions—to communicate orders, and they retained the old administrative divisions and legal system of the shires (counties). The Norman kings also drew from continental institutions. They set up a graded political hierarchy, culminating in the king, whose strength was enforced by

his castles and made visible to all. Because all of England was the king's by conquest, he could treat it as his booty; William kept about 20 percent of the land for himself and divided the rest, distributing it in large but scattered fiefs to a relatively small number of his barons and family members, lay and ecclesiastical, as well as to some lesser men, such as personal servants and soldiers. In turn these men maintained their own vassals; they owed the king military service (and the service of a fixed number of their vassals) along with certain dues, such as **reliefs** (money paid upon inheriting a fief) and **aids** (payments made on important occasions).

Domesday. Apart from the revenues and rights expected from the nobles, the king of England commanded the peasantry as well. Twenty years after his conquest, in 1086, William ordered a survey and census of England, popularly called Domesday because, like the records of people judged at doomsday, it provided facts that could not be appealed. It was the most extensive inventory of land, livestock, taxes, and population that had ever been compiled in Europe. (See "Taking Measure.") The king

> sent his men over all England into every shire and had them find out how many hundred hides [a measure of land] there were in the shire, or what land and cattle the king himself had in the country, or what dues he ought to receive every year from the shire. . . . So very narrowly did he have the survey to be made that there was not a single hide or yard of land, nor indeed . . . an ox or a cow or a pig left out.

The king's men conducted local surveys by consulting Anglo-Saxon tax lists and by taking testimony from local jurors, men sworn to answer a series of formal questions truthfully. From these inquests scribes wrote voluminous reports filled with facts and statements from villagers, sheriffs, priests, and barons. These reports were then summarized in Domesday itself, a concise record of England's resources that supplied the king and his officials with information such as how much and what sort of land England had, who held it, and what revenues—including the lucrative *Danegeld*, which was now in effect a royal tax—could be expected from it.

England and the Continent.   The Norman conquest tied England to the languages, politics, institutions, and culture of the continent. Modern English is an amalgam of Anglo-Saxon and Norman French, the language the Normans spoke. English commerce was linked to the wool industry in Flanders. St. Anselm (1033–1109), the archbishop of Canterbury in England, had been born in Italy and served as the abbot of a monastery in Normandy before crossing the Channel to England.

The barons of England retained their estates in Normandy and elsewhere, and the kings of England often spent more time on the continent than they did on the island. When William's son Henry I (r. 1100–1135) died without male heirs, civil war soon erupted: the throne of England was fought over by two French counts, one married to Henry's

daughter, the other to his sister. The story of England after 1066 was, in miniature, the story of Europe.

Praising the King of France

The twelfth-century kings of France were much less obviously powerful than their English and Byzantine counterparts. Yet they, too, took part in the monarchical revival. Louis VI, called Louis the Fat (r. 1108–1137), so heavy that he had to be hoisted onto his

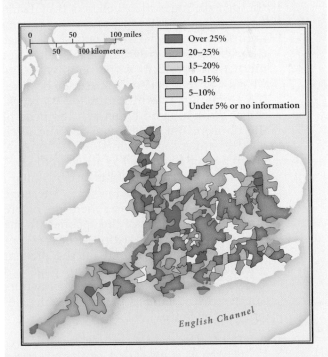

TAKING MEASURE

	Over 25%
	20–25%
	15–20%
	10–15%
	5–10%
	Under 5% or no information

English Channel

Slaves in England in 1086
Domesday provided important data for the English king in 1086, and those data remain important for historians today. We can see from this distribution map based on the data in Domesday, for example, that slavery was an important institution in eleventh-century England. The slaves, who were bought and sold, had no land of their own; they cultivated the land of their lord. Slavery was most important in the west of England, while free peasants dominated in the east. *Adapted from H. C. Darby,* Domesday England *(Cambridge: Cambridge University Press, 1977). Reprinted with the permission of Cambridge University Press.*

horse by a crane, was a tireless defender of royal power. We know a good deal about him and his reputation because a contemporary and close associate, Suger (1081–1152), abbot of St. Denis, wrote Louis's biography. Suger also tutored Louis's son Louis VII (r. 1137–1180) and acted as regent of France when Louis VII left to lead the Second Crusade in 1147.

Suger was a chronicler and propagandist for Louis the Fat. When Louis set himself the task of consolidating his rule in the Île-de-France,◆ Suger portrayed the king as a righteous hero. He thought of the king as the head of a political hierarchy in which Louis had rights over the French nobles because they were his vassals or because they broke the peace. Suger also believed that Louis had a religious role: to protect the church and the poor. He viewed Louis as another Charlemagne, a ruler for all society, not merely an overlord of the nobility. Louis waged war to keep God's peace. To be sure, the Gregorian reform had made its mark: Suger did not claim Louis was the head of the church, but he emphasized the royal dignity and its importance to the papacy. When a pope happened to arrive in France, Louis, not yet king, and his father, Philip I (r. 1052–1108), bowed low, but "the pope lifted them up and made them sit before him like devout sons of the apostles. In the manner of a wise man acting wisely, he conferred with them privately on the present condition of the church." Here the pope was shown needing royal advice. Meanwhile, Suger stressed Louis's piety and active defense of the faith:

> Helped by his powerful band of armed men, or rather by the hand of God, he abruptly seized the castle [of Crécy] and captured its very strong tower as if it were simply the hut of a peasant. Having startled those criminals, he piously slaughtered the impious.

When Louis VI died in 1137, Suger's notion of the might and right of the king of France reflected reality in an extremely small area. Nevertheless, Louis laid the groundwork for the gradual extension of royal power in France. As the lord of vassals, the king

could call upon his men to aid him in times of war, though the most powerful among them sometimes disregarded his wishes and chose not to help. As a king and landlord, he could obtain many dues and taxes. He also drew revenues from Paris, a thriving city not only of commerce but also of scholarship. Officials, called provosts, enforced his royal laws and collected taxes. With money and land, Louis could dispense the favors and give the gifts that added to his prestige and his power. Louis VI and Suger together created the territorial core and royal ideal of the future French monarchy.

> **Review:** Which ruler—Alexius, William the Conqueror, or Louis VI—was the strongest, which the feeblest, and why?

❖ New Forms of Scholarship and Religious Expression

The commercial revolution, the newly organized church, and the revived monarchies of the eleventh and twelfth centuries set the stage for the growth of schools and for new forms of scholarship. Money and career opportunities attracted unheard-of numbers of students to city schools. Worldly motivations were, however, equaled by spiritual ones. The movement for church reform stressed the importance of the church and its beliefs. Many students and teachers in the twelfth century sought knowledge to make their faith clearer and deeper.

Other people in the twelfth century, however, sought to avoid the cities and the schools. Some found refuge in the measured ceremonies and artistic splendor of Benedictine monasteries such as Cluny. Others considered these vast monastic complexes to be ostentatious and worldly. Rejecting the opulence of cities and the splendor of well-endowed monasteries alike, they pursued a monastic life of poverty.

But many people did not choose definitively one place or the other. Some shuttled back and forth between monasteries and city schools. Others, such as Bruno of

◆**Île-de-France:** eel duh FRAHNS

Cologne, imported the learning of the schools into their religious life. Others decidedly did not; yet the new learning, like the new commerce, had a way of seeping into the cracks and crannies of even the most resolutely separate institutions.

Schools and the Liberal Arts

Schools had been connected to monasteries and cathedrals since the Carolingian period. They served to train new recruits to become either monks or priests. Some were better endowed with books and masters (or teachers) than others; a few developed a reputation for a certain kind of theological approach or specialized in a branch of learning, such as literature, medicine, or law. By the end of the eleventh century, the best schools were generally in the larger cities: Reims, Paris, Bologna,◆ Montpellier.◆

Eager students sampled nearly all of them. The young monk Gilbert of Liège◆ was typical: "Instilled with an insatiable thirst for learning, whenever he heard of somebody excelling in the arts, he rushed immediately to that place and drank whatever delightful potion he could draw from the master there." For Gilbert and other students, a good lecture had the excitement of theater. Teachers at cathedral schools found themselves forced to find larger halls to accommodate the crush of students. Other teachers simply declared themselves "masters" and set up shop by renting a room. If they could prove their mettle in the classroom, they had no trouble finding paying students (see A Teacher and His Students, on this page).

"Wandering scholars" like Gilbert were probably all male, and because schools had hitherto been the training ground for clergymen, all students were considered clerics, whether or not they had been ordained. Wandering became a way of life as the consolidation of castellanies, counties, and kingdoms made violence against travelers less frequent. Urban centers soon responded to the needs of transients with markets, taverns, and lodgings.

◆**Bologna:** boh LOH nyuh
◆**Montpellier:** mohn peh LYAY
◆**Liège:** lee EHZH

A Teacher and His Students
This miniature expresses the hierarchical relationship between students and teachers in the twelfth century. But there is more. The miniature appears in a late-twelfth-century manuscript of a commentary written by Gilbert (d. 1154), bishop of Poitiers. Gilbert's ideas in this commentary provoked the ire of St. Bernard, who accused Gilbert of heresy. But Gilbert escaped condemnation. This artist asserts Gilbert's orthodoxy by depicting Gilbert with a halo, in the full dress of a bishop, speaking from his throne. Below Gilbert are three of his disciples, also with halos. The artist's positive view of Gilbert is echoed by modern historians, who recognize Gilbert as a pioneer in his approach to scriptural commentary. *Bibliothèque Municipale de Valenciennes*

Using Latin, Europe's common language, students could drift from, say, Italy to Spain, Germany, England, and France, wherever a noted master had settled. Along with crusaders, pilgrims, and merchants, students made the roads of Europe very crowded indeed.

What the students sought, above all, was knowledge of the seven liberal arts. Grammar, rhetoric, and logic (or dialectic) belonged to the "beginning" arts, the so-called **trivium**.◆ Logic, involving the technical analysis of texts as well as the application and manipulation of mental constructs, was a transitional subject leading to the second part of the liberal arts, the quadrivium. This comprised four areas of study that we might call theoretical math and science: arithmetic, geometry, music (theory rather than practice), and astronomy. Of all these arts, twelfth-century students were most interested in logic. Medieval students and masters were convinced that logic could bring together, order, and clarify every issue, even questions about the nature of God. Thus St. Anselm, who was a major theologian as well as an abbot and archbishop, saw logic as a way for faith to "seek understanding." Emptying his mind of all ideas except that of God, he used the tools of logic to prove God's existence.

After studying the trivium, students went on to schools of medicine, theology, or law. Paris was renowned for theology, Montpellier for medicine, and Bologna for law. All of these schools trained men for jobs. The law schools, for example, taught men who went on to serve popes, bishops, kings, princes, and communes. Scholars interested in the quadrivium, by contrast, tended to pursue those studies outside of the normal school curriculum, and few gained their living through such pursuits.

Scholars of the New Learning

The remarkable renewal of scholarship in the twelfth century had an unexpected benefit: we know a great deal about the men involved in it—and a few of the women—because they wrote so much, often about themselves. Three important figures typify the scholars of the period: Abelard and Heloise, who embraced the new learning wholeheartedly and retired to monasteries only when forced to do so; and Hildegard of Bingen, who happily spent most of her life in a cloister yet wrote knowingly about the world.

Abelard and Heloise. Born into a family of the petty (lesser) French Breton nobility and destined for a career as a warrior and lord, Peter Abelard (1079–1142) instead became one of the twelfth century's greatest thinkers. In his autobiographical account, *Historia calamitatum*◆ (*The Story of My Misfortunes*), Abelard describes his shift from the life of the warrior to the life of the scholar:

> *I was so carried away by my love of learning, that I renounced the glory of a soldier's life, made over my inheritance and rights of the eldest son to my brothers, and withdrew from the court of Mars [war] in order to kneel at the feet of Minerva [learning].*

Arriving eventually at Paris, Abelard studied with William of Champeaux◆ and then challenged his teacher's scholarship. He had nothing but scorn for William's position on "universals," one of the most controversial topics of the day. The question was whether a universal (something that can be said of more than one thing, such as *cat* may be said of Puffy and Fluffy) is real or just a mental category or manner of speaking. William taught that the species (such as *cat*) was indeed real. (We call such thinkers realists.) Others (people who were later called nominalists) claimed that the species was just a word. Abelard took a middle position, maintaining that the species did have a sort of reality, as the common "status" of Puffy and Fluffy.

Later in the twelfth century, scholars discovered that Aristotle had elaborated tools of logic to solve this and other problems. But until midcentury, very little of Aristotle's work was available in Europe because it had not been translated from Greek into Latin. By the end of the century, however, that situation had been rectified by translators who traveled to cities such as Córdoba in Spain and Syracuse in Sicily, where they found Islamic scholars who had already translated Aristotle's Greek into Arabic and could help them translate from Arabic to Latin. (See "Did You Know?," page 387.)

◆**trivium:** TRIH vee uhm

◆***Historia calamitatum:*** hihs TAWR ee uh ka lam ih TAYT uhm
◆**Champeaux:** sham Poh

DID YOU KNOW?

Translations

Tłumaczenie! Do you know what that means? If you don't, it's easy enough to find out. Today there are many dictionaries, translators, and interpreters for almost every one of the world's three thousand languages. But for most of history, this has not been the case. In the Middle Ages, dictionaries and interpreters were very rare. The great writings of the three heirs of the Roman Empire—the Byzantine, Muslim, and European—were largely unavailable across cultures. This kept these societies from knowing about and benefiting from one another. And of the three, Europe was the most isolated.

In the twelfth century this began to change. The same Europeans who flocked to the city schools knew vaguely about Arabic philosophical learning, and they ached to know more. Some of them traveled to the peripheries of Europe, in particular, to Palermo, in Sicily, where Greek, Arabic, and Latin were all official languages. Palermo was unique as a European city that supported a diversity of languages and people who could read and write in a number of them. Some people from France, Germany, England, and northern Italy who wanted to read books in languages other than Latin went to Palermo to learn how to become translators or to find others to do the job.

Others headed to Spain, where they worked with Jewish converts to Christianity. Rather than learn Arabic, they relied on these converts to translate from Arabic into Spanish. Then the Europeans translated from Spanish into Latin. It was in this roundabout way that Aristotle's works were rediscovered in Arabic translation, that Arabic medical treatises were read, that the Qur'an became known outside of the Islamic world, that Arabic love poetry came to inspire medieval songwriters, and that Arabic mathematical breakthroughs, including the discovery of algebra and the use of Arabic numerals, came to Latin-speaking Europe.

By the way, the word *tłumaczenie* (pronounced "twoo-ma-CHAIN-yeh") means "translation" in Polish.

Translating the Qur'an into Latin (mid-twelfth century)
Those who originally translated the Qur'an into Latin wanted not so much to understand the Islamic religion better as to refute it more soundly. In 1142 the abbot of Cluny, Peter the Venerable, made a trip to Spain and commissioned some scholars there to make the first Latin translation of the Qur'an. In the prologue to his *Book Against the Sect or Heresy of the Saracens*, he explained why:

> *Because the Latin-speaking peoples, and most particularly those of recent times, losing their ancient zeal, according to the maxim of the Jews, have not known the various languages of the former wonderful Apostles, but only their own language into which they were born, in that condition they could not know what such an error [as Islam] was or, consequently, put up any resistance to it. For this reason "my heart glowed within me and a flame was enkindled in my meditation" (Ps. 38.4). I was indignant that the Latins did not know the cause of such perdition and, by that ignorance, could not be moved to put up any resistance; for there was no one who replied [to Islam] because there was simply no one who knew [about it].*

Source: Quoted and translated in James Kritzeck, *Peter the Venerable and Islam*, Princeton Oriental Studies 23 (Princeton, N.J., 1964), 30.

After his confrontation with William of Champeaux, Abelard began to lecture and to gather students of his own. Around 1122–1123, he composed a textbook for his students that consisted of opposing positions on 156 subjects, among them "That God is one and the contrary," "That all are permitted to marry and the contrary," "That it is permitted to kill men and the contrary." Arrayed on both sides of each question were passages from the Bible, the church fathers, the letters of popes, and other sources. The juxtaposition of authoritative sentences was nothing new; what was new was calling attention to their contradictions. Abelard's students loved the challenge: they were eager to find the origins of the quotes, consider the context of each one carefully, and seek a reconciliation of the opposing sides. Abelard wrote that his method "excite[d] young readers to the maximum of effort in inquiring into the truth." In fact, in Abelard's view the inquiring student followed the model of Christ himself, who as a boy sat among the rabbis, questioning them.

Abelard's fame as a teacher was such that a Parisian cleric named Fulbert gave Abelard room and board and engaged him as tutor for Heloise (c. 1100–c. 1163/1164), Fulbert's niece. Heloise is one of the few learned women of the period who left written traces. (Hildegard is another.) Brought up under Fulbert's guardianship, Heloise had been sent as a young girl to a convent school, where she received a thorough grounding in literary skills. Her uncle had hoped to continue her education at home by hiring Abelard. Abelard, however, became Heloise's lover as well as her tutor. "Our desires left no stage of love-making untried," wrote Abelard in his *Historia*. At first their love affair was secret. But Heloise became pregnant, and Abelard insisted they marry. They did so clandestinely to prevent damaging Abelard's career, for the new emphasis on clerical celibacy meant that Abelard's professional success and prestige would have been compromised if news of his marriage were made public. After they were married, Heloise and Abelard rarely saw one another; their child, Astrolabe, was raised by Abelarde's sister. Fulbert, suspecting foul play, plotted a cruel punishment: he paid a servant to castrate Abelard. Soon after, both husband and wife entered separate monasteries.

For Heloise, separation from Abelard was a lasting blow. Although she became a successful abbess, carefully tending to the physical and spiritual needs of her nuns, she continued to call on Abelard for "renewal of strength." In a series of letters addressed to him, she poured out her feelings as "his handmaid, or rather his daughter, wife, or rather sister":

You know, beloved, as the whole world knows, how much I have lost in you, how at one wretched stroke of fortune that supreme act

of flagrant treachery robbed me of my very self in robbing me of you. . . . You alone have the power to make me sad, to bring me happiness or comfort.

For Abelard, however, the loss of Heloise and even his castration were not the worst disasters of his life. The cruelest blow came later, and it was directed at his intellect. He wrote a book that applied "human and logical reasons" (as he put it) to the Trinity; the book was condemned at the Council of Soissons in 1121, and he was forced to throw it, page by page, into the flames. Bitterly weeping at the injustice, Abelard lamented, "This open violence had come upon me only because of the purity of my intentions and love of our Faith, which had compelled me to write."

Hildegard of Bingen.   Unlike Abelard and Heloise, Hildegard (1098–1179) did not actively seek to become a scholar. Placed in a German convent at age eight, she received her schooling there and took vows as a nun. In 1136, she was elected abbess of the convent. Shortly thereafter, very abruptly, she began to write and to preach, an activity normally reserved for bishops. In addition, Hildegard addressed fearless letters of advice and admonition to the churchmen and rulers of her day.

Writing and preaching were the external manifestations of an inner life that had been extraordinary from the beginning. Even as a child, Hildegard had had visions—of invisible things, of the future, and (always) of a special kind of light. These visions were intermingled with pain and sickness. Only in her forties did Hildegard interpret her sickness and her visions as gifts from God; she thought her fragility made the visions possible. In her *Scivias*♦ ("Know the Ways of the Lord," 1151), Hildegard describes some of her visions and explains what they meant. She interprets them as containing nothing less than the full story of creation and redemption, a summa, or compendium, of church doctrine.

The *Scivias* was not just a text. Accompanying Hildegard's words were vivid

---

♦*Scivias:* SKIH Vee uhs

Hildegard of Bingen
The illustrations that Hildegard commissioned for her *Scivias* have been lost since the end of World War II, but a hand-drawn copy from 1920 has survived. This image from the copy shows Hildegard at the beginning of the book, where she writes, "Heaven was opened and a fiery light . . . came and permeated my whole brain. . . . And immediately I knew the meaning of the . . . Scriptures." In this miniature, the fiery light comes down in the form of giant red fingers to cover Hildegard's head, while she holds a wax tablet and stylus to write with. The monk peeking through the door is Volmar, who served as Hildegard's secretary. *Photograph by Erich Lessing/Art Resource.*

illustrations—one of which is reproduced here—of her visions, probably painted by a nun under her supervision. For the final vision of the book, Hildegard added fourteen pieces of music. And at the conclusion of the entire *Scivias*, Hildegard appended a play, the leading roles taken by the Virtues, the Soul, and the Devil. She later expanded this and set it to music.

Hildegard's inventiveness was not confined to religious and artistic matters. During the 1150s, she wrote two scientific treatises, one focused on diseases and herbal remedies, the other on subjects ranging from animals and plants to gemstones and metallurgy. For Hildegard, knowledge of God made the world intelligible.

Benedictine Monks and Artistic Splendor

Hildegard's appreciation of worldly things as expressions of God's splendor was typical of Benedictine monks and nuns in the twelfth century. They spent nearly their entire day in large and magnificently outfitted churches singing an expanded and complex liturgy. Hildegard's music was added to the liturgical round at her convent, for example.

In the context of the new monastic movements stressing poverty, the Benedictines were old-fashioned. Yet the "black monks"—so called because they dyed their robes black—reached the height of their popularity in the eleventh century. Monasteries often housed hundreds of monks; convents for nuns were usually less populated. Cluny was one of the largest monasteries, with some four hundred brothers in the mid-eleventh century.

The chief occupation of the monks, as befitted (in their view) citizens of heaven, was prayer. The black monks and nuns devoted themselves to singing the Psalms and other prayers specified in the rule of St. Benedict, adding to them still more Psalms. The rule called for chanting the entire Psalter—150 psalms—over the course of a week, but some monks, like those at Cluny, chanted that number in a day.

Gregorian Chant.   Prayer was neither private nor silent. Black monks had to know not only the words but also the music that went with their prayers; they had to be musicians. The music of the Benedictine monastery was plainchant, also known as Gregorian chant, which consisted of melodies sung in unison and without instrumental accompaniment. Although chant was rhythmically free, lacking a regular beat, its melodies ranged from

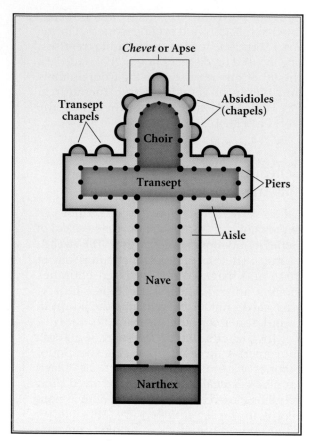

FIGURE 10.1   Floor Plan of a Romanesque Church
As churchgoers entered a Romanesque church, they passed through the narthex, an anteroom decorated with sculptures depicting important scenes from the Bible. Walking through the portal of the narthex, they entered the church's nave, at the east end of which—just after the crossing of the transept and in front of the choir—was the altar. Walking down the nave, they passed massive, tall piers leading up to the vaulting (the ceiling) of the nave. Each of these piers was decorated with sculpture, and the walls were brightly painted. Romanesque churches were both lively and colorful (because of their decoration) and solemn and somber (because of their heavy stones and massive scale).

empire. Musical notation was developed to help monks remember unfamiliar melodies and to ensure that the tunes were sung in approximately the same way in all parts of the Carolingian realm. The melodies were further mastered and organized at this time by fitting them into the Byzantine system of eight modes, or scales. This music survived the dissolution of the Carolingian Empire and remained the core of the music of the Catholic church into the twentieth century.

Romanesque Style.   The new emphasis on the liturgy meant that churches would echo throughout the day to the sounds of chanting monks. The building boom that gave towns their walls and houses extended to churches as well. The style of many of these buildings of the twelfth century was later called **Romanesque**. Although they varied greatly, most Romanesque churches had massive stone and masonry walls decorated on the interior with paintings in bright colors. (See the illustration of St.-Savin, on page 393) The various parts of the church—the chapels in the *chevet* (the east end), for example—were handled as discrete units, retaining the forms of cubes, cones, and cylinders (Figure 10.1). Inventive sculptural reliefs, both inside and outside the church, enlivened these pristine geometrical forms. Emotional and sometimes frenzied, Romanesque sculpture depicted themes ranging from the beauty of Eve (see the sinuous one from the monastery of Autun on this page) to the horrors of the Last Judgment.

In such a setting, gilded reliquaries and altars made of silver, precious gems, and pearls were the fitting accoutrements of worship. Prayer, liturgy, and music in this way complemented the gift economy of the early Middle Ages: richly clad in vestments of the finest materials, intoning the liturgy in the most splendid of churches, monks and priests offered up the gift of prayer to God; in return they begged for the gift of salvation of their souls and the souls of all the faithful.

New Monastic Orders of Poverty

But at the end of the eleventh century the old gift economy was being replaced by a new one, based on profit. Now many people con-

extremely simple to highly ornate and embellished. By the twelfth century, a large repertoire of melodies had grown up, at first through oral composition and transmission and then in written notation, which first appeared in manuscripts of the ninth century.

The melodies preserved by this early notation probably originated in Rome and had been introduced into northern Europe at the command of Charlemagne, who wanted to standardize the liturgical practices of his sidered opulence to be a sign of greed rather than honor. They rejected wealth and embraced poverty as a key element of religious life. The Carthusian order founded by Bruno of Cologne was one such group. Each monk took a vow of silence and lived as a hermit in his own small hut. Monks occasionally joined others for prayer in a common prayer room, or oratory. When not engaged in prayer or meditation, the Carthusians copied manuscripts. They considered this task part of their religious vocation, a way to preach God's word with their hands rather than their mouths. The Carthusian order grew slowly. Each monastery was limited to only twelve monks, the number of the Apostles.

Eve
The Romanesque sculptor of this depiction of Eve delighted in her sinuous curves, which he portrayed as a continuation of the snake from which Eve accepted the apple. Compare this seductive view of Eve with the motherly Eve on page 318. Sculptural figures such as this one, which once adorned the church at Autun, France and the shoemaker on page 363, were typical of the inventive variety of the Romanesque style. © Musée Rodin, Autun, France/Peter Willi/SuperStock.

The Cistercians,♦ in contrast, expanded rapidly. The first Cistercian house, founded in 1098, was at Cîteaux♦ (in Latin, Cistercium) in France. But the guiding spirit and preeminent Cistercian abbot was St. Bernard (c. 1090–1153), who arrived at Cîteaux in 1112 along with about thirty friends and relatives. Soon he became abbot of Clairvaux, one of a cluster of Cistercian monasteries in Burgundy. By the mid-twelfth century, more than three hundred monasteries spread throughout Europe were following what they took to be the customs of Cîteaux. Nuns too—as eager as monks to live the life of simplicity and poverty that they believed the Apostles had enjoyed and endured—adopted Cistercian customs. By the end of the twelfth century, the Cistercians were an order: all of their houses followed rules determined at a General Chapter, a meeting at which the abbots met to hammer out legislation for the whole order.

Although they held up the rule of St. Benedict as the foundation of their monastic life, the Cistercians elaborated a style of life all their own, largely governed by the goal of simplicity. Rejecting even the conceit of blackening their robes, they left them undyed (hence their nickname, the "white monks").

Cistercian churches, though built of stone, were initially unlike the great Romanesque churches of the Benedictines. They were remarkably standardized; the church and the rest of the buildings of any Cistercian monastery were much like those of any other (Figure 10.2). The churches were small, made of smoothly hewn, undecorated stone. Wall paintings and sculpture were prohibited. St. Bernard wrote a scathing attack on Romanesque sculpture in which he acknowledged, in spite of himself, its exceptional allure:

> What is the point of ridiculous monstrosities in the cloister where there are brethren reading— I mean those extraordinary deformed beauties and beautiful deformities? What are those lascivious apes doing, those fierce lions, monstrous centaurs, half-men and spotted leopards? . . . It is more diverting to decipher marble than the text before you.

♦**Cistercians:** sihs TUR shuhns
♦**Cîteaux:** see TOH

FIGURE 10.2 Floor Plan of a Cistercian Monastery
Cistercian monasteries seldom deviated much from this standard plan, which perfectly suited their double lifestyle—one half for the lay brothers, who worked in the fields, the other half for the monks, who performed the devotions. This plan shows the first floor. Above were the dormitories. The lay brothers slept above their cellar and refectory, the monks above their chapter house, common room, and room for novices. No one had a private bedroom, just as the rule of St. Benedict prescribed. *Adapted from Wolfgang Braunfels,* Monasteries of Western Europe *(Princeton, N.J.: Princeton University Press, 1972), 75.*

The Cistercians had no such visual diversions, but the simplicity of their buildings and of their clothing also had its beauty. Illuminated by the pure white light that came through clear glass windows, Cistercian houses like the one at Eberbech, illustrated on this page, were luminous, cool, and serene.

True to this emphasis on purity, the communal liturgy of the Cistercians was simplified and shorn of the many additions found in the houses of the black monks. Only the liturgy as prescribed in the rule of St. Benedict plus one daily Mass were allowed. Even the music for the chant was changed; the Cistercians rigorously suppressed the B-flat, even though doing so made the melody discordant, because of their insistence on strict simplicity.

With their time partly freed from the choir, the white monks dedicated themselves to private prayer and contemplation and to monastic administration. Each house had large and highly organized farms and grazing lands called granges. Cistercian monks spent much of their time managing their estates and flocks, both of which yielded handsome profits by the end of the twelfth century. Clearly part of the agricultural and commercial revolutions of the Middle Ages, the Cistercian order made managerial expertise a part of the monastic life.

At the same time, the Cistercians elaborated a spirituality of intense personal emotion. As St. Bernard said:

> Often enough when we approach the altar to pray our hearts are dry and lukewarm. But if we persevere, there comes an unexpected infusion of grace, our breast expands as it were, and our interior is filled with an overflowing love.

The Cistercians emphasized not only human emotion but also Christ's and Mary's humanity. While pilgrims continued to stream to the tombs and reliquaries of saints, the

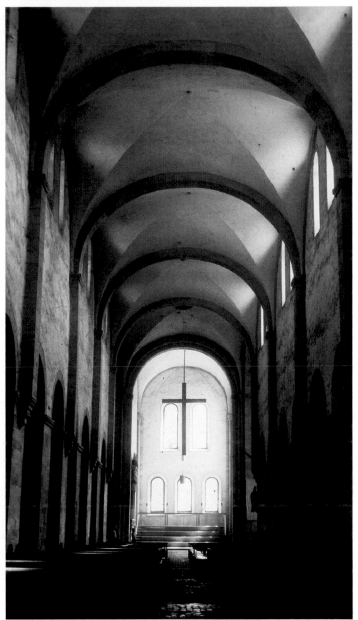

St.-Savin-sur-Gartempe
The nave of the church of St.-Savin was built between 1095 and 1115. Its barrel (or tunnel) vault is typical of Romanesque churches, as is its sense of liveliness, variety, and color. The columns, decorated with striped or wavy patterns, are topped by carved capitals, each different from the next. The entire vault is covered with frescoes painted in shades of browns, ochers, and yellows depicting scenes from the Old Testament. Try to pick out the one that shows Noah's ark. Were such scenes meant to delight the worshipers? How would St. Bernard have answered this question?
Bridgeman–Giraudon/Art Resource, NY.

Eberbech
Compare the nave of Eberbech, a Cistercian church built between 1170 and 1186, with that of St.-Savin. What at St.-Savin was full of variety and color is here subdued by order and calm. There are no wall paintings in a Cistercian church, no variegated columns, no distractions from the interior life of the worshiper. Yet, upon closer look, there are subtle points of interest. How has the architect played with angles, planes, and light in the vaulting? Are the walls utterly smooth? Can you see any decorative elements on the massive piers between the arches? *AKG London/ Stefan Drechsel.*

MAPPING THE WEST Major Religions in the West, c. 1150
The broad washes of color on this map tell a striking story: by 1150, there were three major religions, each corresponding to a broad region. To the west, north of the Mediterranean Sea, Catholic Christianity held sway; to the east, the Greek Orthodox Church was ascendant; all along the southern Mediterranean, Islam triumphed. Only a few places defied this logic: one was a tiny outpost of Catholic crusaders who ruled over a largely Muslim population. What this map does not show, however, are the details: Jewish communities in many cities, lively varieties of Islamic beliefs within the Muslim world, communities of Coptic Christians in Egypt, and scattered groups of heretics in Catholic lands.

Cistercians dedicated all their churches to the Virgin Mary (for whom they had no relics) because for them she signified the model of a loving mother. Indeed, the Cistercians regularly used maternal imagery (as St. Bernard's description invoking the metaphor of a flowing breast illustrates) to describe the nurturing care provided to humans by Jesus himself. The Cistercian Jesus was approachable, human, protective, even mothering.

Similar views of God were held by many who were not members of the Cistercian order; their spirituality signaled wider changes. For example, around 1099, St. Anselm wrote a theological treatise entitled *Why God Became Man* in which he argued that since man had sinned, only a sinless man could redeem him. St. Anselm's work represented a new theological emphasis on the redemptive power of human charity, including that of Jesus as a human being. The crusaders had trodden the very place of Christ's crucifixion, making his humanity both more real and more problematic to people who walked in the holy "place of God's humiliation and our redemption," as one chronicler put it. Yet this new stress on the loving bonds that tied Christians together also led to the persecution of others, like Jews and Muslims, who lived outside the Christian community.

Review: To what degree and in what ways were religious life and thought influenced by the new learning of the schools?

Conclusion

The commercial revolution and the building boom it spurred profoundly changed Europe. New trade, wealth, and business institutions became common in its thriving cities. Merchants and artisans became important people. Mutual and fraternal organizations like the commune expressed and reinforced the solidarity and economic interest of city dwellers.

Political consolidation accompanied economic growth, as kings and popes exerted their authority and tested its limits. The Gregorian reform pitted the emperor against the pope, and two separate political hierarchies emerged, the secular and the ecclesiastical. The two might cooperate, as Suger and Louis VI did in mutual respect, admiration, and dependence; but they might also clash, as did Gregory VII and Henry IV. Secular and religious leaders developed new and largely separate systems of administration, reflecting in political life the new distinctions (such as clerical celibacy and allegiance to the pope) that differentiated clergy from laity. Although in some ways growing apart, the two groups never worked together so closely as in the crusades, military pilgrimages inspired by the pope and led by lay lords.

The commercial economy, political stability, and ecclesiastical needs fostered the growth of schools and the achievements of new scholarship. Young men like Abelard, who a generation before would have become knights, now sought education to enhance their careers and bring personal fulfillment.

Elite women like Heloise could gain an excellent basic education in a convent and then go on to higher studies. Logic fascinated students because it seemed to clarify what was real about themselves, the world, and God. Some churchmen, however, thought that faith could not be analyzed, and they forced Abelard to burn his book on the Trinity.

While Benedictine monks added to their hours of worship, built lavish churches, and devoted themselves to the music of the plainchant, a reformer such as St. Bernard insisted on an intense, interior spiritual life in a monastery austerely and directly based on the rule of St. Benedict. Other reformers, such as Bruno of Cologne, sought the high mountaintop for its isolation and hardship. These reformers repudiated urban society yet unintentionally reflected it: the Cistercians were as invested as any tradesman in the success of their granges, and the Carthusians were dedicated to their books.

The early twelfth century saw a period of renaissance and reform in the church, monarchies, and scholarship. The later twelfth century would be an age when people experimented with and rebelled against the various forms of authority.

Suggested References

The Commercial Revolution

The idea of a commercial revolution in the Middle Ages originated with Lopez. Little discusses some religious consequences. Hyde explores the society and government of the Italian communes.

Hyde, J. K. *Society and Politics in Medieval Italy: The Evolution of Civil Life, 1000–1350.* 1973.

Little, Lester K. *Religious Poverty and the Profit Economy in Medieval Europe.* 1978.

Lopez, Robert S. *The Commercial Revolution of the Middle Ages, 950–1350.* 1976.

*———, and Irving W. Raymond, *Medieval Trade in the Mediterranean World.* 1955.

Church Reform and Its Aftermath

The Investiture Conflict, which pitted the pope against the emperor, has been particularly important to German historians. Blumenthal gives

---

*Primary sources.

a useful overview. The consequences of church reform and the new papal monarchy included both the growth of canon law (see Brundage) and the crusades (see Riley-Smith).

Blumenthal, Uta-Renate. *The Investiture Controversy: Church & Monarchy from the 9th to the 12th Century.* 1991.

Brundage, James A. *Medieval Canon Law.* 1995.

Crusades: http://www.medievalcrusades.com/

*Peters, Edward, ed. *The First Crusade: The Chronicle of Fulcher of Chartres and Other Source Materials.* 1971.

Riley-Smith, Jonathan. *The Crusades. A Short History.* 1987.

———. *The First Crusaders, 1095–1131.* 1997.

Robinson, Ian S. *Henry IV of Germany.* 2000.

*Tierney, Brian, ed. *The Crisis of Church and State, 1050–1300.* 1964.

The Revival of Monarchies

The growth of monarchical power and the development of state institutions are topics of keen interest to historians. Clanchy points to the use of writing and recordkeeping in government. Suger shows the importance of the royal image. Douglas and Hallam discuss different aspects of the Norman conquest of England.

Chibnall, Marjorie. *Anglo-Norman England, 1066–1166.* 1986.

Clanchy, Michael. *From Memory to Written Record: England 1066–1307.* 2nd ed. 1993.

Douglas, David C. *William the Conqueror: The Norman Impact upon England.* 1967.

Dunbabin, Jean. *France in the Making, 843–1180.* 1985.

Grant, Lindy. *Abbot Suger of St-Denis: Church and State in Early Twelfth-Century France.* 1998.

Hallam, Elizabeth M. *Domesday Book through Nine Centuries.* 1986.

*Suger. *The Deeds of Louis the Fat.* Trans. Richard C. Cusimano and John Moorhead. 1992.

New Forms of Scholarship and Religious Expression

The new learning of the twelfth century was first called a renaissance by Haskins. Clanchy's more recent study looks less at the revival of the classics, stressing instead the social and political context of medieval teaching and learning. Recent research on religious developments include discussions of women in the new monastic movements of the twelfth century (Venarde), new views about the development of the Cistercian order (Berman), and new interpretations of the religious fervor of the period as a whole (Constable).

*Abelard's *The Story of My Misfortunes*: http://www.fordham.edu/halsall/basis/abelard-histcal.html.

Berman, Constance Hoffman. *The Cistercian Evolution: The Invention of a Religious Order in Twelfth-Century Europe.* 2000.

Bouchard, Constance Brittain. *"Every Valley Shall Be Exalted": The Discourse of Opposites in Twelfth-Century Thought.* 2003.

Clanchy, Michael. *Abelard: A Medieval Life.* 1997.

Constable, Giles. *The Reformation of the Twelfth Century.* 1996.

Haskins, Charles Homer. *The Renaissance of the Twelfth Century.* 1927.

Hildegard of Bingen: http://www.hildegard.org/

Hildegard von Bingen: Ordo virtutum, Deutsche Harmonia Mundi CD, 77394 (music from Hildegard's *Scivias* and the expanded play at its end).

The Letters of Abelard and Heloise. Trans. Betty Radice. 1974.

Venarde, Bruce L. *Women's Monasticism and Medieval Society: Nunneries in France and England, 890–1215.* 1997.

CHAPTER REVIEW

IMPORTANT EVENTS

910	Foundation of Cluny
1033–1109	St. Anselm, theologian, abbot, and archbishop of Canterbury
1046	Synod of Sutri
1049–1054	Papacy of Leo IX
1054	Great Schism between Latin and Greek church begins
1066	Norman conquest of England under William I
1071	Battle between Byzantines and Seljuk Turks at Manzikert
1073–1085	Papacy of Gregory VII
1077	Henry IV does penance before Gregory VII at Canossa; war breaks out
1079–1142	Peter Abelard
1086	Domesday survey
c. 1090–1153	St. Bernard
1095	Council of Clermont; Pope Urban II calls the First Crusade
1096–1099	First Crusade
1097	Establishment of commune at Milan
1098	Foundation of Cîteaux
1108–1137	Reign of Louis VI (Louis the Fat)
1109	Establishment of the Crusader States
1122	Concordat of Worms ends the Investiture Conflict
c. 1140	Gratian's *Decretum*, a systematic collection of canon law, published
1147–1149	Second Crusade
1151	*Scivias* written by Hildegard of Bingen

KEY TERMS

aids (382)
commercial revolution (360)
commune (364)
Great Schism (367)
Gregorian reform (367)
Investiture Conflict (368)
reconquista (367)
reliefs (382)
Romanesque (390)
Seljuk Turks (372)
simony (366)
trivium (386)

REVIEW QUESTIONS

1. What new professions and institutions arose as a result of the commercial revolution?
2. What were the causes and consequences of the Gregorian reform?
3. Which ruler—Alexius, William the Conqueror, or Louis VI—was the strongest, which the feeblest, and why?
4. To what degree and in what ways were religious life and thought influenced by the new learning of the schools?

MAKING CONNECTIONS

1. What were the similarities—and what were the differences—between the Carolingian renaissance and the twelfth-century schools?
2. What were the similarities—and what were the differences—between the powers wielded by the Carolingian kings and those wielded by twelfth-century rulers?

FOR FURTHER EXPLORATION

To assess your mastery of the material in this chapter, see the Online Study Guide at **bedfordstmartins.com/hunt**.

To read additional primary source material from this period, see Chapter 10 in *Sources of The Making of the West*, Second Edition, Volume I.

An Age of Confidence, 1150–1215

IN 1202, WITH THE MUSLIMS STILL OCCUPYING JERUSALEM, the pope called for a new crusade to the Holy Land. The Venetians fitted out a fine fleet of ships and galleys for the expedition, but when the crusaders arrived in Venice, there were far fewer fighters to pay for the transport than had been anticipated. To defray the costs of the ships and other expenses, the Venetians convinced the crusaders to do them some favors before taking off against the Muslims. First, they had the crusaders attack Zara,♦ a Christian city but Venice's competitor in the Adriatic. Then they had the army attack Constantinople itself, where the Venetians hoped to gain commercial advantage over their rivals. On April 12, 1204, Constantinople fell to the crusaders and the Byzantine Empire was reorganized under Western rule. The Venetians got just what they wanted: the harbor of Constantinople and new bases for an expanded maritime empire.

The planning, organization, assertiveness, and self-confidence of Venice in this episode was characteristic of the age. In the second half of the twelfth century, participants in government, commerce, and religion demanded—and created—permanent institutions and enhanced power. Kings, princes, popes, city dwellers, and even heretics were acutely conscious of themselves as individuals and as members of like-minded groups with identifiable objectives and plans to promote and perpetuate their aims. By about 1200, staffs of literate government officials were preserving both official documents and important papers; lords reckoned their profits with the help of accountants. Craft guilds and religious associations defined and regulated their memberships. The schools, which in the early

---

♦**Zara:** ZAH ruh

The Conquest of Constantinople in 1204
This mosaic, which was originally part of the sumptuous floor of the church of the Benedictine monastery of San Giovanni Evangelista in Ravenna (Italy), is one of several that illustrate episodes of the Fourth Crusade. Here the moment of capturing Constantinople is shown: the windowed tower symbolizes the gate of the city, and the man with the sword signifies a Western knight. The mosaic was produced less than ten years after the event, probably to celebrate the election of Francesco Morosini, the abbot of a monastery closely tied to San Giovanni, as Patriarch—the *Catholic* Patriarch—of Constantinople. *The Art Archive/Dagli Orti.*

twelfth century had crystallized around charismatic teachers like Peter Abelard, became permanent institutions—universities.

The period 1150–1215 was characterized by confidence buttressed by new organizations and institutions. Well-organized rulers exercised control over whole territories through institutions of government that could—if need be—function without them. In the cultural arena, new-style poets boldly used the common language of everyday life, rather than Latin, to write literature of astonishing beauty, humor, and emotional range. Laypeople and those who devoted themselves to religion participated in newly articulate and well-organized groups. But increased confidence and more clearly defined group and individual identities brought with them increased intolerance toward and aggression against those perceived as deviants.

❖ Governments as Institutions

By the end of the twelfth century, western Europeans for the first time spoke of their rulers not as kings of a people (for example, the king of the Franks) but as kings of a territory (for example, the king of France). This new designation reflected an important change in medieval rulership. However strong earlier rulers had been, their political power had been personal (depending on ties of kinship, friendship, and vassalage) rather than territorial (touching all who lived within the borders of their state). The new organization, along with renewed interest in Roman legal concepts, served as a foundation for strong, central rule. The process of state building began to encompass clearly delineated regions.

Western European rulers now began to employ professional administrators; sometimes, as in England, the system was so institutionalized that even when the king left England (as often happened, since he had continental possessions to attend to), his government ran smoothly under his subordinates and appointees. In other regions, such as Germany, bureaucratic administration did not develop so far. In eastern Europe it hardly existed at all.

Germany: The Revived Monarchy of Frederick Barbarossa

The Investiture Conflict and the civil war it generated (1075–1122) strengthened the German princes and weakened the kings, Henry IV and Henry V, who were also the emperors. For decades, the princes enjoyed near independence, building castles on their properties and establishing control over whole territories. To ensure that the emperors who succeeded Henry V (r. 1106–1125) would be weak, the princes supported only those rulers who agreed to give them new lands and powers. A ruler's success depended on balancing the many conflicting interests of his own royal and imperial offices, his family, and the German princes. He also had to contend with the increasing influence of the papacy and the Italian communes, which forged alliances with one another and

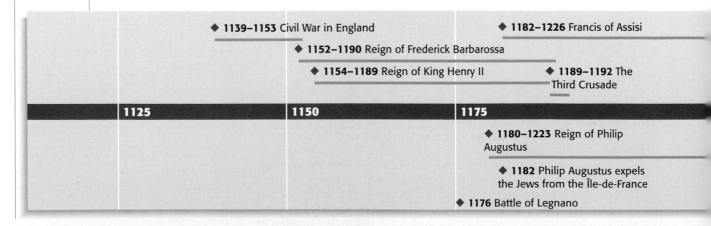

◆ **1139–1153** Civil War in England

◆ **1152–1190** Reign of Frederick Barbarossa

◆ **1154–1189** Reign of King Henry II

◆ **1182–1226** Francis of Assisi

◆ **1189–1192** The Third Crusade

1125	1150	1175

◆ **1180–1223** Reign of Philip Augustus

◆ **1182** Philip Augustus expels the Jews from the Île-de-France

◆ **1176** Battle of Legnano

with the German princes, preventing the consolidation of power under a strong German monarch during the first half of the twelfth century.

During the civil war in Germany, the two sides were represented by two noble families: leading the imperial party were the Staufer, or Hohenstaufen, clan; opposing them were the princely-papal party, the Welfs. (Two later Italian factions, the Ghibellines and the Guelphs, corresponded, respectively, to the Hohenstaufens and the Welfs.) The enmity between these families was legendary, and warfare between the groups raged even after the Concordat of Worms in 1122. Exhausted from constant battles, by 1152 all parties longed for peace. In an act of rare unanimity, they elected as king Frederick I (r. 1152–1190), who was called Barbarossa. In Frederick they seemed to have a candidate who could end the strife: his mother was a Welf, his father a Staufer. Contemporary accounts of the king's career represented Frederick in the image of Christ as the "cornerstone" that joined two houses and reconciled enemies.

New Foundations of Power. Frederick's appearance impressed his contemporaries—the name *Barbarossa* referred to his red-blond hair and beard. But beyond appearances, Frederick impressed those around him by what they called his "firmness." He affirmed royal rights, even when he handed out duchies and allowed others to name bishops, because in return for these political powers Frederick required the princes to concede formally and publicly that they held their

Frederick Barbarossa

In a thirteenth-century manuscript about imperial honor, Frederick Barbarossa is remembered for his firmness. At the top Frederick takes leave of his sons before going on the Third Crusade. They bow in deference to his authority and dignity. At the bottom, Frederick mounts his horse, gesturing a command with his left hand. The caption in Latin reads, "Frederick orders his men to cut down the forest in Hungary." Did Frederick fear retaliation from the Hungarian king? What sort of vision of imperial might did the artist of this miniature want to suggest? *Burgerbibliothek Bern, Cod. 120, II, f. #143r.*

rights and territories from him as their lord. By making them his vassals, although with nearly royal rights within their principalities, Frederick defined the princes' relationship to

- ◆ **1202–1204** The Fourth Crusade
  - ◆ **1204** Fall of Constantinople to Crusaders
    - ◆ **1214** Battle of Bouvines
    - ◆ **1215** Magna Carta

| 1200 | 1225 | 1250 | 1275 |

- ◆ **1204** Philip takes Normandy, Anjou, Maine, Touraine, and Poitou from John
  - ◆ **1209–1229** Albigensian Crusade
    - ◆ **1212** Battle of Las Navas de Tolosa; triumph of the reconquista

Frederick's Reply to the Romans

The confident claims of competing groups to the same rights and powers are well illustrated by Frederick Barbarossa's entry into Rome in 1155. The pope naturally considered it his right to confer the imperial crown on the king. But when Frederick came to Rome, envoys from the new city government that had been established there greeted him with their offer to give him the crown. Frederick reacted forcefully: the crown was not theirs to give; it was his by right. The gist of his reply to the Romans was recorded by his counselor and chronicler, Bishop Otto of Freising.

We have heard much heretofore concerning the wisdom and the valor of the Romans, yet more concerning their wisdom. Wherefore we cannot wonder enough at finding your words insipid with swollen pride rather than seasoned with the salt of wisdom. You set forth the ancient renown of your city. You extoll to the very stars the ancient status of your sacred republic. Granted, granted! To use the words of your own writer, "There was, *there was once*, virtue in this republic." "Once," I say. And O that we might truthfully and freely say "now"! Your Rome—nay, ours also—has experienced the vicissitudes of time. She could not be the only one to escape a fate ordained by the Author of all things for all that dwell beneath the orb of the moon. What shall I say? It is clear how first the strength of your nobility was transferred from this city of ours to the royal city of the East [Constantinople], and how for the course of many years the thirsty Greekling sucked the breasts of your delight. Then came the Frank, truly noble, in deed as in name, and forcibly possessed himself of whatever freedom was still left to you. Do you wish to know the ancient glory of your Rome? The worth of the senatorial dignity? The impregnable disposition of the camp? The virtue and the discipline of the equestrian order, its unmarred and unconquerable boldness when advancing to a conflict? Behold our state. All these things are to be found with us. All these have descended to us, together with the empire.

Source: Brian Tierney, *The Crisis of Church and State, 1050–1300: With Selected Documents* (Englewood Cliffs, NJ: Prentice Hall, 1964), 103–4.

the German king: they were powerful yet personally subordinate to him. In this way Frederick hoped to save the monarchy and to coordinate royal and princely rule, thus ending Germany's chronic civil wars. Frederick used the lord–vassal relationship to give him a free hand to rule while placating the princes.

As the king of Germany, Frederick had the traditional right to claim the imperial crown. When, in 1155, he marched to Rome to be crowned emperor, the fledgling commune there protested that it alone had the right to give him the crown. Frederick interrupted them, asserting that the glory of Rome, together with its crown, came to him by right of conquest. To the pope he was equally insistent: when Hadrian IV (r. 1154–1159) wrote to say that Rome belonged to "St. Peter,"

Frederick replied that his imperial title gave him rights over the city. In part, Frederick was influenced by the revival of knowledge about Roman law—the laws of Theodosius and Justinian—that was taking place in the schools of Italy. In part, too, he was convinced of the sacred—not just secular—origins of the imperial office. Frederick called his empire *sacer*, "sacred," asserting that it was in its own way as precious, worthwhile, and God-given as the church.

Frederick buttressed this high view of his imperial right with worldly power. He married Beatrice of Burgundy, whose vast estates in Burgundy and Provence enabled Frederick to establish a powerful political and territorial base centered in Swabia (today southwestern Germany).

Frederick and Italy. Frederick then looked south to Italy. Its flourishing commercial cities could make him rich. Taxes on agricultural production there alone yielded thirty thousand silver talents annually, an incredible sum equal to the annual income of the richest ruler of the day, the king of England. Finally, Swabia and northern Italy together would give Frederick a compact and centrally located territory.

Furthermore, no emperor could leave Italy alone. The very title came from the Roman emperor, who had controlled the city of Rome and all of Italy. It would have seemed laughable to be "emperor" without holding at least some of this territory. Some historians have faulted Frederick for "entangling" himself in Italy. But Frederick's title demanded he intervene in Italy. To blame him for not concentrating on Germany is to accuse him of lacking modern wisdom, which knows only from hindsight that European polities developed into nation-states, such as France, Germany, and Italy. There was nothing inevitable about the development of nation-states, and Frederick should not be criticized simply because he did not see into the future.

Nevertheless, Frederick's ambitions in Italy were problematic. Since the Investiture Conflict, the emperor had ruled Italy in name only. The communes of the northern cities guarded their liberties jealously, while the pope considered Italy his own sphere of influence. Frederick's territorial base just north of Italy threatened those interests (Map 11.1). In 1157, soon after Frederick's imperial coronation, Hadrian's envoys arrived at a meeting called by the emperor with a letter detailing

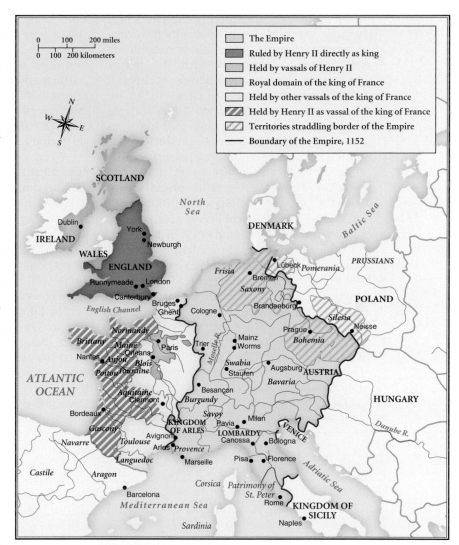

MAP 11.1 Europe in the Age of Frederick Barbarossa and Henry II, 1150–1190
The second half of the twelfth century was dominated by two men, Emperor Frederick Barbarossa and King Henry II. Of the two, Frederick seemed to control more land, but this was deceptive. Although he was emperor, he had great difficulty ruling the territory that was theoretically part of the empire. Frederick's base was in central Germany, and even there he had to contend with very powerful vassals. Henry II's territory was more compact but also more surely under his control.

the dignities, honors, and other *beneficia* the pope had showered on Frederick. The word *beneficia* incensed Frederick's supporters because it meant not only "benefits" but also "fiefs," casting Frederick as the pope's vassal. The incident opened old wounds from the Investiture Conflict and revealed the gulf between papal and imperial conceptions of worldly authority.

Despite the opposition of the cities and the pope, Frederick was determined to conquer northern Italy. Alternatively negotiating and fighting, especially with the major city there, Milan, Frederick achieved military control over the cities in 1158. Adopting an Italian solution for governing the communes—appointing outsiders as *podestà*,♦ or magistrates—Frederick appointed his own men to these powerful positions. Here is where Frederick made his mistake. He chose German officials who lacked a sense of Italian communal traditions. The heavy hand of Frederick's podestà created enormous resentment. For example, the podestà at Milan immediately ordered an inventory of all taxes due the emperor and levied new and demeaning labor duties, even demanding that citizens carry the wood and stones of their plundered city to Pavia, twenty-five miles away, for use in constructing new houses there. By 1167, most of the cities of northern Italy had joined with Pope Alexander III (r. 1159–1181) to form the Lom-

♦**podestà:** po duh STAH

bard League against Frederick. Defeated by the League at the battle of Legnano♦ in 1176, Frederick made peace with Alexander and withdrew most of his forces from Italy. The battle marked the triumph of the city over the crown in Italy, which would not have a centralized government until the nineteenth century; its political history would instead be that of its various regions and their dominant cities.

Frederick Barbarossa was the victim of traditions that were rapidly being outmoded. He based much of his rule in Germany on the bond of lord and vassal at the very moment when rulers elsewhere were relying less on such personal ties and more on salaried officials. He lived up to the meaning of *emperor*, with all its obligations to rule Rome and northern Italy, when other leaders were consolidating their territorial rule bit by bit. In addition, as "universal" emperor, he did not recognize the importance of local pride, language, customs, and traditions; he tried to rule Italian communes with his own men from the outside, and he failed.

Henry the Lion: Lord and Vassal.   Frederick also had problems in Germany, where he had to contend with princes of near-royal status who acted as independent rulers of their principalities, though acknowledging Frederick as their feudal lord. One of the most powerful was Henry the Lion (c. 1130–1195). Married to Matilda, daughter of the English king Henry II and Eleanor of Aquitaine,♦ Henry was duke of Saxony and Bavaria,

Henry the Lion

In 1166, when Henry the Lion was under especially heavy attack by his enemies, he had this giant lion cast out of iron mined in his duchy. A symbol of justice and also of Henry himself, the lion "guarded" Henry's castle at Brunswick. Its pose is probably modeled on that of the she-wolf of Rome, which Henry must have seen near the Lateran Palace when he accompanied Frederick Barbarossa to Rome in 1155. The snarling mouth was meant to suggest ferocity. This lion is the first large freestanding sculpture of the Middle Ages. Compare it with the crusader on page 376 and the shoemaker on page 363.
Erich Lessing/Art Resource.

♦**Legnano:** lehn YAH noh
♦**Aquitaine:** A kwuh tayn

which gave him important bases in both the north and the south of Germany. A self-confident and aggressive ruler, Henry dominated his territory by investing bishops (usurping the role of the emperor as outlined in the Concordat of Worms), collecting dues from his estates, and exercising judicial rights over his duchies. He also actively extended his rule, especially in Slavic regions, pushing northeast past the Elbe River to re-establish dioceses and to build the commercial city of Lübeck.

Henry was lord of many vassals and ministerials (people of unfree status but high prestige). With his army reinforced by Slavs, Henry expanded into new territories. He also organized a staff of clerics and ministerials to collect taxes and tolls and to write up his legal acts. Here, as elsewhere, administration no longer depended entirely on the personal involvement of the ruler.

Yet like kings, princes could fall. Henry's growing power so threatened other princes and even Frederick that in 1179 Frederick called Henry to the king's court for violating the peace. When Henry chose not to appear, Frederick exercised his authority as Henry's lord and charged him with violating his duty as a vassal. Because Henry refused the summons to court and avoided serving his lord in Italy, Frederick condemned him, confiscated his holdings, and drove him out of Germany in 1180.

Late-twelfth-century kings and emperors often found themselves engaged in a balancing act of ruling yet placating their powerful vassals. The process was almost always risky. Successfully challenging one recalcitrant prince-vassal meant negotiating costly deals with the others, since their support was vital. Although he wished to retain Henry's duchy for himself, Frederick had to divide and distribute it to supporters whose aid he needed to enforce his decrees against Henry.

England: Unity through Common Law

In the mid-twelfth century, the government of England was by far the most institutionalized in Europe. The king hardly needed to be present: royal government functioned by itself, with officials handling all the administrative matters and record keeping. The very circumstances of the English king favored the growth of an administrative staff: his frequent travels to and from the continent meant that officials needed to work in his absence, and his enormous wealth meant that he could afford them. King Henry II (r. 1154–1189) was the driving force in extending and strengthening the institutions of English government.

Accession of Henry II, 1154. Like Frederick Barbarossa, Henry II became king in the wake of a terrible civil war. Henry I

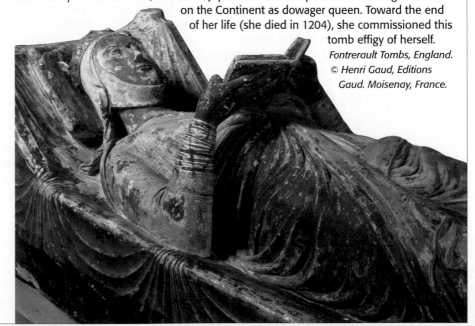

Eleanor of Aquitaine
The life of Eleanor of Aquitaine, queen of France and then of England, illustrates many of the opportunities and limitations available to noblewomen in the twelfth century. Lord of Aquitaine, she was nevertheless herself subject to the lordship of her husbands. Mother of eleven children, she had considerable influence over her sons, but her husband, Henry II, thwarted her and her sons' intrigues by holding her prisoner for fifteen years. With Henry's death in 1189, Eleanor enjoyed considerable power both in England and on the Continent as dowager queen. Toward the end of her life (she died in 1204), she commissioned this tomb effigy of herself.
Fontrerault Tombs, England.
© Henri Gaud, Editions Gaud. Moisenay, France.

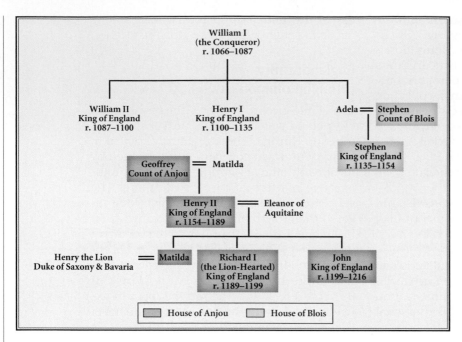

Newly built private castles, already familiar on the continent, now appeared in England as symbols of the rising power of the English barons. But Stephen's coalition of barons, high clergymen, and townsmen eventually fell apart, causing him to agree to the accession of Matilda's son, Henry of Anjou. Thus began what would be known as the **Angevin**♦ (from *Anjou*) dynasty.[1]

Henry's marriage to Eleanor of Aquitaine in 1152 brought the enormous inheritance of the duchy of Aquitaine to the English crown (see Eleanor's tomb effigy). Although he remained the vassal of the king of France for his continental lands, Henry in effect ruled a territory that stretched from England to southern France.

FIGURE 11.1 Genealogy of Henry II
King William I of England was succeeded by his sons William II and Henry I. When Henry died, the succession was disputed by two women and their husbands. One was William I's daughter Adela, married to the count of Blois; the other was Henry's daughter Matilda, wife of the count of Anjou. Although the English crown first went to the house of Blois, it reverted in midcentury to the house of Anjou, headed by Matilda's son Henry. Henry II thus began the Angevin dynasty in England.

(r. 1100–1135), son of William the Conqueror, had no male heir. Before he died, he called on the great barons to swear that his daughter Matilda would rule after him. The effort failed; the Norman barons could not imagine a woman ruling them, and they feared her husband, Geoffrey of Anjou, their perennial enemy on the continent. Many were glad to see Stephen of Blois (r. 1135–1154), the son of Henry's sister Adela, take the throne. With Matilda's son, the future Henry II, only two years old when Stephen took the crown, the struggle for control of England during Stephen's reign became part of a larger territorial contest between the house of Anjou♦ (Henry's family) and the house of Blois (Stephen's family) (Figure 11.1). Continual civil war (1139–1153) in England, as in Germany, benefited the English barons and high churchmen, who gained new privileges and powers as the monarch's authority waned.

Not only did Eleanor bring to Henry the duchy of Aquitaine, but she also bore him sons to maintain his dynasty. Before her marriage to Henry, Eleanor had been married to King Louis VII of France; Louis had the marriage annulled because Eleanor had borne him only daughters. Nevertheless, as queen of France, Eleanor had enjoyed an important position: she disputed with St. Bernard, the Cistercian abbot who was the most renowned churchman of the day, and she accompanied her husband on the Second Crusade, bringing more troops than he did. She had determined to separate from her husband even before he considered leaving her. But she lost much of her power under her English husband, for Henry dominated her just as he came to dominate his barons. Turning

---

♦**Anjou:** AN joo

---

[1]Henry's father, Geoffrey of Anjou, was nicknamed "Plantagenet" from the *genet*, a shrub he liked. Historians sometimes use the name to refer to the entire dynasty, so Henry II was the first Plantagenet as well as the first Angevin king of England.

♦**Angevin:** AN juh vihn

to her offspring in 1173, Eleanor, disguised as a man, tried to join her eldest son, Henry the Younger, in a plot against his father. But the rebellion was put down, and she spent most of her years thereafter, until her husband's death in 1189, confined under guard at Winchester Castle.

Royal Authority and Common Law. When Henry II became king of England, he immediately set to work to undo the damage to the monarchy caused by the civil war. He destroyed or confiscated the new castles and regained crown land. Then he proceeded to extend monarchical power, above all by imposing royal justice.

Henry's judicial reforms built on an already well-developed English system. The Anglo-Saxon kings had royal district courts: the king appointed sheriffs to police the shires, muster military levies, and haul criminals into court. The Norman kings retained these courts, which all the free men of the shire were summoned to attend. To these established institutions, Henry II added a system of judicial visitations called eyres♦ (from the Latin *iter*, "journey"). Under this system, royal justices made regular trips to every locality in England. Henry declared that some crimes, such as murder, arson, and rape, were so heinous as to violate the "king's peace," no matter where they were committed. The king required local representatives of the knightly class to meet during each eyre and either give the sheriff the names of those suspected of committing crimes in the vicinity or arrest the suspects themselves and hand them over to the royal justices.

During the eyres, the justices also heard cases between individuals, today called civil cases. Free men and women (that is, people of the knightly class or above) could bring their disputes over such matters as inheritance, dowries, and property claims to the king's justices. Earlier courts had generally relied on duels between litigants to determine verdicts. Henry's new system offered a different option, an inquest under royal supervision.

The new system of **common law**—law that applied to all of England—was praised

♦**eyres:** ayrs

Hanging Thieves
The development of common law in England meant mobilizing royal agents to bring charges and arrest people throughout the land. In 1124, the royal justice Ralph Basset hanged forty-four thieves. It could not have been very shocking in that context to see, in this miniature from around 1130, eight thieves hanged for breaking into the shrine of St. Edmund. Under Henry II all cases of murder, arson, and rape were considered crimes against the king himself. The result was not just the enhancement of the king's power but also new definitions of crime, more thorough policing, and more systematic punishments. Even so, hanging was probably no more frequent than it had been before. *Pierpont Morgan Library/Art Resource, NY.*

for its efficiency, speed, and conclusiveness by a twelfth-century legal treatise known as *Glanvill* (after its presumed author): "This legal institution emanates from perfect equity. For justice, which after many and long delays is scarcely ever demonstrated by the duel, is advantageously and speedily attained

The Murder of Thomas Becket
Almost immediately after King Henry II's knights murdered Archbishop Thomas Becket in his church at Canterbury, Becket was viewed as a martyr. In this early depiction of the event, one of the murderers knocks off Becket's cap, while another hits the arm of Becket's supporter, who holds the bishop's cross-staff. *British Library, London, UK/Bridgeman Art Library.*

The stiffest opposition to Henry's extension of royal courts came from the church, where a separate system of trial and punishment had long been available to the clergy and to others who enjoyed church protection. The punishments for crimes meted out by these courts were generally quite mild. Jealous of their prerogatives, churchmen refused to submit to the jurisdiction of Henry's courts, and the ensuing contest between Henry II and his appointed archbishop, Thomas Becket (1118–1170), became the greatest battle between the church and the state in the twelfth century. The conflict simmered for six years, until Henry's henchmen murdered Thomas, unintentionally turning him into a martyr. Although Henry's role in the murder remained ambiguous, he was forced by the general outcry to do public penance for the deed. In the end both church and royal courts expanded to address the concerns of an increasingly litigious society. (See The Murder of Thomas Becket on this page.)

Henry II was an English king with an imperial reach. He was lord over almost half of France, though much of this territory was in the hands of his vassals, and he was, at least theoretically, vassal to the French king. In England, he made the king's presence felt everywhere through his system of royal courts that traveled the length and breadth of the country. On the continent, he maintained his position through a combination of war and negotiation, but rebellions begun by his own sons with help from the king of France dogged him throughout his life.

Henry's Successors.   Under Henry and his sons Richard I (r. 1189–1199) and John (r. 1199–1216), the English monarchy was omnipresent and rich. Its omnipresence derived largely from its eyre system of justice and its administrative apparatus. Its wealth came from court fees, income from numerous royal estates both in England and on the continent, taxes from cities, and customary feudal dues (reliefs and aids) collected from barons and knights. These dues were paid on such occasions as the knighting of the king's eldest son and the marriage of the king's eldest daughter. Enriched by the commercial economy of the late twelfth century, the English

through this institution." *Glanvill* might have added that the king also speedily gained a large treasury. The exchequer, as the financial bureau of England was called, recorded all the fines paid for judgments and the sums collected for writs. The amounts, entered on parchment sewn together and stored as rolls, became the Receipt Rolls and Pipe Rolls, the first of many such records of the English monarchy and an indication that writing had become a mechanism for institutionalizing royal power in England.

kings encouraged their knights and barons not to serve them personally in battle but instead to pay the king a tax called **scutage** in lieu of service. The monarchs preferred to hire mercenaries both as troops to fight external enemies and as police to enforce the king's will at home.

Richard I was known as the Lion-Hearted for his boldness. But historians have often criticized him for being an "absentee" king. Yet it is hard to see what he might have done differently. He went on the Third Crusade the very year he was crowned; on his way home, he was captured and held for a long time for ransom by political enemies; and he died defending his possessions on the continent. Richard's real tragedy was that he died young.

Richard's successor, John, has also been widely faulted. Even in his own day, he was accused of asserting his will in a high-handed way. But to understand John, it is necessary to appreciate how desperate he was to keep his continental possessions. In 1204, the king of France, Philip II (r. 1180–1223), confiscated the northern French territories held by John. Between 1204 and 1214, John did everything he could to add to the crown revenues so he could pay for an army to win back the territories. He forced his vassals to pay ever-increasing scutages and extorted money in the form of new feudal dues. He compelled the widows of his vassals to marry men of his choosing or pay him a hefty fee if they refused. Yet despite John's heavy investment in this war effort, his army was defeated in 1214 at the battle of Bouvines. The defeat caused discontented English barons to rebel openly against the king. At Runnymede in June 1215, John was forced to agree to the charter of baronial liberties that has come to be called Magna Carta, or "Great Charter."

Magna Carta, 1215. The English barons intended Magna Carta (so named to distinguish it from a smaller charter issued around the same time concerning the royal forests) to be a conservative document defining the "customary" obligations and rights of the nobility and forbidding the king to break from these customs without consulting his barons. It also maintained that all free men

in the land had certain rights that the king was obligated to uphold. (See "Contrasting Views," page 410.) In this way, Magna Carta implied that the king was not above the law. The growing royal power was matched by the self-confidence of the English barons, certain of their rights and eager to articulate them. In time, as the definition of *free men* expanded to include all the king's subjects, Magna Carta came to be seen as a guarantee of the rights of Englishmen in general.

France: Consolidation and Conquest

Whereas the power of the English king led to a baronial movement to curb it, the weakness of the French monarchy ironically led to its expansion. In 1180, the French crown passed from the Capetian king Louis VII (first husband of Eleanor of Aquitaine) to his young son, Philip II. When the new king came to the throne, the royal domain, the Île-de-France, was sandwiched between territory controlled by the counts of Flanders, Champagne, and Anjou. By far the most powerful ruler on the continent was King Henry II of England. He was the count of Anjou and the duke of Normandy, and he held the duchy of Aquitaine through his wife. He also controlled Poitou♦ and Brittany.

Henry and the counts of Flanders and Champagne vied to control the newly crowned fourteen-year-old king of France. Philip, however, quickly learned to play them off against one another, in

The Consolidation of France under Philip Augustus, 1180–1223

particular by setting the sons of Henry II against their father. Contemporaries were astounded when Philip successfully gained territory: he wrested Vermandois and Artois from Flanders in the 1190s and Normandy, Anjou, Maine, Touraine, and Poitou from King John of England in 1204. After these

♦**Poitou:** pwah TOO

CONTRASTING VIEWS

Magna Carta

Magna Carta, today considered a landmark of constitutional government, began as a demand by English barons and churchmen for specific rights and privileges. Reacting to King John's "abuses," they forced him in 1215 to affix his seal to a "charter of liberties," the "Great Charter" (Magna Carta, Document 1). It set forth the customs that the king was expected to observe and, in its sixty-first clause, in effect allowed the king's subjects to declare war against him if he failed to carry out the charter's provisions.

In 1225, Henry III, John's son, issued a definitive version of the charter. By then it had become more important as a symbol of liberty than for its specific provisions. It was, for example, invoked by the barons in 1242 when they were summoned to one of the first Parliaments (Document 2).

1. MAGNA CARTA, 1215

In these excerpts, the provisions that were dropped in the definitive version of 1225 are starred. Explanatory notes are in brackets. The original charter had sixty-three clauses. In every clause John refers to himself by the royal "we."

1. First of all [we, i.e., John] have granted to God, and by this our present charter confirmed for us and our heirs for ever that the English church shall be free, and shall have its rights undiminished and its liberties unimpaired....

8. No widow shall be forced to marry so long as she wishes to live without a husband, provided that she gives security [a pledge or deposit] not to marry without our consent if she holds [her land] from us, or without the consent of her lord of whom she holds, if she holds of another.

9. Neither we nor our bailiffs will seize for any debt any land or rent, so long as the chattels

[property] of the debtor are sufficient to repay the debt....

*10. If anyone who has borrowed from the Jews any sum, great or small, dies before it is repaid, the debt shall not bear interest as long as the heir is under age, of whomsoever [lord] he holds [his land]; and if the debt falls into our hands [which might happen, as Jews were serfs of the crown], we will not take anything except the principal mentioned in the bond.

*12. No scutage or aid [money payments owed by a vassal to his lord] shall be imposed in our kingdom unless by common counsel of our kingdom, except for ransoming our person, for making our eldest son a knight, and for once marrying our eldest daughter; and for these only a reasonable aid shall be levied....

30. No sheriff, or bailiff of ours, or anyone else shall take the horses or carts of any free man [for the most part, a member of the elite] for transport work save with the agreement of that freeman.

31. Neither we nor our bailiffs will take, for castles or other works of ours, timber which is not ours, except with the agreement of him whose timber it is....

39. No free man shall be arrested or imprisoned or disseised [deprived of his land] or outlawed or exiled or in any way victimized, neither will we attack him or send anyone to attack him, except by the lawful judgment of his peers or by the law of the land....

*61. Since...we have granted all these things aforesaid...we give and grant [the barons] the under-written security, namely, that the barons shall choose any twenty-five barons of the kingdom they wish, who must with all their might observe, hold, and cause to be observed, the peace and liberties which we have granted and confirmed to them by this present charter of ours, so that if we, or our justiciar [the king's chief minister], or our bailiffs or any one of our servants offend in any way against anyone or transgress any of the articles of the peace or the security . . . , [the barons] shall come to us . . . and laying the transgression before us, shall petition us to have that transgression corrected without delay. And if we do not correct the transgression . . . within forty days . . . those twenty-five barons together with the community of the whole land shall distrain and distress us in every way they can, namely, by seizing castles, lands, possessions, and in such other ways as they can, saving [not harming] our person.

Source: *English Historical Documents*, vol. 3, ed. Harry Rothwell (London: Eyre & Spottiswoode, 1975), 317–23.

2. THE BARONS AT PARLIAMENT REFUSE TO GIVE THE KING AN AID, 1242

Henry III convoked the barons to a meeting (parliament), expecting them to ratify his request for money to wage war for his French possessions. As this document makes clear, the barons considered his request an excessive imposition. Magna Carta thus became a justification for their flat rejection of the king's request.

Since he had been their ruler they had many times, at his request, given him aid, namely, a thirteenth of their movable property, and afterwards a fifteenth and a sixteenth and a fortieth. . . . Scarcely, however, had four years or so elapsed from that time, when he again asked them for aid, and, at length, by dint of great entreaties, he obtained a thirtieth, which they granted him on the condition that neither that exaction nor the others before it should in the future be made a precedent of. And regarding that he gave them his charter. Furthermore, he then [at that earlier time] granted them that all the liberties contained in Magna Carta should thence-

John's Seal on Magna Carta

When the rebels at Runnymede got John to assent to their charter, later known as Magna Carta, he did not sign it; he sealed it. From the thirteenth through the fifteenth century, seals were used by kings, queens, aristocrats, guilds, communes, and many other individuals and groups at all levels of society to authenticate their charters— what we would call "legal documents." The seal itself was made out of wax or lead, melted and pressed with a matrix of hard metal, such as gold or brass, that was carved with an image in the negative, designed to produce a raised image. These seals reminded the public of the status as well as the name of the sealer. What image did John wish to project? *British Museum.*

forward be fully observed throughout the whole of his kingdom. . . .

Furthermore, from the time of their giving the said thirtieth, itinerant justices have been continually going on eyre [moving from place to place] through all parts of England, alike for pleas of the forest [to enforce the king's monopoly on forests] and all other pleas, so that all the counties, hundreds, cities, boroughs, and nearly all the vills of England are heavily amerced [fined]; wherefore, from that eyre alone the king has, or ought to have, a very large sum of money, if it were paid, and properly collected. They therefore say with truth that all in the kingdom are so oppressed and impoverished by these amercements and by the other aids given before that they have little or no goods left. And because the king had never, after the granting of the thirtieth, abided by his charter of liberties, nay had since then oppressed them more than usual . . . they told the king flatly that for the present they would not give him an aid.

Source: *English Historical Documents*, 3:355–56.

QUESTIONS TO CONSIDER
1. From the clauses of Magna Carta that say what will henceforth *not* be done, speculate about what the king *had been* doing.
2. How did the barons of 1242 use Magna Carta as a symbol of liberty?

feats a contemporary chronicler dubbed him Philip Augustus, the "augmenter."

After Philip's army confirmed its triumph over most of John's continental territories in 1214, the French monarch could boast that he was the richest and most powerful ruler in France. Unlike Frederick I Barbarossa, who was compelled to divide the territory he had seized from Henry the Lion among the German princes, Philip had sufficient support and resources to keep a tight hold on Normandy.[2] He received homage and fealty from most of the Norman aristocracy; his officers carefully carried out their work there in accordance with Norman customs. For ordinary Normans, the shift from duke to king brought few changes.

Wherever he ruled, Philip instituted a new kind of French administration, run by officials who kept accounts and files. Before Philip's day most French royal arrangements were committed to memory rather than to writing. If decrees were recorded at all, they were saved by the recipient, not by the government. The king did keep some documents, which generally followed him in his travels like personal possessions. But in 1194, in a battle with the king of England, Philip lost his meager cache of documents along with much treasure when he had to abandon his baggage train. After 1194, the king had all his decrees written down, and he established permanent repositories in which to keep them.

Whereas German rulers employed ministerials to do the daily work of government, Philip, like the English king, relied largely on members of the lesser nobility—knights and clerics, many of whom were "masters" educated in the city schools of France. They served as officers of his court, tax collectors, and overseers of the royal estates, making the king's power felt locally as never before.

Eastern Europe and Byzantium: Fragmenting Realms

The importance of institutions such as those developed in England and France is made clear by the experience of regions where they

were not established. In eastern Europe the characteristic pattern was for states to form under the leadership of one great ruler and then to fragment under his successor. For example, King Béla III of Hungary (r. 1172–1196) built up a state that looked superficially like a western European kingdom. He married a French princess, employed at least one scholar from Paris, and built his palace in the French Romanesque style. He enjoyed an annual income from his estates, tolls, dues, and taxes equal to that of the richest western monarchs. But he did not set up enduring government institutions, and in the decades that followed his death, wars between Béla's sons splintered his monarchical holdings, and aristocratic supporters divided the wealth.

Eastern Europe and Byzantium, c. 1200

Russia underwent a similar process. Although twelfth-century Kiev was politically fragmented, autocratic princes to the north constructed Suzdal,◆ the nucleus of the later Muscovite state. The borders of Suzdal were clearly defined, well-to-do towns prospered, monasteries and churches dotted the countryside, and the other princes of Russia recognized its ruler as the "grand prince." Yet in 1212 this nascent state began to crumble as the sons of Grand Prince Vsevolod◆ III (r. 1176–1212) fought one another for territory, much as Béla's sons had done in Hungary.

Although the Byzantine Empire was already a consolidated, bureaucratic state, after the mid-twelfth century it gradually began to show weakness. Traders from the west—the Venetians especially—dominated its commerce. The Byzantine emperors who ruled during the last half of the twelfth century down-

---

[2]Philip was particularly successful in imposing royal control in Normandy; later French kings gave most of the other territories to collateral members of the royal family.

◆**Suzdal:** SOO zduhl
◆**Vsevolod:** TSEV a lid

graded the old civil servants, elevated their relatives to high offices, and favored the military elite. As Byzantine rule grew more personal and European rule became more bureaucratic, the two gradually became more like one another. The final blow came when the crusaders took Constantinople in 1204, parceling out most of the empire among themselves.

Review: What new sources and institutions of power became available to rulers in the twelfth century?

❖ The Growth of a Vernacular High Culture

With their consolidation of territory, wealth, and power in the last half of the twelfth century, kings, barons, princes, and their wives and daughters supported new kinds of literature and music. For the first time on the continent, though long true in England, poems and songs were written in the vernacular, the spoken language, rather than in Latin. They celebrated the lives of the nobility and were meant to be read or sung aloud, sometimes with accompanying musical instruments. They provided a common experience for aristocrats at court. Whether in the cities of Italy or the more isolated courts of northern Europe, patrons and patronesses, enriched by their estates and commerce, now spent their profits on the arts. Their support helped develop and enrich the spoken language while it heightened their prestige as aristocrats.

The Troubadours: Poets of Love and Play

Already at the beginning of the twelfth century, Duke William IX of Aquitaine (1071–1126), the grandfather of Eleanor, had written lyric poems in Occitan, the vernacular of southern France. Perhaps influenced by Arabic and Hebrew love poetry from al-Andalus, his own poetry in turn provided a model for poetic forms that gained popularity through repeated performances. The final four-line stanza of one such poem demonstrates the composer's skill with words:

Per aquesta fri e tremble,	*For this one I shiver and tremble,*
quar de tan bon' amor l'am;	*I love her with such a good love;*
qu'anc no cug qu'en nasques semble	*I do not think the like of her was ever born*
en semblan de gran linh n'Adam.	*in the long line of Lord Adam.*

The rhyme scheme of this poem appears to be simple—*tremble* goes with *semble, l'am* with *n'Adam*—but the entire poem has five earlier verses, all six lines long and all containing the *-am,-am* rhyme in the fourth and sixth lines, while every other line within each verse rhymes as well.

Troubadours, lyric poets who wrote in Occitan, varied their rhymes and meters endlessly to dazzle their audiences with brilliant originality. Most of their rhymes and meters resemble Latin religious poetry of the same time, indicating that the vernacular and Latin religious cultures overlapped. Such similarity is also evident in the troubadours' choice of subjects. The most common topic, love, echoed the twelfth-century church's emphasis on the emotional relationship between God and humans.

The troubadours invented new meanings for old images. When William IX sang of his "good love" for a woman unlike any other born in the line of Adam, the words could be interpreted in two ways. They reminded listeners of the Virgin Mary, a woman unlike any other, but they also referred to William's lover, recalled in another part of the poem, where he had complained

If I do not get help soon
and my lady does not give me love,
by Saint Gregory's holy head I'll die
if she doesn't kiss me in a chamber or under a tree.

His lady's character is ambiguous: she is like the Virgin Mary, but she is also his mistress.

Troubadours, both male and female, expressed prevalent views of love much as popular singers do today. The Contessa de Dia (flourished c. 1160) wrote about her unrequited love for a man:

So bitter do I feel toward him
whom I love more than anything.
With him my mercy and fine manners [cortesia]
are in vain.

Anc no mori per amor ni per al
I Never Died for Love

Anc | no | mo – ri | per | a – mor | ni | per | al,
I | *nev – er* | *died* | *for* | *love* | *or* | *for* | *aught* | *else,*

Mais | ma | vi – da | pot | be | va – ler | mu – rir
But | *my* | *life* | *is* | *surely* | *the* | *e – qual* | *of* | *death*

Quan | vei | la | ren | qu'eu | plus | am | e | de – zir
When | *I* | *see* | *the* | *creature* | *I* | *most* | *love* | *and* | *desire,*

E | ren | no.m | fai | mas | quan | do – lor | e | mal.
And | *it* | *brings* | *me* | *only* | *pain* | *and* | *suf – fer – ing.*

FIGURE 11.2 Troubadour Song: "I Never Died for Love"
This music is the first part of a song that the troubadour poet Peire Vidal wrote sometime between 1175 and 1205. It has been adapted here for the treble clef. There is no time signature, but the music may easily be played by calculating one beat for each note, except for the two-note slurs, which fit into one beat together, a half-beat for each note.
From Samuel N. Rosenberg, Margaret Switten, and Gerard Le Vot, eds., Songs of the Troubadours and Trouvères. *Copyright © 1997 by Samuel N. Rosenberg, Margaret Switten, and Gerard Le Vot. Reprinted by permission of Taylor & Francis/Garland Publishing, http://www.taylorandfrancis.com.*

Aquitaine and other aristocratic women patronized the troubadours: they enjoyed the image that it gave them of themselves. Until recently historians thought that the image was a delusion and that twelfth-century aristocratic women were valuable mainly as heiresses to marry and as mothers of sons. But new research reveals that there were many powerful female lords in southern France. They owned property, had vassals, led battles, decided disputes, and entered into and broke political alliances as their advantage dictated. Both men and women appreciated troubadour poetry, which recognized and praised women's power even as it eroticized it.

Music was part of troubadour poetry, which was always sung, typically by a ♦*jongleur*♦ (musician). Unfortunately, no written troubadour music exists from before the thirteenth century, and even then we have music for only a fraction of the poems. By the thirteenth century, music was written on four- and five-line staves, so scholars can at least determine relative pitches, and modern musicians can sing some troubadour songs with the hope of sounding reasonably like the original. This is the earliest popular music that can be re-created authentically (Figure 11.2).

From southern France the troubadours' songs spread to Italy, northern France, England, and Germany. Similar poetry appeared in other vernacular languages: the *minnesingers*♦ (literally, "love singers") sang in German; the *trouvères*♦ sang in the Old French of northern France. One trouvère was the English king Richard the Lion-Hearted. Taken

The key to troubadour verse is the idea of *cortesia*. It refers to courtesy, the refinement of people living at court, and to their struggle to achieve an ideal of virtue.

Historians and literary critics used to use the term *courtly love* to emphasize one of the themes of courtly literature: overwhelming love for a beautiful married noblewoman who is far above the poet in status and utterly unattainable. But this was only one of many aspects of love that the troubadours sang about: some boasted of sexual conquests, others played with the notion of equality between lovers, and still others preached that love was the source of virtue. The real overall theme of this literature is not courtly love; it is the power of women. No wonder Eleanor of

♦*jongleur:* zhon GLUR
♦*minnesinger:* MIH nuh sihn gur
♦*trouvère:* troo VEHR

prisoner on his return from the Third Crusade, Richard wrote a poem expressing his longing not for a lady but for the good companions of war, the knightly "youths" he had joined in battle:

> They know well, the men of Anjou and Touraine, those bachelors, now so magnificent and safe, that I am arrested, far from them, in another's hands.
> They used to love me much, now they love me not at all.
> There's no lordly fighting now on the barren plains,
> because I am a prisoner.

The Literature of Epic and Romance

The yearning for the battlefield was not as common a topic in lyric poetry as love, but long narrative poems about heroic deeds (**chansons de geste**)♦ appeared frequently in vernacular writing. Such poems followed a long oral tradition and appeared at about the same time as love poems. Like the songs of the troubadours, these epic poems implied a code of behavior for aristocrats, in this case on the battlefield.

By the end of the twelfth century, warriors wanted a guide for conduct and a common class identity. Nobles and knights had begun to merge into one class because they felt threatened from below by newly rich merchants and from above by newly powerful kings. Their ascendancy on the battlefield, where they unhorsed one another with lances and long swords and took prisoners rather than kill their opponents, was also beginning to wane in the face of mercenary infantrymen who wielded long hooks and knives that ripped easily through chain mail. A knightly ethos and sense of group solidarity emerged in the face of these social, political, and military changes.

Thus, the protagonists of heroic poems yearned not for love but for battle:

> The armies are in sight of one another. . . . The cowards tremble as they march, but the brave hearts rejoice for the battle.

Examining the moral issues that made war both tragic and inevitable, poets played on the contradictory values of their society, such as the conflicting loyalties of friendship and

vassalage or a vassal's right to a fief versus a son's right to his father's land.

These vernacular narrative poems, later called epics, focused on war. Other long poems, later called romances, explored the relationships between men and women. Romances reached their zenith of popularity during the late twelfth and early thirteenth centuries. The legend of King Arthur inspired a romance by Chrétien de Troyes♦ (c. 1150–1190) in which a heroic knight, Lancelot, in love with Queen Guinevere, the wife of his lord, comes across a comb bearing some strands of her radiant hair:

> Never will the eye of man see anything receive such honour as when [Lancelot] begins to adore these tresses. . . . Even for St. Martin and St. James he has no need.

Chrétien is evoking the familiar imagery of relics, such as bits of hair or the bones of saints, as items of devotion. Making Guinevere's hair an object of adoration not only conveys the depth of Lancelot's feeling but also pokes a bit of fun at him. Like the troubadours, the romantic poets delighted in the interplay between religious and amorous feelings. Just as the ideal monk merged his will in God's will, Chrétien's Lancelot loses his will to Guinevere. When she sees Lancelot—the greatest knight in Christendom—fighting in a tournament, she tests him by asking him to do his "worst." The poor knight is obliged to lose all his battles until she changes her mind.

Lancelot was the perfect chivalric knight. The word **chivalry** derives from the French word *cheval* ("horse"); the fact that the knight was a horseman marked him as a warrior of the most prestigious sort. Perched high on his horse, his heavy lance couched in his right arm, the knight was an imposing and menacing figure. Chivalry made him gentle—except to his enemies on the battlefield. The chivalric hero was a knight constrained by a code of refinement, fair play, piety, and devotion to an ideal. Historians debate whether real knights lived up to the codes implicit in epics and romances. But there is no doubt that knights saw themselves mirrored in the codes. They were the poets' audience; sometimes they were the poets' subject as well.

♦**chansons de geste:** shahn SOHN duh ZHEST

♦**Chrétien de Troyes:** kray TYAN duh TWAH

For example, when the knight William the Marshal died, his son commissioned a poet to write his biography. In it, William was depicted as a model knight, courteous with the ladies and brave on the battlefield.

> **Review:** What does the work of the troubadours and vernacular poets reveal about the nature of entertainment—its themes, its audience, its performers—in the twelfth century?

❖ New Lay and Religious Associations

The new vernacular culture was merely one reflection of the growing wealth, sophistication, and self-confidence of twelfth-century society. At every level, people were creating new and well-defined institutions to implement their goals. Great lords hired estate managers; townspeople joined guilds that regulated their lives according to impersonal rules; and students and teachers came together to form universities. Many of these associations reflected the developing commercialization of the economy.

The Commercial Revolution Penetrates the Countryside

The earlier commercial revolution had created cities and networks of trade. Now the countryside itself was caught in the web. By 1150, rural life was increasingly organized for the marketplace. The commercialization of the countryside opened up opportunities for both peasants and lords, but it also burdened some with unwelcome obligations.

Great lords hired trained, literate agents to administer their estates, calculate profits and losses, and make marketing decisions. Aristocrats needed money not only because they relished luxuries but also because their honor and authority continued to depend on their personal generosity, patronage, and displays of wealth. In the late twelfth century, when some townsmen could boast fortunes that rivaled the riches of the landed aristocracy, the economic pressures on the nobles increased as their extravagance exceeded their income. Most went into debt.

The lord's need for money changed peasant life, as peasants too became more integrated into the developing commercial economy. The population continued to increase in the twelfth century, and the greater demand for food required more farmland. By the middle of the century, isolated and sporadic attempts to cultivate new land had become a regular and coordinated activity. Great lords offered special privileges to peasants who would do the backbreaking work of plowing marginal land. In 1154, the bishop of Neisse♦ (today in Germany) called for settlers from Flanders and established a village for them. Experts in drainage, these new settlers got rights to the land they reclaimed and owed only light monetary obligations to the bishop, who nevertheless expected to reap a profit from their tolls and tithes. Similar encouragement came from lords throughout Europe, especially in northern Italy, England, Flanders, and Germany. In Flanders, where land was regularly inundated by seawater, the great monasteries sponsored drainage projects. Canals linking the cities to the agricultural districts let boats ply the waters to virtually every nook and cranny of the region. With its dense population, Flanders provided not only a natural meeting ground for long-distance traders from England and France but also numerous markets for local traders.

Sometimes free peasants acted on their own to clear land and relieve the pressure of overpopulation, as when the small freeholders in England's Fenland region cooperated to build banks and dikes to reclaim the land that led out to the North Sea. Villages were founded on the drained land, and villagers shared responsibility for repairing and maintaining the dikes even as each peasant family farmed its new holding individually.

On old estates the rise in population strained to the breaking point the manse organization that had developed in Carolingian Europe, where each household was settled on the land that supported it. Now in the twelfth century, twenty peasant families might live on what had been, in the tenth century, the manse of one family. With the manse supporting so many more people,

♦**Neisse:** NY suh

labor services and dues had to be recalculated, and peasants and their lords often turned services and dues into money rents, payable once a year. With this change, peasant men gained more control over their plots—they could sell them, will them to their sons, or even designate a small portion for their daughters. However, for these privileges, they had either to pay extra taxes or, like communes, to join together to buy their collective liberty for a high price, paid out over many years to their lord. Peasants, like town citizens, gained a new sense of identity and solidarity as they bargained with a lord keen to increase his income at their expense.

Peasants now owed more taxes to support the new administrative apparatuses of monarchs and princes. Kings' demands for money from their subjects filtered to the lowest classes either directly or indirectly. In northern Italy the cities themselves often imposed and enforced dues on the peasants, normally tenant farmers who leased their plots in the countryside surrounding each city. In the mid-twelfth century the urban officials at Florence, working closely with the bishop, dominated the countryside, collecting taxes from its cultivators, calling up its men to fight, and importing its food into the city. Therefore, peasants' gains from rising prices, access to markets, greater productivity, and increased personal freedom were partially canceled out by their cash burdens. Peasants of the late twelfth century ate better than their forebears, but they also had more responsibilities.

Guilds for Commerce and Scholarship

Many **guilds**—associations of craftspeople, merchants, or professionals—began as religious associations. In Ferrara, Italy, for example, the shoemakers' guild started as a prayer confraternity, an association whose members gathered and prayed for one another. But in the second half of the twelfth century, guilds became professional corporations defined by statutes and rules. They negotiated with lords and town governments, set the standards of their trade, and controlled their membership. Universities were also a special kind of guild, defined by statutes and devoted to setting standards

and controlling membership. But in the case of the universities, the standards concerned scholarship, and the members consisted of masters (teachers) and students.

Trade Guilds. As guilds became formally organized, they drew up statutes to determine dues, working hours, wages, and standards for materials and products. Sometimes they came into conflict with town government, as for example in northern Italy, where some communes considered bread too important a commodity to allow bakers to form a guild. At other times the communes supported guild efforts to control wages, reinforcing guild regulations with statutes of their own. When great lords rather than communes governed

A Weaving Workshop
A series of pen-and-ink drawings of various crafts was made in an early-thirteenth-century manuscript produced at Cistercian monastery of Reun, in Austria. In this depiction of a weavers' workshop, a woman (at left) works a carpet loom. She holds a spindle in her left hand and a beater in her right. Two men nearby use other implements of the weaver's trade: shuttles, scissors, and a beater. *Österreichische Nationalbibliothek, Vienna.*

a city, they too tried to control and protect the guilds. King Henry II of England, for example, eagerly gave some guilds in his Norman duchy special privileges so that they would depend on him.

The manufacture of finished products often required the cooperation of several guilds. Producing wool cloth involved numerous guilds—shearers, weavers, fullers (who thickened the cloth), dyers—generally working under the supervision of the merchant guild that imported the raw wool (see the illustration of weavers on the previous page). Some guilds were more prestigious than others: in Florence, for example, professional guilds of notaries and judges ranked above craft guilds. Within each guild of artisans or merchants existed another kind of hierarchy. Apprentices were at the bottom, journeymen and journeywomen in the middle, and masters at the top. Apprentices were boys and occasionally girls placed under the tutelage of a master for a number of years to learn a trade. At Paris, it took four years of apprenticeship to become a baker; at Genoa, it took ten to become a silversmith. Learning a trade was not the same as becoming a master. A young person would spend many years as a day laborer hired by a master who needed extra help. Unlike apprentices, these journeymen and journeywomen did not live with their masters; they worked for them for a wage. This marked an important stage in the economic history of the West. For the first time, many workers were neither slaves nor dependents but free and independent wage earners. At least a few day workers were female; invariably they received wages far lower than those of their male counterparts. Sometimes a married couple worked at the same trade and hired themselves out as a team. Often journeymen and journeywomen were required to be guild members—so that they would pay dues and so their masters could keep tabs on them.

Masters occupied the top of the guild hierarchy, dominating the offices and policies of the guild. They drew up the guild regulations and served as its chief overseers, inspectors, and treasurers. Because the number of masters was few and the turnover of official posts frequent, most masters eventually had a chance to serve as guild officers.

Occasionally they were elected, but more often they were appointed from among the masters of the craft by the ruler—whether a prince or a commune—of the city.

During the late twelfth century, women's labor in some trades gradually declined in importance. In Flanders, for example, as the manufacture of woolen cloth shifted from rural areas to cities, women participated less in the process. Only isolated manors still needed a *gynaeceum*, the women's quarter where female dependents spun, wove, and sewed garments. Instead, large, new-style looms in cities like Ypres♦ and Ghent were run by men working in pairs. They produced a heavy-weight cloth superior to the fabric made on the lighter looms that women had worked. Similarly, water mills and animal-powered mills gradually took the place of female labor in grinding flour by hand. Some women were certainly artisans and traders, and their names occasionally appeared in guild memberships. But they rarely became guild officers.

Universities.   Guilds of masters and students developed at the beginning of the thirteenth century at places such as Paris, Bologna, and Oxford. Each guild (*universitas* in Latin) was so tightly connected to the schools at which the masters taught and the students learned that eventually the term *university* came to include the school as well as the guild.

The universities regulated student discipline, scholastic proficiency, and housing while determining the masters' behavior in equal detail. For example, at the University of Paris the masters were required to wear long black gowns, follow a particular order in their lectures, and set the standards by which students could become masters themselves. The University of Bologna was unique in having two guilds, one of students and one of masters. At Bologna, the students participated in the appointment of masters and paid their salaries.

The University of Bologna was unusual because it was principally a school of law, where the students were often older men, well along in their careers and used to wielding power. The University of Paris, however, at-

♦**Ypres:** EEP ruh

tracted younger students, drawn particularly by its renown in the liberal arts and theology. The Universities of Salerno and Montpellier specialized in medicine. Oxford, once a sleepy town where students clustered around one or two masters, became a center of royal administration, and its university soon developed a reputation for teaching the liberal arts, theology and—very extraordinarily—science.

University curricula differed in content and duration. At the University of Paris in the early thirteenth century, for example, a student had to spend at least six years studying the liberal arts before he could begin to teach. If he wanted to continue his studies with theology, he had to attend lectures on the subject for at least another five years. Lectures were clearly the most important way in which material was conveyed to students. Books were very expensive and not readily available, so students committed their teachers' lectures to memory. The lectures were organized around important texts: the master read an excerpt aloud, delivered his commentary on it, and disputed any contrary commentaries that rival masters might have proposed.

Within the larger association of the university, students found more intimate groups with which to live. These groups, called nations, were linked to the students' place of origin. At Bologna, for example, students incorporated themselves into two nations, the Italians and the non-Italians. Each nation protected its members, wrote statutes, and elected officers.

With few exceptions, masters and students were considered clerics. This had two important consequences. First, it meant that there were no university women. And second, it ensured that university men would be subject to church courts rather than the secular jurisdiction of towns or lords. Many universities could also boast generous privileges from popes and kings, who valued the services of scholars. The combination of clerical status and special privileges made universities virtually self-governing corporations within the towns. This sometimes led to friction. For example, when a student at Oxford was suspected of killing his mistress and the townspeople tried to punish him, the masters protested by refusing to teach and leaving town. Incidents such as this explain why historians speak of the hostility between "town" and "gown." Yet university towns depended on scholars to patronize local restaurants, shops, and hostels. Town and gown normally learned to negotiate with each other to their mutual advantage.

Religious Fervor and Dissent

Around the same time as universities were forming, renewed religious fervor led to the formation of new religious movements that galvanized individual piety and involved great numbers of laypeople. Unlike the reformed orders of the early twelfth century, which had fled the cities, the new religious groups of the late twelfth century embraced (and were embraced by) urban populations. Rich and poor, male and female joined these movements. They criticized the existing church as too wealthy, impersonal, and spiritually superficial. Intensely focused on the life of Christ, men and women in the late twelfth century made his childhood, agony, death, and presence in the Eucharist—the bread and wine that became the body and blood of Christ in the Mass—the most important experiences of their own lives.

For women in particular, common involvement in new sorts of piety was unprecedented, even in the monasteries of the past. Now beckoning to women of every age and every walk of life, the new piety spread beyond the convent, punctuating the routines of daily life with scriptural reading, fasting, and charity. Some of this intense religious response developed into official, orthodox movements within the church; other religious movements so threatened established doctrine that church leaders declared them heretical.

Francis and the Franciscans.   St. Francis (c. 1182–1226) founded the most famous orthodox religious movement—the Franciscans. Francis was a child of city life and commerce. Although expected to follow his well-to-do father in the cloth trade at Assisi in Italy, Francis began to experience doubts, dreams, and illnesses, which spurred him to religious self-examination. Eventually he renounced his family's wealth, dramatically marking the decision by casting off all his clothes and standing naked before his father, a crowd of spectators, and the bishop of

Assisi. Francis then put on a simple robe and went about preaching penance to anyone who would listen. Clinging to poverty as if, in his words, "she" were his "lady" (and thus borrowing the vocabulary of chivalry), he accepted no money, walked without shoes, and wore only one coarse tunic. Francis brought religious devotion out of the cloister and into the streets. Intending to follow the model of Christ, he received, as his biographers put it, a miraculous gift of grace: the stigmata, bleeding sores corresponding to the wounds Christ suffered on the cross.

By all accounts Francis was a spellbinding speaker, and he attracted many followers. Because they went about begging, they were called mendicants, from the Latin verb *mendicare,* meaning "to beg." Recognized as a religious order by the pope, the Brothers of St. Francis (or **friars**, from the Latin term for "brothers") spent their time preaching, ministering to lepers, and doing manual labor. Eventually they dispersed, setting up fraternal groups throughout Italy and then in France, Spain, the Holy Land, Germany, and England. Rather than reject the cities, the friars sought town life, preaching to crowds and begging for their daily bread. St. Francis converted both men and women. In 1212 an eighteen-year-old noblewoman, Clare, formed the nucleus of a community of pious women, which became the Order of the Sisters of St. Francis. At first the women worked alongside the friars; but both Francis and the church hierarchy disapproved of their activities in the world, and soon Franciscan sisters were confined to cloisters under the rule of St. Benedict.

The Beguines. Clare was one of many women who sought a new kind of religious expression. Some women joined convents; others became recluses, living alone, like hermits; still others sought membership in new lay sisterhoods. In northern Europe at the end of the twelfth century, laywomen who lived together in informal pious communities were called **Beguines.**♦ Without permanent vows or an established rule, the Beguines chose to be celibate (though they were free to leave and marry) and often made

their living by weaving cloth or working with the sick and old. Although their daily occupations were ordinary, the Beguines' spiritual lives were often emotional and ecstatic, infused with the combined imagery of love and religion so pervasive in both monasteries and courts. One renowned Beguine, Mary of Oignies♦ (1177–1213), who, like St. Francis, was said to have received stigmata, felt herself to be a pious mother entrusted with the Christ child. As her biographer, Jacques de Vitry, wrote, "Sometimes it seemed to her that for three or more days she held [Christ] close to her so that He nestled between her breasts like a baby, and she hid Him there lest He be seen by others."

Heresies. In addition to the orthodox religious movements that formed at the end of the twelfth century, there was a veritable explosion of ideas and doctrines that contradicted those officially accepted by church authorities and were therefore labeled heresies. Heresies were not new in the twelfth century. But the eleventh-century Gregorian reform had created for the first time in the West a clear church hierarchy headed by a pope who could enforce a single doctrine and discipline. Clearly defined orthodoxy meant that people in western Europe now perceived heresy as a serious problem. When intense religious feeling led to the fervent espousal of new religious ideas, established authorities often felt threatened and took steps to preserve their power.

Among the most visible heretics were dualists, who saw the world as being torn between two great forces, one good, the other evil. Already important in Bulgaria and Asia Minor, dualism became a prominent ingredient in religious life in Italy and the Rhineland by the end of the twelfth century. Another center of dualism was Languedoc,♦ an area of southern France; there the dualists were called **Albigensians,**♦ a name derived from the town of Albi.

Calling themselves "Christ's poor"—though modern historians have given them the collective name Cathars—these men and

♦**Beguine:** beh GEEN

♦**Oignies:** WAHN yee
♦**Languedoc:** lan guh DAHK
♦**Albigensians:** al buh JEHN see ans

women believed that the devil had created the material world. Therefore they renounced the world, abjuring wealth, meat, and sex. Their repudiation of sex reflected some of the attitudes of eleventh-century church reformers (whose orthodoxy, however, was never in doubt), while their rejection of wealth echoed the same concerns that moved St. Francis to embrace poverty. In many ways the dualists simply took these attitudes to an extreme; but unlike orthodox reformers, they also challenged the efficacy and legitimacy of the church hierarchy. Attracting both men and women, young and old, literate and un-lettered, and giving women access to all but the highest positions in their hierarchy, the dualists saw themselves as followers of Christ's original message. But the church called them heretics.

The church also condemned other, non-dualist groups as heretical, not on doctrinal grounds but because these groups allowed their lay members to preach, challenging the authority of the church hierarchy. In Lyon (in southeastern France) in the 1170s, for example, a rich merchant named Waldo decided to take literally the Gospel message "If you wish to be perfect, then go and sell everything you have, and give to the poor" (Matt. 19:21). The same message had inspired countless monks and would worry the church far less several decades later, when St. Francis established his new order. But when Waldo went into the street and gave away his belongings, announcing, "I am not really insane, as you think," he scandalized not only the bystanders but the church as well. Refusing to retire to a monastery, Waldo and his followers—men and women who called themselves the Poor of Lyons but were called Waldensians by their enemies—lived in poverty. They spent their time preaching, quoting the Gospel in the vernacular so that everyone would understand. But the papacy rebuffed Waldo's bid to preach freely; and his community—denounced, excommunicated, and expelled from Lyon—wandered to Languedoc, Italy, northern Spain, and the Moselle valley in Germany. Most were persecuted and eventually exterminated, but a few remnants survived and their descendents were absorbed into the sixteenth-century Protestant Reformation.

> **Review:** Why did guilds develop in medieval European cities?

❖ European Aggression Within and Without

New associations and allegiances gave European men and women a greater sense of identity, confidence, and assertiveness. Those perceived as different, however, became the focus of prejudice, intolerance, and aggression. The legacy of this period of aggression lasted long past the Middle Ages. It marked the beginning of anti-Semitism and the near end of Byzantium.

Classifying a particular group as a threat to society was a common method of asserting political and religious control within Europe in the second half of the twelfth century. Segregated from Christian society, vilified, and persecuted, those who were singled out, principally Jews and heretics, provided a rallying point for popes, princes, and Christian armies. Taking the offensive against those defined as different also meant launching campaigns to defeat people on Christendom's borders, a trend begun earlier with the First Crusade and the *reconquista* of Spain. In the early thirteenth century, wars against the Muslims to the south, the pagans to the north, and the Byzantine Empire to the east made warfare against "the infidel" a permanent feature of medieval life. Even western Europe did not escape: the crusade waged against the Albigensians starting in 1208 in southern France replaced the ruling class and eclipsed the court culture of the troubadours there.

Jews as Strangers

The sentiment against Jews grew over time. Ever since the Roman Empire had become Christian, Jews had been seen as different from Christians, and imperial law had prohibited them, for example, from owning Christian slaves or marrying Christian women. In the Islamic world, Jews were allowed to worship as they pleased, but they were, never-

NEW SOURCES, NEW PERSPECTIVES

The Cairo Geniza

What do historians know about the daily life of ordinary people in the Middle Ages? Generally speaking, very little. We have writings from the intellectual elite and administrative documents from monasteries, churches, and courts. But these rarely mention ordinary folk, and if they do, it is always from the standpoint of those who are not ordinary themselves. Glimpsing the concerns, occupations, and family relations of medieval people as they went about their daily lives is very difficult—except at old Cairo (now called Fustat), in Egypt.

Cairo is exceptional because of a cache of unusual sources that were discovered in the *geniza*, or "depository" of the Jewish synagogue near the city. Because their writings might include the name of God, members of the Jewish community left everything that they wrote, including their notes, letters, and even shopping lists, in the geniza to await ceremonial burial. Cairo was not the only place where this was the practice. But by chance at Cairo, the papers were left untouched in the depository and not buried. In 1890, when the synagogue was remodeled, workers tore down the walls of the geniza and discovered literally heaps of documents.

Many of these documents were purchased by American and English collectors and ended up in libraries in New York, Philadelphia, and Cambridge, England, where they remain. As is often the case in historical research, the questions that scholars ask are just as important as the sources themselves. At first, historians did not ask what the documents could tell them about everyday life. They wanted to know how to transcribe and read them; they wanted to study the evolution of their writing style (a dicipline called paleography). They also needed to organize the material. Dispersed among various libraries, the documents were a hodgepodge of lists, books, pages, and fragments. For example, the first page of a personal letter might be in one library, the second page in a completely different location. For decades, scholars were busy simply transcribing the documents with a view to printing and publishing their contents. Not until 1964 was a bibliography of these published materials made available.

Only then, when they knew where to find the sources and how to piece them together, did historians, most notably S. D. Goitein, begin to work through the papers for their historical interest. What Goitein learned through the remains of the

theless, heavily taxed. (See "New Sources, New Perspectives," above.) In western Europe, scholars had elaborated objections against Jewish doctrine in the twelfth century. Socially isolated and branded as outcasts, Jews served as scapegoats who helped define the larger western society as orthodox. Like lepers, whose disease cut them off from ordinary communities, Jews were believed to threaten the health of those around them. Lepers had to wear a special costume, were forbidden to touch children, could not eat with those not afflicted, and were housed in hospices called leprosaria.◆ Jews were similarly segregated from emerging Christian institutions, though they were not confined to hospices.

Forced off their lands during the eleventh century, most Jews ended up in the cities as craftsmen, merchants, or moneylenders, providing capital for the developing commercial society, whose Christian members were prohibited from charging interest, considering it to be usury, which was forbidden by the

◆**leprosaria:** leh pruh SAIR ee uh

geniza amplified historians' understanding of the everyday life of much of the Mediterranean world. He discovered a cosmopolitan community occupied with trade, schooling, marriages, divorces, poetry, litigation—all the common issues and activities of a middle-class society. For example, some documents showed that middle-class Jewish women disposed of their own property and that widows often reared and educated their children on their own.

The documents from the Cairo geniza also challenged accepted ideas. For example, historians tended to think that the special tax Christians and Jews were obliged to pay under Muslim rule was paltry, but that was because they did not realize how many Jews and Christians lived on the edge of poverty. This financial hardship is revealed in a letter found in the Cairo geniza, written on behalf of a man named Isaac by Moses Maimonides, who is best known as a major Jewish philosopher but was also a very down-to-earth leader of the Jews in Egypt, 1165–1204. Isaac seems not to have been registered as a taxpayer in any particular place, and Moses is here trying to get him registered in Minyat Ziftā, a provincial town where the rates were lower than elsewhere.

Kindly assist the bearer of this letter, Isaac of Der'a [a town in Morocco], for he is an acquaintance of mine. Ask the hāvēr [the local spiritual leader] to make the community care for him, so that he will get the money for his poll tax in your place. He has to pay two [poll taxes], one for

himself and one for his son. If possible, enable him to pay the tax in your town, Minyat Ziftā. For he is a newcomer and thus far has not paid anywhere. He is now on his way to Damietta on an errand important for me. On his way back, action should be taken for him according to your means.

So think twice the next time you throw away a piece of paper. If a historian of the year 3000 were to read your notes, lists, or letters, what would he or she learn about your culture?

QUESTIONS TO CONSIDER

1. Why do the documents in the geniza tell us about Muslim as well as Jewish life in medieval Cairo?
2. Why was it impossible for historians to begin to write about daily life in medieval Cairo immediately after the discovery of the geniza?

FURTHER READING

Constable, Olivia Remie. *Trade and Traders in Muslim Spain: The Commercial Realignment of the Iberian Peninsula, 900–1500.* 1994.

Goitein, S. D. *A Mediterranean Society: The Jewish Communities of the Arab World as Portrayed in the Documents of the Cairo Geniza.* 6 vols. 1967–1983.

Source: Quoted in S. D. Goitein, *A Mediterranean Society: The Jewish Communities of the Arab World as Portrayed in the Documents of the Cairo Geniza*, vol. 2: *The Community* (Berkeley: University of California Press, 1971), 382.

Gospel. The growing monopoly of the guilds, which prohibited Jewish members, pushed Jews out of the crafts and trades: in effect, Jews were compelled to become "usurers" because other fields were closed to them. Even with Christian moneylenders available (for some existed despite the prohibitions), lords, especially kings, borrowed from Jews and encouraged others to do so because, along with their newly asserted powers, European rulers claimed the Jews as their serfs and Jewish property as their own. In England a special royal exchequer of the Jews created

in 1194 collected unpaid debts due after the death of a Jewish creditor.

Even before 1194, Henry II had imposed new and arbitrary taxes on the Jewish community. Similarly in France, persecuting Jews and confiscating their property benefited both the treasury and the authoritative image of the king. For example, early in his reign Philip Augustus's agents surprised Jews at Sabbath worship in their synagogues and seized their goods, demanding that they redeem their own property for a large sum of money. Shortly thereafter, Philip declared forfeit 80 percent of all debts owed to Jews; the remaining 20 percent was to be paid directly to the king. About a year later, in 1182, Philip expelled the Jews from the Île-de-France:

> The king gave them leave to sell each his movable goods. . . . But their real estate, that is, houses, fields, vineyards, barns, winepresses, and such like, he reserved for himself and his successors, the kings of the French.

When he allowed the Jews to return, in 1198, he intended for them to be moneylenders or money changers exclusively, and their activities were to be taxed and monitored by officials.

Limiting Jews to moneylending in an increasingly commercial economy also served the interests of lords in debt to Jewish creditors. For example, in 1190, local nobles orchestrated a brutal attack on the Jews of York (in England) to rid themselves of their debts and of the Jews to whom they owed money. Churchmen too used credit in a money economy but resented the fiscal obligations it imposed. With their drive to create centralized territorial states and their desire to make their authority known and felt, powerful rulers of Europe—churchmen and laymen alike—exploited and coerced the Jews while drawing on and encouraging a wellspring of elite and popular anti-Jewish feeling. Although they must have looked exactly like Christians in reality, Jews now became clearly identified in sculpture and in drawings by markers such as conical hats and, increasingly, by demeaning features (see the illustration "Jews as the Other," on this page).

Attacks against Jews were inspired by more than resentment against Jewish money and the desire for power and control. They also, ironically, grew out of the codification of Christian religious doctrine and Christians' anxiety about their own institutions. For example, in the twelfth century, a newly rigorous definition of the Eucharist was promulgated. This held that when the bread and wine were blessed by the priest during Mass, they became the true body and blood of Christ. For some this meant, in effect, that Christ, wounded and bleeding, lay upon the altar. Reflecting Christian anxi-

Jews as the Other

In medieval art, people were often portrayed not as individuals but rather as "types" who could be identified by physical markers. In the second half of the twelfth century, Jews were increasingly portrayed as looking different from Christians. In this illustration, clerics are shown borrowing money from a Jew. What physical features do all the clerics have in common? (Be sure to look at the clothes as well as the hairstyles.) What distinguishes the laymen from the clerics? How do you know who is meant to be the Jew? In fact, Jews did not regularly wear this type of pointed hat until they were forced to do so in some regions of Europe in the late thirteenth century. *Bayerische Staatsbibliothek.*

eties about real flesh upon the altar, sensational stories, originating in clerical circles but soon widely circulated, told of Jews who secretly sacrificed Christian children in a morbid revisiting of the crucifixion of Jesus. This charge, called blood libel by historians, led to massacres of Jews in cities in England, France, Spain, and Germany. Jews had no rituals involving blood sacrifice at all, but they were convenient and vulnerable scapegoats for Christian guilt and anxiety.

Persecuting Heretics

Attacks against Jews coincided with campaigns against heretics those who deviated from the orthodox teachings of the Catholic Church. Heretical beliefs spread in regions where political control was less centralized, as, for example, in southern France. By the end of the twelfth century, church and secular powers combined to stamp out heresies.

Papal missions to Languedoc to address the heretical Albigensians led to the establishment of the Dominican order. Its founder, St. Dominic (1170–1221), recognized that preachers of Christ's word who came on horseback, followed by a crowd of servants and wearing fine clothes, had no moral leverage with their audience. Dominic and his followers, like their adversaries the Albigensians, rejected material riches and instead went about on foot, preaching and begging. They resembled the Franciscans both organizationally and spiritually and were also called friars.

Sometimes the church resorted to armed force in its campaign against heretics. In 1208, the murder of a papal legate in southern France prompted the pope to demand that northern princes take up the sword, invade Languedoc, wrest the land from the heretics, and populate it with orthodox Christians. This Albigensian Crusade (1209–1229) marked the first time the pope offered warriors fighting an enemy in Christian Europe all the spiritual and temporal benefits of a crusade to the Holy Land. The crusaders' monetary debts were suspended, and they were promised that their sins would be forgiven after forty days' service. Like all crusades, the Albigensian Crusade had political as well as religious dimensions. It pitted southern French princes who often had heretical sympathies against northern leaders eager to demonstrate their piety and win new possessions. After twenty years of fighting, leadership of the crusade was taken over in 1229 by the Capetian kings of France. Southern resistance was broken, and Languedoc was brought under the French crown.

The Albigensian Crusade, 1209–1229

Disastrous Crusades to the Holy Land

The second half of the twelfth century saw new crusades aimed at the Holy Land (Map 11.2). Following the crushing defeat of the crusaders in the Second Crusade, the Muslim hero Nur al-Din united Syria and presided over a renewal of Sunni Islam. His successor, Saladin (1138–1193), fought the Christian king of Jerusalem over Egypt, which Saladin ruled, together with Syria, by 1186. Caught in a pincer, Jerusalem fell to Saladin's armies in 1187. The Third Crusade was called to retake Jerusalem, and it marked a military and political watershed for the crusader states. The European outpost survived, but it was reduced to a narrow strip of land. Christians could continue to enter Jerusalem as pilgrims, but Islamic hegemony over the Holy Land would remain a fact of life for centuries.

Blood Libel Charges in France and England, c. 1100–1300

Adapted from Angus Mackay with David Ditchburn, eds., Atlas of Medieval Europe (New York: Routledge, 1997).

MAP 11.2 Crusades and Anti-Heretic Campaigns, 1150–1204
Europeans aggressively expanded their territory during the second half of the twelfth century. To the north, German knights pushed into Pomerania; to the south, Spanish warriors moved into the remaining strip of Islamic Iberia; to the east, new crusades were undertaken to shore up the tiny European outpost in the Holy Land. Although most of these aggressive activities had the establishment of Christianity as at least one motive, the conquest of Constantinople in 1204 had no such justification. It grew in part out of general European hostility toward Byzantium but mainly out of Venice's commercial ambitions.

The Third Crusade, 1189–1192. Called by the pope and led by the greatest rulers of Europe—Emperor Frederick I Barbarossa, Philip II of France, Leopold of Austria, and Richard I of England—the Third Crusade reflected political tensions among the European ruling class. Richard in particular seemed to cultivate enemies. The most serious of these was Leopold, whom he offended at the siege of Acre. But the apparent personal tensions indicated a broader hostility between the kings of England and France. Leopold, for example, was Philip's ally. On his return home, Richard was captured by Leopold and held for a huge ransom. He had good reason to write his plaintive poem bemoaning his captivity and the lost "love" of former friends.

The Third Crusade accomplished little and exacerbated tensions with Byzantium.

Frederick I went overland on the crusade, passing through Hungary and Bulgaria and descending into the Byzantine Empire. Before his untimely death by drowning in Turkey, he spent most of his time harassing the Byzantines.

The Fourth Crusade, 1202–1204. The hostilities that surfaced during the Third Crusade made it a dress rehearsal for the Fourth. Prejudice, religious zeal, and self-confidence had become characteristic of western European attitudes toward the Byzantine Greeks. The capture of Constantinople by the crusading army, recounted at the beginning of this chapter, was the logical outcome of these attitudes. Convinced of the rightness of their cause, the crusaders plundered, killed, and ransacked the city for treasure and relics. "Never," wrote a contemporary, "was so great an enterprise undertaken by any people since the creation of the world." When one crusader discovered a cache of relics, a chronicler recalled, "he plunged both hands in and, girding up his loins, he filled the folds of his gown with the holy booty of the Church." The Byzantines, naturally enough, saw the same events as a great tragedy. The bishop of Ephesus wrote:

> And so the streets, squares, houses of two and three stores, sacred places, nunneries, houses for nuns and monks, sacred churches, even the Great Church of God and the imperial palace, were filled with men of the enemy, all of them maddened by war and murderous in spirit. . . . [T]hey tore children from their mothers and mothers from their children, and they defiled the virgins in the holy chapels, fearing neither God's anger nor man's vengeance.

The pope decried the sacking of Constantinople, but he also took advantage of it, ordering the crusaders to stay there for a year to consolidate their gains. Plans to go on to the Holy Land were never carried out. The crusade leaders chose one of themselves—Baldwin of Flanders—to be Byzantine emperor, and he, the other princes, and the Venetians divided the empire among themselves. The new Latin empire of Constantinople lasted until 1261, when the Byzantines recaptured the city and some of its outlying territory.

Popes continued to call crusades to the Holy Land until the mid-fifteenth century, but the Fourth Crusade marked the last major mobilization of men and leaders for such an enterprise. Working against these expeditions were the new values of the late twelfth century, which placed a premium on the interior pilgrimage of the soul and valued rulers who stayed home to care for their people. The crusades served as an outlet for religious

Reconquista
In the north of Spain, the Christians adopted the figure of St. James, considered the Apostle to Spain, as the supernatural leader of their armies against the Muslims to the south. On this tympanum from the cathedral of St. James (Santiago) at Compostela, James is shown as a knight on horseback, holding a flag and a sword. He was known as "the Moor-slayer"—slayer of Muslims. Was the reconquista a holy war? How was it like the crusades, and how was it different? *Institut Amatller d'Art Hispanic, Barcelona.*

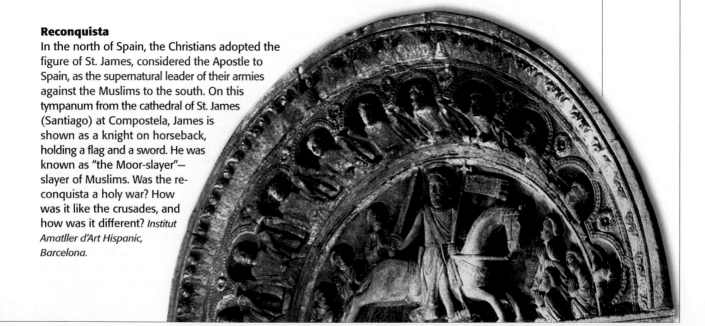

The Children's Crusade (1212)

In some regions intense lay piety led uncoordinated groups of young people to attempt making a pilgrimage to or capturing the Holy Land. Chroniclers recorded their activities, some with dismay, others with amusement or admiration. The account below comes from the Ebersheim Chronicle, *written in Germany.*

Unheard-of events appeal to us from their outset, challenging us to preserve their memory. A certain little boy named Nicholas, who came from the region of Cologne, spurred on a great gathering of children through some unknown counsel, claiming that he could walk across the waves of the sea without wetting his feet and could provide sufficient provisions for those following him. The rumor of such a marvelous deed resounded through the cities and towns, and however many heard him, boys or girls, they abandoned their parents, marked themselves as crusaders, and prepared to cross the sea. And so throughout all Germany and France an infinite number of serving-boys, hand-maids, and maidens followed their leader and came to Vienne, which is a city by the sea [*sic*]. There they were taken on board some ships, carried off by pirates, and sold to the Saracens. Some who tried to return home wasted away with hunger; and many girls who were virgins when they left were pregnant when they returned. Thus, one can clearly see that this journey issued from the deception of the devil because it caused so much loss.

Source: *Medieval Popular Religion 1000–1500: A Reader,* ed. John Shinners (Peterborough, Ontario: Broadview Press, 1997), 398.

---

fervor, self-confidence, ambition, prejudice, and aggression and were a dress rehearsal for the next wave of European colonization, which began in the sixteenth century. But they had in themselves very little lasting positive effect. They marginally stimulated the European economy, taught Europeans about the importance of stone fortifications, and inspired a vast literature of songs and chronicles. Such achievements must be weighed against the lives lost (on both sides) and the religious polarization and prejudices that the crusades fed on and fortified.

Victorious Crusades on the Borders of Europe

Armed expeditions against those perceived as infidels were launched not only against the Holy Land but also much nearer to home. In the second half of the twelfth century, the Spanish reconquista continued with increasing success and virulence while new wars of conquest were waged at the northern edge of Europe.

The Reconquista Triumphs, 1212.   In the second half of the twelfth century, Christian Spain achieved the political configuration that would last for centuries, dominated to the east by the kingdom of Aragon; in the middle by Castile, whose ruler styled himself emperor; and in the west by Portugal, whose ruler similarly transformed his title from prince to king. The three leaders competed for territory and power, but above all they sought an advantage against the Muslims to the south (Map 11.3).

Muslim disunity aided the Christian conquest of Spain. The Muslims of al-Andalus were themselves beset from the south by a new group of Muslims from North Africa, the Almohades.♦ Claiming religious purity, the Almohades declared their own holy war against the Andalusians. These simultaneous threats caused alliances in Spain to be based on political as well as religious considerations. The Muslim ruler of Valencia, for example, declared himself a vassal of the king of

---

♦**Almohades:** AL moh hadz

Castile and bitterly opposed the Almohades' expansion.

But the crusading ideal held no room for such subtleties. During the 1140s, armies under the command of the kings of Portugal, Castile, and Aragon scored resounding victories against Muslim cities. Enlisting the aid of crusaders on their way to the Holy Land in 1147, the king of Portugal promised land, plunder, and protection to all who would help him attack Lisbon. His efforts succeeded, and Lisbon's Muslim inhabitants fled or were slain. Its Mozarabic bishop (the bishop of the Christians under Muslim rule) was killed, and a crusader from England was put in his place. In the 1170s, when the Almohades conquered the Muslim south and advanced toward the cities taken by the Christians, their exertions had no lasting effect. In 1212, a Christian crusading army of Spaniards led by the kings of Aragon and Castile defeated the Almohades decisively at Las Navas de Tolosa.♦ "On their

MAP 11.3 The Reconquista, 1150–1212
Slowly but surely the Christian kingdoms of Spain encroached on al-Andalus, taking Las Navas de Tolosa, deep in Islamic territory, in 1212. At the center of this activity was Castile. It had originally been a tributary of León, but in the course of the twelfth century it became a power in its own right. (In 1230, León and Castile merged into one kingdom.) Meanwhile, the ruler of Portugal, who had also been dependent on León, began to claim the title of king, which was recognized officially in 1179, when he put Portugal under the protection of the papacy. Navarre was joined to Aragon until 1134, when it became, briefly, an independent kingdom. (In 1234 the count of Champagne came to the throne of Navarre, and thereafter its history was as much tied to France as to Spain.)

side 100,000 armed men or more fell in the battle," the king of Castile wrote afterward, "but of the army of the Lord . . . incredible though it may be, unless it be a miracle, hardly 25 or 30 Christians of our whole army fell. O what happiness! O what thanksgiving!" The decisive turning point in the reconquista was reached, though all of Spain came under Christian control only in 1492.

The Northern Crusades. Christians flexed their military muscle along Europe's northern frontiers as well. By the twelfth century, the peoples living along the Baltic coast—partly pagan, mostly Slavic- or Baltic-speaking—had learned to glean a living and a profit from the inhospitable soil and climate. Through fishing and trading, they supplied the rest of Europe and Russia with slaves, furs, amber, wax, and dried fish. Like the earlier Vikings, they combined commercial competition with outright raiding, so that the Danes and the Germans of Saxony both benefited and suffered from their presence. When St. Bernard began to preach the Second Crusade in Germany, he discovered that the Germans were indeed eager to attack the infidels—the ones right next door, that is. St. Bernard pressed the pope to add these northern heathens to the list of those against whom holy war should be launched and urged their conversion or extermination. Thus began the Northern Crusades, which continued intermittently until the early fifteenth century.

♦**Las Navas de Tolosa:** lahs NAH vahs zay toh LOH suh

MAPPING THE WEST Europe and Byzantium, c. 1215
The major transformation in the map of the West between 1150 and 1215 was the conquest of
Constantinople and the setting up of European rule there until 1261. The Byzantine Empire was
now a mere shell. A new state, Epirus, emerged in the power vacuum to dominate Thrace. Bulgaria once again gained its independence. If Venice had hoped to control the Adriatic by conquering Constantinople, it must have been disappointed, for Hungary became its rival over the
ports of the Dalmatian coast.

The Danish king Valdemar I (r. 1157–
1182) and the Saxon duke Henry the Lion led
the first phase of the Northern Crusades.
Their initial attacks on the Slavs were uncoordinated—in some instances they even
fought each other. But in key raids in the
1160s and 1170s, the two leaders worked together briefly to bring much of the region
west of the Oder River under their control.
They took some land outright—Henry the
Lion apportioned conquered territory to his
followers, for example—but more often the
Slavic princes surrendered and had their
territories reinstated once they became vassals of the Christian rulers. Meanwhile,

churchmen arrived: the Cistercians came
long before the first phase of fighting had
ended, confidently building their monasteries
to the very banks of the Oder River. Slavic
peasants surely suffered from the conquerors'
fire and pillage, but the Slavic ruling classes
ultimately benefited from the crusades. Once
converted to Christianity, they found it advantageous for both their eternal salvation
and their worldly profit to join new crusades
to areas still farther east.

Meanwhile German traders, craftspeople,
and colonists poured in, populating new
towns and cities along the Baltic coast and
dominating the shipping that had once been

controlled by non-Christians. The leaders of the crusades gave these townsmen some political independence but demanded a large share of the cities' wealth in return.

Although less well known than the crusades to the Holy Land, the Northern Crusades had far more lasting effects: they settled the Baltic region with German-speaking lords and peasants and forged a permanent relationship between northeastern Europe and its neighbors to the south and west. With the Baltic dotted with churches and monasteries and its peoples dipped into baptismal waters, the region would gradually adopt the institutions of western medieval society—cities, guilds, universities, castles, and manors. The Livs (whose region was eventually known as Livonia) were conquered by 1208, and their bishop sent knights northward to conquer the Estonians. The Prussians would be conquered with the cooperation between the Polish and German aristocracy; German peasants eventually settled Prussia. Only the Lithuanians managed to successfully resist western conquest, settlement, and conversion.

Review: In what ways was Europe's increasing hostility toward the Jews linked to its crusading movements?

Conclusion

In the second half of the twelfth century, Christian Europe expanded from the Baltic Sea to the southern Iberian peninsula. European settlements in the Holy Land, by contrast, were nearly obliterated. When western Europeans sacked Constantinople in 1204, Europe and the Islamic world became the dominant political forces in the West.

Powerful territorial kings and princes expressed their new self-confidence by supporting a lay vernacular culture that celebrated their achievements and power. They also began to establish institutions of bureaucratic authority. They hired staffs to handle their accounts, record acts, collect taxes, issue writs, and preside over courts. Flourishing cities, a growing money economy, and trade and manufacturing provided the finances necessary to support the per-

sonnel now hired by medieval governments. Clerical schools and, by the end of the twelfth century, universities became the training grounds for the new administrators.

Rulers were not alone in their quest to document, define, and institutionalize their power. The second half of the twelfth and the early thirteenth centuries were a great age of organization. Craft guilds and universities drew up statutes providing clearly specified rights, obligations, and privileges to their members. Developing out of the commercial revolution, such organizations in turn made commercial activities a permanent part of medieval life.

Religious associations also formed. Franciscans, Dominicans, and heretics—however dissimilar their beliefs—all rejected wealth and material possessions, revealing how deeply the commercial revolution had affected the moral life of some Europeans, who could not accept the profit motive inherent in a money economy. In emphasizing preaching, these religious associations showed that a lay population, already Christian, now yearned for a more intense and personal spirituality.

New piety, new exclusivity, and new power arose in a society both more confident and less tolerant. Crusaders fought more often and against an increasing variety of foes, not only in the Holy Land but also in Spain, in southern France, and on Europe's northern frontiers. With heretics voicing criticisms and maintaining their beliefs, the church, led by the papacy, now defined orthodoxy and declared dissenters its enemies. The Jews, who had once been fairly well integrated into the Christian community, were treated ambivalently, alternately used and abused. The Slavs and Balts became targets for new evangelical zeal; the Greeks became the butt of envy, hostility, and finally enmity. European Christians still considered Muslims arrogant heathens, and the deflection of the Fourth Crusade did not stem the zeal of popes to call for new crusades to the Holy Land.

Confident and aggressive, the leaders of Christian Europe in the thirteenth century would attempt to impose their rule, legislate morality, and create a unified worldview impregnable to attack. But this drive for order would be countered by unexpected varieties of thought and action, by political and social tensions, and by intensely personal religious quests.

Suggested References

Governments as Institutions

The medieval origins of modern state institutions is a traditional interest of historians studying the medieval period. Hudson explores the growth of royal institutions of justice. Baldwin gives a carefully focused account of the French experience. Bartlett, however, insists on the differences between medieval and modern politics.

Baldwin, John W. *The Government of Philip Augustus: Foundations of French Royal Power in the Middle Ages.* 1986.

Bartlett, Robert. *England under the Norman and Angevin Kings, 1075–1225.* 2000.

Evergates, Theodore, ed. *Aristocratic Women in Medieval France.* 1999.

Fuhrmann, Horst. *Germany in the High Middle Ages, c. 1050–1200.* Trans. T. Reuter. 1986.

Hudson, John. *The Formation of the English Common Law: Law and Society in England from the Norman Conquest to Magna Carta.* 1996.

Jordan, Karl. *Henry the Lion: A Biography.* Trans. P. S. Falla. 1986.

*Otto of Freising. *The Deeds of Frederick Barbarossa.* Trans. C. C. Mierow. 1953.

The Growth of a Vernacular High Culture

Chrétien de Troyes's *Yvain* is a good example of a twelfth-century romance, while troubadour poetry is collected in Goldin's anthology. Cheyette gives an illuminating account of one southern French ruler and her world, and Wheeler and Parsons's collection sheds light on another.

Bouchard, Constance B. *"Strong of Body, Brave and Noble": Chivalry and Society in Medieval France.* 1998.

Cheyette, Fredric L. *Ermengard of Narbonne and the World of the Troubadours.* 2001.

*Chrétien de Troyes. *Yvain: The Knight of the Lion.* Trans. Burton Raffel. 1987.

Crouch, David. *William Marshal: Court, Career, and Chivalry in the Angevin Empire, 1147–1219.* 1990.

*Goldin, Frederick. *Lyrics of the Troubadors and Trouvères: Original Texts, with Translations.* 1973.

The Song of Roland. Trans. P. Terry. 1965.

Wheeler, Bonnie and John Carmi Parsons, ed. *Eleanor of Aquitaine: Lord and Lady.* 2003.

New Lay and Religious Associations

The Little Flowers of Saint Francis gives a good idea of Franciscan spirituality, while the Franciscans are explored as part of wider religious, social, and economic movements in Little's study. Audisio's study looks sympathetically at one heretical group.

Audisio, Gabriel. *The Waldensian Dissent: Persecution and Survival, c. 1170–c. 1570.* Trans. Claire Davison. 1999.

Epstein, Steven. *Wage Labor and Guilds in Medieval Europe.* 1991.

Ferruolo, Stephen C. *The Origins of the University: The Schools of Paris and Their Critics, 1100–1215.* 1985.

The Little Flowers of Saint Francis. Trans. L. Sherley-Price. 1959.

Little, Lester K. *Religious Poverty and the Profit Economy in Medieval Europe.* 1978.

European Aggression Within and Without

Bartlett looks at expansion on all the frontiers of Europe, connecting movement outward with the creation of internal identity. Christiansen's book is the essential source for the Northern Crusades, Wakefield's for the Albigensian Crusade. There are numerous books on the crusades to the east; Riley-Smith gives a good overview. Tolan considers attitudes and prejudices.

Bartlett, Robert. *The Making of Europe: Conquest, Colonization, and Cultural Change, 950–1350.* 1993.

*Blood libel: **http://www.fordham.edu/halsall/source/1173williamnorwich.html**.

Christiansen, Eric. *The Northern Crusades.* 2nd ed. 1998.

Queller, Donald E., and Thomas F. Madden. *The Fourth Crusade: The Conquest of Constantinople, 1201–1204.* 2nd ed. 1999.

Riley-Smith, Jonathan. *The Crusades: A Short History.* 1987.

Tolan, John V. *Saracens: Islam in the Medieval European Imagination.* 2002.

Wakefield, Walter L. *Heresy, Crusade, and Inquisition in Southern France, 1100–1250.* 1974.

*Primary sources.

CHAPTER REVIEW

IMPORTANT EVENTS

1139–1153	Civil War in England
1152–1190	Reign of Frederick Barbarossa
1154–1189	Reign of King Henry II
1176	Battle of Legnano
1180–1223	Reign of Philip II Augustus
1182	Philip Augustus expels the Jews from the Île-de-France
1182–1226	Francis of Assisi
1189–1192	The Third Crusade
1202–1204	The Fourth Crusade
1204	Fall of Constantinople to Crusaders
1204	Philip takes Normandy, Anjou, Maine, Touraine, and Poitou from John
1209–1229	Albigensian Crusade
1212	Battle of Las Navas de Tolosa; triumph of the reconquista
1214	Battle of Bouvines
1215	Magna Carta

KEY TERMS

Albigensians (420)

Angevin (406)

Beguines (420)

chansons de geste (415)

chivalry (415)

common law (407)

friars (420)

guilds (417)

jongleur (414)

scutage (409)

troubadours (413)

REVIEW QUESTIONS

1. What new sources and institutions of power became available to rulers in the twelfth century?
2. What does the work of the troubadours and vernacular poets reveal about the nature of entertainment—its themes, its audience, its performers—in the twelfth century?
3. Why did guilds develop in medieval European cities?
4. In what ways was Europe's increasing hostility toward the Jews linked to its crusading movements?

MAKING CONNECTIONS

1. What were the chief differences that separated the ideals of the religious life in the period 1150–1215 from those of the period 1050–1150?
2. How did commercial interests enter into the crusading movements of the thirteenth century?

FOR FURTHER EXPLORATION

To assess your mastery of the material in this chapter, see the Online Study Guide at **bedfordstmartins.com/hunt**.

To read additional primary-source material from this period, see Chapter 11 in *Sources of The Making of the West*, Second Edition, Volume I.

The Medieval Search for Order and Harmony,
1215–1320

IN THE SECOND half of the thirteenth century, a wealthy patron asked a Parisian workshop specializing in manuscript illuminations to decorate Aristotle's *On the Length and Shortness of Life*. Most Parisian illuminators knew very well how to illustrate the Bible, liturgical books, and patristic writings. But Aristotle was a Greek who had lived before the time of Christ, and he was skeptical about the possibility of an afterlife. His treatise on the length of life ended with death. The workshop's artists did not care about this fact. They proceeded to illustrate Aristotle's work as if he had been a Christian and had believed in the immortal soul. As may be seen in the illustration opposite this page, for the first initial of the book (the large, highly decorated letter that opened the text), the artists depicted the Christian Mass for the dead, a rite that is performed for the eternal salvation of Christians. In this way, the artists subtly but surely forced Aristotle's treatise into the prevailing system of Christian belief and practice.

In the period 1215 to 1320, people at all levels, from workshop artisans to kings and popes, expected to find harmony, order, and unity in a world they believed was created by God. Sometimes, as in the case of the illumination made for Aristotle's work or in the Gothic cathedrals built in the cities, such harmony was made manifest. Because of this, historians sometimes speak of the "medieval synthesis." But often unity was a delusion. For example, kings and popes debated the limits of their power, while theologians fought over the place of reason in matters of faith. Discord continually threatened expectations of unity, harmony, and synthesis.

Christianizing Aristotle
This illumination was created for a thirteenth-century Latin translation of Aristotle's book *On the Length and Shortness of Life.* Although Aristotle did not believe in the eternity of the soul, the artists nevertheless placed a depiction of the Christian Mass for the dead in one of the book's initials, in this way revealing their conviction that the ancient teachings of Aristotle and Christian practice were harmonious. *Biblioteca Apostolica Vaticana.*

New institutions of power and control were created to ensure unity. The church set up tribunals to root out religious dissidents, and kings and other rulers extended their influence over their subjects. Yet these tribunals did not end heresy, and kings did not gain all the power that they wanted. Diversity and opposition continually threatened attempts at control from above.

❖ The Church's Mission of Reform

The church had long sought to reform the secular world. In the eleventh century, during the Gregorian reform, that effort had focused on the king. In the thirteenth century,

however, the church focused on purifying all of society. It looked to strengthened institutions of justice to combat heresy and heretics, and it supported preachers who would bring the official views of the church to the streets. In this way, the church attempted to reorder the world in the image of heaven, with everyone following one rule of God in order and harmony. To some degree, the church succeeded in this endeavor; but it also came up against the limits of control, as dissident voices and forces clashed with its vision.

Innocent III and the Fourth Lateran Council, 1215

Innocent III (r. 1198–1216), whose portrait appears on this page, was the most powerful, respected, and prestigious of medieval popes.

Innocent III
Pope Innocent III appears young, aristocratic, and impassive in this thirteenth-century fresco in the lower church of Sacro Speco, Subiaco, about thirty miles east of Rome and not far from Innocent's birthplace. Innocent claimed full power over the whole church, in any region. Moreover, he thought the pope had the right to intervene in any issue where sin might be involved—and that meant most matters. While these were only theoretical claims, difficult to put into practice given his meager resources and inefficient staff, Innocent was a major force in his day. *Scala/Art Resource, NY.*

1175	1200	1225
	◆ **1188** King Alfonso IX summons townsmen to the *cortes*	◆ **1240** Mongols capture Kiev
	◆ **1212–1250** Reign of Frederick II	
	◆ **1215** Fourth Lateran Council	
		◆ **1226–1270** Reign of Louis IX (St. Louis)
		◆ **1232** Frederick II, "Statute in Favor of the Princes"
		◆ **1233** First permanent Inquisition

He was the pope who allowed St. Francis's group of impoverished followers to become a new church order, and he was the pope who called the Fourth Crusade, the last to mobilize a large force drawn from every level of European society. The first pope to be trained at universities, Innocent studied theology at Paris and law at Bologna. From theology, he learned to tease new meaning out of canonical writings to magnify papal authority: he thought of himself as ruling in the place of Christ the King, with kings and emperors existing to help the pope. From law, Innocent gained his conception of the pope as lawmaker and of law as an instrument of moral reformation.

Innocent utilized the traditional method of declaring church law: a council. Presided over by Innocent, the Fourth Lateran Council (1215) attempted to regulate all aspects of Christian life. The comprehensive legislation it produced in only three days—the pope and his committees had prepared almost all the provisions beforehand—aimed at reforming both the clergy and the laity. Innocent and the other members of the council hoped in this way to create a society united under the authority of the church and its priesthood. They expected that Christians, lay and clerical alike, would work together harmoniously to achieve the common goal of salvation. They

Host Mold

One of the most important decisions of the Fourth Lateran Council was to declare that the body and blood of Christ were "transubstantiated" in the Eucharist: that is, they were transformed into the actual body and blood of Christ. Veneration of the host began to supplant veneration of saints, and increasingly people desired to gaze at the host. Albertus Magnus wrote: "Showing the host to good people impels them to the good." Molds such as the one shown here, made in the fourteenth century, impressed inspiring images into the bread, in this case the image of Christ surrounded by the twelve apostles.

did not anticipate either the sheer variety of responses to their message or the persistence of those who defied it altogether.

The Laity and the Sacraments. For laymen and laywomen, perhaps the most important canons of the Fourth Lateran Council concerned the sacraments, the rites the church believed Jesus had instituted to confer sanctifying grace. Building on the reforms of the eleventh century, the council made the obligations that the sacraments imposed on the laity more precise and detailed. One canon required Christians to attend Mass and to confess their sins to a priest at

◆ **1265** English commons summoned to Parliament

◆ **1265–1321** Dante Alighieri

◆ **1273** Thomas Aquinas, *Summa Theologiae*

| 1250 | 1275 | 1300 | 1325 |

◆ **1302** First Meeting of the French Estates

◆ **1309–1378** Avignon Papacy (Babylonian Captivity)

least once a year. The increasing importance of the Eucharist as God's potent salvific instrument was reinforced by the council's definition:

> [Christ's] body and blood are truly contained in the sacrament of the altar under the forms of bread and wine, the bread and wine having been changed in substance [transubstantiated], by God's power, into his body and blood, so that in order to achieve this mystery of unity we receive from God what he received from us. Nobody can effect this sacrament except a priest who has been properly ordained according to the church's keys, which Jesus Christ himself gave to the apostles and their successors.

The Council's emphasis on this moment of transformation strengthened the role of the priest, for only he could celebrate this mystery.

Other canons of the Fourth Lateran Council codified the traditions of marriage. The church declared that it had the right to discover any impediments to a union, and it claimed jurisdiction over any marital disputes. The canons further insisted that children conceived within clandestine or forbidden marriages be declared illegitimate; they were not to inherit from their parents or become priests.

The impact of these provisions was perhaps less dramatic than church leaders hoped. Well-to-do London fathers included their bastard children in their wills. On English manors, sons conceived out of wedlock regularly took over their parents' land. Men and women continued to marry in secret, and even churchmen had to admit that the consent of both parties made any marriage valid. Nevertheless, many men and women took to heart the obligation to take communion (the Eucharist consecrated by a priest) and confess once a year, and priests proceeded to call out the bans (announcements of marriages) to discover any impediments to them.

The Labeling of the Jews. Innocent III had wanted the council to condemn Christian men who had sexual intercourse with Jewish women and then claimed ignorance as their excuse. But, building on the anti-Jewish feelings that had been mounting throughout the twelfth century, the Fourth Lateran Council went even further, requiring all Jews to advertise their religion by some outward sign: "We decree that [Jews] of either sex in every Christian province at all times shall be distinguished from other people by the character of their dress in public."

As with all church rules, these took effect only when local rulers enforced them. In many instances, they did so with zeal, not so much because they were eager to humiliate Jews but rather because they could make money selling exemptions to Jews who were willing to pay to avoid the requirements. Nonetheless, sooner or later Jews almost everywhere had to wear a badge as a sign of their second-class status.

In southern France and in a few places in Spain, Jews were supposed to wear round badges. In England, Oxford required a badge, while Salisbury demanded that Jews wear special clothing. In Vienna they were told to put on pointed hats (see the illustration on page 424).

The Suppression of Heretics. The Fourth Lateran Council's longest decree blasted heretics: "Those condemned as heretics shall be handed over to the secular authorities for punishment." If the secular authority did not "purge his or her lands of heretical filth," the heretic was to be excommunicated. If he or she had vassals, they were to be released from their oaths of fealty. The land of heretics were to be taken over by orthodox Christians.

Rulers heeded these declarations. Already some had taken up arms against heretics in the Albigensian Crusade (1209–1229). As a result of this crusade, southern France, which had been the home of most Albigensians, came under French royal control. The continuing presence of heretics there and elsewhere led church authorities inspired by the Fourth Lateran Council to set up a court of papal inquisitors. The Inquisition became permanent in 1233.

The Inquisition

The word *inquisition* simply means "inquiry"; the method had long been used by secular rulers to summon people together, either to discover facts or to uncover and punish crimes. In its zeal to end heresy and save souls, the thirteenth-century church used the **Inquisition** to ferret out "heretical depravity." Calling suspects to testify, inquisitors, aided by secular authorities, rounded up virtually entire villages and interrogated everyone. (See "New Sources, New Perspectives," page 440.)

First the inquisitors typically called the people of a district to a "preaching," where they gave a sermon and promised clemency to those who confessed their heresy promptly. Then, at a general inquest, they questioned each man and woman who seemed to know something about heresy: "Have you ever seen any heretics...? Have you heard them preach? Attended any of their ceremonies? Adored heretics?" The judges assigned relatively lenient penalties to those who were not aware that they held heretical beliefs and to heretics who quickly recanted. But unrepentant heretics were punished severely because the church believed that such people threatened the salvation of all. (See "Taking Measure," on this page.)

In the thirteenth century, for the first time, long-term imprisonment became a tool to repress heresy, even if the heretic confessed. "It is our will," wrote one tribunal, "that [Raymond Maurin and Arnalda, his wife,] because they have rashly transgressed against God and holy church . . . be thrust into perpetual prison to do [appropriate] penance, and we command them to remain there in perpetuity." The inquisitors also used imprisonment to force people to recant, to give the names of other heretics, or to admit a plot. As the quest for religious control spawned wild fantasies of conspiracy, the inquisitors pinned their fears on real people.

Lay Piety

The church's zeal to reform the laity was matched by the desire of many laypeople to become more involved in their religion. They flocked to hear the preaching of friars and took what they heard to heart. Some women found new outlets for their piety by focusing on the Eucharist.

Preaching Friars and Receptive Townspeople. The friars made themselves a permanent feature of the towns. At night they slept in their convents, but they spent their

TAKING MEASURE

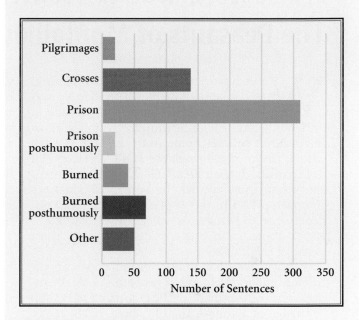

Sentences Imposed by an Inquisitor, 1308–1323
How harsh was the Inquisition? Did its agents regularly burn people alive? How frequently did they imprison people, or order them to go on pilgrimage or wear crosses on their clothing? Statistical data to answer these sorts of questions are normally lacking for the medieval period. But there are exceptions. One comes from a register of offenses and punishments kept by Bernard Gui, an inquisitor in Languedoc from 1308 to 1323. Of 633 punishments handed down by Gui's tribunal, only a relatively small number of people were burned alive. (Those "burned posthumously" would have been burned alive but died beforehand.) Nearly half of the guilty were sentenced to prison, usually for life. (Some were sent to prison posthumously; that is, they would have gone to prison had they not died in the meantime.) Many historians conclude that the Inquisition was not particularly harsh, for capital punishment at the time was regularly meted out to criminals under secular law. *From J. Given, "A Medieval Inquisitor at Work," in* Portraits of Medieval and Renaissance Living, *ed. S. K. Cohn and S. A. Epstein (Ann Arbor: University of Michigan Press, 1996), 215.*

days preaching. So too did other men, often trained in the universities and willing to take to the road to speak to throngs of townsfolk. When Berthold,♦ a Franciscan who traveled the length and breadth of Germany giving

♦**Berthold:** BEHR tohlt

NEW SOURCES, NEW PERSPECTIVES

The Peasants of Montaillou

While historians can know from material evidence how medieval peasants lived and worked, it is nearly impossible to find out what peasants thought. Almost all of our written sources come from the elite classes who, if they noticed peasants at all, certainly did not care about their ideas. How, then, can historians hear and record the voices of peasants themselves? Until the 1960s, historians did not much care to hear those voices. They wanted to know about economic structures rather than peasant mentalities.

That is why historians did not notice an extremely important source of peasant voices, the Inquisition register made at the command of Bishop Fournier of Pamiers in the years 1318–1325. Fournier was a zealous anti-heretic, and when he became bishop of a diocese that harbored many Albigensians, he put the full weight of his office behind rounding them up. He concentrated on one particularly "heretic-infested" village, Montaillou, in the south of France near the Spanish border. Interrogating a total of 114 people, including 48 women, over seven years, he committed their confessions and testimony to parchment with a view to punishing those who were heretics. Fournier was not interested in the peasants' "voices": he wanted to know their religious beliefs and every other detail of their lives and thoughts. However, the long-term result of Fournier's zealous inquest—though he would not be happy to hear it—was to preserve the words of a whole village of peasants, shepherds, artisans, and shopkeepers.

Fournier's register sat in the Vatican archives for centuries, gathering dust, until it was transcribed and published in 1965. Only in 1975 was its great potential for peasant history made clear; in that year, Emmanuel Le Roy Ladurie published *Montaillou: The Promised Land of Error*, which for the first time made a medieval peasant village come to life.

Le Roy Ladurie's book reveals the myths, beliefs, rivalries, tensions, love affairs, tendernesses, and duplicities of a small peasant community where all the people, even those who were better off, worked with their hands; where wealth was calculated by the size of a family's herd of livestock; and where the church's demands for tithes seemed outrageously unfair.

The register shows a community torn apart by the opportunities the Inquisition gave to informers. The village priest, from a well-off family, was very clear about why he was denouncing his parishioners. He liked the Albigensians, he said (he was probably one himself), but "I want to be revenged on the peasants of Montaillou, who have done me harm, and I will avenge myself in every possible way." But the register also shows a community united by love: parents cared about their children, husbands and wives loved one another, and illicit lovers were caught up in passion. One affair took place between the village priest and Béatrice, a woman of somewhat higher rank. The priest courted her for half a year, and after she gave in, they met two or three nights a week. In the end, though, Béatrice decided to marry someone else and left the village.

Béatrice was not the only independent-minded person in Montaillou. Many people there were indeed heretics in the sense that their beliefs defied the teachings of the church. But they called themselves "good Christians." Other villagers re-

sermons, came to a town, a high tower was set up for him outside the city walls. A pennant advertised his presence and let people know which way the wind would blow his voice. St. Anthony of Padua preached in Italian to huge audiences that had lined up hours in advance to be sure they would have a place to hear him.

Townspeople flocked to such preachers because they wanted to know how the Christian message applied to their daily lives. They were concerned, for example, about mained in the Catholic fold. And still others in the region had their own ideas, as may be seen from Raimond de l'Aire's testimony.

Fournier's register became a "new" source because Le Roy Ladurie had new questions and sought a way to answer them, treating his evidence the way ethnographers treat reports by native peoples they have interviewed. Today some historians question Le Roy Ladurie's approach, arguing that an Inquisition record cannot be handled in the same way that ethnographers consider information from their informants. For example, they point out that the words of the peasants were translated from Occitan, the language they spoke, to Latin for the official record. What readers hear are not the voices of the peasants but rather their ideas filtered through the vocabulary and summaries of the elite. Moreover, the peasants called before the tribunal were held in prison, feared for their lives, and were forced to talk about events that had taken place ten or more years earlier. In light of these circumstances, to what extent is their testimony a direct window onto their lives? Nevertheless, the register remains a precious source for learning at least something about what ordinary people thought and felt in a small village about seven hundred years ago.

Raimond de l'Aire's Testimony   One of the witnesses recorded by Jacques Fournier was Raimond de l'Aire. He was not from Montaillou but rather from Tignac, a small town in Fournier's diocese. In this testimony he reports on the beliefs of one of his acquaintances.

> An older man told [Raimond de l'Aire] that a mule has a soul as good as a man's; "and from this belief he had by himself deduced that his own soul and those of other men are nothing but blood, because when a person's blood is taken away, he dies. He also believed that a dead person's soul and body both die, and that after death nothing human remains. . . . From this he believed that the human soul after death [is] neither good nor evil, and that there is no hell or paradise in another world where human souls are rewarded or punished."

QUESTIONS TO CONSIDER

1. In what ways are modern court cases like the Inquisition register of Fournier? In what ways are they unlike such a source? Could you use modern court cases to reconstruct the life of a community?
2. What are the advantages and the pitfalls of using a source such as the register for historical research?
3. Do you think that Raimond might have made up his testimony? Why or why not?
4. What does this testimony suggest about the impact of church doctrines in the French countryside?

FURTHER READING

Boyle, Leonard. "Montaillou Revisited: Mentalité and Methodology." In J. A. Raftis, ed., *Pathways to Medieval Peasants*. 1981.

Le Roy Ladurie, Emmanuel. *Montaillou: The Promised Land of Error*. 1978. The original French version was published in 1975.

Resaldo, Renato. "From the Door of His Tent: The Fieldworker and the Inquisitor." In James Clifford and George E. Marcus, eds., *Writing Culture: The Poetics and Politics of Ethnography*. 1986.

Source: *Heresy and Authority in Medieval Europe: Documents in Translation*, ed. Edward Peters (Philadelphia: University of Pennsylvania Press, 1980), 253.

the ethics of moneymaking, sex in marriage, and family life. In turn, the preachers represented the front line of the church. They met the laity on their own turf and taught them to shape their behaviors to church teachings.

Laypeople further tied their lives to the mendicants, particularly the Franciscans, by becoming **tertiaries**.♦ They adopted the practices of the friars—prayer and works of

♦**tertiaries:** Tur shee eh reez

Friars and Usurers

As the illustration on page 424 reveals, clerics sometimes borrowed money. The friars had a different attitude. St. Francis, son of a merchant, refused to touch money altogether. Instead, he and his friars begged for food and shelter. Even when their numbers grew and they began forming communities and living in monasteries, the friars still insisted on personal poverty, while ministering to city dwellers, who had to deal with money in some way to make a living. In this illumination from about 1250, a Franciscan (in light-colored robes) and a Dominican (in black) reject offers from two usurers, whose profession they are thus shown to condemn. Other friars, including Thomas Aquinas, worked out justifications for some kinds of moneymaking professions, though not usury.

Bibliothèque Nationale, Paris.

churching—the ritual of purification after a pregnancy. In the cities, working women scratched out a meager living. They sometimes made pilgrimages to relic shrines to seek help or cures. Religion was a part of these women's lives, but it did not dominate them.

For some urban women, however, religion was the focus of life, and the church's attempt to define and control the Eucharist had some unintended results. The new emphasis on the holiness of the transformed wine and bread induced some of these pious women to eat nothing but the Eucharist. One such woman, Angela of Foligno,◆ reported that the consecrated bread swelled in her mouth, tasting sweeter than any other food. For these women, eating the Eucharist was truly eating God. This is how they understood the church's teaching that the consecrated bread was actually Christ's body. In the minds of these holy women, Christ's crucifixion was the literal sacrifice of his body, to be eaten by sinful men and women as the way to redeem themselves and others. Renouncing all other foods became part of a life of service, because many of these devout women gave the poor the food that they refused to eat.

These women both accepted and challenged the pronouncements of the Fourth Lateran Council about the meaning of the Eucharist. They agreed that only priests could say Mass, but some of them bypassed their own priests, receiving the Eucharist (as they explained) directly from Christ in the form of a vision. Although men dominated the institutions that governed political, religious, and economic affairs, these women found ways to control their own lives and to some extent the lives of those around them, both those whom they served and those they

charity, for example—while continuing to live in the world, raising families and tending to the normal tasks of daily life, whatever their occupation. Even kings and queens became tertiaries.

The Piety of Women. All across Europe, women in the thirteenth century sought outlets for their intense piety. As in previous centuries, powerful families founded new nunneries, especially within towns and cities. On the whole, these were set up for the daughters of the very wealthy. Ordinary women found different modes of religious expression. Some sought the lives of quiet activity and rapturous mysticism of the Beguines, others the lives of charity and service of women's mendicant orders, and still others domestic lives of marriage and family punctuated by religious devotions. Elisabeth of Hungary, who married a German prince at the age of fourteen, raised three children. At the same time, she devoted her life to fasting, prayer, and service to the poor.

Many women were not as devout as Elisabeth. In the countryside, they cooked their porridge, brewed their ale, and raised their children. They attended church regularly, but only on major feast days or for

◆**Angela of Foligno:** AN jehl uh (of) foh LEE nyoh

A Lady and Her Loving Falcon
This sumptuous velvet-and-silk pouch, made by an embroideress in about 1320, shows a lady in the position of falconer. The falcon—a bird ordinarily used as an aid in hunting—is here depicted as her lover. He is flying toward her to place a crown of greenery on her head, while she touches him tenderly on the shoulder. In her other hand she holds the leash with which she trained him. © *Musée de Tissus, Lyon.*

lived with. Typically involved with meal preparation and feeding, like other women of the time, these holy women found a way to use their control over ordinary food to gain new kinds of social and religious power that could force the clergy to confront female piety.

Review: How did people respond to the teachings and laws of the church in the early thirteenth century?

❖ Cultural Harmonies

Just as the church saw itself as regulating worldly life in accordance with God's plan for salvation, so contemporary thinkers, writers, musicians, and artists sought to harmonize the secular with the sacred. Scholars wrote treatises that reconciled faith with reason, poets and musicians sang of the links between heaven and human life on earth, and artists expressed the same ideas in stone and sculpture. Even in the face of many contradictions, all of these groups were largely successful in communicating a harmonious image of the world.

Scholasticism: Harmonizing Faith and Reason

Scholasticism was the method of logical inquiry and exposition pioneered by Peter Abelard and other twelfth-century teachers. In the thirteenth century, the method was used to summarize and reconcile all knowledge. Many of the thirteenth-century scholastics (the name given to the scholars who used this method) were members of the Dominican and Franciscan orders and taught in the universities. On the whole, they were confident that knowledge obtained through the senses and reason was compatible with the knowledge derived from faith and revelation. One of their goals was to demonstrate this harmony. The scholastic **summa**, or summary of knowledge, was a systematic exposition of the answer to every possible question about human morality, the physical world, society, belief, action, and theology. Another goal of the scholastics was to preach the conclusions of these treatises. As one scholastic put it, "First the bow is bent in study, then the arrow is released in preaching": first you study the summa and then you hit your mark—convert people—by preaching. Many of the preachers who came to the towns were students and disciples of scholastic university teachers.

The method of the summa borrowed much of the vocabulary and many of the rules of logic long ago outlined by Aristotle. Even though Aristotle was a pagan, scholastics considered his coherent and rational body of thought the most perfect that human reason alone could devise. Because they had the benefit of Christ's revelations, the scholastics considered themselves able to take Aristotle's philosophy one necessary step further and reconcile human reason with Christian faith. Full of confidence in their method and conclusions, scholastics embraced the world and its issues.

Some scholastics considered questions about the natural world. Albertus Magnus

(c. 1200–1280), a major theologian, also contributed to the fields of biology, botany, astronomy, and physics. His reconsideration of Aristotle's views on motion led the way to distinctions that helped scientists in the sixteenth and seventeenth centuries arrive at the modern notion of inertia.

St. Thomas Aquinas (c. 1225–1274) was perhaps the most famous scholastic. Huge of build, renowned for his composure in debate, Thomas came from a noble Neapolitan family that had hoped to see him become a powerful bishop rather than a poor university professor. When he was about eighteen years old, he thwarted his family's wishes and joined the Dominicans. Soon he was studying at Cologne with Albertus Magnus. At thirty-two he became a master at the University of Paris.

Like many other scholastics, Thomas considered Aristotle "the Philosopher," the authoritative voice of human reason, which he sought to reconcile with divine revelation in a universal and harmonious scheme. In 1273, he published his monumental *Summa Theologiae* (sometimes called the *Summa Theologica*), which covered all important topics, human and divine. He divided these topics into questions, exploring each one thoroughly and systematically and concluding with a decisive position and a refutation of opposing views. Yet even Thomas departed from Aristotle, who had explained the universe through human reason alone. In Thomas's view, God, nature, and reason were in harmony, so Aristotle's arguments could be used to explore both the human and the divine order, but with some exceptions. "Certain things that are true about God wholly surpass the capability of human reason, for instance that God is three and one," Thomas wrote. But he thought these exceptions rarely occurred.

Many of Thomas's questions spoke to the keenest concerns of his day. He asked, for example, whether it was lawful to sell something for more than its worth. Thomas arranged his argument systematically, quoting first authorities that seemed to declare every sort of selling practice, even deceptive ones, to be lawful. This was the *sic* (or "yes") position. Then he quoted an authority that opposed selling something for more than its worth. This was the *non*. Following that, he gave his own argument, prefaced by the words "I answer that." Unlike Abelard, whose *Sic et Non* inspired this method but left differences unresolved, Thomas wanted to harmonize the two points of view, and so he pointed out that price and worth depended on the circumstances of the buyer and seller and concluded that charging more than a seller had originally paid could be legitimate at times.

For townspeople engaged in commerce and worried about biblical prohibitions on moneymaking, Thomas's ideas about selling practices addressed burning questions. Hoping to go to heaven as well as reap the profits of their business ventures, laypeople listened eagerly to preachers who delivered their sermons in the vernacular but who based their ideas on the Latin summae◆ of Thomas and other scholastics. Thomas's conclusions aided townspeople in justifying their worldly activities.

The work of the thirteenth-century scholastics to unite the secular with the sacred continued for another generation after Thomas. Yet at the beginning of the fourteenth century, fissures began to appear. In the summae of John Duns Scotus (c. 1266–1308), for example, the world and God were less compatible. John, whose name Duns Scotus betrays his Scottish origin, was a Franciscan who taught at both Oxford and Paris. For John, human reason could know truth only through the "special illumination of the uncreated light," that is, by divine illumination. But unlike his predecessors, John believed that this illumination came not as a matter of course but only when God chose to intervene. John—and others—experienced God as sometimes willful rather than reasonable. Human reason could not soar to God; God's will alone determined whether or not a person could know Him. In this way, John separated the divine and secular realms.

Scholastics like Thomas were enormous optimists. They believed that everything had a place in God's scheme of things, that the world was orderly, and that human beings could make rational sense of it. This optimism filled the classrooms, spilled into

◆**summae:** SU my

the friars' convents, and found its way to the streets where artisans and shopkeepers lived and worked. Scholastic philosophy helped give ordinary people a sense of purpose and a guide to behavior. Yet even among scholastics, unity was elusive. In his own day, Thomas was accused of placing too much emphasis on reason, and later scholastics argued pessimistically that reason could not find truth through its own faculties and energies. Once again, harmony was challenged by discord.

New Syntheses in Writing and Music

Thirteenth-century writers and musicians, like scholastics, presented complicated ideas and feelings as harmonious and unified syntheses. Writers explored the relations between this world and the next; musicians found ways to bridge sacred and secular forms of music.

Vernacular Literature Comes of Age. Vernacular literature may be said to have reached its full development with the work of Dante Alighieri♦ (1265–1321), who harmonized the scholastic universe with the mysteries of faith and the poetry of love. Born in Florence in a time of political turmoil, Dante incorporated the major figures of history and his own day into his most famous poem, the *Commedia*, written between 1313 and 1321. Later known as the *Divine Comedy*, Dante's poem describes the poet taking an imaginary journey from Hell to Purgatory and finally to Paradise.

The poem is an allegory in which every person and object must be read at more than one level. At the most literal level, the poem is about Dante's travels. At a deeper level, it is about the soul's search for meaning and enlightenment and its ultimate discovery of God in the light of divine love. Just as Thomas Aquinas thought that Aristotle's logic could lead to important truths, so Dante used the pagan poet Virgil as his guide through Hell and Purgatory. And just as Thomas believed that faith went beyond reason to even higher truths, so Dante found a new guide representing earthly love to lead

him through most of Paradise. That guide was Beatrice, a Florentine girl with whom Dante had fallen in love as a boy and whom he never forgot. But only faith, in the form of the divine love of the Virgin Mary, could bring Dante to the culmination of his journey—a blinding and inexpressibly awesome vision of God:

> What I then saw is more than tongue can say.
> Our human speech is dark before the vision.
> The ravished memory swoons and falls away.

Dante's poem electrified a wide audience. By elevating one dialect of Italian—the language that ordinary Florentines used in their everyday life—to a language of exquisite poetry, Dante was able to communicate the scholastics' harmonious and optimistic vision of the universe in an even more exciting and accessible way. So influential was his work that it is no exaggeration to say that modern Italian is based on Dante's Florentine dialect.

Other writers of the period used different methods to express the harmony of heaven and earth. The anonymous author of the *Quest of the Holy Grail* (c. 1225), for example, wrote about the adventures of some of the knights of King Arthur's Round Table to convey the doctrine of transubstantiation and the wonder of the vision of God. In *The Romance of the Rose*, begun by one author (Guillaume de Lorris, a poet in the romantic tradition) and finished by another (Jean de Meun, a poet in the scholastic tradition), a lover seeks the rose, his true love. In the long dream that the poem describes, the narrator's search for the rose is thwarted by personifications of Love, Shame, Reason, Abstinence, and so on. They present him with arguments for and against love. In the end, sexual love is made part of the divine scheme—and the lover plucks the rose. (See "The Debate between Reason and the Lover," page 446.)

The Motet. Musicians, like poets, developed new compositions that bridged sacred and secular subjects in the thirteenth and fourteenth centuries. This connection appears in the most distinctive musical form of the thirteenth century, the **motet**♦ (from the

♦**Dante Alighieri:** DAHN tay ahl eeg YEH ree

♦**motet:** moh TEHT

The Debate between Reason and the Lover

Jean de Meun's portion of the Romance of the Rose *is organized as a dialogue between the Lover and various figures he meets on his quest for the rose. Reason gives this jaundiced definition of love:*

If I know anything of love, it is
Imaginary illness freely spread
Between two persons of opposing sex,
Originating from disordered sight,
Producing great desire to hug and kiss
And see enjoyment in a mutual lust.
To which the lover responds:
Madam, you would betray me; should I scorn
All folk because the God of Love now frowns?
Shall I no more experience true love,
But live in hate? Truly, so help me God,
Then were I moral sinner worse than thief!

Source: Guillaume de Lorris and Jean de Meun, *The Romance of the Rose,* trans. Harry W. Robbins (New York: Dutton, 1962), 97, 102.

French *mot,* meaning "word"). The motet is an example of **polyphony,**♦ music that consists of two or more melodies performed simultaneously. Before about 1215, most polyphony was sacred; purely secular polyphony was not common before the fourteenth century. The motet, a unique merging of the sacred and the secular, evidently originated in Paris, the center of scholastic culture as well.

The typical thirteenth-century motet has two or three melody lines (or "voices"). The lowest, usually from a liturgical chant melody, has only one or two words; it may have been played on an instrument rather than sung. The remaining melodies have different texts, either Latin or French (or one of each), which are sung simultaneously. Latin texts are usually sacred, whereas French

♦**polyphony:** puh LIH fuh nee

ones are secular, dealing with themes such as love and springtime. The motet thus weaves the sacred (the chant melody in the lowest voice) and the secular (the French texts in the upper voices) into a sophisticated tapestry of words and music. Like the scholastic summae, the motets were written by and for a clerical elite. Yet they incorporated the music of ordinary people, such as the calls of street vendors and the boisterous songs of students. In turn they touched the lives of everyone, for polyphony influenced every form of music, from the Mass to popular songs that entertained and diverted laypeople and churchmen alike.

Complementing the motet's complexity was the development of a new notation for rhythm. By the eleventh century, musical notation could indicate pitch but had no way to denote the duration of the notes. Music theorists of the thirteenth century, however, developed increasingly precise methods to indicate rhythm. Franco of Cologne, for example, in his *Art of Measurable Song* (c. 1280), used different shapes to mark the number of beats each note should be held. His system became the basis of modern musical notation. Because each note could now be allotted a specific duration, written music could express new and complicated rhythms. The music of the thirteenth century reflected both the melding of the secular and the sacred and the possibilities of greater order and control.

The Gothic Revolution in Art and Architecture

Just as polyphonic music united the sacred with the secular, so **Gothic** architecture, sculpture, and painting expressed the order and harmony of the universe.[1] This new style, which was popular from the twelfth to fifteenth centuries, was characterized by pointed arches. These began as architectural motifs but were soon adopted in every art form. Gothic churches appealed to the senses the way that scholastic argument appealed to human reason: both were designed

[1]*Gothic* is a modern term. It was originally meant to denigrate the style's "barbarity," but most contemporary observers now use the word admiringly.

to lead people to knowledge that touched the divine. Being in a Gothic church was a foretaste of heaven.

Architecture. Gothic architecture began around 1135, with the project of Abbot Suger, the close associate of King Louis the Fat of France (see page 384), to remodel portions of the church of St. Denis. Suger's rebuilding of St. Denis was part of the fruitful melding of royal and ecclesiastical interests and ideals in the north of France. At the west end of his church, the point where the faithful entered, Suger decorated the portals with figures of Old Testament kings, queens, and patriarchs, signaling the links between the present king and his illustrious predecessors. Within the church, Suger rebuilt the *chevet*, or choir area, using pointed arches and stained glass to let in light, which Suger believed would transport the worshiper from the "slime of earth" to the "purity of Heaven." Suger said that the Father of lights, God himself, "illuminated" the minds of the beholders through the light that filtered through the stained-glass windows.

Soon the style that Suger pioneered was taken up all across France and Europe. Gothic was an urban architecture, reflecting—in its grand size, jewel-like windows, and bright ornaments—the aspirations, pride, and confidence of rich and powerful merchants, artisans, and bishops. A Gothic church, usually a cathedral (the bishop's principal church), was the religious, social, and commercial focal point of a city. Building Gothic cathedrals was a community project, enlisting the labor and support of an entire urban center. New cathedrals required a small army of quarrymen, builders, carpenters, and glass cutters. Bishops, papal legates, and clerics planned and helped pay for these grand churches, but townspeople also generously financed them and filled them to attend Mass and visit relics. Guilds raised money to pay for stained-glass windows that depicted and celebrated their own patron saints. In turn, towns made money when pilgrims came to visit relics and sightseers arrived to marvel at their great churches.

The technologies making Gothic churches possible were all known before the twelfth century. But Suger's church showed how they could be used together to achieve a particularly dazzling effect. Gothic techniques included ribbed vaulting, which gave a sense of precision and order; the pointed arch, which produced a feeling of soaring height; and flying buttresses, which took the weight of the vault off the walls (Figure 12.1 on page 448). The buttresses permitted much of the wall to be cut away and the open spaces to be filled with glass.

Unlike Romanesque churches, whose exteriors prepare visitors for what they will see within them, Gothic cathedrals surprise. The exterior of a Gothic church has an opaque, bristling, and forbidding look owing to the dark surface of its stained glass and its flying buttresses. The interior, however, is just the opposite. All is soaring lightness, harmony, and order, as the photograph of Ste.-Chapelle illustrates. Just as a scholastic presented his

French Gothic: Ste.-Chapelle
Gothic architecture opened up the walls of the church to windows. Filled with "stained" glass—actually the colors were added to the ingredients of the glass before they were heated, melted, and blown—the windows glowed like jewels. Moreover, each had a story to tell: the life of Christ, major events from the Old Testament, the lives of saints. Ste.-Chapelle, commissioned by King Louis IX (St. Louis) and consecrated in 1248, was built to house Christ's crown of thorns and other relics of the Passion. Compare the use of windows, walls, vault, and piers here to that of a Romanesque church such as St.-Savin (see page 393). *Bridgeman-Giraudon/Art Resource, NY.*

boss

high vault

transverse rib

diagonal rib

springing

clerestory

flying buttress

mullion

light

string course

triforium

gargoyle

spandrel

arcade arch

capital

main arcade

buttress

pier

base

aisle

central or main vessel

FIGURE 12.1 Elements of a Gothic Cathedral
Bristling on the outside with stone flying buttresses, Gothic cathedrals were lofty and serene on the inside. The buttresses, which held the weight of the vault, allowed Gothic architects to pierce the walls with windows running the full length of the church. Within, thick piers anchored on sturdy bases became thin columns as they mounted over the triforium and clerestory, blossoming into ribs at the top. Whether plain or ornate, the ribs gave definition and drew attention to the high pointed vault. *Figure adapted from Michael Camille,* Gothic Art: Glorious Visions *(New York: Abrams, 1996).*

At Sant'Andrea in Vercelli, shown on the next page, for example, there are only two stories, and light filters in from small windows. Yet this is considered a Gothic church, for it uses pointed arches and ribbed vaulting. With no flying buttresses and relatively little portal sculpture, the Italian version of Gothic conveys a spirit of austerity.

Art. Gothic art, both painting and sculpture, decorated the Gothic cathedral. Liberated from their background and sculpted in the round, Gothic figures turned, moved, and interacted with one another. Taken together, they were often meant to be "read" like a scholastic summa. The south portal complex of Chartres cathedral is a good example. Each massive doorway tells a separate story through sculpture: the left depicts the martyrs, the right the confessors, and the center the Last Judgment. Like Dante's *Divine Comedy,* these portals taken together show the soul's pilgrimage from the suffering of this world to eternal life.

argument with utter clarity, so the interior of a Gothic church revealed its structure through its skeleton of ribbed vaults and piers. And just as a scholastic bridged the gap between earthly and celestial realms, so the cathedral elicited a response beyond reason, evoking a sense of awe.

By the mid-thirteenth century, Gothic architecture had spread from France to other European countries. Yet the style varied by region, most dramatically in Italy.

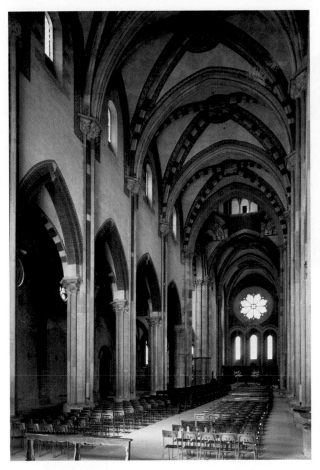

Sant'Andrea

The church of Sant'Andrea at Vercelli was begun about twenty years before Ste.-Chapelle (see page 447). It suggests that Italian church architects and patrons adopted what they liked of French Gothic, particularly its pointed arches, while remaining uninterested in soaring heights and grand stained-glass windows. The real interest of the interior of Sant'Andrea is its inventive and lively use of contrasting light and dark stone. *Scala/Art Resource, NY.*

Giotto's *Last Judgment*

The theme of the Last Judgment fills the west wall of the Arena Chapel in Padua, painted by Giotto between 1304 and 1313. In the center is Christ, surrounded by angels and saints. Beneath him is the cross, symbol of his passion and triumph. Under the cross, to Christ's right, is the donor of church, Enrico Scrovegni, kneeling as he offers a scale model of the chapel to the Virgin Mary, mother of Jesus. Behind and above him are the blessed of heaven. The funnel-like space to Christ's left shows hell, with the devil contentedly munching on the souls of the damned. *Cameraphoto Arte, Venice/Art Resource, NY.*

Like architecture, Gothic sculpture began in France and was adopted, with many variations, elsewhere in Europe during the thirteenth century. The Italian sculptor Nicola Pisano (c. 1220–1278?), for example, crafted dignified figures inspired by classical forms. German sculptors, in contrast, created excited, emotional figures that sometimes gestured dramatically to one another. (See page 450 for an example of German Gothic.)

By the early fourteenth century, the expansive sculptures so prominent in architecture were reflected in painting as well. This new style is evident in the work of Giotto◆ (1266–1337), a Florentine artist who changed the emphasis of painting, which had been predominantly symbolic, decorative, and intellectual. When Giotto filled the walls of a private chapel at Padua with paintings de-

◆**Giotto:** JAHT toh

German Gothic: Strasbourg
The Virgin is mourned in this tympanum over the portal of the Strasbourg cathedral's south transept (the arm that crosses the church from north to south). Here, in German Gothic, the emphasis is on emotion and expressivity. Why do you suppose that Christ stands in the center of the tympanum, as if he is one of the mourners? What is he holding in the crook of his arm? (Hint: The souls of the dead are often shown as miniature people.) *Foto Marburg/Art Resource, NY.*

picting scenes of Christ's life, he experimented with the illusion of depth. Giotto's figures, appearing weighty and voluminous, express a range of emotions as they seem to move across interior and exterior spaces. In bringing sculptural naturalism to a flat surface, Giotto stressed three-dimensionality, illusional space, and human emotion. By fusing earthly forms with religious meaning, Giotto found yet another way to bring together the natural and divine realms.

> **Review:** How did artists, architects, musicians, and scholastics try to link this world with the divine?

❖ The Politics of Control

The quest for order, control, and harmony also became part of the political agendas of princes, popes, and cities. These rulers and institutions imposed—or tried to impose—their authority ever more fully and systematically through taxes, courts, and sometimes representative institutions. The ancestors of modern European parliaments and of the U.S. Congress can be traced to this era.

The Weakening of the Empire

During the thirteenth century, both popes and emperors sought to dominate Italy. In the end, the emperor lost control not only of Italy but of Germany as well.

The clash of the emperor and papacy had its origins in Frederick Barbarossa's failure to control northern Italy, which was crucial to imperial policy. The model of Charlemagne required his imperial successors to exercise hegemony there. Moreover, Italy's prosperous cities beckoned as rich sources of income. When Barbarossa failed in the north, his son Henry VI (r. 1190–1197) tried a new approach to gain Italy: he married the heiress of Sicily, Constance. From this base near the southern tip of Italy, Henry hoped to make good his imperial title. But Henry died suddenly, leaving a three-year-old son, Frederick II, to take up his plan. It was a perilous moment.

While Frederick was a child, the imperial office became the plaything of the German princes and the papacy. Both wanted an emperor, but a virtually powerless one. Thus, when Frederick's uncle Duke Philip of Swabia◆ attempted to become interim king until Frederick reached his majority, many princes and the papacy blocked the move. They supported Otto of Brunswick, the son of Henry the Lion and an implacable foe of Frederick's Staufer family. Otto promised the pope that he would not intervene in Italy, and Pope Innocent III, revealing yet another side of his policy, crowned him emperor in return.

◆**Swabia:** SWAY bee uh

But Innocent had miscalculated. No emperor worthy of the name could leave Italy alone. Almost immediately after his coronation, Otto invaded Sicily, and Innocent excommunicated him in 1211. In 1212, Innocent gave the imperial crown to Frederick II (r. 1212–1250), now a young man ready to take up the reins of power.

Frederick was an amazing ruler: *stupor mundi*—"wonder of the world"—his contemporaries called him. Heir to two cultures, Sicilian on his mother's side and German on his father's, he cut a worldly and sophisticated figure. In Sicily he moved easily within a diverse culture of Jews, Muslims, and Christians. Here he could play the role of all-powerful ruler. In Germany he was less at home. There

Christian princes, often churchmen with ministerial retinues, were acutely aware of their crucial role in royal elections and jealously guarded their rights and privileges.

Both emperor and pope needed to dominate Italy to maintain their power and position (Map 12.1). The papacy under Innocent III was expansionist, gathering money and troops to make good its claim to the Papal States. From this region the pope expected dues and taxes, military service, and the profits of justice. To ensure its survival, the pope refused to tolerate any imperial claims to Italy.

Frederick, in turn, could not imagine ruling as an emperor unless he controlled Italy. He attempted to do this throughout his life, as

MAP 12.1 Europe in the Time of Frederick II, r. 1212–1250
King of Sicily and Germany and emperor as well, Frederick ruled over territory that encircled—and threatened—the papacy. Excommunicated several times, Frederick spent much of his career fighting the pope's forces. In the process he conceded so many powers to the German princes that the emperor thenceforth had little power in Germany. Meanwhile rulers of smaller states, such as England, France, and León-Castile, were increasing their power and authority.

did his heirs. Frederick had a three-pronged strategy. First, he revamped the government of Sicily to give him more control and yield greater profits. His *Constitutions of Melfi* (1231), an eclectic body of laws, set up a system of salaried governors who worked according to uniform procedures. The *Constitutions* called for nearly all court cases to be heard by royal courts, regularized commercial privileges, and set up a system of taxation. Second, to ensure that he would not be hounded by opponents in Germany, Frederick granted them important concessions in his "Statute in Favor of the Princes," finalized in 1232. These privileges allowed the German princes to turn their principalities into virtually independent states. Third, Frederick sought to enter Italy through Lombardy, as his grandfather had done.

The four popes who came between the deaths of Innocent (1216) and Frederick (1250) followed Frederick's every move and excommunicated the emperor a number of times. The most serious of these condemnations came in 1245, when the pope and other churchmen, assembled at the Council of Lyon, excommunicated and deposed Frederick, absolving his vassals and subjects of their fealty to him and, indeed, forbidding anyone to support him. By 1248 papal legates were preaching a crusade against Frederick and all his followers. Frederick's death soon after ensured their triumph.

Italy at the End of the Thirteenth Century

The fact that Frederick's vision of the empire failed is of less long-term importance than the way it failed. His concessions to the German princes meant that Germany would not be united until the nineteenth century. The political entity now called Germany was simply a geographical expression, divided under many independent princes. Between 1254 and 1273, the princes kept the German throne empty. Splintered into factions, they elected two different foreigners, who spent their time fighting each other. In one of history's great ironies, it was during this low point of the German monarchy that the term *Holy Roman Empire* was coined. In 1273, the princes at last united and elected a German, Rudolph (r. 1273–1291), whose family, the Habsburgs, was new to imperial power. Rudolf used the imperial title to help him consolidate control over his own principality, Swabia, but he did not try to fulfill the meaning of the imperial title elsewhere. For the first time, the word *emperor* was freed from its association with Italy and Rome. For the Habsburgs, the title Holy Roman Emperor was a prestigious but otherwise meaningless honorific.

The Staufer failure in Italy meant that the Italian cities would continue their independent course. In Sicily, the papacy ensured that the heirs of Frederick would not continue their rule by calling successively on other rulers to take over the island—first Henry III of England and then Charles of Anjou. Forces loyal to the Staufer family turned to the king of Aragon (Spain). The move left two enduring claimants to Sicily's crown: the kings of Aragon and the house of Anjou. And it spawned a long war impoverishing the region.

The popes won the war against Frederick, but at a cost. Even the king of France criticized the popes for doing "new and unheard-of things." By making its war against Frederick part of its crusade against heresy, the papacy came under attack for using religion as a political tool. (See Municipal Legislation at Pisa, on page 455.)

Louis IX and a New Ideal of Kingship

In hindsight, we can see that Frederick's fight for an empire that would stretch from Germany to Sicily was doomed. The successful rulers of medieval Europe were those content with smaller, more compact, more united polities. The future was reserved for "national" states, like France and England. (Of course, that too may just be one phase of Western civilization.) In France the new ideal of a "stay-at-home" monarch started in the thirteenth century with the reign of Louis IX (r. 1226–1270). His two crusades to the Holy

Land made clear to his subjects just how much they needed him in France, even though his place was ably filled the first time by his mother, Blanche of Castile. The two are pictured on this page.

Louis was revered not because he was a military leader but because he was an administrator, judge, and "just father" of his people. On warm summer days, he would sit under a tree in the woods near his castle at Vincennes on the outskirts of Paris, hearing disputes and dispensing justice personally. Through his administrators, he vigorously imposed his laws and justice over much of France. At Paris he appointed a salaried chief magistrate, who could be supervised and fired if necessary. During his reign the influence of the parlement of Paris, the royal court of justice, increased significantly. Originally a changeable

Louis IX and Blanche of Castile
This miniature probably shows St. Louis, portrayed as a young boy, sitting opposite his mother, Blanche of Castile. Blanche served as regent twice in Louis's lifetime, once when he was too young to rule and a second time when he was away on crusade. The emphasis on the equality of queen and king may be evidence of Blanche's influence on and patronage of the artist. Note that the artist has set both royal figures in a Gothic windowlike setting. **For more help analyzing this image**, see the visual activity for this chapter in the Online Study Guide at **bedfordstmartins.com/hunt**. *The Pierpont Morgan Library/ Art Resource, NY.*

and movable body, part of the king's personal entourage when he dealt with litigation, it was now permanently housed in Paris and staffed by professional judges who heard cases and recorded their decisions.

Unlike his grandfather Philip Augustus, Louis did not try to expand his territory. He inherited a large kingdom that included Poitou and Languedoc (Map 12.2 on page 454), and he was content. Although Henry III, the king of England, attacked him continually to try to regain territory lost under Philip Augustus, Louis remained unprovoked. Rather than prolong the fighting, he conceded a bit and made peace in 1259. At the same time, Louis was a zealous crusader. He took seriously the need to defend

the Holy Land when most of his contemporaries were weary of the idea.

Louis was respectful of the church and the pope; he accepted limits on his power in relation to the church and never claimed power over spiritual matters. Nevertheless, he vigorously maintained the dignity of the king and his rights. He expected royal and ecclesiastical power to work in harmony, and he refused to let the church dictate how he should use his temporal authority. For example, French bishops wanted royal officers to support the church's sentences of excommunication. But Louis declared that he would authorize his officials to do so only if he were able to judge each case for himself, to see if the excommunication had been

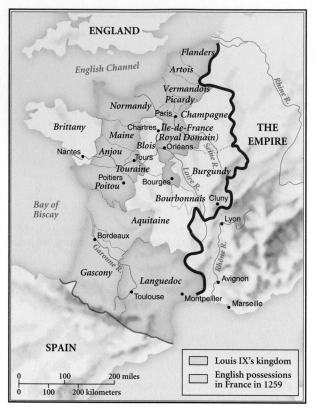

MAP 12.2 France under Louis IX, r. 1226–1270
Louis IX did not expand his kingdom as dramatically as his grandfather Philip Augustus had done. He was greatly admired nevertheless, for he was seen by contemporaries as a model of Christian piety and justice. After his death, he was recognized as a saint and thus posthumously enhanced the prestige of the French monarchy.

justly pronounced or not. The bishops refused, and Louis held his ground. Royal and ecclesiastical power would work side by side, neither subservient to the other.

Many modern historians fault Louis for his policies toward the Jews. His hatred of them was well known. He did not exactly advocate violence against them, but he sometimes subjected them to arrest, canceling the debts owed to them (but collecting part into the royal treasury), and confiscating their belongings. In 1253, he ordered them to live "by the labor of their hands" or leave France. He meant that they should no longer lend money, in effect taking away their one means of livelihood. Louis's contemporaries

did not criticize him for his Jewish policies. If anything, his hatred of Jews enhanced his reputation.

In fact, many of Louis's contemporaries considered him a saint, praising his care for the poor and sick, the pains and penances he inflicted on himself, and his regular participation in church services. In 1297 Pope Boniface VIII canonized him as St. Louis. The result was enormous prestige for the French monarchy. This prestige, joined with the renown of Paris as the center of scholarship and the repute of French courts as the hubs of chivalry, made France the cultural model of Europe.

The Birth of Representative Institutions

As thirteenth-century monarchs and princes expanded their powers, they devised a new political tool to enlist more broadly based support: all across Europe, from Spain to Poland, from England to Hungary, rulers summoned parliaments. These grew out of the ad hoc advisory sessions kings had held in the past with men from the two most powerful classes, or "orders," of medieval society—the nobility and the clergy. In the thirteenth century, the advisory sessions turned into solemn, formal meetings of representatives of the orders to the kings' chief councils—the precursor of parliamentary sessions. Eventually these bodies became organs through which people not ordinarily present at court could articulate their wishes.

In practice, thirteenth-century kings did not so much command representatives of the orders to come to court as they simply summoned the most powerful members of their realm—whether clerics, nobles, or important townsmen—to support their policies. In thirteenth-century León (part of present-day Spain), for example, the king sometimes called only the clergy and nobles; sometimes he sent for representatives of the towns, especially when he wanted the help of town militias. As townsmen gradually began to participate regularly in advisory sessions, kings came to depend on them and their support. In turn, commoners became more fully integrated into the work of royal government.

Municipal Legislation at Pisa (1286)

Large and prosperous cities like Pisa were concerned with controlling the sexual activities of their inhabitants. They prohibited prostitution in the "better" parts of the city, though they allowed it in the medieval version of a red-light district. Sometimes, as at Pisa, homosexuality was seen as a form of heresy.

III. Concerning apostolic regulations against heretics and sodomites:

We will take heed of apostolic regulations which have been laid down against heretics, will observe them to the letter, and will have others do likewise during the entire period of our governance. We and others will harass and threaten sodomites, buggers, and other persons found guilty of the depravity of heresy, proceeding against them in accordance with the form of the law. . . .

IV. Concerning prostitutes and men of ill-fame:

We will not allow any public prostitute or female go-between, or one who receives prostitutes, or pimps, male or female to remain within the walls of the city of Pisa, in "good" public places, from which we will have them expelled in accordance with the desires of the local residents, or at least three of them, who are of good reputation, neither near, inside or outside the walls of the city of Pisa[1] . . . and they are not to stay or dwell in any street or public square. The podestà and captains [local officials charged with prosecuting criminals] are to do and observe this. If they don't they are to forfeit one hundred *denarii*. . . .

Persons may expel such prostitutes by force if necessary from the aforementioned places without incurring any punishment. No prostitute may presume to enter a bathhouse, except on Wednesday, under penalty of a fine of fifty *solidi*, to be paid every time they break the law. The bathhouse attendants (or owners) are to pay the same fine, and this is to be announced throughout the city. No public prostitute may wear a cloak, under penalty of the same fine; this is to be overseen by the police. Any Pisan who allows his home to serve as a dwelling for a prostitute or for any of the aforementioned persons, male or female, that is, persons of ill fame, reputation, class or conduct; who received thieves, buggers, sodomites, gamblers, dice throwers or other persons of ill fame, should be condemned to pay one hundred *denarii*.

---

[1]This is followed by a very detailed list of the boundaries of those parts of the city of Pisa from which they are excluded.

Source: Michael Goodich, ed., *Other Middle Ages: Witnesses at the Margins of Medieval Society*, (Philadelphia: University of Pennsylvania Press, 1998), 116–17.

Spanish Cortes. The *cortes*◆ of Castile-León were among the earliest representative assemblies called to the king's court and the first to include townsmen. Enriched by plunder, fledgling villages soon burgeoned into major commercial centers. Like the cities of Italy, Spanish towns dominated the countryside. Their leaders—called *caballeros*◆ *villanos*, or "city horsemen," because they were rich enough to fight on horseback—monopolized municipal offices. In 1188, when King Alfonso IX (r. 1188–1230) summoned townsmen to the cortes for the first time on record, the city caballeros served as

---

◆*cortes:* kawr TEHZ

◆*caballeros:* ka buh YEHR os

their representatives, agreeing to Alfonso's plea for military and financial support and for help in consolidating his rule. Once convened at court, these wealthy townsmen joined bishops and noblemen in formally counseling the king and assenting to royal decisions. Beginning with Alfonso X (r. 1252–1284), Castilian monarchs regularly called on the cortes to participate in major political and military decisions and to assent to new taxes to finance them.

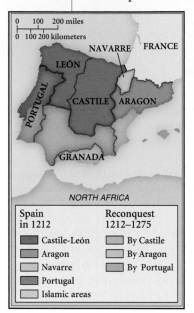

Spain in the Thirteenth Century

0 100 200 miles
0 100 200 kilometers

FRANCE
NAVARRE
LEÓN
PORTUGAL
CASTILE ARAGON
GRANADA

NORTH AFRICA

Spain in 1212
- Castile-León
- Aragon
- Navarre
- Portugal
- Islamic areas

Reconquest 1212–1275
- By Castile
- By Aragon
- By Portugal

English Parliament.

The English Parliament also developed as a new tool of royal government.[2] In this case, however, the king's control was complicated by the power of the barons, manifested, for example, in Magna Carta. In the twelfth century, King Henry II had consulted prelates and barons at Great Councils, using these parliaments as his tool to ratify and gain support for his policies. Although Magna Carta had nothing to do with such councils, the barons thought the document gave them an important and permanent role in royal government as the king's advisers and a solid guarantee of their customary rights and privileges. Henry III (r. 1216–1272) was crowned at the age of nine and therefore was king in name only for the first sixteen years of his reign. Instead, England was governed by a council consisting of a few barons, university-trained administrators, and a papal legate. Although not quite "government by

Parliament," this council set a precedent for baronial participation in government.

A parliament that included commoners came only in the midst of war and as a result of political weakness. Henry so alienated nobles and commoners alike by his wars, debts, choice of advisers, and demands for money that the barons threatened to rebel. At a meeting at Oxford in 1258, they forced Henry to dismiss his foreign advisers, rule with the advice of a Council of Fifteen chosen jointly by the barons and the king, and limit the terms of his chief officers. However, this new government was itself riven by strife among the barons, and civil war erupted in 1264. At the battle of Lewes in the same year, the leader of the baronial opposition, Simon de Montfort (c. 1208–1265), routed the king's forces, captured the king, and became England's de facto ruler. Because only a minority of the barons followed Simon, he sought new support by convening a parliament in 1265, to which he summoned not only the earls, barons, and churchmen who backed him but also representatives from the towns, the "commons"—and he appealed for their help. Thus, for the first time the commons were given a voice in government. Even though Simon's brief rule ended that very year and Henry's son Edward I (r. 1272–1307) became a rallying point for royalists, the idea of representative government in England had emerged, born out of the interplay between royal initiatives and baronial revolts.

The Weakening of the Papacy

In France, the development of representative institutions originated in the conflict between Pope Boniface VIII (r. 1294–1303) and King Philip IV (r. 1285–1314), known as Philip the Fair. At the time, this confrontation seemed to be just one more episode in the ongoing struggle between medieval popes and rulers for power and authority. But in fact, at the end of the thirteenth century kings had more power, and the standoff between Boniface and Philip became a turning point that weakened the papacy and strengthened the monarchy.

Taxing the Clergy. For centuries the clergy had maintained a special status within the medieval state. Since the twelfth century

---

[2]Although *Parlement* and *Parliament* are similar words, both deriving from the French word *parler* ("to speak"), the institutions they named were very different. The Parlement of France was a law court, whereas the English Parliament, although beginning as a court to redress grievances, had by 1327 become above all a representative institution. The major French representative assembly, the Estates General, first convened at the beginning of the fourteenth century.

popes had declared the clergy under their jurisdiction. Clerics were not taxed except in the case of religious wars; they were not tried except in clerical courts. At the end of the thirteenth century, royal challenges to these principles were met by angry papal responses. The clashes began over taxing the clergy. Philip the Fair and the English king Edward I both financed their wars (mainly against one another) by taxing the clergy along with everyone else. The new principle of national sovereignty that they were claiming led them to assert jurisdiction over all people, even churchmen, who lived within their borders. For the pope, however, the principle at stake was his role as head of the clergy. Thus, Pope Boniface VIII, whose heavy, dignified image is illustrated on this page, declared that only the pope could authorize taxes on clerics. Threatening to excommunicate kings who taxed prelates without papal permission, he called on clerics to disobey any such royal orders.

Edward and Philip reacted swiftly. Taking advantage of the important role English courts played in protecting the peace, Edward declared that all clerics who refused to pay his taxes would be considered outlaws—literally "outside the law." Clergymen who were robbed, for example, would have no recourse against their attackers; if accused of crimes, they would have no defense in court. Relying on a different strategy, Philip forbade the exportation of precious metals, money, or jewels, effectively sealing French borders. Immediately the English clergy cried out for legal protection, while the papacy itself cried out for the revenues it had long enjoyed from French pilgrims, litigants, and travelers. Boniface was forced to back down, conceding in 1297 that kings had the right to tax their clergy in emergencies. But this did not end the confrontation.

The King's New Tools: Propaganda and Popular Opinion. In 1301, Philip the Fair tested his jurisdiction in southern France by arresting Bernard Saisset,◆ the bishop of Pamiers, on a charge of treason for slandering the king by comparing him to an owl, "the handsomest of birds which is worth abso-

lutely nothing." Saisset's imprisonment violated the principle, maintained both by the pope and by French law, that a clergyman was not subject to lay justice. Boniface reacted angrily, and Philip seized the opportunity to deride and humiliate him, orchestrating a public relations campaign against Boniface. He convened representatives of the clergy, nobles, and townspeople to explain, justify, and propagandize his position. This new assembly, which met in 1302, was the ancestor of the French representative institution, the Estates General. The pope's reply, the

Boniface VIII
For the sculptor who depicted Pope Boniface VIII, Arnolfo di Cambio (d. 1302), not much had changed since the time of Innocent III. Look at the picture of Innocent on page 436 and compare the two popes: both are depicted as young, majestic, authoritative, sober, and calm. Yet Boniface could not have been very calm, for his authority was challenged at every turn. He was forced to withdraw his opposition to royal taxation of the clergy. He tried to placate the French king, Philip the Fair, by canonizing Philip's grandfather, St. Louis. Even so, Philip arrested the bishop of Pamiers and brought him to trial. When Boniface protested, he was proclaimed a heretic by the French. A few months later he was dead. *Scala/Art Resource, NY.*

◆**Bernard Saisset:** bair NAHR say SAY

bull[3] *Unam Sanctam*♦ (1302), intensified the situation to fever pitch by declaring bluntly "that it is altogether necessary to salvation for every human creature to be subject to the Roman Pontiff." At meetings of the king's inner circle, Philip's agents declared Boniface a false pope, accusing him of sexual perversion, various crimes, and heresy.

Papal Defeat. In 1303, royal agents, acting under Philip's orders, invaded Boniface's palace at Anagni (southeast of Rome) to capture the pope, bring him to France, and try him. Fearing for the pope's life, however, the people of Anagni joined forces and drove the French agents out of town. Yet even after such public support for the pope, the king made his power felt. Boniface died very shortly thereafter, and the next two popes quickly pardoned Philip and his agents for their actions.

Just as Frederick II's defeat showed the weakness of the empire, so Boniface's humiliation showed the limits of papal control. The two powers that claimed "universal" authority had very little weight in the face of new, limited, but tightly controlled national states such as France and England. After 1303, popes continued to fulminate against kings and emperors, but henceforth their words had less and less impact. In the face of newly powerful medieval states—undergirded by vast revenues, judicial apparatuses, representative institutions, and even the loyalty of churchmen—the papacy could make little headway. The delicate balance between church and state, a hallmark of the years of St. Louis that reflected a search for harmony as well as a drive for power, had broken down by the end of the thirteenth century. The quest for control led not to harmony but to confrontation and extremism.

In 1309, forced from Rome by civil strife, the papacy settled at Avignon, a city technically in the Holy Roman Empire but very close to, and influenced by, France. Here the popes remained until 1378. The period 1309–1378 came to be called the Baby-lonian Captivity by Europeans sensitive to having the popes live far from Rome, on the Rhône River.[4] The Avignon popes, many of them French, established a sober and efficient organization that took in regular revenues and gave the papacy more say than ever before in the appointment of churchmen. They would, however, slowly abandon the idea of leading all of Christendom and would tacitly recognize the growing power of the secular states to regulate their internal affairs.

The Road to the Signori

In the course of the thirteenth century, new groups, generally made up of the non-noble classes—the *popolo*, the "people," who fought on foot—attempted to take over the reins of power in many Italian communes. The popolo incorporated members of city associations such as craft and merchant guilds, parishes, and the commune itself. In fact, the popolo was a kind of alternative commune. Armed and militant, the popolo demanded a share in city government, particularly to gain a voice in matters of taxation. In 1222 at Piacenza, for example, the popolo's members won half the government offices; a year later they and the nobles worked out a plan to share the election of their city's government. Such power sharing was a typical result of the popolo's struggle. In some cities, however, nobles overcame and dissolved the popolo, while in others the popolo virtually excluded the nobles from government. Constantly confronting one another, quarreling, feuding, and compromising, such factions turned northern Italian cities into centers of civil discord.

Weakened by this constant friction, the communes were tempting prey for great regional nobles who, allying with one or another faction, often succeeded in establishing themselves as *signori*♦ (singular *signore*, "lord") of the cities, keeping the peace at the

---

[3]An official papal document is called a bull, from the *bulla*, or seal, that was used to authenticate it.

[4]The term *Babylonian Captivity* refers to the biblical story of the forced deportation of the people of Judea to Babylon and their long exile there. See 2 Kings 24–25.

♦*Unam Sanctam:* UN ahm SANKT ahm

♦*signori:* see noh REE ah

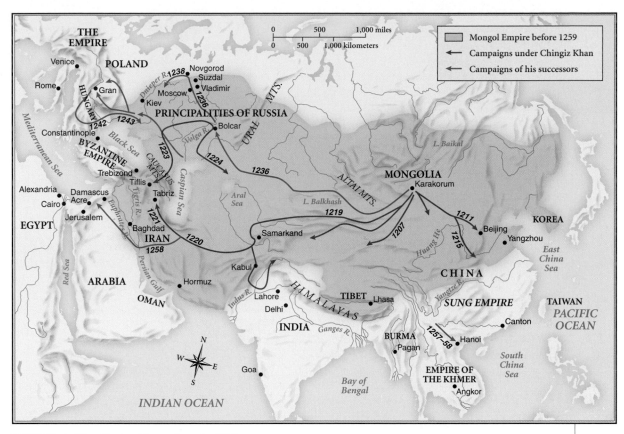

MAP 12.3 The Mongol Invasions to 1259
The Mongols were the first people to tie the eastern world to the west. Their conquest of China, which took place at about the same time as their invasions of Russia and Iran, created a Eurasian economy, opening up trade relations across regions that had long been separated by language, religion, and political regimes.

price of repression. In these circumstances, many communes gave way to lordships, with one family dominating the government. The fate of Piacenza over the course of the thirteenth century was typical: first dominated by nobles, its commune granted the popolo a voice by 1225; but then by midcentury both the nobles and the popolo were eclipsed by the power of a signore.

The Mongol Takeover

Europeans were not the only warring society in the thirteenth century: to the east the Mongols (sometimes called Tatars or Tartars) created an aggressive army under the leadership of Chingiz (or Genghis) Khan

(c. 1162–1227) and his sons. In part, economic necessity drove them out of Mongolia: climatic changes had reduced the grasslands that sustained their animals and their nomadic way of life. But they were also inspired by Chingiz's hope of conquering the world. By 1215, the Mongols held Beijing and most of northern China. Some years later they moved through central Asia and skirted the Caspian Sea (Map 12.3).

The Golden Horde in Russia. In the 1230s, the Mongols began concerted attacks in Europe—in Russia, Poland, and Hungary, where weak native princes were no match for the Mongols' formidable armies and tactics. Only the death of their Great Khan, Chingiz's

MAPPING THE WEST Europe, c. 1320
The empire, now called the Holy Roman Empire, still dominated the map of Europe in 1320, but the emperor himself had little power. Each principality—often each city—was ruled separately and independently. To the east, the Ottoman Turks were just beginning to make themselves felt. In the course of the next century they would disrupt the Mongol hegemony and become a great power.

son Ogodei (1186–1241)—styled the *khagan*, or khan of khans—and disputes over his succession prevented a concentrated assault on Germany. In the 1250s, the Mongols took Iran, Iraq, and Syria.

The Mongols' sophisticated and devastating military tactics contributed to their overwhelming success. They devised two- and three-flank operations. The invasion of Hungary, for example, was two-pronged: one division of their army arrived from Russia while the other moved through Poland and Germany. Many Hungarians perished

in the assault as the Mongols, fighting mainly on horseback, with heavy lances and powerful bows and arrows whose shots traveled far and penetrated deeply, crushed the Hungarian army of mixed infantry and cavalry.

In the West, the Mongol rule in Russia lasted the longest. At Vladimir in the north, they broke through the defensive walls of the city and burned the populace huddled for protection inside the cathedral. Their most important victory in Russia was the capture of Kiev in 1240. Making the mouth of the

Volga River the center of their power in Russia, the Mongols dominated all of Russia's principalities for about two hundred years.

The Mongol Empire in Russia, later called the **Golden Horde** (*golden* probably from the color of their leader's tent; *horde* from a Turkish word meaning "camp"), adopted much of the local government apparatus and left many of the old institutions in place. They allowed Russian princes to continue ruling as long as they paid homage and tribute to the khan, and they tolerated the Russian church, exempting it from taxes. The Mongol's chief undertaking was a series of population censuses on the basis of which they recalculated taxes and recruited troops.

Opening of China to Europeans. The Mongol invasion changed the political configuration of Europe and Asia. Because the Mongols were willing to deal with westerners, one effect of their conquests was to open China to European travelers for the first time. Some missionaries, diplomats, and merchants went to China by overland routes; others set sail from the Persian Gulf (controlled by the Mongols) and rounded India before arriving in China. Some of these voyagers hoped to enlist the aid of the Mongols against the Muslims; others expected to make new converts to Christianity; still others dreamed of lucrative trade routes.

The most famous of these travelers was Marco Polo (1254–1324), son of a merchant family from Venice. Marco's father and uncle had already been to China once and returned when Marco joined them on a second expedition. He stayed in China for nearly two years, as did other westerners. In fact, evidence suggests that an entire community of Venetian traders—women, men, and children—lived in the city of Yangzhou in the mid-fourteenth century.

Merchants paved the way for missionaries. Friars, preachers to the cities of Europe, became missionaries to new continents as well. In 1289, the pope made the Franciscan John of Monte Corvino his envoy to China. Preaching in India along the way, John arrived in China four or five years after setting out, converting one local ruler, and building a church. A few years later, now at Beijing, he boasted that he had converted six thousand people, constructed two churches, and translated the New Testament and Psalms into the native language.

The long-term effect of the Mongols on the West was to open up new land routes to the East that helped bind the two halves of the known world together. Travel stories such as Marco Polo's stimulated others to seek out the fabulous riches—textiles, ginger, ceramics, copper—of China and other regions of the East. In a sense, the Mongols initiated the search for exotic goods and missionary opportunities that culminated in the European "discovery" of a new world, the Americas.

Review: In what ways did the secular rulers of the period 1215–1320 cooperate with the church; in what ways did they not—and why?

Conclusion

The thirteenth century sought harmony but discovered how elusive it could be. Theoretically, the universal papacy and empire were supposed to work together; instead they clashed in bitter warfare, leaving the government of Germany to the princes and northern Italy to its communes and *signori*. Theoretically, faith and reason were supposed to arrive at the same truths. In the hands of scholastics they sometimes did so, but not always. Theoretically, all Christians were expected to practice the same rites and follow the teachings of the church. In fact, local enforcement determined which church laws took effect—and to what extent. Moreover, the quest for harmony was never able to bring together all the diverse peoples, ideas, and interests of thirteenth-century society. Far from integrating, Jews found themselves set apart from everyone else through legislation and visible markers. Heretics were pursued with zeal; there was no question here of unity.

The quest for harmony worked more surely in the arts. Artists and architects integrated sculpture, stone, and glass to depict religious themes and fill the light-infused space of Gothic churches. Musicians wove together disparate melodic and poetic lines into motets. Writers melded heroic and romantic themes with theological truths and mystical visions.

Political leaders also aimed at order and control: to increase their revenues, expand their territories, and enhance their prestige. The kings of England and France and the governments of northern and central Italian cities partially succeeded in achieving these goals, while the king of Germany (who was also the emperor) failed miserably. Germany remained fragmented until the nineteenth century. Within the new, compact governments, however, the quest for harmony succeeded to a degree. Kings and representative institutions worked well together on the whole, and clergy and laymen came to feel that they were part of the same political entity, whether that entity was France or a German principality. Ironically, the Mongols, who began as invaders in the west, helped unify areas that were far apart through opening trade routes.

The harmonies became even more discordant toward the end of the thirteenth century. The balance between church and state achieved under St. Louis in France, for example, disintegrated into irreconcilable claims to power in the time of Pope Boniface and Philip the Fair. The carefully constructed tapestry of St. Thomas's summae, which wove together Aristotle's secular philosophy and divine Scripture, began to unravel in the teachings of John Duns Scotus. The eclectic Italian Gothic style, which gathered indigenous as well as northern elements, gave way to a new style, that of Giotto, whose work, rooted in the medieval search for harmony, also heralded the Renaissance art of the fourteenth century.

Suggested References

The Church's Mission of Reform

While historians continue to explore the traditional and important political figures behind the thirteenth-century church (Sayers), other scholars have begun to trace the impact of new church doctrine on the laity and the way the laity actively interpreted it (Bynum).

Bynum, Caroline Walker. *Holy Feast and Holy Fast: The Religious Significance of Food to Medieval Women.* 1987.

*Fourth Lateran Council: http://abbey.apana.org.au/councils/ecum12.htm.

Logan, F. Donald. *A History of the Church in the Middle Ages.* 2002.

Sayers, Jane. *Innocent III: Leader of Europe, 1198–1216.* 1994.

Cultural Harmonies

Most studies of the art and thought of the period specialize in one or the other, but the pioneering synthesis by Panofsky demonstrates that a wider view is possible. Duby attempts to place Gothic architecture in the context of the culture and society that produced it.

*Amiens cathedral: http://www.learn.columbia.edu/MCAHweb/index-frame.html.

*Dante. *The Divine Comedy.* Many editions; recommended are translations by Mark Musa and John Ciardi. The *Inferno* has been particularly well translated by Robert Pinsky and, most recently, by Robert Hollander and Jean Hollander.

Duby, Georges. *The Age of the Cathedrals: Art and Society, 980–1420.* Trans. Eleanor Levieux and Barbara Thompson. 1981.

Katzenellenbogen, Adolf. *The Sculptural Programs of Chartres Cathedral.* 1959.

Panofsky, Erwin. *Gothic Architecture and Scholasticism.* 1951.

Sargent, Steven D., ed. and trans. *On the Threshold of Exact Science: Selected Writings of Anneliese Maier on Late Medieval Natural Philosophy.* 1982.

Smart, Alastair. *The Dawn of Italian Painting, 1250–1400.* 1978.

*Thomas Aquinas: http://www.newadvent.org/summa.

The Politics of Control

Thirteenth-century states used to be seen as harbingers of modern ones, but the newest history suggests that this is anachronistic. Thus, Abulafia argues that Frederick II followed models of medieval rulership, and O'Callaghan shows how far different medieval representative institutions were from their modern counterparts.

*Primary sources.

Only in the last ten or so years have historians studied the prelude to Columbus's voyages by looking at medieval precedents.

Abulafia, David. *Frederick II: A Medieval Emperor*. 1988.

Campbell, Mary B. *The Witness and the Other World: Exotic European Travel Writing, 400–1600*. 1989.

Farmer, Sharon. *Surviving Poverty in Medieval Paris: Gender, Ideology, and the Daily Lives of the Poor*. 2002.

Fernández-Armesto, Felipe. *Before Columbus: Exploration and Colonization from the Mediterranean to the Atlantic, 1229–1492*. 1987.

*Joinville, Jean de, and Geoffroy de Villehardouin. *Chronicles of the Crusades*. Trans. M. R. B. Shaw. 1963.

Jordan, William Chester. *The French Monarchy and the Jews: From Philip Augustus to the Late Capetians*. 1989.

Morgan, David. *The Mongols*. 1986.

O'Callaghan, Joseph F. *The Cortes of Castille-León, 1188–1350*. 1989.

Richard, Jean. *Saint Louis: Crusader King of France*. Trans. Jean Birrell. 1992.

Strayer, Joseph R. *The Reign of Philip the Fair*. 1980.

*Wood, Charles T. *Philip the Fair and Boniface VIII: State vs. Papacy*. 2nd ed. 1971.

CHAPTER REVIEW

IMPORTANT EVENTS

1188	King Alfonso IX summons townsmen to the *cortes*
1212–1250	Reign of Frederick II
1215	Fourth Lateran Council
1273	Thomas Aquinas publishes the *Summa Theologiae*
1226–1270	Reign of Louis IX (St. Louis)
1232	"Statute in Favor of the Princes"
1233	First permanent Inquisition
1240	Mongols capture Kiev
1265	English commons summoned to Parliament
1265–1321	Dante Alighieri
1302	First Meeting of the French Estates
1309–1378	Avignon Papacy (Babylonian Captivity)

KEY TERMS

Golden Horde (461)

Gothic (446)

Inquisition (438)

motet (445)

polyphony (446)

scholasticism (443)

summa (443)

tertiaries (441)

REVIEW QUESTIONS

1. How did people respond to the teachings and laws of the church in the early thirteenth century?

2. How did artists, architects, musicians, and scholastics try to link this world with the divine?

3. In what ways did the secular rulers of the period 1215–1320 cooperate with the church; in what ways did they not—and why?

MAKING CONNECTIONS

1. Why was Innocent III more successful than Boniface VIII in carrying out his objectives?

2. What impact did the Mongolian invasions have on the medieval economy?

FOR FURTHER EXPLORATION

To assess your mastery of the material in this chapter, see the Online Study Guide at **bedfordstmartins.com/hunt**.

To read additional primary-source material from this period, see Chapter 12 in *Sources of The Making of the West*, Second Edition, Volume I.

The Crisis of Late Medieval Society, 1320–1430

Political Crises across Europe
- The Changing Nature of Warfare
- The Hundred Years' War, 1337–1453
- Popular Uprisings
- Imperial Fragmentation and Eastern European State Building
- Multiethnic States on the Frontiers

The Plague and Society
- Rise and Spread of the Plague
- Responses to the Plague: Flagellants and Anti-Semitism
- Consequences of the Plague

Challenges to Spiritual Authority
- The Papal Monarchy and Its Critics
- The Great Schism, 1378–1417
- The Conciliar Movement
- Dissenters and Heretics
- The Hussite Revolution

The Social Order and Cultural Change
- The Household
- The Underclass
- Hard Times for Trade
- The Flourishing of Vernacular Literature and the Birth of Humanism

"IN THE YEAR OF OUR LORD 1349," begins the chronicle kept by the Nuremberg citizen Ulman Stromer, "the Jews resided in the middle of the square, and their houses lined its sides as well as a street behind where Our Lady's now stands. And the Jews were burned on the evening of St. Nicholas's as it has been described." These terse words belie the horror experienced by the Jewish community. Robbed of their belongings in an uprising, the Jews of Nuremberg were later rounded up by the city magistrates and required to convert to Christianity. Those who refused were burned at the stake. The new church of Our Lady went up on the site where the Jewish synagogue was razed.

Nuremberg, in central Germany, was but one of numerous sites of anti-Jewish furor in 1349. After decades in which religious and political institutions had gained control, the violence of 1349 represented the breakdown of authority in the face of widespread warfare, catastrophic losses of population from disease, and unprecedented challenges to religious authority. The coming together of these political, demographic, and religious developments resulted in a general crisis of late medieval society.

The political aspect of the crisis centered on the conflict between the English and the French that came to be called the Hundred Years' War (1337–1453). High taxes and widespread devastation also led to popular revolts that shook political establishments. But the loss of life in war paled in comparison to deaths by disease and famine.

In the mid-fourteenth century a series of disasters—famine, climatic changes, and disease—scourged a society already weakened by overpopulation, economic stagnation, social conflicts, and war.

The Burning of Jews
While townspeople watch, an executioner carries more firewood to the pyre of Jews, an example of the horrible persecutions against Jewish communities during the plague years of 1348–1350. This religious violence, arising out of the confrontation between Christianity and Judaism, had the opposite effect to that intended by Christians. Instead of converting, most Jews honored their martyrs and felt less incentive to accept the faith of their oppressors. © *Brussels, Royal Library of Belgium.*

The plague, or Black Death, wiped out at least a third of Europe's population. With recurring bouts of the plague and continuous warfare through the second half of the fourteenth century, population density would not reach thirteenth-century levels again until the sixteenth century, and in many areas not until the eighteenth century.

In society at large, order gave way to chaos and violence. Groups of flagellants, who whipped themselves as a form of penance, roamed central Europe. Jews were persecuted on a scale not surpassed until the twentieth century. Anti-Jewish persecutions, or pogroms, broke out in the Holy Roman Empire, southern France, Aragon, and Castile, ravaging the once-flourishing Jewish culture of the Middle Ages.

Dynastic conflicts, popular uprisings, and the steady advances of the Muslim Ottoman Turks in southeastern Europe undermined political authority and threatened the social order. During the late Middle Ages, the idea of universal Christendom that had fueled and sustained the crusades receded, while loyalties to state, community, and social groups deepened. The papacy, the very symbol of Christian unity and authority, remained divided by the claims of rival popes and challenged by heretical movements.

The word *crisis* implies a turning point, a decisive moment, and during the hundred-plus years between 1320 and 1430, European civilization faced such a time. Departing from the path of expansion, it entered a period of uncertainty, disunity, and contraction.

❖ Political Crises across Europe

The crises of the fourteenth century affected political allegiances and exacerbated social and religious tensions. Just as many people came to reject the church's dictates, so did citizens refuse to trust rulers to serve the ordinary person's best interests. The idea of Christian unity, always stronger in theory than in practice, dissolved in the face of national rivalries. The conflict between the English and the French known as the Hundred Years' War destroyed the lives of countless thousands of noncombatants as well as soldiers. Commoners—town residents and peasants—challenged the political status quo in hopes of gaining a share of the power their rulers wielded over them or at least a voice in how they were governed. Beyond the frontiers of Christendom, the Muslim Ottoman Turks steadily encroached on the Balkans and the Mediterranean. The political crises of the late Middle Ages shaped the pattern of conflicts for the next two hundred years.

The Changing Nature of Warfare

Although nobles continued to dominate European society in the late-Middle Ages, their social and political roles were gradually but fundamentally transformed. The ranks of the nobility encompassed a wide range of people—from powerful magnates whose wealth rivaled that of kings to humble knights who lived much like peasants—yet

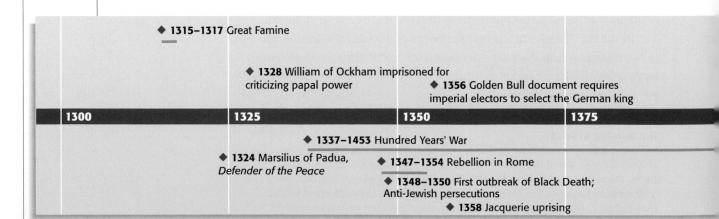

◆ **1315–1317** Great Famine

◆ **1328** William of Ockham imprisoned for criticizing papal power

◆ **1356** Golden Bull document requires imperial electors to select the German king

| 1300 | 1325 | 1350 | 1375 |

◆ **1337–1453** Hundred Years' War

◆ **1324** Marsilius of Padua, *Defender of the Peace*

◆ **1347–1354** Rebellion in Rome

◆ **1348–1350** First outbreak of Black Death; Anti-Jewish persecutions

◆ **1358** Jacquerie uprising

two developments in this period affected all of them: an agrarian crisis and a change in the nature of warfare.

Traditionally the nobles had comprised the warrior class and had lived on the profits from the land they owned. In the wake of the Black Death, their income from their land dwindled as food prices declined because of the dramatic drop in population. Forced to seek additional revenues, knights turned enthusiastically to war. Motivated solely by material gain, noblemen from many nations served willingly in foreign campaigns, forming units at their own expense. The English knight John Hawkwood put it best: "Do you not know that I live by war, and peace would be my undoing?" Captain of an army that sold its services to various Italian states vying for power, Hawkwood represented the new soldier: the **mercenary** who lived a life of violence and gave his loyalty to the side that paid the most.

As if to compensate for the cynical reality of mercenary warfare, the European nobility emphasized the traditional knightly codes of behavior in an effort to bolster their authority. Romances associated with King Arthur and his chivalrous knights became a vogue, not only in reading but also in life. Edward III of England, for example, created the Order of the Garter in 1344 to revive the idea of chivalry. During truces in the Hundred Years' War, English and French knights jousted, engaging in mock combat according to the rules of chivalry.

Yet chivalric combat waged by knights on horseback was quickly yielding to new military realities. Commoners, criminals, and adventurers often joined the ranks of the new mercenary armies. In addition, new military technologies—firearms, siege equipment, and stronger fortifications, for example—undermined the nobility's preeminence as a fighting force (see Siege Warfare on page 470). By the last decades of the fourteenth century, cannons were becoming common in European warfare. Equipment counted more than valor and often determined the outcome of battles.

The Hundred Years' War, 1337–1453

The Hundred Years' War was a protracted struggle in western Europe that involved the nobility of many nations. It was sparked by conflicting French and English interests in southwestern France. As part of the French royal policy of centralizing jurisdiction, Philip VI in 1337 confiscated the southwestern province of Aquitaine, which had until then been held by the English monarchs as a fief of the French crown. To recover his lands, Edward III of England in turn laid claim to the French throne.

The Combatants.   To rally Englishmen to their cause, English kings spread anti-French propaganda throughout their realm. Yeomen (freemen farmers) as well as the nobility rallied to serve their king, fired by patriotism and the lust for plunder. Spectacular victories won by the English further fueled popular fervor for war, as knights, yeomen, and adventurers returned home with booty,

- ◆ **1378** Ciompi rebellion; Wycliffe, *On the Church*
- ◆ **1378–1417** Great Schism
- ◆ **1415** Jan Hus executed; Hussite revolution begins
- ◆ **1381** English peasant uprising
- ◆ **1429** Joan of Arc leads French to victory at siege of Orléans
- ◆ **1386** Union of Poland and Lithuania

1400   **1425**   **1450**

- ◆ **1389** Ottomans defeat Serbs at Kosovo
- ◆ **1391** Attack on Jews, forced conversion in Spain
- ◆ **1414–1417** Council of Constance

Siege Warfare
Siege warfare during the Hundred Years' War pitted cannons against fortifications. As cannons grew in caliber, walls became thicker, and protruding battlements and gun emplacements were added to provide counter-firepower. Late-medieval sieges were time-consuming affairs that often lasted for years. *Bibliothèque Nationale de France.*

hostages, and tales of bloody slaughter and amorous conquests. War became its own engine. Mercenary companies came to replace freemen in the English army. These companies remained in France during the long intervals of armistice between short, destructive campaigns punctuated by a few spectacular battles.

Elaborate chivalric behavior, savage brutality, and unabashed profiteering permeated the fighting in the Hundred Years' War. This warfare involved definite rules whose application depended on social status. English and French knights took one another prisoner and showed all the formal courtesy

required by chivalry—but they slaughtered captured common soldiers like cattle. Overall the war consisted not of pitched battles but rather of a series of raids in which English fighters plundered cities and villages, causing terrible destruction. English knights financed their own campaigns, and war was expected to turn a profit either in captured booty or in ransom paid to free captured nobles.

Ruling over a more populous realm and commanding far larger armies, the French kings were nevertheless hindered in the war by the independent actions of their powerful barons. Against the accurate and deadly English freemen archers, the French knights met repeated defeats. Yet perhaps even more than they despised their English adversaries, the French nobles feared their own peasants and the urban middle classes. Their fears of peasant rebellion were not unfounded, for a deep chasm separated the warrior class from their social inferiors in medieval Europe.

The Course of the War. Historians divide the Hundred Years' War into three periods: the first marked by English triumphs, the second in which France slowly gained the upper hand, and the third ending in the English expulsion from France (Map 13.1). The final, most important phase saw two key developments: the rise of Burgundy, a hodgepodge of territories held together only by the political machinations of its dukes, and the rise of France as a distinct nation.

The final phase began when the English king Henry V (r. 1413–1422) launched a full-scale invasion of France and crushed the French at Agincourt (1415). Three parties then struggled for domination in France. Henry occupied Normandy and claimed the French throne; the dauphin (heir apparent to the French throne), later Charles VII (r. 1422–1461), ruled central France;[1] and the duke of Burgundy held a vast territory in the northeast that included the Low Countries. Burgundy was thus able to broker war or peace by shifting support first to the

_____
[1]Although the dauphin was not crowned until 1429, he assumed the title Charles VII in 1422, following the death of his father.

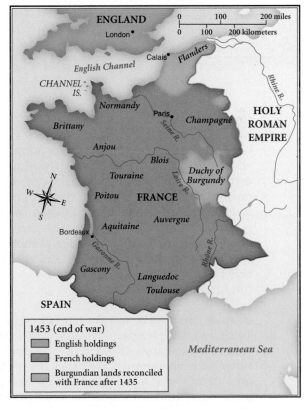

MAP 13.1 The Hundred Years' War, 1337–1453

As rulers of Aquitaine, English kings contested the French monarchy for the domination of France. Squeezed between England and Burgundy, the effective possession of the French kings was vastly reduced after the battle of Poitiers.

The Spoils of War
This illustration from Jean Froissart's *Chronicles* depicts soldiers pillaging a conquered city. Looting in the Hundred Years' War became the main income for mercenary troops and contributed to the general misery of late-medieval society. Food, furniture, and even everyday household items were looted. War had come to feed on itself. *Bibliothèque Nationale de France.*

English and then to the French. But even with Burgundian support the English could not establish firm control. In Normandy, a savage guerrilla war harassed the English army. Driven from their villages by pillaging and murdering soldiers, the Norman peasants retreated into forests, formed armed bands, and attacked the English. The miseries of war inspired prophecies of miraculous salvation; among the predictions was the belief that a virgin would deliver France from the English invaders.

Joan of Arc. At the court of the dauphin, in 1429, a sixteen-year-old peasant girl presented herself and her vision to save France. Born in a village in Lorraine, Joan of Arc grew up in a war-ravaged country that longed for divine deliverance. (See "Contrasting Views," page 474.) The young maid had first presented herself as God's messenger to the local noble, who was sufficiently impressed to equip Joan with a horse, armor, and a ret-

inue to send her to the dauphin's court. (According to her later testimony, Joan ran away from home when her father threatened to drown her because she refused an arranged marriage.) Joan of Arc's extraordinary appearance inspired the beleaguered French to trust in divine providence. In that same year, she accompanied the French army that laid a prolonged but successful siege on Orléans, was wounded, and showed great courage in battle. Upon her urging, the dauphin traveled deep into hostile Burgundian territory to be anointed King Charles VII of France at the cathedral in Reims, thus strengthening his legitimacy by following the traditional ritual of coronation.

Joan's fortunes declined after Reims. She promised to capture Paris, but the Anglo-Burgundian defenders drove back her troops and the French began to lose faith in the Maid, as she was known. When the Burgundians captured Joan in 1430, Charles and his forces did little to save her. Still, Joan was a powerful symbol, and the English were determined to undermine her claim to divine guidance. In a trial conducted by French theologians in Anglo-Burgundian service, Joan was accused of false prophecy and witchcraft because she wore men's clothes and led armies (see Joan of Arc, on this page). Tricked into recanting her prophetic mission, she retracted her confessions, returned the female attire given her after an English soldier had raped her in prison, and reaffirmed her divine mission. The English then burned her at the stake as a relapsed heretic in 1431.

After Joan's death, the English position slowly crumbled and their alliance with the Burgundians fell apart in 1435. The duke of Burgundy then recognized Charles VII as king of France. Skirmish by skirmish, the English were driven from French soil, retaining only the port of Calais when hostilities ceased in 1453. Two years later, the French church rescinded the 1431 verdict that had condemned Joan of Arc as a heretic. Some five centuries later, she was canonized and declared the patron saint of France.

Consequences of the War.   The Hundred Years' War had four major impacts. First, the long years of warfare aggravated the demographic and economic crises of the fourteenth century. Recurrent plagues (discussed later in this chapter) and pillage further ravaged the population. Constant insecurity caused by marauding bands of soldiers prevented farmers from cultivating fields even in times of truce. In Normandy, perhaps up to half the population had perished by the end of the war, victims of disease, famine, and warfare.

Second, the war prevented a quick resolution of the crisis in spiritual authority. As we will see, the collapse of papal authority known as the Great Schism owed much to the fact that rival popes could call on the respective belligerents to support their own claims. Locked in combat, the French, English, and Burgundian rulers could not agree to restore papal authority.

Third, the political landscape of western Europe changed. The necessity of mobilization strengthened the hand of the French mon-

Joan of Arc, c. 1420
Painted in the style of the French-Flemish school, this manuscript illustration contrasts the metallic hardness of Joan's armor and sword with the soft fluttering banner depicting God and two angels. With her right arm upturned clasping a sword and her left turned down to support the banner, Joan strikes a perfect pose as a messenger of God, similar to the angels depicted above. © *AKG-Images, London.*

archy. Under Charles VII, a standing army was established to supplement the feudal noble levies, financed by increased taxation and expanded royal judicial claims. By 1500, the French monarchy would emerge as one of the leading powers of Europe, ready to battle Burgundy and the empire for the domination of Europe. Burgundy also emerged as a strong power from the Hundred Years' War. By absorbing the Low Countries, this French duchy was evolving into an independent state, a rich power situated between France and Germany and commanding the fabulous wealth of Flemish cities. The Burgundian dukes became

Joan of Arc: Who Was "the Maid"?

The figure of Joan of Arc looms above the confused events and personalities of the Hundred Years' War. But who was this slender young woman from the Lorraine? Calling herself La Pucelle◆ ("the Maid"), Joan left home after she was instructed in a vision to present herself as God's messenger at the court of Charles, the dauphin of France (Document 1). Either captivated by her piety and bravery or threatened by her power and actions, contemporaries labeled Joan everything from a divine symbol to a relapsed heretic (Documents 2–3). Her capture and her year-long imprisonment, torture, interrogation, and subsequent execution generated documentation and ensured her immortality (Document 4).

1. JOAN'S VISION

Joan first spoke of her visions at length after her capture by her enemies, who were eager to prove that she was inspired by the devil. This document is the only information we have from Joan herself about her childhood. Notice three things: first, the references to light and voice, a standard representation by medieval visionaries; second, the instruction not to tell her father about her mission, which implied that she left home without his consent; and third, the reference to the siege of Orléans, which might have been an addition to her memory after the momentous events of her career. It was likely that she first thought of her mission in a more general way of saving France.

When I was thirteen years old, I had a voice from God to help me govern my conduct. And the first time I was very fearful. And came this voice, about the hour of noon, in the summer-time, in my father's garden; I had not fasted on the eve preceding that day. I heard the voice on the right-hand side, towards the church; and rarely do I hear it without a brightness. This brightness comes from the same side as the voice is heard. It is usually a great light. When I came to France, often I heard this voice.... The voice was sent to me by God and, after I had thrice heard this voice, I knew that it was the voice of an angel. This voice has always guarded me well and I have always understood it clearly....

It has taught me to conduct myself well, to go habitually to church. It told me that I, Joan, should come into France....This voice told me, twice or thrice a week, that I, Joan, must go away and that I must come to France and that my father must know nothing of my leaving. The voice told me that I should go to France and I could not bear to stay where I was. The voice told me that I should raise the siege laid to the city of Orléans....And me, I answered it that I was a poor girl who knew not how to ride nor lead in war.

Source: Régine Pernoud, ed., *Joan of Arc: By Herself and Her Witnesses* (Lanham, Md.: Scarborough House, 1994), 30.

2. MESSENGER OF GOD?

When Joan appeared at the court of the dauphin, her reputation as the messenger of God had preceded her. The French court received her with a mixture of wonder, curiosity, and outright skepticism. The political and military situation looked so desperate that many had been hoping for a divine deliverance when Joan made her arrival in history. There was debate among the dauphin's counselors whether Joan should be taken seriously, however, and the dauphin referred the case to a panel of theologians to determine whether Joan's mission was of divine origin. The following account of Joan's first visit to the dauphin was recorded by Simon Charles, president of the Chamber of Accounts.

I know that, when Joan arrived in [the castle and town of] Chinon, there was deliberation in counsel to decide whether the King should hear her or not. To start with they sent to ask her why she was

---

◆ *La Pucelle:* lah poo SEHL

come and what she was asking for. She was unwilling to say anything without having spoken to the King, yet was she constrained by the King to say the reasons for her mission. She said that she had two [reasons] for which she had a mandate from the King of Heaven; one, to raise the siege of Orléans, the other to lead the King to Rheims for his [coronation]. Which being heard, some of the King's counsellors said that the King should on no account have faith in Joan, and the others that since she said that she was sent by God, and that she had something to say to the King, the King should at least hear her.

Source: Pernoud, 48–49.

3. NORMAL GIRL?

This memoir, written by Marguerite la Touroulde, one of the women who lived with Joan and took care of her after the dauphin had accepted Joan's services to save France, testifies to Joan's ordinariness. The messenger of God appears in these words as a normal, devout young girl whose only remarkable quality seems to be her physical and martial prowess.

Joan was then brought to Bourges and, by command of the lord d'Albret, she was lodged in my house. . . . She was in my house for a period of three weeks, sleeping, drinking and eating, and almost every day I slept with Joan and I neither saw in her nor perceived anything of any kind of unquietness, but she behaved herself as an honest and Catholic woman, for she went very often to confession, willingly heard mass and often asked me to go to Matins. And at her instance I went, and took her with me several times.

Sometimes we talked together and some said to Joan that doubtless she was not afraid to go into battle because she knew well that she would not be killed. She answered that she was no safer than any other combatant. . . . Joan was very simple and ignorant and knew absolutely nothing, it seems to me, excepting in the matter of war. . . . She was open-handed in almsgiving and most willingly gave to the indigent and to the poor, saying that she had been sent for the consolation of the poor and the indigent.

And several times I saw her at the bath and in the bath-houses, and so far as I was able to see, she was a virgin, and from all that I know she was all innocence, excepting in arms, for I saw her riding on horseback and bearing a lance as the best of soldiers would have done it, and at that the men-at-arms marvelled.

Source: Pernoud, 64–65.

4. SACRED MARTYR?

After her capture, Joan was condemned to burn at the stake. She went to her death in 1431 clutching a crucifix and uttering the name of Christ. Her actions and demeanor moved many to remember the event. Their testimonies ten years later provided the evidence for judges to overturn her conviction. Her good name restored, Joan would live on in the memory of France as its greatest heroine. Pierre Cusquel, a stonemason from Orléans, offered the following testimony.

I heard say that Master Jean Tressard, secretary to the King of England, returning from Joan's execution afflicted and groaning, wept lamentably over what he had seen in that place and said indeed: "We are all lost, for we have burnt a good and holy person," and that he believed that her soul was in God's hands and that, when she was in the midst of the flames, she had still declaimed the name of the Lord Jesus. That was common repute and more or less all the people murmured that a great wrong and injustice had been done to Joan. . . . After Joan's death the English had the ashes gathered up and thrown into the Seine because they feared lest she escape or lest some say she had escaped.

Source: Pernoud, 233.

QUESTIONS TO CONSIDER
1. What was Joan's vision? Was her vision understood differently by the French king or by herself during her trial?
2. What was the source of Joan's charisma? Why did she inspire such a wide range of responses?

rivals of French kings after about 1450 and established a brilliant court culture. As for England, defeat abroad spread discontent at home. The English monarchy suffered through decades of disunity and strife, and from the 1460s to 1485, England was torn by civil war—the War of the Roses (described in Chapter 14).

Further, the heavy financial burden of warfare also destabilized the banking system. Default on war loans by England's Edward III precipitated the collapse of several of the largest banks in Europe, all based in Italy. The political crisis of the Hundred Years' War thus had a direct impact on the economic crisis of the fourteenth century.

Popular Uprisings

English and French knights waged war at the expense of the common people. While French peasants and townsfolk were taxed, robbed, raped, and murdered by marauding bands of

Outbreak of the Jacquerie
Soldiers massacre unarmed peasants during the 1358 Jacquerie, or peasant insurrection, in this illustration from Jean Froissart's *Chronicles.* Wielding swords, spears, and daggers, the soldiers brutally repress the peasantry. © *The British Library/Topham-HIP/The Image Works.*

mercenaries, their English counterparts had to pay ever higher taxes to support the wars. Widespread resentment fueled popular uprisings, which contributed to the general disintegration of political and social order. In 1358, a short but savage rebellion erupted in the area around Paris, shocking the nobility. And in 1381, a more widespread and broadly based revolt broke out in England. In the cities, the social and economic dislocations of the war deepened the general crisis of mid-century and sparked insurrections in the cities of France, Flanders, and Italy.

Jacquerie Uprising in Paris. Historians traditionally described the 1358 rebellion—named the Jacquerie♦ after the jacket (*jacque*) worn by serfs—as a "peasant fury," implying that it represented simply a spontaneous outburst of aimless violence. More recent research, however, has revealed the complex social origins of the movement. The revolt broke out after the English captured King John at the battle of Poitiers,♦ when the estates of France (the representatives of the clergy, nobility, and the cities) met in Paris to discuss monarchical reform and national defense. Unhappy with the heavy war taxes, the incompetence of the warrior nobility, and the brutality of marauding mercenaries, the townspeople sought greater political influence. Political conflict between commoner and nobles soon turned into a massive uprising.

The rebels, under Étienne Marcel, the leader of the merchants of Paris, began to destroy manor houses and castles near the city, massacring entire noble families in a savage class war. Contemporaries were astonished at the intensity and violence of the Jacquerie. The chronicler Jean Froissart, sympathetic to the nobility, said the rebels aimed "to destroy all the nobles and gentry in the world." Repression by nobles was even more savage, however, as thousands of rebels died in battles or were executed. In Paris the rebel leader Marcel was killed in factional strife, but urban rebellions continued to flicker.

English Peasant Revolt. In England, rural and urban discontent intensified as land-

♦**Jacquerie:** zhah kuh REE
♦**Poitiers:** pwah TYAY

lords, peasants, and workers pursued increasingly opposing interests. The trigger for outright rebellion was the imposition of a poll tax (per capita tax) passed by Parliament in 1377 to raise money for the war against France. In May 1381, a revolt broke out. Rebels in Essex and Kent joined bands in London to confront the king. A famous couplet by the radical preacher John Ball, who was executed after the revolt, expresses the rebels' egalitarian, antinoble sentiment:

> When Adam delved [dug] and Eve span [spun]
> Who was then a gentleman?

Forced to address the rebels, young King Richard II agreed to abolish serfdom and impose a ceiling on land rent, concessions immediately rescinded after the rebels' defeat in a suppression as bloody as that in France.

Unrest in Flanders. Popular uprisings also took place in the Low Countries, especially in the cities of Flanders, the most densely populated and urbanized region of Europe. For more than a century, Flanders had been Europe's industrial and financial heartland, importing raw wool from England, manufacturing fine cloth, and exporting woolen goods to all parts of Europe.

Because the region depended on trade for food and goods, Flanders was especially sensitive to the larger political and economic changes. The Hundred Years' War undermined the woolen industry as Edward III of England declared a trade embargo, thus halting shipments of raw materials to Flemish industries. Although Flanders was a French fief, weavers and other artisans opposed their count's pro-French policy because they depended on English wool. From 1338 to 1345, the citizens of the large industrial city of Ghent rebelled against their prince. In the late 1370s, the townspeople of Ghent sought an alliance with the people of Paris and fielded an army to battle the count. Though they suffered a disastrous defeat in 1382, they were not completely subdued until the fifteenth century.

Urban Insurrections in Italy. Revolts in Rome and Florence resulted in part from the long absence of the popes during the Avignon papacy, which had been established in 1309 after civil strife forced the pope out of Rome. Factional violence between powerful noble families in Rome fueled popular hatred of local magnates and provided the background for a popular revolt. The Florentine chronicler Giovanni Villani wrote that "on May 20, 1347. . . . a certain Cola di Rienzo had just returned to Rome from a mission on behalf of the Roman people to the court of the Pope, to beg him to come and live, with his court, in the bishopric of St. Peter, as he should do." Although unsuccessful in his mission to Avignon, Rienzo so impressed the Romans with his speech that they proclaimed him "tribune of the people," a title harking back to the plebeians' representatives in the ancient Roman republic. "Certain of the Orsini and the Colonna [families]," continued Villani, "as well as other nobles, fled from the city to their lands and castles to escape the fury of the tribune and the people." Rienzo and his followers took advantage of the nobles' flight and tried to remake their city in the image of classical Roman republicanism. But like the revolts in Paris and Ghent, the Roman uprising (1347–1354) was suppressed by the nobility.

The pattern of social conflict behind these urban revolts is best exemplified by the Ciompi◆ uprising in Florence. One of the largest European cities in the fourteenth century, Florence was a center of banking and the woolen industry in southern Europe. As the wool industry declined because of falling demand, unemployment became an explosive social problem. During the summer of 1378, the lower classes, many of them woolworkers, rose against the regime. Joined by artisans and merchants, they demanded more equitable power sharing with the bankers and wealthy merchants who controlled city government. By midsummer, crowds thronged the streets, and woolworkers set fire to the palaces of the rich and demanded the right to form their own guild. The insurrection was subsequently called the Ciompi uprising (meaning "uprising by the little people"). Alarmed by the radical turn of events, the guild artisans turned against their worker allies and defeated them in fierce street battles. The revolt ended

---

◆**Ciompi:** CHAHM pee

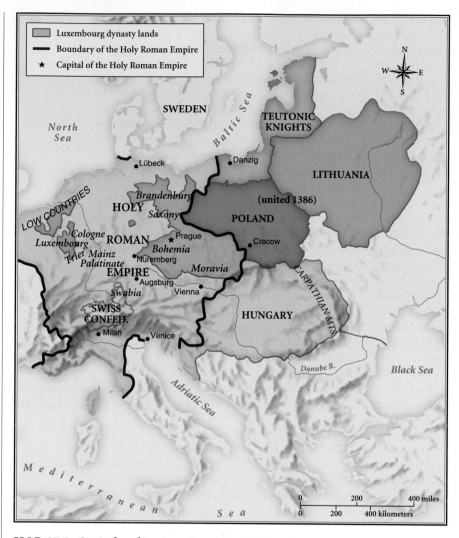

MAP 13.2 Central and Eastern Europe, c. 1400

Through the Holy Roman Empire and the Teutonic Knights, Germanic influence extended far into eastern Europe including Bohemia, Moravia, and the Baltic coast. The Polish-Lithuanian Commonwealth, united in 1386, and the Kingdom of Hungary were the other great powers in eastern Europe.

Europe, nor did they significantly alter the distribution of power. Instead they were subsumed by larger political transformations, from which the princely states would emerge as the major political forces in European civilization in the next centuries.

Imperial Fragmentation and Eastern European State Building

While England and France struggled for domination in western Europe, the Holy Roman Empire, unified in name only, became an arena in which princes and cities assumed more power in their own hands. This political fragmentation, together with a stronger orientation toward the Slavic lands of eastern Europe, signified a growing separation between central and western Europe (see Map 13.2 on this page). Within the empire, the four most significant developments were the shift of political focus from the south and west to the east, the changing balance of power between the emperor and the princes, the development of cities, and the rise of self-governing communes in the Alps.

Three of the five Holy Roman Emperors in the period from 1350 to 1450 belonged to the House of Luxembourg: Charles IV (r. 1355–1378), Wenceslas (r. 1378–1400), and Sigismund (r. 1410–1437). Having obtained Bohemia by marriage, the Luxembourg dynasty based its power in the east, and Prague became the imperial capital. This move initiated a shift of power within the Holy Roman Empire away from the Rhineland and Swabia toward east-central Europe. Except for a continuous involvement with northern Italy, theoretically a part of the Holy

with a restoration of the patrician regime, although Ciompi exiles continued to plot worker revolts into the 1380s.

The Ciompi rebellion, like the uprisings in Paris, Ghent, and Rome, were part of a larger set of changes in late medieval Europe. The rebels were motivated by social and economic depression, which in turn was caused by the general crisis of warfare, economic stagnation, and disease. But as significant as their motivations was their failure. Urban revolts did not redraw the political map of

Roman Empire, German institutions became more closely allied with eastern rather than western Europe. For example, the Holy Roman Empire's first university, Charles University (named after its royal founder, Charles IV), was established in 1348 in Prague. Bohemians and Hungarians also began to exert more influence in imperial politics.

Another development that separated central from western Europe was the fragmentation of political authority in the Holy Roman Empire at a time when French, English, and Castilian monarchs were consolidating their power. Charles IV's coronation as emperor in 1355 did not translate into more power at home. The Bohemian nobility refused to recognize his supreme authority, and the German princes secured from him a constitutional guarantee for their own sovereignty. In 1356, Charles was forced to agree to the Golden Bull, a document that required the German king to be chosen by seven electors: the archbishops of Mainz, Cologne, and Trier, the king of Bohemia, the elector of Saxony, the count of the Palatinate, and the margrave of Brandenburg. The imperial electoral college also guaranteed the existence of numerous local and regional power centers, a distinctive feature in German history that continued into the modern age.

Although no single German city rivaled Paris, London, Florence, or Ghent in population, its large number of cities made Germany an economic power. But rivalry among powerful princes prevented the cities from evolving into republics like those in Italy. Nevertheless, the cities were at the forefront of economic growth. Nuremberg and Augsburg became centers of the north–south trade, linking Poland, Bohemia, and the German lands with the Mediterranean. In northern Germany, the Hanseatic League (from *Hansa*, a German merchant guild or trading association), under the leadership of Lübeck, united the many towns trading between the Baltic and the North Sea. At its zenith in the fifteenth century, the Hanseatic fleet controlled the Baltic, and the league was a power to be reckoned with by kings and princes.

Another sign of political fragmentation was the growth of self-governing peasant and town communes in the high Alpine valleys that united in the Swiss Confederation. In

1291, the peasants of Uri, Schwyz, and Unterwalden had sworn a perpetual alliance against their oppressive Habsburg overlord. After defeating a Habsburg army in 1315, these free peasants took the name Confederates and developed a new alliance that would become Switzerland. In the process, the Swiss enshrined their freedom in the legend of William Tell, their national hero who was forced by a Habsburg official to prove his archery skills by successfully shooting an arrow through an apple placed on the head of his own son. This challenge so outraged the citizens that they rose up in arms against the Habsburg rule. By 1353, Lucerne, Zurich, and Bern had joined the confederation. The Swiss Confederation continued to acquire new members into the sixteenth century, defeating armies sent by different princes.

Growth of the Swiss Confederation to 1353

Also in the mid-fourteenth century, two large monarchies took shape in northeastern Europe— Poland and Lithuania. In the early twelfth century, Poland had splintered into petty duchies, and the Mongol invasion of the 1240s had caused frightful devastation. But recovery was under way by 1300, and unlike almost every other part of Europe, Poland experienced an era of demographic and economic expansion in the fourteenth century. Both Jewish and German settlers, for example, helped build thriving towns like Cracow. Monarchical consolidation followed. King Casimir♦ III (r. 1333–1370) won recognition in most of the country's regions for his royal authority, embodied in comprehensive law codes. A problem that persisted throughout his reign, however, was conflict with the neighboring princes of Lithuania, Europe's last pagan rulers, who for centuries fiercely resisted Christianization by the German crusading order, the Teutonic Knights. After the Mongols overran Russia, Lithuania extended its rule southward, offering western Russian princes protection against Mongol and Musco-

♦**Casimir:** KAH zuh mihr

vite rule. By the late fourteenth century, a vast Lithuanian principality had arisen, embracing modern Lithuania, Belarus, and Ukraine.

Casimir III died in 1370 without a son; the failure of a new dynasty to take hold opened the way for the unification of Poland and Lithuania. In 1386, the Lithuanian prince Jogailo accepted Roman Catholic baptism, married the young queen of Poland, and later assumed the Polish crown. Under the Jagiellonian dynasty, Poland and Lithuania kept separate legal systems. Catholicism and Polish culture prevailed among the principality's upper class, while most native Lithuanian village folk remained pagan for several centuries. With only a few interruptions, the Polish-Lithuanian federation would last for five centuries.

Multiethnic States on the Frontiers

While some Christian princes were battling one another, others were fighting Muslim foes at the frontiers of Christian Europe. Two regions at opposite ends of the Mediterranean—Spain and the Ottoman Empire—were unusual in medieval Europe for their religious and ethnic diversity. As a result of the Spanish **reconquista** of the twelfth and thirteenth centuries, the Iberian Christian kingdoms contained large religious and ethnic minorities. In Castile, where historians estimate the population before the outbreak of the plague in 1348 at four to five million, 7 percent of the inhabitants were Muslims or Jews. In Aragon, of the approximately one million people at midcentury, perhaps 3 to 4 percent belonged to these two religious minorities. In the Iberian peninsula, the Christian kingdoms consolidated their gains against Muslim Granada, bringing sizable minority populations into newly Christian regions. At the same time, the orthodox Byzantine Empire, hardly recovered from the Fourth Crusade, fought for survival against the Ottoman

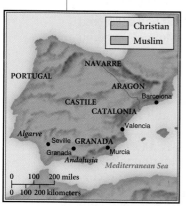

Christian Territory in Iberia, c. 1350

Turks. In the Balkans and Anatolia, the Ottomans created a multiethnic state, but one different from the Iberian kingdoms.

The Iberian Peninsula. In the mid-fourteenth century, the Iberian peninsula encompassed six areas: Portugal, Castile, Navarre, Aragon, and Catalonia—all Christian—and Muslim Granada. Among these territories, Castile and Aragon were the most important, both politically and economically. The Muslim population was concentrated in the south. Initially, the Iberian Muslims, called **Moors**, under Christian rule could own property, practice their religion, and elect their own judges, but conditions worsened for them in the fifteenth century as fears of rebellions and religious prejudices intensified among Christians. As Christian conquerors and settlers advanced, most Muslims were driven out of the cities or confined to specific neighborhoods. Many Muslims were captured and enslaved by Christian armies. These slaves worked in Christian households or on large estates called **latifundia**, which were granted by the Castilian kings to the crusading orders, the church, and powerful noble families. Slavery existed on a fairly large scale in Mediterranean areas where Christian and Muslim civilizations confronted one another: in Iberia, North Africa, Anatolia, and in the Balkans.

Jews congregated mostly in cities, where they practiced many professions and encountered few social obstacles to advancement. Jewish physicians and tax collectors made up part of the administration of Castile, but the Christian populace resented their social prominence and wealth. Moreover, the religious fervor and sense of crisis in the later fourteenth century intensified the ever-present intolerance toward Jews. In June 1391, incited by the sermons of the priest Fernandon Martínez, a mob attacked the Jewish community in Seville, plundering, burning, and killing all who refused baptism. The anti-Semitic violence spread to other cities in the peninsula. Sometimes the authorities tried to protect the Jews, who were legally the king's property. About half of the 200,000 Castilian Jews converted to Christianity to save themselves; another 25,000 were murdered or fled to

Portugal and Granada. The survivors were to face even more discrimination and violence in the fifteenth century.

The Ottoman and Byzantine Empires. The fourteenth century also saw a great power rise at the other end of the Mediterranean. Under Osman I (r. 1280–1324) and his son Orhan Gazi (r. 1324–1359), the Ottoman dynasty became a formidable force in Anatolia and the Balkans, where political disunity opened the door for Ottoman advances (Map 13.3). The Ottomans were one of several Turkish tribal confederations in central Asia. As converts to Islam and as warriors, the Ottoman cavalry raided Byzantine territory in an Islamic jihad, or holy war.

Under Murat I (r. 1360–1389), the Ottomans reduced the Byzantine Empire to the city of Constantinople and the status of a vassal state. In 1364, Murat defeated a joint Hungarian-Serbian army at the Maritsa River, alerting Europe for the first time to the new threat of an Islamic invasion. Pope Urban V called for a crusade, but the Christian kingdoms in the west were already fighting in the Hundred Years' War. In the Balkans, the Ottomans skillfully exploited Christian disunity, playing

Janissaries in the Ottoman Army
Janissaries (literally "new infantry") were recruited from among Christian boys raised by the sultan. They were distinguished by their high ornamental headgear and their use of firearms, which made them a particularly effective component of the Ottoman forces. Here a squad of Janissaries is shown on parade, with a model of a Turkish war galley. *Österreichische National bibliothek.*

Serbian, Albanian, Wallachian,♦ Bulgarian, and Byzantine interests against one another. Moreover, Venice, Genoa, and Ragusa each pursued separate commercial interests. Thus, an Ottoman army allied not only with the Bulgarians but even with some Serbian princes won the battle of Kosovo (1389), destroying the last organized Christian resistance south of the Danube. The Ottomans secured control of southeastern Europe after 1396, when at Nicopolis they crushed a crusading army.

The Ottoman invasion was more than a continuation of the struggle between Christendom and Islam. The battle for territory transcended the boundaries of faith. Christian princes also served the Ottoman Empire as vassals to the sultan. The **Janissaries** (above), Christian slave children raised by the sultan

MAP 13.3 Ottoman Expansion in the Fourteenth and Fifteenth Centuries
The Balkans were the major theater of expansion for the Ottoman Empire, whose conquests also included Egypt and the North African coast. The Byzantine Empire was long reduced to the city of Constantinople and surrounded by the Ottomans before its final fall in 1453.

♦**Wallachian:** wah LAY kee uhn

as Muslims, constituted the fundamental backbone of the Ottoman army. They formed a service class, the *devshirme*, which was both dependent on and loyal to the ruler. At the sultan's court, Christian women were prominent in the harem; thus, many Ottoman princes had Greek or Serbian mothers. In addition to the Janissaries, Christian princes and converts to Islam served in the emerging Ottoman administration. In conquered areas, existing religious and social structures remained intact when local people accepted Ottoman overlordship and paid taxes. Only in areas of persistent resistance did the Ottomans drive out or massacre the inhabitants, settling Turkish tribes in their place. A distinctive pattern of Balkan history was thus established at the beginning of the Ottoman conquest: extremely diverse ethnic and religious communities were woven together into the fabric of an efficient central state.

By the mid-fourteenth century, the territory of the Byzantine Empire consisted of only Constantinople, Thessalonika, and a narrow strip of land in modern-day Greece. During the century, the Black Death, three civil wars between rivals to the throne, and numerous Ottoman incursions devastated Byzantine land and population. Constantinople was saved in 1402 from a five-year Ottoman siege only when Mongol invaders crushed another Ottoman army near Ankara in Anatolia. Although the empire's fortunes declined, Byzantium experienced a religious and cultural ferment, as the elites compensated for their loss of power in a search for past glory. The majority asserted the superiority of the Greek Orthodox faith and opposed the reunion of the Roman and Greek churches, the political price for western European military aid. Many adhered to tradition, attacking any departures from ancient literary models and Byzantine institutions. A handful, such as the scholar George Gemistos (1353–1452), abandoned Christianity and embraced Platonic philosophy. Gemistos even changed his name (meaning "full" in Greek) to Plethon, its classical equivalent. The scholar Manuel Chrysoloras◆ became professor of Greek in Florence in 1397, thus establishing the study of ancient Greece in

◆**Chrysoloras:** krihs uh LOHR uhs

western Europe. This revival of interest in Greek antiquity eventually became part of the broad cultural movement known as the Renaissance.

> **Review:** How were dynastic warfare and popular uprisings related in the fourteenth century?

❖ The Plague and Society

Confronted with the rise of the Ottoman Empire, Latin Christendom faced a series of internal crises that wrought havoc on its population and economy. In the fifty years after 1348, Europe lost one-third of its population to repeated outbreaks of the bubonic plague, which originated in central Asia. A healthy population could have resisted the plague, but Europeans were far from healthy: they had been suffering from famines and hunger for two generations before the first outbreak. In the face of massive deaths, a new climate of fear settled on the landscape. Some people tried to avert the "scourge of God" in rituals of religious fanaticism; others searched out scapegoats, killing Jews and burning synagogues.

The demographic crisis also had important consequences for the economy, causing falling demands for food and goods and economic contraction. Further symptoms of this social and economic crisis were social unrest, labor strife, rising wages, and falling investments. A mood of uncertainty prevailed in business, and women were excluded more and more from the urban economy.

Rise and Spread of the Plague

Well before the plague struck, European economic growth had slowed and then stopped. By 1300, the economy could no longer support Europe's swollen population. Having cleared forests and drained swamps, the peasant masses now farmed marginal lands and divided their plots into ever smaller parcels; as a result, their income and the quality of their diet eroded. In the great urban centers, where thousands depended on steady employment and cheap bread, a bad harvest, always followed by sharply rising food prices, meant hunger and eventual famine. A cooling of the European climate also contributed to the crisis in the food supply. Modern studies of tree rings indicate that fourteenth-century Europe entered a colder period, with a succession of severe winters beginning in 1315. The extreme cold upset an ecological system already overtaxed by human civilization. Crop failures were widespread. In many cities of northwestern Europe, the price of bread tripled in a month, and thousands starved to death. Some Flemish cities, for example, lost 10 percent of their population. But the Great Famine of 1315–1317 was only the first in a series of catastrophes confronting the overpopulated and undernourished society of fourteenth-century Europe. In midcentury, death mowed down masses of weakened bodies.

From its breeding ground in central Asia, the bubonic plague passed eastward into China, where it decimated the population and wiped out the remnants of the tiny Italian merchant community in Yangzhou. Bacteria-carrying fleas, living on black rats, transmitted the disease. The disease traveled back to Europe alongside valuable cargoes of silk, porcelain, and spices. In 1347, the Genoese colony in Caffa in the Crimea contracted the plague from the Mongols. Fleeing by ship in a desperate but futile attempt to escape the disease, the Genoese in turn communicated the plague to other Mediterranean seaports. By January 1348, the plague had infected Sicily, Sardinia, Corsica, and Marseilles. Six months later, it had spread to Aragon, all of Italy, the Balkans, and most of France. The disease then crept northward to Germany, England, and Scandinavia, reaching the Russian city of Novgorod in 1350 (Map 13.4 on page 484).

Nothing like the Black Death (1348–1350), as this epidemic came to be called, had struck Europe since the great plague of the sixth century. The Italian writer Giovanni Boccaccio◆ (1313–1375) reported that the plague

> first betrayed itself by the emergence of certain tumors in the groin or the armpits, some of which grew as large as a common apple, others as an egg.... From the two said parts of the

---

◆**Giovanni Boccaccio:** joh VAHN nee bohk KAHT choh

Death Strangling a Plague Victim
In this graphic and terrifying illustration from a fourteenth-century Czech manuscript, the plague is personified as Death choking a sick man to death in his bed. Note the black running sore on the side of the body under the right armpit, which corresponds to contemporary descriptions of symptoms of the plague. *Werner Forman/Art Resource, NY.*

> body this ... began to propagate and spread itself in all directions indifferently; after which the form of the malady began to change, black spots or livid making their appearance in many cases on the arm or the thigh or elsewhere, now few and large, now minute and numerous.

Most cities, where crowding and filth increased the chances of contagion, lost roughly half their population in less than a year. Florence lost almost two-thirds of its population of ninety thousand; Siena lost half its people. Paris, the largest city of western Europe, came off relatively well, losing only a quarter of its 200,000 inhabitants. Rural areas seem to have suffered fewer deaths, but regional differences were pronounced. (See "Taking Measure," page 485.)

Helplessness and incomprehension worsened the terror wrought by the plague. The Black Death was not particular: old and young, poor and rich were equally affected, although the wealthy had a better chance of avoiding the disease if they escaped to their country estates before the epidemic hit their city. Medical knowledge of the time could not explain the plague's causes. The physicians at the University of Paris blamed the calamity on the stars. In a report prepared for King Philip VI of France in 1348, the professors of medicine described a conjunction of Saturn, Mars, and Jupiter in the house of Aquarius in 1345, resulting in widespread death and pestilence on earth. Various treatments were used in an attempt to combat the plague, ranging from bloodletting, a traditional cure to balance the body's four humors, to the commonsense remedy of lying quietly in bed and the desperate suggestion of breathing in the vapors of latrines. Many people believed that poisoned air caused the disease, and upon hearing of an outbreak, they walled in their neighbors, hoping in vain to contain the epidemic.

The devastation of 1348 was only the beginning. The plague cut down Europeans repeatedly. Further outbreaks occurred in 1361, 1368–1369, 1371, 1375, 1390, and 1405; they continued, with longer dormant intervals, into the eighteenth century.

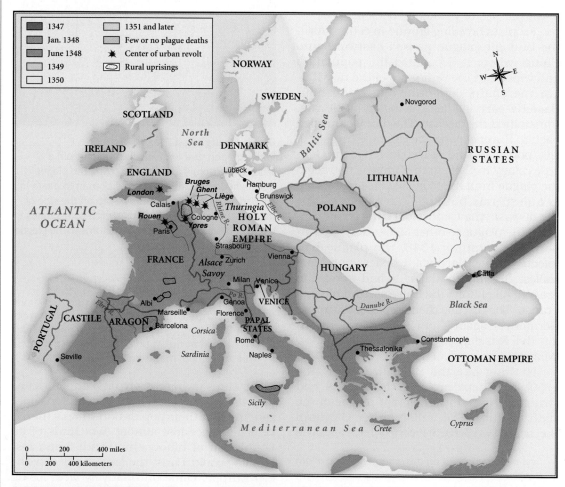

MAP 13.4 Advance of the Plague, 1347–1350
The gradual but deadly spread of the plague followed the roads and rivers of Europe. Note the earlier transmission by sea from the Crimea to the ports of the Mediterranean before the general spread to northern Europe.

TAKING MEASURE

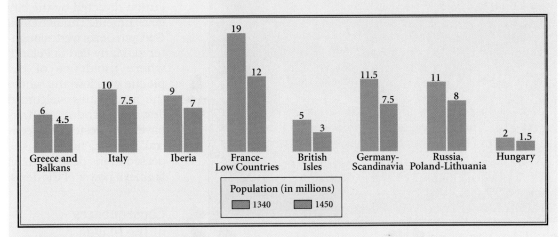

Population Losses and the Plague
The bar chart represents dramatically the impact of the Black Death and the recurrent plagues between 1340 and 1450. More than a century after the Black Death, none of the regions of Europe had made up for the losses of population. The population of 1450 stood at about 75–80 percent of the pre-plague population. The hardest hit areas were France and the Low Countries, which also suffered from the devastations of the Hundred Years' War. *From Carlo M. Cipolla, ed.,* Fontana Economic History of Europe: The Middle Ages *(Great Britain: Collins/Fontana Books, 1974), 36.*

Responses to the Plague: Flagellants and Anti-Semitism

Some believed the plague was God's way of chastising a sinful world and sought to save themselves by repenting their sins. In 1349, bands of men and women wearing tattered clothes, marching in pairs, carrying flags, and following their own leaders appeared in southern Germany. When they reached a town or village, they visited the local church and, to the great astonishment of the congregation and the alarm of the clergy, sang hymns while publicly whipping themselves, according to strict rituals, until blood flowed. They soon came to be called **flagellants**◆ (see Flagellants, page 486).

From southern Germany the flagellants moved throughout the Holy Roman Empire. In groups of several dozen to many hundred, they traveled and attracted great excitement. The flagellants' flamboyant piety moved many laypeople, but most of the clergy

◆**flagellants:** FLA juh luhnts

distrusted a lay movement that did not originate within the church hierarchy. At the inception of the movement, the flagellants recruited only from respectable social groups, such as artisans and merchants. Converts who joined the wandering bands, however, often came from the margins of society, and discipline began to break down. In 1350, the church declared the flagellants heretical and suppressed them.

In some communities the flagellants spawned violence against Jews. From 1348 to 1350, anti-Semitic persecutions, beginning in southern France and spreading through Savoy to the Holy Roman Empire, destroyed many Jewish communities in central and western Europe. Sometimes the clergy incited the attacks against the Jews, calling them Christ-killers, accusing them of poisoning wells and kidnapping and ritually slaughtering Christian children, and charging them with stealing and desecrating the host (the communion wafer that Catholics believed became the body of Christ during Mass). In towns throughout Europe, economic resentment

Flagellants

The penitential brothers of the cross carried a banner depicting the instruments of Christ's torture and a crucifix as they scourged themselves on their exposed backs with whips (shown in their right hands), chanting for God's forgiveness and an end to the plague. The Latin text beneath this illustration (not shown) explained the flagellant procession in 1349 in Tournai: "The preceding year on the day of the Assumption of the Virgin, some two hundred men came from the town of Bruges, and almost every hour they whipped themselves and called on God to bestow grace on their penance." Both Tournai and Bruges are in today's Belgium. © ARPL/Topham/The Image Works.

fueled anti-Semitism as those in debt turned on creditors, often Jews who had become rich from the commercial revolution of the thirteenth century. Perhaps most cynical were the nobility of Alsace, heavily indebted to Jewish bankers, who sanctioned the murder of Jews to avoid repaying their debts.

Many anti-Semitic incidents were spontaneous, with mobs plundering Jewish quarters and killing anyone who refused baptism. Authorities seeking a focus for the widespread anger and fear orchestrated some of the violence. Relying on chronicles, historians have long linked the arrival of the Black Death with anti-Jewish violence. More recent historical research shows that in some cities the anti-Semitic violence actually preceded the epidemic. This revised chronology of events demonstrates official complicity and even careful premeditation in the destruction of some Jewish communities, exploiting popular hysteria about the plague. For example, the magistrates of Nuremberg

obtained approval from Emperor Charles IV before organizing the 1349 persecution directed by the city government. Thousands of German Jews were slaughtered. Many fled to Poland, where incidence of the plague was low and where the authorities welcomed Jews as productive taxpayers. In western and central Europe, however, the persecutions destroyed the financial power of the Jews.

Consequences of the Plague

Although the Black Death took a horrible human toll, some people profited from the disaster. In an overpopulated society with limited resources, massive death opened the ranks for advancement. For example, after 1350, landlords had difficulty acquiring new tenant farmers without making concessions in land contracts; fewer priests now competed for the same number of **benefices** (ecclesiastical offices funded by an endowment), and workers received much higher wages because the supply of laborers had plummeted. The Black Death and the resulting decline in urban population meant a lower demand for grain relative to the supply and thus a drop in cereal prices. All across Europe noble landlords, whose revenues dropped as prices dropped, had to adjust to these new circumstances. Some revived feudal demands for labor services; others looked to their central government for legislation to regulate wages; and still others granted favorable terms to peasant proprietors, often after bloody peasant revolts. Many noblemen lost a portion of their wealth and a measure of their autonomy and political influence. Consequently, European nobles became more dependent on their monarchs and on war to supplement their incomes and enhance their power.

For the peasantry and the urban working population, the higher wages generally meant an improvement in living standards. To compensate for the lower demand and price for grain, many peasants and landlords turned to stock breeding and grape and barley cultivation. As European agriculture diversified, peasants and artisans consumed more beer, wine, meat, cheese, and vegetables—a better and more varied diet than their thirteenth-century forebears had eaten. The reduced cereal prices also stimulated sheep raising in place of farming, and thus a portion of the settled population, especially in the English Midlands and in Castile, became migratory.

Because of the shrinking population and decreased demand for food, cultivating marginal fields was no longer profitable and many settlements were simply abandoned. By 1450, for example, some 450 large English villages and many smaller hamlets had disappeared. In central Europe east of the Elbe River, where German peasants had migrated, large tracts of cultivated land reverted to forest. Estimates suggest that some 80 percent of all villages in parts of Thuringia♦ (Germany) vanished.

Also as a result of the plague, the focus of manufacturing shifted from a mass market to a highly lucrative, if small, luxury market. The drastic loss in urban population had reduced the demand for such mass-manufactured goods as cloth, one of the causes for the Ciompi uprising in Florence. Fewer people now possessed proportionately greater concentrations of wealth. In the southern French city of Albi, for example, the proportion of citizens with possessions worth more than a hundred French pounds doubled between 1343 and 1357, while the number of poor people, those with less than ten pounds, declined by half.

Faced with the possibility of imminent and untimely death, some of the urban populace sought immediate gratification. The Florentine Matteo Villani described the newfound desire for luxury in his native city in 1351: "The common people ... wanted the dearest and most delicate foods ... while children and common women clad themselves in all the fair and costly garments of the illustrious who had died." Those with means increased their consumption of luxuries: silk clothing, hats, doublets (snug-fitting men's jackets), and boots from Italy as well as expensive jewelry and spices from Asia became fashionable in northwestern Europe. Whereas agricultural prices continued to decline, prices of manufactured goods, particularly luxury items, remained constant and even rose as demand for them outstripped supply.

The long-term consequences of this new consumption pattern spelled the end for the traditional woolen industry that had produced for a mass market. Diminishing demand for wool caused hardships for woolworkers, and social and political unrest shook many older industrial centers dependent on the cloth industry. In the Flemish clothing center of Ypres,♦ for example, production figures fell from a high of ninety thousand pieces of cloth in 1320 to fewer than twenty-five thousand by 1390. In Ghent, where 44 percent of all households were woolworkers and where some 60 percent of the working population depended on the textile industry, the woolen market's slump meant constant labor unrest.

Much more difficult to measure was the sense of economic insecurity. One trend, however, seemed clear: the increasingly restrictive labor market for women in the urban economy in this age of crisis. In the German city of Cologne, for example, more and more artisan guilds excluded women from their ranks. By the late fifteenth century, the independent women's guilds had become a relic of the past. Everywhere, fathers favored sons and sons-in-law to succeed them in their crafts. Daughters and widows, however, resisted this patriarchal regime in the urban economy. They were most successful in industries with the least regulations, such as in beer brewing—where in Munich, for example, women held productive positions amid the economic recession.

Review: What were the demographic, economic, and psychological consequences of the plague?

♦**Thuringia:** thu RIHN jee uh

♦**Ypres:** EEP ruh

❖ Challenges to Spiritual Authority

The crises of confidence and control that swept late medieval Europe extended to the papacy, the very symbol of Christian unity and authority. The popes' claim to supremacy in Christendom had never been unchallenged. Kings and princes contested the popes' dual authority as spiritual and temporal rulers; friars and preachers questioned their wealth and power; theologians doubted the monarchical pretensions of popes over general church councils; heretics and dissenters denied outright their claims of apostolic succession. While some voices opposed papal authority within the church, other movements offered alternative visions and institutions for the faithful's guidance and salvation.

The Papal Monarchy and Its Critics

Papal government continued to grow even after the papal residence moved to Avignon in 1309. In the fourteenth century, the papacy's government and institutions were more sophisticated than those of secular states. A succession of popes, all lawyers by training, concentrated on consolidating the financial and legal powers of the church, mainly through appointments and taxes. Claiming the right to assign all benefices, the popes gradually secured authority over the clergy throughout western and central Europe. Under the skillful guidance of John XXII (r. 1316–1334), papal rights increased incrementally without causing much protest. By 1350, the popes had secured the right to appoint all major benefices and many minor ones. To gain these lucrative positions, potential candidates often made gifts to the papal court. This imposition of papal taxes on all benefice holders developed from taxation to finance the Crusades. Out of these precedents the papacy instituted a regular system of papal taxation that produced the money it needed to consolidate papal government.

Papal government consisted of the pope's personal household, the College of Cardinals, and the church's financial and judicial apparatus. Combining elements of monarchy and oligarchy, the curia developed a bureaucracy that paralleled the organization of secular government. The pope's relatives often played a major role in his household; many popes came from extended noble lineages, and they often gave their family members preferential treatment.

After the pope, the cardinals, as a collective body, were the most elevated entity in the church. Like great nobles in royal courts, the cardinals, many of them nobles themselves, advised and aided the pope. They maintained their own households, employing scores of scribes, servants, and retainers. Most posts in the papal bureaucracy went to clerics with legal training, thus accentuating the juristic and administrative character of the highest spiritual authority in Christendom. During the fourteenth and fifteenth centuries, the papal army also grew, as the popes sought to restore and control the Papal States in Italy.

This growing papal monarchy was sharply criticized by members of the mendicant orders, who denounced the papal pretension to worldly power and wealth. William of Ockham◆ (c. 1285–1349), an English Franciscan who was one of the most eminent theologians of his age, believed that church power derived from the congregation of the faithful, both laity and clergy, not from the pope or a church council. Rejecting the confident synthesis of Christian doctrine and Aristotelian philosophy by Thomas Aquinas, Ockham believed that universal concepts had no reality in nature but instead existed only as mere representations, names in the mind—a philosophy that came to be called **nominalism**. Perceiving and analyzing such concepts as "man" or "papal infallibility" offered no assurance that the concepts expressed truth. Observation and human reason were limited as the means to understand the universe and to know God. Ockham emphasized the covenant between God and his faithful. God promises to act consistently—for example, to reward virtue and punish vice. Ockham stressed simplicity in his explanations of universal concepts. His insistence that simple explanations were superior to complex ones became known as Ockham's razor. Imprisoned by Pope John XXII for

◆**Ockham:** AH kuhm

heresy in 1328, Ockham escaped in 1328 and found refuge with Emperor Louis of Bavaria.

Another antipapal refugee at the imperial court was Marsilius of Padua, a citizen of an Italian commune, a physician and lawyer by training, and rector of the University of Paris. Marsilius attacked the very basis of papal power in *The Defender of the Peace* (1324). The true church, Marsilius argued, was constituted by the people, who had the right to select the head of the church, either through the body of the faithful or through a "human legislator." Papal power, Marsilius asserted, was the result of historical usurpation, and its exercise represented tyranny. In 1327, John XXII, the living target of the treatise, decreed the work heretical.

The Great Schism, 1378–1417

By the second half of the fourteenth century, the Avignon papacy had taken on a definitive French character. All five popes elected between 1305 and 1378 were natives of southern France, as were many of the cardinals and most of the curia. Moreover, French parishes provided half of the papacy's income. Subjected to pressure from the French monarchy and turning increasingly secular in its opulence and splendor, the papacy was lambasted by the Italian poet Francesco Petrarch as being "in Babylonian Captivity," like the Jews of ancient Israel who were exiled by their Babylonian conquerors. Nonetheless, Gregory XI, elected pope in 1371, was determined to return to Rome, where he expected to exert greater moral force to organize a crusade against the Ottomans. Before he could carry out his plans, however, Florence declared war against the Papal States in 1375, and Gregory hastened to Rome to prevent the collapse of his territorial power in Italy.

When Gregory died in 1378, sixteen cardinals—one Spanish, four Italian, and eleven French—met in Rome to elect the new pope. Although many in the curia were homesick for Avignon, the Roman people, determined to keep the papacy and its revenues in Rome, clamored for the election of a Roman. An unruly crowd rioted outside the conclave, drowning out the cardinals' discussions. Fearing for their lives, the cardinals

elected the archbishop of Bari, an Italian, who took the title Urban VI. If the cardinals thought they had elected a weak man who would both do their bidding and satisfy the Romans, they were wrong: Urban immediately tried to curb the cardinals' power. In response, thirteen cardinals elected another pope, Clement VII, and returned to Avignon.

Thus began the second **Great Schism** in the Christian church (see page 367 for the first Great Schism, in 1054), which was perpetuated by political divisions in Europe (Map 13.5 on page 490). Charles V of France, who did not want the papacy to return to Rome, immediately recognized Clement, his cousin, as did several other rulers. An enemy of Charles V, Richard II of England, professed allegiance to Urban, as did the rulers of other areas. Faithful Christians were equally divided in their loyalties. Even the greatest mystic of the age—Catherine of Siena (1347–1380), who told of her mystical unions with God and spiritual ecstasies in more than 350 letters and was later canonized a saint—found herself forced to take sides. Catherine supported Urban. But another holy man, Vincent Ferrer (1350–1419), a popular Dominican preacher, supported Clement. All Christians theoretically found themselves deprived of the means of salvation, as bans from Rome and Avignon each placed a part of Christian Europe under interdict, or censure from participation in most sacraments and from Christian burial. Because neither pope would step down willingly, the leading intellectuals in the church tried to end the schism. Success would elude them for nearly forty years.

The Conciliar Movement

According to canon law, only a pope could summon a general council of the church, a sort of parliament of all Christians. But given the state of confusion in Christendom, many intellectuals argued that the crisis justified calling a general council to represent the body of the faithful, over and against the head of the church. Jean Gerson, chancellor of the University of Paris, asserted that "the pope can be removed by a general council celebrated without his consent and against his will." He justified his claim by reasoning

MAP 13.5 The Great Schism, 1378–1417
The allegiances to Roman and Avignon popes followed the political divisions between the European monarchs. The Great Schism weakened the Latin West during a period of Islamic expansion through the Ottoman Empire.

that "normally a council is not legally... celebrated without papal calling....But, as in grammar and in morals, general rules have exceptions."

The first attempt to resolve the question of church authority came in 1409, at the Council of Pisa, attended by cardinals who had defected from the two popes. The council asserted its supremacy by declaring both popes deposed and electing a new pontiff, Alexander V. When the popes at Rome and Avignon refused to yield to the authority of the council, Christian Europe found itself in the embarrassing position of choosing

among three popes. Pressure to hold another council then came from central Europe, where a new heretical movement, ultimately known as Hussitism, undermined orthodoxy from Bohemia to central Germany. Threatened politically by challenges to church authority, Emperor Sigismund pressed Pope John XXIII, the successor to Alexander (who had died ten months after being elected), to convene a church council at Constance in 1414–1417.

The cardinals, bishops, and theologians assembled in Constance felt compelled to combat heresy and heal the schism. As described later in this chapter, they ordered Jan Hus, leader of the Hussite movement, burned at the stake. They deposed John XXIII, the "Pisan pope," because of tyrannical behavior, condemning him as an antipope. The Roman pope, Gregory XII, accepted the council's authority and resigned in 1415 (having been elected in 1406). At its closing in 1417, the council also deposed Benedict XIII (Clement's successor), who refused to abdicate the Avignon papacy. The rest of Christendom, however, hailed Martin V, the council's appointment, as the new pope, thus ending the Great Schism.

Dissenters and Heretics

Religious conflict in the late Middle Ages took a variety of forms. The papacy struggled with its critics within the church but found religious dissension outside the church even more threatening.

Free Spirits, Beguines, and Beghards. The Free Spirits, found mostly in northern Europe, practiced an extreme form of **mysticism**. They asserted that humans and God were of the same essence and that individual believers could attain salvation, even sanctity, without the church and its sacraments. In the fourteenth century, the Free Spirits found converts among the Beguines,◆ pious laywomen who lived together, and the Beghards, men who did not belong to a particular religious order but who led pious lives and begged for their sustenance. Living in community houses (*beguinages*), the Beguines imitated the convent lives of nuns but did not submit to clerical control. First prevalent in northern Europe, beguinages sprang up rapidly in the Low Countries and the Rhineland, regions of heavy urbanization. This essentially urban development represented the desire by many urban women to achieve salvation through piety and good works, as many began to feel that the clergy did not adequately address their spiritual needs.

For the church, the existence of Free Spirits among the Beghards and Beguines raised the larger question of ecclesiastical control, for this development threatened to eliminate the boundary between the laity and the

◆**Beguines:** bay GEENS

Burning of a Heretic
Execution by fire was the usual method of killing heretics. This illustration shows the burning of a Lollard, a follower of the teachings of Wycliffe, who opposed the established church. While heretics were condemned by the church, their executions were at the hands of secular authorities, who are present here.
Hulton Getty/Liaison Agency.

clergy. In the 1360s, Emperor Charles IV and Pope Urban V extended the Inquisition to Germany in a move to crush this heresy. In the cities of the Rhineland, fifteen mass trials took place, most around the turn of the fifteenth century. By condemning the heretics and requiring beguinages to be under the control of the mendicant orders, the church contained potential dissent. Throughout the fifteenth century the number of beguinages continued to drop.

Lollards. In England, intellectual dissent, social unrest, and nationalist sentiment combined to create a powerful anticlerical movement that the church hierarchy labeled Lollardy (from *lollar*, meaning "idler"). John Wycliffe (c. 1330–1384), who inspired the movement, was an Oxford professor. Initially employed as a royal apologist in the struggle between state and church, Wycliffe gradually developed ideas that challenged the very foundations of the Roman church. His treatise *On the Church*, composed in 1378, advanced the view that the true church was a community of believers rather than a clerical hierarchy. In other writings, Wycliffe repudiated monasticism, excommunication, the Mass, and the priesthood, substituting reliance on Bible reading and individual conscience in place of the official church as the path to salvation. Responsibility for church reform, Wycliffe believed, rested with the king, whose authority he claimed exceeded that of the pope.

At Oxford, Wycliffe gathered around him like-minded intellectuals, and together they influenced and reflected a widespread anticlericalism in late medieval England. Wycliffe actively promoted the use of English in religious writing. His supporters included members of the gentry, but most were artisans and other humbler people who had some literacy. Religious dissent was key in motivating the 1381 peasant uprising in England, and the radical preacher John Ball was only one of the many common priests who supported the revolt. Real income for parish priests had fallen steadily after the Black Death, and as a result the sympathy of the impoverished clergy lay with the common folk against the great bishops, abbots, and lords of the realm.

After Wycliffe's death, the English bishops suppressed intellectual dissent at Oxford. But in spite of persistent persecutions, Lollard ideas, such as clandestine English Bibles, survived underground during the fifteenth century, to resurface during the convulsive religious conflict of the early sixteenth century known as the Reformation.

The Hussite Revolution

The most profound challenge to papal authority in the late Middle Ages came from Bohemia. Here the spiritual, intellectual, political, and economic criticisms of the papacy that sprang up in other countries fused in one explosive spark. Religious dissent quickly became the vehicle for a nationalist uprising and a social revolution.

Under Emperor Charles IV the pace of economic development and social change in the Holy Roman Empire had quickened in the mid-fourteenth century. Prague, the capital, became one of Europe's great cities: the new silver mine at Kutná Hora boosted Prague's economic growth, and the first uni-

versity in the empire was founded there in 1348. Prague was located in Bohemia, a part of the Holy Roman Empire settled by a Slavic people, the Czechs, since the early Middle Ages. Later, many German merchants and artisans migrated to Bohemian cities, and Czech peasants, uprooted from the land, flocked to the cities in search of employment. This diverse society became a potentially explosive mass when heightened expectations of commercial and intellectual growth collided with the grim realities of the plague and economic problems in the late fourteenth century. Tax protests, urban riots, and ethnic conflicts signaled growing unrest, but it was religious discontent that became the focus for popular revolt.

Critics of the clergy, often clergy themselves, decried the moral conduct of priests and prelates who held multiple benefices, led dissolute lives, and ignored their pastoral duties. Critics asked how the clergy, living in a state of mortal sin, could legitimately perform the sacraments. Advocating greater lay participation in the Mass and in the reading of Scripture, religious dissenters drew some of their ideas from the writings of Wycliffe. Among those influenced by Wycliffe's ideas were Jan Hus (d. 1415) and his follower Jerome of Prague (d. 1416), both Prague professors, ethnic Czechs, and leaders of a group of reformers. Although the reform party attracted adherents from all Czech-speaking social groups, the German minority, who dominated the university and urban elites in Prague, opposed it out of ethnic rivalry. The Bohemian nobility protected Hus; the common clergy rebelled against the bishops; and the artisans and workers in Prague were ready to back the reform party by force. These disparate social interests all focused on one symbolic but passionately felt religious demand: the ability to receive the Eucharist as both bread and wine at Mass. In traditional Roman liturgy, the chalice was reserved for the clergy; the Utraquists, as their opponents called them (from *utraque*, Latin for "both"), also wanted to drink wine from the chalice, to achieve a measure of equality between laity and clergy.

Despite a guarantee of safety from Emperor Sigismund, Hus was burned at the stake while attending the Council of Constance in 1415. Hus's death caused a national uproar, and the reform movement, which had thus far focused only on religious issues, burst forth as a national revolution.

Sigismund's initial repression of the revolt in the provinces was brutal, and many dissenters were massacred. To organize their defense, Hussites gathered at a mountain in southern Bohemia, which they called Mount Tabor after the mountain in the New Testament where the transfiguration of Christ took place. Now called Taborites, they began to restructure their community according to biblical injunctions. Like the first Christian church, they initially practiced communal ownership of goods and thought of themselves as the only true Christians awaiting the return of Christ and the end of the world. As their influence spread, the Taborites compromised with the surrounding social order, collecting tithes from peasants and retaining magistrates in towns under their control. Taborite leaders were radical priests who ministered to the community in the Czech language, exercised moral and judicial leadership, and even led the people into battle.

Modeling themselves after the Israelites of the Old Testament and the first Christians of the New Testament, the Taborites impressed even their enemies. Aeneas Sylvius Piccolomini, the future Pope Pius II (r. 1458–1464), observed that "among the Taborites you will hardly find a woman who cannot demonstrate familiarity with the Old and New Testaments." The Taborite army, drawn from many social classes and led by priests, repelled five attacks by the "crusader" armies from neighboring Germany, triumphing over their enemies using a mixture of religious fervor and military technology, such as a wagon train to protect the infantry from cavalry charges. Resisting all attempts to crush them, the Czech revolu-

The Hussite Revolution, 1415–1436

tionaries eventually gained the right from the papacy to receive the Eucharist as both bread and wine, a practice that continued until the sixteenth century.

Review: How did the papacy lose and then recover authority in the late Middle Ages?

❖ The Social Order and Cultural Change

An abundance of written and visual records documenting the lives of all social groups has survived from the fourteenth century. Sources ranging from chronicles of dynastic conflicts and noble chivalry to police records of criminality paint a vivid picture of late medieval society, showing the changed relations between town and country, noble and commoner, and men and women. These sources reveal Europeans' struggles to adjust to uncertainties and changes related to the plague, war, and religious dissent (see "Piers the Ploughman" page 494). New material wealth allowed some to enjoy more comfortable lives, but the disruptions and dislocations caused by various crises forced many on the margins of society—the poor, beggars, and prostitutes—into a violent underworld of criminality.

One response to the upheavals of the later Middle Ages was the blossoming of a broad cultural movement. As the Byzantines recovered their appreciation of Greek antiquity, so did Italians revive ancient Roman culture. This movement focused initially on imitating classical Latin rhetoric, but it later extended to other disciplines, such as the study of history. The brilliant achievements in the visual arts and vernacular literature realized at this time were the beginnings of the great movement known as the Renaissance (French for "rebirth").

The Household

Family life and the household economy formed the fabric of late medieval society. Most Europeans lived in a confined social world, surrounded by families and neighbors. The focus of their lives was the house, where parents and children, and occasionally a grandparent or other relative, lived together. This pattern generally characterized both urban and rural society. In some peasant societies, such as in Languedoc (southern France), brothers and their families shared the same roof; but the nuclear family was by far the norm.

For artisans and peasants of medium wealth, the family dwelling usually consisted of a two- or three-story building in the city and a single farmhouse in the countryside. For these social groups the household generally served as both work and private space; shopkeepers and craftspeople used their ground floors as workshops and storefronts, reserving the upper stories for family life. By today's standards, late medieval urban life was intolerably crowded, with little privacy. Neighbors could easily spy on each other from adjoining windows. In rural areas the family house served a variety of purposes, not least to shelter the farm animals during the winter.

In a society with an unequal distribution of power between women and men, the worlds of commerce and agriculture were those in which women came closest to partnership with their husbands. Even though women were excluded from privileged guilds in some cities such as Cologne, many women worked in the unorganized retail trade. They sold dairy products, meat, cloth, salt, flour, and fish; brewed beer; spun and wove cloth; and often acted informally as their husbands' business partners. Fourteenth-century women played a crucial role in the urban economy.

Piers the Ploughman

In Piers the Ploughman, *English cleric William Langland blends prophecy and satirical comedy in his fourteenth-century poem about the failures of society to live up to Christianity's ideals. This selection from the prologue describes the narrator's dream in which unscrupulous clergy appear prominently. His observations on the state of the Church reflect the mood of discontent in an age that gave rise to the English Peasants Uprising as well as the Great Schism.*

I saw the Friars there too—all four Orders of them—preaching to the people for what they could get. In their greed for fine clothes, they interpreted the Scriptures to suit themselves and their patrons. Many of these Doctors of Divinity can dress as handsomely as they please, for as their trade advances, so their profits increase. And now that Charity has gone into business, and become confessor-in-chief to wealthy lords, many strange things have happened in the last few years; unless the Friars and Holy Church mend their quarrel, the worst evil in the world will soon be upon us.

There was also *a* Pardoner,[1] preaching like a priest. He produced a document covered with Bishops' seals, and claimed to have power to absolve all the people from broken fasts and vows of every kind. The ignorant folk believed him and were delighted. They came up and knelt to kiss his documents, while he, blinding them with letters of indulgence[2] thrust in their faces, raked in their rings and jewellery with his roll of parchment!—So the people give their gold to support these gluttons, and put their trust in dirty-minded scoundrels. If the Bishop were worthy of the name, if he kept his ears open to what went on around him, his seal would not be sent out like this to deceive the people. But it is not by the Bishop's leave that this rogue preaches; for the parish priest is in league with the Pardoner, and they divide the proceeds between them—money which, but for them, would go to the poor of the parish.

---

[1]Church official who raised money by selling waivers to absolve sins.
[2]Means by which a person could perform certain religious tasks or pay fees to avoid purgatory after death.

Source: William Langland, *Piers the Ploughman* (New York: Penguin Classics, 1986), 26–27.

June

Real farmwork in fourteenth-century France was never as genteel as in this miniature painting, part of a series illustrating the months of the year in the beautiful devotional book, the *Book of Hours* of the Duke de Berry. Nevertheless, the scene does faithfully represent haying and suggests the gendered division of village labor, as the men swing their scythes and the women wield rakes. **For more help analyzing this image**, please see the visual activity for this chapter in the Online Study Guide at **bedfordstmartins.com/hunt**. *Bridgeman-Giraudon/Art Resource, NY.*

February

As in all the miniatures in the Duke de Berry's prayer book, this cozy scene shows that the late-medieval nobility liked to imagine their peasants and livestock securely housed in warm, separate shelters, while the customary work of rural society goes on peacefully. But in reality, peasants led a hard life, faced with the uncertainties of weather and the depredations of war. *Bridgeman-Giraudon/Art Resource, NY.*

The degree to which women participated in public life, however, varied with class and region. Women in Mediterranean Europe, especially in upper-class families, lived more circumscribed lives than their counterparts in northern Europe. In the southern regions, for example, women could not dispose of personal property without the consent of males, be they fathers, husbands, or grown sons. In the north, women regularly represented themselves in legal transactions and testified in court.

Partnership characterized the peasant marriage. Although men and women performed different tasks, such as plowing and spinning, many chores required mutual effort. During harvests, all family members were mobilized. The men usually reaped with sickles, while the women picked the fields. Viticulture (the cultivation of grapes for wine-making) called for full cooperation between the sexes: both men and women worked equally in picking grapes and trampling them to make wine.

Because the rural household constituted the basic unit of agricultural production, most men and women remarried quickly after a spouse died. The incidence of households headed by a single person, usually a poor widow, was much lower in villages than in cities. Studies of court records for fourteenth-century English villages show relatively few reports of domestic violence, a result perhaps of the economic dependency between the sexes. Violence against women was more visible in urban societies, where many women worked as servants and prostitutes.

The improved material life of the middle classes was represented in many visual images of the later Middle Ages. Italian and Flemish paintings of the late fourteenth and early fifteenth centuries depict the new comforts of urban life such as fireplaces and private latrines and show an interest in material objects: beds, chests, rooms, curtains, and buildings provide the ubiquitous background of Italian paintings of the period.

The Underclass

If family life and the household economy formed the fabric of late medieval society, the world of poverty and criminality represented its torn fringes. Fourteenth-century society rested on a broad base of underclass—poor peasants and laborers in the countryside, workers and servants in the cities. Lower still were the marginal elements of society, straddling the line between legality and criminality.

Organized gangs prowled the larger cities. In Paris, a city teeming with thieves, thugs, beggars, prostitutes, and vagabonds, the Hundred Years' War led to a sharp rise in crime. Gang members were mostly artisans who vacillated between work and crime. Sometimes disguised as clerics, they robbed, murdered, and extorted from prostitutes. Many soldiers, having been initiated into a life of plunder and killing, turned to crime.

Those on society's fringes were mostly young people who lacked stable families; they wandered extensively, begging and steal-

ing. Criminals were even present among the clergy. Some clerics turned to crime to make ends meet during an age of steadily declining clerical income. "Decent society" treated these marginal elements with suspicion and hatred. New laws restricted vagabonds and begging clerics, although cities and guilds also began building hospitals and alms-houses to deal with these social problems.

Women featured prominently in the underclass, reflecting the unequal distribution of power between the sexes. In Mediterranean Europe, some 90 percent of slaves were women in domestic servitude. Their actual numbers were small—several hundred in fourteenth-century Florence, for example—because only rich households could afford slaves. The women came from Muslim or Greek Orthodox countries and usually served in upper-class households in the great commercial city republics of Venice, Florence, and Ragusa. Urban domestic service was also the major employment for girls from the countryside, who worked to save money for their dowries. In addition to the usual household chores, women also worked as wet nurses.

Given their exclusion from many professions and their powerlessness, many poor women found prostitution the only way to make a living. Male violence also forced some women into prostitution: rape stripped away their social respectability and any prospects for marriage. Though condemned by the church, prostitutes were tolerated throughout the Middle Ages. In the fourteenth and fifteenth centuries, however, governments intensified their attempts to control sexuality by institutionalizing prostitution. Restricted to particular quarters in cities, supervised by officials, sometimes under direct government management, prostitutes found themselves confined to brothels, increasingly controlled by males. In legalizing and controlling prostitution, officials aimed to maintain the public order.

Hard Times for Trade

Compared with the commercial prosperity of the twelfth and thirteenth centuries, the later Middle Ages was an age of retrenchment for business. As the fourteenth-century crises afflicted the business community, a climate of pessimism and caution permeated commerce, especially during the second half of the century.

The first major crisis that undermined Italian banks was caused by the Hundred Years' War, during which England's Edward III borrowed heavily from the largest Italian banking houses, the Bardi and Peruzzi of Florence. In the early 1340s, however, Edward defaulted. Adding to their problems, the Florentine bankers were forced to make war loans to their own government. The once-powerful banks could not rebound from the losses they incurred, and both of them fell.

This breakdown in the most advanced economic sector reflected the general recession in the European economy. Merchants were less likely to take risks and more willing to invest their money in government bonds than in production and commerce. Fewer merchants traveled to Asia, partly because of the danger of attack by Ottoman Turks on the overland routes that had once been protected by the Mongols. The Medici of Florence, who would dominate Florentine politics in the next century, stuck close to home, investing part of their banking profits in art and politics and relying mostly on business agents to conduct their affairs in other European cities.

Historians have argued that this fourteenth-century economic depression diverted capital away from manufacturing and into investments in the arts and luxuries for immediate consumption. Instead of plowing their profits back into their businesses, merchants acquired land, built sumptuous townhouses, purchased luxury items, and invested in bonds.

The most important trade axis continued to link Italy with the Low Countries. Italian cities produced silk, wool, jewelry, and other luxury goods that northern Europeans desired, and Italian merchants also imported spices, gold, and other coveted products from Asia and Africa. Traveling either by land through Lyon or by sea around Gibraltar, these products reached Bruges, Ghent, and Antwerp, where they were shipped to England, northern Germany, Poland, and Scandinavia. The reverse flow carried raw materials and silver, the latter to help balance the trade between northern Europe and the Mediter-

ranean. Diminished production and trade eventually caused turmoil in northern Europe and a crisis for financiers in the Low Countries. Bruges, the financial center for northwestern Europe, saw its power fade during the fifteenth century when a succession of its money changers went bankrupt. The Burgundian dukes eventually enacted a series of monetary laws that undermined Bruges's financial and banking community and, by extension, the city's political autonomy as well.

The Flourishing of Vernacular Literature and the Birth of Humanism

Vernacular literature blossomed in the fourteenth century. Poetry, stories, and chronicles composed in Italian, French, English, and other national languages helped articulate a new sense of aesthetics. No longer did Latin and church culture dominate the intellectual life of Europe, and no longer were writers principally clerics or aristocrats. Also located in the cities, a new intellectual movement, humanisme, a return to the study of Greek and Roman texts, and an emulation of the civic values expressed by authors of classical antiquity.

Middle-Class Writers and Noble Patrons. The great writers of late medieval Europe were of urban middle-class origins, from families that had done well in government or church service or commercial enterprises, unlike the medieval troubadours, who had aristocratic backgrounds. The audience of these new writers was the literate laity. Francesco Petrarch (1304–1374), the poet laureate of Italy's vernacular literature, and his younger contemporary and friend Giovanni Boccaccio (1313–1375) were both Florentine. Petrarch was born in Arezzo, where his father, a notary, lived in political exile from Florence. Boccaccio's father worked for the Florentine banking firm of Bardi in Paris, where Boccaccio was born. Geoffrey Chaucer (c. 1342–1400) was the first great vernacular poet of medieval England. His father was a wealthy wine merchant; Chaucer worked as a servant to the king and controller of customs in London. Even writers who celebrated the life of the nobility were children of commoners. Although born in Valenciennes to a family of moneylenders and merchants, Jean Froissart (1333?–c. 1405), whose chronicle vividly describes the events of the Hundred Years' War, was an ardent admirer of chivalry. Christine de Pizan (1364–c. 1430), the official biographer of the French king, was the daughter of a Venetian municipal councilor.

Life in all its facets found expression in the flourishing vernacular literature, as writers told of love, greed, and salvation. Boccaccio's *Decameron* popularized the short story, as the characters in this novella tell sensual and bizarre tales in the shadow of the Black Death. Members of different social orders parade themselves in Chaucer's *Canterbury Tales*, journeying together on a pilgrimage. Chaucer describes a merchant on horseback as follows:

> A marchant was ther with a forked berd
> In mottelee, and hye on horse he sat
> up-on his heed a Flaundrish bever hat
> his botes clasped faire and fetisly....
> For sothe he was a worthy man withalle
> but sooth to seyn, I noot how men him calle.

Chaucer also vividly portrayed other social classes—yeomen, London guildsmen, and minor officials.

Noble patronage was crucial to the growth of vernacular literature, a fact reflected in the careers of the most famous writers. Perhaps closest to the model of an

The Book of the City of Ladies (1405)

In The Book of the City of Ladies, *Christine de Pizan confronts a long tradition of misogyny by male writers. Each chapter recounts the accomplishments and capabilities of remarkable women—both mythical and historic—who reside within her fictional city. In this section from the book's opening, de Pizan expresses her distress at widespread works that disparage women's abilities, which prompts her to write her own account.*

...given that I could scarcely find a moral work by any author which didn't devote some chapter or paragraph to attacking the female sex, I had to accept their unfavourable opinion of women since it was unlikely that so many learned men, who seemed to be endowed with such great intelligence and insight into all things, could possibly have lied on so many different occasions. It was on the basis of this one simple argument that I was forced to conclude that, although my understanding was too crude and ill-informed to recognize the great flaws in myself and other women, these men had to be in the right. Thus I preferred to give more weight to what others said than to trust my own judgement and experience.

I dwelt on these thoughts at such length that it was as if I had sunk into a deep trance. My mind became flooded with an endless stream of names as I recalled all the authors who had written on this subject. I came to the conclusion that God had surely created a vile thing when He created woman. Indeed, I was astounded that such a fine craftsman could have wished to make such an appalling object which, as these writers would have it, is like a vessel in which all the sin and evil of the world has been collected and preserved. This thought inspired such a great sense of disgust and sadness in me that I began to despise myself and the whole of my sex as an aberration in nature.

With a deep sigh, I called out to God: 'Oh Lord, how can this be? Unless I commit an error of faith, I cannot doubt that you, in your infinite wisdom and perfect goodness, could make anything that wasn't good. Didn't you yourself create woman especially and then endow her with all the qualities that you wished her to have? How could you possibly have made a mistake in anything? Yet here stand women not simply accused, but already judged, sentenced and condemned! I just cannot understand this contradiction.

Source: Christine de Pizan, *The Book of the City of Ladies* (London: Penguin Classics, 1999), 6–7.

independent man of letters, Petrarch nonetheless relied on powerful patrons at various times. His early career began at the papal court in Avignon, where his father worked; during the 1350s, he enjoyed the protection and patronage of the duke of Milan. For Boccaccio, who started out in the world of commerce, the court of King Robert of Naples initiated him into the world of letters. Chaucer served the English crown in administrative posts and on many diplomatic missions, during which he met his two Italian counterparts. Noble patronage also shaped the literary creations of Froissart and Christine de Pizan. Commissioned to write the official biography of King Charles V, Christine would have been unable to produce most of her writings without the patronage of women in the royal household. She presented her most famous work, *The Book of the City of Ladies* (1405), a defense of women's reputation and virtue, to Isabella of Bavaria, the queen of France and wife of Charles VI (see excerpt on page 498).

Classical Revival. Vernacular literature blossomed not at the expense of Latin but alongside a classical revival. In spite of the renown of their Italian writings, Petrarch and Boccaccio, for example, took great pride in their Latin works. Latin represented the language of salvation and was also the international language of learning. Professors taught and wrote in Latin; students spoke it as best they could; priests celebrated Mass and dispensed sacraments in Latin; and theologians composed learned treatises in Latin. Church Latin was very different from the Latin of the ancient Romans, both in syntax and in vocabulary. In the second half of the fourteenth century, writers began to imitate the "classical" Latin of Roman literature. In the forefront of this literary and intellectual movement, Petrarch traveled to many monasteries in search of long-ignored Latin manuscripts. For writers like Petrarch, medieval church Latin was an artificial, awkward language, whereas classical Latin and, after its revival, Greek were the mother tongues of the ancients. Thus the classical writings of Rome and Greece represented true vernacular literature, only more authentic, vivid, and glorious than the poetry

Poet and Queen
Christine de Pizan, kneeling, presents a manuscript of her poems to Isabelle of Bavaria, the queen of France. Isabelle's royal status is marked by the French coat of arms, the fleur-de-lis that decorates the bedroom walls. The sumptuous interior (chairs, cushions, tapestry, paneled ceiling, glazed and shuttered windows) was typical of aristocratic domestic architecture. Even in the intimacy of her bedroom, Queen Isabelle, like all royal personages, was constantly attended and almost never alone (note her ladies-in-waiting). *The British Library Picture Library, London.*

and prose written in Italian and other contemporary European languages. Classical allusions and literary influences abound in the works of Boccaccio, Chaucer, Christine de Pizan, and others. The new intellectual fascination with the ancient past also stimulated translations of classical works into the vernacular.

This attempt to emulate the virtues and learning of the ancients gave rise to a new intellectual movement: humanism. For humanists the study of history and literature was the chief means of identifying with the glories of the ancient world. By the early fifteenth century, the study of classical Latin had become fashionable among a small intellectual elite, first in Italy and gradually throughout Europe. Reacting against the painstaking logic and abstract language of the scholastic philosophy that predominated in the medieval period, the humanists of the Renaissance preferred eloquence and style in their discourse, imitating the writings of Cicero and other great Roman authors.

Paradise Lost

This fourteenth-century painting by the Sienese Giovanni di Paolo depicts the expulsion of Adam and Eve from the Garden of Eden. At right, an angel chases away the ancestors of humanity. At left, Paradise is the core around which the seven celestial spheres rotate, propelled by the action of God. By positioning Adam and Eve to the right-hand side of the panel, Paolo dramatically represents their expulsion. *The Metropolitan Museum of Art, Robert Lehman Collection, 1975. (1975.1.31) Photograph © 1981 the Metropolitan Museum of Art.*

Italian lawyers and notaries had a long-standing interest in classical rhetoric because eloquence was a skill essential to their professions. Gradually the imitation of ancient Roman rhetoric led to the absorption of ancient ideas. In the writings of Roman historians such as Livy and Tacitus, fifteenth-century Italian civic elites (many of them lawyers) found echoes of their own devout patriotism. Between 1400 and 1430 in Florence, a time of war and crisis, the study of the humanities evolved into a republican ideology that historians call "civic humanism." In the early fifteenth century, the Florentines waged a highly successful propaganda war on behalf of virtuous republican Florence against tyrannical Milan, invoking the memory of the overthrow of Etruscan tyrants by the first Romans. Thus the study of ancient civilization was not only an antiquarian quest but also a call to public service and political action.

Review: What were examples of the new secular culture of the fourteenth century?

Conclusion

Between 1320 and 1430, European civilization was in crisis. The traditional order, achieved during the optimism and growth of the High Middle Ages, was undercut first—and most severely—by the Hundred Years' War and the Black Death, which combined to cause a drastic reduction in population and contraction of the economy. Faced with massive death and destruction, some people sought escape in rituals of religious fanaticism. Others searched out scapegoats, spawning a wave of anti-Jewish persecutions that reached from southern France throughout the Holy Roman Empire; the Nuremberg pogrom of 1349 was only one example. Empire and papacy, long symbols of unity, collapsed into political disintegration and spiritual malaise.

The disintegration of European order hastened the consolidation of some states, such as France. Other areas, such as Spain and the Ottoman Empire, included different linguistic and religious groups under one political authority. Still other regions, principally central Europe and Italy, remained divided into competing principalities and city-states characterized more by the sense of local differences than by their linguistic similarity.

In the eastern Mediterranean, European civilization retreated in the face of Ottoman Turk advances. Christian Europe continued to grow, however, in the Iberian peninsula; for the next three centuries the Mediterranean would be the arena for struggles between Christian and Islamic empires. The papacy called for new crusades, but divisions among European powers largely thwarted this effort.

The conciliar movement, although instrumental in ending the Great Schism, failed to limit supreme papal power, identified by its critics as the source of spiritual discontent. Successful in repressing or compromising

MAPPING THE WEST Europe, c. 1430
Two of the dynamic regions of expansion lie in the southeastern and southwestern sectors of this map: the Ottoman Empire, which continued its attacks into central Europe and the Mediterranean, and the Iberian countries that opposed Muslim advances by their own crusades and maritime expansions. While England, France, Iberia, and the Balkans were consolidated into large political entities, central Europe and Italy remained fragmented. Yet it was these two fragmented regions that gave Europe the cultural and technological innovations of the age.

with the Lollard, Hussite, and other heretical movements, the church survived the crisis of the later Middle Ages but left unresolved issues of spiritual authority.

In the world of letters, vernacular literature and humanism prepared the ground for a golden age of culture that would spread from the Italian cities to other areas of Europe.

Suggested References

Political Crises across Europe

The scholarship on the political conflicts of late medieval Europe has shifted from narrative of military campaigns and diplomacy to focus on peasant uprisings, urban revolts, and their relationship to the larger struggles between dynasties and countries. In addition to the Hundred

Years' War, southeastern Europe and Iberia have also come into focus.

Allmand, Christopher. *The Hundred Years' War: England and France at War, c. 1300–1450.* 1988.

*Froissart: **http://www.nipissings.ca/department/ history/muhlberger/froissart/tales.htm**.

*Froissart, Jean. *Chronicles.* Trans. Geoffrey Brereton. 1968.

Hilton, R. H., and T. H. Aston, eds. *The English Rising of 1381.* 1984.

Index of Late Medieval Maps: **http://www .henry-davis.com/MAPS/LMwebpages/ LML.html**.

Leuschner, Joachim. *Germany in the Late Middle Ages.* 1980.

Mollat, Michel, and Philippe Wolff. *The Popular Revolutions of the Late Middle Ages.* 1973.

Nichols, David. *The van Arteveldes of Ghent: The Varieties of Vendetta and the Hero in History.* 1988.

O'Callaghan, Joseph F. *A History of Medieval Spain.* 1975.

*Pernoud, Régine ed. *Joan of Arc: By Herself and Her Witnesses.* 1966.

Shaw, Stanford J. *History of the Ottoman Empire and Modern Turkey.* Vol. 1, *Empire of the Gazia: The Rise and Decline of the Ottoman Empire, 1280–1808.* 1976.

Vale, Malcolm. *War and Chivalry: Warfare and Aristocratic Culture in England, France, and Burgundy at the End of the Middle Ages.* 1981.

Warner, Marina. *Joan of Arc: The Image of Female Heroism.* 1981.

The Plague and Society

Recent scholarship stresses the social, economic, and cultural impact of the plague. One particularly exciting direction of research focuses on the persecution of religious minorities as a result of the Black Death.

Bois, Guy. *The Crisis of Feudalism: Economy and Society in Eastern Normandy, c. 1300–1550.* 1984.

Cohn, Samuel K. "The Black Death: End of a Paradigm." *American Historical Review* 107, no. 3 (2002), pp. 703–38.

Herlihy, David. *The Black Death and the Transformation of the West.* 1997.

Nicholas, David. *The Later Medieval City 1300–1500.* 1997.

Nirenberg, David. *Communities of Violence: Persecution of Minorities in the Middle Ages.* 1996.

Plague and public health in Renaissance Europe: **http://jefferson.village.virginia.edu/osheim/ intro.html**.

Rörig, Fritz. *The Medieval Town.* 1967.

Ziegler, Philip. *The Black Death.* 1970.

Challenges to Spiritual Authority

While there continues to be a great deal of interest in dissident thinkers who challenged the authority of the medieval church, much recent scholarship is devoted to the popular movements of dissent against papal and ecclesiastical authority.

Ashton, Margaret. *Lollards and Reformers.* 1989.

———. *Lollardy and the Gentry in the Later Middle Ages.* 1997.

Fudge, Thomas A. *The Magnificent Ride: The First Reformation in Hussite Bohemia.* 1998.

Kaminsky, Howard. *A History of the Hussite Revolution.* 1967.

Leff, Gordon. *Heresy in the Later Middle Ages: The Relation of Heterodoxy to Dissent, c. 1250–1450.* 1967.

Oakley, Francis. *Council over Pope? Towards a Provisional Ecclesiology.* 1969.

Ozment, Steven. *The Age of Reform, 1250–1550: An Intellectual and Religious History of Late Medieval and Reformation Europe.* 1980.

Renouard, Yves. *The Avignon Papacy, 1305–1403.* 1970.

The Social Order and Cultural Change

In addition to the importance of Italy, other research examines the household, gender, and women's work during this period. Literary scholarship continues to explore the relationship between vernacular literature and humanism.

Duby, Georges. *A History of Private Life.* Vol. 2, *Revelations of the Medieval World.* 1988.

Fubini, Riccardo. *Humanism and Secularization: From Petrarch to Valla.* 2003.

Geremek, Bronislaw. *The Margins of Society in Late Medieval Paris.* 1987.

Gersh, Stephen, and Bert Roest, eds. *Medieval and Renaissance Humanism: Rhetoric, Representation and Reform.* 2003.

Hanawalt, Barbara A., ed. *Women and Work in Preindustrial Europe.* 1986.

Herlihy, David. *Women, Family, and Society in Medieval Europe.* 1995.

———. *Opera muliebria. Women and Work in Medieval Europe.* 1990.

Miskimim, Harry A. *The Economy of Early Renaissance Europe, 1300–1460.* 1975.

*Primary source.

CHAPTER REVIEW

IMPORTANT EVENTS

1315–1317	Great Famine in Europe
1324	Marsilius of Padua denies the legitimacy of papal supremacy in *The Defender of the Peace*
1328	Pope John XXII imprisons the English theologian William of Ockham for criticizing papal power
1337–1453	Hundred Years' War between the English and French
1347–1354	Rebellion in Rome
1348–1350	First outbreak in Europe of the Black Death
1349–1351	Anti-Jewish persecutions in the empire
1356	Charles IV agrees to Golden Bull document requiring imperial electors to select the German king
1358	Jacquerie uprising in France
1378	Ciompi rebellion in Florence; John Wycliffe's treatise *On the Church* asserts that the true church is a community of believers
1378–1417	Great Schism divides papacy
1381	English peasant uprising
1386	Union of Poland and Lithuania
1389	Ottomans defeat Serbs at Kosovo
1391	Attack on Jews and forced conversion in Spain
1414–1417	Council of Constance ends the Great Schism
1415	Execution of Jan Hus; Hussite revolution begins
1429	Joan of Arc leads French to victory at siege of Orléans

KEY TERMS

benefices (486)

flagellants (485)

Great Schism (489)

Janissaries (481)

latifundia (480)

mercenary (469)

Moors (480)

mysticism (491)

nominalism (488)

reconquista (480)

vernacular literature (497)

REVIEW QUESTIONS

1. How were dynastic warfare and popular uprisings related in the fourteenth century?
2. What were the demographic, economic, and psychological consequences of the plague?
3. How did the papacy lose and then recover authority in the late Middle Ages?
4. What were examples of the new secular culture of the fourteenth century?

MAKING CONNECTIONS

1. Is it reasonable to say that the late Middle Ages experienced a general crisis in society? Why or why not?
2. To what extent was Christendom less tolerant and open in the fourteenth century than in the high Middle Ages?

FOR FURTHER EXPLORATION

To assess your mastery of the material in this chapter, see the Online Study Guide at **bedfordstmartins.com/hunt**.

To read additional primary-source material from this period, see Chapter 13 in *Sources of The Making of the West*, Second Edition.

Renaissance Europe, 1400–1500

IN 1461, THE OTTOMAN RULER MEHMED II sent a letter to Sigismondo Malatesta, the lord of the Italian city-state of Rimini, asking the Italian prince to lend him court painter and architect Matteo de Pasti. The Ottoman sultan was planning to build a new palace in the recently conquered capital, Constantinople (modern Istanbul), as a fitting symbol of his imperial dominion, and he had heard of de Pasti's reputation. The Rimini painter had not only produced illuminated manuscripts and portrait medals of Sigismondo's mistress but also designed a monument to the prince's military glory, which was modeled after the principles described in Vitruvius's treatise *On Architecture* (first century B.C.E.). This was a work rediscovered in Italy in 1414.

Armed with a letter from Sigismondo, maps, and gifts, de Pasti set out for Constantinople, ready to court favors for his patron, who was eager to form an alliance with the Turkish ruler. Venetian authorities, however, intercepted the artist in Crete. Anxious to prevent a political connection between another Italian power and the sultan, the Venetians confiscated the gifts and sent de Pasti back to Rimini. Thus, Mehmed's new palace was constructed without de Pasti's help—but with the aid of several Venetian painters instead. The palace came to be called the Topkapi Saray and still stands today looking across the Bosporus, the strait that divides European and Asian Turkey.

The story of Matteo de Pasti's failed mission illustrates the central theme of the Renaissance: the connection among power, culture, and fame in an age that was rediscovering the arts and the worldview of classical antiquity. This rediscovery, which scholars in the sixteenth century labeled the **Renaissance** (French for "rebirth"),

Sacred and Social Body
The fifteenth-century Venetian state used lavish, dignified ceremony to impress citizens and visitors with its grandeur and to symbolize its divine protection. Here the great Venetian Renaissance painter Gentile Bellini depicts one such scene, a procession of the Eucharist across the Piazza San Marco uniting in common purpose the clergy and the Venetian governing elite.
Scala/Art Resource, NY.

signified the revival of forms of classical learning and the arts following the long interval they characterized as the Middle Ages. (See "Terms of History," page 508.) After the crisis of the fourteenth century, European civilization seemed to rise in the fifteenth like a phoenix from the ashes of the Black Death. The Renaissance had two main trajectories: a revolution in culture that originated in Italy and gradually expanded north to other countries of Europe, and (even more profound and far-reaching) the expansion of European control to the non-European world.

The story of de Pasti's mission further illustrates three secondary themes: First, it shows how specific Renaissance artistic practices were based on the revival of classical learning. Second, it reflects the competition among Italian city-states set against a larger backdrop of changing relations between Christian Europe and the non-Christian world. Third, it demonstrates the significance of culture in the political representation of power.

The rebirth of culture took many forms: in learning, in the visual arts, in architecture, and in music. Portraits, palaces, and poetry commemorated the glory of the rich and powerful, while a new philosophy called humanism advocated classical learning and argued for the active participation of the individual in civic affairs. Family, honor, social status, and individual distinction—these were the goals that fueled the ambitions of Renaissance men and women.

A new feeling of power characterized the spirit of the Renaissance, as Europeans recovered their sense of control over the world after the crisis of the fourteenth century. The quest for power by families and individuals duplicated on a smaller scale the enhanced power of the state. Like individuals, the Renaissance states competed for wealth, glory, and honor. While warfare and diplomacy channeled the restless energy of the Italian states, monarchies and empires outside of Italy also expanded their power through conquests and institutional reforms. The European world changed drastically as new powers such as the Ottoman Empire and Muscovy rose to prominence in the east, while the Iberian kingdoms of Portugal and Spain expanded European domination to Africa, Asia, and the Americas.

❖ Widening Intellectual Horizons

A revolution in the arts and learning was in the making. Europeans' rediscovery of Greek and Roman writers reflected an expanded interest in human achievements and glory. New secular voices celebrating human glory were added to the old prayers for salvation in the afterlife. While the intense study of Latin and Greek writings focused on rhetoric and eloquence in learning, revolutionary techniques in bookmaking, painting, architecture, and music created original forms and expressed a new excitement with the beauty of nature. In the center of this fascinating nature was humanity.

◆ **1434** Medici establish influence in Florence

◆ **1453** Ottoman conquest of Constantinople; end of Byzantine Empire

◆ **1454** Treaty of Lodi balances power among major Italian States

◆ **1440s** Printing press with metallic type invented

◆ **1462** Ivan III becomes tsar

1420   **1440**   **1460**

◆ **1415** Portugal captures Ceuta

◆ **1438** Pragmatic Sanction of Bourges allows French kings to control church revenue and appoint bishop

◆ **1450** Sforza seizes Milan

◆ **1460–1485** Wars of the roses; Tudor Dynasty ascendant

◆ **c. 1450–1500** Height of Florentine Renaissance

The Humanist Renewal

Europeans' fascination with the ancient past in turn gave rise to a new intellectual movement: **humanism**, so called because its practitioners studied and supported the liberal arts, or humanities. As a group, the humanists were far from homogeneous: some were professional scholars, others high-ranking civil servants; some worked as notaries, and still others were rich patricians who had acquired a taste for learning. Nonetheless, all humanists focused on classical history and literature in their attempt to emulate the glories of the ancient world.

By the early fifteenth century the study of classical Latin (which had begun in the late fourteenth century) as well as classical and biblical Greek had become fashionable among a small intellectual elite, first in Italy and gradually throughout Europe. The fall of Constantinople in 1453 sent Greek scholars to Italy for refuge, giving extra impetus to the revival of Greek learning in the West. Venice and Florence assumed leadership in this new field—the former by virtue of its commercial and political ties to the eastern Mediterranean, the latter thanks to the patronage of Cosimo de' Medici,♦ who sponsored the Platonic Academy, a discussion group dedicated to the study of Plato and his followers under the intellectual leadership of Marsilio Ficino (1433–1499). Thinkers of the second half of the fifteenth century had more curiosity

---

♦**Cosimo de' Medici:** KAW zee moh day MEH dih chee

about Platonic and various mystical neo-Platonic ideas—particularly alchemy, numerology, and natural magic—than about the serious study of natural phenomena and universal principles.

Most humanists did not consider the study of ancient cultures a conflict with their Christian faith. In "returning to the sources"—a famous slogan of the time—philosophers attempted to harmonize the disciplines of Christian faith and ancient learning. Ficino, the foremost Platonic scholar of the Renaissance, was deeply attracted to natural magic and was also a priest. He argued that the immortality of the soul, a Platonic idea, was perfectly compatible with Christian doctrine and that much of ancient wisdom actually foreshadowed later Christian teachings.

In Latin learning, the fifteenth century continued in the tradition of Petrarch. Reacting against the painstaking logic and abstract language of scholastic philosophy, the humanists of the Renaissance advocated eloquence and style in their discourse, imitating the writings of Cicero and other great Roman authors (see Chapter 13). Through their activities as educators and civil servants, professional humanists gave new vigor to the humanist curriculum of grammar, rhetoric, poetry, history, and moral philosophy. By the end of the fifteenth century, European intellectuals considered a good command of classical Latin, with perhaps some knowledge of Greek, as one of the requirements of an educated man. This humanist revolution would influence school curricula up to the middle of the nineteenth century and even beyond.

◆ **1471–1484** Pope Sixtus IV; Renaissance in Rome

◆ **1474–1516** Spain unified under Isabella and Ferdinand

◆ **1477** Death of Charles the Bold begins decline of Burgundy

◆ **1519** Spain conquers Mexico

◆ **1530** Fall of Florentine Republic

1480　　　　**1500**　　　　**1520**

◆ **1478** Inquisition carried out in Spain

◆ **1485** End of civil wars in England

◆ **1492** Spain conquers Granada, expels Jews; Columbus sails for Americas

◆ **1494** France invades Italy

TERMS OF HISTORY

Renaissance

The word *renaissance*, which is French for "rebirth," has been employed numerous times in this book. Recall the Macedonian renaissance, the Islamic renaissance, the renaissance of the twelfth century. All those *renaissances* refer to the rebirth of classical culture—or aspects of classical culture—in the medieval period.

Renaissance was first used in the sixteenth century to refer to a historical moment. At that time it meant the rebirth of classical poetry, prose, and art of that period alone. Only later did historians borrow the word to refer to earlier rebirths. The first person to herald the fifteenth-century Renaissance was the Italian painter and architect Giorgio Vasari (1511–1574) in his *Lives of the Most Excellent Italian Architects, Painters, and Sculptors* (1550). Vasari argues that Greco-Roman art declined after the dissolution of the Roman Empire, to be followed by a long period of barbaric insensitivity to classical monuments. Only in the past generations had Italian artists begun to restore the perfection of the arts, according to Vasari, a development he called *rinascita*, the Italian for "rebirth." It was the French equivalent—*renaissance*—that stuck.

Referring initially to a rebirth in the arts and literature, the word *Renaissance* came to define a consciousness of modernity. The writings of the Florentines Petrarch and Boccaccio in the fourteenth century showed that they thought of themselves as living in an age distinct from a long preceding period—which they dubbed the "middle age"—with values different from those of the classical civilizations of Greece and Rome. Petrarch, Boccaccio, and other Florentines began to consider their civilization a revival of the classical model in art, architecture, and language, the latter evidenced by an increased interest in classical Latin and Greek. From Florence and Italy, the Renaissance spread to France, Spain, the Low Countries, and central Europe by the fifteenth century. It inspired a golden age of vernacular literature in those countries during the second half of the sixteenth century; scholars speak of a "Northern Renaissance" as late as 1600.

The word *Renaissance* acquired widespread recognition with the publication of Jakob Burckhardt's *The Civilization of the Renaissance in Italy* in 1860. A historian at the University of Basel, Burckhardt considered the Renaissance a watershed in Western civilization. For him, the Renaissance ushered in a spirit of modernity, freeing the individual from the domination of society and creative impulses from the repression of the church; the Renaissance represented the beginning of secular society and the preeminence of individual creative geniuses.

Dominant for a long time, Burckhardt's ideas have been strongly revised by scholars. Some point out the many continuities between the Middle Ages and the Renaissance; others argue that the Renaissance was not a secular but a profoundly religious age; and still others see the Renaissance as only the beginning of a long period of transition from the Middle Ages to modernity. The consensus among scholars is that the Renaissance represents a distinct cultural period lasting from the fourteenth to the sixteenth century, centered on the revival of classical learning and spreading from Italy to northern Europe. Historians disagree about the significance of this cultural rebirth for society at large, but they generally understand it to represent some of the complex changes that characterized the passing of medieval society to modernity.

FURTHER READING

Burckhardt, Jakob. *The Civilization of the Renaissance in Italy.* 1860.

Ferguson, Wallace K. *The Renaissance in Historical Thought.* 1948.

Hay, Denis. "Idea of Renaissance." In *Dictionary of the History of Ideas.* 1973.

Ruggiero, Guido, ed. *The Blackwell Companion to the World of the Renaissance.* 2001.

The Advent of Printing

The invention of mechanical printing aided greatly in making the classical texts widely available. Printing with movable type—a revolutionary departure from the old practice of copying by hand—was invented in the 1440s by Johannes Gutenberg, a German goldsmith (c. 1400–1470). Mass production of books and pamphlets made the world of letters more accessible to a literate audience. Two preconditions proved essential for the advent of printing: the industrial production of paper and the commercial production of manuscripts. Papermaking came to Europe from China via Arab intermediaries. By the fourteenth century, paper mills were operating in Italy, producing paper that was more fragile but much cheaper than parchment or vellum, the animal skins that Europeans had previously used for writing.

By the fifteenth century, a brisk industry in manuscript books was flourishing in Europe's university towns and major cities. Production was in the hands of stationers, who organized copying of the manuscripts in workshops known as scriptoria, and who acted as retail booksellers. The largest stationers, in Paris or Florence, were extensive operations by fifteenth-century standards.

The invention of movable type was an enormous technological breakthrough that took bookmaking out of the hands of human copyists. Printing—or "mechanically writing," as contemporaries called it—was not new: the Chinese had been printing by woodblock since the tenth century, and woodcut pictures made their appearance in Europe in the early fifteenth century. Movable type, however, allowed entire manuscripts to be printed more quickly than by copying. The process involved casting durable metal molds to represent the letters of the alphabet. The letters were arranged to represent the text on a page and then pressed in ink against a sheet of paper. The imprint could be repeated numerous times with only a small amount of human labor (see the illustration, Printing Press, on this page). In 1467, two German printers established the first press in Rome and produced twelve thousand volumes in five years, a feat that in the past would have required a thousand scribes working full-time for the same number of years.

Printing Press
This illustration from a French manuscript of 1537 depicts typical printing equipment of the sixteenth century. To the left an artisan is using the screw press to apply the paper to the inked type. Also shown are the composed type secured in a chase, the printed sheet (four pages of text printed on one sheet) held by the seated proofreader, and the bound volume. When two pages of text were printed on one standard-sized sheet, the bound book was called a folio. A bound book with four pages of text on one sheet was called a quarto ("in four"), and a book with eight pages of text on one sheet was called an octavo ("in eight"). The last is a pocket-size book, smaller than today's paperback. *Bridgeman-Giraudon/Art Resource, NY.*

After the 1440s, printing spread rapidly from Germany to other European countries (Map 14.1, page 510). In the 1490s, the German city of Frankfurt-am-Main became an international meeting place for printers and booksellers, establishing a book fair that remains an unbroken tradition to this day. Early books from the presses were exclusive and inaccessible, especially to a largely illiterate population. Gutenberg's famous two-volume Latin Bible was unmistakably a luxury item. Altogether 185 copies were printed. First priced at well over what a fifteenth-century professor could earn in a year, the Gutenberg Bible has always been

MAP 14.1 The Spread of Printing in the Fifteenth Century
The Holy Roman Empire formed the center of printing. Presses in other countries were often established by migrant German printers, especially in Italy. Printing did not reach Muscovy until the sixteenth century.

one of the most expensive books in history, for both its rarity and its exquisite crafting.

Some historians argue that the invention of mechanical printing gave rise to a communications revolution as significant as, for example, the widespread use of the personal computer today. The multiplication of standardized texts altered the thinking habits of Europeans by freeing individuals from having to memorize everything they learned; it certainly made possible the relatively speedy and inexpensive dissemination of knowledge, and it created a wider community of scholars, no longer dependent on personal patronage or church sponsorship for texts. Printing facilitated the free expression and exchange of ideas, and its disruptive potential did not go unnoticed by political and ecclesiastical au-

thorities. Emperors and bishops in Germany, the homeland of the printing industry, moved quickly to issue censorship regulations.

Review: How did humanism and the printing press influence learning in the Renaissance?

❖ Revolution in the Arts

The Renaissance was one of the most creative periods in the European arts. New techniques in painting, architecture, and musical performance fostered original styles and new subjects. Three transformations were particularly significant. First, artists, previously seen as artisans, acquired a more prominent social status, as individual talent and genius were recognized by a society hungry for culture. Second, sculptors and painters developed a more naturalistic style, especially in representing the human body. And finally, the use of perspective in Renaissance art reflected a new mathematical and scientific basis for artistic creation, which was manifest not only in the visual arts but also in architecture and musical composition.

From Artisan to Artist

The artist was a new social type in the Renaissance. Leonardo da Vinci (1452–1519)—a painter, architect, and inventor trained in the artisanal tradition—described his freedom to create as a gentleman of leisure: "The painter sits at his ease in front of his work, dresses as he pleases, and moves his light brush with the beautiful colors...often accompanied by musicians or readers of various beautiful works." If this picture fits with today's image of the creative genius, so do the stories about Renaissance painters and their eccentricities: some were violent, others absentminded; some worked as hermits, while others cared little for money.

The point of stories about "genius," often told by Renaissance artists themselves, was to convince society that the artists' works were unique and their talents priceless. The artist, as opposed to the artisan, was an individual with innate talents who created works of art according to his imagination rather than following the blueprints of a patron. Of course, the reality was that most artists still relied on wealthy patrons for support. And although they wished to create as their genius dictated, not all patrons of the arts allowed artists to work without restrictions. While the duke of Milan appreciated Leonardo's genius, the duke of Ferrara paid for his art by the square foot. For every successful artist—such as the painter Andrea Mantegna (1431–1506), who was exalted by Pope Innocent VIII—there were many others who painted marriage chests and look-alike Madonnas for middle-class homes.

A successful artist who did fit the new vision of unfettered genius was the Florentine sculptor Donatello (1386–1466), one of the heroes Giorgio Vasari described in his *Lives of the Artists*, a seventeenth-century book of biographies of the greatest artists of the Renaissance. Not only did Donatello's sculptures evoke classical Greek and Roman models, but the grace and movement of his work inspired Cosimo de' Medici, the ruler of Florence, to excavate antique works of art. Moreover, Donatello transcended material preoccupations. According to Vasari:

> Donatello was free, affectionate, and courteous ...and more so to his friends than to himself. He thought nothing of money, keeping it in a basket suspended by a rope from the ceiling, so that all his workmen and friends took what they wanted without saying anything to him.

A favorite artist of the most powerful man in fifteenth-century Florence, Donatello owed his ability to be generous in large part to Medici patronage.

Renaissance artists worked under any of three conditions: long-term service in princely courts, commissioned piecework, and production for the market. Mantegna, for example, worked from 1460 until his death in 1506 for the princes of Mantua. In return for a monthly salary and other gifts, he promised to paint panels and frescoes (paintings on a wet plaster surface). His masterpieces—fresco scenes of courtly life with vivid and accurate portraits of members of the princely family—decorated the walls of the palace. In practice, however, Mantegna sometimes was treated more as a skilled worker than as an independent artist: he was once asked to adorn his majestic tapestries with life sketches of farm animals.

The workshop—the norm of artistic production in Renaissance Florence and in northern European cities such as Nuremberg and Antwerp—afforded the artist greater autonomy. As heads of workshops, artists trained apprentices and negotiated contracts with clients. Famous artists developed followings, and wealthy consumers came to pay a premium for work done by a master instead of apprentices. Studies of art contracts show that in the course of the fifteenth century artists gained greater control over their work. Early in the century clients routinely stipulated detailed conditions for works of art. Clients might also determine the arrangement of figures in a picture, leaving the artist little more than the execution. After mid-century, however, such specific directions became less common. In 1487, for example, the Florentine painter Filippo Lippi (1457–1504), in his contract to paint frescoes in the Strozzi chapel, specified that the work should be "all from his own hand and particularly the figures." The shift underscores the increasing recognition of the unique skills of individual artists.

In the fifteenth century, most large-scale work was commissioned by specific patrons, but the art market, for which artists produced works without prior arrangement for sale, developed initially in the Low Countries.

Limited at first to smaller altarpieces, woodcuts, engravings, sculpture, and pottery paintings, this market began to extend to larger panel paintings. The commercialization of art celebrated the new context of artistic creation itself: artists working in an open, competitive, urban civilization.

The Human Figure

If the individual artist is a man of genius, what greater subject for the expression of beauty is there than the human body itelf? From the fourteenth-century Florentine painter Giotto (see Chapter 12), Renais-

Masaccio's *Trembling Man*
Renaissance paintings differ from medieval paintings in many ways, one of which is their use of naturalism, in which subjects—human and nature—are depicted in a realistic rather than a symbolic way. Here, the important subject is baptism, but Masaccio's representation emphasizes the feeling of cold water, a naturalistic treatment intended to connect the subject of the painting and the viewer. *Erich Lessing/Art Resource, NY.*

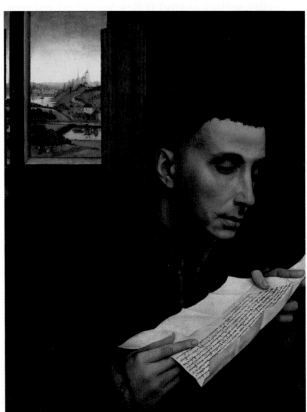

St. Ivo by Rogier van der Weyden
This painting of St. Ivo of Chartres (c.1040–1116) by Rogier van der Weyden (1400?–64) exemplifies the Flemish School style of detailed realistic human portraits shown against the backdrop of a landscape or city scene. Born in Tournai, Weyden spent most of his life as the official city painter of Brussels. The Flemish School exerted a significant influence on painting in France, Portugal, and Castile in the 15th century. © *National Gallery Collection; by kind permission of the Trustees of the National Gallery/CORBIS.*

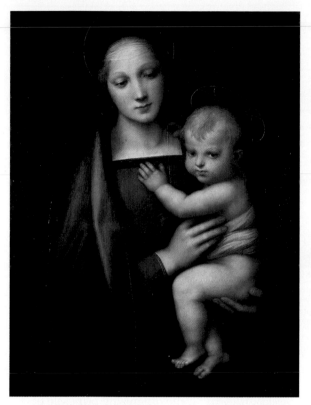

Madonna and Child
Raphael's *Madonna and Child* flows with natural grace: Jesus and the Virgin Mary are unfrozen from their static representations in Byzantine and medieval art. This naturalistic portrayal reflects how religious feelings were permeated by the everyday in the Renaissance. *Scala/Art Resource, NY.*

Botticelli's *Spring*
This detail from Botticelli's *Spring* depicts the graceful movements of dance and the beauty of the female body through the naturalistic technique of Renaissance art. Note the contrast between the stillness of the formal composition, with the figures anchored by the trees in the background, and the movement conveyed by the gently flowing robes and the swirling motion of the dancing figures. *Scala/Art Resource, NY.*

sance artists learned to depict ever more expressive human emotions and movements. The work of the short-lived but brilliant painter Masaccio◆ (1401–1428) exemplifies this development. His painting *Expulsion from Paradise* shows Adam and Eve grieving in shame and despair.

Feminine beauty also found many masterpiece representations in Renaissance art. These representations range from the graceful movements of classical pagan figures and allegories, as in Sandro Botticelli's (c. 1445–1510) *The Birth of Venus* and *Springtime*, to Raphael's (1483–1520) numerous tender depictions of the Virgin Mary and the infant

Jesus. In addition to rendering homage to classical and biblical figures, Renaissance artists painted portraits of their contemporaries. The increasing number of portraits in Renaissance painting illustrates the new, elevated view of human existence. Initially limited to representations of pontiffs, monarchs, princes, and patricians, portraiture of the middle classes became more widespread as the century advanced. Painters from the Low Countries such as Jan van Eyck◆ (1390?–1441) distinguished themselves in this genre; their portraits achieved a sense of detail and reality unsurpassed until the advent of photography.

◆**Masaccio:** muh ZAH chee oh

◆**Jan van Eyck:** yahn vahn EYEK

The ideal of a universal man was elaborated in the writings of Giovanni Pico della Mirandola (1463–1494). Born to a noble family, Pico avidly studied Latin and Greek philosophy. He befriended Ficino, Florence's leading Platonic philosopher, and enjoyed the patronage of Lorenzo de' Medici (1449–1492), who provided him with a villa after the papacy condemned some of his writings. Pico's oration *On the Dignity of Man* embodied the optimism of Renaissance philosophy. To express his marvel at the human species, Pico imagined God's words at his creation of Adam: "In conformity with your free judgment, in whose hands I have placed them, you are confined by no bounds, and you will fix limits of nature for yourself." Pico's construct placed mankind at the center of the universe as the measure of all things and "the molder and maker of himself." In his efforts to reconcile Platonic and Christian philosophy, Pico stressed both the classical emphasis on human responsibility in shaping society and the religious trust in God's divine plan.

For the first time after classical antiquity, sculptors again cast the human body in bronze, in life-size or larger freestanding statues. Donatello's equestrian statue of a Venetian general, one of the finest examples of this new endeavor, was consciously based on Roman statues of mounted emperors. Free from fabric and armor, the human body was idealized in the eighteen-foot-tall marble sculpture *David*, the work of the great Michelangelo Buonarroti♦ (1475–1564).

Order through Perspective

Renaissance art was distinguished from that of earlier eras by its depiction of the world as the eye perceives it. The use of visual perspective—an illusory three-dimensional space on a two-dimensional surface and the ordered arrangement of painted objects from one viewpoint—became one of the distinctive features of Western art. Neither Persian, Chinese, Byzantine, nor medieval Western art—all of which had been more concerned with conveying symbolism than reality—expressed this aesthetic for order through the use of perspective. Underlying the idea of perspective was a new Renaissance worldview: humans asserting themselves over nature in painting and design by controlling space. Optics became the organizing principle of the natural world in that it detected the "objective" order in nature. The Italian painters were keenly aware of their new technique, and they criticized the Byzantine and the northern Gothic stylists for "flat" depiction of the human body and the natural world. The highest accolade for a Renaissance artist was to be described as an "imitator of nature": the artist's teacher was nature, not design books or master painters. Leonardo described how "painting...compels the mind of the painter to transform itself into the mind of nature itself and to translate between nature and art, setting out, with nature, the causes of nature's phenomena regulated by nature's laws."

Michelangelo's *David*
Commissioned of the great Florentine artist when he was twenty-six, *David* (1501–1504) represents a masterpiece of sculpture that equaled the glory of ancient human sculpture. This huge marble figure—the earliest monumental statue of the Renaissance—depicts David larger than life-size in the full beauty and strength of the male body. *Nimatallah/Art Resource, NY.*

♦**Buonarroti:** bwoh nahr RAW tee

The perspectival representation that now dominated art is illustrated aptly by the work of three artists: Lorenzo Ghiberti♦ (c. 1378–1455), Andrea Mantegna, and Piero della Francesca (1420–1492). In 1401, the sculptor and goldsmith Ghiberti won a contest to design bronze doors for the San Giovanni Baptistry in Florence, a project that would occupy <u>him</u> the rest of his life. Choosing stories from the Old and New Testaments as his themes, Ghiberti used linear perspective to create a sense of depth and space in his bronze panels. His doors were so moving that Michelangelo in the sixteenth century described them as "the Gates of Paradise."

The Sacrifice of Isaac
Ghiberti's brilliant work (1401–1402) forms one of the panels on the door of the San Giovanni Baptistry in Florence. Technically difficult to execute, this bronze relief captures the violence of movement when the angel intervenes as Abraham prepares to slit the throat of Isaac, a story told in the Hebrew Scriptures.
Scala/Art Resource, NY.

Mantegna's most brilliant achievement, his frescoes in the bridal chamber of the Gonzaga Palace, completed between 1465 and 1474, created an illusory extension of reality, a three-dimensional representation of life, as the actual living space in the chamber "opened out" to the painted landscape on the walls. By contrast, the painter Piero della Francesca set his detached and expressionless figures in a geometrical world of columns and tiles, framed by intersecting lines and angles. Human existence, if della Francesca's painting can be taken as a reflection of his times, was shaped by human design, in accordance with the faculties of reason and observation. Thus, the artificially constructed urban society of the Renaissance was the ideal context in which to understand the ordered universe.

Perhaps even more than the visual artists, fifteenth-century architects embodied the Renaissance ideals of uniting artistic creativity and scientific knowledge. Among the greatest talents of the day was Filippo Brunelleschi♦ (1377–1446), a Florentine architect whose designs included the dome of the city's cathedral, modeled after ancient Roman ruins; the Ospedale degli Innocenti (a hospital for orphans); and the interiors of several Florentine churches.

One of the first buildings designed by the Florentine architect Leon Battista Alberti (1404–1472), the Rucellai Palace in Florence, shows a strong classical influence and inaugurated a trend in the construction of urban palaces for the Florentine ruling elite. Although Alberti undertook architectural designs for many princes, his significance lies more in his theoretical works, which strongly influenced his contemporaries. In a book on painting dedicated to Brunelleschi, Alberti analyzed the technique of perspective as the method of imitating nature. In *On Architecture* (1415), modeled after the Roman Vitruvius, Alberti argued for large-scale urban planning, with monumental buildings set on open squares, harmonious and beautiful in their proportions. His ideas were put into action by Pope Sixtus IV (r. 1471–1484) and his successors in the urban renewal of Rome, and they

♦**Lorenzo Ghiberti:** loh REHNT soh gee BEHR tee

♦**Brunelleschi:** broo nuhl EHS kee

Frescoes of the Camera degli Sposi
Andrea Mantegna's frescoes in the ducal palace depict members of the Gonzaga family, together with their court and animals, in various festive scenes. In masterly use of the perspective techniques, four painted walls lead to a vaulted ceiling decorated as heaven. The landscape view to the left of the door reflects the Renaissance idea of a painting as a window to the real world. *Scala/Art Resource, NY.*

Piero della Francesca, *The Flagellation of Christ*
Active in Urbino in the mid-fifteenth century, the Tuscan artist Piero della Francesca was a master of dramatic perspective design, as exemplified in this small panel painting. His use of cool colors and his imaginative manipulation of geometric space have led many art historians to regard Piero as the earliest forebear of the abstract artists of our own time. *Scala/Art Resource, NY.*

served to transform that unruly medieval town into a geometrically constructed monument to architectural brilliance by recalling the grandeur of its ancient origins.

New Musical Harmonies

Italy set the standards for the visual arts in Europe, but in musical styles it was more influenced by the northern countries. Around 1430, a new style of music appeared in the Low Countries that would dominate composition for the next two centuries. Instead of writing pieces with one major melodic line, composers wrote for three or four instrumental or human voices, each equally important in expressing a melody in harmony with the others.

The leader of this new style, known as polyphonic ("many sounds") music, was Guillaume Dufay (1400–1474), whose musical training began in the cathedral choir of his hometown, Cambrai in the Low Countries. His successful career took him to all the cultural centers of the Renaissance, where nobles sponsored new compositions and maintained a corps of musicians for court and religious functions. In 1438, Dufay composed festive music to celebrate the completion of the cathedral dome in Florence designed by Brunelleschi. Dufay expressed the harmonic relationship among four voices in ratios that matched the mathematically precise dimensions of Brunelleschi's architecture. After a period of employment at the papal court, Dufay returned to his native north and composed music for the Burgundian and French courts.

Although his younger counterpart Johannes Ockeghem♦ (c. 1420–1495), whose influence rivaled Dufay's, worked almost exclusively at the French court, Dufay's mobile career was typical. Josquin des Prez♦ (1440–1521), another Netherlander, wrote music in Milan, Ferrara, Florence, and Paris and at the papal court. The new style of music was beloved by the elites.

Within Renaissance polyphony were three main musical genres: the canon (central texts) of the Catholic Mass; the motet, which used both sacred and secular texts; and the secular chanson, often using the tunes of folk dances. Composers often adapted familiar folk melodies for sacred music, expressing religious feeling primarily through human voices instead of instruments. The tambourine and the lute were indispensable for dances, however, and small ensembles of wind and string instruments with contrasting sounds performed with singers in the fashionable courts of Europe. Also in use in the fifteenth century were new keyboard instruments—the harpsichord and clavichord—which could play several harmonic lines at once.

Review: How did the shift from artisan to artist, a new naturalistic style, and the use of perspective in art reflect and influence a Renaissance mentality?

♦**Johannes Ockeghem:** yoh HAHN uhs OH kuh gehm
♦**Josquin des Prez:** zhaw SKAN deh PRAY

❖ The Intersection of Private and Public Lives

Lineage and descent shaped political power in dynastic states. In the fourteenth century, the state itself, through its institutions and laws, attempted to shape private life. Nowhere was this process more evident than in Florence. Considerations of state power intruded into the most intimate personal concerns: sexual intimacy, marriage, and childbirth could not be separated from the values of the ruling classes. With a society dominated by upper-class, patriarchal households, Renaissance Italy specified rigid roles for men and women, subordinating women and making marriage a vehicle for consolidating social hierarchy.

Renaissance Social Hierarchy

To deal with a mounting fiscal crisis, in 1427 the government of Florence ordered that a comprehensive tax record of households in the city and territory be compiled. Completed in 1430, this survey represented the most detailed population census then taken in European history. From this mass of data, historians have been able to reconstruct a picture of the Florentine state, particularly its capital.

The state of Florence, roughly the size of Massachusetts, had a population of more than 260,000. Tuscany, the area in which the Florentine state was located, was one of the most urbanized regions of Europe. With 38,000 inhabitants, the capital city of Florence claimed 14 percent of the total population and an enormous 67 percent of the state's wealth. Straddling the Arno River, Florence was a beautiful, thriving city with a defined social hierarchy. Some 60 percent of all households belonged to what the Florentines called the "little people"—workers, artisans, small merchants. The Florentines' "fat people" (roughly our middle class) made up 30 percent of the urban population and included the wealthier merchants, the leading artisans, notaries, doctors, and other professionals (see "A Merchant's Advice to His Sons" on the next page). At the very bottom of the hierarchy were slaves and servants,

A Merchant's Advice to His Sons

Giovanni Rucellai, one of the most successful merchants of fifteenth-century Florence, kept an extensive diary that reveals life among the city's urban elite. In this selection, Rucellai warns his sons against pursuing political power for self-serving reasons. Rucellai's comments on political office reflect a strong sentiment of support for the Florentine Republic and an implicit critique of the Medici, who dominated the city by means of their enormous wealth.

I do not deny that participation in the republic's affairs is not a most worthy enterprise, nor do I castigate him who, because of his excellence and his good works, honours his country by being just and honest. In fact, I say that a true honour is one which is appreciated by all citizens. But to do as they do: submit to this one, line up behind that one, form alliances, factions and conspiracies in order to surpass the most sagacious citizens; to desire to administer the state as if it were one's shop, appropriating its wealth and considering it as dowry for one's daughters, competing with one group of citizens while despising another; all these are dishonest things in a city. Therefore, my sons, I wish that you never desire an important political position

in order to convert the treasure of the state into your own, for such an action is not good and I shall not approve it. He who aspires to a political position with this goal in mind has always been destroyed by the state itself regardless of the power of ingenuity which he might command. Everyone who has tried to ride this horse has always fallen from it, and the higher his position, the greater his blow and the more complete his ruin....

Let me repeat that the act of governing is notable and praiseworthy. He is a true citizen who assumes office not of his own will, not for his own advancement or grandeur, but when guided by reason, justice, prudence and has the approval of the good citizens–not with a view to becoming an overlord and superior to others, but in order to be of greater service. The good citizen wishes the good of all, he loves peace, equality, honesty, humility, the tranquility of the entire city, is happy in the pursuit of his own affairs, scorns avarice and uncontrollable passions and seeks to advance good understanding in his household and even more in his country.

Source: Anthony Molho, ed., *Social and Economic Foundations of the Italian Renaissance* (New York: John Wiley, 1969), 197–98.

largely women from the surrounding countryside employed in domestic service. At the top, a tiny elite of very wealthy patricians, bankers, and wool merchants controlled the state. In fact, the richest 1 percent of urban households (approximately one hundred families) owned more than one-quarter of the city's wealth and one-sixth of Tuscany's total wealth. The patricians in particular owned almost all government bonds, a lucrative investment guaranteed by a state they dominated.

Surprisingly, men seem to have outnumbered women in the 1427 survey. For every 100 women there were 110 men, unlike most past and present populations, in which women are the majority. In addition to

female infanticide, which was occasionally practiced, the persistent underreporting of women probably explains the statistical abnormality.

Most people, men and women alike, lived in households with at least six inhabitants, although the form of family unit—nuclear or extended—varied, depending mainly on wealth, with poor people rarely able to support extended families. Among urban patricians and landowning peasants, the extended family held sway. The number of children in a family, it seems, reflected class differences as well. Wealthier families had more children; childless couples existed almost exclusively among the poor, who were also more likely to abandon the infants they could not feed.

Family Alliances

Wealth and class clearly determined family structure and the pattern of marriage and childbearing. In a letter to her eldest son, Filippo, dated 1447, Alessandra Strozzi announced the marriage of her daughter Caterina to the son of Parente Parenti. She described the young groom, Marco Parenti, as "a worthy and virtuous young man, and... the only son, and rich, 25 years old, and keeps a silk workshop; and they have a little political standing." The dowry was set at one thousand florins, a substantial sum—but for four to five hundred florins more, Alessandra admitted to Filippo, Caterina would have fetched a husband from a more prominent family.

The Strozzi belonged to one of Florence's most distinguished traditional families, but at the time of Caterina's betrothal the family had fallen into political disgrace. Alessandra's husband, an enemy of the Medici, was exiled in 1434; Filippo, a rich merchant in Naples, lived under the same political ban. Although Caterina was clearly marrying beneath her social station, the marriage represented an alliance in which money, political status, and family standing all balanced out. More an alliance between families than the consummation of love, an Italian Renaissance marriage was usually orchestrated by the male head of a household. In this case, Alessandra, as a widow, shared the matchmaking responsibility with her eldest son and other male relatives. Eighteen years later, when it came time to find a wife for Filippo, who had by then accumulated enough wealth to start his own household, Marco Parenti, his brother-in-law, would serve as matchmaker.

The upper-class Florentine family traced descent and determined inheritance through the male line. Because the distribution of wealth depended on this patriarchal system, women occupied an ambivalent position in the household. A daughter could claim inheritance only through her dowry, and she often disappeared from family records after her marriage. A wife seldom emerged from the shadow of her husband, and consequently the lives of many women have been lost to history.

In the course of a woman's life, her family often pressured her to conform to conventional expectations. At the birth of a daughter, most wealthy Florentine fathers opened an account at the Dowry Fund, a public fund established in 1425 to raise state revenues and a major investment instrument for the upper classes. In 1433, the fund paid annual interest of between 15 and 21 percent, and fathers could hope to raise handsome dowries to marry their daughters to more prominent men when the daughters reached their late teens. The Dowry Fund supported the structure of the marriage market, in which the circulation of wealth and women consolidated the social coherence of the ruling classes. (See "Taking Measure," on the next page.)

Women's subordination in marriage often reflected the age differences between spouses. The Italian marriage pattern, in which young women married older men, contrasted sharply with the northern European model, in which partners were much closer in age. Significant age disparity also left many women widowed in their twenties and thirties, and remarriage often created hard choices. A widow's father and brothers frequently pressed her to remarry to form a new family alliance. A widow, however, could not bring her children into her new marriage because they belonged to her first husband's family. Faced with the choice between her children and her paternal family, not to mention the question of her own happiness, a widow could hope to gain greater autonomy only in her old age, when, like Alessandra, she might assume matchmaking responsibilities to advance her family's fortunes.

In northern Europe, however, women enjoyed a relatively more secure position. In England, the Low Countries, and Germany, for example, women played a significant role in the economy—not only in the peasant household, in which everyone worked, but especially in the town, serving as peddlers, weavers, seamstresses, shopkeepers, midwives, and brewers. In Cologne, for example, women could join one of several artisans' guilds, and in Munich they ranked among some of the richest brewers. Women in northern Europe shared inheritances with their brothers, retained control of their dowries, and had the right to

TAKING MEASURE

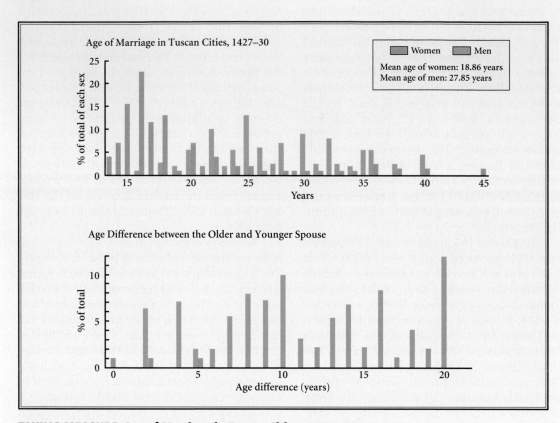

Age of Marriage in Tuscan Cities, 1427–30

Women   Men
Mean age of women: 18.86 years
Mean age of men: 27.85 years

Age Difference between the Older and Younger Spouse

TAKING MEASURE Age of Marriage in Tuscan Cities, 1427–1430

The 1427–1430 Florentine tax and census records indicate two distinctly different marriage patterns for men and women. While the mean marriage age for women was 18.86 years, that for men was 27.85 years. This difference reflected the considerable difficulty for young men to amass enough wealth to start a household. More revealing is the chart showing the differences in age between the spouses. Some 12 percent of all spouses had a difference of twenty years. While the great majority of these marriages involved older, wealthier, established males, often in second marriages after the death of their first spouses, a small number involved younger men marrying up in the social ladder to widows of guild members to acquire a position. Together these charts give important information on gender relations and reflect the underlying class and gender inequalities in Renaissance society. *From David Herlihy and Christiane Klapisch-Zuber,* Tuscans and Their Families: A Study of Florentine Catasto of 1427 *(New Haven: Yale University Press, 1985), 205. Reprinted by permission of Yale University Press.*

represent themselves before the law. Italian men who traveled to the north were appalled at the differences in gender relations, criticizing English women as violent and brazen and disapproving of the mixing of the sexes in German public baths.

The Regulation of Sexuality

Along with marriage patterns, child care and attitudes toward sexuality also reflected class differences in Renaissance life. Florentine middle- and upper-class fathers arranged business contracts with wet nurses to breast-feed their infants; babies thus spent prolonged periods of time away from their families. Such elaborate child care was beyond the reach of the poor, who often abandoned their children to strangers or to public charity.

By the beginning of the fifteenth century, Florence's two hospitals were accepting large numbers of abandoned children in addition to the sick and infirm. In 1445, the government opened the Ospedale degli Innocenti to deal with the large number of abandoned children. These unfortunate children came from two sources: poor families who were unable to feed another mouth, especially in times of famine, war, and economic depression; and women who had given birth out of wedlock. A large number of the latter were domestic slaves or servants who had been impregnated by their masters; in 1445, one-third of the first hundred foundlings at the new hospital were children of such liaisons. For some women the foundling hospital provided an alternative to infanticide. More than two-thirds of abandoned infants were girls, a clear indicator of the inequality between the sexes. The large number of abandoned infants overtaxed the hospital's limited resources—the death rate for infants there was much higher than the already high infant mortality rate of the time.

Illegitimacy in itself did not necessarily carry a social stigma in fifteenth-century Europe. Most upper-class men acknowledged and supported their illegitimate children as a sign of virility, and illegitimate children of noble lineage often rose to social and political prominence. Any social stigma was borne primarily by the woman, whose ability to marry became compromised. Shame and guilt drove some poor single mothers to kill their infants, a crime for which they paid with their own lives if discovered.

In addition to prosecuting infanticide, the public regulation of sexuality focused on prostitution and homosexuality. Intended "to eliminate a worse evil by a lesser one," a 1415 statute established government brothels in Florence. Concurrent with its higher tolerance of prostitution, the Renaissance state had a low tolerance of homosexuality. In 1432, the Florentine state appointed mag-istrates "to discover—whether by means of secret denunciation, accusations, notification, or any other method—those who commit the vice of sodomy, whether actively or passively." The government set fines for homosexual acts and carried out death sentences against pederasts (men who have sex with boys).

Fifteenth-century European magistrates took violence against women less seriously than illegal male sexual behavior, as the different punishments indicate. In Renaissance Venice, for example, the typical jail sentence for rape or attempted rape was only six months. Magistrates often treated noblemen with great leniency and handled rape cases according to class distinctions. For example, Agneta, a young girl living with a government official, was abducted and raped by two millers, who were sentenced to five years in prison; several servants who abducted and raped a slave woman were sentenced to three to four months in jail; and a nobleman who abducted and raped Anna, a slave woman, was freed. The brilliant civilization of the Renaissance was experienced very differently by men and women.

> **Review:** In what ways did the Renaissance state shape the private sphere?

❖ The Renaissance State and the Art of Politics

Among the achievements of the Renaissance, the state seemed to represent a work of art. For the Florentine political theorist Niccolò Machiavelli✦ (1469–1527), the state was an artifice of human creation to be conquered, shaped, and administered by princes according to the principles of power politics. Machiavelli laid out these principles in *The Prince*: "It can be observed that men use various methods in pursuing their own personal objectives, that is glory and riches....I believe that...fortune is the arbiter of half the things we do,

✦**Niccolò Machiavelli:** neek koh LOH mah kee uh VEHL ee

MAP 14.2 Italy, c. 1450
The political divisions of Italy reflected powerful city-centered republics and duchies in the north and the larger but economically more backward south. Local and regional identities remained strong into the modern age.

leaving the other half or so to be controlled by ourselves." *The Prince* was the first treatment of the science of politics to discuss the acquisition and exercise of power without reference to an ultimate moral or ethical end. Machiavelli's keen observations of power, scandalous to his contemporaries, were based on a careful study of Italian politics during the Renaissance. Though a republican at heart, Machiavelli recognized the necessity of power in founding a state, whose survival ultimately rested on republican virtue. Outside of Italy, other European states also furnished many examples to illustrate the ruthless nature of power politics and the artifice of state building. In general, a mid-century period of turmoil gave way to the restructuring of central monarchical power in the last decades of the fifteenth century.

Many states developed stronger, institutionally more complex central governments in which middle-class lawyers played an increasingly prominent role. The expanded Renaissance state paved the way for the development of the nation-state in later centuries.

Republics and Principalities in Italy

The Italian states of the Renaissance can be divided into two broad categories: republics, which preserved the traditional institutions of the medieval commune by allowing a civic elite to control political and economic life, and principalities, which were ruled by a dynasty. The most powerful and influential states were the republics of Venice and Florence and the principalities of Milan and Naples. In addition to these four, a handful of smaller states, such as Siena, Ferrara, and Mantua stood out as important cultural centers during the Renaissance (Map 14.2).

Venice.   Venice, a city built on a lagoon, ruled an extensive colonial empire that extended from the Adriatic to the Aegean Sea. Venetian merchant ships sailed the Mediterranean, the Atlantic coast, and the Black Sea; Christian pilgrims to Palestine booked passage on Venetian ships; in 1430, the Venetian navy numbered more than three thousand ships. Symbolizing their intimacy with and dominion over the sea, the Venetians celebrated an annual "Wedding of the Sea." Amid throngs of spectators and foreign dignitaries, the Venetian doge (the elected duke) sailed out to the Adriatic, threw a golden ring into its waters to renew the union, and intoned, "Hear us with favor, O Lord. We worthily entreat Thee to grant that this sea be tranquil and quiet for our men and all others who sail upon it."

In the early fifteenth century, however, Venetians faced threats on both sides. From 1425 to 1454, Venice fought expanding Milan on land. The second, and greater, danger came from the eastern Mediterranean, where the Ottoman Turks finally captured Byzantine Constantinople in 1453. Faced by these external threats, Venice drew strength from its internal social cohesion. Under the rule of an oligarchy of aristocratic merchants,

Venice enjoyed stability; and its maritime empire benefited citizens of all social classes, who joined efforts to defend the interests of the "Most Serene Republic," a contemporary name that reflected Venice's lack of social strife.

Florence. Compared with serene Venice, the republic of Florence was in constant agitation, responsive to political conflicts, new ideas, and artistic styles. Like Venice, Florence described its government in the humanist language of ancient Roman republicanism. Unlike Venice, Florentine society was turbulent as social classes and political factions engaged in constant civic strife. By 1434, a single family had emerged dominant in this fractious city: the Medici. Cosimo de' Medici (1388–1464), the head of the family, was ruthless. His contemporary Pope Pius II did not mince words in describing Medici power: "Cosimo, having thus disposed of his rivals, proceeded to administer the state at his pleasure and amassed wealth." Even though he did not hold any formal political office, Cosimo wielded influence in government through business associates and clients who were indebted to him for loans, political appointments, and other favors.

The Medici Bank handled papal finances and established branch offices in many Italian cities and the major northern European financial centers. Backed by immense private wealth, Cosimo became the arbiter of war and peace, the regulator of law, more master than citizen. Yet the prosperity and security that Florence enjoyed made him popular as well. At his death, Cosimo was lauded as the "father of his country."

Cosimo's grandson Lorenzo ("the Magnificent"), who assumed power in 1467, bolstered the regime's legitimacy with his lavish patronage of the arts. But opponents were not lacking. In 1478, Lorenzo narrowly escaped an assassination attempt. Two years after Lorenzo's death in 1494, partisans who opposed the Medici drove them from Florence. The Medici returned to power in 1512, only to be driven out again in 1527. In 1530, the republic fell and the Medici once again seized control, declaring Florence a **duchy** (a state ruled by dukes) and naming themselves its dukes.

Milan. Unlike Florence, with its republican aspirations, the duchy of Milan had been under dynastic rule since the fourteenth century. The most powerful Italian principality, Milan was a military state; it was relatively uninterested in the support of the arts but had first-class armaments and textile industries in the capital city and rich farmlands in Lombardy. Until 1447, the duchy was ruled by the Visconti dynasty, a group of powerful lords whose plans to unify all of northern and central Italy failed because of combined opposition from Venice, Florence, and other Italian powers. In 1447, the last Visconti duke died without a male heir, and the nobility proclaimed Milan to be a republic.

For three years the new republic struggled to maintain Milan's political and military strength. Cities that the Visconti family had subdued rebelled against Milan, and the two great republics of Venice and Florence plotted its downfall. Milan's ruling nobility, seeking further defense, appointed Francesco Sforza,♦ who had married the illegitimate daughter of the last Visconti duke, to the post of general. Sforza promptly turned against his employers, claiming the duchy as his own. A bitter struggle between the nobility and the townspeople in Milan further undermined the republican cause, and in 1450 Sforza entered Milan in triumph.

The power of the Sforza dynasty reached its height during the 1490s. In 1493, Duke Ludovico married his niece Bianca Maria to Maximilian, the newly elected Holy Roman Emperor, promising an immense dowry in exchange for the emperor's recognition of his rule. But the newfound Milanese glory was soon swept aside by France's invasion of Italy in 1494, and the duchy itself eventually came under Spanish rule.

The Papal States. In the violent arena of Italian politics, the papacy, an uneasy mixture of worldly splendor and religious authority, was a player like the other states. The vicars of Christ negotiated treaties, made war, and built palaces; a few led scandalous lives. Pope Alexander VI (r. 1492–1503), the most notorious pontiff, kept a mistress and

♦**Francesco Sforza:** frahn CHEHS kaw SFAWR tsah

fathered children, one of whom, Cesare Borgia, served as Machiavelli's model for a ruthless ruler in *The Prince.*

The popes' concern with politics stemmed from their desire to restore papal authority, greatly undermined by the Great Schism of 1378–1417 and the conciliar movement. To that end, the popes used both politics and culture to enhance their authority. Politically, they curbed local power, expanded papal government, increased taxation, enlarged the papal army and navy, and extended papal diplomacy. Culturally, the popes renovated churches, created the Vatican Library, sponsored artists, and patronized writers to glorify their role and power as St. Peter's successors. In undertaking these measures, the Renaissance papacy merely exemplified the larger trend toward the centralization of power evident in the development of monarchies and empires outside of Italy as well.

Naples.   After a struggle for succession between Alfonso of Aragon and René d'Anjou, a cousin of the king of France, the kingdoms of Naples and Sicily came under Aragonese rule between 1435 and 1494. Unlike the northern Italian states, Naples was dominated by powerful feudal barons who retained jurisdiction and taxation over their own vast estates. Alfonso I (r. 1435–1458), called Alfonso the Magnanimous for his generous patronage of the arts, promoted the urban middle class to counter baronial rule, using as his base Naples, the only large city in a relatively rural kingdom. Alfonso's son Ferante I (r. 1458–1494) continued his father's policies: two of his chief ministers hailed from humble backgrounds. With their private armies and estates intact, however, the barons constantly threatened royal power, and in 1462 many rebelled against Ferante. More ruthless than his father, Ferante handily crushed the opposition.

Embroiled in Italian politics, Alfonso and Ferante shifted their alliances among the papacy, Milan, and Florence. But the greater threat to Neapolitan security was external. In 1480, Ottoman forces captured the Adriatic port of Otranto, where they massacred the entire male population. And in 1494, a French invasion ended the Aragonese dynasty in Naples, although, as in Milan, France's claim would eventually be superseded by that of Spain.

Renaissance Diplomacy

Many features of diplomacy characteristic of today's nation-states first appeared in fifteenth-century Europe. By midcentury, competition between states and the extension of warfare raised the practice of diplomacy to nearly an art form. The first diplomatic handbook, composed in 1436 by Frenchman Bernard du Rosier, later archbishop of Toulouse, declared that the business of the diplomat was "to pay honor to religion... and the Imperial crown, to protect the rights of kingdoms, to offer obedience...to confirm friendships...make peace...to arrange past disputes and remove the cause for future unpleasantness."

The emphasis on ceremonies, elegance, and eloquence (Italians referred to ambassadors as orators) masked the complex game of diplomatic intrigue and spying. In the fifteenth century, a resident ambassador was expected to keep a continuous stream of foreign political news flowing to the home government, not just to conduct temporary diplomatic missions, as earlier ambassadors had done. In some cases the presence of semiofficial agents developed into full-fledged ambassadorships: the Venetian embassy to the sultan's court in Constantinople developed out of the merchant-consulate that had represented all Venetian merchants, and Medici Bank branch managers eventually acted as political agents for the Florentine republic.

Foremost in the development of diplomacy was Milan, a state with political ambition and military might. Under the Visconti dukes, Milan sent ambassadors to Aragon, Burgundy, the Holy Roman Empire, and the Ottoman Empire. Under the Sforza dynasty, Milanese diplomacy continued to function. For generations Milanese diplomats at the French court sent home an incessant flow of information on the rivalry between France and Burgundy. Francesco Sforza also used his diplomatic corps to extend his political patronage. In letters of recommendation to the papacy, Francesco commented on the political desirability of potential ecclesiastical candidates by using code words, sometimes supplemented with instructions to his ambassador to indicate his true intent regardless of the coded letter of recommendation. In more sensitive diplomatic reports, ciphers (codes) were used to prevent the messages from being understood by hostile powers if they were captured.

As the center of Christendom, Rome became the diplomatic hub of Europe. During the 1490s, well over two hundred diplomats were stationed in Rome. The papacy sent out far fewer envoys than it received; only at the end of the fifteenth century were papal nuncios, or envoys, permanently established in the European states.

The most outstanding achievement of Italy's Renaissance diplomacy was the negotiation of a general peace treaty that settled the decades of warfare engendered by Milanese expansion and civil war. The Treaty of Lodi (1454) established a complex balance of power among the major Italian states and maintained relative stability in the peninsula for half a century. Renaissance diplomacy eventually failed, however, when France invaded in 1494, leading to the collapse of the whole Italian state system.

Monarchies and Empires

Locked in fierce competition among themselves, the Italian states paid little attention to the large territorial states emerging in the rest of Europe that would soon overshadow Italy with their military power and economic resources. Whether in Burgundy, England, Spain, France, the Ottoman Empire, or Muscovy, rulers employed various stratagems to expand or enhance their power. In central Europe, by contrast, rulers failed to centralize power.

Burgundy. The expansion of Burgundy during the fifteenth century was a result of military might and careful statecraft. The spectacular success of the Burgundian dukes and their equally dramatic demise both bear testimony to the artful creation of the Renaissance state, paving the way for the development of the European nation-state.

Part of the French royal house, the Burgundian dynasty expanded its power

rapidly by acquiring land, primarily in the Netherlands. Between 1384 and 1476, the Burgundian state filled the territorial gap between France and Germany, extending from the Swiss border in the south to Friesland (Germany) in the north. Through purchases, inheritance, and conquests, the dukes ruled over French-, Dutch-, and German-speaking subjects, creating a state that resembled a patchwork of provinces and regions, each jealously guarding its laws and traditions. The Low Countries, with their flourishing cities, constituted the state's economic heartland, and the region of Burgundy itself, which gave the state its name, offered rich farmlands and vineyards. Unlike England, whose island geography made it a natural political unit; or France, whose borders were forged in the national experience of repelling English invaders; or Castile, whose national identity came from centuries of warfare against Islam, Burgundy was an artificial creation whose coherence depended entirely on the skillful exercise of statecraft.

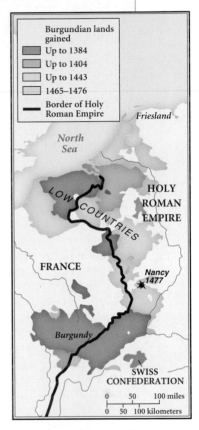

Expansion of Burgundy, 1384–1476

At the heart of Burgundian politics was the personal cult of its dukes. Philip the Good (r. 1418–1467) and his son Charles the Bold (r. 1467–1477) were very different kinds of rulers, but both were devoted to enhancing the prestige of their dynasty and the security of their dominion. A bon vivant who fathered many illegitimate children, Philip was a lavish patron of the arts who commissioned numerous illuminated manuscripts, chronicles, tapestries, paintings, and music in his efforts to glorify Burgundy. Charles, by contrast, spent more time on war than at court. Renowned for his courage

The Burgundian Court

The ideals of late-medieval courtly style found fullest expression in fifteenth-century Burgundy. This painting of the wedding of Philip the Good and Isabella of Portugal was executed in the workshop of the Flemish master Jan van Eyck. It conveys the atmosphere of chivalric fantasy in which the Burgundian dynasty enveloped itself. *Bridgeman-Giraudon/Art Resource, NY.*

another, they also staged elaborate ceremonies to enhance their power and promote their legitimacy (see The Burgundian Court, on this page). Their entries into cities and their presence at weddings, births, and funerals became the centerpieces of a "theater" state in which the dynasty provided the only link among very diverse territories. New rituals became propaganda tools. Philip's revival of chivalry at court transformed the semi-independent nobility into courtiers closely tied to the prince.

In addition to sponsoring political propaganda, the Burgundian rulers controlled their geographically dispersed state by developing a financial bureaucracy and a standing army. But maintaining the army, one of the largest in Europe, left the dukes chronically short of money. They were forced to sell political offices to raise funds, a practice that led to an inefficient and corrupt bureaucracy. The demise of the Burgundian state had two sources: the loss of Charles the Bold, who died without a male heir, and an alliance between France and the Holy Roman Empire. When Charles fell in battle in 1477, France seized the duchy of Burgundy. The Netherlands remained loyal to Mary, Charles's daughter, and through her husband, the future Holy Roman Emperor Maximilian, some of the Burgundian lands and the dynasty's political and artistic legacy passed on to the Habsburgs.

England.   In England, defeat in the Hundred Years' War was followed by civil war at home. Henry VI (r. 1422–1461), who ascended to the throne as a child, proved in maturity to be a weak and, on occasion, mentally unstable monarch. He was unable to control the great lords of the realm, who wrought anarchy with their numerous private feuds. In 1460, Richard of York rebelled;

(hence his nickname), he died in 1477 when his army was routed by the Swiss at Nancy, a loss that began the decline of Burgundian power.

The Burgundians' success depended in large part on their personal relationship with their subjects. Not only did the dukes travel constantly from one part of their dominion to his son defeated Henry and was then crowned Edward IV (r. 1461–1483). England's intermittent civil wars, later called the Wars of the Roses continued until 1485, fueled at home by factions among nobles and regional discontent and abroad by Franco-Burgundian intervention. The ultimate victor was Henry Tudor, who took the title of Henry VII (r. 1485–1509).

The Wars of the Roses did relatively little damage to England's soil. The battles were generally short and, in the words of the French chronicler Philippe de Commynes (c. 1447–1511), "England enjoyed this peculiar mercy above all other kingdoms, that neither the country, nor the people nor the houses, were wasted, destroyed or demolished, but the calamities and misfortunes of the war fell only upon the soldiers, and especially on the nobility." As a result, the English economy continued to grow during the fifteenth century. The cloth industry expanded considerably, and the English now used much of the raw wool that they had been exporting to the Low Countries to manufacture goods at home. London merchants, taking a vigorous role in trade, also assumed greater political prominence not only in governing London but also as bankers to kings and members of Parliament. In the countryside the landed classes—the nobility, the gentry (a kind of lesser nobility), and the yeomanry (free farmers)—benefited from rising farm and land-rent income as the population increased slowly but steadily.

Spain. In the Iberian monarchies, decades of civil war over the royal successions began to wane only in 1469, when Isabella of Castile and Ferdinand of Aragon married. Retaining their separate titles, the two monarchs ruled jointly over their dominions, each of which adhered to its traditional laws and privileges. Their union represented the first step toward the creation of a unified Spain. Isabella and Ferdinand limited the privileges of the nobility and allied themselves with the cities, relying on the Hermandad (civic militia) to enforce justice and on lawyers to staff the royal council.

The united strength of Castile and Aragon brought the reconquista to a close with a final crusade against the Muslims.

Isabella I of Spain, c. 1500
In 1474 Isabella became queen of Castile, and in 1479 her husband Ferdinand took control of the kingdom of Aragon. The union of these crowns would lead to the creation of a unified Spain under "Catholic monarchs." This detail from the retable in a Spanish church (the ledge raised above the back of altars) shows her in pious devotion with her hands clasped next to a prayer book. *The Granger Collection, NY.*

After more than a century of peace, war broke out in 1478 between Granada, the last Iberian Muslim state, and the Catholic royal forces. Weakened by internal strife, Granada finally fell in 1492. Two years later, in recognition of the crusade, Pope Alexander VI bestowed the title "Catholic monarchs" on Isabella and Ferdinand, ringing in an era in which militant Catholicism became an instrument of state authority and shaped the national consciousness.

The relative religious tolerance of the Middle Ages in Iberia, in which Muslims, Jews, and Christians had generally lived side by side, now yielded to the demand for religious conformity. The practice of Catholicism became a test of one's loyalty to the church and to the Spanish monarchy. In 1478, royal jurisdiction introduced the Inquisition to Spain, primarily as a means to control the **conversos** (Jewish converts to Christianity), whose elevated positions in the economy and the government aroused widespread resentment from the so-called Old Christians. Conversos often were suspected of practicing their ancestral religion in secret while pretending to adhere to their new Christian faith. Appointed by the monarchs, the clergy (called inquisitors) presided over tribunals set up to investigate those suspected of religious lapses. The accused could defend themselves but not confront their accusers, who were often anonymous. The wide spectrum of punishments ranged from monetary fines to the ritual of public confession called **auto da fé**◆ (literally, "demonstration of faith") to burning at the stake. After the fall of Granada, many Moors were forced to convert or resettle in Castile, and in 1492 Ferdinand and Isabella ordered all Jews in their kingdoms to choose between exile or conversion.

The single most dramatic event for the Jews of Renaissance Europe was their expulsion from Spain, the country with the largest and most vibrant Jewish communities, and their subsequent dispersion throughout the Mediterranean world. On the eve of the expulsion, approximately 200,000 Jews and 300,000 conversos were living in

Spain Just before Unification, Late Fifteenth Century

◆**auto da fé:** ow toh duh FAY

Castile and Aragon. Well over 100,000 Jews chose exile. The priest Andrés Bernáldez described the expulsion:

> Just as with a strong hand and outstretched arm, and much honor and riches, God through Moses had miraculously taken the other people of Israel from Egypt, so in these parts of Spain they had . . . to go out with much honor and riches, without losing any of their goods, to possess the holy promised land, which they confessed to have lost through their great and abominable sins which their ancestors had committed against God.

France. France, too, was recovering from war. Although France won the Hundred Years' War, it emerged from that conflict in the shadow of the brilliant Burgundian court. Under Charles VII (r. 1422–1461) and Louis XI (r. 1461–1483), the French monarchy began the slow process of expansion and recovery. Abroad, Louis fomented rebellion in England. At home, however, lay the more dangerous enemy, Burgundy. In 1477, with the death of Charles the Bold, Louis seized large tracts of Burgundian territory. France's horizons expanded even more when Louis inherited most of southern France after the Anjou dynasty died out. By the end of the century, France had doubled its territory, assuming close to its modern-day boundaries.

To strengthen royal power at home, Louis promoted industry and commerce, imposed permanent salt and land taxes, maintained western Europe's first standing army (created by his predecessor), and dispensed with the meeting of the Estates General, which included the clergy, the nobility, and representatives from the major towns of France. The French kings further increased their power with important concessions from the papacy. With the 1438 Pragmatic Sanction of Bourges, Charles asserted the superiority of a general church council over the pope. Harking back to a long tradition of the high Middle Ages, the Sanction of Bourges established what would come to be known as **Gallicanism** (after Gaul, the ancient Roman name for France), in which the French king would effectively control ecclesiastical revenues and the appointment of French bishops.

Central and Eastern Europe. The rise of strong, new monarchies in western Europe contrasted sharply with the weakness of state authority in central and eastern Europe, where developments in Hungary, Bohemia, and Poland resembled the Burgundian model of personal dynastic authority (Map 14.3). Under Matthias Corvinus (r. 1456–1490), the Hungarian king who briefly united the Bohemian and Hungarian crowns, an east-central European empire seemed to be emerging. A patron of the arts and a humanist, Matthias created a great library in Hungary. He repeatedly defeated the encroaching Austrian Habsburgs and even occupied Vienna in 1485. His empire did not outlast his death in 1490, however. The powerful Hungarian magnates, who enjoyed the constitutional right to elect the king, ended it by refusing to acknowledge his son's claim to the throne.

In Poland, the nobility preserved their power under the monarchy by maintaining their right to elect kings. By selecting weak monarchs and fiercely defending noble liberties, the Polish nobility ruled a land of serfs and frustrated any attempt at the centralization of power and state building. Only in 1506 would Poland and Lithuania again form a loosely united "commonwealth" under a single king.

The Ottoman Empire. In the Balkans, the Ottoman Empire, under Sultan Mehmed II (r. 1451–1481), became a serious threat to all of Christian Europe. After Mehmed ascended the throne, he proclaimed a holy war and laid siege to Constantinople in 1453. A city of 100,000, the Byzantine capital could muster only 6,000 defenders (including a small contingent of Genoese) against an Ottoman force estimated at between 200,000 and 400,000 men. The city's fortifications, many of which dated from Emperor Justinian's rule in the sixth century, were no match for fifteenth-century cannons. The defenders held out for fifty-three days: while the Christians confessed their sins and prayed for divine deliverance, in desperate anticipation of the Second Coming, the Muslim besiegers pressed forward, urged on by the certainty of rich spoils and Allah's promise of a final victory over the infidel Rome. Finally the de-

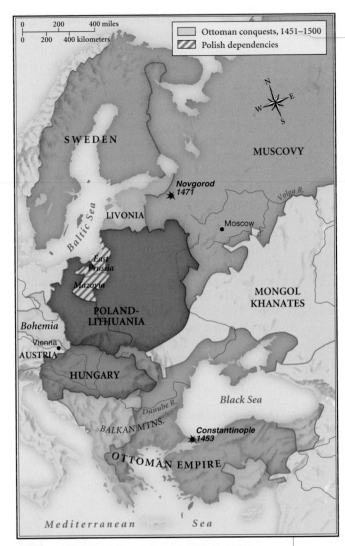

MAP 14.3 Eastern Europe in the Fifteenth Century
The rise of Muscovy and the Ottomans shaped the map of eastern Europe. Some Christian monarchies such as Serbia lost their independence. Others, such as Hungary, held off the Ottomans until the early sixteenth century.

fenders were overwhelmed, and the last Byzantine emperor, Constantine Palaeologus,♦ died in battle. Some sixty thousand residents were carried off in slavery, and the city was sacked. Mehmed entered Constantinople in triumph, rendered thanks to Allah in Justinian's Church of St. Sophia, which became a mosque, and was remembered as "the Conqueror."

♦**Palaeologus:** pay lee AHL uh guhs

Muscovy. North of the Black Sea and east of Poland-Lithuania, a very different polity was taking shape. In the second half of the fifteenth century, the princes of Muscovy embarked on a spectacular path of success that would make their state the largest on earth. Subservient to the Mongols in the fourteenth century, the Muscovite princes began to assert their independence with the collapse of Mongol power. Ivan III (r. 1462–1505) was the first Muscovite prince to claim an imperial title, referring to himself as **tsar** (or czar, from the name Caesar). In 1471, Ivan defeated the city-state of Novgorod, whose territories encompassed a vast region in northern Russia. Six years later he abolished the local civic government of this proudly independent city, which had enjoyed trade with the thriving cities of central Europe. To consolidate his autocratic rule and wipe out memories of past freedoms, in 1484 and 1489 Ivan forcibly relocated thousands of leading Novgorod families to lands around Moscow. He also expanded his territory to the south and east when his forces pushed back the Mongols to the Volga River.

Unlike other European monarchies, whose powers were bound by collective rights and laws, Ivan's Russian monarchy claimed absolute property rights over all lands and subjects. The expansionist Muscovite state was shaped by two traditions: religion and service. After the fall of the Byzantine Empire, the tsar was the Russian Orthodox church's only defender of the faith against Islam and Catholicism. Orthodox propaganda thus legitimized the tsar's rule by proclaiming Moscow the "Third Rome" (the first two being Rome itself and Constantinople) and praising the tsar's autocratic power as the best protector of the faith. The Mongol system of service to rulers, by which the prince's subjects were bound to him by life and blood and not by a contract of loyalty, also deeply informed Muscovite statecraft. In their conception of the state as private dominion,

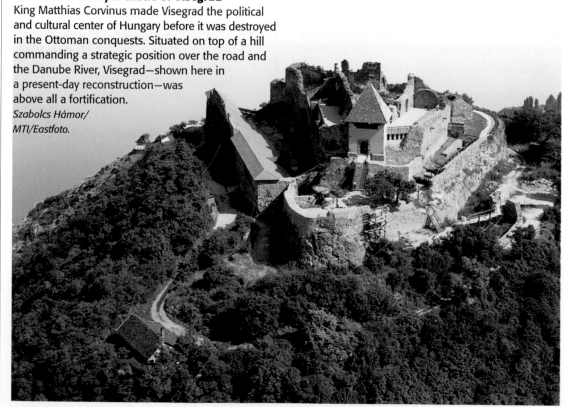

The Medieval Royal Castle of Visegrad
King Matthias Corvinus made Visegrad the political and cultural center of Hungary before it was destroyed in the Ottoman conquests. Situated on top of a hill commanding a strategic position over the road and the Danube River, Visegrad—shown here in a present-day reconstruction—was above all a fortification.
Szabolcs Hámor/ MTI/Eastfoto.

A View of Moscow
This image comes from the travel book of the Habsburg ambassador to Moscow, Sigismund
von Herberstein, who engraved it himself in 1547. Note the representation of Muscovite soldiers
with bows and arrows, weapons long since outdated in western Europe. Note also the domination of the Kremlin (in the middle) over a city that consisted mostly of modest wooden houses.
Bridgeman-Giraudon/Art Resource, NY.

their emphasis on autocratic power, and
their division of the populace into a land-
holding elite in service to the tsar and a vast
majority of taxpaying subjects, the Muscovite
princes created a state more in the despotic
political tradition of the central Asian steppes
and the Ottoman Empire than of western
Europe.

In state building, Muscovy joined England,
France, and Spain as examples of success, in
sharp contrast to Burgundy and Poland. Yet
far more significant was the expansion of
the boundary of Europe itself, as maritime
explorations brought Europeans into contact with indigenous civilizations in Africa,
the Americas, and Asia.

Review: How did Renaissance princes increase
their power at the expense of the nobility and
their subjects?

❖ On the Threshold of World History: Widening Geographic Horizons

The fifteenth century constituted the first
era of world history. The significance of the
century lies not so much in the European
"discovery" of Africa and the Americas as in
the breakdown of cultural frontiers inaugurated by European colonial expansion. Before
the maritime explorations of Portugal and
Spain, Europe had remained at the periphery
of world history. Fourteenth-century Mongols
had been more interested in conquering
China and Persia—lands with sophisticated
cultures—than in invading Europe; Persian
historians of the early fifteenth century dismissed Europeans as "barbaric Franks"; and
China's Ming dynasty rulers, who sent maritime expeditions to Southeast Asia and East

Africa around 1400, seemed unaware of the Europeans, even though Marco Polo and other Italian merchants had appeared at the court of the preceding Mongol Yuan dynasty. In the fifteenth century, the Portuguese and Spanish, inspired by the search for profit (from spices and gold) and by a crusading spirit against Islam, sailed across the Atlantic, Indian, and Pacific Oceans; they were followed a century later by the English, French, and Dutch, bringing people, merchandise, crops, and diseases in a global exchange that would shape the modern world. For the first time the people of the Americas were brought into contact with a larger historical force that threatened to destroy not only their culture but their existence as well. European exploitation, conquest, and racism defined this historical era of transition from the medieval to the modern world.

The Divided Mediterranean

In the second half of the fifteenth century, the Mediterranean Sea, which had dominated medieval maritime trade, began to lose its preeminence to the Atlantic Ocean. To win control over the Mediterranean, the Ottomans embarked on an ambitious naval program to transform their empire into a major maritime power. War and piracy disrupted the flow of Christian trade: the Venetians mobilized all their resources to fight off Turkish advances, and the Genoese largely abandoned the eastern Mediterranean for trade opportunities presented by the Atlantic voyage.

The Mediterranean states used ships made with relatively backward naval technology, compared with that of Portugal and Spain. The most common ship, the galley—a flat-bottomed vessel propelled by sails and oars—dated from the time of ancient Rome. Most galleys could not withstand open-ocean voyages, although Florentine and Genoese galleys still made long journeys to Flanders and England, hugging the coast for protection. The galley's dependence on human labor was a more serious handicap. Because prisoners of war and convicted criminals toiled as oarsmen in both Christian and Muslim ships, victory in war or the enforcement of criminal penalties was crucial to a state's ability to float

Engraving of Katharina, an African Woman
Like other artists in early-sixteenth-century Europe, Albrecht Dürer would have seen in person Africans who went to Portugal and Spain as students, servants, and slaves. Note Katharina's noble expression and dignified attire. Before the rise of the slave trade in the seventeenth century, most Africans in Europe were household servants of the aristocracy. Considered prestigious symbols, such servants were not employed primarily for economic production. *Foto Marburg/Art Resource, NY.*

large numbers of galleys. Slavery, too, a traditional Mediterranean institution, sometimes provided the necessary labor.

Although the Mediterranean was divided into Muslim and Christian zones, it still offered a significant opportunity for exchange. Sugarcane was transported to the western Mediterranean from western Asia. From the Balearic Islands off Spain (under Aragonese rule), the crop then traveled to the Canary Islands in the Atlantic, where the Spanish enslaved the native population to work the new sugar plantations. Eventually sugar—and slavery—were exported to the Americas.

Different ethnic groups also moved across the maritime frontier. After Granada fell in 1492, many Muslims fled to North Africa and continued to raid the Spanish coast. When Castile expelled the Jews, some of them settled in North Africa, more in Italy, and many in the Ottoman Empire, Greek-speaking Thessalonika, and Palestine. Conversant in two or three languages, Spanish Jews often served as intermediaries between the Christian West and Muslim East. Greeks occupied a similar position. Most Greeks in the homeland adhered to the Greek Orthodox church under Ottoman protection, but some converted to Islam and entered imperial service, making up a large part of the Ottoman navy. The Greeks on Crete, Chios, and other Aegean islands, however, lived under Italian rule, some of them converting to Roman Catholicism and entering Venetian, Genoese, and Spanish service. A region with warring 0states and competing religions, the Mediterranean remained a divided zone as more and more Europeans turned instead to the unknown oceans.

Portuguese Explorations

The first phase of European overseas expansion began in 1433 with Portugal's systematic exploration of the West African coast and culminated in 1519–1522 with Spain's circumnavigation of the globe (Map 14.4, page 537). Looking back, the sixteenth-century Spanish historian Francisco López de Gómora described the Iberian maritime voyages to the East and West Indies as "the greatest event since the creation of the world, apart from the incarnation and death of him who created it." (See "New Sources, New Perspectives," page 534.)

In many ways a continuation of the struggle against Muslims in the Iberian peninsula, Portugal's maritime voyages displayed that country's mixed motives of piety, glory, and greed. The Atlantic explorations depended for their success on several technological breakthroughs, such as the lateen sail adapted from the Arabs (it permitted a ship to tack against headwinds), new types of sailing vessels, and better charts and instruments. What motivated these explorers was a combination of crusading zeal against Muslims and medieval adventure stories, such as the tales of the Venetian traveler Marco Polo (1254–1324). Behind the spirit of the crusade lurked vistas of vast gold mines in West Africa (the trade across the Sahara was controlled by Arabs) and a mysterious Christian kingdom established by Prester John (actually the Coptic Christian kingdom of Abyssinia, or Ethiopia, in East Africa). The Portuguese hoped to reach the spice-producing lands of South and Southeast Asia by sea to bypass the Ottoman Turks, who controlled the traditional land routes between Europe and Asia.

By 1415, the Portuguese had captured Ceuta on the Moroccan coast, thus establishing a foothold in Africa. Thereafter, Portuguese voyages sailed farther and farther down the West African coast. By midcentury, the Portuguese chain of forts had reached Guinea and could protect the gold and slave trades. At home the royal house of Portugal financed the fleets, with crucial roles played by Prince Peter, regent of the throne between 1440 and 1448; his more famous younger brother, Prince Henry the Navigator; and King John II (r. 1481–1495). Henry financed many voyages out of the revenues of a noble crusading order. Private monies also helped; leading Lisbon merchants participated in financing the gold and slave trades off the Guinea coast.

In 1455, Pope Nicholas V (r. 1447–1455) sanctioned Portuguese overseas expansion, commending King John II's crusading spirit and granting him and his successors the monopoly on trade with inhabitants of the newly "discovered" regions. In 1487–1488, Bartholomeu Dias took advantage of the prevailing winds in the South Atlantic to reach the Cape of Good Hope. A mere ten years later (1497–1499), under the captainship of Vasco da Gama, a Portuguese fleet rounded the cape and reached Calicut, India, the center of the spice trade. Twenty-three years later, in 1512, Ferdinand Magellan, a Portuguese sailor in Spanish service, led the first expedition to circumnavigate the globe. By 1517, a chain of Portuguese forts dotted the Indian Ocean: at Mozambique, Hormuz (at the mouth of the Persian Gulf), Goa (in India), Colombo (in modern Sri Lanka), and Malacca (modern Malaysia).

NEW SOURCES, NEW PERSPECTIVES

Portuguese Voyages of Discovery

The quincentennial celebration of Vasco da Gama's 1499 voyage to India took place in the same year (1998) that Lisbon staged a World Exposition—thus inspiring the theme of "Discoveries of the Oceans" in Portugal's presentation of its past and its contributions to civilization. The celebration of Portugal and the oceans strengthened interest in Portuguese maritime history and traditions, but it also inspired examination and criticism of that country's history. The result has been a rich mix of new sources and perspectives, presented in publications and exhibitions.

The traditional historical approach emphasizes the technical innovations of Portuguese seamanship. Inventions of new sailing vessels, such as the caravel, a high-sided ship capable of carrying a large load and maintaining balance in rough seas, enabled Portuguese sailors to venture ever farther into the oceans. Other nautical instruments reflected a cumulative knowledge of seamanship and geography that reduced the risks of long-distance travel. Sailors compiled nautical guides showing the time of tides (see A Nautical Tide Calendar) and the position of the sun in the sky at different latitudes at different seasons (see A Nautical Solar Guide). Most valuable of all were the pilots' books, or *roteiros* (books of sailing directions), often accompanied by detailed maps of maritime regions and coasts. These books of routes and maritime charts lessened but did not eliminate

Portuguese Ships
Maritime voyagers in Portugal were sponsored by the highest authorities in the land, the best known of whom was Prince Henry, nicknamed "the Navigator." This detail from the altarpiece of Santa Ana depicts monarchs, noblemen, and bishops against a backdrop of different types of sailing vessels. The caravel, the largest ship in the background, was the main type of vessel for Portuguese voyages in the fifteenth and sixteenth centuries.

A Nautical Tide Calendar
A high-tide chart, showing at which hour and at which fifth (the hour is divided into twelve-minute segments) high tide will recur from the day of the new moon. The left column in black starts with the date of the new moon and day. The red columns indicate first the hour and then the fifth of high tide.

A Nautical Solar Guide
From the codex of Bastiao Lopes (c. 1568), this guide shows the declination angle of the sun for different days in the months of April, May, and June.

the dangers of the oceans. The roteiro of Diogo Alfonso (1535), for example, gave these directions for the voyage to India:

> Setting forth from Lisbon you steer to the southwest until you catch sight of the island of Porto Santo or the island of Madeira. And from thence go southward in search of the Canaries; and as soon as you pass the Canaries set course southwest and south until you reach 15 degrees, that is 50 leagues from Cape Verde.

After passing through the mid-Atlantic, Alfonso advised the pilots to seek the most important landmark of all:

> If you come 35 degrees more or less, seeking the Cape of Good Hope, when you come upon cliff-faces, you may know that they are those of the Cape of Good Hope. . . . From hence you should set course northeast by north to $19\frac{1}{4}$ degrees. Then north-northeast, until you reach the latitude of $16\frac{3}{4}$ degrees.

(Continued)

(*Continued*)

Portugal's historical memory, solidified in the centuries since its earliest explorers, has celebrated its national heroes and discoverers as it mourned the numerous ships and men lost at sea. But much of this commemoration developed in the late nineteenth and early twentieth centuries as a justification for Portuguese colonialism, a fact now being examined by scholars in the wake of the Vasco da Gama quincentennial. How did Muslims and Indians see the arrival of the Portuguese, for example? The Indian historian Sanjay Subrahmanyam has argued that Vasco da Gama brought a new level of maritime violence to the Indian Ocean in 1499 with his attacks on Muslim shipping. Still other scholars, such as Antonio Manuel Hespanha, director of the Scientific Committee of the Discoveries, has called Portuguese scholars to examine their own past with a critical eye.

The many volumes and expositions sponsored by the committee have highlighted the multicultural aspects of the Portuguese encounter with Asia, America, and Africa, one that was too complex and ambivalent to be reduced to a simple heroic narrative.

QUESTIONS TO CONSIDER
1. What do the two quotes suggest about the dangers faced by Portuguese sailors?
2. What were the motives behind the Portuguese voyages to India?

FURTHER READING
Russell-Wood, A. J. R. *A World on the Move: The Portuguese in Africa, Asia, and America, 1415–1800.* 1992.
Subrahmanyam, Sanjay. *The Career and Legend of Vasco da Gama.* 1997.

After the voyages of Christopher Columbus, Portugal's interests clashed with Spain's. Mediated by Pope Alexander VI, the 1494 Treaty of Tordesillas settled disputes between Portugal and Spain by dividing the Atlantic world between the two royal houses. A demarcation 370 leagues west of the Cape Verde Islands divided the Atlantic Ocean, reserving for Portugal the West African coast and the route to India and giving Spain the oceans and lands to the west (see Map 14.4). Unwittingly, this agreement also allowed Portugal to claim Brazil in 1500, which was accidentally "discovered" by Pedro Alvares Cabral (1467–1520) on his voyage to India.

The Voyages of Columbus

Historians agree that Christopher Columbus (1451–1506) was born to Genoese parents; beyond that, we have little accurate information about this man who brought together the history of Europe and the Americas. In 1476, he arrived in Portugal, apparently a survivor of a naval battle between a Franco-Portuguese and a Genoese fleet; in 1479, he married a Portuguese noblewoman. He spent the next few years mostly in Portuguese service, gaining valuable experience in regular voyages down the west coast of Africa. In 1485, after the death of his wife, Columbus settled in Spain.

Fifteenth-century Europeans already knew that Asia lay beyond the vast Atlantic Ocean, and that the world was round. *The Travels of Marco Polo*, written more than a century earlier, still exerted a powerful hold on European images of the East. Columbus read it many times, along with other travel books, and proposed to sail west across the Atlantic to reach the lands of the khan, unaware that the Mongol Empire had already collapsed in eastern Asia. Vastly underestimating the distances, he dreamed of finding a new route to the East's gold and spices and partook of the larger European vision that had inspired the Portuguese voyages. (His critics had a much more accurate idea of the globe's size and of the

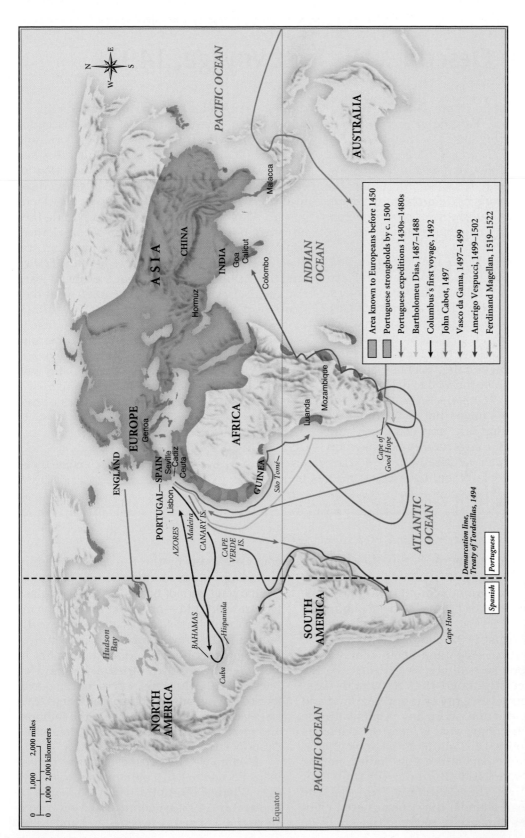

MAP 14.4 Early Voyages of World Exploration
Over the course of the fifteenth and early sixteenth centuries, the Atlantic Ocean was dominated by European shipping following the pioneering voyages of the Portuguese, who also first sailed around the Cape of Good Hope to the Indian Ocean and the Cape Horn to the Pacific. The search for spices and the need to circumnavigate the Ottoman Empire inspired these voyages.

Columbus Describes His First Voyage, 1493

In this famous letter to Raphael Sanchez, treasurer to his patrons, Ferdinand and Isabella, Columbus recounts his initial journey to the Bahamas, Cuba, and Hispaniola (today Haiti and the Dominican Republic), and tells of his achievements. This passage reflects the first contact between Native Americans and Europeans; already the themes of trade, subjugation, gold, and conversion all emerge in Columbus's own words.

Indians would give whatever the seller required; . . . Thus they bartered, like idiots, cotton and gold for fragments of bows, glasses, bottles, and jars; which I forbad as being unjust, and myself gave them many beautiful and acceptable articles which I had brought with me, taking nothing from them in return; I did this in order that I might the more easily conciliate them, that they might be led to become Christians, and be inclined to entertain a regard for the King and Queen, our Princes and all Spaniards, and that I might induce them to take an interest in seeking out, and collecting, and delivering to us such things as they possessed in abundance, but which we greatly needed. They practise no kind of idolatry, but have a firm belief that all strength and power, and indeed all good things, are in heaven, and that I had descended from thence with these ships and sailors, and under this impression was I received after they had thrown aside their fears. Nor are they slow or stupid, but of very clear understanding; and those men who have crossed to the neighbouring islands give an admirable description of everything they observed; but they never saw any people clothed, nor any ships like ours. On my arrival at that sea, I had taken some Indians by force from the first island that I came to, in order that they might learn our language, and communicate to us what they know respecting the country; which plan succeeded excellently, and was a great advantage to us, for in a short time, either by gestures and signs, or by words, we were enabled to understand each other. These men are still travelling with me, and although they have been with us now a long time, they continue to entertain the idea that I have descended from heaven.

Source: Christopher Columbus, *Four Voyages to the New World*. Translated by R. H. Major (New York: Corinth Books, 1961), 8–9.

difficulty of the venture.) But after the Portuguese and French monarchs rejected his proposal, Columbus found royal patronage with Isabella of Castile and Ferdinand of Aragon.

In August 1492, equipped with a modest fleet of three ships and about ninety men, Columbus set sail across the Atlantic. His contract stipulated that he would claim Castilian sovereignty over any new land and inhabitants and share any profits with the crown. Reaching what is today the Bahamas on October 12, Columbus mistook the islands to be part of the East Indies, not far from Japan and "the lands of the Great Khan." As the Castilians explored the Caribbean islands, they encountered communities of peaceful Indians, the Arawaks, who were awed by the Europeans' military technology, not to mention their appearance. Exchanging gifts of beads and broken glass for Arawak gold—an exchange that convinced Columbus of the trusting nature of the Indians—the crew established peaceful relationships with many communities. Yet in spite of many positive entries in the ship's log referring to Columbus's personal goodwill toward the Indians, the Europeans' objectives were clear: find gold, subjugate the Indians, and propagate Christianity. (See "Columbus Describes His First Voyage," above.)

Excited by the prospect of easy riches, many flocked to join Columbus's second voyage. When Columbus departed Cádiz in September 1493, he commanded seventeen ships that carried between 1,200 and 1,500 men, many believing that all they had to do was "to load the gold into the ships." Failing to find the imaginary gold mines and spices, however, the colonial enterprise quickly switched its focus to finding slaves. Columbus and his crew first enslaved the Caribs, enemies of the Arawaks; in 1494, Columbus proposed a regular slave trade based in Hispaniola. The Spaniards exported enslaved Indians to Spain, and slave traders sold them in Seville. Soon the Spaniards began importing sugarcane from Madeira, forcing large numbers of Indians to work on plantations to produce enough sugar for export to Europe. Columbus himself was edged out of this new enterprise. When the Spanish monarchs

Columbus in the Caribbean

realized the vast potential for material gain that lay in their new dominions, they asserted direct royal authority by sending officials and priests to the Americas, which were named after the Italian Amerigo Vespucci, who led a voyage across the Atlantic in 1499–1502.

Columbus's place in history embodies the fundamental transformations of his age. A Genoese in the service of Portuguese and Spanish employers, Columbus had a career illustrating the changing balance between the Mediterranean and the Atlantic. As the fifteenth-century Ottomans drove Genoese merchants out of the eastern Mediterranean, the Genoese turned to the Iberian peninsula. Columbus was one of many such adventurers who served the Spanish and Portuguese crowns.

A New Era in Slavery

The European voyages of discovery initiated a new era in slavery, both in expanding the economic scale of slave labor and in attaching race and color to servitude. Slavery had existed since antiquity. During the Renaissance, slavery was practiced in many

diverse forms. Nearly all slaves arrived as strangers in the Mediterranean ports of Barcelona, Marseille, Venice, and Genoa. Some were captured in war or by piracy; others—Africans—were sold by other Africans and Bedouin traders to Christian buyers; in western Asia, parents sold their children into servitude out of poverty; and many in the Balkans became slaves when their land was devastated by Ottoman invasions. Slaves were Greek, Slav, European, African, and Turk. Many served as domestic slaves in the leading European cities of the Mediterranean. Others sweated as galley slaves in Ottoman and Christian fleets. Still others worked as agricultural laborers on Mediterranean islands. In the Ottoman army, slaves even formed an important elite contingent.

The Portuguese maritime voyages changed this picture. From the fifteenth century, Africans increasingly filled the ranks of slaves. Exploiting warfare in West Africa, the Portuguese traded in gold and "pieces," as African slaves were called, a practice condemned at home by some conscientious clergy. One, Manoel Severim de Faria, observed that "one cannot yet see any good effect resulting from so much butchery; for this is not the way in which commerce can flourish and the preaching of the gospel progress." Critical voices, however, could not deny the enormous profits that the slave trade brought to Portugal. Most slaves toiled in the sugar plantations of the Portuguese Atlantic islands and in Brazil. A fortunate few labored as domestic servants in Portugal, where African freedmen and slaves, some 35,000 in the early sixteenth century, constituted almost 3 percent of the population, a percentage that was much higher than in other European countries. In the Americas, slavery would truly flourish as an institution of exploitation.

Europeans in the New World

In 1500, on the eve of European invasion, the native peoples of the Americas were divided into many societies, both sedentary and nomadic. Among the settled peoples, the largest political and social organizations centered in the Mexican and Peruvian highlands. The

MAP 14.5 European Explorations in the Americas in the Sixteenth Century
While Spanish and Portuguese explorers claimed Central and South America for the
Iberian crowns, there were relatively few voyages to North America. The discovery of
precious metals fueled the explorations and settlements of Central and South America,
establishing the foundations of European colonial empires in the New World.

Aztecs and the Incas ruled over subjugated
Indian populations in their respective empires. With an elaborate religious culture
and a rigid social and political hierarchy,
the Aztecs and Incas based their civilizations in large urban capitals.

The Spanish explorers organized their
expeditions to the mainland from a base in
the Caribbean (Map 14.5). Two prominent
leaders, Hernán Cortés (1485–1547) and
Francisco Pizarro (c. 1475–1541), gathered
men and arms and set off in search of gold.
Catholic priests accompanied the fortune
hunters to bring Christianity to allegedly
uncivilized peoples and thus to justify brutal
conquests. His small band swelled by peoples who had been subjugated by the
Aztecs, Cortés captured the Aztec capital,
Tenochtitlán, in 1519. Two years later

Mexico, then named New Spain, was added
to Charles V's empire. To the south, Pizarro
conquered the Andean highlands, exploiting a civil war between rival Incan kings.

By the mid-sixteenth century the Spanish empire, built on greed and justified by its
self-proclaimed Catholic mission, stretched
unbroken from Mexico to Chile. In addition
to the Aztecs and Incas, the Spaniards also
subdued the Mayas on the Yucatán peninsula, a people with a sophisticated knowledge
of cosmology and arithmetic. The gold and
silver mines in Mexico proved a treasure
trove for the Spanish crown, but the real
prize was the discovery of vast silver deposits
in Potosí (today in Bolivia).

Not to be outdone by the Spaniards,
other European powers joined the scramble
for gold in the New World. In North America,

the French went in search of a "northwest passage" to China. By 1504, French fishermen had appeared in Newfoundland. Thirty years later Jacques Cartier led three voyages that explored the St. Lawrence River as far as Montreal. An early attempt in 1541 to settle Canada failed because of the harsh winter and Indian hostility, and John Cabot's 1497 voyage to find a northern route to Asia also failed. More permanent settlements in Canada and the present-day United States would succeed only in the seventeenth century.

Review: What European countries led the way in maritime expansion and what were their motives?

Conclusion

During the Renaissance, Western civilization expanded in several important aspects: in the intellectual horizons of Europeans through the rediscovery of classical civilization and a renewed appreciation of human potential and achievement; in the greater centralization and institutionalization of expanded power of the state; and, finally, in the widened geographic horizons of an age of maritime exploration. Above all, the Renaissance was one of the most brilliant periods in artistic activity, one that glorified both God and humanity. A new spirit of confidence spurred Renaissance artists to develop a new appreciation for the

MAPPING THE WEST Renaissance Europe, c. 1500
By 1500, the shape of early modern Europe was largely consolidated and would remain stable until the eighteenth century. The only exception was the disappearance of an independent Hungarian kingdom after 1529.

human body and a new visual perspective in art and to apply mathematics and science to architecture, music, and artistic composition.

Highlighting the intensity of cultural production was the competition between burgeoning states and between Christian Europe and the Muslim Ottoman Empire. That competition fostered an expansion of the frontiers of Europe first to Africa and then across the Atlantic Ocean to the Americas. While centered in Italy, the Renaissance spread throughout Europe—in fact, historians view it as the first global movement in history—eventually shifting the center of European civilization from the Mediterranean to the Atlantic seaboard. But while Europeans of the Renaissance recovered from the deprivations of the late Middle Ages, they would soon enter yet another period of turmoil, one brought about not by demographic and economic collapse but by a profound crisis of conscience that the brilliance of Renaissance civilization had tended to obscure.

Suggested References

Widening Intellectual Horizons

In addition to the study of great artists and writers, recent scholarship has turned its attention to the "consumption" of cultural goods. Its focus has been on issues of education, art markets, and the different habits of reading and seeing in the past.

Burke, Peter. *The Italian Renaissance: Culture and Society in Italy.* 1986.

Eisenstein, Elizabeth. *The Printing Revolution in Early Modern Europe.* 1993.

Grafton, Anthony, and Lisa Jardine. *From Humanism to the Humanities: Education and the Liberal Arts in Fifteenth and Sixteenth Century Europe.* 1986.

Hankins, James, ed. *Renaissance Civic Humanism: Reappraisals and Reflections.* 2000.

Martin, Henri-Jean, and Lucien Febvre. *The Coming of the Book: The Impact of Printing, 1450–1800.* 1976.

Rabil, Albert, ed. *Renaissance Humanism: Foundations, Forms, and Legacy.* 1997.

Revolution in the Arts

Scholarship in Renaissance art history advances along two time-honored axes of research: studies of individual artists that focus heavily on Italy, and interpretations of art history within the larger cultural history of the period, with themes such as cross-cultural comparisons, patronage, and markets.

Baxandall, Michael. *Painting and Experience in Fifteenth Century Italy: A Primer in the Social History of Pictorial Style.* 1972.

Goffen, Rona. *Renaissance Rivals: Michelangelo, Leonardo, Raphael.* 2002.

Jardine, Lisa, and Jerry Brotton. *Global Interests: Renaissance Art between East and West.* 2000.

Mulryne, J. R., and Elizabeth Goldring, eds. *Court Festivals of the European Renaissance: Art, Politics, and Performance.* 2002.

The Intersection of Private and Public Lives

Much scholarship has focused on Italy and the Low Countries, where historical sources from this period are abundant. The investigation of legal records, population censuses, and tax rolls have yielded fascinating insights into the daily life of the period and the relationship between private life and the political process.

Brucker, Gene A., ed. *The Society of Renaissance Florence: A Documentary Study.* 1971.

Dean, Trevor, and K. J. P. Lowe, eds. *Marriage in Italy, 1300–1650.* 1998.

Herlihy, David, and Christiane Klapisch-Zuber. *Tuscans and Their Families: A Study of the Florentine Catasto of 1427.* 1978.

Pitkin, Hanna Fenichel. *Fortune Is a Woman: Gender and Politics in the Thought of Niccolò Machiavelli.* 1984.

Po-chia Hsia, R. *Trent 1475: Stories of a Ritual Murder Trial.* 1992.

Ruggiero, Guido. *Boundaries of Eros: Sex Crime and Sexuality in Renaissance Venice.* 1985.

The Renaissance State and the Art of Politics

Scholarship on the Renaissance state had concentrated on the study of Florence, but recent scholarship has broadened to include Venice, Milan, and smaller Italian city-states as well. Outside of Italian history, research on the Burgundian state gives a valuable comparative perspective.

Blockmans, Wim. *A History of Power in Europe: Peoples, Markets, States.* 1997.

Goffman, Daniel. *The Ottoman Empire and Early Modern Europe.* 2001.

Imber, Colin. *The Ottoman Empire 1300–1650: The Structure of Power.* 2002.

Kollmann, Nancy. *Kinship and Politics: The Making of the Muscovite Political System, 1345–1547.* 1987.

Liss, Peggy K. *Isabel the Queen: Life and Times.* 1992.

Lowe, Kate J. P., ed. *Cultural Links between Portugal and Italy in the Renaissance.* 2000.

Martines, Lauro. *Power and Imagination: City-States in Renaissance Italy.* 1979.

Prevenier, Walter, and Wim Blockmans. *The Burgundian Netherlands.* 1986.

On the Threshold of World History: Widening Geographic Horizons

The recent celebrations of the overseas voyages of Christopher Columbus and Vasco da Gama have inspired studies with new perspectives. The traditional view of "Europe discovers the world" has been replaced by a more nuanced and complex picture that takes in non-European views and uses Asian, African, and Mesoamerican sources.

Boxer, Charles R. *Four Centuries of Portuguese Expansion, 1415–1826.* 1969.

*Fuson, Robert H., ed. *The Log of Christopher Columbus.* 1987.

Russell-Wood, A. J. R. *A World on the Move: The Portuguese in Africa, Asia, and America, 1415–1808.* 1992.

Subrahmanyam, Sanjay. *The Career and Legend of Vasco da Gama.* 1997.

---

*Primary source.

CHAPTER REVIEW

IMPORTANT EVENTS

1415	Portugal captures Ceuta, establishing foothold in Africa
1434	Medici establish influence in Florence
1438	Pragmatic Sanction of Bourges allows French kings to control church revenue and appoint bishops
1440s	Printing press invented
1450	General Francesco Sforza seizes Milan
c. 1450–1500	Height of Florentine Renaissance
1453	Ottoman conquest of Constantinople; end of Byzantine Empire
1454	Treaty of Lodi balances power among major Italian states
1460–1485	Wars of the Roses; Tudor dynasty ascendant
1462	Ivan III becomes tsar
1471–1484	Pope Sixtus IV; Renaissance in Rome
1474–1516	Spain unified under Isabella and Ferdinand
1477	Death of Charles the Bold begins decline of Burgundy
1478	Inquisition carried out in Spain
1485	End of civil wars in England
1492	Spain conquers Granada, expels Jews; Columbus sails for Americas
1494	France invades Italy, beginning of more than fifty years of Habsburg-Valois conflict
1519	Spain conquers Mexico
1531	Fall of Florentine Republic

KEY TERMS

auto da fé (528)

conversos (528)

duchy (523)

Gallicanism (528)

humanism (507)

Renaissance (505)

tsar (530)

REVIEW QUESTIONS

1. How did humanism and the printing press influence learning in the Renaissance?

2. How did the shift from artisan to artist, a new naturalistic style, and the use of perspective in art reflect and influence a Renaissance mentality?

3. In what ways did the Renaissance state shape the private sphere?

4. How did Renaissance princes increase their power at the expense of the nobility and their subjects?

5. What European countries led the way in maritime expansion and what were their motives?

MAKING CONNECTIONS

1. Where were the centers of Renaissance creativity and why did this movement arise in those places?

2. How did Renaissance and medieval culture and society differ? How were they similar?

3. Compare the relative strengths of economic and religious motives in European voyages of exploration.

FOR FURTHER EXPLORATION

To assess your mastery of the material in this chapter, see the Online Study Guide at bedfordstmartins.com/hunt.

To read additional primary-source material from this period, see Chapter 14 in *Sources of The Making of the West*, Second Edition.

The Struggle for Reformation Europe, 1500–1560

HILLE FEIKEN LEFT THE CITY OF MÜNSTER, Germany, on June 16, 1534, elegantly dressed, bedecked with jewels, and determined to kill. Münster, which religious radicals had seized and declared a holy city, lay under siege by armies loyal to its bishop, Franz von Waldeck. Hille, one of the radicals, was attempting to rescue her city by imitating the ancient Israelite heroine Judith, who according to the Book of Judith delivered Jerusalem from an invading Assyrian army. The Assyrian commander Holofernes, charmed by Judith's beauty, tried to seduce her; but after he had fallen into a drunken sleep, Judith cut off his head, inducing the terrified Assyrian forces to flee Jerusalem. Inspired by this story, Hille crossed enemy lines and tried to persuade the commander of the besieging troops to take her to the bishop, promising to reveal a secret means of capturing the city without further fighting. Unfortunately, a defector recognized Hille and betrayed her. She was beheaded.

Hille Feiken and the other radicals in Münster were part of a sect known as Anabaptists, whose members believed they were a community of saints amid a hopelessly sinful world. The Anabaptists' efforts to form a separate holy community tore at the foundations of social order, and they met merciless persecution from the political and religious authorities. Anabaptism was only one dimension of the Protestant Reformation, which had been set in motion by the German reformer Martin Luther in 1517 and had become a sweeping movement to uproot church abuses and restore early Christian teachings. When Luther first criticized the practices and doctrines of the Catholic church, he had not wished to break away from Rome. As the breach widened, however, Luther and his followers referred

---

Vincenzo Catena, Judith
The Book of Judith tells the story of a beautiful young Israelite who presents herself to Holofernes, the general of an army besieging Jerusalem. His guard lowered by wine and Judith's charms, Judith assassinates Holofernes and cuts off his head, thus frightening off the enemy and saving her people. In this early 16th century painting, Venetian artist Vincenzo Catena conveys Judith's strength, beauty, and commitment to her task—one that Hille Feiken sought to reenact so that she might free her own besieged city of Münster. *Venice, Pinacoteca Querini-Stampalia/AKG Images/Cameraphoto.*

to their camp as the evangelical movement, emphasizing its adherence to the Gospels.[1] Supporters of Luther were called **Evangelicals** until 1529, when German princes and city delegates lodged a formal protest against imperial authorities who had declared Luther's cause criminal. From that point on, they were called **Protestants**, those who protested.

Hille Feiken's story was a sign of the times. Inspired by Luther—but often going far beyond what he would condone—ordinary men and women attempted to gain control over their salvation. Their stories intertwined with bloody struggles among princes for domination in Europe, an age-old conflict now complicated by the clash of rival faiths. In the end the princes would prevail over both a divided Christendom and a restless people. Protestant or Catholic, European monarchs expanded their power at the expense of the church and disciplined their subjects in the name of piety and order.

❖ A New Heaven and a New Earth

The last book of the Bible, Revelation (also known as the Apocalypse), foretells the passing of the old world and the coming of a new heaven and earth presided over by Christ.

---

[1]The word *gospel*, meaning "good tidings," comes from the Old English translation of the Greek word *euangelion*.

In 1500, some Europeans expected the Last Judgment to arrive soon. Indeed, the times seemed desperate. Muslim Turks were advancing on Europe while Christian princes fought among themselves. Some critics of the church labeled the pope as none other than the terrifying Antichrist, whose evil reign (according to Revelation) would end with Christ's return to earth.

In this frightening atmosphere, many people intensified their search for religious comfort. At the same time, important intellectuals within the church sharply criticized its leaders and the clergy for failing to provide the authority the people sought. Committed to a gradual reform of the Roman church, these intellectuals, known as Christian humanists for their devotion to both Christian and pagan antiquity, envisioned a better world based on education.

The Crisis of Faith

It was the church hierarchy, not the Christian religion, that proved deficient to believers in Europe. Numerous signs pointed to an intense spiritual anxiety among the laity. People went on pilgrimages, new shrines sprang up, and prayer books printed in vernacular languages as well as Latin sold briskly. Alongside the sacraments and rituals of the official church, laypeople practiced their own rituals for healing and salvation.

Only a thin line separated miracles, which the church accepted, and magic, which it rejected. Clerics who wanted to reform the church denounced superstitions,

◆ **1494** Italian Wars begin

◆ **1516** Erasmus publishes Greek New Testament; More, *Utopia*

◆ **1517** Luther's, ninety-five theses challenge church profiteering

◆ **1529** German Protestants; Colloquy of Marburg assembles to address disagreements between German and Swiss church reformers

| 1500 | 1510 | 1520 | 1530 |

◆ **1520** Luther publishes three treatises; Zwingli breaks from Rome

◆ **1527** Charles V's imperial troops sack Rome

◆ **1525** German Peasants' War

but other clergy readily exploited gullible laypeople. Perhaps the most notorious scandal prior to the Reformation occurred in the Swiss city of Basel. In 1510, several Dominicans claimed that the Virgin Mary had worked miracles there, though they themselves had in fact concocted the events. For a while their plot brought in crowds of pilgrims, but when the deception was uncovered, the perpetrators were burned at the stake.

Often the church gave external behavior more weight than spiritual intentions. Numerous regulations defined the different levels of human sinfulness. For example, even married couples could sin by having intercourse on one of the church's many holy days or by making love out of "lust" instead of out of an intent to conceive a child. The church similarly regulated other behaviors, prohibiting the eating of meat on certain days and censoring blasphemous language.

In receiving the sacrament of penance—one of the central pillars of the Roman church—sinners were expected to examine their consciences, sincerely confess their sins to a priest, and receive forgiveness. In practice, however, confession proved highly unsatisfactory to many Christians. For those with religious scruples, the demands of confession intensified their anxiety about salvation. Some believers were not sure they had remembered to confess all their sins; others trembled before God's anger and doubted his mercy. Also, some priests abused their authority by demanding sexual or monetary favors in return for forgiveness. Such incidents, although by no means widespread, seriously compromised the sanctity of the priestly office and the sacrament.

Although a sincere confession saved a sinner from hell, he or she still faced doing penance in either this life or the next. To alleviate suffering after death in purgatory, a person could earn an **indulgence**, a remission of sin, by performing certain religious tasks—going on pilgrimage, attending Mass, doing holy works. The common church practice of selling indulgences as a substitution for performing good works suggested that the church was more interested in making money than in saving souls.

Dissatisfaction with the official church prompted several reform efforts by bishops and leading clerics prior to the Reformation; these were, however, limited to certain monastic houses and dioceses. More important, there existed a gulf between clerical privileges and the religious needs of the laypeople. Urban merchants and artisans yearned for a religion more meaningful to their daily lives and for a clergy more responsive to their needs. They wanted priests to preach edifying sermons, to administer the sacraments conscientiously, and to lead moral lives. They criticized the church's rich endowments that provided income for children of the nobility. And they generously donated money to establish new preacherships for university-trained clerics, overwhelmingly from urban backgrounds and often from their own social classes. Most of these young clerics, who criticized the established church and hoped for reform, were schooled in Christian humanism.

◆ **1534** Henry VIII breaks with Rome; Affair of the Placards in France

◆ **1536** Calvin, *Institutes*

◆ **1540** Jesuits established as new Catholic order

◆ **1555** Peace of Augsburg ends religious wars in Germany and recognizes Lutherans

◆ **1559** Treaty of Cateau-Cambrésis ends conflict between Habsburg and Valois

| 1540 | 1550 | 1560 |

◆ **1541** Calvin installed in Geneva

◆ **1545–1563** Catholic Council of Trent condemns Protesant beliefs; confirms church doctrine and sacrament

◆ **1547** Charles V defeats Protestants at Mühlberg

Christian Humanism

Outraged by the abuse of power **Christian humanists** dreamed of ideal societies based on peace and morality. These intellectuals also sought to realize the ethical ideals of the classical world. Scholarship and social reform became inseparable goals. Two men, the Dutch scholar Desiderius Erasmus (c. 1466–1536) and the English lawyer Thomas More (1478–1535), stood out as representatives of these Christian humanists, who coupled their love of classical learning with the emphasis on Christian piety.

Erasmus. Erasmus dominated the humanist world of early-sixteenth-century Europe, just as Cicero had dominated ancient Roman letters. He was on intimate terms with kings and popes, and his reputation extended across Europe.

Through his books and letters, disseminated by the printing press, Erasmus's fame spread. In the *Adages* (1500), a collection of quotations from ancient literature offering his witty and wise commentaries on the human experience, Erasmus established a reputation as a superb humanist dedicated to educational reform. In the *Colloquies* (1523), a compilation of Latin dialogues intended as language-learning exercises, Erasmus exerted his sharp wit to criticize the morals and customs of his time. Lamenting poor table manners, for example, Erasmus advised his cultivated readers not to pick their noses at meals, not to share half-eaten chicken legs, and not to speak while stuffing their mouths. Turning to political matters, he mocked the clergy's corruption and Christian princes' bloody ambitions.

Only through education, Erasmus believed, could individuals reform themselves and society. His goal was a unified, peaceful Christendom in which charity and good works, not empty ceremonies, would mark true religion and in which learning and piety would dispel the darkness of ignorance. He elaborated many of these ideas in his *Handbook of the Militant Christian* (1503), an eloquent plea for a simple religion devoid of greed and the lust for power (see the illustration on this page). In *The Praise of Folly* (1509), Erasmus satirized values held dear by his con-temporaries. Modesty, humility, and poverty represented the true Christian virtues in a world that worshiped pomposity, power, and wealth. The wise appeared foolish, he concluded, for their wisdom and values were not of this world.

Erasmus devoted years to preparing an edition of the New Testament from the original Greek; it was finally published in 1516. Moved by the pacifism of the apostolic church,

Albrecht Dürer, *The Knight, Death, and the Devil*
Dürer's 1513 engraving of the knight depicts a grim and determined warrior advancing in the face of devils, one of whom holds out an hourglass with a grimace while another wields a menacing pike. An illustration for Erasmus's *The Handbook of the Militant Christian,* this scene is often interpreted as portraying a Christian clad in the armor of righteousness on a path through life beset by death and demonic temptations. Yet the knight in early-sixteenth-century Germany had become a mercenary, selling his martial skills to princes. Some waylaid merchants, robbed rich clerics, and held citizens for ransom. The most notorious of these robber-knights, Franz von Sickingen, was declared an outlaw by the emperor and murdered in 1522. **For more help analyzing this image,** see the visual activity for this chapter in the Online Study Guide at **bedfordstmartins.com/hunt**. *Bridgeman-Giraudon/Art Resource, NY.*

Thomas More, *Utopia* (1516)

More's entertaining description of Utopia, a fictional island inhabited by a self-sufficient and contented people, was intended as a critique of contemporary English society. In this passage he explains Utopia's social organization and economic structure, which is devoid of poverty and greed.

Each household, as I said, comes under the authority of the oldest male. Wives are subordinate to their husbands, children to their parents, and younger people generally to their elders. Every town is divided into four districts of equal size, each with its own shopping centre in the middle of it. There the products of every household are collected in warehouses, and then distributed according to type among various shops. When the head of a household needs anything for himself or his family, he just goes to one of these shops and asks for it. And whatever he asks for, he's allowed to take away without any sort of payment, either in money or in kind. After all, why shouldn't he? There's more than enough of everything to go round, so there's no risk of his asking for more than he needs—for why should anyone want to start hoarding, when he knows he'll never have to go short of anything? No living creature is naturally greedy, except from fear of want—or in the case of human beings, from vanity, the notion that you're better than people if you can display more superfluous property than they can. But there's no scope for that sort of thing in Utopia.

Source: Thomas More, *Utopia* (New York: Penguin Classics, 1965), 80–82.

Erasmus instructed the young future emperor Charles V to rule as a just Christian prince. He vented his anger by ridiculing the warrior-pope Julius II and expressed deep sorrow for the brutal warfare that had been ravaging Europe for decades.

A man of peace and moderation, Erasmus found himself challenged by angry younger men and radical ideas once the Reformation took hold; he eventually chose Christian unity over reform and schism. His dream of Christian pacifism shattered, he lived to see dissenters executed—by Catholics and Protestants alike—for speaking their conscience. Erasmus spent his last years in Freiburg and Basel, isolated from the Protestant community, his writings condemned by many in the Catholic church.

Thomas More. If Erasmus found himself abandoned by his times, his good friend Thomas More, to whom *The Praise of Folly* was dedicated,[2] met with even greater suffering. Having attended Oxford and trained in the law, More had legal talents that served him well in government. As a member of Parliament and then a royal ambassador, he proved a competent and loyal servant to Henry VIII. In 1529, he became lord chancellor, the chief official in government, but, tired of court intrigue and in protest against Henry's control of the clergy, More resigned his position in 1532. He would later pay with his life for upholding conscience over political expediency.

More's best-known work, *Utopia* (1516) (see excerpt above), describes an imaginary land and was intended as a critique of his own society. A just, equitable, and hardworking community, Utopia (meaning both "no place" and "best place" in Greek) was the opposite of England. In Utopia everyone worked the land for two years; and since Utopians enjoyed public schools, communal kitchens, hospitals, and nurseries, they had no need for money or private property. Dedicated to the pursuit of knowledge and natural religion, with equal distribution of goods and few laws, Utopia knew neither crime nor war. More believed that politics,

---

[2]The Latin title, *Encomium Moriae* (The Praise of Folly), was a pun on More's name and the Latin word for folly.

property, and war fueled human misery, whereas for his Utopians, "fighting was a thing they absolutely loathe. They say it's a quite subhuman form of activity, although human beings are more addicted to it than any of the lower animals."

More's tolerant and rational society did have a few oddities—voluntary slavery, for instance, and strictly controlled travel. Although premarital sex brought severe punishment, prospective marriage partners could examine each other naked before making their final decisions. Men headed Utopia's households and exercised authority over women and children. And Utopians did not shy away from declaring war on their neighbors to protect their way of life. Nevertheless, this imaginary society was paradise compared with a Christian Europe battered by division and violence. The Christian humanists dreamed beautiful visions for a better future, but they lived in a time that called for violent and radical changes to solve a profound crisis of faith.

> **Review:** How did the Christian humanists combine classical learning with their goals of Christian renewal?

❖ Protestant Reformers

At the beginning of the sixteenth century, widespread popular piety and anticlericalism created a volatile mixture of need and resentment. A young German friar, tormented by his own religious doubts, was to become the spokesman for a generation. From its origins as a theological dispute in 1517, Martin Luther's reform movement sparked explosive protests. By the time Luther died in 1546, half of western Europe had renounced allegiance to the Roman Catholic church.

While Luther opened the first act of the Reformation in Germany, Huldrych Zwingli◆ extended the Reformation to Switzerland. The French theologian John Calvin continued the work of religious reform in a later generation. Calvin's challenge to the Catholic church extended far beyond the German-

◆**Huldrych Zwingli:** hullrich ZWIHN lee

speaking lands of central Europe, eventually shaping Protestantism in England, Scotland, the Low Countries, France, and eastern Europe.

Martin Luther and the German Nation

Son of a miner and entrepreneur, Martin Luther (1483–1546) began his studies in the law, pursuing a career open to ambitious young men from middle-class families and urged on him by his father. His true calling, however, lay with the church. Caught in a storm on a lonely road one midsummer's night, the young student grew terrified by the thunder and lightning. He implored the help of St. Anne, the mother of the Virgin Mary, and promised to enter a monastery if she protected him. To the chagrin of his father, Luther abandoned law for a religious life and entered the Augustinian order.

In the monastery the young Luther experienced a religious crisis. Appalled at his own sense of sinfulness and the weakness of human nature, he lived in terror of God's justice in spite of frequent confessions and penance. A pilgrimage to Rome only deepened his unease with the institutional church. A sympathetic superior came to Luther's aid and sent him to study theology, a discipline that gradually led him to experience grace and gain insight into salvation. Shortly before his death, Luther recalled his monastic days:

> *Though I lived as a monk without reproach, I felt that I was a sinner before God with an extremely disturbed conscience. I could not believe that he was placated by my satisfaction [in penance]. I did not love, yes, I hated the righteous God who punishes sinners, and secretly . . . I was angry with God. . . . Nevertheless, I beat importunately upon Paul [in Romans 1:17]. . . . At last, by the mercy of God, meditating day and night, I gave heed to the context of the words, namely, "In [the gospel] the righteousness of God is revealed, as it is written, 'He who through faith is righteous shall live.'" There I began to understand that the righteousness of God is that by which the righteous live by a gift of God, namely by faith.*

Subsequent events made Luther, now a professor of theology in the town of Wittenberg, a public figure. In 1516, the new archbishop of Mainz, Albrecht of Brandenburg, commissioned the Dominican friar Johann Tetzel to sell indulgences in his archdiocese (which included Saxony). The proceeds would help cover the cost of constructing St. Peter's Basilica in Rome and also partly defray Archbishop Albrecht's expenses in procuring his archbishopric. Such blatant profiteering outraged many, including Luther. In 1517, Luther composed ninety-five theses—propositions for an academic debate—that questioned indulgence peddling and the purchase of church offices. Once they became public, the theses unleashed a torrent of pent-up resentment and frustration among the laypeople.

What began as a theological debate in a provincial university soon engulfed the Holy Roman Empire. (See "Contrasting Views," page 554.) Luther's earliest supporters included younger Christian humanists and clerics who shared his critical attitude toward the church establishment. None of these Evangelicals, as they called themselves, came from the upper echelons of the church; many were from urban middle-class backgrounds, and most were university-trained. As a group, their profile differed from that of the poorly educated rural clergy or from their noble clerical superiors, who often owed their positions to family influence rather than theological learning. The Evangelicals represented those social groups most ready to challenge clerical authority—merchants, artisans, and literate urban laypeople.

Initially, Luther presented himself as the pope's "loyal opposition." In 1520, he composed three treatises. In *Freedom of a Christian*, written in Latin for the learned and addressed to Pope Leo X, Luther argued that the Roman church's numerous rules and its stress on "good works" were useless. He insisted that faith, not good works, saves sinners from damnation, and he sharply distinguished between true Gospel teachings and invented church doctrines. Luther suggested instead "the priesthood of all believers," arguing that the Bible provided all the teachings necessary for Christian living and that a professional caste of clerics should not hold sway over laypeople. *Freedom of a Christian* was immediately translated into German and was circulated widely. Its principles "by

faith alone," "by Scripture alone," and "the priesthood of all believers" became central features of the reform movement. In his second treatise, *To the Nobility of the German Nation*, which he wrote in German, Luther appealed to German nationalism. He denounced the corrupt Italians in Rome who were cheating and exploiting his compatriots and called on the German princes to defend their nation and reform the church. The third, *On the Babylonian Captivity of the Church*, which he composed in Latin mainly for a clerical audience, condemned the papacy as the embodiment of the Antichrist.

From Rome's perspective, the "Luther Affair," as church officials called it, was essentially a matter of clerical discipline. Rome ordered Luther to obey his superiors and keep quiet. But the church establishment had very seriously misjudged the extent of Luther's influence (see "Erasmus Writes to Luther," page 556). Luther's ideas spread rapidly throughout the Holy Roman Empire, unleashing forces that neither the church nor Luther could control. Social, nationalist, and religious protests fused into an explosive mass very similar to the Czech revolution that Jan Hus had inspired a century

Luther's World in the Early Sixteenth Century

earlier (see Chapter 13). Like Hus, Luther appeared before an emperor: in 1521, he defended his faith before Charles V (r. 1520–1558), the newly elected Holy Roman Emperor who at the age of nineteen was the ruler of the Low Countries, Spain, Spain's Italian and New World dominions, and the Austrian Habsburg lands. At the Imperial Diet of Worms, the formal assembly presided over by this powerful ruler, Luther shocked Germans by declaring his admiration for the Czech heretic (a heretic is a dissenter from the right teachings of the church). But unlike Hus, Luther did not suffer martyrdom because he enjoyed the protection of Frederick the Wise, the elector of Saxony (one of the seven German electors entitled to choose the German king) and Luther's lord.

Martin Luther: Holy Man or Heretic?

When Martin Luther criticized the papacy and the Catholic church, he was hailed as a godly prophet by some and condemned as a heretic by others. Both Protestants and Catholics used popular propaganda to argue their cause. They spread their message to a largely illiterate or semiliterate society through pamphlets, woodcuts, and broadsheets in which visual images took on increasing importance, to appeal to a wide public. These polemical works were produced in the thousands and distributed to cities and market towns throughout the Holy Roman Empire. A few were even translated into Latin to reach an audience outside of Germany.

The 1521 woodcut by Matthias Gnidias represents Luther standing above his Catholic opponent, the Franciscan friar Thomas Murner, who is depicted here as a crawling dragon, Leviathan, the biblical monster (Document 1). Another positive image of Luther, also published in 1521, depicts him as inspired by the Holy Spirit (Document 2). An anti-Luther image from a few years later represents him as a seven-headed monster (Document 3), signifying that the reformer is the source of discord within Christianity. This image appeared in a book published in 1529 by the Dominican friar Johannes Cochlaeus, one of Luther's strongest opponents.

Both Protestants and Catholics used woodcuts and

illustrations extensively as propaganda to appeal to the vast majority of people who were illiterate. Visual examples of religious propaganda worked effectively to demonize enemies and to contrast sharply good and evil. The 1520s saw the most intense production of these cheap polemical visual prints, but the use of visual propaganda would last for more than a century in the confessional struggles.

1. MATTHIAS GNIDIAS'S REPRESENTATION OF LUTHER AND LEVIATHAN, 1521

Dressed in a friar's robes, the Murner-Leviathan monster breathes "ignis, sumus, & sulphur"—fire, smoke, and sulphur. The good friar, Luther, holds the Bible in his hands, and is represented here as a prophet (foretelling the end of the world). The vertical Latin caption declares that the Lord will visit the earth with his sword and kill the Leviathan monster; he will trample underfoot lions and dragons; and the dragon, with a halter around its nostrils, will be dragged away on a hook.

Luther and Leviathan

During the 1520s, the anti-Roman evangelicals included many German princes, city officials, professors, priests, and ordinary men and women, particularly in the cities. As centers of publishing and commerce, German towns became natural distribution

points for Lutheran propaganda. Moreover, urban people proved particularly receptive to Luther's teachings. Many were literate and were eager to read the Scriptures, and merchants and artisans resented the clergy's tax-exempt status and the competition from

Luther as Monk *The Granger Collection.*

2. LUTHER AS MONK, DOCTOR, MAN OF THE BIBLE, AND SAINT, 1521

This woodcut by an anonymous artist appeared in a volume that the Strasbourg printer Johann Schott published in 1521. In addition to being one of the major centers of printing, Strasbourg was also a stronghold of the reform movement. Note the use of traditional symbols to signify Luther's holiness: the Bible in his hands, the halo, the Holy Spirit in the form of a dove, and his friar's robes. Although the cult of saints and monasticism came under severe criticism during the Reformation, the representation of Luther in traditional symbols of sanctity stressed his conservative values instead of his radical challenge to church authorities.

3. THE SEVEN-HEADED MARTIN LUTHER BY JOHANNES COCHLAEUS, 1529

The seven heads are labeled (from left to right) doctor, Martin, Luther, ecclesiast, enthusiast, visitirer, and Barrabas. The term enthusiast *represented a name of abuse, applied usually by the Catholic church to Anabaptists and religious radicals of all sorts.* Visitirer *is a pun in German on the*

Seven-Headed Luther *The Granger Collection.*

word Tier, *meaning "animal." Cochlaeus also mocks the new practice of Protestant clergy visiting parishes to check up on pastors' and parishioners' adherence to reformed doctrines and rituals in order to enforce Christian discipline. From left to right Luther's many heads gradually reveal him to be a rebel, as Barrabas was condemned to die as a rabble-rouser by the Romans but instead was freed and his place taken by Jesus at the crucifixion. The number seven also alludes to the seven deadly sins.*

QUESTIONS TO CONSIDER

1. Why did Johannes Cochlaeus condemn Martin Luther? How did he construct a negative image of Luther?
2. Evaluate the visual and the textual representations of Luther as a godly man: which medium is more effective?

monasteries and nunneries that produced their own goods. Magistrates began to curtail clerical privileges and subordinate the clergy to municipal authority. Luther's message—that each Christian could appeal directly to God for salvation—spoke to townspeople's spiritual needs and social vision. Thus inspired, many reform priests led their urban parishioners away from Roman liturgy. From Wittenberg, the reform movement quickly emerged into a torrent of many streams.

Erasmus Writes to Martin Luther (1519)

Prior to Luther's formal excommunication by Pope Leo X in January 1521, it was still possible for the Christian humanist Erasmus to see the fierce critic of Rome as a kindred spirit. Erasmus wrote from Leuven in the Spanish Netherlands (today in Belgium), the site of a university whose theologians were among the first to condemn the opinions of Luther.

Leuven, May 30, 1519

Greetings, dearest brother in Christ. Your letter was most delightful, revealing as it did the clarity of your intellect and breathing as it did a Christian spirit. No words of mine could make clear the tragedies which your books are causing here. These people cannot even rid their minds of the completely false supposition that your reflections were written with my assistance, and that I am the standard-bearer of your party, as they call it. They believe they have a handle to destroy humane letters, which they mortally detest, as being likely to infringe upon the supremacy of theology, which to them is far more important than Christ. They also think they can destroy me, whom they regard as having contributed some impetus to the revival of interest in studies. The whole business is carried in with ranting, impertinence, tricks, insults, and deceit. If I had not seen it with my own eyes, or rather felt it, I would never have believed anyone who told me that theologians could rave in such fashion. You might say it is a plague sent by fate. And yet this poison, which originated among a few, has spread among many others, so that a great part of this academy may be said to be infected with the contagion of the common disease.

I have sworn that you are completely unknown to me, that I have not even read your books; hence that I neither approve nor disapprove. But I did warn them not to heap such public opprobrium on your books before they had read them. I added that this was of particular importance for them, whose judgment ought to be carefully weighed. They should, I said, consider whether it was right to vilify before the common herd matters which should rather be refuted in published books and discussed among learned men, especially when the life of the author is unanimously praised. It was all to no purpose. They still rave with their hostile, indeed slanderous discussions. How often we have met to agree on peace! How often they have started new trouble as the result of baseless suspicions! And these people claim to be theologians.

Source: W. T. H. Jackson, ed., *Essential Works of Erasmus* (New York: Bantam, 1965), 317.

Huldrych Zwingli and the Swiss Confederation

While Luther provided the religious leadership for northern Germany, the south came under the strong influence of a reform movement that had emerged in Switzerland. In the late fifteenth and early sixteenth centuries, Switzerland's chief source of income was the export of soldiers; hardy Swiss peasants fought as mercenaries in papal, French, and imperial armies, earning respect as fierce pikemen. Many young Swiss men died in battle, and many others returned maimed for life. In 1520, the chief preacher of the Swiss city of Zurich, Huldrych Zwingli (1484–1531), criticized his superior, Cardinal Matthew Schinner, for sending the country's young men off to serve in papal armies.

The son of a Swiss village leader, Zwingli became a reformer independent of Martin Luther. After completing his university studies, Zwingli was ordained a priest and served as an army chaplain for several years. Deeply influenced by Erasmus, whom he met in 1515, Zwingli adopted the Dutch humanist's vision of social renewal through education. In 1520, he openly declared himself a reformer and attacked not only corruption among the ecclesiastical (church) hierarchy but also the church rituals of fasting and clerical celibacy.

Under Zwingli's leadership, Zurich served as the center for the Swiss reform movement.

Guided by his vision of a theocratic (church-directed) society that would unite religion, politics, and morality, Zwingli refused to draw any distinction between the ideal citizen and the perfect Christian—an idea radically different from Luther's—and rooted out internal dissent. Theologically, Luther insisted that Christ was both truly and symbolically present in the Eucharist, the central Christian sacrament; Zwingli, however, viewed the Eucharist as simply a ceremony symbolizing Christ's union with believers.

In 1529, troubled by these differences and other disagreements, Evangelical princes and magistrates assembled the major reformers in the Colloquy of Marburg, in central Germany. After several days of intense discussions, the North German and Swiss reformers managed to resolve many differences over doctrine, but Luther and Zwingli failed to agree on the meaning of the Eucharist. Thus, the German and Swiss reform movements continued on separate paths. The issue of the Eucharist would later divide Lutherans and Calvinists as well.

John Calvin and Christian Discipline

Under the leadership of John Calvin (1509–1564), another wave of reform pounded at the gates of Rome. Born in Picardy, in northern France, to the secretary of the bishop of Noyon, Calvin studied in Paris and Orléans, where he took a law degree. A gifted intellectual who was attracted to humanism, Calvin could have enjoyed a brilliant career in government or the church. Instead, experiencing a crisis of faith, like Luther, he sought salvation through intense theological study.

Calvin read the works of the leading French humanists who sought to reform the church from within and gradually came to question fundamental Catholic teachings. Unlike Luther, who described his life in vivid detail, Calvin generally revealed nothing about the personal struggle that brought him to this point.

During Calvin's long religious development, the Reformation steadily gained adherents in France. On Sunday, October 18, 1534, Parisians found church doors posted with ribald broadsheets denouncing the Catholic Mass. Smuggled into France from the Protestant and French-speaking parts of Switzerland, the broadsheets unleashed a wave of royal repression in the capital. This so-called Affair of the Placards provoked a national crackdown on church dissenters, who had until then been left alone. Hundreds of French Protestants were arrested, scores were executed, and many more, including Calvin, fled abroad.

On his way to Strasbourg, Germany, a haven for religious dissidents, Calvin detoured to Geneva—the French-speaking city-republic where he would find his life's work. Geneva had renounced allegiance to its bishop, and the local reformer Guillaume Farel threatened Calvin with God's curse if he did not stay and labor there. This frightening appeal succeeded. Under Calvin and Farel, the reform party became embroiled in a political struggle between two civic factions: their supporters, many of whom were

THE PROGRESS OF THE REFORMATION

1517	Martin Luther disseminates ninety-five theses attacking the sale of indulgences and other church practices
1520	Reformer Huldrych Zwingli breaks with Rome
1525	Radical reformer Thomas Müntzer killed in Peasants' War
1529	Lutheran German princes protest the condemnation of religious reform by Charles V; genesis of the term *Protestants*
1534	The English Parliament establishes King Henry VIII as head of the Anglican church, severing ties to Rome
1534–1535	Anabaptists control the city of Münster, Germany, in a failed experiment to create a holy community
1541	John Calvin establishes himself permanently in Geneva, making that city a model of Christian reform and discipline

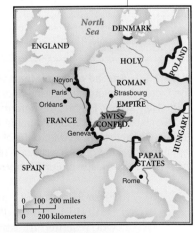

Calvin's World in the Mid-Sixteenth Century

MAP 15.1 Spread of Protestantism in the Sixteenth Century
The Protestant Reformation divided northern and southern Europe. From its heartland in the Holy Roman Empire, the Reformation won the allegiance of Scandinavia, England, and Scotland and made considerable inroads in the Low Countries, France, eastern Europe, Switzerland, and even parts of northern Italy. While the Mediterranean countries remained loyal to Rome, a vast zone of confessional divisions and strife characterized the religious landscape of Europe from Britain in the west to Poland in the east.

Geneva, but Calvin returned in 1541, after his supporters triumphed. He remained there until his death in 1564.

Under Calvin's inspiration and moral authority, Geneva became a disciplined Christian republic, modeled after the ideas in his *The Institutes of the Christian Religion*, first published in 1536. No reformer prior to Calvin had expounded on the doctrines, organization, history, and practices of Christianity in such a systematic, logical, and coherent manner. Calvin followed Luther's doctrine of salvation to its ultimate logical conclusion: if God is almighty and humans cannot earn their salvation by good works, then no Christian can be certain of salvation. Developing the doctrine of **predestination**, Calvin argued that God had ordained every man, woman, and child to salvation or damnation—even before the creation of the world. Thus, the "elect," in Calvinist theology, were known only to God. In practice, however, Calvinist doctrine demanded rigorous discipline: the knowledge that only the elect, a small group, would be saved should guide the actions of the godly in an uncertain world. Fusing church and society into what followers named the Reformed church, Geneva became a single moral community, as reflected in its very low rate of extramarital births in the sixteenth century. The community was praised by advocates as less troubled by crime and sin than other cities and attacked by critics as despotic.

This charge of despotism came from Calvin's treatment of dissenters. Like Zwingli, he did not tolerate them. While passing through

French refugees, and the opposition, represented by the leading old Genevan families, who resented the strict moral regulations of the new, foreign-born clerical regime. A political setback in 1538 drove Calvin and Farel from

Geneva in 1553, the Spanish physician Michael Servetus was arrested because he had published books attacking Calvin and questioning the doctrine of the Trinity, the belief that God exists in three persons—the Father, Son (Christ), and Holy Spirit. Upon Calvin's advice, Servetus was executed by the authorities. (Calvin did not approve, however, of the method of execution: burning at the stake.) Although Calvin came under criticism for Servetus's death, Geneva became the new center of the Reformation, the place where pastors trained for mission work and from which books expressing Calvinist doctrines were exported. The Calvinist movement spread to France, the Netherlands, England, Scotland, Germany, Poland, Hungary, and eventually New England, becoming the established form of the Reformation in many of these countries (Map 15.1 on page 558).

Review: In what ways did Luther, Zwingli, and Calvin challenge the Roman Catholic church?

❖ Reshaping Society through Religion

The religious upheavals of the sixteenth century affected European society in two major ways. First, those who challenged the social order were crushed by the political and religious authorities. Such was the fate of the Anabaptists and peasant rebels in the Holy Roman Empire, who tried in vain to establish new, biblically inspired social orders. As a result of these radical movements, both Protestant and Catholic authorities became alarmed by the subversive potential of religious reforms. They viewed religious reforms, instead, as ways of instilling greater discipline in Christian worship and in social behavior. Hence, the second and most lasting impact of the Reformation was in the realm of church discipline and piety. Protestant reformers and their supporters worked to create a God-fearing, pious, and disciplined Christian.

Challenging the Social Order

The freedom of the Christian proclaimed by Luther resonated with those who suffered oppression, and the corruption of sin decried by

the reformers inspired others to seek Christian perfection. During the early 1520s, two movements emerged in the Holy Roman Empire to challenge the foundations of religious and political order. While peasants and urban artisans staged massive revolts against church and nobility, the Anabaptists attempted to re-create the perfect Christian community on earth.

The Peasants' War of 1525. Between 1520 and 1525, many city governments, often under intense popular pressure and sometimes in sympathy with the Evangelicals, allowed the reform movement to sweep away church authority. Local officials appointed new clerics who were committed to reforming Christian doctrine and ritual. The turning point came in 1525, when the crisis of church authority exploded in the Peasants' War, a massive rural uprising that threatened the entire social order (Map 15.2 on the next page).

German Peasants' War of 1525
This colored woodcut depicts peasants attacking the pope, a monk, and a nobleman during the massive rural uprisings against the church that took place in southern and central Germany in 1525. Even the heavens show signs of trouble: a comet and clouds in the shape of a goat signify bloodshed and sin. *The Granger Collection, NY.*

The church was the largest landowner in the Holy Roman Empire: about one-seventh of the empire's territory consisted of ecclesiastical principalities in which bishops and abbots exercised both secular and churchly power. Luther's anticlerical message struck home with peasants who were paying taxes to both their lord and the church. In the spring of 1525, many peasants in southern and central Germany rose in rebellion, sometimes inspired by wandering preachers. Some urban workers and artisans joined the peasant bands, which plundered monasteries, refused to pay church taxes, and demanded village autonomy, the abolition of serfdom, and the right to appoint their own pastors. The more radical rebels called for the destruction of the entire ruling class. In Thuringia, the rebels were led by an ex-priest, Thomas Müntzer (1468?–1525), who promised to chastise the wicked and thus clear the way for the Last Judgment.

The Peasants' War split the reform movement. Princes and city authorities turned against the rebels. The Catholic and evangelical princes of Thuringia joined hands to crush Müntzer and his supporters. All over the empire, princes defeated peasant armies, hunted down their leaders, and uprooted all opposition. By the end of the year, more than 100,000 rebels had been killed and many others maimed, imprisoned, or exiled. Luther had tried to mediate the conflict initially, criticizing the princes for their brutality toward the peasants but also warning the rebels against mixing religion and social protest. Luther believed that rulers were ordained by God and thus must be obeyed even if they were tyrants. The Kingdom of God belonged not to this world but to the next, he insisted. Luther considered Müntzer's mixing of religion and politics the greatest danger to the Reformation, nothing less than "the devil's work." When the rebels ignored Luther's appeal and continued to follow more radical preachers, Luther called on the princes to restore the divinely ordained social order and slaughter the rebels. Fundamentally conservative in its political philosophy, the Lutheran church would henceforth depend on established political authority for its protection.

Emerging as the champions of an orderly religious reform, many German princes eventually confronted Emperor Charles V, who supported Rome. In 1529, Charles declared the Roman Catholic faith the empire's only legitimate religion.

MAP 15.2 The Peasants' War of 1525
The centers of uprisings clustered in southern and central Germany, where the density of cities encouraged the spread of discontent and allowed for alliances between urban masses and rural rebels. The proximity to the Swiss Confederation, a stronghold of the Reformation movement, also inspired antiestablishment uprisings.

Proclaiming their allegiance to the re-form cause, the Lutheran German princes protested, and thus came to be called Protestants.

Anabaptists.   While Zwingli was challenging the Roman Catholic church, some laypeople in Zurich were secretly pursuing their own path to reform. Taking their cue from the New Testament's descriptions of the first Christian community, these men and women believed that true faith was based on reason and free will. How could a baby knowingly choose Christ? Only adults could believe and accept baptism; hence the invalidity of Catholic infant baptism and the need for a new rite. These people came to be called **Anabaptists**—those who were rebaptized. As pacifists, they rejected the authority of courts and considered themselves a community of true Christians unblemished by sin. The Anabaptist movement drew its leadership primarily from the artisan class and its members from the middle and lower classes— men and women attracted by a simple message of peace and salvation.

Persecution of the Anabaptists
A large number of the more than one thousand martyrs killed for their faith in the Low Countries were Anabaptists. Until persecutions stopped in the 1580s, the authorities executed hundreds of Anabaptist men by beheading and women by drowning. This drawing is from the 1685 Dutch Anabaptist martyrology (a collection of books dedicated to the study and remembrance of martyrs) titled *The Bloody Theater,* compiled by Tilleman van Bracht. *Beinecke Rare Book and Manuscript Library, Yale University.*

Zwingli immediately attacked the Anabaptists for their refusal to bear arms and swear oaths of allegiance, sensing accurately that they were repudiating his theocratic order. When persuasion failed to convince the Anabaptists, Zwingli urged Zurich magistrates to impose the death sentence. Thus, the Reformation's first martyrs of conscience were victims of its evangelical reformers.

Nevertheless, Anabaptism spread quickly from Zurich to many cities in southern Germany, despite the Holy Roman Empire's general condemnation of the movement in 1529. In 1534, one Anabaptist group, believing that the end of the world was imminent, seized control of the northwestern city of Münster. Proclaiming themselves a community of saints and imitating the ancient Israelites, the Münster Anabaptists abolished private property in imitation of the early Christian church and dissolved traditional marriages, allowing men, like Old Testament patriarchs, to have multiple wives, to the consternation of many women. Besieged by a combined Protestant and Catholic army,

the city fell in June 1535. The leaders died in battle or were horribly executed. The Anabaptist movement in northwestern Europe nonetheless survived under the determined pacifist leadership of the Dutch reformer Menno Simons (1469–1561), whose followers were eventually named Mennonites. Defeated in their bid for revolution, the common people became the subject of religious reforms and discipline. The Reformation strengthened rather than loosened social control in a vast effort to instill religious conformity and moral behavior orchestrated by secular rulers and a new clerical elite.

New Forms of Discipline

The emergence of a new urban, middle-class culture was one result of the religious cataclysms of the sixteenth century. Appearing first in Protestant Europe, it included an emphasis on literacy, a new educational agenda, and a new work ethic, all of which came together as a watershed in European civilization. Other changes, although sparked by the Protestant

Reformation, represented the culmination of developments that stretched back to the Middle Ages: the advent of public relief for the poor, the condemnation of vagrancy, and a general disciplining of society, from marriage reforms to changes in musical composition.

Reading the Bible. Prior to the Reformation, the Latin **Vulgate** was the only Bible authorized by the church, although many vernacular translations of parts of the Bible circulated. The Vulgate contains errors of translation from the Greek and Hebrew, as humanists such as Erasmus pointed out. Nevertheless, textual authority was predicated on church authority, and textual revisions were potentially subversive. The Bible had the potential to subvert the established order.

In 1522, Martin Luther translated Erasmus's Greek New Testament into German, the first full vernacular translation in that language. The new translation was illustrated with woodcuts, and more than 200,000 copies of Luther's New Testament were printed over twelve years, an immense number for the time. In 1534, Luther completed a translation of the Old Testament. Peppered with witty phrases and colloquial expressions, Luther's Bible was a treasure chest of the German language. Because of a huge appetite for the story of salvation, the popular reception of Luther's Bible was virtually assured. Widespread among urban households, the German Bible occupied a central place in a family's history. Generations passed on valuable editions; pious citizens often bound the Scriptures with family papers or other reading material. To counter Protestant success, Catholic German Bibles appeared, thus authorizing and encouraging Bible reading by the Catholic laity, a sharp departure from medieval church practice.

The relationship between Scripture reading and religious reform also highlighted the history of early French and English Bibles. In the same year that Luther's German New Testament appeared in print, the French humanist Jacques Lefèvre d'Étaples (c. 1455–1536) translated the Vulgate New Testament into French. Sponsored by Guillaume Briçonnet,◆ the bishop of Meaux,◆ who wanted

to distribute free copies of the New Testament to the poor of the region, the enterprise represented an early attempt to reform the French church without breaking with Rome.

Sensing a potentially dangerous association between the vernacular Bible and heresy, England's church hierarchy reacted swiftly against English-language Bibles. Nevertheless, the Englishman William Tyndale (1495–1536), inspired by Luther's Bible during a visit to Wittenberg, translated the Bible into English. Since England had few printing presses, he had his translation printed in Germany and the Low Countries and then smuggled into England. Tyndale was burned at the stake as a hated heretic. Later, following Henry VIII's break with Rome and adoption of the Reformation, the government promoted an English Bible based on Tyndale's translation.

Although the vernacular Bible occupied a central role in Protestantism, Bible reading did not become widespread until the early seventeenth century. Educational reform proceeded slowly throughout the sixteenth century, limiting the number of literate people. Furthermore, the complete Bible was an expensive book out of the reach of poor households. Perhaps most important of all, the Protestant clergy, like their Catholic counterparts, grew suspicious of unsupervised Bible reading. Just as the first reformers cited Scripture against Rome, ordinary men and women, drawing their own lessons from the Bible, questioned and challenged the authority of the new Protestant establishment.

Indoctrinating the Young. To enter the Kingdom of God, Luther warned the princes and magistrates of the Holy Roman Empire, they must change hearts and minds. He encouraged them to establish schools, supported by confiscated church property, and educate children in the knowledge and fear of God. The ordinance for a girls' school in Göttingen spelled out that the school's purpose was "to initiate and hold girls in propriety and the fear of God. To fear God, they must learn their catechism, beautiful psalms, sayings, and other fine Christian and holy songs and little prayers."

The Protestant Reformation replaced late-medieval church schools with a state school system. Controlled by state officials

---

◆**Guillaume Briçonnet:** gee YOHM BREE sah neh
◆**Meaux:** moh

who examined, appointed, and paid teachers, the new educational system aimed to train obedient, pious, and hardworking Christian citizens. Discipline, not new ideas, informed sixteenth-century pedagogy. Teachers frequently used the rod to enforce discipline while students memorized their lessons. The curriculum of girls' schools included domestic skills in addition to reading and writing.

A two-tiered system existed in Protestant education. Every **parish** (the basic territorial unit of the Catholic church) had its primary school for children between six and twelve. A secondary system of humanist schools aimed to train future pastors, scholars, and officials. These higher schools for boys, called gymnasia (from the Greek *gymnasion*), were intended to prepare students for university study. Greek and Latin classics constituted the core of the curriculum, to which was added religious instruction.

In Catholic Europe, educational reforms at the primary level proceeded unevenly. In northern and central Italian cities, most girls and boys received some education, in a strong pedagogic tradition dating to at least the thirteenth century. For Spain, France, and southern Germany, our knowledge is fragmentary. Catholics did succeed in developing an excellent system of secondary education through the colleges established by the new Society of Jesus, whose members were known as Jesuits, the most important religious order of Catholic Europe in the sixteenth century. Established to compete with the Protestant gymnasia, hundreds of Jesuit colleges dotted Catholic Europe by the late sixteenth century. Among their alumni would be princes, philosophers, lawyers, churchmen, and officials—the elite of Catholic Europe. The different Christian schools helped to perpetuate the religious divisions of Reformation Europe for many generations.

Public Relief for the Poor.   In the early sixteenth century, secular governments began to take over institutions of public charity from the church. This development, which took place in both Catholic and Protestant Europe, marked two trends that had become apparent during the later Middle Ages: the rise of a work ethic simultaneous with a growing hostility toward the poor and the

widespread poverty brought about by population growth and spiraling inflation.

Given Europe's agrarian economy with severe technological limitations, population growth put pressure on society's food resources. By 1500, the cycle of demographic collapse and economic depression triggered by the Black Death of 1348 had passed. Between 1500 and 1560, a new cycle of rapid economic and population growth created prosperity for some and stress—caused or heightened by increased inflation—for many. Wanderers and urban beggars were by no means novel, but the reaction to poverty was new.

Sixteenth-century moralists decried the crime and sloth of vagabonds. Rejecting the notion that the poor played a central role in the Christian idea of salvation and that charity and prayers united rich and poor, these moralists cautioned against charlatans and criminals who brought disease in their wake. Instead, they said, people should distinguish between the genuine poor, or "God's Poor," and vagabonds; the latter, who were able-bodied, should be forced to work.

The Reformation provided an opportunity to restructure relief for the poor. In Nuremberg (1522) and Strasbourg (1523), magistrates centralized poor relief with church funds. Instead of using decentralized, private initiative, magistrates appointed officials to head urban agencies that would certify the genuine poor and distribute welfare funds to them. This development progressed rapidly in urban areas, where poverty was most visible, and transcended religious divisions. During the 1520s, cities in the Low Countries, Italy, and Spain passed ordinances that prohibited begging and instituted public charity. In 1526, the Spanish humanist Juan Luis Vives, a Catholic, wrote *On the Support of the Poor*, a Latin treatise urging authorities to establish public poor relief; the work was soon translated into French, Italian, German, and English. National laws followed. In 1531, Henry VIII asked justices of the peace (unpaid local magistrates) to license the poor in England and to differentiate between those capable of working and those who could not. In 1540, Charles V (who ruled Spain as Charles I) imposed a welfare tax in Spain to augment that country's inadequate system of private charity.

New Marriage Ordinances. In their effort to establish order and discipline in worship and in society, the Protestant reformers decried sexual immorality and glorified the family. The idealized patriarchal family provided a bulwark against the forces of disorder. Protestant magistrates established marital courts, passed new marriage laws, closed brothels, and inflicted harsher punishments for sexual deviance.

Prior to the Reformation, marriages had been private affairs between families; some couples never even registered with the church. Under canon law, the Catholic church recognized any promise made between two consenting adults (with the legal age of twelve for females, fourteen for males) as a valid marriage. In rural areas and among the urban poor, most couples simply lived together as common-law husband and wife. The problem with the old marriage laws had been their complexity and the difficulties of enforcement. Often young men readily promised marriage in a passionate moment, only to renege later. The overwhelming number of cases in Catholic church courts involved young women seeking to enforce promises after they had exchanged their personal honor—that is, their virginity—for the greater honor of marriage.

The Reformation proved more effective than the late medieval church in suppressing common-law marriages. Protestant governments asserted greater official control over marriage, and Catholic governments followed suit. A marriage was legitimate only if it had been registered by both a government official and a member of the clergy. In many Protestant countries, the new marriage ordinances also required parental consent, thus giving householders immense power in regulating not only marriage but also the transmission of family property.

Women approached this new sexual regime with ambivalence. The laws stipulated that women could seek divorce for desertion, impotence, and flagrant abuse, although in practice the marital courts encouraged reconciliation. These changes came with a price, however: a woman's role took on the more limited definition of obedient wife, helpful companion, and loving mother. Now the path to religious power was closed to

The Disciplined Home
Proper table manners reflected discipline and morality in the godly household, an ideal of the religious reformers of the sixteenth century. The householder, the father-patriarch, leads his wife and children in prayer before a meal. The orderly behavior parallels the comfort (oven, smoked glass windows, chandeliers, timber ceiling, and cabinets) of a well-off patrician family. *Woodcut by Abraham Bach, Staatsbibliothek Bamberg, Germany.*

women. Unlike pious Catholic women, Protestant women could not renounce family, marriage, and sexuality to attain recognition and power in the church.

In the fervor of the early Reformation years, the first generation of Protestant women attained greater marital equality than those of subsequent generations. Katharina Zell, wife of the reformer Matthew Zell, defended her equality by citing Scripture when a critic used St. Paul to support his argument that women should remain silent in church. Katharina retorted, "I would remind you of the word of this same apostle that in Christ there is no male nor female." Further quoting the Book of Joel, she recited the prophecy that "[God] will pour forth [his] spirit upon all flesh and your sons and daughters will prophesy."

Katharina helped feed and clothe the thousands of refugees who flooded Strasbourg after their defeat in the Peasants' War. In 1534, she published a collection of hymns. She encouraged her husband to oppose Protestant persecution of dissenters. After Matthew's death in 1548, Katharina continued to feed the sick, the poor, and the imprisoned. Outraged by the intolerance of a new breed of Protestant clergy, she reprimanded a prominent Lutheran pastor for his persecution of dissenters: "You young fellows tread on the graves of the first fathers of this church in Strasbourg and punish all who disagree with you, but faith cannot be forced."

A more typical role model was Katharina von Bora (1499–1550), who married Martin Luther in 1525. Sent to a Catholic nunnery at the age of ten, the adult Katharina responded to the reformers' attack on monasticism. With the help of Luther, she and other nuns escaped by hiding in empty barrels that had contained smoked herring. After their marriage, Katie, as Luther affectionately called her, ran the home, feeding their children, relatives, and student boarders. Although she deferred to Luther—she addressed him as Herr Doktor—Katharina defended a woman's right as an equal in marriage. When Luther teased her about Old Testament examples of polygamy, Katharina retorted, "Well, if it comes to that, I'll leave you and the children and go back to the cloister." Accepting her prescribed role in a patriarchal household—one of the three Protestant estates of politics, household, and church—Katharina von Bora represented the ideal Protestant woman.

The Sacred and Secular Patronage of Music. Religious reform left its imprint on musical composition as it did on other aspects of social and cultural life. In Catholic Europe, the church and, to a lesser extent, the princely courts still employed and commissioned musicians. The two leading composers of the sixteenth century, Orlando de Lassus (1532–1594) and Giovanni Pierluigi da Palestrina (1525–1594), were both in papal service as choirmasters. Lassus, a Fleming by birth, went to Munich in 1556 to enter the service of the court of Bavaria, the most important German Catholic principality in the Holy Roman Empire. A prolific composer, Lassus left 390 secular songs in Italian, French, and German, as well as approximately 500 motets and other substantial sacred vocal works. The Italian Palestrina is remembered for his sacred music, especially for his polyphonies that accompanied

the Mass, in which he reaffirmed Catholic tradition by using themes from Gregorian chants of medieval times.

In Protestant Europe the chorale—or harmonized hymn—emerged as a new musical form. Unlike Catholic services, for which professional musicians sang in Latin, Protestant services urged the entire congregation to sing in unison. To encourage participation, Martin Luther, an accomplished lute player, composed many hymns in German. Drawing from Catholic sacred music as well as folk tunes, Luther and his collaborators wrote words to accompany familiar melodies. The best known of Luther's hymns, "Ein' feste Burg," became the beloved English Protestant hymn "A Mighty Fortress" and inspired many subsequent variations.

Protestants sang hymns to signify their new faith. During the Peasants' War of 1525, for example, Thomas Müntzer and the peasant rebels implored God's intercession by singing the hymn "Oh Come, Thou Holy Spirit" before they were mowed down by the knights and mercenaries in a one-sided slaughter. Eyewitnesses also reported Protestant martyrs singing hymns before their executions. In Lutheran Germany, hymnals and prayer books adorned many urban households; the intimate relationship among religious devotion, bourgeois culture, and musical literacy would become a characteristic of Germany in later centuries.

Review: How did the forces for radical change unleashed by the Protestant Reformation interact with the urge for social order and stability?

❖ A Struggle for Mastery

In the sixteenth century, new patterns of conflicts generated by the Reformation superimposed themselves on traditional dynastic strife. Two developments came together to create instability almost everywhere in Europe: the ambitions of powerful princes and the passions of religious reformers. And almost everywhere, violence failed to settle religious differences. By 1560, an exhausted Europe found itself in a state of compromised peace, but one fraught with the seeds of future conflict.

The Court

At the center of this politics of dynasty and religion was the court, the focus of princely power and intrigue. European princes used the institution of the royal court to bind their nobility and impress their subjects. Briefly defined, the court was the prince's household. Around the ruling family, however, coalesced a small community of household servants, noble attendants, councilors, officials, artists, and soldiers. During the sixteenth century, this political elite developed a sophisticated culture.

The French court of Francis I (r. 1515–1547) became the largest in Europe after the demise of the Burgundian dukes. In addition to the prince's household, the royal family set up households for other members: the queen and the queen mother each had her own staff of maids and chefs, as did each of the royal children. The royal household employed officials to handle finances, guard duty, clothing, and food; in addition, physicians, librarians, musicians, dwarfs, animal trainers, and a multitude of hangers-on bloated its size. By 1535, the French court numbered 1,622 members.

Although Francis built many palaces (the most magnificent at Fontainebleau), the French court was often on the move. It took no fewer than eighteen thousand horses to transport the people, furniture, and documents—not to mention the dogs and falcons for the royal hunt. Hunting, in fact, was a passion for the men at court; it represented a form of mock combat, essential in the training of a military elite. Francis himself loved war games and almost lost his own life when, storming a house during one mock battle, he was hit on the head by a burning log.

Two writers, both Italian, were the most eloquent spokesmen for the culture of courtesy, or proper court behavior: Ludovico Ariosto (1474–1533), in service at the Este court in Ferrara, and Baldassare Castiglione (1478–1529), a servant of the duke of Urbino and the pope. Considered one of the greatest Renaissance poets, Ariosto composed a long epic poem, *Orlando Furioso*, which represented court culture as the highest synthesis of Christian and classical values. Set against the historic struggle between Charlemagne and the Arabs, the poem tells the love story of Bradamante and Ruggiero. Before the separated lovers are reunited, the reader meets scores of characters who have hundreds of adventures. Modeled after Greek and Roman epics, *Orlando Furioso* also followed the tradition of the medieval chivalric romance. The tales of combat, valor, love, and magic captivated the court's noble readers, who, through this highly idealized fantasy, enjoyed a glorified view of their own world.

Equally popular was *The Courtier* by the suave diplomat Castiglione. Like Ariosto, Castiglione tried to represent court culture as a synthesis of military virtues and literary and artistic cultivation. Speaking in eloquent dialogues, Castiglione's characters debate the qualities of an ideal courtier. The true courtier, Castiglione asserts, is a gentleman who speaks in a refined language and carries himself with nobility and dignity in the service of his prince and his lady. Clothing assumes a significant symbolism in *The Courtier*; in the words of one character, "I am not saying that clothes provide the basis for making hard and fast judgments about a man's character. . . . But I do maintain that a man's attire is also no small evidence for what kind of personality he has." All the formalities of court culture, however, could not mask the smoldering religious passions within, and the chivalry of Ariosto's *Orlando Furioso* had its real-life counterpart in the savage wars between Christianity and Islam in the sixteenth century.

Art and the Christian Knight

Through their patronage of artists, the Habsburg emperors and the Catholic popes created idealized self-images, representations of their era's hopes. The use of art for political glorification was nothing new, but below the surface of sixteenth-century art flowed an undercurrent of idealism. For all his political limitations, Emperor Maximilian I (r. 1493–1519), for example, was a visionary who dreamed of restoring Christian chivalry and even toyed with the idea of ruling as pope and emperor. He appointed the Nuremberg artist Albrecht Dürer (1471–1528) as court painter, to represent the Habsburg vision of universal Christian emperorship. Dürer's design for Maximilian's triumphal carriage in

1518 positioned the figures of Justice, Temperance, Prudence, and Fortitude at a level above the seated emperor, with other important allegorical figures—Reason, Nobility, and Power—also in attendance.

For many artists and humanists, such as Erasmus, Emperor Charles V embodied the ideal Christian knight. The Venetian painter Titian (1477–1576) captured the emperor's life on canvas four times (see the illustrations on this page). His 1532 portrait depicts a grand prince in his early thirties. Two portraits from 1548 and 1550 show him victorious over Protestants. Charles's favorite was the final portrait, *Gloria,* one of two Titians he took with him to his monastic retirement: it shows the kneeling emperor wrapped in a white death shroud joining the throng of the saved to worship the Trinity.

The Habsburg dynasty did not monopolize artistic self-glorification, however. The Florentine Michelangelo Buonarroti (1475–1564) matured his multiple talents in the service of the Medici family. After the overthrow of the Medici, Michelangelo became Pope Julius II's favorite artist, painting with furious energy the Sistine Chapel and working on a never-finished tomb and sculpture for the warrior-pope. Later Michelangelo was commissioned by Pope Paul III to design palaces in Rome; in 1547, he became the chief architect of St. Peter's Basilica. Michelangelo's work signified the transition from the Renaissance to the age of religious conflicts. His artistic talents served to glorify a papacy under siege, just as Titian lent his hand in defending the Habsburg cause against **infidels** (unbelievers) and heretics.

Titian, *Charles V at Mühlberg* **and** *Gloria*
The Venetian artist Titian was commissioned by Charles V to paint a series of portraits of the emperor at four stages of his career to show events in his long life for which he wished to be remembered. In the first painting, Titian captures the emperor's sense of victory at having finally crushed the German Protestant princes in battle in 1547. In the detail from *Gloria* (right), Titian vividly shows that all military glory and earthly power is doomed to fade away. Emperor Charles V, dressed in a white robe, turns to the Trinity in the heavens. Painted after his abdication in 1556, *Gloria* is a reminder to Charles of the transience of earthly glory. Compare these two very different images of Charles V. What impression does his attire in each convey? *Scala/Art Resource, NY/Institut Amatller d'Art Hispanic.*

Wars Among Habsburgs, Valois, and Ottomans

While the Reformation was taking hold in Germany, the great powers of Spain and France fought each other for the domination of Europe (Map 15.3). French claims over Italian territories provided the fuse for this conflict. The Italian Wars, started in 1494, escalated into a general conflict that involved most Christian monarchs and the Muslim Ottoman sultan as well. From 1494 to 1559 the Valois and Habsburg dynasties remained implacable enemies; only in 1559 did the French king acknowledge defeat and sign the Treaty of Cateau-Cambrésis♦ that established peace. This basic Franco-Spanish (Valois-Habsburg) struggle drew in many other belligerents, who fought on one side or the other for their own benefits. Some acted purely out of power considerations, such as England, first siding

♦**Cateau-Cambrésis:** ka TOH kahn bray ZEE

with France and then with Spain. Others fought for their independence, such as the papacy and the Italian states, who did not want any one power, particularly Spain, to dominate Italy. Still others chose sides for religious reasons, such as the Protestant princes in Germany, who exploited the Valois-Habsburg conflict to extract religious liberties from the emperor in 1555. Finally, the Ottoman Turks saw in this fight an opportunity to further their territorial expanse.

The Ottoman Empire reached its height of power under Sultan Suleiman I, known as Suleiman the Magnificent (r. 1520–1566). In 1526, a Turkish expedition destroyed the Hungarian army at Mohács (see the illustration on page 570). Three years later, the Ottoman army laid siege to Vienna; though unsuccessful, the siege sent shock waves throughout Christian Europe. In 1535, Charles V led a campaign to capture Tunis, the lair of North African pirates loyal to the Ottomans. Desperate to overcome Charles's

MAP 15.3 Habsburg-Valois-Ottoman Wars, 1494–1559
As the dominant European power, the Habsburg dynasty fought on two fronts: a religious war against the Islamic Ottoman Empire and a political war against the French Valois, who challenged Habsburg hegemony. The Mediterranean, the Balkans, and the Low Countries all became theaters of war.

superior forces, Francis I eagerly forged an alliance with the Turkish sultan. Coming to the aid of the French, the Turkish fleet besieged the imperial troops holding Nice, on the southern coast of France. Francis even ordered all inhabitants of nearby Toulon to vacate the town so that he could turn it into a Muslim colony for eight months, complete with a mosque and slave market.

Many Christians were scandalized that France would ally itself with the Turks to make war on another Christian king. This brief Franco-Turkish alliance, however, reflected the spirit of the times: the age-old idea of the Christian crusade against Islam was in competition with a new political strategy that saw religion as but one factor in power politics.

While the Mediterranean served as the theater of war between Habsburgs and Ottomans, most Habsburg-Valois battles were fought in Italy and the Low Countries. There were spectacular and bloody victories, but none led to a speedy and decisive end to the war. During the 1520s, the Habsburgs seemed triumphant. In 1525, the troops of Charles V crushed the French army at Pavia, Italy, counting among their captives the French king, Francis I. Treated with great honor by Charles, Francis was kept in Spain until he agreed to a treaty renouncing all claims to Italy. Furious at this humiliation, Francis repudiated the treaty the moment he reached France, reigniting the conflict. In 1527, Charles's troops captured Rome because the pope had allied with the French. Many of the imperial troops were German Protestant mercenaries, who pillaged Catholic churches and tortured the Catholic clergy. Protestants and Catholics alike interpreted the sack of Rome by imperial forces as a punishment of God; this disaster spurred the Catholic church to enact reforms.

The 1530s and 1540s saw more indecisive battles. Constantly distracted by the challenges of the Ottomans and the German Protestants, Charles V could not crush France

The Field of the Cloth of Gold
This painting by an unknown artist shows the meeting of Henry VIII of England and Francis I of France near Calais for the sealing of an Anglo-French alliance. Note the prominent figure of Henry on horseback among his entourage. The meeting was a scene of ritual display of power and pomp, with tents and canopies laid out over a vast area for the royal receptions, hence the name of the painting, *The Field of the Cloth of Gold. The Royal Collection © 2004 Her Majesty Queen Elizabeth II.*

The Battle at Mohács
This Ottoman painting shows the 1529 victory of the sultan's army over the Hungarians at Mohács. The battle resulted in the end of the Hungarian kingdom, which would be divided into three realms under Ottoman, Habsburg, and Transylvanian rule. Note the prominence of artillery and the Janissaries with muskets. The Ottomans commanded a vast army with modern equipment, a key to their military prowess in the sixteenth century. *Topkapi Palace Museum.*

in one swift blow. Years of conflict drained the treasuries of all monarchs because warfare was becoming more expensive.

The Finance and Technologies of War

The sixteenth century marked the beginning of superior Western military technology. All armies grew in size and their firepower became ever more deadly, increasing the cost of war. For example, heavier artillery pieces meant that the rectangular walls of medieval cities had to be transformed into fortresses with jutting forts and gun emplacements. England had a war expenditure more than double its royal revenues in the 1540s. To pay these bills, the government devalued its coinage (the sixteenth-century equivalent of printing more paper money), causing prices to rise rapidly.

Other European powers fell into similar predicaments. Charles V boasted the largest army in Europe—but he also sank deeper into debt. Between 1520 and 1532, Charles borrowed 5.4 million ducats, primarily to pay his troops; from 1552 to 1556, his war loans soared to 9.6 million ducats. On his death in 1547, Francis I owed the bankers of Lyon almost 7 million French pounds— approximately the entire royal income for that year. The European powers literally fought themselves into bankruptcy. Taxation, the sale of offices, and outright confiscation failed to bring in enough money to satisfy the war machine. Both the Habsburg and the Valois kings looked to the leading bankers to finance their costly wars.

Foremost among these financiers was the Fugger bank, the largest such enterprise in sixteenth-century Europe. Based in the southern German imperial city of Augsburg, the Fugger family and their associates built an international financial empire that helped to make kings. The enterprise began with Jakob Fugger (1459–1525), who became personal banker to Charles V's grandfather Maximilian I. Constantly short of cash, Maximilian had granted the Fugger family numerous mining and minting concessions. The Fugger enterprise reaped handsome profits from its Habsburg connections. To pay for the service of providing and accepting bills of exchange, the Fuggers charged substantial fees. By the end of his life, Maximilian was so deeply in debt to Jakob Fugger that he had to pawn the royal jewels.

In 1519, Fugger assembled a consortium of German and Italian bankers to secure the election of Charles V as Holy Roman Emperor. For the next three decades, the alliance between Europe's largest international bank and its largest empire tightened. Between 1527 and 1547, the Fugger bank's assets grew from three million guldens (German currency) to over seven million; roughly 55 percent of the assets were from loans to the Habsburgs, with the Spanish branch taking the lion's share.

A STRUGGLE FOR MASTERY   **571**

1500–1560

Charles barely stayed one step ahead of his creditors, and his successor in Spain gradually lost control of the Spanish state finances. To service debts, European monarchs sought revenues in war and tax increases. But paying for troops and crushing rebellions took more money and more loans. Debt forced Spain and France to sign the Treaty of Cateau-Cambrésis in 1559, thus ending more than sixty years of warfare, but the cycle of financial crises and warfare persisted until the late eighteenth century.

Divided Realms

Throughout Europe, rulers viewed religious divisions as a dangerous challenge to the unity of their realms and the stability of their rule. A subject could very well swear greater allegiance to God than to his lord. Moreover, the Peasants' War of 1525 showed that religious dissent could lead to rebellion. In addition, religious differences intensified the formation of noble factions, which exploited the situation when weak monarchs or children ruled.

France. In France, Francis I tolerated Protestants until the Affair of the Placards in 1534. Persecutions of Huguenots—as Protestants were called in France—were only sporadic, however, and the Reformed church grew steadily. During the 1540s and 1550s, many French noble families—including some of the most powerful—converted to Calvinism. Under their protection, the Reformed church was able to organize openly and hold synods (church meetings), especially in southern and western France. Francis and his successor, Henry II (r. 1547–1559), succeeded in maintaining a balance of power between Catholic and Huguenot and between hostile noble factions. But after Henry's death the weakened monarchy could no longer hold together the fragile realm. The real drama of the Reformation in France took place after 1560, when the country plunged into decades of religious wars, whose savagery was unparalleled elsewhere in Europe.

England. The English monarchy played the central role in shaping that country's religious reform. During the 1520s, English

Protestants were few in number. King Henry VIII (r. 1509–1547) changed all that.

In the first eighteen years of his reign, Henry firmly opposed the Reformation, even receiving the title "Defender of the Faith" from Pope Leo X for a treatise Henry wrote against Luther. A robust, ambitious, and well-educated man, Henry wanted to make his mark on history and, with the aid of his chancellors Cardinal Thomas Wolsey and Thomas More, he vigorously suppressed Protestantism and executed its leaders.

But by 1527, the king wanted to divorce his wife, Catherine of Aragon (d. 1536), the daughter of Ferdinand and Isabella of Spain and the aunt of Charles V. The eighteen-year marriage had produced a daughter, Princess Mary (known as Mary Tudor), but Henry desperately needed a male heir to consolidate the rule of the still-new Tudor dynasty. Moreover, he was in love with Anne Boleyn, a lady at court and a strong supporter of the Reformation. Henry claimed that his marriage to Catherine had never been valid because she was the widow of his older brother, Arthur. Arthur and Catherine's marriage, which apparently was never consummated, had been annulled by Pope Julius II to allow the marriage between Henry and Catherine to take place. Now Henry asked the reigning pope, Clement VII, to declare his marriage to Catherine invalid.

Around "the king's great matter" unfolded a struggle for political and religious control. When Henry failed to secure papal approval of his divorce, he chose two Protestants as his new loyal servants: Thomas Cromwell (1485–1540) as chancellor and Thomas Cranmer (1489–1556) as archbishop of Canterbury. Under their leadership the English Parliament passed a number of acts between 1529 and 1536 that severed ties between the English church and Rome. The Act of Supremacy of 1529 made Henry the head of the so-called Anglican church (the Church of England), invalidated the claims of Catherine's daughter, Princess Mary, to the throne, recognized Henry's marriage to Anne Boleyn, and allowed the English crown to confiscate the properties of the monasteries.

By 1536, Henry had grown tired of Anne Boleyn, who had given birth to the future

Queen Elizabeth I but had produced no sons. The king, who would go on to marry four other wives but father only one son, Edward, had Anne beheaded on the charge of adultery, an act that he defined as treason. Thomas More also had gone to the block in 1535 for treason—in his case, for refusing to recognize Henry as "the only supreme head on earth of the Church of England"—and Cromwell suffered the same fate in 1540 when he lost favor. When Henry died in 1547, the Anglican church, nominally Protestant, still retained much traditional Catholic doctrine and ritual. But the principle of royal supremacy in religious matters would remain a lasting feature of Henry's reforms.

The boy king Edward VI (r. 1547–1553) furthered the Reformation by welcoming prominent religious refugees from the continent. With the accession of Mary Tudor (r. 1553–1558), however, Catholicism was restored and Protestants persecuted. Close to three hundred Protestants perished at the stake, and more than eight hundred fled to Germany and Switzerland. Finally, after Anne Boleyn's daughter, Elizabeth, succeeded her half-sister Mary to the throne in 1558, the Anglican cause again gained momentum; it eventually defined the character of the English nation, and Catholic missionaries were ruthlessly hunted down and executed as traitors to a Protestant nation.

Scotland. Still another pattern of religious politics unfolded in Scotland, where powerful noble clans directly challenged royal power. Until the 1550s, Protestants had been a small minority in Scotland. The most prominent Scottish reformer, John Knox (1514–1572), spent many of his early years in exile in England and on the continent. For Knox, God's cause was obstructed by a woman, who became his greatest enemy.

The queen regent Mary of Guise (d. 1560) stood at the center of Scotland's conflict. After the death of her husband, James V, in 1542, Mary of Guise, a Catholic, cultivated the support of her native France. Her daughter and heir to the throne, Mary Stuart (also a Catholic), had been educated in France and was married to the French dauphin Francis, son of Henry II. The queen regent surrounded herself with French advisers and soldiers.

Alienated by this pro-French atmosphere, many Scottish noblemen had joined the pro-English, anti-French Protestant cause.

The era's suspicion of female rulers and regents also played a part in Protestant propaganda. In 1558, John Knox published *The First Blast of the Trumpet against the Monstrous Regiment [Rule] of Women,* a diatribe against both Mary Tudor of England and Mary of Guise. Knox declared that "to promote a woman to bear rule, superiority, dominion, or empire above any realm, nation, or city is repugnant to nature, contumely to God, a thing most contrary to his revealed will and approved ordinance and, finally, it is the subversion of good order, of all equality and justice." In 1560, the Protestants assumed control of the Scottish Parliament, and dethroned the regent Mary of Guise. They later forced her daughter, Mary, queen of Scots, to flee to England, and installed Mary's infant son James as king.

The German States. In the German states, the Protestant princes and cities formed the Schmalkaldic♦ League in 1531. Headed by the elector of Saxony and Philip of Hesse (the two leading Protestant princes), the league included most of the imperial cities, the chief source of the empire's wealth. On the other side, allied with Emperor Charles V, were the bishops and the few remaining Catholic princes. Although Charles had to concentrate on fighting the French and the Turks during the 1530s, he had by now temporarily secured the western Mediterranean; thus, he turned to central Europe to try to resolve the growing religious differences there.

In 1541, Charles convened an Imperial Diet at Regensburg to patch up the theological differences between Protestants and Catholics, only to see negotiations between the two sides break down rapidly. The schism threatened to become permanent. Vowing to crush the Schmalkaldic League, the emperor secured French neutrality in 1544 and papal support in 1545. Luther died in 1546. In the following year, war broke out. Using seasoned Spanish veterans and German allies, Charles occupied the German imperial cities in the south, restoring Catholic elites and

♦**Schmalkaldic:** shmahl KAHL dihk

suppressing the Reformation. In 1547, he defeated the Schmalkaldic League armies at Mühlberg and captured the leading Lutheran princes. Jubilant, Charles proclaimed a decree, the "Interim," which restored Catholics' right to worship in Protestant lands while permitting Lutherans to keep their own rites. Protestant resistance to the Interim was deep and widespread: many pastors went into exile, and riots broke out in many cities.

For Charles V, the reaction of his former allies proved far more alarming than Protestant resistance. His success frightened some Catholic powers. With Spanish troops controlling Milan and Naples, Pope Julius III (r. 1550–1552) feared that papal authority would be subjugated by imperial might. In the Holy Roman Empire, Protestant princes spoke out against "imperial tyranny." Jealously defending their traditional liberties against an over-mighty emperor, the Protestant princes, led by Duke Maurice of Saxony, a former ally, raised arms against Charles. The princes declared war in 1552, chasing a surprised, unprepared, and practically bankrupt emperor back to Italy.

Forced to construct an accord, Charles V agreed to the Peace of Augsburg in 1555. The settlement recognized the Lutheran church in the empire, accepted the secularization of church lands but "reserved" the remaining ecclesiastical territories (mainly the bishoprics) for Catholics, and, most important, established the principle that all princes, whether Catholic or Lutheran, enjoyed the sole right to determine the religion of their lands and subjects. Significantly, Calvinist, Anabaptist, and other dissenting groups were excluded from the settlement. The religious revolt of the common people had culminated in a princes' Reformation. As the constitutional framework for the Holy Roman Empire, the Augsburg settlement preserved a fragile peace in central Europe until 1618, but the exclusion of Calvinists would plant the seed for future conflict.

Exhausted by decades of war and disappointed by the disunity in Christian Europe, Emperor Charles V resigned his many thrones in 1555 and 1556, leaving his Netherlandish-Burgundian and Spanish dominions to his son, Philip II, and his Austrian lands to his brother, Ferdinand (who was also elected Holy Roman Emperor to succeed Charles). Retiring to a monastery in southern Spain, the most powerful of the Christian monarchs spent his last years quietly seeking salvation (Figure 15.1).

> **Review:** How did European rulers attempt to stabilize their territories in the face of religious divisions?

❖ A Continuing Reformation

Reacting to the waves of Protestant challenge, the Catholic church mobilized for defense. Drawing on traditions from before the Reformation, Catholicism offered hopes of renewal in the 1540s and 1550s. The Council of Trent defined the beliefs and practices of the Catholic church and condemned Protestant beliefs, while new religious orders, most notably the Society of Jesus, began a vigorous campaign for the reclamation of souls. Christian Europe was transformed. Not only had the old religious unity passed

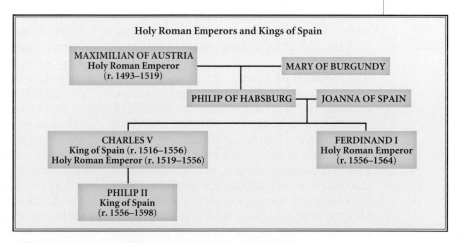

FIGURE 15.1 The Habsburg Succession, 1493–1556
The reign of Charles V ended with the splintering of the largest empire in Europe. Saddled with debts inherited from his grandfather and accrued from perpetual warfare, Charles ceded the Holy Roman Empire to his brother Ferdinand and gave Spain to his son Philip.

forever, but a new earth emerged under the canopy of a new heaven, as missionaries from Catholic Europe traveled to other parts of the world to win converts who might compensate for the millions lost to the Protestant Reformation.

Catholic Renewal

Many voices for reform had echoed within the Catholic church long before Luther, but the papacy had failed to sponsor any significant change in the decades before the Reformation. Nevertheless, a Catholic reform movement gathered momentum in Italy during the 1530s and 1540s. Drawn from the elite, especially the Venetian upper class, the Catholic reformers stressed biblical ethics and moral discipline. Gian Matteo Giberti, bishop of Verona from 1524 to 1543, resigned his position in the Roman curia to concentrate on his pastoral duties. Gasparo Contarini♦ (1483–1542), who was descended from a Venetian noble family and had served the republic as ambassador to Charles V, subsequently was elevated to cardinal, in which position he labored to heal the schism within the church.

Under Pope Paul III (r. 1534–1549) and his successors, the papacy finally took the lead in church reform. The Italian nobility also played a leading role, and Spaniards and Italians of all classes provided the backbone for this movement, sometimes called the Catholic Reform. Its crowning achievements were the calling of a general church council and the founding of new religious orders.

The Council of Trent.   In 1545, Pope Paul III and Charles V convened a general church council at Trent, a town on the border between the Holy Roman Empire and Italy. The Council of Trent, 1545–1563, which met sporadically over the next seventeen years before completing its work, shaped the essential character of Catholicism until the 1960s. It reasserted the supremacy of clerical authority over the laity and stipulated that bishops reside in their dioceses and that seminaries be established in each diocese to train priests. The council also confirmed

♦**Gasparo Contarini:** GAHS pahr oh kohn tah REE nee

and clarified church doctrine and sacraments. On the sacrament of the Eucharist, the council reaffirmed that the bread actually becomes Christ's body—a rejection of all Protestant positions on this issue sufficiently emphatic as to preclude compromise. For the sacrament of marriage, the council specified that all weddings must henceforth take place in churches and be registered by the parish clergy; it further rejected the Protestant allowance for divorce.

The Council of Trent marked a watershed; henceforth, the schism between Protestant and Catholic remained permanent, and all hopes of reconciliation faded. The focus of the Catholic church turned now to rolling back the tide of dissent.

The Society of Jesus.   The energy of the Catholic renewal expressed itself most vigorously in the founding of new religious orders. The most important of these, the Society of Jesus, or Jesuits, was established by a Spanish nobleman, Ignatius of Loyola (1491–1556). Imbued with tales of chivalric romances and the national glory of the *reconquista,* Ignatius eagerly sought to prove his mettle as a soldier. In 1521, while defending a Spanish border fortress against French attack, he sustained a severe injury. During his convalescence, Ignatius read lives of the saints; once he recovered, he abandoned his quest for military glory in favor of serving the church.

Attracted by his austerity and piety, young men gravitated to this charismatic figure. Thanks to his noble birth and a cardinal's intercession, Ignatius gained a hearing before the pope, and in 1540 the church recognized his small band. With Ignatius as its first general, the Jesuits became the most vigorous defenders of papal authority. The society quickly expanded; by the time of Ignatius's death in 1556, Europe had one thousand Jesuits. Jesuits established hundreds of colleges throughout the Catholic world, educating future generations of Catholic leaders. Jesuit missionaries played a key role in the global Portuguese maritime empire and brought Roman Catholicism to Africans, Asians, and native Americans. Together with other new religious orders, the Jesuits restored the confidence of the faithful in the dedication and power of the Catholic church.

Missionary Zeal

To win new souls, Catholic missionaries set sail throughout the globe. They saw their effort as proof of the truth of Roman Catholicism and the success of their missions as a sign of divine favor, both particularly important in the face of Protestant challenge. But the missionary zeal of Catholics brought different messages to indigenous peoples: for some the message of a repressive and coercive alien religion, for others a sweet sign of reason and faith. Frustrated in his efforts to convert Brazilian Indians, a Jesuit missionary wrote to his superior in Rome in 1563 that "for this kind of people it is better to be preaching with the sword and rod of iron." This attitude was common among Christian missionaries in the Americas and Africa, despite the isolated missionary voices that condemned Europeans' abuse of native populations.

The Dominican Bartolomé de Las Casas (1474–1566) was perhaps the most severe critic of colonial brutality in Spanish America, yet even he argued that Africans were constitutionally more suitable for labor than native Americans and should be imported to the plantations in the Americas to relieve the indigenous peoples, who were being worked to death. Under the influence of Las Casas and his followers, the Spanish crown tried to protect the indigenous peoples against exploitation by European settlers, a policy whose success was

The Portuguese in Japan
In this sixteenth-century Japanese black-lacquer screen painting of Portuguese missionaries, the Jesuits are dressed in black and the Franciscans in brown. At the lower right corner is a Portuguese nobleman depicted with exaggerated "Western" features. The Japanese considered themselves lighter in skin color than the Portuguese, whom they classified as "barbarians." In turn, the Portuguese classified Japanese (and Chinese) as "whites." The perception of ethnic differences in the sixteenth century depended less on skin color than on clothing, eating habits, and other cultural signals. Color classifications were unstable and changed over time: by the late seventeenth century, Europeans no longer regarded Asians as "whites." *Laurie Platt Winfrey, Inc.*

determined by the struggle among missionaries, conquistadores (Spanish conquerors in the Americas), and royal officials for the bodies and souls of native populations.

To ensure rapid Christianization, European missionaries focused initially on winning over local elites. The recommendation of a Spanish royal official in Mexico City was typical. He wrote to the crown in 1525:

> In order that the sons of caciques [chiefs] and native lords may be instructed in the faith, Your Majesty must command that a college be founded wherein they may be taught . . . to the end that they may be ordained priests. For he who shall become such among them, will be of greater profit in attracting others to the faith than will fifty [European] Christians.

Legend:
- Lutheran
- Anglican
- Calvinist
- Calvinist influenced
- Roman Catholic
- Mixed confessional area
- ▲ Anabaptist minorities

MAPPING THE WEST Reformation Europe, c. 1560
The fortunes of Roman Catholicism were at their lowest point around 1560. Northern Germany and Scandinavia owed allegiance to the Lutheran church, England broke away under a national church headed by its monarchs, and the Calvinist Reformation would extend across large areas of western, central, and eastern Europe. Southern Europe remained solidly Catholic.

Nevertheless, this recommendation was not adopted and the Catholic clergy in Spanish America remained overwhelmingly European.

The Portuguese were more willing than the Spanish to train indigenous peoples as missionaries. A number of young African nobles went to Portugal to be trained in theology, among them Dom Henry, a son of King Afonso I of Kongo, a Portuguese ally. In East Asia, Christian missionaries under Portuguese protection concentrated their efforts on the elites, preaching the Gospel to

Confucian scholar-officials in China and to the samurai (the warrior aristocracy) in Japan. The missionary enterprise seemed highly successful: by the second half of the sixteenth century, vast multitudes of native Americans had become nominal Christians, and thirty years after Francis Xavier's 1549 landing in Japan the Jesuits could claim more than 100,000 Japanese converts.

After an initial period of relatively little racial discrimination, the Catholic church in the Americas and Africa adopted strict rules based on color. For example, the first Mexican Ecclesiastical Provincial Council in 1555 declared that holy orders were not to be conferred on Indians, mestizos (people of mixed European-Indian parentage), and mulattoes (people of mixed European-African heritage); along with descendants of Moors, Jews, and persons who had been sentenced by the Spanish Inquisition, these groups were deemed "inherently unworthy of the sacerdotal [priestly] office." Europeans reinforced their sense of racial superiority with their perception of the "treachery" that native Americans and Africans exhibited whenever they resisted domination.

A different conversion tactic applied to Asia. There, European missionaries, who admired Chinese and Japanese civilization and were not backed by military power, used the sermon rather than the sword to win converts (see the illustration on page 575). The Jesuit Francis Xavier preached in India and Japan, his work vastly assisted by a network of Portuguese trading stations. He died in 1552, awaiting permission to travel to China. A pioneer missionary in Asia, Xavier had prepared the ground for future missionary successes in Japan and China.

Review: How did the Catholic church maintain and, in the wake of the Reformation, regain its influence?

Conclusion

Mocking the warlike popes, the Dutch humanist Erasmus compared his times to those of the early Christian church. In *The Praise of Folly,* he satirized Christian prelates and princes, who "continued to shed Christian blood," the same blood as that of the martyrs who had built the foundations of Christianity. Turning from the papacy to the empire, Erasmus and many intellectuals and artists of his generation saw in Emperor Charles V the model Christian prince. As the most powerful ruler in all Europe, Charles was hailed as the harbinger of peace, the protector of justice, and the foe of the infidel Turks. For the generation that came of age before the Reformation, Christian humanism—and its imperial embodiment—represented an ideal for political and moral reform that would save Christendom from corruption and strife.

The Reformation changed this dream of peace, justice, and unity. Instead of leading a crusade against Islam, Charles V wore himself out in ceaseless struggle against Francis I of France and the German Protestants. Instead of the Christian faith of charity and learning that Erasmus had envisioned, Christianity split into a number of hostile camps that battled one another with words and swords. Instead of the intellectual unity of the generation of Erasmus and Thomas More, the mid-sixteenth-century cultural landscape erupted in a burst of conflicting doctrinal statements and left in its wake a climate of censorship, repression, division, and inflexibility.

After the brutal suppression of popular revolts in the 1520s and 1530s, religious persecution became a Christian institution: Luther called on the princes to kill rebellious peasants in 1525, Zwingli advocated the drowning of Anabaptists, and Calvin supported the death sentence for Michael Servetus. Meanwhile, persecutions and executions in Catholic lands provided Protestants with a steady stream of martyrs. The two peace settlements in the 1550s failed to provide long-term solutions: the Peace of Augsburg gradually disintegrated as the religious struggles in the empire intensified, and the Treaty of Cateau-Cambrésis was but a brief respite in a century of crisis. In the following generations, civil war and national conflicts would set Catholics against Protestants in numerous futile attempts to restore a single faith.

Suggested References

A New Heaven and a New Earth

Recent scholarship on the Reformation era has emphasized the connected nature of religious, political, social, economic, and cultural history. Another new direction is to connect the study of Christian reform movements with Christian-Jewish relations prior to the Reformation.

Brady, Thomas A. *Turning Swiss: Cities and Empire, 1450–1550.* 1985.

Essential Works of Erasmus. Ed. W. T. H. Jackson. 1965.

Hsia, R. Po-chia. *The Myth of Ritual Murder: Jews and Magic in the Reformation.* 1988.

Jardine, Lisa. *Erasmus: Man of Letters.* 1993.

Protestant Reformers

While continuing to refine our understanding of the leading Protestant reformers, recent scholars have also offered new interpretations that take into consideration the popular impact of the reformers' teachings.

Bouwsma, William J. *John Calvin: A Sixteenth-Century Portrait.* 1988.

Haigh, Christopher. *English Reformations: Religion, Politics, and Society under the Tudors.* 1993.

*Hillerbrand, Hans J., ed. *The Protestant Reformation.* 1969.

Martin Luther's life and thought: http://www.wsu.edu/~dee/REFORM/LUTHER.htm.

Oberman, Heiko A. *Luther: Man between God and Devil.* 1990.

Puritan and Reformed sermons and other writings: http://www.puritansermons.com/poetry.htm.

Scribner, R. W. *For the Sake of Simple Folk: Popular Propaganda for the German Reformation.* 1981.

Scribner, R. W., et al., eds. *The Reformation in a National Context.* 1994.

Reshaping Society through Religion

The most important trend in recent scholarship has been the consideration of the impact of the Reformation on society and culture. Many studies have shown the limited influence of the ideas of reformers; others document the persistence of traditional religious habits and practices well past the sixteenth century.

Bainton, Roland. *Women of the Reformation in Germany and Italy.* 1971.

Blickle, Peter. *The Revolution of 1525.* 1981.

Elton, G. R. *Reformation Europe, 1517–1559.* 1963.

Hsia, R. Po-chia. *The German People and the Reformation.* 1988.

Ozment, Steven E. *The Reformation in the Cities.* 1975.

Strauss, Gerald. *Luther's House of Learning: Indoctrination of the Young in the German Reformation.* 1978.

Wiesner, Merry. *Christianity and the Regulation of Sexuality in the Early Modern World.* 2000.

A Struggle for Mastery

Still focused on the struggle between the Habsburg and Valois dynasties, historical scholarship has also moved out in the direction of cultural and military history. Recent works have studied military innovations and artistic representations of the sixteenth-century monarchs.

Elliott, J. H. *The Old World and the New, 1492–1650.* 1970.

*Guicciardini, Francesco. *The History of Italy.* Trans. Sidney Alexander. 1969.

Knecht, R. J. *Francis I.* 1982.

Parker, Geoffrey. *The Military Revolution: Military Innovation and the Rise of the West, 1500–1800.* 1988.

Partridge, Loren, and Randolph Starn. *A Renaissance Likeness: Art and Culture in Raphael's Julius II.* 1980.

Trevor-Roper, Hugh. *Princes and Artists: Patronage and Ideology at Four Habsburg Courts, 1517–1633.* 1976.

A Continuing Reformation

Current scholarship suggests that by comparing the Protestant Reformation and the Catholic Reforms, we can gain insight into the underlying social and cultural changes that affected all of Christian Europe. Another new direction of research brings the study of Christianity into the non-European realm by focusing on missions.

Crosby, Alfred W. *The Colombian Exchange: Biological and Cultural Consequences of 1492.* 1972.

Evennet, Henry Outram. *The Spirit of the Counter-Reformation.* 1968.

Hsia, R. Po-chia. *The World of the Catholic Renewal.* 1997.

O'Malley, John W. *Trent and All That.* 2000.

Prodi, Paolo. *The Papal Prince, One Body and Two Souls: The Papal Monarchy in Early Modern Europe.* 1982.

*Primary source.

CHAPTER REVIEW

IMPORTANT EVENTS

1494 Italian Wars begin

1516 Erasmus publishes Greek edition of the New Testament; More writes *Utopia*

1517 Martin Luther composes ninety-five theses to challenge church profiteering

1520 Luther publishes three treatises; Zwingli breaks from Rome

1525 German Peasants' War

1527 Charles V's imperial troops sack Rome

1529 German Protestants; Colloquy of Marburg assembles to address disagreements between German and Swiss church reformers

1534 Act of Supremacy Henry VIII breaks with Rome; Affair of the Placards in France

1536 Calvin publishes first edition of *Institutes*

1540 Jesuits established as new Catholic order

1541 Calvin installed in Geneva

1545–1563 Catholic Council of Trent condemns Protestant beliefs and confirms church doctrine and sacraments

1547 Charles V defeats Protestants at Mühlberg

1555 Peace of Augsburg ends religious wars in Germany and recognizes Lutherans

1559 Treaty of Cateau-Cambrésis ends conflict between Habsburg and Valois

KEY TERMS

Anabaptist (561)

Christian humanists (550)

Evangelicals (548)

indulgence (549)

infidel (567)

parish (563)

predestination (558)

Protestants (548)

Vulgate (562)

REVIEW QUESTIONS

1. How did the Christian humanists combine classical learning with their goals of Christian renewal?

2. In what ways did Luther, Zwingli, and Calvin challenge the Roman Catholic Church?

3. How did the forces for radical change unleashed by the Protestant Reformation interact with the urge for social order and stability?

4. How did European rulers attempt to stabilize their territories in the face of religious divisions?

5. How did the Catholic church maintain and, in the wake of the Reformation, regain its influence?

MAKING CONNECTIONS

1. Contrast the ways in which the Christian humanists and the Protestant reformers tried to change society.

2. How were the religious and political conflicts of the early sixteenth century related?

FOR FURTHER EXPLORATION

To assess your mastery of the material in this chapter, see the Online Study Guide at bedfordstmartins.com/hunt.

To read additional primary-source material from this period, see Chapter 15 in *Sources of The Making of the West*, Second Edition.

A Century of Crisis,
1560–1648

IN MAY 1618, PROTESTANTS IN THE KINGDOM of Bohemia furiously protested the Holy Roman Emperor's attempts to curtail their hard-won religious freedoms. Protestants wanted to build new churches; the Catholic emperor wanted to stop them. Tensions boiled over when two Catholic deputy governors tried to dissolve the meetings of Protestants. On May 23, a crowd of angry Protestants surged up the stairs of the royal castle in Prague, trapped the two Catholic deputies, dragged them screaming for mercy to the windows, and hurled them to the pavement below. One of the rebels jeered: "We will see if your [Virgin] Mary can help you!" But because they landed in a dung heap, the Catholic deputies survived. One of the two limped off on his own; the other was carried away by his servants to safety. Although no one died, this "defenestration" (from the French for "window," *la fenêtre*) of Prague touched off the Thirty Years' War (1618–1648), which eventually involved almost every major power in Europe. Before it ended, the fighting had devastated the lands of central Europe and produced permanent changes in European politics and culture.

The Thirty Years' War grew out of the religious conflicts initiated by the Reformation. When Martin Luther began the Protestant Reformation in 1517, he had no idea that he would be unleashing such dangerous forces, but religious turmoil and warfare followed almost immediately upon his break with the Catholic church. Until the early 1600s, the Peace of Augsburg of 1555 maintained relative calm in the lands of the Holy Roman Empire by granting each ruler the right to determine the religion of his territory. But in western Europe, religious strife increased dramatically after 1560 as Protestants made inroads in France, the Spanish-ruled Netherlands, and England. All in all, nearly constant warfare marked the century between 1560 and 1648. These struggles most often began as religious conflicts, but religion was never the sole motive; political power entered into every equation and raised the stakes of conflict.

Religious Conflicts and State Power, 1560–1618
- French Wars of Religion, 1562–1598
- Challenges to Spanish Power
- Elizabeth I's Defense of English Protestantism
- The Clash of Faiths and Empires in Eastern Europe

The Thirty Years' War and the Balance of Power, 1618–1648
- Origins and Course of the War
- The Effects of Constant Fighting
- The Peace of Westphalia, 1648

Economic Crisis and Realignment
- From Growth to Recession
- Consequences for Daily Life
- The Economic Balance of Power

A Clash of Worldviews
- The Arts in an Age of Crisis
- The Natural Laws of Politics
- Origins of the Scientific Revolution
- Magic and Witchcraft

The Defenestration of Prague, 1618
In this detail from a copper-plate engraving by Swiss artist Matthäus Merian (1593–1650), Czech Protestants attack the Catholic deputies sent to disband their meeting. The attackers are about to throw the two Catholics out of the windows of the royal castle (that is, the Catholics are about to suffer "defenestration"). The defenestration touched off the Thirty Years' War. *Mary Evans Picture Library.*

The Bohemian Protestants, for example, wanted both freedom to practice their religion as Protestants and national independence for the Czechs, the largest ethnic group in Bohemia. Since Bohemia had many Catholics, religious and political aims inevitably came into conflict.

Although particularly dramatic and deadly, the church-state crisis was only one of a series of upheavals that shaped this era. In the early seventeenth century, a major economic downturn led to food shortages, famine, and disease in much of Europe. These hit especially hard in the central European lands devastated by the fighting of the Thirty Years' War and helped shift the balance of economic power to northwestern Europe, away from the Mediterranean and central Europe. The deepening sense of crisis prompted some to seek new, nonreligious grounds for all forms of authority, whether artistic, political, or philosophical. A clash of worldviews was in the making. The development of new scientific methods of research would ultimately reshape Western attitudes over the long term.

❖ Religious Conflicts and State Power, 1560–1618

The Peace of Augsburg of 1555 made Lutheranism a legal religion in the predominantly Catholic Holy Roman Empire, but it did not extend recognition to Calvinists. Although the followers of Martin Luther (Lutherans) and those of John Calvin (Calvinists) similarly refused the authority of the Catholic church, they disagreed with each other about religious doctrine and church organization. The rapid expansion of Calvinism after 1560 threatened to alter the religious balance of power in much of Europe. Calvinists challenged Catholic dominance in France, the Spanish-ruled Netherlands, Scotland, and Poland-Lithuania. In England they sought to influence the new Protestant monarch, Elizabeth I. Calvinists were not the only source of religious contention, however. Philip II of Spain also fought the Muslim Ottoman Turks in the Mediterranean and expelled the remnants of the Muslim population in Spain. To the east, the Russian tsar Ivan IV fought to make Muscovy the center of an empire based on Russian Orthodox Christianity. He had to compete with Lutheran Sweden and Poland-Lithuania, itself divided by conflicts among Catholics, Lutherans, and Calvinists.

French Wars of Religion, 1562–1598

Calvinist inroads in France had begun in 1555, when the Genevan Company of Pastors took charge of missionary work. Supplied with false passports and often disguised as merchants, the Calvinist pastors moved rapidly among their growing congregations, which gathered in secret in towns near Paris or in the south. Calvinist nobles provided military protection to local congregations and helped set up a national organization for the French Calvinist—or **Huguenot**◆—church. In 1562, rival Huguenot and Catholic armies

◆**Huguenot:** HYOO guh no

◆ **1562** French Wars of Religion

◆ **1566** Calvinist revolt against Spain

◆ **1569** Poland-Lithuania formed

◆ **1571** Battle of Lepanto

◆ **1598** Edict of Nantes

◆ **1618** Thirty Years' War

| 1560 | 1580 | 1600 |

◆ **1572** St. Bartholomew's Day Massacre

◆ **1588** England defeats Spanish Armada

◆ **1601** Shakespeare, *Hamlet*

began fighting a series of wars that threatened to tear the French nation into shreds (Map 16.1).

Religious Division in the Nobility. Conversion to Calvinism in French noble families often began with the noblewomen, some of whom sought intellectual independence as well as spiritual renewal in the new faith. Charlotte de Bourbon, for example, fled from a Catholic convent and eventually married William of Orange, the leader of the anti-Spanish resistance in the Netherlands. Calvinist noblewomen protected pastors, provided money and advice, and helped found schools and establish relief for the poor.

Religious divisions in France often reflected political disputes among noble families. At least one-third of the nobles—a much larger proportion than in the general population—joined the Huguenots, who usually followed the lead of the Bourbon family. The Bourbons were close relatives of the French king and stood first in line to inherit the throne if the Valois♦ kings failed to produce a male heir. The most militantly Catholic nobles took their cues from the Guise♦ family, who aimed to block Bourbon ambitions. The Catholic Valois were caught between these two powerful factions, each with its own military organization. The situation grew even more volatile when King Henry II was accidentally killed during a jousting tournament in 1559 and his fifteen-year-old son, Francis, died soon after. Ten-

year-old Charles IX (r. 1560–1574) became king, with his mother, Catherine de Médicis, as regent. An ambassador commented on the weakness of Catherine's hold: "It is sufficient to say that she is a woman, a foreigner, and a Florentine to boot, born of a simple house, altogether beneath the dignity of the Kingdom of France." The Bourbon and Guise factions consolidated their forces, and civil war erupted in 1562. Both sides committed terrible atrocities. Priests and pastors were murdered, and massacres of whole congregations became frighteningly commonplace.

St. Bartholomew's Day Massacre, 1572. Although a Catholic herself, Catherine aimed to preserve the throne for her son by playing the Guise and Bourbon factions off each other. To this end she arranged the marriage of the king's Catholic sister, Marguerite de Valois, to Henry of Navarre,♦ a Huguenot and Bourbon. Just four days after the wedding in August 1572, assassins tried but failed to kill one of the Huguenot nobles allied with the Bourbons, Gaspard de Coligny. Panicked at the thought of Huguenot revenge and perhaps herself implicated in the botched plot, Catherine convinced her son to order the killing of leading Huguenots. On St. Bartholomew's Day, August 24, a bloodbath began, fueled by years of growing animosity between Catholics and Protestants. (See Massacre Motivated by Religion page 585.) The duke of Guise himself killed Coligny. Each side viewed the other as less than human, as a source of moral pollution

♦**Valois:** VAL wah
♦**Guise:** geez

♦**Navarre:** nuh VAHR

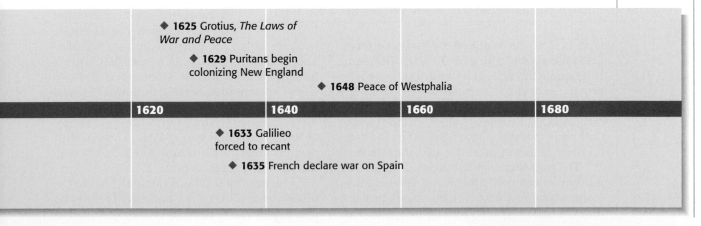

♦ **1625** Grotius, *The Laws of War and Peace*

♦ **1629** Puritans begin colonizing New England

♦ **1648** Peace of Westphalia

| 1620 | 1640 | 1660 | 1680 |

♦ **1633** Galilieo forced to recant

♦ **1635** French declare war on Spain

MAP 16.1 Protestant Churches in France, 1562
Calvinist missionaries took their message from their headquarters in Geneva across the border into France. The strongest concentration of Protestants was in southern France. The Bourbons, leaders of the Protestants in France, had their family lands in Navarre, a region in southwestern France that had been divided between France and Spain.

right of resistance was linked to a notion of contract; upholding the true religion was part of the contract imagined as binding the ruler to his subjects. Both the right of resistance and the idea of a contract fed into the larger doctrine of constitutionalism—that a government's legitimacy rested on its upholding a constitution or contract between ruler and ruled. Constitutionalism justified resistance movements from the sixteenth century onward. Protestants and Catholics alike now saw the conflict as an international struggle for survival that required aid to coreligionists in other countries. In this way, the French Wars of Religion paved the way for wider international conflicts over religion in the decades to come.

Henry IV and the Edict of Nantes. The religious division in France grew even more dangerous when Charles IX died and his brother Henry III (r. 1574–1589) became king. Like his brothers before him, Henry III failed to produce an heir. Next in line to the throne was none other than the Protestant Bourbon leader Henry of Navarre. Convinced that Henry III lacked the will to root out Protestantism, the Guises formed the Catholic League, which requested help from Spanish king Philip II. Henry III responded with a fatal trick: in 1588 he summoned the two Guise leaders to a meeting and had his men kill them. A few months later a fanatical monk stabbed Henry III to death, and Henry of Navarre became Henry IV (r. 1589–1610), despite Philip II's attempt to block his way with military intervention.

that had to be eradicated. In three days, Catholic mobs murdered three thousand Huguenots in Paris. Ten thousand died in the provinces over the next six weeks. The pope joyfully ordered the church bells rung throughout Catholic Europe; Spain's Philip II wrote Catherine that it was "the best and most cheerful news which at present could come to me."

The massacre settled nothing. Huguenot pamphleteers now proclaimed their right to resist a tyrant who worshiped idols (a practice that Calvinists equated with Catholicism). This

The new king soon concluded that to establish control over the war-weary country he had to place the interests of the French state

Massacre Motivated by Religion

The Italian artist Giorgio Vasari painted *St. Bartholomew's Night: The Massacre of the Huguenots* for a public room in Pope Gregory XIII's residence. In what ways did the artist celebrate what he saw as a Catholic victory over Protestant heresy? *Scala/Art Resource.*

ahead of his Protestant faith. In 1593, Henry IV publicly embraced Catholicism, reputedly explaining his conversion with the statement "Paris is worth a Mass." Within a few years he defeated the ultra-Catholic opposition and drove out the Spanish. In 1598, he made peace with Spain and issued the Edict of Nantes, in which he granted the Huguenots a large measure of religious toleration. The approximately 1.25 million Huguenots became a legally protected minority within an officially Catholic kingdom of some 20 million people. Protestants were free to worship in specified towns and were allowed their own troops, fortresses, and even courts. Few believed in religious toleration, but Henry IV followed the advice of those neutral Catholics and Calvinists called ***politiques***✦ who urged him to give priority to the development of a durable state. Although their opponents hated them for their compromising spirit, the politiques believed that religious disputes could be resolved only in the peace provided by strong government.

The Edict of Nantes ended the French Wars of Religion, but Henry still needed to reestablish monarchical authority. He used court festivities and royal processions to rally subjects around him, and he developed a new class of royal officials to counterbalance the fractious nobility. In exchange for an annual payment, officials who had purchased their offices could pass them on to heirs or sell them to someone else. By buying offices that eventually ennobled their holders, rich middle-class merchants and lawyers could become part of a new social elite known as the "nobility of the robe" (named after the robes that magistrates wore, much like those judges wear today). New income raised by the increased sale of offices reduced the state debt and helped Henry build the base for a strong monarchy. His efforts did not, however, prevent his own assassination in 1610 after nineteen unsuccessful attempts.

✦**politiques:** paw LUH teek

Challenges to Spanish Power

Although he failed to prevent Henry IV from taking the French throne, Philip II of Spain (r. 1556–1598) was the most powerful ruler in Europe (Map 16.2). In addition to the western Habsburg lands in Spain and the Netherlands, he had inherited from his father, Charles V, all the Spanish colonies recently settled in the New World of the Americas. Gold and silver funneled from the colonies supported his campaigns against the Ottoman Turks and French and English Protestants. But all of the money of the New

World could not prevent Philip's eventual defeat in the Netherlands, where Calvinist rebels established an independent Dutch Republic that soon vied with Spain, France, and England for commercial supremacy.

Philip II, the Catholic King.   A deeply devout Catholic, Philip II came to the Spanish throne at age twenty-eight determined to restore Catholic unity in Europe and lead the Christian defense against the Muslims. In his quest Philip benefited from a series of misfortunes. His four wives all died, but through them he became part of four royal families:

MAP 16.2 The Empire of Philip II, r. 1556–1598
Spanish king Philip II drew revenues from a truly worldwide empire. In 1580 he was the richest European ruler, but the demands of governing such far-flung territories eventually drained many of his resources.

Portuguese, English, French, and Austrian. His brief marriage to Mary Tudor (Mary I of England) did not produce an heir, but it and his subsequent marriage to Elisabeth de Valois, the sister of Charles IX and Henry III of France, gave him reason enough for involvement in English and French affairs. In 1580, when the king of Portugal died without a direct heir, Philip took over this neighboring realm with its rich empire in Africa, India, and the Americas.

Philip insisted on Catholic unity in his own possessions and worked to forge an international Christian coalition against the Ottoman Turks. In 1571, he achieved the single greatest military victory of his reign when he joined with Venice and the papacy to defeat the Turks in a great sea battle off the Greek coast at Lepanto.♦ Fifty thousand sailors and soldiers fought on the allied side, and eight thousand died. Spain now controlled the western Mediterranean. But Philip could not rest on his laurels. Between 1568 and 1570, the **Moriscos**♦—Muslim converts to Christianity who remained secretly faithful to Islam—had revolted in the south of Spain, killing 90 priests and 1,500 Christians. The victory at Lepanto destroyed any prospect that the Turks might come to their aid, yet Philip took stern measures against the Moriscos. He forced 50,000 to leave their villages and resettle in other regions. In 1609, his successor, Philip III, ordered their expulsion, and by 1614 some 300,000 Moriscos had been forced to relocate to North Africa.

The Revolt of the Netherlands.

The Calvinists of the Netherlands were less easily intimidated than the Moriscos: they were far from Spain and accustomed to being left alone. In 1566, Calvinists in the Netherlands attacked Catholic churches, smashing stained-glass windows and statues of the Virgin Mary. Philip sent an army, which executed more than 1,100 people during the next six years. Prince William of Orange (whose name came from the lands he owned in southern France) took the lead of the anti-Spanish resistance. He encouraged adventurers and pirates known as the Sea Beggars

♦**Lepanto:** lee PAHN toh
♦**Moriscos:** muh RIHS kohs

to invade the northern ports. The Spanish responded with more force, culminating in November 1576 when Philip's long-unpaid mercenary armies sacked Antwerp, then Europe's wealthiest commercial city. In eleven days of horror known as the Spanish Fury, the Spanish soldiers slaughtered seven thousand people. Shocked into response, the Netherlands' ten largely Catholic southern provinces formally allied with the seven largely Protestant northern provinces and expelled the Spaniards.

Important religious, ethnic, and linguistic differences promoted a federation rather than a union of Dutch states. The southern provinces remained Catholic, French-speaking in parts, and suspicious of the increasingly strict Calvinism in the north. In 1579, the southern provinces returned to the Spanish fold. Despite the assassination in 1584 of William of Orange, Spanish troops never regained control in the north. Spain would not formally recognize Dutch independence until

The Netherlands during the Revolt, c. 1580

1648, but by the end of the sixteenth century the Dutch Republic was a self-governing state sheltering a variety of religious groups.

The Dutch Republic.

The princes of Orange resembled a ruling family in the Dutch Republic (sometimes incorrectly called Holland after the most populous of the seven provinces), but their powers paled next to those of local elites. Urban merchant and professional families known as regents controlled the towns and provinces. In the absence of a national bureaucracy, a single legal system, or a central court, each province governed itself and sent delegates to the one common institution, the States General, which carried out the wishes of the strongest individual provinces and their ruling families.

Well situated for maritime commerce, the Dutch Republic developed a thriving economy based on shipping and shipbuilding. Whereas elites in other countries focused on their landholdings, the Dutch looked for

Rembrandt van Rijn's✦ Depiction of Dutch Life
Rembrandt's painting known as *The Night Watch* (1642) shows members of a voluntary militia company in action. In fact, it is a group portrait, probably commissioned by the guardsmen themselves. Once responsible for defending the city, the militia companies had become eating and drinking clubs for prosperous businessmen. The painting demonstrates Rembrandt's interest in every aspect of daily life in the Dutch Republic. *Rijksmuseum, Amsterdam.*

investments in trade. After the Dutch gained independence, Amsterdam became the main European money market for two centuries. The city was also a primary commodities market and a chief supplier of arms—to allies, neutrals, and even enemies. Dutch entrepreneurs produced goods at lower prices than anyone else and marketed them more efficiently. Dutch merchants favored free trade in Europe because they could compete at an advantage. They controlled many

overseas markets thanks to their preeminence in seaborne commerce: by 1670, the Dutch commercial fleet was larger than the English, French, Spanish, Portuguese, and Austrian fleets combined.

Since the Dutch traded with anyone anywhere, it is perhaps not surprising that Dutch society tolerated more religious diversity than the other European states. One-third of the Dutch population remained Catholic, and the secular authorities allowed them to worship as they chose in private. Because Protestant sects could generally count

✦**Rembrandt van Rijn:** REHM brant van ryn

on toleration from local regents, they remained peaceful. The Dutch Republic also had a relatively large Jewish population because many Jews had settled there after being driven out of Spain and Portugal; from 1597, Jews could worship openly in their synagogues. This openness to various religions helped make the Dutch Republic one of Europe's chief intellectual and scientific centers in the seventeenth and eighteenth centuries.

Elizabeth I's Defense of English Protestantism

As the Dutch revolt unfolded, Philip II became increasingly infuriated with Elizabeth I (r. 1558–1603), who had succeeded her half-sister Mary Tudor as queen of England. Philip had been married to Mary and had enthusiastically seconded Mary's efforts to return England to Catholicism. When Mary died in 1558, Elizabeth rejected Philip's proposal of marriage and promptly brought Protestantism back to England. Eventually she provided funds and troops to the Dutch Protestant cause. As Elizabeth moved to solidify her personal power and the authority of the Anglican church (Church of England), she had to squash uprisings by Catholics in the north and at least two serious plots against her life. In the long run, however, her greater challenges came from the Calvinist Puritans and Philip II.

Puritanism and the Church of England. The **Puritans** were strict Calvinists who opposed all vestiges of Catholic ritual in the Church of England. After Elizabeth became queen, many Puritans returned from exile abroad, but Elizabeth resisted their demands for drastic changes in church ritual and governance. The Church of England's Thirty-Nine Articles of Religion, issued under her authority in 1563, incorporated elements of Catholic ritual along with Calvinist doctrines. Puritan ministers angrily denounced the Church of England's "popish attire and foolish disguising, . . . tithings, holy days, and a thousand more abominations." To accomplish their reforms, Puritans tried to undercut the crown-appointed bishops' authority by placing control of church administration in the hands of a local presbytery made up of the minister

and the elders of the congregation. Elizabeth rejected this Calvinist "presbyterianism."

The Puritans nonetheless steadily gained influence. Known for their emphasis on strict moral lives, the Puritans tried to close England's theaters and Sunday fairs. Every Puritan father—with the help of his wife—was to "make his house a little church" by teaching the children to read the Bible. At Puritan urging, a new translation of the Bible, known as the King James Bible after Elizabeth's successor, James I, was authorized in 1604. Believing themselves God's elect and England an "elect nation," the Puritans also pushed Elizabeth to help Protestants on the continent.

Queen Elizabeth I of England
The Anglican (Church of England) Prayerbook of 1569 included a handcolored print of Queen Elizabeth saying her prayers. As queen, Elizabeth was also official head of the Church of England (the scepter or sword at her feet symbolizes her power). She named bishops and made final decisions about every aspect of church governance. *Bridgeman Art Library.*

Triumph over Spain. Although enraged by Elizabeth's aid to the Dutch rebels, Philip II bided his time as long as Elizabeth remained unmarried and her Catholic cousin Mary Stuart, better known as Mary, Queen of Scots, stood next in line to inherit the English throne. In 1568, Scottish Calvinists forced Mary to abdicate the throne of Scotland in favor of her year-old son James (eventually James I of England), who was then raised as a Protestant. After her abdication, Mary spent nearly twenty years under house arrest in England, fomenting plots against Elizabeth. In 1587, when a letter from Mary offering her succession rights to Philip was discovered, Elizabeth overcame her reluctance to execute a fellow monarch and ordered Mary's beheading.

In response, Pope Sixtus V decided to subsidize a Catholic crusade under Philip's leadership against the heretical queen, "the English Jezebel." At the end of May 1588, Philip II sent his armada (Spanish for "fleet") of 130 ships from Lisbon toward the English Channel. The English scattered the Spanish Armada by sending blazing fire ships into its midst. A great gale then forced the Spanish to flee around Scotland. When the armada limped home in September, half the ships had been lost and thousands of sailors were dead or starving. Protestants throughout Europe rejoiced. In his play *King John* a few years later (1596), William Shakespeare wrote, "This England never did, nor never shall,/Lie at the proud foot of a conqueror." Philip and Catholic Spain suffered a crushing psychological blow. A Spanish monk lamented, "Almost the whole of Spain went into mourning."

By the time Philip II died in 1598, his great empire had begun to lose its luster. The costs of fighting the Dutch, the English, and the French had mounted, and an overbur-

Retreat of the Spanish Armada, 1588

dened peasantry could no longer pay the taxes required to meet rising expenses. In his novel *Don Quixote*◆ (1605), the Spanish writer Miguel de Cervantes captured the sadness of Spain's loss of grandeur. Cervantes himself had been wounded at Lepanto, been held captive in Algiers, and then served as a royal tax collector. His novel's hero, a minor nobleman, wants to understand "this thing they call reason of state," but he reads so many romances and books of chivalry that he loses his wits and wanders the countryside hoping to re-create the heroic deeds of times past. Don Quixote's futile adventures incarnated the thwarted ambitions of a declining military aristocracy.

England could never have defeated Spain in a head-to-head battle on land, but Elizabeth made the most of her limited means and consolidated the country's position as a Protestant power. In her early years, she held out the prospect of marriage to many political suitors; but in order to maintain her—and England's—independence, she never married. She cajoled Parliament with references to her female weaknesses, but she showed steely-eyed determination in protecting the monarchy's interests. Her chosen successor, James I (r. 1603–1625), came to the throne as king of both Scotland and England. Shakespeare's tragedies *Hamlet* (1601), *King Lear* (1605), and *Macbeth* (1606), written around the time of James's succession, might all be read as commentaries on the uncertainties faced by Elizabeth and James. But Elizabeth's story, unlike those of Shakespeare's tragedies, had a happy ending; she left James secure in a kingdom of growing weight in world politics.

The Clash of Faiths and Empires in Eastern Europe

In the east, the most contentious border divided Christian Europe from the Islamic realm of the Ottoman Turks. After their defeat at Lepanto in 1571, the Ottomans were down but far from out. They continued their attacks, seizing Venetian-held Cyprus in 1573. In the Balkans, the Turks allowed their Christian subjects to cling to the

◆**Don Quixote:** dahn kee HOH tee

Orthodox faith rather than forcibly converting them to Islam. They also tolerated many prosperous Jewish communities, which grew with the influx of Jews expelled from Spain.

The Muscovite tsars officially protected the Russian Orthodox church, which faced no competition within Russian lands. Building on the base laid by his grandfather Ivan III, Tsar Ivan IV (r. 1533–1584) stopped at nothing in his endeavor to make Muscovy the center of a mighty Russian empire. Given to unpredictable fits of rage, Ivan tortured priests, killed numerous *boyars* (nobles), and murdered his own son with an iron rod during a quarrel. His epithet "the Terrible" reflects not only the terror he unleashed but also the awesome impression he evoked. Cunning, intelligent, morbidly suspicious, and cruel, Ivan came to embody barbarism in the eyes of westerners. An English visitor wrote that Ivan's actions had bred "a general hatred, distreccion [distraction], fear and discontentment throw [throughout] his kingdom.... God has a great plague in store for this people." Such warnings did not keep away the many westerners drawn to Moscow by opportunities to buy furs and sell western cloth and military hardware.

Ivan brought the entire Volga valley under Muscovite control and initiated Russian expansion eastward into Siberia. In 1558, he struck out to the west, vainly attempting to seize the decaying state of the German crusader (Teutonic) knights in present-day Estonia and Latvia to provide Russia direct access to the Baltic Sea. Two formidable foes blocked Ivan's plans for expansion: Sweden (which then included much of present-day Finland) and Poland-Lithuania. Their rulers hoped to annex the eastern Baltic provinces themselves. Poland and the grand duchy of Lithuania united into a single commonwealth in 1569 and controlled territory stretching from the Baltic Sea to deep within present-day Ukraine and Belarus.♦ It was the largest state lying wholly within the boundaries of Europe.

Poland-Lithuania, like the Dutch Republic, constituted one of the great exceptions to the general trend in early modern Europe

♦**Belarus:** bee luh ROOS

toward greater monarchical authority; the Polish and Lithuanian nobles elected their king and severely circumscribed his authority. Noble converts to Lutheranism or Calvinism feared religious persecution by the Catholic majority, so the Polish-Lithuanian nobility insisted that their kings accept the principle of religious toleration as a prerequisite for election. The numerous Jewish communities prospered under the protection of the king and nobles.

Poland-Lithuania threatened the rule of Ivan's successors in Russia. After Ivan IV died in 1584, a terrible period of chaos known as the Time of Troubles ensued, during which the king of Poland-Lithuania tried to put his son on the Russian throne. In 1613, an army of nobles, townspeople, and peasants finally drove out the intruders and put on the throne a nobleman, Michael Romanov (r. 1613–1645), who established an enduring new dynasty. With the return of peace, Muscovite Russia resumed the process of state building.

Russia, Poland-Lithuania, and Sweden in the Late 1500s

> **Review:** In what ways did the power of states depend on unity in religion?

❖ The Thirty Years' War and the Balance of Power, 1618–1648

Although the eastern states managed to avoid civil wars over religion, the rest of Europe was drawn into the final and most deadly of the wars of religion, the Thirty Years' War. It began in 1618 with conflicts between Catholics and Protestants within the Holy Roman Empire and eventually involved most European states. By its end in 1648, many central European lands lay in ruins and the balance of power had shifted away from the Habsburg powers—Spain and Austria—toward France, England, and the Dutch Republic. Constant warfare created immediate turmoil, but it also fostered the growth of armies and bureaucracies; out of the carnage would emerge centralized and powerful states that made increasing demands on ordinary people.

Origins and Course of the War

The fighting that devastated central Europe had its origins in a combination of political weakness, ethnic competition, and religious conflict. The Austrian Habsburgs officially ruled over the huge Holy Roman Empire, which comprised eight major ethnic groups. The emperor and four of the seven electors who chose him were Catholic; the other three electors were Protestants. The Peace of Augsburg of 1555 was supposed to maintain the balance between Catholics and Lutherans, but it had no mechanism for resolving conflicts; tensions rose as the new Catholic religious order, the Jesuits, won many Lutheran cities back to Catholicism and as Calvinism, unrecognized under the Peace, made inroads into Lutheran areas. By 1613, two of the three Protestant electors had become Calvinists.

War first broke out in Bohemia after the defenestration of Prague in May 1618. The Austrian Habsburgs held not only the imperial crown of the Holy Roman Empire but also a collection of separately administered royal crowns, of which Bohemia was one. When the Catholic Habsburg heir Archduke Ferdinand was crowned king of Bohemia in 1617, he began to curtail the religious freedom previously granted to Protestants. After the defenestration, the Czechs, the largest ethnic group in Bohemia, established a Protestant assembly to spearhead resistance. A year later, when Ferdinand was elected emperor (as Ferdinand II, r. 1619–1637), the rebellious Bohemians deposed him and chose in his place the young Calvinist Frederick V of the Palatinate (r. 1616–1623). A quick series of clashes ended in 1620 when the imperial armies defeated the outmanned Czechs at the battle of White Mountain, near Prague. Like the martyrdom of the religious reformer Jan Hus in 1415, White Mountain

became an enduring symbol of the Czechs' desire for self-determination. They would not gain their independence until 1918.

White Mountain did not end the war. Private mercenary armies (armies for hire) began to form during the fighting, and the emperor had virtually no control over them. The meteoric rise of one commander, Albrecht von Wallenstein (1583–1634), showed how political ambition could trump religious conviction. A Czech Protestant by birth, Wallenstein offered in 1625 to raise an army for the Catholic emperor and soon had in his employ 125,000 soldiers, who occupied and plundered much of Protestant Germany with the emperor's approval.

The Lutheran king of Denmark Christian IV (r. 1596–1648) responded by invading northern Germany to protect the Protestants and to extend his own influence. Despite Dutch and English encouragement, Christian lacked adequate military support, and Wallenstein's forces defeated him. Emboldened by his general's victories, Ferdinand issued the Edict of Restitution in 1629, which outlawed Calvinism in the empire and reclaimed Catholic church properties confiscated by the Lutherans.

With Protestant interests in serious jeopardy, Gustavus Adolphus (r. 1611–1632) of Sweden marched into Germany in 1630. Declaring his support for the Protestant cause, he also intended to gain control over trade in northern Europe. His highly trained army of some 100,000 soldiers made Sweden, with a population of only one million, the supreme power of northern Europe. Now the primacy of political motives became obvious: the Catholic French government under the leadership of Cardinal Richelieu♦ offered to subsidize the Lutheran Gustavus. Richelieu hoped to block Spanish intervention in the war and win influence and perhaps territory in the Holy Roman Empire. The agreement between the Lutheran and Catholic powers to fight the Catholic Habsburgs showed that state interests now outweighed all other considerations.

Gustavus defeated the imperial army and occupied the Catholic parts of southern Germany before he was killed at the battle of

---

♦**Richelieu:** RIH shuh loo

Lützen in 1632. Once again the tide turned, but this time it swept Wallenstein with it. Because Wallenstein was rumored to be negotiating with Protestant powers, Ferdinand dismissed his general and had his henchmen assassinate him.

France openly joined the fray in 1635 by declaring war on Spain and soon after forged an alliance with the Calvinist Dutch to aid them in their struggle for independence from Spain. The French king Louis XIII (r. 1610–1643) and his chief minister Richelieu (1585–1642) had hoped to profit from the troubles of Spain in the Netherlands and from the conflicts between the Austrian emperor and his Protestant subjects. Religion took a backseat as the two Catholic powers France and Spain pummeled each other. The Swedes kept up their pressure in Germany, the Dutch attacked the Spanish fleet, and a series of internal revolts shook the cash-strapped Spanish crown. In 1640, peasants in the rich northeastern province of Catalonia rebelled, overrunning Barcelona and killing the viceroy; the Catalans resented government confiscation of their crops and demands that they house and feed soldiers on their way to the French frontier. The Portuguese revolted in 1640 and proclaimed independence like the Dutch. In 1643, the Spanish

suffered their first major defeat at French hands. Although the Spanish were forced to concede independence to Portugal (part of Spain only since 1580), they eventually suppressed the Catalan revolt.

France too faced exhaustion after years of rising taxes and recurrent revolts. In 1642 Richelieu died. Louis XIII followed him a few months later and was succeeded by his five-year-old son Louis XIV. With an Austrian queen mother serving as regent and an Italian cardinal, Mazarin, providing advice, French politics once again moved into a period of instability, rumor, and crisis. All sides were ready for peace.

The Effects of Constant Fighting

When peace negotiations began in the 1640s, they did not come a moment too soon for the ordinary people of Europe. Some towns had faced up to ten or eleven prolonged sieges during the fighting. In 1648, as negotiations dragged on, a Swedish army sacked the rich cultural capital Prague, plundered its churches and castles, and effectively eliminated it as a center of culture and learning.

Even worse suffering took place in the countryside. One of the earliest German novels, *The Adventures of a Simpleton* (1669)

The Violence of the Thirty Years' War
The French artist Jacques Collot produced this engraving of the Thirty Years' War as part of a series called *The Miseries and Misfortunes of War* (1633). The actions depicted resemble those in Hans Grimmelshausen's novel *The Adventures of a Simpleton*. *The Granger Collection.*

The Horrors of the Thirty Years' War

Hans Grimmelshausen experienced the Thirty Years' War firsthand and then wrote about it in his novel, The Adventures of a Simpleton *(published in 1669). He had been a Lutheran schoolboy when soldiers from an unidentified army looted his town. Later he served as a musketeer in the Catholic imperial armies and converted to Catholicism. In the novel, he writes from the point of view of a "simpleton," a naive peasant who does not understand what is happening around him as a group of cavalrymen ransack the village.*

What they did not intend to take along they broke and spoiled. Some ran their swords into the hay and straw, as if there hadn't been hogs enough to stick. Some shook the feathers out of beds and put bacon slabs, hams, and other stuff in the ticking, as if they might sleep better on these. Others knocked down the hearth and broke the windows, as if announcing an everlasting summer. They flattened out copper and pewter dishes and baled the ruined goods. They burned up bedsteads, tables, chairs, and benches, though there were yards of dry firewood outside the kitchen. Jars and crocks, pots and casseroles all were broken, either because they preferred their meat broiled or because they thought they'd eat only one meal with us. In the barn, the hired girl was handled so roughly that she was unable to walk away, I am ashamed to report. They stretched the hired man out flat on the ground, stuck a wooden wedge in his mouth to keep it open, and emptied a milk bucket full of stinking manure drippings down his throat; they called it a Swedish cocktail. He didn't relish it and made a very wry face.... Then they used thumbscrews, which they cleverly made out of their pistols, to torture the peasants, as if they wanted to burn witches. Though he had confessed to nothing as yet, they put one of the captured hayseeds in the bake-oven and lighted a fire in it. They put a rope around someone else's head and tightened it like a tourniquet until blood came out of his mouth, nose, and ears. In short, every soldier had his favorite method of making life miserable for peasants, and every peasant had his own misery.

Source: *The Adventures of Simplicius Simpliccissimus*, 2nd ed. Trans. George Schulz-Behrend (Columbia, S.C.: Camden House, 1993), 6–7.

by Hans Grimmelshausen,◆ recounts the horror of the war in detail (see excerpt above). In one scene, the boy Simplicius has to watch while unidentified enemy cavalrymen ransack the house; rape the maid, his mother, and his sister; and hold the feet of his father to the fire until he tells where he hid his gold and jewels. Peasants fled their villages, which were often burned down. At times, desperate peasants revolted and attacked nearby castles and monasteries. War and intermittent outbreaks of plague cost some German towns one-third or more of their population. One-third of the inhabitants of Bohemia also perished.

Soldiers did not fare all that much better. An Englishman who fought for the Dutch army in 1633 described how he slept on the wet ground, got his boots full of water, and "at peep of day looked like a drowned ratt." Governments increasingly short of funds often failed to pay the troops, and frequent mutinies, looting, and pillaging resulted. Armies attracted all sorts of displaced people desperately in need of provisions. In the last year of the Thirty Years' War, the Imperial-Bavarian Army had 40,000 men entitled to draw rations—and more than 100,000 wives, prostitutes, servants, children, maids, and other camp followers forced to scrounge for their own food. The result was scenes like those witnessed by Simplicius.

Although foreign mercenaries still predominated in many armies, rulers began to recruit more of their own subjects. Volunteers proved easiest to find in hard times, when the threat of starvation induced men to accept the bonus offered for signing up. A Venetian general

◆**Grimmelshausen:** GRIHM uhls how zuhn

explained the motives for enlisting: "To escape from being craftsmen [or] working in a shop; to avoid a criminal sentence; to see new things; to pursue honour (though these are very few)... all in the hope of having enough to live on and a bit over for shoes, or some other trifle."

The Peace of Westphalia, 1648

The comprehensive settlement provided by the Peace of Westphalia♦—named after the German province where negotiations took place—would serve as a model for resolving conflict among warring European states.

♦**Westphalia:** wehst FAYL yuh

For the first time, a diplomatic congress addressed international disputes, and the signatories to the treaties guaranteed the resulting settlement. A method still in use, the congress was the first to bring *all* parties together, rather than two or three at a time.

The Winners and Losers. France and Sweden gained most from the Peace of Westphalia. Although France and Spain continued fighting until 1659, France acquired parts of Alsace and replaced Spain as the prevailing power on the continent. Baltic conflicts would not be resolved until 1661, but Sweden took several northern territories from the Holy Roman Empire (Map 16.3).

MAP 16.3 The Thirty Years' War and the Peace of Westphalia, 1648

The Thirty Years' War involved many of the major continental European powers. The arrows marking invasion routes show that most of the fighting took place in central Europe in the lands of the Holy Roman Empire. The German states and Bohemia sustained the greatest damage during the fighting. None of the combatants emerged unscathed because even ultimate winners such as Sweden and France depleted their resources of men and money.

The Arts and State Power
Diego Velázquez painted King Philip IV of Spain and many members of his court. This painting of 1634–1635 shows Philip on horseback. In the seventeenth century, many rulers hired court painters to embellish the image of royal majesty. Philip IV commissioned this painting for his new palace called Buen Retiro.

The Habsburgs lost the most. The Spanish Habsburgs recognized Dutch independence after eighty years of war. The Swiss Confederation and the German princes demanded autonomy from the Austrian Habsburg rulers of the Holy Roman Empire. Each German prince gained the right to establish Lutheranism, Catholicism, or Calvinism in his state, a right denied to Calvinist rulers by the Peace of Augsburg in 1555. The independence ceded to German princes sustained political divisions that would remain until the nineteenth century and prepared the way for the emergence of a new power, the Hohenzollern♦ Elector of Brandenburg, who increased his territories and developed a small but effective standing army. After losing considerable territory in

♦**Hohenzollern:** hoh uhn ZOH lurn

the west, the Austrian Habsburgs turned eastward to concentrate on restoring Catholicism to Bohemia and wresting Hungary from the Turks.

The Peace of Westphalia permanently settled the distributions of the main religions in the Holy Roman Empire: Lutheranism would dominate in the north, Calvinism in the area of the Rhine River, and Catholicism in the south. Most of the territorial changes in Europe remained intact until the nineteenth century. In the future, international warfare would be undertaken for reasons of national security, commercial ambition, or dynastic pride rather than to enforce religious uniformity. As the politiques of the late sixteenth century had hoped, state interests now outweighed motivations of faith in political affairs.

Growth of State Authority.
Warfare increased the reach of states: as the size of armies increased, governments needed more men, more money, and more supervisory officials. Most armies in the 1550s had fewer than 50,000 men, but Gustavus Adolphus had 100,000 men under arms in 1631. In France the rate of land tax paid by peasants doubled in the eight years after France joined the war. In addition to raising taxes, governments deliberately depreciated the value of the currency, which often resulted in inflation and soaring prices. Rulers also sold new offices and manipulated the embryonic stock and bond markets. When all else failed, they declared bankruptcy. The Spanish government, for example, did so three times in the first half of the seventeenth century. From Portugal to Muscovy, ordinary people resisted new taxes by forming makeshift armies and battling royal forces. With their colorful banners, unlikely leaders, strange names (the Nu-Pieds, or "Barefooted," in

France, for instance), and crude weapons, the rebels usually proved no match for state armies, but they did keep officials worried and troops occupied.

As the demand for soldiers and for the money to supply them rose, the number of state employees multiplied, paperwork proliferated, and appointment to office began to depend on university education in the law. Monarchs relied on advisers who now took on the role of modern prime ministers. Axel Oxenstierna,◆ for example, played a central part in Swedish governments between 1611 and 1654; continuity in Swedish affairs, especially after the death of Gustavus Adolphus, largely depended on him. As Louis XIII's chief minister, Richelieu arranged support for the Lutheran Gustavus even though Richelieu was a cardinal of the Catholic church. His priority was ***raison d'état***◆ ("reason of state"), that is, the state's interest above all else. He silenced Protestants within France because they had become too independent and crushed noble and popular resistance to Louis's policies. He set up intendants—delegates from the king's council dispatched to the provinces—to oversee police, army, and financial affairs.

To justify the growth of state authority and the expansion of government bureaucracies, rulers carefully cultivated their royal images. (See The Arts and State Power, left.) James I of England explicitly argued that he ruled by divine right and was accountable only to God: "The state of monarchy is the supremest thing on earth; for kings are not only God's lieutenant on earth, but even by God himself they are called gods." He advised his son to maintain a manly appearance (his own well-known homosexual liaisons did not make him seem less manly to his subjects): "Eschew to be effeminate in your clothes, in perfuming, preening, or such like, and fail never in time of wars to be galliardest and bravest, both in clothes and countenance." Clothes counted for so much that most rulers regulated who could wear which kinds of cloth and decoration, reserving the richest and rarest such as ermine and gold for themselves.

◆**Axel Oxenstierna:** AK suhl OOK sehn stehr nah
◆**raison d'état:** ray zohn DAY TAH

Just as soldiers had to learn new drills for combat, courtiers had to learn to follow precise rituals at court. In Spain, court regulations set the wages, duties, and ceremonial functions of every official. Hundreds, even thousands, of people made up such a court. The court of Philip IV (r. 1621–1665), for example, numbered seventeen hundred. In the 1630s Philip built a new palace near Madrid. There the courtiers lived amid extensive parks and formal gardens, artificial ponds and grottoes, an iron aviary (which led some critics to call the whole thing a chicken coop), a wild animal cage, a courtyard for bullfights, and rooms filled with sculptures and paintings. State funerals, public festivities, and court display, like the acquisition of art and the building of sumptuous palaces, served to underline the power and glory of the ruler.

Review: Why did a war fought over religious differences result in stronger states?

❖ Economic Crisis and Realignment

The devastation caused by the Thirty Years' War deepened an economic crisis that was already under way. After a century of rising prices, caused partly by massive transfers of gold and silver from the New World and partly by population growth, in the early 1600s prices began to level off and even to drop, and in most places population growth slowed. With fewer goods being produced, international trade fell into recession. Agricultural yields also declined. Just when states attempted to field ever-expanding standing armies, peasants and townspeople alike were less able to pay the escalating taxes needed to finance the wars. Famine and disease trailed grimly behind economic crisis and war, in some areas causing large-scale uprisings and revolts. Behind the scenes, the economic balance of power gradually shifted as northwestern Europe began to dominate international trade and broke the stranglehold of Spain and Portugal in the New World.

From Growth to Recession

Population grew and prices rose in the second half of the sixteenth century. Even though religious and political turbulence led to population decline in some cities, such as war-torn Antwerp, overall rates of growth remained impressive: in the sixteenth century, parts of Spain doubled in population and England's population grew by 70 percent. The supply of precious metals swelled too. Improvements in mining techniques in central Europe raised the output of silver and copper mines, and in the 1540s new silver mines had been discovered in Mexico and Peru. Spanish gold imports peaked in the 1550s, silver in the 1590s. (See "Taking Measure," below.) This flood of precious metals combined with population growth to fuel an astounding inflation in food prices in western Europe—400 percent in the sixteenth century—and a more moderate rise in the cost of manufactured goods. Wages rose much more slowly, at about half the rate of the increase in food prices. Governments always overspent revenues and by the end of the century most of Europe's rulers faced deep deficits.

Recession did not strike everywhere at the same time, but the warning signs were unmistakable. From the Baltic to the East Indies, foreign trade slumped as war and an uncertain money supply made business riskier. After 1625, silver imports to Spain declined, in part because so many of the native Americans who worked in Spanish colonial mines died from disease and in part because the ready supply of precious metals was progressively exhausted. Textile production fell in many countries and in some places nearly collapsed, largely because of decreased demand and a shrinking labor force. Even the relatively limited trade in African slaves stagnated, though its growth would resume after 1650 and skyrocket after 1700. African slaves were first transported to the new colony of Virginia in 1619, foreshadowing a major transformation of economic life in the New World colonies.

Demographic slowdown also signaled economic trouble. Overall, Europe's population may actually have declined, from 85 million in 1550 to 80 million in 1650. In the Mediterranean, growth apparently stopped in the 1570s. The most sudden reversal occurred in central Europe as a result of the Thirty Years' War: one-fourth of the inhabitants of the Holy Roman Empire perished in the 1630s and 1640s. The population continued to increase only in England and Wales, the Dutch Republic and the Spanish Netherlands, and Scandinavia.

Where the population stagnated or declined, agricultural prices dropped because of less demand, and farmers who produced for the market suffered. The price of grain fell most precipitously, causing many farmers to convert grain-growing land to pasture or vineyards.

TAKING MEASURE

The Rise and Fall of Silver Imports to Spain, 1550–1660
Gold and silver from the New World enabled the king of Spain to pursue aggressive policies in Europe and around the world. At what point did silver imports reach their highest level? Was the fall in silver imports precipitous or gradual? What can we conclude about the resources available to the Spanish king? *From Earl J. Hamilton,* American Revolution and the Price Revolution in Spain, 1501–1650 *(Cambridge, MA: Harvard University Press, 1934).*

Interest in improvement of the land diminished. In some places, peasants abandoned their villages and left land to waste, as had happened during the plague epidemic of the late fourteenth century. The only country that emerged unscathed from this downturn was the Dutch Republic, principally because it had long excelled in agricultural innovation. Inhabiting Europe's most densely populated area, the Dutch developed systems of field drainage, crop rotation, and animal husbandry that provided high yields of grain for both people and animals. Their foreign trade, textile industry, crop production, and population all grew. After the Dutch, the English fared best; unlike the Spanish, the English never depended on New World gold and silver, and unlike most continental European countries, England escaped the direct impact of the Thirty Years' War.

Historians have long disagreed about the causes of the early-seventeenth-century recession. Some cite the inability of agriculture to support a growing population by the end of the sixteenth century; others blame the Thirty Years' War, the states' demands for more taxes, the irregularities in money supply resulting from rudimentary banking practices, or the waste caused by middle-class expenditures in the desire to emulate the nobility. To this list of causes, recent researchers have added climatic changes. (See "New Sources, New Perspectives," page 600.) Cold winters and wet summers meant bad harvests, and these natural disasters ushered in a host of social catastrophes. When the harvest was bad, prices shot back up and many could not afford to feed themselves.

Consequences for Daily Life

The recession of the early 1600s had both short-term and long-term effects. In the short term it aggravated the threat of food shortages and increased the outbreaks of famine and disease. In the long term it deepened the division between prosperous and poor peasants and fostered the development of a new pattern of late marriages and smaller families.

Famine and Disease. When grain harvests fell short, peasants immediately suffered because, outside of England and the Dutch

Republic, grain had replaced more expensive meat as the essential staple of most Europeans' diets. The average adult European now ate more than four hundred pounds of grain per year. Peasants lived on bread, soup with a little fat or oil, peas or lentils, garden vegetables in season, and only occasionally a piece of meat or fish. Usually the adverse years differed from place to place, but from 1594 to 1597 most of Europe suffered from shortages; the resulting famine triggered revolts from

The Life of the Poor
This mid-seventeenth-century painting by the Dutch artist Adriaen Pietersz van de Venne depicts the poor peasant weighed down by his wife and child. An empty food bowl signifies their hunger. In retrospect, this painting seems unfair to the wife of the family; she is shown in clothes that are not nearly as tattered as her husband's and is portrayed entirely as a burden, rather than as a help in getting by in hard times. In reality, many poor men abandoned their homes in search of work, leaving their wives behind to cope with hungry children and what remained of the family farm. *Allen Memorial Art Museum, Oberlin College, Oberlin, Ohio, Mrs. F. F. Prentiss Fund, 1960.*

NEW SOURCES, NEW PERSPECTIVES

Tree Rings and the Little Ice Age

Global cooling helped bring about the economic crisis of the seventeenth century. Glaciers advanced, average temperatures fell, and winters were often exceptionally severe. Canals and rivers essential to markets froze over. Great storms disrupted ocean traffic (one storm changed the escape route of the Spanish Armada). Even in the valleys far from the mountain glaciers, cooler weather meant lower crop yields, which quickly translated into hunger and greater susceptibility to disease, leading in turn to population decline. Some historians of climate refer to the entire period 1600–1850 as the little ice age because glaciers advanced during this time and retreated only after 1850; others argue for the period 1550–1700 as the coldest, but either time frame includes the seventeenth century. Since systematic records of European temperatures were kept only from the 1700s onward, how do historians know that the weather was cooler? Given the current debates about global warming, how can we sift through the evidence to come up with a reliable interpretation?

Information about climate comes from various sources. The advance of glaciers can be seen in letters complaining to the authorities. In 1601, for example, panic-stricken villagers in Savoy (in the French Alps) wrote, "We are terrified of the glaciers . . .

which are moving forward all the time and have just buried two of our villages." Yearly temperature fluctuations can be determined from the dates of wine harvests; growers harvested their grapes earliest when the weather was warmest and latest when it was coolest. Scientists study ice cores taken from Greenland to determine temperature variations; such studies seem to indicate that the coolest times were the periods 1160–1300; the 1600s; and 1820–1850. The period 1730–1800 appears to have been warmer. Recently, scientists have developed techniques for sampling corals in the tropics and sediments on oceanic shelves.

But the most striking are data gathered from tree rings (the science is called dendrochronology or dendroclimatology). Timber samples have been taken from very old oak trees and also from ancient beams in buildings and archaeological digs and from logs left long undisturbed in northern bogs and riverbeds. In cold summers, trees lay down thinner growth rings; in warm ones, thicker rings. Information about tree rings confirms the conclusions drawn from wine harvest and ice core samples: the seventeenth century was relatively cold. Recent tree ring studies have shown that some of the coldest summers were caused by volcanic eruptions; according to a study of more

Ireland to Muscovy. To head off social disorder, the English government drew up a new Poor Law in 1597 that required each community to support its poor. Many other governments also increased relief efforts.

Most people, however, did not respond to their dismal circumstances by rebelling or mounting insurrections. They simply left their huts and hovels and took to the road in search of food and charity. Overwhelmed officials recorded pitiful tales of suffering. Women and children died while waiting in line for food at convents or churches. Husbands left their wives and families to search

for better conditions in other parishes or even other countries. Those left behind might be reduced to eating chestnuts, roots, bark, and grass. In eastern France in 1637, a witness reported, "The roads were paved with people. . . . Finally it came to cannibalism." Eventually compassion gave way to fear as these hungry vagabonds, who sometimes banded together to beg for bread, became more aggressive, occasionally threatening to burn a barn if they were not given food.

Successive bad harvests led to malnutrition, which weakened people and made them more susceptible to such epidemic

The Frozen Thames
This painting by Abraham Hondius of the frozen Thames River in London dates to 1677. In the 1670s and 1680s the Thames froze several times. Hondius himself depicted another such view in 1684. Diarists recorded that shopkeepers even set up their stalls on the ice. In other words, the expected routines of daily life changed during the cooling down of the seventeenth century. Contemporaries were shocked enough by the changes to record them for posterity. *Museum of London.*

than one hundred sites in North America and Europe, the five coldest summers in the past four hundred years were in 1601, 1641, 1669, 1699, and 1912 (four out of five in the seventeenth century), and all but the summer of 1699 came in years following recorded eruptions.

QUESTIONS TO CONSIDER

1. What were the historical consequences of global cooling in the seventeenth century?

2. Why would trees be especially valuable sources of information about climate?

FURTHER READING

Galloway, Patrick R. "Long-Term Fluctuations in Climate and Population in the Preindustrial Era." *Population and Development Review* 12 (1986): 1–24.

Lamb, H. H. *Climate, History and the Modern World*, 2nd ed. 1995.

diseases as the plague, typhoid fever, typhus, dysentery, smallpox, and influenza. Disease did not spare the rich, although many epidemics hit the poor hardest. The plague was feared most: in one year it could cause the death of up to half of a town's or village's population, and it struck with no discernible pattern. Nearly 5 percent of France's entire population died just in the plague of 1628–1632.

The Changing Status of the Peasantry. Economic crisis heightened the contrast between prosperity and poverty. Peasants faced many obligations, including rent and various fees for inheriting or selling land and tolls for using mills, wine presses, or ovens. States collected direct taxes on land and sales taxes on such consumer goods as salt, an essential preservative. Protestant and Catholic churches alike exacted a **tithe**◆ (a tax equivalent to one-tenth of the parishioner's annual income); often the clergy took their tithe in the form of crops and collected it directly during the harvest. Any reversal of fortune could force peasants into the home-

◆**tithe:** tyth

The Figure Explained:

Being a Diffection of the WOMB, with the ufual manner how the CHILD lies therein near the time of its Birth.

B B. The inner parts of the *Chorion* extended and branched out.

C. The *Amnios* extended.

D D. The Membrane of the Womb extended and branched.

E. The Flefhy fubftance call'd the *Cake* or *Placenta*, which nourifhes the Infant, it is full of Veffels.

F. The Veffels appointed for the Navel ftring.

G. The Navel ftring carrying nourifhment from the *Placenta* to the Navel.

H H H. The manner how the Infant lieth in the Womb near the time of its Birth.

I. The Navel ftring how it enters into the Navel.

The *Midwives Book* (1671)
The English woman Jane Sharp wrote the first book on midwifery by a woman. She endeavored to provide as much scientific information about the female body as was available at the time. *British Library.*

less world of vagrants and beggars, who numbered as much as 1 to 2 percent of the total population.

In England, the Dutch Republic, northern France, and northwestern Germany, the peasantry was disappearing: improvements gave some peasants the means to become farmers who rented substantial holdings, produced for the market, and in good times enjoyed relative comfort and higher status. Those who could not afford to plant new crops such as maize (American corn) or buckwheat or to use techniques that ensured higher yields became simple laborers with little or no land of their own. One-half to four-fifths of the peasants did not have enough land to support a family. They descended deeper into debt during difficult times and often lost their land to wealthier farmers or to city officials intent on developing rural estates.

As the recession deepened, women lost some of their economic opportunities. Widows who had been able to take over their late husbands' trade now found themselves excluded by the urban guilds or limited to short tenures. Many women went into domestic service until they married, some for their entire lives. When town governments began to fear the effects of increased mobility from country to town and town to town, they carefully regulated the work of female servants, requiring women to stay in their positions unless they could prove mistreatment by a master.

Effects on Marriage and Childbearing. Demographic historians have shown that European families reacted almost immediately to economic crisis. During bad harvests they postponed marriages and had fewer children. When hard times passed, more people married and had more children. But even in the best of times, one-fifth to one-quarter of all children died in their first year, and half died before age twenty. In 1636, an Englishman described his grief when his twenty-one-month-old son died: "We both found the sorrow for the loss of this child, on whom we had bestowed so much care and affection . . . far to surpass our grief for the decease of his three elder brothers, who dying almost as soon as they were born, were not so endeared to us as this [one] was."

Childbirth still carried great risks for women, about 10 percent of whom died in the process. Even in the richest and most enlightened homes, childbirth often occasioned an atmosphere of panic. To allay their fears, women sometimes depended on magic stones and special pilgrimages and prayers. Midwives delivered most babies; physicians were scarce, and even if they did attend a birth they were generally less helpful than the midwife. The Englishwoman Alice Thornton described in her diary how a doctor bled her to prevent a miscarriage after a fall (bloodletting, often by the application of leeches, was a common medical treatment); her son died anyway in a breech birth that almost killed her too.

It might be assumed that families would have more children to compensate for high death rates, but beginning in the early seventeenth century and continuing until the end of the eighteenth, families in all ranks of society started to limit the number of children. Because methods of contraception were not widely known, they did this for the most part by marrying later; the average age at marriage during the seventeenth century rose from the early twenties to the late twenties. The average family had about four children. Poorer families seem to have had fewer children, wealthier ones more. Peasant couples, especially in eastern and southeastern Europe, had more children than urban couples because cultivation still required intensive manual labor—and having children was the most economical means of securing enough laborers.

The consequences of late marriage were profound. Young men and women were expected to put off marriage (and sexual intercourse) until their mid to late twenties—if they were among the lucky 50 percent who lived that long and not among the 10 percent who never married. Because both the Reformation and the Counter-Reformation had stressed sexual fidelity and abstinence before marriage, the number of births out of wedlock was relatively small (2–5 percent of births); premarital intercourse was generally tolerated only after a couple had announced their engagement.

The Economic Balance of Power

Just as the recession produced winners and losers among ordinary people, so too it created winners and losers among the competing states of Europe. The economies of southern Europe declined, whereas those of the northwest emerged stronger. Competition in the New World reflected and reinforced

this shift as the English, Dutch, and French rushed to establish trading outposts and permanent settlements to compete with the Spanish and Portuguese.

Regional Differences.   The crisis of the seventeenth century ended the dominance of Mediterranean economies, which had endured since the time of the Greeks and Romans, and ushered in the new powers of northwestern Europe with their growing Atlantic economies. With expanding populations and geographical positions that promoted Atlantic trade, England and the Dutch Republic vied with France to become the leading mercantile powers. Northern Italian industries were eclipsed; Spanish commerce with the New World dropped. Amsterdam replaced Seville, Venice, Genoa, and Antwerp as the center of European trade and commerce. The plague also had differing effects. Whereas central Europe and the Mediterranean countries took generations to recover from its ravages, northwestern Europe quickly replaced its lost population, no doubt because this area's people had suffered less from the effects of the Thirty Years' War and from the malnutrition related to the economic crisis.

All but the remnants of serfdom had disappeared in western Europe, yet in eastern Europe nobles reinforced their dominance over peasants, and the burden of serfdom increased. The price rise of the sixteenth century prompted Polish and eastern German nobles to increase their holdings and step up their production of grain for western markets. To raise production, they demanded more rent and dues from their peasants, whom the government decreed must stay in their villages. Although noble landlords lost income in the economic downturn of the first half of the seventeenth century, their peasants gained nothing. Those who were already dependent became serfs—completely tied to the land. A local official might complain of "this barbaric and as it were Egyptian servitude," but he had no power to fight the nobles. In Muscovy the complete enserfment of the peasantry would eventually be recognized in the Code of Laws in 1649. Although enserfment produced short-term profits for landlords, in the long run it

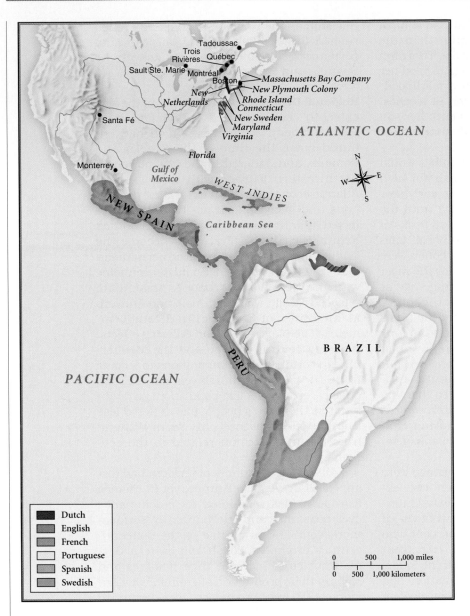

MAP 16.4 European Colonization of the Americas, c. 1640
Europeans established themselves first in coastal areas. The English, French, and Dutch set up most of their colonies in the Caribbean and North America because the Spanish and Portuguese had already colonized the easily accessible regions in South America. Vast inland areas still remained unexplored and uncolonized in 1640.

petition as a way of increasing national wealth. To this end, they chartered private joint-stock companies to enrich investors by importing fish, furs, tobacco, and precious metals, if they could be found, and to develop new markets for European products. Because Spain and Portugal had divided among themselves the rich spoils of South America, other prospective colonizers had to carve niches in seemingly less hospitable places, especially North America and the Caribbean (Map 16.4). Eventually the English, French, and Dutch would dominate commerce with these colonies.

In establishing permanent colonies, the Europeans created whole new communities across the Atlantic. Careful plans often fell afoul of the hazards of transatlantic shipping, however. Originally, the warm climate of Virginia made it an attractive destination for the Pilgrims, a small English sect that, unlike the Puritans, attempted to separate from the Church of England. But the *Mayflower*, which had sailed for Virginia with Pilgrim emigrants, landed far to the north in Massachusetts, where in 1620 the settlers founded New Plymouth Colony. As the religious situation for English Puritans worsened, wealthier people became willing to emigrate, and in 1629 a prominent group of Puritans incorporated themselves as the Massachusetts Bay Company. They founded a virtually self-governing colony headquartered in Boston.

Colonization in North America grew steadily. By the 1640s, the British North American colonies had more than fifty thousand people—not including the Indians, whose numbers had been decimated in epi-

retarded economic development in eastern Europe and kept most of the population in a stranglehold of illiteracy and hardship.

Competition in the New World. Many European states, including Sweden and Denmark, rushed to join the colonial comdemics and wars—and the foundations of representative government in locally chosen colonial assemblies. By contrast, French Canada had only about three thousand European inhabitants by 1640. Because the French government refused to let Protestants emigrate from France and establish a foothold in the New World, it denied itself a ready population for the settling of permanent colonies abroad. Both England and France turned their attention to the Caribbean in the 1620s and 1630s when they occupied the islands of the West Indies after driving off the native Caribs. These islands would prove ideal for a plantation economy of tobacco and sugarcane.

Some colonists justified their mission by promising to convert the native population to Christianity. As the English colonizer John Smith told his followers in Virginia, "The growing provinces addeth to the King's Crown; but the reducing heathen people to civility and true religion bringeth honour to the King of Heaven." Catholic France and Spain were more successful, however, than Protestant England in their efforts to convert American natives. Protestantism did not mesh well with native American cultures because it demanded an individual conversion experience based on a Christian notion of sin. Catholicism, in contrast, stressed shared rituals, which were more accessible to the native populations.

Spain did not stand still while the British and French moved into North America and the Caribbean. Even while developing silver mines in Mexico and South America with compulsory Indian labor, the Spanish explored the Pacific coast up to northern California and pushed as far north as New Mexico. On the other side of the world, in the Philippines, they competed with local Muslim rulers and indigenous tribal leaders to extend their control. Catholic missionaries printed tracts in Spanish and the island's native Tagalog and established a university in 1611. Spanish officials worked closely with the missionaries to rule over a colony composed of indigenous peoples, Spaniards, and some Chinese merchants. By 1600 they had gained control of much of the area.

> **Review:** What were the consequences of economic recession in the early 1600s?

"Savages" of the New World

The half-dressed savage appears much like a noble Italian in Paolo Farinati's 1595 painting *America;* he holds a crucifix in his right hand, signifying his conversion to Christianity. But to his left his comrades are roasting human flesh. Europeans were convinced that many native peoples were cannibals. What can we conclude from this painting about European attitudes toward peoples of the New World? *Villa della Torre, Mezzane de Sotto, Verona.*

❖ A Clash of Worldviews

The countries that moved ahead economically in this period—England, the Dutch Republic, and to some extent France—turned out to be the most receptive to new secular worldviews. In the long-term process known as **secularization**, religion became a matter of private conscience rather than public policy. Secularization did not entail a loss of religious faith, but it did prompt a search for nonreligious explanations for political authority and natural phenomena. During the late sixteenth and early seventeenth centuries, art, political theory, and science all began to break some of their bonds with religion. The visual arts, for example, more frequently depicted secular subjects. Scientists and scholars sought laws in nature to explain politics as well as movements in the heavens and on earth. A scientific revolution was in the making. Yet traditional attitudes did not disappear. Belief in magic and witchcraft pervaded every level of society. People of all classes accepted supernatural explanations for natural phenomena, a view only gradually and partially undermined by new ideas.

The Arts in an Age of Crisis

Two new forms of artistic expression—professional theater and opera—developed to express secular values in an age of conflict over religious beliefs. The greatest playwright of the English language, William Shakespeare, never referred to religious disputes in his plays, and he always set his most personal reflections on political turmoil and uncertainty in faraway times or places. Religion played an important role in the new mannerist and baroque styles of painting, however, even though many rulers commissioned paintings on secular subjects for their own uses.

Theater in the Age of Shakespeare. Permanent professional theater companies appeared for the first time in Europe in the last quarter of the sixteenth century. In previous centuries, traveling companies made their living by playing at major religious festivals and by repeating their performances in small towns and villages along the way. In London, Seville, and Madrid, the first professional acting companies performed before paying audiences in the 1570s. A huge outpouring of playwriting followed. The Spanish playwright Lope de Vega◆ (1562–1635) alone wrote more than fifteen hundred plays. Between 1580 and 1640, three hundred English playwrights produced works for a hundred different acting companies. Theaters did a banner business despite Puritan opposition in England and Catholic objections in Spain. Shopkeepers, apprentices, lawyers, and court nobles crowded into open-air theaters to see everything from bawdy farces to profound tragedies.

The most enduring and influential playwright of the time was the Englishman William Shakespeare (1564–1616), son of a glovemaker, who wrote three dozen plays and acted in one of the chief troupes. Although Shakespeare's plays were not set in contemporary England, they reflected the concerns of his age: the nature of power and the crisis of authority. As noted earlier in this chapter, three of his greatest tragedies—*Hamlet* (1601), *King Lear* (1605), and *Macbeth* (1606)—show the uncertainty and even chaos that result when power is misappropriated or misused. In each play, family relationships are linked to questions about the legitimacy of government, just as they were for Elizabeth I herself. Hamlet's mother marries the man who murdered his royal father and usurped the crown; two of Lear's daughters betray him when he tries to divide his kingdom; Macbeth's wife persuades him to murder the king and seize the throne. One character in the final act describes the tragic story of Prince Hamlet as one "Of carnal, bloody, and unnatural acts;/Of accidental judgments, casual slaughters;/Of deaths put on by cunning and forced cause." Like many real-life people, Shakespeare's tragic characters found little peace in the turmoil of their times.

Mannerism and the Baroque in Art. New styles of painting departed abruptly from Renaissance perspective, which had emphasized precise and harmonious lines. In the late sixteenth century the artistic style

◆**Lope de Vega:** LOH pay day VAY gah

known as **mannerism** emerged in the Italian states and soon spread across Europe. Mannerism was an almost theatrical style that allowed painters to distort perspective to convey a message or emphasize a theme. The most famous mannerist painter, called El Greco because he was of Greek origin, trained in Venice and Rome before he moved to Spain in the 1570s. His paintings encapsulated the mannerist style: he crowded figures or objects into every available space, used larger-than-life or elongated figures, and created new and often bizarre visual effects. The religious intensity of El Greco's pictures shows that faith still motivated many artists, as it did much political conflict. (See Mannerist Painting, right column.)

The most important new style was the **baroque**,◆ which, like mannerism, originated in the Italian states. Like many historical categories, the word *baroque* was not used as a label by people living at the time; in the eighteenth century, art critics coined the word to mean shockingly bizarre, confused, and extravagant, and until the late nineteenth century, art historians and collectors largely disdained the baroque. In place of the Renaissance emphasis on harmonious design, unity, and clarity, the baroque featured curves, exaggerated lighting, intense emotions, release from restraint, and even a kind of artistic sensationalism.

Closely tied to the Counter-Reformation, the baroque melodramatically reaffirmed the emotional depths of the Catholic faith and glorified both church and monarchy. The style spread from Rome to other Italian states and then into central Europe. The Catholic Habsburg territories, including Spain and the Spanish Netherlands, embraced the style. The Spanish built baroque churches in their American colonies as part of their massive conversion campaign. Within Europe, Protestant countries largely resisted the baroque, as we can see by comparing Flemish painters from the Spanish Netherlands with Dutch artists. The first great baroque painter was an Italian-trained Fleming, Peter Paul Rubens (1577–1640). A devout Catholic, Rubens painted vivid, exuberant pictures on religious themes, packed with figures. His style

◆**baroque:** buh ROHK

Mannerist Painting
With its distortion of perspective, crowding of figures, and mysterious allusions, El Greco's painting *The Dream of Philip II* (1577) is a typical mannerist painting. What can we conclude about Philip II's character from the way he is depicted here? © *National Gallery, London.*

was an extension of the theatrical baroque style, conveying ideas through broad gestures and dramatic poses. (See Baroque Style of Painting, on the next page.) The great Dutch Protestant painters of the next generation, such as Rembrandt van Rijn (1606–1669), sometimes used biblical subjects, but their pictures were more realistic and focused on everyday scenes. Many of them

Baroque Style of Painting
Although the subject matter here is secular and not religious, *The Hippo Hunt* (1615–1616) by the Flemish painter Peter Paul Rubens displays many of the elements that define the baroque style: dramatic action, intense emotions, and an emphasis on curves and violent contrasts. Rubens painted this scene for Duke Maximilian of Bavaria. The picture also shows European interest in exotic places; the Turks are hunting animals not seen in Europe. *Alte Pinakothek, Munich/Giraudon, Paris/SuperStock.*

suggested the Protestant concern for an inner life and personal faith rather than the public expression of religiosity.

Opera. A new secular musical form, the opera, grew up parallel to the baroque style in the visual arts. First influential in the Italian states, opera combined music, drama, dance, and scenery in a grand sensual display, often with themes chosen to please the ruler and the aristocracy. Operas could be based on typically baroque sacred subjects or on traditional stories. Like Shakespeare, opera composers often turned to familiar stories their audiences would recognize and readily follow. One of the most innovative composers of

opera was Claudio Monteverdi (1567–1643), whose work contributed to the development of both opera and the orchestra. His earliest operatic production, *Orfeo* (1607), was the first to require an orchestra of about forty instruments and to include instrumental as well as vocal sections.

The Natural Laws of Politics

In reaction to the religious wars, jurists and scholars not only began to defend the primacy of state interests over those of religious conformity but also insisted on secular explanations for politics. Machiavelli had pointed in this direction with his prescriptions for

Renaissance princes in the early sixteenth century, but the intellectual movement gathered steam in the aftermath of the religious violence unleashed by the Reformation. Religious toleration could not take hold until government could be organized on some principle other than one king, one faith. The French politiques Michel de Montaigne and Jean Bodin started the search for those principles, and the Dutch jurist Hugo Grotius developed ideas on government that would influence John Locke and the American revolutionaries of the eighteenth century.

Montaigne and Bodin.   Michel de Montaigne◆ (1533–1592) was a French magistrate who resigned his office in the midst of the wars of religion to write about the need for tolerance and open-mindedness. Although himself a Catholic, Montaigne painted on the beams of his study the statement "All that is certain is that nothing is certain." To capture this need for personal reflection in a tumultuous age of religious discord, he invented the essay as a short and pithy form of expression. He revived the ancient doctrine of skepticism, which held that total certainty is never attainable—a doctrine, like toleration of religious differences, that was repugnant to Protestants and Catholics alike, both of whom were certain that their religion was the right one. He also questioned the common European habit of calling newly discovered peoples in the New World barbarous and savage: "Everyone gives the title of barbarism to everything that is not in use in his own country."

The French Catholic lawyer Jean Bodin◆ (1530–1596) sought systematic secular answers to the problem of disorder in *The Six Books of the Republic* (1576). Comparing the different forms of government throughout history, he concluded that there were three basic types of sovereignty: monarchy, aristocracy, and democracy. Only strong monarchical power offered hope for maintaining order, he insisted. Bodin rejected any doctrine of the right to resist tyrannical authority: "I denied that it was the function of a good man or of a good citizen to offer violence to his prince for any reason, however great a

tyrant he might be" (and, it might be added, whatever his ideas on religion). Bodin's ideas helped lay the foundation for absolutism, the idea that the monarch should be the sole and uncontested source of power. Nonetheless, the very discussion of types of governments in the abstract implied that they might be subject to choice rather than simply being God-given, as most rulers maintained.

Grotius and Natural Law.   During the Dutch revolt against Spain, the jurist Hugo Grotius◆ (1583–1645) gave new meaning to the notion of "natural law"—laws of nature that give legitimacy to government and stand above the actions of any particular ruler or religious group. Grotius argued that natural law stood beyond the reach of either secular or divine authority; it would be valid even if God did not exist. By this account, natural law, not Scripture, religious authority, or tradition, should govern politics. Such ideas got Grotius into trouble with both Catholics and Protestants. His work, *The Laws of War and Peace* (1625), was condemned by the Catholic church. The Dutch Protestant government arrested him for his part in religious controversies; his wife helped him escape prison by hiding him in a chest of books. He fled to Paris, where he got a small pension from Louis XIII and served as his ambassador to Sweden. The Swedish king Gustavus Adolphus claimed that he kept Grotius's book under his pillow even while at battle. Grotius was one of the first to argue that international conventions should govern the treatment of prisoners of war and the making of peace treaties.

At the same time that Grotius expanded the principles of natural law, most jurists worked on codifying the huge amount of legislation and jurisprudence devoted to legal forms of torture. Most states and the courts of the Catholic church used torture when the crime was very serious and the evidence seemed to point to a particular defendant but no definitive proof had been established. The judges ordered torture—hanging the accused by the hands with a rope thrown over a beam, pressing the legs in a leg screw, or just tying the hands very tightly—to extract

---

◆**Montaigne:** mahn TAYN
◆**Bodin:** baw DAN

◆**Grotius:** GROH shee uhs

DID YOU KNOW?

The Gregorian Calendar: 1582

The Catholic church relied on the work of astronomers when it undertook a major reform of the calendar in 1582. Every culture has some kind of calendar by which it groups days to mark time, but the length of the day, the week, and the month have varied throughout human history. At different moments in the past, West Africans, for example, used four-day weeks, central Asians five-day weeks, and Egyptians ten-day weeks. These different systems became uniform when most of the world's countries adopted the Gregorian calendar. The spread of the use of the Gregorian calendar, which happened only very gradually after its introduction in 1582, marked the extension of Western influence in the world.

The Gregorian calendar got its name from Pope Gregory XIII, who ordered calendar reform to compute more accurately the exact date on which Easter—the Christian holiday commemorating the resurrection of Jesus—should fall. Easter was supposed to fall on the first Sunday after the first full moon after the vernal equinox. But over the years the dates had become confused because no one had been able to calculate the exact

length of a solar year (365.242199 days). As a result, the calendar had become increasingly out of phase with the seasons; by 1545, the vernal (spring) equinox had moved ten days from its proper date. In 1582, when the reform took effect, October 5 became October 15, thus omitting ten days and setting the vernal equinox straight—but causing any number of legal complications.

Although the Gregorian calendar was based on a truer calculation of the length of a year and thus required less adjustment than previous calendars, it was not immediately adopted, even in Christian Europe, in part because any change would have been difficult to enforce given the state of communications at the time. Because the pope had sponsored the reform, the Catholic countries embraced it first; Protestant countries used it only after 1700. England accepted it in 1752. Adoption followed in Japan in 1873, Egypt in 1875, Russia in 1918, and Greece in 1923. The Greek Orthodox church never accepted it, so Easter in that church is about one week later than elsewhere in Christianity.

Even though the Gregorian calendar is astronomically correct, it still has bothersome

a confession, which had to be given with a medical expert and notary present and had to be repeated without torture. Children, pregnant women, the elderly, aristocrats, kings, and even professors were exempt.

Grotius's conception of natural law directly challenged the use of torture. To be in accord with natural law, Grotius argued, governments had to defend natural rights, which he defined as life, body, freedom, and honor. Grotius did not encourage rebellion in the name of natural law or rights, but he did hope that someday all governments would adhere to these principles and stop killing their own and one another's subjects in the name of religion. Natural law and natural rights would play an important role in the founding

of constitutional governments from the 1640s forward and in the establishment of various charters of human rights in our own time.

Origins of the Scientific Revolution

Although the Catholic and Protestant churches encouraged the study of science and many prominent scientists were themselves clerics, the search for a secular, scientific method of determining the laws of nature eventually challenged the traditional accounts of natural phenomena. (See "Did You Know?", above.) Christian doctrine had incorporated the scientific teachings of ancient philosophers, especially Ptolemy and Aristotle; now these came into question. A

Calendar
This painting by Aldo Durazzi shows Gregory XIII presiding over the council of 1582 that reformed the calendar. The Catholic church sponsored the work of many astronomers and other scientists.
Archivio di Stato, Siena. Photo Lensini Fabrio.

defects: the months are different in length, and holidays do not fall on the same day in each year. Two other calendars have been proposed. The International Fixed Calendar would divide the year into thirteen months of twenty-eight days with an additional day at the end. The World Calendar would divide the year into four quarters of ninety-one days, each with an additional day at the end of the year; the first month in each quarter would have thirty-one days, and the second and third thirty days each. Neither has been adopted. Logic does not always win this kind of argument, for changing the length of the months seems almost equivalent to changing which side of the road you drive on; once a system is learned, no one really wants to give it up and start all over again. The same is true for the numbering of the years, which was set by the Council of Nicaea in 325. The year 1 was designated as the year it was believed Jesus was born. Today scholars have determined that the date was wrong by several years, and many object in any case to the use of a calendar based on the birth of Jesus. But if that dating system were eliminated, what would replace it? Where should a common calendar begin?

revolution in astronomy challenged the Ptolemaic view, endorsed by the Catholic church, which held that the sun revolved around the earth. Startling breakthroughs took place in medicine, too, which laid the foundations for modern anatomy and pharmacology. By the early seventeenth century, a new **scientific method** had been established based on a combination of experimental observation and mathematical deduction. Conflicts between the new science and religion followed almost immediately.

The Revolution in Astronomy.   The traditional account of the movement of the heavens derived from the second-century Greek astronomer Ptolemy, who put the earth at the center of the cosmos. Above the earth were fixed the moon, the stars, and the planets in concentric crystalline spheres; beyond these fixed spheres dwelt God and the angels. The planets revolved around the earth at the command of God. In this view, the sun revolved around the earth; the heavens were perfect and unchanging, and the earth was "corrupted." Ptolemy insisted that the planets revolved in perfectly circular orbits (because circles were more "perfect" than other figures). To account for the actual elliptical paths that could be observed and calculated, he posited orbits within orbits, or epicycles.

In 1543, the Polish clergyman Nicolaus Copernicus (1473–1543) began the revolution in astronomy by publishing his treatise *On the Revolution of the Celestial Spheres.* Copernicus attacked the Ptolemaic account, arguing that the earth and planets revolved around the sun, a view known as **heliocentrism** (a sun-centered universe). He discovered that by placing the sun instead of the earth at the center of the system of spheres, he could eliminate many epicycles from the calculations. In other words, he claimed that the heliocentric view simplified the mathematics. Copernicus died soon after publishing his theories, but when the Italian monk Giordano Bruno (1548–1600) taught heliocentrism, perhaps with the aim of establishing a new religion, the Catholic Inquisition (set up to seek out heretics) arrested him and burned him at the stake.

Copernicus's views began to attract widespread attention in the early seventeenth century, when astronomers systematically collected evidence that undermined the Ptolemaic view. A leader among them was the Danish astronomer Tycho Brahe♦ (1546–1601). While at university he lost part of his nose in a duel and for the rest of his life he wore a metal insert to replace the missing part. Brahe designed and built new instruments for observing the heavens and trained a whole generation of astronomers. His observation of a new star in 1572 and a comet in 1577 called into question the Aristotelian view that the universe was unchanging. Brahe still rejected heliocentrism, but the assistant he employed when he moved to Prague in 1599, Johannes Kepler (1571–1630), was converted to the Copernican view. Kepler continued Brahe's collection of planetary observations and used the evidence to develop his three laws of planetary motion, published between 1609 and 1619. Kepler's laws provided mathematical backing for heliocentrism and directly challenged the claim long held, even by Copernicus, that planetary motion was circular. Kepler's first law stated that the orbits of the planets are ellipses, with the sun always at one focus of the ellipse.

The Italian Galileo Galilei (1564–1642) provided more evidence to support the heliocentric view and also challenged the doctrine that the heavens were perfect and unchanging. In 1609, he learned that two Dutch astronomers had built a telescope. He quickly invented a better one and observed the earth's moon, four satellites of Jupiter, the phases of Venus (a cycle of changing physical appearances), and sunspots. The moon, the planets, and the sun were no more perfect than the earth, he insisted, and the shadows he could see on the moon could only be the product of hills and valleys like those on earth. Galileo portrayed the earth as a moving part of a larger system, only one of

The Trial of Galileo
In this anonymous painting of the trial held in 1633, Galileo appears seated on a chair in the center facing the church officials who accused him of heresy for insisting that the sun, not the earth, was the center of the universe (heliocentrism). Catholic officials forced him to recant or suffer the death penalty. What do you think the painter thought of Galileo? *Private collection, New York. © Photograph by Erich Lessing/Art Resource.*

♦**Brahe:** BRAH hee

Galileo Writes to Kepler about Their Common Interests in Astronomy

Galileo Galilei and Johannes Kepler were two of the pioneers of the scientific revolution. In this letter, written before either of them became famous, Galileo writes to Kepler about his interest in the German astronomer's work. It shows that experimenters knew of each other's work even across considerable distances. Galileo expresses his worries about embracing Copernicanism, worries that turned out to be well founded when the Inquisition sentenced him in 1633 to house arrest for his views.

Padua, August 4, 1597

I received your book, most learned sir, which you sent me by Paulus Amberger, not some days since, but only a few hours ago. And as this Paulus has notified me of his return to Germany, I would consider myself ungrateful if I did not now send you my thanks in the present letter. I thank you, therefore, and most especially because you have judged me worthy of such a token of your friendship. So far I have read only the introduction of your work, but I have to some extent gathered your plan from it, and I congratulate myself on the exceptional good fortune of having such a man as a comrade in the pursuit of truth. For it is too bad that there are so few who seek the truth and so few who do not follow a mistaken method in philosophy. This is not, however, the place to lament the misery of our century, but to rejoice with you over such beautiful ideas for proving the truth. So I add only, and I promise, that I shall read your book at leisure; for I am certain that I shall find the noblest things in it. And this I shall do the more gladly, because I accepted the view of Copernicus many years ago, and from this standpoint I have discovered from their origins many natural phenomena, which doubtless cannot be explained on the basis of the more commonly accepted hypothesis. I have written many direct and indirect arguments for the Copernican view, but until now I have not dared to publish them, alarmed by the fate of Copernicus himself, our master. He has won for himself undying fame in the eyes of a few, but he has been mocked and hooted at by an infinite multitude (for so large is the number of fools). I would dare to come forward publicly with my ideas if there were more people of your way of thinking. As this is not the case, I shall refrain. The shortness of time and my eager desire to read your book compel me to close, but I assure you of my sympathy, and I shall always gladly be at your service. Farewell and do not neglect to send me further good news of yourself.

Source: Translation by Mary Martin McLaughlin, from *The Portable Medieval Reader* by James Bruce Ross and Mary Martin McLaughlin. Copyright © 1953 by Viking Penguin, Inc., renewed © 1981 by James Bruce Ross and Mary Martin McLaughlin. Reprinted with the permission of Viking Penguin, a division of Penguin Putnam Inc.

many planets revolving around the sun, not as the fixed center of a single, closed universe. (See Galileo Writes to Kepler, above.)

Because he recognized the utility of the new science for everyday projects, Galileo published his work in Italian, rather than Latin, to appeal to a lay audience of merchants and aristocrats. But he meant only to instruct an educated elite. The new science, he claimed, suited "the minds of the wise," not "the shallow minds of the common people." After all, his discoveries challenged the commonsensical view that it is the sun that rises and sets while the earth stands still. If the Bible were wrong about motion in the universe, as Galileo's position implied, the error came from the Bible's use of common language to appeal to the lower orders. The Catholic church was not mollified by this explanation. In 1616 the church forbade Galileo to teach that the earth moves, and in 1633 accused him of not obeying the earlier order. Forced to appear before the Inquisition, he agreed to publicly recant his assertion about the movement of the earth to save himself from torture and death. (See the Trial of Galileo, on page 612.) Afterward he lived under house arrest and could publish his work only in the Dutch Republic, which had become a haven for iconoclastic scientists and thinkers.

Breakthroughs in Medicine. Until the mid-sixteenth century, medical knowledge in Europe had been based on the writings of the second-century Greek physician Galen, who was a contemporary of Ptolemy. Galen derived his knowledge of the anatomy of the human body from partial dissections. In the same year that Copernicus challenged the traditional account in astronomy (1543), the Flemish scientist Andreas Vesalius♦ (1514–1564) did the same for anatomy. Drawing on public dissections in the medical faculties of European universities, Vesalius eventually refuted Galen's work in his illustrated anatomical text, *On the Construction of the Human Body.* Theophrastus Bombastus von Hohenheim, better known as Paracelsus♦ (1493–1541), went even further than Vesalius. He burned Galen's text at the University of Basel, where he was a professor of medicine. Paracelsus experimented with new drugs; performed operations (at the time, most academic physicians taught medical theory, not practice); and pursued his interests in magic, alchemy, and astrology. He helped establish the modern science of pharmacology.

The Englishman William Harvey (1578–1657) also used dissection to examine the circulation of blood within the body, demonstrating how the heart worked as a pump. The heart and its valves were "a piece of machinery," Harvey insisted. They obeyed mechanical laws just as the planets and earth revolved around the sun in a mechanical universe. Nature could be understood by experiment and rational deduction, not by following traditional authorities.

Scientific Method: Bacon and Descartes. In the 1630s, the European intellectual elite began to accept the new scientific views. Ancient learning, the churches and their

theologians, and even cherished popular beliefs seemed to be undermined by a new standard of truth—the scientific method, which was based on systematic experiments and rational deduction. Two men were chiefly responsible for spreading the prestige of scientific method: the English politician Sir Francis Bacon (1561–1626) and the French mathematician and philosopher René Descartes♦ (1596–1650). They represented the two essential halves of scientific method: respectively, inductive reasoning through observation and experimental research and deductive reasoning from self-evident principles.

In *The Advancement of Learning* (1605), Bacon attacked reliance on ancient writers and optimistically predicted that scientific method would lead to social progress. The minds of the medieval scholars, he said, had been "shut up in the cells of a few authors (chiefly Aristotle, their dictator) as their persons were shut up in the cells of monasteries and colleges," and they could therefore produce only "cobwebs of learning" that were "of no substance or profit." Advancement would take place only through the collection, comparison, and analysis of information. Knowledge, in Bacon's view, must be empirically based (that is, gained by observation and experiment). Bacon ardently supported the scientific method over popular beliefs, which he rejected as "fables and popular errors." Claiming that God had called the Catholic church "to account for their degenerate manners and ceremonies," Bacon looked to the Protestant English state, which he served as lord chancellor, for leadership on the road to scientific advancement.

Although Descartes agreed with Bacon's denunciation of traditional learning, he saw that the attack on tradition might only replace the dogmatism of the churches with the skepticism of Montaigne—that nothing at all was certain. A Catholic who served in the Thirty Years' War, Descartes aimed to establish the new science on more secure philosophical foundations, those of mathematics and logic (Descartes invented analytic geometry). In his *Discourse on Method* (1637), he argued that mathematical and mechanical principles provided the key to under-

---

♦**Vesalius:** vuh SAY lee uhs
♦**Paracelsus:** pa ruh SEHL suhs

♦**Descartes:** day KAHRT

standing all of nature, including the actions of people and states. All prior assumptions must be repudiated in favor of one elementary principle: "I think, therefore I am." Everything else could—and should—be doubted, but even doubt showed the certain existence of someone thinking. Begin with the simple and go on to the complex, he asserted, and believe only those ideas that present themselves "clearly and distinctly." Descartes believed that rational individuals would see the necessity of strong state power and that only "meddling and restless spirits" would plot against it. He insisted that human reason could not only unravel the secrets of nature but also prove the existence of God. Although he hoped to secure the authority of both church and state, his reliance on human reason alone irritated authorities, and his books were banned in many places. He moved to the Dutch Republic to work in peace. Scientific research, like economic growth, became centered in the northern, Protestant countries, where it was less constrained by church control than in the Catholic south.

Magic and Witchcraft

Despite the new emphasis on clear reasoning, observation, and independence from past authorities, science had not yet become separate from magic. Many scholars, like Paracelsus, studied alchemy alongside other scientific pursuits. Elizabeth I maintained a court astrologer who was also a serious mathematician, and many writers distinguished between "natural magic," which was close to experimental science, and demonic "black magic." The astronomer Tycho Brahe defended his studies of alchemy and astrology as part of natural magic. For many of the greatest minds, magic and science were still closely linked.

In a world in which most people believed in astrology, magical healing, prophecy, and ghosts, it is hardly surprising that many of Europe's learned people also firmly believed in witchcraft, the exercise of magical powers gained by a pact with the devil. The same Jean Bodin who argued against religious fanaticism insisted on death for witches—and for those magistrates who would not prosecute them. In France alone, 345 books and

The Witches' Sabbath
This English woodcut from about 1600 shows witches dining with the devil and his demons. Many believed that witches made a pact with the devil to carry out his evil deeds. It is hard to tell whether or not all the witches in this picture are women. *Mary Evans Picture Library.*

pamphlets on witchcraft appeared between 1550 and 1650. Trials of witches peaked in Europe between 1560 and 1640, the very time of the celebrated breakthroughs of the new science. Montaigne was one of the few to speak out against executing accused witches: "It is taking one's conjectures rather seriously to roast someone alive for them," he wrote in 1580.

Belief in witches was not new in the sixteenth century. Witches had long been thought capable of almost anything: passing through walls, flying through the air, destroying crops, and causing personal catastrophes from miscarriage to demonic possession. What was new was the official persecution, justified by the notion that witches were agents of Satan whom the righteous must oppose. In a time of economic crisis, plague, warfare, and the clash of religious differences, witchcraft trials provided an outlet for social stress and anxiety, legitimated by state power. Denunciation and persecution of witches coincided with the spread of reform, both Protestant and Catholic. The

MAPPING THE WEST The Religious Divisions of Europe, c. 1648
The Peace of Westphalia recognized major religious divisions within Europe that have endured
for the most part to the present day. Catholicism dominated in southern Europe, Lutheranism
had its stronghold in northern Europe, and Calvinism flourished along the Rhine River. In southeastern Europe, the Islamic Ottoman Turks accommodated the Greek Orthodox Christians under
their rule but bitterly fought the Catholic Austrian Habsburgs for control of Hungary.

trials concentrated especially in the German
lands of the Holy Roman Empire, the boiling
cauldron of the Thirty Years' War.

The victims of the persecution were
overwhelmingly female: women accounted
for 80 percent of the accused witches in about
100,000 trials in Europe and North America
during the sixteenth and seventeenth centuries. About one-third were sentenced to
death. Before 1400, when witchcraft trials
were rare, nearly half of those accused had
been men. Explanations for this gender difference have raised many controversies.

Some historians argue that the trials expressed a fundamental hatred of women that
came to a head during conflicts over the Reformation. Official descriptions of witchcraft
oozed lurid details of sexual orgies, incest, homosexuality, and cannibalism, in which
women acted as the devil's sexual slaves. In
this view, Catholic and Protestant reforming
clergy attacked the presumably wild and
undisciplined sexuality of women as the most
obvious manifestation of popular unruliness
and heretical tendencies. Lawyers and judges
followed their lead.

Other historians point to a social dimension that helps explain the prominence of women among the accused. Accusers were almost always better off than those they accused. The poorest and most socially marginal people in most communities were elderly spinsters and widows. Because they were thought likely to hanker after revenge on those more fortunate, they were singled out as witches. Another commonly accused woman was the midwife, who was a prime target for suspicion when a baby or mother died in childbirth. Although sometimes venerated for their special skill, midwives also numbered among the thousands of largely powerless women persecuted for their supposed consorting with the devil.

Witchcraft trials declined when scientific thinking about causes and effects raised questions about the evidence used in court: how could judges or jurors be certain that someone was a witch? The tide turned everywhere at about the same time, as physicians, lawyers, judges, and even clergy came to suspect that accusations were based on popular superstition and peasant untrustworthiness. As early as the 1640s, French courts ordered the arrest of witch-hunters and released suspected witches. In 1682, a French royal decree treated witchcraft as fraud and imposture, meaning that the law did not recognize anyone as a witch. In 1693, the jurors who had convicted twenty witches in Salem, Massachusetts, recanted, claiming: "We confess that we ourselves were not capable to understand. . . . We justly fear that we were sadly deluded and mistaken." The Salem jurors had not stopped believing in witches; they had simply lost confidence in their ability to identify them. This was a general pattern. Popular attitudes had not changed; what had changed was the attitudes of the elites. When physicians and judges had believed in witches and carried out official persecutions, with torture, those accused of witchcraft had gone to their deaths in record numbers. But when the same groups distanced themselves from popular beliefs, the trials and the executions stopped.

Review: How could belief in witchcraft and the rising prestige of scientific method coexist?

Conclusion

The witchcraft persecutions of the late sixteenth and early seventeenth centuries reflected the traumas of these times of religious war, economic decline, and crises of political authority. Faced with new threats, some people blamed the poor widow or upstart midwife for their problems; others joined desperate revolts, and still others emigrated to the New World to seek a better life. Even rulers confronted frightening choices: forced abdication, death in battle, or assassination often accompanied their religious decisions, and economic shocks could threaten the stability of their governments.

Religious conflicts shaped the destinies of every European power in this period. These conflicts came to a head in the Thirty Years' War (1618–1648), which cut a path of destruction through central Europe and involved most of the European powers. Repulsed by the effects of religious violence on international relations, European rulers agreed to a peace that effectively removed disputes between Catholics and Protestants from the international arena. The growing separation of political motives from religious ones did not mean that violence or conflict had ended, however. Struggles for religious uniformity within states would continue, though on a smaller scale. Bigger armies required more state involvement, and almost everywhere rulers emerged from these decades of conflict with expanded powers. The growth of state power directly changed the lives of ordinary people: more men went into the armies, and most families paid higher taxes. The constant extension of state power is one of the defining themes of modern history; religious warfare gave it a jump-start.

For all their power, rulers could not control economic, social, or intellectual trends, much as they often tried. The economic downturn of the seventeenth century produced unexpected consequences for European states even while it made life miserable for many ordinary people; economic power and vibrancy shifted from the Mediterranean world to the northwest because the countries of northwestern Europe—England, France, and the Dutch Republic especially—suffered less from the fighting of the Thirty Years' War and recovered more quickly from the loss of population and production during bad times.

In the face of violence and uncertainty, some began to look for secular alternatives in art, politics, and science. Although it would be foolish to claim that everyone's mental universe changed because of the clash between religious and secular worldviews, a truly monumental shift in attitudes had begun. Secularization combined a growing interest in nonreligious forms of art, such as theater and opera, the search for nonreligious foundations of political authority, and the establishment of scientific method as the standard of truth. Proponents of these changes did not renounce their religious beliefs or even hold them less fervently, but they did insist that attention to state interests and scientific knowledge could serve as a brake on religious violence and popular superstitions.

Suggested References

Religious Conflicts and State Power, 1560–1618

The personalities of rulers such as Elizabeth I of England and Philip II of Spain remain central to the religious and political conflicts of this period.

Benedict, Philip. *Christ's Churches Purely Reformed: A Social History of Calvinism.* 2002.

Holt, Mack P. *The French Wars of Religion, 1562–1629.* 1995.

Israel, Jonathan. *The Dutch Republic: Its Rise, Greatness, and Fall, 1477–1806.* 1995.

Kamen, Henry. *Philip of Spain.* 1997.

*Marcus, Leah S., Janel Mueller, and Mary Beth Rose. *Elizabeth I: Collected Works.* 2000.

Mattingly, Garrett. *The Defeat of the Spanish Armada.* 2nd ed. 1988.

Philip II: http://www.historylearningsite.co.uk/Phillip.htm.

The Thirty Years' War and the Balance of Power, 1618–1648

As ethnic conflicts erupt again in eastern Europe, historians have traced their roots back to the intertwined religious, ethnic, and dynastic struggles of the Thirty Years' War.

*Primary sources.

Asch, Ronald G. *The Thirty Years' War: The Holy Roman Empire and Europe, 1618–1648.* 1997.

Osborne, Toby. *Dynasty and Diplomacy in the Court of Savoy: Political Culture and the Thirty Years' War.* 2002.

Parker, Geoffrey. *The Military Revolution: Military Innovation and the Rise of the West, 1500–1800.* 1988.

Parrott, David. *Richelieu's Army: War, Government and Society in France, 1624–1642.* 2001.

Economic Crisis and Realignment

Painstaking archival research has enabled historians to reconstruct the demographic, economic, and social history of the period discussed in this chapter. Recently, attention has focused more specifically on women, the family, and the early history of slavery.

Ashton, Trevor H., ed. *Crisis in Europe.* 1965.

Braudel, Fernand. *The Mediterranean and the Mediterranean World in the Age of Philip the Second.* 2 vols. Trans. Siân Reynolds. 1972–1973.

Ringrose, David R. *Expansion and Global Interaction, 1200–1700.* 2001.

Rublack, Ulinka. *The Crimes of Women in Early Modern Germany.* 1999.

Wiesner, Merry E. *Women and Gender in Early Modern Europe*, 2nd ed. 2000.

A Clash of Worldviews

The transformation of intellectual and cultural life has long fascinated scholars. Recent works have developed a new kind of study called microhistory, which focuses on one person (like Ginzburg's Italian miller).

Butterfield, Sir Herbert. *The Origins of Modern Science: 1300–1800.* Rev. ed. 1965.

Clark, Stuart, ed. *Languages of Witchcraft: Narrative, Ideology, and Meaning in Early Modern Culture.* 2001.

The Galileo Project: http://riceinfo.rice.edu/Galileo.

Ginzburg, Carlo. *The Cheese and the Worms: The Cosmos of a Sixteenth-Century Miller.* Trans. John Tedeschi and Anne Tedeschi. 1992.

Jacob, James. *The Scientific Revolution.* 1998.

Thomas, Keith. *Religion and the Decline of Magic.* 1971.

CHAPTER REVIEW

IMPORTANT EVENTS

1562 French Wars of Religion begin

1566 Revolt of Calvinists in the Netherlands against Spain begins

1569 Formation of commonwealth of Poland-Lithuania

1571 Battle of Lepanto marks victory of West over Ottomans at sea

1572 St. Bartholomew's Day Massacre of French Protestants

1588 Defeat of the Spanish Armada by England

1598 French Wars of Religion end with Edict of Nantes

1601 William Shakespeare, *Hamlet*

1618 Thirty Years' War begins

1625 Hugo Grotius publishes *The Laws of War and Peace*

1629 English Puritans set up the Massachusetts Bay Company and begin to colonize New England

1633 Galileo Galilei is forced to recant his support of heliocentrism

1635 French join the Thirty Years' War by declaring war on Spain

1648 Peace of Westphalia ends the Thirty Years' War

KEY TERMS

baroque (607)

heliocentrism (612)

Huguenot (582)

mannerism (607)

Moriscos (587)

politiques (585)

Puritans (589)

raison d'état (597)

scientific method (611)

secularization (606)

tithe (601)

REVIEW QUESTIONS

1. In what ways did the power of states depend on unity in religion?

2. Why did a war fought over religious differences result in stronger states?

3. What were the consequences of economic recession in the early 1600s?

4. How could belief in witchcraft and the rising prestige of scientific method coexist?

MAKING CONNECTIONS

1. How did the balance of power shift in Europe between 1560 and 1648? What were the main reasons for the shift?

2. Relate the new developments in the arts and sciences to the political and economic changes of this period of crisis.

FOR FURTHER EXPLORATION

To assess your mastery of the material in this chapter, see the Online Study Guide at **bedfordstmartins.com/hunt**.

To read additional primary-source material from this period, see Chapter 16 in *Sources of The Making of the West*, Second Edition.

State Building and the Search for Order, 1648–1690

IN ONE OF HER HUNDREDS of letters to her daughter, the French noblewoman Marie de Sévigné♦ (1626–1696) told a disturbing story about François Vatel, the organizer of a three-day celebration for King Louis XIV and three thousand other guests. Vatel got upset when he did not have enough roast for everyone who appeared for dinner. Early the next morning, when the fish he had ordered did not arrive, Vatel rushed up to his room, put his sword against the door, and on the third try, ran it through his heart. The fish arrived soon after. The king expressed his regrets for the trouble caused by his visit, but the celebration continued. That evening, Sévigné wrote, there was "a very good dinner, light refreshments later, and then supper, a walk, cards, hunting, everything scented with daffodils, everything magical."

It is difficult now for us to comprehend how anyone could care that much about a shipment of fish. The story nonetheless reveals an important aspect of state building in the seventeenth century: to extend state authority, which had been challenged during the wars over religion and threatened by economic recession, many rulers created an aura of overwhelming power and brilliance around themselves. Louis XIV, like many other rulers, believed that he reigned by divine right. He served as God's lieutenant on earth and even claimed certain godlike qualities. As part of his campaign to underline his majesty, Louis encouraged leading nobles, like Vatel's employer, the prince de Condé, to dispense huge sums to entertain him and his court. The effort succeeded: noblemen and noblewomen such as Sévigné came to see the king and his court as somehow "magical."

Louis XIV's model of state building was known as **absolutism**, a system of government in which the ruler claimed sole and uncontestable power. Although absolutism exerted great influence, especially

---

♦**Marie de Sévigné:** ma ree duh say veen nyay

Louis XIV and His Bodyguards
One of Louis XIV's court painters, the Flemish artist Adam Frans van der Meulen, depicted the king arriving at the palace of Versailles, still under construction (the painting dates from 1669). None of the gardens, pools, or statues had been installed. Louis is the only figure facing the viewer, and his dress is much more colorful than that of anyone else in the painting. *Réunion des Musées Nationaux/ Art Resource, NY. Photo: Gérard Blot.*

in central and eastern Europe, it faced competition from **constitutionalism**, a system in which the ruler had to share power with parliaments made up of elected representatives. Constitutionalism led to weakness in Poland-Lithuania, but it provided a strong foundation for state power in England, the British North American colonies, and the Dutch Republic. Constitutionalism triumphed in England, however, only after one king had been executed as a traitor and another had been deposed.

Both methods of state building faced similar challenges in the mid-seventeenth century. Competition in the international arena required resources, and all states raised taxes in this period, provoking popular protests and rebellions. The wars over religion that culminated in the Thirty Years' War left many economies in dire straits, and, even more significant, they created a need for new explanations of political authority. Monarchs still relied on religion to justify their divine right to rule, but they increasingly sought secular defenses of their powers too. Absolutism and constitutionalism were the two main responses to the threat of disorder and breakdown left as a legacy of the wars over religion.

The search for order took place not only at the level of states and rulers but also in intellectual, cultural, and social life. In science, the Englishman Isaac Newton explained the regular movement of the universe with the law of gravitation and thereby consolidated the scientific revolution. Artists sought means of glorifying power and expressing order and symmetry in new fashion. As states

consolidated their power, elites endeavored to distinguish themselves more clearly from the lower orders. The upper classes emulated the manners developed at court and tried in every way to distance themselves from anything viewed as vulgar or lower class. Officials, clergy, and laypeople all worked to reform the poor, now seen as a major source of disorder. Whether absolutist or constitutionalist, seventeenth-century states all aimed to extend control over their subjects' lives.

❖ Louis XIV: Model of Absolutism

French king Louis XIV (r. 1643–1715) personified the absolutist ruler who in theory shared his power with no one. Louis personally made all important state decisions and left no room for dissent. In 1651, he reputedly told the Paris high court of justice, *"L'état, c'est moi"* ("I am the state"), emphasizing that state authority rested in him personally. Louis cleverly manipulated the affections and ambitions of his courtiers, chose as his ministers middle-class men who owed everything to him, built up Europe's largest army, and snuffed out every hint of religious or political opposition. Yet the absoluteness of his power should not be exaggerated. Like all other rulers of his time, Louis depended on the cooperation of many people: local officials who enforced his decrees, peasants and artisans who joined his armies and paid his taxes, creditors who loaned crucial funds, clergy

◆ **1642–1646** English civil war

◆ **1648** Peace of Westphalia, Fronde revolt in France; Ukranian Cossacks rebel; Dutch Republic recognized as independent

◆ **1649** Charles I beheaded; new Russian legal code

1640	**1650**	**1660**

◆ **1651** Hobbes, *Leviathan*

◆ **1660** Monarchy restored in England

◆ **1661** Barbados institutes slave code

◆ **1667** First of Louis XIV's many wars

who preached his notion of Catholicism, and nobles who joined court festivities rather than staying home and causing trouble.

The Fronde, 1648–1653

Louis XIV built on a long French tradition of increasing centralization of state authority, but before he could do so he had to weather a series of revolts known as the **Fronde.**♦ Derived from the French word for a child's slingshot, the term was used by critics to signify that the revolts were mere child's play. In fact, however, they posed an unprecedented threat to the French crown. Louis was only five when he came to the throne in 1643 upon the death of his father, Louis XIII, who with his chief minister Cardinal Richelieu had steered France through increasing involvement in the Thirty Years' War, rapidly climbing taxes, and innumerable tax revolts. Louis XIV's mother, Anne of Austria, and her Italian-born adviser and rumored lover Cardinal Mazarin (1602–1661) ruled in the young monarch's name.

To meet the financial pressure of fighting the Thirty Years' War, Mazarin sold new offices, raised taxes, and forced creditors to extend loans to the government. In 1648, a coalition of his opponents presented him with a charter of demands that, if granted, would have given the **parlements**♦ (high courts) a form of constitutional power with the right to approve new taxes. Mazarin re-

♦**Fronde:** frohnd
♦**parlements:** PAHR luh muhnts

sponded by arresting the leaders of the parlements. He soon faced a series of revolts that at one time or another involved nearly every social group in France.

The Fronde posed an immediate menace to the young king. Fearing for his safety, his mother and members of his court took Louis and fled Paris. With civil war threatening, Mazarin and Anne agreed to compromise with the parlements. The nobles saw an opportunity to reassert their claims to power against the weakened monarchy and renewed their demands for greater local control, which they had lost when the religious wars ended in 1598. Leading noblewomen often played key roles in the opposition to Mazarin, carrying messages and forging alliances, especially when male family members were in prison. While the nobles sought to regain power and local influence, the middle and lower classes chafed at the constant tax increases. Conflicts erupted throughout the kingdom as nobles, parlements, and city councils all raised their own armies to fight either the crown or each other, and rampaging soldiers devastated rural areas and disrupted commerce. In places, such as the southwestern city of Bordeaux, the urban poor revolted as well.

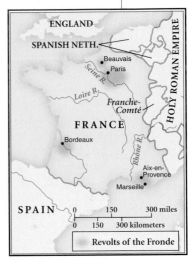

The Fronde, 1648–1653

♦ **1670** Molière, *The Middle-Class Gentleman*

♦ **1678** Madame de Lafayette, *The Princess of Clèves*

♦ **1683** Austrian Habsburgs break Turkish siege of Vienna

♦ **1685** Louis XIV revokes Edict of Nantes

1670   1680   1690

♦ **1687** Newton, *Principia Mathematica*

♦ **1688** William and Mary crowned

♦ **1690** Locke, *Two Treatises of Government; Essay Concerning Human Understanding*

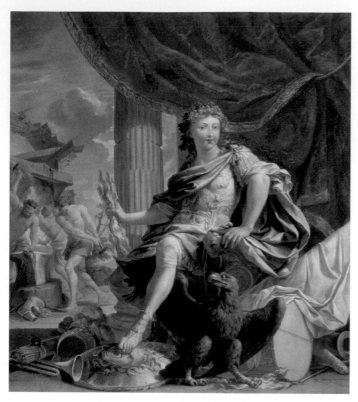

Louis XIV, Conqueror of the Fronde
In this painting of 1654, Louis XIV is depicted as the Roman god Jupiter, who crushes the discord of the Fronde (represented on the shield by the Medusa's head made up of snakes). When the Fronde began, Louis was only ten years old; at the time of this painting, he was sixteen. The propaganda about his divine qualities had already begun. *Réunion des Musées Nationaux/Art Resource, NY. Photo: Gérard Blot.*

memoirs he wrote later for his son's instruction: "Everywhere was disorder. My Court as a whole was still very far removed from the sentiments in which I trust you will find it." Louis listed many other problems in the kingdom, but none occupied him more than his attempts to control France's leading nobles, some of whom came from families that had opposed him militarily during the Fronde.

Typically quarrelsome, the French nobles had long exercised local authority by maintaining their own fighting forces, meting out justice on their estates, arranging jobs for underlings, and resolving their own conflicts through dueling. Louis set out to domesticate the warrior nobles by replacing violence with court ritual, such as the three-day festival described by Marie de Sévigné. Using a systematic policy of bestowing pensions, offices, honors, gifts, and the threat of disfavor or punishment, Louis induced the nobles to cooperate with him and made himself the center of French power and culture. The aristocracy vied for his favor, attended the ballets and theatricals he put on, and learned the rules of etiquette he supervised—in short, became his clients, dependent on him for advancement. Great nobles competed for the honor of holding his shirt when he dressed, foreign ambassadors squabbled for places near him, and royal mistresses basked in the glow of his personal favor.

Participation at court required constant study. The preferred styles changed without notice, and the tiniest lapse in attention to etiquette could lead to ruin. Madame de Lafayette described the court in her novel *The Princess of Clèves* (1678): "The Court gravitated around ambition. Nobody was tranquil or indifferent—everybody was busily trying to better his or her position by pleasing, by helping, or by hindering somebody else." Occasionally the results were tragic, as in the suicide of Vatel recounted by Marie de Sévigné. Elisabeth Charlotte, duchess of Orléans, the German-born sister-in-law of Louis, complained that "everything here is pure self-interest and deviousness."

Neither the nobles nor the judges of the parlements really wanted to overthrow the king; they simply wanted a greater share in power. But Louis XIV never forgot the humiliation and uncertainty that marred his childhood. Years later he recalled an incident in which a band of Parisians invaded his bedchamber to determine whether he had fled the city, and he declared the event an affront not only to himself but also to the state. His own policies as ruler would be designed to prevent the repetition of any such revolts.

Court Culture as an Element of Absolutism

When Cardinal Mazarin died in 1661, Louis XIV decided to rule without a first minister. He described the dangers of his situation in the

Politics and the Arts. Louis XIV appreciated the political uses of every form of art. Mock battles, extravaganzas, theatrical performances, even the king's dinner—Louis's daily life was a public performance designed to enhance his prestige. Calling himself the Sun King, after Apollo, Greek god of the sun, Louis stopped at nothing to burnish this radiant image. He played Apollo in ballets performed at court; posed for portraits with the emblems of Apollo (laurel, lyre, and tripod); and adorned his palaces with statues of the god. He also emulated the style and methods of ancient Roman emperors. At a celebration for the birth of his first son in 1662, Louis dressed in Roman attire, and many engravings and paintings showed him as a Roman emperor. Commissioned histories vaunted his achievements, and coins and medals spread his likeness throughout the realm.

The king's officials treated the arts as a branch of government. The king gave pensions to artists who worked for him and sometimes protected writers from clerical critics. The most famous of these was the playwright Molière,◆ whose comedy *Tartuffe* (1664) made fun of religious hypocrites and was loudly condemned by church leaders. Louis forced Molière to delay public performances of the play but resisted calls for his dismissal. Louis's ministers set up royal academies of dance, painting, architecture, music, and science and took control of the Académie française (French Academy), which to this day decides on correct usage of the French language. Louis's government also regulated the number and locations of theaters and closely censored all forms of publication.

Music and theater enjoyed special prominence. Louis commissioned operas to celebrate royal marriages, baptisms, and military victories. His favorite composer, Jean-Baptiste Lully, an Italian who began as a cook's assistant and rose to be virtual dictator of French musical taste, wrote sixteen operas for court performances as well

◆**Molière:** mohl YEHR

as many ballets. Louis himself danced in the ballets if a role seemed especially important. Playwrights presented their new plays directly to the court. Pierre Corneille and Jean-Baptiste Racine wrote tragedies set in Greece or Rome that celebrated the new aristocratic virtues that Louis aimed to inculcate: a reverence for order and self-control. All the characters were regal or noble, all the language lofty, all the behavior aristocratic.

The Palace of Versailles. Louis glorified his image as well through massive public works projects. Veterans' hospitals and new fortified towns on the frontiers represented his military might. Urban improvements, such as the reconstruction of the Louvre palace in Paris, proved his wealth. But his most ambitious project was the construction of a new palace at Versailles,◆ twelve miles from the turbulent capital (see illustration on the next page).

Building began in the 1660s. By 1685, the frenzied effort engaged 36,000 workers, not including the thousands of troops who diverted a local river to supply water for pools

◆**Versailles:** vur SY

Louis XIV Visits the Royal Tapestry Workshop
This tapestry was woven at the Gobelins tapestry workshop between 1673 and 1680. It shows Louis XIV (wearing a red hat) and his minister Colbert (dressed in black, holding his hat) visiting the workshop on the outskirts of Paris. The workshop artisans scurry to show Louis all the luxury objects they manufacture. Louis bought the workshop in 1662 and made it a national enterprise for making tapestries and furniture. *Bridgeman-Giraudon/Art Resource, NY.*

The Palace of Versailles
This view of the palace from 1675 shows the central section of the newly reconstructed palace. The entire building was still not complete at this date, but some sense of King Louis XIV's emphasis on majesty and order is already apparent. *Réunion des Musées Nationaux/Art Resource, NY. Photo: Gérard Blot.*

and fountains. The gardens designed by landscape architect André Le Nôtre reflected the spirit of Louis XIV's rule: their geometrical arrangements and clear lines showed that art and design could tame nature and that order and control defined the exercise of power. Le Nôtre's geometrical landscapes were imitated in places as far away as St. Petersburg in Russia and Washington, D.C. Versailles symbolized Louis's success in reining in the nobility and dominating Europe, and other monarchs eagerly mimicked French fashion and often conducted their business in French.

Yet for all its apparent luxury and frivolity, life at Versailles was often cramped and cold. Fifteen thousand people crowded into the palace's apartments, including all the highest military officers, the ministers of state, and the separate households of each member of the royal family. Refuse collected in the corridors during the incessant building, and thieves and prostitutes overran the grounds.

By the time Louis actually moved from the Louvre to Versailles in 1682, he had reigned as monarch for thirty-nine years. After his wife's death in 1683, he secretly married his mistress, Françoise d'Aubigné, marquise de Maintenon, and conducted most state affairs from her apartments at the palace. Her opponents at court complained that she controlled all the appointments, but her efforts focused on her own projects, including her favorite: the founding in 1686 of a royal school for girls from impoverished noble families. She also inspired Louis XIV to increase his devotion to Catholicism.

Enforcing Religious Orthodoxy

Louis believed that he ruled by divine right. As Bishop Jacques-Benigne Bossuet♦ (1627–1704) explained, "We have seen that kings

♦**Bossuet:** baw SWAY

take the place of God, who is the true father of the human species. We have also seen that the first idea of power which exists among men is that of the paternal power; and that kings are modeled on fathers." The king, like a father, should instruct his subjects in the true religion, or at least make sure that others did so.

Louis's campaign for religious conformity first focused on the Jansenists, Catholics whose doctrines and practices resembled some aspects of Protestantism. Following the posthumous publication of the book *Augustinus* (1640) by the Flemish theologian Cornelius Jansen (1585–1638), the Jansenists stressed the need for God's grace in achieving salvation. They emphasized the importance of original sin and, in their austere religious practice, resembled the English Puritans. Prominent among the Jansenists was Blaise Pascal (1623–1662), a mathematician of genius, who wrote his *Provincial Letters* (1656–1657) to defend Jansenism against charges of heresy. Many judges in the parlements likewise endorsed Jansenist doctrine.

Some questioned Louis's understanding of the finer points of doctrine: according to his sister-in-law, Louis himself "has never read anything about religion, nor the Bible either, and just goes along believing whatever he is told." But Louis rejected any doctrine that gave priority to considerations of individual conscience over the demands of the official church hierarchy, especially when that doctrine had been embraced by some noble supporters of the Fronde. Louis preferred teachings that stressed obedience to authority. Therefore, in 1660 he began enforcing various papal bulls (decrees) against Jansenism and closed down Jansenist theological centers. Jansenists were forced underground for the rest of his reign.

After many years of escalating pressure on the Calvinist Huguenots, Louis revoked the Edict of Nantes in 1685 and eliminated all of the Calvinists' rights. Louis considered the Edict (1598), by which his grandfather Henry IV granted the Protestants religious freedom and a degree of political independence, a temporary measure, and he fervently hoped to reconvert the Huguenots to Catholicism. He closed their churches and schools, banned all their public activities, and exiled those who refused to embrace the state religion. Thousands of Huguenots emigrated to England, Brandenburg-Prussia, the Dutch Republic, or North America. Many now wrote for publications attacking Louis XIV's absolutism. Protestant European countries were shocked by this crackdown on religious dissent and would cite it in justification of their wars against Louis.

> **Review:** How "absolute" was the power of Louis XIV?

Extending State Authority at Home and Abroad

Louis XIV could not have enforced his religious policies without the services of a nationwide bureaucracy. **Bureaucracy**—a network of state officials carrying out orders according to a regular and routine line of authority—comes from the French word *bureau*, for "desk," which came to mean "office," both in the sense of a physical space and a position of authority. Louis personally supervised the activities of his bureaucrats and worked to ensure his supremacy in all matters. But he always had to negotiate with nobles and local officials in order to achieve his ends.

Bureaucracy and Mercantilism. Louis extended the bureaucratic forms his predecessors had developed, especially the use of intendants, officials who held their positions directly from the king rather than owning their offices, as crown officials had traditionally done. Louis handpicked an intendant for each region to represent his will against entrenched local interests such as the parlements, provincial estates, and noble governors; they supervised the collection of taxes, the financing of public works, and the provisioning of the army. In 1673 Louis decreed that the parlements could no longer vote against his proposed laws or even speak against them. His intendants reduced local powers over finances and insisted on more efficient tax collection. Despite the doubling of taxes in Louis's reign, the local rebellions that had so beset the crown from the 1620s to the 1640s subsided in the face of these better-organized state forces.

Louis's success in consolidating his authority depended on hard work, an eye for detail, and an ear to the ground. In his memoirs he described the tasks he set for himself:

> to learn each hour the news concerning every province and every nation, the secrets of every court, the mood and weaknesses of each Prince and of every foreign minister; to be well-informed on an infinite number of matters about which we are supposed to know nothing; to elicit from our subjects what they hide from us with the greatest care; to discover the most remote opinions of our courtiers and the most hidden interests of those who come to us with quite contrary professions [claims].

To gather all this information, Louis relied on a series of talented ministers, usually of modest origins, who gained fame, fortune, and even noble status from serving the king. Most important among them was Jean-Baptiste Colbert (1619–1683), the son of a wool merchant turned royal official. Colbert had managed Mazarin's personal finances and worked his way up under Louis XIV to become head of royal finances, public works, and the navy. He founded a family dynasty that eventually produced five ministers of state, an archbishop, two bishops, and three generals.

Colbert used the bureaucracy to establish a new economic doctrine, **mercantilism**. According to mercantilist policy, governments must intervene to increase national wealth by whatever means possible. Such government intervention inevitably increased the role and eventually the number of bureaucrats needed. Under Colbert, the French government established overseas trading companies, granted manufacturing monopolies, and standardized production methods for textiles, paper, and soap. A government inspection system regulated the quality of finished goods and compelled all craftsmen to organize into guilds, in which masters could supervise the work of the journeymen and apprentices. To protect French production, Colbert rescinded many internal customs fees but enacted high foreign tariffs, which cut imports of competing goods. To compete more effectively with England and the Dutch Republic, Colbert also subsidized shipbuilding, a policy that dramatically expanded the number of seaworthy vessels. Such mercantilist measures aimed to ensure France's prominence in world markets and to provide the resources needed to fight wars against the increasingly long list of enemies. Although later economists questioned the value of this state intervention in the economy, virtually every government in Europe embraced mercantilism.

Colbert's mercantilist projects extended to Canada, where in 1663 he took control of the trading company that had founded New France. He transplanted several thousand peasants from western France to the present-day province of Quebec, which France had claimed since 1608. To guard his investment, Colbert sent fifteen hundred soldiers to join the settlers. Of particular concern to the French government were the Iroquois, who regularly interrupted French fur-trading convoys. Shows of French military force, including the burning of Indian villages and winter food supplies, forced the Iroquois to make peace with New France; and from 1666 to 1680, French traders moved westward with minimal interference. In 1672, fur trader Louis Jolliet and Jesuit missionary Jacques Marquette reached the upper Mississippi River and traveled downstream as far as Arkansas. In 1684, French explorer Sieur de La Salle went all the way down to the Gulf of Mexico, claiming a vast territory for Louis XIV and calling it Louisiana after him. Louis and Colbert encouraged colonial settlement as part of their rivalry with the English and the Dutch in the New World.

The Army and War. Colonial settlement occupied only a small portion of Louis XIV's attention, however, for his main foreign policy goal was to extend French power in Europe. In pursuing this purpose, he inevitably came up against the Spanish and Austrian Habsburgs, whose lands encircled his. To expand French power, Louis needed the biggest possible army. His powerful ministry of war centralized the organization of French troops. Barracks built in major towns received supplies from a central distribution system. The state began to provide uniforms for the soldiers and to offer veterans some hospital care. A militia draft instituted in 1688 supplemented the army in times of war and enrolled a hundred thousand men. Louis's wartime army could field a force as large as that of all his enemies combined.

Absolutist governments always tried to increase their territorial holdings, and as Louis extended his reach, he gained new enemies. In 1667–1668, in the War of Devolution (so called because Louis claimed that lands in the Spanish Netherlands should devolve to him because the Spanish king had failed to pay the dowry of Louis's Spanish bride), Louis defeated the Spanish armies but had to make peace when England, Sweden, and the Dutch Republic joined the war. In the Treaty of Aix-la-Chapelle◆ in 1668, he gained control of a few towns on the border of the Spanish Netherlands. Pamphlets sponsored by the Habsburgs accused Louis of aiming for "universal monarchy," or domination of Europe. The chorus of denunciation would only grow over the years.

In 1672, Louis XIV opened hostilities against the Dutch because they stood in the way of his acquisition of more territory in the Spanish Netherlands. He declared war again on Spain in 1673. By now the Dutch had allied themselves with their former Spanish masters to hold off the French. Louis also marched his troops into territories of the Holy Roman Empire, provoking many of the German princes to join with the emperor, the Spanish, and the Dutch in an alliance against Louis, now denounced as a "Christian Turk" for his imperialist ambitions. But the French armies more than held their own. Faced with bloody but inconclusive results on the battlefield, the parties agreed to the Treaty of Nijmegen◆ of 1678–1679, which ceded several Flemish towns and Franche-Comté to Louis, linking Alsace to the rest of France. French government deficits soared, and in 1675 increases in taxes touched off the most serious antitax revolt of Louis's reign.

Louis had no intention of standing still. Heartened by the Habsburgs' seeming weakness, he pushed eastward, seizing the city of Strasbourg in 1681 and invading the province of Lorraine in 1684. In 1688, he attacked some of the small German cities of the Holy

WARS OF LOUIS XIV

1667–1668	**War of Devolution** Enemies: Spain, Dutch Republic, England, Sweden Ended by Treaty of Aix-la-Chapelle in 1668, with France gaining towns in Spanish Netherlands (Flanders)
1672–1678	**Dutch War** Enemies: Dutch Republic, Spain, Holy Roman Empire Ended by Treaty of Nijmegen, 1678–1679, which gave several towns in Spanish Netherlands and Franche-Comté to France
1688–1697	**War of the League of Augsburg** Enemies: Holy Roman Empire, Sweden, Spain, England Ended by Peace of Rijswijk, 1697, with Louis returning all his conquests made since 1678 except Strasbourg

Roman Empire. As Louis's own mental powers diminished with age, he seems to have lost all sense of measure. His armies laid waste to German cities such as Mannheim; his government ordered the local military commander to "kill all those who would still wish to build houses there." Between 1689 and 1697, a coalition known as the League of Augsburg—made up of England, Spain, Sweden, the Dutch Republic, the Austrian emperor, and various German princes—fought Louis XIV to a stalemate. When hostilities ended in the Peace of Rijswijk◆ in 1697, Louis returned many of his conquests made since 1678 with the exception of Strasbourg (Map 17.1). Louis never lost his taste for war, but his allies learned how to set limits on his ambitions.

Louis was the last French ruler before Napoleon to accompany his troops to the battlefield. In later generations, as the military became more professional, French rulers left the fighting to their generals. Although Louis had eliminated the private armies of his noble courtiers, he constantly promoted his own military prowess in order to keep his noble officers under his sway. He had minia-

◆**Aix-la-Chapelle:** ayks lah shah PEHL
◆**Nijmegen:** NY may guhn

◆**Rijswijk:** RYS vyk

MAP 17.1 Louis XIV's Acquisitions, 1668–1697
Every ruler in Europe hoped to extend his or her territorial control, and war was often the result. Louis XIV steadily encroached on the Spanish Netherlands to the north and the lands of the Holy Roman Empire to the east. Although coalitions of European powers reined in Louis's grander ambitions, he nonetheless incorporated many neighboring territories into the French crown.

ture battle scenes painted on his high heels and commissioned tapestries showing his military processions into cities, even those he did not take by force. He seized every occasion to assert his supremacy, insisting that other fleets salute his ships first.

War required money and men, which Louis obtained by expanding state control over finances, conscription, and military supply. Thus, absolutism and warfare fed each other as the bureaucracy created new ways to raise and maintain an army and the army's success in war justified further expansion of state power. But constant warfare also eroded the state's resources. Further administrative and legal reform, the elimination of the buying and selling of offices, and the lowering of taxes—all were made impossible by the need for more money.

The playwright Corneille wrote, no doubt optimistically, "The people are very happy when they die for their kings." What is certain is that the wars touched many peasant and urban families. The people who lived on the routes leading to the battlefields had to house and feed soldiers; only nobles were exempt from this requirement. Everyone, moreover, paid the higher taxes that were necessary to support the army. By the end of Louis's reign, one in six Frenchmen had served in the military.

❖ Absolutism in Central and Eastern Europe

Central and eastern European rulers saw in Louis XIV a powerful model of absolutist state building, yet they did not blindly emulate the Sun King, in part because they confronted conditions peculiar to their regions. The ruler of Brandenburg-Prussia had to rebuild lands ravaged by the Thirty Years' War and unite far-flung territories. The Austrian Habsburgs needed to govern a mosaic of ethnic and religious groups while fighting off the Ottoman Turks. The Russian tsars wanted to extend their power over an extensive but relatively impoverished empire. The great exception to absolutism in eastern Europe was Poland-Lithuania, where a long crisis virtually destroyed central authority and pulled much of eastern Europe into its turbulent wake.

Brandenburg-Prussia and Sweden: Militaristic Absolutism

Brandenburg-Prussia began as a puny state on the Elbe River, but it had a remarkable future. In the nineteenth century, it would unify the disparate German states into modern-day Germany. The ruler of Brandenburg was an elector, one of the seven German princes entitled to select the Holy Roman Emperor. Since the sixteenth century the ruler of Brandenburg had also controlled the duchy of East Prussia; after 1618 the state was called Brandenburg-Prussia. Despite meager resources, Frederick William of Hohenzollern, the Great Elector of Brandenburg-Prussia (r. 1640–1688), succeeded in welding his scattered lands into an absolutist state.

Pressured first by the necessities of fighting the Thirty Years' War and then by the demands of reconstruction, Frederick William determined to force his territories' estates (representative assemblies) to grant him a dependable income. The Great Elector struck a deal with the Junkers◆ (nobles) of each province: in exchange for allowing him to collect taxes, he gave them complete control over their enserfed peasants and exempted them from taxation. The tactic worked. By the end of his reign, the estates met only on ceremonial occasions.

Supplied with a steady income, Frederick William could devote his attention to military and bureaucratic consolidation. Over

forty years he expanded his army from eight thousand to thirty thousand men. (See "Taking Measure" below.) The army mirrored the rigid domination of nobles over peasants that characterized Brandenburg-Prussian society: peasants filled the ranks, and Junkers became officers. Nobles also took positions as bureaucratic officials, but military needs always had priority. The elector named special war commissars to take charge not only of military affairs but also of tax collection. To hasten military dispatches, he also established one of Europe's first state postal systems.

As a Calvinist ruler, Frederick William avoided the ostentation of the French court, even while following the absolutist model of centralizing state power. He boldly rebuffed Louis XIV by welcoming twenty thousand French Huguenot refugees after Louis's revocation of the Edict of Nantes. In pursuing foreign and domestic policies that promoted state power and prestige, Frederick William adroitly switched sides in Louis's wars and would stop at almost nothing to crush resistance at home.

TAKING MEASURE

State	Soldiers	Population	Ratio of soldiers/total population
France	300,000	20 million	1:66
Russia	220,000	14 million	1:64
Austria	100,000	8 million	1:80
Sweden	40,000	1 million	1:25
Brandenburg-Prussia	30,000	2 million	1:66
England	24,000	10 million	1:410

*Figures for the end of the seventeenth century, ranging from 1688 for Prussia to 1710 for France

The Seventeenth-Century Army

The figures in this chart are only approximate, but they tell an important story. What conclusions can be drawn about the relative weight of the military in the different European states? Why would England have such a smaller army than the others? Is the absolute or the relative size of the military the most important indicator? *From André Corvisier, Armées et sociétés en Europe de 1494 à 1789 (Paris: Presses Universitaires de France, 1976), 126.*

◆**Junkers:** YUN kurs

In 1701, his son Frederick I (r. 1688–1713) persuaded Holy Roman Emperor Leopold I to grant him the title "king in Prussia." Prussia had arrived as an important power.

Across the Baltic, Sweden also stood out as an example of absolutist consolidation. In the Thirty Years' War, King Gustavus Adolphus's superb generalship and highly trained army had made Sweden the supreme power of northern Europe. The huge but sparsely populated state included not only most of present-day Sweden but also Finland, Estonia, half of Latvia, and much of the Baltic coastline of modern Poland and Germany. The Baltic, in short, was a Swedish lake. After Gustavus Adolphus died, his daughter Queen Christina (r. 1632–1654) conceded much authority to the estates. Absorbed by religion and philosophy, Christina eventually abdicated and converted to Catholicism. Her successors temporarily made Sweden an absolute monarchy.

In Sweden (as in neighboring Denmark-Norway), absolutism meant the estates standing aside while the king led the army in lucrative foreign campaigns. The aristocracy went along because it staffed the bureaucracy and reaped war profits. Intrigued by French culture, Swedes also gleamed with national pride. In 1668, the nobility demanded the introduction of a distinctive national costume: should we Swedes, they asked, "who are so glorious and renowned a nation. . . . let ourselves be led by the nose by a parcel of French dancing-masters"? Sweden spent the forty years after 1654 continuously warring with its neighbors. By the 1690s, war expenses began to outrun the small Swedish population's ability to pay, threatening the continuation of absolutism.

An Uneasy Balance: Austrian Habsburgs and Ottoman Turks

Holy Roman Emperor Leopold I (r. 1658–1705) ruled over a variety of territories of different ethnicities, languages, and religions, yet in ways similar to his French and Prussian counterparts, he gradually consolidated his power. Like all the Holy Roman emperors since 1438, Leopold was an Austrian Habsburg. He was simultaneously duke of Upper and Lower Silesia,♦ count of Tyrol,

archduke of Upper and Lower Austria, king of Bohemia, king of Hungary and Croatia, and ruler of Styria♦ and Moravia (Map 17.2). Some of these territories were provinces in the Holy Roman Empire; others were simply ruled from Vienna as Habsburg family holdings.

The Austrian Version of Absolutism. Leopold needed to build up his armies and state authority in order to defend the Holy Roman Empire's international position, which had been weakened by the Thirty Years' War. The emperor and his closest officials took control over recruiting, provisioning, and strategic planning and worked to replace the mercenaries hired during the Thirty Years' War with a permanent standing army that promoted professional discipline. To pay for the army and staff his growing bureaucracy, Leopold had to gain the support of local aristocrats and chip away at provincial institutions' powers.

Intent on replacing Bohemian nobles who had supported the 1618 revolt against Austrian authority, the Habsburgs promoted a new nobility made up of Czechs, Germans, Italians, Spaniards, and even Irish who used German as their common tongue, professed Catholicism, and loyally served the Austrian dynasty. Bohemia became a virtual Austrian colony. "You have utterly destroyed our home, our ancient kingdom, and have built us no new one in its place," lamented a Czech Jesuit in 1670, addressing Leopold. "Woe to you! . . . The nobles you have oppressed, great cities made small. Of smiling towns you have made straggling villages." Austrian censors prohibited publication of this protest for over a century.

Battle for Hungary. In addition to holding Louis XIV in check on his western frontiers, Leopold had to confront the ever-present challenge of the Ottoman Turks to his east. Hungary was the chief battle zone between Austria and the Turks for more than 150 years. In 1682, when war broke out again, Austria controlled the northwest section of Hungary; the Turks occupied the center; and in the east, the Turks demanded tribute from the Hungarian princes who ruled Transylvania. In 1683, the Turks pushed all the way to the gates of Vienna and laid siege to the Austrian

♦**Silesia:** sy LEE zhee uh

♦**Styria:** STIHR ee uh

Brandenburg-Prussian territory in 1640
Brandenburg-Prussian territory acquired to 1688
Austrian Habsburg territory in 1648
Lands taken from Turks by Austrian Habsburgs, to 1699

MAP 17.2 State Building in Central and Eastern Europe, 1648–1699
The Austrian Habsburgs had long contested the Ottoman Turks for dominance of eastern Europe, and by 1699 they had pushed the Turks out of Hungary. In central Europe, the Austrian Habsburgs confronted the growing power of Brandenburg-Prussia, which had emerged from relative obscurity after the Thirty Years' War to begin an aggressive program of expanding its military and its territorial base. As emperor of the Holy Roman Empire, the Austrian Habsburg ruler governed a huge expanse of territory, but the emperor's control was in fact only partial because of guarantees of local autonomy.

capital; after reaching this high-water mark, however, Turkish power ebbed. With the help of Polish cavalry, the Austrians finally broke the siege and turned the tide in a major counteroffensive (see illustration on the next page). By the Treaty of Karlowitz♦ of 1699, the Ottoman Turks surrendered almost all of Hungary to the Austrians.

Hungary's "liberation" from the Turks came at a high price. The fighting laid waste vast stretches of Hungary's central plain, and the population may have declined by as much as 65 percent after 1600. Once the Turks had been beaten back, Austrian rule over Hungary tightened. In 1687, the Habsburg dynasty's hereditary right to

the Hungarian crown was acknowledged by the Hungarian diet, a parliament revived by Leopold in 1681 to gain the support of Hungarian nobles. The diet was dominated by nobles who had amassed huge holdings in the liberated territories. They formed the core of a pro-Habsburg Hungarian aristocracy that would buttress the dynasty until it fell in 1918; Austrians and Hungarians dominated the other ethnic groups such as Croats and Romanians who had enjoyed considerable autonomy under the Ottoman Turks. To root out remaining Turkish influence and assert Austrian superiority, Leopold systematically destroyed Turkish buildings and rebuilt Catholic churches, monasteries, roadside shrines, and monuments in the flamboyant Austrian baroque style.

♦**Karlowitz:** KAHR luh vihts

The Siege of Vienna, 1683
This detail from a painting by Franz Geffels shows the camp of the Ottoman Turks. The Turkish armies had surrounded Vienna since July 14, 1683. Jan Sobieski led an army of Poles which joined with Austrians and Germans to beat back the Turks on September 12, 1683. © *Archivo Iconografico, S.A./CORBIS.*

Ottoman State Authority. The Ottoman Turks also pursued state consolidation, but in a very different fashion from the Europeans. The Ottoman state extended its authority through a combination of settlement and military control. Hundreds of thousands of Turkish families moved with Turkish soldiers into the Balkan peninsula in the 1400s and 1500s. As locals converted to Islam, administration passed gradually into their hands. To this day, the Croatian language, for example, includes many Turkish words. In the Ottoman homeland of Anatolia, the sultans, the Ottoman rulers, were often challenged by mutinous army officers. Despite frequent palace coups and assassinations of sultans, the Ottoman state survived. Un-

like its European counterparts, it rarely faced peasant revolts. Rather than resisting state authorities, Ottoman peasants periodically worked for the state as mercenaries. Similarly, the Ottomans played the elites off each other, absorbing some into the state bureaucracy and pitting one level of authority against another. This constantly shifting social and political system explains how the coup-ridden Ottoman state could appear weak in Western eyes and still pose a massive military threat on Europe's southeastern borders. In the end, the Ottoman state lasted longer than Louis XIV's absolute monarchy. Nevertheless, the seventeenth century marked a period of cultural decline in the eyes of the Turks themselves; they looked back to the sixteenth century as their golden age in poetry and architecture.

Russia: Foundations of Bureaucratic Absolutism

Seventeenth-century Russia seemed a world apart from the Europe of Louis XIV. Straddling Europe and Asia, it stretched across Siberia to the Pacific Ocean. Western visitors either sneered or shuddered at the "barbarism" of Russian life, and Russians reciprocated by nursing deep suspicions of everything foreign. But under the surface, Russia was evolving along paths much like the rest of absolutist Europe; the tsars wanted to claim unlimited autocratic power, but they had to surmount internal disorder and come to an accommodation with noble landlords.

Serfdom and the Code of 1649. When Tsar Alexei (r. 1645–1676) tried to extend state authority by imposing new administrative structures and taxes in 1648, Moscow and other cities erupted in bloody rioting. The government immediately doused the fire. In 1649, Alexei convoked the Assembly of the Land (consisting of noble delegates from the provinces) to consult on a sweeping law code to organize Russian society in a strict social hierarchy that would last for nearly two centuries. The code of 1649 assigned all subjects to a hereditary class according to their current occupation or state needs. Slaves and free peasants were merged into a serf class. As serfs they could not change occupations or move; they were tightly tied to the soil and to their noble masters. To prevent tax evasion, the code also forbade townspeople to move from the community where they resided. Nobles owed absolute obedience to the tsar and were required to serve in the army, but in return no other group could own estates worked by serfs. Serfs became the chattel of their lord, who could sell them like horses or land. Their conditions of life differed little from those of the slaves on the plantations in the Americas.

Some peasants resisted enserfment. In 1667, Stenka Razin, a Cossack from the Don region in southern Russia, led a rebellion that promised liberation from "the traitors and bloodsuckers of the peasant communes"—the great noble landowners, local governors, and Moscow courtiers. Captured four years later by the tsar's army, Razin was dismembered, his head and limbs publicly displayed, and his body thrown to the dogs (see the illustration on this page). Thousands of his followers also suffered grisly deaths, but his memory lived on in folk songs and legends. Landlords successfully petitioned for the abolition of the statute of limitations on runaway serfs, the use of state agents in searching for runaways, and harsh penalties against those who harbored runaways. The increase in Russian state authority went hand in hand with the enforcement of serfdom.

The Tsar's Absolute Powers.   To extend his power and emulate his western rivals, Tsar Alexei wanted a bigger army, exclusive control over state policy, and a greater say in religious matters. The size of the army increased dramatically from 35,000 in the 1630s to 220,000 by the end of the century. The Assembly of the Land, once an important source of noble consultation, never met again after 1653. Alexei also imposed firm control over the Russian Orthodox church. In 1666, a church council reaffirmed the tsar's role as God's direct representative on earth. The state-dominated church took action against a religious group called the **Old Believers**, who rejected church efforts to bring Russian worship in line with Byzantine tradition. Old Believer leaders, including the noblewoman Fedosia Morozova, endured exile, prison, and torture; whole communities of

Stenka Razin in Captivity
After leading a revolt of thousands of serfs, peasants, and members of non-Russian tribes of the middle and lower Volga region, Stenka Razin was captured by Russian forces and led off to Moscow, as shown here, where he was executed in 1671. He has been the subject of songs, legends, and poems ever since. *Novosti Photo Library (London).*

Old Believers starved or burned themselves to death rather than submit. Religious schism opened a gulf between the Russian people and the crown.

Nevertheless, modernizing trends prevailed. As the state bureaucracy expanded, adding more officials and establishing regulations and routines, the government intervened more and more in daily life. Decrees regulated tobacco smoking, card playing, and alcohol consumption and even dictated how people should leash and fence their pet dogs. Nobles and ordinary citizens commissioned portraits of themselves instead of only buying religious icons. Tsar Alexei set up the first Western-style theater in the Kremlin, and his daughter Sophia translated French plays. The most adventurous nobles began to wear German-style clothing. Some even argued that service and not just birth should determine rank. A long struggle over Western influences had begun.

Poland-Lithuania Overwhelmed

Unlike the other eastern European powers, Poland-Lithuania did not follow the absolutist model. Decades of war weakened the monarchy and made the great nobles into virtually autonomous warlords. They used the parliament and demands for constitutionalism to stymie monarchical power. The result was a precipitous slide into political disarray and weakness.

In 1648, Ukrainian Cossack warriors revolted against the king of Poland-Lithuania, inaugurating two decades of tumult known as the Deluge. Cossack bands had formed from runaway peasants and poor nobles in the no-man's-land of southern Russia and Ukraine. The Polish nobles who claimed this potentially rich land scorned the Cossacks as troublemakers, but to the Ukrainian peasant population they were liberators. In 1654, the Cossacks offered Ukraine to Russian rule, provoking a Russo-Polish war that ended in 1667 when the tsar annexed eastern Ukraine and Kiev. Neighboring powers tried to profit from the chaos in Poland-Lithuania; Sweden, Brandenburg-Prussia, and Transylvania sent armies to seize territory.

Many towns were destroyed in the fighting, and as much as a third of the Polish population perished. The once prosperous Jewish and Protestant minorities suffered greatly: some fifty-six thousand Jews were killed by either the Cossacks, Polish peasants, or Russian troops, and thousands more had to flee or convert to Christianity. One rabbi wrote, "We were slaughtered each day, in a more agonizing way than cattle: they are butchered quickly, while we were being executed slowly." Surviving Jews moved from towns to shtetls◆ (Jewish villages), where they took up petty trading, moneylending, tax gathering, and tavern leasing—activities that fanned peasant anti-Semitism. Desperate for protection amid the war, most Protestants backed the violently anti-Catholic Swedes, and the victorious Catholic majority branded them as traitors. Some Protestant refugees fled to the Dutch Republic and England. In Poland-Lithuania it came to be assumed that a good Pole was a Catholic. The commonwealth had ceased to be an outpost of toleration.

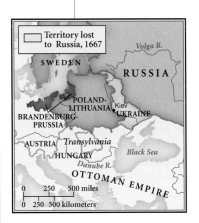

Poland-Lithuania in the Seventeenth Century

◆**shtetls:** SHTEH tuhls

The commonwealth revived briefly when a man of ability and ambition, Jan Sobieski (r. 1674–1696), was elected king. He gained a reputation throughout Europe when he led twenty-five thousand Polish cavalrymen into battle in the siege of Vienna in 1683. His cavalry helped rout the Turks and turned the tide against the Ottomans. Married to a politically shrewd French princess, Sobieski openly admired Louis XIV's France. Despite his efforts to rebuild the monarchy, he could not halt Poland-Lithuania's decline into powerlessness.

Elsewhere the ravages of war had created opportunities for kings to increase their power, but in Poland-Lithuania the great nobles gained all the advantage. They dominated the Sejm (parliament), and to maintain an equilibrium among themselves, they each wielded an absolute veto power. This "free veto" constitutional system deadlocked parliamentary government. The monarchy lost its room to maneuver, and with it much of its remaining power. An appalled Croat visitor in 1658 commented on the situation:

> Among the Poles there is no order in the state, and the subjects are not afraid either of the king or the judge. Everybody who is stronger thinks to have the right to oppress the weaker, just as the wolves and bears are free to capture and kill cattle.... Such abominable depravity is called by the Poles "aristocratic freedom."

The Polish version of constitutionalism fatally weakened the state and made it prey to neighboring powers.

Review: Why did absolutism succeed everywhere in eastern Europe except Poland-Lithuania?

❖ Constitutionalism in England

In the second half of the seventeenth century, western and eastern Europe began to move in different directions. In general, the farther east one traveled, the more absolutist the style of government (with the exception of Poland-Lithuania) and the greater the gulf between landlord and peasant. In eastern Europe, nobles lorded over their serfs but owed almost slavish obedience in turn to their rulers. In western Europe, even in absolutist France, serfdom had almost entirely disappeared and nobles and rulers alike faced greater challenges to their control. The greatest challenges of all would come in England.

This outcome might seem surprising, for the English monarchs enjoyed many advantages compared with their continental rivals: they needed less money for their armies because they had stayed out of the Thirty Years' War, and their island kingdom was in theory easier to rule because its population was only one-fourth the size of France's and of relatively homogeneous ethnicity. Yet the English rulers failed in their efforts to install absolutist policies. The English revolutions of 1642–1660 and 1688–1689 overturned two kings, confirmed the constitutional powers of an elected parliament, and laid the foundation for the idea that government must guarantee certain rights under the law.

England Turned Upside Down, 1642–1660

Disputes about the right to levy taxes and the nature of authority in the Church of England had long troubled the relationship between the English crown and Parliament. For more than a hundred years, wealthy English landowners had been accustomed to participating in government through Parliament and expected to be consulted on royal policy. Although England had no one constitutional document, a variety of laws, judicial decisions, charters and petitions granted by the king, and customary procedures all regulated relations between king and Parliament. When Charles I tried to assert his authority over Parliament, a civil war broke out. It set in motion an unpredictable chain of events, which included an extraordinary ferment of religious and political ideas. Some historians view the English civil war of 1642–1646 as the last great war of religion because it pitted Puritans against those trying to push the Anglican church toward Catholicism; others see in it the first modern revolution because it gave birth to democratic political and religious movements.

Charles I versus Parliament. When Charles I (r. 1625–1649) succeeded his father, James I, he faced an increasingly aggressive Parliament that resisted new taxes and resented the king's efforts to extend his personal control. In 1628, Parliament forced Charles to agree to the Petition of Right, by which he promised not to levy taxes without

Artemisia Gentileschi, *Painting*
Among the many paintings commissioned by King Charles I of England was this painting by the Italian artist Artemisia Gentileschi (1630s), which shows the artist herself at work. Gentileschi lived at the English court and worked for Charles between 1638 and 1641. She painted as well for King Philip IV of Spain and for many Italian patrons. Coming from the hand of a woman, the painting must be seen as a kind of wry commentary on women's exclusion from most cultural endeavors. The figure supposedly represents an allegory of painting. Most allegories—symbolic figures standing for abstract concepts—relied on female figures, not because women did these things but because women could be imagined as symbols. The Italian word for "painting," moreover, like many Romance-language words for abstractions, is gendered female *(la pittura)*. But Gentileschi portrays herself, not an abstract female figure, as if to say that real women can paint too. *The Royal Collection. © 2004 Her Majesty Queen Elizabeth II.*

its consent. Charles hoped to avoid further interference with his plans by simply refusing to call Parliament into session between 1629 and 1640. Without it, the king's ministers had to find every loophole possible to raise revenues. They tried to turn "ship money," a levy on seaports in times of emergency, into an annual tax collected everywhere in the country. The crown won the ensuing court case, but many subjects still refused to pay what they considered to be an illegal tax.

Religious tensions brought conflicts over the king's authority to a head. The Puritans had long agitated for the removal of any vestiges of Catholicism, but Charles, married to a French Catholic, moved in the opposite direction. With Charles's encouragement, the archbishop of Canterbury, William Laud (1573–1645), imposed increasingly elaborate ceremonies on the Anglican church. Angered by these moves toward "popery," the Puritans poured forth reproving pamphlets and sermons. In response Laud hauled them before the feared Court of Star Chamber, which the king personally controlled. The court ordered harsh sentences for Laud's Puritan critics; they were whipped, pilloried, branded, and even had their ears cut off and their noses split. When Laud tried to apply his policies to Scotland, however, they backfired completely: the stubborn Presbyterian Scots rioted against the imposition of the Anglican prayer book—the Book of Common Prayer—and in 1640 they invaded the north of England. To raise money to fight the war, Charles called Parliament into session and unwittingly opened the door to a constitutional and religious crisis.

The Parliament of 1640 did not intend revolution, but reformers in the House of Commons (the lower house of Parliament) wanted to undo what they saw as the royal tyranny of the 1630s. Parliament removed Laud from office, ordered the execution of an unpopular royal commander, abolished the Court of Star Chamber, repealed recently levied taxes, and provided for a parliamentary assembly at least once every three years, thus establishing a constitutional check on royal authority. Moderate reformers expected to stop there and resisted Puritan pressure to abolish bishops and eliminate the Anglican prayer book. But their hand was forced in

January 1642, when Charles and his soldiers invaded Parliament and tried unsuccessfully to arrest those leaders who had moved to curb his power. Faced with mounting opposition within London, Charles quickly withdrew from the city and organized an army.

Civil War and the Challenge to All Authorities. The ensuing civil war between king and Parliament lasted four years (1642–1646) and divided the country. The king's army of royalists, known as Cavaliers, enjoyed the most support in northern and western England. The parliamentary forces, called Roundheads because they cut their hair short, had their stronghold in the southeast, including London. Although Puritans dominated on the parliamentary side, they were divided among themselves about the proper form of church government: the Presbyterians wanted a Calvinist church with some central authority, whereas the Independents favored entirely autonomous congregations free from other church government (hence the term *congregationalism,* often associated with the Independents). Putting aside their differences for the sake of military unity, the Puritans united under an obscure member of the House of Commons, the country gentleman Oliver Cromwell (1599–1658), who sympathized with the Independents. After Cromwell skillfully reorganized the parliamentary troops, his New Model Army defeated the Cavaliers at the battle of Naseby in 1645. Charles surrendered in 1646.

Although the civil war between king and Parliament had ended in victory for Parliament, divisions within the Puritan

England during the Civil War

ranks now came to the fore: the Presbyterians dominated Parliament, but the Independents controlled the army. The disputes between elites drew lower-class groups into the debate. (See "Contrasting Views," page 640.) When Parliament tried to disband the New Model Army in 1647, disgruntled soldiers protested. Called **Levellers** because of their insistence on leveling social differences, the soldiers took on their officers in a series of debates about the nature of political authority. The Levellers demanded that Parliament meet annually, that members be paid so as to allow common people to participate, and that all male heads of households be allowed to vote. Their ideal of political participation excluded servants, the propertyless, and women but offered access to artisans, shopkeepers, and modest farmers. Cromwell and other army leaders rejected the Levellers' demands as threatening to property owners. Cromwell insisted, "You have no other way to deal with these men but to break them in pieces.... If you do not break them they will break you."

Just as political differences between Presbyterians and Independents helped spark new political movements, so too their conflicts over church organization fostered the emergence of new religious doctrines. The new sects had in common only their emphasis on the "inner light" of individual religious inspiration and a disdain for hierarchical authority (see the illustration). Their emphasis on equality before God and greater participation in church governance appealed to the middle and lower classes. The Baptists, for example, insisted on adult baptism because they believed

that Christians should choose their own church and that every child should not automatically become a member of the Church of England. The Quakers demonstrated their beliefs in equality and the inner light by refusing to doff their hats to men in authority. Manifesting their religious experience by trembling, or "quaking," the Quakers believed that anyone—man or woman—inspired by a direct experience of God could preach.

Parliamentary leaders feared that the new sects would overturn the whole social hierarchy. Rumors abounded, for example, of naked Quakers running through the streets waiting

Religious Radicals

The Puritans in Parliament had opposed the Catholic leanings of the Church of England (shown as the Arminian here) and worried that Catholic missionary groups, such as the Jesuits (top left), might gain access to England. But they also detested the nonconformist Protestant sects that sprang up during the civil war: some individuals, called Ranters or Seekers, supposedly claimed they were Jesus come again; Arians rejected the doctrine of the Trinity; libertines attacked all sacramental objects of religion; anti-scripturians rejected the authority of the Bible; soul sleepers believed that souls of the dead remained "asleep" until the Second Coming; Anabaptists refused infant baptism; the family of love did not keep the sabbath; and some advocated easier divorce. It should be remembered that pamphlets such as the one from which this illustration was taken represented the views of those who opposed these tendencies. It is questionable, for example, whether Arians believed in free love, libertines attacked religious objects, or those in favor of easier divorce beat their wives. *British Library.*

The English Civil War

The civil war between Charles I and Parliament (1642–1646) excited furious debates about the proper forms of political authority, debates that influenced political thought for two centuries or more. The Levellers, who served in the parliamentary army, wanted Parliament to be more accountable to ordinary men like themselves (Document 1). After the restoration of the monarchy in 1660, Lucy Hutchinson wrote a memoir in which she complained that Puritan *had become a term of political slander. Her memoir shows how religious terms had been politicized by the upheaval (Document 2). Thomas Hobbes, in his famous political treatise* Leviathan *(1651), develops the consequences of the civil war for political theory (Document 3).*

1. THE LEVELLERS, "THE AGREEMENT OF THE PEOPLE, AS PRESENTED TO THE COUNCIL OF THE ARMY" (OCTOBER 28, 1647)

Note especially two things about this document: (1) it focuses on Parliament as the chief instrument of reform, and (2) it claims that government depends on the consent of the people.

...Since, therefore, our former oppressions and scarce-yet-ended troubles have been occasioned, either by want of frequent national meetings in Council [Parliament], or by rendering those meetings ineffectual, we are fully agreed and resolved to provide that hereafter our representatives be neither left to an uncertainty for the time nor made useless to the ends for which they are intended. In order whereunto we declare:— That the people of England, being at this day very unequally distributed by Counties, Cities, and Borough for the election of their deputies in Parliament, ought to be more indifferently [equally] proportioned according to the number of the inhabitants....That the power of this, and all future Representatives of this Nation, is inferior only to theirs who choose them, and doth extend, without the consent or concurrence of any other person or persons [the king], to the enacting, altering, and repealing of laws, to the erecting and abolishing of offices and courts, to the appointing, removing, and calling to account magistrates and officers of all degrees, to the making of war and peace, to the treating with foreign States [in other words, Parliament is the supreme power, not the king]....These things we declare to be our native rights, and therefore are agreed and resolved to maintain them with our utmost possibilities against all opposition whatsoever....

Source: Samuel Rawson Gardiner, ed., *The Constitutional Documents of the Puritan Revolution, 1625–1660* (Oxford: Clarendon Press, 1906), 333–35.

2. LUCY HUTCHINSON, MEMOIRS OF THE LIFE OF COLONEL HUTCHINSON (1664–1671)

Lucy Hutchinson wrote her memoir to defend her Puritan husband, who had been imprisoned upon the restoration of the monarchy.

for "a sign." Some sects did advocate sweeping change. The Diggers promoted rural communism—collective ownership of all property. Seekers and Ranters questioned just about everything. One notorious Ranter, John Robins, even claimed to be God. A few men advocated free love. These developments convinced the political elite that tolerating the new sects would lead to skepticism, anarchism, and debauchery.

In keeping with their notions of equality and individual inspiration, many of the new sects provided opportunities for women to become preachers and prophets. The Quakers thought women especially capable of prophecy. One prophet, Anna Trapnel, explained her vocation: "For in all that was said by me, I was nothing, the Lord put all in my mouth, and told me what I should say." Women pre-

If any were grieved at the dishonour of the kingdom, or the griping of the poor, or the unjust oppressions of the subject by a thousand ways invented to maintain the riots of the courtiers and the swarms of needy Scots the king had brought in to devour like locusts the plenty of this land, he was a puritan; if any showed favour to any godly, honest person, kept them company, relieved them in want, or protected them against violent and unjust oppression, he was a puritan.... In short, all that crossed the views of the needy courtiers, the proud encroaching priests, the thievish projectors, the lewd nobility and gentry... all these were puritans; and if puritans, then enemies to the king and his government, seditious, factious hypocrites, ambitious disturbers of the public peace, and finally the pest of the kingdom.

Source: Christopher Hill and Edmund Dell, eds., *The Good Old Cause: The English Revolution of 1640–1660, Its Causes, Course and Consequences* (London: Lawrence and Wishart, 1949), 179–80.

3. THOMAS HOBBES, *LEVIATHAN* (1651)

In this excerpt, Hobbes depicts the anarchy of a society without a strong central authority, but he leaves open the question of whether that authority should be vested in "one Man" or "one Assembly of men," that is, a king or a parliament.

During the time men live without a common Power to keep them all in awe, they are in that condition which is called Warre; and such a warre, as is of every man, against every man.... In such condition, there is no place for Industry; because the fruit thereof is uncertain: and consequently no Culture of the Earth; no Navigation, nor use of the commodities that may be imported by Sea; no commodious Building; no Instrument of moving, and removing such things as require much force; no Knowledge of the face of the Earth; no account of Time; no Arts; no Letters; no Society; and which is worst of all, continuall feare, and danger of violent death; and the life of man, solitary, poore, nasty, brutish, and short.

The only way to erect such a Common Power, as may be able to defend them from the invasion of Forraigners, and the injuries of one another, and thereby to secure them in such sort, as that by their owne industrie, and by the Fruites of the Earth, they may nourish themselves and live contentedly; is, to conferre all their power and strength upon one Man, or upon one Assembly of men, that may reduce all their wills, by plurality of voices, unto one Will.... This is more than Consent, or Concord; it is a reall Unitie of them all, in one and the same Person, made by Covenant of every man with every man.... This done, the Multitude so united in one Person, is called a COMMON-WEALTH, in latine CIVITAS. This is the Generation of that great LEVIATHAN, or rather (to speake more reverently) of that *Mortall God*, to which wee owe under the *Immortall God*, our peace and defence.

Source: Thomas Hobbes, *Leviathan*, ed. Richard E. Flathman and David Johnston (New York: Norton, 1997), 70, 95.

QUESTIONS TO CONSIDER
1. Why would both the king and the parliamentary leaders find the Levellers' views disturbing?
2. Why did Hobbes's arguments about political authority upset supporters of both monarchy and Parliament?

sented petitions, participated prominently in street demonstrations, distributed tracts, and occasionally even dressed as men, wearing swords and joining armies. The duchess of Newcastle complained in 1650 that women were "affecting a Masculinacy... practicing the behaviour... of men." The outspoken women in new sects like the Quakers underscored the threat of a social order turning upside down.

Oliver Cromwell. At the heart of the continuing political struggle was the question of what to do with the king, who tried to negotiate with the Presbyterians in Parliament. In late 1648, Independents in the army purged the Presbyterians from Parliament, leaving a "rump" of about seventy members. This Rump Parliament then created a high court to try Charles I. The court found him guilty

Oliver Cromwell
In this painting of 1649, Robert Walker deliberately evokes previous portraits of English kings. Cromwell is shown preparing for battle in Ireland (note the shore and sea on Cromwell's right); he holds the baton of military command, and a young page is tying on a sash, symbol of his rank. Cromwell lived an austere life; he is depicted here without any sign of luxury. When he died, he was buried in Westminster Abbey, but in 1661 his body was exhumed and hanged in its shroud. His head was cut off and displayed outside Westminster Hall for nearly twenty years. *Courtesy of the National Portrait Gallery, London.*

of attempting to establish "an unlimited and tyrannical power" and pronounced a death sentence. On January 30, 1649, Charles was beheaded before an enormous crowd, which reportedly groaned as one when the axe fell. Although many had objected to Charles's autocratic rule, few had wanted him killed. For royalists, Charles immediately became a martyr, and reports of miracles, such as the curing of blindness by the touch of a handkerchief soaked in his blood, soon circulated.

The Rump Parliament abolished the monarchy and the House of Lords (the upper house of Parliament) and set up a Puritan republic with Oliver Cromwell (see the illustration on this page) as chairman of the Council of State. Cromwell did not tolerate

dissent from his policies. He saw the hand of God in events and himself as God's agent. Pamphleteers and songwriters ridiculed his red nose and accused him of wanting to be king, but few challenged his leadership. When his agents discovered plans for mutiny within the army, they executed the perpetrators; new decrees silenced the Levellers. Although Cromwell allowed the various Puritan sects to worship rather freely and permitted Jews with needed skills to return to England for the first time since the thirteenth century, Catholics could not worship publicly, nor could Anglicans use the Book of Common Prayer. The elites—many of them were still Anglican—were troubled by Cromwell's religious policies but pleased to see some social order reestablished.

The new regime aimed to extend state power just as Charles I had before. Cromwell laid the foundation for a Great Britain made up of England, Ireland, and Scotland by reconquering Scotland and subduing Ireland. Anti-English rebels in Ireland had seized the occasion of troubles between king and Parliament to revolt in 1641. When his position was secured in 1649, Cromwell went to Ireland with a large force and easily defeated the rebels, massacring whole garrisons and their priests. He encouraged expropriating the lands of the Irish "barbarous wretches," and Scottish immigrants resettled the northern county of Ulster. This seventeenth-century English conquest left a legacy of bitterness that the Irish even today call "the curse of Cromwell." In 1651, Parliament turned its attention overseas, putting mercantilist ideas into practice in the first Navigation Act, which allowed imports only if they were carried on English ships or came directly from the producers of goods. The Navigation Act was aimed at the Dutch, who dominated world trade; Cromwell tried to carry the policy further by waging naval war on the Dutch from 1652 to 1654.

At home, however, Cromwell faced growing resistance. His wars required a budget twice the size of Charles I's, and his increases in property taxes and customs duties alienated landowners and merchants. The conflict reached a crisis in 1653: Parliament considered disbanding the army, whereupon Cromwell abolished the Rump Parliament in a military coup and made himself Lord

Protector. He now silenced his critics by banning newspapers and using networks of spies and mail readers to keep tabs on his enemies. When Cromwell died in 1658, the diarist John Evelyn claimed, "There were none that cried but dogs." Cromwell intended that his son should succeed him, but his death only revived the prospect of civil war and political chaos. In 1660, a newly elected, staunchly Anglican Parliament invited Charles II, the son of the executed king, to return from exile.

The Glorious Revolution of 1688

The traditional monarchical form of government was reinstated in 1660, restoring the king to full partnership with Parliament. Charles II (r. 1660–1685) promised "a liberty to tender consciences" in an attempt to extend religious toleration, especially to Catholics, with whom he sympathized. Yet in the first years of his reign more than a thousand Puritan ministers lost their positions, and after 1664, attending a service other than one conforming with the Anglican prayer book was illegal. Natural disasters also marred the early years of Charles II's reign. The plague stalked London's rat-infested streets in May 1665 and claimed more than thirty thousand victims by September. Then in 1666, the Great Fire (see the illustration below) swept the city. The crown now had a city as well as a monarchy to rebuild.

The Restored Monarchy.   The restoration of monarchy made some in Parliament fear that the English government would come to resemble French absolutism. This fear was

Great Fire of London, 1666
This view of London shows the three-day fire at its height. The writer John Evelyn described the scene in his diary: "All the sky was of a fiery aspect, like the top of a burning oven, and the light seen above 40 miles round about for many nights. God grant mine eyes may never behold the like, who now saw above 10,000 houses all in one flame; the noise and cracking and thunder of people, the fall of towers, houses, and churches, was like an hideous storm." Everyone in London at the time felt overwhelmed by the catastrophe, and many attributed it to God's punishment for the upheavals of the 1640s and 1650s. *Museum of London Photographic Library.*

not unfounded. In 1670, Charles II made a secret agreement, soon leaked, with Louis XIV in which he promised to announce his conversion to Catholicism in exchange for money for a war against the Dutch. Charles never proclaimed himself a Catholic, but in his Declaration of Indulgence (1673) he did suspend all laws against Catholics and Protestant dissenters. Parliament refused to continue funding the Dutch war unless Charles rescinded his Declaration of Indulgence. Asserting its authority further, Parliament passed the Test Act in 1673, requiring all government officials to profess allegiance to the Church of England and in effect disavow Catholic doctrine. Then in 1678, Parliament precipitated the so-called Exclusion Crisis by explicitly denying the throne to a Roman Catholic. This action was aimed at the king's brother and heir, James, an open convert to Catholicism. Charles refused to allow it to become law.

The dynastic crisis over the succession of a Catholic gave rise to two distinct factions in Parliament: the Tories, who supported a strong, hereditary monarchy and the restored ceremony of the Anglican church, and the Whigs, who advocated parliamentary supremacy and toleration for Protestant dissenters such as Presbyterians. Both labels were originally derogatory: *Tory* meant an Irish Catholic bandit; *Whig* was the Irish Catholic designation for a Presbyterian Scot. The Tories favored James's succession despite his Catholicism, whereas the Whigs opposed a Catholic monarch. The loose moral atmosphere of Charles's court also offended some Whigs, who complained tongue in cheek that Charles was father of his country in much too literal a fashion (he had fathered more than one child by his mistresses but produced no legitimate heir).

Parliament's Revolt against James II. Upon Charles's death, James succeeded to the throne as James II (r. 1685–1688). James pursued pro-Catholic and absolutist policies even more aggressively than his brother. When a male heir—who would take precedence over James's two adult Protestant daughters—was born to James's second wife, an Italian Catholic, Tories and Whigs banded together. They invited the

Dutch ruler William, prince of Orange, and his wife, James's older daughter Mary, to invade England. Mary was brought up as a Protestant and willing to act with her husband against her father's pro-Catholic policies. James fled to France and hardly any blood was shed. Parliament offered the throne jointly to William (r. 1689–1702) and Mary (r. 1689–1694) on the condition that they accept a bill of rights guaranteeing Parliament's full partnership in a constitutional government.

In the Bill of Rights (1689), William and Mary agreed not to raise a standing army or to levy taxes without Parliament's consent. They also agreed to call meetings of Parliament at least every three years, to guarantee free elections to parliamentary seats, and to abide by Parliament's decisions and not suspend duly passed laws. The agreement gave England's constitutional government a written, legal basis by formally recognizing Parliament as a self-contained, independent body that shared power with the rulers. Victorious supporters of the coup declared it the **Glorious Revolution**. Constitutionalism had triumphed over absolutism in England.

The propertied classes who controlled Parliament prevented any resurgence of the popular turmoil of the 1640s. The Toleration Act of 1689 granted all Protestants freedom of worship, though non-Anglicans were still excluded from the universities; Catholics got no rights but were more often left alone to worship privately. When the Catholics in Ireland rose to defend James II, William and Mary's troops brutally suppressed them. With the Whigs in power and the Tories in opposition, wealthy landowners now controlled political life throughout the realm. The factions' differences, however, were minor; essentially, the Tories had less access to the king's patronage. A contemporary reported that King William had said "that if he had good places [honors and land] enough to bestow, he should soon unite the two parties."

Review: What differences over religion and politics caused the conflict between king and Parliament in England?

❖ Constitutionalism in the Dutch Republic and the Overseas Colonies

When William and Mary came to the throne in England in 1689, the Dutch and the English put aside the rivalries that had brought them to war against each other in 1652–1654, 1665–1667, and 1672–1674. Under William, the Dutch and the English together led the coalition that blocked Louis XIV's efforts to dominate continental Europe. The English and Dutch had much in common: oriented toward commerce, especially overseas, they were the successful exceptions to absolutism in Europe. Also among the few outposts of constitutionalism in the seventeenth century were the British North American colonies, which developed representative government while the English were preoccupied with their revolutions at home. Constitutionalism was not the only factor shaping this Atlantic world; as constitutionalism developed in the colonies, so too did the enslavement of black Africans as a new labor force.

The Dutch Republic

When the Dutch Republic gained formal independence from Spain in 1648, it had already established a decentralized, constitutional state. Rich merchants called regents effectively controlled the internal affairs of each province and through the Estates General named the *stadholder*,◆ the executive officer responsible for defense and for representing the state at all ceremonial occasions. They almost always chose one of the princes of the house of Orange, but the prince of Orange resembled a president more than a king.

The decentralized state encouraged and protected trade, and the Dutch Republic soon became Europe's financial capital. The Bank of Amsterdam offered interest rates less than half those available in England and France. Praised for their industriousness, thrift, and cleanliness—and maligned as greedy, dull "butter-boxes"—the Dutch dominated overseas commerce with their

shipping (Map 17.3). They imported products from all over the world: spices, tea, and silk from Asia; sugar and tobacco from the Americas; wool from England and Spain; timber and furs from Scandinavia; grain from eastern Europe. (See "Did You Know?" on page 647.) A widely reprinted history of Amsterdam that appeared in 1662 described the city as "risen through the hand of God to the peak of prosperity and greatness. . . . The whole world stands amazed at its riches and from east and west, north and south they come to behold it."

The Dutch rapidly became the most prosperous and best-educated people in Europe. Middle-class people supported the visual arts, especially painting, to an unprecedented degree. Artists and engravers produced thousands of works, and Dutch artists were among the first to sell to a mass market. Whereas in other countries kings, nobles, and churches bought art, Dutch buyers were merchants, artisans, and shopkeepers. Engravings, illustrated histories, and oil paintings, even those of Rembrandt van Rijn (1606–1669), were all relatively inexpensive. One foreigner commented that "pictures are very common here, there being scarce an ordinary tradesman whose house is not decorated with them." Dutch artists focused on familiar daily details (see the illustration on page 648) because for them ordinary people had religious as well as political significance; even children at play could be infused with radiant beauty. The family household, not the royal court, determined the moral character of this intensely commercial society. Relative prosperity decreased the need for married women to work, so Dutch society developed the clear contrast between middle-class male and female roles that would become prevalent elsewhere in Europe and in America more than a century later. As one contemporary Dutch writer explained, "The husband must be on the street to practice his trade; the wife must stay at home to be in the kitchen."

Extraordinarily high levels of urbanization and literacy created a large reading public. Dutch presses printed books censored elsewhere (printers or authors censored in one province simply shifted operations to another), and the University of Leiden attracted students

---

◆ *stadholder*: STAT hohl dur

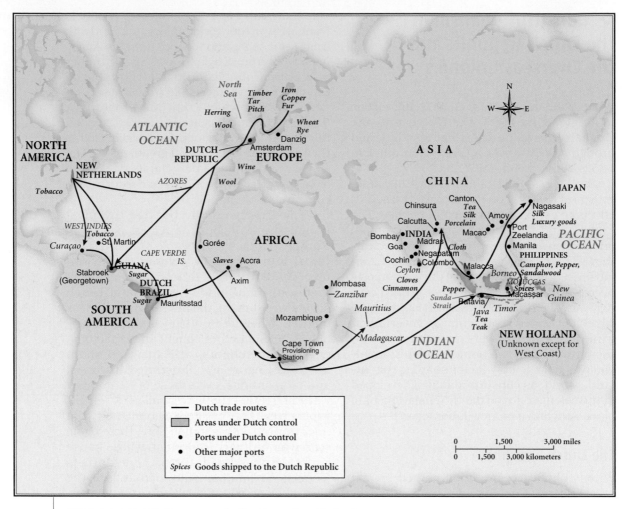

MAP 17.3 Dutch Commerce in the Seventeenth Century

Even before gaining formal independence from the Spanish in 1648, the Dutch had begun to compete with the Spanish and Portuguese all over the world. In 1602, a group of merchants established the Dutch East India Company, which soon offered investors an annual rate of return of 35 percent on the trade in spices with countries located on the Indian Ocean. Global commerce gave the Dutch the highest standard of living in Europe and soon attracted the envy of the French and the English.

and professors from all over Europe. Dutch tolerance extended to the works of Benedict Spinoza (1633–1677), a Jewish philosopher and biblical scholar who was expelled by his synagogue for alleged atheism but left alone by the Dutch authorities. Spinoza strove to reconcile religion with science and mathematics, but his work scandalized many Christians and Jews because he seemed to equate God and nature. Like nature, Spinoza's God followed unchangeable laws and could not be influenced by human actions, prayers, or faith.

Dutch learning, painting, and commerce all enjoyed wide renown in the seventeenth century, but this luster proved hard to maintain. The Dutch lived in a world of international rivalries in which strong central authority gave their enemies an advantage. Though inconclusive, the naval wars with England drained the state's revenues. Even more dangerous were the land wars with France, which continued into the eighteenth century. The Dutch survived these challenges but increasingly depended on alliances with other powers, especially England. At

DID YOU KNOW?

Tobacco and the Invention of "Smoking"

In the early seventeenth century, a "new astonishing fashion," wrote a German ambassador, came to the Dutch Republic from the New World. The term *smoking* gradually evolved in the seventeenth century out of "a fog-drinking bout," "drinking smoke," or "drinking tobacco." One Jesuit preacher called it "dry drunkenness." The analogy to inebriation is not entirely far-fetched, for nicotine (named after the French ambassador to Portugal, Jean Nicot, who brought tobacco to France in the mid-sixteenth century) does have an effect more comparable to alcohol than to caffeine; nicotine is a nerve toxin that dulls the nervous system. It is not known exactly where in the Americas tobacco had its birthplace, but its use was widespread by the time the Europeans arrived. Mayans and Aztecs smoked ceremonial pipes, Incas used tobacco as a medicine, and Indians in Brazil took snuff.

Spain began exporting tobacco to other European countries in the sixteenth century. The Spanish did not exploit the possibilities of producing tobacco on plantations; tobacco growing began in earnest in the seventeenth century only with the spread of black slavery. Virginia and Maryland ex-panded their exports of tobacco sixfold between 1663 and 1699. Until 1700, Amsterdam dominated the curing process; half the tobacco factories in Amsterdam were owned by Jewish merchants of Spanish or Portuguese descent.

Smoking spread geographically from western to eastern Europe, socially from the upper classes downward, and from men to women. At first the Spanish preferred cigars, the British pipes, and the French snuff. In the eighteenth century, both upper- and middle-class women took snuff, which was considered an aristocratic taste. Before the end of the nineteenth century, women did not regularly take tobacco in any form other than snuff. A woman smoking a pipe or cigar was a favorite target of cartoonists in the eighteenth and nineteenth centuries. This changed with the Russian invention of the cigarette in the mid-nineteenth century. Women began to smoke cigarettes in the late 1800s as a sign of emancipation.

Source: Wolfgang Schivelbusch, *Tastes of Paradise: A Social History of Spices, Stimulants, and Intoxicants*, trans. David Jacobson (New York: Vintage Books, 1992).

The Vice of Tobacco
In this engraving of 1628, *The Vice of Tobacco,* the Dutch artist Gillis van Scheyndel portrays smoking as similar to excessive drinking, a habit that makes people sick and leads them astray. Pipes often symbolized the folly and futility of a life given over to materialistic pleasures. The company of revelers is led on by a pipe-smoking ape who has features like a devil. *Koninklijke Bibliotheek.*

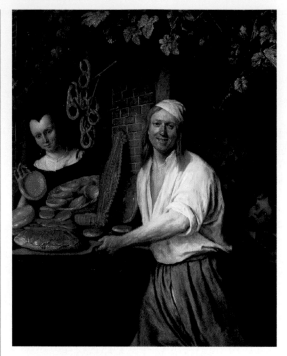

A Typical Dutch Scene from Daily Life
Jan Steen painted *The Baker Arent Oostward and His
Wife* in 1658. Steen ran a brewery and tavern in addition
to painting, and he was known for his interest in the
details of daily life. Dutch artists popularized this kind
of "genre" painting, which showed ordinary people at
work and play. How does this typically Dutch approach
differ from Baroque painting as seen in Chapter 16, page
608? **For more help analyzing this image**, see the
visual activity for this chapter in the Online Study Guide at
bedfordstmartins.com/hunt. *Rijksmuseum, Amsterdam.*

the end of the seventeenth century, the regent elite became more exclusive, more preoccupied with ostentation, less tolerant of
deviations from strict Calvinism, and more
concerned with imitating French styles than
with encouraging their own.

> **Review:** What social factors explain Dutch will-
> ingness to tolerate religious differences?

Freedom and Slavery in the New World

The French and English also increasingly
overshadowed the Dutch in the New World
colonies. While the Dutch concentrated on
shipping, including the slave trade, the
seventeenth-century French and English established settler colonies that would eventually provide fabulous revenues to the home
countries. Many European governments encouraged private companies to vie for their
share of the slave trade, and slavery began to
take clear institutional form in the New World
in this period. Even as slavery offered only a
degrading form of despotism to black
Africans, whites found in the colonies greater
political and religious freedom than in
Europe.

The Rise of the Slave Trade. After the
Spanish and Portuguese had shown that
African slaves could be transported and
forced to labor in South and Central America,
the English and French endeavored to set up
similar labor systems in their new Caribbean
island colonies. White planters with large
tracts of land bought African slaves to work
fields of sugarcane; and as they gradually
built up their holdings, the planters displaced most of the original white settlers,
who moved to mainland North American
colonies. After 1661, when Barbados instituted a slave code that stripped all Africans
of rights under English law, slavery became
codified as an inherited status that applied
only to blacks. The result was a society of ex-
tremes: the very wealthy whites, about 7
percent of the population in Barbados; and
the enslaved, powerless black majority. The
English brought few of their religious or constitutional practices to the Caribbean. Other
Caribbean colonies followed a similar pattern
of development. Louis XIV promulgated a "black
code" in 1685 to regulate the legal status of
slaves in the French colonies. Although one
of his aims was to prevent non-Catholics
from owning slaves in the French colonies,
the code had much the same effect as the
English codes on the slaves themselves: they
had no legal rights.

The highest church and government authorities in Catholic and Protestant countries alike condoned the gradually expanding
slave trade; the governments of England,
France, Spain, Portugal, the Dutch Republic,
and Denmark all encouraged private companies to traffic in black Africans. The Dutch
West India Company was the most successful of them. In 1600, about 9,500 Africans
were exported from Africa to the New World

every year; by 1700, this number had increased nearly fourfold to 36,000 annually. Historians advance several different ideas about which factors increased the slave trade: some claim that improvements in muskets made European slavers more formidable; others cite the rising price for slaves, which made their sale more attractive for Africans; still others focus on factors internal to Africa such as the increasing size of African armies and their use of muskets in fighting and capturing other Africans for sale as slaves. Whatever the reason, the way had been prepared for the development of an Atlantic economy based on slavery.

Constitutional Freedoms in the English Colonies. Virtually left to themselves during the upheavals in England, the fledgling English colonies in North America developed representative government on their own. Almost every colony had a governor and a two-house legislature. The colonial legislatures constantly sought to increase their power and resisted the efforts of Charles II and James II to reaffirm royal control. William and Mary reluctantly allowed emerging colonial elites more control over local affairs. The social and political elite among the settlers hoped to impose an English social hierarchy dominated by rich landowners. Ordinary immigrants to the colonies, however, took advantage of plentiful land to carve out their own farms using white servants and, later, in some colonies, African slaves.

For native Americans, the expanding European presence meant something else altogether. They faced death through disease and warfare and the accelerating loss of their homelands. Unlike white settlers, many native Americans believed that land was a divine gift provided for their collective use and not subject to individual ownership. Europeans' claims that they owned exclusive land rights consequently resulted in frequent skirmishes. In 1675–1676, for instance, three tribes allied under Metacomet♦ (called King Philip by the English) threatened the survival of New England settlers, who savagely repulsed the attacks and sold their captives as slaves. Whites could portray native Americans as "noble savages," but when threatened they often depicted them as conspiring villains and sneaky heathens who were akin to Africans in their savagery.

❖ The Search for Order in Elite and Popular Culture

The early success of constitutionalism in England, the Dutch Republic, and the English North American colonies would help to shape a distinctive Atlantic world in the eighteenth century. Just how constitutionalism was linked to the growing commerce with the colonies remains open to debate, however, since the constitutional governments, like the absolutist ones, avidly pursued profits in the burgeoning slave trade. Freedom did not mean liberty for everyone. One of the great debates of the time—and thereafter—concerned the meaning of freedom: for whom, under what conditions, with what justifiable limitations could freedom be claimed?

There was no freedom without order to sustain it, and most Europeans feared disorder above all else. In 1669, the English writer Margaret Cavendish, duchess of Newcastle, cataloged some of the sources of disorder in her time: "I wish Men were as Harmless as most Beasts are, then surely the World would be more Quiet and Happy than it is, for then there would not be such Pride, Vanity, Ambition, Covetousness, Faction, Treachery, and Treason, as is now." Cavendish wrote not long after the restoration of the monarchy in England, and her thoughts echoed the titanic struggles that had taken place over the nature of authority, not only in England but throughout Europe. Political theories, science, poetry, painting, and architecture all reflected in some measure the attempts to ground authority—to define the relation between freedom and order—in new ways. Authority concerned not just rulers and subjects but also the hierarchy of groups in society. As European states consolidated their powers, elites worked to distinguish themselves from the lower classes. They developed new codes of correct behavior for themselves and tried to teach order and discipline to their social inferiors.

♦**Metacomet:** MEH TAH caw MEHT

Social Contract Theory: Hobbes and Locke

The turmoil of the times prompted a major rethinking of the foundations of all authority. Two figures stood out prominently amid the cacophony of voices: Thomas Hobbes and John Locke. Their writings fundamentally shaped the modern subject of political science. Hobbes justified absolute authority; Locke provided the rationale for constitutionalism. Yet both argued that all authority came not from divine right but from a **social contract** among citizens.

Hobbes.   Thomas Hobbes (1588–1679) was a royalist who sat out the English civil war of the 1640s in France, where he tutored the future king Charles II. Returning to England in 1651, he published his masterpiece, *Leviathan* (1651), in which he argued for unlimited authority in a ruler. Absolute authority could be vested in either a king or a parliament; it had to be absolute, he insisted, in order to overcome the defects of human nature. Believing that people are essentially self-centered and driven by the "right to self-preservation," Hobbes made his case by referring to science, not religion. To Hobbes, human life in a state of nature—that is, any situation without firm authority—was "solitary, poor, nasty, brutish, and short." He believed that the desire for power and natural greed would inevitably lead to unfettered competition. Only the assurance of social order could make people secure enough to act according to law; consequently, giving up personal liberty, he maintained, was the price of collective security. Rulers derived their power, he concluded, from a contract in which absolute authority protects people's rights.

Hobbes's notion of rule by an absolute authority left no room for political dissent or nonconformity, and it infuriated both royalists and supporters of Parliament. He enraged royalists by arguing that authority came not from divine right but from the social contract. Parliamentary supporters resisted Hobbes's claim that rulers must possess absolute authority to prevent the greater evil of anarchy; they believed that a constitution should guarantee shared power between king and parliament and protect individual rights under the law. Like Machiavelli before him, Hobbes became associated with a cynical, pessimistic view of human nature, and future political theorists often began their arguments by refuting Hobbes.

Locke.   Rejecting both Hobbes and the more traditional royalist defenses of absolute authority, John Locke (1632–1704) used the notion of a social contract to provide a foundation for constitutionalism. Locke experienced political life firsthand as physician, secretary, and intellectual companion to the earl of Shaftesbury, a leading English Whig. In 1683, during the Exclusion Crisis, Locke fled with Shaftesbury to the Dutch Republic. There he continued work on his *Two Treatises of Government*, which, when published in 1690, served to justify the Glorious Revolution of 1688. Locke's position was thoroughly anti-absolutist. He denied the divine right of kings and ridiculed the common royalist idea that political power in the state mirrored the father's authority in the family. Like Hobbes, he posited a state of nature that applied to all people. Unlike Hobbes, however, he thought people were reasonable and the state of nature peaceful.

Locke insisted that government's only purpose was to protect life, liberty, and property, a notion that linked economic and political freedom. Ultimate authority rested in the will of a majority of men who owned property, and government should be limited to its basic purpose of protection. A ruler who failed to uphold his part of the social contract between the ruler and the populace could be justifiably resisted, an idea that would become crucial for the leaders of the American Revolution a century later. For England's landowners, however, Locke helped validate a revolution that consolidated their interests and ensured their privileges in the social hierarchy. Although Locke himself owned shares in the Royal African Company and justified slavery, his writings were later used by abolitionists in their campaign against slavery.

Locke defended his optimistic view of human nature in the immensely influential *Essay Concerning Human Understanding* (1690). He denied the existence of any innate ideas and asserted instead that each human is born with a mind that is a tabula rasa (blank slate). Everything humans know, he claimed, comes from sensory experience, not from anything inherent in human nature. Locke's views promoted the belief that "all men are created equal," a belief that challenged absolutist forms of rule and ultimately raised questions about women's roles as well. Not surprisingly, Locke devoted considerable energy to rethinking educational practices; he believed that education crucially shaped the human personality by channeling all sensory experience.

Newton and the Consolidation of the Scientific Revolution

New breakthroughs in science lent support to Locke's optimistic view of human potential. Building on the work of Copernicus, Kepler, and Galileo (see Chapter 16), the English natural philosopher Isaac Newton finally synthesized the laws of movement found among bodies on earth and related them to planetary motion. He united the mechanics of heavenly motion in a single **law of universal gravitation**, and in a stroke further enhanced the prestige of the new science. Almost immediately, upper-class men and women realized that being truly educated required a knowledge of the new science, while monarchs spied in science a new form of power that should not be ignored.

Newton. A Cambridge University student at the time of Charles II's restoration, Isaac Newton (1642–1727) learned mathematics and natural philosophy from his tutors and through his extraordinary application of his own mind. Sent home to weather the plague in 1665 and 1666, he attacked various problems in mathematics and established the basis for the new mathematics of moving bodies, the infinitesimal calculus. Over the next twenty years, he labored on an astounding variety of problems in mechanics and optics. In 1687 he finally brought his most significant mathematical and mechanical discoveries together in his masterwork, *Principia Mathematica*. Newton united celestial and terrestrial mechanics with his law of universal gravitation. According to Newton, the planets as well as the earth's moon move

Isaac Newton Analyzing the Nature of Light
To study the refraction of light, Newton made a hole in a window shutter, darkened the room, and let in a column of light, which he passed through a prism. In this way, he discovered that light is not homogeneous; violet refracts more light than any of the other colors, while red refracts less than orange, and orange refracts less than yellow. Newton used this knowledge to construct a reflecting telescope, which used mirrors to eliminate the distortion introduced by the spectrum of colors in light. © *The Image Works Archive.*

at uniform speeds proportional to their weight and to their distance from the sun. His law held that every body in the universe exerts over every other body an attractive force directly proportional to the product of their masses and inversely proportional to the square of the distance between them. The law of universal gravitation explained Kepler's elliptical planetary orbits just as it accounted for the motion of ordinary objects as they descend toward the earth.

Newton proved that a universal force acts at a distance between the sun and all the planets and that the same mathematical formula applies to all the movements at all times. To establish his law of universal gravitation, Newton first applied mathematical principles to formulate three fundamental physical laws: (1) in the absence of force, motion continues in a straight line; (2) the rate of change in the motion of an object is a result of the forces acting on it; and (3) the action and reaction between two objects are equal and opposite. Newtonian physics thus combined mass, inertia, force, velocity, and acceleration—all key concepts in modern science—and made them quantifiable. Newton showed that these laws of motion explained the orbiting of the planets as well as the fall of an apple to the ground: "From the same principles [of motion] I now demonstrate the frame of the System of the World."

Once set in motion, in Newton's view, the universe operated like a masterpiece made possible by the ingenuity of God. Others, less devout than Newton, could see it as a clockwork, with no need for God's continuing intervention. Gravity, although a mysterious force, could be expressed mathematically. Newton saw no conflict between faith and science. He believed that by demonstrating that the physical universe followed rational principles, natural philosophers could prove the existence of God and so liberate humans from doubt and the fear of chaos. The English poet Alexander Pope later valorized Newton, as did many others among his contemporaries:

> Nature and Nature's laws lay hid in night
> God said, Let Newton be! and all was light.

Even while laying the foundation for modern physics, optics and mechanics, Newton carried out alchemical experiments in his rooms at Cambridge University and spent long hours trying to calculate the date of the beginning of the world and its end with the second coming of Jesus. Not all scientists accepted Newton's planetary theories immediately, especially on the continent; the Dutch scientist Christian Huygens, for example, declared the concept of attraction (action at a distance) "absurd." But within a couple of generations Newton's work gained widespread assent, partly because of experimental verification.

Public Interest in Science. Despite the initial controversies about the possibility of universal gravitation at a distance, absolutist rulers quickly saw the potential of the new science for enhancing their prestige and glory. Frederick William, the Great Elector of Brandenburg-Prussia, for example, set up agricultural experiments in front of his Berlin palace, and various German princes supported the work of Gottfried Wilhelm Leibniz♦ (1646–1716), who claimed that he, and not Newton, had invented the calculus. A lawyer, diplomat, mathematician, and scholar who wrote about metaphysics, cosmology, and history, Leibniz also helped establish scientific societies in the German states. Government involvement in science was greatest in France, where it became an arm of mercantilist policy; in 1666, Colbert founded the Royal Academy of Sciences, which supplied fifteen scientists with government stipends. It met in the King's Library in Paris, where for the first years the members devoted themselves to alchemical experiments and the study of mechanical devices.

Constitutional states supported science informally but provided an environment that encouraged its spread. The Royal Society of London, the counterpart to the one in Paris, grew out of informal meetings of scientists at London and Oxford rather than direct government involvement. It received a royal charter in 1662 but maintained complete independence; its members arranged for the publication of Newton's *Principia*. The society's secretary described its business to be "in the first place, to scrutinize the whole of Nature and to investigate its activity and powers by means of observations and experiments; and then in course of time to hammer out a more solid philosophy and more ample amenities of civilization." Whether the state paid for the work or not, thinkers of the day now tied science explicitly to social progress.

Because of their exclusion from most universities, women only rarely participated in the new scientific discoveries. In 1667, nonetheless, the Royal Society of London invited Margaret Cavendish, a writer of poems, essays, letters, and philosophical treatises, to attend a meeting to watch the exhibition of experiments. Labeled "mad" by her peers, she attacked the use of telescopes and microscopes because she detected in the new experimentalism a mechanistic view of the world that exalted masculine prowess and challenged the Christian belief in freedom of

♦**Leibniz:** LYB nits

the will. Yet she urged the formal education of women, complaining that "we are kept like birds in cages to hop up and down in our houses." "Many of our Sex may have as much wit, and be capable of Learning as well as men," she insisted, "but since they want Instructions [lack education], it is not possible they should attain to it."

Freedom and Order in the Arts

Like Newton, Locke, and Hobbes, most artists and intellectuals had experienced enough of the upheavals of the seventeenth century to fear the prospect of chaos and disintegration. The French mathematician Blaise Pascal vividly captured their worries in his *Pensées*♦ (Thoughts) of 1660: "I look on all sides, and I see only darkness everywhere." But Pascal was more skeptical than most about man's ability to forge order out of chaos: "Nature presents to me nothing which is not a matter of doubt and concern.... It is incomprehensible that God should exist, and incomprehensible that He should not exist." Poets, painters, and architects all tried to make sense of the individual's place within what Pascal called "the eternal silence of these infinite spaces."

Milton.   The English Puritan poet John Milton (1608–1674) gave priority to individual liberty. In 1643, in the midst of the civil war between king and Parliament, he published writings in favor of divorce. When Parliament enacted a censorship law aimed at such literature, Milton responded in 1644 with one of the first defenses of freedom of the press, *Areopagitica.*♦ (See the excerpt on page 654.) Milton served as secretary to the Council of State during Cromwell's rule and earned the enmity of Charles II by writing a justification for the execution of his father, Charles I.

Forced into retirement after the restoration of the monarchy, Milton published in 1667 his epic poem *Paradise Lost.* He used Adam and Eve's Fall to meditate on human freedom and the tragedies of rebellion. Although Milton wanted to "justify the ways of God to man," his Satan, the proud angel who challenges God, is so compelling as to be heroic. In the

end, Adam and Eve learn to accept moral responsibility. Individuals learn the limits to their freedom, yet personal liberty remains essential to their definition as human.

The Varieties of Artistic Style.   The dominant artistic styles of the time—the baroque and the classical—both submerged the ordinary individual in a grander design. The baroque style proved to be especially suitable for public displays of faith and power that overawed individual beholders. The combination of religious and political purposes in baroque art is best exemplified in the architecture and sculpture of Gian Lorenzo Bernini (1598–1680), the papacy's official

Gian Lorenzo Bernini, *Ecstasy of St. Teresa of Ávila* (c. 1650)
This ultimate statement of baroque sculpture captures all the drama and even sensationalism of a mystical religious faith. Bernini based his figures on a vision reported by St. Teresa in which she saw an angel: "In his hands I saw a great golden spear, and at the iron tip there appeared to be a point of fire. This he plunged into my heart several times so that it penetrated my entrails. When he pulled it out I felt that he took them with it, and left me utterly consumed by the great love of God." *Scala/Art Resource, NY.*

♦*Pensées:* pahn SAYS
♦*Areopagitica:* ar ee oh puh JIHT ih kuh

John Milton's Defense of Freedom of the Press

In Areopagitica *(1644), the English poet John Milton rebuked Parliament for passing a bill to restrict freedom of the press by requiring licensing of every publication. The title came from Areopagus, the name of a court in ancient Athens. Milton argued that freedom of thought was essential to human dignity.*

I deny not but that it is of greatest concernment in the church and commonwealth to have a vigilant eye how books demean themselves as well as men; and thereafter to confine, imprison, and do sharpest justice on them as malefactors. For books are not absolutely dead things, but do contain a potency of life in them to be as active as that soul was whose progeny they are; nay, they do preserve as in a vial the purest efficacy and extraction of that living intellect that bred them. I know they are as lively and as vigorously productive as those fabulous dragon's teeth; and being sown up and down, may chance to spring up armed men. And yet, on the other hand, unless wariness be used, as good almost kill a man as kill a good book: who kills a man kills a reasonable creature, God's image; but he who destroys a good book, kills reason itself, kills the image of God, as it were, in the eye. Many a man lives a burden to the earth; but a good book is the precious lifeblood of a master spirit, embalmed and treasured up on purpose to a life beyond life. 'Tis true, no age can restore a life, whereof perhaps there is no great loss; and revolutions of ages do not oft recover the loss of a rejected truth, for the want of which whole nations fare the worse. We should be wary, therefore, what persecution we raise against the living labors of public

men, how we spill that seasoned life of man preserved and stored up in books; since we see a kind of homicide may be thus committed, sometimes a martyrdom; and if it extend to the whole impression, a kind of massacre, whereof the execution ends not in the slaying of an elemental life, but strikes at that ethereal and fifth essence, the breath of reason itself, slays an immortality rather than a life. But lest I should be condemned of introducing license, while I oppose licensing, I refuse not the pains to be so much historical as will serve to show what hath been done by ancient and famous commonwealths against this disorder, till the very time that this project of licensing crept out of the Inquisition, was caught up by our prelates, and hath caught some of our presbyters. [...]

As therefore the state of man now is, what wisdom can there be to choose, what continence to forbear without the knowledge of evil? He that can apprehend and consider vice with all her baits and seeming pleasures, and yet abstain, and yet distinguish, and yet prefer that which is truly better, he is the true warfaring Christian. I cannot praise a fugitive and cloistered virtue, unexercised and unbreathed, that never sallies out and sees her adversary, but slinks out of the race where that immortal garland is to be run for, not without dust and heat. Assuredly we bring not innocence into the world, we bring impurity much rather: that which purifies us is trial, and trial is by what is contrary.

Source: John Milton, *Milton's Prose Writing* (London: J.M. Dant, 1961), 149–50, 158.

---

artist. His architectural masterpiece was the gigantic square facing St. Peter's Basilica in Rome (1656–1671). His use of freestanding colonnades and a huge open space is meant to impress the individual observer with the power of the popes and the Catholic religion. Bernini also sculpted tombs for the popes and a large statue of Constantine, the first Christian emperor of Rome—perfect ex-

amples of the marriage of power and religion. In 1665, Louis XIV hired Bernini to plan the rebuilding of the Louvre palace in Paris but then rejected his ideas as incompatible with French tastes.

Although France was a Catholic country, French painters, sculptors, and architects, like their patron Louis XIV, preferred the standards of **classicism** to those of the

French Classicism
This painting by Nicolas Poussin, *Discovery of Achilles on Skyros* (1649–1650), shows the French interest in classical themes and ideals. In the Greek story, Thetis dressed her son Achilles as a young woman and hid him on the island of Skyros so he would not have to fight in the Trojan War. When a chest of treasures is offered to the women, Achilles reveals himself (he is the figure on the far right) because he cannot resist the sword. In telling the story, Poussin emphasizes harmony and almost a sedateness of composition, avoiding the exuberance and emotionalism of the baroque style. *Photograph © 2003 Museum of Fine Arts, Boston.*

baroque. French artists developed classicism to be a French national style, distinct from the baroque style that was closely associated with France's enemies, the Austrian and Spanish Habsburgs. As its name suggests, classicism reflected the ideals of the art of antiquity: geometric shapes, order, and harmony of lines took precedence over the sensuous, exuberant, and emotional forms of the baroque. Rather than being overshadowed by the sheer power of emotional display, in classicism the individual could be found at the intersection of converging, symmetrical, straight lines (see illustration above). These influences were apparent in the work of the leading French painters of the period, Nicolas Poussin (1594–1665) and Claude Lorrain (1600–1682), both of whom worked in Rome and tried to re-create classical Roman values in their mythological scenes and Roman landscapes.

Dutch painters found the baroque and classical styles less suited to their private market, where buyers sought smaller-scale works with ordinary subjects. Dutch artists came from common stock themselves— Rembrandt's father was a miller, and the father of Jan Vermeer (1632–1675) was a silk worker. Their clients were people like themselves who purchased paintings much as they bought tables and chairs. Although he occasionally worked on commission for the prince of Orange, even Rembrandt painted ordinary people, suffusing his canvases with a radiant, otherworldly light that made the plainest people and objects appear deeply spiritual. Vermeer's best-known paintings show women working at home; like Rembrandt, Vermeer made ordinary activities seem precious and beautiful.

Art might also serve the interests of science. One of the most skilled illustrators of insects and flowers was Maria Sibylla Merian (1646–1717), a German-born painter-scholar whose engravings were widely celebrated for their brilliant realism and microscopic clarity. Merian eventually separated from her husband and joined a sect called the Labadists (after its French founder, Jean de Labadie), whose members did not believe in formal marriage ties. After moving with her daughters to the Labadists' community in the northern Dutch province of Friesland, Merian went with missionaries from the sect to the Dutch colony of Surinam in South America and painted watercolors (see the illustration on page 656) of the exotic flowers, birds, and insects she found in the jungle around the cocoa and sugarcane plantations. In the seventeenth century, many women became known for their still lifes and

Dutch Art

Dutch artists went their own way, following neither the baroque nor the classical style. *Officer with a Laughing Girl* (1657) by Jan Vermeer shows a scene that captures the Dutch fascination with the details of ordinary life. Note for example the richness of the texture of the girl's clothing, the delicacy of the glass in the window, and the presence of a map as decoration on the wall. As worldwide traders, the Dutch gave great value to maps. *Copyright © The Frick Collection, New York.*

European Fascination with Products of the New World

In this painting of a banana plant, Maria Sibylla Merian offers a scientific study of one of the many exotic plants and animals found by Europeans who traveled to the colonies overseas. Merian was fifty-one when she traveled to the Dutch South American colony of Surinam with her daughter. *Courtesy of Hunt Institute for Botanical Documentation, Carnegie Mellon University, Pittsburgh, PA.*

especially their paintings of flowers. Paintings by the Dutch artist Rachel Ruysch, for example, fetched higher prices than those received by Rembrandt.

Women and Manners

Poetry and painting imaginatively explored the place of the individual within a larger whole, but real-life individuals had to learn to navigate their own social worlds. Manners—which involved individual self-discipline—were essential skills of social navigation, and women usually took the lead in teaching them. Women's importance in refining social relationships quickly became a subject of controversy.

The Cultivation of Manners. The court had long been a central arena for the development of manners. Under the tutelage of their mothers and wives, nobles learned to hide all that was crass and to maintain a fine sense of social distinction. In some ways, aristocratic men were expected to act more like women; just as women had long been expected to please men, now aristocratic men had to please their monarch or patron by displaying proper manners and conversing with elegance and wit. The art of pleasing included foreign languages (especially French), dance, a taste for fine music, and attention to dress.

As part of the evolution of new aristocratic ideals, nobles learned to disdain all that was lowly. The upper classes began to reject popular festivals and fairs in favor of private theaters, where seats were relatively expensive and behavior was formal. Clowns and buffoons now seemed vulgar; the last king of England to keep a court fool was Charles I. Chivalric romances that had entranced the nobility down to the time of Cervantes's *Don Quixote* (1605) now passed into popular literature.

The greatest French playwright of the seventeenth century, Molière (the pen name of Jean-Baptiste Poquelin, 1622–1673), wrote sparkling comedies of manners that revealed much about the new aristocratic behavior. His play *The Middle-Class Gentleman*, first performed for Louis XIV in 1670, revolves around the yearning of a rich, middle-class Frenchman, Monsieur Jourdain, to learn to act like a *gentilhomme*♦ (meaning both "gentleman" and "nobleman"). Monsieur Jourdain buys fancy clothes; hires private instructors in dancing, music, fencing, and philosophy; and lends money to a debt-ridden noble in hopes that the noble will marry his daughter. Only his sensible wife and his daughter's love for a worthier commoner stand in his way. The message for the king's courtiers seemed to be a reassuring one: only true nobles by blood can hope to act like nobles. But the play also showed how the middle classes were learning to emulate the nobility; if one could learn to act nobly through self-discipline, could not anyone with some education and money pass himself off as noble?

As Molière's play demonstrated, new attention to manners trickled down from the court to the middle class. A French treatise on manners written in 1672 explained proper behavior:

> If everyone is eating from the same dish, you should take care not to put your hand into it before those of higher rank have done so. . . . Formerly one was permitted . . . to dip one's bread into the sauce, provided only that one had not already bitten it. Nowadays that would be a kind of rusticity. Formerly one was allowed to take from one's mouth what one could not eat and drop it on the floor, provided it was done skillfully. Now that would be very disgusting.

The key words *rusticity* and *disgusting* reveal the association of unacceptable social behavior with the peasantry, dirt, and repulsion. Similar rules governed spitting and blowing one's nose in public. Once the elite had successfully distinguished itself from the lower classes through manners, scholars became more interested in studying popular expressions. They avidly collected proverbs, folktales, and songs—all of these now curiosities. In fact, many nobles at Louis XIV's court read fairy tales.

Debates about Women's Roles. Courtly manners often permeated the upper reaches of society by means of the salon,♦ an informal gathering held regularly in private homes and presided over by a socially eminent woman. In 1661, one French author claimed to have identified 251 Parisian women as hostesses of salons. Although the French government occasionally worried that these gatherings might challenge its authority, the three main topics of conversation were love, literature, and philosophy. Hostesses often worked hard to encourage the careers of budding authors. Before publishing a manuscript, many authors would read their compositions to a salon gathering. Corneille, Racine, and even Bishop Bossuet sought women's approval for their writings.

Some women went beyond encouraging male authors and began to write on their own, but they faced many obstacles. Marie-Madeleine de La Vergne, known as Madame de Lafayette, wrote several short novels that were published anonymously because it was considered inappropriate for aristocratic women to appear in print. Following the publication of *The Princess of Clèves* in 1678, she denied having written it. Hannah Wooley, the English author of many books on domestic conduct, published under the name of her first husband. Women were known for writing wonderful letters (Marie de Sévigné was a prime example), but the correspondence circulated only in handwritten form. In the 1650s, despite these limitations, French women began to turn out best sellers in a new type of literature, the novel. Their success prompted the philosopher Pierre

---

♦*gentilhomme*: ZHOHN tee ohm

♦**salon**: SA lahn

Bayle to remark in 1697 that "our best French novels for a long time have been written by women."

The new importance of women in the world of manners and letters did not sit well with everyone. Although the French writer François Poulain de la Barre (1647–1723), in a series of works published in the 1670s, used the new science to assert the equality of women's minds, most men resisted the idea. Clergy, lawyers, scholars, and playwrights attacked women's growing public influence. Women, they complained, were corrupting forces and needed restraint. Only marriage, "this salutary yoke," could control their passions and weaknesses. Women were accused of raising "the banner of prostitution in the salons, in the promenades, and in the streets." Molière wrote plays denouncing women's pretension to judge literary merit. English playwrights derided learned women by creating characters with names such as Lady Knowall, Lady Meanwell, and Mrs. Lovewit.

A real-life target of the English playwrights was Aphra Behn (1640–1689), one of the first professional woman authors, who supported herself by journalism and wrote plays and poetry. She also translated scientific works and defended Copernicanism. Her short novel *Oroonoko*♦ (1688) told the story of an African prince wrongly sold into slavery. (See the excerpt on the next page.) The story was so successful that it was adapted by playwrights and performed repeatedly in England and France for the next hundred years. Behn responded to her critics by arguing that there was "no reason why women should not write as well as men." Women also played important roles in the new colonies. In order to establish more permanent and settled colonies, governments promoted the emigration of women so that male colonists would set up orderly Christian white households rather than pursuing sexual relations with native or slave women.

Reforming Popular Culture

The illiterate peasants who made up most of Europe's population had little or no knowledge of the law of gravitation, upper-class

♦*Oroonoko*: OH roo noh koh

manners, or novels, no matter who authored them. Their culture had three main elements: the knowledge needed to work at farming or in a trade; popular forms of entertainment such as village fairs and dances; and their religion, which shaped every aspect of life and death. What changed most noticeably in the seventeenth century was the social elites' attitude toward lower-class culture. The division between elite and popular culture widened as elites insisted on their difference from the lower orders and tried to instill new forms of discipline in their social inferiors.

Popular Religion. In the seventeenth century, Protestant and Catholic churches alike pushed hard to change popular religious practices. Their campaigns against popular "paganism" began during the sixteenth-century Protestant Reformation and Catholic Counter-Reformation but reached much of rural Europe only in the seventeenth century. Puritans in England tried to root out maypole dances, Sunday village fairs, gambling, taverns, and bawdy ballads because they interfered with sober observance of the Sabbath. In Lutheran Norway, pastors denounced a widespread belief in the miracle-working powers of St. Olaf. The word *superstition* previously meant "false religion" (Protestantism was a superstition for Catholics, Catholicism for Protestants); in the seventeenth century it took on its modern meaning of irrational fears, beliefs, and practices, which anyone educated or refined would avoid.

The Catholic campaign against superstitious practices found a ready ally in Louis XIV. While the Sun King reformed the nobles at court through etiquette and manners, Catholic bishops in the French provinces trained parish priests to reform their flocks by using catechisms in local dialects and insisting that parishioners attend Mass. The church faced a formidable challenge. One bishop in France complained in 1671, "Can you believe that there are in this diocese entire villages where no one has even heard of Jesus Christ?" In some places, believers sacrificed animals to the Virgin, prayed to the new moon, and worshiped at the sources of streams as in pre-Christian times.

Like its Protestant counterpart, the Catholic campaign against ignorance and

Aphra Behn, *Oroonoko*

Aphra Behn wrote poetry, plays, and novels— though writing was denounced by some men as an indecent activity for women. Behn also traveled to Surinam, where she set her novel Oroonoko *(1688). In this passage, she describes the "royal slave" (an African prince tricked into slavery) as very much like a European aristocrat. His physical appearance made him seem like an ancient Roman rather than a seventeenth-century African slave.*

I have often seen and conversed with this great man, and been a witness to many of his mighty actions; and do assure my reader, the most illustrious courts could not have produced a braver man, both for greatness of courage and mind, a judgment more solid, a wit more quick, and a conversation more sweet and diverting. He knew almost as much as if he had read much: he had heard of, and admired the Romans; he had heard of the late Civil Wars in England, and the deplorable death of our great monarch, and would discourse of it with all the sense and abhorrence of the injustice imaginable. He had an extreme good and graceful mien, and all the civility of a well-bred great man. He had nothing of barbarity in his nature, but in all points addressed himself as if his education had been in some European court.

This great and just character of Oroonoko gave me an extreme curiosity to see him, especially when I knew he spoke French and English, and that I could talk with him. But though I had heard so much of him, I was as greatly surprised when I saw him as if I had heard nothing of him, so beyond all report I found him. He came into the room, and addressed himself to me, and some other women, with the best grace in the world. He was pretty tall, but of a shape the most exact that can be fancied; the most famous statuary could not form the figure of a man more admirably turned from head to foot. His face was not of that brown, rusty black which most of that nation are, but a perfect ebony, or polished jet. His eyes were the most awful that could be seen, and very piercing; the white of them being like snow, as were his teeth. His nose was rising and Roman, instead of African and flat. His mouth, the finest shaped that could be seen; far from those great turned lips, which are so natural to the rest of the Negroes. The whole proportion and air of his face was so noble, and exactly formed, that, bating his colour, there could be nothing in nature more beautiful, agreeable, and handsome.

Source: Aphra Behn, *Oroonoko, The Rover, and Other Works* (New York: Penguin, 1992), 80–81.

---

superstition helped extend state power. Clergy, officials, and local police worked together to limit carnival celebrations, to regulate pilgrimages to shrines, and to replace "indecent" images of saints with more restrained and decorous ones. In Catholicism, the cult of the Virgin Mary and devotions closely connected with Jesus, such as the Holy Sacrament and the Sacred Heart, took precedence over the celebration of popular saints who seemed to have pagan origins or were credited with unverified miracles. Reformers everywhere tried to limit the number of feast days on the grounds that they encouraged lewd behavior.

New Attitudes toward Poverty. The campaign for more disciplined religious practices helped generate a new attitude toward the poor. Poverty previously had been closely linked with charity and virtue in Christianity; it was a Christian duty to give alms to the poor, and Jesus and many of the saints had purposely chosen lives of poverty. In the sixteenth and seventeenth centuries, the upper classes, the church, and the state increasingly regarded the poor as dangerous, deceitful, and lacking in character. "Criminal laziness is the source of all their vices," wrote a Jesuit expert on the poor. The courts had previously expelled beggars from cities; now local leaders,

MAPPING THE WEST Europe at the End of the Seventeenth Century
A map can be deceiving. Although Poland-Lithuania looks like a large country on this map, it had been fatally weakened by internal conflicts. In the next century it would disappear entirely. The Ottoman Empire still controlled an extensive territory, but outside of Anatolia its rule depended on intermediaries. The Austrian Habsburgs had pushed the Turks out of Hungary and back into the Balkans. At the other end of the scale, the very small Dutch Republic had become very rich through international commerce. Size did not always prove to be an advantage.

both Catholic and Protestant, tried to reform their character. Municipal magistrates collected taxes for poor relief, and local notables organized charities; together they transformed hospitals into houses of confinement for beggars. In Catholic France, upperclass women's religious associations, known as confraternities, set up asylums that confined prostitutes (by arrest if necessary) and rehabilitated them. Confraternities also

founded hospices where orphans learned order and respect. Such groups advocated harsh discipline as the cure for poverty.

As hard times increased the numbers of the poor and the rates of violent crime as well, attitudes toward the poor hardened. The elites wanted to separate the very poor from society either to change them or to keep them from contaminating others. Hospitals became holding pens for society's unwanted members; in them, the poor joined the disabled, the incurably diseased, and the insane. The founding of hospitals demonstrates the connection between elites' attitudes and state building. In 1676, Louis XIV ordered every French city to establish a hospital, and his government took charge of the finances. Other rulers soon followed the same path.

> **Review:** In what ways did elite and popular culture become more separate in this period?

Conclusion

The search for order took place on various levels, from the reform of the disorderly poor to the establishment of more regular bureaucratic routines in government. The absolutist government of Louis XIV served as a model for all those who aimed to increase the power of the central state. Even Louis's rivals—such as the Holy Roman Emperor Leopold I and Frederick William, the Great Elector of Brandenburg-Prussia—followed his lead in centralizing authority and building up their armies. Whether absolutist or constitutionalist in form, seventeenth-century states aimed to penetrate more deeply into the lives of their subjects. They wanted more men for their armed forces; higher taxes to support their projects; and more control over foreign trade, religious dissent, and society's unwanted.

Some tears had begun to appear, however, in the seamless fabric of state power. The civil war between Charles I and Parliament in England in the 1640s opened the way to new demands for political participation. When Parliament overthrew James II in 1688, it also insisted that the new king and queen, William and Mary, agree to a Bill of Rights. Left on their own during the turmoil in England, the English North American colonies developed distinctive forms of representative government. In the eighteenth century, new levels of economic growth and the appearance of new social groups would exert pressures on the European state system. The success of seventeenth-century rulers created the political and economic conditions in which their critics would flourish.

Suggested References

Louis XIV: Model of Absolutism

Recent studies have insisted that absolutism could never be entirely absolute because the king depended on collaboration and cooperation to enforce his policies. Some of the best sources for Louis XIV's reign are the letters written by important noblewomen. The Web site of the Château of Versailles includes views of rooms in the castle.

*Beik, William. *Louis XIV and Absolutism: A Brief Study with Documents.* 2000.

*Forster, Elborg, trans. *A Woman's Life in the Court of the Sun King: Elisabeth Charlotte, Duchesse d'Orléans.* 1984.

Hurt, John J. *Louis XIV and the Parlements.* 2002.

*Sévigné, Madame de. *Selected Letters.* Trans. Leonard Tancock. 1982.

Treasure, Geoffrey. *Louis XIV.* 2001.

Versailles: **http://www.chateauversailles.fr**.

Absolutism in Central and Eastern Europe

Too often central and eastern European forms of state development have been characterized as backward in comparison with those of western Europe. Now historians emphasize the patterns of ruler-elite cooperation shared with western Europe, but they also underscore the weight of serfdom in eastern economies and political systems.

Barkey, Karen. *The Ottoman Route to State Centralization.* 1994.

Çiçek, Kemal, ed. *The Great Ottoman-Turkish Civilisation,* 4 vols. 2000.

Kivelson, Valerie A. *Autocracy in the Provinces: The Muscovite Gentry and Political Culture in the Seventeenth Century.* 1996.

Vierhaus, Rudolf. *Germany in the Age of Absolutism.* Trans. Jonathan B. Knudsen. 1988.

Wilson, Peter H. *German Armies: War and German Politics, 1648–1806.* 1998.

Constitutionalism in England

Though recent interpretations of the English revolutions emphasize the limits on radical change, Hill's portrayal of the radical ferment of ideas remains fundamental.

Cromwell: **http://www.cromwell.org**.

*Primary sources.

*Graham, Elspeth, et al., eds. *Her Own Life: Autobiographical Writings by Seventeenth-Century English Women.* 1989.

*Haller, William, and Godfrey Davies, eds. *The Leveller Tracts, 1647–1653.* 1944.

Hill, Christopher. *The World Turned Upside Down: Radical Ideas during the English Revolution.* 1972.

Israel, Jonathan, ed. *The Anglo-Dutch Moment: Essays on the Glorious Revolution and Its World Impact.* 1991.

Knoppers, Laura Lunger. *Constructing Cromwell: Ceremony, Portrait, and Print, 1645–1661.* 2000.

Constitutionalism in the Dutch Republic and the Overseas Colonies

Studies of the Dutch Republic emphasize the importance of trade and consumerism. Recent work on the colonies has begun to explore the intersecting experiences of settlers, native Americans, and African slaves.

*Campbell, P. F. *Some Early Barbadian History.* 1993.

Israel, Jonathan. *Dutch Primacy in World Trade, 1585–1740.* 1989.

Price, J. L. *The Dutch Republic in the Seventeenth Century.* 1998.

Schama, Simon. *The Embarrassment of Riches: An Interpretation of Dutch Culture in the Golden Age.* 1988.

Taylor, Alan. *American Colonies.* 2002.

Thornton, John. *Africa and Africans in the Making of the Atlantic World, 1400–1800.* 1992.

The Search for Order in Elite and Popular Culture

Historians do not always agree about the meaning of popular culture: Was it something widely shared by all social classes or a set of activities increasingly identified with the lower classes, as Burke argues? The central Web site for Dutch museums allows the visitor to tour rooms and see paintings in scores of Dutch museums, many of which have important holdings of paintings by Rembrandt and Vermeer. The Web site on Isaac Newton links to many other sites on his scientific and mathematical discoveries.

Burke, Peter. *Popular Culture in Early Modern Europe.* 1978.

Davis, Natalie Zemon. *Women on the Margins: Three Seventeenth-Century Lives.* 1995.

Dutch Museums: http://www.hollandmuseums .nl.

*Fitzmaurice, James, ed. *Margaret Cavendish: Sociable Letters.* 1997.

Jardine, Lisa. *On a Grander Scale: The Outstanding Life of Sir Christopher Wren.* 2003.

Newton: http://www-history.mcs.st-andrews.ac .uk/history/Mathematicians/Newton.html.

Westfall, Richard S. *The Life of Isaac Newton.* 1993.

*Primary sources.

CHAPTER REVIEW

IMPORTANT EVENTS

1642–1646 Civil war between King Charles I and Parliament in England

1648 Peace of Westphalia ends Thirty Years' War; the Fronde revolt challenges royal authority in France; Ukrainian Cossack warriors rebel against the king of Poland-Lithuania; Spain formally recognizes independence of the Dutch Republic

1649 Execution of Charles I of England; new Russian legal code

1651 Thomas Hobbes publishes *Leviathan*

1660 Monarchy restored in England

1661 Slave code set up in Barbados

1667 Louis XIV begins first of many wars that continue throughout his reign

1670 Molière's play, *The Middle-Class Gentleman*

1678 Marie-Madeline de La Vergne (Madame de Lafayette) anonymously publishes her novel *The Princess of Clèves*

1683 Austrian Habsburgs break the Turkish siege of Vienna

1685 Louis XIV revokes toleration for French Protestants granted by the Edict of Nantes

1687 Isaac Newton publishes *Principia Mathematica*

1688 Parliament deposes James II and invites his daughter, Mary, and her husband, William of Orange, to take the throne

1690 John Locke's *Two Treatises of Government, Essay Concerning Human Understanding*

KEY TERMS

absolutism (621)

bureaucracy (627)

classicism (654)

constitutionalism (622)

Fronde (623)

Glorious Revolution (644)

law of universal gravitation (651)

Levellers (639)

mercantilism (628)

Old Believers (635)

parlements (623)

social contract (650)

REVIEW QUESTIONS

1. How "absolute" was the power of Louis XIV?
2. Why did absolutism succeed everywhere in eastern Europe except Poland-Lithuania?
3. What differences over religion and politics caused the conflict between king and Parliament in England?
4. What social factors explain Dutch willingness to tolerate religious differences?
5. In what ways did elite and popular culture become more separate in this period?

MAKING CONNECTIONS

1. What are the most important differences between absolutism and constitutionalism as political systems?
2. In what ways did religious differences still cause political conflict?
3. Why was the search for order a major theme in science, politics, and the arts?

FOR FURTHER EXPLORATION

To assess your mastery of the material in this chapter, see the Online Study Guide at **bedfordstmartins.com/hunt**.

To read additional primary-source material from this period, see Chapter 17 in *Sources of The Making of the West*, Second Edition.

The Atlantic System and Its Consequences, 1690–1740

JOHANN SEBASTIAN BACH (1685–1750), composer of mighty organ fugues◆ and church cantatas, was not above amusing his Leipzig audiences, many of them university students. In 1732 he produced a cantata about a young woman in love—with coffee. Her old-fashioned father rages that he won't find her a husband unless she gives up the fad. She agrees, secretly vowing to admit no suitor who will not promise in the marriage contract to let her brew coffee whenever she wants. Bach offers this conclusion:

> *The cat won't give up its mouse,*
> *Girls stay faithful coffee-sisters*
> *Mother loves her coffee habit,*
> *Grandma sips it gladly too—*
> *Why then shout at the daughters?*

Bach's era might well be called the age of coffee. European travelers at the end of the sixteenth century had noticed Middle Eastern people drinking a "black drink," *kavah*, and the Turks took coffee beans with them on their military campaigns in eastern Europe. Few Europeans sampled the drink at first, and the Arab monopoly on its production kept prices high. This changed around 1700 when the Dutch East India Company introduced coffee plants to Java and other Indonesian islands. Coffee production then spread to the French Caribbean, where African slaves provided the plantation labor. In Europe, imported coffee spurred the development of a new kind of meeting place: the first coffeehouse opened in London in 1652, and the idea spread quickly to other European cities. The coffeehouses became gathering places for men to drink, read

---

◆**fugues:** fyoogs

London Coffeehouse
This gouache (a variant on watercolor painting) from about 1725 depicts a scene from a London coffeehouse located in the courtyard of the Royal Exchange (merchants' bank). Middle-class men (wearing wigs) read newspapers, drink coffee, smoke pipes, and discuss the news of the day. The coffeehouse draws them out of their homes into a new public space. *British Museum, Bridgeman Art Library, NY.*

newspapers, and talk politics. As a London newspaper commented in 1737, "There's scarce an Alley in City and Suburbs but has a Coffeehouse in it, which may be called the School of Public Spirit, where every Man over Daily and Weekly Journals, a Mug, or a Dram . . . devotes himself to that glorious one, his Country."

European consumption of coffee, tea, chocolate, and other novelties increased dramatically as European nations forged worldwide economic links. At the center of this new global economy was the **Atlantic system**, the triangular pattern of trade that bound together western Europe, Africa, and the Americas. Europeans bought slaves in western Africa, transported and sold them in their colonies in North and South America and the Caribbean, bought the commodities such as coffee and sugar that were produced by the new colonial plantations, and then sold the goods in European ports for refining and reshipment. This Atlantic system first took clear shape in the early eighteenth century; it was the hub of European expansion all over the world.

Coffee drinking was one example among many of the new social and cultural patterns that took root between 1690 and 1740. Improvements in agricultural production at home reinforced the effects of trade overseas; Europeans now had more disposable income for extras, and they spent their money not only in the new coffeehouses and cafés that sprang up all over Europe but also on newspapers, musical concerts, paintings, and novels. A new middle-class public began to make its presence felt in every domain of culture and social life.

Although the rise of the Atlantic system gave Europe new prominence in the global context, European rulers still focused most of their political, diplomatic, and military energies on their rivalries within Europe. A coalition of countries succeeded in containing French aggression, and a more balanced diplomatic system emerged. In eastern Europe, Prussia and Austria had to contend with the rising power of Russia under Peter the Great. In western Europe, both Spain and the Dutch Republic declined in influence but continued to vie with Britain and France for colonial spoils in the Atlantic. The more evenly matched competition among the great powers encouraged the development of diplomatic skills and drew attention to public health as a way of encouraging population growth.

In the aftermath of Louis XIV's revocation of the Edict of Nantes in 1685, a new intellectual movement known as the Enlightenment began to germinate. An initial impetus came from French Protestant refugees who published works critical of absolutism in politics and religion. Increased prosperity, the growth of a middle-class public, and the decline in warfare after Louis XIV's death in 1715 helped fuel this new critical spirit. Fed by the popularization of science and the growing interest in travel literature, the Enlightenment encouraged greater skepticism about religious and state authority. Eventually the movement would question almost every aspect of social and political life in

◆ **1690s** Development of Caribbean plantations

◆ **1694** Bank of England established; Astell, *A Serious Proposal to the Ladies*

◆ **1697** Bayle, *Historical and Critical Dictionary*

◆ **1714–1727** King George I of England

◆ **1715** Death of Louis XIV

◆ **1719** Defoe, *Robinson Crusoe*

1690 | **1700** | **1710**

◆ **1699** Turks forced to recognize Austrian rule over Hungary, Transylvania

◆ **1703** Building of St. Petersburg begins; first Russian newspaper

◆ **1713–1714** Peace of Utrecht

Europe. The Enlightenment began in western Europe in those countries—Britain, France, and the Dutch Republic—most affected by the new Atlantic system. It too was a product of the age of coffee.

❖ The Atlantic System and the World Economy

Although their ships had been circling the globe since the early 1500s, Europeans did not draw most of the world into their economic orbit until the 1700s. Western European trading nations sent ships loaded with goods to buy slaves from local rulers on the western coast of Africa; then transported the slaves to the colonies in North and South America and the Caribbean and sold them to the owners of plantations producing coffee, sugar, cotton, and tobacco; and bought the raw commodities produced in the colonies and shipped them back to Europe, where they were refined or processed and then sold to other parts of Europe and the world. The Atlantic system and the growth of international trade helped create a new consumer society.

Slavery and the Atlantic System

Spain and Portugal dominated Atlantic trade in the sixteenth and seventeenth centuries, but in the eighteenth century European trade in the Atlantic rapidly expanded and became more systematically interconnected (Map 18.1, page 668). By 1630, Portugal had already sent 60,000 African slaves to Brazil to work on the new **plantations** (large tracts of lands producing staple crops, farmed by slave labor, and owned by colonial settlers from western Europe), which were producing some 15,000 tons of sugar a year. Realizing that plantations producing staples for Europeans could bring fabulous wealth, the European powers grew less interested in the dwindling trade in precious metals and more eager to colonize. In the 1690s large-scale planters of sugar, tobacco, and coffee began displacing small farmers who relied on one or two servants. Planters and their plantations won out because cheap slave labor allowed them to produce mass quantities of commodities at low prices.

State-chartered private companies from Portugal, France, Britain, the Dutch Republic, Prussia, and even Denmark exploited the 3,500-mile coastline of West Africa for slaves. Before 1675, most blacks taken from Africa had been sent to Brazil, but by 1700 half of the African slaves landed in the Caribbean (Figure 18.1). Thereafter, the plantation economy began to expand on the North American mainland. The numbers stagger the imagination. Before 1650, slave traders transported about 7,000 Africans each year across the Atlantic; this rate doubled between 1650 and 1675, nearly doubled again in the next twenty-five years, and kept going until the 1780s (Figure 18.2, page 670). In all, more than 11 million Africans, not counting those who died at sea or in Africa, were transported to the Americas before the slave trade

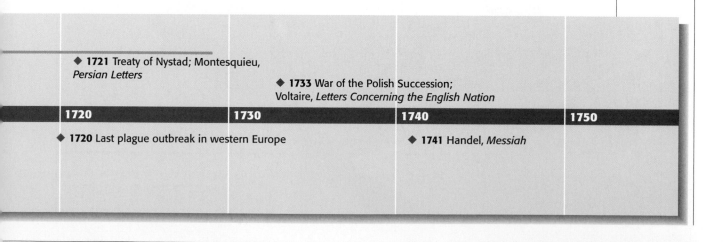

◆ **1721** Treaty of Nystad; Montesquieu, *Persian Letters*

◆ **1733** War of the Polish Succession; Voltaire, *Letters Concerning the English Nation*

| 1720 | 1730 | 1740 | 1750 |

◆ **1720** Last plague outbreak in western Europe

◆ **1741** Handel, *Messiah*

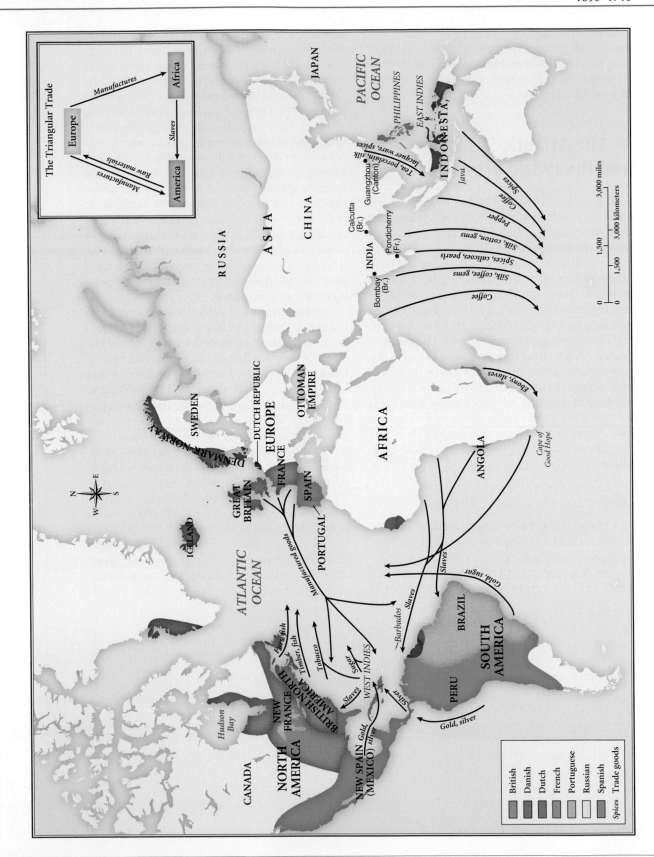

◀ **MAP 18.1 European Trade Patterns, c. 1740**

By 1740, the European powers had colonized much of North and South America and incorporated their colonies there into a worldwide system of commerce centered on the slave trade and plantation production of staple crops. Europeans still sought spices and luxury goods in China and the East Indies, but outside of Java, few Europeans had settled permanently in these areas. How did control over colonies determine dominance in international trade in this period?

began to wind down after 1850. Many traders gained spectacular wealth, but companies did not always make profits. The English Royal African Company, for example, delivered 100,000 slaves to the Caribbean, imported 30,000 tons of sugar to Britain, yet lost money after the few profitable years following its founding in 1672.

The Life of the Slaves. The balance of white and black populations in the New World colonies was determined by the staples produced. Because they did not own plantations, New England merchants and farmers bought few slaves. Blacks—both slave and free—made up only 3 percent of the population in eighteenth-century New England, compared with 60 percent in South Carolina. On the whole, the British North American colonies contained a higher proportion of African Americans from 1730 to 1765 than at any other time in American history. The imbalance of whites and blacks was even more extreme in the Caribbean; by 1713, the French Caribbean colony of Saint Domingue had four times as many black slaves as whites,

and by 1754 slaves outnumbered whites more than ten to one. Most indigenous people had died fighting Europeans or the diseases brought by them.

Enslaved women and men suffered terribly. Most had been sold to European traders by Africans from the west coast who acquired them through warfare or kidnapping. The vast majority were between fourteen and thirty-five years old. Before they were crammed onto the ships for the three-month trip, their heads were shaved, they were stripped naked, and some were branded with red-hot irons. Men and women were separated. Men were shackled with leg irons. Sailors and officers raped the women whenever they wished and beat those who refused their advances. In the cramped and appalling conditions of the voyage, as many as one-fourth of the slaves died.

Those who survived the transit were forced into degrading and oppressive conditions. As soon as masters bought slaves, they gave them new names, often only first names, and in some colonies branded them as personal property. Slaves had no social

FIGURE 18.1 African Slaves Imported into American Territories, 1701–1810

During the eighteenth century, planters in the newly established Caribbean colonies imported millions of African slaves to work the new plantations that produced sugar, coffee, indigo, and cotton for the European market. The vast majority of African slaves transported to the Americas ended up in either the Caribbean or Brazil. Why were so many slaves transported to the Caribbean islands, which are relatively small compared to Spanish or British North America? *Adapted from Philip D. Curtin, The Atlantic Slave Trade: A Census (Madison: University of Wisconsin Press, 1969).*

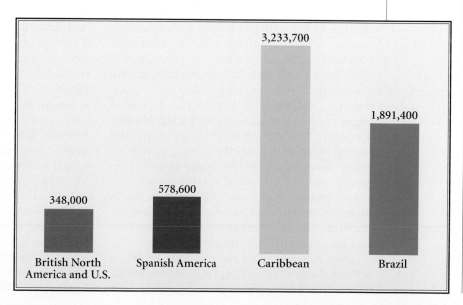

3,233,700

1,891,400

348,000

578,600

British North America and U.S.   Spanish America   Caribbean   Brazil

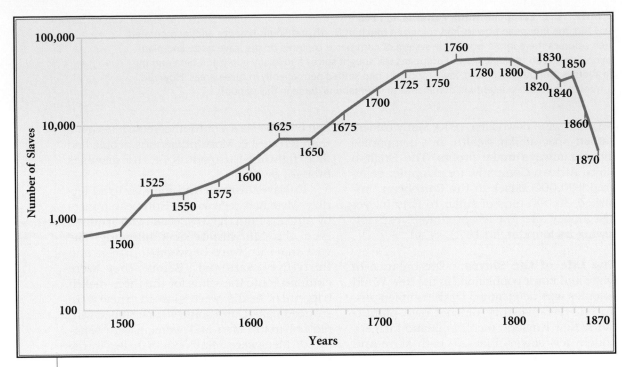

FIGURE 18.2 Annual Imports in the Atlantic Slave Trade, 1450–1870
The importation of slaves to the American territories reached its height in the second half of the eighteenth century and began to decline around 1800. Yet despite the abolition of the slave trade by the British in 1807, commerce in slaves did not seriously diminish until after the revolutions of 1848. *Adapted from Philip D. Curtin,* The Atlantic Slave Trade: A Census *(Madison: University of Wisconsin Press, 1969). Reprinted by permission of the University of Wisconsin Press.*

identities of their own; they were expected to learn their master's language and to do any job assigned. Slaves worked fifteen- to seventeen-hour days and were fed only enough to keep them on their feet. Brazilian slaves consumed more calories than the poorest Brazilians do today, but that hardly made them well fed. The death rate among slaves was high, especially on the sugar plantations, where slaves had to cut and haul sugar cane to the grinders and boilers before it spoiled. During the harvest, grinding and boiling went on around the clock. Because so many slaves died in the sugar-growing regions, more and more slaves, especially strong males, had to be imported. In North America, in contrast, where sugar was a minor crop, the slave population increased tenfold by 1863 through natural growth.

Not surprisingly, despite the threat of torture or death on recapture, slaves sometimes ran away. (See "New Sources, New

Perspectives," page 672.) In Brazil, runaways hid in *quilombos*◆ (hideouts) in the forests or backcountry. When it was discovered and destroyed in 1695, the quilombo of Palmares had thirty thousand fugitives who had formed their own social organization complete with elected kings and councils of elders. Outright revolt was uncommon, especially before the nineteenth century, but other forms of resistance included stealing food, breaking tools, and feigning illness or stupidity. Slaveholders' fears about conspiracy and revolt lurked beneath the surface of every slave-based society. In 1710, the royal governor of Virginia reminded the colonial legislature of the need for unceasing vigilance: "We are not to Depend on Either Their Stupidity, or that Babel of Languages among 'em; freedom Wears a Cap which Can Without a Tongue, Call Togather all Those who Long to Shake off

---

◆**quilombos:** kih LOM bos

the fetters of Slavery." Masters defended whipping and other forms of physical punishment as essential to maintaining discipline. Laws called for the castration of a slave who struck a white person.

Effects on Europe. Plantation owners often left their colonial possessions in the care of agents and collected the revenue to live as wealthy landowners back home, where they built opulent mansions and gained influence in local and national politics. William Beckford, for example, had been sent from Jamaica to school in England as a young boy. When he inherited sugar plantations and shipping companies from his father and older brother, he moved the headquarters of the family business to London in the 1730s to be close to the government and financial markets. His holdings formed the single most powerful economic interest in Jamaica, but he preferred to live in England where he could buy works of art for his many luxurious homes, hold political office (he served as lord mayor of London and in Parliament), and even lend money to the government.

The slave trade permanently altered consumption patterns for ordinary people. Sugar had been prescribed as a medicine before the end of the sixteenth century, but the development of plantations in Brazil and the Caribbean made it a standard food item. By 1700, the British sent home 50 million pounds of sugar a year, a figure that doubled by 1730. During the French Revolution of the 1790s, sugar shortages would become a cause for rioting in Paris. Equally pervasive was the spread of tobacco; by the 1720s, Britain imported two hundred shiploads of tobacco from Virginia and Maryland every year, and men of every country and class smoked pipes or took snuff.

The Origins of Modern Racism. The traffic in slaves disturbed many Europeans. As a government memorandum to the Spanish king explained in 1610: "Modern theologians in published books commonly report on, and condemn as unjust, the acts of enslavement which take place in provinces of this Royal Empire." Between 1667 and 1671, the French Dominican monk Father Du Tertre published three volumes in which he denounced the mistreatment of slaves in the French colonies.

In the 1700s, however, slaveholders began to justify their actions by demeaning the mental and spiritual qualities of the

Caribbean Sugar Mill

This seventeenth-century engraving of a sugar mill or grinder makes the work seem much less difficult than it was in practice. Slaves cut the sugar cane and then hauled it from the fields to the mill where it was crushed. Many slaves lost fingers or hands in the process. The slaves then collected the juice (bottom center) and carried it to the boilers, shown at the bottom left and right. The sap was poured into molds and dried. Then the bricks of raw sugar were exported to Europe for refining. *The Granger Collection, NY.*

Oral History and the Life of Slaves

Historians have found it difficult to reconstruct slave life from the point of view of the slaves themselves, in part because slaves newly imported from Africa to the New World did not speak the language of their captors. Scholars have attempted to fill in this blank by using a variety of overlapping sources. The most interesting and controversial of these sources are oral histories taken from descendants of slaves. In some former slave societies, these descendants still tell stories about their ancestors' first days under slavery. The controversy comes from using present-day memories to get at eighteenth-century lives.

One of the regions most intensively studied in this fashion is Dutch Surinam, on the northeast coast of South America between present-day Guyana and French Guiana. This region is a good source of oral histories because 10 percent of the African slaves transported there between the 1680s and the 1750s escaped from the plantations and fled into the nearby rain forests. There they set up their own societies and developed their own language, in which they carried on the oral traditions of the first runaway slaves. The descendants of the runaway slaves recount:

In slavery, there was hardly anything to eat. It was at the place called Providence Plantation. They whipped you there till your ass was burning. Then they would give you a bit of plain rice in a calabash [a bowl made from the tropical American tree known as calabash]. . . . And the gods told them that this is no way for human beings to live. They would help them. Let each person go where he could. So they ran.

Slaves of Surinam in the 1770s
John Gabriel Stedman published an account of his participation in a five-year expedition against the runaway slaves of Surinam that took place in the 1770s. He provided drawings such as the one reproduced here, which shows Africans who have just come off a slave ship. *Schomburg Center for Research in Black Culture/New York Public Library/Art Resource, NY.*

enslaved Africans. White Europeans and colonists sometimes described black slaves as animal-like, akin to apes. A leading New England Puritan asserted about the slaves: "Indeed their *Stupidity* is a *Discouragement*. It may seem, unto as little purpose, to *Teach*, as to *wash an Aethiopian* [Ethiopian]." One of the great paradoxes of this time was that talk of liberty and self-evident rights, especially prevalent in Britain and its North American colonies, coexisted with the belief that some people were meant to be slaves. Although Christians believed in principle in a kind of spiritual equality between blacks and whites, the churches often defended or at least did not oppose the inequities of slavery.

From other sources, historians have learned that there was a major slave rebellion at Providence Plantation in Surinam, in 1693.

By comparing such oral histories to written accounts of plantation owners, missionaries, and Dutch colonial officials, historians have been able to paint a richly detailed picture not only of slavery but also of runaway slave societies, which were especially numerous in South America. At the end of the eighteenth century, a Portuguese-speaking Jew wrote his own history of plantation life based on records from the local Jewish community that are now lost. Because the Dutch, unlike most other Europeans, allowed Jews to own slaves, Portuguese-speaking Jews from Brazil owned about one-third of the plantations and slaves in Surinam. This eighteenth-century chronicler, David de Ishak Cohen Nassy, wrote his version of Surinam's first slave revolt:

> There was in the year 1690 a revolt on a plantation situated on the Cassewinica Creek, behind Jews Savannah, belonging to a Jew named Imanuël Machado, where, having killed their master, they fled, carrying away with them everything that was there. . . . The Jews . . . in an expedition which they undertook against the rebels, killed many of them and brought back several who were punished by death on the very spot.

The oral histories told about the revolt from the runaway slaves' perspective:

> There had been a great council meeting [of runaway slaves] in the forest. . . . They decided to burn a different one of his plantations from the place where he had whipped Lanu [one of the runaway slaves] because they would find more tools there. This was the Cassewinica Plantation, which had many slaves. They knew all about this plantation from slavery times. So, they attacked. It was at night. They killed

> the head of the plantation, a white man. They took all the things, everything they needed.

The runaway slaves saw the attack as part of their ongoing effort to build a life in the rain forest, away from the whites.

Over the next decades, the runaway slaves fought a constant series of battles with plantation owners and Dutch officials. Finally in 1762, the Dutch granted the runaway slaves their freedom in a peace agreement and allowed them to trade in the main town of the colony in exchange for agreeing to return all future runaways. The runaways had not destroyed the slave system, but they had gained their own independence alongside it. From their oral histories it is possible to retrace their efforts to build new lives in a strange place, in which they combined African practices with New World experiences.

Source: Richard Price, *Alabi's World* (Baltimore: Johns Hopkins University Press, 1990), 17, 9.

QUESTIONS TO CONSIDER
1. What did runaway slaves aim to accomplish when they attacked plantations?
2. Why would runaway slaves make an agreement with the Dutch colonial officials to return future runaways?
3. Can oral histories recorded in the twentieth century be considered accurate versions of events that took place in the eighteenth century? How can they be tested?

FURTHER READING
Price, Richard. *Alabi's World.* 1990.
Stedman, John Gabriel. *Narrative of a Five Years' Expedition Against the Revolted Negroes of Surinam.* Edited, and with an introduction and notes, by Richard Price and Sally Price. 1988.

World Trade and Settlement

The Atlantic system helped extend European trade relations across the globe. The textiles that Atlantic shippers exchanged for slaves on the west coast of Africa, for example, were manufactured in India and exported by the British and French East India Companies. As much as one-quarter of the British exports to Africa in the eighteenth century were actually re-exports from India. To expand its trade in the rest of the world, Europeans seized territories and tried to establish permanent settlements. The eighteenth-century extension of European power prepared the way for western global domination in the nineteenth and twentieth centuries.

The Americas. In contrast to the sparsely inhabited trading outposts in Asia and Africa, the colonies in the Americas bulged with settlers. The British North American colonies, for example, contained about 1.5 million nonnative (that is, white settler and black slave) residents by 1750. While the Spanish competed with the Portuguese for control of South America, the French competed with the British for control of North America. Spanish and British settlers came to blows over the boundary between the British colonies and Florida, which was held by Spain.

Local economies shaped colonial social relations; men in French trapper communities in Canada, for example, had little in common with the men and women of the plantation societies in Barbados or Brazil. Racial attitudes also differed from place to place. The Spanish and Portuguese tolerated intermarriage with the native populations in both America and Asia. Sexual contact, both inside and outside marriage, fostered greater racial variety in the Spanish and Portuguese colonies than in the French or the English territories (though mixed-race people could be found everywhere). By 1800, **mestizos**, children of Spanish men and Indian women, accounted for more than a quarter of the population in the Spanish colonies, and many of them aspired to join the local elite. Greater racial diversity seems not to have improved the treatment of slaves.

Where intermarriage between colonizers and natives was common, conversion to Christianity proved most successful. Although the Indians maintained many of their native religious beliefs, many Indians in the Spanish colonies had come to consider themselves devout Catholics by 1700. Indian carpenters and artisans in the villages produced innumerable altars, retables (painted panels), and sculpted images to adorn their local churches, and individual families put up domestic shrines. Yet the clergy remained overwhelmingly Spanish: the church hierarchy concluded that the Indians' humility and innocence made them unsuitable for the priesthood.

In the early years of American colonization, many more men than women emigrated from Europe. Although the sex imbalance began to decline at the end of the seventeenth century, it remained substantial; two and a half times as many men as women were among the immigrants leaving Liverpool, England, between 1697 and 1707, for example. Women who emigrated as indentured servants ran great risks: if they did not die of disease during the voyage, they were likely to give birth to illegitimate children (the fate of at least one in five servant women) or be virtually sold into marriage. Many upper-class women were kept in seclusion, especially in the Spanish and Portuguese colonies.

The uncertainties of life in the American colonies provided new opportunities for European women and men willing to live outside the law, however. In the 1500s and 1600s, the English and Dutch governments had routinely authorized pirates to prey on the ships of their rivals, the Spanish and Portuguese. Then, in the late 1600s, English, French, and Dutch bands made up of deserters and crews from wrecked vessels began to form their own associations of pirates, especially in the Caribbean. Called **buccaneers** from their custom of curing strips of beef, called *boucan* by the native Caribs of the islands, the pirates governed themselves and preyed on everyone's shipping without regard to national origin. In 1720, the trial of buccaneers associated with Calico Jack Rackham in Jamaica revealed that two women had dressed as men and joined the pirates in looting and plundering English ships. Mary Read and Anne Bonny escaped death by hanging only because they were pregnant. After 1700, the colonial governments tried to stamp out piracy. As one British judge argued in 1705, "A pirate is in perpetual war with every individual and every state. . . . They are worse than ravenous beasts."

Africa and Asia. White settlements in Africa and Asia remained small and almost insignificant, except for their long-term potential. Europeans had little contact with East Africa and almost none with Africa's vast interior. A few Portuguese trading posts in Angola and Dutch farms on the Cape of Good Hope provided the only toeholds for future expansion. In China the emperors had welcomed Catholic missionaries at court in the seventeenth century, but the priests' credibility diminished as they squabbled among themselves and associated with

European merchants, whom the Chinese considered pirates. "The barbarians [Europeans] are like wild beasts," one Chinese official concluded. In 1720, only one thousand Europeans resided in Guangzhou (Canton), the sole place where foreigners could legally trade for spices, tea, and silk (see Map 18.1 page 668).

Europeans exercised more influence in Java (in what was then called the East Indies) and in India. Dutch coffee production in Java and nearby islands increased phenomenally in the early 1700s, and many Dutch settled there to oversee production and trade. Dutch, English, French, Portuguese, and Danish companies competed in India for spices, cotton, and silk; by the 1740s the English and French had become the leading rivals in India, just as they were in North America. Both countries extended their power as India's Muslim rulers lost control to local Hindu princes, rebellious Sikhs, invading Persians, and their own provincial governors. A few thousand Europeans lived in India, though many thousand more soldiers were stationed there to protect them. The staple of trade with India in the early 1700s was calico—lightweight, brightly colored cotton cloth that caught on as a fashion in Europe (see the image on this page).

Europeans who visited India were especially struck by what they viewed as exotic religious practices. In a book published in 1696 of his travels to western India, an Anglican minister described the fakirs♦ (religious mendicants or beggars of alms), "some of whom show their devotion by a shameless appearance, walking naked, without the least rag of clothes to cover them." Such writings increased European interest in the outside world but also fed a European sense of superiority that helped excuse the more violent forms of colonial domination (see The Exotic as Consumer Item on the next page).

♦**fakirs:** fuh KEER

India Cottons and Trade with the East
This colored cotton cloth (now faded with age) was painted and embroidered in Madras in southern India sometime in the late 1600s. The male figure with a mustache may be a European, but the female figures are clearly Asian. Europeans—especially the British—discovered that they could make big profits on the export of Indian cotton cloth to Europe. They also traded Indian cottons in Africa for slaves and sold large quantities in the colonies. *Victoria and Albert Museum, London.*

The Birth of Consumer Society

As worldwide colonization produced new supplies of goods, from coffee to calico, population growth in Europe fueled demand for them. Beginning first in Britain, then in France and the Italian states, and finally in eastern Europe, population surged, growing by about 20 percent between 1700 and 1750. The gap between a fast-growing northwest and a more stagnant south and central Europe now diminished as regions that had lost population during the seventeenth-century downturn recovered. Cities, in particular, grew. Between 1600 and 1750, London's population more than tripled and Paris's more than doubled.

Although contemporaries could not have realized it then, this was the start of the modern population explosion. It appears that a decline in the death rate, rather than a rise in the birthrate, explains the turnaround. Three main factors contributed to increased longevity: better weather and hence more bountiful harvests,

The Exotic as Consumer Item
This painting by the Venetian artist Rosalba Carriera (1675–1757) is titled *Africa*. The young black girl wearing a turban represents the African continent. Carriera was known for her use of pastels. In 1720, she journeyed to Paris where she became an associate of Antoine Watteau and helped inaugurate the rococo style in painting. Why did the artist choose to paint an African girl for this picture? **For more help analyzing this image**, see the visual activity for this chapter in the Online Study Guide at **bedfordstmartins.com/hunt**. *Staatliche Kunstsammlungen Dresden, Gemaldegalerie Alte Meister.*

improved agricultural techniques, and the plague's disappearance after 1720.

By the early eighteenth century, the effects of economic expansion and population growth brought about a **consumer revolution**. The British East India Company began to import into Britain huge quantities of calicoes. British imports of tobacco doubled between 1672 and 1700; at Nantes, the center of the French sugar trade, imports quadrupled between 1698 and 1733. Tea, chocolate, and coffee became virtual necessities. In the 1670s, only a trickle of tea reached London, but by 1720 the East India Company sent 9 million pounds to England—a figure that rose to 37 million pounds by 1750. By 1700, England had two thousand coffeehouses; by 1740, every English country town had at least

two. Paris got its first cafés at the end of the seventeenth century; Berlin opened its first coffeehouse in 1714; Bach's Leipzig boasted eight by 1725. In the English economic literature of the 1690s, writers reacted to these developments by expressing a new view of humans as consuming animals with boundless appetites. Many authors attacked the new doctrine of consumerism, but they could not hold back the fast-growing market for consumption.

Review: How is consumerism related to slavery?

❖ New Social and Cultural Patterns

The impact of the Atlantic system and world trade was most apparent in the cities, where people had more money for consumer goods. But rural changes also had significant long-term influence, as a revolution in agricultural techniques made it possible to feed more and more people with a smaller agricultural workforce. As population increased, more people moved to the cities, where they found themselves caught up in innovative urban customs such as attending musical concerts and reading novels. Along with a general increase in literacy, these activities helped create a public that responded to new writers and artists. Social and cultural changes were not uniform across Europe, however; as usual, people's experiences varied depending on whether they lived in wealth or poverty, in urban or rural areas, or in eastern or western Europe.

Agricultural Revolution

Although Britain, France, and the Dutch Republic shared the enthusiasm for consumer goods, Britain's domestic market grew most quickly. In Britain, as agricultural output increased 43 percent over the course of the 1700s, the population increased by 70 percent. The British imported grain to feed the growing population, but they also benefited from the development of techniques that together constituted an **agricultural revolution**. No new machinery propelled this revolution—just increasingly aggressive attitudes toward investment and management. The Dutch and the Flemish had pioneered many of these techniques in the 1600s, but the British took them further.

Four major changes occurred in British agriculture that eventually spread to other countries. First, farmers increased the amount of land under cultivation by draining wetlands and by growing crops on previously uncultivated common lands (acreage maintained by the community for grazing). Second, those farmers who could afford it consolidated small, scattered plots into larger, more efficient units. Third, livestock raising became more closely linked to crop growing, and the yields of each increased. (See "Taking Measure," opposite.) For centuries, most farmers had rotated their fields in and out of production to replenish the soil. Now farmers planted carefully chosen fodder crops such as clover and turnips that added nutrients to the soil, thereby eliminating the need to leave a field fallow (unplanted) every two or three years. With more fodder available, farmers could raise more livestock, which in turn produced more manure to fertilize grain fields. Fourth, selective breeding of animals combined with the increase in fodder to improve the quality and size of herds. New crops had only a slight impact; potatoes, for example, were introduced to Europe from South America in the 1500s, but because people feared they might cause leprosy, tuberculosis, or fevers, they were not grown in quantity until the late 1700s. By the 1730s and 1740s, agricultural output had increased dramatically, and prices for food had fallen because of these interconnected innovations.

Changes in agricultural practices did not benefit all landowners equally. The biggest British landowners consolidated their holdings in the "enclosure movement." They put pressure on small farmers and villagers to sell their land or give up their common lands. The big landlords then fenced off (enclosed) their property. Because enclosure eliminated community grazing rights, it frequently sparked a struggle between the big landlords and villagers, and in Britain it normally required an act of Parliament. Such acts became increasingly common in the

second half of the eighteenth century, and by the century's end six million acres of common lands had been enclosed and developed. "Improvers" produced more food more efficiently than small farmers could and thus supported a growing population.

TAKING MEASURE

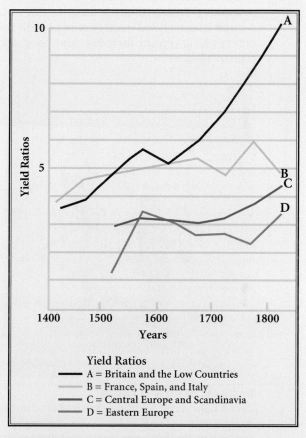

Yield Ratios
- A = Britain and the Low Countries
- B = France, Spain, and Italy
- C = Central Europe and Scandinavia
- D = Eastern Europe

Relationship of Crop Harvested to Seed Used, 1400–1800
The impact and even the timing of the agricultural revolution can be determined by this figure, based on yield ratios (the number of grains produced for each seed planted). Britain, the Dutch Republic, and the Austrian Netherlands all experienced huge increases in crop yields after 1700. Other European regions lagged behind right into the 1800s. Why is crop yield such an important measure? *From Peter J. Hugill,* World Trade since 1431: Geography, Technology, and Capitalism *(Johns Hopkins University Press, 1995), p. 56. Reprinted by permission of Johns Hopkins University Press.*

Contrary to the fears of contemporaries, small farmers and cottagers (those with little or no property) were not forced off the land all at once. But most villagers could not afford the litigation involved in resisting enclosure, and small landholders consequently had to sell out to landlords or farmers with larger plots. Landlords with large holdings leased their estates to tenant farmers at constantly increasing rents, and the tenant farmers in turn employed the cottagers as salaried agricultural workers. In this way the English peasantry largely disappeared, replaced by a more hierarchical society of big landlords, enterprising tenant farmers, and poor agricultural laborers.

Treatment of Serfs in Russia
Visitors from western Europe often remarked on the cruel treatment of serfs in Russia. This drawing by one such visitor shows the punishment that could be inflicted by landowners. Serfs could be whipped for almost any reason, even for making a soup too salty or neglecting to bow when the lord's family passed by. Their condition actually deteriorated in the 1700s, as landowners began to sell serfs much like slaves. New decrees made it illegal for serfs to contract loans, enter into leases, or work for anyone other than their lord. Some landlords kept harems of serf girls. Although the Russian landlords' treatment of serfs was even more brutal than that in the German states and Poland, upper classes in every country regarded the serfs as dirty, deceitful, brutish, and superstitious. *New York Public Library Slavonic Division/Art Resource, NY.*

The new agricultural techniques spread slowly from Britain and the Low Countries (the Dutch Republic and the Austrian Netherlands) to the rest of western Europe. Outside a few pockets in northern France and the western German states, however, subsistence agriculture (producing just enough to get by rather than surpluses for the market) continued to dominate farming in western Europe and Scandinavia. In southwestern Germany, for example, 80 percent of the peasants produced no surplus because their plots were too small. Unlike the populations of the highly urbanized Low Countries (where half the people lived in towns and cities), most Europeans, western and eastern, eked out their existence in the countryside.

In eastern Europe, the condition of peasants worsened in the areas where landlords tried hardest to improve crop yields. To produce more for the Baltic grain market, aristocratic landholders in Prussia, Poland, and parts of Russia drained wetlands, cultivated moors, and built dikes. They also forced peasants off lands that the peasants had worked for themselves, increased compulsory labor services (the critical element in serfdom), and began to manage their estates directly. Some eastern landowners grew fabulously wealthy. The Potocki family in the Polish Ukraine, for example, owned three million acres of land and had 130,000 serfs. In parts of Poland and Russia the serfs hardly differed from slaves in status, and their "masters" ran their huge estates much like American plantations (see the image on this page).

Social Life in the Cities

Because of emigration from the countryside, cities grew in population and consequently exercised more influence on culture and social life. Between 1650 and 1750, cities with at least ten thousand inhabitants increased in population by 44 percent. From the eighteenth century onward, urban growth would be continuous. Along with the general growth of cities, an important south-to-north shift occurred in the pattern of urbanization. Around 1500, half of the people in cities of at least ten thousand residents could be found in the Italian states, Spain, or Portugal; by 1700, the urbanization of northwestern and southern Europe was roughly equal. Eastern Europe, despite the huge cities of Istanbul and Moscow, was still less urban than western Europe. London was by far the most populous European city, with 675,000 inhabitants in 1750; Berlin had 90,000 people, Warsaw only 23,000.

Urban Social Classes. Many landowners kept a residence in town, so the separation between rural and city life was not as extreme as might be imagined, at least not for the very rich. At the top of the ladder in the big cities were the landed nobles. Some of them filled their lives only with conspicuous consumption of fine food, extravagant clothing, coaches, books, and opera; others held key political, administrative, or judicial offices. However they spent their time, these rich families employed thousands of artisans, shopkeepers, and domestic servants. Many English peers (highest-ranking nobles) had thirty or forty servants at each of their homes.

The middle classes of officials, merchants, professionals, and landowners occupied the next rung down on the social ladder. London's population, for example, included about 20,000 middle-class families (constituting, at most, one-sixth of the city's population). In this period the middle classes began to develop distinctive ways of life that set them apart from both the rich noble landowners and the lower classes. Unlike the rich nobles, the middle classes lived primarily in the cities and towns, even if they owned small country estates. They ate more moderately than nobles but much better than peasants or laborers. For breakfast the British middle classes ate toast and rolls and, after 1700, drank tea. Dinner, served midday, consisted of roasted or boiled beef or mutton, poultry or pork, and vegetables. Supper was a light meal of bread and cheese with cake or pie. Beer was the main drink in London, and many families brewed their own. Even children drank beer because of the lack of fresh water.

In contrast to the gigantic and sprawling country seats of the richest English peers, middle-class houses in town had about seven rooms, including four or five bedrooms and one or two living rooms, still many more than the poor agricultural worker. New household items reflected society's increasing wealth and its exposure to colonial imports: by 1700, a middle-class house in London typically had mirrors in every room, a coffeepot and coffee mill, numerous pictures and ornaments, a china collection, and several clocks. Life for the middle classes on the continent was quite similar, though wine replaced beer in France.

Below the middle classes came the artisans and shopkeepers (most of whom were organized in professional guilds), then the journeymen, apprentices, servants, and laborers. At the bottom of the social scale were the unemployed poor, who survived by intermittent work and charity. Women married to artisans and shopkeepers often kept the accounts, supervised employees, and ran the household as well. Every middle-class and upper-class family employed servants; artisans and shopkeepers frequently hired them too. Women from poorer families usually worked as domestic servants until they married. Four out of five domestic servants in the city were female. In large cities such as London, the servant population grew faster than the population of the city as a whole.

Signs of Social Distinction. Social status in the cities was readily visible. Wide, spacious streets graced rich districts; the houses had gardens, and the air was relatively fresh. In poor districts the streets were narrow, dirty, dark, humid, and smelly, and the houses were damp and crowded. The poorest people were homeless, sleeping under bridges or in abandoned homes. A Neapolitan prince described his homeless neighbors as "lying like filthy animals, with no distinction of age or sex." In some districts, rich and poor lived in the same buildings; the poor clambered up to shabby, cramped apartments on the top floors.

Like shelter, clothing was a reliable social indicator. The poorest workingwomen in Paris wore woolen skirts and blouses of dark colors over petticoats, a bodice, and a corset. They also donned caps of various sorts, cotton stockings, and shoes (probably their only pair). Workingmen dressed even more drably. Many occupations could be recognized by their dress: no one could confuse lawyers in their dark robes with masons or butchers in their special aprons, for example. People higher on the social ladder were more likely to sport a variety of fabrics, colors, and unusual designs in their clothing

Gin Lane, London

The English painter and engraver William Hogarth chronicled every aspect of social life in London. In this engraving from 1751, he shows the appalling effects of cheap gin on lower-class London families. In the front center, a drunken woman is taking snuff while her unwatched baby falls to his death. Everywhere violence and mayhem reign. The only buildings of substance are the pawnbroker and the gin shop. In the same year, Parliament passed a gin act regulating the sale of alcohol. Hogarth's depiction reveals as much about middle-class fears as it does of actual lower-class behavior. © *Archivo Iconografico, S.A./CORBIS.*

and to own many different outfits. Social status was not an abstract idea; it permeated every detail of daily life.

The Growth of a Literate Public

The ability to read and write also reflected social differences. People in the upper classes were more literate than those in the lower classes; city people were more literate than peasants. Protestant countries appear to have been more successful at promoting education and literacy than Catholic countries, perhaps because of the Protestant emphasis on Bible reading. Widespread literacy among the lower classes was first achieved in the Protes-

tant areas of Switzerland and in Presbyterian Scotland, and rates were also very high in the New England colonies and the Scandinavian countries. In France, literacy doubled in the eighteenth century thanks to the spread of parish schools, but still only one in two men and one in four women could read and write. Most peasants remained illiterate. Despite the efforts of some Protestant German states to encourage primary education, primary schooling remained woefully inadequate almost everywhere in Europe: few schools existed, teachers received low wages, and no country had yet established a national system of control or supervision.

Despite the deficiencies of primary education, a new literate public arose especially among the middle classes of the cities. More books and periodicals were published than ever before. Britain and the Dutch Republic led the way in this powerful outpouring of printed words. The trend began in the 1690s and gradually accelerated. In 1695, the British government allowed the licensing system, through which it controlled publications, to lapse, and new newspapers and magazines appeared almost immediately. The first London daily newspaper came out in 1702, and in 1709 Joseph Addison and Richard Steele published the first literary magazine, *The Spectator.* They devoted their magazine to the cultural improvement of the increasingly influential middle class. By the 1720s, twenty-four provincial newspapers were published in England. In the London coffeehouses, an edition of a single newspaper might reach ten thousand male readers. Women did their reading at home. Newspapers on the continent lagged behind and often consisted mainly of advertising with little critical commentary. France, for example, had no daily paper until 1777.

Review: What were the social and cultural consequences of the agricultural revolution?

New Tastes in the Arts

The new literate public did not just read newspapers; its members now pursued an interest in painting, attended concerts, and besieged booksellers in search of popular

Rococo Painting

Painted originally as a shop sign for an art merchant, *Gersaint's Shopsign* (1721) by Antoine Watteau demonstrates the new rococo style. The colors are muted and the atmosphere is light and airy. The subject matter—the sale of art, gilded mirrors, and toiletries to the new urban aristocrats and middle classes—is entirely secular and even commercial. The canvas reflects the new urban market for art and slyly notes the passing of a era: a portrait of the recently deceased Louis XIV is being packed away on the left-hand side of the painting. Watteau painted the sign in eight days while suffering from the tuberculosis that would kill him just a few months later. *Scala/Art Resource, NY.*

novels. Because increased trade and prosperity put money into the hands of the growing middle classes, a new urban audience began to compete with the churches, rulers, and courtiers as chief patrons for new work. As the public for the arts expanded, printed commentary on them emerged, setting the stage for the appearance of political and social criticism. New artistic tastes thus had effects far beyond the realm of the arts.

Rococo Painting. Developments in painting reflected the tastes of the new public, as the **rococo**◆ style challenged the hold of the baroque and classical schools, especially in France. Like the baroque, the rococo emphasized irregularity and asymmetry, movement and curvature, but it did so on a much smaller, subtler scale. Many rococo paintings depicted scenes of intimate sensuality rather than the monumental, emotional grandeur favored by classical and baroque painters.

Personal portraits and pastoral paintings took the place of heroic landscapes and grand, ceremonial canvases. Rococo paintings adorned homes as well as palaces and served as a form of interior decoration rather than as a statement of piety. (See the painting above for an example of a painting of a shop sign.) Its decorative quality made rococo art an ideal complement to newly discovered materials such as stucco and porcelain, especially the porcelain vases now imported from China.

Rococo, like *baroque*, was an invented word (from the French word *rocaille*, meaning "shellwork") and originally a derogatory label, meaning "frivolous decoration." But the great French rococo painters, such as Antoine Watteau◆ (1684–1721) and François Boucher◆ (1703–1770), were much more than mere decorators. Although both emphasized the erotic in their depictions, Watteau

◆**rococo:** ruh KOH koh

◆**Watteau:** vah TOH
◆**Boucher:** boo SHAY

captured the melancholy side of a passing aristocratic style of life, and Boucher painted middle-class people at home during their daily activities. Both painters thereby contributed to the emergence of new sensibilities in art that increasingly attracted a middle-class public.

Music for the Public. The first public music concerts were performed in England in the 1670s, becoming much more regular and frequent in the 1690s. City concert halls typically seated about two hundred, but the relatively high price of tickets limited attendance to the better-off. Music clubs provided entertainment in smaller towns and villages. On the continent, Frankfurt organized the first regular public concerts in 1712; Hamburg and Paris began holding them within a few years. Opera continued to spread in the eighteenth century; Venice had sixteen public opera houses by 1700, and in 1732 Covent Garden opera house opened in London.

The growth of a public that appreciated and supported music had much the same effect as the extension of the reading public: like authors, composers could now begin to liberate themselves from court patronage and work for a paying audience. This development took time to solidify, however, and court or church patrons still commissioned much eighteenth-century music. Bach, a German Lutheran, wrote his *St. Matthew Passion* for Good Friday services in 1729 while he was organist and choirmaster for the leading church in Leipzig. He composed secular works (like the "Coffee Cantata") for the public and a variety of private patrons.

The composer George Frederick Handel (1685–1759) was among the first to grasp the new directions in music. A German by birth, he wrote operas in Italy and then moved in 1710 to Britain, where he wrote music for the court and began composing oratorios, a form he introduced in Britain. The oratorio combined the drama of opera with the majesty of religious and ceremonial music and featured the chorus over the soloists. The "Hallelujah Chorus" from Handel's oratorio *Messiah* (1741) is perhaps the single best-known piece of Western classical music. It reflected the composer's personal, deeply felt piety but also his willingness to combine musical materials into a dramatic form that captured the enthusiasm of the new public. In 1740, a poem about Handel published in the *Gentleman's Magazine* exulted: "His art so modulates the sounds in all, / Our passions, as he pleases, rise and fall." Music had become an integral part of the new middle-class public's culture.

Novels. Nothing captured the imagination of the new public more than the novel, the literary genre whose very name underscored the eighteenth-century taste for novelty. More than three hundred French novels appeared between 1700 and 1730. During this unprecedented explosion, the novel took on its modern form and became more concerned with individual psychology and social description than with the adventure tales popular earlier (such as Cervantes's *Don Quixote*). The novel's popularity was closely tied to the expansion of the reading public, and novels were available in serial form in periodicals or from the many booksellers who popped up to serve the new market.

Women figured prominently in novels as characters, and women writers abounded. The English novel *Love in Excess* (1719) quickly reached a sixth printing, and its author, Eliza Haywood (1693?–1756), earned her living turning out a stream of novels with titles such as *Persecuted Virtue, Constancy Rewarded,* and *The History of Betsy Thoughtless*—all showing a concern for the proper place of women as models of virtue in a changing world. When her husband deserted her and her two children, Haywood first worked as an actress but soon turned to writing plays and novels. In the 1740s, she began publishing a magazine, *The Female Spectator*, which argued in favor of higher education for women.

Haywood's male counterpart was Daniel Defoe (1660–1731), a merchant's son who had a diverse and colorful career as a manufacturer, political spy, novelist, and social commentator. Defoe wrote about schemes for national improvement, the state of English trade, the economic condition of the countryside, the effects of the plague, and the history of pirates; he is most well known, however, for his novels *Robinson Crusoe* (1719) and *Moll Flanders* (1722). The story of the adventures of a shipwrecked sailor,

Robinson Crusoe portrayed the new values of the time: to survive, Crusoe had to employ fearless entrepreneurial ingenuity. He had to be ready for the unexpected and be able to improvise in every situation. He was, in short, the model for the new man in an expanding economy. Crusoe's patronizing attitude toward the black man Friday now draws much critical attention, but his discovery of Friday shows how the fate of blacks and whites had become intertwined in the new colonial environment.

Religious Revivals

Despite the novel's growing popularity, religious books and pamphlets still sold in huge numbers, and most Europeans remained devout, even as their religions were changing. In this period, a Protestant revivalist movement known as **Pietism**♦ rocked the complacency of the established churches in the German Lutheran states, the Dutch Republic, and Scandinavia. Pietists believed in a mystical religion of the heart; they wanted a deeply emotional, even ecstatic religion. They urged intense Bible study, which in turn promoted popular education and contributed to the increase in literacy. Many Pietists attended catechism instruction every day and also went to morning and evening prayer meetings in addition to regular Sunday services.

As a grassroots movement, Pietism appealed to both Lutherans and Calvinists, some of whom left their churches to form new sects. One of the most remarkable disciples of Pietism was the Englishwoman Jane Leade (1623–1704), who founded the sect of Philadelphians (from the Greek for "brotherly love"), which soon spread to the Dutch Republic and the German states. Leade's visions and studies of mysticism led her to advocate a universal, nondogmatic church that would be open to all Christians. Philadelphic societies maintained only loose ties to one another, however, and despite Leade's organizational aims they soon went off in different directions.

Catholicism also had its versions of religious revival, especially in France. A Frenchwoman, Jeanne Marie Guyon♦ (1648–1717),

attracted many noblewomen and a few leading clergymen to her own Catholic brand of Pietism, known as Quietism. Claiming miraculous visions and astounding prophecies, she urged a mystical union with God through prayer and simple devotion. Despite papal condemnation and intense controversy within Catholic circles in France, Guyon had followers all over Europe.

Even more influential were the Jansenists, who gained many new adherents to their austere form of Catholicism despite Louis XIV's harassment and repeated condemnation by the papacy. Under the pressure of religious and political persecution, Jansenism took a revivalist turn in the 1720s. At the funeral of a Jansenist priest in Paris in 1727, the crowd who flocked to the grave claimed to witness a series of miraculous healings. Within a few years a cult formed around the priest's tomb, and clandestine Jansenist presses reported new miracles to the reading public. When the French government tried to suppress the cult, one enraged wit placed a sign at the tomb that read, "By order of the king, God is forbidden to work miracles here." Some believers fell into frenzied convulsions, claiming to be inspired by the Holy Spirit through the intercession of the dead priest. After midcentury, Jansenism became even more politically active as its adherents joined in opposition to crown policies on religion.

❖ Consolidation of the European State System

The spread of Pietism and Jansenism reflected the emergence of a middle-class public that now participated in every new development, including religion. The middle classes could pursue these interests because the European state system gradually stabilized despite the increasing competition for wealth in the Atlantic system. Warfare settled three main issues between 1690 and 1740: a coalition of powers held Louis XIV's France in check on the continent, Great Britain emerged from the wars against Louis as the preeminent maritime power, and Russia defeated Sweden in the contest for supremacy in the Baltic. After

♦**Pietism:** PY uh tih zuhm
♦**Guyon:** gwee yohn

Louis XIV's death in 1715, Europe enjoyed the fruits of a more balanced diplomatic system, in which warfare became less frequent and less widespread. States could then spend their resources establishing and expanding control over their own populations, both at home and in their colonies.

The Limits of French Absolutism

Lying on his deathbed in 1715, the seventy-six-year-old Louis XIV watched helplessly as his accomplishments began to unravel. Not only had his plans for territorial expansion been thwarted, but his incessant wars had exhausted the treasury, despite new taxes. In 1689, Louis's rival, William III, prince of Orange and king of England and Scotland (r. 1689–1702), had set out to forge a European alliance that eventually included Britain, the Dutch Republic, Sweden, Austria, and Spain. The allies fought Louis to a stalemate in the War of the League of Augsburg, sometimes called the Nine Years' War (1689–1697), and when hostilities resumed four years later, they finally put an end to Louis's expansionist ambitions.

The War of the Spanish Succession, 1701–1713. When the mentally and physically feeble Charles II (r. 1665–1700) of Spain died without a direct heir, all of Europe poised for a fight over the spoils. The Spanish succession could not help but be a burning issue. Even though Spanish power had declined since Spain's golden age in the sixteenth century, Spain still had extensive territories in Italy and the Netherlands as well as colonies overseas. Before Charles died, he named Louis XIV's second grandson, Philip, duke of Anjou, as his heir, but the Austrian emperor Leopold I refused to accept Charles's deathbed will.

In the ensuing war, the French lost several major battles and had to accept disadvantageous terms in the Peace of Utrecht◆ of 1713–1714 (Map 18.2). Although Philip was recognized as king of Spain, he had to renounce any future claim to the French crown, thus barring unification of the two kingdoms. Spain surrendered its territories in Italy and the Netherlands to the Austrians and Gibraltar

to the British; France ceded possessions in North America (Newfoundland, the Hudson Bay area, and most of Nova Scotia) to Britain. France no longer threatened to dominate European power politics.

The Death of Louis XIV and the Regency. At home, Louis's policy of absolutism had fomented bitter hostility. Nobles fiercely resented his promotions of commoners to high office. The duke of Saint-Simon◆ complained that "falseness, servility, admiring glances, combined with a dependent and cringing attitude, above all, an appearance of being nothing without him, were the only ways of pleasing him." Archbishop Fénelon,◆ who tutored the king's grandson, called for reform. An admirer of Guyon's Quietism, Fénelon severely criticized the "steady stream of extravagant adulation, which reaches the point of idolatry"; the constant, bloody wars; and the misery of the people.

On his deathbed, Louis XIV offered sound advice to his five-year-old great-grandson and successor, Louis XV (r. 1715–1774): "Do not imitate my love of building nor my liking for war." After being named regent, the duke of Orléans (1674–1723), nephew of the dead king, revived some of the parlements' powers and tried to give leading nobles a greater say in political affairs. To raise much-needed funds, in 1719 the regent encouraged the Scottish financier John Law to set up an official trading company for North America and a state bank that issued paper money and stock (without them, trade depended on the available supply of gold and silver). The bank was supposed to offer lower interest rates to the state, thus cutting the cost of financing the government's debts. The value of the stock rose rapidly in a frenzy of speculation, only to crash a few months later. With it vanished any hope of establishing a state bank or issuing paper money for nearly a century.

France finally achieved a measure of financial stability under the leadership of Cardinal Hercule de Fleury (1653–1743), the most powerful member of the government after the death of the regent. Fleury aimed to avoid adventure abroad and keep social

---

◆**Utrecht:** OO trehkt

◆**Saint-Simon:** san see MOHN
◆**Fénelon:** fehn LOHN

MAP 18.2 Europe, c. 1715

Although Louis XIV succeeded in putting his grandson Philip on the Spanish throne, France emerged considerably weakened from the War of Spanish Succession. France ceded large territories in Canada to Britain, which also gained key Mediterranean outposts from Spain, as well as a monopoly on providing slaves to the Spanish colonies. Spanish losses were catastrophic. Philip had to renounce any future claim to the French crown and give up considerable territories in the Netherlands and Italy to the Austrians. How did the competing English and French claims in North America around 1715 create potential conflicts for the future?

peace at home; he balanced the budget and carried out a large project for road and canal construction. Colonial trade boomed. Peace and the acceptance of limits on territorial expansion inaugurated a century of French prosperity.

British Rise and Dutch Decline

The British and the Dutch had formed a coalition against Louis XIV under their joint ruler William III, who was simultaneously stadholder (elected head) of the Dutch Republic and, with his English wife, Mary (d. 1694), ruler of England, Wales, and Scotland. After William's death in 1702, the British and Dutch went their separate ways. Over the next decades, England incorporated Scotland and subjugated Ireland, becoming "Great Britain." At the same time Dutch imperial power declined; by 1700, Great Britain dominated the seas and the Dutch, with their small population of less than two million, came to depend on alliances with bigger powers.

From England to Great Britain. English relations with Scotland and Ireland were complicated by the problem of succession: William and Mary had no children. To ensure a Protestant succession, Parliament ruled that Mary's sister, Anne, would succeed William and Mary and that the Protestant House of Hanover in Germany would succeed Anne if she had no surviving heirs. Catholics were excluded. When Queen Anne (r. 1702–1714) died leaving no children, the elector of Hanover, a Protestant great-grandson of James I, consequently became King George I (r. 1714–1727). The House of Hanover— renamed the House of Windsor during World War I—still occupies the British throne.

Support from the Scots and Irish for this solution did not come easily because many in Scotland and Ireland supported the claims to the throne of the deposed Catholic king, James II, and, after his death in 1701, his son James Edward. Out of fear of this **Jacobitism** (from the Latin *Jacobus* for "James"), Scottish Protestant leaders agreed to the Act of Union of 1707, which abolished the Scottish Parliament and affirmed the Scots' recognition of the Protestant Hanoverian succession. The Scots agreed to obey the Parliament of Great Britain, which would include Scottish members in the House of Commons and the House of Lords. A Jacobite rebellion in Scotland in 1715, aiming to restore the Stuart line, was suppressed. The threat of Jacobitism nonetheless continued into the 1740s (see Map 18.2 on page 685).

The Irish—90 percent of whom were Catholic—proved even more difficult to subdue. When James II had gone to Ireland in 1689 to raise a Catholic rebellion against the new monarchs of England, William III responded by taking command of the joint English and Dutch forces and defeating James's Irish supporters. James fled to France, and the Catholics in Ireland faced yet more confiscation and legal restrictions. By 1700, Irish Catholics, who in 1640 had owned 60 percent of the land in Ireland, owned just 14 percent. The Protestant-controlled Irish Parliament passed a series of laws limiting the rights of the Catholic majority: Catholics could not bear arms, send their children abroad for education, establish Catholic schools at home, or marry Protestants. Catholics could not sit in Parliament, nor could they vote for its members unless they took an oath renouncing Catholic doctrine. These and a host of other laws reduced Catholic Ireland to the status of a colony; one English official commented in 1745, "The poor people of Ireland are used worse than negroes." Most of the Irish were peasants who lived in primitive housing and subsisted on a meager diet that included no meat.

The Parliament of Great Britain was soon dominated by the Whigs. In Britain's constitutional system, the monarch ruled with Parliament. The crown chose the ministers, directed policy, and supervised administration, while Parliament raised revenue, passed laws, and represented the interests of the people to the crown. The powers of Parliament were reaffirmed by the Triennial Act in 1694, which provided that Parliaments meet at least once every three years (this was extended to seven years in 1716, after the Whigs had established their ascendancy). Only 200,000 propertied men could vote, out of a population of more than 5 million, and, not surprisingly, most members of Parliament came from the landed gentry. In fact, a few hundred families controlled all the important political offices.

George I and George II (r. 1727–1760) relied on one man, Sir Robert Walpole (1676–1745), to help them manage their relations with Parliament. From his position as First Lord of the Treasury, Walpole made himself into the first, or "prime," minister, leading the House of Commons from 1721 to 1742 (see the illustration on this page). Although appointed initially by the king, Walpole established an enduring pattern of parliamentary government in which a prime minister from the leading party guided legislation through the House of Commons. Walpole also built a vast patronage machine that dispensed government jobs to win support for the crown's policies. Walpole's successors relied more and more on the patronage system and eventually alienated not only the Tories but also the middle classes in London and even the North American colonies.

The partisan division between the Whigs, who supported the Hanoverian succession and the rights of dissenting Protestants, and the Tories, who had backed the Stuart line and the Anglican church, did not hamper Great Britain's pursuit of economic, military, and colonial power. In this period, Great Britain became a great power on the world stage by virtue of its navy and its ability to finance major military involvement in the wars against Louis XIV. The founding in 1694 of the Bank of England—which, unlike the French bank, endured—enabled the government to raise money at low interest for foreign wars. By the 1740s, the government could borrow more than four times what it could in the 1690s.

The Dutch Eclipse. When William of Orange (William III of England) died in 1702, he left no heirs, and for forty-five years the Dutch lived without a stadholder. The merchant ruling class of some two thousand families dominated the Dutch Republic more than ever, but they presided over a country that counted for less in international power politics. In some areas, Dutch decline was only relative: the Dutch population was not growing as fast as others, for example, and the Dutch share of the Baltic trade decreased from 50 percent in 1720 to less than 30 percent by the 1770s. After 1720, the Baltic countries—Prussia, Russia, Denmark, and

Sir Robert Walpole at a Cabinet Meeting
Sir Robert Walpole and George II developed the institution of a cabinet, which brought together the important heads of departments. The cabinet included Walpole as first lord of the treasury, the two secretaries of state, the lord chancellor, the chancellor of the exchequer, the lord privy seal, and the lord president of the council. Walpole's cabinet was the ancestor of modern cabinets in both Great Britain and the United States. Its similarities to modern forms should not be overstated, however. The entire staff of the two secretaries of state, who had charge of all foreign and domestic affairs other than taxation, numbered twenty-four in 1726. How would discussions in the new coffeehouses (shown in the opening illustration to this chapter) influence the kinds of decisions made by Walpole and his cabinets?
The Fotomas Index, U.K.

Sweden—began to ban imports of manufactured goods to protect their own industries, and Dutch trade in particular suffered. The output of Leiden textiles dropped to one-third of its 1700 level by 1740. Shipbuilding, paper manufacturing, tobacco processing, salt refining, and pottery production all dwindled as well. The Dutch East India Company saw its political and military grip loosened in India, Ceylon, and Java.

The biggest exception to the downward trend was trade with the New World, which increased with escalating demands for sugar and tobacco. The Dutch shifted their interest away from great power rivalries toward those areas of international trade and finance where they could establish an enduring presence.

Russia's Emergence as a European Power

The commerce and shipbuilding of the Dutch and British so impressed Russian tsar Peter I (r. 1689–1725) that he traveled incognito to their shipyards in 1697 to learn their methods firsthand. Known to history as Peter the Great, he dragged Russia kicking and screaming all the way to great-power status. Although he came to the throne while still a minor (on the eve of his tenth birthday), grew up under the threat of a palace coup, and enjoyed little formal education, his accomplishments soon matched his seven-foot-tall stature. Peter transformed public life in Russia and established an absolutist state on the western model. His attempts to create a society that resembled western Europe known as **Westernization**, ignited an enduring controversy: did Peter set Russia on a course of inevitable Westernization required to compete with the West, or did he forever and fatally disrupt Russia's natural evolution into a distinctive Slavic society?

Westernization. To pursue his goal of Westernizing Russian culture, Peter set up the first greenhouses, laboratories, and technical schools and founded the Russian Academy of Sciences. He ordered translations of western classics and hired a German theater company to perform the French plays of Molière. He replaced the traditional Russian calendar with the western one,* introduced Arabic numerals, and brought out the first public newspaper. He ordered his

---

*Peter introduced the Julian calendar, then still used in Protestant but not Catholic countries. Later in the eighteenth century, Protestant Europe abandoned the Julian for the Gregorian calendar. Not until 1918 was the Julian calendar abolished in Russia, at which point it had fallen thirteen days behind Europe's Gregorian calendar.

Peter the Great Modernizes Russia
In this popular print, a barber forces a protesting noble to conform to western fashions. (The barber is sometimes erroneously identified as Peter himself.) Peter ordered all nobles, merchants, and middle-class professionals to cut off their beards or pay a huge tax to keep them. An early biographer of Peter, the French writer Jean Rousset de Missy (1730), claimed that those who lost their beards saved them to put in their coffins, in fear that they would not enter heaven without them. Most western Europeans applauded these attempts to change Russian customs, but many Russians deeply resented the attack on traditional ways. Why was everyday dress such a contested issue in Russia? *Carole Frohlich Archive.*

officials and the nobles to shave their beards (see the illustration above) and dress in western fashion, and he even issued precise regulations about the suitable style of jacket, boots, and cap (generally French or German). He published a book on manners for young noblemen and experimented with dentistry on his courtiers.

Peter encouraged foreigners to move to Russia to offer their advice and skills, especially for building the capital city. Named St. Petersburg after the tsar, the new capital symbolized Russia's opening to the West. Construction began in 1703 in a Baltic province that had been recently conquered from Sweden. By the end of 1709, forty thousand recruits a year found themselves assigned to the work. Peter ordered skilled workers to move to the new city and commanded all landowners possessing more than forty serf households to build houses there. In the 1720s, a German minister described St. Petersburg "as a wonder of the world, considering its magnificent palaces, . . . and the short time that was employed in the building of it." By 1710, the permanent population of the capital reached eight thousand. At Peter's death in 1725, it had forty thousand residents.

As a new city far from the Russian heartland around Moscow, St. Petersburg represented a decisive break with Russia's past. Peter widened that gap by every means possible. At his new capital he tried to improve the traditionally denigrated, secluded status of women by ordering them to dress in European styles and appear publicly at his dinners for diplomatic representatives. Imitating French manners, he decreed that women attend his new social salons of officials, officers, and merchants for conversation and dancing. A foreigner headed every one of Peter's new technical and vocational schools, and for its first eight years the new Academy of Sciences included no Russians. Every ministry was assigned a foreign adviser. Upper-class Russians learned French or German, which they spoke even at home. Such changes affected only the very top of Russian society, however; the mass of the population had no contact with the new ideas and ended up paying for the innovations either in ruinous new taxation or by building St. Petersburg, a project that cost the lives of thousands of workers. Serfs remained tied to the land, completely dominated by their noble lords.

The Great Peterhof Palace
Peter the Great wanted a residence that could compete with the palace at Versailles, and in 1714 work began at a site 18 miles from Saint Petersburg. Peter's daughter Elizabeth replaced the original building with this more elaborate one in the late 1740s. Peter built the canal in front as a way of linking the palace to the nearby Gulf of Finland. He also ordered the installation of a hydraulic system to feed water to the fountains whose statuary is much like that of western palaces. © *Didier Roland/Imapress/The Image Works.*

Peter the Great's Brand of Absolutism.
Peter also reorganized government and finance on western models and, like other absolute rulers, strengthened his army. With ruthless recruiting methods, which included branding a cross on every recruit's left hand to prevent desertion, he forged an army of 200,000 men and equipped it with modern weapons. He created schools for artillery, engineering, and military medicine and built the first navy in Russian history. Not surprisingly, taxes tripled.

The tsar allowed nothing to stand in his way. He did not hesitate to use torture, and he executed thousands. He allowed a special guards regiment unprecedented power to expedite cases against those suspected of rebellion, espionage, pretensions to the throne, or just "unseemly utterances" against him. Opposition to his policies reached into his own family: because his only son, Alexei, had allied himself with Peter's critics, the tsar threw him into prison, where the young man mysteriously died.

To control the often restive nobility, Peter insisted that all noblemen engage in state service. A Table of Ranks (1722) classified them into military, administrative, and court categories, a codification of social and legal relationships in Russia that would last for nearly two centuries. All social and material advantages now depended on serving the crown. Because the nobles lacked a secure independent status, Peter could command them to a degree that was unimaginable in western Europe. State service was not only compulsory but also permanent. Moreover, the male children of those in service had to be registered by the age of ten and begin serving at fifteen. To increase his authority over the Russian Orthodox church, Peter allowed the office of patriarch (supreme head) to remain vacant, and in 1721 he replaced it with the Holy Synod, a bureaucracy of laymen under his supervision. To many Russians, Peter was the devil incarnate.

Peter's achievements could not ensure his succession. In the thirty-seven years after his death in 1725, Russia endured six different rulers, none of whom established firm control. Recurrent palace coups weakened the monarchy and enabled the nobility to loosen Peter's rigid code of state service. In

the process the serfs' status only worsened. Serfs ceased to be counted as legal subjects; the criminal code of 1754 listed them as property. They not only were bought and sold like cattle but also had become legally indistinguishable from them. Westernization had not yet touched their lives.

> **Review:** How did Peter the Great's government compare to those of Britain and France?

The Balance of Power in the East

Peter the Great's success in building up state power changed the balance of power in eastern Europe. Overcoming initial military setbacks, Russia eventually defeated Sweden and took its place as the leading power in the Baltic region. Russia could then turn its attention to eastern Europe, where it competed with Austria and Prussia. Once-mighty Poland-Lithuania became the playground for great power rivalries.

The Decline of Sweden. Sweden had dominated the Baltic region since the Thirty Years' War (1618–1648) and did not easily give up its preeminence. When Peter the Great joined an anti-Swedish coalition in 1700 with Denmark, Saxony, and Poland, Sweden's Charles XII (r. 1697–1718) stood up to the test. Still in his teens at the beginning of the Great Northern War, Charles first defeated Denmark, then destroyed the new Russian army, and quickly marched into Poland and Saxony. After defeating the Poles and occupying Saxony, Charles invaded Russia. Here Peter's rebuilt army finally defeated him at the battle of Poltava (1709).

The Russian victory resounded everywhere. The Russian ambassador to Vienna reported, "It is commonly said that the tsar will be formidable to all Europe, that he will be a kind of northern Turk." Prussia and other German states joined the anti-Swedish alliance, and war resumed. Charles XII died in battle in 1718, and complex negotiations finally ended the Great Northern War. By the terms of the Treaty of Nystad (1721), Sweden ceded its eastern Baltic provinces—Livonia, Estonia, Ingria, and southern Karelia—to Russia. Sweden also lost territories on the north German coast to Prussia and the other allied German states (Map 18.3). An aristocratic reaction against Charles XII's incessant demands for war supplies swept away Sweden's absolutist regime, essentially removing Sweden from great power competition.

Prussian Militarization. Prussia had to make the most of every military opportunity, as it did in the Great Northern War, because it was much smaller in size and population than Russia, Austria, or France. King Frederick William I (r. 1713–1740) doubled the size of the Prussian army; though much smaller than those of his rivals, it was the best-trained and most up-to-date force in Europe. By 1740, Prussia had Europe's highest proportion of men at arms (1 of every 28 people, versus 1 in 157 in France and 1 in 64 in Russia) and the highest proportion of nobles in the military (1 in 7 noblemen, as compared with 1 in 33 in France and 1 in 50 in Russia).

The army so dominated life in Prussia that the country earned the label "a large army with a small state attached." So obsessed was Frederick William with his soldiers that the five-foot-five-inch-tall king formed a regiment of "giants," the Grenadiers, composed exclusively of men over six feet tall. Royal agents scoured Europe trying to find such men and sometimes kidnapped them right off the street. Frederick William, the "Sergeant King," was one of the first rulers to wear a military uniform as his everyday dress. He subordinated the entire domestic administration to the army's needs. He also installed a system for recruiting soldiers by local district quotas. He financed the army's growth by subjecting all the provinces to an excise tax on food, drink, and manufactured goods and by increasing rents on crown lands. Prussia was now poised to become one of the major players on the continent.

The War of Polish Succession, 1733–1735. Prussia did not enter into military conflict foolishly. During the War of Polish Succession it stood on the sidelines, content to watch the bigger powers fight each other. The war showed how the balance of power had changed since the heyday of Louis XIV: France had to maneuver within a complex great-power system that now included Russia, and Poland-Lithuania no longer controlled its own destiny. When the king of Poland-Lithuania died in 1733, France, Spain, and Sardinia went to war against Austria and Russia, each side supporting rival claimants to the Polish throne. After Russia

MAP 18.3 Russia and Sweden after the Great Northern War, 1721

After the Great Northern War, Russia supplanted Sweden as the major power in the north. Although Russia had a much larger population from which to draw its armies, Sweden made the most of its advantages and gave way only after a great military struggle.

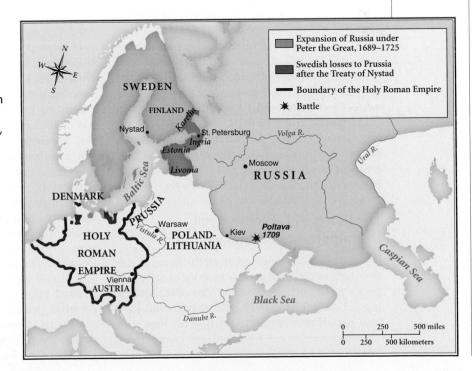

drove the French candidate out of Poland-Lithuania, France agreed to accept the Austrian candidate; in exchange, Austria gave the province of Lorraine to the French candidate, the father-in-law of Louis XV, with the promise that the province would pass to France on his death. France and Britain went back to pursuing their colonial rivalries. Prussia and Russia concentrated on shoring up their influence within Poland-Lithuania.

Austria did not want to become mired in a long struggle in Poland-Lithuania because its armies still faced the Turks on its southeastern border. Even though the Austrians had forced the Turks to recognize their rule over all of Hungary and Transylvania in 1699 and occupied Belgrade in 1717, the Turks did not stop fighting. In the 1730s, the Turks retook Belgrade, and Russia now claimed a role in the struggle against the Turks. Moreover, Hungary, though "liberated" from Turkish rule, proved less than enthusiastic about submitting to Austria. In 1703, the wealthiest Hungarian noble landlord, Ferenc Rákóczi♦ (1676–1735), raised an army of seventy thousand men who fought for "God, Fatherland, and Liberty" until 1711. They forced the Austrians to recognize local Hungarian institutions, grant amnesty, and restore confiscated estates in exchange for confirming hereditary Austrian rule.

The Power of Diplomacy and the Importance of Numbers

No single power emerged from the wars of the first half of the eighteenth century clearly superior to the others, and the idea of maintaining a balance of power guided both military and diplomatic maneuvering. The Peace of

♦**Rákóczi:** RA koht see

Austrian Conquest of Hungary, 1657–1730

Legend:
- Habsburg dominions, 1657
- Habsburg Hungary, 1657
- Expansion to 1699
- Expansion to 1718
- Regained by Ottoman Empire
- ★ Battle

POLAND-LITHUANIA
AUSTRIA
HUNGARY
Vienna 1683
Transylvania
Belgrade 1717
Adriatic Sea
OTTOMAN EMPIRE

0 250 500 miles
0 250 500 kilometers

Utrecht had explicitly declared that such a balance was crucial to maintaining peace in Europe, and in 1720 a British pamphleteer wrote, "There is not, I believe, any doctrine in the law of nations, of more certain truth... than this of the balance of power." This system of equilibrium often rested on military force, such as the leagues formed against Louis XIV or the coalition against Sweden. All states counted on diplomacy, however, to resolve issues even after fighting had begun.

To meet the new demands placed on it, the diplomatic service, like the military and financial bureaucracies before it, had to develop regular procedures. The French set a pattern of diplomatic service that the other European states soon imitated. By 1685, France had embassies in all the important capitals. Nobles of ancient families served as ambassadors to Rome, Madrid, Vienna, and London, whereas royal officials were chosen for Switzerland, the Dutch Republic, and Venice. The ambassador selected and paid for his own staff. This practice could make the journey to a new post very cumbersome, because the staff might be as large as eighty people, and they brought along all their own furniture, pictures, silverware, and tapestries. It took one French ambassador ten weeks to get from Paris to Stockholm.

Despite a new emphasis on honest and informed negotiation, rulers still employed secret agents and often sent secret instructions that negated the official ones sent by their own foreign offices. Secret diplomacy had some advantages because it allowed rulers to break with past alliances, but it also led to confusion and, sometimes, scandal, for the rulers often employed unreliable adventurers as their confidential agents. Still, the diplomatic system in the early eighteenth century proved successful enough to ensure a continuation of the principles of the Peace of Westphalia (1648); in the midst of every crisis and war, the great powers would convene and hammer out a written agreement detailing the requirements for peace.

Adroit diplomacy could smooth the road toward peace, but success in war still depended on sheer numbers—of men and muskets. Because each state's strength depended largely on the size of its army, the growth and health of the population increasingly entered into government calculations. The publication in 1690 of the Englishman William Petty's *Political Arithmetick* quickened the interest of government officials everywhere. Petty offered statistical estimates of human capital—that is, of population and wages—to determine Britain's national wealth. A large, growing population could be as vital to a state's future as access to silver mines or overseas trade, so government officials devoted increased effort to the statistical estimation of total population and rates of births, deaths, marriages, and fertility. In 1727, Frederick William I of Prussia founded two university chairs to encourage population studies, and textbooks and handbooks advocated state intervention to improve the population's health and welfare.

Public Hygiene and Health Care

Physicians used the new population statistics to explain the environmental causes of disease, another new preoccupation in this period. Petty devised a quantitative scale that distinguished healthy from unhealthy places largely on the basis of air quality, an early precursor of modern environmental studies. Cities were the unhealthiest places because excrement (animal and human) and garbage accumulated where people lived densely packed together. Paris seemed to a visitor "so detestable that it is impossible to remain there" because of the smell; even the facade of the Louvre palace in Paris was soiled by the contents of night commodes that servants routinely dumped out of windows. Only the wealthy could escape walking in mucky streets, by hiring men to carry them in sedan chairs or to drive them in coaches.

After investigating specific cities, medical geographers urged government campaigns to improve public sanitation. Everywhere, environmentalists gathered and analyzed data on climate, disease, and population, searching for correlations to help direct policy. As a result of these efforts, local governments undertook such measures as draining low-lying areas, burying refuse, and cleaning wells, all of which eventually helped lower the death rates from epidemic diseases.

Hospitals and medical care underwent lasting transformations. Founded originally as charities concerned foremost with the moral worthiness of the poor, hospitals gradually evolved into medical institutions that defined patients by their diseases. The process of diagnosis changed as physicians began to use specialized Latin terms for illnesses. The gap between medical experts and their patients increased, as physicians now also relied on postmortem dissections in the hospital to gain better knowledge, a practice most patients' families resented. Press reports of body snatching and grave robbing by surgeons and their apprentices outraged the public well into the 1800s.

Despite the change in hospitals, individual health care remained something of a free-for-all in which physicians competed with bloodletters, itinerant venereal-disease doctors, bonesetters, druggists, midwives, and "cunning women," who specialized in home remedies. The medical profession, with nationwide organizations and licensing, had not yet emerged, and no clear line separated trained physicians from quacks. Physicians often followed popular prescriptions for illnesses because they had nothing better to offer. Patients were as likely to die of diseases caught in the hospital as to be cured there. Antiseptics were virtually unknown.

The various "medical" opinions about childbirth highlight the confusion people faced. Midwives delivered most babies, though they sometimes encountered criticism, even from within their own ranks. One consulting midwife complained that ordinary midwives in Bristol, England, made women in labor drink a mixture of their husband's urine and leek juice. By the 1730s, female midwives faced competition from male midwives, who were known for using instruments such as forceps to pull the baby out of the birth canal. Women rarely sought a physician's help in giving birth, however; they preferred the advice and assistance of trusted local midwives. In any case, trained physicians were few in number and almost nonexistent outside cities.

Insanity was treated as a physical rather than an emotional ailment. Doctors believed most madness was caused by "melancholia,"♦ a condition they attributed to disorders in the

---

♦**melancholia:** meh luhn KOH lee uh

Lady Mary Wortley Montagu, Smallpox Inoculation in the Ottoman Empire

In this letter of 1718 Lady Mary described the Turkish practice of deliberately stimulating a mild form of smallpox in order to confer immunity to the disease. Lady Mary had herself suffered the disfiguring ravages of the disease in 1715, and her brother had died of it. She was so impressed by the Turkish example that she inoculated her own children. Her letters show her to be an astute observer of foreign customs. They also reflect the growing interest in foreign travel in the eighteenth century.

A propos of distempers, I am going to tell you a thing, that will make you wish yourself here. The small-pox, so fatal, and so general amongst us, is here entirely harmless, by the invention of engrafting, which is the term they give it. There is a set of old women, who make it their business to perform the operation, every autumn, in the month of September, when the great heat is abated. People send to one another to know if any of their family has a mind to have the small-pox; they make parties for this purpose, and when they are met (commonly fifteen or sixteen together) the old woman comes with a nut-shell full of the matter of the best sort of small-pox, and asks what vein you please to have opened. She immediately rips open that you offer to her, with a large needle (which gives you no more pain than a common scratch) and puts into the vein as much matter as can ly [lie] upon the head of her needle, and after that, binds up the little wound with a hollow bit of shell, and in this manner opens four or five veins. The Grecians have commonly the superstition of opening one in the middle of the forehead, one in each arm, and one on the breast, to mark the sign of the Cross; but this has a very ill effect, all these wounds leaving little scars, and is not done by those that are not superstitious, who chuse [choose] to have them in the legs, or that part of the arm that is concealed. The children or young patients play together all the rest of the day, and are in perfect health to the eighth. Then the fever begins to seize them, and they keep their beds two days, very seldom three. They have very rarely above twenty or thirty in their faces, which never mark, and in eight days time they are as well as before their illness. Where they are wounded, there remains running sores during the distemper, which I don't doubt is a great relief to it. Every year, thousands undergo this operation, and the French Ambassador says pleasantly, that they take the small-pox here by way of diversion, as they take the waters in other countries. There is no example of any one that has died in it, and you may believe I am well satisfied of the safety of this experiment, since I intend to try it on my dear little son. I am patriot enough to take the pains to bring this useful invention into fashion in England, and I should not fail to write to some of our doctors very particularly about it, if I knew any one of them that I thought had virtue enough to destroy such a considerable branch of their revenue, for the good of mankind. But that distemper is too beneficial to them, not to expose to all their resentment, the hardy wight that should undertake to put an end to it. Perhaps if I live to return, I may, however, have courage to war with them. Upon this occasion, admire the heroism in the heart of . . .

Source: From letter 31, to Mrs. S. C. from Adrianople, April 1, 1718, in *Letters of the Right Honourable Lady M—y W—y M—e: Written During her Travels in Europe, Asia and Africa* . . . (London: A. Homer, 1764), 113–16.

system of bodily "humors." Their prescribed treatments included blood transfusions; ingestion of bitter substances such as coffee, quinine, and even soap; immersion in water; various forms of exercise; and burning or cauterizing the body to allow black vapors to escape.

Hardly any infectious diseases could be cured, though inoculation against smallpox spread from the Middle East to Europe in the early eighteenth century, thanks largely to the efforts of Lady Mary Wortley Montagu (1689–1762). In 1716 Montagu accompanied her husband to Constantinople, where he took up a post as British ambassador to the Ottoman Empire. She returned in 1718, after witnessing firsthand the Turkish use of inoculation (see "Lady Mary Wortley Montagu, Smallpox Inoculation in the Ottoman Empire", opposite). When a new smallpox epidemic threatened England in 1721, she called on her physician to inoculate her daughter. Two patients died after inoculation in the following months, prompting clergymen and physicians to attack the practice, which remained in dispute for decades. Inoculation against smallpox began to spread more widely after 1796 when the English physician Edward Jenner developed a serum based on cowpox, a milder disease. Many other diseases spread quickly in the unsanitary conditions of urban life. Ordinary people washed or changed clothes rarely, lived in overcrowded housing with poor ventilation, and got their water from contaminated sources such as refuse-filled rivers.

Until the mid-1700s, most people considered bathing dangerous. Public bathhouses had disappeared from cities in the sixteenth and seventeenth centuries because they seemed a source of disorderly behavior and epidemic illness. In the eighteenth century, even private bathing came into disfavor because people feared the effects of contact with water. Fewer than one in ten newly built private mansions in Paris had baths. Bathing was hazardous, physicians insisted, because it opened the body to disease. One manners manual of 1736 admonished, "It is correct to clean the face every morning by using a white cloth to cleanse it. It is less good to wash with water, because it renders the face susceptible to cold in winter and sun in summer." The upper classes associated cleanliness not with baths but with frequently changed linens, powdered hair, and perfume, which was thought to strengthen the body and refresh the brain by counteracting corrupt and foul air.

❖ The Birth of the Enlightenment

Economic expansion, the emergence of a new consumer society, and the stabilization of the European state system all generated optimism about the future. The intellectual corollary was the **Enlightenment**, a term used later in the eighteenth century to describe the loosely knit group of writers and scholars who believed that human beings could apply a critical, reasoning spirit to every problem they encountered in this world. The new secular, scientific, and critical attitude first emerged in the 1690s, scrutinizing everything from the absolutism of Louis XIV to the traditional role of women in society. After 1740, criticism took a more systematic turn as writers provided new theories for the organization of society and politics; but as early as the 1720s, established authorities realized they faced a new set of challenges. Even while slavery expanded in the Atlantic system, Enlightenment writers began to insist on the need for new freedoms in Europe.

Popularization of Science and Challenges to Religion

The writers of the Enlightenment glorified the geniuses of the new science and championed the scientific method as the solution for all social problems. (See "Terms of History," page 696.) One of the most influential popularizations was the French writer Bernard de Fontenelle's *Conversations on the Plurality of Worlds* (1686). Presented as a dialogue between an aristocratic woman and a man of the world, the book made the Copernican, heliocentric view of the universe available to the literate public. By 1700, mathematics and science had become fashionable pastimes in high society, and the public flocked to lectures explaining scientific discoveries. Journals complained that scientific learning had become the

TERMS OF HISTORY

Progress

Believing as they did in the possibilities of improvement, many Enlightenment writers preached a new doctrine about the meaning of human history. They challenged the traditional Christian belief that the original sin of Adam and Eve condemned human beings to unhappiness in this world and offered instead an optimistic vision: human nature, they claimed, was inherently good, and progress would be continuous if education developed human capacities to the utmost. Science and reason could bring happiness in this world. The idea of novelty or newness itself now seemed positive rather than threatening. Europeans began to imagine that they could surpass all those who preceded them in history, and they began to think of themselves as more "advanced" than the "backward" cultures they encountered in other parts of the world.

More than an intellectual concept, the idea of progress included a new conception of historical time and of Europeans' place within world history. Europeans stopped looking back, whether to a lost Garden of Eden or to the writings of Greek and Roman antiquity. Growing prosperity, European dominance overseas, and the scientific revolution oriented them toward the future. Europeans began to apply the word *modern* to their epoch, to distinguish it from the Middle Ages (a new term), and they considered their modern period superior in achievement. Consequently, Europeans took it as their mission to bring their modern, enlightened ways of progress to the areas they colonized.

The economic and ecological catastrophes, destructive wars, and genocides of the twentieth century cast much doubt on this rosy vision of continuing progress. As the philosopher George Santayana (1863–1952) complained, "The cry was for vacant freedom and indeterminate progress: *Vorwarts! Avanti! Onward! Full Speed Ahead!*, without asking whether directly before you was a bottomless pit." In the movement toward postmodernism, which began in the 1970s, critics argued that we should no longer be satisfied with the modern; the modern brought us calamity and disaster, not reason and freedom. They wanted to go beyond the modern, hence the term *postmodernism*. The most influential postmodern historian, the Frenchman Michel Foucault, argued in the 1970s and 1980s that history did not reveal a steady progress toward enlightenment, freedom, and humanitarianism but rather a descent into greater and greater social control, what he called a "carceral [prisonlike] society." He analyzed the replacement of torture with the prison, the birth of the medical clinic, and the movements for sexual liberation and declared that all simply ended up teaching people to watch themselves more closely and to cooperate in the state's efforts to control their lives.

Historians are now chastened in their claims about progress. They would no longer side with the German philosopher Georg W. F. Hegel, who proclaimed in 1832, "The history of the world is none other than the progress of the consciousness of freedom." They worry about the nationalistic claims inherent, for example, in the English historian Thomas Babington Macaulay's insistence that "the history of England is emphatically the history of progress" (1843). But most would not go so far as Foucault in denouncing modern developments. As with many other historical questions, the final word is not yet in: Is there a direction in human history that can correctly be called progress? Or is history, as many in ancient times thought, a set of repeating cycles?

FURTHER READING

Bury, J. B. *The Idea of Progress: An Inquiry into Its Origin and Growth.* 1932.

Foucault, Michel. *Discipline and Punish: The Birth of the Prison.* Trans. Alan Sheridan. 1977.

passport to female affection: "There were two young ladies in Paris whose heads had been so turned by this branch of learning that one of them declined to listen to a proposal of marriage unless the candidate for her hand undertook to learn how to make telescopes." Such writings poked fun at women with intellectual interests, but they also demonstrated that women now participated in discussions of science.

The New Skepticism.   Interest in science spread in literate circles because it offered a model for all forms of knowledge. As the prestige of science increased, some developed a skeptical attitude toward attempts to enforce religious conformity. A French Huguenot refugee from Louis XIV's persecutions, Pierre Bayle (1647–1706), launched an internationally influential campaign against religious intolerance from his safe haven in the Dutch Republic. His *News from the Republic of Letters* (first published in 1684) bitterly criticized the policies of Louis XIV and was quickly banned in Paris and condemned in Rome. After attacking Louis XIV's anti-Protestant policies, Bayle took a more general stand in favor of religious toleration. No state in Europe officially offered complete tolerance, though the Dutch Republic came closest with its tacit acceptance of Catholics, dissident Protestant groups, and open Jewish communities. In 1697, Bayle published the *Historical and Critical Dictionary*, which cited all the errors and delusions that he could find in past and present writers of all religions. Even religion must meet the test of reasonableness: "Any particular dogma, whatever it may be, whether it is advanced on the authority of the Scriptures, or whatever else may be its origins, is to be regarded as false if it clashes with the clear and definite conclusions of the natural understanding [reason]."

Although Bayle claimed to be a believer himself, his insistence on rational investigation seemed to challenge the authority of faith. As one critic complained, "It is notorious that the works of M. Bayle have unsettled a large number of readers, and cast doubt on some of the most widely accepted principles of morality and religion." Bayle asserted, for example, that atheists might possess moral codes as effective as those

A Budding Scientist
In this engraving, *Astrologia,* by the Dutch artist Jacob Gole (c. 1660–1723), an upper-class woman looks through a telescope to do her own astronomical investigations. Women with intellectual interests were often disparaged by men, yet some middle- and upper-class women managed to pursue serious interests in science. One of the best known of these was the Italian Laura Bassi (1711–1778), who was a professor of physics at the University of Bologna. Such a position was all but impossible to attain since women were not allowed to attend university classes in any European country. Yet because many astronomical observatories were set up in private homes rather than public buildings or universities, wives and daughters of scientists could make observations and even publish their own findings. *Bibliotèque Nationale de France.*

of the devout. Bayle's *Dictionary* became a model of critical thought in the West.

Other scholars challenged the authority of the Bible by subjecting it to historical criticism. Discoveries in geology in the early eighteenth century showed that marine fossils dated immensely further back than the biblical flood. Investigations of miracles, comets, and oracles, like the growing literature against belief in witchcraft, urged the use of reason to combat superstition and prejudice. Comets, for example, should not be considered evil omens just because earlier generations had passed down such a belief. Defenders of church and state published books warning of the new skepticism's dangers. The spokesman for Louis XIV's absolutism, Bishop Bossuet, warned that "reason is the guide of their choice, but reason only brings them face to face with vague conjectures and baffling perplexities." Human beings, the traditionalists held, were simply incapable of subjecting everything to reason, especially in the realm of religion.

State authorities found religious skepticism particularly unsettling because it threatened to undermine state power too. The extensive literature of criticism was not limited to France, but much of it was published in French, and the French government took the lead in suppressing the more outspoken works. Forbidden books were then often published in the Dutch Republic, Britain, or Switzerland and smuggled back across the border to a public whose appetite was only whetted by censorship.

The Young Voltaire. The most influential writer of the early Enlightenment was a Frenchman born into the upper middle class, François-Marie Arouet,♦ known by his pen name, Voltaire (1694–1778). Voltaire took inspiration from Bayle: "He gives facts with such odious fidelity, he exposes the arguments for and against with such dastardly impartiality, he is so intolerably intelligible, that he leads people of only ordinary common sense to judge and even to doubt." In his early years Voltaire suffered arrest, imprisonment, and exile, but he eventually achieved wealth and acclaim. His tangles with church and state began in the early 1730s, when he published his *Letters Concerning the English Nation* (the English version appeared in 1733), in which he devoted several chapters to Newton and Locke and used the virtues of the British as a way to attack Catholic bigotry and government rigidity in France (see the extract on page 699). Impressed by British toleration of religious dissent (at least among

Protestants), Voltaire spent two years in exile in Britain when the French state responded to his book with yet another order for his arrest.

Voltaire also popularized Newton's scientific discoveries in his *Elements of the Philosophy of Newton* (1738). The French state and many European theologians considered Newtonianism threatening because it glorified the human mind and seemed to reduce God to an abstract, external, rationalistic force. So sensational was the success of Voltaire's book on Newton that a hostile Jesuit reported, "The great Newton, was, it is said, buried in the abyss, in the shop of the first publisher who dared to print him. . . . M. de Voltaire finally appeared, and at once Newton is understood or is in the process of being understood; all Paris resounds with Newton, all Paris stammers Newton, all Paris studies and learns Newton." The success was international too. Before long, Voltaire was elected a fellow of the Royal Society in London and in Edinburgh, as well as to twenty other scientific academies. Voltaire's fame continued to grow, reaching truly astounding proportions in the 1750s and 1760s (see Chapter 19).

Travel Literature and the Challenge to Custom and Tradition

Just as scientific method could be used to question religious and even state authority, a more general skepticism also emerged from the expanding knowledge about the world outside of Europe. During the seventeenth and eighteenth centuries, the number of travel accounts dramatically increased as travel writers used the contrast between their home societies and other cultures to criticize the customs of European society.

Visitors to the new colonies sought something resembling "the state of nature," that is, ways of life that preceded sophisticated social and political organization—although they often misinterpreted different forms of society and politics as having no organization at all. Travelers to the Americas found "noble savages" (native peoples) who appeared to live in conditions of great freedom and equality; they were "naturally good" and "happy" without taxes, lawsuits, or much organized government. In China, in contrast, travelers

---

♦**Arouet:** ahr WEH

Voltaire, *Letters Concerning the English Nation* (1733)

In the 1720s, Voltaire (1694–1778) visited both the Dutch Republic and England. He learned English and came to admire English political institutions and customs, using comparison with them to criticize religious intolerance and Catholic censorship in France. In this selection from a letter on Locke, Voltaire develops the argument that religion should be considered a matter of faith and conscience and be separated from arguments concerning philosophy. He also shows his disdain for the common people.

We must not be apprehensive that any philosophical opinion will ever prejudice the religion of a country. Though our demonstrations clash directly with our mysteries, that's nothing to the purpose, for the latter are not less revered upon that account by our Christian philosophers, who know very well that objects of reason and those of faith are of a very different nature. Philosophers will never form a religious sect, the reason of which is, their writings are not calculated for the vulgar, and they themselves are free from enthusiasm. If we divide mankind into twenty parts, it will be found that nineteen of these consist of persons employed in manual labour, who will never know that such a man as Mr. Locke existed. In the remaining twentieth part how few are readers? And among such as are so, twenty amuse themselves with romances to one who studies philosophy. The thinking part of mankind are confined to a very small number, and these will never disturb the peace and tranquillity of the world.

Neither Montaigne, Locke, Bayle, Spinoza, Hobbes, Lord Shaftesbury, Collins nor Toland lightened up the firebrand of discord in their countries; this has generally been the work of divines, who, being at first puffed up with the ambition of becoming chiefs of a sect, soon grew very desirous of being at the head of a party. But what do I say? All the works of the modern philosophers put together will never make so much noise as even the dispute which arose among the Franciscans [a Catholic religious order] merely about the fashion of their sleeves and of their cowls.

Source: Peter Gay, ed., *The Enlightenment: A Comprehensive Anthology* (New York: Simon & Schuster, 1973), 166.

found a people who enjoyed prosperity and an ancient civilization. Christian missionaries made little headway in China, and visitors had to admit that China's religious systems had flourished for four or five thousand years with no input from Europe or from Christianity. The basic lesson of travel literature in the 1700s, then, was that customs varied: justice, freedom, property, good government, religion, and morality all were relative to the place. One critic complained that travel encouraged free thinking and the destruction of religion: "Some complete their demoralization by extensive travel, and lose whatever shreds of religion remained to them.

Every day they see a new religion, new customs, new rites."

Travel literature turned explicitly political in Montesquieu's *Persian Letters* (1721). Charles-Louis de Secondat, baron of Montesquieu♦ (1689–1755), the son of an eminent judicial family, was a high-ranking judge in a French court. He published *Persian Letters* anonymously in the Dutch Republic, and the book went into ten printings in just one year—a best seller for the times. Montesquieu tells the story of two Persians, Rica and Usbek, who leave their country "for love

♦**Montesquieu:** mahn thus KYOO

of knowledge" and travel to Europe. They visit France in the last years of Louis XIV's reign, writing of the king: "He has a minister who is only eighteen years old, and a mistress of eighty. . . . Although he avoids the bustle of towns, and is rarely seen in company, his one concern, from morning till night, is to get himself talked about." Other passages ridicule the pope. Beneath the satire, however, was a serious investigation into the foundation of good government and morality. Montesquieu chose Persians for his travelers because they came from what was widely considered the most despotic of all governments, in which rulers had life-and-death powers over their subjects. In the book, the Persians constantly compare France to Persia, suggesting that the French monarchy might verge on despotism.

The paradox of a judge publishing an anonymous work attacking the regime that employed him demonstrates the complications of the intellectual scene in this period. Montesquieu's anonymity did not last long, and soon Parisian society lionized him. In the late 1720s, he sold his judgeship and traveled extensively in Europe, staying eighteen months in Britain. In 1748, he published a widely influential work on comparative government, *The Spirit of Laws*. The Vatican soon listed both *Persian Letters* and *The Spirit of Laws* on its index of forbidden books.

Raising the Woman Question

Many of the letters exchanged in *Persian Letters* focused on women, marriage, and the family because Montesquieu considered the position of women a sure indicator of the nature of government and morality. Although Montesquieu was not a feminist, his depiction of Roxana, the favorite wife in Usbek's harem, struck a chord with many women. Roxana revolts against the authority of Usbek's eunuchs and writes a final letter to her husband announcing her impending suicide: "I may have lived in servitude, but I have always been free, I have amended your laws according to the laws of nature, and my mind has always remained independent." Women writers used the same language of tyranny and freedom to argue for concrete changes in their status. Feminist ideas were not entirely

new, but they were presented systematically for the first time during the Enlightenment and represented a fundamental challenge to the ways of traditional societies.

The most systematic of these women writers was the English author Mary Astell (1666–1731), the daughter of a businessman and herself a supporter of the Tory party and the Anglican religious establishment. In 1694, she published *A Serious Proposal to the Ladies*, in which she advocated founding a private women's college to remedy women's lack of education. Addressing women, she asked, "How can you be content to be in the World like Tulips in a Garden, to make a fine *shew* [show] and be good for nothing?" Astell argued for intellectual training based on Descartes's principles, in which reason, debate, and careful consideration of the issues took priority over custom or tradition. Her book was an immediate success: five printings appeared by 1701. In later works such as *Reflections upon Marriage* (1706), Astell criticized the relationship between the sexes within marriage: "If absolute sovereignty be not necessary in a state, how comes it to be so in a family? . . . *If all men are born free*, how is it that all women are born slaves?" Her critics accused her of promoting subversive ideas and of contradicting the Scriptures.

Astell's work inspired other women to write in a similar vein. The anonymous *Essay in Defence of the Female Sex* (1696) attacked "the Usurpation of Men; and the Tyranny of Custom," which prevented women from getting an education. In 1709, Elizabeth Elstob published a detailed account of the prominent role women played in promoting Christianity in English history. She criticized men who "would declare openly they hated any Woman who knew more than themselves." In the introduction to the work of one of the best-known female poets, Elizabeth Singer Rowe, a friend of the author, complained of the "notorious Violations on the Liberties of Freeborn English Women" that came from "a plain and an open design to render us meer [mere] Slaves, perfect Turkish Wives."

Most male writers unequivocally stuck to the traditional view of women, which held that women were less capable of reasoning than men and therefore did not need

MAPPING THE WEST Europe in 1740

By 1740, Europe had achieved a kind of diplomatic equilibrium in which no one power predominated. But the relative balance should not deflect attention from important underlying changes: Spain, the Dutch Republic, Poland-Lithuania, and Sweden had all declined in power and influence while Great Britain, Russia, Prussia, and Austria had solidified their positions, each in a different way. France's ambitions had been thwarted, but its combination of a big army and rich overseas possessions made it a major player for a long time to come.

systematic education. Such opinions often rested on biological suppositions. The long-dominant Aristotelian view of reproduction held that only the male seed carried spirit and individuality. At the beginning of the eighteenth century, however, scientists began to undermine this belief. Physicians and surgeons began to champion the doctrine of *ovism*—that the female egg was essential in making new humans. During the decades that followed, male Enlightenment writers would continue to debate women's nature and appropriate social roles.

Review: What were the major issues in the early decades of the Enlightenment?

Conclusion

Europeans crossed a major threshold in the first half of the eighteenth century. They moved silently but nonetheless momentously from an economy governed by scarcity and the threat of famine to one of ever-increasing growth and the prospect of continuing improvement. Expansion of colonies overseas and economic development at home created greater wealth, longer life spans, and higher expectations for the future. In these better times for many, a spirit of optimism prevailed. People could now spend money on newspapers, novels, and travel literature as well as on coffee, tea, and cotton cloth. The growing literate public avidly followed the latest trends in religious debates, art, and music. Not everyone shared equally in the benefits, however: slaves toiled in misery for their masters in the Americas, eastern European serfs found themselves ever more closely bound to their noble lords, and rural folk almost everywhere tasted fewer fruits of consumer society.

Politics changed too as population and production increased and cities grew. Experts urged government intervention to improve public health, and states found it in their interest to settle many international disputes by diplomacy, which itself became more regular and routine. The consolidation of the European state system allowed a tide of criticism and new thinking about society to swell in Great Britain and France and begin to spill throughout Europe. Ultimately, the combination of the Atlantic system and the Enlightenment would give rise to a series of Atlantic revolutions.

Suggested References

The Atlantic System and the World Economy

It is easier to find sources on individual parts of the system than on the workings of the interlocking trade as a whole, but work has been rapidly increasing in this area. The Dunn book remains one of the classic studies of how the plantation system took root.

Blackburn, Robin. *The Making of New World Slavery: From the Baroque to the Modern, 1492–1800.* 1997.

Dunn, Richard S. *Sugar and Slaves: The Rise of the Planter Class in the English West Indies, 1624–1713.* 1972.

Harms, Robert. *The Diligent: A Voyage Through the Worlds of the Slave Trade.* 2003.

Slave movement during the eighteenth and nineteenth centuries: **http://dpls.dacc.wisc.edu/slavedata**.

Smith, Alan K. *Creating a World Economy: Merchant Capital, Colonialism, and World Trade, 1400–1825.* 1991.

Tadman, Michael. "The Demographic Cost of Sugar: Debates on Slave Societies and Natural Increase in the Americas," *American Historical Review* 105 (December 2000): 1534–1575.

New Social and Cultural Patterns

Many of the novels of the early eighteenth century provide fascinating insights into the development of new social attitudes and customs. In particular, see Daniel Defoe's *Robinson Crusoe* (1719) and *Moll Flanders* (1722); the many novels of Eliza Haywood; and Antoine François Prévost's *Manon Lescaut* (1731), a French psychological novel about a nobleman's fatal love for an unfaithful woman, which became the basis for an opera in the nineteenth century.

Age of Enlightenment (with sections on art, architecture, music, literature, and daily life): **http://history.evansville.net/enlighte.html**.

Earle, Peter. *The Making of the English Middle Class: Business, Society, and Family Life in London, 1660–1730.* 1989.

Handel's Messiah: The New Interactive Edition (CD-ROM). 1997.

Roche, Daniel. *The People of Paris: An Essay in Popular Culture in the Eighteenth Century.* Trans. Marie Evans. 1987.

Consolidation of the European State System

Studies of rulers and states can be supplemented by work on "political arithmetic" and public health.

Aspromourgos, Tony. *On the Origins of Classical Economics: Distribution and Value from William Petty to Adam Smith.* 1996.

Brewer, John. *The Sinews of Power: War, Money, and the English State, 1688–1783.* 1990.

Brockliss, Laurence, and Colin Jones. *The Medical World of Early Modern France.* 1997.

Frey, Linda, and Marsha Frey. *Societies in Upheaval: Insurrections in France, Hungary, and Spain in the Early Eighteenth Century.* 1987.

Hughes, Lindsey. *Peter the Great: A Biography.* 2002.

Porter, Roy. *Madness: A Brief History.* 2002.

Raeff, Marc. *Understanding Imperial Russia: State and Society in the Old Regime.* Trans. Arthur Goldhammer. 1984.

The Birth of the Enlightenment

The definitive study of the early Enlightenment is the book by Hazard, but many others have contributed biographies of individual figures or, more recently, studies of women writers.

Besterman, Theodore. *Voltaire.* 1969.

Grendy, Isobel. *Lady Mary Wortley Montagu.* 1999.

Hazard, Paul. *The European Mind: The Critical Years, 1680–1715.* 1990.

*Hill, Bridget, ed. *The First English Feminist: Reflections upon Marriage and Other Writings by Mary Astell.* 1986.

Israel, Jonathan I. *Radical Enlightenment: Philosophy and the Making of Modernity, 1650–1750.* 2001.

*Jacob, Margaret C. *The Enlightenment: A Brief History with Selected Readings.* 2000.

*Primary sources.

CHAPTER REVIEW

IMPORTANT EVENTS

1690s	Beginning of rapid development of plantations in Caribbean
1694	Bank of England established; Mary Astell's *A Serious Proposal to the Ladies* argues for the founding of a private women's college
1697	Pierre Bayle publishes *Historical and Critical Dictionary*, detailing errors of religious writers
1699	Turks forced to recognize Habsburg rule over Hungary and Transylvania
1703	Peter the Great of Russia begins construction of St. Petersburg, founds first Russian newspaper
1713–1714	Peace of Utrecht
1714	Elector of Hanover becomes King George I of England
1715	Death of Louis XIV
1719	Daniel Defoe publishes *Robinson Crusoe*
1720	Last outbreak of bubonic plague in western Europe
1721	Treaty of Nystad; Montesquieu publishes *Persian Letters* anonymously in the Dutch Republic
1733	War of the Polish Succession; Voltaire's *Letters Concerning the English Nation* attacks French intolerance and narrow-mindedness
1741	George Frederick Handel composes the *Messiah*

KEY TERMS

agricultural revolution (676)

Atlantic system (666)

buccaneers (674)

consumer revolution (676)

Enlightenment (695)

Jacobitism (686)

mestizo (674)

Pietism (683)

plantation (667)

rococo (681)

Westernization (688)

REVIEW QUESTIONS

1. How is consumerism related to slavery?
2. What were the social and cultural consequences of the agricultural revolution?
3. How did Peter the Great's government compare to those of Britain and France?
4. What were the major issues in the early decades of the Enlightenment?

MAKING CONNECTIONS

1. In what ways did the rise of slavery and the plantation system change European politics and society?
2. Why was the Enlightenment born just at the moment that the Atlantic system took shape?
3. What were the major differences between the wars of the first half of the eighteenth century and those of the seventeenth century? (Refer to Chapters 16 and 17.)

FOR FURTHER EXPLORATION

For additional help mastering the material in this chapter, see the Online Study Guide at bedfordstmartins.com/hunt.

For additional primary-sources material from this period, see Chapter 18 in *Sources of The Making of the West*, Second Edition.

Appendix

Useful Facts and Figures

PROMINENT ROMAN EMPERORS

Julio-Claudians

27 B.C.E.–14 C.E.	Augustus
14–37	Tiberius
37–41	Gaius (Caligula)
41–54	Claudius
54–68	Nero

Flavian Dynasty

69–79	Vespasian
79–81	Titus
81–96	Domitian

Golden Age Emperors

96–98	Nerva
98–117	Trajan
117–138	Hadrian
138–161	Antonius Pius
161–180	Marcus Aurelius

Severan Emperors

193–211	Septimius Severus
211–217	Antoninus (Caracalla)
217–218	Macrinus
222–235	Severus Alexander

Period of Instability

235–238	Maximinus Thrax
238–244	Gordian III
244–249	Philip the Arab
249–251	Decius
251–253	Trebonianus Gallus
253–260	Valerian
270–275	Aurelian
275–276	Tacitus
276–282	Probus
283–285	Carinus

Dominate

284–305	Diocletian
306	Constantius
306–337	Constantine I
337–340	Constantine II
337–350	Constans I

(Continued)

337–361	Constantius II
361–363	Julian
363–364	Jovian
364–375	Valentinian I
364–378	Valens
367–383	Gratian
375–392	Valentinian II
378–395	Theodosius I (the Great)

The Western Empire

395–423	Honorius
406–407	Marcus
407–411	Constantine III

409–411	Maximus
411–413	Jovinus
412–413	Sebastianus
423–425	Johannes
425–455	Valentinian III
455–456	Avitus
457–461	Majorian
461–465	Libius Severus
467–472	Anthemius
473–474	Glycerius
474–475	Julius Nepos
475–476	Romulus Augustulus

PROMINENT BYZANTINE EMPERORS

Dynasty of Theodosius

395–408	Arcadius
408–450	Theodosius II
450–457	Marcian

Dynasty of Leo

457–474	Leo I
474	Leo II
474–491	Zeno
475–476	Basiliscus
484–488	Leontius
491–518	Anastasius

Dynasty of Justinian

518–527	Justin
527–565	Justinian I
565–578	Justin II
578–582	Tiberius II
578–582	Tiberius II (I) Constantine
582–602	Maurice
602–610	Phocas

Dynasty of Heraclius

610–641	Heraclius
641	Heraclonas
641	Constantine III
641–668	Constans II
646–647	Gregory
649–653	Olympius
669	Mezezius
668–685	Constantine IV
685–695	Justinian II (banished)
695–698	Leontius

698–705	Tiberius III (II)
705–711	Justinian II (restored)
711–713	Bardanes
713–716	Anastasius II
716–717	Theodosius III

Isaurian Dynasty

717–741	Leo III
741–775	Constantine V Copronymus
775–780	Leo IV
780–797	Constantine VI
797–802	Irene
802–811	Nicephorus I
811	Strauracius
811–813	Michael I
813–820	Leo V

Phrygian Dynasty

820–829	Michael II
821–823	Thomas
829–842	Theophilus
842–867	Michael III

Macedonian Dynasty

867–886	Basil I
869–879	Constantine
887–912	Leo VI
912–913	Alexander
913–959	Constantine VII Porphrogenitos
920–944	Romanus I Lecapenus
921–931	Christopher
924–945	Stephen
959–963	Romanus II

963–969	Nicephorus II Phocas
976–1025	Basil II
1025–1028	Constantine VIII (IX) alone
1028–1034	Romanus III Argyrus
1034–1041	Michael IV the Paphlagonian
1041–1042	Michael V Calaphates
1042	Zoe and Theodora
1042–1055	Constantine IX Monomchus
1055–1066	Theodora alone
1056–1057	Michael VI Stratioticus

Prelude to the Comnenian Dynasty

1057–1059	Isaac I Comnenos
1059–1067	Constantine X (IX) Ducas
1068–1071	Romanus IV Diogenes
1071–1078	Michael VII Ducas
1078–1081	Nicephorus III Botaniates
1080–1081	Nicephorus Melissenus

Comnenian Dynasty

1081–1118	Alexius I
1118–1143	John II
1143–1180	Manuel I
1180–1183	Alexius II
1183–1185	Andronieus I
1183–1191	Isaac, Emperor of Cyprus

Dynasty of the Angeli

1185–1195	Isaac II
1195–1203	Alexius III
1203–1204	Isaac II (restored) with Alexius IV
1204	Alexius V Ducas Murtzuphlus

Lascarid Dynasty in Nicaea

1204–1222	Theodore I Lascaris
1222–1254	John III Ducas Vatatzes
1254–1258	Theodore II Lascaris
1258–1261	John IV Lascaris

Dynasty of the Paleologi

1259–1289	Michael VIII Paleologus
1282–1328	Andronicus II
1328–1341	Andronicus III
1341–1391	John V
1347–1354	John VI Cantancuzenus
1376–1379	Andronicus IV
1379–1391	John V (restored)
1390	John VII
1391–1425	Manuel II
1425–1448	John VIII
1449–1453	Constantine XI (XIII) Dragases

PROMINENT POPES

314–335	Sylvester
440–461	Leo I
590–604	Gregory I (the Great)
687–701	Sergius I
741–752	Zachary
858–867	Nicholas I
1049–1054	Leo IX
1059–1061	Nicholas II
1073–1085	Gregory VII
1088–1099	Urban II
1099–1118	Paschal II
1159–1181	Alexander III
1198–1216	Innocent III
1227–1241	Gregory IX
1243–1254	Innocent IV
1294–1303	Boniface VIII
1316–1334	John XXII
1447–1455	Nicholas V
1458–1464	Pius II
1492–1503	Alexander VI
1503–1513	Julius II
1513–1521	Leo X
1534–1549	Paul III
1555–1559	Paul IV
1585–1590	Sixtus V
1623–1644	Urban VIII
1831–1846	Gregory XVI
1846–1878	Pius IX
1878–1903	Leo XIII
1903–1914	Pius X
1914–1922	Benedict XV
1922–1939	Pius XI
1939–1958	Pius XII
1958–1963	John XXIII
1963–1978	Paul VI
1978	John Paul I
1978–	John Paul II

THE CAROLINGIAN DYNASTY

687–714	Pepin of Heristal, Mayor of the Palace
715–741	Charles Martel, Mayor of the Palace
741–751	Pepin III, Mayor of the Palace
751–768	Pepin III, King
768–814	Charlemagne, King
800–814	Charlemagne, Emperor
814–840	Louis the Pious

West Francia

840–877	Charles the Bald, King
875–877	Charles the Bald, Emperor
877–879	Louis II, King

879–882	Louis III, King
879–884	Carloman, King

Middle Kingdoms

840–855	Lothair, Emperor
855–875	Louis (Italy), Emperor
855–863	Charles (Provence), King
855–869	Lothair II (Lorraine), King

East Francia

840–876	Ludwig, King
876–880	Carloman, King
876–882	Ludwig, King
876–887	Charles the Fat, Emperor

GERMAN KINGS CROWNED EMPEROR

Saxon Dynasty

962–973	Otto I
973–983	Otto II
983–1002	Otto III
1002–1024	Henry II

Franconian Dynasty

1024–1039	Conrad II
1039–1056	Henry III
1056–1106	Henry IV
1106–1125	Henry V
1125–1137	Lothair II (Saxony)

Hohenstaufen Dynasty

1138–1152	Conrad III
1152–1190	Frederick I (Barbarossa)
1190–1197	Henry VI
1198–1208	Philip of Swabia
1198–1215	Otto IV (Welf)
1220–1250	Frederick II
1250–1254	Conrad IV

Interregnum, 1254–1273: Emperors from Various Dynasties

1273–1291	Rudolf I (Habsburg)
1292–1298	Adolf (Nassau)

1298–1308	Albert I (Habsburg)
1308–1313	Henry VII (Luxemburg)
1314–1347	Ludwig IV (Wittelsbach)
1347–1378	Charles IV (Luxemburg)
1378–1400	Wenceslas (Luxemburg)
1400–1410	Rupert (Wittelsbach)
1410–1437	Sigismund (Luxemburg)

Habsburg Dynasty

1438–1439	Albert II
1440–1493	Frederick III
1493–1519	Maximilian I
1519–1556	Charles V
1556–1564	Ferdinand I
1564–1576	Maximilian II
1576–1612	Rudolf II
1612–1619	Matthias
1619–1637	Ferdinand II
1637–1657	Ferdinand III
1658–1705	Leopold I
1705–1711	Joseph I
1711–1740	Charles VI
1742–1745	Charles VII (not a Habsburg)
1745–1765	Francis I
1765–1790	Joseph II
1790–1792	Leopold II
1792–1806	Francis II

RULERS OF FRANCE

Capetian Dynasty

987–996	Hugh Capet
996–1031	Robert II
1031–1060	Henry I
1060–1108	Philip I
1108–1137	Louis VI
1137–1180	Louis VII
1180–1223	Philip II (Augustus)
1223–1226	Louis VIII
1226–1270	Louis IX (St. Louis)
1270–1285	Philip III
1285–1314	Philip IV
1314–1316	Louis X
1316–1322	Philip V
1322–1328	Charles IV

Valois Dynasty

1328–1350	Philip VI
1350–1364	John
1364–1380	Charles V
1380–1422	Charles VI
1422–1461	Charles VII
1461–1483	Louis XI
1483–1498	Charles VIII
1498–1515	Louis XII
1515–1547	Francis I
1547–1559	Henry II
1559–1560	Francis II
1560–1574	Charles IX
1574–1589	Henry III

Bourbon Dynasty

1589–1610	Henry IV
1610–1643	Louis XIII
1643–1715	Louis XIV
1715–1774	Louis XV
1774–1792	Louis XVI

After 1792

1792–1799	First Republic
1799–1804	Napoleon Bonaparte, First Consul
1804–1814	Napoleon I, Emperor
1814–1824	Louis XVIII (Bourbon Dynasty)
1824–1830	Charles X (Bourbon Dynasty)
1830–1848	Louis Philippe
1848–1852	Second Republic
1852–1870	Napoleon III, Emperor
1870–1940	Third Republic
1940–1944	Vichy government, Pétain regime
1944–1946	Provisional government
1946–1958	Fourth Republic
1958–	Fifth Republic

MONARCHS OF ENGLAND AND GREAT BRITAIN

Anglo-Saxon Monarchs

829–839	Egbert
839–858	Ethelwulf
858–860	Ethelbald
860–866	Ethelbert
866–871	Ethelred I
871–899	Alfred the Great
899–924	Edward the Elder
924–939	Ethelstan
939–946	Edmund I
946–955	Edred
955–959	Edwy
959–975	Edgar
975–978	Edward the Martyr
978–1016	Ethelred the Unready
1016–1035	Canute (Danish nationality)
1035–1040	Harold I
1040–1042	Hardicanute
1042–1066	Edward the Confessor
1066	Harold II

Norman Monarchs

1066–1087	William I (the Conqueror)
1087–1100	William II
1100–1135	Henry I

House of Blois

1135–1154	Stephen

House of Plantagenet

1154–1189	Henry II
1189–1199	Richard I

(Continued)

1199–1216	John
1216–1272	Henry III
1272–1307	Edward I
1307–1327	Edward II
1327–1377	Edward III
1377–1399	Richard II

House of Lancaster

1399–1413	Henry IV
1413–1422	Henry V
1422–1461	Henry VI

House of York

1461–1483	Edward IV
1483	Edward V
1483–1485	Richard III

House of Tudor

1485–1509	Henry VII
1509–1547	Henry VIII
1547–1553	Edward VI
1553–1558	Mary
1558–1603	Elizabeth I

House of Stuart

1603–1625	James I
1625–1649	Charles I

Commonwealth and Protectorate (1649–1660)

1653–1658	Oliver Cromwell
1658–1659	Richard Cromwell

House of Stuart (Restored)

1660–1685	Charles II
1685–1688	James II
1689–1694	William III and Mary II
1694–1702	William III (alone)
1702–1714	Anne

House of Hanover

1714–1727	George I
1727–1760	George II
1760–1820	George III
1820–1830	George IV
1830–1837	William IV
1837–1901	Victoria

House of Saxe-Coburg-Gotha

1901–1910	Edward VII

House of Windsor

1910–1936	George V
1936	Edward VIII
1936–1952	George VI
1952–	Elizabeth II

PRIME MINISTERS OF GREAT BRITAIN

Term	Prime Minister	Government
1721–1742	Sir Robert Walpole	Whig
1742–1743	Spencer Compton, Earl of Wilmington	Whig
1743–1754	Henry Pelham	Whig
1754–1756	Thomas Pelham-Holles, Duke of Newcastle	Whig
1756–1757	William Cavendish, Duke of Devonshire	Whig
1757–1761	William Pitt (the Elder), Earl of Chatham	Whig
1761–1762	Thomas Pelham-Holles, Duke of Newcastle	Whig
1762–1763	John Stuart, Earl of Bute	Tory
1763–1765	George Grenville	Whig
1765–1766	Charles Watson-Wentworth, Marquess of Rockingham	Whig
1766–1768	William Pitt, Earl of Chatham (the Elder)	Whig
1768–1770	Augustus Henry Fitzroy, Duke of Grafton	Whig
1770–1782	Frederick North (Lord North)	Tory
1782	Charles Watson-Wentworth, Marquess of Rockingham	Whig

1782–1783	William Petty FitzMaurice, Earl of Shelburn	Whig
1783	William Henry Cavendish Bentinck, Duke of Portland	Whig
1783–1801	William Pitt (the Younger)	Tory
1801–1804	Henry Addington	Tory
1804–1806	William Pitt (the Younger)	Tory
1806–1807	William Wyndham Grenville (Baron Grenville)	Whig
1807–1809	William Henry Cavendish Bentinck, Duke of Portland	Tory
1809–1812	Spencer Perceval	Tory
1812–1827	Robert Banks Jenkinson, Earl of Liverpool	Tory
1827	George Canning	Tory
1827–1828	Frederick John Robinson (Viscount Goderich)	Tory
1828–1830	Arthur Wellesley, Duke of Wellington	Tory
1830–1834	Charles Grey (Earl Grey)	Whig
1834	William Lamb, Viscount Melbourne	Whig
1834–1835	Sir Robert Peel	Tory
1835–1841	William Lamb, Viscount Melbourne	Whig
1841–1846	Sir Robert Peel	Tory
1846–1852	John Russell (Lord)	Whig
1852	Edward Geoffrey–Smith Stanley Derby, Earl of Derby	Whig
1852–1855	George Hamilton Gordon Aberdeen, Earl of Aberdeen	Peelite
1855–1858	Henry John Temple Palmerston, Viscount Palmerston	Tory
1858–1859	Edward Geoffrey–Smith Stanley Derby, Earl of Derby	Whig
1859–1865	Henry John Temple Palmerston, Viscount Palmerston	Tory
1865–1866	John Russell (Earl)	Liberal
1866–1868	Edward Geoffrey–Smith Stanley Derby, Earl of Derby	Tory
1868	Benjamin Disraeli, Earl of Beaconfield	Conservative
1868–1874	William Ewart Gladstone	Liberal
1874–1880	Benjamin Disraeli, Earl of Beaconfield	Conservative
1880–1885	William Ewart Gladstone	Liberal
1885–1886	Robert Arthur Talbot, Marquess of Salisbury	Conservative
1886	William Ewart Gladstone	Liberal
1886–1892	Robert Arthur Talbot, Marquess of Salisbury	Conservative
1892–1894	William Ewart Gladstone	Liberal
1894–1895	Archibald Philip–Primrose Rosebery, Earl of Rosebery	Liberal
1895–1902	Robert Arthur Talbot, Marquess of Salisbury	Conservative
1902–1905	Arthur James Balfour, Earl of Balfour	Conservative
1905–1908	Sir Henry Campbell-Bannerman	Liberal
1908–1915	Herbert Henry Asquith	Liberal
1915–1916	Herbert Henry Asquith	Coalition
1916–1922	David Lloyd George, Earl Lloyd-George of Dwyfor	Coalition
1922–1923	Andrew Bonar Law	Conservative
1923–1924	Stanley Baldwin, Earl Baldwin of Bewdley	Conservative
1924	James Ramsay MacDonald	Labour
1924–1929	Stanley Baldwin, Earl Baldwin of Bewdley	Conservative
1929–1931	James Ramsay MacDonald	Labour
1931–1935	James Ramsay MacDonald	Coalition
1935–1937	Stanley Baldwin, Earl Baldwin of Bewdley	Coalition
1937–1940	Neville Chamberlain	Coalition
1940–1945	Winston Churchill	Coalition
1945	Winston Churchill	Conservative
1945–1951	Clement Attlee, Earl Attlee	Labour
1951–1955	Sir Winston Churchill	Conservative

(Continued)

PRIME MINISTERS OF GREAT BRITAIN (continued)

Term	Prime Minister	Government
1955–1957	Sir Anthony Eden, Earl of Avon	Conservative
1957–1963	Harold Macmillan, Earl of Stockton	Conservative
1963–1964	Sir Alec Frederick Douglas-Home, Lord Home of the Hirsel	Conservative
1964–1970	Harold Wilson, Lord Wilson of Rievaulx	Labour
1970–1974	Edward Heath	Conservative
1974–1976	Harold Wilson, Lord Wilson of Rievaulx	Labour
1976–1979	James Callaghan, Lord Callaghan of Cardiff	Labour
1979–1990	Margaret Thatcher (Baroness)	Conservative
1990–1997	John Major	Conservative
1997–	Tony Blair	Labour

RULERS OF PRUSSIA AND GERMANY

1701–1713	*Frederick I
1713–1740	*Frederick William I
1740–1786	*Frederick II (the Great)
1786–1797	*Frederick William II
1797–1840	*Frederick William III
1840–1861	*Frederick William IV
1861–1888	*William I (German emperor after 1871)
1888	Frederick III
1888–1918	*William II
1918–1933	Weimar Republic
1933–1945	Third Reich (Nazi dictatorship under Adolf Hitler)
1945–1952	Allied occupation
1949–1990	Division of Federal Republic of Germany in west and German Democratic Republic in east
1990–	Federal Republic of Germany (reunited)

*King of Prussia

RULERS OF AUSTRIA AND AUSTRIA-HUNGARY

1493–1519	*Maximilian I (Archduke)
1519–1556	*Charles V
1556–1564	*Ferdinand I
1564–1576	*Maximilian II
1576–1612	*Rudolf II
1612–1619	*Matthias
1619–1637	*Ferdinand II
1637–1657	*Ferdinand III
1658–1705	*Leopold I
1705–1711	*Joseph I
1711–1740	*Charles VI
1740–1780	Maria Theresa
1780–1790	*Joseph II
1790–1792	*Leopold II

1792–1835	*Francis II (emperor of Austria as Francis I after 1804)
1835–1848	Ferdinand I
1848–1916	Francis Joseph (after 1867 emperor of Austria and king of Hungary)
1916–1918	Charles I (emperor of Austria and king of Hungary)
1918–1938	Republic of Austria (dictatorship after 1934)
1945–1956	Republic restored, under Allied occupation
1956–	Free Republic

*Also bore title of Holy Roman Emperor

LEADERS OF POST-WORLD WAR II GERMANY

West Germany (Federal Republic of Germany), 1949–1990

Years	Chancellor	Party
1949–1963	Konrad Adenauer	Christian Democratic Union (CDU)
1963–1966	Ludwig Erhard	Christian Democratic Union (CDU)
1966–1969	Kurt Georg Kiesinger	Christian Democratic Union (CDU)
1969–1974	Willy Brandt	Social Democratic Party (SPD)
1974–1982	Helmut Schmidt	Social Democratic Party (SPD)
1982–1990	Helmut Kohl	Christian Democratic Union (CDU)

East Germany (German Democratic Republic), 1949–1990

Years	Communist Party Leader
1946–1971	Walter Ulbricht
1971–1989	Erich Honecker
1989–1990	Egon Krenz

Federal Republic of Germany (reunited), 1990–

| 1990–1998 | Helmut Kohl | Christian Democratic Union (CDU) |
| 1998– | Gerhard Schroeder | Social Democratic Party (SPD) |

RULERS OF RUSSIA, THE USSR, AND THE RUSSIAN FEDERATION

c. 980–1015	Vladimir
1019–1054	Yaroslav the Wise
1176–1212	Vsevolod III
1462–1505	Ivan III
1505–1553	Vasily III
1553–1584	Ivan IV
1584–1598	Theodore I
1598–1605	Boris Godunov
1605	Theodore II
1606–1610	Vasily IV
1613–1645	Michael
1645–1676	Alexius
1676–1682	Theodore III
1682–1689	Ivan V and Peter I
1689–1725	Peter I (the Great)
1725–1727	Catherine I
1727–1730	Peter II
1730–1740	Anna
1740–1741	Ivan VI
1741–1762	Elizabeth
1762	Peter III
1762–1796	Catherine II (the Great)
1796–1801	Paul
1801–1825	Alexander I
1825–1855	Nicholas I
1855–1881	Alexander II
1881–1894	Alexander III
1894–1917	Nicholas II

Union of Soviet Socialist Republics (USSR)*

1917–1924	Vladimir Ilyich Lenin
1924–1953	Joseph Stalin
1953–1964	Nikita Khrushchev
1964–1982	Leonid Brezhnev
1982–1984	Yuri Andropov
1984–1985	Konstantin Chernenko
1985–1991	Mikhail Gorbachev

Russian Federation

1991–1999	Boris Yeltsin
1999–	Vladimir Putin

*USSR established in 1922

RULERS OF SPAIN

1479–1504	Ferdinand and Isabella
1504–1506	Ferdinand and Philip I
1506–1516	Ferdinand and Charles I
1516–1556	Charles I (Holy Roman Emperor Charles V)
1556–1598	Philip II
1598–1621	Philip III
1621–1665	Philip IV
1665–1700	Charles II
1700–1746	Philip V
1746–1759	Ferdinand VI
1759–1788	Charles III
1788–1808	Charles IV
1808	Ferdinand VII
1808–1813	Joseph Bonaparte
1814–1833	Ferdinand VII (restored)
1833–1868	Isabella II
1868–1870	Republic
1870–1873	Amadeo
1873–1874	Republic
1874–1885	Alfonso XII
1886–1931	Alfonso XIII
1931–1939	Republic
1939–1975	Fascist dictatorship under Francisco Franco
1975–	Juan Carlos I

RULERS OF ITALY

1861–1878	Victor Emmanuel II
1878–1900	Humbert I
1900–1946	Victor Emmanuel III
1922–1943	Fascist dictatorship under Benito Mussolini (maintained in northern Italy until 1945)
1946 (May 9–June 13)	Humbert II
1946–	Republic

SECRETARIES-GENERAL OF THE UNITED NATIONS

		Nationality
1946–1952	Trygve Lie	Norway
1953–1961	Dag Hammarskjöld	Sweden
1961–1971	U Thant	Myanmar
1972–1981	Kurt Waldheim	Austria
1982–1991	Javier Pérez de Cuéllar	Peru
1992–1996	Boutros Boutros-Ghali	Egypt
1997–	Kofi A. Annan	Ghana

UNITED STATES PRESIDENTIAL ADMINISTRATIONS

Term(s)	President	Political Party
1789–1797	George Washington	No party designation
1797–1801	John Adams	Federalist
1801–1809	Thomas Jefferson	Democratic-Republican
1809–1817	James Madison	Democratic-Republican
1817–1825	James Monroe	Democratic-Republican
1825–1829	John Quincy Adams	Democratic-Republican
1829–1837	Andrew Jackson	Democratic
1837–1841	Martin Van Buren	Democratic
1841	William H. Harrison	Whig
1841–1845	John Tyler	Whig
1845–1849	James K. Polk	Democratic
1849–1850	Zachary Taylor	Whig
1850–1853	Millard Filmore	Whig
1853–1857	Franklin Pierce	Democratic
1857–1861	James Buchanan	Democratic
1861–1865	Abraham Lincoln	Republican
1865–1869	Andrew Johnson	Republican
1869–1877	Ulysses S. Grant	Republican
1877–1881	Rutherford B. Hayes	Republican
1881	James A. Garfield	Republican
1881–1885	Chester A. Arthur	Republican
1885–1889	Grover Cleveland	Democratic
1889–1893	Benjamin Harrison	Republican
1893–1897	Grover Cleveland	Democratic
1897–1901	William McKinley	Republican
1901–1909	Theodore Roosevelt	Republican
1909–1913	William H. Taft	Republican
1913–1921	Woodrow Wilson	Democratic
1921–1923	Warren G. Harding	Republican
1923–1929	Calvin Coolidge	Republican
1929–1933	Herbert C. Hoover	Republican
1933–1945	Franklin D. Roosevelt	Democratic
1945–1953	Harry S. Truman	Democratic
1953–1961	Dwight D. Eisenhower	Republican
1961–1963	John F. Kennedy	Democratic
1963–1969	Lyndon B. Johnson	Democratic
1969–1974	Richard M. Nixon	Republican
1974–1977	Gerald R. Ford	Republican
1977–1981	Jimmy Carter	Democratic
1981–1989	Ronald W. Reagan	Republican
1989–1993	George H. W. Bush	Republican
1993–2001	William J. Clinton	Democratic
2001–	George W. Bush	Republican

MAJOR WARS OF THE MODERN ERA

1546–1555	German Wars of Religion
1526–1571	Ottoman wars
1562–1598	French Wars of Religion
1566–1609, 1621–1648	Revolt of the Netherlands
1618–1648	Thirty Years' War
1642–1648	English Civil War
1652–1678	Anglo-Dutch Wars
1667–1697	Wars of Louis XIV
1683–1697	Ottoman wars
1689–1697	War of the League of Augsburg
1702–1714	War of Spanish Succession
1702–1721	Great Northern War
1714–1718	Ottoman wars
1740–1748	War of Austrian Succession
1756–1763	Seven Years' War
1775–1781	American Revolution
1796–1815	Napoleonic wars
1846–1848	Mexican-American War
1853–1856	Crimean War
1861–1865	United States Civil War
1870–1871	Franco-Prussian War
1894–1895	Sino-Japanese War
1898	Spanish-American War
1904–1905	Russo-Japanese War
1914–1918	World War I
1939–1945	World War II
1946–1975	Vietnam wars
1950–1953	Korean War
1990–1991	Persian Gulf War
1991–1997	Civil War in the former Yugoslavia
2003	Iraq War

Glossary of Key Terms

This glossary of key terms contains definitions of words and ideas that are central to your understanding of the material covered in this textbook. Each term in the glossary is in boldface in the text when it is first defined, then listed again in the corresponding Chapter Review section to signal its importance. We have also included the page number on which the full discussion of the term appears so that you can easily locate the complete explanation to strengthen your historical vocabulary.

For words not defined here, two additional resources may be useful: the index, which will direct you to many more topics discussed in the text, and a good dictionary.

Abbasids (326): The caliphal dynasty that came to power in 750. The Abbasids built their capital at Baghdad, where they exercised considerable power over the entire Islamic world until the late ninth century.

Absolutism (621): A system of government in which the ruler claimed sole and uncontestable power.

agora (93): The central market square of a Greek city-state, a popular place to gather for conversation.

agricultural revolution (676): Increasingly aggressive attitudes toward investment in and management of land that increased production of food in the 1700s; this revolution developed first in England and then spread to the continent.

aids (382): Payments paid by a vassal to his lord on important occasions, such as the knighting of the lord's eldest son or the marriage of his eldest daughter.

Albigensians (420): The name given by its opponents to a religious movement of dualists centered in Albi, in southern France. The Albigensians were considered heretics, and a crusade was launched against them.

Anabaptists (561): Sixteenth-century religious dissenters who believed that humans have free will and that people must knowingly select the Christian faith through rebaptism as adults. They advocated radical separation from society; though originally pacifist, some chose violent paths to religious renewal.

Angevins (406): The dynasty from Anjou that came to the English throne with Henry II. Also called Plantagenets.

Anglo-Saxon England (308): England *after* the invasions of the Angles and Saxons (which began in the 440s) and *before* the Norman conquest in 1066.

apocalypticism (51): A religious belief about the end of the world; literally, "uncovering the future."

apostate (254): Literally, "renegade from the faith"; the emperor Julian (r. 361–363), who rejected Christianity and tried to restore traditional religion as the state religion, was given the nickname "the Apostate."

apostolic succession (228): The principle by which Christian bishops traced their authority back to Jesus's apostles.

aretê (53): Greek for "excellence"; a competitive value that defined the Greek social elite.

Arianism (257): The Christian doctrine named after Arius, who argued that Jesus was "begotten" by God and did not have an identical nature with his Father.

asceticism (260): The practice of self-denial (from the Greek *askesis*, "training"), as in the lives of monks; a doctrine for Christians emphasized by Augustine.

Atlantic system (666): The triangular pattern of trade established in the 1700s that bound together western Europe, Africa, and the Americas. Europeans sold slaves from western Africa and bought commodities such as coffee and sugar that were produced by the new colonial plantations in North and South America and the Caribbean.

auctoritas (207): Literally, "moral authority"; the authority derived from respect on which the Roman princeps' power rested.

Augustus (206): The title meaning "divinely favored" that Rome's Senate granted Octavian and that became shorthand for "Roman imperial ruler."

auto da fé (528): Literally, "demonstration of faith"; the ritual of public confession that was one of the punishments given to heretics by the Inquisition in the fifteenth century.

ban (347): The rights to collect taxes, hear court cases, levy fines, and muster men for defense. It was largely understood as a complex of royal rights, but around 1000, local rulers as well as kings began exercising them.

baroque (607): An artistic style of the seventeenth century that featured curves, exaggerated lighting, intense emotions, release from restraint, and even a kind of artistic sensationalism; like mannerism, it departed from the Renaissance emphasis on harmonious design, unity, and clarity.

Beguines (420): Women in northern Europe who chose a life of celibacy outside of a cloister. Taking no permanent vows, the women lived in community houses and earned their living as laundresses and the like.

benefices (486): In the Catholic church, ecclesiastical offices funded by an endowment.

buccaneers (674): Pirates of the Caribbean who governed themselves and preyed on international shipping.

bureaucracy (627): A network of state officials carrying out orders according to a regular and routine line of authority.

Byzantine Empire (272): Historians' name for the eastern Roman Empire from about 500 to 1453, derived from Byzantium, the original name of Constantinople.

castellan (347): A person who controlled a castle. After around 1000, these castles were the seats of local power in France.

chansons de geste (415): Long vernacular poems about knightly and heroic deeds.

chivalry (415): The proper, ideal comportment of a knight, who was constrained by a code of refinement, fair play, and piety.

Christ (226): Greek for "anointed one" (the corresponding Hebrew word is *Messiah*); in apocalyptic religious thinking, the agent of God sent to conquer the forces of evil.

Christian humanists (550): Humanists who in the sixteenth century dreamed of ideal societies based on peace and morality, and who sought to realize the ethical ideals of the classical world. Desiderius Erasmus (c. 1466–1536) and Thomas More (1478–1535) are representative of these thinkers.

city-state (9): A state consisting of an urban center exercising political and economic control over the countryside around it.

civilization (4): A way of life that includes political states based on cities with dense populations, large buildings constructed for communal activities, diverse economies, a sense of local identity, and some knowledge of writing.

classicism (654): A style of painting and architecture that reflected the ideals of the art of antiquity; in classicism, geometric shapes, order, and harmony of lines took precedence over the sensuous, exuberant, and emotional forms of the baroque.

coloni (251): Tenant farmers in the Roman Empire who became bound by law to the land they worked and whose children were legally required to continue to farm the same land.

Colosseum (218): Rome's giant amphitheater for gladiatorial shows and other spectacles.

commercial revolution (360): Historians' term to describe the collective effect of the development of a profit economy, growth of cities, increased trade, and the rise of powerful new groups of merchants and artisans at the end of the eleventh/beginning of the twelfth century.

common law (407): The law of all of England. Its first chief architect was King Henry II, who sent his justices to every locality in his realm, declared certain crimes to be under his jurisdiction, and opened up new possibilities for property litigation under royal aegis.

commune (364): Sworn associations of citizens who formed a legal corporate body. Communes were the normal institution of self-government in medieval towns.

constitutionalism (622): A system of government in which rulers had to share power with parliaments made up of elected representatives.

consumer revolution (676): The rapid increase in consumption of new staples produced in the Atlantic system as well as of other items of daily life, such as mirrors, that were previously unavailable or beyond the reach of ordinary people.

conversos (528): Jews in the Iberian peninsula who converted to Christianity in the fifteenth century.

cuneiform (12): The earliest form of writing, invented in Mesopotamia and done with wedge-shaped characters.

curials (251): The social elite in the Roman Empire's towns who were responsible for collecting taxes for the imperial government and paying for any shortfalls themselves.

Dark Age (45): An extended period of economic depression and depopulation.

debasement of coinage (235): Putting less silver in a coin without changing its face value; practiced during the third-century crisis in Rome.

decurions (220): Municipal senate members in the Roman Empire responsible for collecting local taxes.

Delian League (88): The naval alliance headed by Athens after the Persian Wars, and the basis of Athenian empire.

demography (P-11): The study of the size, growth, density, distribution, and vital statistics of the human population.

Diaspora (51): The dispersion of the Jewish population outside of ancient Israel.

dominate (246): Roman rule from Diocletian (r. 284–305) onward; a blatantly authoritarian style of rule; derived from *dominus* ("master"; "lord") and contrasted with principate.

dualism (128): The concept that spiritual being and physical being are separate.

duchy (523): A state ruled by dukes; Florence, for example, became a duchy in 1530.

dynatoi (324): A new hereditary elite, largely made of military families, that developed in the Byzantine Empire, especially in Anatolia, in the course of the tenth and eleventh centuries.

Edict of Milan (253): Constantine's and Licinius's proclamation of religious toleration that also expressed their favoring of Christianity.

empire (14): A political unit in which one or more formerly independent territories or peoples are ruled by a single sovereign power.

Enlightenment (695): The eighteenth-century intellectual movement whose proponents believed that human beings could apply a critical, reasoning spirit to every problem. Based on a popularization of scientific discoveries, the movement often challenged religious and secular authorities.

Epicureanism (151): The philosophy initiated by Epicurus of Athens to help people achieve pleasure (meaning an "absence of disturbance") in their lives.

epigrams (147): Short poems covering a variety of themes, especially love, and a favorite genre of Hellenistic women poets.

equites (189): Literally, "equestrians" or "knights"; wealthy Roman businessmen who chose not to pursue a government career.

Evangelicals (548): Supporters of Martin Luther and religious reform in the 1520s; the word refers to the Gospels.

feudalism (343): A term sometimes used by historians to speak of the relationship between lords, vassals, fiefs, and fragmented rulership in western Europe during the Middle Ages.

First Triumvirate (196): The coalition formed in 60 B.C.E. by Gnaeus Pompey, Lucinius Crossus, and Julius Caesar (the word *triumvirate* means "a group of three").

flagellants (485): A group of Christians who whipped themselves publicly as a form of penance during the fourteenth century.

friars (420): "Brothers" of the mendicant orders, such as the Franciscans and Dominicans.

frieze (95): A continuous band of figures sculpted in relief, as on an ancient Greek temple.

Fronde (623): A series of revolts in France, 1648–1653, that challenged the authority of young Louis XIV and his minister Mazarin.

Gallicanism (528): The higher loyalty of the French clergy to the interests of the French church and monarchy than to the papacy; established by the Pragmatic Sanction of Bourges in 1438.

Glorious Revolution (644): The events when the English Parliament deposed King James II in 1688 and replaced him with William, prince of Orange, and James's daughter Mary.

Golden Horde (461): A name for the Mongol Empire in Russia.

Gothic (446): A style of architecture characterized by pointed arches, ribbed vaults, and large stained-glass windows.

Great Persecution (251): The violent program initiated by Diocletian in 303 to make Christians convert to traditional religion or risk confiscation of their property and even death.

Great Schism (367, 489): The term *Great Schism* refers to two different periods in the history of the Christian church. The first, in 1054, refers to the separation of the Latin Catholic church and the Greek Orthodox church; the second, to the period from 1378 to 1417, when the church had two separate popes, one in Rome and one in Avignon, France.

Gregorian Reform (367): The movement for church reform—including clerical celibacy and an end to lay investiture—associated with Pope Gregory VII.

guilds (417): Religious, economic, and trade associations. They regulated, protected, and policed their membership, setting up standards for professional practices.

heliocentrism (612): The view articulated by Polish clergyman Nicolaus Copernicus that the earth and planets revolve around the sun; Galileo Galilei was condemned by the Catholic church for supporting this view.

Hellenistic (124): An adjective meaning "Greek-like" that is today used as a chronological term for the period 323–30 B.C.E.

hetaira (99): A witty and attractive woman who charged fees to entertain at symposia.

hierarchies (P-7): Social systems ranking certain people as more important and more dominant than others; the earliest evidence of social differentiation comes from the Paleolithic period.

hieroglyphs (19): The Egyptian form of writing using pictures as its characters.

Hijra (294): The emigration of Muhammad and his followers from Mecca to Medina. Its date, 622, begins the Islamic calendar.

Homo sapiens (P-3): Literally, "wise human being"; the scientific term for human beings similar, but not identical, to modern human beings.

hoplite (66): A heavily armed Greek infantryman. Hoplites constituted the main strike force of a city-state's militia.

hubris (114): The Greek term for excessive arrogance, especially when an overconfident human being went against the will of the gods.

Huguenot (582): The name given to Calvinists in France after 1560; its linguistic origin remains uncertain.

humanism (507): A literary and intellectual movement that arose in the early fifteenth century to valorize the writings of Greco-Roman antiquity; it was so named because its practitioners studied and supported the liberal arts, or humanities.

humanitas (186): Cicero's ideal of "humaneness," meaning generous and honest treatment of others based on natural law.

hunter-gatherers (P-5): Paleolithic people who roamed to find their food in the wild and did not live in a permanent location.

iconoclasm (291): Literally, "icon breaking"; the destruction of icons, or images of holy people (e.g., Christ, Mary, the saints). Byzantine emperors banned icons from 726 to 787; a modified ban was revived in 815 and lasted until 843.

indulgence (549): In Roman Catholic doctrine, a remission of sin earned by performing certain religious tasks to avoid purgatory after death; indulgences were in use by the thirteenth century. The Catholic clergy's practice of selling indulgences came under fire during the Reformation.

infidel (567): Someone outside of the particular faith.

Inquisition (438): The court of inquiry permanently set up by the church in 1233; its purpose was to ferret out and punish heretics.

Investiture Conflict (368): The conflict between Pope Gregory VII and Henry IV over the right of laymen to appoint bishops and install them in their office.

Jacobitism (686): The movement of support for deposed British king James II (from the Latin *Jacobus* for "James") that had substantial support in Scotland and Ireland in the early eighteenth century.

Janissaries (481): Christian slave children who were raised by the Ottoman sultan as Muslims and served in the Ottoman army during the fourteenth century.

jongleur (414): A musician. Jongleurs sang the songs of troubadours and played musical instruments. Ordinarily they moved from court to court.

Koine (155): The "common" or "shared" form of the Greek language that became the international language in the Hellenistic period.

ladder of offices (178): The series of Roman elective government offices from quaestor to consul.

latifundia (187, 480): Rich landowners' huge farms worked by gangs of slaves.

law of universal gravitation (651): Newton's law uniting celestial and terrestrial mechanics held that every body in the universe exerts over every other body an attractive force directly proportional to the product of their masses and inversely proportional to the square of the distance between them.

Levellers (639): Disgruntled soldiers in Cromwell's New Model Army who wanted to "level" social differences and extend political participation to all male property owners.

Linear B (36): The Mycenaeans' pictographic script for writing Greek.

Lombard Italy (311): Northern Italy (and some inland parts of the south) under the rule of the Lombards. Beginning in the 570s, Lombard rule ended with Charlemagne's conquest of northern Italy in 774.

lyric poetry (76): Greek poetry sung with the accompaniment of the lyre and stressing the expression of emotion.

Maat (21): The Egyptian goddess ("What Is Right") embodying truth, justice, and cosmic order.

madrasa (330): A school located within or attached to a mosque.

mannerism (607): A late-sixteenth-century style of painting in which a distorted perspective created bizarre and theatrical effects that contrasted with the precise, harmonious lines of Renaissance painting.

manor (357): A great estate consisting (normally) of arable fields, vineyards, meadows, and woodland, ordinarily owned by a lord (which could as easily be a monastery or a church as a layperson) and cultivated by serfs.

martyr (228): Greek for "witness," designating someone who dies for his or her religious belief.

materialism (150): The philosophical doctrine that only things made of matter truly exist.

mean (130): Aristotle's term for the balance in desires that people needed to achieve to live just and worthwhile lives.

Mediterranean polyculture (33): The cultivation of olives, grapes, and grains in a single, interrelated agricultural system.

mercantilism (628): The doctrine that governments must intervene to increase national wealth by whatever means possible.

mercenary (469): A soldier who fights for money. Mercenaries first appeared in the fourteenth century after the Black Death caused nobles to seek new sources of revenue; they stood in contrast to citizens who fought for their cities or peasants conscripted to serve their lords.

Merovingian dynasty (307): The dynasty that ruled as kings of the Franks from about 486 to 751.

mestizo (674): A person born to a Spanish father and Native American mother.

metaphysics (128): Ideas about the ultimate nature of reality beyond the reach of human senses.

metic (97): A foreigner granted a permanent residency permit in a Greek city-state in return for obligations to pay taxes and do military service.

monotheism (25): The belief in only one god, as in Judaism, Christianity, and Islam.

Moors (480): Muslims in Spain and Portugal under Christian rule in the mid-fourteenth century.

moral dualism (50): The concept that the world is the arena of an ongoing battle between the opposing divine forces of good and evil.

Moriscos (587): Muslim converts to Christianity in Spain who remained secretly faithful to Islam; they were expelled from Spain in 1614.

mos maiorum (165): Literally, "the way of the elders"; the set of Roman traditional values.

motet (445): A two- or three-part polyphonic song that interweaves vernacular and sacred texts.

mystery cult (97): A set of prayers, hymns, ritual purification, sacrifice, and other forms of worship undertaken to gain divine protection; each cult was connected to a particular divinity and centered on initiation into secret knowledge about the divine and human worlds.

mysticism (491): A belief that the emotional and individual experience with God is more important than external religious behavior. The Free Spirits of the late Middle Ages practiced an extreme form of mysticism.

Neolithic [period] (P-4): "New Stone" period; the period of the Stone Age during which people developed agriculture and domesticated animals.

Neolithic Revolution (P-8): The changes in human life in the New Stone Age produced by the invention of agriculture and the domestication of animals.

Neoplatonism (233): The spiritual philosophy developed by Plotinus (c. 205–270) that was based on Plato's ideas and very influential for Christian intellectuals.

nominalism (488): A late medieval philosophy that holds that concepts have no reality in nature but exist only as representations, or merely as words.

Old Believers (635): A Russian Orthodox religious group that rejected church efforts to bring Russian worship in line with Byzantine tradition.

optimates (189): The Roman political faction supporting the "best," or highest, social class; established during the late republic.

orders (176): The two groups of people in the Roman republic—the patricians (aristocratic families) and the plebeians (everyone else).

ostracism (91): Athenian democracy's annual procedure to block tyranny by sending a citizen into exile for ten years by a vote of six thousand citizens in the assembly.

palace society (33): The political and social organization of Minoan and Mycenaean civilization, with palace complexes as their administrative centers.

Paleolithic [period] (P-4): "Old Stone" period; the period of the Stone Age before people farmed for a living.

parish (563): The basic territorial organization of the Catholic and main Protestant churches.

parlements (623): High courts in France (the term comes from the French *parler*, "to speak"). Each region had its parlement; the parlements could not propose laws, but they could review laws presented by the king and refuse to register them (the king could also insist on their registration).

patria potestas (167): Literally, "father's power"; the legal right of a father in ancient Rome to own the property of his children and slaves and to control their lives.

patron-client system (166): The interlocking network of mutual obligations between Roman patrons (social superiors) and clients (social inferiors).

Pax Romana (204): The period of "Roman peace" under the principate in the first and second centuries C.E.

Peace of God (349): A movement begun by bishops in the south of France first to limit the violence done to property and later (with the Truce of God) to limit fighting between warriors.

Pietism (683): The Protestant revivalist movement that emphasized deeply emotional individual religious experience.

plantation (667): A large tract of land producing staple crops such as sugar, coffee, and tobacco; farmed by slave labor; and owned by a colonial settler who emigrated from western Europe.

plebiscites (179): Laws passed by the Plebeian Assembly in the Roman republic.

polis (57): The Greek term for an independent city-state based on citizenship.

political states (P-15): People living in a definite territory and organized under a system of government with powerful leaders, officials, and judges.

politiques (585): Political advisers during the French Wars of Religion who argued that compromise in matters of religion—limited toleration for the Calvinists—would strengthen the monarchy.

polyphony (446): Music that consists of two or more melodies performed simultaneously.

polytheism (12): The worship of multiple gods.

populares (189): The Roman political faction supporting the common people established during the late republic.

praetorian guard (207): The group of soldiers stationed in Rome under the emperor's control; first formed by Augustus.

predestination (558): John Calvin's doctrine that God preordained salvation or damnation for each person before creation; those chosen for salvation were considered the "elect."

primogeniture (348): The right to inheritance of the firstborn.

principate (204): The political system invented by Augustus as a disguised monarchy with the *princeps* ("first man") as emperor.

proletarians (179): In the Roman republic, the mass of people so poor they owned no property.

proscription (192): The procedure devised under Roman general Lucius Cornelius Sulla of posting a list of those supposedly guilty of treasonable crimes so that they could be executed and their property confiscated.

Protestants (548): Members of the Christian branch that formed when Martin Luther and his followers broke from the Catholic church in 1517; the name was first used in 1529 in an imperial diet by German princes who protested Emperor Charles V's edict to repress religious dissent.

Puritans (589): Strict Calvinists who opposed all vestiges of Catholic ritual in the Church of England.

radical democracy (90): The ancient Athenian system of democracy, established in the 460s and 450s B.C.E., that extended direct political power and participation in the court system to the mass of adult male citizens.

raison d'état (597): French for "reason of state." The political doctrine, first proposed by Cardinal Richelieu of France, which held that the state's interests should prevail over those of religion; Richelieu, for example, allied with the Lutheran king of Sweden even though he himself was a leading official of the Catholic Church.

rationalism (77): The philosophic idea that people must justify their claims by logic and reason.

reconquista (367, 480): The Christian reconquest of Spain.

redistributive economy (15): A system in which state officials control the production and distribution of goods.

reliefs (382): Money payments made by a vassal to his lord upon inheriting a fief.

Renaissance (505): The rebirth of classical poetry, prose, and art in Europe that began in the fourteenth century; the word *renaissance* can also refer to other earlier cultural rebirths.

res publica (172): Literally, "the people's matter" or "the public business"; the Romans' name for their republic.

rococo (681): A style of painting that emphasized irregularity and asymmetry, movement and curvature, but on a smaller, more intimate scale than the baroque.

Romanesque (390): The term for the art and architecture in western Europe of the period before around 1150, characterized by monumentality and solidity enlivened by sculpture and painting.

Romanization (221): The spread of Roman law and culture in the provinces of the Roman Empire.

ruler cults (155): Cults that involved worship of a Hellenistic ruler as a savior god.

Sassanid Empire (284): The empire of the Sassanid dynasty of Persia, which lasted from 224 until its conquest by Islamic armies in 637–651.

satrap (49): A regional governor in the Persian empire.

scholasticism (443): The body of theological and philosophical thought of the scholastics, the scholars of the medieval universities, which combined the authority of the church fathers with that of Aristotle.

scientific method (611): A combination of experimental observation and mathematical deduction to determine the laws of nature; it became the secular standard of truth and as such challenged the hold of both the churches and popular beliefs.

scutage (409): A money payment paid by a vassal in lieu of military service. King John of England demanded scutage rather than service because vassals owed service for only forty days whereas hired soldiers would work as long as they were paid.

Sea Peoples (37): The diverse groups of raiders who devastated the eastern Mediterranean in the period of calamities around 1200–1000 B.C.E.

secularization (606): The trend toward making religious faith a private domain rather than one directly connected to state power and science; it prompted a search for nonreligious explanations for political authority and natural phenomena.

Seljuk Turks (372): A Sunni Muslim Turkic group whose migration westward, into areas that had been controlled by Byzantium and various local Muslim rulers, set off the First Crusade.

serfs (345): Semifree peasants. Serfs could not legally leave the land they tilled; they owed labor services and either produce or money to their lord whose land it was. Yet they were not slaves: they had the right to marry, to keep part of their produce, and to remain on the land.

simony (366): Derived from the name of Simon Magus, a magician in the New Testament who offers St. Peter money to have the power to confer the Holy Spirit (Acts 8:9–24), the term came to mean the giving of gifts or money for church offices.

social contract (650): The doctrine found in the writings of Hobbes and Locke that all political authority derives not from divine right but from an implicit contract between citizens and their rulers.

Socratic method (109): Socrates' method of conversation, in which he asked probing questions to make his listeners examine their most cherished assumptions before drawing conclusions.

Sophists (106): Competitive intellectuals and teachers who offered a new form of education and new philosophical and religious ideas beginning about 450 B.C.E.

Stoicism (151): The most influential Hellenistic philosophy, which taught the goal of living a virtuous life in harmony with nature.

subjectivism (106): The belief, especially associated with the Sophist Protagoras, that there is no absolute reality behind and independent of appearances.

successor kings (139): Alexander's commanders (Antigonus, Seleucus, and Ptolemy) who took over portions of his empire to create personal monarchies after his death.

summa (443): A scholastic treatise. These characteristically took up a topic and explored it exhaustively, resulting in a "summary" of all opinions and their resolution.

symposium (plural: symposia) (99): A drinking party for Greek men with entertainment ranging from philosophical conversation to hired female companions (see *hetaira*).

tertiaries (441): Laypeople who affiliated themselves with the friars and adopted many of their pious practices while living in the world.

tetrarchy (247): Literally, "rule by four"; devised by Diocletian to put into practice his principle of subdivision of power in ruling the Roman Empire.

tithe (347, 601): A tax equivalent to one-tenth of the parishioner's annual income taken by the church.

Torah (51): The first five books of the Hebrew Bible; also referred to as the Pentateuch. It contains early Jewish law.

trireme (89): An ancient Greek warship rowed by 170 oarsmen sitting on three levels and equipped with a ram.

trivium (386): The first three—the foundational subjects—of the seven liberal arts: grammar, rhetoric, and logic (or dialectic).

troubadours (413): Vernacular poets in southern France who sang of love, longing, and courtesy.

tsar (530): The Russian imperial title first taken by Muscovite prince Ivan III (r. 1462–1505); also spelled *czar*, from Caesar.

Twelve Tables (177): The first written Roman law code, enacted between 451 and 449 B.C.E.

Umayyad caliphate (298): The successors of Muhammad who traced their ancestry to Umayyah, a member of Muhammad's tribe. The first of these caliphs was related to Muhammad because he married two of the Prophet's daughters. The dynasty lasted from 661 to 750.

ummah (294): The community of believers following Muhammad.

vassalage (344): The rights and duties of a vassal, a free warrior who was nevertheless the dependent of another, his lord.

vernacular literature (497): Works written in the languages spoken by the people as opposed to being written in Latin; such literature blossomed in the fourteenth century.

Visigothic Spain (310): Spain under the Visigoths. Beginning in the mid-fifth century, Visigothic rule ended with the conquest of most of Spain by Islamic armies in 711.

Vulgate (562): The authoritative Latin version of the Catholic Bible, the only one authorized prior to the Protestant Reformation.

wergild (270): Under Frankish law, money or goods a murderer had to pay as compensation for his crime; most went to the victim's kin, but the king received about one-third.

Westernization (688): The effort, especially in Peter the Great's Russia, to make society and social customs resemble counterparts in western Europe, especially France, Britain and the Dutch Republic.

wisdom literature (23): Fables, proverbs, essays, and prophecies teaching morality and proper behavior.

ziggurat (10): A large Mesopotamian temple with a stair-step design.

Additional Credits

Chapter 1, page 17: "Hammurabi's Laws for Physicians." From translation adapted in *Ancient Near Eastern Texts Relating to the Old Testament*, 3rd. ed. with supplement, by James B. Pritchard. Copyright © 1950, 1955, 1969, renewed 1978 by Princeton University Press. Reprinted by permission of Princeton University Press. **Page 26:** "Declaring Innocence on Judgement Day in Ancient Egypt." From *The Book of the Dead.* Reprinted in *Ancient Egyptian Literature: A Book of Readings*, translated by Miriam Lichtheim, Vol II: *The New Kingdom.* Published by the University of California Press (1976). © 1973–1980 by the Regents of the University of California. Reprinted courtesy of the University of California Press.

Chapter 3, page 107: "Sophists Arguing both Sides of a Case." Excerpt from *Dissoi Logio* 1. 1-6. Translation adapted from *The Older Sophists* by Rosamund Kent Sprague, ed. Copyright © 1972 by Rosamund Kent Sprague. Reprinted by permission of the University of South Carolina Press. **Page 117:** Taking Measure: "Military Forces of Athens and Sparta at the Beginning of the Peloponnesian War." Adapted from Fig. 4.10 in *Risk and Survival in Ancient Greece: Reconstructing the Rural Domestic Economy* by Thomas W. Gallant. Copyright © 1991 by Thomas W. Gallant. Courtesy of Stanford University Press.

Chapter 4, page 141: "Ethnic Tension in Ptolemaic Egypt." From *Greeks in Ptolemaic Egypt: Case Studies in the Social History of the Hellenistic World,* with translation adapted by Naphtali Lewis. Copyright © 1986 by Naphtali Lewis. Reprinted by permission of Oxford University Press.

Chapter 8, page 288: Taking Measure: "Church Repair." Adaptation of three figures (8a, 8b, and 8c) from *The Sixth Century: Production, Distribution and Demand* by Richard Hodges and William Bowden. Copyright © 1998, Brill Publishers, via Copyright Clearance Center. Reprinted by permission.

Chapter 9, page 337: "Dhuoda's Handbook for Her Son." From *Handbook for William: A Carolingian Woman's Counsel for Her Son.* Translated with Introductions and Notes by Carol Neel. Copyright © 1991. University of Nebraska Press. Reprinted by permission. **Page 345:** "The Chronicle of Fulcher of Chartres." Edited text from pp. 35–37 in *The First Crusade: The Chronicle of Fulcher of Chartres and Other Source Materials*, edited Edward Peters. Copyright © 1971 Edward Peters. Reprinted by permission of the University of Pennsylvania Press.

Chapter 10, page 370: "A Byzantine View of Papal Primacy." From *Byzantium: Church, Society, and Civilization Seen through Contemporary Eyes* by Deno John Geanakoplos. Quoting from *Byzantium and the Roman Primacy*, translated by Edwin A. Quain, S.J.

Copyright © 1966/79 Fordham University Press. Reprinted by permission of the publisher. **Page 378:** "Genoese Traders in Palestine." Excerpt from pp. 88–89 in *Medieval Trade* in the Mediterranean World: Illustrative Documents. Translated with Introductions and Notes by Robert S. Lopez & Irving W. Raymond. Copyright © 1955 by Columbia University Press. Reprinted with the permission of the publisher. **Page 374:** "The Jewish Experience, as told by Solomon Bar Simson." Edited text from pp. 21–23 in *The Jews and the Crusaders: The Hebrew Chronicles of the First and Second Crusaders*, translated and edited by Shlomo Eidelberg. Copyright © Shlomo Eidelberg. Reprinted by permission of the author. **Page 383:** Taking Measure: "Slaves in England in 1086 as Reported in Domesday." Excerpted data from appendices 1, 3, 13, and 14 (for map w/table) in *Domesday England* by H.C. Darby. Copyright © 1977 by H.C. Darby. Reprinted with the permission of Cambridge University Press.

Chapter 11, page 425: Adaptation of 2 maps from p. 146 in *Atlas of Medieval Europe*, edited by Angus Mackay and David Ditchburn. Copyright © Routledge. Reprinted with the permission of Taylor & Francis, Ltd.

Chapter 13, page 474: Edited text from pp. 30, 48–49, 64–65, 223–24, 233 in *Joan of Arc: By Herself and Her Witnesses* by Regine Pernoud. © 1994 by Regine Pernoud. Reprinted by permission of Madison Books. **Page 494:** Excerpt from *Piers the Ploughman* by William Langland, translated by J.F. Goodridge (Penguin Classics, 1959, Revised Edition, 1966). Copyright © J.F. Goodrich, 1959, 1966. Reprinted by permission of Penguin Books, Ltd. **Page 485:** Taking Measure: "Population Losses and the Plague." Excerpted text from table 1, p. 36 in *The Fontana Economic History of Europe: The Middle Ages* by Carlo M. Cipolla, ed. © 1974 by Carlo M. Cipolla/ Fontana Books. Reprinted by permission of HarperCollins Publishers, Ltd. **Page 498:** Excerpt from *The Book of the City of Ladies* by Christine de Pizan, translated by Rosalind Brown-Grant (Penguin Classics, 1999). Translation © Rosalind Brown-Grant, 1999. Reprinted by permission of Penguin Group Ltd.

Chapter 15, page 551: Excerpt from *Utopia* by Thomas More, translated by Paul Turner (Penguin Classics, 1961). Copyright © Paul Turner, 1961. Reprinted by permission of Penguin Books, Ltd. **Page 556:** "Erasmus Writes to Martin Luther" Excerpt from p. 317 in *Essential Works of Erasmus*, edited by W.T.H. Jackson. © 1965 Bantam, Doubleday Dell a division of Random House, Inc.

Chapter 16, page 594: "The Horrors of the Thirty Years' War." Excerpt from pp. 6–7 in *The Adventures of Simplicius Simplicissimus*, translated by George Schulz-Behrend, 2nd ed. Copyright © 1993 by George Schulz-Behrend. Reprinted by permission of Camden House. **Page 613:** "Galileo Writes to Kepler." From *The*

Index

Wooley, Hannah, 657
Wool industry and trade
  effect of diminishing
    demand, 487
  effect of Hundred Years' War
    on, 477
  in England, 527
  guilds and, 418
  linking England and
    Flanders, 383
  manufacture in eleventh and
    twelfth centuries, 364
Workers
  in ancient Egypt
    New Kingdom, 26–27
    Old Kingdom, 22–23
  in Athens, 126
Works and Days (Hesiod), 56
Worms, Concordat of (1122), 369,
  401
Worms, Imperial Diet of (1521),
  553
Worms, Jewish cemetery in,
  377 *(i)*
Writing. *See also* Alphabet
  Anglo-Saxon becoming a
    written language, 310
  Caroline minuscule, 335

cuneiform, 12 *(f)*
demotic, 20 *(f)*
Greek loss of knowledge of, 52
hieroglyphs, 19, 20 *(f)*
invention of, 11–12
Kufic script, 294 *(i)*
Linear A, 32
Linear B, 36, 52
of Minoan Crete, 32
Rosetta stone, 122 *(i)*
Writs, 382
Wycliffe, John (c. 1330–1384),
  491–492

Xavier, Francis, St., 577
Xenophanes of Colophon
  (c. 580–480 B.C.E.), 78
Xenophon (c. 430–355 B.C.E.),
  102, 132
  on homosexuality, 72
Xerxes I (Persian king;
  r. 486–465 B.C.E.), 87

Yahweh (Hebrew god), 28
Yangzhou, European traders
  in, 461
York, Jews of, 424
York helmet, 308 *(i)*

Ypres, 487

Zachary (pope; r. 741–752), 314
  and Pippin III, 331
Zama, Battle of (202 B.C.E.),
  182
Zara, 399
Zarathustra, 50
  and cult of Mithras, 232
Zell, Katharina, 564
Zell, Matthew (1477–1548),
  564
Zengi (Seljuk chieftain), 379
Zeno (333–262 B.C.E.), 151
Zeno (Byzantine emperor;
  r. 474–491), 267
Zenobia (queen of Palmyra,
  r. 269–272), 237
  territory of, 236 *(m)*
Zeus (Greek god), 63
Ziggurats, 10
  Ur in Sumer, 10 *(i)*
Zoroastrianism, 50, 287
Zurich, 479
  Zwingli in, 556–557
Zwingli, Huldrych (1484–1531),
  552, 556–557
  and Anabaptists, 561